"This book does a good job of looking at the big picture and the interaction of different cultures that helped form our global world." — Ken Faunce, *University of Idaho*

"Students will not be overwhelmed by a rash of details and will take away a big picture about the history of the world that raises interesting questions about today." — Laura A. Smoller, *University of Arkansas at Little Rock*

"After reading the brief sections, one comes away with a better understanding of these societies than if one had waded through a conventional text." — Barbara A. Moss, *Clark Atlanta University*

"Strayer's text is characterized by a commitment to thematic focus and clarity that should be of great assistance to students as they prepare for essays and analytical questions." — Abel Alves, *Ball State University*

"The class using the Strayer chapters saw an increase of ten points, or an entire grade, when compared to classes of the last twelve years. It was remarkable. I have never been forced to give so many A grades before." — Eric Mayer, *Victor Valley College*

"Unlike most world history texts, it avoids the chronological/geographic formula and instead embraces comparison, connections, and change in a deliberately brief text: quite an achievement." — Timothy J. Coates, *College of Charleston*

"Strayer's engaging book discusses world history not as separate threads that connect and entangle at some points, but as a tapestry where complex events and issues are contextualized in a big-picture approach that emphasizes change, connection, and comparison." — Charles Didier Gondola, *Indiana University–Purdue University Indianapolis*

"An entirely new and engaging approach to the topic. Instead of the traditional chronological slog through various 'civilizations,' the author offers a unique cross-continents examination of world systems of trade and social organization." — Theresa Jordan, *Washington State University*

"The author shows a remarkable agility and flexibility in dealing with cases and examples from all over the planet." — James A. Wood, *North Carolina A&T State University*

2

De Eſpañol, y Meſtiſa; Caſtiſ

Ways of the World

A Brief Global History

ROBERT W. STRAYER

California State University, Monterey Bay

Bedford/St. Martin's

Boston • New York

To Alisa and her generation

For Bedford/St. Martin's
Publisher for History: Mary Dougherty
Director of Development for History:
   Jane Knetzger
Developmental Editor: Jim Strandberg
Senior Production Editor: Bridget Leahy
Senior Production Supervisor: Joe Ford
Executive Marketing Manager: Jenna Bookin
   Barry
Editorial Assistant: Lynn Sternberger
Production Assistant: Lidia MacDonald-Carr
Copyeditor: Linda McLatchie
Text and Cover Design: Joyce Weston
Cover Art: Codex Duran: Fol. 208v. *Meeting
   between Hernán Cortés and Moctezuma.*
   Bridgeman Art Library

Frontispiece: Mestizo family. Scala/Art
   Resource, NY
Cartography: Mapping Specialists Limited
Indexer: EdIndex
Composition: Aptara®, Inc.
Printing and Binding: RR Donnelley
   and Sons

President: Joan E. Feinberg
Editorial Director: Denise B. Wydra
Director of Marketing: Karen R. Soeltz
Director of Editing, Design, and Production:
   Marcia Cohen
*Assistant Director of Editing, Design, and
   Production:* Elise S. Kaiser
Managing Editor: Elizabeth M. Schaaf

Library of Congress Control Number: 2008925891

Manufactured in the United States of America.

1   2   3   4   5   6   12   11   10   09   08

For information, write: Bedford/St. Martin's
75 Arlington Street, Boston, MA 02116
(617-399-4000)

ISBN-10: 0-312-45287-X   ISBN-13: 978-0-312-45287-2 (combined edition)
ISBN-10: 0-312-45288-8   ISBN-13: 978-0-312-45288-9 (Vol. 1)
ISBN-10: 0-312-45289-6   ISBN-13: 978-0-312-45289-6 (Vol. 2)
ISBN-10: 0-312-55728-0   ISBN-13: 978-0-312-55728-7 (high school edition)

Acknowledgments: Acknowledgments and copyrights can be found at the back of the book on pages 773-74, which constitute an extension of the copyright page.

Preface

WHEN I ENTERED COLLEGE IN 1960, there was no such thing as a world history course, either in my school or almost anywhere else in the country. When I started teaching at the college level in 1970, the study of world history was just beginning to make itself felt, and the State University of New York College at Brockport, where I taught for many years, was among the first to offer an introductory world history course. By the time I began teaching in California in 2002, world history had become an established and rapidly growing enterprise, in both secondary schools and universities, all across the country. Thus, as a teaching field, world history is a relatively new entry in the course lists of American universities, and as a subject for research and writing, it represents a new agenda within the historical profession.

This flowering of world history has coincided almost precisely with my own career in the academy. Over the course of several decades, I have been able to roam the world with history—as a student, a teacher, a scholar and writer, a traveler, and an active participant in the world history movement. My involvement in the more specialized fields of African and, later, Soviet history has likewise contributed much to the more central focus of my academic life, which is world history.

Like many others who have been attracted to this most exciting field of study, I have become something of a "specialist of the whole" rather than a specialist in one of its parts. No teacher or writer, of course, can be master of the vast array of cultures, themes, and time periods that world history encompasses. However, those of us interested in world history read widely; we look for the big picture processes and changes that have marked the human journey; we are alert to the possibilities of comparison across cultural boundaries; and we pay special attention to the multiple interactions among human communities. Students, the wider public, and professional scholars alike need the larger integrated view of the past that world history provides as well as the more focused and specialized understandings of particular countries, cultures, and peoples that most history courses offer.

On a professional level, world history has afforded me a distinctive and fulfilling career, allowing me to sample a variety of specialized fields, to interact with a remarkable community of scholars and teachers, and to engage thousands of students with the larger trajectory of the human story. More personally, my career in world history has been an immensely fruitful journey, for I have encountered times, places, and peoples that otherwise would have lain well outside my own experience. The writing of *Ways of the World* has provided an opportunity to crystallize the work of my adult life and to share it with others. Doing so has been a rare and rich privilege.

What's in a Title?

The title of a book should evoke something of its character and outlook. *Ways of the World* is intended to suggest at least three dimensions of this text.

The first is **diversity** or **variation**, for the "ways of the world," or the ways of being human in the world, have been many and constantly changing. World history, or global history as it is sometimes called, was conceived in part to counteract a Eurocentric perspective on the human past, deriving from several centuries of Western dominance on the world stage. This book seeks to embrace the experience of humankind in its vast diversity, while noticing the changing location of particular centers of innovation and wider influence.

A second meaning attached to the title *Ways of the World* involves an emphasis on major **panoramas**, **patterns**, or **pathways**, as opposed to highly detailed narratives. This reflects my own observation in the classroom, and that of many world history instructors, that students can easily feel overwhelmed by the sheer quantity of data that a course in global history can require of them. In this book, the larger patterns of world history appear in the foreground on center stage, while the plentiful details, data, and facts occupy the background, serving in supporting roles.

A third implication of the book's title lies in a certain **reflective** or **musing quality** of *Ways of the World*. It is a product of my own growing appreciation that history of any kind, and world history in particular, offers endless raw material for contemplating large questions. And so a final section in each chapter, titled "Reflections," raises questions about the nature of the historical enterprise and of the human processes it explores.

- Chapter 3, for example, about First Civilizations, ponders their ambiguous legacy—great achievements in size, complexity, innovation, and culture and equally great oppression, experienced in massive inequality, patriarchy, slavery, and war.

- Chapter 5, which deals with cultural traditions of the classical era, muses on the tensions or misunderstandings that sometimes arise between historians and the believers of various religious traditions.

- The Reflections section of Chapter 18, on the Industrial Revolution, asks whether we are presenting history as a horse race to the finish line of modernity and unduly celebrating those who arrived there first.

- Chapter 21, about the era of the world wars during the first half of the twentieth century, probes the possibility of deriving specific "lessons" from these conflicts and expresses some skepticism about the familiar notion that "history repeats itself."

Other chapters invite students to reflect on issues such as surprise or unexpectedness in the historical record and contingency or accident as modes of explanation. These Reflections sections seek to engage student readers with the larger and perhaps quasi-philosophical issues with which historians constantly grapple.

Achieving Coherence

The great virtue of world history lies in its inclusiveness, for it allows us to see the world and to see it whole, an obvious necessity given the demands of contemporary life. But that virtue is also the source of world history's greatest difficulty—telling a coherent story. How can we meaningfully present the planet's many and distinct peoples and their intersections with one another in the confines of a single book or a single term? What prevents that telling from bogging down in the endless detail of various civilizations or cultures, from losing the forest for the trees, from implying that history is just "one damned thing after another"?

Less Can Be More

Ways of the World seeks to cope with that fundamental conundrum of world history—the challenge of condensing the history of the world into a single text—in several ways. The first is relative brevity and a corresponding selectivity. This means, of course, leaving some things out or treating them more succinctly than some instructors might expect. The positive side of this brevity is that the textbook need not dominate the pedagogy of the course or overwhelm students with facts. It allows for more professorial creativity in constructing individual world history courses and in mixing and matching various reading materials. And wouldn't it be wonderful if we found students asking for "more," rather than complaining about "too much"?

Brevity also encourages a "themes and cases" rather than a "civilization-by-civilization" approach to the global past. Thus, most chapters in this book focus on a broad theme, explored on a global or transregional scale:

- classical-era empires in Chapter 4
- comparative social structures in Chapter 6
- long-distance commerce in Chapters 8 and 15
- the colonial experience in Chapter 20
- the communist experiment in Chapter 22
- twentieth-century globalization in Chapter 24

Such chapters explore a given theme in general while illustrating it with a few particular cases.

The Three Cs of World History:
Change, Comparison, Connection

As a further aid to achieving coherence on a global scale, *Ways of the World* refers repeatedly to what I call the "**three Cs**" of world history. They represent some of

the distinctive perspectives of world history as an academic discipline and are introduced more extensively in the prologue.

The first "C" emphasizes large-scale **changes**, both within and especially across
major regions of the world. Change, of course, is a central theme in all historical
study and serves to challenge "essentialist" descriptions of particular cultures or
peoples. Among the macrochanges highlighted in *Ways of the World* are

- agriculture in Chapter 2
- civilization in Chapter 3
- the rise of universal religions in Chapter 5
- the changing shape of the Islamic world in Chapter 11
- industrialization in Chapter 18
- European global dominance in Chapter 19
- the rise and fall of world communism in Chapter 22

The second "C" involves frequent **comparison**. It is a technique of integration through juxtaposition, of bringing several regions or cultures into our field of
vision at the same time. It encourages reflection both on the common elements of
the human experience and on the many variations in that experience. Such comparisons are a prominent feature of virtually every chapter of the book. We examine the difference, for example,

- between the Agricultural Revolution in the Eastern Hemisphere and that in
  the Western Hemisphere (Chapter 2)
- between early Mesopotamian and Egyptian civilizations (Chapter 3)
- between the beginnings of Buddhism and the early period of Christianity
  (Chapter 5)
- between European and Asian empires of the early modern era (Chapter 14)
- between the Chinese and the Japanese response to European intrusion
  (Chapter 19)
- between Iran and Turkey within the twentieth-century Islamic world
  (Chapter 23)

The final "C" emphasizes **connections**, networks of communication and
exchange that increasingly shaped the character of those societies that participated
in them. For world historians, cross-cultural interaction becomes one of the major
motors of historical change. Such connections are addressed in nearly every chapter. For example:

- Chapter 3 explores the clash of the Greeks and the Persians during the
  classical era.
- Chapter 8 highlights the long-distance commercial networks that linked
  the Afro-Eurasian world and, less extensively, the Western Hemisphere in
  premodern times.

- Chapter 11 focuses attention on the transregional world of Islam.
- Chapter 12 turns the spotlight on the multiple interactions of the Mongol era.
- Chapters 14 and 15 explore various facets of the transhemispheric Columbian exchange of the early modern era.
- Chapter 17 probes the linkages among the Atlantic revolutions of the late eighteenth and early nineteenth centuries.
- Chapter 24 concludes the book with an examination of globalization, highlighting its economic, feminist, religious, and environmental dimensions.

Organizing World History: Chronology, Theme, and Region

Organizing a world history textbook is, to put it mildly, a daunting task. How should we divide up the seamless stream of human experience into manageable and accessible pieces, while recognizing always that such divisions are both artificial and to some extent arbitrary? Historians, of course, debate the issue endlessly. In structuring *Ways of the World*, I have drawn on my own sense of "what works" in the classroom, on a personal penchant for organizational clarity, and on established practice in the field. The outcome has been an effort to balance three principles of organization—chronology, theme, and region—in a flexible format that can accommodate a variety of teaching approaches and organizational strategies.

The chronological principle is expressed most clearly in the overall structure of the book, which divides world history into six major periods. Each of these six parts begins with a brief **Big Picture essay** that introduces the general patterns of a particular period and raises questions about the problems historians face in dividing up the human past into meaningful chunks of time.

Part One (to 500 B.C.E.) deals in three separate chapters with beginnings—of human migration and social construction in the Paleolithic era, of agriculture, and of civilization. Each of them pursues an important theme on a global scale and illustrates that theme with regional examples treated comparatively.

Part Two, on the classical era (500 B.C.E. to 500 C.E.), likewise employs the thematic principle in exploring the major civilizations of Eurasia (Chinese, Indian, Persian, and Mediterranean), with separate chapters focusing on their empires (Chapter 4), cultural traditions (Chapter 5), and social organization (Chapter 6). This structure represents a departure from conventional practice, which usually treats the classical era on a civilization-by-civilization basis, but it allows for more effective and pointed comparison. These Eurasian chapters are followed by a single chapter (Chapter 7) that examines regionally the classical era in sub-Saharan Africa and the Americas, while asking whether their histories largely follow Eurasian patterns or depart from them.

Part Three embraces the thousand years between 500 and 1500 C.E., often known simply, and not very helpfully, as the "postclassical" era. The Big Picture essay for Part Three spotlights and seeks to explain a certain vagueness in our descriptions of this period of time, pointing out the various distinctive civilizational patterns of that millennium as well as the accelerating interactions among them. The six chapters of Part Three reflect a mix of thematic and regional principles. Chapter 8 focuses topically on commercial networks, while Chapters 9, 10, and 11 deal regionally with the Chinese, Christian, and Islamic worlds respectively. Chapter 12 treats pastoral societies as a broad theme and the Mongols as the most dramatic illustration of their impact on the larger stage of world history. Chapter 13, which bridges the two volumes of the book, presents an around-the-world tour in the fifteenth century, which serves both to conclude Volume 1 and to open Volume 2.

In considering the early modern era (1450–1750), **Part Four** treats each of its three constituent chapters thematically. Chapter 14 compares European and Asian empires; Chapter 15 lays out the major patterns of global commerce and their consequences (trade in spices, silver, furs, and slaves); and Chapter 16 focuses on cultural patterns, including the globalization of Christianity and the rise of modern science.

Part Five takes up the era of maximum European influence in the world, from 1750 to 1914. Here the Big Picture essay probes how we might avoid Eurocentrism, while describing a period of time in which Europeans were in fact increasingly central to the global story. Part Five, which charts the emergence of a distinctively modern society in Europe, devotes separate chapters to the Atlantic revolutions (Chapter 17) and the Industrial Revolution (Chapter 18). Then it turns to the growing impact of those societies on the rest of humankind—on China, the Ottoman Empire, and Japan, which are treated comparatively in Chapter 19; and on the world of formal colonies in Chapter 20.

The most recent century (1914–2008), which is treated in **Part Six**, is perhaps the most problematic for world historians, given the abundance of data and the absence of time to sort out what is fundamental and what is peripheral. The Big Picture essay that opens Part Six explores this difficulty, asking whether that century deserves the status of a separate period in the human story. Chapters 21, 22, and 23 examine respectively three major regions of the world in that century—the Western or industrial world, the communist world, and the third or developing world—while Chapter 24 explores the multiple processes of globalization, which have both linked and divided the human community in new ways.

Promoting Active Learning: Focus on Features

As all instructors know, students can often "do the assignment" or read the required chapter and yet have nearly no understanding of it when they come to class. The problem, frequently, is passive studying—a quick once-over, perhaps some highlighting of the text—but little sustained involvement with the material. A central pedagogical problem in all teaching at every level is how to encourage more active, engaged styles of learning. How can we push students to articulate in their own words the major ideas of a particular chapter or section of the text? How can we encourage them to recognize arguments, even in a textbook, and to identify and evaluate the evidence on which those arguments are based? Active learning seeks to enable students to manipulate the information of the book, using its ideas and data to answer questions, to make comparisons, to draw conclusions, to criticize assumptions, and to infer implications that are not explicitly disclosed in the book itself. This ability to use and rearrange the material of a text, not simply to recall it, lies at the heart of active college-level learning.

Ways of the World incorporates a number of features or learning aids that are designed to promote active learning, to assist students in reading the text and instructors in teaching it, and to generate more lively classroom exchanges.

- The part-opening **Big Picture essays** preview for students what follows in the subsequent chapters. In doing so, they provide a larger context for those chapters; they enable students to make comparisons with greater ease; they facilitate making connections across several chapters; and they raise questions about periodization.

- Each Big Picture essay is followed by a **Landmarks timeline**, providing a chronological overview of what follows in that particular part of the book. Each of these Landmarks is organized in a series of parallel regional timelines, allowing students to see at a glance significant developments in various regions of the world during the same time.

- A **contemporary vignette** opens each chapter with a story that links the past and the present. Chapter 1, for example, presents Gudo Mahiya, a twenty-first-century member of a gathering and hunting society in Tanzania, who rejects an opportunity to become a settled farmer or herder. Chapter 15, which describes the Atlantic slave trade, opens with a brief account of an African American woman who in 2002 visited what had been a slave port in Ghana. These vignettes seek to show the continuing resonance of the past in the lives of contemporary people.

- To encourage active learning explicitly, a series of **questions in the margins** provides students with "something to look for" as they read particular sections. Those notations also indicate what kind of question is being asked—about change, comparison, or connection, for example. Such questions relate directly to the material that follows. In Chapter 5, for example, beside a discussion of the major schools of thought in classical-era China, a marginal question asks: "Comparison: What different answers to the problem of disorder arose in classical China?" And in Chapter 17, just before a discussion of Latin American independence movements, there appears this marginal question: "Connection: How were the Spanish American revolutions shaped by the American, French, and Haitian revolutions that happened earlier?"

- To further foster active learning, the **Second Thoughts** section at the end of each chapter provides a list of particulars (people, places, events, processes, concepts) under the heading "**What's the Significance?**" inviting students to check their grasp of that chapter's material. The next part of the Second Thoughts section is a set of **Big Picture Questions**. Unlike the marginal questions, which are keyed specifically to the adjacent material, these Big Picture Questions are not directly addressed in the text. Instead, they provide opportunities for integration, comparison, analysis, and sometimes speculation. Such questions might well become the basis for engaging writing assignments, class discussions, or exam items. Finally, a limited **list of suggested readings**—books, articles, and Web sites—invites further exploration of the material in the chapter.

- **Snapshots** appear in every chapter and present succinct glimpses of particular themes, regions, or time periods, adding some trees to the forest of world history. A Snapshot in Chapter 3, for example, compares six different early writing systems, while another in Chapter 11 summarizes key achievements in Islamic science and scholarship. In Chapter 15, a Snapshot briefly summarizes the numerical dimensions of the Atlantic slave trade, and in Chapter 22, yet another Snapshot illustrates with statistical data the accomplishments, limitations, and tragedies of China under Maoist communism.

- As is always true of books published by Bedford/St. Martin's, a **rich program of maps and images** accompanies the narrative. Because history and geography are so closely related, more than 100 maps have been included in the two volumes of the book. They have been carefully chosen to orient the reader to the parts of the world described in the text. About 150 images, most of them contemporary to the times and places they illustrate, provide visual evidence of the ways people understood their worlds and their lives.

Supplements

A comprehensive collection of print and electronic resources for students and instructors accompanies this book. Developed with my collaboration, they are designed to provide a host of practical learning and teaching aids.

For Students

Print Resources

World History Matters: A Student Guide to World History Online.   Based on the popular "World History Matters" Web site produced by the Center for History and New Media, this unique resource, written by Kristin Lehner (The Johns Hopkins University), Kelly Schrum (George Mason University), and T. Mills Kelly (George Mason University), combines reviews of 150 of the most useful and reliable world history Web sites, with an introduction that guides students in locating, evaluating, and correctly citing online sources. The Web sites offer opportunities for researching broad themes as well as special topics and regions and feature a range of sources, including primary documents, maps, art, photographs, statistics, and audio and video recordings. This resource is available free when packaged with the text.

Bedford Series in History and Culture.   More than 100 titles in this highly praised series combine first-rate scholarship, historical narrative, and important primary documents for undergraduate courses. Each book is brief, inexpensive, and focused on a specific topic or period. Package discounts are available.

Trade Books.   Titles published by sister companies Farrar, Straus and Giroux; Henry Holt and Company; Hill and Wang; Picador; and St. Martin's Press are available at a 50 percent discount when packaged with Bedford/St. Martin's textbooks. For more information, visit bedfordstmartins.com/tradeup.

New Media Resources

Online Study Guide at bedfordstmartins.com/strayer.   The Online Study Guide helps students synthesize the material covered in *Ways of the World*. For each chapter, it provides a multiple-choice self-test that focuses on important conceptual ideas; an identification quiz that helps students remember key people, places, and events; a flashcard activity that tests students' knowledge of key terms; and two interactive map activities intended to strengthen students' geographic skills. Instructors can monitor students' progress through an online Quiz Gradebook or receive e-mail updates.

Jules Benjamin, **A Student's Online Guide to History Reference Sources at bedfordstmartins.com/strayer.**   This Web site provides links to history-related databases, indexes, and journals, plus contact information for state, provincial, local, and professional history organizations.

The Bedford Bibliographer at bedfordstmartins.com/strayer.   *The Bedford Bibliographer*, a simple but powerful Web-based tool, assists students with the process of collecting sources and generates bibliographies in four commonly used documentation styles.

The Bedford Research Room at bedfordstmartins.com/strayer.   The Research Room, drawn from Mike Palmquist's *The Bedford Researcher*, offers a wealth of resources—including interactive tutorials, research activities, student writing samples, and links to hundreds of other places online—to support students in courses across the disciplines. The site also offers instructors a library of helpful instructional tools.

Diana Hacker's **Research and Documentation Online at bedfordstmartins .com/strayer.** This Web site provides clear advice on how to integrate primary and secondary sources into research papers, how to cite sources correctly, and how to format in MLA, APA, *Chicago*, or CBE style.

The St. Martin's Tutorial on Avoiding Plagiarism at bedfordstmartins .com/strayer. This online tutorial reviews the consequences of plagiarism and explains what sources to acknowledge, how to keep good notes, how to organize research, and how to integrate sources appropriately. The tutorial includes exercises to help students practice integrating sources and recognize acceptable summaries.

For Instructors

Print Resources

Instructor's Resource Manual. This extensive manual by Eric W. Nelson (Missouri State University) and Phyllis G. Jestice (University of Southern Mississippi) offers both experienced and first-time instructors tools for presenting textbook material in exciting and engaging ways—chapter learning objectives; annotated chapter outlines; lecture strategies; tips for helping students with common misconceptions and difficult topics; a list of key terms and definitions; answer guidelines for in-text chapter questions; and suggestions for in-class activities (including using film, video, and literature), ways to start discussions, topics for debate, and analyzing primary sources. Each chapter concludes with a guide to all the chapter-specific supplements available with *Ways of the World*. A guide for first-time teaching assistants, two sample syllabi, a list of useful books for a first-time world history professor, and a list of books that form the basis of a world history reference library are also included.

New Media Resources

Instructor's Resource CD-ROM. This disc provides instructors with ready-made and customizable PowerPoint multimedia presentations built around chapter outlines, maps, figures, and all images from the textbook, plus jpeg versions of all maps, figures, and images. The disc also contains chapter-related multiple-choice questions that can be used with the i-clicker personal response system.

Computerized Test Bank. Written by Eric W. Nelson (Missouri State University) and Phyllis G. Jestice (University of Southern Mississippi), the test bank provides more than thirty exercises per chapter, including multiple-choice, fill-in-the-blank, short-answer, and full-length essay questions. Instructors can customize quizzes, add or edit both questions and answers, and export questions and answers to a variety of formats, including WebCT and Blackboard. The disc includes correct answers and essay outlines.

Book Companion Site at bedfordstmartins.com/strayer. The companion Web site gathers all the electronic resources for *Ways of the World*, including the Online Study Guide and related Quiz Gradebook, at a single Web address and provides convenient links to lecture, assignment, and research materials, such as PowerPoint chapter outlines and the digital libraries at Make History.

Make History at bedfordstmartins.com/strayer. Comprising the content of Bedford/St. Martin's five acclaimed online libraries—Map Central, the Bedford History Image Library, DocLinks, HistoryLinks, and PlaceLinks—Make History provides one-stop access to relevant digital content, including maps, images, documents, and Web links. Students and instructors alike can search this free, easy-to-use database by keyword, topic, date, or specific chapter of *Ways of the World* and download the content they find. Instructors can also create collections of content and store them online for later use or post them to the Web to share with students.

Content for Course Management Systems. A variety of student and instructor resources developed for this textbook is ready for use in course management systems such as Blackboard, WebCT, and other platforms. This e-content includes nearly all the offerings from the book's Online Study Guide as well as the book's test bank.

Videos and Multimedia. A wide assortment of videos and multimedia CD-ROMs on various topics in world history is available to qualified adopters.

"It Takes a Village"

In any enterprise of significance, "it takes a village," as they say. Bringing *Ways of the World* to life, it seems, has occupied the energies of several villages.

The largest of these villages consists of those many people who read the manuscript at various stages, and commented on it, sometimes at great length. I continue to be surprised at the power of this kind of collaboration. Frequently, I find that passages I had regarded as polished to a gleaming perfection benefited greatly from the collective wisdom and experience of these thoughtful reviewers. Many of the readers were commissioned by Bedford/St. Martin's and are listed here in alphabetical order, with my great thanks:

Hedrick Alixopulos, *Santa Rosa Junior College*
Abel Alves, *Ball State University*
Monty Armstrong, *Cerritos High School*
Eva Baham, *Southern University*
Cheryl Barkey, *Cabrillo College*
Eric Bobo, *Hinds Community College*
Robert W. Brown, *University of North Carolina at Pembroke*

Deborah Buffton, *University of Wisconsin–La Crosse*

Mark W. Chavalas, *University of Wisconsin–La Crosse*

Katherine Clark, *SUNY Brockport*

Timothy J. Coates, *College of Charleston*

John Hillas Cole, *Hawaii Community College*

Melinda S. Courtney, *Saddleback College*

Michael R. Davidson, *Southern Illinois University, Carbondale*

Kyle Eidahl, *Florida A&M University*

Ken Faunce, *University of Idaho*

Nancy Fitch, *California State University, Fullerton*

J. Arch Getty, *University of California, Los Angeles*

Trevor Getz, *San Francisco State University*

Charles Didier Gondola, *Indiana University–Purdue University Indianapolis*

Stephen S. Gosch, *University of Wisconsin–Eau Claire*

Howell H. Gwin Jr., *Lamar University*

John K. Hayden, *Southwestern Oklahoma State University*

Beth Hodges, *Lenoir Community College*

Bryan Jack, *Winston–Salem State University*

Michele G. Scott James, *Mira Costa College*

Theresa Jordan, *Washington State University*

Theodore Kallman, *San Joaquin Delta College*

Carol A. Keller, *San Antonio College*

John Lavalle, *Western New Mexico University*

John Mack, *Labette Community College*

Moira Maguire, *University of Arkansas at Little Rock*

Susan Maneck, *Jackson State University*

Michael Markowski, *Westminster College*

Eric Martin, *Lewis-Clark State College*

Morag Martin, *SUNY Brockport*

Eric Mayer, *Victor Valley College*

Brendan McManus, *Bemidji State University*

Eben Miller, *Southern Maine Community College*

Barbara A. Moss, *Clark Atlanta University*

Andrew Muldoon, *Metropolitan State College of Denver*

Eric Nelson, *Missouri State University*

Leonora Neville, *The Catholic University of America*

Theodore A. Nitz, *Gonzaga University*

Patricia O'Neill, *Central Oregon Community College*

Bill Palmer, *Marshall University*

Stephen Rapp, *Georgia State University*

David Rayson, *Normandale Community College*

Salvador Rivera, *SUNY Cobleskill*

Eric C. Rust, *Baylor University*

David P. Sandgren, *Concordia College*
Daniel Sarefield, *Ohio State University*
Jane Scimeca, *Brookdale Community College*
Kenneth P. Serbin, *University of San Diego*
Robert P. Sherwood, *Georgia Military College*
John M. Simpson, *Pierce College*
Laura A. Smoller, *University of Arkansas at Little Rock*
William Storey, *Millsaps College*
Mark B. Tauger, *West Virginia University*
Donna A. Vinson, *Salem State College*
Frank J. Wetta, *Ocean County College*
James A. Wood, *North Carolina Agricultural and Technical State University*
Eloy Zárate, *Pasadena City College*

Others in the village of reviewers have been friends, family, and colleagues who graciously agreed to read portions of the manuscript and offer helpful counsel: Kabir Helminski, James Horn, Elisabeth Jay, David Northrup, Lynn Parsons, Katherine Poethig, Kevin Reilly, and Julie Shackford-Bradley.

The "Bedford village" has been a second community sustaining this enterprise and the one most directly responsible for the book's appearance in print. Its unofficial chief, at least for this project, has been Jim Strandberg, the development editor assigned to this book. He has read and reread every word, perused every map, and examined every image, all with exegetical care, offering suggestions, encouragement, praise, and useful criticism. As a student and teacher of history himself, Jim has brought to this delicate task the sensitivity of a fine historian as well as the competence of an outstanding editor.

Publisher Mary Dougherty first broached the possibility of this volume and, with a manner as lovely as it is professional, has provided overall editorial leadership and a calming balm to authorial anxieties. Jane Knetzger, director of development, has overseen the project from its beginning, bore my many questions with forbearance, and, even better, provided timely answers. Company president Joan Feinberg has, to my surprise and delight, periodically kept her own experienced hand in this pot, while executive editor Beth Welch, though fully engaged in her own projects, has served as counselor from the sidelines. Photo researcher Carole Frohlich identified and acquired the many images that grace *Ways of the World* and did so with amazing efficiency and courtesy. Senior editor Louise Townsend provided initial guidance as the project got under way, and Denise Wydra, the editorial director, has offered helpful encouragement.

Operating more behind the scenes in the Bedford village, a series of highly competent and always supportive people have shepherded this book along its way. A succession of capable editorial assistants—Holly Dye, Alix Roy, and Lynn Sternberger—provided invaluable assistance in handling the manuscript, contacting reviewers, and keeping on top of the endless details that such an enterprise demands. Bridget Leahy served as project editor during the book's production and, often under considerable pressure, did so with both grace and efficiency. Copy editor Linda McLatchie polished the prose and sorted out my inconsistent usages with a seasoned and perceptive eye.

Jenna Bookin Barry and Sally Constable have overseen the marketing process, while history specialist John Hunger and a cadre of humanities specialists and sales representatives have introduced the book to the academic world. Heidi Hood and Jack Cashman supervised the development of ancillary materials to support the book, and Donna Dennison ably coordinated research for the lovely covers that mark *Ways of the World*.

A final and much smaller community sustained this project and its author. It is that most intimate of villages that we know as a marriage. Here I pay wholly inadequate tribute to its other member, my wife, Suzanne Sturn. She knows how I feel, and no one else needs to.

To all my fellow villagers, I offer deep thanks for perhaps the richest intellectual experience of my professional life. I am grateful beyond measure.

Robert Strayer
La Selva Beach, California

Brief Contents

Contents

PART TWO   The Classical Era in World History, 500 B.C.E.–500 C.E.   *86*

PART THREE   An Age of Accelerating Connections, 500–1500   *208*

THE BIG PICTURE   Defining a Millennium   *209*

8   Commerce and Culture, 500–1500   *217*

PART FOUR   The Early Modern World, 1450–1750 *396*

15 Global Commerce, 1450–1750   *433*

16 Religion and Science, 1450–1750   *461*

PART FIVE   The European Moment in World History, 1750–1914   *490*

17 Atlantic Revolutions and Their Echoes, 1750–1914   *499*

18 Revolutions of Industrialization, 1750–1914   *527*

19 Internal Troubles, External Threats: China, the Ottoman Empire, and Japan, 1800–1914   559

20 Colonial Encounters, 1750–1914   589

Maps

Special Features

Landmarks

Snapshots

Prologue

From Cosmic History to Human History

IN THE BEGINNING, ACCORDING TO THE NAVAHO, the world was created by Holy People, who had long lived underground and were forced to the surface by a great flood, from which they escaped through a hollow reed. First Man and First Woman were later formed from ears of white and yellow corn. To the ancient Greeks, an original Cosmic Egg, floating on a formless mixture of air, water, and matter, gave birth to the deities of Earth and Sky, who then created the earth and all its living creatures, as well as the sun, moon, and stars. For the Hebrews of biblical times, God brought order out of a primordial chaos, creating light and darkness, the earth, and all its living creatures. Pronouncing it good, God then made the first humans, placing them in the Garden of Eden, where they soon encountered temptation and choice in the form of a serpent.

These are among the multitude of stories, or myths of origin, that seek to answer that fundamentally human question: what happened in the beginning? Such stories seek to anchor particular societies in a larger context, providing their people with a sense of place, purpose, and belonging. World historians are among the modern scholars who, like earlier tellers of creation stories, also seek to puzzle out the beginnings of the cosmos, of the earth, of life, and of humankind. Unlike myths of origin, though, modern creation stories rely largely on those fields of study that emerged from the Scientific Revolution of the sixteenth century and later—astronomy, physics, geology, biology. Such accounts claim to be truer and more certain, at least in a literal sense, for they can be checked and verified rather than simply accepted and believed. They are, however, stronger on *how* things began than on *why*. Although they provide a more factually detailed account of beginnings, they may have less to offer about the meaning of it all. Therefore, many people in the modern world have tried hard to reconcile scientifically derived understandings of "in the beginning" with the meaning-based accounts contained in long-standing religious traditions.

The History of the Universe

The very largest of these modern frameworks is sometimes called "big history." It is really the "history of everything" from the big bang to the present, and it extends over the enormous, almost unimaginable timescale of some 13.7 billion years, the current

$\mathcal{S}$napshot   The History of the Universe as a Cosmic Calendar[1]

Big bang	January 1	13.7 billion years ago
Stars and galaxies begin to form	End of January/ mid-February	12 billion years ago
Milky Way galaxy forms	March/early April	10 billion years ago
Origin of the solar system	September 9	4.7 billion years ago
Formation of the earth	September 15	4.5 billion years ago
Earliest life on earth	Late September/ early October	4 billion years ago
Oxygen forms on earth	December 1	1.3 billion years ago
First worms	December 16	658 million years ago
First fish, first vertebrates	December 19	534 million years ago
First reptiles, first trees	December 23	370 million years ago
Age of dinosaurs	December 24–28	329–164 million years ago
First humanlike creatures	December 31 (late evening)	2.7 million years ago
First agriculture	December 31: 11:59:35	12,000 years ago
Birth of the Buddha/ Greek civilization	December 31: 11:59:55	2,500 years ago
Birth of Jesus	December 31: 11:59:56	2,000 years ago
Aztec and Inca empires	December 31: 11:59:59	500 years ago

■ Change

What have been the major turning points in the prehuman phases of "big history"?

rough estimate of the age of the universe.[2] Big history provides the largest possible context in which the more familiar story of the human journey might be situated.

To make this vast expanse of time even remotely comprehensible, some scholars have depicted the history of the cosmos as if it were a single calendar year (see the Snapshot). On that cosmic calendar, most of the action took place in the first few milliseconds of January 1. As astronomers, physicists, and chemists tell it, the universe that we know began in an eruption of inconceivable power and heat. Out of that explosion of creation emerged matter, energy, gravity, electromagnetism, and the "strong" and "weak" forces that govern the behavior of atomic nuclei. As gravity pulled the rapidly expanding cosmic gases into increasingly dense masses, stars formed, with the first ones lighting up around 1 to 2 billion years after the big bang, or the end of January to mid-February on the cosmic calendar.

Hundreds of billions of stars followed, each with its own history, though following common patterns. Over eons of time, these stars came together in galaxies, such as our own Milky Way, which probably emerged in March or early April, and in even larger structures called groups, clusters, and superclusters. Within the stars, enormous nuclear reactions gave rise to the elements that are reflected in the periodic table known to all students of chemistry. But stars also collapse and die, and in doing so they sometimes generate supernova, black holes, and pulsars—phenomena at least as fantastic as the most exotic of earlier creation stories. Adding to the strangeness of our picture of the cosmos is the recent and controversial notion that perhaps 90 percent or more of the total mass of the universe is invisible to us, consisting of a mysterious and mathematically predicted substance known to scholars only as "dark matter."

The contemplation of cosmic history has prompted profound religious or philosophical questions about the meaning of human life. For some, it has engendered a sense of great insignificance in the face of cosmic vastness. In disputing the earth- and human-centered view of the Catholic Church, Voltaire, an eighteenth-century French thinker, wrote: "This little globe, nothing more than a point, rolls in space like so many other globes; we are lost in this immensity."[3] Nonetheless, human awareness of the mystery of this immeasurable universe renders us unique and generates for many people feelings of awe and humility that are almost religious. As tiny but knowing observers of this majestic cosmos, we have found ourselves living in a grander home than ever we knew before.

The History of a Planet

For most of us, one star, our own sun, is far more important than all the others, despite its quite ordinary standing among the billions of stars in the universe and its somewhat remote location on the outer edge of the Milky Way galaxy. Circling that star are a series of planets, formed of leftover materials from the sun's birth. One of those planets, the third from the sun and the fifth largest, is home to all of us. Human history—our history—takes place not only on the earth but also as part of the planet's history.

That history began with the emergence of the entire solar system about two-thirds of the way through cosmic history, some 4.7 billion years ago, or early September on the cosmic calendar. Geologists have learned a great deal about the history of the earth—the formation of its rocks and atmosphere, the movement of its continents, the collision of the tectonic plates that make up its crust, and the constantly changing landscape as mountains formed, volcanoes erupted, and erosion transformed the surface of the planet. All of this has been happening for more than 4 billion years and continues still.

The most remarkable feature of the earth's history—and so far as we know unrepeated elsewhere—was the emergence of life from the chemical soup of the early planet. It happened rather quickly, only about 600 million years after the earth itself took shape, or late September on the cosmic calendar. Then for some 3 billion years, life remained at the level of microscopic single-celled organisms. According to biologists, the many species of larger multicelled creatures—all of the flowers, shrubs, and trees as well as all of the animals of land, sea, and air—have evolved in an explosive proliferation of life-forms, punctuated by massive die-offs as well, over the past 600 million years, or since mid-December on the cosmic calendar.

Each of these species also has had a history as it struggled to find resources, cope with changing environments, and deal with competitors. The history of dinosaurs, for example, from their rise to their extinction, occupied about 165 million years, or about five days in late December on the cosmic calendar. Egocentric creatures that we are, however, virtually all of our history books and history courses focus entirely on a single species—our own, *Homo sapiens*, humankind. On the cosmic calendar, *Homo sapiens* is an upstart primate whose entire history occurred in the last few minutes of December 31. Almost all of what we normally study in history courses—agriculture, writing, civilizations, empires, industrialization—took place in the very last minute of that cosmic year.

Yet during that brief time, humankind has had a career more remarkable and arguably more consequential for the planet than any other species. At the heart of human uniqueness lies our amazing capacity for accumulating knowledge and skills. Other animals learn, of course, but they learn the same things over and over again. Twenty-first-century chimpanzees in the wild master the same skills as their ancestors did a million years ago, but the exceptional communication abilities provided by human language allow us to learn from one another, to express that learning in abstract symbols, and then to pass it on, cumulatively, to future generations. Thus we have moved from stone-tipped spears to nuclear weapons, from "talking drums" to the Internet, from ox-drawn carts to the family car.

This extraordinary ability has translated into a human impact on the earth that is unprecedented among all living species.[4] Human populations have multiplied far more extensively and have come to occupy a far greater range of environments than has any other large animal. Through our ingenious technologies, we have appropriated for ourselves, according to recent calculations, some 25 to 40 percent of the solar energy that enters the food chain. We have recently gained access to the stored solar energy of coal, gas, and oil, all of which have been millions of years in the making, and we have the capacity to deplete these resources in a few hundred or a few thousand years. Other forms of life have felt the impact of human activity, as numerous extinct or threatened species testify. Human beings have even affected the atmosphere itself as global warming alters the climate of the planet. Thus human history has been, and remains, of great significance not for ourselves alone, but also for the earth itself and for the many other living creatures with which we share it.

The History of the Human Species ... in a Single Paragraph: A Preview

The history of our species has occupied roughly the last 250,000 years, conventionally divided into three major phases, based on the kind of technology that was most widely practiced. The enormously long Paleolithic age, with its gathering and hunting way of life, accounts for 95 percent or more of the time that humans have occupied the planet. People utilizing a Paleolithic technology initially settled every major landmass on the planet and constructed the first human societies (see Chapter 1). Then beginning about 12,000 years ago with the first Agricultural Revolution, the domestication of plants and animals increasingly became the primary means of sustaining human life and societies. In giving rise to farming village societies, to pastoral communities depending on their herds of animals, and to state- and city-based civilizations, this agrarian way of life changed virtually everything and fundamentally shaped the human experience ever since. Finally around 1750, a quite sudden spurt in the rate of technological change, which we know as the Industrial Revolution, took hold. That vast increase in productivity, wealth, and human control over nature once again transformed almost every aspect of human life and gave rise to new kinds of societies that we call "modern."

Here then, in a single paragraph, is the history of humankind—the Paleolithic era, the agricultural era, and, most recently and briefly, the modern industrial era. Clearly this is a world history perspective, encompassing the human species as a whole rather than focusing solely on one or another of its particular and distinctive cultures. That perspective—known variously as planetary, global, or world history—has become increasingly prominent among students of the past. Why should this be so?

Why World History?

Not long ago—in the mid-twentieth century, for example—virtually all college-level history courses were organized in terms of particular civilizations or nations. In the United States, courses such as Western Civilization or some version of American History served to introduce students to the study of the past. Since then, however, a set of profound changes has pushed much of the historical profession in a different direction.

The world wars of the twentieth century, revealing as they did the horrendous consequences of unchecked nationalism, persuaded some historians that a broader view of the past might contribute to a notion of global citizenship. Economic and cultural globalization has highlighted both the interdependence of the world's peoples and their very unequal positions within that world. Moreover, we are aware as never before that our problems—whether they involve economic well-being, environmental deterioration, disease, or terrorism—respect no national boundaries. To many thoughtful people, a global present seemed to call for a global past. Furthermore, as colonial empires shrank and newly defined third world peoples

■ Change
Why has world history achieved an increasingly prominent place in American education in recent decades?

asserted themselves on the world stage, these people also insisted that their histories be accorded equivalent treatment with those of Europe. An explosion of new knowledge about the histories of Asia, Africa, and pre-Columbian America erupted from the research of scholars around the world. All of this has generated a "world history movement," reflected in college and high school curricula, in numerous conferences and specialized studies, and in a proliferation of textbooks, of which this is one.

This world history movement has attempted to create a global understanding of the human past that highlights broad patterns cutting across particular civilizations and countries, while acknowledging in an inclusive fashion the distinctive histories of its many peoples. This is, to put it mildly, a tall order. How is it possible to encompass within a single book or course the separate stories of the world's various peoples? Surely it must be something more than just recounting the history of one civilization or culture after another. How can we distill a common history of humankind as a whole from the distinct trajectories of particular peoples? Because no world history book or course can cover everything, what criteria should we use for deciding what to include and what to leave out? Such questions have ensured no end of controversy among students, teachers, and scholars of world history, making it one of the most exciting fields of historical inquiry.

Comparison, Connection, and Change: The Three Cs of World History

Despite much debate and argument, most world historians would probably agree on three major issues or questions that define their field of study. Each of them confronts a particular problem in our understanding of the past.

The first involves constant **comparison**. Whatever else it may be, world history is a comparative discipline, seeking to identify similarities and differences in the experience of the world's peoples. What is the difference between the development of agriculture in the Middle East and in Mesoamerica? Was the experience of women largely the same in all patriarchal societies? What did the Roman Empire and Han dynasty China have in common? Why did the Industrial Revolution and a modern way of life evolve first in Western Europe rather than somewhere else? What distinguished the Russian and Chinese revolutions? What different postures toward modernity emerged within the Islamic world? Describing and, if possible, explaining such similarities and differences are among the major tasks of world history. Comparison, then, is a recurring theme in this book, with expressions in every chapter.

Comparison has proven an effective tool in the struggle against Eurocentrism, the notion that Europeans or people of European descent have long been the primary movers and shakers of the historical process. That notion arose in recent centuries when Europeans were in fact the major source of innovation in the world and did for a time exercise something close to world domination. This temporary preeminence decisively shaped the way Europeans thought and wrote about their own histories and those of other people. In their own eyes, Europeans alone were progressive people, thanks to some cultural or racial superiority. Everyone else was stagnant, backward, savage, or barbarian. The unusual power of Europeans allowed them for a time to act on those beliefs and to impose such ways of thinking on much of the world. World historians have been among the critics of such Eurocentric views, for world history sets European achievements in a comparative and global context, helping us to sort out what was distinctive about its historical development and what similarities it bore to other major regions of the world.

The art of comparison is a learned skill, entailing several steps. It requires, first of all, asking explicitly comparative questions and determining what particular cases will be involved. If you want to compare revolutions, for example, you would need to decide which ones you are considering—American, French, Russian, Chinese, Cuban. Defining categories of comparison is a further step. Precisely which characteristics of these revolutions will you compare—their origins, their ideologies, the social classes involved, their outcomes? Finally, how will you present your comparison? You might choose a case-by-case analysis in which you would describe, say, the American Revolution first, followed by an account of the Cuban Revolution, which makes explicit comparisons with the former. Or you might choose a thematic approach in which you would consider first the origins of both revolutions, followed by a comparison of their ideologies, and so on. You will find examples of both approaches in this book.

A second major theme of world history involves the interaction, encounters, and **connections** among different and often distant peoples. What happened when people of distinct civilizations or cultures met? Focusing on cross-cultural connections represents an effort to counteract a habit of thinking about particular peoples, states, or cultures as self-contained and isolated communities. Despite the historical emergence of separate and distinct societies, none of them developed alone. Each was embedded in a network of relationships with both near and more distant peoples. Moreover, these cross-cultural connections did not begin with the voyages of Columbus. The Chinese, for example, interacted continuously with the nomadic peoples on their northern border; generated technologies that diffused across all of Eurasia; transmitted elements of their culture to Japan, Korea, and Vietnam; and assimilated a foreign religious tradition, Buddhism, which had originated in India. Though clearly distinctive, China was not a self-contained or isolated civilization. The encounter with strangers, or at least with strange ideas and practices, was everywhere one of the most powerful motors of change in human societies. Thus world history pays attention not only to the internal developments of particular civilizations or peoples but also to the networks, webs, and cross-cultural encounters in which they were enmeshed.

Third, historians of every kind are concerned always with what changes, what persists, and why. In world history, it is the "big picture" **changes**—those that impact large segments of humankind—that are of greatest interest. How did the transition from a gathering and hunting economy to one based on agriculture take place? How did cities, empires, and civilizations take shape in various parts of the world? What generated the amazing transformations of the "revolution of modernity" in recent centuries? World historians also pay attention to the changes that occur within and between particular civilizations. How can we explain the dramatic collapse of Maya civilization or the fall of the Roman Empire? How did Buddhism change when it entered China? How was Islam transformed when it encountered West African societies? What lay behind the emergence of a new balance of global power after 1500, one that featured the growing prominence of Europe on the world stage?

Both change and comparison provide an antidote to a persistent tendency of human thinking that historians call "essentialism." A more common term is "stereotyping." It refers to our inclination to define particular groups of people with an unchanging or essential set of characteristics. Women are nurturing; peasants are conservative; Americans are aggressive; Hindus are religious. Serious students of history soon become aware that every significant category of people contains endless divisions and conflicts and that human communities are constantly in flux. Peasants may often accept the status quo, except of course when they rebel, as they frequently have. Americans have experienced periods of isolationism and withdrawal from the world as well as times of aggressive engagement with it. Things change.

But some things persist, even if they also change. We should not allow an emphasis on change to blind us to the continuities of human experience. A recognizably Chinese state has operated for more than 2,000 years. Slavery and patriarchy persisted as human institutions for thousands of years until they were challenged in recent centuries, and in various forms they exist still. The teachings of Buddhism, Christianity, and Islam have endured for centuries, though with endless variations and transformations.

Comparisons, connections, and changes—all of them operating on a global scale—represent three ways of bringing some coherence to the multiple and complex stories of world history. They will recur repeatedly in the pages that follow.

Second Thoughts

To assess your mastery of the material in this prologue, see the **Online Study Guide** at bedfordstmartins.com/strayer.

What's the Significance?

myths of origin	big history	the three Cs
cosmic calendar	comparative history	

Big Picture Questions

1. What is the difference between religiously based myths of origin and creation stories derived from scientific accounts?
2. How do you respond personally to modern notions of the immense size and age of the universe?
3. What examples of comparison, connection, and change in world history would you like to explore further as your course unfolds?

Next Steps: For Further Study

For Web sites and documents related to this prologue, see **Make History** at bedfordstmartins.com/strayer.

David Christian, *Maps of Time* (2004). A brilliant survey of "big history" by a leading world historian.

Ross Dunn, ed., *The New World History* (2000). A collection of articles dealing with the teaching of world history.

Patrick Manning, *Navigating World History* (2003). An up-to-date overview of the growth of world history, the field's achievements, and the debates within it.

J. R. McNeill and William H. McNeill, *The Human Web* (2003). An approach to world history that emphasizes the changing webs of connection among human communities.

David Northrup, "Globalization and the Great Convergence: Rethinking World History in the Long Term," *Journal of World History* (September 2005). A thoughtful essay identifying broad patterns of human history.

"The Cosmic Time-Line," http://visav.phys.uvic.ca/~babul/AstroCourses/P303/BB-slide.htm. A more detailed cosmic calendar.

"World History for Us All," http://worldhistoryforusall.sdsu.edu/dev/default.htm. A model world history curriculum for high school courses.

Ways of the World

A Brief Global History

PART ONE
First Things First
Beginnings in History

TO 500 B.C.E.

Contents

Turning Points in Early World History

Both the ancient sages who developed their societies' creation myths and the grandparents who still relate the histories of their families have had to decide at what point to begin their stories and what major turning points in those stories to highlight. So too must historians, whether they narrate the tale of a village, a city, a nation, a civilization, or the entire human community. For world historians, concerned with humankind as a whole, four major "beginnings," each of them an extended historical process, have charted the initial stages of the human journey.

The Emergence of Humankind

Ever since Charles Darwin, most scholars have come to view human beginnings in the context of biological change on the planet. In considering this enormous process, we operate on a timescale quite different from the billions of years that mark the history of the universe and of the earth. According to archeologists and anthropologists, the evolutionary line of descent leading to *Homo sapiens* diverged from that leading to chimpanzees, our closest primate relatives, some 5 million to 6 million years ago, and it happened in eastern and southern Africa. There, perhaps twenty or thirty different species emerged, all of them members of the Homininae (or hominid) family of humanlike creatures. What they all shared was bipedalism, the ability to walk upright on two legs. In 1976, the archeologist Mary Leakey uncovered in what is now Tanzania a series of footprints of three such hominid individuals, preserved in cooling volcanic ash about 3.5 million years ago. Two of them walked side by side, apparently holding hands.

Over time, these hominid species changed. Their brains grew larger, as evidenced by the size of their skulls. About 2.3 million years ago, a hominid creature known as *Homo habilis* began to make and use simple stone tools. Others started to eat meat, at least occasionally. By 1 million years ago, some hominid species, especially *Homo erectus*, began to migrate out of Africa, and their remains have been found in various parts of Eurasia. This species is also associated with the first controlled use of fire.

Eventually all of these earlier hominid species died out, except one: *Homo sapiens*, ourselves. We too emerged first in Africa and quite recently, probably no more than 250,000 years ago, although there is constant debate among specialists about these matters. For a long time, all of the small number of *Homo sapiens* lived in Africa, but sometime after 100,000 years ago, they too began to migrate out of Africa onto the Eurasian landmass, then to Australia, and ultimately into the Western Hemisphere and the Pacific islands. The great experiment of human history had begun.

The Global Dispersion of
Humankind (p. 14)

The Globalization of Humankind

Today, every significant landmass on earth is occupied by human beings, but it was not always so. A mere half million years ago our species did not exist, and only 100,000 years ago that species was limited to Africa and numbered, some scholars believe, fewer than 10,000 individuals. These ancient ancestors of ours were armed with a very limited technology of stone tools with which to confront the dangers of the natural world. How did *Homo sapiens* move from such a modest role in the scheme of things to a worldwide and increasingly dominant presence? What kind of societies, technologies, and understandings of the world accompanied, and perhaps facilitated, this globalization of humankind?

The phase of human history during which these initial migrations took place is known to scholars as the *Paleolithic* era. The term "Paleolithic" literally means the "old stone age," but it refers more generally to a food-collecting or gathering and hunting way of life, before agriculture allowed people to grow food or raise animals deliberately. Lasting until roughly 11,000 years ago, the Paleolithic era represents over 95 percent of the time that human beings have inhabited the earth, although it accounts for only about 12 percent of the total number of people who have lived on the planet.

It was during this time that *Homo sapiens* colonized the world, making themselves at home in every environmental niche, from the frigid Arctic to the rain forests of Central Africa and Brazil, in mountains, deserts, and plains. It was an amazing achievement, accomplished by no other large species. Accompanying this global migration were slow changes in the technological tool kits of early humankind as well as early attempts to impose meaning on the world through art, ritual, and religion. Although often neglected by historians and history textbooks, this long period of the human experience merits greater attention and is the focus of Chapter 1.

The Revolution of Farming and Herding

In early 2008, almost all of the world's 6.6 billion people lived from the food grown on farms and gardens and from domesticated animals raised for their

Teosinte

Modern Corn

Teosinte and Maize/Corn
(p. 42)

meat, milk, or eggs, but this was not always so. In fact, before 11,000 years ago, no one survived in this fashion. Then, repeatedly and fairly rapidly, at least in world history terms, human communities in parts of the Middle East, Asia, Africa, and the Americas began the laborious process of domesticating animals and selecting seeds to be planted. This momentous accomplishment represents another "first" in the human story. After countless millennia of relying on the gathering of wild foods and the hunting of wild animals, why and how did human societies begin to practice agriculture and herding? What changes to human life did this new technology bring with it?

This food-producing revolution, considered in Chapter 2, surely marks the single most significant and enduring transformation of the human condition, providing the foundation for virtually everything that followed. The entire period from the beginning of agriculture to the Industrial Revolution around 1750 might be considered a single phase of the human story—the age of agriculture—calculated now on a timescale of millennia or centuries rather than the more extended periods of earlier eras. Although the age of agriculture was far shorter than the immense Paleolithic era that preceded it, farming and herding allowed for a substantial increase in human numbers.

In the various beginnings of food production lay the foundations for some of the most enduring divisions within the larger human community. Much depended on the luck of the draw—on the climate and soils, on the various wild plants and animals that were available for domestication. Many agricultural peoples lived in small settled villages, independent of larger political structures, while drawing their food supply from their own gardens and farms. Some depended on root crops, such as potatoes in the Andes; others relied on tree crops, such as the banana; the most favored areas were those where highly nutritious wild grains such as rice, wheat, or corn could be domesticated. In more arid regions where farming was impossible, some peoples, known as pastoralists, came to depend heavily on their herds of domesticated animals. Because they moved frequently and in regular patterns, in search of pasturelands, they are often referred to as nomads. In terms of animal husbandry, the Americas were at a distinct disadvantage, for there were few large animals that could be tamed—no goats, sheep, pigs, horses, camels, or cattle. In the Afro-Eurasian world, conflicts between settled agricultural peoples and more mobile pastoral peoples represented an enduring pattern of interaction across the region.

The Turning Point of Civilization

The most prominent and powerful human communities to emerge from the Agricultural Revolution were those we often designate as "civilizations," societies that were based in bustling cities and governed by powerful states. Virtually all of the world's people now live in a state with a formal political authority that controls a particular territory, whether it is a tiny country such as The Gambia, a single city such as Singapore, or a huge territory such as Russia. The political, economic, and cultural life of state-based societies everywhere gives prominence to cities. By the early twenty-first century, about half of the world's population lived in urban centers. States and cities have become so common as to seem almost natural.

In world history terms, however, the appearance of states and cities is a rather recent phenomenon. Not until several thousand years *after* the beginning of agriculture did the first cities and states emerge, around 3500 B.C.E. Well after 1000 C.E., substantial numbers of people still lived in communities without any state or urban structures. Nonetheless, people living in state- and city-based societies or civilizations have long constituted the most powerful and innovative human communities on the planet. They gave rise to empires of increasing size, to enduring cultural and religious traditions, to new technologies, to sharp class inequalities, to male domination (patriarchy), and to large-scale warfare.

For all of these reasons, civilizations have featured prominently in accounts of world history, sometimes crowding out the stories of other kinds of human communities. The earliest civilizations, which emerged between 3500 and 500 B.C.E., have long fascinated professional historians and lovers of history everywhere. In at least six separate places—Mesopotamia (present-day Iraq), Egypt, Pakistan and northern India, China, Peru, and Mexico—such state- and city-based societies emerged. What was their relationship to the Agricultural Revolution? What new ways of life did they bring to the experience of humankind? These are the questions that are examined in Chapter 3.

A Note on Dates

Recently it has become standard in the Western world to refer to dates prior to the birth of Christ as B.C.E. (before the Common Era), replacing the earlier B.C. (before Christ) usage. This convention is an effort to become less Christian-centered and

Eurocentric in our use of language, although the chronology remains linked to the birth of Jesus. Similarly the time following the birth of Christ is referred to as C.E. (the Common Era) rather than A.D. (*Anno Domini*, Latin for "year of the Lord"). Dates in the more distant past are designated in this book simply as so many "years ago." Of course, these conventions are only some of the many ways that human societies have reckoned time. The Chinese frequently dated important events in terms of the reign of particular emperors, while Muslims created a new calendar beginning with Year 1, marking Muhammad's emigration to Medina in 622 C.E. As with so much else, the ways that we measure time reflect the cultures in which we have been born and the historical experience of our societies.

Landmarks of Early World History, to 500 B.C.E.

27,000	26,000	25,000	24,000	23,000	22,000	21,000	20,000	19,000	18,000	17,000	16,000	15,000	14,000

Africa

250,000 years ago
Emergence of *Homo sapiens*

100,000 years ago
Human migration out of Africa into Eurasia

16,000–9000 B.C.E.
Development of distinctive regional cultures

Eurasia

60,000 years ago
Human entry into Australia

40,000 years ago
Human entry into Europe

15,000 B.C.E.
Lascaux cave paintings in southern France

The Americas

30,000–15,000 years ago
Human entry into the Americas

13,000	12,000	11,000	10,000	9000	8000	7000	6000	5000	4000	3000	2000	1000	900

3000–2000 B.C.E.
Agricultural breakthroughs
in sub-Saharan Africa

13,000–11,000 B.C.E.
Harvesting of wild grains
in northeastern Africa

9000 B.C.E.
Cattle herding in
Sudanic Africa

3100 B.C.E.
Unification
of Egypt

1000 B.C.E.
Beginning of
ironworking in
sub-Saharan
Africa

3500 B.C.E.
Emergence
of Nubian
civilization

2000 B.C.E. Beginnings
of Bantu migrations

1650 B.C.E. Hyksos
invasion of Egypt

14,000–8000 B.C.E.
End of last Ice Age

9000–7000 B.C.E. First agricultural
breakthrough (Fertile Crescent)

4000 B.C.E.
Domestication
of horses in
Ukraine/south-
ern Russia

2000 B.C.E. Beginnings
of Indus Valley and
Chinese civilizations

1792–1750 B.C.E.
Reign of Hammurabi
in Babylonian Empire

3000–1000 B.C.E.
Indo-European migrations

3500 B.C.E.
Beginning of
Mesopotamian
civilization

1500–1000 B.C.E.
Beginnings of
ironworking in
Anatolia

10,000–9000 B.C.E.
Flourishing of Clovis culture

9000 B.C.E.
Extinction of various large
mammals in North America

3000–2000 B.C.E.
Cultivation of maize, squash, and
beans in Mesoamerica

3000–2000 B.C.E.
Cultivation of potatoes, quinoa,
and manioc in the Andes

3000–1800 B.C.E.
Norte Chico ("mother
civilization" of the Andes)

1000 B.C.E.
Beginnings
of Olmec
civilization

900 B.C.E.
Chavín religious
cult in Peru

CHAPTER ONE

First Peoples

Populating the Planet

TO 10,000 B.C.E.

"We do not want cattle, just wild animals to hunt and water that we can drink."[1] That was the view of Gudo Mahiya, a prominent member of the Hadza people of northern Tanzania, when he was questioned in 1997 about his interest in a settled life of farming and cattle raising. With only about 1,000 total members, the Hadza represent one of the very last peoples on earth to continue a way of life that was universal among humankind until 10,000 to 12,000 years ago. At the beginning of the twenty-first century, several hundred Hadza still made a living by hunting game, collecting honey, digging up roots, and gathering berries and fruit. They lived in quickly assembled grass huts located in small mobile camps averaging eighteen people and moved frequently around their remote region. Almost certainly their way of life is doomed, as farmers, governments, missionaries, and now tourists descend on them. The likely disappearance of their culture parallels the experience of many other such societies, which have been on the defensive against more numerous and powerful neighbors for 10,000 years.

NONETHELESS, THAT WAY OF LIFE SUSTAINED HUMANKIND for more than 95 percent of the time that our species has inhabited the earth. During countless centuries, human beings successfully adapted to a wide variety of environments without benefit of deliberate farming or animal husbandry. Instead, our early ancestors wrested a livelihood by gathering wild foods such as berries, nuts, roots, and grain; by scavenging dead animals; by hunting live animals; and by fishing. Known to scholars as "gathering and hunting" peoples, they were foragers or food collectors

---

Paleolithic Art: The rock art of gathering and hunting peoples has been found in Africa, Europe, Australia, and elsewhere. This image from the San people of southern Africa represents aspects of their outer life in the form of wild animals and hunters with bows as well as the inner life of their shamans during a trance, reflected in the elongated figures with both human and animal features. (Image courtesy of S.A. Tourism) rather than food producers. Instead of requiring the earth to produce what they wanted, they took—or perhaps borrowed—what nature had to offer. Because they used stone rather than metal tools, they also have been labeled "Paleolithic," or "old stone age," peoples.

History courses and history books often neglect this long phase of the human journey and instead choose to begin the story with the coming of agriculture about 12,000 years ago or with the advent of civilizations about 5,000 years ago. Some historians identify "real history" with writing and so dismiss the Paleolithic era as largely unknowable because its people did not write. Others, impressed with the rapid pace of change in human affairs since the coming of agriculture, assume that nothing much of real significance happened in the Paleolithic era—and no change meant no history.

But does it make sense to ignore the first 200,000 years or more of human experience? Although written records are absent, scholars have learned a great deal about these people through their material remains: stones and bones, fossilized seeds, rock paintings and engravings, and much more. Archeologists, biologists, botanists, demographers, linguists, and anthropologists have contributed much to our growing understanding of gathering and hunting peoples. Furthermore, the achievements of Paleolithic peoples—the initial settlement of the planet, the creation of the earliest human societies, the beginning of reflection on the great questions of life and death—deserve our attention. The changes they wrought, though far more slowly than we are accustomed to, provided the foundation on which all subsequent human history was constructed. Our grasp of the human past is incomplete—massively so—if we choose to disregard them.

Out of Africa to the Ends of the Earth: First Migrations

The first 150,000 years or more of human experience was an exclusively African story. Around 250,000 years ago, in the grasslands of eastern and southern Africa, *Homo sapiens* first emerged, following in the footsteps of many other hominid species before it. Time and climate have erased much of the record of these early people, and Africa has witnessed much less archeological research than have other parts of the world, especially Europe. Nonetheless, scholars have turned up evidence of distinctly human behavior in Africa long before its appearance elsewhere. Africa, almost certainly, was the place where the "human revolution" occurred, where "culture," defined as learned or invented ways of living, became more important than biology in shaping behavior.

What kinds of uniquely human activity show up in the early African record?[2] In the first place, human beings began to inhabit new environments within Africa—forests and deserts—where no hominids had lived before. Accompanying these movements of people were technological innovations of various kinds: stone blades and points fastened to shafts replaced the earlier "hand axes"; tools made from bones appeared, and so did grindstones. Evidence of hunting and fishing, not just the scavenging of dead animals, marks a new phase in human food collection.

$\mathcal{S}$napshot   **The Long Road to the Global Presence of Humankind**

(all dates approximate)	Years Ago
Earliest bipedal hominids (walking upright on two legs)	7 million to 6 million
Homo habilis (earliest use of stone tools)	2.5 million
Homo erectus (first controlled use of fire and first hominid migrations out of Africa)	1.9 million to 200,000
Earliest *Homo sapiens* in Africa	250,000
Beginnings of human migration out of Africa	100,000
Human entry into eastern Asia	70,000
Human entry into Australia (first use of boats)	60,000–40,000
Human entry into Europe	40,000
Extinction of large mammals in Australia	30,000
Human entry into the Americas	30,000–15,000
Cave art in Europe	25,000
Extinction of Neanderthals	25,000
End of last Ice Age (global warming)	16,000–10,000
Earliest agricultural revolutions	12,000–10,000
Extinction of large mammals in North America	11,000
Austronesian migration to Pacific islands and Madagascar	3,500–1,000
Human entry into New Zealand (last major region to receive human settlers)	1,000

Settlements were planned around the seasonal movement of game and fish. Patterns of exchange over a distance of almost 200 miles indicate larger networks of human communication. The use of body ornaments, beads, and pigments such as ochre as well as possible planned burials suggest the kind of social and symbolic behavior that has characterized human activity ever since. All of this occurred before 100,000 years ago and, based on current evidence, long before such activity surfaced elsewhere in the world.

Then, sometime after 100,000 years ago, human beings began their long trek out of Africa and into Eurasia, Australia, the Americas, and, much later, the islands of the Pacific (see Map 1.1). In occupying the planet, members of our species accomplished

Map 1.1   The Global Dispersion of Humankind

With origins in Africa perhaps 250,000 years ago, members of our species (*Homo sapiens*) have migrated to every environmental niche on the planet over the past 100,000 years.

(30,000–15,000 years ago)

GREENLAND

NORTH AMERICA

(40,000

ATLANTIC OCEAN

PACIFIC OCEAN

Equator

Easter Island

(1500 years ago)

SOUTH AMERICA

(by 12,500 years ago)

0   1,000   2,000 miles

0   1,000   2,000 kilometers

CHAPTER 1 / FIRST PEOPLES: POPULATING THE PLANET, TO 10,000 B.C.E.

15

EUROPE
years ago)

ASIA

(70,000 years ago)

PACIFIC OCEAN

(100,000 years ago)

AFRICA

Equator

(3500 years ago)

(1500 years ago)

(60,000–40,000 years ago)

AUSTRALIA

INDIAN OCEAN

(1000 years ago)
NEW ZEALAND

Ice sheet (20,000 years ago)
Land bridges (20,000 years ago)
Human expansion (dates for earliest human occupation)

ANTARCTICA

the remarkable feat of learning to live in virtually every environmental niche on earth, something that no other large animal had done; and they did it with only stone tools and a gathering and hunting technology to aid them. Furthermore, much of this long journey occurred during the difficult climatic conditions of the last Ice Age (at its peak around 20,000 years ago), when thick ice sheets covered much of northern Eurasia and North America. The Ice Age did give these outward-bound human beings one advantage, however: the amount of water frozen in northern glaciers lowered sea levels around the planet, creating land bridges among various regions that were separated after the glaciers melted. Britain was then joined to Europe; eastern Siberia was connected to Alaska; and New Guinea, Australia, and Tasmania were all part of a huge supercontinent known as Sahul.

Into Eurasia

■ Change
What was the sequence of human migration across the planet?

Human migration out of Africa led first to the Middle East and from there westward into Europe about 40,000 years ago and eastward into Asia. Among the most carefully researched areas of early human settlement in Eurasia are those in southern France and northern Spain. Colder Ice Age climates around 20,000 years ago apparently pushed more northerly European peoples southward into warmer regions. There they altered their hunting habits, focusing on reindeer and horses, and developed new technologies such as spear throwers and perhaps the bow and arrow as well as many different kinds of stone tools.[3] Most remarkably, they also left a record of their world in hundreds of cave paintings, depicting reindeer, bulls, horses, and other animals, brilliantly portrayed in colors of red, yellow, brown, and black. Images of human beings, impressions of human hands, and various abstract designs, perhaps an early form of writing, often accompanied the cave paintings.

The Lascaux Caves
Discovered by four teenage boys in 1940, the Lascaux caves in southern France contain some 2,000 images, dating to perhaps 17,000 years ago. Many of them depict in quite realistic form the wild animals of the region—oxen, bulls, horses, ibex, and birds. (JM Labat/ Photo Researchers, Inc.)

Scholars have debated endlessly what insights these remarkable images might provide into the mental world of Paleolithic Europeans.[4] Were they examples of "totemic" thinking—the belief that particular groups of people were associated with, or descended from, particular animals? Did they represent a form of "hunting magic" intended to enhance the success of these early hunters? Because many of the paintings were located deep within caves, were they perhaps part of religious or ritual practices or rites of passage? Were they designed to pass on information to future generations? Or did they symbolize, as some recent scholars contend, a coded representation of a Paleolithic worldview divided into male and female realms, both opposed to and balancing each other? We simply do not know. Nonetheless, these images excite our imagination still, 20,000 years or more after they were created. In them we sense a kinship with the humanity of our distant ancestors.

Farther east, archeologists have uncovered still other remarkable Paleolithic adaptations to Ice Age conditions. Across the vast plains of Central Europe, Ukraine, and Russia, new technologies emerged, including bone needles, multilayered clothing, weaving, nets, storage pits, baskets, and pottery. Partially underground dwellings constructed from the bones and tusks of mammoths compensated for the absence of caves and rock shelters. All of this suggests that some of these people settled down in more permanent settlements, at least temporarily abandoning their nomadic journeys. Associated with these Eastern European peoples were numerous female figurines. Carved from stone, antlers, mammoth tusks, or, occasionally, baked clay, these so-called Venus figurines depict the female form, often with exaggerated breasts, buttocks, hips, and stomachs. They were not limited to a single region but have been found all across Europe, from Spain to Russia, suggesting a network of human communication and cultural diffusion over a wide area.

Into Australia

Early human migration to Australia, currently dated to around 60,000 years ago, came from Indonesia and involved another "first" in human affairs—the use of boats. Over time, people settled in most regions of this huge continent, though quite sparsely. Scholars estimate the population of Australia at about 300,000 people in 1788, when the first Europeans arrived. Over tens of thousands of years, these people had developed perhaps 250 languages; collected a wide variety of bulbs, tubers, roots, seeds, and cereal grasses; and hunted large and small animals, as well as birds, fish, and other marine life. A relatively simple technology, appropriate to a gathering and hunting economy, sustained Australia's Aboriginal people into modern times. When outsiders arrived in the late eighteenth century, all of the continent's people still practiced that ancient way of life, despite the presence of agriculture in nearby New Guinea.

Accompanying their technological simplicity and traditionalism was the development of an elaborate and complex outlook on the world, known as the Dreamtime. Expressed in endless stories, in extended ceremonies, and in the evocative rock art of the continent's peoples, the Dreamtime recounted the beginning of things; how ancestral beings crisscrossed the land, creating its rivers, hills, rocks, and waterholes; how various peoples came to inhabit the land; and how they relate to animals and to one another. In this view of the world, everything in the natural order was a vibration, an echo, a footprint of these ancient happenings, which link the current inhabitants intimately to particular places and to timeless events in the past.

The journeys of the Dreamtime's ancestral beings reflect in a general way the networks of migration, communication, and exchange that linked the continent's many Paleolithic peoples. Far from isolated groups, they had long exchanged particular stones, pigments, materials for ropes and baskets, wood for spears, feathers and shells for ornaments, and an addictive psychoactive drug known as *pituri* over distances of hundreds of miles.[5] Songs, dances, stories, and rituals likewise circulated. Precisely how far back in time these networks extend is difficult to pinpoint, but it seems clear that Paleolithic Australia, like ancient Europe, was both many separate worlds and, at the same time, one loosely connected world.

Into the Americas

The earliest settlement of the Western Hemisphere occurred much later than that of Australia, for it took some time for human beings to penetrate the frigid lands of eastern Siberia, which was the jumping-off point for the move into the Americas. Experts continue to argue about precisely when the first migrations occurred (somewhere between 30,000 and 15,000 years ago), about the route of migration (by land across the Bering Strait or by sea down the west coast of North America), about how many separate migrations took place, and about how long it took for people to penetrate to the tip of South America.[6] There is, however, good evidence of human activity in southern Chile by 12,500 years ago.

The first clearly defined and widespread cultural tradition in the Americas is associated with people who made a distinctive projectile point, known to archeologists as a Clovis point. Scattered all over North America, Clovis culture flourished around 12,000 to 11,000 years ago. Scattered bands of Clovis people ranged over huge areas, camping along rivers, springs, and waterholes, where large animals congregated. Although they certainly hunted smaller animals and gathered many wild plants, Clovis people show up in the archeological record most dramatically as hunters of very large mammals, such as mammoths and bison. Killing a single mammoth could provide food for many weeks or, in cold weather, for much of the winter. The wide distribution of Clovis point technology suggests yet again a regional pattern of cultural diffusion and at least indirect communication over a large area.

Then, about 10,900 years ago, all trace of the Clovis people disappears from the archeological record at the same time that many species of large animals, including the mammoth and several species of horses and camels, also became extinct. Did the Clovis people hunt these animals to extinction and then vanish themselves as their source of food disappeared? Or did the drier climate that came with the end of the Ice Age cause this "megafaunal extinction"? Experts disagree, but what happened next was the creation of a much greater diversity of cultures as people adapted to this new situation in various ways. Hunters on the Great Plains continued to pursue bison, which largely avoided the fate of the mammoths. Others learned to live in the desert, taking advantage of seasonal plants and smaller animals, while those who lived near the sea, lakes, or streams drew on indigenous fish and birds. Many peoples retained their gathering and hunting way of life into modern times, while others became farmers and, in a few favored regions, later developed cities and large-scale states.[7]

Into the Pacific

The last phase of the great human migration to the ends of the earth took place in the Pacific Ocean and was distinctive in many ways. In the first place, it occurred quite recently, jumping off only about 3,500 years ago from the Bismarck and Solomon islands near New Guinea as well as from the islands of the Philippines. It was everywhere a waterborne migration, making use of oceangoing canoes and remarkable navigational skills, and it happened very quickly and over a huge area of the planet. Speaking Austronesian languages that trace back to southern China, these oceanic voyagers had settled every habitable piece of land in the Pacific basin within about 2,500 years. Other Austronesians had sailed west from Indonesia across the Indian Ocean to settle the island of Madagascar off the coast of eastern Africa. This extraordinary process of expansion—both rapid and extensive—made the Austronesian family of languages the most widespread in the world. With the occupation of Aotearoa (New Zealand) about 1200 C.E., the initial human settlement of the planet was finally complete (see Map 1.2).

In contrast with all of the other migrations, these Pacific voyages were undertaken by people with an agricultural technology, who carried both domesticated plants and animals in their canoes. Both men and women made these journeys, suggesting a deliberate intention to colonize new lands. Virtually everywhere they went, two developments followed. One was the creation of highly stratified societies or chiefdoms, of which ancient Hawaiian society is a prime example. In Hawaii, an elite class of chiefs with political and military power ruled over a mass of commoners. The other development was the dramatic impact that these migrations had on the environment of previously uninhabited islands. Many species of

■ **Comparison**
How did Austronesian migrations differ from other early patterns of human movement?

Map 1.2 Migration of Austronesian-Speaking People
People speaking Austronesian languages completed the human settlement of the earth quite recently as they settled the islands of the vast Pacific and penetrated the Indian Ocean to Madagascar, off the coast of southeast Africa.

animals quickly became extinct, especially large flightless birds. The destruction of the forests of Rapa Nui (Easter Island) between the fifteenth and seventeenth centuries C.E. brought famine, violent conflict, and a sharp population decline to this small island society, while the absence of large trees ensured that no one could leave the island, for they could no longer build the canoes that had brought them there.[8]

The Ways We Were

During their long journeys across the earth, Paleolithic people created a multitude of separate and distinct societies, each with its own history, culture, language, identity, stories, and rituals, but the limitations of a gathering and hunting technology using stone tools imposed some commonalities on these ancient people. Based on the archeological record and on the example of gathering and hunting societies that still existed in modern times, scholars have sketched out some of the common features of these early societies.

The First Human Societies

■ Change

In what ways did a gathering and hunting economy shape other aspects of Paleolithic societies?

Above all else, these Paleolithic societies were small, consisting of bands of twenty-five to fifty people, in which all relationships were intensely personal and thought of normally in terms of kinship. No anonymity or "hiding in the crowd" was possible in a society of relatives. The available technology permitted only a very low population density and ensured an extremely slow rate of population growth. Scholars estimate that world population may have been as low as 10,000 people around 100,000 years ago and grew slowly to 500,000 by 30,000 years ago and then to 6 million by 10,000 years ago.[9] These Paleolithic bands were seasonally mobile or nomadic, moving frequently and in regular patterns to exploit the resources of wild plants and animals on which they depended. The low productivity of a gathering and hunting economy normally did not allow the production of much surplus, and because they were on the move so often, transporting an accumulation of goods was out of the question.

All of this meant highly egalitarian societies, lacking the many inequalities of wealth and power that came with later agricultural and urban life. With no formal chiefs, kings, bureaucrats, soldiers, nobles, or priests, these people were perhaps freer of tyranny and oppression than any subsequent kind of human society, even if they were more constrained by the forces of nature. Without specialists, most people possessed the same set of skills, although male and female tasks often differed sharply. Relationships between women and men usually were far more equal than in later societies. As the primary food gatherers, women provided the bulk of the family "income." One study of a modern gathering and hunting society in southern Africa found that plants, normally gathered by women, provided 70 percent of the diet, while meat, hunted by men, accounted for just 30 percent.[10]

When the British navigator and explorer Captain James Cook first encountered the gathering and hunting peoples of Australia in 1770, he described them, perhaps a little enviously, in this way:

> They live in a Tranquillity which is not disturb'd by the Inequality of Conditions: The Earth and sea of their own accord furnishes them with all things necessary for life, they covet not Magnificient houses, Household-stuff.... In short they seem'd to set no value upon any thing we gave them.... They think themselves provided with all the necessarys of Life.[11]

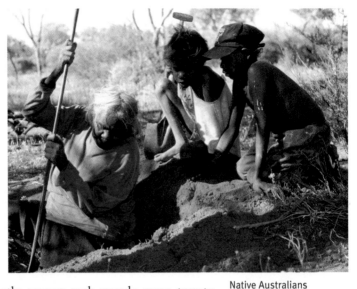

Native Australians
A number of Aboriginal Australians maintained their gathering and hunting way of life well into the twentieth century. Here an older woman shows two young boys how to dig for honey ants, a popular food. (Bill Bachman/Alamy)

The Europeans who settled permanently among such people some twenty years later, however, found a society in which physical competition among men was expressed in frequent one-on-one combat and in formalized but bloody battles. It also meant recurrent, public, and quite brutal beatings of wives by their husbands.[12] Although sometimes romanticized by Europeans, the relative social equality of Paleolithic peoples did not always generate a utopia of social harmony.

Like all human cultures, Paleolithic societies had rules and structures. A gender-based division of labor usually cast men as hunters and women as gatherers. Values emphasizing reciprocal sharing of goods resulted in clearly defined rules about distributing the meat from an animal kill. Rules about incest and adultery governed sexual behavior, while understandings about who could hunt or gather in particular territories regulated economic activity. Leaders arose as needed to organize a task such as a hunt, but without conferring permanent power on individuals.

Economy and the Environment

For a long time, gathering and hunting peoples were viewed as "primitive," impoverished, barely eking out a living from the land. In more recent decades, anthropologists studying contemporary Paleolithic societies—those that survived into the twentieth century—began to paint a different picture. They noted that gathering and hunting people frequently worked fewer hours to meet their material needs than did people in agricultural or industrial societies and so had more "leisure time." One scholar referred to them as "the original affluent society," not because they had so much, but because they wanted or needed so little.[13] Nonetheless, life expectancy was low, probably little more than thirty-five years on average; life in the wild was surely dangerous; and dependency on the vagaries of nature rendered it insecure as well.

Paleolithic people were not always at the mercy of nature; at times, they acted to alter the natural environment substantially. The use of deliberately set fires to encourage the growth of particular plants certainly changed the landscape and in Australia led to the proliferation of fire-resistant eucalyptus trees at the expense of other plant species. In many parts of the world—Australia, North America, Siberia, Madagascar, Pacific islands—the extinction of various large animals followed fairly quickly after the arrival of human beings, leading scholars to suggest that Paleolithic humankind played a major role, coupled perhaps with changing climates, in the disappearance of these animals. Other hominid, or humanlike, species, such as the Neanderthals in Europe or the recently discovered Flores man in Indonesia, also perished after living side by side with *Homo sapiens* for millennia. Whether their disappearance occurred through massacre, interbreeding, or peaceful competition, they were among the casualties of the rise of humankind. Thus the biological environment inhabited by gathering and hunting peoples was not wholly "natural" but was shaped in part by their own hands.

The Realm of the Spirit

The religious or spiritual dimension of Paleolithic culture has been very hard to pin down because bones and stones tell us little about what people thought, art is subject to many interpretations, and the experience of contemporary gathering and hunting peoples may not reflect the more distant past. There is, however, clear evidence for a rich ceremonial life. The presence of rock art deep inside caves and far from living spaces suggests a "ceremonial space" separate from ordinary living. The extended rituals of contemporary Australian Aboriginal people, which sometimes last for weeks, confirm this impression, as do numerous and elaborate burial sites found throughout the world. No full-time religious specialists or priests led these ceremonies, but part-time shamans, people believed to be especially skilled at dealing with the spirit world, emerged as the need arose. Such people often entered an altered state of consciousness or a trance while performing the ceremonies, often with the aid of psychoactive drugs.

Precisely how these people understood the nonmaterial world is hard to reconstruct, and speculation abounds. Evidence from ancient Africa suggests a variety of understandings: some Paleolithic societies were apparently monotheistic; others saw several levels of supernatural beings, including a Creator Deity, various territorial spirits, and the spirits of dead ancestors; still others believed in an impersonal force suffused throughout the natural order that could be accessed by shamans during a trance dance.[14] The prevalence of Venus figurines and other symbols all across Europe has convinced some scholars, but not all, that Paleolithic religious thought had a strongly feminine dimension, embodied in a Great Goddess and concerned with the regeneration and renewal of life.[15] It seems likely that many gathering and hunting peoples developed a cyclical view of time that drew on the changing phases of the moon and on the cycles of female fertility—birth, menstruation, pregnancy,

The Willendorf Venus
Less than four and a half inches in height and dating to about 25,000 years ago, this female figure, which was found near the town of Willendorf in Austria, has become the most famous of the many Venus figurines. Certain features—the absence of both face and feet, the coils of hair around her head, the prominence of her breasts and sexual organs—have prompted much speculation among scholars about the significance of these intriguing carvings. (Naturhistorisches Museum, Vienna, Austria/The Bridgeman Art Library)

Snapshot **The Paleolithic Era in Perspective**[16]

	Paleolithic Era (from 250,000 to 10,000 years ago)	Agricultural Era (from 10,000 to 200 years ago)	Modern Industrial Era (since 1800)
Duration of each era, as a percentage of 250,000 years	96%	4%	0.08%
Percent of people who lived, out of 80 billion total	12%	68%	20%
Percent of years lived in each era (reflects changing life expectancies)	9%	62%	29%

new birth, and death. Such understandings of the cosmos, which saw endlessly repeated patterns of regeneration and disintegration, were very different than later Western views, which saw time moving in a straight line toward some predetermined goal.[17]

Settling Down: "The Great Transition"

Though glacially slow by contemporary standards, Paleolithic cultures changed over time as people moved into new environments, as populations slowly grew, as climates altered, and as different human groups interacted with one another. For example, all over the Afro-Eurasian world after 25,000 years ago, a tendency toward the miniaturization of stone tools is evident. Known as "micro-blades," these smaller and more refined spear points, arrowheads, knives, and scrapers were carefully struck from larger cores and often mounted in antler, bone, or wooden handles.[18] This ancient and global technological change was similar perhaps to the miniaturization of electronic components in the twentieth century. Another important change in the strategies of Paleolithic people was the collection of wild grains, which represented a major addition to the food supply beyond the use of roots, berries, and nuts. This innovation originated in northeastern Africa around 16,000 years ago.

But the most striking and significant change in the lives of Paleolithic peoples occurred as the last Ice Age came to an end between 16,000 and 10,000 years ago. What followed was a general global warming, though one with periodic fluctuations and cold snaps. Unlike the contemporary global warming, generated by human activity and especially the burning of fossil fuels, this ancient warming phase was a wholly natural phenomenon, part of a long cycle of repeated heating and

■ **Change**

Why did some Paleolithic peoples abandon earlier, more nomadic ways and begin to live a more settled life?

cooling characteristic of the earth's climatic history. Plants and animals unable to survive in the Ice Age climate now flourished and increased their range, providing a much richer and more diverse environment for many human societies. Under these improved conditions, human populations grew, and some previously nomadic gathering and hunting communities, but not all of them, found it possible to settle down and live in more permanent settlements or villages. These societies were becoming both larger and more complex, and it was less possible to simply move away if trouble struck. Settlement also meant that households could store and accumulate goods to a greater degree than their nomadic ancestors. Because some people were more energetic, talented, or lucky than others, the thin edge of inequality very gradually began to wear away the egalitarianism of Paleolithic communities.

Changes along these lines emerged in many places. Paleolithic societies in Japan, known as Jomon, settled down in villages by the sea, where they greatly expanded the number of animals, both land and marine, that they consumed. They also created some of the world's first pottery, along with dugout canoes, paddles, bows, bowls, and tool handles, all made from wood. A similar pattern of permanent settlement, a broader range of food sources, and specialized technologies is evident in Scandinavia, Southeast Asia, North America, and the Middle East between 12,000 and 4,000 years ago. Bows and arrows seem to have been invented separately in Europe, Africa, and the Middle East during this period and spread later to the Americas. In Labrador, longhouses accommodating 100 people appear in the archeological record. Far more elaborate burial sites in many places testify to the growing complexity of human communities and the kinship systems that bound them together. Separate cemeteries for dogs suggest that humankind's best friend was also our first domesticated animal friend.

This process of settling down among gathering and hunting peoples—and the changes that followed from it—marked a major turn in human history, away from countless millennia of nomadic journeys by very small communities. It also provided the setting within which the next great transition would occur. Growing numbers of people, living in settled communities, placed a much greater demand on the environment than did small bands of wandering people. Therefore, it is perhaps not surprising that among the innovations that emerged in these more complex gathering and hunting societies was yet another way for increasing the food supply—agriculture. That epic transition is the subject of the next chapter.

Comparing Paleolithic Societies

Over the 200,000 years or more of the Paleolithic era, human societies naturally differed from one another—in their tool kits, their adaptation to the environment, their beliefs, their social organization, and much more. Here we examine more carefully two such societies, the San of southern Africa and the Chumash of southern California. What they shared was a gathering and hunting way of life and a continuing existence into modern times. Unlike many other such peoples who succumbed

Jomon Figurines
Female figurines, dating to perhaps 4,000 years ago, have been found among Japan's Paleolithic people, known as the Jomon. Many scholars believe these carvings had a ritual function, associated with fertility. (Tokyo National Museum, Collection of Mrs. Kane Yamazaka)

to the relentless expansion of agricultural or industrial societies, the San and the Chumash maintained their ancient way of life into the eighteenth, nineteenth, and twentieth centuries. Even though modern gathering and hunting societies studied by anthropologists surely differed in many ways from their ancient counterparts, they do allow us to see the human face of a way of life long vanished from most parts of the earth.

The San of Southern Africa

On the northern fringe of the Kalahari Desert, in Angola, Namibia, and Botswana, lies the country of the San people, who numbered 50,000 to 80,000 at the start of the twenty-first century. Linguistically, they are related to one of the great language families of Africa, Khoisan, whose speakers have lived throughout eastern and southern Africa for many millennia. The immediate ancestors of the San have inhabited southern Africa for at least 5,000 years. Economically, Khoisan-speaking peoples practiced a gathering and hunting way of life with a technology of stone tools that was recognizable to their twentieth-century San descendants. Another cultural practice of long standing was the remarkable rock art of southern Africa, depicting people and animals, especially the antelope, in thousands of naturalistic scenes of hunts, battles, and dances. Dating to as early as 26,000 years ago, this tradition persisted into the nineteenth century, making it the "oldest artistic tradition of humankind."[19] Modern scholars suggest that this art reflected the religious experience of trance healers, who were likely the artists who painted these images. When a late-nineteenth-century anthropologist showed some of these rock paintings to an elderly San couple, the woman began to sing and dance, while the man became sad, remembering the old songs.[20] In these and other ways, contemporary San people are linked to an ancient cultural tradition that is deeply rooted in the African past.

Most Khoisan gathering and hunting peoples had long ago been absorbed or displaced by the arrival of Bantu-speaking peoples bearing agriculture, domesticated animals, and iron tools, but the San, who lived in a relatively remote location, endured. Even the colonization of southern Africa by Europeans left the San largely intact until the 1960s and later, but not completely, for they traded with their agricultural neighbors and sometimes worked for them. The San also began to use iron arrowheads, fashioned from metals introduced by the newcomers. Drums, borrowed from their Bantu-speaking neighbors, now supplemented their own stringed instruments and became part of San musical tradition. Despite these borrowings, when anthropologists descended on the San in the 1950s and 1960s and studied every aspect of their culture, they found a people still practicing an ancient way of life. The following account of San life is drawn largely from the work of Richard Lee, an anthropologist who lived with and was adopted by one of the San groups who called themselves the Ju/'hoansi.[21] The term literally

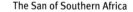

■ Description
What are the most prominent features of San life?

The San of Southern Africa

means "real people"; the virgule (slash) and the apostrophe in the name denote "clicks," which are a distinctive sound in the San language.

In the semidesert conditions of the northern Kalahari, the Ju/'hoansi have drawn a livelihood from a harsh land using some twenty-eight tools for gathering, hunting, and preparing food. The most important implements include an all-purpose wooden digging stick, a large leather garment used for carrying things and also as a blanket, a knife, a spear, a bow and arrow tipped with a potent poison, woven ropes, and nets. The Ju/'hoansi have identified and named some 260 species of wild animals, of which the kudu, wildebeest, and gemsbok are the most commonly hunted, entirely by men. More than 100 species of wild plants, including various nuts, berries, roots, fruits, melons, and greens, were collected, largely by women.

What kind of life did they create for themselves with this modest technology? According to Richard Lee, it was a "happy combination of an adequate diet and a short workweek." He calculated that the Jo/'hoansi consumed 2,355 calories on average every day, about 30 percent from meat and 70 percent from vegetables, well balanced with sufficient protein, vitamins, and minerals—and, he concluded, they "[did] not have to work very hard" to achieve this standard of living. An average workweek involved about seventeen hours of labor in getting food and another twenty-five hours in housework and making and fixing tools, with the total work divided quite equally between men and women. This left plenty of leisure time for resting, visiting, endless conversation, and conducting rituals and ceremonies. Still, it was an uncertain and perpetually anxious life, with fluctuating rainfall, periodic droughts, seasonal depletion of plants, and the unpredictable movement of animals.

What made this way of life possible was a particular kind of society, one characterized by mobility, sharing, and equality. The basic unit of social organization was a band or camp of roughly ten to thirty people, who were connected by ties of exchange and kinship with similar camps across a wide area. The membership of a camp fluctuated over time as many people claimed membership in more than one band. Furthermore, the camps themselves, consisting of quickly built grass huts, were moved frequently, with the Jo/'hoansi seldom staying more than a few months in any one place. The flexibility of this arrangement allowed them to adjust rapidly to the changing seasonal patterns of their desert environment.

At one level, Jo/'hoansi society was extremely simple. No formal leaders, chiefs, headmen, priests, or craft specialists existed, and decisions were made by individual families and camps after much discussion. On another level, social relationships were extremely complex, and it took Richard Lee several years to penetrate them. In addition to common kinship relations of marriage and descent, there were "joking" and "avoidance" relationships that determined the degree of familiarity with which people engaged one another. A further element of complexity lay in a unique "naming" system, which created a deep bond among people with the same name, even though they were not biologically related. For example, a man could not marry any woman who bore the same name as his mother or sister.

At the heart of such a small-scale society of intense personal relationships were values of modesty, cooperation, and equality, which the Jo/'hoansi went to great lengths to inculcate and maintain. One technique, known as "insulting the meat," involved highly negative comments about the size or quality of an animal killed by a hunter and the expectation that a successful hunter would disparage his own kill. As one man put it:

> When a young man kills much meat, he comes to think of himself as a chief or a big man, and he thinks of the rest of us as his servants or inferiors. We can't accept this. We refuse one who boasts, for someday his pride will make him kill someone. So we always speak of his meat as worthless. In this way we cool his heart and make him gentle.

Another practice tending toward equality was the principle that the owner of the arrow that killed an animal, not the successful hunter himself, had the right to distribute the meat from that animal. Because arrows were widely shared, and sometimes owned by women, this custom spread the prestige of meat distribution widely within the society and countered any possibility that the hunter might regard the meat as his private property.

Beyond the sharing of food within a camp was a system of unequal gift exchange among members of different camps. For example, I give you something today, and many months later, you may give me a gift that need not be equivalent in value. When Richard Lee appeared puzzled by the inequality of the exchange, he was told: "we don't trade with things; we trade with people." This system of exchange had more to do with establishing social relations than with accumulating goods. One famous and highly respected hunter named Toma "gave away everything that came into his hands. . . . [I]n exchange for his self-imposed poverty, he won the respect and following of all the people."[22] It was an economic system that aimed at leveling wealth, not accumulating it, and that defined success in terms of possessing friends or people with obligations to oneself, rather than possessing goods.

Social equality extended also to relations between women and men. Richard Lee noted "relative equality between the sexes with no-one having the upper hand." Teenagers engaged quite freely in sex play, and the concept of female virginity was apparently unknown, as were rape, wife beating, and the sexual double standard. Although polygamy was permitted, most marriages were in fact monogamous because women strongly resisted sharing a husband with another wife. Frequent divorce among very young couples allowed women to leave unsatisfactory marriages easily. Lee found that longer-term marriages seemed to be generally fulfilling and stable. Both men and women expected a satisfying sexual relationship, and both occasionally took lovers, although discreetly.

But not all was sweetness and light among the Jo/'hoansi. Frequent arguments about the distribution of meat or the laziness or stinginess of particular people generated conflict, as did rivalries among men over women. Lee identified twenty-two murders that had occurred between 1920 and 1955 and several cases in which the community came together to conduct an execution of particularly disruptive individuals. Lesser tensions were handled through talk; more serious disputes might result in separation, with some people leaving to join another camp or to start their own.

In confronting the world beyond material and social life, the Jo/'hoansi reflected beliefs and practices that were arguably tens of thousands of years old. Unlike later peoples with their many gods, goddesses, spirits, and powers, the San populated the spiritual universe in a quite limited way. A Creator God, *Gao Na*, gave rise to the earth, men, women, animals, waterholes, and all other things; but like the Greek gods, this was a capricious deity, who often visited misfortune on humankind, simply because he chose to. A lesser god, *Gauwa*, was even more destructive, spreading disease, conflict, and death, but also on occasion providing assistance to beleaguered humans. The most serious threat to human welfare came from the ghosts of dead ancestors, the *gauwasi,* who were viewed as primarily malevolent. Asked why the ancestral spirits were so destructive, one woman healer replied:

> Longing for the living is what drives the dead to make people sick. . . . They are very very sad. . . . They miss their people on earth. And so they come back to us. They hover near the villages and put sickness into people, saying "Come, come here to me."

The Jo/'hoansi had one powerful resource for counteracting these evil influences from the world of the gods and ancestors. It was *n/um*, a spiritual potency that lies in the stomach and becomes activated during "curing dances," powerful nightlong rituals held frequently, especially during the dry season when several camps converged on the remaining waterholes. Around a fire, an inner circle of women clapped and sang, while men danced in a circle behind them. Then someone went into a trance and, in that altered state of consciousness, sought to share his or her activated *n/um* with everyone in the camp, pulling the evil out of them. Doing so had the power to heal the sick, to bring harmony to the community, to affect the rainfall and the supply of animals, and to protect everyone from the evil designs of the ancestors.[23]

Recent analysis suggests that the rock art of southern Africa represents the visions achieved by ancient trance dancers as they did battle with the supernatural world. If so, the Jo/'hoansi of the twentieth century were participating in the longest and most continuous religious tradition in world history.

The trance dance was in many ways a distinctive tradition. It did not seek communion with the supernatural; no gifts or sacrifices were offered to the gods or the ancestors, and few prayers were made for their assistance. Viewing the gods as the source of disease, conflict, and death, the Jo/'hoansi hurled at them words of reproach, abuse, and rejection, seeking to ward them off, to expel them from society. It was, as one scholar put it, a "war with God."[24] The leaders of this war, the trance dancers, were not possessed by any supernatural being but used the trance state to activate their own internal *n/um*. Nor were they a priestly elite. Men and women alike could become healers, although a fearful and extended process of spiritual preparation awaited them. Almost half of the men and one-third of the women whom Lee encountered had entered the trance state. It was a much-sought-after role, but it conveyed no permanent power or authority. Finally, Jo/'hoansi religious thinking located the source of evil and misfortune outside of the community in the activity of the gods and ancestors rather than within society in the form of sorcerers or witches. The curing dances brought the community together, united against the external and supernatural enemy.

The Chumash of Southern California

If the San Jo/'hoansi people provide a window into the life of at least one nomadic and long-established gathering and hunting society, the Chumash are more representative of those later post–Ice Age Paleolithic peoples who settled in permanent villages and constructed more complex societies. Together the San and the Chumash illustrate the immense variation that was possible within the limits of a gathering and hunting way of life.

Located in southern California in the vicinity of present-day Santa Barbara, the Chumash occupied a richer and more varied environment than did the San. Speaking a series of related dialects, they lived along the coast, in the immediate interior, and on a series of offshore islands. Thus they were able to draw on the resources of the sea as well as those of the land to support a much more densely settled population of perhaps 20,000 people when they encountered the Spanish in the sixteenth century.

Although the area had been sparsely occupied for about 10,000 years, the history of its people comes into sharper focus only in the centuries of the Common Era. The first millennium C.E. witnessed a growing population, the overhunting and depletion of deer herds in the interior, likely food shortages, and consequently increasing levels of violence and warfare among rival groups. Evidence for this violence is found in the large number of skeletons with bashed-in skulls or arrow and spear wounds. Then, in the several centuries after 1150 C.E., the Chumash, according to a noted scholar, "created an entirely new society."[25] Whereas the history of the San is marked by long-term continuities with a distant past, the Chumash experienced an extraordinary transformation.

A major element of that transformation lay in a remarkable technological innovation—the creation of a planked canoe, or *tomol*—an oceangoing vessel some twenty to thirty feet long and with a cargo capacity of two tons. Called "the most technically sophisticated watercraft developed in the New World," this new craft came into general use around 1000 C.E.[26] Its creation brought immense prestige, wealth, and power to those who built and owned these vessels, injecting a new element of inequality into Chumash society. The boatbuilders organized themselves into an elite craft

■ Comparison
In what ways, and why, did Chumash culture differ from that of the San?

The Chumash of Southern California

A Chumash Tomol
A technologically sophisticated seagoing canoe, the tomol, shown here in a contemporary drawing, was constructed from redwood or pine planks sewn together and caulked with hard tar and pine pitch. In recent decades, Chumash descendants have built several tomols and paddled them from the California mainland to the Channel Islands, re-creating a voyage that their distant ancestors had made many times. These reenactments were part of an effort to preserve for future generations the culture and traditions of the ancient Chumash. (Gaviota Coast Conservancy/Redrawn by © Elizabeth Leahy)

guild, the Brotherhood of the Tomol, which monopolized canoe production and held the tools, knowledge, and sacred medicine associated with these boats. The tomol stimulated a blossoming of trade along the coast and between the coast and the islands as plant food, animal products, tools, and beads now moved regularly among Chumash communities. The boats also made possible deep-sea fishing, with swordfish, central to Chumash religious practice, being the most highly prized and prestigious catch.

In other ways as well, the material life of the Chumash was far more elaborate than that of the San. They lived in round, permanent, substantial houses, covered by grass or reeds, some of them fifty feet in diameter and able to hold up to seventy people. Every village had its own sweathouse, built partially underground and entered through an opening in the roof. Soapstone bowls, wooden plates, beautifully decorated reed baskets, and a variety of items made from bone or shell reflected a pattern of technological innovation far beyond that of the San.

A resource-rich environment, a growing and settled population, flourishing commerce, and technological innovation combined to produce something that scholars not long ago would have considered impossible—a market economy among a gathering and hunting people. Whereas the economic life of the San was regulated almost entirely by custom and tradition, that of the Chumash involved important elements of a market-based system: individuals acting out of a profit motive; the use of money in the form of stringed beads; regulation of the supply of money to prevent inflation; specialized production of goods such as beads, stone tools, canoes, and baskets; prices attached to various items; payment for services provided by dancers, healers, and buriers; and private ownership of canoes, stores of food, and some tools. This is how an early Spanish observer described the Chumash in 1792:

> All these Indians are fond of traffic and commerce. They trade frequently with those of the mountains, bringing them fish and beadwork which they exchange for seeds and shawls of foxskin and a kind of blanket.... When they trade for profit, beads circulate among them as if they were money, being strung on long threads, according to the greater or smaller wealth of each one.... These strings of beads ... are used by the men to adorn their heads and for collars.... They all make a show of their wealth which they always wear in sight on their heads, whence it is taken for gambling and trafficking.[27]

How different is all this from the life of the Jo/'hoansi! Permanently settled villages, ranging in size from several hundred to a thousand people, would have struck the San as unsustainably large compared to their own mobile camps of twenty-five to fifty people. The specialized skills of the Chumash probably would have surprised the Jo/'hoansi, because all San people possessed pretty much the same set of skills. The San no doubt would have been appalled by the public display of wealth, the impulse toward private accumulation, and the inequalities of Chumash society. A bearskin cape, worn only by the elite of canoe owners and village chiefs, marked the beginnings of class distinctions, as did burials, which were far more elaborate for the wealthy and their children than for commoners. Members of the Brotherhood of the Tomol often were buried with parts of their canoes.

Perhaps most offensive to the egalitarian and independent Jo/'hoansi would have been the emergence of a permanent and hereditary political elite among the Chumash. High-ranking Chumash chiefs, who inherited their positions through the male line, exercised control over a number of communities, but each village also had its own chief, some of whom were women. These political leaders, all of whom were also canoe owners, led their people in war, presided over religious rituals, and regulated the flourishing trade that followed the invention of the tomol. They also named the dates for periodic feasts, during which donations and collections from the wealthy were used to feed the poor and to set aside something for a rainy day. This effort at redistributing wealth might have earned the approval of the Jo/'hoansi, who continually sought to level any social and economic distinctions among themselves.

Whatever the Jo/'hoansi might have thought, these transformations—technological, economic, social, and political—created a more unified and more peaceful life among the Chumash in the several centuries after 1150. Earlier patterns of violence apparently subsided as specialized crafts and enhanced trade evened out the distribution of food, making various Chumash communities dependent on one another. More formal political leadership enabled the peaceful resolution of disputes, which formerly had been resolved in battle. Frequent celebrations served to bring various Chumash villages together, while a society-wide organization of ritual experts provided yet another integrating mechanism. These transformations represent a remarkable achievement, especially because they introduced in a gathering and hunting society many social elements normally associated only with agricultural peoples. However, the coming of the Europeans, with their guns, diseases, and missionaries, largely destroyed Chumash society in the centuries following that epic encounter. The mobile San, in their remote location, were able to preserve their ways of life far longer than the more settled, and therefore vulnerable, Chumash, who were unable to avoid the powerful newcomers.

Reflections: The Uses of the Paleolithic

Even when it is about a past as distant as the Paleolithic era, the study of history is also about those who tell it in the present. We search the past, always, for our own purposes. For a long time, modern people were inclined to view their Paleolithic ancestors as "primitive," "superstitious," unevolved, unable to exercise control over nature, and ignorant of its workings. Such a view was, of course, a kind of self-congratulation, designed to highlight the "progress" of modern humankind. It was a way of saying, "Look how far we have come."

In more recent decades, growing numbers of people, disillusioned with modernity, have looked to the Paleolithic era for material with which to criticize, rather than celebrate, contemporary life. Feminists have found in gathering and hunting peoples a much more gender-equal society and religious thinking that featured the "divine feminine," qualities that encouragingly suggested that patriarchy was neither inevitable nor eternal. Environmentalists have sometimes identified peoples in the distant past who were uniquely in tune with the natural environment rather than seeking to dominate it. Some nutritionists have advocated a "Paleolithic diet" of wild plants and animals as better adapted to our physiology. Critics of modern materialism and competitive capitalism have been delighted to discover societies in which values of sharing and equality predominated over those of accumulation and hierarchy. Still others have asked, in light of the long Paleolithic era, whether the explosive population and economic growth of recent centuries should be considered "normal" or "natural." Perhaps it should be regarded as extraordinary, possibly even pathological. Finally, research about the Paleolithic era has been extremely important in efforts by contemporary gathering and hunting peoples, or their descendants, to maintain or recover their older identities amid the conflicting currents of modern life. All of these uses of the Paleolithic have been a way of asking, "What have we lost in the mad rush to modernity, and how can we recover it?"

Both those who look with disdain on Paleolithic "backwardness" and those who praise, often quite romantically, its simplicity and equality seek to use these ancient people for their own purposes. In our efforts to puzzle out the past, all of us—historians and students of history very much included—stand somewhere. None of us can be entirely detached and "outside of it all" when we view the past. Nor is this necessarily a matter for regret. What we may lose in objectivity, we gain in passionate involvement with the historical record and the many people who inhabit it. Despite its remoteness in time and manner of living, the Paleolithic era resonates still in the twenty-first century, reminding us of our kinship with these distant people and the significance of that kinship in finding our own way in a very different world.

Second Thoughts

What's the Significance?

To assess your mastery of the material in this chapter, see the **Online Study Guide** at bedfordstmartins.com/strayer.

Paleolithic rock art
Venus figurines
Dreamtime
Clovis culture
megafaunal extinction

Austronesian migrations
"the original affluent society"
shamans
trance dance

Paleolithic "settling down"
San culture
"insulting the meat"
Chumash culture
Brotherhood of the Tomol

Big Picture Questions

1. What is the significance of the Paleolithic era in world history?
2. In what ways did various Paleolithic societies differ from one another, and how did they change over time?
3. What statements in this chapter seem to be reliable and solidly based on facts, and which ones are more speculative and uncertain?
4. How might our attitudes toward the modern world influence our assessment of Paleolithic societies?

Next Steps: For Further Study

David Christian, *This Fleeting World: A Short History of Humanity* (2008). The first part of this lovely essay by a leading world historian provides a succinct survey of the Paleolithic era.

Brian M. Fagan, *People of the Earth: An Introduction to World Prehistory* (2006). A global account of early human history, written by a leading archeologist.

Clive Gamble, *Timewalkers: The Prehistory of Global Colonization* (2003). A beautifully written account of the initial human settlement of the earth.

Sally McBreatry and Alison S. Brooks, "The Revolution That Wasn't: A New Interpretation of the Origin of Modern Human Behavior," *Journal of Human Evolution* 39 (2000). A long scholarly article laying out the archeological evidence for the emergence of humankind in Africa.

Marjorie Shostak, *Nisa: The Life and Words of an !Kung Woman* (2000). A vivid first-person account of a San woman's life in a twentieth-century gathering and hunting society.

"Prehistoric Art," http://witcombe.sbc.edu/ARTHprehistoric.html#general. An art history Web site with a wealth of links to Paleolithic art around the world.

For Web sites and documents related to this chapter, see **Make History** at bedfordstmartins.com/strayer.

CHAPTER TWO

First Farmers

The Revolutions of Agriculture

10,000 B.C.E. – 3000 B.C.E.

"After me, I suppose there will be nothing here," remarked seventy-two-year-old Elsie Eiler in 2005. At the time, she was the sole remaining resident of the farm town of Monowi, Nebraska. "There is just no employment for people. Farming is hard and all the small farms have had to merge into bigger ones, and the young people just want to go away to college and a city. Few of them come back." Founded in 1902 by Czech immigrants, Monowi in the early twentieth century boasted a post office, two banks, a high school, a church, and rows of well-built homes. By the early twenty-first century, the church was boarded up, many houses had collapsed, deer and wild elk roamed the town's empty spaces, and flocks of birds nested in thick weeds of what had once been Main Street. With the death of her husband in 2004, Mrs. Eiler became the only living soul in Monowi, where she served as the town's mayor and ran its only business, a tavern whose customers came from passing traffic and nearby settlements.[1]

MRS. EILER'S STORY AND THAT OF HER TOWN were part of a much larger global process taking place over the past several centuries of the industrial age—a dramatic decline in the number of people directly earning their living as farmers. The United States represents an extreme case of this worldwide phenomenon: at the beginning of the twenty-first century, only about 5 percent of Americans lived on farms, and many of them were over the age of sixty-five. Despite the small number of American farmers, modern agriculture was so productive

Chinese Neolithic Pottery: Associated everywhere with the Agricultural Revolution was an explosion of pottery making, because settled farmers needed storage capacity to a much greater extent than did nomadic gatherers and hunters. Pottery also provided an outlet for creative expression in the designs and images that decorated many of these early pots. This painted pottery urn, more than 5,000 years old, is from the Yangshao cultural region in northern China, where one of the world's early agricultural breakthroughs occurred. (The National Museum of China, Beijing) that those few people were able to feed the entire country and to export a large amount of food as well. This modern retreat from the farm marked a dramatic reversal of a much more ancient pattern in which growing numbers of people began to farm and agriculture became for the first time the primary occupation for the vast majority of humankind. The beginnings of that epic process represent the central theme of this chapter.

The Agricultural Revolution in World History

The chief feature of the long Paleolithic era—and the first human process to operate on a global scale—was the initial settlement of the earth. Then, beginning around 12,000 years ago, a second global pattern began to unfold—agriculture. Often called the Neolithic or Agricultural Revolution, it referred to the deliberate cultivation of particular plants as well as the taming and breeding of particular animals. Thus a whole new way of life gradually replaced the earlier practices of gathering and hunting in most parts of the world. Although it took place over centuries and millennia, the coming of agriculture represented a genuinely revolutionary transformation of human life all across the planet and provided the foundation for almost everything that followed: growing populations, settled villages, animal-borne diseases, horse-drawn chariot warfare, cities, states, empires, civilizations, writing, literature, and much more.

Among the most revolutionary aspects of the age of agriculture was a new relationship between humankind and other living things, for now men and women were not simply using what they found in nature but were actively changing it as well. They were consciously "directing" the process of evolution. The actions of farmers in the Americas, for example, transformed corn from a plant with a cob of an inch or so to one measuring about six inches by 1500. Later efforts more than doubled that length. Farmers everywhere stamped the landscape with a human imprint in the form of fields with boundaries, terraced hillsides, irrigation ditches, and canals. Animals too were transformed as selective breeding produced sheep that grew more wool, cows that gave more milk, and chickens that laid more eggs than their wild counterparts.

This was "domestication"—the taming, and the changing, of nature for the benefit of humankind—but it created a new kind of mutual dependence. Many domesticated plants and animals could no longer survive in the wild and relied on human action or protection in order to reproduce successfully. Similarly, human beings in the agricultural era lost the skills of their gathering and hunting ancestors, and in any event there were now too many of them to live in that older fashion. As a consequence, farmers and herders became dependent on their domesticated plants and animals. From an outside point of view, it might well seem that corn and cows had tamed human beings, using people to ensure their own survival and growth as a species, as much as the other way around.

A further revolutionary aspect of the Neolithic age is summed up in the term "intensification." It means getting more for less, in this case more food and resources—far more—from a much smaller area of land than was possible with a gathering and hunting technology. More food meant more people. Growing populations in turn required an even greater need for the intensive exploitation of the environment. And so was launched the continuing human effort to "subdue the earth" and to "have dominion over it," as the biblical story in Genesis recorded God's command to Adam and Eve.

Comparing Agricultural Beginnings

Perhaps the most extraordinary feature of the Agricultural or Neolithic Revolution was that it occurred, separately and independently, in many widely scattered parts of the world: the Fertile Crescent of Southwest Asia, several places in sub-Saharan Africa, China, New Guinea, Mesoamerica, the Andes, and eastern North America (see the Snapshot on p. 38 and Map 2.2). Even more remarkably, all of this took place at roughly the same time (at least as measured by the 250,000-year span of human history on the planet)—between 12,000 and 4,000 years ago. These facts have generated many questions with which historians and other scholars have long struggled. Why was the Agricultural Revolution so late in the history of humankind? What was unique about the period after 10,000 B.C.E. that may have triggered or facilitated this vast upheaval? In what different ways did the Agricultural Revolution take shape in its various locations? How did it spread from its several points of origin to the rest of the earth? And what impact did it have on the shaping of human societies?

Common Patterns

It is no accident that the Agricultural Revolution coincided with the end of the last Ice Age, a process of global warming that began some 16,000 years ago. By about 11,000 years ago, the Ice Age was over, and climatic conditions similar to those of our own time generally prevailed. This was but the latest of some twenty-five periods of glaciation and warming that have occurred over the past several million years of the earth's history and which are caused by minor periodic changes in the earth's orbit around the sun. The end of the last Ice Age, however, coincided with the migration of *Homo sapiens* across the planet and created new conditions that made agriculture possible. Combined with active hunting by human societies, climate change in some areas helped to push into extinction various species of large mammals on which Paleolithic people had depended, thus adding to the pressure to find new food sources. The warmer, wetter, and more stable conditions, particularly in the tropical and temperate regions of the earth, also permitted the flourishing of more wild plants, especially cereal grasses, which were the ancestors of many domesticated crops. What climate change took away with one hand, it apparently gave back with the other.

■ **Change**
What accounts for the emergence of agriculture after countless millennia of human life without it?

Snapshot   **Agricultural Breakthroughs**[2]

Location	Dates (B.C.E.)	Plants	Animals
Southwest Asia (Fertile Crescent)	9000–7000	barley, wheat, lentils, figs	goats, sheep, cattle, pigs
China	6500–5000	rice, millet, soybeans	pigs, chickens, water buffalo
Saharan and sub-Saharan Africa	3000–2000	sorghum, millet, yams, teff	cattle (perhaps 8000 B.C.E.)
Highland New Guinea	7000–4000	taro, bananas, yams, sugarcane	—
Andes region	3000–2000	potatoes, quinoa, manioc	llamas, alpaca, guinea pig
Mesoamerica	3000–2000	maize, squash (perhaps 7000 B.C.E.), beans	turkey
Eastern woodlands of North America	2000–1000	sunflower, goosefoot, sumpweed	—

Over their long history, gathering and hunting peoples had already developed a deep knowledge of the natural world and in some cases an ability to manage it actively. They had learned to make use of a large number of plants and to hunt and eat both small and large animals, creating what archeologists call a "broad spectrum diet." In the Middle East, people had developed sickles for cutting newly available wild grain, baskets to carry it, mortars and pestles to remove the husk, and storage pits to preserve it. Peoples of the Amazon and elsewhere had learned to cut back some plants to encourage the growth of their favorites. Native Australians had built elaborate traps in which they could capture, store, and harvest large numbers of eels.

In hindsight, much of this looks like a kind of preparation for agriculture. Because women in particular had long been intimately associated with collecting wild plants, most scholars believe that they were the likely innovators who led the way to deliberate farming, with men perhaps taking the lead in domesticating animals. Clearly the knowledge and technology necessary for agriculture were part of a longer process of more intense human exploitation of the earth. Nowhere was agriculture an overnight invention.

Using such technologies, and benefiting from the global warming at the end of the last Ice Age, gathering and hunting peoples in various places were able to settle down and establish more permanent villages, abandoning their nomadic ways and more intensively exploiting the local area. This was particularly the case in resource-rich areas close to seas, lakes, marshes, and rivers. In settling down, however, they soon lost some of the skills of their ancestors and found themselves now required to support growing populations. Evidence for increasing human numbers around the world during this period of global warming has persuaded some scholars that agriculture was a response to an impending "food crisis."[3] If the number of people outstripped the local resources, or if sudden fluctuations in climate—prolonged drought or a cold snap, for example—diminished those resources, these newly settled communities were in trouble. It was no longer so easy to simply move away. These vagaries surely were strong motives to experiment and to innovate in an effort to increase the food supply. Clearly, many of the breakthroughs to agriculture occurred only *after* gathering and hunting peoples had already grown substantially in numbers and had established a sedentary way of life.

These were some of the common patterns that facilitated the Agricultural Revolution. New opportunities appeared with the improved conditions that came at the end of the Ice Age. New knowledge and technology emerged as human communities explored and exploited that changed environment. The disappearance of many large mammals, growing populations, newly settled ways of life, and fluctuations in the process of global warming—all of these represented pressures or incentives to increase food production and thus to minimize the risks of life in a new era.[4] From some combination of these opportunities and incentives emerged the profoundly transforming process of the Agricultural Revolution.

This new way of life operated everywhere with a simple technology—the digging stick or hoe (the plow was developed only later). But the several transitions to this hoe-based agriculture, commonly known as horticulture, varied considerably, depending on what plants and animals were available locally. For example, potatoes were found in the Andes region, but not in Africa or Asia; wheat and wild pigs existed in the Fertile Crescent, but not in the Americas. Furthermore, of the world's 200,000 plant species, only several hundred have been domesticated, and just five of these—wheat, corn, rice, barley, and sorghum—supply more than half of the calories that sustain human life. Only fourteen species of large mammals have been successfully domesticated, of which sheep, pigs, goats, cattle, and horses have been the most important. Because they are stubborn, nervous, solitary, or finicky, many animals simply cannot be readily domesticated.[5] In short, the kind of Agricultural Revolution that unfolded in particular places depended very much on what happened to be available locally, and that in turn depended on sheer luck.

Variations

Among the most favored areas—and the first to experience a full Agricultural Revolution—was the Fertile Crescent, an area sometimes known as Southwest Asia, consisting of present-day Iraq, Syria, Israel/Palestine, and southern Turkey (see Map 2.1). In this region, an extraordinary variety of wild plants and animals capable of domestication provided a rich array of species on which the now largely settled gathering and hunting people could draw. What triggered the transition to agriculture, it seems, was a cold and dry spell between 11,000 and 9500 B.C.E., a

■ **Comparison**
In what different ways did the Agricultural Revolution take shape in various parts of the world?

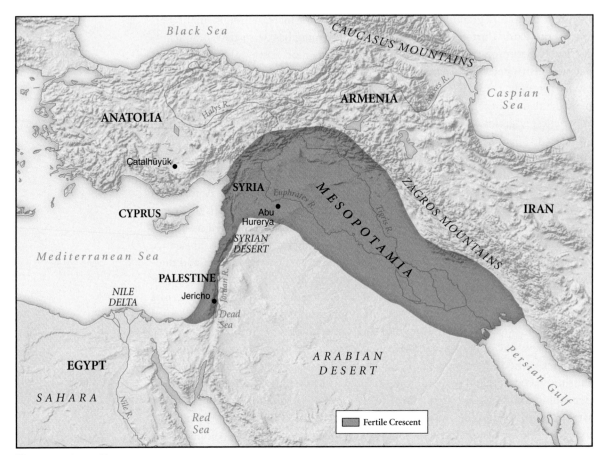

Map 2.1 The Fertile Crescent

Located in what is now called the Middle East, the Fertile Crescent was the site of many significant processes in early world history, including the first breakthrough to agriculture and later the development of some of the First Civilizations.

temporary interruption in the general process of global warming. Larger settled populations were now threatened with the loss of the wild plants and animals on which they had come to depend. Their solution was domestication. In the millennium or so after 9000 B.C.E., figs, wheat, barley, rye, peas, lentils, sheep, goats, pigs, and cattle all came under human control, providing the foundation for the world's first, and most productive, agricultural societies.

Archeological evidence suggests that the transition to a fully agricultural way of life in this region sometimes took place quite quickly, within as few as 500 years. Signs of that transformation included large increases in the size of settlements, which now housed as many as several thousand people. In these agricultural settings, archeologists have found major innovations: the use of sun-dried mud bricks; the appearance of monuments or shrinelike buildings; displays of cattle skulls; more elaborate human burials, including the removal of the skull; and more sophisticated tools, such as sickles, polished axes, and awls.[6] Environmental deterioration in ecologically fragile regions was yet another indication of this new way of life. Numerous settlements in the Jordan River valley and Palestine were abandoned as growing populations of people and goats stripped the area of trees and ground cover, leading to soil erosion and food shortages, which required their human inhabitants to scatter.[7]

At roughly the same time, perhaps a bit later, another process of domestication was unfolding on the African continent in a most unlikely place—the eastern part of what is now the Sahara in present-day Sudan. Between 10,000 and 5,000 years ago, however, "the Saharan desert . . . effectively did not exist," according to scholars, as the region received more rainfall than currently, had extensive grassland vegetation, and was "relatively hospitable to human life."[8] It seems likely that cattle were domesticated in this region about 1,000 years before they were separately brought under human control in the Middle East and India. At about the same time, the donkey also was domesticated in northeastern Africa near the Red Sea and spread from there into Southwest Asia, even as the practice of raising sheep and goats moved in the other direction. In Africa, animal domestication thus preceded the domestication of plants, while elsewhere in the world it was the other way around.

In terms of farming, the African pattern again was somewhat different. Unlike the Fertile Crescent, where a number of plants were domesticated in a small area, sub-Saharan Africa witnessed the emergence of several widely scattered farming practices. Sorghum, which grows well in arid conditions, was the first grain to be "tamed" in the eastern Sahara region. In the highlands of Ethiopia, teff, a tiny, highly nutritious grain, as well as enset, a relative of the banana, came under cultivation. In the forested region of West Africa, yams, oil palm trees, okra, and the kola nut (still used as a flavoring for Coca-Cola and Pepsi) emerged as important crops. The scattered location of these domestications generated a less productive agriculture than in the more favored and compact Fertile Crescent, but a number of the African domesticates—sorghum, castor beans, gourds, millet, the donkey—subsequently spread to enrich the agricultural practices of Eurasian peoples.

Yet another pattern of agricultural development took shape in the Americas. Like the Agricultural Revolution in Africa, the domestication of plants in the Americas occurred separately in a number of locations—in the coastal Andean regions of western South America, in Mesoamerica, in the Mississippi valley, and perhaps in the Amazon basin—but surely its most distinctive feature lay in the absence of animals that could be domesticated. Of the fourteen major species of large mammals that have been brought under human control, only one, the llama/alpaca, existed in the Western Hemisphere. Without goats, sheep, pigs, cattle, or horses, the peoples of the Americas lacked the sources of protein, manure, and power (to draw plows or pull carts, for example) that were widely available to societies in the Afro-Eurasian world. Because they could not depend on domesticated animals for meat, agricultural peoples in the Americas relied more on hunting and fishing than did peoples in the Eastern Hemisphere.

Furthermore, the Americas lacked the rich cereal grains that were widely available in Afro-Eurasia. Instead they had maize or corn, first domesticated in southern Mexico by 4000 to 3000 B.C.E. Unlike the cereal grains of the Fertile Crescent, which closely resemble their wild predecessors, the ancestor of corn, a mountain grass called *teosinte*, looks nothing like what we now know as corn or maize.

Teosinte   Modern Corn

Teosinte and Maize/Corn
The sharp difference in size
between the tiny cobs of
teosinte, a wild grass, and
usable forms of domesti-
cated maize meant that the
Agricultural Revolution took
place more slowly in
Mesoamerica than it had in
Mesopotamia. (Nicolle Rager
Fuller, National Science
Foundation)

Thousands of years of selective adaptation were required to develop a sufficiently large cob and number of kernels
to sustain a productive agriculture, an
achievement that one geneticist has
called "arguably man's first, and perhaps
his greatest, feat of genetic engineering."[9] Even then, corn was nutritionally
poorer than the protein-rich cereals of
the Fertile Crescent. To provide sufficient dietary protein, corn had to be
supplemented with squash and beans,
which were also domesticated in the
Americas. Thus while Middle Eastern
societies quite rapidly replaced their
gathering and hunting economy with agriculture, that process took 3,500 years in
Mesoamerica.

Another difference in the progress of the Agricultural Revolution lay in the
north/south orientation of the Americas, which required agricultural practices to
move through, and adapt to, quite distinct climatic and vegetation zones if they were
to spread. The east/west axis of Eurasia meant that agricultural innovations could
spread more rapidly because they were entering roughly similar environments. Thus
corn, beans, and squash, which were first domesticated in Mesoamerica, took several
thousand years to travel the few hundred miles from their Mexican homeland to the
southwestern United States and another thousand years or more to arrive in eastern
North America. The llama, guinea pig, and potato, which were domesticated in the
Andean highlands, never reached Mesoamerica.[10]

The Globalization of Agriculture

■ Connection
In what ways did
agriculture spread?
Where and why was it
sometimes resisted?

From the various places where it originated, agriculture spread to much of the rest
of the earth, although for a long time it coexisted with gathering and hunting ways
of life (see Map 2.2). Broadly speaking, this extension of farming occurred in two
ways. The first is called *diffusion*, which refers to the gradual spread of agricultural
techniques, and perhaps of the plants and animals themselves, but without the
extensive movement of agricultural people. Neighboring groups exchanged ideas
and products in a "down-the-line" pattern of communication. A second process
involved the slow colonization or migration of agricultural peoples as growing
populations and pressures to expand pushed them outward. Often this meant the
conquest, absorption, or displacement of the earlier gatherers and hunters, along
with the spread of the languages and cultures of the migrating farmers. In many
places, both processes took place.[11] The spread of corn-based agriculture in the
Americas, highlighted in the Snapshot on page 43, illustrates the process.

Snapshot   **The History of Maize/Corn**[12]

The earliest domestication of teosinte—a grass from which modern maize/corn subsequently developed in a process of adaptation and "genetic engineering" over thousands of years—occurs, in southern Mexico. It may have been used for the sugary syrup found in its stalk as well as the nutritional value of its kernels.	9000–8000 B.C.E.
Maize cultivation spreads to South America (Ecuador, Peru).	2300–1000 B.C.E.
Maize cob reaches length of about six centimeters. There is evidence that corn was ground with stone mortars and baked in flat bread.	by 2000 B.C.E.
Maize becomes the staple of Mesoamerican agriculture. Its cultural importance was reflected in its prominence in various myths of origin. Such stories among the Maya, for example, held that humankind was made first of mud, then of wood, and finally, and most successfully, from maize dough.	1500 B.C.E.
Maize spreads to the southwestern United States, along with the migration of farming people	1000 B.C.E.
In Peru, the average size of a maize cob doubles. Maize is used for making maize beer.	500 B.C.E.–1 C.E.
Maize cultivation reaches the eastern woodlands of the Mississippi River valley, largely through diffusion, although people of this region had already domesticated several minor crops, such as sunflowers.	500 C.E.
Maize farming is introduced in New England and is widespread by 1300, about 300 years before the arrival of the Pilgrims.	1000 C.E.
Maize spreads to Europe, Africa, and Asia, following European conquest of the Americas.	16th–18th centuries C.E.

Triumph and Resistance

Some combination of diffusion and migration took the original agricultural package of Southwest Asia and spread it widely into Europe, Central Asia, Egypt, and North Africa between 6500 and 4000 B.C.E. Languages originating in the core region accompanied this movement of people and farming practices. Thus Indo-European languages, which originated probably in Turkey and are widely spoken even today from India to Europe, reflect this movement of culture associated with the spread of agriculture. In a similar process, the Chinese farming system moved into Southeast Asia and elsewhere, and with it a number of related language families developed. India received agricultural influences from the Middle East, Africa, and China alike.

Map 2.2   The Global
Spread of Agriculture
From ten or more separate
points of origin, agriculture
spread to adjacent areas,
eventually encompassing
almost all of the world's
peoples.

Bantu Migrations

Within Africa, the development of agricultural societies in the south-ern half of the continent is associated with the migration of peoples speak-ing one or another of the some 400 Bantu languages. Beginning from what is now southern Nigeria or Cameroon around 3000 B.C.E., Bantu-speaking people moved east and south over the next several millennia, tak-ing with them their agricultural, cattle-raising, and, later, ironworking skills, as well as their languages. The Bantus generally absorbed, killed, or drove away the indigenous Paleolithic peoples or exposed them to animal-borne diseases to which they had no immunities. A similar process brought agricultural Austronesian-speaking people, who originated in southern China, to the Philippine and Indonesian islands, with similar consequences for their earlier inhabitants. Later, Austronesian speakers carried agriculture to the uninhabited islands of the Pacific and to Madagascar off the coast of southeastern Africa (see Map 1.2 on p. 19).

The globalization of agriculture was a prolonged process, lasting 10,000 years or more after its first emergence in the Fertile Crescent, but it was not successful everywhere. The Agricultural Revolution in New Guinea, for example, did not spread much beyond its core region. In particular, it did not pass to the nearby peo-ples of Australia, who remained steadfastly committed to gathering and hunting ways of life. The people of the west coast of North America, arctic regions, and southwestern Africa also maintained their gathering and hunting way of life into the modern era. A very few, such as the Hadza, described at the beginning of Chapter 1, practice it still.

Some of those who resisted the swelling tide of agriculture lived in areas unsuit-able to farming, such as harsh desert or arctic environments; others lived in regions of particular natural abundance, like the territory of the Chumash, so they felt lit-tle need for agriculture. Such people found it easier to resist agriculture if they were not in the direct line of advance of more powerful agricultural people. But the fact that many of the remaining gathering and hunting peoples knew about agricultural practices from nearby farming neighbors suggests that they quite deliberately chose to resist it, preferring the freer life of their Paleolithic ancestors.

Nonetheless, by the beginning of the Common Era, the global spread of agriculture had reduced gathering and hunting peoples to a small and dwindling minority of humankind. If that process meant "progress" in certain ways, it also claimed many victims as the relentlessly expanding agricultural frontier slowly destroyed gathering and hunting societies. Whether this process occurred through the peaceful diffusion of new technologies, through intermarriage, through disease, or through the violent displacement of earlier peoples, the steady erosion of this ancient way of life has been a persistent thread of the human story over the past 10,000 years. The final chapters of that long story are being written in our own century. After the Agricultural Revolution, the future, almost everywhere, lay with the farmers and herders and with the distinctive societies that they created.

The Culture of Agriculture

What did that future look like? In what ways did societies based on the domestication of plants and animals differ from those rooted in a gathering and hunting economy? In the first place, the Agricultural Revolution led to an increase in human population, as the greater productivity of agriculture was able to support much larger numbers. An early agricultural settlement uncovered near Jericho in present-day Israel probably had 2,000 people, a vast increase in the size of human communities compared to much smaller Paleolithic bands. On a global level, scholars estimate that the world's population was about 6 million around 10,000 years ago, before the Agricultural Revolution got under way, and shot up to some 50 million by 5,000 years ago and 250 million by the beginning of the Common Era. Here was the real beginning of the human dominance over other forms of life on the planet.

But larger communities and more people did not necessarily mean an improved life for ordinary people. Farming involved hard work and more of it than in many earlier gathering and hunting societies. The remains of early agricultural people show some deterioration in health—more tooth decay and anemia, a shorter physical stature, and diminished life expectancy. Living close to animals subjected humans to new diseases—smallpox, flu, measles, chicken pox, malaria, tuberculosis, rabies—while living in larger communities generated epidemics for the first time in human history.[13] Furthermore, relying on a small number of plants or animals rendered early agricultural societies vulnerable to famine, in case of crop failure, drought, or other catastrophes. The advent of agriculture bore costs as well as benefits.

Agriculture also imposed constraints on human communities. Some Paleolithic people had settled in permanent villages, but all agricultural people did so, as farming required a settled life. A good example of an early agricultural settlement comes from northern China, one of the original independent sources of agriculture, where rice, millet, pig, and chicken farming gave rise to settled communities by about 7,000 years ago. In 1953, workers digging the foundation for a factory uncovered the remains of an ancient village, now called Banpo, near the present-day city of Xian. Millet, pigs, and dogs had been domesticated, but diets were supplemented with wild plants, animals, and fish. Some forty-five houses covered with thatch laid over wooden beams provided homes to perhaps 500 people. More than 200 storage pits permitted the accumulation of grain, and six kilns and pottery wheels enabled the production of various pots, vases, and dishes, many decorated with geometric designs and human and animal images. A large central space suggests an area for public religious or political activity, and a trench surrounding the village indicates some common effort to defend the community.

Early agricultural villages such as Banpo reveal another feature of the age of agriculture—an explosion of technological innovation. Mobile Paleolithic peoples had little use for pots, but such vessels were essential for settled societies, and their creation and elaboration accompanied agriculture everywhere, as did the weaving of textiles, made possible by collecting the fibers of domesticated plants (cotton and

■ Change
What was revolutionary about the Agricultural Revolution?

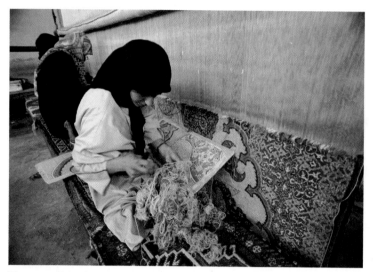

Women and Weaving
During the Paleolithic era and beyond, the weaving of cloth was widely regarded as "women's work." It still is in many places, as this picture from an early twenty-first-century carpet-weaving workshop in Isfahn (Iran) illustrates. (Phil Weymout/Lonely Planet Images/Getty Images)

flax, for example) and animals such as sheep. Evidence for the invention of looms of several kinds dates back to 7,000 years ago, and textiles, some elaborately decorated, show up in Peru, Switzerland, China, and Egypt. Like agriculture itself, weaving clearly seems to be a technology in which women were the primary innovators. It was a task that was compatible with child-rearing responsibilities, which virtually all human societies assigned primarily to women.[14] Another technology associated with the Agricultural Revolution was metallurgy. The working of gold and copper, then bronze, and, later, iron became part of the jewelry-, tool-, and weapon-making skill set of humankind. The long "stone age" of human technological history was coming to an end, and the age of metals was beginning.

A further set of technological changes, beginning around 4000 B.C.E., has been labeled the "secondary products revolution."[15] These technological innovations involved new uses for domesticated animals, beyond their meat and hides. Agricultural people in parts of Europe, Asia, and Africa learned to milk their animals, to harvest their wool, and to enrich the soil with their manure. Even more important, they learned to ride horses and camels and to hitch various animals to plows and carts. Because these types of animals did not exist in the Americas, this revolutionary new source of power and transportation was available only in the Eastern Hemisphere.

A final feature of early agricultural societies lay in their growing impact on the environment, as farming and herding peoples deliberately altered the natural ecosystem by removing the natural ground cover for their fields, by making use of irrigation, and by grazing their now-domesticated animals. In parts of the Middle East within a thousand years after the beginning of settled agricultural life, some villages were abandoned when soil erosion and deforestation led to declining crop yields, which could not support mounting populations.[16] The advent of more intensive agriculture associated with city-based civilizations only heightened this human impact on the landscape (see Chapter 3).

Social Variation in the Age of Agriculture

■ **Comparison**
What different kinds of societies emerged out of the Agricultural Revolution?

The resources generated by the Agricultural Revolution opened up vast new possibilities for the construction of human societies, but they led to no single or common outcome. Differences in the natural environment, the encounter with strangers, and sometimes deliberate choices gave rise to several distinct kinds of societies early on in the age of agriculture, all of which have endured into modern times.

Pastoral Societies

One variation of great significance grew out of the difference between the domestication of plants and the domestication of animals. Many societies made use of both, but in regions where farming was difficult or impossible—arctic tundra, some grasslands, and deserts—some people came to depend far more extensively on their animals, such as sheep, goats, cattle, horses, camels, or reindeer. Animal husbandry was a "distinct form of food-producing economy," relying on the milk, meat, and blood of animals.[17] Known as herders, pastoralists, or nomads, such people emerged in Central Asia, the Arabian Peninsula, the Sahara, and in parts of eastern and southern Africa. What they had in common was mobility, for they moved seasonally as they followed the changing patterns of vegetation necessary as pasture for their animals.

The particular animals central to pastoral economies differed from region to region. The domestication of horses by 4000 B.C.E. and the later mastery of horseback-riding skills enabled the growth of pastoral peoples all across the steppes of Central Asia by the first millennium B.C.E. Although organized primarily in kinship-based clans or tribes, these nomads periodically created powerful military confederations, which played a major role in the history of Eurasia for thousands of years. In the Inner Asian, Arabian, and Saharan deserts, domesticated camels made possible the human occupation of forbidding environments. The grasslands south of the Sahara and in parts of eastern Africa supported cattle-raising pastoralists. The absence of large animals capable of domestication meant that no pastoral societies emerged in the Americas.

The relationship between nomadic herders and their farming neighbors has been one of the enduring themes of Afro-Eurasian history. Frequently, it was a relationship of conflict as pastoral peoples, unable to produce their own agricultural products, were attracted to the wealth and sophistication of agrarian societies and sought access to their richer grazing lands as well as their food crops and manufactured products. The biblical story of the deadly rivalry between two brothers—Cain, a "tiller of the ground," and Abel, a "keeper of sheep"—reflects this ancient conflict, which persisted well into modern times. But not all was conflict between pastoral and agricultural peoples. The more peaceful exchange of technologies, ideas, products, and people across the ecological frontier of pastoral and agricultural societies also served to enrich and to change both sides. In the chapters that follow, and especially in Chapter 12, we will encounter pastoral

The Domestication of Animals

Although farming often gets top billing in discussions of the Neolithic Revolution, the raising of animals was equally important, for they provided meat, pulling power, transportation (in the case of horses and camels), and manure. Animal husbandry also made possible pastoral societies, which were largely dependent on their domesticated animals. In this Egyptian carving, dating to about 2380 B.C.E., two workers lead a prime bull to the fields. (G. Dagli Orti/The Art Archive)

societies repeatedly, particularly as they interact with neighboring agricultural and "civilized" peoples.

Agricultural Village Societies

The most characteristic early agricultural societies were those of settled village-based farmers, such as those living in Banpo or Jericho. Such societies retained much of the equality and freedom of gathering and hunting communities, as they continued to do without kings, chiefs, bureaucrats, or aristocracies.

An example of this type of social order can be found at Çatalhüyük, a very early agricultural village in southern Turkey. A careful excavation of the site revealed a population of several thousand people who buried their dead under their houses and then filled the houses with dirt and built new ones on top, layer upon layer. No streets divided the houses, which were constructed adjacent to one another. People moved about the village on adjoining rooftops, from which they entered their homes. Despite the presence of many specialized crafts, few signs of inherited social inequality have surfaced. Nor is there any indication of male or female dominance, although men were more closely associated with hunting wild animals and women with plants and agriculture. "Both men and women," concludes one scholar, "could carry out a series of roles and enjoy a range of positions, from making tools to grinding grain and baking to heading a household."[18]

Many such village-based agricultural societies flourished well into the modern era, usually organizing themselves in terms of kinship groups or lineages, which incorporated large numbers of people well beyond the immediate or extended family. Such people traced their descent through either the male or the female line to some common ancestor, real or mythical. In many African societies, for example, a lineage system provided the framework within which large numbers of people could make and enforce rules, maintain order, and settle disputes without going to war. In short, the lineage system performed the functions of government, but without the formal apparatus of government, and thus did not require kings or queens, chiefs, or permanent officials associated with a state organization. The Tiv of central Nigeria organized close to a million people in this fashion at the end of the nineteenth century. Theirs was a system in which power was dispersed throughout the society rather than being concentrated in particular people or institutions. In fact, the Tiv had no word for "politics" as a separate aspect of life, for there was no state that specialized in political matters.

Çatalhüyük
Since the 1960s, archeologists have uncovered the connected homes of Çatalhüyük, shown here in a photo of the excavation, as well as many artifacts, murals, and sculptures from this early agricultural settlement in southern Turkey. (Courtesy, James Mellaart/Çatalhöyük Research Project)

Despite their democratic qualities and the absence of centralized authority, village-based lineage societies sometimes developed modest social and economic inequalities. Elders could exploit the labor of junior members of the community and sought particularly to control women's reproductive powers, which were essential for the growth of the lineage. Among the Igbo of southern Nigeria, "title societies" enabled men and women of wealth and character to earn a series of increasingly prestigious "titles" that set them apart from other members of their community, although these honors could not be inherited. Lineages also sought to expand their numbers, and hence their prestige and power, by incorporating war captives or migrants in subordinate positions, sometimes as slaves.

Many agricultural societies, in Africa and elsewhere, conducted their affairs without formal centralized states or full-time rulers, even when they were aware of these institutions and practices from nearby peoples. Given the frequent oppressiveness of organized political power in human history, such experiments with "stateless" forms of social organization represent an intriguing alternative to states, kingdoms, and empires, so frequently highlighted in the historical record. These agricultural village societies pioneered the human settlement of vast areas; adapted to a variety of environments; created numerous cultural, artistic, and religious traditions; incorporated new crops, institutions, and people into their cultures; and interacted continuously with their neighbors.

Chiefdoms

In other places, agricultural societies gave rise to chiefdoms, in which inherited positions of power and privilege introduced a more distinct element of inequality, but unlike later "kings," chiefs could seldom use force to compel the obedience of their subjects. Instead they relied on their generosity or gift giving, their ritual status, or their personal charisma to persuade their followers. The earliest such chiefdoms seem to have emerged in the Tigris-Euphrates river valley called Mesopotamia (present-day Iraq), sometime after 6000 B.C.E., when temple priests organized irrigation systems and controlled trade with nearby societies.

■ **Comparison**

How did chiefdoms differ from stateless agricultural village societies?

Many chiefdoms followed in all parts of the world, and the more recent ones have been much studied by anthropologists. For example, chiefdoms emerged everywhere in the Pacific islands, which had been colonized by agricultural Polynesian peoples. Chiefs usually derived from a senior lineage, tracing their descent to the first son of an imagined ancestor. With both religious and secular functions, chiefs led important rituals and ceremonies, organized the community for warfare, directed its economic life, and sought to resolve internal conflicts. They collected tribute from commoners in the form of food, manufactured goods, and raw materials. These items in turn were redistributed to warriors, craftsmen, religious specialists, and other subordinates, while the chief kept enough to maintain his prestigious position and his imposing lifestyle.[19] In North America as well, a remarkable series of chiefdoms emerged in the eastern woodlands, where an extensive array of large earthen

Cahokia
Pictured here in an artist's reconstruction, Cahokia (near St. Louis, Missouri) was the center of an important agricultural chiefdom around 1100 C.E. See Chapter 7 for details. (Cahokia Mounds State Historic Site, Illinois. Painting by Lloyd K. Townsend)

mounds testify to the organizational capacity of these early societies. The largest of them, known as Cahokia, flourished around 1100 C.E. In such agricultural chiefdoms—both ancient and more recent—the distinction between elite and commoner, based on birth rather than age or achievement, began to take root. It was a fateful turn in the organization of human societies—one that was replicated, elaborated, and assumed to be natural in all later states and civilizations.

⊔ Reflections: The Legacies of Agriculture

Because it is practiced around the world and has achieved virtually universal acceptance, agriculture or "domestication" may seem to be a "natural" or inevitable feature of the human story. In terms of world history, however, it is a recent development, an adaptation to the unique conditions of the latest interglacial period. Who can say how long those conditions will last or whether agriculture would remain a viable way of life in a renewed Ice Age?

No matter how it turns out in the very long run, during the last 10,000 years or so, the Agricultural Revolution has radically transformed both the trajectory of the human journey and the evolution of life on the planet. This epic transformation granted to one species, *Homo sapiens*, a growing power over many other species of plants and animals. Agriculture made possible an increase in human numbers far beyond what a gathering and hunting economy could support, and it enabled human beings to control and manipulate both plants and animals for their own purposes far more than ever before.

But if agriculture provided humankind with the power to dominate nature, it also, increasingly, enabled some people to dominate others. This was not immediately apparent, and for several thousand years, and much longer in some places, agricultural villages retained much of the social equality that had characterized

Paleolithic life. Slowly, though, many of the resources released by the Agricultural Revolution accumulated in the hands of a few. Rich and poor, chiefs and commoners, landowners and dependent peasants, rulers and subjects, dominant men and subordinate women, slaves and free people—these distinctions, so common in the record of world history, took shape most extensively in productive agricultural settings, which generated an economic surplus. The endless elaboration of such distinctions, for better or worse, is a major element in the story of civilization.

Second Thoughts

What's the Significance?

end of the last Ice Age	Bantu migration	pastoral societies
broad spectrum diet	native Australians	Çatalhüyük
Fertile Crescent	Banpo	stateless societies
teosinte	secondary products	chiefdoms
diffusion	revolution	

To assess your mastery of the material in this chapter, see the **Online Study Guide** at bedfordstmartins.com/strayer.

Big Picture Questions

1. The Agricultural Revolution marked a decisive turning point in human history. What evidence might you offer to support this claim, and how might you argue against it?
2. How did early agricultural societies differ from those of the Paleolithic era? How does the example of settled gathering and hunting peoples such as the Chumash complicate this comparison?
3. Was the Agricultural Revolution inevitable? Why did it occur so late in the story of humankind?
4. "The Agricultural Revolution provides evidence for 'progress' in human affairs." Do you agree with this statement?

Next Steps: For Further Study

Elizabeth Wayland Barber, *Women's Work: The First 20,000 Years* (1994). Explores the role of women in early technological development, particularly textile making.

Peter Bellwood, *First Farmers* (2005). The most recent and up-to-date account of the Agricultural Revolution, considered on a global basis.

Mark Nathan Cohen, *The Food Crisis in Prehistory* (1977). An older work arguing that mounting human population triggered the breakthrough to agriculture.

Jared Diamond, *Guns, Germs, and Steel* (1998). A provocative and much-publicized explanation for regional economic differences, based on variations among early agricultural revolutions.

Steven Mithen, *After the Ice: A Global Human History, 20,000–5000 B.C.* (2004). An imaginative tour of world archeological sites during the Agricultural Revolution.

Neil Roberts, *The Holocene: An Environmental History* (1998). Explores the role of climate change and human activity in shaping the global environment during the age of agriculture.

"The Agricultural Revolution," http://www.wsu.edu/gened/learn-modules/top_agrev/agrev-index .html. A Web-based tutorial from Washington State University.

For Web sites and documents related to this chapter, see **Make History** at bedfordstmartins.com/strayer.

CHAPTER THREE

First Civilizations

Cities, States, and Unequal Societies

3500 B.C.E. - 500 B.C.E.

"Over 100 miles of wilderness, deep exploration into pristine lands, the solitude of backcountry camping, 4×4 trails, and ancient American Indian rock art and ruins. You can't find a better way to escape civilization!"[1] So goes an advertisement for a vacation in Utah's Canyonlands National Park, one of thousands of similar attempts to lure apparently constrained, beleaguered, and "civilized" city-dwellers into the spacious freedom of the wild and the imagined simplicity of earlier times. This urge to "escape from civilization" has long been a central feature in modern life. It is a major theme in Mark Twain's famous novel *Huck Finn*, in which the restless and rebellious Huck resists all efforts to "sivilize" him by fleeing to the freedom of life on the river. It is a large part of the "cowboy" image in American culture, and it permeates environmentalist efforts to protect the remaining wilderness areas of the country. Nor has this impulse been limited to modern societies and the Western world. The ancient Chinese teachers of Daoism likewise urged their followers to abandon the structured and demanding world of urban and civilized life and to immerse themselves in the eternal patterns of the natural order. It is a strange paradox that we count the creation of civilization among the major achievements of humankind and yet people within these civilizations have often sought to escape the constraints, artificiality, hierarchies, and other discontents of city living.

WHAT EXACTLY ARE THESE CIVILIZATIONS that have generated such ambivalent responses among their inhabitants? When, where, and how did they first arise in human history? What changes did they bring to

Raherka and Mersankh: Writing was among the defining features of civilizations almost everywhere. In ancient Egyptian civilization, the scribes who possessed this skill enjoyed both social prestige and political influence. This famous statue shows Raherka, the chief of the scribes during Egypt's Fifth Dynasty (about 2350 B.C.E.), in an affectionate pose with his wife, Mersankh. (Réunion des Musées Nationaux/Art Resource, NY) the people who lived within them? Why might some people criticize or seek to escape from them? These are the issues addressed in this chapter.

As historians commonly use the term, civilization represents a new and particular type of human society, made possible by the immense productivity of the Agricultural Revolution. Such societies encompassed far larger populations than any earlier form of human community and for the first time concentrated some of those people in sizable cities, numbering in the many tens of thousands. In these cities, people were organized and controlled by powerful states whose leaders could use force to compel obedience. Profound differences in economic function, skill, wealth, and status sharply divided the people of civilizations, making them far less equal, and subject to much greater oppression, than had been the case in earlier agricultural villages, pastoral societies, and chiefdoms. Pyramids, temples, palaces, elaborate sculptures, written literature, complex calendars, as well as class, slavery, patriarchy, and large-scale warfare—all of these have been among the cultural products of civilization.

Something New: The Emergence of Civilizations

■ Change
When and where did the First Civilizations emerge?

Like agriculture, civilization was a global phenomenon, showing up independently in six major locations scattered around the world during the several millennia after 3500 B.C.E. and in a number of other smaller expressions as well (see Map 3.1). At the time, these breakthroughs to a new way of life were small islands of innovation in a sea of people living in much older ways. In the long run of human history, however, civilizations gradually absorbed, overran, or displaced people practicing other ways of living. Over the next 5,000 years, civilization, as a unique kind of human community, gradually encompassed ever-larger numbers of people and extended over ever-larger territories, even as particular civilizations rose, fell, revived, and changed.

Introducing the First Civilizations

The earliest of these civilizations emerged around 3500 B.C.E. to 3000 B.C.E. in three places. One was the "cradle" of Middle Eastern civilization, expressed in the many and competing city-states of Sumer, in southern Mesopotamia (located in present-day Iraq). Much studied by archeologists and historians, Sumerian civilization gave rise to the world's earliest written language, which was used initially by officials to record the goods received by various temples. Almost simultaneously, the Nile River valley in northeastern Africa witnessed the emergence of Egyptian civilization, famous for its pharaohs and pyramids, as well as a separate civilization known as Nubia, farther south along the Nile. Unlike the city-states of Sumer, Egyptian civilization took shape as a unified territorial state in which cities were rather less prominent. Later in this chapter, we will explore these two First Civilizations in greater detail.

Less well known and only recently investigated by scholars was a third early civilization that was developing along the central coast of Peru from roughly 3000 B.C.E. to 1800 B.C.E., at about the same time as the civilizations of Egypt and Sumer. This desert region received very little rainfall, but it was punctuated by dozens of rivers that brought the snowmelt of the adjacent Andes Mountains to the Pacific Ocean. Along a thirty-mile stretch of that coast and in the nearby interior, a series of some twenty-five urban centers emerged in an area known as Norte Chico, the largest of which was Caral, in the Supe River valley. In Norte Chico, archeologists have found monumental architecture in the form of earthen platform mounds, one of them measuring 60 feet tall and 500 feet long, as well as large public ceremonial structures, stone buildings with residential apartments, and other signs of urban life.

Norte Chico was a distinctive civilization in many ways. Its cities were smaller than those of Mesopotamia and show less evidence of economic specialization. The economy was based to an unusual degree on an extremely rich fishing industry in anchovies and sardines along the coast. These items apparently were exchanged for cotton, essential for fishing nets, as well as food crops such as squash, beans, and guava, all of which were grown by inland people in the river valleys using irrigation agriculture. Unlike Egypt and Mesopotamia, Peruvian civilization did not rest upon grain-based farming, the people of Norte Chico did not develop pottery or writing, and few sculptures, carvings, or drawings have been uncovered so far. Archeologists have, however, found a 5,000-year-old *quipu* (a series of knotted cords, later used extensively by the Inca for accounting purposes), which some scholars have suggested may have been an alternative form of writing. Furthermore, the cities of Norte Chico lacked defensive walls, and archeologists have discovered little evidence of warfare, such as burned buildings and mutilated corpses. It was also an unusually self-contained civilization. Whereas Egypt and Mesopotamia had long interacted with each other, the only import from the outside world evident in Norte Chico, or in Andean civilization generally, was maize (corn), which was derived ultimately from Mesoamerica, though without direct contact between the two regions. Norte Chico apparently "lighted a cultural fire" in the Andes and established a pattern for the many Andean civilizations that followed— Chavín, Moche, Nazca, and, much later, the Inca.[2]

Somewhat later, three additional First Civilizations made their appearance. In the Indus and Saraswati river valleys of what is now Pakistan, a remarkable civilization arose during the third millennium B.C.E. By 2000 B.C.E., it embraced a far larger area than Mesopotamia, Egypt, or coastal Peru and was expressed primarily in its elaborately planned cities. All across this huge area, about twice the size of Texas, common patterns prevailed: standardized weights, measures, architectural styles, even the size of bricks. As elsewhere, irrigated agriculture provided the economic foundation for the civilization, and a written language, thus far undeciphered, provides evidence of a literate culture.

Unlike its Middle Eastern counterparts, the Indus Valley civilization apparently generated no palaces, temples, elaborate graves, kings, or warrior classes. In short,

Map 3.1   First Civilizations

Six First Civilizations emerged independently in locations scattered across the planet, all within a few thousand years, from 3500 to 1000 B.C.E.

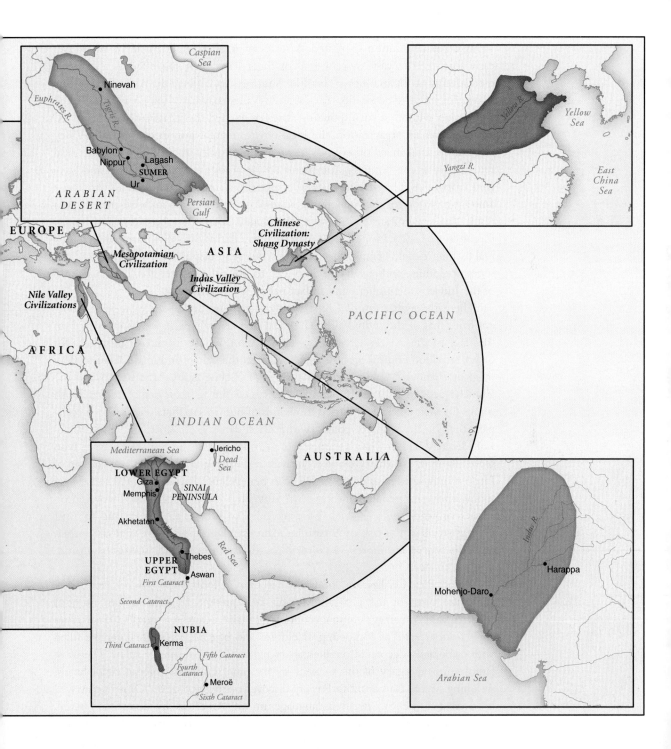

the archeological evidence provides little indication of a political hierarchy or centralized state. This absence of evidence has sent scholars scrambling to provide an explanation for the obvious specialization, coordination, and complexity that the Indus Valley civilization exhibited. A series of small republics, rule by priests, an early form of the caste system—all of these have been suggested as alternative mechanisms of integration in this first South Asian civilization. Although no one knows for sure, the possibility that the Indus Valley may have housed a sophisticated civilization without a corresponding state has excited the imagination of scholars.

Whatever its organization, the local environmental impact of the Indus Valley civilization, as in many others, was heavy and eventually undermined its ecological foundations. Repeated irrigation increased the amount of salt in the soil and lowered crop yields. The making of mud bricks, dried in ovens, required an enormous amount of wood for fuel, generating large-scale deforestation and soil erosion. As a result, these magnificent cities were abandoned by about 1700 B.C.E. and largely forgotten thereafter. Nonetheless, many features of this early civilization—ceremonial bathing, ritual burning, yoga positions, bulls and elephants as religious symbols, styles of clothing and jewelry—continued to nourish the later classical civilization of the Indian subcontinent and in fact persist into the present.[3]

The early civilization of China, dating to perhaps 2200 B.C.E., was very different from that of the Indus Valley. The ideal of a centralized state was evident from the days of the Xia dynasty (2200–1766 B.C.E.), whose legendary monarch Wu organized flood control projects that "mastered the waters and made them to flow in great channels." Subsequent dynasties—the Shang (1766–1122 B.C.E.) and the Zhou (1122–256 B.C.E.)—substantially enlarged the Chinese state, erected lavish tombs for their rulers, and buried thousands of human sacrificial victims to accompany them in the world to come. By the Zhou dynasty, a distinctive Chinese political ideology had emerged, featuring a ruler, known as the Son of Heaven, who served as an intermediary between heaven and earth and ruled by the Mandate of Heaven only so long as he governed with benevolence and maintained social harmony among his people. An early form of written Chinese has been discovered on numerous oracle bones, which were intended to predict the future and to assist China's rulers in the task of governing. Chinese civilization, more than any other, has experienced an impressive cultural continuity from its earliest expression into modern times.

A final First Civilization, known as the Olmec, took shape around 1200 B.C.E. along the coast of the Gulf of Mexico near present-day Veracruz in southern Mexico. Based on an agricultural economy of maize, beans, and squash, Olmec cities arose from a series of competing chiefdoms and became ceremonial centers filled with elaborately decorated temples, altars, pyramids, and tombs of rulers. The most famous artistic legacy of the Olmecs lay in some seventeen colossal basalt heads, weighing twenty tons or more. Recent discoveries suggest that the Olmecs may well have created the first written language in the Americas by about 900 B.C.E. Sometimes regarded as the "mother civilization" of Mesoamerica, Olmec cultural patterns—mound building, artistic styles, urban planning, a game played with a rubber ball, ritual sacrifice, and bloodletting by rulers—spread widely throughout the region and influenced subsequent civilizations, such as the Maya and Teotihuacán.

Beyond these six First Civilizations, other smaller civilizations also flourished. Lying south of Egypt in the Nile Valley, Nubian civilization was clearly distinctive and independent of its northern neighbor, although Nubia was involved in a long and often contentious relationship with Egypt. Likewise in China, a large city known as Sanxingdui, rich in bronze sculptures and much else, arose separately but at the same time as the more well-known Shang dynasty. As a new way of living and a new form of human society, civilization was beginning its long march toward encompassing almost all of humankind by the twentieth century.

Shang Dynasty Bronze
This bronze tiger, created around 1100 B.C.E., illustrates Chinese skill in working with bronze and the mythological or religious significance of the tiger as a messenger between heaven and the human world. (Jiangxi Provincial Museum, Nanchang/Visual Connection Archive)

The Question of Origins

The first question that historians ask about almost everything is "How did it get started?" Scholars of all kinds—archeologists, anthropologists, sociologists, and historians—have been arguing about the origins of civilization for a very long time, with no end in sight.[4] Amid all the controversy, one thing seems reasonably clear: civilizations had their roots in the Agricultural Revolution. That is the reason they appeared so late in the human story, for only an agricultural technology permitted human communities to produce sufficient surplus to support large populations and the specialized or elite minorities who did not themselves produce food. Furthermore, all of the First Civilizations emerged from earlier and competing chiefdoms, in which some social ranking and economic specialization had already developed. It was a gradual and evolutionary process. However, not all agricultural societies or chiefdoms developed into civilizations, so something else must have been involved. It is the search for this "something else" that has provoked such great debate among scholars.

Some scholars have emphasized the need to organize large-scale irrigation projects as a stimulus for the earliest civilizations, but archeologists have found that the more complex water control systems appeared long after states and civilizations had already been established. Others have suggested that powerful states were

■ **Change**
What accounts for the initial breakthroughs to civilization?

useful in protecting the privileges of favored groups. Warfare and trade have figured in still other explanations for the rise of civilizations. Anthropologist Robert Carneiro combined several of these factors in a thoughtful approach to the question.[5] He argued that a growing density of population, producing more congested and competitive societies, was a fundamental motor of change, and especially in areas where rich agricultural land was limited, either by geography (oceans, deserts, mountains) or by powerful competing societies. Such settings provided incentives for innovations, such as irrigation or plows that could produce more food, because opportunities for territorial expansion were not readily available. But circumscribed environments with dense populations also generated intense competition among rival groups, which led to repeated warfare. A strong and highly organized state was a decided advantage in such competition. Because losers could not easily flee to new lands, they were absorbed into the winner's society as a lower class. Successful leaders of the winning side emerged as an elite with an enlarged base of land, a class of subordinated workers, and a powerful state at their disposal—in short, a civilization.

Although such a process was relatively rapid by world history standards, it took many generations, centuries, or perhaps millennia to evolve. It was, of course, an unconscious undertaking in which the participants had little sense of the long-term outcome as they coped with the practical problems of survival on a day-to-day basis. What is surprising, though, is the rough similarity of the result in many widely separated places from about 3000 B.C.E. to the beginning of the Common Era.

However they got started (and much about this is still guesswork), the First Civilizations, once established, represented a very different kind of human society than anything that came before. All of them were based on highly productive agricultural economies. Various forms of irrigation, drainage, terracing, and flood control enabled these early civilizations to tap the food-producing potential of their regions. In dry lands with good soil, such as northern China and southern Iraq, water made all the difference and vastly increased the agricultural output. In all these civilizations, pottery likewise enhanced the productivity of farming, as did animal-drawn plows and metalworking in Afro-Eurasia. Ritual sacrifice, often of people, usually accompanied the growth of civilization, and the new rulers normally served as high priests or were seen as divine beings, their right to rule legitimated by association with the sacred.

An Urban Revolution

■ Change
What was the role of cities in the early civilizations?

It was these resources from agriculture that made possible one of the most distinctive features of the First Civilizations—cities. What would an agricultural villager have made of Uruk, ancient Mesopotamia's largest city? Uruk had walls more than twenty feet tall and a population around 50,000 in the third millennium B.C.E. The city's center, visible for miles around, was a stepped pyramid, or *ziggurat*, topped with a temple. Inside the city, our village visitor would have found other temples as well, serving as centers of worship and as places for the redistribution of stored food. Numerous craftspeople labored as masons, copper workers, weavers, and many other specialties, while bureaucrats helped administer the city. It was, surely, a "vibrant, noisy, smelly, sometimes bewildering and dangerous, but also exciting place."[6] Here is how the *Epic of Gilgamesh*, Mesopotamia's ancient epic poem, describes the city:

> Come then, Enkidu, to ramparted Uruk,
> Where fellows are resplendent in holiday clothing,
> Where every day is set for celebration,
> Where harps and drums are played.
> And the harlots too, they are fairest of form,
> Rich in beauty, full of delights,
> Even the great gods are kept from sleeping at night.[7]

Equally impressive to a village visitor would have been the city of Mohenjo Daro, which flourished along the banks of the Indus River around 2000 B.C.E. With a population of perhaps 40,000, Mohenjo Daro and its sister city of Harappa featured large, richly built houses of two or three stories, complete with indoor plumbing, luxurious bathrooms, and private wells. Streets were laid out in a gridlike pattern, and beneath the streets ran a complex sewage system. Workers lived in row upon row of standardized two-room houses. Grand public buildings, including what seems to be a huge public bath, graced the city, while an enormous citadel was surrounded by a brick wall some forty-five feet high.

Even larger, though considerably later, was the Mesoamerican city of Teotihuacán, located in the central valley of Mexico. It housed perhaps 200,000 people in the middle of the first millennium C.E. Broad avenues, dozens of temples, two huge pyramids, endless stone carvings and many bright frescoes, small apartments for the ordinary, palatial homes for the wealthy—all of this must have seemed another world for a new visitor from a distant village. In shopping for obsidian blades, how was she to decide among the 350 workshops in the city? In seeking relatives, how could she find her way among many different compounds, each surrounded by a wall and housing a different lineage? And what would she make of a neighborhood composed entirely of Mayan merchants from the distant coastal lowlands?

Cities, then, lay at the heart of all of the First Civilizations. They were political/administrative capitals; they were centers for the production of

Mohenjo Daro
Flourishing around 2000 B.C.E., Mohenjo Daro was by far the largest city of the Indus Valley civilization, covering more than 600 acres. Here is a picture of a small part of that city as it has been uncovered by archeologists during the past century. (Paolo Koch/Photo Researchers, Inc.)

culture, including art, architecture, literature, ritual, and ceremony; they served as marketplaces for both local and long-distance exchange; and they housed most manufacturing activity. Everywhere they generated a unique kind of society, compared to earlier agricultural villages. Urban society was impersonal, for it was no longer possible to know everyone. Relationships of class and occupation were at least as important as those of kinship and village loyalty. Most notably, the degree of specialization and inequality far surpassed that of all preceding human communities.

The Erosion of Equality

Among the most novel features of early urban life, at least to our imaginary village visitor, was the amazing specialization of work. In an amusing Egyptian document from about 1200 B.C.E., a teacher tries to persuade a reluctant student, preparing to be a scribe (a literate public official), to take his lessons seriously by pointing out the disadvantages of the many other occupations that await him. His lazy pupil might wind up as a washerman, potter, maker of boots and shoes, watchman, merchant, crewman on a ship, field worker, peasant, soldier, or unskilled worker, possibly hauling stones for the pyramids. All of these jobs he describes as dirty, demeaning, or laborious and concludes: "If you have any sense, be a scribe."[8] In ancient Mesopotamia, even scribes were subdivided into many categories: junior and senior scribes, temple scribes and royal scribes, scribes for particular administrative or official functions.[9] None of these people, of course, grew their own food; they were supported by the highly productive agriculture of farmers.

Hierarchies of Class

■ **Change**
In what ways was social inequality expressed in early civilizations?

Alongside the occupational specialization of the First Civilizations lay their vast inequalities—in wealth, status, and power. Here we confront a remarkable and persistent feature of the human journey. As ingenuity and technology created more-productive economies, the greater wealth now available to societies was everywhere piled up rather than spread out. Early signs of this erosion of equality were evident in the more settled and complex gathering and hunting societies such as the Chumash and in agricultural chiefdoms such as Cahokia, but the advent of urban-based civilizations multiplied and magnified these inequalities many times over, as the egalitarian values of earlier cultures were everywhere displaced. This transition represents one of the major turning points in the social history of humankind.

As the First Civilizations took shape, inequality and hierarchy soon came to be regarded as normal and natural. Upper classes everywhere enjoyed great wealth in land or salaries, were able to avoid physical labor, had the finest of everything, and occupied the top positions in political, military, and religious life.

Frequently, they were distinguished by the clothing they wore, the houses they lived in, and the manner of their burial. Early Chinese kings bestowed special clothing, banners, chariots, weapons, and ornaments on their regional officials, and all of these items were graded according to the officials' precise location in the hierarchy. In Mesopotamia, the punishments prescribed in the famous Code of Hammurabi depended on social status. A free-born commoner who struck a person of equal rank had to pay a small fine, but if he struck "a man who is his superior, he shall receive 60 strokes with an oxtail whip in public." Clearly, class had consequences.

In all civilizations, free commoners represented the vast majority of the population and included artisans of all kinds, lower-level officials, soldiers and police, servants, and, most numerous of all, farmers. It was their surplus production—appropriated through a variety of taxes, rents, required labor, and tribute payments—that supported the upper classes. At least some of these people were aware of, and resented, these forced extractions and their position in the social hierarchy. Most Chinese peasants, for example, owned little land of their own and worked on plots granted to them by royal or aristocratic landowners. An ancient poem compared the exploiting landlords to rats and expressed the farmers' vision of a better life.

> Large rats! Large rats!
> Do not eat our spring grain!
> Three years have we had to do with you.
> And you have not been willing to think of our toil.
> We will leave you,
> And go to those happy borders.
> Happy borders, happy borders!
> Who will there make us always to groan?[10]

At the bottom of social hierarchies everywhere were slaves. Slavery and civilization, in fact, seem to have emerged together. The Code of Hammurabi, dating to almost 2000 B.C.E., mentions slavery in a casual, accepted, matter-of-fact way. Female slaves, captured in the many wars among rival Mesopotamian cities, were put to work in large-scale semi-industrial weaving enterprises, while males helped to maintain irrigation canals and construct ziggurats. Others worked as domestic servants in the households of their owners. In all of the First Civilizations, slaves—derived from prisoners of war, criminals, and debtors—were available for sale; for work in the fields, mines, homes, and shops of their owner; or on occasion for sacrifice. From the days of the earliest civilizations until the nineteenth century, the practice of "people owning people" has been an enduring feature of state-based societies everywhere.

The practice of slavery in ancient times varied considerably from place to place. Egypt and the Indus Valley civilizations initially had far fewer slaves than did Mesopotamia, which was highly militarized. Later, the Greeks of Athens and the Romans employed slaves far more extensively than did the Chinese or Indians (see Chapter 6). Furthermore, most ancient slavery differed from the type of slavery practiced in the Americas during recent centuries; in the early civilizations, slaves were not a primary agricultural labor force, many children of slaves could become free people, and slavery was not associated primarily with "blackness" or with Africa.

Hierarchies of Gender

■ Change

In what ways have historians tried to explain the origins of patriarchy?

Accompanying the hierarchies of class were those of gender, as civilizations everywhere undermined the earlier and more equal relationships between men and women. Most scholars agree that early horticultural societies, those using a hoe or digging stick, continued the relative gender equality that had characterized Paleolithic peoples. In such societies, women were much involved in agricultural labor, which generated most of the food for the village. Women were also engaged in spinning, weaving, and making pots—activities that were compatible with their role as mothers. Their central economic function, together with their amazing capacity to produce new life, gave women considerable respect and, arguably, a status generally equal to that of men. Some scholars have seen this respect and status reflected, at least in Europe and the Middle East, in a proliferation of figurines, masks, signs, symbols, and myths, all featuring women and feminine themes dealing with birth, growth, death, and regeneration.[11]

But as the First Civilizations took shape, the institutions and values of male dominance, often referred to as patriarchy, gradually emerged. The big question, of course, lies in trying to explain this momentous change. What was it about civilization that seemed to generate patriarchy?

One approach to answering this question highlights the role of a new and more intensive form of agriculture, involving the use of animal-drawn plows and the keeping and milking of large herds of animals. Unlike earlier farming practices that relied on a hoe or digging stick, plow-based agriculture meant heavier work, which men were better able to perform. Taking place at a distance from the village, this new form of agriculture was perhaps less compatible with women's primary responsibility for child rearing. Furthermore, the growing population of civilizations meant that women were more often pregnant and even more deeply involved in child care than before. Thus, in plow-based communities, men took over most of the farming work, and the status of women declined correspondingly, even though their other productive activities—weaving and food preparation, for example—continued. "As women were increasingly relegated to secondary tasks . . . ," writes archeologist Margaret Ehrenberg, "they had fewer personal resources with which to assert their status."[12]

Patriarchy also developed in civilizations untouched by plow agriculture, such as those of Mesoamerica and the Andes. Perhaps something else was at work. Historian David Christian suggests that the declining position of women was connected more generally to the growth of social complexity in civilizations as economic, religious, and political "specialists" became more prominent. Because men were less important in the household, they may have been more available to assume the powerful and prestigious specialist roles. From these positions of authority, men were able to shape the values and practices of their societies in ways that benefited themselves at the expense of women. Here, perhaps, lies the origin of an ancient distinction between the realm of the home, defined as the domain of women, and the world of public life, associated with men.[13]

Women have long been identified not only with the home but also with nature, for they are intimately involved in the fundamental natural process of reproduction. But civilization seemed to highlight culture, or the human mastery of nature, through agriculture, monumental art and architecture, and the creation of large-scale cities and states. Did this mean, as some scholars have suggested, that women were now associated with an inferior dimension of human life (nature), while men assumed responsibility for the higher order of culture?[14]

A further aspect of civilization that may well have contributed to patriarchy was warfare. Large-scale military conflict with professionally led armies was a feature of almost all of the First Civilizations, and female prisoners of war often were the first slaves. With military service largely restricted to men, its growing prominence in the affairs of civilizations served to enhance the power and prestige of a male warrior class. So too, perhaps, did private property and commerce, central elements of the First Civilizations. Without sharp restrictions on women's sexual activity, how could a father be certain that family property would be inherited by his offspring? In addition, the buying and selling associated with commerce was soon applied to male rights over women, as female slaves, concubines, and wives were exchanged among men.

Patriarchy in Practice

Whatever the precise origins of patriarchy, male dominance permeated the First Civilizations, marking a gradual change from the more equal relationships of men and women within agricultural villages or Paleolithic bands. Historian Gerda Lerner documented this transition in ancient Mesopotamian civilization. By the second millennium B.C.E., various written laws codified and sought to enforce a patriarchal family life that offered women a measure of paternalistic protection while insisting on their submission to the unquestioned authority of men. Central to these laws was the regulation of female sexuality. A wife caught sleeping with another man might be drowned at her husband's discretion, whereas he was permitted to enjoy sexual relations with his female servants, though not with another man's wife. Divorce was far easier for a man than for his wife. Rape was a serious offense, but the injured party was primarily the father or the husband of the victim, rather than the violated woman herself. Even elite women, who were often

■ Comparison
How did Mesopotamian and Egyptian patriarchy differ from each other?

allowed to act on behalf of their powerful husbands, saw themselves as dependent. "Let all be well with [my husband]," prayed one such wife, "that I may prosper under his protection."[15]

Furthermore, women in Mesopotamian civilization were sometimes divided into two sharply distinguished categories. Respectable women, those under the protection and sexual control of one man, were required to be veiled when outside the home, whereas nonrespectable women, such as slaves and prostitutes, were forbidden to do so and were subject to severe punishment if they presumed to cover their heads.

Finally, the powerful goddesses of earlier times were gradually relegated to the home and hearth and were replaced by dominant male deities, who now were credited with the power of creation and fertility and viewed as the patrons of wisdom and learning. The culmination of this "demotion of the goddess," argues Gilda Lerner, lies in the Hebrew Scriptures, in which a single male deity, Yahweh, alone undertakes the act of creation without any participation of a female goddess.

Patriarchy was not everywhere the same, however. Egypt, while clearly patriarchal, afforded its women greater opportunities than did most other First Civilizations. In Egypt, women were recognized as legal equals to men, able to own property and slaves, to administer and sell land, to make their own wills, to sign their own marriage contracts, and to initiate divorce. Royal women occasionally exercised significant political power, acting as regents for their young sons or more rarely as queens in their own right. Clearly, though, this was seen as abnormal, for Egypt's most famous queen, Hatshepsut (reigned 1472–1457 B.C.E.), was sometimes portrayed in statues as a man, dressed in male clothing and sporting the traditional false beard of the pharaoh. Moreover, married women in Egypt were not veiled as in Mesopotamia. Statues and paintings often showed men and women in affectionate poses and as equal partners, as can be seen in the photo at the beginning of this chapter. Although marriages were clearly arranged by parents, the love poetry of New Kingdom Egypt (1550–1064 B.C.E.) suggests an element of romance and longing. One lovesick boy lamented the absence of his beloved, referred to as a "sister."

> Seven days since I saw my sister,
> and sickness invaded me; . . .
> The sight of her makes me well . . .
> Her speaking makes me strong;
> Embracing her expels my malady. . . .

And a young woman exults at the sight of her love:

> I passed before his house,
> I found his door ajar;
> My brother stood by his mother; . . .

He looked at me as I passed by, . . .
How my heart exulted in gladness,
My brother, at your sight[16]

The Rise of the State

What, we might reasonably ask, held ancient civilizations together despite the many tensions and complexities of urban living and the vast inequalities of civilized societies? Why did they not fly apart amid the resentments born of class and gender hierarchies? The answer, in large part, lay in yet another distinctive feature of the First Civilizations—states. Organized around particular cities or larger territories, early states were headed almost everywhere by kings, who employed a variety of ranked officials, exercised a measure of control over society, and defended it against external enemies. To modern people, the state is such a familiar reality that we find it difficult to imagine life without it. Nonetheless, it is a quite recent invention in human history, with the state replacing, or at least supplementing, kinship as the basic organizing principle of society and exercising far greater authority than earlier chiefdoms.

Coercion and Consent

Early states in Mesopotamia, Egypt, China, Mesoamerica, and elsewhere drew their power from various sources, all of which assisted in providing cohesion for the First Civilizations. One basis of power was the recognition that the complexity of life in cities or densely populated territories required some authority to coordinate and regulate the community. Someone had to organize the irrigation systems of river valley civilizations. Someone had to adjudicate conflicts among the many different peoples, unrelated to one another, who rubbed elbows in the early cities. Someone had to direct efforts to defend the city or territory against aggressive outsiders. The state, in short, solved certain widely shared problems and therefore had a measure of voluntary support among the population. For many people, it was surely useful.

■ **Change**
What were the sources of state authority in the First Civilizations?

The state, however, was more useful for some people than for others, for it also served to protect the privileges of the upper classes, to require farmers to give up a portion of their product to support city-dwellers, and to demand work on large public projects such as pyramids and fortifications. If necessary, state authorities had the ability, and the willingness, to use force to compel obedience. The Egyptian teacher mentioned earlier described to his reluctant student what happens to a peasant unable to pay his tax in grain.

> Now the scribe lands on the shore. He surveys the harvest. Attendants are behind him with staffs, Nubians with clubs. One says [to the peasant], "Give grain." There is none. He is beaten savagely. He is bound, thrown into a well, submerged head

A Mesopotamian Ziggurat
This massive ziggurat/temple to the Mesopotamian moon god Nanna was built around 2100 B.C.E. in the city of Ur. The solitary figure standing atop the staircase illustrates the size of this huge structure. (Richard Ashworth/Robert Harding World Imagery/Corbis)

down. His wife is bound in his presence. His children are in fetters. His neighbors abandon them and flee.[17]

Such was the power of the state, as rulers accumulated the resources to pay for officials, soldiers, police, and attendants. This capacity for violence and coercion marked off the states of the First Civilizations from earlier chiefdoms, whose leaders had only persuasion, prestige, and gifts to back up their authority.

Force, however, was not always necessary, for the First Civilizations soon generated ideas suggesting that state authority and class and gender inequalities were normal, natural, and ordained by the gods. Kingship everywhere was associated with the sacred. Ancient Chinese kings were known as the Son of Heaven, and they alone could perform the rituals and sacrifices necessary to keep the cosmos in balance. Mesopotamian rulers were thought to be the stewards of their city's patron gods. Their symbols of kingship—crown, throne, scepter, mace—were said to be of divine origin, sent to earth when the gods established monarchy. Egyptians, most of all, invested their pharaohs with divine qualities. Rulers claimed to embody all the major gods of Egypt, and their supernatural power ensured the regular flooding of the Nile and the defeat of the country's enemies.

But if religion served most often to justify unequal power and privilege, it might also on occasion be used to restrain, or even undermine, the established order. Hammurabi claimed that his law code was inspired by Marduk, the chief god of Babylon, and was intended to "bring about the rule of righteousness in the land, to destroy the wicked and the evil-doers; so that the strong should not harm the weak."[18] Another Mesopotamian monarch, Urukagina from the city of Lagash, claimed authority from the city's patron god for reforms aimed at ending the corruption and tyranny of a previous ruler. In China during the Zhou dynasty (1122–256 B.C.E.), emperors ruled by the Mandate of Heaven, but their bad behavior could result in the removal of that mandate and the overthrow of the ruler.

Writing and Accounting

A further support for state authority lay in the remarkable invention of writing. It was a powerful and transforming innovation, regarded almost everywhere as a gift

Snapshot　　Writing in Ancient Civilizations

Most of the early writing systems were "logophonetic," using symbols to designate both whole words and particular sounds or syllables. Chinese characters, which indicated only words, were an exception. None of them employed alphabets.

Location	Type	Initial Use	Example	Comment
Sumer	Cuneiform: wedge-shaped symbols on clay tablets representing objects, abstract ideas, sounds, and syllables	Records of economic transactions, such as temple payments and taxes	bird	Regarded as the world's first written language; other languages such as Babylonian and Assryian were written with Sumerian script
Egypt	Hieroglyphs ("sacred carvings"): a series of signs that denote words and consonants (but not vowels or syllables)	Business and administrative purposes; later used for religious inscriptions, stories, poetry, hymns, and mathematics	rain, dew, storm	For everyday use, less formal systems of cursive writing (known as "hieratic" and "demotic") were developed
Andean	Quipu: a complex system of knotted cords in which the color, length, type, and location of knots conveyed mostly numerical meaning	Various accounting functions; perhaps also used to express words	numerical data (possibly in codes), words and ideas	Widely used in the Inca Empire; recent discoveries place quipus in Caral some 5,000 years ago
Indus River Valley	Some 400 pictographic symbols representing sounds and words, probably expressing a Dravidian language currently spoken in southern India	Found on thousands of clay seals and pottery; probably used to mark merchandise	6 fish	As yet undeciphered
China	Oracle bone script: pictographs (stylized drawings) with no phonetic meaning	Inscribed on turtle shells or animal bones; used for divination (predicting the future) in the royal court of Shang dynasty rulers	horse	Direct ancestor of contemporary Chinese characters
Olmec	Signs that represent sounds (syllables) and words; numbering system using bars and dots	Used to record the names and deeds of rulers and shamans, as well as battles and astronomical data	jaguar	Structurally similar to later Mayan script; Olmec calendars were highly accurate and the basis for later Mesoamerican calendars

from the gods, while people without writing often saw it as something magical or supernatural. Distinctive forms of writing emerged in all of the First Civilizations except the Andes, although some scholars now regard their knotted strings, or quipus, as a kind of writing.[19]

Writing sustained the First Civilizations and their successors in many ways. Literacy defined elite status and conveyed enormous prestige to those who possessed it. Because it can be learned, writing also provided a means for some commoners to join the charmed circle of the literate. Writing as propaganda, celebrating the great deeds of the kings, featured prominently, especially among the Egyptians and later among the Maya. A hymn to the pharaoh, dating to about 1850 B.C.E., extravagantly praised the ruler.

> He has come unto us . . . and has given peace to the two Riverbanks
> . . . and has made Egypt to live; he hath banished its suffering;
> . . . he has caused the throat of the subjects to breathe
> . . . and has trodden down foreign countries
> . . . he has delivered them that were robbed
> . . . he has come unto us, that we may (nurture up?) our children and
> bury our aged ones.[20]

In Mesopotamia and elsewhere, writing served an accounting function, recording who had paid their taxes, who owed what to the temple, and how much workers had earned. Thus it immensely strengthened bureaucracy. Complex calendars indicated precisely when certain rituals should be performed. Writing also gave weight and specificity to orders, regulations, and laws. Hammurabi's famous law code, while correcting certain abuses, made crystal clear that fundamental distinctions divided men and women and separated slaves, commoners, and people of higher rank.

Once it had been developed, writing, like religion, proved hard to control and operated as a "wild card" in human affairs. It gave rise to literature and philosophy, to astronomy and mathematics, and, in some places, to history. On occasion, the written word proved threatening, rather than supportive, to rulers. China's so-called First Emperor, Qin Shihuangdi (reigned 221–210 B.C.E.), allegedly buried alive some 460 scholars and burned their books when they challenged his brutal efforts to unify China's many warring states, or so his later critics claimed. Thus writing became a major arena for social and political conflict, and rulers always have sought to control it.

The Grandeur of Kings

Yet another source of state authority derived from the lavish lifestyle of elites, the impressive rituals they arranged, and the imposing structures they created. Everywhere, kings, high officials, and their families lived in luxurious palaces, dressed in splendid clothing, bedecked themselves with the loveliest jewelry, and were attended by endless servants. Their deaths triggered elaborate burials, of which the pyramids of the Egyptian pharaohs were perhaps the most ostentatious. Almost all of the First Civilizations accompanied high-status funerals with the human sacrifice of numerous retainers, who would nourish the souls or serve the needs of their rulers in the afterlife. Monumental palaces, temples, ziggurats, pyramids, and statues conveyed the immense power of the state and its elite rulers. The Olmec civilization of Mesoamerica (1200–400 B.C.E.) erected enormous human heads, more than ten feet tall and weighing at least twenty tons, carved from blocks of basalt and probably representing particular rulers. Somewhat later the Maya Temple of the Giant Jaguar, towering 154 feet tall, was the most impressive among many temples, pyramids, and palaces that graced the city of Tikal. All of this must have seemed overwhelming to common people in the cities and villages of the First Civilizations.

Olmec Head

This colossal statue, some six feet high and five feet wide, is one of seventeen such carvings, dating to the first millennium B.C.E., that were discovered in the territory of the ancient Olmec civilization. Thought to represent individual rulers, each of the statues has a distinct and realistically portrayed face. (Danny Lehman/Corbis)

Comparing Mesopotamia and Egypt

A productive agricultural technology, city living, immense class inequalities, patriarchy, the emerging power of states—all of these were common features of First Civilizations across the world and also of those that followed. Still, these civilizations were not everywhere the same, for differences in political organization, religious beliefs and practices, the role of women, and much more gave rise to distinctive traditions. Nor were they static. Like all human communities, they changed over the centuries. Finally, these civilizations did not exist in isolation, for they participated in networks of interactions with near and sometimes more distant neighbors. In looking more closely at two of these First Civilizations—Mesopotamia and Egypt—we can catch a glimpse of the differences, changes, and connections that characterized early civilizations.

■ **Comparison**

In what ways did Mesopotamian and Egyptian civilizations differ from each other?

Environment and Culture

The civilizations of both Mesopotamia and Egypt grew up in river valleys and depended on their rivers to sustain a productive agriculture in otherwise arid lands. Those rivers, however, had radically different characteristics. At the heart of Egyptian life was the Nile, "that green gash of teeming life," which rose predictably every year to bring the soil and water that nurtured a rich Egyptian agriculture. The

Snapshot   **Key Moments in Mesopotamian History**

Beginning of irrigated agriculture	6000 B.C.E.
Period of independent Sumerian city-states	3200–2350 B.C.E
Earliest cuneiform texts	3000 B.C.E.
First Sumerian law codes	2500 B.C.E.
First Mesopotamian empire: conquest of Sumer by Sargon of Akkad	2350 B.C.E.
Epic of Gilgamesh compiled	after 2000 B.C.E.
Babylonian empire	1900–1500 B.C.E.
Reign of Hammurabi	1792–1750 B.C.E.
Assyrian rule in Mesopotamia	900–612 B.C.E.
Assyrian conquest of Israel	722 B.C.E.
Babylonian conquest of Judah by King Nebuchadnezzar	586 B.C.E.
Mesopotamia incorporated into Persian empire	by 500 B.C.E.

Tigris and Euphrates rivers, which gave life to Mesopotamian civilization, also rose annually, but "unpredictably and fitfully, breaking man's dikes and submerging his crops."[21] (See Map 3.2.) Furthermore, an open environment without serious obstacles to travel made Mesopotamia far more vulnerable to invasion than the much more protected space of Egypt, which was surrounded by deserts, mountains, seas, and cataracts. For long periods of its history, Egypt enjoyed a kind of "free security" from external attack that Mesopotamians could only have envied.

Does the physical environment shape the human cultures that develop within it? Most historians are reluctant to endorse any kind of "determinism," especially one suggesting that "geography is destiny," but in the case of Mesopotamia and Egypt, many scholars have seen at least some relationship between the physical setting and culture.

In at least some of its literature, the Mesopotamian outlook on life, which developed within a precarious, unpredictable, and often violent environment, viewed humankind as caught in an inherently disorderly world, subject to the whims of capricious and quarreling gods, and facing death without much hope of a life beyond. A Mesopotamian poet complained: "I have prayed to the gods and sacrificed, but who can understand the gods in heaven? Who knows what they plan for us? Who has ever been able to understand a god's conduct?"[22] In the *Epic of Gilgamesh*, Mesopotamia's most famous literary work, death is described as a journey "down the road from which there is no turning back." The afterworld is a "house whose people sit in darkness; dust is their food and clay is their meat." In a futile effort to avoid this fate, the hero Gilgamesh sets out on a search for eternal

Map 3.2 Mesopotamia
After about 1,000 years of independent and competitive existence, the city-states of Sumer were incorporated into a number of larger imperial states based in Akkad, Babylon, and then Assyria.

life, but after many adventures and false starts, he is told, "[Y]ou will never find that life for which you are looking. When the gods created man, they allotted to him death, but life they retained in their own keeping." Nonetheless, not all is despair.

> As for you, Gilgamesh, fill your belly with good things; day and night, night and day, dance and be merry, feast and rejoice. Let your clothes be fresh, bathe yourself in water, cherish the little child that holds your hand, and make your wife happy in your embrace; for this too is the lot of man.[23]

By contrast, elite literate culture in Egypt, developing in a more stable, predictable, and beneficent environment, produced a rather more cheerful and hopeful outlook on the world. The rebirth of the sun every day and of the river every year seemed to assure Egyptians that life would prevail over death. The amazing pyramids, constructed during Egypt's Old Kingdom (2663–2195 B.C.E.), reflected the firm belief that at least the pharaohs and other high-ranking people could successfully make the journey to eternal life in the Land of the West. Incantations carved in royal burial chambers of the pharaohs describe an afterlife that Gilgamesh could only have envied.

> The gatekeeper comes out to you,
> He grasps your hand,
> Takes you into heaven, to your father, Geb.
> He rejoices at your coming,
> Gives you his hand,
> Kisses you, caresses you,
> Sets before you the spirits, the imperishable stars.
> The hidden ones worship you,
> The great ones surround you,
> The watchers wait on you,
> Barley is threshed for you . . .
> Rise up, O Teti, you shall not die.

Over time, larger groups of people, beyond the pharaoh and his entourage, gained access to the afterlife, if they followed proper procedures. By the New Kingdom (1550–1064 B.C.E.), a moral element had entered the equation for eternal life as claims on immortality were now made on the basis of ethical living. One text used in burial ceremonies required "a negative confession" of those seeking entrance to the afterlife: "I have not done crimes against the people; I have not mistreated cattle . . . ; I have not robbed the poor . . . ; I have not made anyone suffer."[24] Thus Egyptian civilization not only affirmed the possibility of eternal life but also democratized access to it.

If the different environments of Mesopotamia and Egypt shaped their societies and cultures, those civilizations, with their mounting populations and growing demand for resources, likewise had an impact on the environment.[25] In Sumer (southern Mesopotamia), deforestation and soil erosion decreased crop yields by some 65 percent between 2400 and 1700 B.C.E. Also contributing to this disaster was the increasing salinization of the soil, a long-term outcome of intensive irrigation. By 2000 B.C.E., there were reports that "the earth turned white" as salt accumulated in the soil. As a result, wheat was largely replaced by barley, which is far more tolerant of salty conditions. This ecological deterioration clearly weakened Sumerian city-states, facilitated their conquest by foreigners, and shifted the center of Mesopotamian civilization permanently to the north.

Egypt, by contrast, created a more sustainable agricultural system, which lasted for thousands of years and contributed to the remarkable continuity of its civilization. Whereas Sumerian irrigation involved a complex and artificial network of canals and dikes that led to the salinization of the soil, its Egyptian counterpart was much less intrusive, simply regulating the natural flow of the Nile. Such a system avoided the problem of salty soils, allowing Egyptian agriculture to emphasize wheat production, but it depended on the general regularity and relative gentleness of the Nile's annual flooding. On occasion, that pattern was interrupted, with serious consequences for Egyptian society. An extended period of low floods between 2250 and 1950 B.C.E. led to sharply reduced agricultural output, large-scale starvation, the loss of livestock, and, consequently, social upheaval and political disruption. Nonetheless, Egypt's ability to work *with* its more favorable natural environment enabled a degree of stability and continuity that proved impossible in Sumer, where human action intruded more heavily into a less benevolent natural setting.

Cities and States

Politically as well as culturally and environmentally, Mesopotamian and Egyptian civilizations differed sharply. For its first thousand years (3200–2350 B.C.E.), Mesopotamian civilization, located in the southern Tigris-Euphrates region known as Sumer, was organized in a dozen or more separate and independent city-states. Each city-state was ruled by a king, who claimed to represent the city's patron deity and who controlled the affairs of the walled city and surrounding rural area. Quite remarkably, some 80 percent of the population of Sumer lived in one or another of these city-states, making Mesopotamia the most thoroughly urbanized society of ancient times. The chief reason for this massive urbanization, however, lay in the great flaw of this system, for frequent warfare among these Sumerian city-states caused people living in rural areas to flee to the walled cities for protection. With no overarching authority, rivalry over land and water often led to violent conflict. After one such conflict destroyed the city of Ur and desecrated its temple, a poet lamented the city's sad fate.

> After your city had been destroyed, how now can you exist!
> After your house had been destroyed, how has your heart led you on!
> Your city has become a strange city . . .
> Your house has become a house of tears.[26]

These conflicts, together with environmental devastation, eventually left Sumerian cities vulnerable to outside forces, and after about 2350 B.C.E., stronger peoples from northern Mesopotamia conquered Sumer's warring cities, bringing an end to the Sumerian phase of Mesopotamian civilization. First the Akkadians (2350–2000 B.C.E.) and later the Babylonians (1900–1500 B.C.E.) and the Assyrians (900–612 B.C.E.) created larger territorial states or bureaucratic empires that encompassed all or most of Mesopotamia. Periods of political unity now descended upon this First Civilization, but it was unity imposed from outside. Much later, a similar process befell the Greek city-states, whose endemic warfare invited Macedonian invasion and their subsequent incorporation into the empires of Alexander the Great and then of the Romans (see Chapter 4).

Egyptian civilization, by contrast, began its history around 3100 B.C.E., with the merger of several earlier states or chiefdoms into a unified territory that stretched some 1,000 miles along the Nile. For an amazing 3,000 years, Egypt maintained that unity and independence, though with occasional interruptions. A combination

of wind patterns that made it easy to sail south along the Nile and a current flow-
ing north facilitated communication, exchange, unity, and stability within the Nile
Valley. Here was a record of political longevity and continuity that the
Mesopotamians and many other ancient peoples might well have envied.

Cities in Egypt were far less important than in Mesopotamia, although political capitals, market centers, and major burial sites gave it an urban presence as well.
Most people lived in agricultural villages along the river rather than in urban centers, perhaps because Egypt's greater security made it less necessary for people to
gather in fortified towns. The focus of the Egyptian state resided in the pharaoh,
believed to be a god in human form. He alone ensured the daily rising of the sun
and the annual flooding of the Nile. All of the country's many officials served at his
pleasure; the law of the land was simply the pharaoh's edict; and access to the afterlife lay in proximity to him and burial in or near his towering pyramids.

This image of the pharaoh and his role as an enduring symbol of Egyptian civilization persisted over the course of three millennia, but the realities of Egyptian
political life changed over time. By 2400 B.C.E., the power of the pharaoh had
diminished, as local officials and nobles, who had been awarded their own land and

Snapshot   Key Moments in Nile Valley Civilizations

Small-scale states in Sudanic Africa	5000 B.C.E.
Nubian kingdom of Ta-Seti	3400–3200 B.C.E.
Unification of Egypt as a single state	3100 B.C.E.
Frequent warfare between Egypt and Nubian states	3100–2600 B.C.E.
Old Kingdom Egypt (high point of pharaohs' power and pyramid building)	2663–2195 B.C.E.
Nubian kingdom of Kush established	2500 B.C.E.
Egyptian commercial expeditions to Nubia	2300 B.C.E.
Hyksos invasion and rule of Egypt	1650–1550 B.C.E.
New Kingdom Egypt	1550–1064 B.C.E.
Emergence of Egyptian empire	1500 B.C.E.
Queen Hatshepsut launches expeditions to Land of Punt, probably along the East African coast	1473–1458 B.C.E.
Kush conquest of Egypt	760–660 B.C.E.
Assyrian conquest of Egypt	671–651 B.C.E.
Persian rule in Egypt	525–404 B.C.E.
Roman conquest of Egypt	30 B.C.E.

were able to pass their positions on to their sons, assumed greater authority. When changes in the weather resulted in the Nile's repeated failure to flood properly around 2200 B.C.E., the authority of the pharaoh was severely discredited, and Egypt dissolved for several centuries into a series of local principalities.

Even when centralized rule was restored around 2000 B.C.E., the pharaohs never regained their old power and prestige. Kings were now warned that they too would have to account for their actions at the Day of Judgment. Nobles no longer sought to be buried near the pharaoh's pyramid but instead created their own more modest tombs in their own areas. Osiris, the god of the dead, became increasingly prominent, and "all men who were worthy . . . not merely those who had known the pharaoh in life" could aspire to immortality in his realm.[27]

Interaction and Exchange

Although Mesopotamia and Egypt represented separate and distinct civilizations, they interacted frequently with each other and with both near and more distant neighbors. Even in these ancient times, the First Civilizations were embedded in larger networks of commerce, culture, and power. None of them stood alone.

The early beginnings of Egyptian civilization illustrate the point. Its agriculture drew upon wheat and barley, which reached Egypt from Mesopotamia, as well as gourds, watermelon, domesticated donkeys, and cattle, which derived from Sudan. Some scholars argue that Egypt's step pyramids and its system of writing were stimulated by Mesopotamian models. The practice of "divine kingship" seems to have derived from the central or eastern Sudan, where small-scale agricultural communities had long viewed their rulers as sacred and buried them with various servants and officials. From this complex of influences, the Egyptians created something distinct and unique, but that civilization had roots in both Africa and Southwest Asia.[28]

Furthermore, once they were established, both Mesopotamia and Egypt carried on extensive long-distance trade. Sumerian merchants had established seaborne contact with the Indus Valley civilization as early as 2300 B.C.E. Other trade routes connected it to Anatolia (present-day Turkey), Egypt, Iran, and Afghanistan. During Akkadian rule over Mesopotamia, a Sumerian poet described its capital of Agade.

> In those days the dwellings of Agade were filled with gold,
> its bright-shining houses were filled with silver,
> into its granaries were brought copper, tin, slabs of
> lapis lazuli [a blue gemstone], its silos bulged at the sides . . .
> its quay where the boats docked were all bustle. . . .[29]

All of this and more came from far away.

Egyptian trade likewise extended far afield. Beyond its involvement with the Mediterranean and the Middle East, Egyptian trading journeys extended deep into

■ **Connection**

In what ways were Mesopotamian and Egyptian civilizations shaped by their interactions with near and distant neighbors?

Egypt and Nubia
By the fourteenth century B.C.E., Nubia was a part of an Egyptian empire. This wall painting shows Nubian princes bringing gifts or tribute, including rings and bags of gold, to Huy, the Egyptian viceroy of Nubia. The mural comes from Huy's tomb. (Courtesy of the Trustees of the British Museum)

Africa, including Nubia, south of Egypt in the Nile Valley, and Punt, along the East African coast of Ethiopia and Somalia. One Egyptian official described his return from an expedition to Nubia: "I came down with three hundred donkeys laden with incense, ebony . . . panther skins, elephant tusks, throw sticks, and all sorts of good products."[30] What most intrigued the very young pharaoh who sent him, however, was a dancing dwarf that accompanied the expedition back to Egypt.

Along with trade goods went cultural influence from the civilizations of Mesopotamia and Egypt. Among the smaller societies of the region to feel this influence were the Hebrews, who had migrated from Mesopotamia to Palestine and Egypt early in their history. Their sacred writings, recorded in the Old Testament, showed the influence of Mesopotamia in the "eye for an eye" principle of their legal system and in the story of a flood that destroyed the world. Unique to the Hebrews, however, was their emerging awareness of a merciful and single deity, Yahweh, who demanded an ethical life from his people. This conception subsequently achieved global significance when it was taken over by Christianity and Islam.

The Phoenicians, who were commercially active in the Mediterranean basin from their homeland in present-day Lebanon, also were influenced by Mesopotamian civilization. They adopted the Mesopotamian fertility goddess Ishtar, renaming her Astarte. They also adapted the Sumerian cuneiform method of writing to a much easier alphabetic system, which later became the basis for Greek and Latin writing. Various Indo-European peoples, dispersing probably from north-central Anatolia, also incorporated Sumerian deities into their own religions as well as bronze metallurgy and the wheel into their economies. When their widespread migrations carried them across much of Eurasia, they took these Sumerian cultural artifacts with them.

Egyptian cultural influence likewise spread in several directions. Nubian civilization, located to the south of Egypt in the Nile Valley, not only traded with its more powerful neighbor but also was subject to periodic military intervention and political control from Egypt. Skilled Nubian archers were actively recruited for service as mercenaries in Egyptian armies. They often married Egyptian women and were buried in Egyptian style. All of this led to the diffusion of Egyptian culture in Nubia, expressed in building Egyptian-style pyramids, worshipping Egyptian gods and goddesses, and making use of Egyptian hieroglyphic writing. Despite this cultural borrowing, Nubia remained a distinct civilization, developing its own alphabetic script, retaining many of its own gods, developing a major ironworking industry by 500 B.C.E., and asserting its political independence whenever possible. The Nubian kingdom of Kush, in fact, invaded Egypt in 760 B.C.E. and ruled it for about 100 years.

In the Mediterranean basin, clear Egyptian influence is visible in the art of the Minoan civilization, which emerged on the island of Crete about 2500 B.C.E. More controversial has been the claim by historian Martin Bernal in a much-publicized book, *Black Athena* (1987), that ancient Greek culture—its art, religion, philosophy, and language—drew heavily upon Egyptian as well as Mesopotamian precedents. His book lit up a passionate debate among scholars. To some of his critics, Bernal seemed to undermine the originality of Greek civilization by suggesting that it had an Afro-Asian origin. His supporters accused the critics of Eurocentrism. Whatever its outcome, the academic controversy surrounding Bernal's book served to focus attention on Egypt's relationship to black Africa and to the world of the Mediterranean basin.

Influence was not a one-way street, however, as Egypt and Mesopotamia likewise felt the impact of neighboring peoples. Pastoral peoples, speaking Indo-European languages and living in what is now southern Russia, had domesticated the horse by perhaps 4000 B.C.E. and later learned to tie that powerful animal to wheeled carts and chariots. This new technology provided a fearsome military potential that enabled various chariot-driving peoples to temporarily overwhelm ancient civilizations. Based in Anatolia, the Hittites overran the powerful Babylonian empire of Mesopotamia in 1595 B.C.E. About the same time, another pastoral group with chariots, the Hyksos, invaded Egypt and ruled it for more than a century (1650–1535 B.C.E.). But chariot technology was portable, and soon both the Egyptians and the Mesopotamians incorporated it into their own military forces. In fact, this powerful military innovation, together with the knowledge of bronze metallurgy, spread quickly and widely, reaching China by 1200 B.C.E. There it enabled the creation of a strong Chinese state ruled by the Shang dynasty. All of these developments provide evidence of at least indirect connections across the entire Eurasian landmass in ancient times. Even then, no civilization was wholly isolated from larger patterns of interaction.

In Egypt, the intrusion of the chariot-driving Hyksos shattered the sense of security that this Nile Valley civilization had long enjoyed. It also stimulated the normally complacent Egyptians to adopt a number of technologies pioneered earlier in Asia, including the horse-drawn chariot; new kinds of armor, bows, daggers, and swords; improved methods of spinning and weaving; new musical instruments; and olive and pomegranate trees. Absorbing these foreign innovations, Egyptians expelled the Hyksos and went on to create their own empire, both in Nubia and in the eastern Mediterranean regions of Syria and Palestine. By 1500 B.C.E., the previously self-contained Egypt became for several centuries an imperial state bridging Africa and Asia, ruling over substantial numbers of non-Egyptian peoples (see Map 3.3). It also

Map 3.3   An Egyptian Empire
During the New Kingdom period after 1550 B.C.E., Egypt became for several centuries an empire, extending its political control southward into Nubia and northward into Palestine.

became part of an international political system that included the Babylonian and later Assyrian empires of Mesopotamia as well as many other peoples of the region. Egyptian and Babylonian rulers engaged in regular diplomatic correspondence, referred to one another as "brother," exchanged gifts, and married their daughters into one another's families. One Babylonian king complained to an Egyptian pharaoh that the delegation that had come to take his daughter to Egypt contained only five carriages. What would his courtiers say about the daughter of a great ruler traveling with such a paltry escort?[31]

Reflections: "Civilization": What's in a Word?

In examining the cultures of Mesopotamia and Egypt, we are worlds away from life in agricultural villages or Paleolithic bands. Much the same holds for those of the Indus Valley, China, Mesoamerica, and the Andes. Strangely enough, historians have been somewhat uncertain as to how to refer to these new forms of human community. Following common practice, I have called them "civilizations," but scholars have reservations about the term for two reasons. The first is its implication of superiority. In popular usage, "civilization" suggests refined behavior, a "higher" form of society, something unreservedly positive. The opposite of "civilized"—barbarian, savage, or "uncivilized"—is normally understood as an insult implying inferiority, and that, of course, is precisely how the inhabitants of many civilizations have viewed those outside their own societies, particularly those neighboring peoples living without the alleged benefit of cities and states.

Modern assessments of the First Civilizations reveal a profound ambiguity about these new, larger, and more complex societies. On the one hand, these civilizations have given us inspiring art, profound reflections on the meaning of life, more productive technologies, increased control over nature, and the art of writing—all of which have been cause for celebration. On the other hand, as anthropologist Marvin Harris noted, "[H]uman beings learned for the first time how to bow, grovel, kneel, and kowtow."[32] Massive inequalities, state oppression, slavery, large-scale warfare, the subordination of women, and epidemic disease also accompanied the rise of civilization, generating discontent, rebellion, and sometimes the urge to escape. This ambiguity about the character of civilizations has led some historians to avoid the word, referring to early Egypt, Mesopotamia, and other regions instead as complex societies, urban-based societies, state-organized societies, or some more neutral term.

A second reservation about using the term "civilization" derives from its implication of solidity—the idea that civilizations represent distinct and widely shared identities with clear boundaries that mark them off from other such units. It is unlikely, however, that many people living in Mesopotamia, Norte Chico, or ancient China felt themselves part of a shared culture. Local communities defined by occupation, clan affiliation, village, city, or region were surely more important for most people than those of some larger civilization. At best, members of an educated upper class who shared a common literary tradition may have felt themselves part of some more inclusive civilization, but that left out most of the population. Moreover, unlike modern nations, none of the earlier civilizations had definite borders. Any identification with that civilization surely faded as distance from its core region increased. Finally, the line between civilizations and other kinds of societies is not always clear. Just when does a village or town become a city? At what point does a chiefdom become a state? Scholars continue to argue about these distinctions.

Given these reservations, should historians discard the notion of civilization? Maybe so, but this book continues to use it both because it is so deeply embedded in our way of thinking about the world and because no alternative concept has achieved widespread usage for making distinctions among different kinds of human communities. When the term appears in the text, try to keep in mind two points. First, as used by historians, "civilization" is a purely descriptive term, designating a particular type of human society—one with cities and states—and does not imply any judgment or assessment, any sense of superiority or inferiority. Second, it is used to define broad cultural patterns in particular geographic regions—Mesopotamia, the Peruvian coast, or China, for example—even though many people living in those regions may have been more aware of differences and conflicts than of those commonalities.

Second Thoughts

What's the Significance?

To assess your mastery of the material in this chapter, see the **Online Study Guide** at bedfordstmartins.com/strayer.

Norte Chico/Caral	Mohenjo Daro/Harappa	*Epic of Gilgamesh*
Indus Valley civilization	Code of Hammurabi	Egypt: "the gift of the Nile"
Olmec civilization	patriarchy	Nubia
Uruk	rise of the state	Hyksos

Big Picture Questions

1. What distinguished civilizations from other forms of human community?
2. How does the use of the term "civilization" by historians differ from that of popular usage? How do you use the term?
3. "Civilizations were held together largely by force." Do you agree with this assessment, or were there other mechanisms of integration as well?
4. In the development of the First Civilizations, what was gained for humankind, and what was lost?

Next Steps: For Further Study

Cyril Aldred, *The Egyptians* (1998). A brief and up-to-date account from a widely recognized expert.

Samuel Noah Kramer, *History Begins at Sumer* (1981). A classic account of Sumerian civilization, filled with wonderful stories and anecdotes.

David B. O'Connor, *Ancient Nubia: Egypt's Rival in Africa* (1994). An overview of this ancient African civilization, with lovely illustrations based on a museum exhibit.

Christopher A. Pool, *Olmec Archeology and Early Mesoamerica* (2007). A scholarly and up-to-date account of the earliest civilization in Mesoamerica.

Lauren Ristvet, *In the Beginning* (2007). A sweeping examination of the early phases of world history, from human evolution to the First Civilizations.

"The Ancient Indus Civilization," http://www.harappa.com/har/haro.html. Hundreds of vivid pictures and several brief essays on the Indus Valley civilization.

The British Museum, "Ancient Egypt," http://www.ancientegypt.co.uk/menu.html. An interactive exploration of Egyptian civilization.

For Web sites and documents related to this chapter, see **Make History** at bedfordstmartins.com/strayer.

PART TWO

The Classical Era in World History

500 B.C.E.–500 C.E.

Contents

After the First Civilizations:
What Changed and What Didn't?

Studying world history has much in common with using the zoom lens of a camera. Sometimes, we pull the lens back in order to get a picture of the broadest possible panorama. At other times, we zoom in a bit for a middle-range shot, or even further for a close-up of some particular feature of the historical landscape. Students of world history soon become comfortable with moving back and forth among these several perspectives.

As we bid farewell to the First Civilizations, we will take the opportunity to pull back the lens and look broadly, and briefly, at the entire age of agricultural civilizations, a period from about 3500 B.C.E., when the earliest of the First Civilizations arose, to about 1750 C.E., when the first Industrial Revolution launched a new and distinctively modern phase of world history. During these more than 5,000 years, the most prominent large-scale trend was the globalization of civilization as this new form of human community increasingly spread across the planet, encompassing more people and larger territories.

The first wave of that process, addressed in Chapter 3, was already global in scope, with expressions in Asia, Africa, and the Americas. Those First Civilizations generated the most impressive and powerful human societies created thus far, but they proved fragile and vulnerable as well. The always-quarreling city-states of ancient Mesopotamia had long ago been absorbed into the larger empires of Babylon and Assyria. During the first millennium B.C.E., Egypt too fell victim to a series of foreign invaders, including the forces of Nubia, Assyria, Alexander the Great, and the Roman Empire. The Indus Valley civilization likewise declined sharply, as deforestation, topsoil erosion, and decreased rainfall led to desertification and political collapse by 1500 B.C.E. Norte Chico civilization seems to have faded away by 1800 B.C.E. The end of Olmec civilization around 400 B.C.E. has long puzzled historians, for it seems that the Olmecs themselves razed and then abandoned their major cities, even as their civilizational style spread to neighboring peoples. About the same time, China's unified political system fragmented into a series of warring states.

Even if particular First Civilizations broke down, there was no going back. Civilization as a form of human community proved durable and resilient as well as periodically fragile. Thus, in the thousand years between 500 B.C.E. and 500 C.E., new or enlarged urban-centered and state-based societies emerged to replace the First Civilizations in the Mediterranean basin, the Middle East, India, China, Mesoamerica, and the Andes. Furthermore, smaller expressions of civilization began to take shape elsewhere—in Ethiopia and West Africa, in Japan and Indonesia, in Vietnam and Cambodia. In short, the development of civilization was becoming a global process.

Many of these "second wave" civilizations likewise perished in time, as the collapse of the Roman Empire, Han dynasty China, and the Mayan cities remind us. They were followed by yet a "third wave" of civilizations (roughly 500 to 1500 C.E.; see Part Three). Some of them represented the persistence or renewal of older patterns (China, Byzantium, the Aztecs, and the Incas, for example). Others, such as those in Western Europe, Russia, Japan, and West Africa, marked new expressions of civilization, all of which borrowed heavily from more-established neighboring civilizations. The largest of these, Islamic civilization, incorporated a number of older centers of civilization, Egypt and Mesopotamia for example, under the umbrella of a new religion. The globalization of civilization continued apace.

The size and prominence of these civilizations sometimes lead historians and history textbooks to ignore those cultures that did not embrace the city- and state-centered characteristic of civilizations. World history, as a field of study, has often been slanted in the direction of civilizations at the expense of other forms of human community. To counteract that tendency, the following chapters will, on occasion, point out the continuing historical development of gathering and hunting peoples, agricultural societies organized around kinship principles and village life, emerging chiefdoms, and pastoral peoples.

Continuities in Civilization

The renewal and expansion of civilization, however, remains the leading story. As this account of the human journey moves into the second and third waves of civilization, the question arises as to how they differed from the first ones. From a panoramic perspective, the answer is "not much." States and empires rose, expanded, and collapsed with a tiresome regularity, requiring history students to remember who was up and who was down at various times. It is arguable, however, that little fundamental change occurred amid these constant fluctuations. Monarchs continued to rule most of the new civilizations; men continued to dominate women; a sharp divide between the elite and everyone else persisted almost everywhere, as did the practice of slavery.[1]

Furthermore, no technological or economic breakthrough occurred to create new kinds of human societies as the Agricultural Revolution had done earlier or as the Industrial Revolution would do in later centuries. Landowning elites had little incentive to innovate, for they benefited enormously from simply expropriating the surplus that peasant farmers produced. Nor would peasants have any reason to invest much effort in creating new forms of production when they knew full well that any gains they might generate would be seized by their social superiors. Merchants, who often were risk takers, might have spawned innovations, but they usually were dominated by powerful states and were viewed with suspicion and condescension by more prestigious social groups.

Many fluctuations, repetitive cycles, and minor changes characterize this long era of agricultural civilization, but no fundamental or revolutionary transformation of social or economic life took place. The major turning points in human history had occurred earlier with the emergence of agriculture and the birth of the First Civilizations and would occur later with the breakthrough of industrialization.

Changes in Civilization

While this panoramic perspective allows us to see the broadest outlines of the human journey, it also obscures much of great importance that took place during the second and third waves of the age of agrarian civilization. If we zoom in a bit more closely, significant changes emerge, even if they did not result in a thorough transformation of human life. Population, for example, grew more rapidly than ever before during this period, as the Snapshot illustrates. Even though the overall trend was up, important fluctuations interrupted the pattern, especially during the first millennium C.E., when no overall growth took place. Moreover, the rate of growth, though rapid in comparison with Paleolithic times, was quite slow if we measure it against the explosive expansion of recent centuries, when human numbers quadrupled in the twentieth century alone. This modest and interrupted pattern of population growth during the age of agrarian civilization reflected the absence of any fundamental economic breakthrough, which could have supported much larger numbers.

Snapshot   **World Population during the Age of Agricultural Civilization[2]**

The Roman Empire (p. 110)

Another change lies in the growing size of the states or empires that structured civilizations. The Roman, Persian, Indian, and Chinese empires of second-wave civilizations, as well as the Arab, Mongol, and Inca empires of the third wave, all dwarfed the city-states of Mesopotamia and the Egypt of the pharaohs. Each of these empires brought together in a single political system a vast diversity of peoples. Even so, just to keep things in perspective, as late as the seventeenth century C.E., only one-third of the world's landmass was under the control of any state-based system, although these societies now encompassed a considerable majority of the world's people.

The rise and fall of these empires likewise represented very consequential changes to the people who experienced them. In the course of its growth, the Roman Empire utterly destroyed the city of Carthage in North Africa, with the conquerors allegedly sowing the ground with salt so that nothing would ever grow there again. Similar bloodshed and destruction accompanied the creation of other much-celebrated states. Their collapse also had a dramatic impact on the lives of their people. Scholars have estimated that the large population of Mayan civilization shrank by some 85 percent in less than a century as that society dissolved around 840 C.E. It is difficult to imagine the sense of trauma and bewilderment associated with a collapse of this magnitude.

Second- and third-wave civilizations also generated important innovations in many spheres. Those in the cultural realm have been perhaps the most widespread and enduring. Distinctive "wisdom traditions"—the great philosophical/religious systems of Confucianism and Daoism in China, Hinduism and Buddhism in India, Greek rationalism in the Mediterranean, and Judaism, Zoroastrianism, Christianity, and Islam in the Middle East—have provided the moral and spiritual framework within which people have sought to order their lives and define their relationship to the mysteries of life and death. All of these philosophical and religious systems are the product of second- and third-wave civilizations.

Although no technological breakthrough equivalent to the Agricultural or Industrial Revolution took place during the second and third waves of agrarian civilizations, more modest innovations considerably enhanced human potential for manipulating the environment. China was a primary source of such technological change, though by no means the only one. "Chinese inventions and discoveries," wrote one prominent historian, "passed in a continuous flood from East to West for twenty centuries before the scientific revolution."[3] They included piston bellows, the draw-loom, silk-handling machinery, the wheelbarrow, a better harness for draft animals, the crossbow, iron casting, the iron-chain suspension bridge, gunpowder, firearms, the magnetic compass, paper, printing, and porcelain. India pioneered the crystallization of sugar and techniques for the manufacture of cotton textiles. Roman technological achievements were particularly apparent in construction and civil engineering—the building of roads, bridges, aqueducts, and fortifications—and in the art of glassblowing.

A further process of change following the end of the First Civilizations lay in the emergence of far more elaborate, widespread, and dense networks of communication and exchange that connected many of the world's peoples to one another. Many of the technologies mentioned here diffused widely across large areas. Sugar production provides a telling example. The syrup from sugarcane, which was initially domesticated in New Guinea early in the age of agriculture, was first processed into crystallized sugar in India by 500 C.E. During the early centuries of the Islamic era, Arab traders brought this technology from India to the Middle East and the Mediterranean, where Europeans learned about it during the Crusades. Europeans then transferred the practice of making sugar to the Atlantic islands and finally to the Americas, where it played a major role in stimulating a plantation economy and the Atlantic slave trade.[4]

Long-distance trade routes represented another form of transregional interaction. Caravan trade across northern Eurasia, seaborne commerce within the Indian Ocean basin, the exchange of goods across the Sahara, river-based commerce in the eastern woodlands of North America, various trading networks radiating from Mesoamerica—all of these carried goods, and sometimes culture as well. Buddhism, Hinduism, Christianity, and especially Islam spread widely beyond their places of origin, often carried on the camels and ships of merchants, creating ties of culture and religion among distant peoples within the Afro-Eurasian zone. Disease also increasingly linked distant human communities. According to the famous Greek historian Thucydides, a mysterious plague "from parts of Ethiopia above Egypt" descended on Athens in 430 B.C.E. and decimated the city, "inflicting a blow on Athenian society from which it never entirely recovered."[5]

Thus the second and third waves of civilization gave rise to much larger empires, new and distinctive cultural/religious traditions, any number of technological innovations, and novel patterns of interaction among far-flung societies. In these ways, the world became quite different from what it had been in the age of the First Civilizations, even though fundamental economic and social patterns had not substantially changed.

Classical Civilizations

At this point, and in the four chapters that follow, our historical lens zooms in to a middle-range focus on the major second-wave civilizations during the thousand years between 500 B.C.E. and 500 C.E. Historians frequently refer to this period of time as the "classical era" of world history, a term that highlights enduring traditions that have lasted into modern times and persist still in the twenty-first century. Confucianism, Hinduism, Buddhism, Judaism, and Christianity all took shape during this era of second-wave civilizations, and all of them remain very much alive at the dawn of the third millennium C.E. Despite the many and profound transformations of modernity, billions of people in the contemporary world still guide their lives, or at least claim to, according to teachings that first appeared 2,000 or more years ago.

Beyond the practices of individuals, the current identities of entire countries, regions, and civilizations are still linked to the achievements of the classical era. In 1971, a largely Muslim Iran mounted a lavish and much-criticized celebration of the 2,500th anniversary of the ancient Persian Empire. In 2004, a still communist China permitted public celebrations to mark the 2,555th birthday of its ancient sage Confucius. Students in Western schools and universities continue to read the works of Plato and Aristotle, produce the plays of Aeschylus and Sophocles, and admire the accomplishments of Athens. Many Indians still embrace the ancient religious texts called the Vedas and the Upanishads and continue to deal with the realities of caste. These are the continuities and enduring legacies that are reflected in the notion of "classical civilizations."

Designating the millennium between 500 B.C.E. and 500 C.E. as a "classical era" in world history is derived largely from the experience of Eurasian peoples, for it was on the outer rim of that huge continent that the largest and most influential civilizations took shape—in China, India, Persia, and the Mediterranean basin. Furthermore, that continent housed the vast majority of the world's people, some 80 percent or more.[6] Thus the first three chapters of Part Two focus exclusively on these Eurasian civilizations. Chapter 4 introduces them by examining and comparing their political frameworks and especially the empires (great or terrible, depending on your point of view) in which most of them were expressed. Chapter 5 looks at the cultural or religious traditions that each of them generated, while Chapter 6 probes their social organization—class, caste, slavery, and gender. Chapter 7 turns the spotlight on Africa and the Americas, asking whether their histories during the classical era followed Eurasian patterns or explored alternative possibilities.

In recalling the classical era, we will have occasion to compare the experiences of its various peoples, to note their remarkable achievements, to lament the tragedies that befell them and the suffering to which they gave rise, and to ponder their continuing power to fascinate us still.

Landmarks of the Classical Era, 500 B.C.E.–500 C.E.

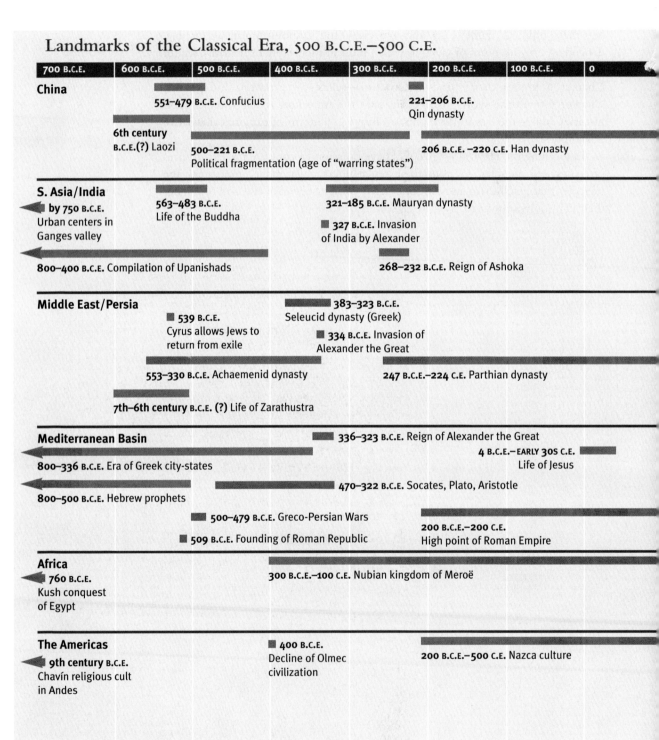

| 700 B.C.E. | 600 B.C.E. | 500 B.C.E. | 400 B.C.E. | 300 B.C.E. | 200 B.C.E. | 100 B.C.E. | 0 |

China

551–479 B.C.E. Confucius

221–206 B.C.E. Qin dynasty

6th century B.C.E.(?) Laozi

500–221 B.C.E. Political fragmentation (age of "warring states")

206 B.C.E.–220 C.E. Han dynasty

S. Asia/India

by 750 B.C.E. Urban centers in Ganges valley

563–483 B.C.E. Life of the Buddha

321–185 B.C.E. Mauryan dynasty

327 B.C.E. Invasion of India by Alexander

800–400 B.C.E. Compilation of Upanishads

268–232 B.C.E. Reign of Ashoka

Middle East/Persia

539 B.C.E. Cyrus allows Jews to return from exile

383–323 B.C.E. Seleucid dynasty (Greek)

334 B.C.E. Invasion of Alexander the Great

553–330 B.C.E. Achaemenid dynasty

247 B.C.E.–224 C.E. Parthian dynasty

7th–6th century B.C.E. (?) Life of Zarathustra

Mediterranean Basin

336–323 B.C.E. Reign of Alexander the Great

4 B.C.E.–EARLY 30S C.E. Life of Jesus

800–336 B.C.E. Era of Greek city-states

470–322 B.C.E. Socates, Plato, Aristotle

800–500 B.C.E. Hebrew prophets

500–479 B.C.E. Greco-Persian Wars

509 B.C.E. Founding of Roman Republic

200 B.C.E.–200 C.E. High point of Roman Empire

Africa

760 B.C.E. Kush conquest of Egypt

300 B.C.E.–100 C.E. Nubian kingdom of Meroë

The Americas

9th century B.C.E. Chavín religious cult in Andes

400 B.C.E. Decline of Olmec civilization

200 B.C.E.–500 C.E. Nazca culture

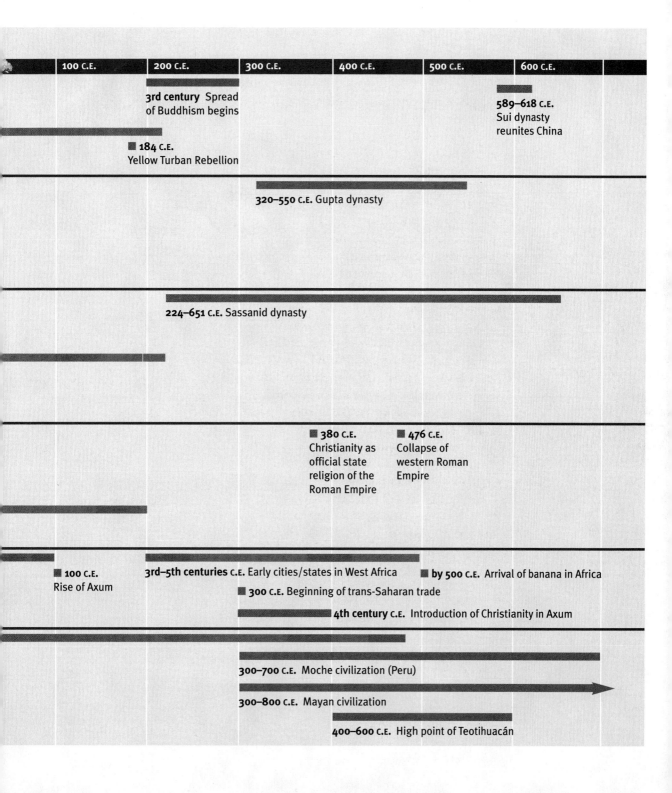

| 100 C.E. | 200 C.E. | 300 C.E. | 400 C.E. | 500 C.E. | 600 C.E. |

3rd century Spread of Buddhism begins

589–618 C.E. Sui dynasty reunites China

■ **184** C.E. Yellow Turban Rebellion

320–550 C.E. Gupta dynasty

224–651 C.E. Sassanid dynasty

■ **380** C.E. Christianity as official state religion of the Roman Empire

■ **476** C.E. Collapse of western Roman Empire

■ **100** C.E. Rise of Axum

3rd–5th centuries C.E. Early cities/states in West Africa

■ **by 500** C.E. Arrival of banana in Africa

■ **300** C.E. Beginning of trans-Saharan trade

4th century C.E. Introduction of Christianity in Axum

300–700 C.E. Moche civilization (Peru)

300–800 C.E. Mayan civilization

400–600 C.E. High point of Teotihuacán

CHAPTER FOUR

Eurasian Empires

500 B.C.E. – 500 C.E.

Are We Rome? It was the title of a thoughtful book, published in 2007, asking what had become a familiar question in the early twenty-first century: "Is the United States the new Roman Empire?"[1] With the collapse of the Soviet Union by 1991 and the subsequent U.S. invasions of Afghanistan and Iraq, some commentators began to make the comparison. The United States' enormous multicultural society, its technological achievements, its economically draining and overstretched armed forces, its sense of itself as unique and endowed with a global mission, its concern about foreigners penetrating its borders, its apparent determination to maintain military superiority—all of this invited comparison with the Roman Empire. Supporters of a dominant role for the United States argue that Americans must face up to their responsibilities as "the undisputed master of the world" as the Romans did in their time. Critics warn that the Roman Empire became overextended abroad and corrupt and dictatorial at home and then collapsed, suggesting that a similar fate may await the American empire. Either way, the point of reference was an empire that had passed into history some 1,500 years earlier, a continuing reminder of the relevance of the distant past to our contemporary world. In fact, for at least several centuries, that empire has been a source of metaphors and "lessons" about personal morality, corruption, political life, military expansion, and much more.

Even in a world largely critical of empires, they still excite the imagination of historians and readers of history. The earliest ones show up in the era of the First Civilizations when Akkadian, Babylonian, and Assyrian empires encompassed the city-states of Mesopotamia and established an enduring imperial tradition in the Middle East. Egypt

China's Terra-Cotta Army: Ranking as one of the most spectacular archeological finds of the twentieth century, this collection of terra-cotta soldiers and horses was part of an immense funerary complex of China's "first emperor," Qin Shihuangdi, who died in 210 B.C.E. (Dennis Cox/ChinaStock)

became an imperial state when it temporarily ruled Nubia and the lands of the eastern Mediterranean. Following in their wake were many more empires, whose rise and fall have been a central feature of world history for the past 4,000 years.

BUT WHAT EXACTLY IS AN EMPIRE? At one level, empires are simply states, political systems that exercise coercive power. The term, however, is normally reserved for larger and more aggressive states, those that conquer, rule, and extract resources from other states and peoples. Thus empires have generally encompassed a considerable variety of peoples and cultures within a single political system, and they have often been associated with political and cultural oppression. No clear line divides empires and small multiethnic states, and the distinction between them is arbitrary and subjective. Frequently, empires have given political expression to a civilization or culture, as in the Chinese and Persian empires. Civilizations have also flourished without a single all-encompassing state or empire, as in the competing city-states of Mesopotamia, Greece, and the Maya or the many rival states of post-Roman Europe. In such cases, civilizations were expressed in elements of a common culture rather than in a unified political system.

The Eurasian empires of the classical era—those of Persia, Greece under Alexander the Great, Rome, China during the Qin and Han dynasties, India during the Mauryan and Gupta dynasties—shared a set of common problems. Would they seek to impose the culture of the imperial heartland on their varied subjects? Would they rule conquered people directly or through established local authorities? How could they extract the wealth of empire in the form of taxes, tribute, and labor while maintaining order in conquered territories? And, no matter how impressive they were at their peak, they all sooner or later collapsed, providing a useful reminder to their descendants of the fleeting nature of all human creation.

Why have these and other empires been of such lasting fascination to both ancient and modern people? Perhaps in part because they were so big, creating a looming presence in their respective regions. Their armies and their tax collectors were hard to avoid. Maybe also because they were so bloody. Conquest and the violence that accompanies it easily grab our attention, and certainly, all of these empires were founded and sustained at a great cost in human life. The collapse of these once-powerful states is likewise intriguing, for the fall of the mighty seems somehow satisfying, perhaps even a delayed form of justice. The study of empires also sets off by contrast those times and places in which civilizations have prospered without an enduring imperial state.

But empires have also commanded attention simply because they were important. Very large numbers of people—probably the majority of humankind before the twentieth century—have lived out their lives in empires, where they were often governed by rulers culturally different from themselves. These imperial states brought together people of quite different traditions and religions and so stimulated the exchange of ideas, cultures, and values. The Roman Empire, for example, provided the vehicle within which Christianity was transformed from a small Jewish sect into a world religion. Despite their violence, exploitation, and oppression, empires also imposed substantial periods of peace and security, which fostered economic and artistic development, commercial exchange, and cultural mixing.

Empires and Civilizations in Collision: The Persians and the Greeks

The classical era in Eurasia witnessed the flowering of second-wave civilizations in the Mediterranean world, the Middle East, India, and China. For the most part, these distant civilizations did not directly encounter one another, as each established its own political system, cultural values, and ways of organizing society. A great exception to that rule lay in the Mediterranean world and in the Middle East, where the emerging Persian Empire and Greek civilization, physically adjacent to each other, experienced a centuries-long interaction and clash. It was one of the most consequential cultural encounters of the classical world.

The Persian Empire

In 500 B.C.E., the largest and most impressive of the world's empires was that of the Persians, an Indo-European people whose homeland lay on the Iranian plateau just north of the Persian Gulf. Living on the margins of the earlier Mesopotamian civilization, the Persians constructed an imperial system that drew upon previous examples, such as the Babylonian and Assyrian empires, but far surpassed them all in size and splendor. Under the leadership of the famous monarchs Cyrus (reigned 557–530 B.C.E.) and Darius (reigned 522–486 B.C.E.), Persian conquests quickly reached from Egypt to India, encompassing in a single state some 35 million people, an immensely diverse realm containing dozens of peoples, states, languages, and cultural traditions (see Map 4.1).

■ **Comparison**

How did Persian and Greek civilizations differ in their political organization and values?

The Persian Empire centered on an elaborate cult of kingship in which the monarch, secluded in royal magnificence, could be approached only through an elaborate ritual. When the king died, sacred fires all across the land were extinguished, Persians were expected to shave their hair in mourning, and the manes of horses were cut short. Ruling by the will of the great Persian god Ahura Mazda, kings were absolute monarchs, more than willing to crush rebellious regions or officials. Interrupted on one occasion while he was with his wife, Darius ordered the offender, a high-ranking nobleman, killed, along with his entire clan. In the eyes of many, Persian monarchs fully deserved their effusive title—"Great king, King of kings, King of countries containing all kinds of men, King in this great earth far and wide." Darius himself best expressed the authority of the Persian ruler when he observed: "what was said to them by me, night and day, it was done."[2]

Map 4.1   The Persian Empire

At its height, the Persian Empire was the largest in the world. It dominated the lands of the First Civilizations in the Middle East and was commercially connected to neighboring regions.

But more than conquest and royal decree held the empire together. An effective administrative system placed Persian governors, called *satraps,* in each of the empire's twenty-three provinces, while lower-level officials were drawn from local authorities. A system of imperial spies, known as the "eyes and ears of the King," represented a further imperial presence in the far reaches of the empire. A general policy of respect for the empire's many non-Persian cultural traditions also cemented the state's authority. Cyrus won the gratitude of the Jews when in 539 B.C.E. he allowed those exiled in Babylon to return to their homeland and rebuild their temple in Jerusalem. In Egypt and Babylon, Persian kings took care to uphold local religious cults in an effort to gain the support of their followers and officials. The Greek historian Herodotus commented that "there is no nation which so readily adopts foreign customs. They have taken the dress of the Medes and in war they wear the Egyptian breastplate. As soon as they hear of any luxury, they instantly make it their own."[3] For the next 1,000 years or more, Persian imperial bureaucracy and court life, replete with administrators, tax collectors, record keepers, and translators, provided a model for all subsequent regimes in the region, including, later, those of the Islamic world.

The infrastructure of empire included a system of standardized coinage, predictable taxes levied on each province, and a newly dug canal linking the Nile with the Red Sea, which greatly expanded commerce and enriched Egypt. A "royal road," some 1,700 miles in length, facilitated communication and commerce across this vast empire. Caravans of merchants could traverse this highway in three months, but agents of the imperial courier service, using a fresh supply of horses every twenty-five to thirty miles, could carry a message from one end of the road to another in a week or two. Herodotus

Persepolis
The largest palace in Persepolis, the Persian Empire's ancient capital, was the Audience Hall. The emperor officially greeted visiting dignitaries at this palace, which was constructed around 500 B.C.E. This relief, which shows a lion attacking a bull and Persian guards at attention, adorns a staircase leading to the Audience Hall. (Gianni Dagli Orti/Corbis)

was impressed. "Neither snow, nor rain, nor heat, nor darkness of night," he wrote, "prevents them from accomplishing the task proposed to them with utmost speed." That description of the imperial Persian postal system was much later adopted as the unofficial motto for its counterpart in the United States Postal Service.

The immense wealth and power of the Persian Empire were reflected in the construction of elaborate imperial centers, particularly Susa and Persepolis. Palaces, audience halls, quarters for the harem, monuments, and carvings made these cities into powerful symbols of imperial authority. Materials and workers alike were drawn from all corners of the empire and beyond. Inscribed in the foundation of Persepolis was Darius's commentary on what he had set in motion: "And Ahuramazda was of such a mind, together with all the other gods, that this fortress (should) be built. And (so) I built it. And I built it secure and beautiful and adequate, just as I was intending to."[4]

The Greeks

It would be hard to imagine a sharper contrast than that between the huge and centralized Persian Empire, governed by an absolute and almost unapproachable monarch, and the small competing city-states of classical Greece, which allowed varying degrees of popular participation in political life. Like the Persians, the Greeks were an Indo-European people whose early history drew on the legacy of the First Civilizations. The classical Greece of historical fame emerged around 750 B.C.E. as a new civilization and flourished for about 400 years before it was incorporated into a succession of foreign empires. During that relatively short period of time, the civilization of Athens and Sparta, of Plato and Aristotle, of Zeus and Apollo took shape and collided with its giant neighbor to the east.

Calling themselves Hellenes, the Greeks created a civilization that was distinctive in many ways, particularly in comparison with the Persians. The total population of

■ **Change**
Why did semidemocratic governments emerge in some of the Greek city-states?

Greece and the Aegean basin was just 2 million to 3 million, a fraction of that of the Persian Empire. Furthermore, Greek civilization took shape on a small peninsula, deeply divided by steep mountains and valleys. Its geography certainly contributed to the political shape of that civilization, which found expression, not in a Persian-style empire, but in hundreds of city-states or small settlements (see Map 4.2). Most were quite modest in size, with between 500 and 5,000 male citizens. Each of these city-states was fiercely independent and in frequent conflict with its neighbors, yet they had much in common, speaking the same language and worshipping the same gods. Every four years they temporarily suspended their persisting rivalries to participate together in the Olympic Games, which had begun in 776 B.C.E. Despite this emerging sense of Greek cultural identity, it did

Map 4.2   Classical Greece
The classical civilization of Greece was centered on a small peninsula of southeastern Europe, but Greek settlers spread that civilization along the coasts of the Mediterranean and Black seas.

little to overcome the endemic political rivalries of the larger city-states—Athens, Sparta, Thebes, Corinth, and many others.

Like the Persians, the Greeks were an expansive people, but their expansion took the form of settlement in distant places rather than conquest and empire. Pushed by a growing population, Greek traders in search of iron and impoverished Greek farmers in search of land stimulated a remarkable emigration. Between 750 and 500 B.C.E., Greek settlements were established all around the Mediterranean basin and the rim of the Black Sea. Settlers brought Greek culture, language, and building styles to these new lands, even as they fought, traded, and intermarried with their non-Greek neighbors.

The most distinctive feature of Greek civilization, and the greatest contrast with Persia, lay in the extent of popular participation in political life that occurred within the city-states. It was the idea of "citizenship," of free people running the affairs of state, of equality for all citizens before the law, that was so unique. A foreign king, observing the operation of the public assembly in Athens, was amazed that male citizens as a whole actually voted on matters of policy: "I find it astonishing," he noted, "that here wise men speak on public affairs, while fools decide them."[5] Compared to the rigid hierarchies, inequalities, and absolute monarchies of Persia and other ancient civilizations, the Athenian experiment was remarkable. This is how one modern scholar defined it:

> Among the Greeks the question of who should reign arose in a new way. Previously the most that had been asked was whether one man or another should govern and whether one alone or several together. But now the question was whether all the citizens, including the poor, might govern and whether it would be possible for them to govern as citizens, without specializing in politics. In other words, should the governed themselves actively participate in politics on a regular basis?[6]

The extent of participation and the role of "citizens" varied considerably, both over time and from city to city. Early in Greek history, only the wealthy and well-born had the rights of full citizenship, such as speaking and voting in the assembly, holding public office, and fighting in the army. Gradually, middle- and lower-class men, mostly small-scale farmers, also obtained these rights. At least in part, this broadening of political rights was associated with the growing number of men able to afford the armor and weapons that would allow them to serve as *hoplites*, or infantrymen, in the armies of the city-states. In many places, dictators known as *tyrants* emerged for a time, usually with the support of the poorer classes, to challenge the prerogatives of the wealthy. Sparta—famous for its extreme forms of military discipline and its large population of *helots*, conquered people who lived in slavelike conditions—vested most political authority in its Council of Elders. The council was composed of twenty-eight men over the age of sixty, derived from the wealthier and more influential segment of society, who served for life and provided political leadership for Sparta.

Snapshot   **Key Moments in Classical Greek History**

Traditional date for first Olympic Games	776 B.C.E.
Emergence of Greek city-states and overseas colonization	750–700 B.C.E.
Evolution of hoplite military tactics	700–650 B.C.E.
Tyrants rule in many city-states	670–500 B.C.E.
Sparta dominant in Peloponnesus	550 B.C.E.
Cleisthenes' political reforms in Athens	507 B.C.E.
Greco-Persian Wars	490–479 B.C.E.
Golden Age of Athens (building of Parthenon; Athenian democracy, rule of Pericles)	479–429 B.C.E.
Helot rebellion in Sparta	463 B.C.E.
Peloponnesian War	431–404 B.C.E.
Macedonian conquest of Greece	338 B.C.E.
Conquests of Alexander the Great	333–323 B.C.E.
Hellenistic era	323–30 B.C.E.
Greece comes under Roman control	2nd century B.C.E.

It was in Athens that the Greek experiment in political participation achieved its most distinctive expression. Early steps in this direction were the product of intense class conflict, leading almost to civil war. A reforming leader named Solon emerged in 594 B.C.E. to push Athenian politics in a more democratic direction, breaking the hold of a small group of aristocratic families. Debt slavery was abolished, access to public office was opened to a wider group of men, and all citizens were allowed to take part in the Assembly. Later reformers such as Cleisthenes and Pericles extended the rights of citizens even further. By 450 B.C.E., all holders of public office were chosen by lot and were paid, so that even the poorest could serve. The Assembly, where all citizens could participate, became the center of political life.

Athenian democracy, however, was different from modern democracy. It was direct, rather than representative, democracy, and it was distinctly limited. Women, slaves, and foreigners, together far more than half of the population, were wholly excluded from political participation. Nonetheless, political life in Athens was a world away from that of the Persian Empire and even from that of many other Greek cities.

■ Connection
What were the consequences for both sides of the encounter between the Persians and the Greeks?

Collision: The Greco-Persian Wars

If ever there was an unequal conflict between civilizations, surely it was the collision of the Greeks and the Persians. The confrontation between the small and divided Greek cities and Persia, the world's largest empire, grew out of their respective patterns of expansion. A number of Greek settlements on the Anatolian seacoast, known to the Greeks as Ionia, came under Persian control as that empire extended its domination to the west. In 499 B.C.E., some of these Ionian Greek cities revolted against Persian domination and found support from Athens on the Greek mainland. Outraged by this assault from the remote and upstart Greeks, the Persians twice in ten years (490 and 480 B.C.E.) launched major military expeditions to punish the Greeks in general and Athens in particular. Against all odds and all expectations, the Greeks held them off, defeating the Persians on both land and sea.

Though no doubt embarrassing, this defeat on the far western fringes of its empire had little effect on the Persians, but it had a profound impact on the Greeks and especially on Athens, whose forces had led the way to victory. Beating the Persians in battle was a source of enormous pride for Greece. Years later, elderly Athenian men asked one another how old they had been when the Greeks triumphed in the momentous Battle of Marathon in 490 B.C.E. In their view, this victory was the product of Greek freedoms, because those freedoms had motivated men to fight with extraordinary courage for what they valued so highly. It led to a worldview in which Persia represented Asia and despotism, whereas Greece signified Europe and freedom. Thus was born the notion of an East / West divide, which has shaped European thinking about the world into the twentieth century and beyond.

The Greeks' victory also radicalized Athenian democracy, for it had been men of the poorer classes who had rowed their ships to victory, and now they were in a position to insist on full citizenship. The fifty years or so after the Greco-Persian Wars were not only the high point of Athenian democracy but also the Golden Age of Greek culture. During this period, the Parthenon, that marvelous temple to the Greek goddess Athena, was built; Greek theater was born from the work of Aeschylus, Sophocles, and Euripides; and Socrates was beginning his career as a philosopher and an irritant in Athens. The great Athenian statesman Pericles celebrated the uniqueness of Athens in a famous speech.

> It is true that we are called a democracy, for the administration is in the hands of the many and not of the few. But while the law secures equal justice to all alike in their private disputes, the claim of excellence is also recognized.... Neither is poverty a bar, but a man may benefit his country whatever be the obscurity of his condition.... We alone regard a man who takes no interest in public affairs, not as a harmless, but as a useless character.[7]

But Athens's Golden Age was also an era of incipient empire. In the Greco-Persian Wars, Athens had led a coalition of more than thirty Greek city-states on the basis of its naval power, but Athenian leadership in the struggle against Persian aggression had spawned an imperialism of its own. After the war, Athenian efforts to solidify its dominant position among the allies led to intense resentment and finally to a bitter civil war (431–404 B.C.E.), with Sparta taking the lead in defending the traditional independence of Greek city-states. In this bloody conflict, known as the Peloponnesian War, Athens was defeated, while the Greeks exhausted themselves and magnified their distrust of one another. Thus the way was open to their eventual takeover by the growing forces of Macedonia, a frontier region on the northern fringes of the Greek world. The glory days of the Greek experiment were over, but the spread of Greek culture was just beginning.

■ **Connection**
What changes did Alexander's conquests bring in their wake?

Collision: Alexander and the Hellenistic Era

The Macedonian conquest of Greece, led by Philip II, finally accomplished by 338 B.C.E. what the Greeks themselves had been unable to achieve—the political unification of Greece, but at the cost of much of the prized independence of its various city-states. It also set in motion a second round in the collision of Greece and Persia as Philip's son, Alexander, prepared to lead a massive Greek expedition against the Persian Empire. Such a project appealed to those who sought vengeance for the earlier Persian assault on Greece, but it also served to unify the fractious Greeks in a war against their common enemy.

Map 4.3 Alexander's Empire and Successor States
Alexander's conquests, though enormous, did not long remain within a single empire, for his generals divided them into three successor states shortly after his death. This was the Hellenistic world within which Greek culture spread.

The story of this ten-year expedition (333–323 B.C.E.), accomplished while Alexander was still in his twenties, has become the stuff of legend (see Map 4.3). Surely it was among the greatest military feats of the classical world in that it created a Greek empire from Egypt and Anatolia in the west to Afghanistan and India in the east. In the process, the great Persian Empire was thoroughly defeated; its

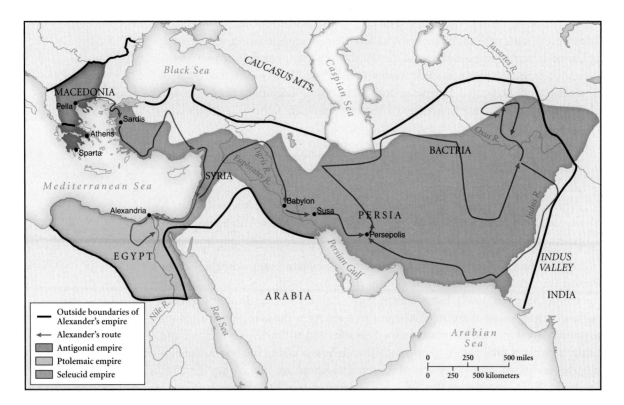

capital, Persepolis, was looted and burned; and Alexander was hailed as the "king of Asia." In Egypt, Alexander, then just twenty-four years old, was celebrated as a liberator from Persian domination, was anointed as pharaoh, and was declared by Egyptian priests to be the "son of the gods." Arrian, a later Greek historian, described Alexander in this way:

> His passion was for glory only, and in that he was insatiable.... Noble indeed was his power of inspiring his men, of filling them with confidence, and in the moment of danger, of sweeping away their fear by the spectacle of his own fearlessness.[8]

Alexander died in 323 B.C.E., without returning to Greece, and his empire was soon divided into three kingdoms, ruled by leading Macedonian generals.

From the viewpoint of world history, the chief significance of Alexander's amazing conquests lay in the widespread dissemination of Greek culture during what historians call the Hellenistic era (323–30 B.C.E.). Elements of that culture, generated in a small and remote Mediterranean peninsula, now penetrated the lands of the First Civilizations—Egypt, Mesopotamia, and India—resulting in one of the great cultural encounters of the classical world.

The major avenue for the spread of Greek culture lay in the many cities that Alexander and later Hellenistic rulers established throughout the empire. Complete with Greek monuments and sculptures, Greek theaters and markets, Greek councils and assemblies, these cities attracted many thousands of Greek settlers serving as state officials, soldiers, or traders. Alexandria in Egypt—the largest of these cities, with half a million people—was an enormous cosmopolitan center where Egyptians, Greeks, Jews, Babylonians, Syrians, Persians, and many others rubbed elbows. A harbor with space for 1,200 ships facilitated long-distance commerce.

Alexander the Great
This mosaic of Alexander on horseback comes from the Roman city of Pompeii. It depicts the Battle of Issus (333 B.C.E.), in which Greek forces, although considerably outnumbered, defeated the Persian army, led personally by Emperor Darius III. (Scala/Art Resource, NY)

Greek learning flourished thanks to a library of some 700,000 volumes and the Museum, which sponsored scholars and writers of all kinds.

From cities such as these, Greek culture spread. A simplified form of the Greek language was widely spoken from the Mediterranean to India. The Indian monarch Ashoka published some of his decrees in Greek, while an independent Greek state was established in Bactria in what is now northern Afghanistan. The attraction of many young Jews to Greek culture prompted the Pharisees to develop their own school system, as this highly conservative Jewish sect feared for the very survival of Judaism.

Cities such as Alexandria were very different from the original city-states of Greece, both in their cultural diversity and in the absence of the independence so valued by Athens and Sparta. Now they were part of large conquest states ruled by Greeks: the Ptolemaic empire in Egypt and the Seleucid empire in Persia. These were imperial states, which, in their determination to preserve order, raise taxes, and maintain the authority of the monarch, resembled the much older empires of Mesopotamia, Egypt, Assyria, and Persia. Macedonians and Greeks, representing perhaps 10 percent of the population in these Hellenistic kingdoms, were clearly the elite and sought to keep themselves separate. In Egypt, different legal systems for Greeks and native Egyptians maintained this separation. An Egyptian worker complained that his supervisors despised him and refused to pay him simply because he was an Egyptian.[9] Periodic rebellions expressed the resentment at Greek arrogance, condescension, and exploitation.

But the separation between the Greeks and native populations was by no means complete, and a fair amount of cultural interaction and blending occurred. Alexander himself had taken several Persian princesses as his wives and actively encouraged intermarriage between his troops and Asian women. In both Egypt and Mesopotamia, Greek rulers patronized the building of temples to local gods and actively supported their priests. A growing number of native peoples were able to become Greek citizens by getting a Greek education, speaking the language, dressing appropriately, and assuming a Greek name. In India, Greeks were assimilated into the hierarchy of the caste system as members of the Ksatriya (warrior) caste, while in Bactria a substantial number of Greeks converted to Buddhism, including one of their kings, Menander. A school of Buddhist art that emerged in the early centuries of the Common Era depicted the Buddha in human form for the first time, but in Greek-like garb with a face resembling the god Apollo. Clearly, not all was conflict between the Greeks and the peoples of the East.

In the long run, much of this Greek cultural influence disappeared as the Hellenistic kingdoms that had promoted it weakened and vanished by the first century B.C.E. While it lasted, however, it represented a remarkable cultural encounter, born of the collision of two empires and two classical civilizations. In the western part of that Hellenistic world, Greek rule was replaced by that of the Romans, whose empire, like Alexander's, also served as a vehicle for the continued spread of Greek culture and ideas.

Comparing Empires: Roman and Chinese

While the adjacent civilizations of the Greeks and the Persians collided, two other classical empires were taking shape—the Roman Empire on the far western side of Eurasia and China's imperial state on the far eastern end. They flourished at roughly the same time (200 B.C.E.–200 C.E.); they occupied a similar area (about 1.5 million square miles); and they encompassed populations of a similar size (50 million to 60 million people). They were the giant empires of their time, shaping the lives of close to half of the world's population. Unlike the Greeks and the Persians, the Romans and the Chinese were only dimly aware of each other and had almost no direct contact. Historians, however, have seen them as fascinating variations on an imperial theme and have long explored their similarities and differences.

Rome: From City-State to Empire

How do empires arise? This is one of the perennial questions that historians tackle. Like the Persian Empire, that of the Romans took shape initially on the margins of the civilized world and was an unlikely rags-to-riches story. Rome began as a small and impoverished city-state on the western side of central Italy in the eighth century B.C.E., so weak, according to legend, that Romans were reduced to kidnapping neighboring women in order to reproduce. In a transformation of epic proportions, Rome became an enormous imperial state that encompassed the Mediterranean basin and included parts of continental Europe, Britain, North Africa, and the Middle East.

■ **Change**
How did Rome grow from a single city to the center of a huge empire?

Originally ruled by a king, Roman aristocrats around 509 B.C.E. threw off the monarchy and established a republic in which the wealthy class, known as *patricians*, dominated. Executive authority was exercised by two consuls, who were advised by a patrician assembly, the Senate. Deepening conflict with the poorer classes, called *plebeians*, led to important changes in Roman political life. A written code of law offered plebeians some protection from abuse; a system of public assemblies provided an opportunity for lower classes to shape public policy; and a new office of *tribune*, who represented plebeians, allowed them to block unfavorable legislation. Romans took great pride in this political system, believing that they enjoyed greater freedom than did many of their more autocratic neighbors. The values of the republic—rule of law, the rights of citizens, the absence of pretension, upright moral behavior, keeping one's word—were later idealized as "the way of the ancestors."

With this political system and these values, the Romans launched their empire-building enterprise, a prolonged process that took more than 500 years (see Map 4.4). It began in the 490s B.C.E. with Roman control over its Latin neighbors in central Italy and over the next several hundred years encompassed most of the Italian peninsula. Between 264 and 146 B.C.E., victory in the Punic Wars with Carthage, a powerful empire with its capital in North Africa, extended Roman control over the western Mediterranean and made Rome a naval power. Subsequent expansion in the eastern Mediterranean brought the ancient civilizations of Greece, Egypt, and Mesopotamia under Roman domination. Rome also expanded into territories in Southern and Western Europe, including present-day Spain, France, and Britain. By early in the second century C.E., the Roman Empire had reached its maximum extent.

No overall design or blueprint drove the building of empire, nor were there any precedents to guide the Romans. What they created was something wholly new— an empire that encompassed the entire Mediterranean basin and beyond. It was a

Map 4.4   The Roman Empire
At its height in the second century C.E., the Roman Empire incorporated the entire Mediterranean basin, including the lands of the Carthaginian Empire, the less developed region of Western Europe, the heartland of Greek civilization, and the ancient civilizations of Egypt and Mesopotamia.

piecemeal process, which the Romans invariably saw as defensive. Each addition of territory created new vulnerabilities, which could be assuaged only by more conquests. For some, the growth of empire represented opportunity. Poor soldiers hoped for land, loot, or salaries that might lift their families out of poverty. The well-to-do or well-connected gained great estates, earned promotion, and sometimes achieved public acclaim and high political office. The wealth of long-established societies in the eastern Mediterranean (Greece and Egypt, for example) beckoned, as did the resources and food supplies of the less developed western regions, such as Carthage and Spain. There was no shortage of motivation for the creation of the Roman Empire.

Snapshot   **Key Moments in the History of the Roman Empire**

Traditional date of Rome's founding as a monarchy	753 B.C.E.
Establishment of Roman Republic	509 B.C.E.
Turmoil between patricians and plebeians ("struggle of the orders")	509–287 B.C.E.
Twelve Tables (Rome's first written law code)	450 B.C.E.
Punic Wars	264–146 B.C.E.
Civil war; Julius Caesar appointed dictator and then assassinated	49–44 B.C.E.
Reign of Caesar Augustus	27 B.C.E.–14 C.E.
Great fire in Rome; Emperor Nero blames Christians	64 C.E.
Roman citizenship extended to almost all free subjects	212 C.E.
Constantine converts to Christianity	312 C.E.
Founding of Constantinople as the "New Rome"	324 C.E.
Roman Empire split into eastern and western halves	395 C.E.
"Barbarian" invasions	4th–5th centuries C.E.
Collapse of western Roman Empire	476 C.E.

Although Rome's central location in the Mediterranean basin provided a convenient launching pad for empire, it was the army, "well-trained, well-fed, and well-rewarded," that built the empire.[10] Drawing on the growing population of Italy, that army was often brutal in war. Carthage, for example, was utterly destroyed; the city was razed to the ground, and its inhabitants were either killed or sold into slavery. Nonetheless, Roman authorities could be generous to former enemies. Some were granted Roman citizenship; others were treated as allies and allowed to maintain their local rulers. As the empire grew, so too did political forces in Rome that favored its continued expansion and were willing to commit the necessary manpower and resources.

The relentless expansion of empire raised a profound question for Rome: could republican government and values survive the acquisition of a huge empire? The wealth of empire enriched a few, enabling them to acquire large estates and slaves to work those estates, while pushing growing numbers of free farmers into the cities and poverty. Imperial riches also empowered a small group of military leaders—Marius, Sulla, Pompey, Julius Caesar—who recruited their troops directly from the ranks of the poor and whose fierce rivalries brought civil war to Rome during the first century B.C.E. Traditionalists lamented the apparent decline of republican values—simplicity, service, free farmers as the backbone of the army, the

Queen Boudica
This statue in London commemorates the resistance of the Celtic people of eastern Britain against Roman rule during a revolt in 60–61 C.E., led by Queen Boudica. A later Roman historian lamented that "all this ruin was brought upon the Romans by a woman, a fact which in itself caused them the greatest shame." (Daniel Boulet, photographer)

■ **Comparison**
How and why did the making of the Chinese empire differ from that of the Roman Empire?

authority of the Senate—amid the self-seeking ambition of the newly rich and powerful. When the dust settled from the civil war, Rome was clearly changing, for authority was now vested primarily in an emperor, the first of whom was Caesar Augustus (reigned 27 B.C.E.–14 C.E.). The republic was history; Rome was becoming an empire.

But it was an empire with an uneasy conscience, for many felt that in acquiring an empire, Rome had betrayed and abandoned its republican origins. Augustus was careful to maintain the forms of the republic—the Senate, consuls, public assemblies—and referred to himself as "first man" rather than "king" or "emperor." And in a bow to republican values, he spoke of the empire's conquests as reflecting the "power of the Roman people" rather than of the Roman state. Despite this rhetoric, he was emperor in practice, if not in name, for he was able to exercise sole authority, backed up by his command of a professional army. Later emperors were less reluctant to flaunt their imperial prerogatives. During the first two centuries C.E., this empire in disguise provided security, grandeur, and relative prosperity for the Mediterranean world. This was the *pax Romana*, the Roman peace, the era of imperial Rome's greatest extent and greatest authority.

China: From Warring States to Empire

About the same time, on the other side of Eurasia, another huge imperial state was in the making—China. Here, however, the task was understood differently. It was not a matter of creating something new, as in the case of the Roman Empire, but of restoring something old. As one of the First Civilizations, a Chinese state had emerged as early as 2200 B.C.E. and under the Xia, Shang, and Zhou dynasties had grown progressively larger, but by 500 B.C.E. this Chinese state was in shambles. Any earlier unity vanished in an age of warring states, featuring the endless rivalries of seven competing kingdoms.

To many Chinese, this was a wholly unnatural and unacceptable condition, and rulers in various states vied to reunify China. One of them, known to history as Shihuangdi from the state of Qin, succeeded brilliantly. That state had already developed an effective bureaucracy, had subordinated its aristocracy, had equipped its army with iron weapons, and enjoyed rapidly rising agricultural output and a growing population. It also had adopted a political philosophy called Legalism, which advocated clear rules and harsh punishments as a means of enforcing the authority of the state. With these resources, Shihuangdi (ruled 221–210 B.C.E.) launched a military campaign to reunify China and in just ten years soundly defeated the other warring states. Believing that he had created a universal and eternal empire, he grandly named himself Shihuangdi, which means the "first emperor." Unlike Caesar Augustus, he showed little ambivalence about empire. Subsequent conquests extended China's boundaries far to the south into the northern part of Vietnam, to the northeast into Korea, and to the northwest, where the Chinese pushed back the nomadic pastoral people of the steppes. Although the boundaries fluctuated over time, Shihuangdi laid the foundations for a unified Chinese state, which has endured, with periodic interruptions, to the present (see Map 4.5).

Building on earlier precedents, the Chinese process of empire formation was far more compressed than the centuries-long Roman effort, but it was no less dependent on military force and no less brutal. Scholars who opposed Shihuangdi's policies

Map 4.5   Classical China

The brief Qin dynasty brought unity to the heartland of Chinese civilization, and the much longer Han dynasty extended its territorial reach south toward Vietnam, east to Korea, and west into Central Asia. To the north lay the military confederacy of the nomadic Xiongnu.

were executed and their books burned. Aristocrats who might oppose his centralizing policies were moved physically to the capital. Hundreds of thousands of laborers were recruited to construct the Great Wall of China, designed to keep out northern "barbarians," and to erect a monumental mausoleum as the emperor's final resting place, which included some 7,500 life-size ceramic soldiers (shown in the photo at the beginning of this chapter). More positively, Shihuangdi imposed a uniform system of weights, measures, and currency and standardized the length of axles for carts and the written form of the Chinese language.

As in Rome, the creation of the Chinese empire had domestic repercussions, but they were brief and superficial compared to Rome's transition from republic to empire. The speed and brutality of Shihuangdi's policies ensured that his own Qin dynasty did not last long, and it collapsed unmourned in 206 B.C.E. The Han dynasty that followed (206 B.C.E–220 C.E.) retained the centralized features of Shihuangdi's creation, although it moderated the harshness of his policies. It was Han dynasty rulers who consolidated China's imperial state and established the political patterns that lasted into the twentieth century.

Consolidating the Roman and Chinese Empires

■ **Comparison**

In comparing the Roman and Chinese empires, which do you find more striking—their similarities or their differences?

Once established, these two huge imperial systems shared a number of common features. Both, for example, defined themselves in universal terms. The Roman writer Polybius spoke of bringing "almost the entire world" under the control of Rome,[11] while the Chinese state was said to encompass "all under heaven." Both of them invested heavily in public works—roads, bridges, aqueducts, canals, protective walls—all designed to integrate their respective domains militarily and commercially.

Furthermore, Roman and Chinese authorities both invoked supernatural sanctions to support their rule. By the first century C.E., Romans began to regard their deceased emperors as gods and established a religious cult to bolster the authority of living emperors. It was the refusal of early Christians to take part in this cult that provoked their periodic persecution by Roman authorities.

In China, a much older tradition had long linked events on earth with affairs in heaven. In this conception, heaven was neither a place nor a supreme being but rather an impersonal moral force that regulated the universe. Emperors were called the Son of Heaven and were said to govern by the Mandate of Heaven so long as they ruled morally and with benevolence. Peasant rebellions, "barbarian" invasions, or disastrous floods were viewed as signs that the emperor had ruled badly and thus had lost the Mandate of Heaven. Among the chief duties of the emperor was the performance of various rituals thought to maintain the appropriate relationship between heaven and earth. What moral government meant in practice was spelled out in the writings of Confucius and his followers, which became the official ideology of the empire (see Chapter 5).

Both of these classical civilizations also absorbed a foreign religious tradition—Christianity in the Roman Empire and Buddhism in China—although the process unfolded somewhat differently. In the case of Rome, Christianity was born as a small sect of a small province in a remote corner of the empire. From there, it spread slowly for several centuries, mostly among the poor and lower classes; this process was considerably aided by the *pax Romana* and Roman roads. After suffering intermittent persecution, Christianity in the fourth century C.E. obtained state support from emperors who hoped to shore up a tottering empire with a common religion, and thereafter the religion spread quite rapidly.

In the case of China, by contrast, Buddhism came from India, far beyond the Chinese world. It was introduced to China by Central Asian traders and received little support from Han dynasty rulers. In fact, the religion spread only modestly among Chinese until after the Han dynasty collapsed (220 C.E.), when it appealed to people who felt bewildered by the loss of a predictable and stable society. Not until the Sui dynasty emperor Wendi (581–604 C.E.) reunified China did the new religion gain state support, and then only temporarily. Buddhism thus became one of several religious strands in a complex Chinese mix, while Christianity, though divided internally, ultimately became the dominant religious tradition throughout Europe.

The Roman and Chinese empires also had a different relationship to the societies they governed. Rome's beginnings as a small city-state meant that Romans, and even Italians, were always a distinct minority within the empire. The Chinese empire, by contrast, grew out of a much larger cultural heartland, already ethnically Chinese. Furthermore, as the Chinese state expanded, especially to the south, it actively assimilated the non-Chinese or "barbarian" people. In short, they became Chinese, culturally, linguistically, through intermarriage, and in physical appearance as well. Many Chinese in modern times are in fact descended from people who at one point or another were not Chinese at all.

The Roman Empire also offered a kind of assimilation to its subject peoples. Gradually and somewhat reluctantly, the empire granted Roman citizenship to various individuals, families, or whole communities for their service to the empire or in recognition of their adoption of Roman culture. In 212 C.E., Roman citizenship was bestowed on almost all free people of the empire. Citizenship offered clear advantages—the right to hold public office, to serve in the Roman military units known as legions, to wear a toga, and more—but it conveyed a legal status, rather than cultural assimilation, and certainly did not erase other identities, such as being Greek, Egyptian, or a citizen of a particular city.

Various elements of Roman culture—its public buildings, its religious rituals, its Latin language, its style of city life—were attractive, especially in Western Europe, where urban civilization was something new. In the eastern half of the empire, however, things Greek retained tremendous prestige. Many elite Romans in fact regarded Greek culture—its literature, philosophy, and art—as superior to their own and proudly sent their sons to Athens for a Greek education. To some extent, the two blended into a mixed Greco-Roman tradition, which the empire served to disseminate throughout the realm. Other non-Roman cultural traditions—such as the cult of the Persian god Mithra or the compassionate Egyptian goddess Isis, and, most extensively, the Jewish-derived religion of Christianity—also spread throughout the empire. Nothing similar occurred in Han dynasty China, except for

Buddhism, which established a modest presence, largely among foreigners. Chinese culture, widely recognized as the model to which others should conform, experienced little competition from an older, venerated, or foreign tradition.

Language served these two empires in important but contrasting ways. Latin, an alphabetic language depicting sounds, gave rise to various distinct languages— Spanish, Portuguese, French, Italian, Romanian—whereas Chinese did not. Chinese characters, which represented words or ideas more than sounds, were not easily transferable to other languages, but written Chinese could be understood by all literate people, no matter which spoken dialect of the language they used. Thus Chinese, more than Latin, served as an instrument of elite assimilation. For all of these reasons, the various peoples of the Roman Empire were able to maintain their separate cultural identities far more than was the case in China.

Politically, both empires established effective centralized control over vast regions and huge populations, but the Chinese, far more than the Romans, developed an elaborate bureaucracy to hold the empire together. The Han emperor Wudi (reigned 141–87 B.C.E.) established an imperial academy for training officials for an emerging bureaucracy with a curriculum based on the writings of Confucius. This was the beginning of a civil service system, complete with examinations and selection by merit, which did much to integrate the Chinese empire and lasted into the early twentieth century. Roman administration was a somewhat ramshackle affair, relying more on regional elites and the army to provide cohesion. Unlike the Chinese, however, the Romans developed an elaborate body of law, applicable equally to all people of the realm, dealing with matters of justice, property, commerce, and family life. Chinese and Roman political development thus generated different answers to the question of what made for good government. For those who inherited

Snapshot   **Key Moments in Classical Chinese History**

Political fragmentation ("warring states" period)	500–221 B.C.E.
Unification of China: Shihuangdi and Qin dynasty	221–206 B.C.E.
Beginning of Han dynasty, with Liu Bang as its first emperor	206–195 B.C.E.
Reign of Emperor Wudi, who established Confucian Academy for training imperial bureaucrats	141–87 B.C.E.
Emperor Wang Mang attempts land reform, without success	9–23 C.E.
Yellow Turban peasant revolt	184 C.E.
Collapse of Han dynasty	220 C.E.
Renewed political fragmentation	220–581 C.E.
China's unity is restored (Sui dynasty)	589–618 C.E.
Tang dynasty	618–907 C.E.

the Roman tradition, it was good laws, whereas for those in the Chinese tradition, it was good men.

The Collapse of Empires

Empires rise, and then, with some apparent regularity, they fall, and in doing so, they provide historians with one of their most intriguing questions: What causes the collapse of these once-mighty structures? In China, the Han dynasty empire came to an end in 220 C.E.; the traditional date for the final disintegration of the Roman Empire is 476 C.E., although a process of decline had been under way for several centuries. In the Roman case, however, only the western half of the empire collapsed, while the eastern part, subsequently known as the Byzantine Empire, maintained the tradition of imperial Rome for another thousand years.

■ **Comparison**

How did the collapse of empire play out differently in the Roman world and in China?

Despite this difference, a number of common factors have been associated with the end of these imperial states. At one level, they simply got too big, too overextended, and too expensive to be sustained by the available resources, and no fundamental technological breakthrough was available to enlarge these resources. Furthermore, the growth of large landowning families with huge estates enabled them to avoid paying taxes, turned free peasants into impoverished tenant farmers, and diminished the authority of the central government. In China, such conditions led to a major peasant revolt, known as the Yellow Turban Rebellion, in 184 C.E.

Rivalry among elite factions created instability in both empires and eroded imperial authority. In China, persistent tension between castrated court officials (*eunuchs*) loyal to the emperor and Confucian-educated scholar-bureaucrats weakened the state. In the Roman Empire between 235 and 284 C.E., some twenty-six individuals claimed the title of Roman emperor, only one of whom died of natural causes. In addition, epidemic disease ravaged both societies. The population of the Roman Empire declined by 25 percent in the two centuries following 250 C.E., a demographic disaster that meant diminished production, less revenue for the state, and fewer men available for the defense of the empire's long frontiers.

To these mounting internal problems was added a growing threat from nomadic or semi-agricultural peoples occupying the frontier regions of both empires. The Chinese had long developed various ways of dealing with the Xiongnu and other nomadic people to the north—building the Great Wall to keep them out, offering them trading opportunities at border markets, buying them off with lavish gifts, contracting marriage alliances with nomadic leaders, and conducting periodic military campaigns against them. But as the Han dynasty weakened in the second and third centuries C.E., such peoples more easily breached the frontier defenses and set up a succession of "barbarian states" in north China. Culturally, however, many of these foreign rulers gradually became Chinese, encouraging intermarriage, adopting Chinese dress, and setting up their courts in Chinese fashion.

A weakening Roman Empire likewise faced serious problems from Germanic-speaking peoples living on its northern frontier. Growing numbers of these people

Meeting of Attila and Pope Leo I
Among the "barbarian" invaders of the Roman Empire, none were more feared than the Huns, led by the infamous Attila. In a celebrated meeting in 452 C.E., Pope Leo I persuaded Attila to spare the city of Rome and to withdraw from Italy. This painting from about 1360 C.E. records that remarkable meeting. (National Szechenyi Library, Budapest)

began to enter the empire in the fourth century C.E.—some as mercenaries in Roman armies and others as refugees fleeing the invasions of the ferocious Huns, who were penetrating Europe from Central Asia. Once inside the declining empire, various Germanic groups established their own kingdoms, at first controlling Roman emperors and then displacing them altogether by 476 C.E. Unlike the nomadic groups in China, who largely assimilated Chinese culture, Germanic kingdoms in Europe developed their own ethnic identity—Visigoths, Franks, Anglo-Saxons, and others—even as they drew on Roman law and adopted Roman Christianity. Far more than in China, the fall of the Roman Empire produced a new culture, blending Latin and Germanic elements, which provided the foundation for the hybrid civilization that would arise in Western Europe.

The collapse of empire meant more than the disappearance of centralized government and endemic conflict. In both China and post-Roman Europe, it also meant the decline of urban life, a contracting population, less area under cultivation, diminishing international trade, and vast insecurity for ordinary people. It must have seemed that civilization itself was unraveling.

The most significant difference between the collapse of empire in China and that in the Mediterranean basin lay in what happened next. In China, after about 350 years of disunion, disorder, frequent warfare, and political chaos, a Chinese imperial state, similar to that of the Han dynasty, was reassembled under the Sui (589–618 C.E.), Tang (618–907), and Song (960–1279) dynasties. Once again, a single emperor ruled; a bureaucracy selected by examinations governed; and the ideas of Confucius informed the political system. Such a Chinese empire persisted into the early twentieth century, establishing one of the most continuous political traditions of any civilization in world history.

The story line of European history following the end of the Roman Empire was very different indeed. No large-scale, centralized, imperial authority, encompassing all of Western Europe, has ever been successfully reestablished there for any length of time. The memory of Roman imperial unity certainly persisted, and many subsequently tried unsuccessfully to re-create it. But most of Western Europe dissolved into a highly decentralized political system involving kings with little authority, nobles, knights and vassals, various city-states in Italy, and small territories ruled by princes, bishops, or the pope. From this point on, Europe would be a civilization without an encompassing imperial state.

From a Chinese point of view, Western Europe's post-Roman history must seem an enormous failure. Why were Europeans unable to reconstruct something of the unity of their classical empire, while the Chinese clearly did? Surely the greater cultural homogeneity of Chinese civilization made that task easier than it was amid the vast ethnic and linguistic diversity of Europe. The absence in the Roman legacy of a strong bureaucratic tradition also contributed to European difficulties, whereas in China the bureaucracy provided stability even as dynasties came and went. The Chinese also had in Confucianism a largely secular ideology that placed great value on political matters in the here and now. The Roman Catholic Church in Europe, however, was frequently at odds with state authorities, and its "otherworldliness" did little to support the creation of large-scale empires. Finally, Chinese agriculture was much more productive than that of Europe, and for a long time its metallurgy was more advanced.[12] These conditions gave Chinese state-builders more resources to work with than were available to their European counterparts.

Intermittent Empire: The Case of India

Among the classical civilizations of Eurasia, empire loomed large in Persian, Mediterranean, and Chinese history, but it played a much less prominent role in India. In the Indus River valley flourished the largest of the First Civilizations, embodied in exquisitely planned cities such as Harappa but with little evidence of any central political authority. The demise of this early civilization by 1500 B.C.E. was followed over the next thousand years by the creation of a new civilization based farther east, along the Ganges River on India's northern plain. That process has occasioned considerable scholarly debate, which has focused on the role of the Aryans, a pastoral Indo-European people long thought to have invaded and destroyed the Indus Valley civilization and created the new one along the Ganges. More recent research has called this view into question. Did the Aryans invade suddenly, or did they migrate slowly into the Indus River valley, or were they already there as a part of the Indus Valley population? Was the new civilization largely the work of Aryans, or did it evolve gradually from Indus Valley culture? About all of this, scholars have yet to reach agreement.[13]

> ■ **Comparison**
> Why were centralized empires so much less prominent in India than in China?

However it occurred, by 600 B.C.E. what would become the classic civilization of South Asia had begun to take shape across northern India. Politically, that civilization emerged as a fragmented collection of towns and cities, some small republics governed by public assemblies, and a number of regional states ruled by kings. An astonishing range of ethnic, cultural, and linguistic diversity also characterized this civilization, as an endless variety of peoples migrated into India from Central Asia across the mountain passes in the northwest. These features of Indian civilization—political fragmentation and vast cultural diversity—have informed much of South Asian history throughout many centuries, offering a sharp contrast to the pattern of development in China. What gave Indian civilization a recognizable identity and character was neither an imperial tradition nor ethnolinguistic commonality, but rather a distinctive religious tradition, known later to outsiders as Hinduism, and a unique social organization, the caste system. These features of Indian life are explored further in Chapters 5 and 6.

Nonetheless, empires and emperors were not entirely unknown in India's long history. Northwestern India had been briefly ruled by the Persian Empire and then conquered by Alexander the Great. These Persian and Greek influences helped stimulate

Map 4.6 Empire in South Asia

Large-scale empires in the Indian subcontinent were less frequent and less enduring than in China. Two of the largest efforts were those of the Mauryan and Gupta dynasties.

Legend:
- Mauryan Empire, 250 B.C.E.
- Gupta Empire, 420 C.E.
- ▲ Rock and pillar edicts and inscriptions of Ashoka

the first and largest of India's short experiments with a large-scale political system, the Mauryan Empire (326–184 B.C.E.), which encompassed all but the southern tip of the subcontinent (see Map 4.6).

The Mauryan Empire was an impressive political structure, equivalent to the Persian, Chinese, and Roman empires, though not nearly as long-lasting. With a population of perhaps 50 million, the Mauryan Empire boasted a large military force, reported to include 600,000 infantry soldiers, 30,000 cavalry, 8,000 chariots, and 9,000 elephants. A civilian bureaucracy featured various ministries and a large contingent of spies to provide the rulers with local information. The state also operated many industries—spinning, weaving, mining, shipbuilding, and armaments. This complex apparatus was financed by taxes on trade, on herds of animals, and especially on land, from which the monarch claimed a quarter or more of the crop.[14]

Mauryan India is perhaps best known for one of its emperors, Ashoka (reigned 268–232 B.C.E.), who left a record of his activities and his thinking in a series of edicts carved on rocks and pillars throughout the kingdom. Ashoka's reign began in a familiar fashion—ruthless consolidation of his own power and vigorous expansion of the state's frontiers. A particularly bloody battle against the state of Kalinga marked a turning point in Ashoka's reign. Apparently repulsed by the destruction, Ashoka converted to Buddhism and turned his attention to more peaceful ways of governing his huge empire. His carved edicts outlined a philosophy of nonviolence and of toleration for the many sects of the immensely varied religious culture of India. Referring to all Indians as "my children," he urged the "advancement of all sects" and promised to work for "every kind of happiness in this world and the next."

In pursuit of this philosophy, Ashoka abandoned his much-beloved royal hunts, ended animal sacrifices in the capital, eliminated most meat from the royal menu, and was particularly generous in his support of Buddhist monasteries as well as stupas, which housed relics of major Buddhist figures. In addition, he ordered the digging of wells, the planting of shade trees, and the building of rest stops along the empire's major highways—all of which served to integrate the kingdom's economy.

But he did not completely abandon the prerogatives of a ruler, for the edicts reminded people that he retained the power to punish wrongdoing, and the death penalty remained intact. Nonetheless, Ashoka's reign certainly had a different tone than that of China's Shihuangdi or of Alexander the Great, who, according to legend, wept because he had no more worlds to conquer. Of course, Ashoka's policies were good politics as well as good morality. They were an effort to develop an inclusive and integrative moral code for an extremely diverse realm.

Despite their good intentions, these policies ultimately were not very successful. Shortly after Ashoka's death, the Mauryan Empire broke apart into a more common Indian pattern of competing regional states that rose and fell with some regularity. Several other short-lived imperial experiments, such as the Gupta Empire (320–550 C.E.), also marked India's history, but none lasted long. India's political history thus resembled that of Western Europe after the collapse of the Roman Empire far more than that of China or Persia. Neither imperial nor regional states commanded the kind of loyalty or exercised the degree of influence that they did in other classical civilizations. India's unparalleled cultural diversity surely was one reason, as was the frequency of invasions from Central Asia, which repeatedly smashed states that might have provided the nucleus for an all-India empire. Finally, India's social structure, embodied in a caste system linked to occupational groups, made for intensely local loyalties at the expense of wider identities (see Chapter 6).

Nonetheless, a frequently vibrant economy fostered a lively internal commerce and made India the focal point of an extensive network of trade in the Indian Ocean basin. In particular, its cotton textile industry long supplied cloth throughout the Afro-Eurasian world. Strong guilds of merchants and artisans provided political leadership in major towns and cities, and their wealth patronized lavish temples, public buildings, and religious festivals. Great creativity in religious matters generated Hindu and Buddhist traditions that later penetrated much of Asia. Indian mathematics and science, especially astronomy, also were impressive; Indian scientists plotted the movements of stars and planets and recognized quite early that the earth was round. Clearly, the absence of consistent imperial unity did not prevent the evolution of an enduring civilization.

Ashoka of India
This twelfth-century stone relief provides a visual image of the Mauryan dynasty's best-known ruler. (Philip Baird/ www.anthroarcheart.org)

Reflections: Classical Empires and the Twentieth Century

The classical empires discussed in this chapter have long ago passed into history, but we have kept them alive in memory, for they have proven useful, even in the twentieth and early twenty-first centuries. Those empires have provided legitimacy for contemporary states, inspiration for new imperial ventures, and abundant warnings and cautions for those seeking to criticize more recent empires. For example, in bringing communism to China in the twentieth century, the Chinese leader Mao Zedong compared himself to Shihuangdi, the unifier of China and the brutal founder of its Qin dynasty. Reflecting on his campaign against intellectuals in general and Confucianism in particular, Mao declared to a Communist Party conference: "Emperor Qin Shihuang was not that outstanding. He only buried alive 460 Confucian scholars. We buried 460 thousand Confucian scholars.... To the charge of being like Emperor Qin, of being a dictator, we plead guilty."[15]

In contrast, modern-day Indians, who have sought to present their country as a model of cultural tolerance and nonviolence, have been quick to link themselves to Ashoka and his policies of inclusiveness. When the country became independent from British colonial rule in 1947, India soon placed an image of Ashoka's Pillar on the new nation's currency.

In the West, it has been the Roman Empire that has provided a template for thinking about political life. Many in Great Britain celebrated their own global empire as a modern version of the Roman Empire. In the early twentieth century, African students in a mission school in British-ruled Kenya were asked on a history exam to list the benefits that Roman occupation brought to Britain. The implication was obvious. If the British had been "civilized" by Roman rule, then surely Africans would benefit from falling under the control of the "superior" British. Likewise, to the Italian fascist dictator Benito Mussolini, his country's territorial expansion during the 1930s and World War II represented the creation of a new Roman Empire. Most recently, of course, America's dominant role in the world has prompted the question: are the Americans the new Romans?

Historians frequently cringe as politicians and students use (and perhaps misuse) historical analogies to make their case for particular points of view in the present. But we have little else to go on except history in making our way through the complexities of contemporary life, and historians themselves seldom agree on the "lessons" of the past. Lively debate about the continuing relevance of classical empires shows that although the past may be gone, it surely is not dead.

Second Thoughts

What's the Significance?

To assess your mastery of the material in this chapter, see the **Online Study Guide** at bedfordstmartins.com/strayer.

Persian Empire	Alexander the Great	Qin Shihuangdi
Athenian democracy	Hellenistic era	Han dynasty
Greco-Persian Wars	Caesar Augustus	Mauryan Empire
	pax Romana	Ashoka

Big Picture Questions

1. What common features can you identify in the empires described in this chapter?
2. In what ways did these empires differ from one another? What accounts for those differences?
3. Are you more impressed with the "greatness" of empires or with their destructive and oppressive features? Why?
4. Do you think that the classical empires hold "lessons" for the present, or are contemporary circumstances sufficiently unique as to render the distant past irrelevant?

Next Steps: For Further Study

Norman F. Cantor, *Antiquity* (2003). An overview of ancient and classical civilizations.

Arthur Cotterell, *The First Emperor of China* (1988). A biography of Shihuangdi.

Christopher Kelley, *The Roman Empire: A Very Short Introduction* (2006). A brief, up-to-date, and accessible account of the Roman achievement.

Cullen Murphy, *Are We Rome? The Fall of an Empire and the Fate of America* (2007). A reflection on the usefulness and the dangers of comparing the Roman Empire to the present-day United States.

Sarah Pomeroy et al., *Ancient Greece* (1999). A highly readable survey of Greek history by a team of distinguished scholars.

Romila Thapar, *Ashoka and the Decline of the Mauryas* (1961). A classic study of India's early empire builder.

Illustrated History of the Roman Empire. http://www.roman-empire.net. An interactive Web site with maps, pictures, and much information about the Roman Empire.

For Web sites and documents related to this chapter, see **Make History** at bedfordstmartins.com/strayer.

Eurasian Cultural Traditions

500 B.C.E.–500 C.E.

In 2004, some 180 married couples in Beijing, China, stood before a picture of their country's ancient sage, Confucius, and took an oath, pledging fidelity to each other and promising never to divorce. This was a small part of a nationwide celebration of the 2,555th anniversary of the birth of Confucius. A public memorial service was held in his hometown of Qufu, while high government officials warmly welcomed delegates attending an international symposium devoted to his teaching. What made this celebration remarkable was that it took place in a country still ruled by the Communist Party, which had long devoted enormous efforts to discrediting Confucius and his teachings. In the view of communist China's revolutionary leader, Mao Zedong, Confucianism was associated with class inequality, patriarchy, feudalism, superstition, and all things old and backward, but the country's ancient teacher and philosopher, apparently, had outlasted its revolutionary hero. High-ranking political leaders, all officially communist, have begun to invoke Confucius and to urge "social harmony," rather than class conflict, as China rapidly modernizes. Many anxious parents offer prayers at Confucian temples when their children are taking the national college entrance exams.

Buddhism also has experienced something of a revival in China, as thousands of temples, destroyed during the heyday of communism, have been repaired and reopened. Christianity too has grown rapidly since the death of Mao in 1976, with professing Christians numbering some 7 percent of China's huge population by the early twenty-first century. Here are reminders, in a Chinese context, of the continuing appeal of cultural traditions forged during the classical era. Those traditions are

---

China's Cultural Traditions: In this idealized painting, attributed to the Chinese artist Wang Shugu (1649–1730), the Chinese teacher Confucius presents a baby Buddha to the Daoist master Laozi. The image illustrates the assimilation of a major Indian religion into China as well as the generally peaceful coexistence of these three traditions. (British Museum/The Art Archive) among the most enduring legacies that second-wave civilizations have bequeathed to the modern world.

IN THE SEVERAL CENTURIES SURROUNDING 500 B.C.E., something quite remarkable happened all across Eurasia. More or less simultaneously, in China, India, the Middle East, and Greece, there emerged cultural traditions that spread widely, have persisted in various forms into the twenty-first century, and have shaped the values and outlooks of most people who have inhabited the planet over the past 2,500 years.

In China, it was the time of Kong Fuzi (Confucius) and Laozi, whose teachings gave rise to Confucianism and Daoism respectively. In India, a series of religious writings known as the *Upanishads* gave expression to the classical philosophy of Hinduism, while a religious reformer, Siddhartha Gautama, set in motion a separate religion known later as Buddhism. In the Middle East, a distinctively monotheistic religious tradition appeared. It was expressed in Zoroastrianism, derived from the teachings of the Persian prophet Zarathustra, and in Judaism, articulated in Israel by a number of Jewish prophets such as Amos, Jeremiah, and Isaiah. Finally, in Greece, a rational and humanistic tradition found expression in the writings of Socrates, Plato, Aristotle, and many others.

These cultural traditions differed greatly. Chinese and Greek thinkers focused more on the affairs of this world and credited human rationality with the power to understand that reality. Indian, Persian, and Jewish intellectuals, who explored the realm of the divine and its relationship to human life, were much more religious. All of these traditions sought an alternative to an earlier polytheism, in which the activities of various gods and spirits explained what happened in this world. These gods and spirits had generally been seen as similar to human beings, though much more powerful. Through ritual and sacrifice, men and women might placate the gods or persuade them to do human bidding. In contrast, the new cultural traditions of the classical era sought to define a single source of order and meaning in the universe, some moral or religious realm, sharply different from and higher than the sphere of human life. The task of humankind, according to these new ways of thinking, was personal moral or spiritual transformation—often expressed as the development of compassion—by aligning ourselves with that higher order.[1] These enormously rich and varied traditions have collectively posed the great questions of human life and society that have haunted and inspired much of humankind ever since. They also defined the distinctive cultures that distinguished the various classical civilizations from one another.

Why did these traditions all emerge at roughly the same time? Here we encounter an enduring issue of historical analysis: What is the relationship between ideas and the circumstances in which they arise? Are ideas generated by particular political, social, and economic conditions? Or are they the product of creative human imagination independent of the material environment? Or do they derive from some combination of the two? In the case of the classical cultural traditions, many historians have

Snapshot   **Thinkers and Philosophies of the Classical Era**

Person	Date	Location	Religion/Philosophy	Key Ideas
Zoroaster	7th century B.C.E. (?)	Persia (present-day Iran)	Zoroastrianism	Single High God; cosmic conflict of good and evil
Hebrew prophets (Isaiah, Amos, Jeremiah)	9th–6th centuries B.C.E.	Eastern Mediterranean/Palestine/Israel	Judaism	Transcendent High God; covenant with chosen people; social justice
Anonymous writers of Upanishads	800–400 B.C.E.	India	Brahmanism/Hinduism	Brahma (the single impersonal divine reality); karma; rebirth; goal of liberation (moksha)
Confucius	6th century B.C.E.	China	Confucianism	Social harmony through moral example; secular outlook; importance of education; family as model of the state
Mahavira	6th century B.C.E.	India	Jainism	All creatures have souls; purification through nonviolence; opposed to caste
Siddhartha Gautama	6th century B.C.E.	India	Buddhism	Suffering caused by desire/attachment; end of suffering through modest and moral living and meditation practice
Laozi, Zhuangzi	6th–3rd centuries B.C.E.	China	Daoism	Withdrawal from the world into contemplation of nature; simple living; end of striving
Socrates, Plato, Aristotle	5th–4th centuries B.C.E.	Greece	Greek rationalism	Style of persistent questioning; secular explanation of nature and human life
Jesus	early 1st century C.E.	Palestine/Israel	Christianity	Supreme importance of love based on intimate relationship with God; at odds with established authorities
Saint Paul	1st century C.E.	Palestine/Israel/eastern Roman Empire	Christianity	Christianity as a religion for all; salvation through faith in Christ

noted the tumultuous social changes that accompanied the emergence of these new teachings. An iron-age technology, available since roughly 1000 B.C.E., made possible more productive economies and more deadly warfare. Growing cities, increased trade, the prominence of merchant classes, the emergence of new states and empires, new contacts among civilizations—all of these disruptions, occurring in already-literate societies, led thinkers to question older outlooks and to come up with new solutions to fundamental questions: What is the purpose of life? How should human society be ordered? What is the relationship between human life in this world and the moral or spiritual realms that lie beyond? But precisely why various societies developed their own distinctive answers to these questions remains an elusive mystery—a tribute, perhaps, to the unpredictable genius of the human imagination.

China and the Search for Order

As one of the First Civilizations, China had a tradition of state building that historians have traced back to around 2000 B.C.E. or before. By the time the Zhou dynasty took power in 1122 B.C.E., the notion of the Mandate of Heaven had taken root, as had the idea that the normal and appropriate condition of China was one of political unity. By the eighth century B.C.E., the authority of the Zhou dynasty and its royal court had substantially weakened, and by 500 B.C.E. any unity that China had earlier enjoyed was long gone. What followed was a period of chaos, growing violence, and disharmony that became known as the "age of warring states" (403–221 B.C.E.). During these dreadful centuries of disorder and turmoil, a number of Chinese thinkers began to consider how order might be restored, how the apparent tranquillity of an earlier time could be realized again. From their reflections emerged classical cultural traditions of Chinese civilization.

The Legalist Answer

■ Comparison
What different answers to the problem of disorder arose in classical China?

One answer to the problem of disorder—though not the first to emerge—was a hardheaded and practical philosophy known as "Legalism." To Legalist thinkers, the solution to China's problems lay in rules or laws, clearly spelled out and strictly enforced through a system of rewards and punishments. "If rewards are high," wrote Han Feizi, one of the most prominent Legalist philosophers, "then what the ruler wants will be quickly effected; if punishments are heavy, what he does not want will be swiftly prevented."[2] Legalists generally entertained a rather pessimistic view of human nature. Most people were stupid and shortsighted. Only the state and its rulers could act in their long-term interests. Doing so meant promoting farmers and soldiers, the only two groups in society who performed essential functions, while suppressing artisans, merchants, aristocrats, scholars, and other classes regarded as useless.

Legalist thinking provided inspiration and methods for the harsh reunification of China under Shihuangdi and the Qin dynasty (221–206 B.C.E.), but the brutality of that short dynasty thoroughly discredited Legalism. Although its techniques and practices played a role in subsequent Chinese statecraft, no philosopher or ruler ever again openly advocated its ideas. The Han and all subsequent dynasties drew instead on the teachings of China's greatest sage—Confucius.

The Confucian Answer

Born to an aristocratic family in the state of Lu in northern China, Confucius (551–479 B.C.E.) was both learned and ambitious. Believing that he had found the key to solving China's problem of disorder, he spent much of his adult life seeking a political position from which he might put his ideas into action. But no such opportunity came his way. Perhaps it was just as well, for it was as a thinker and a teacher that Confucius left a profound imprint on Chinese history and culture and on other East Asian societies, such as Korea and Japan. After his death, his students collected his teachings in a short book called the *Analects*, and later scholars elaborated and commented endlessly on his ideas, creating a body of thought known as Confucianism.

The Confucian answer to the problem of China's disorder was very different from that of the Legalists. Not laws and punishments, but the moral example of superiors was the Confucian key to a restored social harmony. For Confucius, human society consisted primarily of unequal relationships: the father was superior to the son; the husband to the wife; the older brother to the younger brother; and, of course, the ruler to the subject. If the superior party in each of these relationships behaved with sincerity, benevolence, and genuine concern for others, then the inferior party would be motivated to respond with deference and obedience. Harmony then would prevail. As Confucius put it, "The relation between superiors and inferiors is like that between the wind and the grass. The grass must bend when the wind blows across it." Thus, in both family life and in political life, the cultivation of *ren*—translated as human-heartedness, benevolence, goodness, nobility of heart—was the essential ingredient of a tranquil society.

But how are these humane virtues to be nurtured? Believing that people have a capacity for improvement, Confucius emphasized education as the key to moral betterment. He prescribed a broad liberal arts education emphasizing language, literature, history, philosophy, and ethics, all applied to the practical problems of government. Ritual and ceremonies were also important, for they conveyed the rules of appropriate behavior in the many and varying circumstances of life. For the "superior person," or "gentleman" in Confucian

■ **Description**
Why has Confucianism been defined as a "humanistic philosophy" rather than a supernatural religion?

Filial Piety
This Song dynasty painting served as an illustration of an ancient Chinese text in the Confucian tradition called the "Classic of Filial Piety," originally composed sometime around the fourth century B.C.E. and subsequently reissued many times. Here, a son kneels submissively in front of his parents. The long-enduring social order that Confucius advocated began at home with unquestioning obedience and the utmost respect for parents and other senior members of the family. (National Palace Museum, Taipei, Taiwan, Republic of China)

terms, this process of improvement involved serious personal reflection and a willingness to strive continuously to perfect his moral character.

Such ideas left a deep mark on Chinese culture. The discrediting of Legalism during the Qin dynasty opened the door to the adoption of Confucianism as the official ideology of the Chinese state, to such an extent that Confucianism became almost synonymous with Chinese culture. As China's bureaucracy took shape during the Han dynasty and after, Confucianism became the central element of the educational system, which prepared students for the series of examinations required to gain official positions. In those examinations, candidates were required to apply the principles of Confucianism to specific situations that they might encounter once in office. Thus generation after generation of China's male elite was steeped in the ideas and values of Confucianism.

Family life had long been central to Chinese popular culture, expressed in the practice of ancestor veneration, including visiting the graves of the deceased, presenting them with offerings, and erecting commemorative tablets and shrines in their honor. In Confucian thinking, the family became a model for political life, a kind of miniature state. Filial piety, the honoring of one's ancestors and parents, was both an end in itself and a training ground for the reverence due to the emperor and state officials. Confucianism also set the tone for defining the lives of women. A somewhat later woman writer, Ban Zhao (45–116 C.E.), penned a famous work called *Lessons for Women*, which spelled out the implication of Confucian thinking for women.

> Let a woman modestly yield to others. . . . Always let her seem to tremble and to fear. . . . Then she may be said to humble herself before others. . . . To guard carefully her chastity . . . to choose her words with care . . . , to wash and scrub filth away . . . , with whole-hearted devotion to sew and to weave, to love not gossip and silly laughter, in cleanliness and order to prepare the wine and food for serving guests: [These] may be called the characteristics of womanly work.[3]

Ban Zhao called for greater attention to education for young girls, not because they were equal to boys, but so that a young woman might be better prepared to serve her husband.

Confucianism also placed great importance on history, for the ideal good society lay in the past. Confucian ideas were reformist, perhaps even revolutionary, but they were consistently presented as an effort to restore a past golden age. Those ideas also injected a certain democratic element into Chinese elite culture, for the great sage had emphasized that "superior men" and potential government officials were those of outstanding moral character and intellectual achievement, not simply those of aristocratic background. Usually only young men from wealthy families could afford the education necessary for passing examinations, but on occasion villagers could find the resources to sponsor one of their bright sons. Thus the Confucian-based examination system provided a modest element of social mobility in an otherwise hierarchical society. Confucian values clearly justified the many inequalities of Chinese society, but they also established certain expectations for government. Emperors should keep taxes low, administer justice, and provide for the material needs of the people. Those who failed to govern by the moral norms of Confucian values forfeited the Mandate of Heaven and invited upheaval and their replacement by another dynasty.

Finally, Confucianism marked Chinese elite culture by its secular, or nonreligious, character. Confucius did not deny the reality of gods and spirits. In fact, he advised people to participate in family and state rituals "as if the spirits were present," and he believed that the universe had a moral character with which human beings should align themselves. But the thrust of Confucian teaching was distinctly this-worldly and practical, concerned with human relationships, effective government, and social harmony. Asked on one occasion about his view of death and the spirits, Confucius replied that because we do not fully understand this life, we cannot possibly know anything about the life beyond. Although members of the Chinese elite generally acknowledged that magic, the gods, and spirits were perhaps necessary for the lower orders of society, they felt that educated people would find them of little help in striving for moral improvement and in establishing a harmonious society.

The Daoist Answer

No civilization has ever painted its cultural outlook in a single color. As Confucian thinking became generally known in China, a quite different school of thought also took shape. Known as Daoism, it was associated with the legendary figure Laozi, who, according to tradition, was a sixth-century B.C.E. archivist. He is said to have penned a short poetic volume, the *Daodejing* (*The Way and Its Power*), before vanishing in the wilderness to the west of China on his water buffalo. Daoist ideas were later expressed in a more explicit fashion by the philosopher Zhuangzi (369–286 B.C.E.).

In many ways, Daoist thinking ran counter to that of Confucius, who had emphasized the importance of education and earnest striving for moral improvement and good government. The Daoists ridiculed such efforts as artificial and useless, generally making things worse. In the face of China's disorder and chaos, they urged withdrawal into the world of nature and encouraged behavior that was spontaneous, individualistic, and natural. Whereas

Chinese Landscape Paintings
Focused largely on mountains and water, Chinese landscape paintings were much influenced by the Daoist search for harmony with nature. Thus human figures and buildings were usually eclipsed by towering peaks, waterfalls, clouds, and trees. This seventeenth-century painting entitled *Temple on a Mountain Ledge* shows a Buddhist monastery in such a setting, while the poem in the upper right refers to the artist's earlier wanderings, a metaphor for the Buddhist quest for enlightenment. (Mr. and Mrs. John D. Rockefeller 3rd Collection of Asian Art/Asia Society 179.124)

■ **Comparison**
How did the Daoist outlook differ from that of Confucianism?

Confucius focused on the world of human relationships, the Daoists turned the spotlight on the immense realm of nature and its mysterious unfolding patterns. Confucius roams within society, the Chinese have often said; Laozi wanders beyond.

The central concept of Daoist thinking is *dao*, an elusive notion that refers to the way of nature, the underlying and unchanging principle that governs all natural phenomena. According to the *Daodejing*, the dao "moves around and around, but does not on this account suffer. All life comes from it. It wraps everything with its love as in a garment, and yet it claims no honor, for it does not demand to be lord. I do not know its name and so I call it the Dao, the Way, and I rejoice in its power."[4]

Applied to human life, Daoism invited people to withdraw from the world of political and social activism, to disengage from the public life so important to Confucius, and to align themselves with the way of nature. It meant simplicity in living, small self-sufficient communities, limited government, and the abandonment of education and active efforts at self-improvement. "Give up learning," declares the *Daodejing*, "and put an end to your troubles." The flavor of the Daoist approach to life is evident in this passage from the *Daodejing*:

> A small country has few people.
> Though there are machines that can work ten to a hundred times faster
> than man, they are not needed. . . .
> Though they have boats and carriages, no one uses them. . . .
> Men return to the knotting of ropes in place of writing.
> Their food is plain and good, their clothes fine but simple. . . .
> They are happy in their ways.
> Though they live within sight of their neighbors,
> And crowing cocks and barking dogs are heard across the way,
> Yet they leave each other in peace while they grow old and die.[5]

The yin yang symbol

Despite its sharp differences with the ideas of Confucianism, the Daoist perspective was widely regarded by elite Chinese as complementing rather than contradicting Confucian values. Such an outlook was facilitated by the ancient Chinese concept of yin and yang, which expressed a belief in the unity of opposites.

Thus a scholar-official might pursue the Confucian project of "government by goodness" during the day, but upon returning home in the evening or following his retirement, he might well behave in a more Daoist fashion—pursuing the simple life, reading Daoist philosophy, practicing Daoist meditation and breathing exercises, or enjoying landscape paintings in which tiny human figures are dwarfed by the vast peaks and valleys of the natural world. Daoism also shaped the culture of ordinary people as it entered popular religion. This kind of Daoism sought to tap the power of the dao for practical uses and came to include magic, fortune-telling, and the search for immortality. It also on occasion provided an ideology for peasant uprisings, such as the Yellow Turban Rebellion (184–204 C.E.; see Chapter 6), which imagined a utopian society without the oppression of governments and landlords. In its many and varied forms, Daoism, like Confucianism, became an enduring element of Chinese cultural tradition.

Cultural Traditions of Classical India

The cultural development of Indian civilization was far different from that of China. Whereas Confucianism paid little attention to the gods, spirits, and speculation about religious matters, Indian elite culture embraced the divine and all things spiritual with enthusiasm and generated elaborate philosophical visions about the nature of ultimate reality. Still, the Indian religious tradition, known to us as Hinduism, differed from other world religions. Unlike Buddhism, Christianity, or Islam, Hinduism had no historical founder; rather, it grew up over many centuries along with Indian civilization. Although it later spread into Southeast Asia, Hinduism was not a missionary religion seeking converts but was, like Judaism, associated with a particular people and territory.

In fact, "Hinduism" was never a single tradition at all, and the term itself derived from outsiders — Greeks, Muslims, and later the British — who sought to reduce the infinite variety of Indian cultural patterns into a recognizable system. From the inside, however, Hinduism dissolved into a vast diversity of gods, spirits, beliefs, practices, rituals, and philosophies. This endlessly variegated Hinduism served to incorporate into Indian civilization the many diverse peoples who migrated into or invaded the South Asian peninsula over many centuries and several millennia. Its ability to accommodate this diversity gave India's cultural development a distinctive quality.

South Asian Religion: From Ritual Sacrifice to Philosophical Speculation

Despite the fragmentation and variety of Indian cultural and religious patterns, an evolving set of widely recognized sacred texts provided some commonality. The earliest of these texts, known as the *Vedas*, were collections of poems, hymns, prayers, and rituals. Compiled by priests called *Brahmins*, the Vedas were for centuries transmitted orally and were reduced to writing in Sanskrit around 600 B.C.E. In the Vedas, historians have caught fleeting glimpses of classical Indian civilization in its formative centuries (1500–600 B.C.E.). Those sacred writings tell of small competing chiefdoms or kingdoms, of sacred sounds and fires, of numerous gods, rising and falling in importance over the centuries, and of the elaborate ritual sacrifices that they required. Performing these sacrifices and rituals with great precision enabled the Brahmins to acquire enormous power and wealth, sometimes exceeding even that of kings and warriors, but also generated growing criticism, as ritual became mechanical and formal and as Brahmins required heavy fees to perform them.

From this dissatisfaction arose another body of sacred texts, the *Upanishads*. Composed by largely anonymous thinkers between 800 and 400 B.C.E., these were

■ **Change**
In what ways did the religious traditions of South Asia change over the centuries?

Hindu Ascetics
Hinduism called for men in the final stage of life to leave ordinary ways of living and withdraw into the forests to seek spiritual liberation, or moksha. Here, in an illustration from an early thirteenth-century Indian manuscript, a holy man explores a text with three disciples in a secluded rural setting. (Réunion des Musées Nationaux/Art Resource, NY)

mystical and highly philosophical works that sought to probe the inner meaning of the sacrifices prescribed in the Vedas. In the Upanishads, external ritual gave way to introspective thinking, which expressed in many and varied formulations the central concepts of philosophical Hinduism that have persisted into modern times. Chief among them was the idea of *Brahman*, the World Soul, the final and ultimate reality. Beyond the multiplicity of material objects and individual persons and beyond even the various gods themselves lay this primal unitary energy or divine reality infusing all things, similar in some ways to the Chinese notion of the dao. This alone was real; the immense diversity of existence that human beings perceived with their senses was but an illusion.

The fundamental assertion of philosophical Hinduism was that the individual human soul, or *atman*, was in fact a part of Brahman. Beyond the quest for pleasure, wealth, power, and social position, all of which were perfectly normal and quite legitimate, lay the effort to achieve the final goal of humankind—union with Brahman, an end to our illusory perception of a separate existence. This was *moksha*, or liberation, compared sometimes to a bubble in a glass of water breaking through the surface and becoming one with the surrounding atmosphere.

Achieving this exalted state was held to involve many lifetimes, as the notion of *samsara*, or rebirth/reincarnation, became a central feature of Hindu thinking. Human souls migrated from body to body over many lifetimes, depending on one's actions. This was the law of *karma*. Pure actions, appropriate to one's station in life, resulted in rebirth in a higher social position or caste. Thus the caste system of distinct and ranked groups, each with its own duties, became a register of spiritual progress. Birth in a higher caste was evidence of "good karma," based on actions in a previous life, and offered a better chance to achieve moksha, which brought with it an end to the painful cycle of rebirth.

Various ways to this final release, appropriate to people of different temperaments, were spelled out in Hindu teachings. Some might achieve moksha through knowledge or study; others by means of detached action in the world, doing one's work without regard to consequences; still others through passionate devotion to some deity or through extended meditation practice. Such ideas—carried by Brahmin priests and even more by wandering ascetics, who had withdrawn from ordinary life to pursue their spiritual development—became widely known throughout India.

The Buddhist Challenge

About the same time as philosophical Hinduism was taking shape, there emerged another movement that soon became a distinct and separate religious tradition—Buddhism. Unlike Hinduism, this new faith had a historical founder, Siddhartha Gautama (ca. 566–ca. 486 B.C.E.), a prince from a small north Indian state. According to Buddhist tradition, the prince had enjoyed a sheltered and delightful youth but was shocked to his core upon encountering old age, sickness, and death. Leaving family and fortune behind, he then set out on a six-year spiritual quest, finally achieving insight, or "enlightenment," at the age of thirty-five. For the rest of his life, he taught what he had learned and gathered a small but growing community whose members came to see him as the Buddha, the Enlightened One.

"I teach but one thing," the Buddha said, "suffering and the end of suffering." To the Buddha, suffering or sorrow—experiencing life as imperfect, impermanent, and unsatisfactory—was the central and universal feature of human life. Its cause was desire or craving for individual fulfillment and particularly attachment to the notion of a core self or ego that is uniquely and solidly "me." The cure for this "dis-ease" lay in living a modest and moral life combined with meditation practice. Those who followed the Buddhist path most fully could expect to achieve enlightenment or *nirvana*, a virtually indescribable state in which individual identity would be "extinguished" along with all greed, hatred, and delusion. With the pain of unnecessary suffering finally ended, the enlightened person would experience an overwhelming serenity, even in the midst of difficulty, as well as an immense loving-kindness, or compassion, for all beings. It was a simple message, elaborated endlessly and in various forms by those who followed him.

Much of the Buddha's teaching reflected the Hindu traditions from which it sprang. The idea that ordinary life is an illusion, the concepts of karma and rebirth, the goal of overcoming the incessant demands of the ego, the practice of meditation, the hope for final release from the cycle of rebirth—all of these Hindu elements found their way into Buddhist teaching. In this respect, Buddhism was a simplified and more accessible version of Hinduism.

Other elements of Buddhist teaching, however, sharply challenged prevailing Hindu thinking. Rejecting the religious authority of the Brahmins, the Buddha ridiculed their rituals and sacrifices as

■ **Comparison**
In what ways did Buddhism reflect Hindu traditions, and in what ways did it challenge them?

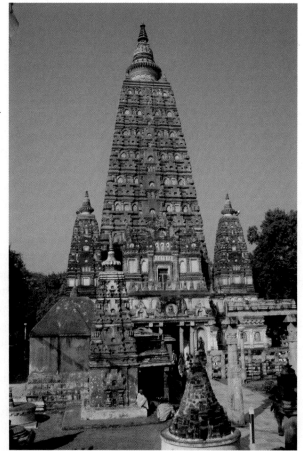

The Mahabodhi Temple Constructed on the traditional site of the Buddha's enlightenment in northern India, the Mahabodhi temple became a major pilgrimage site and was lavishly patronized by local rulers. (Alison Wright/Robert Harding World Imagery/Getty Images)

irrelevant to the hard work of dealing with one's suffering. Nor was he much interested in abstract speculation about the creation of the world or the existence of God, for such questions, he declared, "are not useful in the quest for holiness; they do not lead to peace and to the direct knowledge of *nirvana*." Individuals had to take responsibility for their own spiritual development with no help from human authorities or supernatural beings. "Be a lamp unto yourselves," counseled the dying Buddha. "Work out your own salvation." It was a religion of intense self-effort, based on personal experience. The Buddha also challenged the inequalities of a Hindu-based caste system, arguing that neither caste position nor gender was a barrier to enlightenment. The possibility of "awakening" was available to all.

When it came to establishing a formal organization of the Buddha's most devoted followers, though, the prevailing patriarchy of Indian society made itself felt. Buddhist texts recount that the Buddha's foster mother, Prajapati Gotami, sought to enter the newly created order of monks but was repeatedly refused admission by the Buddha himself. Only after the intervention of the Buddha's attendant, Ananda, did he relent and allow women to join a separate order of nuns. Even then, these nuns were subjected to a series of rules that clearly subordinated them to men. Male monks, for example, could officially admonish the nuns, but the reverse was forbidden.

Nonetheless, thousands of women flocked to join the Buddhist order of nuns, where they found a degree of freedom and independence unavailable elsewhere in Indian society. The classic Hindu text, "The Laws of Manu," had clearly defined the position of women: "In childhood a female must be subject to her father; in youth to her husband; when her lord is dead to her sons; a woman must never be independent." But Buddhist nuns delighted in the relative freedom of their order, where they largely ran their own affairs, were forbidden to do household chores, and devoted themselves wholly to the search for "awakening," which many apparently achieved. A nun named Mutta declared: "I am free from the three crooked things: mortar, pestle, and my crooked husband. I am free from birth and death and all that dragged me back."[6]

Gradually, Buddhist teachings found an audience in India. Its egalitarian message appealed especially to lower-caste groups and to women. The availability of its teaching in the local language of Pali, rather than the classical Sanskrit, made it accessible. Establishing monasteries and stupas containing relics of the Buddha on the site of neighborhood shrines to earth spirits or near a sacred tree linked the new religion to local traditions. The most dedicated followers joined monasteries, devoting their lives to religious practice and spreading the message among nearby people. State support during the reign of Ashoka (268–232 B.C.E.) likewise helped the new religion gain a foothold in India as a distinct tradition separate from Hinduism.

As Buddhism spread, both within and beyond India, differences in understanding soon emerged, particularly as to how nirvana could be achieved or, in a common Buddhist metaphor, how to cross the river to the far shore of enlightenment. The Buddha had taught a rather austere doctrine of intense self-effort, undertaken

■ Comparison
What is the difference between the Theravada and Mahayana expressions of Buddhism?

most actively by monks and nuns who withdrew from society to devote them-selves fully to the quest. This early version of the new religion, known as *Theravada* (the Teaching of the Elders), portrayed the Buddha as an immensely wise teacher and model, but certainly not divine. It was more psychological than religious, a set of practices rather than a set of beliefs. The gods, though never completely denied, played little role in assisting believers in their search for enlightenment. In short, individuals were on their own in crossing the river. Clearly this was not for everyone.

By the early centuries of the Common Era, a modified form of Buddhism called *Mahayana* (Great Vehicle) had taken root in parts of India, proclaiming that help was available for the strenuous voyage. Buddhist thinkers developed the idea of *bodhisattvas*, spiritually developed people who postponed their own entry into nirvana in order to assist those who were still suffering. The Buddha himself became something of a god, and both earlier and future Buddhas were available to offer help. Elaborate descriptions of these supernatural beings, together with vari-ous levels of heavens and hells, transformed Buddhism into a popular religion of salvation. Furthermore, religious merit, leading to salvation, might now be earned by acts of piety and devotion, such as contributing to the support of a monastery, and that merit might be transferred to others. This was the Great Vehicle, allowing far more people to make the voyage across the river.

Hinduism as a Religion of Duty and Devotion

Strangely enough, Buddhism as a distinct religious practice ultimately died out in the land of its birth as it was reincorporated into a broader Hindu tradition, but it spread widely and flourished, particularly in its Mahayana form, in other parts of Asia. Buddhism declined in India perhaps in part because the mounting wealth of monasteries and the economic interests of their leading figures separated them from ordinary people. Competition from Islam after 1000 C.E. also may have played a role. The most important reason for Buddhism's decline in India, however, was the growth during the first millennium C.E. of a new kind of popular Hinduism, which the masses found more accessible than the elaborate sacrifices of the Brahmins or the philosophical speculations of intellectuals. Some scholars have seen this phase of Hinduism as a response to the challenge of Buddhism. Expressed in the widely known epic poems of the *Mahabharata* and the *Ramayana*, this revived Hinduism indicated more clearly that action in the world and the detached performance of caste duties might also provide a path to liberation.

In the much-beloved Hindu text known as the *Bhagavad Gita*, itself an episode within the *Mahabharata*, the troubled warrior-hero Arjuna is in anguish over the necessity of killing his kinsmen as a decisive battle approaches. But he is assured by his charioteer Lord Krishna, an incarnation of the god Vishnu, that performing his duty as a warrior, and doing so selflessly without regard to consequences, is an act of devotion that would lead to "release from the shackles of repeated rebirth."

■ **Change**
What new emphases characterized Hinduism as it responded to the challenge of Buddhism?

This was not an invitation to militarism, but rather an affirmation that ordinary people, not just Brahmins, could also make spiritual progress by selflessly performing the ordinary duties of their lives. "The man who, casting off all desires, lives free from attachments, who is free from egoism, and from the feeling that this or that is mine, obtains tranquility." Withdrawal and asceticism were not the only ways to moksha.

Also becoming increasingly prominent was yet another religious path—the way of devotion to one or another of India's many gods and goddesses. Beginning in south India and moving northward, this *bhakti* (worship) movement involved the intense adoration of and identification with a particular deity through songs, prayers, and rituals associated with the many cults that emerged throughout India. By far the most popular deities were Vishnu, the protector and preserver of creation and associated with mercy and goodness, and Shiva, representing the divine in its destructive aspect, but many others also had their followers. This proliferation of gods and goddesses, and of their *bhakti* cults, occasioned very little friction or serious religious conflict. "Hinduism," writes a leading scholar, "is essentially tolerant, and would rather assimilate than rigidly exclude."[7] This capacity for assimilation extended to an already-declining Buddhism, which for many people had become yet another cult worshipping yet another god. The Buddha in fact was incorporated into the Hindu pantheon as the ninth incarnation of Vishnu. By 1000 C.E., Buddhism had largely disappeared as a separate religious tradition within India.

Thus a constantly evolving and enormously varied South Asian religious tradition had transformed itself from a religion of ritual sacrifice to one of philosophical speculation, to one of devotional worship and detached action in the world. In the process, it had generated Buddhism, which became the first of the great universal religions of world history, and then had absorbed that new religion back into the fold of an emerging popular Hinduism.

Moving toward Monotheism: The Search for God in the Middle East

Paralleling the evolution of Chinese and Indian cultural traditions was the movement toward a distinctive monotheistic religious tradition in the Middle East, which found expression in Persian Zoroastrianism and in Judaism. Neither of these religions themselves spread very widely, but the monotheism that they nurtured became the basis for both Christianity and Islam, which have shaped so much of world history over the past 2,000 years. Amid the proliferation of gods and spirits that had long characterized religious life throughout the ancient world, the idea of a single supreme Deity, the sole source of all creation and goodness, was a radical cultural innovation. That conception created the possibility of a universal religion, open to all of humankind, but it could also mean an exclusive and intolerant faith, committed to the worship of the one true God.

Zoroastrianism

During the glory years of the powerful Persian Empire, a new religion arose to challenge the polytheism of earlier times. Tradition dates its Persian prophet, Zarathustra (Zoroaster to the Greeks), to the sixth or seventh century B.C.E., although some scholars place him hundreds of years earlier. Whenever he actually lived, his ideas took hold in Persia and received a degree of state support during the Achaemenid dynasty (558–330 B.C.E.). Appalled by the endemic violence of recurring cattle raids, Zarathustra recast the traditional Persian polytheism into a vision of a single unique god, Ahura Mazda, who ruled the world and was the source of all truth, light, and goodness. This benevolent deity was engaged in a cosmic struggle with the forces of evil, embodied in an equivalent supernatural figure, Angra Mainyu. Ultimately this struggle would be decided in favor of Ahura Mazda, aided by the arrival of a final Savior who would restore the world to its earlier purity and peace. At a day of judgment, those who had aligned with Ahura Mazda would be granted new resurrected bodies and rewarded with eternal life in Paradise. Those who had sided with evil and the "Lie" were condemned to everlasting punishment. Zoroastrian teaching thus placed great emphasis on the free will of humankind and the necessity for each individual to choose between good and evil.

The Zoroastrian faith achieved widespread support within the Persian heartland, although it also found adherents in other parts of the empire, such as Egypt, Mesopotamia, and Anatolia. Because it never became an active missionary religion, it did not spread widely beyond the region. Alexander the Great's invasion of the Persian Empire and the subsequent Greek-ruled Seleucid dynasty (330–155 B.C.E.) were disastrous for Zoroastrianism, as temples were plundered, priests slaughtered, and sacred writings burned. But the new faith managed to survive this onslaught and flourished again during the Parthian (247 B.C.E.–224 C.E.) and Sassanid (224–651 C.E.) dynasties. It was the arrival of Islam and an Arab empire that occasioned the final decline of Zoroastrianism in Persia, although a few believers fled to India, where they became known as Parsis ("Persians") and continue their faith into present times.

Like Buddhism, the Zoroastrian faith vanished from its place of origin, but unlike Buddhism, it did not spread beyond Persia in a recognizable form. Some parts of the Zoroastrian belief system, however, did become incorporated into other religious traditions. The presence of many Jews in the Persian Empire meant that they surely became aware of Zoroastrian ideas. Many of those ideas— including the conflict of God and an evil counterpart (Satan); the notion of a last judgment and resurrected bodies; and a belief in the final defeat of evil, the arrival of a savior (Messiah), and the remaking of the world at the end of time—found a place in an evolving Judaism. Some of these teachings, especially the concepts of heaven and hell, later became prominent in those enormously

■ **Connection**
What aspects of Zoroastrianism and Judaism subsequently found a place in Christianity and Islam?

Zoroastrian Fire Altar
Representing the energy of the Creator God Ahura Mazda, the fire altar became an important symbol of Zoroastrianism and was often depicted on Persian coins in association with images of Persian rulers. This particular coin dates from the third century C.E. (©AAAC/Topham/The Image Works)

influential successors to Judaism—Christianity and Islam.[8] Thus the Persian tradition of Zoroastrianism continued to echo well beyond its disappearance in the land of its birth.

Judaism

■ **Description**
What was distinctive about the Jewish religious tradition?

While Zoroastrianism emerged in the greatest empire of its time, Judaism, the Middle East's other ancient monotheistic tradition, was born among one of the region's smaller and, at the time, less significant peoples—the Hebrews. Their traditions, recorded in the Old Testament, tell of an early migration from Mesopotamia to Palestine under the leadership of Abraham. Those same traditions report that a portion of these people later fled to Egypt, where they were first enslaved and then miraculously escaped to rejoin their kinfolk in Palestine. There, around 1000 B.C.E., they established a small state, which soon split into two parts—a northern kingdom called Israel and a southern state of Judah.

In a region politically dominated by the large empires of Assyria, Babylon, and Persia, these tiny Hebrew communities lived a precarious existence. Israel was conquered by Assyria in 722 B.C.E., and many of its inhabitants were deported to distant regions, where they assimilated into the local culture. In 586 B.C.E., the kingdom of Judah likewise came under Babylonian control, and its elite class was shipped off to exile. In Babylon, these people, now calling themselves Jews, retained their cultural identity and later were able to return to their homeland. A large part of that identity lay in their unique religious ideas. It was in creating that religious tradition, rather than in building a powerful empire, that this small people cast a long shadow in world history.

From their unique historical experience of exodus from Egypt and exile in Babylon, the Jews evolved over many centuries a distinctive conception of God. Unlike the peoples of Mesopotamia with their many gods and goddesses, the Jews found in their god, whom they called Yahweh, a powerful and jealous deity, who demanded their exclusive loyalty. "Thou shalt have no other gods before me"—this was the first of the Ten Commandments. It was a difficult requirement, for as the Jews turned from a pastoral life to agriculture, many of them were continually attracted by the fertility gods of neighboring peoples. Their neighbors' goddesses also were attractive, offering a kind of spiritual support that the primarily masculine Yahweh could not. This was not quite monotheism, for the repeated demands of the Hebrew prophets to turn away from other gods show that those deities remained real for many Jews. Over time, however, Yahweh triumphed. The Jews came to understand their relationship to him as a contract or a covenant. In return for their sole devotion and obedience, Yahweh would consider the Jews his chosen people, favoring them in battle, causing them to grow in numbers, and bringing them prosperity and blessing.

Ancient Israel

Unlike the bickering, arbitrary, polytheistic gods of Mesopotamia or ancient Greece, which were associated with the forces of nature and behaved in quite human fashion, Yahweh was increasingly seen as a lofty, transcendent deity of utter holiness and purity, set far above the world of nature, which he had created. But unlike the impersonal conceptions of ultimate reality found in Daoism and Hinduism, Yahweh was encountered as a divine person with whom people could actively communicate. He was also a god who acted within the historical process, bringing the Jews out of Egypt or using foreign empires to punish them for their disobedience.

Furthermore, Yahweh was transformed from a god of war, who ordered his people to "utterly destroy" the original inhabitants of the Promised Land, to a god of social justice and compassion for the poor and the marginalized, especially in the passionate pronouncements of Jewish prophets such as Amos and Isaiah. The prophet Isaiah describes Yahweh as rejecting the empty rituals of his chosen but sinful people: "What to me is the multitude of your sacrifices, says the Lord. . . . Wash yourselves, make yourselves clean . . . cease to do evil, learn to do good . . . ; seek justice; correct oppression; defend the fatherless; plead for the widow."[9]

Here was a distinctive conception of the divine—singular, transcendent, personal, separate from nature, engaged in history, and demanding social justice and moral righteousness above sacrifices and rituals. This set of ideas sustained a separate Jewish identity in both ancient and modern times, and it was this understanding of God that provided the foundation on which both Christianity and Islam were built.

The Cultural Tradition of Classical Greece: The Search for a Rational Order

Unlike the Jews, the Persians, or the civilization of India, Greek thinkers of the classical era generated no lasting religious tradition of world historical importance. The religion of these city-states brought together the unpredictable, quarreling, and lustful gods of Mount Olympus, secret fertility cults, oracles predicting the future, and the ecstatic worship of Dionysus, the god of wine. The distinctive feature of the classical Greek cultural tradition was the willingness of many Greek intellectuals to abandon this mythological framework, to affirm that the world was a physical reality governed by natural laws, and to assert that human rationality could both understand these laws and work out a system of moral and ethical life. In separating science and philosophy from conventional religion, the Greeks developed a way of thinking that bore some similarity to the secularism of Confucian thought in China.

Precisely why Greek thought evolved in this direction is hard to say. Perhaps the diversity and incoherence of Greek religious mythology presented its intellectuals with a challenge to bring some order to their understanding of the world. Greece's geographic position on the margins of the great civilizations of Mesopotamia,

■ **Description**
What are the distinctive features of the Greek intellectual tradition?

Egypt, and Persia certainly provided intellectual stimulation. Furthermore, the growing role of law in the political life of Athens possibly suggested that a similar regularity also underlay the natural order.

The Greek Way of Knowing

The foundations of this distinctive cultural tradition emerged in the three centuries between 600 and 300 B.C.E., coinciding with the flourishing of Greek city-states, especially Athens, and with the growth of its artistic, literary, and theatrical traditions. The enduring significance of Greek thinking lay not so much in the answers it provided to life's great issues, for the Greeks seldom agreed with one another, but rather in its way of asking questions. Its emphasis on argument, logic, and the relentless questioning of received wisdom; its confidence in human reason; its enthusiasm for puzzling out the world without much reference to the gods—these were the defining characteristics of the Greek cultural tradition.

The great exemplar of this approach to knowledge was Socrates (469–399 B.C.E.), an Athenian philosopher who walked about the city engaging others in conversation about the good life. He wrote nothing, and his preferred manner of teaching was not the lecture or exposition of his own ideas but rather a constant questioning of the

The Death of Socrates
Condemned to death by an Athenian jury, Socrates declined to go into exile, voluntarily drank a cup of poison hemlock, and died in 399 B.C.E. in the presence of his friends. The dramatic scene was famously described by Plato and much later was immortalized on canvas by the French painter Jacques-Louis David in 1787. (Image copyright © The Metropolitan Museum of Art/Art Resource, NY)

assumptions and logic of his students' thinking. Concerned always to puncture the pretentious, he challenged conventional ideas about the importance of wealth and power in living well, urging instead the pursuit of wisdom and virtue. He was critical of Athenian democracy and on occasion had positive things to say about Sparta, the great enemy of his own city. Such behavior brought him into conflict with city authorities, who accused him of corrupting the youth of Athens and sentenced him to death. At his trial, he defended himself as the "gadfly" of Athens, stinging its citizens into awareness. To any and all, he declared, "I shall question, and examine and cross-examine him, and if I find that he does not possess virtue, but says he does, I shall rebuke him for scorning the things that are most important and caring more for what is of less worth."[10]

The earliest of the classical Greek thinkers, many of them living on the Ionian coast of Anatolia, applied this rational and questioning way of knowing to the world of nature. For example, Thales, drawing on Babylonian astronomy, predicted an eclipse of the sun and argued that the moon simply reflected the sun's light. He also was one of the first Greeks to ask about the fundamental nature of the universe and came up with the idea that water was the basic stuff from which all else derived, for it existed as solid, liquid, and gas. Others argued in favor of air or fire or some combination. Democritus suggested that atoms, tiny "uncuttable" particles, collided in various configurations to form visible matter. Pythagoras believed that beneath the chaos and complexity of the visible world lay a simple, unchanging mathematical order. What these thinkers had in common was a commitment to a rational and nonreligious explanation for the material world.

Such thinking also served to explain the functioning of the human body and its diseases. Hippocrates and his followers came to believe that the body was composed of four fluids, or "humors," which, when out of proper balance, caused various ailments. He also traced the origins of epilepsy, known to the Greeks as "the sacred disease," to simple heredity: "It seems to me to be no more divine or sacred than other diseases, but has a natural cause from which it originates, like other afflictions."[11] The Hippocratic Oath taken by all new doctors is named for this ancient Greek scientist.

A similar approach informed Greek thinking about the ways of humankind. Herodotus, who wrote about the Greco-Persian Wars, explained his project as an effort to discover "the reason why they fought one another." This assumption that human reasons lay behind the conflict, not simply the whims of the gods, was what made Herodotus a historian in the modern sense of that word. Ethics and government also figured importantly in Greek thinking. Plato (429–348 B.C.E.) famously sketched out in *The Republic* a design for a good society. It would be ruled by a class of highly educated "guardians" led by a "philosopher-king." Such people would be able to penetrate the many illusions of the material world and to grasp the "world of forms," in which ideas such as goodness, beauty, and justice lived a real and unchanging existence. Only such people, he argued, were fit to rule.

Aristotle (384–322 B.C.E.), a student of Plato and a teacher of Alexander the Great, was perhaps the most complete expression of the Greek way of knowing, for he wrote or commented on practically everything. With an emphasis on empirical observation, he cataloged the constitutions of 158 Greek city-states, identified hundreds of species of animals, and wrote about logic, physics, astronomy, the weather, and much else besides. Famous for his reflections on ethics, he argued that "virtue" was a product of rational training and cultivated habit and could be learned. As to government, he urged a mixed system, combining the principles of monarchy, aristocracy, and democracy.

The Greek Legacy

The rationalism of the Greek tradition was clearly not the whole of Greek culture. The gods of Mount Olympus continued to be a reality for many people, and the ecstatic songs and dances that celebrated Dionysus, the god of wine, were anything but rational and reflective. The death of Socrates at the hands of an Athenian jury showed that philosophy could be a threat as well as an engaging pastime. Nonetheless, Greek rationalism, together with Greek art, literature, and theater, persisted long after the glory days of Athens were over. The Roman Empire facilitated the spread of Greek culture within the Mediterranean basin, and not a few leading Roman figures sent their children to be educated in Athens at the Academy that Plato had founded. An emerging Christian theology was expressed in terms of Greek philosophical concepts, especially those of Plato. Even after the western Roman Empire collapsed, classical Greek texts were preserved in the eastern half, known as Byzantium.

In the West, however, direct access to Greek texts was far more difficult in the chaotic conditions of post-Roman Europe, and for centuries classical scholarship was neglected in favor of Christian writers. Much of that legacy was subsequently rediscovered after the twelfth century C.E. as European scholars gained access to classical Greek texts. From that point on, the Greek legacy has been viewed as a central element of an emerging "Western" civilization. It played a role in formulating an updated Christian theology, in fostering Europe's Scientific Revolution, and in providing a point of departure for much of European philosophy.

Long before this European rediscovery, the Greek legacy had also entered Islamic culture. Systematic translations of Greek works of science and philosophy into Arabic, together with Indian and Persian learning, stimulated Muslim thinkers and scientists, especially in the fields of medicine, astronomy, mathematics, geography, and chemistry. It was in fact largely from Arabic translations of Greek writers that Europeans became reacquainted with the legacy of classical Greece, especially during the twelfth and thirteenth centuries. Despite the many centuries that have passed since the flourishing of classical Greek culture, that tradition has remained, especially in the West, an inspiration for those who celebrate the powers of the human mind to probe the mysteries of the universe and to explore the equally challenging domain of human life.

Snapshot   **Reflections on Human Love from Mediterranean Civilization**

From the Jews: The Song of Solomon

My beloved speaks and says to me: "Arise my love, my fair one and come away; for lo, the winter is past; the rain is over and gone. The flowers appear on the earth; the time of singing has come, and the voice of the turtle dove is heard in our land. The fig tree puts forth its figs; and the vines are in blossom; they give fragrance. Arise my love, my fair one, and come away."

From the Greeks: Fragments from Sappho of Lesbos

If you will come, I shall put out new pillows for you to rest on.
I was so happy. Believe me, I prayed that that night might be doubled for us.
Now I know why Eros, of all the progeny of Earth and Heaven, has been most dearly loved.

From the Romans: Ovid Giving Advice to a Young Man on the Art of Love

Add gifts of mind to bodily advantage. A frail advantage is beauty, that grows less as time draws on and is devoured by its own years. . . . O handsome youth, will soon come hoary hairs; soon will come furrows to make wrinkles in your body. Now make thee a soul that will abide, and add to it thy beauty; only that endures to the ultimate pyre. Nor let it be a slight care to cultivate your mind in the liberal arts, or to learn the two languages well. Ulysses was not comely, but he was eloquent; yet he fired two goddesses of the sea with love.

From the Christians: Saint Paul on Love: 1 Corinthians 13

Love is patient and kind; love is not jealous or boastful; it is not arrogant or rude. Love does not insist on its own way; it is not irritable or resentful; it does not rejoice at wrong, but rejoices in the right. Love bears all things, believes all things, hopes all things, endures all things. Love never ends. . . . So faith, hope and love abide, these three, but the greatest of these is love.

Comparing Jesus and the Buddha

About 500 years after the time of Confucius, the Buddha, Zarathustra, and Socrates, a young Jewish peasant/carpenter in the remote province of Judaea in the Roman Empire began a brief three-year career of teaching and miracle-working before he got in trouble with local authorities and was executed. In one of history's most unlikely stories, the teachings of that obscure man, barely noted in the historical records of the time, became the basis of the world's second great universal religion. This man, Jesus of Nazareth, and the religion of Christianity, which grew out of his life and teaching, had a dramatic impact on world history, similar to and often compared with that of India's Siddhartha Gautama, the Buddha.

■ Comparison

How would you compare the lives and teachings of Jesus and the Buddha? In what different ways did the two religions evolve after the deaths of their founders?

The Lives of the Founders

The family background of the two teachers could hardly have been more different. Gautama was born to royalty and luxury, whereas Jesus was a rural or small-town worker from a distinctly lower-class family. But both became spiritual seekers, mystics in their respective traditions, who claimed to have personally experienced another level of reality. Those powerful religious experiences provided the motivation for their life's work and the personal authenticity that attracted their growing band of followers.

Both were "wisdom teachers," challenging the conventional values of their time, urging the renunciation of wealth, and emphasizing the supreme importance of love or compassion as the basis for a moral life. The Buddha had instructed his followers in the practice of *metta*, or loving-kindness: "Just as a mother would protect her only child at the risk of her own life, even so, let [my followers] cultivate a boundless heart towards all beings."[12] In a similar vein during his famous Sermon on the Mount, Jesus told his followers: "You have heard that it was said 'Love your neighbor and hate your enemy,' but I tell you 'Love your enemies and pray for those who persecute you.'"[13] Both Jesus and the Buddha called for the personal transformation of their followers, through "letting go" of the grasping that causes suffering, in the Buddha's teaching, or "losing one's life in order to save it," in the language of Jesus.[14]

Despite these similarities, there were also some differences in their teachings and their life stories. Jesus inherited from his Jewish tradition an intense devotion to a single personal deity with whom he was on intimate terms, referring to him as *Abba* ("papa" or "daddy"). According to the New Testament, the miracles he performed reflected the power of God available to him as a result of that relationship. The Buddha's original message, by contrast, largely ignored the supernatural, involved no miracles, and taught a path of intense self-effort aimed at ethical living and mindfulness as a means of ending suffering. Furthermore, Jesus' teachings had a sharper social and political edge than did those of the Buddha. Jesus spoke more clearly on behalf of the poor and the oppressed, directly criticized the hypocrisies of the powerful, and deliberately associated with lepers, adulterous women, and tax collectors, all of whom were regarded as "impure." In doing so, Jesus reflected his own lower-class background, the Jewish tradition of social criticism, and the reality of Roman imperial rule over his people, none of which corresponded to the Buddha's experience. Finally, Jesus' public life was very brief, probably less than three years, compared to more than forty years for the Buddha. His teachings had so antagonized both Jewish and Roman authorities that he was crucified as a common criminal. The Buddha's message was apparently less threatening to the politically powerful, and he died a natural death at age eighty.

■ Change
In what ways was Christianity transformed in the five centuries following the death of Jesus?

Establishing New Religions

It seems likely that neither Jesus nor the Buddha had any intention of founding a new religion; rather they sought to reform the traditions from which they had come. Nonetheless, Christianity and Buddhism soon emerged as separate religions, distinct from Judaism and Hinduism, proclaiming their messages to a much wider and more inclusive audience. In the process, both teachers were transformed by their followers into gods. According to many scholars, Jesus never claimed divine status, seeing himself as a teacher or a prophet, whose close relationship to God could be imitated by anyone.[15] The Buddha likewise viewed himself as an enlightened but fully human person, an example of what was possible for anyone who followed the path. But in Mahayana Buddhism, the Buddha became a supernatural being, who could be worshipped and prayed to and was spiritually available to his followers. Jesus too soon became divine in the eyes of his followers, "the Son of God, Very God of Very God," according to one of the creeds of the early Church, while his death and resurrection made possible the forgiveness of sins and the eternal salvation of those who believed.

The transformation of Christianity from a small Jewish sect to a world religion began with Saint Paul (10-65 C.E.), an early convert whose missionary journeys in the eastern Roman Empire led to the founding of small Christian communities that included non-Jews. The Good News of Jesus, Paul argued, was for everyone, and Gentile (non-Jewish) converts need not follow Jewish laws or rituals such as circumcision. In one of his many letters to these new communities, later collected as part of the New Testament, Paul wrote, "There is neither Jew nor Greek . . . neither slave nor free . . . neither male nor female, for you are all one in Christ Jesus."[16] Despite Paul's egalitarian pronouncement, early Christianity, like Buddhism, reflected prevailing patriarchal values, even as they both offered women new opportunities. Although women apparently played leadership roles in the "house churches" of the first century C.E., Paul counseled women to "be subject to your husbands" and declared that "it is shameful for a woman to speak in church."[17]

Nonetheless, the inclusive message of early Christianity was one of the attractions of the new faith as it spread very gradually within the Roman Empire during the several centuries after Jesus' death. The earliest converts were usually lower-stratum people—artisans, traders, and a considerable number of women—mostly from towns and cities, while a scattering of wealthier, more prominent, and better-educated people subsequently joined the ranks of Christians.[18] The spread of the faith often was accompanied by reports of miracles, healings, and the casting out of demons—all of which were impressive to people thoroughly accustomed to seeing the supernatural behind the

Women in the Early Church
This third-century C.E. fresco from a Roman catacomb is called the *Fractio Panis*, "the breaking of the bread" or Holy Communion. Some scholars argue that the figures are those of women, suggesting that women held priestly office in the early Church and were only later excluded from it. (Scala/Art Resource, NY)

events of ordinary life.[19] Christian communities also attracted converts by the way their members cared for one another. In the middle of the third century C.E., the church in Rome supported 154 priests (of whom 52 were exorcists) and some 1,500 widows, orphans, and destitute people.[20] By 300 C.E., perhaps 10 percent of the Roman Empire's population (some 5 million people) identified themselves as Christians.

In the Roman world, the strangest and most offensive feature of the new faith was its exclusive monotheism and its antagonism to all other supernatural powers, particularly the cult of the emperors. Christians' denial of these other gods caused them to be tagged as "atheists" and was one reason behind the empire's intermittent persecution of Christians during the first three centuries of the Common Era. All of that ended with Emperor Constantine's conversion in the early fourth century C.E. and with growing levels of state support for the new religion in the decades that followed.

Roman rulers sought to use an increasingly popular Christianity as glue to hold together a very diverse population in a weakening imperial state. Constantine and his successors thus provided Christians with newfound security and opportunities. The emperor Theodosius (reigned 379–395 C.E.) enforced a ban on all polytheistic ritual sacrifices and ordered their temples closed. Christians by contrast received patronage for their buildings, official approval for their doctrines, suppression of their rivals, prestige from imperial recognition, and, during the late fourth century, the proclamation of Christianity as the official state religion. All of this set in motion a process by which the Roman Empire, and later all of Europe, became overwhelmingly Christian. Beyond the Roman world, the new religion also found a home in various parts of Africa, the Middle East, and Asia (see Map 5.1).

The situation in India was quite different. Even though Ashoka's support gave Buddhism a considerable boost, it was never promoted to the exclusion of other faiths. He sought harmony among India's diverse population through religious tolerance rather than uniformity. The kind of monotheistic intolerance that Christianity exhibited was quite foreign to Indian patterns of religious practice. Although Buddhism subsequently died out in India as it was absorbed into a reviving Hinduism, no renewal of Roman polytheism occurred, and Christianity became an enduring element of European civilization. Nonetheless, Christianity did adopt some elements of religious practice from the Roman world, including perhaps the cult of saints and the dating of the birth of Jesus to the winter solstice. In both cases, however, these new religions spread widely beyond their places of origin. Buddhism provided a network of cultural connections in much of Asia, and Christianity did the same for western Eurasia and parts of Africa (see Map 5.1).

Creating Institutions

As Christianity spread within the Roman Empire and beyond, it developed a hierarchical organization, with patriarchs, bishops, and priests—all men—replacing

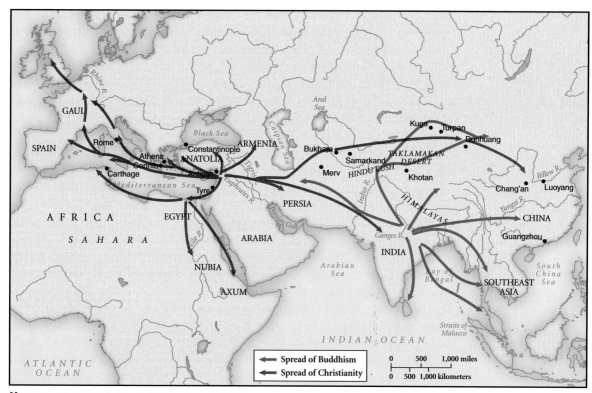

Map 5.1 The Spread of Early Christianity and Buddhism
In the five centuries after the birth of Jesus, Christianity found converts from Spain to northeast Africa, Central Asia, and India. In the Roman Empire, Axum, and Armenia, the new religion enjoyed state support as well. Subsequently Christianity took root solidly in Europe and after 1000 C.E. in Russia as well. Meanwhile, Buddhism was spreading from its South Asian homeland to various parts of Asia, even as it was weakening in India itself.

the house churches of the early years, in which women played a more prominent part. At least in some places, however, women continued to exercise leadership and even priestly roles, prompting Pope Gelasius in 494 to speak out sharply against those who encouraged women "to officiate at the sacred altars, and to take part in all matters imputed to the offices of the male sex, to which they do not belong."[21] In general, though, the exclusion of women from the priesthood established a male-dominated clergy and a patriarchal church, which has lasted into the twenty-first century.

This emerging hierarchical structure of the Church, together with its monotheistic faith, also generated a great concern for unity in matters of doctrine and practice. The bishop of Rome gradually emerged as the dominant leader, or pope, of the Church in the western half of the empire, but this role was not recognized in the east. This division contributed to the later split between Roman Catholic and Eastern Orthodox branches of Christendom, a schism that continues to the present (see Chapter 10). Doctrinal differences also tore at the unity of Christianity and embroiled the Church in frequent controversy about the nature of Jesus (was he human, divine, or both?), his relationship to God (equal or inferior?), and the always-perplexing doctrine of the Trinity (God as Father, Son, and Holy Spirit). A series of church councils—at Nicaea (325 C.E.), Chalcedon (451 C.E.), and Constantinople (553 C.E.), for example—sought to define an "orthodox," or correct, position on these and other issues, declaring those who disagreed as *anathema*, completely expelled from the Church.

Buddhists too clashed over their various interpretations of the Buddha's teachings, and a series of councils failed to prevent the division between Theravada, Mahayana, and other approaches. A considerable proliferation of different sects, practices, teachings, and meditation techniques subsequently emerged within the Buddhist world, but these divisions generally lacked the "clear-cut distinction between 'right' and 'wrong' ideas" that characterized conflicts within the Christian world.[22] Although Buddhist states and warrior classes (such as the famous samurai of Japan) sometimes engaged in warfare, religious differences among Buddhists seldom provided the basis for the kind of bitterness and violence that often accompanied religious conflict within Christendom, such as the Thirty Years' War (1618–1648) between Catholic and Protestant states in Europe. Nor did Buddhists develop the kind of overall church hierarchy that characterized Christianity, although communities of monks and nuns, organized in monasteries, created elaborate rules to govern their internal affairs.

Reflections: Religion and Historians

To put it mildly, religion has always been a sensitive subject, and no less so for historians than for anyone else. For believers or followers of particular traditions, religion partakes of another world—that of the sacred or the divine—which is not accessible to historians or other scholars, who depend on evidence available in this world. This situation has generated various tensions or misunderstandings between historians and religious practitioners.

One of these tensions involves the question of change. Most religions present themselves as timeless, partaking of eternity or at least reflecting ancient practice. In the eyes of historians, however, the religious aspect of human life changes as much as any other. The Hindu tradition changed from a religion of ritual and sacrifice to one of devotion and worship. Buddhism became more conventionally religious, with an emphasis on the supernatural, as it evolved from Theravada to Mahayana forms. A male-dominated hierarchical Christian Church, with its pope, bishops, priests, and state support, was very different from the small house churches, which suffered persecution by imperial authorities in the early Christian centuries. The implication—that religions are at least in part a human phenomenon—has been troublesome to some believers.

Historians, on the other hand, have sometimes been uncomfortable in the face of claims by believers that they have actually experienced a divine reality. Some secular scholars have been inclined to dismiss such claims as unprovable at best. Even the biographical details of the lives of the Buddha and Jesus are difficult to prove by the standards of historians. Certainly, modern historians are in no position to validate or refute the spiritual claims of these teachers, but we need to take them seriously. Although we will never know precisely what happened to the Buddha as he sat in meditation in northern India or what transpired when Jesus spent forty days in the wilderness, clearly those experiences changed the two men and motivated their subsequent actions. Later, Muhammad likewise claimed to have received revelations from God in the caves outside Mecca. Millions of the followers of these religious leaders have also acted on the basis of what they perceived to be an encounter with the divine or other levels of reality. This interior dimension of human experience, though difficult to grasp with any precision, has been a significant mover and shaper of the historical process.

Yet a third problem arises from debates within particular religious traditions about which group most accurately represents the "real" or authentic version of the faith. Historians usually refuse to take sides in such disputes. They simply notice with interest that most human cultural traditions generate conflicting views, some of which become the basis for serious conflict in their societies.

Reconciling personal religious convictions with the perspectives of modern historical scholarship is no easy task. At the very least, all of us can appreciate the immense human effort that has gone into the making of classical religious traditions, and we can acknowledge the enormous significance of these traditions in the unfolding of the human story. They have shaped the meanings that billions of people over thousands of years have attached to the world they inhabit. These religious traditions have justified the vast social inequalities and oppressive states of human civilizations, but they also have enabled human beings to endure those difficulties and on occasion have stimulated reform and rebellion. And they have guided much of humankind in our endless efforts to penetrate the mysteries of the world beyond and of the world within.

Second Thoughts

What's the Significance?

Legalism
Confucianism
Daoism
Ban Zhao
Vedas
Upanishads

Siddhartha Gautama (the
   Buddha)
Theravada/Mahayana
Bhagavad Gita
Zoroastrianism
Judaism

Greek rationalism
Socrates, Plato, Aristotle
Jesus of Nazareth
Saint Paul

To assess your mastery of the material in this chapter, see the **Online Study Guide** at bedfordstmartins.com/strayer.

Big Picture Questions

1. "Religions are fundamentally alike." Does the material in this chapter support or undermine this idea?
2. Is a secular outlook on the world an essentially modern phenomenon, or does it have precedents in the classical era?
3. "Religion is a double-edged sword, both supporting and undermining political authority and social elites." How would you support both sides of this statement?
4. How would you define the appeal of the religious/cultural traditions discussed in this chapter? To what groups were they attractive, and why?

For Web sites and documents related to this chapter, see **Make History** at bedfordstmartins.com/strayer.

Next Steps: For Further Study

Karen Armstrong, *The Great Transformation* (2006). A comparative and historical study of the major classical-era religions by a well-known scholar.

Peter Brown, *The Rise of Western Christendom* (2003). A history of the first 1,000 years of Christianity, cast in a global framework.

Don Johnson and Jean Johnson, *Universal Religions in World History* (2007). A comparative study of the historical development of Buddhism, Christianity, and Islam.

Huston Smith, *An Illustrated World's Religions* (1994). A sympathetic account of major world religions, beautifully illustrated, by a prominent scholar of comparative religion.

Arthur Waley, *Three Ways of Thought in Ancient China* (1983). A classic work, first published more than half a century ago, about the major philosophies of old China.

Jonathan S. Walters, *Finding Buddhists in Global History* (1998). A brief account that situates Buddhism in a world history framework.

"Religions of the World," http://www.mnsu.edu/emuseum/cultural/religion. A succinct and attractively illustrated introduction to six major world religious traditions.

Eurasian Social Hierarchies

500 B.C.E–500 C.E.

She is a twenty-six-year-old Hindu woman from Goa, on India's west coast. She speaks the Marathi language, has a high school education, is not currently employed, neither smokes nor drinks, but occasionally eats meat. Like millions of other Indians, she is seeking a partner by placing a personal ad in the newspaper or on the Internet. In addition to the personal and professional data found everywhere in such ads, in India they almost always contain another piece of information— the caste of the seeker. The young woman from Goa lists herself as a member of a "scheduled caste" known as Chambar, formerly called "untouchables," the lowest category in the hierarchy of India's ranked society. That personal ads in twenty-first-century India still refer to caste points out how deeply entrenched and enduring ancient patterns of social life can be.

THE MOST RECENT 250 YEARS OF WORLD HISTORY have called into question social structures long assumed to be natural and permanent. The French, Russian, and Chinese revolutions challenged and destroyed ancient monarchies and class hierarchies; the abolitionist movement of the nineteenth century attacked slavery, largely unquestioned for millennia; the women's movement confronted long and deeply held patriarchal assumptions about the proper relationship between women and men; and Mahatma Gandhi, during India's struggle for independence in the twentieth century, sought to raise the status of "untouchables," referring to them as *Harijan*, or "children of God." Nevertheless, caste, class, patriarchy, and even slavery have certainly not vanished from human society, even now. During the era of "second wave" civilizations

---

Indian Society: A fresco from the time of India's Gupta dynasty (320–600 C.E.) shows townspeople in a royal procession. (© Benoy K. Behl)

in Eurasia, these patterns of inequality found expressions and generated social tensions that remain recognizable to the contemporary descendants of these classical societies.

Millions of individual people, inhabiting the classical civilizations of Eurasia, lived within a political framework of states or empires. They occupied as well a world of ideas, religions, and values that derived both from local folkways and from the teaching of the great religious or cultural traditions of their civilizations. They also lived within established societies that defined relationships between rich and poor, powerful and powerless, slaves and free people, and men and women. Those social relationships shaped the daily lives and the life chances of everyone; they provided the foundation for political authority as well as challenges to it; they were both justified and challenged by the religious and cultural traditions of these civilizations.

Like the First Civilizations, those of the classical era were sharply divided along class lines, and they too were patriarchal, with women clearly subordinated to men in most domains of life. In constructing their societies, however, the classical civilizations differed substantially from one another. Chinese, Indian, and Mediterranean civilizations provide numerous illustrations of the many and varied ways in which peoples of the classical era organized their social life. The assumptions, tensions, and conflicts accompanying these social patterns provided much of the distinctive character and texture that distinguished these diverse civilizations from one another.

Society and the State in Classical China

Chinese society was unique in the ancient world in the extent to which it was shaped by the actions of the state. Nowhere was this more apparent than in the political power and immense social prestige of Chinese state officials. For more than 2,000 years, these officials, bureaucrats acting in the name of the emperor both in the capital and in the provinces, represented the cultural and social elite of Chinese civilization. This class had its origins in the efforts of early Chinese rulers to find administrators loyal to the central state rather than to their own families or regions. Philosophers such as Confucius had long advocated selecting such officials on the basis of merit and personal morality rather than birth or wealth. As the Han dynasty established its authority in China around 200 B.C.E., its rulers required each province to send men of promise to the capital, where they were examined and chosen for official positions on the basis of their performance.

An Elite of Officials

■ Description
How would you describe the social hierarchy of classical China?

Over time, this system of selecting administrators evolved into the world's first professional civil service. In 124 B.C.E., Emperor Wu Di established an imperial academy where potential officials were trained as scholars and immersed in Chinese classical texts dealing with history, literature, art, and mathematics, with an emphasis on Confucian teachings. By the end of the Han dynasty, it enrolled some 30,000 students, who were by then subjected to a series of written examinations to select officials of various grades. Private schools in the provinces funneled still more aspiring candidates into this examination system, which persisted until the early twentieth century. In theory open to all men, this system in practice favored those whose families were wealthy enough to provide the years of education required to pass even the lower-level exams. Proximity to the capital and family connections to the imperial court also helped in gaining a position in this highest of Chinese elites. Nonetheless, village communities or a local landowner might sponsor the education of a bright young man from a commoner family, enabling him to enter the charmed circle of officialdom. One rags-to-riches story told of a pig farmer who became an adviser to the emperor himself. Thus the examination system provided a modest measure of social mobility in an otherwise quite hierarchical society.

In later dynasties, that system grew to be even more elaborate and became an enduring and distinguishing feature of Chinese civilization. During the Tang dynasty, the famous poet and official Po Chu-I (772–846 C.E.) wrote a poem entitled "After Passing the Examination," which shows something of the fame and fortune that awaited an accomplished student as well as the continuing loyalty to family and home that ideally marked those who succeeded.

> For ten years I never left my books,
> I went up . . . and won unmerited praise.
> My high place I do not much prize;
> The joy of my parents will first make me proud.
> Fellow students, six or seven men,
> See me off as I leave the City gate.
> My covered coach is ready to drive away;
> Flutes and strings blend their parting tune.
> Hopes achieved dull the pains of parting;
> Fumes of wine shorten the long road . . .
> Shod with wings is the horse of him who rides
> On a Spring day the road that leads to home.[1]

Those who made it into the bureaucracy entered a realm of high privilege and enormous prestige. Senior officials moved about in carriages and were bedecked with robes, ribbons, seals, and headdresses appropriate to their rank. Even lower officials who served in the provinces rather than the capital were distinguished by their polished speech, their cultural sophistication, and their urban manners as well as their political authority. Proud of their learning, they were the bearers, and often the makers, of Chinese culture. "Officials are the leaders of the populace," stated an imperial edict of 144 B.C.E., "and it is right and proper that the carriages they ride in and the robes that they wear should correspond to the degrees of their dignity."[2]

The Landlord Class

Most officials came from wealthy families, and in China wealth meant land. When the Qin dynasty unified China by 210 B.C.E., most land was held by small-scale peasant farmers. But by the first century B.C.E., the pressures of population growth, taxation, and indebtedness had generated a class of large landowners as impoverished peasants found it necessary to sell their lands to more prosperous neighbors. This accumulation of land in large estates was a persistent theme in Chinese history, and one that was persistently, though not very successfully, opposed by state authorities. Landlords of large estates often were able to avoid paying taxes, thus decreasing state revenues and increasing the tax burden for the remaining peasants. In some cases, they could also mount their own military forces to challenge the authority of the emperor.

One of the most dramatic state efforts to counteract the growing power of large landowners is associated with Wang Mang, a high court official of the Han dynasty who usurped the emperor's throne in 8 C.E. and immediately launched a series of startling reforms. A firm believer in Confucian good government, Wang Mang saw his reforms as re-creating a golden age of long ago in which small-scale peasant farmers represented the backbone of Chinese society. Accordingly, he ordered the great private estates to be nationalized and divided up among the landless. Government loans to peasant families, limits on the amount of land a family might own, and an end to private slavery were all part of his reform program, but these measures proved impossible to enforce. Opposition from wealthy landowners, nomadic invasions, poor harvests, floods, and famines led to the collapse of Wang Mang's reforms and his assassination in 23 C.E.

Large landowning families, therefore, remained a central feature of Chinese society, although the fate of individual families rose and fell as the wheel of fortune raised them to great prominence or plunged them into poverty and disgrace. As a class, they benefited both from the wealth that their estates generated and from the power and prestige that accompanied membership in the official elite. The term "scholar-gentry" reflected their twin sources of privilege. With homes in both urban and rural areas, members of the scholar-gentry class lived luxuriously. Multistoried houses, the finest of silk clothing, gleaming carriages, private orchestras, high-stakes gambling—all of this was part of the life of China's landlord class.

Peasants

■ Change
What class conflicts disrupted Chinese society?

Throughout the history of China's civilization, the vast majority of its population has been peasants, living in households of four to five people, representing two or three generations. Some owned enough land to support their families and perhaps even sell something on the local market. Many others could barely survive. Nature, the state, and landlords combined to make the life of most peasants extremely vulnerable. Famines, floods, droughts, hail, and pests could wreak havoc without warning. State authorities required the payment of taxes, demanded about a month's labor every year on various public projects, and conscripted young men for two years of military service. During the Han dynasty, growing numbers of impoverished and desperate peasants had to sell out to large land-lords and work as tenants or sharecrop-pers on their estates, where rents could run as high as one-half to two-thirds of the crop. Other peasants fled, taking to a life of begging or joining a gang of bandits in a remote area.

An eighth-century C.E. Chinese poem by Li Shen reflects poignantly on the enduring hardships of peasant life.[3]

Chinese Peasants
For many centuries, the normal activities of Chinese peasant farmers included plowing, planting, and threshing grain, as shown in this painting from China's Song dynasty (960–1279 C.E.). (*Farmers at Work*, Northern Song Dynasty, 960–1279 [wall painting]/ Mogao Caves, Dunhuang/The Bridgeman Art Library)

The cob of corn in springtime sown
In autumn yields a hundredfold.
No fields are seen that fallow lie:
And yet of hunger peasants die.

As at noontide they hoe their crops,
Sweat on the grain to earth down drops.
How many tears, how many a groan,
Each morsel on thy dish did mould!

Such conditions generated periodic peasant rebellions, which punctuated Chinese history over the past 2,000 years. Toward the end of the second century C.E., wandering bands of peasants began to join together as floods along the Yellow River and resulting epidemics compounded the misery of land-lessness and poverty. What emerged was a massive peasant uprising known as the Yellow Turban Rebellion because of the yellow scarves the peasants wore around their heads. That movement, which swelled to about 360,000 armed followers by 184 C.E., found leaders, organization, and a unifying ideology in a popular form of Daoism. Featuring super-natural healings, collective trances, and public confessions of sin, the Yellow Turban movement looked forward to the "Great Peace"—a golden age of complete equality, social harmony, and common owner-ship of property. Although the rebellion was suppressed by the military forces of the Han dynasty, the Yellow Turban and other peasant upheavals devastated the economy, weakened the state, and contributed to the overthrow of the dynasty a few decades later. Repeatedly in Chinese history, such peasant movements, often expressed in religious terms,

Yellow Turban Rebellion

registered the sharp class antagonisms of Chinese society and led to the collapse of more than one ruling dynasty.

Merchants

Peasants were oppressed in China and certainly exploited, but they were also honored and celebrated in the official ideology of the state. In the eyes of the scholar-gentry, peasants were the solid productive backbone of the country, and their hard work and endurance in the face of difficulties were worthy of praise. Merchants, however, did not enjoy such a favorable reputation in the eyes of China's cultural elite. They were widely viewed as unproductive, making a shameful profit from selling the work of others. Stereotyped as greedy, luxury-loving, and materialistic, merchants stood in contrast to the alleged frugality, altruism, and cultured tastes of the scholar-gentry. They were also seen as a social threat, as their ill-gained wealth impoverished others, deprived the state of needed revenues, and fostered resentments.

Such views lay behind periodic efforts by state authorities to rein in merchant activity and to keep them under control. Early in the Han dynasty, merchants were forbidden to wear silk clothing, ride horses, or carry arms. Nor were they permitted to sit for civil service examinations or hold public office. State monopolies on profitable industries such as salt, iron, and alcohol served to limit merchant opportunities. Later dynasties sometimes forced merchants to loan large sums of money to the state. Despite this active discrimination, merchants frequently became quite wealthy. Some tried to achieve a more respectable elite status by purchasing landed estates or educating their sons for the civil service examinations. Many had back-door relationships with state officials and landlords who found them useful and were not averse to profiting from business connections with merchants, despite their unsavory reputation.

Class and Caste in India

India's social organization shared certain broad features with that of China. In both civilizations, birth determined social status for most people; little social mobility was available for the vast majority; sharp distinctions and great inequalities characterized social life; and religious or cultural traditions defined these inequalities as natural, eternal, and ordained by the gods. Despite these similarities, the organization, flavor, and texture of ancient Indian society were distinctive compared to almost all other classical civilizations. These unique aspects of Indian society have long been embodied in what we now call the *caste system*, a term that comes from the Portuguese word *casta*, which means "race" or "purity of blood." That social organization emerged over thousands of years and in some respects has endured into modern times.

■ **Description**
What set of ideas underlies India's caste-based society?

Caste as Varna

The origins of the caste system are at best hazy. An earlier theory—that caste evolved from a racially defined encounter between light-skinned Aryan invaders and the darker-hued native peoples—has been challenged in recent years, but no clear alternative has emerged. Perhaps the best we can say at this point is that the distinctive social system of classical India grew out of the interaction of many culturally different peoples on the South Asian peninsula together with the development of economic and social differences among these peoples as the inequalities of "civilization" spread in the Ganges River valley and beyond. Notions of race, however, seem less central to the growth of the caste system than those of economic specialization and of culture.

By the beginning of the classical era, around 500 B.C.E., the idea that society was forever divided into four great classes known as *varna* was deeply embedded in Indian thinking. Everyone was born into and remained within one of these classes for life. At the top of this hierarchical system were the Brahmins, priests whose rituals and sacrifices alone could ensure the proper functioning of the world. They were followed by the Ksatriya class, warriors and rulers charged with protecting and governing society. Next was the Vaisya class, originally commoners who cultivated the land. These three classes came to be regarded as pure Aryans and were called the "twice-born," for they experienced not only a physical birth but also formal initiation into their respective varnas and status as people of Aryan descent. Far below these twice-born in the hierarchy of varna groups were the Sudras, native peoples incorporated into the margins of Aryan society in very subordinate positions. Regarded as servants of their social betters, they were not allowed to hear or repeat the Vedas or to take part in Aryan rituals. So little were they valued that a Brahmin who killed a Sudra was penalized as if he had killed a cat or a dog.

According to varna theory, these four classes were formed from the body of the god Purusha and were therefore eternal and changeless. Although these divisions are widely recognized in India even today, historians have noted considerable social flux in ancient Indian history. Members of the Brahmin and Ksatriya groups, for example, were frequently in conflict over which ranked highest in the varna hierarchy, and only slowly did the Brahmins emerge clearly in the top position. Both of them, although theoretically purely Aryan, absorbed various tribal peoples as classical Indian civilization expanded. Tribal medicine men or sorcerers found a place as Brahmins, while warrior groups entered the Ksatriya varna. The Vaisya varna, originally defined as cultivators, evolved into a business class with a prominent place for

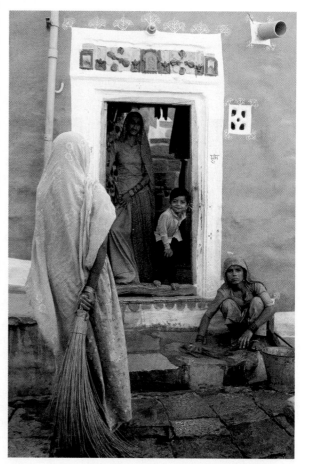

India's Untouchables
Although the Indian constitution of 1950 legally abolished "untouchability," active discrimination persists against this lowest group in the caste hierarchy, now known as Dalits, or the oppressed. Sweeping is just one of many Dalit occupations; here several sweepers perform their tasks in front of an upper-caste home. (Lindsay Hebberd/Corbis)

merchants, while the Sudra varna became the domain of peasant farmers. Finally a whole new category, ranking lower even than the Sudras, emerged in the so-called untouchables, people who did the work considered most unclean and polluting, such as cremating corpses, dealing with the skins of dead animals, and serving as executioners.

Snapshot   **Social Life and Duty in Classical India**

Much personal behavior in classical India, at least ideally, was regulated according to caste. Each caste was associated with a particular color, with a part of the body of the god Purusha, and with a set of duties.

Caste (Varna)	Color/Symbolism	Part of Purusha	Duties
Brahmin	white/spirituality	head	priests, teachers
Ksatriya	red/courage	shoulders	warriors, rulers
Vaisya	yellow/wealth	thighs	farmers, merchants, artisans
Sudra	black/ignorance	feet	labor
Untouchables (outside of the varna system; thus no color and not associated with Purusha)	—	—	polluted labor

Beyond caste, behavior was ideally defined in terms of four stages of life, at least for the first three varna groups. Each new stage was marked by a *samskara*, a ritual initiating the person into this new phase of life.

Stage of Life	Duties
Student	Boys live with a teacher (guru); learn Sanskrit, rituals, Vedas; practice obedience, respect, celibacy, nonviolence.
Householder	Marriage and family; men practice caste-based career/occupation; women serve as wives and mothers, perform household rituals and sacrifices, actively support children and elders.
Retirement	Both husband and wife withdraw to the forests following birth of grandchildren; diminished household duties; greater focus on spiritual practice; sex permitted once a month.
Wandering ascetic	Only for men (women return to household); total rejection of ordinary existence; life as wandering hermit without shelter or possessions; caste becomes irrelevant; focus on achieving *moksha* and avoiding future rebirth.

Caste as Jati

As the varna system took shape in India, another set of social distinctions also arose, deriving largely from specific occupations. In India as elsewhere, urban-based civilization gave rise to specialized occupations, many organized in guilds that regulated their own affairs in a particular region. Over time, these occupationally based groups, known as *jatis*, blended with the varna system to create classical India's unique caste-based society.

The many thousands of jatis became the primary cell of India's social life beyond the family or household, but each of them was associated with one of the great classes (varnas). Thus Brahmins were divided into many separate jatis, or subcastes, as were each of the other varnas as well as the untouchables. In a particular region or village, each jati was ranked in a hierarchy known to all, from the highest of the Brahmins to the lowest of the untouchables. Marriage and eating together were permitted only within an individual's own jati. Each jati was associated with a particular set of duties, rules, and obligations, which defined its members' unique and separate place in the larger society. Brahmins, for example, were forbidden to eat meat, while Ksatriyas were permitted to do so. Upper-caste women, of course, covered their breasts, while some lower-caste women were forbidden to do so as a sign of their lower ranking. "It is better to do one's own duty badly than another's well"—this frequently quoted saying summed up the underlying idea of Indian society.[4]

With its many separate, distinct, and hierarchically ranked social groups, Indian society was quite different from that of China or the Greco-Roman world. It was also unique in the set of ideas that explained and justified that social system. Foremost among them was the notion of ritual purity and pollution applied to caste groups. Brahmins or other high-caste people who came in contact with members of lower castes, especially those who cleaned latrines, handled corpses, or butchered and skinned dead animals, were in great danger of being polluted, or made ritually unclean. Thus untouchables were forbidden to use the same wells or to enter the temples designated for higher-caste people. Sometimes they were required to wear a wooden clapper to warn others of their approach. A great body of Indian religious writing defined various forms of impurity and the ritual means of purification.

A further support for this idea of inherent inequality and permanent difference derived from emerging Hindu notions of *karma, dharma*, and rebirth. Being born into a particular caste was generally regarded as reflecting the good or bad deeds (karma) of a previous life. Thus an individual's own prior actions were responsible for his or her current status. Any hope for rebirth in a higher caste rested on the faithful and selfless performance of one's present caste duties (dharma) in this life. Doing so contributed to spiritual progress by subduing the relentless demands of the ego. Such teachings, like that of permanent impurity, provided powerful ideological support for the inequalities of Indian society. So too did the threat of social

■ **Comparison**

What is the difference between varna and jati as expressions of classical India's caste system?

ostracism, because each jati had the authority to expel members who violated its rules. No greater catastrophe could befall a person than this, for it meant the end of any recognized social life and the loss of all social support.

As caste restrictions tightened, it became increasingly difficult—virtually impossible—for individuals to raise their social status during their lifetimes, but another kind of upward mobility enabled entire jatis, over several generations, to raise their standing in the local hierarchy of caste groups. By acquiring land or wealth, by adopting the behaviors of higher-caste groups, by finding some previously overlooked "ancestor" of a higher caste, a particular jati might slowly be redefined in a higher category. Thus India's caste system was in practice rather more fluid and changing than the theory of caste might suggest.

■ Comparison
How did India's caste system differ from China's class system?

India's social system thus differed from that of China in several ways. It gave priority to religious status and ritual purity (the Brahmins), whereas China elevated political officials to the highest of elite positions. The caste system divided Indian society into vast numbers of distinct social groups; China had fewer, but broader, categories of society—scholar-gentry, landlords, peasants, merchants. Finally, India's caste society defined these social groups far more rigidly and with even less opportunity for social mobility than in China.

The Functions of Caste

A caste-based social structure shaped India's classical civilization in various ways. Because caste (jati) was a very local phenomenon, rooted in particular regions or villages, it focused the loyalties of most people on a quite restricted territory and weakened the appeal or authority of larger all-Indian states. This localization is one reason that India, unlike China, seldom experienced an empire that encompassed the entire subcontinent (see Chapter 4). Caste, together with the shared culture of Hinduism, provided a substitute for the state as an integrative mechanism for Indian civilization. It offered a distinct and socially recognized place for almost everyone. In looking after widows, orphans, and the destitute, jatis provided a modest measure of social security and support. Even the lowest-ranking jatis had the right to certain payments from the social superiors whom they served.

Furthermore, caste represented a means of accommodating the many migrating or invading peoples who entered the subcontinent. The cellular, or honeycomb, structure of caste society allowed various peoples, cultures, and traditions to find a place within a larger Indian civilization while retaining something of their unique identity. The process of assimilation was quite different in China, however; incorporation into Chinese civilization meant becoming Chinese ethnically, linguistically, and culturally. Finally, India's caste system facilitated the exploitation of the poor by the wealthy and powerful. The multitude of separate groups into which it divided the impoverished and oppressed majority of the population made class consciousness and organized resistance across caste lines much more difficult to achieve.

Slavery in the Classical Era:
The Case of the Roman Empire

Beyond the inequalities of class and caste lay those of slavery, a social institution with deep roots in human history. One scholar has suggested that the early domestication of animals provided the model for enslaving people.[5] Certainly slave owners have everywhere compared their slaves to tamed animals. Aristotle, for example, observed that the ox is "the poor man's slave." War, patriarchy, and the notion of private property, all of which accompanied the First Civilizations, also contributed to the growth of slavery. Large-scale warfare generated numerous prisoners, and everywhere in the ancient world capture in war meant the possibility of enslavement. Early records suggest that women captives were the first slaves, usually raped and then enslaved as concubines, whereas male captives were killed. Patriarchal societies, in which men sharply controlled and perhaps even "owned" women, may have suggested the possibility of using other people, men as well as women, as slaves. The class inequalities of early civilizations, which were based on great differences in privately owned property, also made it possible to imagine people owning other people.

Slavery and Civilization

Whatever its precise origins, slavery generally meant ownership by a master, the possibility of being sold, working without pay, and the status of an "outsider" at the bottom of the social hierarchy. For most, it was a kind of "social death,"[6] for slaves usually lacked any rights or independent personal identity recognized by the larger society. By the time Hammurabi's law code casually referred to Mesopotamian slavery (around 1750 B.C.E.), it was already a long-established tradition in the region and in all of the First Civilizations. Likewise, virtually all subsequent civilizations — in the Americas, Africa, and Eurasia — practiced some form of slavery.

■ **Comparison**
How did the inequalities of slavery differ from those of caste?

Slave systems throughout history have varied considerably. In some times and places, such as classical Greece and Rome, a fair number of slaves might be emancipated in their own lifetimes, through the generosity or religious convictions of their owners, or to avoid caring for them in old age, or by allowing slaves to purchase their freedom with their own funds. In some societies, the children of slaves inherited the status of their parents, while in others, such as the Aztec Empire, they were considered free people. Slaves likewise varied considerably in the labor they were required to do, with some working for the state in high positions, others performing domestic duties in their owner's household, and still others toiling in fields or mines in large work gangs.

The classical civilizations of Eurasia differed considerably in the prominence and extent of slavery in their societies. In China, it was a minor element, amounting to perhaps 1 percent of the population. Convicted criminals and their families, confiscated by the government and sometimes sold to wealthy private individuals, were among the earliest slaves in Han dynasty China. In desperate circumstances, impoverished or indebted peasants might sell their children into slavery. In southern China, teenage boys of poor families could be purchased by the wealthy, for whom they served as status symbols. Chinese slavery, however, was never very widespread and did not become a major source of labor for agriculture or manufacturing.

In India as well, people could fall into slavery as criminals, debtors, or prisoners of war and served their masters largely in domestic settings, but religious writings and secular law offered, at least in theory, some protection for slaves. Owners were required to provide adequately for their slaves and were forbidden to abandon them in old age. According to one ancient text, "a man may go short himself or stint his

$Snapshot$ **Comparing Greco-Roman and American Slavery**

	Greco-Roman Slavery (500 B.C.E.–500 C.E.)	**Slavery in the Americas (1500–1888)**
Source of slaves	Majority were prisoners from Roman wars of conquest; victims of pirate kidnapping; obtained through networks of long-distance trade; result of natural reproduction; abandoned children	Derived almost entirely from transatlantic slave trade; many were prisoners of African wars, debtors, or criminals in African societies
Race	Not a major factor	Came to be associated with Africa and "blackness"
Manumission (granting legal freedom to slaves)	Quite common; freed slaves received citizenship in Roman Empire but not in Greece	Much less common, especially in North America; freed slaves were long feared and discriminated against in North America, but less so in Latin America
Roles/Work	No distinction between slave and wage labor; slaves worked at wide variety of jobs, from poets, physicians, scholars, and teachers to field hands and mine laborers	Majority worked as agricultural laborers on plantations producing for export; few held elite occupations
Fate of slavery	Gradual transformation from slavery to serfdom as Roman Empire collapsed; no abolitionist movements; Christianity provided general support for slavery, though some encouragement for manumission	Ended in nineteenth century as a result of slave rebellions, industrialization, and abolitionist movements, some based in Christian teaching; replaced by sharecropping or indentured labor

wife and children, but never his slave who does his dirty work for him."[7] Slaves in India could inherit and own property and earn money in their spare time. A master who raped a slave woman was required to set her free and pay compensation. The law encouraged owners to free their slaves and allowed slaves to buy their freedom. All of this suggests that Indian slavery was more restrained than that of other ancient civilizations. Nor did Indian civilization depend economically on slavery, for most work was performed by lower-caste, though free, people.

The Making of a Slave Society: The Case of Rome

In sharp contrast to other classical civilizations, slavery played an immense role in the Mediterranean, or Western, world. Although slavery was practiced in Chinese, Indian, and Persian civilizations, the Greco-Roman world can be described as a slave society. By a conservative estimate, classical Athens alone was home to perhaps 60,000 slaves, or about one-third of the total population. In Athens, ironically, the growth of democracy and status as a free person were defined and accompanied by the simultaneous growth of slavery on a mass scale. The greatest of the Greek philosophers, Aristotle, developed the notion that some people were "slaves by nature" and should be enslaved for their own good and for that of the larger society.

■ Comparison

How did Greco-Roman slavery differ from that of other classical civilizations?

"The ancient Greek attitude toward slavery was simple," writes one modern scholar. "It was a terrible thing to become a slave, but a good thing to own a slave."[8] Even poor households usually had at least one or two female slaves, providing domestic work and sexual services for their owners. Although substantial numbers of Greek slaves were granted freedom by their owners, they usually did not become citizens or gain political rights. Nor could they own land or marry citizens, and particularly in Athens they had to pay a special tax. Their status remained "halfway between slavery and freedom."[9]

Practiced on an even larger scale, slavery was a defining element of Roman society. By the time of Christ, the Italian heartland of the Roman Empire had some 2 to 3 million slaves, representing 33 to 40 percent of the population.[10] Not until the modern slave societies of the Caribbean, Brazil, and the southern United States was slavery practiced again on such an enormous scale. Wealthy Romans could own many hundreds or even thousands of slaves. One woman in the fifth century C.E. freed 8,000 slaves when she withdrew into a life of Christian monastic practice.

Roman Slavery
This Roman mosaic from the third century C.E. shows the slave Myro serving a drink to his master, Fructus. (Bardo Museum Tunis/Gianni Dagli Orti/The Art Archive)

Even people of modest means frequently owned two or three slaves. In doing so, they confirmed their own position as free people, demonstrated their social status, and expressed their ability to exercise power. Slaves and former slaves also might be slave owners. One freedman during the reign of Caesar Augustus owned 4,116 slaves at the time of his death.

The vast majority of Roman slaves had been prisoners captured in the many wars that accompanied the creation of the empire. In 146 B.C.E., following the destruction of the North African city of Carthage, some 55,000 people were enslaved en masse. From all over the Mediterranean basin, such people were funneled into the major slave-owning regions of Italy and Sicily. Pirates also furnished slaves, kidnapping tens of thousands of people and selling them to Roman slave traders on the island of Delos. Roman merchants purchased still other slaves through networks of long-distance commerce extending to the Black Sea, the East African coast, and northwestern Europe. The supply of slaves also occurred through natural reproduction, as the children of slave mothers were regarded as slaves themselves. Such "home-born" slaves had a certain prestige and were thought to be less troublesome than those who had known freedom earlier in their lives. Finally, abandoned or exposed children could legally become the slave of anyone who rescued them.

Unlike New World slavery of later times, Roman slavery was not identified with a particular racial or ethnic group. Egyptians, Syrians, Jews, Greeks, Gauls, North Africans, and many other people found themselves alike enslaved. From within the empire and its adjacent regions, an enormous diversity of people were bought and sold at Roman slave markets.

Like slave owners everywhere, Romans regarded their slaves as "barbarians"— lazy, unreliable, immoral, prone to thieving—and came to think of certain peoples, such as Asiatic Greeks, Syrians, and Jews, as slaves by nature. Nor was there any serious criticism of slavery in principle, although on occasion owners were urged to treat their slaves in a more benevolent way. Even the triumph of Christianity within the Roman Empire did little to undermine slavery, for Christian teaching held that slaves should be "submissive to [their] masters with all fear, not only to the good and gentle, but also to the harsh."[11] In fact, Saint Paul used the metaphor of slavery to describe the relationship of believers to God, styling them as "slaves of Christ," while Saint Augustine described slavery as God's punishment for sin. Thus slavery was deeply embedded in the religious thinking and social outlook of elite Romans.

Similarly, slavery was entrenched throughout the Roman economy. No occupation was off-limits to slaves except military service, and no distinction existed between jobs for slaves and those for free people. Frequently they labored side by side. In rural areas, slaves provided much of the labor force on the huge estates, or *latifundia*, which produced grain, olive oil, and wine, mostly for export, much like the later plantations in the Americas. There they often worked chained together. In the cities, slaves worked in their owners' households, but also as skilled artisans, teachers, doctors, business agents, entertainers, and actors. In the empire's many mines and quarries, slaves and criminals labored under brutal conditions. Slaves in the service of the emperor provided manpower for the state bureaucracy, maintained temples and shrines, and kept Rome's water supply system functioning. Trained in special schools, they also served as gladiators in the violent spectacles of Roman public life. Thus slaves were represented among the highest and most prestigious occupations and in the lowest and most degraded.

Slave owners in the Roman Empire were supposed to provide the necessities of life to their slaves. When this occurred, slaves may have had a more secure life than was available to impoverished free people, who had to fend for themselves, but the price of this security was absolute subjection to the will of the master. Beatings, sexual abuse, and sale to another owner were constant possibilities. Lacking all rights in the law, slaves could not legally marry, although many contracted unofficial unions. Slaves often accumulated money or possessions, but such property legally belonged to their masters and could be seized at any time. If a slave murdered his master, Roman law demanded the lives of all of the victim's slaves. When one Roman official was killed by a slave in 61 C.E., every one of his 400 slaves was condemned to death. For an individual slave, the quality of life depended almost entirely on the character of the master. Brutal owners made it a living hell. Benevolent owners made life tolerable and might even grant favored slaves their freedom or permit them to buy that freedom. As in Greece, manumission of slaves was a widespread practice, and in the Roman Empire, unlike Greece, freedom was accompanied by citizenship.

Resistance and Rebellion

Roman slaves, like their counterparts in other societies, responded to enslavement in many ways. Most, no doubt, did what they had to simply to survive, but there are recorded cases of Roman prisoners of war who chose to commit mass suicide rather than face the horrors of slavery. Others, once enslaved, resorted to the "weapons of the weak"—small-scale theft, sabotage, pretending illness, working poorly, and placing curses on their masters. Fleeing to the anonymous crowds of the city or to remote rural areas prompted owners to post notices in public places, asking for information about their runaways. Catching runaway slaves became an organized private business. Occasional murders of slave owners made masters conscious of the dangers they faced. "Every slave we own is an enemy we harbor" ran one Roman saying.[12]

On several notable occasions, the slaves themselves rose in rebellion. The most famous uprising occurred in 73 B.C.E. when a slave gladiator named Spartacus led seventy other slaves from a school for gladiators in a desperate bid for freedom. The surprising initial success of their revolt attracted a growing following of rebellious slaves, numbering perhaps 120,000 at the height of the uprising. For two years, they set Italy ablaze. In a dramatic reversal of roles, they crucified some captured slave owners and set others to fighting one another in the style of gladiators. Following a series of remarkable military victories, the movement split and eventually succumbed

The Rebellion of Spartacus

to the vastly superior numbers of the Roman legions. A terrible vengeance followed as some 6,000 rebel slaves were nailed to crosses along the Appian Way from Rome to Capua, where the revolt had begun.

Nothing on the scale of the Spartacus rebellion occurred again in the Western world of slavery until the Haitian Revolution of the 1790s. But Haitian rebels sought the creation of a new society free of slavery altogether. None of the Roman slave rebellions, including that of Spartacus, had any such overall plan or goal. They simply wanted to escape Roman slavery themselves. Although rebellions created a perpetual fear in the minds of slave owners, the slave system itself was hardly affected.

Comparing Patriarchies of the Classical Era

No division of human society has had greater significance for the lives of individuals than that between male and female. Every human community has elaborated that basic biological difference into a gender system that sought to define masculinity and femininity and to determine the appropriate roles and positions of men and women in the larger society. At least since the emergence of the First Civilizations, those gender systems have been everywhere patriarchal, featuring the dominance of men over women in the family and in society generally. More widespread than slavery, these inequalities of gender, like those of class or caste, shaped the character of the classical civilizations.

In all of them, men were regarded as superior to women, and sons were generally preferred over daughters. Men had legal and property rights unknown to most women. Public life in general was a male domain, while women's roles—both productive and reproductive—took place mostly in domestic settings. Frequently men could marry more than one woman and claimed the right to regulate the social and sexual lives of the wives, daughters, and sisters in their families. Widely seen as weak and feared as potentially disruptive, women required the protection and control of men.

These common elements of patriarchy have been so widespread and pervasive that historians have been slow to recognize that gender systems evolved, changing over time. New agricultural technologies, the rise or decline of powerful states, the incorporation of world religions, interaction with culturally different peoples—all of these developments and more generated significant change in gender systems. Nor has patriarchy been everywhere the same. Restrictions on women were far sharper in classical civilizations than in those pastoral or agricultural societies that lay beyond the reach of urban centers and powerful empires. The degree and expression of patriarchy also varied from one civilization to another, as the earlier discussion of Mesopotamia and Egypt illustrated (see Chapter 3).

Within particular civilizations, patriarchy interacted with class to generate usually a more restricted life for upper-class women, who were largely limited to the home and the management of servants. In contrast, lower-class women often had a somewhat freer but more burdensome life, for economic necessity required them to work in the fields, to shop in the streets, or to serve in the homes of their social superiors. China provides a fascinating example of how patriarchy changed over time, while the contrasting patriarchies of Athens and Sparta illustrate clear variations even within the limited world of Greek civilization.

A Changing Patriarchy: The Case of China

As Chinese civilization took shape during the Han dynasty, elite thinking about gender issues became more explicitly patriarchal, more clearly defined, and linked to an emerging Confucian ideology. Long-established patterns of thinking in terms of pairs of opposites were now described in gendered and unequal

Chinese Women Musicians
This tenth-century rendering by the painter Gu Hongzhong shows these upper-class women serving as musicians for a high official of a Tang dynasty emperor. It was titled *The Night Revels of Han Xizai*. The painter was apparently sent by the emperor to spy on the suspicious behavior of the minister, who in various tellings was suspected of either rebellion or undignified activity. (Werner Forman/Art Resource, NY)

terms. The superior principle of *yang* was viewed as masculine and related to heaven, rulers, strength, rationality, and light, whereas *yin*, the lower feminine principle, was associated with the earth, subjects, weakness, emotion, and darkness. Thus female inferiority was permanent and embedded in the workings of the universe.

■ **Change**
In what ways did the expression of Chinese patriarchy change over time, and why did it change?

What this meant more practically was spelled out repeatedly over the centuries in various Confucian texts. Two notions in particular summarized the ideal position of women, at least in the eyes of elite male writers. The adage "Men go out, women stay in" emphasized the public and political roles of men in contrast to the domestic and private domain of women. A second idea, known as the "three obediences," emphasized a woman's subordination first to her father, then to her husband, and finally to her son. "Why is it," asked one text, "that according to the rites the man takes his wife, whereas the woman leaves her house [to join her husband's family]? It is because the *yin* is lowly, and should not have the initiative; it proceeds to the *yang* in order to be completed."[13]

The Chinese woman writer and court official Ban Zhou (45–116 C.E.) observed that the ancients had practiced three customs when a baby girl was born. She was placed below the bed to show that she was "lowly and weak," required always to "humble herself before others." Then she was given a piece of broken pottery to play with, signifying that "her primary duty [was] to be industrious." Finally, her birth was announced to the ancestors with an offering to indicate that she was responsible for "the continuation of [ancestor] worship in the home."[14]

Yet such notions of passivity, inferiority, and subordination were not the whole story of women's lives in classical China. A few women, particularly the wives,

Chinese Women at Work
For a long time, the spinning and weaving of cloth were part of women's domestic work in China. So too was fishing, as illustrated by the woman at the bottom right of this Chinese painting. (Palace Museum, Beijing)

concubines, or widows of emperors, were able on occasion to exercise considerable political authority. In doing so, they provoked much antifemale hostility on the part of male officials, who often blamed the collapse of a dynasty or natural disasters on the "unnatural" and "disruptive" influence of women in political affairs. A number of writers, however, praised women of virtue as wise counselors to their fathers, husbands, and rulers and depicted them positively as active agents.[15]

Within her husband's family, a young woman was clearly subordinate as a wife and daughter-in-law, but as a mother of sons, she was accorded considerable honor for her role in producing the next generation of male heirs to carry on her husband's lineage. When her sons married, she was able to exercise the significant authority of a mother-in-law. Furthermore, a woman, at least in the upper classes, often brought with her a considerable dowry, which was regarded as her own property and gave her some leverage within her marriage. Women's roles in the production of textiles, often used to pay taxes or to sell commercially, made her labor quite valuable to the family economy. And a man's wife was sharply distinguished from his concubines, for the wife alone produced the legitimate heirs who could carry on the family tradition. Thus women's lives were more complex and varied than the prescriptions of Confucian orthodoxy might suggest.

Much changed in China following the collapse of the Han dynasty in the third century C.E. Centralized government vanished amid much political fragmentation and conflict. Confucianism, the main ideology of Han China, was discredited, while Daoism and Buddhism attracted a growing following. Pastoral and nomadic people invaded northern China and ruled a number of the small states that had replaced the Han government. These new conditions resulted in some loosening of the strict patriarchy of classical China over the next five or six centuries.

The cultural influence of nomadic peoples, whose women were far less restricted than those of China, was noticed, and criticized, by more Confucian-minded male observers. One of them lamented the sad deterioration of gender roles under the influence of nomadic peoples.

> In the north of the Yellow river it is usually the wife who runs the household. She will not dispense with good clothing or expensive jewelry. The husband has to settle for old horses and sickly servants. The traditional niceties between husband and wife are seldom observed, and from time to time he even has to put up with her insults.[16]

Others criticized the adoption of nomadic styles of dress, makeup, and music. By the time of the Tang dynasty (618-907), writers and artists depicted elite women as capable of handling legal and business affairs on their own and on occasion riding horses and playing polo, bareheaded and wearing men's clothing. Tang legal codes even recognized a married daughter's right to inherit property from her family of birth. Such images of women were quite different from those of Han dynasty China.

A further sign of a weakening patriarchy and the cause of great distress to advocates of Confucian orthodoxy lay in the unusual reign of Empress Wu (reigned 690-705 C.E.), a former high-ranking concubine in the imperial court, who came to power amid much palace intrigue and was the only woman ever to rule China with the title of emperor. With the support of China's growing Buddhist establishment, Empress Wu governed despotically, but she also consolidated China's civil service examination system for the selection of public officials and actively patronized scholarship and the arts. Some of her actions seem deliberately designed to elevate the position of women. She commissioned the biographies of famous women, decreed that the mourning period for mothers be made equal to that for fathers, and ordered the creation of a Chinese character for "human being" that suggested the process of birth flowing from one woman without a prominent male role. Her reign was brief and unrepeated.

The growing popularity of Daoism provided new images of the feminine and new roles for women. Daoist texts referred to the *dao* as "mother" and urged the traditionally feminine virtues of yielding and passive acceptance rather than the male-oriented striving of Confucianism. Daoist sects often featured women as priests, nuns, or reclusive meditators, able to receive cosmic truth and to use it for the benefit of others. A variety of female deities from Daoist or Buddhist traditions found a place in Chinese village religion,[17] while growing numbers of women found an alternative to family life in Buddhist monasteries. None of this meant an end to patriarchy, but it does suggest some change in the tone and expression of that patriarchy.

Contrasting Patriarchies in Athens and Sparta

The patriarchies of the classical era not only fluctuated over time but also varied considerably from place to place. Nowhere is this variation more apparent than in the contrasting cases of Athens and Sparta, two of the leading city-states of classical Greek civilization (see Map 4.2). Even within the small area of classical Greece, the opportunities available to women and the restrictions imposed on them differed substantially. Although Athens has been celebrated as a major source of Western democracy and rationalism, its posture toward women was far more negative and restrictive than that of the highly militaristic and much less democratic Sparta.

In the several centuries between about 700 and 400 B.C.E., as the men of Athens moved toward unprecedented freedom and participation in political life, the city's

■ **Comparison**
How did the patriarchies of Athens and Sparta differ from each other?

Women of Athens
This painting on a seventh-century B.C.E. ceramic vase shows Athenian women gathering water at a fountain. (Museo di Villa Giulia Rome/ Gianni Dagli Orti/The Art Archive)

women experienced growing limitations. They had no role whatsoever in the assembly, the councils, or the juries of Athens, which were increasingly the focus of life for free men. In legal matters, women had to be represented by a guardian, and court proceedings did not even refer to them by name, but only as someone's wife or mother.

Greek thinkers, especially Aristotle, provided a set of ideas that justified women's exclusion from public life and their general subordination to men. According to Aristotle, "a woman is, as it were, an infertile male. She is female in fact on account of a kind of inadequacy." That inadequacy lay in her inability to generate sperm, which contained the "form" or the "soul" of a new human being. Her role in the reproductive process was passive, providing a receptacle for the vital male contribution. Compared often to children or domesticated animals, women were associated with instinct and passion and lacked the rationality to take part in public life. "It is the best for all tame animals to be ruled by human beings," wrote Aristotle. "For this is how they are kept alive. In the same way, the relationship between the male and the female is by nature such that the male is higher, the female lower, that the male rules and the female is ruled."[18]

As in China, proper Greek women were expected to remain inside the home, except perhaps for religious festivals or funerals. Even within the home, women's space was quite separate from that of men. Although poorer women, courtesans, and prostitutes had to leave their homes to earn money, collect water, or shop, ideal behavior for upper-class women assigned these tasks to slaves or to men and involved a radical segregation of male and female space. "What causes women a bad reputation," wrote the Greek playwright Euripides in *The Trojan Women*, "is not remaining inside."

Within the domestic realm, Athenian women were generally married in their mid-teens to men ten to fifteen years older than themselves. Their main function was the management of domestic affairs and the producti on of sons who would become citizens. These sons were expected to become literate, while their sisters were normally limited to learning spinning, weaving, and other household tasks. The Greek writer Menander exclaimed: "Teaching a woman to read and write? What a terrible thing to do! Like feeding a vile snake on more poison." Nor did women have much economic power. Although they could own personal property obtained through dowry, gifts, or inheritance, land was passed through male heirs, with a few exceptions. By law, women were forbidden to buy or sell land and could negotiate contracts only if the sum involved was valued at less than a bushel of barley.

There were exceptions, although rare, to the restricted lives of Athenian women, the most notable of which was Aspasia (ca. 470–400 B.C.E.). She was born in the Greek city of Miletus, on the western coast of Turkey, to a wealthy family that believed in educating its daughters. As a young woman, Aspasia found her way to Athens, where her foreign birth gave her somewhat more freedom than was normally available to the women of that city. She soon attracted the attention of Pericles, Athens's leading political figure. The two lived together as husband and wife until Pericles' death in 429 B.C.E., although they were not officially married. Treated as an equal partner by Pericles, Aspasia proved to be a learned and witty conversationalist who moved freely in the cultured circles of Athens. Her foreign birth and her apparent influence on Pericles provoked critics to suggest that she was a *hetaera,* a professional, educated, high-class entertainer and sexual companion, similar to a Japanese geisha. Although little is known about her, a number of major Athenian writers commented about her, both positively and negatively. She was, by all accounts, a rare and remarkable woman in a city that offered little opportunity for individuality or achievement to its female population.

The evolution of Sparta differed in many ways from that of Athens. Early on, Sparta solved the problem of feeding a growing population, not by creating overseas colonies as did many Greek city-states, but by conquering their neighbors and reducing them to a status of permanent servitude, not far removed from slavery. Called *helots,* these dependents far outnumbered the free citizens of Sparta and represented a permanent threat of rebellion. Solving this problem shaped Spartan society decisively. Sparta's answer was a militaristic regime, constantly ready for war to keep the helots in their place. To maintain such a system, all boys were removed from their families at the age of seven to be trained by the state in military camps, where they learned the ways of war. There they remained until the age of thirty. The ideal Spartan male was a warrior, skilled in battle, able to endure hardship, and willing to die for his city. Mothers are said to have told their sons departing for battle to "come back with your shield . . . or on it." Although economic equality for men was the ideal, it was never completely realized in practice. And unlike Athens, political power was exercised primarily by a small group of wealthy men.

This militaristic and far-from-democratic system had implications for women that, strangely enough, offered them greater freedoms and fewer restrictions. Their central task was reproduction—bearing warrior sons for Sparta. To strengthen their bodies for childbearing, girls were encouraged to take part in sporting events— running, wrestling, throwing the discus and javelin, even driving chariots. At times, they competed in the nude before mixed audiences. Their education, like that of boys, was prescribed by the state, which also insisted that newly married women cut their hair short, unlike adult Greek women elsewhere. Thus Spartan women were not secluded or segregated, as were their Athenian counterparts. Furthermore,

A Girl of Sparta
This figurine portrays a young female Spartan athlete or runner. Compare her clothing with that worn by the Athenian women depicted on the vase (shown on page 174. (National Archaeological Museum, Athens/Archaeological Receipts Fund)

Spartan young women, unlike those of Athens, usually married men of their own age, about eighteen years old, thus putting the new couple on a more equal basis. Marriage often began with a trial period to make sure the new couple could produce children, with divorce and remarriage readily available if they could not. Because men were so often away at war or preparing for it, women exercised much more authority in the household than was the case in Athens.

It is little wonder that the freedom of Spartan women appalled other Greeks, who believed that it undermined good order and state authority. Aristotle complained that the more egalitarian inheritance practices of Spartans led to their women controlling some 40 percent of landed estates. In Sparta, he declared, women "live in every sort of intemperance and luxury" and "the [male] rulers are ruled by women." Plutarch, a Greek writer during the heyday of the Roman Empire, observed critically that "the men of Sparta always obeyed their wives." The clothing worn by Spartan women to give them greater freedom of movement seemed immodest to other Greeks.

Nonetheless, in another way, Sparta may have been more restrictive than Athens and other Greek city-states, particularly in its apparent prohibition of homosexuality. At least this was the assertion of the Athenian writer Xenophon (427–355 B.C.E.), who stated that Sparta's legendary founder Lycurgus "caused lovers to abstain from sexual intercourse with boys."[19] Elsewhere, however, homoerotic relationships were culturally approved and fairly common for both men and women, although this did not prevent their participants from entering heterosexual marriages as well. The ideal homosexual relationship—between an older man and a young adolescent boy—was viewed as limited in time, for it was supposed to end when the boy's beard began to grow. Unlike contemporary Western societies where sexuality is largely seen as an identity, the ancient Greeks viewed sexual choice more casually and as a matter of taste.

Sparta clearly was a patriarchy, with women serving as breeding machines for its military system and lacking any formal role in public life, but it was a lighter patriarchy than that of Athens. The joint efforts of men and women seemed necessary to maintain a huge class of helots in permanent subjugation. Death in childbirth was considered the equivalent of death in battle, for both contributed to the defense of Sparta, and both were honored alike. In Athens, on the other hand, growing freedom and democracy were associated with the strengthening of the male-dominated, property-owning household, and within that household men, the cornerstone of Athenian society, were expected to exercise authority. Doing so required increasingly severe limitations and restrictions on the lives of women. Together, the cases of Athens and Sparta illustrate how the historical record appears different when viewed through the lens of gender. Athens, so celebrated for its democracy and philosophical rationalism, offered little to its women, whereas Sparta, often condemned for its militarism and virtual enslavement of the helots, provided a somewhat wider scope for the free women of the city.

Reflections: Arguing with Solomon and the Buddha

"What has been will be again; what has been done will be done again; there is nothing new under the sun." Recorded in the Old Testament book of Ecclesiastes and generally attributed to King Solomon, this was a despairing view about the essential changelessness and futility of human life. In contrast, central to Buddhist teachings has been the concept of "impermanence"—the notion that "everything changes; nothing remains without change." These observations from classical-era thinkers were intended to point to other levels of reality that lay beyond the dreary constancy or the endless changeability of this world. For students of history, however, these comments from Solomon and the Buddha serve to focus attention on issues of change and continuity in the historical record of classical Eurasian civilizations. What is more impressive—the innovations and changes or the enduring patterns and lasting features of these civilizations?

Clearly there were some new things under the sun, even if they had roots in earlier times. The Greek conquest of the Persian Empire under the leadership of Alexander the Great was both novel and unexpected. The Roman Empire encompassed the entire Mediterranean basin in a single political system for the first time. Buddhism and Christianity emerged as new, distinct, and universal religious traditions, although both bore the marks of their origin in Hindu and Jewish religious thinking respectively. The collapse of dynasties, empires, and civilizations long thought to be solidly entrenched—the Chinese and Roman, for example—must surely have seemed to people of the time as something new under the sun. Historians therefore might take issue with Solomon's dictum, should we seek to apply it to the history of the classical era.

Students of the past might also argue a little with the Buddha and his insistence on the "impermanence" of everything. Much that was created in the classical era—particularly its social and cultural patterns—has demonstrated an impressive continuity over many centuries, even if it also changed in particular ways over time. China's scholar-gentry class retained its prominence throughout the ups and downs of changing dynasties and into the twentieth century. India's caste-based social structure still endures as a way of thinking and behaving for hundreds of millions of people on the South Asian peninsula. Although slavery gave way to serfdom in the post-Roman world, it was massively revived in Europe's American colonies after 1500 and remained an important and largely unquestioned part of all civilizations until the nineteenth century. Patriarchy, with its assumptions of male superiority and dominance, has surely been the most fundamental, long-lasting, and taken-for-granted feature of all civilizations. Not until the twentieth century were those assumptions effectively challenged, but even then patriarchy has continued to shape the lives and the thinking of the vast majority of humankind. And many hundreds of millions of people in the twenty-first century still honor or practice religious and cultural traditions begun during the classical era.

Neither the insight of Solomon nor that of the Buddha, taken alone, offers an effective guide to the study of history, for continuity and change alike have long provided the inextricable warp and woof of historical analysis. Untangling their elusive relationship has figured prominently in the task of historians and has contributed much to the enduring fascination of historical study.

Second Thoughts

What's the Significance?

To assess your mastery of the material in this chapter, see the **Online Study Guide** at bedfordstmartins.com/strayer.

Wang Mang
China's scholar-gentry class
Yellow Turban Rebellion
caste as varna and jati

"ritual purity" in Indian social practice
Greek and Roman slavery
Spartacus

the "three obediences"
Empress Wu
Aspasia and Pericles
helots

Big Picture Questions

1. What is the difference between class and caste?
2. Why was slavery so much more prominent in Greco-Roman civilization than in India or China?
3. What philosophical, religious, or cultural ideas served to legitimate the class and gender inequalities of classical civilizations?
4. "Social inequality was both accepted and resisted in classical civilizations." What evidence might support this statement?
5. What changes in the patterns of social life of the classical era can you identify? What accounts for these changes?
6. "Cultural and social patterns of civilizations seem to endure longer than the political framework of states and empires." Based on Chapters 4, 5, and 6, would you agree with this statement?

Next Steps: For Further Study

For Web sites and documents related to this chapter, see **Make History** at bedfordstmartins.com/strayer.

Jeannine Auboyer, *Daily Life in Ancient India* (2002). A social history of classical India, with a focus on caste, ritual, religion, and art.

Sue Blundell, *Women in Ancient Greece* (1999). A well-written academic study, with occasional humorous stories and anecdotes.

Keith Bradley, *Slavery and Society at Rome* (1994). A scholarly but very readable account of slavery in the Roman Empire.

Michael Lowe, *Everyday Life in Early Imperial China* (1968). A vivid description of social life during the Han dynasty.

Bonnie Smith, ed., *Women's History in Global Perspective*, 3 volumes (2004). A collection of thoughtful essays by major scholars covering world history from ancient times to the twentieth century.

"Women in World History," http://chnm.gmu.edu/wwh/index.html. Documents, reviews, and lesson plans for learning and teaching about women's history in a global context.

CHAPTER SEVEN

Classical Era Variations

Africa and the Americas

500 B.C.E. – 1200 C.E.

"In a [Maya] community called Xolep, there was no paper or pencils where I taught. I started by drawing figures in the dirt. We then taught letters by forming them with sticks. One day students brought flower petals to shape the letters. . . . When we were able to gather enough money for notebooks, we gave them to the students and asked them to report the next day to the tree where we were holding school. . . . They proudly filed under the teaching tree, notebooks tucked under their arms, feeling that they were now officially students."[1]

This incident, reported in 1999 by a participant in an independent schools movement among the Maya of southern Mexico, was a tiny part of an ongoing revival of Maya culture. Despite the collapse of their famous classical civilization more than a thousand years ago, Maya language and folkways have persisted among some 6 million people currently living in Mexico, Belize, Guatemala, and Honduras. And despite five centuries of repression, exploitation, and neglect at the hands of Spanish colonizers and the independent governments that followed, they were now in the midst of what one writer called "a new time of the Maya."[2] They were writing their own histories, celebrating their own culture, creating their own organizations, and teaching their children to read. The most dramatic expression of this recent Maya revival was an armed uprising, begun in early 1994 and led by the Zapatista Army of National Liberation. Growing out of long-term social and economic grievances against local landowners and an unresponsive government, that rebellion stunned Mexico and focused global attention on the poverty and misery of the country's indigenous Maya. Once again, some 1,500 years after the high point of their classical civilization, the Maya were making history.

An Elite Maya Woman: In this painted clay statue, the woman carries an infant under her left arm and a monkey in her right. On the left side of the headdress, a bird is drinking from a flower, indicating a high status. (© Justin and Barbara Kerr)

FOR MANY PEOPLE, THE CLASSICAL ERA EVOKES most vividly the civilizations of Eurasia—especially the Greeks and the Romans, the Persians and the Chinese, and the Indians of South Asia—yet those were not the only classical-era civilizations. During this period, the Mesoamerican Maya and the Peruvian Moche thrived, as did several civilizations in Africa, including Meroë, Axum, and the Niger River valley. Furthermore, those peoples who did not organize themselves around cities or states likewise had histories of note and alternative ways of constructing their societies, although they are often neglected in favor of civilizations. This chapter explores the histories of the varied peoples of Africa and the Americas during the classical era. On occasion, those histories will extend some centuries beyond the chronological boundaries of the classical age in Eurasia, because patterns of historical development around the world did not always coincide precisely.

At the broadest level, however, human cultures evolved in quite similar fashion around the world. All, of course, were part of that grand process of human migration that initially peopled the planet. Beginning in Africa, that vast movement of humankind subsequently encompassed Eurasia, Australia, the Americas, and Oceania. Everywhere except Oceania, gathering and hunting long remained the sole basis for sustaining life and society. Then, in the three major supercontinents— Eurasia, Africa, and the Americas—the momentous turn of the Agricultural Revolution took place independently and in several distinct areas of each landmass. That revolutionary transformation of human life subsequently generated, in particularly rich agricultural environments of all three regions, those more complex societies that we know as civilizations, which featured cities, states, monumental architecture, and great social inequality. In these ways, the historical trajectory of the human journey on the earth has a certain unity and similarity across quite distinct continental regions. At the beginning of the Common Era, that trajectory had generated a total world population of about 250 million people, substantially less than the current population of the United States alone. By contemporary standards, it was still a sparsely populated planet.

The world's human population was distributed very unevenly across the three giant continents, as the Snapshot indicates. If these estimates are even reasonably accurate, then during the classical era Eurasia was home to more than 80 percent of the world's people, Africa about 11 percent, and the Americas between 5 and 7 percent. That unevenness in population distribution is part of the reason that world historians focus more attention on Eurasia than on Africa or the Americas. Here lies one of the major differences among the continents.

There were other differences as well. The absence of most animals capable of domestication meant that no pastoral societies developed in the Americas, and no draft animals were available to pull plows or carts or to carry heavy loads for long distances. Africa lacked wild sheep, goats, chickens, horses, and camels, but its proximity to Eurasia meant that these animals, once domesticated, became widely available to African peoples. Metallurgy in the Americas was likewise far less developed than in the Eastern Hemisphere, where iron tools and weapons played such an

Snapshot　**Continental Population in the Classical Era**[3]

(Note: Population figures for such early times are merely estimates and are often controversial among scholars. Percentages do not always total 100 percent due to rounding.)

	Eurasia	Africa	North America	Central/South America	Australia/ Oceania	Total World
Area (in square miles and as percentage of world total)						
	21,049,000 (41%)	11,608,000 (22%)	9,365,000 (18%)	6,880,000 (13%)	2,968,000 (6%)	51,870,000
Population (in millions and as percentage of world total)						
400 B.C.E.	127 (83%)	17 (11%)	1 (0.7%)	7 (5%)	1 (0.7%)	153
10 C.E.	213 (85%)	26 (10%)	2 (0.8%)	10 (4%)	1 (0.4%)	252
200 C.E.	215 (84%)	30 (12%)	2 (0.8%)	9 (4%)	1 (0.4%)	257
600 C.E.	167 (80%)	24 (12%)	2 (1%)	14 (7%)	1 (0.5%)	208
1000 C.E.	195 (77%)	39 (15%)	2 (0.8%)	16 (6%)	1 (0.4%)	253

important role in economic and military life. In the Americas, writing was limited to the Mesoamerican region and was most highly developed among the Maya, whereas in Africa it was confined to the northern and northeastern parts of the continent during the classical era. In Eurasia, writing emerged elaborately in many regions. Classical-era civilizations in Africa and the Americas were fewer in number and generally smaller than those of Eurasia, and larger numbers of their people lived in communities that did not feature cities and states.

To illustrate the historical developments of the classical era beyond Eurasia, this chapter focuses on three regions in Africa and three in the Americas. To what extent did these histories parallel those of Eurasia? In what ways did they forge new or different paths?

The African Northeast

When historians refer to Africa during the classical era, they are speaking generally of a geographic concept, a continental landmass, and not a cultural identity. Certainly no one living on the continent at that time thought of himself or herself as an African. Like Eurasia or the Americas, Africa hosted numerous separate societies, cultures, and civilizations with vast differences among them as well as some interaction between them.

Many of these differences grew out of the continent's environmental variations. Small regions of Mediterranean climate in the northern and southern extremes, large deserts (the Sahara and the Kalahari), even larger regions of savanna grasslands, tropical rain forest in the continent's center, highlands and mountains in eastern Africa — all of these features, combined with the continent's enormous size, ensured variation and difference among Africa's many peoples. Africa did, however, have one distinctive environmental feature: bisected by the equator, it was the most tropical of the world's three supercontinents. Persistent warm temperatures caused the rapid decomposition of vegetable matter called humus, resulting in poorer and less fertile soils and a less productive agriculture than in the more temperate Eurasia. Those climatic conditions also spawned numerous disease-carrying insects and parasites, which have long created serious health problems in many parts of the continent. It was within these environmental constraints that African peoples made their histories.

A further geographic feature shaped African history — its proximity to Eurasia, which allowed parts of Africa to interact with Eurasian civilizations. During the classical era, North Africa was incorporated into the Roman Empire and used to produce wheat and olives on large estates with slave labor. Christianity spread widely, giving rise to some of the early Church's most famous martyrs and to one of its most important theologians, Saint Augustine (354–430 C.E.). The Christian faith found an even more permanent foothold in the lands now known as Ethiopia.

Arabia was another point of contact with the larger world for African peoples. The arrival of the domesticated camel, probably from Arabia, generated a nomadic pastoral way of life among some of the Berber peoples of the western Sahara during the first three centuries C.E. A little later, camels also made possible trans-Saharan commerce, which linked interior West Africa to the world of Mediterranean civilization. Over many centuries, the East African coast was a port of call for Egyptian, Roman, and Arab merchants, and that region subsequently became an integral part of Indian Ocean trading networks.

Both the external connections and, more important, the internal development of African societies generated various patterns of historical change during the classical era. Three regions — northeastern Africa, the Niger River basin in West Africa, and the vast world of Bantu-speaking Africa south of the equator — serve to illustrate these differences and the many social and cultural experiments spawned by the peoples of this continent.

Meroë: Continuing a Nile Valley Civilization

■ Connection
How did the history of Meroë and Axum reflect interaction with neighboring civilizations?

In the Nile Valley south of Egypt lay the lands of Nubian civilization, almost as old as Egypt itself. Over many centuries, Nubians both traded and fought with Egypt, alternately conquering and being conquered by their northern neighbor. While borrowing heavily from Egypt, Nubia remained a distinct and separate civilization

Map 7.1 Africa in the Classical Era

During the classical era, older African civilizations such as Egypt and Nubia persisted and changed, while new civilizations emerged in Axum and the Niger River valley. South of the equator, Bantu-speaking peoples spread rapidly, creating many new societies and identities.

(see Chapter 3). By the classical era, as Egypt fell under foreign control, Nubian civilization came to center on the southern city of Meroë, where it flourished between 300 B.C.E. and 100 C.E. (see Map 7.1).

Politically, the Kingdom of Meroë was governed by an all-powerful and sacred monarch, a position occasionally conferred on women. Rulers were buried, in

A Bracelet from Meroë
This gold bracelet, dating to about 100 B.C.E., illustrates the skill of Meroë's craftsmen as well as the kingdom's reputation as one of the wealthiest states of the ancient world. (Bracelet with image of Hathor, Nubian, Meroitic Period, about 100 B.C.E. Object Place: Sudan, Nubia, Gebel Barkal, Pyramid 8, Gold, enamel. Museum of Fine Arts, Boston, Harvard University–Boston Museum of Fine Arts Expedition, 20.333. Photograph © 2008 Museum of Fine Arts, Boston)

accordance with ancient traditions, along with a number of human sacrificial victims. The city of Meroë and other urban centers housed a wide variety of economic specialties—merchants, weavers, potters, and masons, as well as servants, laborers, and slaves. The smelting of iron and the manufacture of iron tools and weapons were especially prominent industries. The rural areas surrounding Meroë were populated by peoples who practiced some combination of herding and farming and paid periodic tribute to the ruler. Rainfall-based agriculture was possible in Meroë, and consequently farmers were less dependent on irrigation. This meant that the rural population did not need to concentrate so heavily along the Nile and was less directly controlled from the capital than was the case in Egypt, where state authorities were required to supervise an irrigation system serving a dense population along the river.

The wealth and military power of Meroë derived in part from extensive long-distance trading connections, to the north via the Nile and to the east and west by means of camel caravans. Its iron weapons and cotton cloth, as well as its access to gold, ivory, tortoiseshells, and ostrich feathers, gave Meroë a reputation for great riches in the classical world of northeastern Africa and the Mediterranean. The discovery in Meroë of a statue of the Roman emperor Augustus, probably seized during a raid on Roman Egypt, testifies to contact with the Mediterranean world. Culturally, Meroë seemed to move away from the heavy Egyptian influence of earlier times. A local lion god, Apedemek, grew more prominent than Egyptian deities such as Isis and Osiris, while the use of Egyptian-style writing declined as a new and still undeciphered Meroitic script took its place.

In the centuries following 100 C.E., the Kingdom of Meroë declined, in part because of deforestation caused by the need for wood to make charcoal for smelting iron. The effective end of the Meroë phase of Nubian civilization came with the kingdom's conquest in the 340s C.E. by the neighboring and rising state of Axum. In the centuries that followed, three separate Nubian states emerged, and Coptic (Egyptian) Christianity penetrated the region. For almost a thousand years, Nubia was a Christian civilization, using Greek as a liturgical language and constructing churches in Coptic or Byzantine fashion. After 1300 or so, political division, Arab immigration, and the penetration of Islam eroded this Christian civilization, and Nubia became part of the growing world of Islam.

Axum: The Making of a Christian Kingdom

If Meroë and Nubia represented the continuation of an old African civilization, Axum marked the emergence of a new one. Axum lay in the Horn of Africa, in what is now Eritrea and northern Ethiopia (see Map 7.1). Its economic foundation was a highly productive agriculture that used a plow-based farming system, unlike most of the rest of Africa, which relied on the hoe or digging stick. Axum's agriculture generated substantial amounts of wheat, barley, millet, and teff, a highly nutritious grain unique to that region. By 50 C.E. or so, a substantial state had emerged, stimulated by its participation in Red Sea and Indian Ocean commerce. At Adulis, then the largest port on the East African coast, a wide range of merchants sought the products of the African interior—animal hides, rhinoceros horn, ivory, obsidian, tortoiseshells, and slaves. Taxes on this trade provided a major source of revenue for the Axumite state and the complex society that grew up within it.

The interior capital city, also known as Axum, was a center of monumental building and royal patronage for the arts. The most famous of these were huge stone obelisks, which most likely marked royal graves. Some of them were more than 100 feet tall and at the time were the largest structures in the world hewn from a single piece of rock. The language used at court, in the towns, and for commerce was Geez, written in a script derived from South Arabia. The Axumite state exercised a measure of control over the mostly Agaw-speaking people of the country through a loose administrative structure focusing on the collection of tribute payments. To the Romans, Axum was the third major empire within the world they knew, following their own and the Persian Empire.

Through its connections to Red Sea trade and the Roman world, particularly Egypt, Axum was introduced to Christianity in the fourth century C.E. Its monarch at the time, King Ezana, adopted the new religion about the same time as Constantine did in the Roman Empire. Christianity took root in Axum, linking that kingdom religiously to Egypt, where a distinctive Christian church known as Coptic was already well established. Although Egypt subsequently became largely Islamic, reducing its Christian community to a small minority, Christianity maintained a dominant position in the mountainous terrain of highland Ethiopia and in the early twenty-first century still represents the faith of perhaps half of the country's population.

During the fourth through the sixth century C.E., Axum mounted a campaign of imperial expansion that took its forces into the Kingdom of Meroë and across the Red Sea into Yemen in South Arabia. By 571, the traditional date for the birth of Muhammad, an Axumite army, including a number of African war elephants, had reached the gates of Mecca, but it was a fairly short-lived

The Columns of Axum
Dating to the time when Axum first encountered Christianity (300–500 C.E.), this column, measuring some seventy-nine feet tall, probably served as a funeral monument for the kingdom's ancient rulers. (Antonello Langellotto/TIPS Images)

imperial venture. The next several centuries were ones of decline for the Axumite state, owing partly to environmental changes, such as soil exhaustion, erosion, and deforestation, brought about by intensive farming. Equally important was the rise of Islam, which altered trade routes and diminished the revenue available to the Axumite state. Its last coins were struck in the early seventh century. When the state revived several centuries later, it was centered farther south on the Ethiopian plateau. There emerged the Christian church and the state that present-day Ethiopia has inherited, but the link to ancient Axum was long remembered and revered.

With their long-distance trading connections, urban centers, centralized states, complex societies, monumental architecture, written languages, and imperial ambitions, both Meroë and Axum paralleled on a smaller scale the major features of the classical civilizations of Eurasia. Furthermore, both were in direct contact with the world of Mediterranean civilizations. Elsewhere in Africa during the classical era, quite different histories unfolded.

Along the Niger River: Cities without States

■ **Description**
How does the experience of the Niger Valley challenge conventional notions of "civilization"?

In the middle stretches of the Niger River in West Africa, the classical era witnessed the emergence of a remarkable urbanization (see Map 7.1). A prolonged dry period during the five centuries after 500 B.C.E. brought growing numbers of people from the southern Sahara into the fertile floodplain of the middle Niger in search of more reliable access to water. Accompanying them were their domesticated cattle, sheep, and goats; their agricultural skills; and their ironworking technology. Over the centuries of the classical era and beyond (roughly 300 B.C.E.–900 C.E.), the peoples of this region created a distinctive city-based civilization. The most fully studied of the urban clusters that grew up along the middle Niger was the city of Jenne-jeno, which at its high point probably housed more than 40,000 people.

Among the most distinctive features of these cities was the apparent absence of a corresponding state structure. Unlike the cities of Egypt, China, the Roman Empire, or Axum, these middle Niger urban centers were not encompassed within some larger imperial system. Nor were they like the city-states of ancient Mesopotamia, in which each city had its own centralized political structure, embodied in a monarch and his accompanying bureaucracy. According to a leading historian of the region, they were "cities without citadels," complex urban centers that apparently operated without the coercive authority of a state, for archeologists have found in their remains few signs of despotic power, widespread warfare, or deep social inequalities.[4] In this respect, these urban centers resemble the early cities of the Indus Valley civilization, where likewise little archeological evidence of centralized state structures has been found (see Chapter 3).

In place of such hierarchical organization, Jenne-jeno and other cities of the region emerged as clusters of economically specialized settlements surrounding a larger central town. The earliest and most prestigious of these specialized occupations was iron smithing. Working with fire and earth (ore) to produce this highly useful metal, the smiths of the Niger Valley were both feared and revered. Archeologist Roderick McIntosh, a leading figure in the excavation of Jenne-jeno, argued that "their knowledge of the transforming arts—earth to metal, insubstantial fire to the mass of iron—was the key to a secret, occult realm of immense power and immense danger."[5]

Other specializations followed. Villages of cotton weavers, potters, leather workers, and griots (praise-singers who preserved and recited the oral traditions of their societies) grew up around the central towns. Gradually these urban artisan communities became occupational castes, whose members passed their jobs and skills to their children and could marry only within their own group. In the surrounding rural areas, as in all urban-based civilizations, farmers tilled the soil and raised their animals, but specialization also occurred in farming as various ethnic groups focused on fishing, rice cultivation, or some other agricultural pursuit. At least for a time, these middle Niger cities represented an African alternative to an oppressive state, which in many parts of the world accompanied an increasingly complex urban economy and society. A series of distinct and specialized economic groups shared authority and voluntarily used the services of one another, while maintaining their separate identity through physical separation.

Accompanying this unique urbanization, and no doubt stimulating it, was a growing network of indigenous West African commerce. The middle Niger flood-plain supported a rich agriculture and had clay for pottery, but it lacked stone, iron ore, salt, and fuel. This scarcity of resources was the basis for long-distance commerce, which operated by boat along the Niger River and overland by donkey to the north and south. Iron ore from more than 50 miles away, copper from mines 200 miles distant, gold from even more distant sources, stones and salt from the Sahara—all of these items have been found in Jenne-jeno, in return no doubt for grain, fish, smoked meats, iron implements, and other staples. Jenne-jeno itself was an important transshipment point in this commerce, in which goods were transferred from boat to donkey or vice versa. By the 500s C.E., there is evidence of an even wider commerce and at least indirect contact, from Mauritania in the west to present-day Mali and Burkina-Faso in the east.

In the second millennium C.E., new historical patterns developed in West Africa (see Chapter 8). A number of large-scale states or empires emerged in the region—Ghana, Mali, and Songhay, among the most well known. At least partially responsible for this development was the flourishing of a camel-borne trans-Saharan commerce, previously but a trickle across the great desert. As West Africa became more firmly connected to North Africa and the Mediterranean, Islam penetrated the region, marking a gradual but major cultural transformation. All of this awaited West Africa in the postclassical era, submerging, but not completely eliminating, the decentralized city life of the Niger Valley.

South of the Equator: The World of Bantu Africa

In Africa south of the equator, the most significant development of the classical era involved the accelerating movement of Bantu-speaking peoples into this enormous subcontinent. It was a process that had begun many centuries earlier from a homeland region in what is now southeastern Nigeria and the Cameroons. In the long run, that movement of peoples generated some 400 distinct but closely related languages, known collectively as Bantu. By the first century C.E., agricultural peoples speaking Bantu languages had largely occupied the forest regions of equatorial Africa, and at least a few of them had probably reached the East African coast. In the several centuries that followed, they established themselves quite rapidly in most of eastern and southern Africa (see Map 7.1), introducing immense economic and cultural changes to a huge region of the continent.

The spread of Bantu peoples was not a conquest or invasion such as that of Alexander the Great; nor was it a massive and self-conscious migration like that of Europeans to the Americas. Rather it was a slow movement of peoples, perhaps a few extended families at a time, but taken as a whole, it brought to Africa south of the equator a measure of cultural and linguistic commonality, marking it as a distinct region of the continent.

Cultural Encounters

■ Connection

In what ways did the arrival of Bantu-speaking peoples stimulate cross-cultural interaction?

That movement of peoples also generated numerous cross-cultural encounters, as the Bantu-speaking newcomers interacted with already-established societies, changing both of them in the process. Among those encounters, none was more significant than that between the agricultural Bantu and the gathering and hunting peoples who earlier occupied Africa south of the equator. This was part of a long-term global phenomenon in which farmers largely replaced foragers as the dominant people on the planet (see Chapter 2).

In this encounter, Bantu-speaking farmers had various advantages. One was numerical, as agriculture generated a more productive economy, enabling larger numbers to live in a smaller area than was possible with a gathering and hunting way of life. Another advantage was disease, for the farmers brought with them both parasitic and infectious diseases—malaria, for example—to which foraging people had little immunity. A third advantage was iron, so useful for tools and weapons, which Bantu migrants brought to many of their interactions with peoples still operating with stone-age technology. Thus, during the classical era, gathering and hunting peoples were displaced, absorbed, or largely eliminated in most parts of Africa south of the equator—but not everywhere.

In the Kalahari region of southwestern Africa and a few places in East Africa, gathering and hunting peoples such as the San (see Chapter 1) survived into modern times. Furthermore, many of the Bantu languages of southern Africa retain to this day the distinctive "clicks" that they borrowed from the now-vanished gathering and hunting peoples who long preceded them in the region.

In the rain forest region of Central Africa, the foraging Batwa (Pygmy) people, at least some of them, became "forest specialists" who produced honey, wild game, elephant products, animal skins, and medicinal barks and plants, all of which entered regional trading networks in exchange for the agricultural products of their Bantu neighbors. They also adopted Bantu languages, while maintaining a non-agricultural lifestyle and a separate identity. For their part, the Bantu farmers regarded their Batwa neighbors as first-comers to the region and therefore closest to the ancestral and territorial spirits that determined the fertility of the land and people. Thus, as forest-dwelling Bantu peoples grew in numbers and created chiefdoms, those chiefs appropriated the Batwa title of "owners of the land" for themselves, claimed Batwa ancestry, and portrayed the Batwa as the original "civilizers" of the earth.[6]

Khoikhoi of South Africa The Khoikhoi people of South Africa, several of whom are shown here in an 1886 photograph, were originally gatherers and hunters, who adopted cattle and sheep raising from outsiders, perhaps from early Bantu-speaking immigrants to the region, but did not practice agriculture. Living in southern Africa for most of the last two millennia, they illustrate the interaction and selective cultural borrowing that took place among the various peoples of the region. (Hulton-Deutsch Collection/Corbis)

In other ways as well, Bantu cultures changed as they encountered different peoples. In the drier environment of East Africa, the yam-based agriculture of the West African Bantu homeland was unable to support their growing numbers, so Bantu farmers increasingly adopted grains as well as domesticated sheep and cattle from the already-established people of the region. Their agriculture also was enriched by acquiring a variety of food crops from Southeast Asia—coconuts, sugarcane, and especially bananas—which were brought to East Africa by Indonesian sailors and immigrants early in the first millennium C.E. Bantu farmers then spread this agricultural package and their acquired ironworking technology throughout the vast area of eastern and southern Africa, probably reaching present-day South Africa by 400 C.E. They also brought a common set of cultural and social practices, which diffused widely across Bantu Africa. One prominent historian described these practices as encompassing,

> in religion, the centrality of ancestor observances; in philosophy, the problem of evil understood as the consequence of individual malice or of the failure to honor one's ancestors; in music, an emphasis on polyrhythmic performance with drums as the key instrument; in dance, a new form of expression in which a variety of prescribed body movements took preference over footwork; and in agriculture, the pre-eminence of women as the workers and innovators.[7]

All of this became part of the common culture of Bantu Africa.

Society and Religion

In the thousand years or so (500-1500 C.E.) that followed their initial colonization of Africa south of the equator, Bantu-speaking peoples also created a wide variety of quite distinct societies and cultures. Some—in present-day Kenya, for example—organized themselves without any formal political specialists at all. Instead they made decisions, resolved conflicts, and maintained order by using kinship structures or lineage principles supplemented by age grades, which joined men of a particular generation together across various lineages. Elsewhere, lineage heads who acquired a measure of personal wealth or who proved skillful at mediating between the local spirits and the people might evolve into chiefs with a modest political authority. In several areas, such as the region around Lake Victoria or present-day Zimbabwe, larger and more substantial kingdoms evolved. Along the East African coast after 1000 C.E., dozens of rival city-states linked the African interior with the commerce of the Indian Ocean basin (see Chapter 8). The kind of society that developed in any particular area depended on a host of local factors, including population density, trading opportunities, and interaction among culturally different peoples.

In terms of religion, Bantu practice in general placed less emphasis on a High or Creator God, who was viewed as remote and largely uninvolved in ordinary life, and focused instead on ancestral or nature spirits. The power of dead ancestors might be accessed through rituals of sacrifice, especially that of cattle. Supernatural power deriving from ancient heroes, ancestors, or nature spirits also resided in charms, which could be activated by proper rituals and used to control the rains, defend the village, achieve success in hunting, or identify witches. Belief in witches was widespread, reflecting the idea that evil or misfortune was the work of malicious people. Diviners, skilled in penetrating the world of the supernatural, used dreams, visions, charms, or trances to identify the source of misfortune and to prescribe remedies. Was a particular illness the product of broken taboos, a dishonored ancestor, an unhappy nature spirit, or a witch? Was a remedy to be found in a cleansing ceremony, a sacrifice to an ancestor, the activation of a charm, or the elimination of a witch?[8] Such issues constantly confronted the people of Bantu Africa.

Unlike the major monotheistic religions, with their "once and for all" revelations from God through the Christian Bible or the Muslim Quran, Bantu religious practice was predicated on the notion of "continuous revelation"—the possibility of constantly receiving new messages from the world beyond. Moreover, unlike Buddhism, Christianity, or Islam, Bantu religions were geographically confined, intended to explain, predict, and control local affairs, with no missionary impulse or inclination toward universality.

Civilizations of Mesoamerica

Although geography permitted interaction between African and Eurasian peoples, the Atlantic and Pacific oceans ensured that the cultures and societies of the Western Hemisphere had long operated in a world apart from their Afro-Eurasian counterparts.

Nor were the cultures of the Americas stimulated by the kind of fruitful interaction among their own civilizations that played such an important role in the Eastern Hemisphere. Nothing similar to the contact between Egypt and Mesopotamia, or Persia and the Greeks, or the extensive communication along the Silk Road trading network enriched the two major centers of civilization in the Americas—Mesoamerica and the Andes—which had little if any direct contact with each other. Furthermore, the achievements of early American civilizations and cultures occurred without the large domesticated animals or ironworking technologies that were so important throughout the Eastern Hemisphere.

Accounts of pre-Columbian American societies often focus primarily on the Aztec and Inca empires (see Chapter 13), yet these impressive creations, flourishing in the fifteenth and early sixteenth centuries, were but the latest in a long line of civilizations that preceded them in Mesoamerica and the Andes respectively. Although these two regions housed the vast majority of the population of the Americas, the peoples of North America, the Amazon River basin, and elsewhere were the centers of their own worlds and made their own histories. It is the period preceding the Aztecs and Incas that represents the classical era in the history of the Americas.

Stretching from central Mexico to northern Central America, the area known as Mesoamerica was, geographically speaking, one of "extraordinary diversity compressed into a relatively small space."[9] That environment ranged from steamy lowland rain forests to cold and windy highland plateaus, cut by numerous mountains and valleys and generating many microclimates. Such conditions contributed to substantial linguistic and ethnic diversity and to many distinct and competing cities, chiefdoms, and states.

Despite this diversity, Mesoamerica, like Bantu Africa, was also a distinct region, bound together by elements of a common culture. Its many peoples shared an intensive agricultural technology devoted to raising maize, beans, chili peppers, and squash; they prepared maize in a distinctive and highly nutritious fashion; they based their economies on market exchange; they practiced religions featuring a similar pantheon of deities, belief in a cosmic cycle of creation and destruction, human sacrifice, and monumental ceremonial centers; they employed a common ritual calendar of 260 days and hieroglyphic writing; and they interacted frequently among themselves. During the first millennium B.C.E., for example, the various small states and chiefdoms of the region, particularly the Olmec, exchanged a number of luxury goods used to display social status and for ritual purposes—jade, serpentine, obsidian tools, ceramic pottery, shell ornaments, stingray spines, and turtle shells. As a result, aspects of Olmec culture, such as artistic styles, temple pyramids, the calendar system, and rituals involving human sacrifice, spread widely throughout Mesoamerica and influenced many of the civilizations that followed.

Classical Civilizations of Mesoamerica

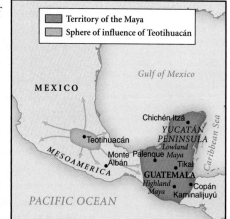

The Maya: Writing and Warfare

■ Comparison
With what Eurasian civilizations might the Maya be compared?

Among the Mesoamerican civilizations, none has attracted more attention than that of the Maya, the major classical civilization of Mesoamerica. Scholars have traced the beginnings of the Maya people to ceremonial centers constructed as early as 2000 B.C.E. in present-day Guatemala and the Yucatán region of Mexico, but it was during the classical phase of Maya civilization, between 250 and 900 C.E., that their most notable cultural achievements emerged. Their intellectuals, probably priests, developed a mathematical system that included the concept of zero and place nota- tion and was capable of complex calculations. They combined this mathematical ability with careful observation of the night skies to plot the cycles of planets, to predict eclipses of the sun and the moon, to construct elaborate calendars, and to calculate accurately the length of the solar year.

Accompanying these intellectual achievements was the creation of the most elaborate writing system in the Americas, which used both pictographs and pho- netic or syllabic elements. Carved on stone and written on bark paper or deerskin books, Mayan writing recorded historical events, masses of astronomical data, and religious or mythological texts. Temples, pyramids, palaces, and public plazas abounded, graced with painted murals and endless stone carving. It is not surpris- ing that early scholars viewed Maya civilization as a peaceful society led by gentle stargazing priest-kings devoted to temple building and intellectual pursuits.

The economic foundations for these cultural achievements were also impres- sive. By 600 C.E., the Maya lived in an "almost totally engineered landscape."[10] They drained swamps, terraced hillsides, flattened ridge tops, and constructed an elabo- rate water management system. Much of this was in support of a flourishing agri- culture, which supported a very rapidly growing and dense population by 750 C.E. This agriculture sustained substantial elite classes of nobles, priests, merchants, archi- tects, and sculptors, as well as specialized artisans producing pottery, tools, and cot- ton textiles. And it was sufficiently productive to free a large labor force for work on the many public structures that continue to amaze contemporary visitors.

We now know that these many achievements took place within a highly frag- mented political system of city-states, local lords, and regional kingdoms with no cen- tral authority, with frequent warfare, and with the extensive capture and sacrifice of prisoners. The larger political units of Maya civilization were densely populated urban and ceremonial centers, ruled by powerful kings, who were divine rulers or "state shamans" able to mediate between humankind and the supernatural. One of these cities, Tikal, contained perhaps 50,000 people, with another 50,000 or so in the sur- rounding countryside, by 750 C.E.[11] Some of these city-states were clearly imperialis- tic, but none succeeded in creating a unified Maya empire. Various centers of Maya civilization rose and fell; fluctuating alliances among them alternated with periods of sporadic warfare; ruling families intermarried; the elite classes sought luxury goods from far away—jade, gold, shells, feathers from exotic birds, cacao—to bolster their authority and status. In its political dimensions, classical Maya civilization more closely resembled the competing city-states of ancient Mesopotamia or classical Greece than the imperial structures of Rome, Persia, or China.

But that imposing civilization collapsed with a completeness and rapidity rare in world history. In less than a century following the onset of a long-term drought in 840, the population of the low-lying southern heartland of the Maya dropped by 85 percent or more as famine, epidemic, and fratricidal warfare reaped a horrific toll. It was a catastrophe from which there was no recovery. Elements of Maya culture survived in scattered settlements, but the great cities were deserted, and large-scale construction and artistic work ceased. The last date inscribed in stone corresponds to 909 C.E. As a complex civilization, the Maya had passed into history.

Explaining this remarkable demise has long kept scholars guessing. It seems clear that neither foreign invasion nor internal rebellion played a major role, as they had in the collapse of the Roman and Chinese empires. One recent account focuses on ecological and political factors.[12] Extremely rapid population growth after 600 C.E. pushed total Maya numbers to perhaps 5 million or more and soon outstripped available resources, resulting in deforestation and the erosion of hillsides. Under such conditions, climate change in the form of prolonged droughts in the 800s may well have triggered the collapse, while political disunity and endemic rivalries prevented a coordinated and effective response to the emerging catastrophe. Maya warfare in fact became more frequent as competition for increasingly scarce land for cultivation became sharper. Whatever the precise explanation, the Maya collapse, like that of the Romans and others, illustrates the fragility of civilizations, whether they are embodied in large empires or organized in a more decentralized fashion.

Teotihuacán: America's Greatest City

At roughly the same time as the Maya flourished in the southern regions of Mesoamerica, the giant city of Teotihuacán, to the north in the Valley of Mexico, was also thriving. Begun around 150 B.C.E. and apparently built to a plan rather than evolving haphazardly, the city came to occupy about eight square miles and by 550 C.E. had a population variously estimated between 100,000 and 200,000. It was by far the largest urban complex in the Americas at the time and one of the six largest in the world. Beyond this, much about Teotihuacán is unknown, such as its original name, the language of its people, the kind of government that ordered its life, and the precise function of its many deities.

Physically, the city was enormously impressive, replete with broad avenues, spacious plazas, huge marketplaces, temples, palaces, apartment complexes, slums, waterways, reservoirs, drainage systems, and colorful murals. Along the main north/south boulevard, now known as the Street of the Dead, were the grand homes of the elite, the headquarters of state authorities, many temples, and two giant pyramids. One of them, the Pyramid of the Sun, had been constructed over an ancient tunnel leading to a cave and may well have been regarded as the site of creation itself, the birthplace

■ **Connection**

In what ways did Teotihuacán shape the history of Mesoamerica?

of the sun and the moon. At the Temple of the Feathered Serpent, archeologists have found the remains of some 200 people, their hands and arms tied behind them; they were the apparently unwilling sacrificial victims meant to accompany into the after-life the high-ranking persons buried there.

Off the main avenues in a gridlike pattern of streets lay thousands of residential apartment compounds, home to the city's commoners, each with its own kitchen area, sleeping quarters, courtyards, and shrines. In these compounds, perhaps in groups of related families or lineages, lived many of the farmers who tilled the lands outside the city. Thousands of Maya specialists—masons, leather workers, potters, construction laborers, merchants, civil servants—also made their homes in these apartments. So too did skilled makers of obsidian blades, who plied their trade in hundreds of separate workshops, generating products that were in great demand throughout Mesoamerica. At least two small sections of the city were reserved exclusively for foreigners.

Buildings, both public and private, were decorated with mural paintings, sculptures, and carvings. Many of these works of art display abstract geometric and stylized images. Others depict gods and goddesses, arrayed in various forms—feathered serpents, starfish, jaguars, flowers, and warriors. One set of murals shows happy people cavorting in a paradise of irrigated fields, playing games, singing, and chasing butterflies, which were thought to represent the souls of the dead. Another portrays dancing warriors carrying elaborate curved knives, to which were attached bleeding human hearts.

The art of Teotihuacán, unlike that of the Maya, has revealed few images of self-glorifying rulers or individuals. Nor did the city have a tradition of written public inscriptions as the Maya did, although a number of glyphs or characters suggest at least a limited form of writing. One scholar has suggested that "the rulers of Teotihuacán might have intentionally avoided the personality cult of the dynastic art and writing" so characteristic of the Maya.[13] Some have argued that those rulers may have constituted an oligarchy or council of high-ranking elites rather than a single monarch.

However it was governed, Teotihuacán cast a huge shadow over Mesoamerica, particularly from 300 to 600 C.E., although scholars disagree as to precisely how its power and influence were exercised. A core region of perhaps 10,000 square miles was administered directly from the city itself, while tribute was no doubt exacted from other areas within its broader sphere of influence. At a greater distance, the power of

A Mural of Teotihuacán
The paradise of the god of the rain, portrayed in this mural, was available only to those who died through drowning, storms, or lightning. The deity in the center presides over the waters, and rain springs from his hands, while at the sides, priests make their offerings. The dating of such murals is uncertain, but most were apparently created between 450 and 650 C.E. (Enrique Franco-Torrijos)

Teotihuacán's armies gave it a presence in the Maya heartland more than 600 miles to the east. At least one Maya city, Kaminalijuyu in the southern highlands, was completely taken over by the Teotihuacán military and organized as a colony. In Tikal, a major lowland Maya city, in the year 378 C.E., agents of Teotihuacán apparently engineered a coup that placed a collaborator on the throne and turned the city for a time into an ally or a satellite. Elsewhere—in the Zapotec capital of Monte Alban, for example—murals show unarmed persons from Teotihuacán engaged in what seems to be more equal diplomatic relationships.

At least some of this political and military activity was no doubt designed to obtain, either by trade or by tribute, valued commodities from afar—food products, cacao beans, tropical bird feathers, honey, salt, medicinal herbs. The presence in Teotihuacán of foreigners, perhaps merchants, from the Gulf Coast and Maya lowlands, as well as much pottery from those regions, provides further evidence of long-distance trade. Furthermore, the sheer size and prestige of Teotihuacán surely persuaded many, all across Mesoamerica, to imitate the architectural and artistic styles of the city. Thus, according to a leading scholar, "Teotihuacan meant something of surpassing importance far beyond its core area."[14] Almost a thousand years after its still-mysterious collapse around 650 C.E., the peoples of the Aztec Empire dubbed the great metropolis as Teotihuacán, the "city of the gods."

Civilizations of the Andes

Yet another center of civilization in the Americas lay in the dramatic landscape of the Andes. Bleak deserts along the coast supported human habitation only because they were cut by dozens of rivers flowing down from the mountains, offering the possibility of irrigation and cultivation. The offshore waters of the Pacific Ocean also provided an enormously rich marine environment with an endless supply of seabirds and fish. The Andes themselves, a towering mountain chain with many highland valleys, afforded numerous distinct ecological niches, depending on altitude. On its steep slopes, people carved out huge staircase terrace systems, which remain impressive in the twenty-first century.

Classical Civilizations of the Andes

The most well known of the civilizations to take shape in this environment was that of the Incas, which encompassed practically the entire region, some 2,500 miles in length, in the fifteenth century. Yet the Incas represented only the most recent and the largest in a long history of civilizations in the area.

The coastal region of central Peru had in fact generated one of the world's First Civilizations, known as Norte Chico, dating back to around 3000 B.C.E. (see Chapter 3). The classical era in Andean civilization, roughly 1000 B.C.E. to 1000 C.E., provides an opportunity to look briefly at several of the cultures that followed Norte Chico and preceded the Inca civilization. Because none of them had developed writing, historians are largely dependent on archeology for an understanding of these civilizations.

Chavín: A Pan-Andean Religious Movement

■ Connection

What kind of influence did Chavín exert in the Andes region?

In both the coastal and highland regions of Peru, archeologists have uncovered numerous local ceremonial centers or temple complexes, dating to between 2000 and 1000 B.C.E. Often constructed in a characteristic U shape, they were associated with small-scale irrigation projects and suggest the growing authority of religious leaders. Human trophy heads indicate raiding, warfare, and violence among these local centers. Then around 900 B.C.E., one of them, located in the Andean highlands at a village called Chavín de Huántar, became the focus of a religious movement that soon swept through both coastal and highland Peru.

Chavín de Huántar enjoyed a strategic location, high in the Andes and situated on trade routes to both the coastal region to the west and the Amazon rain forest to the east. By perhaps 750 B.C.E., it had become a small town of 2,000 to 3,000 people, with clear distinctions between an elite class, who lived in stone houses, and ordinary people, with adobe dwellings. An elaborate temple complex included numerous galleries, hidden passageways, staircases, ventilation shafts, drainage canals, and distinctive carvings. Little is known about the rituals or beliefs that animated Chavín's religious practice, but the artwork suggests that it drew on ideas from both the desert coastal region and the rain forests. Major deities were represented as jaguars, crocodiles, and snakes, all of them native to the Amazon basin. Shamans or priests likely made use of the San Pedro cactus and its hallucinogenic properties to penetrate the supernatural world. Some of the fantastic artwork of this civilization—its jaguar-human images, for example—may well reflect the visions of these religious leaders.

Over the next several centuries, this blended religious movement proved attractive across much of Peru and beyond, as Chavín-style architecture, sculpture, pottery, religious images, and painted textiles were widely imitated within the region. Chavín itself became a pilgrimage site and perhaps a training center for initiates from distant centers. At locations three weeks or more away by llama caravan, temples were remodeled to resemble that of Chavín, although in many cases with locally inspired variations.[15] Much of the spread of Chavín religious imagery and practice paralleled the trade routes that linked highland and coastal Peru. Although there is some evidence for violence and warfare, no Chavín "empire" emerged. Instead, a widespread religious cult, traveling on the back of a trading network, provided for the first time and for several centuries a measure of economic and cultural integration to much of the Peruvian Andes.

Moche: A Regional Andean Civilization

■ Description

What supports scholars' contention that Moche represented a regional civilization in the Andes?

By 200 B.C.E., the pan-Andes Chavín cult had faded, replaced by a number of regional civilizations. Among them, the Moche civilization clearly stands out. Dominating a 250-mile stretch of Peru's northern coast and incorporating thirteen river valleys, the Moche flourished between about 100 and 800 C.E. Their economy was rooted in a complex irrigation system, requiring constant maintenance, which funneled runoff from the Andes into fields of maize, beans, and squash and acres of cotton, all fertilized by rich bird droppings called guano. Moche fishermen also harvested millions of anchovies from the bountiful Pacific.

Politically, Moche was governed by warrior-priests, some of whom lived atop huge pyramids. The largest of these structures, dubbed the Pyramid of the Sun, had been constructed from 143 million sun-dried bricks. There shaman-rulers, often under the influence of hallucinogenic drugs, conducted ancient rituals that mediated between the world of humankind and that of the gods, and they also presided over the ritual sacrifice of human victims, drawn from their many prisoners of war, which became central to the politico-religious life of the Moche. Images on Moche pottery show a ruler attired in a magnificent feather headdress and seated on a pyramid, while a parade of naked prisoners marches past him. Other scenes of decapitation and dismemberment indicate the fate that awaited those destined for sacrifice. For these rulers, the Moche world was apparently one of war, ritual, and diplomacy.

The immense wealth of this warrior-priest elite and the exquisite artistry of Moche craftsmen are reflected in the elaborate burials accorded the rulers. At one site, Peruvian archeologists uncovered the final resting place of three such individuals, whom they named the Lords of Sipan. Laid in adobe burial chambers, one above the other, each was decked out in his ceremonial regalia—elaborate gold masks, necklaces, and headdresses; turquoise and gold bead bracelets; cotton tunics covered with copper plates; a gold rattle showing a Moche warrior smashing a prisoner with his war club; and a copper knife. In 2005, in another remarkable discovery dating to about 450 C.E., archeologists found the burial place of a very high-status woman, who was in her late twenties and heavily tattooed. She had been laid to rest with hundreds of funeral objects, including gold sewing needles; weaving tools; much gold, silver, and copper jewelry; and a female sacrificial victim lying beside her. Even more suggestive were two elaborate war clubs and twenty-three spear throwers. Was she perhaps a warrior, a priest, or a ruler?

The most accessible aspect of Moche life and much of what scholars know about the Moche world derive from the superb skill of their craftspeople, such as metal-workers, potters, weavers, and painters. Face masks, figures of animals, small earrings, and other jewelry, many plated in gold, display amazing technical abilities and artistic sensibility. On their ceramic pottery are naturalistic portraits of noble lords and rulers and images from the life of common people, including the blind and the sick. Battle scenes show warriors confronting their enemies with raised clubs. Erotic encounters between men and women and gods making love to humans likewise represent common themes, as do grotesque images of their many gods and goddesses. Much of this, of course, reflects the culture of the Moche elite. Scholars know much less about the daily life of the farmers, fishermen, weavers, traders, construction workers, and servants whose labor made that elite culture possible.

These cultural achievements, however, rested on fragile environmental foundations, for the region was subject to periodic drought, earthquakes, and occasional

The Lord of Sipan
The Moche ruler in the center of the grave, dating to about 290 C.E., was about forty years old when he died and, at five feet five inches, was quite tall for the time. Except for early signs of arthritis, he was in good health and seems to have performed little physical labor during his life. Accompanying him in death were the four individuals shown here, plus three young women, a priest, a guard, a dog, and considerable food and drink. (Kevin Schafter/Corbis)

torrential rains associated with El Niño episodes. Scholars believe that during the sixth century C.E. some combination of these forces caused extended ecological disruption, which seriously undermined Moche civilization. In these circumstances, the Moche were vulnerable to aggressive neighbors and possibly to internal social tensions as well. By the end of the eighth century C.E., that civilization had passed into history.[16]

The Chavín and Moche civilizations were but two of the many that grew up in the Andes region before the Incas consolidated the entire area into a single empire. The Nazca, for example, on the arid southern coast of Peru, have become famous for their underground irrigation canals, polychrome pottery, and textiles, but especially for their gigantic and mysterious lines in the desert in the form of monkeys, birds, spiders, whales, and various abstract designs. In the interior, a series of larger states emerged. One of them was centered on Tiwanaku, a city of monumental buildings and perhaps 40,000 to 50,000 people that flourished during much of the first millennium C.E. The Huari and Chimu kingdoms were further examples of this Andean civilization, to which the Incas gave a final and spectacular expression before all of the Americas was swallowed up in European empires from across the sea.

North America in the Classical Era: From Chaco to Cahokia

North America in the Classical Era

The peoples of the Americas in the pre-Columbian era might be divided into three large groupings. The most prominent and well known are those of the Mesoamerican and Andean regions, where cities, states, and dense populations created civilizations broadly similar to those of classical Eurasia. Elsewhere, gathering and hunting peoples carried on that most ancient of human adaptations to the environment. Arctic and subarctic cultures; the bison hunters of the Great Plains; the complex and settled communities of the Pacific coast, such as the Chumash (see Chapter 1); nomadic bands living in the arid regions of southern South America—all of these represent the persistence of gathering and hunting peoples in substantial regions of the Americas.

Even larger areas—the eastern woodlands of the United States, Central America, the Amazon basin, the Caribbean islands—were populated by peoples sometimes defined as "semi-sedentary."[17] These were agricultural societies, although less intensive and productive than those of Mesoamerica or the Andes and supporting usually much smaller populations. Nor did they generate large urban centers or inclusive empires.

These peoples who lived beyond the direct reach of the major civilizations also made their own histories, changing in response to their unique environments, their interactions with outsiders, and their own visions of the world. The Anasazi of the southwestern United States, now called the Ancestral Pueblo, and the mound-building cultures of the eastern woodlands provide two illustrations from North America during the classical era.

Pit Houses and Great Houses: The Ancestral Pueblo

The southwestern region of North America, an arid land cut by mountain ranges and large basins, first acquired maize from its place of origin in Mesoamerica during the second millennium B.C.E., but it took roughly 2,000 years for that crop, later supplemented by beans and squash, to become the basis of a settled agricultural way of living. In a desert region, farming was risky, and maize had to be gradually adapted to the local environment. Not until around 600 to 800 C.E. did permanent village life take hold widely. People then lived in pit houses with floors sunk several feet below ground level. Some settlements had only a few such homes, whereas others contained twenty-five or more. By 900 C.E., many of these villages also included kivas, much larger pit structures used for ceremonial purposes, which symbolized the widespread belief that humankind emerged into this world from another world below. Individual settlements were linked to one another in local trading networks and sometimes in wider webs of exchange that brought them buffalo hides, copper, turquoise, seashells, macaw feathers, and coiled baskets from quite distant locations.

■ **Comparison**

In what ways were the histories of the Ancestral Pueblo and the Mound Builders similar to each other, and how did they differ?

Pueblo Bonito
Called Pueblo Bonito ("pretty village") by the Spanish, this great house of the Ancestral Pueblo people was at its high point in the eleventh century C.E. The circular structures, known as kivas, were probably ceremonial sites. Their prominence, and the absence of major trash collections, have persuaded some scholars that Pueblo Bonito was more of a ritual center than a residential town. (Courtesy, Chaco Canyon National Historic Park)

These processes of change—growing dependence on agriculture, increasing population, more intensive patterns of exchange—gave rise to larger settlements and adjacent aboveground structures known as pueblos. The most spectacular of these took shape in Chaco canyon in what is now northwestern New Mexico. There, between 860 and 1130 C.E., five major pueblos emerged. This Chaco Phenomenon encompassed 25,000 square miles and linked some seventy outlying settlements to the main centers. The population was not large, perhaps as few as 5,000 people, although experts continue to debate the issue. The largest of these towns or "great houses," Pueblo Bonito, stood five stories high and contained more than 600 rooms and many kivas. Hundreds of miles of roads, up to forty feet wide, radiated out from Chaco, likewise prompting much debate among scholars. Without wheeled carts or large domesticated animals, such an elaborate road system seems unnecessary for ordinary trade or travel. Did the roads represent, as some scholars speculate, a "sacred landscape which gave order to the world," joining its outlying communities to a Middle Place, an entrance perhaps to the underworld?[18]

Among the Chaco elite were highly skilled astronomers, who constructed an observatory of three large rock slabs situated so as to throw a beam of light across a spiral rock carving behind it at the summer solstice. By the eleventh century, Chaco also had become a dominant center for the production of turquoise ornaments, which became a major item of regional commerce. Not all was sweetness and light, however. Warfare, internal conflict, and occasional cannibalism (a matter of much controversy among scholars) apparently increased in frequency as an extended period of drought in the half century following 1130 brought this flourishing culture to a rather abrupt end. By 1200, the great houses had been abandoned, and their inhabitants became scattered in small communities that later became the Pueblo peoples of more recent times.

The Mound Builders of the Eastern Woodlands

Unlike the Chaco region in the southwest, the eastern woodlands of North America and especially the Mississippi River valley hosted an independent Agricultural Revolution. By 2000 B.C.E., many of its peoples had domesticated local plant species, including sunflowers, sumpweed, goosefoot, some gourds and squashes, and a form of artichoke. These few plants, however, were not sufficient to support a fully settled agricultural village life; rather they supplemented diets derived from gathering and hunting without fundamentally changing that ancient way of life. Such peoples created societies distinguished by arrays of large earthen mounds, found all over the United States east of the Mississippi, prompting archeologists to dub them the Mound Builders.[19] The earliest of them date to around 2000 B.C.E., but the most elaborate and widespread of these mound-building cultures took shape between 200 B.C.E. and 400 C.E. and is known to scholars as the Hopewell culture, after an archeological site in Ohio.

Several features of the Hopewell culture have intrigued archeologists. Particularly significant are the striking burial mounds and geometric earthworks, sometimes covering areas equivalent to several city blocks, and the wide variety of artifacts found within them—smoking pipes, human figurines, mica mirrors, flint blades, fabrics, and jewelry of all kinds. The mounds themselves were no doubt the focus of elaborate burial rituals, but some of them were aligned with the moon with such precision as to allow the prediction of lunar eclipses. Developed most elaborately in the Ohio River valley, Hopewell-style earthworks, artifacts, and ceremonial pottery have also been found throughout the eastern woodlands region of North America. Hopewell centers in Ohio contained mica from the Appalachian mountains, volcanic glass from Yellowstone, conch shells and sharks' teeth from the Gulf of Mexico, and copper from the Great Lakes. All of this suggests an enormous "Hopewell Interaction Sphere," linking this huge region in a loose network of exchange, as well as a measure of cultural borrowing of religious ideas and practices within this immense area.[20]

The next and most spectacular phase in the history of these mound-building peoples took shape as corn-based agriculture, derived ultimately but indirectly from

Mexico, gained ground in the Mississippi valley after 800 C.E., allowing larger populations and more complex societies to emerge. The dominant center was Cahokia, near present-day St. Louis, Missouri, which flourished from about 900 to 1250 C.E. Its central mound, a terraced pyramid of four levels, measured 1,000 feet long by 700 feet wide, rose more than 100 feet above the ground, and occupied fifteen acres. It was the largest structure north of Mexico, the focal point of a community numbering 10,000 or more people, and the center of a widespread trading network (see an artist's reconstruction of Cahokia on p. 52).

Cahokia emerged and flourished at about the same time as did the great houses of Chaco canyon, but its urban presence was far larger than that of its southwestern counterpart. Both were made possible by the arrival of corn-based agriculture, originating in Mesoamerica, though direct contact with Mexico is much more apparent in Chaco. Finally, Cahokia emerged as the climax of a long history of mound-building cultures in the eastern woodlands, whereas Chaco was more of a "start-up" culture, emerging quite quickly "with a relatively shallow history."[21]

Evidence from burials and from later Spanish observers suggests that Cahokia and other centers of this Mississippi culture were stratified societies with a clear elite and with rulers able to mobilize the labor required to build such enormous structures. One high-status male was buried on a platform of 20,000 shell beads, accompanied by 800 arrowheads, sheets of copper and mica, and a number of sacrificed men and women nearby.[22] Well after Cahokia had declined and was abandoned, sixteenth-century Spanish and French explorers encountered another such chiefdom among the Natchez people, located in southwestern Mississippi. Paramount chiefs, known as Great Suns, dressed in knee-length fur coats and lived luxuriously in deerskin-covered homes. An elite class of "principal men" or "honored peoples" clearly occupied a different status from commoners, sometimes referred to as "stinkards." These sharp class distinctions were blunted by the requirement that upper-class people, including the Great Suns, had to marry "stinkards."

The military capacity of these Mississippi chiefdoms greatly impressed European observers, as this Spanish account indicates:

> The next day the cacique [paramount chief] arrived with 200 canoes filled with men, having weapons . . . the warriors standing erect from bow to stern, holding bows and arrows. . . . [F]rom under the canopy where the chief man was, the course was directed and orders issued to the rest. . . . [W]hat with the awnings, the plumes, the shields, the pennons, and the number of people in the fleet, it appeared like a famous armada of galleys.[23]

Here then in the eastern woodlands of North America were peoples who independently generated a modest Agricultural Revolution, assimilated corn and beans from distant sources, developed increasingly complex societies, and created monumental structures, new technologies, and artistic traditions. In doing so, they gave rise to a regional cultural complex that enveloped much of the United

States east of the Mississippi in a network of ceremonial, economic, and cultural exchange.

Reflections: Deciding What's Important: Balance in World History

Among the perennial problems that teachers and writers of world history confront is sorting through the vast record of times past and choosing what to include and what to leave out. A related issue involves the extent to which particular peoples or civilizations will be treated. Should the Persians get as much space as the Greeks? Does Africa merit equal treatment with Eurasia? Where do the Americas fit in the larger human story? What, in short, are the criteria for deciding what is important in telling the story of the human venture?

One standard might be duration. Should ways of living that have endured for longer periods of time receive greater attention than those of lesser length? If only this criterion was followed, then the Paleolithic era of gathering and hunting should occupy 90 percent or more of any world history text. On the other hand, perhaps change is more important than continuity. If so, then something new merits more space than something old. Thus we pay attention to both agriculture and civilizations because they represent significant turning points in human experience. Population provides yet another principle for determining inclusion. That, of course, is the reason that Eurasia, with about 80 percent of the world's population during the classical era, is addressed in three chapters, whereas Africa and the Americas together receive only one chapter. There is also the related issue of influence. Buddhism, Christianity, and Islam spread more widely and shaped the lives of more people than did the religions of the Maya or the Bantu-speaking peoples of Africa. Do they therefore deserve more extended treatment?

A final possible criterion involves the location of the historian and his or her audience. The recent development of world history as a field of study has sought vigorously to counteract a Eurocentric telling of the human story. Still, is there anything inherently wrong with an account of world history that is centered on one's own people? When I taught history in an Ethiopian high school in the mid-1960s, I was guided by an Afrocentric curriculum, which focused first on Ethiopian history, then on Africa as a whole, and finally on the larger world. Might a world historian from the Middle East, for example, legitimately strike a somewhat different balance in the treatment of various civilizations than someone writing for a largely Western audience or for Chinese readers?

Any account of the world's past will mix and match these criteria in various and contested ways. Among scholars, there exists neither a consensus about this question nor any formula to ensure a "proper" balance. You may want to consider whether the balance struck in this chapter, this section, and the book as a whole is appropriate or somehow out of line.

Second Thoughts

What's the Significance?

Meroë

Axum

Niger Valley civilization

Bantu expansion

Maya civilization

Teotihuacán

Chavín

Moche

Chaco Phenomenon

Cahokia

Big Picture Questions

1. "The histories of Africa and the Americas during the classical era largely resemble those of Eurasia." Do you agree with this statement? Explain why or why not.
2. "The particular cultures and societies of Africa and of the Americas discussed in this chapter developed largely in isolation from one another." What evidence would support this statement, and what might challenge it?
3. What generated change in the histories of Africa and the Americas during the classical era?

Next Steps: For Further Study

Richard E. W. Adams, *Ancient Civilizations of the New World* (1997). A broad survey based on current scholarship of the Americas before Columbus.

Christopher Ehret, *The Civilizations of Africa* (2002). A recent overview of African history before 1800 by a prominent scholar.

Brian M. Fagan, *Ancient North America* (2005). A prominent archeologist's account of North American history.

Eric Gilbert and Jonathan T. Reynolds, *Africa in World History* (2004). An accessible account of African history set in a global context.

Guy Gugliotta, "The Maya: Glory and Ruin," *National Geographic* (August 2007). A beautifully illustrated account of the rise and fall of Maya civilization.

Kairn A. Klieman, "*The Pygmies Were Our Compass*" (2003). A scholarly examination of the Pygmies (Batwa) of the Congo River basin and their interaction with Bantu-speaking peoples.

Charles Mann, *1491* (2005). A thoughtful journalist's account, delightfully written, of the controversies surrounding the history of the Americas before 1492.

"Ancient Africa's Black Kingdoms," http://www.homestead.com/wysinger/ancientafrica.html. A Web site exploring the history of Nubia.

"Maya Adventures," http://www.smm.org/sln/ma. A collection of text and pictures about the Maya, past and present.

PART THREE

An Age
of Accelerating
Connections

500–1500

Contents

Defining a Millennium

History seldom turns sharp corners, and historians often have difficulty deciding just when one phase of the human story ends and another begins. Between roughly 200 and 850 C.E., many of the classical states and civilizations of the world (Han dynasty China, the Roman Empire, Gupta India, Meroë, Axum, Maya, Teotihuacán, Moche) experienced severe disruption, decline, or collapse. For many historians, this marks the end of the classical era and the start of some new period of world history. Furthermore, almost everyone agrees that the transatlantic voyages of Columbus around 1500 represent yet another new departure in world history. This coupling of the Eastern and Western hemispheres set in motion historical processes that transformed most of the world and signaled the beginning of the modern era.

How are we to understand the thousand years (roughly 500 to 1500) between the end of the classical era and the beginning of modern world history? Historians, frankly, have had some difficulty in defining a distinct identity for this millennium, and this problem is reflected in the vague terms used to describe it. Many textbooks, including this one on occasion, refer to this 1,000-year period simply as the "postclassical" age, but that, of course, merely indicates that it came after the classical era. Others have termed it "medieval," a middle or intermediate age, something in between the classical and modern eras. Many historians feel uncomfortable with this term because it derives specifically from European history and thus runs the risk of appearing Eurocentric. It also seems to suggest that this millennium was merely a run-up to modernity, rather than something of significance in its own right. This book sometimes uses the concept of "third-wave civilizations," distinguishing, at least chronologically, those that emerged after 500 C.E. from both the First Civilizations and those of the classical era (the second-wave civilizations). At best, these terms indicate where this period falls in the larger time frame of world history, but none of them are very descriptive.

Third-Wave Civilizations: Something New, Something Old, Something Blended

A large part of the problem lies in the rather different trajectories of various regions of the world during this postclassical era. It is not easy to identify clearly defined features that encompass all the major civilizations during this period and distinguish them from what went before, but we can point to several distinct patterns of development among these third-wave societies of the postclassical era.

In some areas, for example, wholly new but smaller civilizations arose where none had existed before. Along the East African coast, Swahili civilization emerged in a string of thirty or more city-states, very much engaged in the commercial life of the Indian Ocean basin. In the area now encompassed by Ukraine and western Russia, another new civilization, known as Kievan Rus, likewise took shape with a good deal of cultural borrowing from Mediterranean civilization. East and Southeast Asia also witnessed new centers of civilization. Those in Japan, Korea, and Vietnam were strongly influenced by China, while Srivijaya on the Indonesian island of Sumatra and later the Angkor kingdom, centered in present-day Cambodia, drew on the Hindu and Buddhist traditions of India.

All of these represent a continuation of a well-established pattern in world history—the globalization of civilization. It began with the First Civilizations of Mesopotamia, Egypt, and elsewhere about 3000 B.C.E. and then took new and larger forms in the classical era (500 B.C.E.–500 C.E.), when Greco-Roman, Persian, Indian, and Chinese civilizations flourished across Eurasia. Each of the new third-wave civilizations was, of course, culturally unique, but like their predecessors, they too featured states, cities, specialized economic roles, sharp class and gender inequalities, and other elements of "civilized" life. They were certainly distinctive, but not fundamentally different from earlier civilizations. As newcomers to the growing number of civilizations, all of them borrowed heavily from larger or more established centers.

The largest, most expansive, and most widely influential of the new third-wave civilizations was surely that of Islam. It began in Arabia in the seventh century C.E., projecting the Arab peoples into a prominent role as builders of an enormous empire while offering a new, vigorous, and attractive religion. Viewed as a new civilization defined by its religion, the world of Islam came to encompass many other centers of civilization, including Egypt, Mesopotamia, Persia, India, the interior of West Africa and the coast of East Africa, Spain, southeastern Europe, and more. Here was a uniquely cosmopolitan or "umbrella" civilization that, according to one leading scholar, "came closer than any had ever come to uniting all mankind under its ideals."[1]

Yet another, and quite different, historical pattern during the postclassical millennium involved older or classical civilizations that persisted or were reconstructed. The Byzantine Empire, embracing the eastern half of the old Roman Empire, continued the patterns of Mediterranean Christian civilization and persisted until 1453, when it was overrun by the Ottoman Turks. In China, following almost four centuries of fragmentation, the Sui, Tang, and Song dynasties (589–1279) restored China's imperial unity and reasserted its Confucian tradition. Indian civilization retained its ancient patterns of caste and Hinduism amid vast cultural diversity, even as parts of India fell under the control of Muslim rulers. The West African savanna kingdoms of Ghana, Mali, and Songhay, stimulated and sustained by long-distance trade across the Sahara, built upon the earlier Niger Valley civilization.

Variations on this theme of continuing or renewing older traditions took shape in the Western Hemisphere, where two centers of civilization—in Mesoamerica and in the Andes—had been long established. In Mesoamerica, the collapse of classical Maya civilization and of the great city-state of Teotihuacán by about 900 C.E. opened the way for other peoples to give new shape to this ancient civilization. The most well known of these efforts was associated with the Mexica or Aztec people, who created a powerful and impressive state in the fifteenth century. About the same time, on the western rim of South America, a Quechua-speaking people, now known as the Inca, incorporated various centers of Andean civilization into a huge bureaucratic empire. Both the Aztecs and the Incas gave a new political expression to much older patterns of civilized life.

A final pattern took shape in Western Europe following the collapse of the Roman Empire. There would-be kings and church leaders alike sought to maintain links with the older Greco-Roman-Christian traditions of classical Mediterranean civilization. In the absence of empire, though, new and far more decentralized societies emerged, led now by Germanic peoples and centered in Northern and Western Europe, considerably removed from the older centers of Rome and Athens. It was a hybrid civilization, combining old and new, classical and Germanic elements, in a unique blending. For five centuries or more, this region was a relative backwater, compared to the more vibrant, prosperous, and powerful civilizations of the Islamic world and of China. During the centuries after 1000 C.E., however, Western European civilization emerged as a rapidly growing and expansive set of competitive states, willing, like other new civilizations, to borrow quite extensively from their more developed neighbors.

The Ties That Bind: Transregional Interaction in the Postclassical Era

These quite different patterns of development within particular civilizations of the postclassical millennium have made it difficult to define that era in a single, all-encompassing fashion. In another way, though, a common theme emerges, for during this time, the world's various regions, cultures, and peoples interacted with one another far more extensively than before. More than ever, change in human societies was the product of contact with strangers, or at least with their ideas, armies, goods, or diseases. In a variety of places—island Southeast Asia, coastal East Africa, Central Asian cities, parts of Western Europe, the Islamic Middle East, and the Inca Empire—local cosmopolitan regions emerged in which trade, migration, or empire had brought peoples of different cultures together in a restricted space. These "miniglobalizations," both larger and more common than in the classical era, became a distinctive feature of third-wave civilizations.

"No man is an island, entire of itself," wrote the seventeenth-century English poet John Donne. "Every man is a piece of the continent, a part of the main." Much the same might be said of every civilization, culture, or region. None of them were wholly isolated or separate from their neighbors, although the range and intensity of cross-cultural interaction certainly varied over time. In limited ways, that was the case for the First Civilizations as well as their classical successors. Both Egyptian and Mesopotamian cultural influence spread well beyond the core regions of those civilizations. Horseback-riding skills and chariot technology diffused widely across Eurasia. The encounter of the Greeks and Persians changed both of those classical civilizations. Cross-cultural mixing in northern India gave rise to the caste system, while the Silk Road trading networks across Eurasia provided some contact among the distant empires of Rome, China, and India.

The scale and pace of such interaction accelerated considerably during the era of third-wave, or postclassical, civilizations. Much of Part Three highlights these intersections and spells out their many and varied consequences. Three major mechanisms of cross-cultural interaction, which we will meet in the chapters that follow, were of particular significance for transforming the lives and societies of those who took part in them.

One such mechanism was trade. The exchange of goods has been everywhere one of the primary means of cross-cultural interaction, and virtually every human society has engaged in it at some level. Although most trade in the premodern world occurred locally among nearby communities, world historians have focused attention especially on long-distance trade, commercial relationships that linked distant human communities. This kind of commerce grew considerably during the postclassical era—along the Silk Roads of Eurasia, within the Indian Ocean basin, across the Sahara, and along the Mississippi and other rivers. Everywhere it acted as an agent of change for all of its participants. In places where long-distance trade was practiced extensively, it required that more people devote their energies to producing for a distant market rather than for the consumption of their own communities. Those who controlled this kind of trade often became extremely wealthy, exciting envy or outrage among those less fortunate. Many societies learned about new products via these trade routes. Europe's knowledge of pepper and other spices, for example, derived from Roman seaborne trade with India beginning in the first century C.E. Many centuries later, Europeans' desire for Asian spices played a part in propelling Western commercial and military expansion into the Indian Ocean.

Such trade also had political consequences as many new states or empires were established on the basis of resources derived from long-distance commerce. The West African kingdoms of Ghana and Mali, the Swahili cities of the East African coast, the early eastern Slavic state known as Rus, and the Indonesian state of Srivijaya are four such examples. Furthermore, far more than goods traveled the trade routes that linked various third-wave civilizations with one another. Religious ideas, technologies, and germs also made their ways along those paths of commerce, bringing significant change to their participants.

Yet another mechanism of cross-cultural interaction lay in large empires. Not only did they incorporate many distinct cultures within a single political system, but their size and stability also provided the security that encouraged travelers and traders to journey long distances from their homelands. Empires, of course, were nothing new in world history, but many of those associated with third-wave civilizations were distinctive. In the first place, they were larger. The Arab Empire, which accompanied the initial spread of Islam, stretched from Spain to India. Even more extensive was the Mongol Empire of the thirteenth and fourteenth centuries. In the Western Hemisphere, the Inca Empire encompassed dozens of distinct peoples in a huge state that ran some 2,500 miles along the spine of the Andes Mountains.

Furthermore, the largest of these empires were the creation of nomadic or pastoral peoples. Classical empires in the Mediterranean basin, China, India, and Persia had been the work of settled farming societies. But now, in the thousand years between 500 and 1500, peoples with a recent history of a nomadic or herding way of life entered the stage of world history as empire builders—Arabs, Turks, Mongols, Aztecs—ruling over agricultural peoples and established civilizations. These empires changed those who created them as well as those who were forcibly incorporated within them. They also did much to foster cross-cultural interaction. Marco Polo, for example, made his way from Italy to China and back in the thirteenth century, thanks largely to the security provided by the Mongol Empire.

Together, large-scale empires and long-distance trade facilitated the spread of ideas, technologies, food crops, and germs far beyond their points of origin. Buddhism spread from India to much of Asia; Christianity encompassed Europe and took root in distant Russia as well as in northeastern Africa, southern India, and western China. Hinduism attracted followers in Southeast Asia; and more than any of the other world religions, Islam became an Afro-Eurasian phenomenon with an enormous reach. Beyond the connections born of commerce and conquest, those of culture and religion generated lasting ties among many peoples of the Eastern Hemisphere.

Technologies, too, were diffused widely. Until the sixth century C.E., China maintained a monopoly on the manufacture of raw silk. Then this technology spread beyond East Asia, allowing the development of a silk industry in the eastern Mediterranean and later in Italy. India too contributed much to the larger world—crystallized sugar, a system of numerals and the concept of zero, techniques for making cotton textiles, and many food crops. Arabs, who were responsible for spreading many of these Indian innovations, found India a "place of marvels."[2] In the Americas, corn gradually diffused from Mesoamerica, where it was initially domesticated, to North America, where it stimulated population growth and the development of more complex societies. Disease also linked distant communities. The plague, or Black Death, decimated many parts of Eurasia and North Africa as it made its deadly way from east to west in the fourteenth century.

A focus on these accelerating connections across cultural boundaries puts the historical spotlight on merchants, travelers, missionaries, migrants, soldiers, and administrators—people who traveled abroad rather than those who stayed at home. Frequently, they stimulated cultural change in the lands they visited, and of course they themselves often were changed by the experience. More than a few of the Christian Crusaders who invaded the Middle East to rescue the holy places from Islamic control wound up as Muslims themselves.

This cross-cultural emphasis in world history also raises provocative questions about what happens when cultures interact or when strangers meet. How did external stimuli operate to produce change within particular societies? How did individuals or societies decide what to accept and what to reject when confronted with new ideas or practices? Were they free to decide such questions, or were they acting under pressure or constraints that limited the possibilities of real choice? In what ways did they alter foreign customs or traditions to better meet their own needs and correspond to their own values? These are some of the questions that will arise as we consider the accelerating connections associated with third-wave civilizations.

Landmarks in the Era of Accelerating Connections, 500–1500

500	600	700	800	900

East Asia

589–618
Sui dynasty;
reunification of China

604
Seventeen Article
Constitution
in Japan

688
Withdrawal of
Chinese military
forces from Korea

845
Suppression
of Buddhism
in China

868
First printed
book in China

939
Vietnam establishes
independence
from China

Islamic World

570–632
Life of
Muhammad

650s
Quran compiled

656
Emergence of
Shia Islam

750–900 High point of Abbasid dynasty

800–1000 Emergence of Sufism

The World of Christendom

476
End of western
Roman Empire

527–565
Justinian rules
Byzantine Empire

726–843 Iconoclasm in Byzantium

800
Charlemagne crowned as
new "Roman emperor"

912–961 Reign of
Abd al-Rahman III

988
Conversion
of Kievan
Rus to
Christianity

Africa

300–500
Beginnings of
trans-Saharan trade

7th–8th centuries Introduction of Islam and
Arab culture in North Africa

869–883
African slave
rebellion
in Iraq

900s Kings of Ghana
convert to Islam

The Americas

500 Flourishing
of Teotihuacán

600–1150 Anasazi culture, Ancestral Pueblo

850 Collapse of
Maya civilization

900–1250 Cahokia

950–1150
Flourishing
of Toltec
civilization

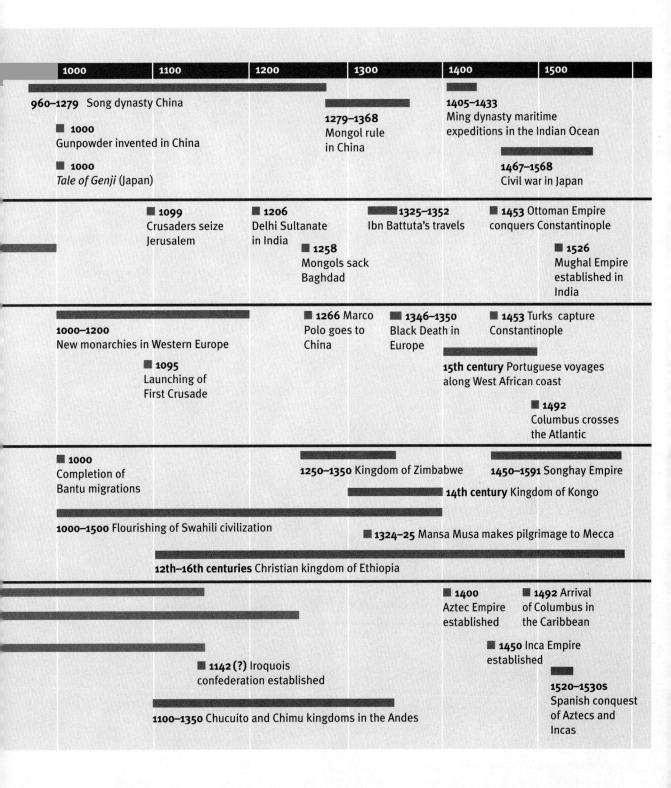

1000	1100	1200	1300	1400	1500

960–1279 Song dynasty China

■ **1000**
Gunpowder invented in China

■ **1000**
Tale of Genji (Japan)

1279–1368
Mongol rule
in China

1405–1433
Ming dynasty maritime
expeditions in the Indian Ocean

1467–1568
Civil war in Japan

■ **1099**
Crusaders seize
Jerusalem

■ **1206**
Delhi Sultanate
in India

■ **1258**
Mongols sack
Baghdad

■ **1325–1352**
Ibn Battuta's travels

■ **1453** Ottoman Empire
conquers Constantinople

■ **1526**
Mughal Empire
established in
India

1000–1200
New monarchies in Western Europe

■ **1095**
Launching of
First Crusade

■ **1266** Marco
Polo goes to
China

■ **1346–1350**
Black Death in
Europe

■ **1453** Turks capture
Constantinople

15th century Portuguese voyages
along West African coast

■ **1492**
Columbus crosses
the Atlantic

■ **1000**
Completion of
Bantu migrations

1250–1350 Kingdom of Zimbabwe

1450–1591 Songhay Empire

14th century Kingdom of Kongo

1000–1500 Flourishing of Swahili civilization

■ **1324–25** Mansa Musa makes pilgrimage to Mecca

12th–16th centuries Christian kingdom of Ethiopia

■ **1400**
Aztec Empire
established

■ **1492** Arrival
of Columbus in
the Caribbean

■ **1450** Inca Empire
established

■ **1142 (?)** Iroquois
confederation established

1520–1530s
Spanish conquest
of Aztecs and
Incas

1100–1350 Chucuito and Chimu kingdoms in the Andes

CHAPTER EIGHT

Commerce and Culture

500–1500

"Forget compass readings, camel caravans, and disorienting, potentially deadly Jeep journeys through the world's most fabled and forbidding desert. Soon it will be possible to take a leisurely drive along a paved two-lane highway from the spot where Europe kisses the tip of this continent into the heart of sub-Saharan Africa. That's the idea, anyway."[1] So wrote a journalist for the *New York Times* in late 2003, describing international plans for a modern highway across the Sahara, linking Europe and North Africa with the vast interior of West Africa. Such a road, its advocates hoped, would not only promote tourism, trade, and economic growth but also provide an alternative route for West African Muslims making the pilgrimage to Mecca. At the same time, in early 2004, some twenty-three nations signed an agreement to build a network of highways all across Asia, ultimately linking Tokyo with Istanbul and enabling a number of landlocked countries of Central Asia to participate more fully in the world economy.

THESE TWO AMBITIOUS PROJECTS OF THE EARLY TWENTY-FIRST CENTURY were part of the accumulating infrastructure of contemporary globalization. But they also evoked much older patterns of global commerce, the famous Silk Road network across Eurasia and the trans-Saharan trade routes, both of which flourished in the postclassical era. Here is a reminder, from the viewpoint of world history, that exchange among distant peoples is not altogether new and that the roots of economic globalization lie deep in the past.

The exchange of goods among communities occupying different ecological zones has long been a prominent feature of human history.

Travels on the Silk Road: This Chinese ceramic figurine from the Tang dynasty (618–907 C.E.) shows a group of musicians riding on a camel along the famous Silk Road commercial network that long linked the civilizations of western and eastern Eurasia. (©Asian Art & Archaeology, Inc./Corbis)

Coastlands and highlands, steppes and farmlands, islands and mainlands, valleys and mountains, deserts and forests—each generates different products desired by others. Furthermore, some societies have been able to monopolize, at least temporarily, the production of particular products, such as silk in China or certain spices in Southeast Asia, that others have found valuable. This uneven distribution of goods and resources, whether natural or resulting from human activity, has long motivated exchange, not only within particular civilizations or regions but among them as well. In the world of 500–1500, long-distance trade became more important than ever before in linking and shaping distant societies and peoples. For the most part, it was indirect, a chain of separate transactions in which goods traveled farther than individual merchants. Nonetheless, a network of exchange and communication extending all across the Afro-Eurasian world, and separately in parts of the Americas as well, slowly came into being.

In what ways was trade significant? How did it generate change within the societies that it connected? Economically speaking, it often altered consumption, enabling West Africans, for example, to import scarce salt, necessary for human diets and useful for seasoning and preserving food, from distant mines in the Sahara in exchange for the gold of their region. Trade also affected the day-to-day working lives of many people, encouraging them to specialize in producing particular products for sale in distant markets rather than for use in their own communities. Trade, in short, diminished the economic self-sufficiency of local societies.

Trade shaped the structure of those societies as well. Traders often became a distinct social group, viewed with suspicion by others because of their impulse to accumulate wealth without actually producing anything themselves. In some societies, trade became a means of social mobility, as Chinese merchants, for example, were able to purchase landed estates and establish themselves within the gentry class. Long-distance trade also enabled elite groups in society to distinguish themselves from commoners by acquiring prestigious goods from a distance—silk, tortoiseshells, rhinoceros horn, or particular feathers, for example. The association with faraway or powerful societies, signaled by the possession of their luxury goods, often conveyed status in communities more remote from major civilizations.

Political life also was sometimes transformed by trade. The wealth available from controlling and taxing trade motivated the creation of states in various parts of the world and sustained those states once they had been constructed. Furthermore, commerce posed a set of problems to governments everywhere. Should trade be left in private hands, as in the Aztec Empire, or should it be controlled by the state, as in the Inca Empire? How should state authorities deal with men of commerce, who were both economically useful and potentially disruptive?

Moreover, the saddlebags of camel caravans or the cargo holds of merchant vessels carried more than goods. Trade became the vehicle for the spread of religious ideas, technological innovations, disease-bearing germs, and plants and animals to regions far from their places of origin. In just this fashion, Buddhism made its way from India to Central and East Asia, and Islam crossed the Sahara into West Africa. So did the pathogens that devastated much of Eurasia during the Black Death. These immense cultural and biological transformations were among the most significant outcomes of the increasingly dense network of long-distance commerce during the era of third-wave civilizations.

Silk Roads: Exchange across Eurasia

The Eurasian landmass has long been home to the majority of humankind as well as to the world's most productive agriculture, largest civilizations, and greatest concentration of pastoral peoples. Beyond its many separate societies and cultures, Eurasia also gave rise to one of the world's most extensive and sustained networks of exchange among its diverse peoples. Known to scholars as the Silk Roads, a reference to its most famous product, these land-based trade routes linked pastoral and agricultural peoples as well as the large civilizations on the continent's outer rim (see Map 8.1). None of its numerous participants knew the full extent of this network's reach, for it was largely a "relay trade" in which goods were passed down the line, changing hands many times before reaching their final destination. Nonetheless, the Silk Roads provide a certain unity and coherence to Eurasian history alongside the distinct stories of its separate civilizations and peoples (see Map 8.1).

Map 8.1 The Silk Roads
For 2,000 years, goods, ideas, technologies, and diseases made their way across Eurasia on the several routes of the Silk Roads.

The Growth of the Silk Roads

■ Change
What lay behind the emergence of Silk Road commerce, and what kept it going for so many centuries?

The beginnings of the Silk Roads lay in both geography and history. As a geographic unit, Eurasia is often divided into inner and outer zones that represent quite different environments. Outer Eurasia consists of relatively warm, well-watered areas, suitable for agriculture, which provided the setting for the great civilizations of China, India, the Middle East, and the Mediterranean. Inner Eurasia, the lands of eastern Russia and Central Asia, lies farther north and has a harsher and drier climate, much of it not conducive to agriculture. Long inhabited by pastoral peoples herding their animals from horseback, the people of this region had for centuries traded with and raided their agricultural neighbors to the south. Products of the forest and of semi-arid northern grasslands known as the steppes—such as hides, furs, livestock, wool, and amber—were exchanged for the agricultural products and manufactured goods of adjacent civilizations. The movement of pastoral peoples for thousands of years also served to diffuse Indo-European languages, bronze metallurgy, horse-based technologies, and more all across Eurasia.

The construction of the classical civilizations and their imperial states during the last five centuries B.C.E. added another element to these earlier Eurasian connections. From the south, the Persian Empire invaded the territory of pastoral peoples in present-day Turkmenistan and Uzbekistan. From the west, Alexander the Great's empire stretched well into Central Asia. From the east, China's Han dynasty extended its authority westward, seeking to control the nomadic Xiongnu and to gain access to the powerful "heavenly horses" that were so important to Chinese military forces. By the early centuries of the Common Era, indirect trading connections, often brokered by pastoral peoples, linked the classical civilizations in a network of transcontinental exchange.

Silk Road trading networks prospered most when large and powerful states provided security for merchants and travelers. Such conditions prevailed during the classical era when the Roman and Chinese empires anchored long-distance commerce at the western and eastern ends of Eurasia. Silk Road trade flourished again during the seventh and eighth centuries C.E. as the Byzantine Empire, the Muslim Abbasid dynasty, and Tang dynasty China created an almost continuous belt of strong states across Eurasia. In the thirteenth and fourteenth centuries, the Mongol Empire briefly encompassed almost the entire route of the Silk Roads in a single state, giving a renewed vitality to long-distance trade.

Goods in Transit

During such times especially, a vast array of goods (detailed in the following Snapshot) made their way across the Silk Roads, often carried in large camel caravans that traversed the harsh and dangerous steppes, deserts, and oases of Central Asia. In high demand and hard to find, most of these goods were luxury products, destined for an elite and wealthy market, rather than staple goods, for only readily moved

$\mathcal{S}$napshot   **Economic Exchange along the Silk Roads**

Region	Products Contributed to Silk Road Commerce
China	silk, bamboo, mirrors, gunpowder, paper, rhubarb, ginger, lacquerware, chrysanthemums
Forest lands of Siberia and grasslands of Central Asia	furs, walrus tusks, amber, livestock, horses, falcons, hides, copper vessels, tents, saddles, slaves
India	cotton, herbal medicine, precious stones, spices
Middle East	dates, nuts, almonds, dried fruit, dyes, lapis lazuli, swords
Mediterranean basin	gold coins, glassware, glazes, grapevines, jewelry, artworks, perfume, wool and linen textiles, olive oil

commodities of great value could compensate for the high costs of transportation across such long and forbidding distances.

Of all these luxury goods, it was silk that came to symbolize this Eurasian exchange system. When China held a monopoly on silk-producing technology, this precious fabric moved generally from east to west. The demand for silk as well as cotton textiles from India was so great in the Roman Empire that various Roman writers were appalled at the drain of resources that it represented. They also were outraged at the moral impact of wearing revealing silk garments. "I can see clothes of silk," lamented Seneca the Younger in the first century C.E., "if materials that do not hide the body, nor even one's decency, can be called clothes....Wretched flocks of maids labour so that the adulteress may be visible through her thin dress, so that her husband has no more acquaintance than any outsider or foreigner with his wife's body."[2] By the sixth century C.E., however, the knowledge and technology for producing raw silk had spread beyond China. An old Chinese story attributes it to a Chinese princess who smuggled out silkworms in her turban when she was married off to a Central Asian ruler. In a European version of the tale, Christian monks living in China did the deed by hiding some silkworms in a bamboo cane, an act of industrial espionage that allowed an independent silk-producing and silk-weaving industry to take hold in the Byzantine Empire. However it happened, Koreans, Japanese, Indians, and Persians likewise learned how to produce this precious fabric.

As the supply of silk increased, its many varieties circulated even more extensively across Eurasian trade routes. In Central Asia, silk was used as currency and as a means of accumulating wealth. In both China and the Byzantine Empire, silk became a symbol of high status, and governments passed laws that restricted silk clothing to members of the elite. Furthermore, silk became associated with the sacred in the expanding world religions of Buddhism and Christianity. Chinese Buddhist pilgrims who made their way to India seeking religious texts and relics took with them large quantities of silk as gifts to the monasteries they visited.

■ **Significance**
What made silk such a highly desired commodity across Eurasia?

Buddhist monks in China received purple silk robes from Tang dynasty emperors as a sign of high honor. In the world of Christendom, silk wall hangings, altar covers, and vestments became highly prestigious signs of devotion and piety. Because no independent silk industry developed in Western Europe until the twelfth century C.E., a considerable market developed for silks imported from the Islamic world. Ironically, the splendor of Christian churches depended in part on Islamic trading networks and on silks manufactured in the Muslim world. Some of those silks were even inscribed with passages in Arabic from the Quran, unbeknownst to their European buyers.[3]

■ **Connection**

What were the major economic, social, and cultural consequences of Silk Road commerce?

Compared to contemporary global commerce, the volume of trade on the Silk Roads was small, and its focus on luxury goods limited its direct impact on most people. Nonetheless, it had important economic and social consequences. Peasants in the Yangzi River delta of southern China sometimes gave up the cultivation of food crops, choosing to focus instead on producing silk, paper, porcelain, lacquerware, or iron tools, much of which was destined for the markets of the Silk Roads. In this way, the impact of long-distance trade trickled down to affect the lives of ordinary farmers. Furthermore, favorably placed individuals could benefit immensely from long-distance trade. The twelfth-century Persian merchant Ramisht made a personal fortune from his long-distance trading business and with his profits purchased an enormously expensive silk covering for the Kaaba, the central shrine of Islam in Mecca.[4]

Cultures in Transit

■ **Change**

What accounted for the spread of Buddhism along the Silk Roads?

More important even than the economic impact of the Silk Roads was their role as a conduit of culture. Buddhism in particular, a cultural product of Indian civilization, spread widely throughout Central and East Asia, owing much to the activities of merchants along the Silk Roads. From its beginnings in India during the sixth century B.C.E., Buddhism had appealed to merchants, who preferred its universal message to that of a Brahmin-dominated Hinduism that privileged the higher castes. Indian traders and Buddhist monks, sometimes supported by rulers such as Ashoka, brought the new religion to the trans-Eurasian trade routes. To the west, Persian Zoroastrianism largely blocked the spread of Buddhism, but in the oasis cities of Central Asia, such as Merv, Samarkand, Khotan, and Dunhuang, Buddhism quickly took hold. By the first century B.C.E., many of the inhabitants of these towns had converted to Buddhism, and foreign merchant communities soon introduced it to northern China as well.[5]

Conversion to Buddhism in the oasis cities was a voluntary process, without the pressure of conquest or foreign rule. Dependent on long-distance trade, the inhabitants and rulers of those sophisticated and prosperous cities found in Buddhism a link to the larger, wealthy, and prestigious civilization of India. Well-to-do Buddhist merchants could earn religious merit by building monasteries and supporting monks. The monasteries in turn provided convenient and culturally familiar places of rest and resupply for merchants making the long and arduous trek across Central Asia. Many of these cities became cosmopolitan centers of learning and commerce. Scholars have found thousands of Buddhist texts in the city of Dunhuang, where several branches of the Silk Roads joined to enter western China, together with hundreds of cave temples, lavishly decorated with murals and statues.

Outside of the oasis communities, Buddhism progressed only slowly among pastoral peoples of Central Asia. The absence of a written language was an obstacle to the penetration of a highly literate religion, and their nomadic ways made the founding of monasteries, so important to Buddhism, quite difficult. But as pastoralists became involved in long-distance trade or came to rule settled agricultural peoples, Buddhism seemed more attractive. The nomadic Jie people, who controlled much of northern China after the collapse of the Han dynasty, are a case in point. Their ruler in the early fourth century C.E., Shi Le, became acquainted with a Buddhist monk called Fotudeng, who had traveled widely on the Silk Roads. The monk's reputation as a miracle worker, a rain-maker, and a fortune-teller and his skills as a military strategist cemented a personal relationship with Shi Le and led to the conversions of thousands and the construction of hundreds of Buddhist temples. In China itself, Buddhism remained for many centuries a religion of foreign merchants or foreign rulers. Only slowly did it become popular among the Chinese themselves, a process examined more closely in Chapter 9.

As Buddhism spread across the Silk Roads from India to Central Asia, China, and beyond, it also changed. The original faith had shunned the material world, but Buddhist monasteries in the rich oasis towns of the Silk Roads found themselves very much involved in secular affairs. Some of them became quite wealthy, receiving gifts from well-to-do merchants, artisans, and local rulers. The begging bowls of the monks became a symbol rather than a daily activity. Sculptures and murals in the monasteries depicted musicians and acrobats, women applying makeup, and even drinking parties.[6]

Doctrines changed as well. It was the more devotional Mahayana form of Buddhism (see Chapter 5)—featuring the Buddha as a deity, numerous bodhisattvas, an emphasis on compassion, and the possibility of earning merit—that flourished on the Silk Roads, rather than the more austere psychological teachings of the original Buddha. Moreover, Buddhism picked up elements of other cultures

Dunhuang

Located in western China at a critical junction of the Silk Road trading network, Dunhuang was also a center of Buddhist learning, painting, and sculpture as that religion made its way from India to China and beyond. In some 492 caves, a remarkable gallery of Buddhist art has been preserved. These images of Buddhist deities and heavenly beings date from the sixth century C.E. (© Benoy K. Behl) while in transit on the Silk Roads. In the area northwest of India that had been influenced by the invasions of Alexander the Great, statues of the Buddha reveal distinctly Greek influences. The Greco-Roman mythological figure of Herakles, the son of Zeus and associated with great strength, courage, masculinity, and sexual prowess, was used to represent Vajrapani, one of the divine protectors of the Buddha. In a similar way, the gods of many peoples along the Silk Roads were incorporated into Buddhist practice as bodhisattvas.

Disease in Transit

■ **Connection**

What was the impact of disease along the Silk Roads?

Beyond goods and cultures, diseases too traveled the trade routes of Eurasia, and with devastating consequences.[7] Each of the major population centers of the Afro-Eurasian world had developed characteristic disease patterns, mechanisms for dealing with them, and in some cases immunity to them. But when contact among human communities occurred, people were exposed to unfamiliar diseases for which they had little immunity or few effective methods of coping. An early example involved Athens, which in 430–429 B.C.E. was suddenly afflicted by a new and still unidentified infectious disease that had entered Greece via seaborne trade from Egypt, killing perhaps 25 percent of its army and permanently weakening the city-state.

Even more widespread diseases affected the Roman Empire and Han dynasty China during the classical era as the Silk Roads promoted contact all across Eurasia. Smallpox and measles devastated the populations of both empires, contributing to their political collapse. Paradoxically, these disasters may well have strengthened the appeal of Christianity in Europe and Buddhism in China, for both of them offered compassion in the face of immense suffering.

Again in the period between 534 and 750 C.E., intermittent outbreaks of bubonic plague ravaged the coastal areas of the Mediterranean Sea as the black rats that carried the disease arrived via the seaborne trade with India, where they originally lived. What followed was catastrophic. Constantinople, the capital city of the Byzantine Empire, lost some 10,000 people per day during a forty-day period in 534 C.E., according to a contemporary historian. Disease played an important role in preventing Byzantium from reintegrating Italy into its version of a renewed Roman Empire encompassing the Mediterranean basin. The repeated recurrence of the disease over the next several centuries also weakened the ability of Christendom to resist the Muslim armies that poured out of Arabia in the seventh century C.E.

The most well-known dissemination of disease was associated with the Mongol Empire, which briefly unified much of the Eurasian landmass during the thirteenth and fourteenth centuries C.E. (see Chapter 12). That era of intensified interaction facilitated the spread of the Black Death—identified variously with the bubonic plague, anthrax, or a package of epidemic diseases—from China to Europe. Its consequences were enormous. Between 1346 and 1350, about one-third of the population of Europe perished from the plague. "A dead man," wrote the Italian writer Boccaccio, "was then of no more account than a dead goat."[8] Despite the terrible human toll, some among the living benefited. Tenant farmers and urban workers, now in short supply, could demand higher wages or better terms. Some landowning nobles, on the other hand, were badly hurt as the price of their grains dropped and the demands of their dependents grew.

A similar death toll afflicted China and parts of the Islamic world. The Central Asian steppes, home to many nomadic peoples including the Mongols, also suffered terribly, undermining Mongol rule and permanently altering the balance between pastoral and agricultural peoples to the advantage of settled farmers. In these and many other ways, disease carried by long-distance trade shaped the lives of millions and altered their historical development.

In the long run of world history, the exchange of diseases gave Europeans a certain advantage when they confronted the peoples of the Western Hemisphere after 1500. Exposure over time had provided them with some degree of immunity to Eurasian diseases. In the Americas, however, the absence of domesticated animals, the less intense interaction among major centers of population, and their isolation from the Eastern Hemisphere ensured that native peoples had little defense against the diseases of Europe and Africa. Thus, when their societies were suddenly invaded by Europeans from across the Atlantic, they perished in appalling numbers. Such was the long-term outcome of the very different histories of the two hemispheres.

Sea Roads: Exchange across the Indian Ocean

If the Silk Roads linked Eurasian societies by land, sea-based trade routes likewise connected distant peoples all across the Eastern Hemisphere. Since the days of the Phoenicians, Greeks, and Romans, the Mediterranean Sea had been an avenue of maritime commerce throughout the region, a pattern that continued during the postclassical era. The Italian city of Venice, for example, emerged by 1000 C.E. as a major center of commerce, with its ships and merchants active in the Mediterranean and Black seas as well as on the Atlantic coast. Much of its wealth derived from control of expensive and profitable imported goods from Asia, many of which came up the Red Sea through the Egyptian port of Alexandria. There Venetian merchants picked up those goods and resold them throughout the Mediterranean basin. This type of transregional exchange linked the maritime commerce of the Mediterranean Sea to the much larger and more extensive network of seaborne trade in the Indian Ocean basin.

Until the creation of a genuinely global oceanic system of trade after 1500, the Indian Ocean represented the world's largest sea-based system of communication and exchange, stretching from southern China to eastern Africa (see Map 8.2). Like the Silk Roads, oceanic trade also grew out of the vast environmental and cultural diversities of the region. The desire for various goods not available at home—such as porcelain from China, spices from the islands of Southeast Asia, cotton goods and pepper from India, ivory and gold from the African coast—provided the incentive for Indian Ocean commerce. Transportation costs were lower on the Sea Roads

■ **Comparison**
How did the operation of the Indian Ocean trading network differ from that of the Silk Roads?

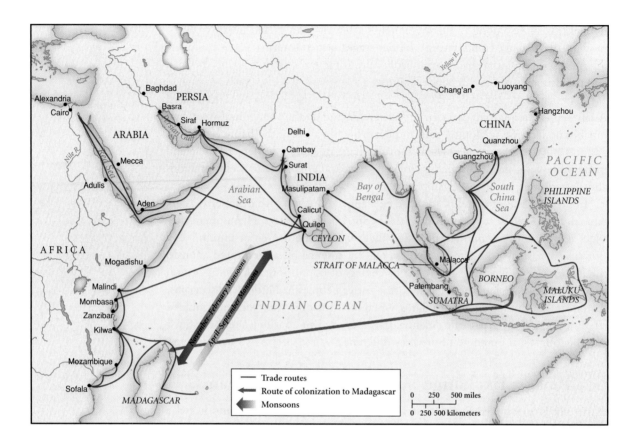

Map 8.2   The Sea Roads
Paralleling the Silk Road trading network, a sea-based commerce in the Indian Ocean basin connected the many peoples between China and East Africa.

than on the Silk Roads, because ships could accommodate larger and heavier cargoes than camels. This meant that the Sea Roads could eventually carry more bulk goods and products destined for a mass market—textiles, pepper, timber, rice, sugar, wheat—whereas the Silk Roads were limited largely to luxury goods for the few.

What made Indian Ocean commerce possible were the *monsoons*, alternating wind currents that blew predictably eastward during the summer months and westward during the winter. An understanding of monsoons and a gradually accumulating technology of shipbuilding and oceanic navigation drew on the ingenuity of many peoples—Chinese, Malays, Indians, Arabs, Swahilis, and others. Collectively they made "an interlocked human world joined by the common highway of the Indian Ocean."[9]

But this world of Indian Ocean commerce did not occur between entire regions and certainly not between "countries," even though historians sometimes write about India, Indonesia, Southeast Asia, or East Africa as a matter of shorthand or convenience. It operated rather across an "archipelago of towns" whose merchants often had more in common with one another than with the people of their own hinterlands.[10] It was these urban centers, strung out around the entire Indian Ocean basin, that provided the nodes of this widespread commercial network.

Weaving the Web of an Indian Ocean World

The world of Indian Ocean commerce was long in the making, dating back to the time of the First Civilizations. Seaborne trade via the Persian Gulf between ancient Mesopotamia and the Indus Valley civilization is reflected in archeological finds in both places. Some scholars believe that the still-undeciphered Indian writing system may have been stimulated by Sumerian cuneiform. The ancient Egyptians, and later the Phoenicians, likewise traded down the Red Sea, exchanging their manufactured goods for gold, ivory, frankincense, and slaves from the coasts of Ethiopia, Somalia, and southern Arabia. These ventures mostly hugged the coast and took place over short distances. An exception was Malay sailors; speaking Austronesian languages, they jumped off from the islands of present-day Indonesia during the first millennium B.C.E. and made their way in double-outrigger canoes across thousands of miles of open ocean to the East African island of Madagascar. There they introduced their language and their crops. Those food crops—bananas, coconuts, and cocoyams—soon spread to the mainland, where they greatly enriched the diets of African peoples. Also spread to the mainland was a Malayo-Polynesian xylophone, which is still played in parts of Africa today.

The tempo of Indian Ocean commerce picked up in the era of classical civilizations during the early centuries of the Common Era, as mariners learned how to ride the monsoons. Merchants from the Roman Empire, mostly Greeks, Syrians, and Jews, established settlements in southern India and along the East African coast. The introduction of Christianity into both Ethiopia and Kerala (in southern India) testifies to the long-term cultural impact of that trade. In the eastern Indian Ocean and the South China Sea, Chinese and Southeast Asian merchants likewise generated a growing commerce, and by 100 C.E. Chinese traders had reached India.

The fulcrum of this growing commercial network lay in India itself. Its ports bulged with goods from both west and east, as illustrated in the Snapshot. Its merchants were in touch with Southeast Asia by the first century C.E., and settled communities of Indian traders appeared throughout the Indian Ocean basin and as far away as

---

Snapshot   **Economic Exchange in the Indian Ocean Basin**

Region	Products Contributed to Indian Ocean Commerce
Mediterranean basin	ceramics, glassware, wine, gold, olive oil
East Africa	ivory, gold, iron goods, slaves, tortoiseshells, quartz, leopard skins
Arabia	frankincense, myrrh, perfumes
India	grain, ivory, precious stones, cotton textiles, spices, timber, tortoiseshells
Southeast Asia	tin, sandlewood, cloves, nutmeg, mace
China	silks, porcelain, tea

Alexandria in Egypt. Indian cultural practices, such as Hinduism and Buddhism, as well as South Asian political ideas began to take root in Southeast Asia.

■ Change
What lay behind the flourishing of Indian Ocean commerce in the postclassical millennium?

In the era of third-wave civilizations between 500 and 1500, two major processes changed the landscape of the Afro-Eurasian world and wove the web of Indian Ocean exchange even more densely than before. One was the economic and political revival of China, some four centuries after the collapse of the Han dynasty. Especially during the Tang and Song dynasties (618–1279), China reestablished an effective and unified state, which actively encouraged maritime trade. Furthermore, the impressive growth of the Chinese economy sent Chinese products pouring into the circuits of Indian Ocean commerce, while providing a vast and attractive market for Indian and Southeast Asian goods. Chinese technological innovations, such as larger ships and the magnetic compass, likewise added to the momentum of commercial growth.

A second transformation in the world of Indian Ocean commerce involved the sudden rise of Islam in the seventh century C.E. and its subsequent spread across much of the Afro-Eurasian world (see Chapter 11). Unlike Confucian culture, which was quite suspicious of merchants, Islam was friendly to commercial life; the Prophet Muhammad himself had been a trader. The creation of an Arab Empire, stretching from the Atlantic Ocean through the Mediterranean basin and all the way to India, brought together in a single political system an immense range of economies and cultural traditions and provided a vast arena for the energies of Muslim traders.

Those energies greatly intensified commercial activity in the Indian Ocean basin in many ways. Middle Eastern gold and silver flowed into southern India to purchase pepper, pearls, textiles, and gemstones. Muslim merchants and sailors, as well as Jews and Christians living within the Islamic world, established communities of traders from East Africa to the southern China coast. Efforts to reclaim wasteland in Mesopotamia to produce sugar and dates for export stimulated a slave trade from East Africa, which landed thousands of Africans in southern Iraq to work on plantations and in salt mines under horrendous conditions. A massive fifteen-year revolt (868–883) among these slaves badly disrupted the Islamic Abbasid Empire before it was brutally crushed.[11]

Beyond these specific outcomes, the expansion of Islam gave rise to an international maritime culture by 1000, shared by individuals living in the widely separated port cities around the Indian Ocean. The immense prestige, power, and prosperity of the Islamic world stimulated widespread conversion, which in turn facilitated commercial transactions. Even those who did not convert to Islam, such as Buddhist rulers in Burma, nonetheless regarded it as commercially useful to assume Muslim names.[12] Thus was created "a maritime Silk Road … a commercial and informational network of unparalleled proportions."[13] After 1000, the culture of this network was increasingly Islamic.

■ Connection
What is the relationship between the rise of Srivijaya and the world of Indian Ocean commerce?

Sea Roads as a Catalyst for Change: Southeast Asia and Srivijaya

Oceanic commerce transformed all of its participants in one way or another, but nowhere more so than in Southeast Asia and East Africa, at opposite ends of the

Indian Ocean network. In both regions, trade stimulated political change as ambitious or aspiring rulers used the wealth derived from commerce to construct larger and more centrally governed states or cities. Both areas likewise experienced cultural change as local people were attracted to foreign religious ideas from Hindu, Buddhist, or Islamic sources. As on the Silk Roads, trade was a conduit for culture.

Located between the major civilizations of China and India, Southeast Asia was situated by geography to play an important role in the evolving world of Indian Ocean commerce. When Malay sailors, long active in the waters around Southeast Asia, opened an all-sea route between India and China through the Straits of Malacca around 350 C.E., the many small ports along the Malay Peninsula and the coast of Sumatra began to compete intensely to attract the growing number of traders and travelers making their way through the straits. From this competition emerged the Malay kingdom of Srivijaya, which dominated this critical choke point of Indian Ocean trade from 670 to 1025. A number of factors—Srivijaya's plentiful supply of gold; its access to the source of highly sought-after spices, such as cloves, nutmeg, and mace; and the taxes levied on passing ships—provided resources to attract supporters, to fund an embryonic bureaucracy, and to create the military and naval forces that brought some security to the area.

Srivijaya monarchs drew upon local beliefs that chiefs possessed magical powers and were responsible for the prosperity of their people, but they also made use of imported Indian political ideas and Buddhist religious concepts, which had been brought to the area by a multitude of Indian merchants and teachers. Some Indians were employed as advisers, clerks, or officials to Srivijaya rulers, who began to assign Sanskrit titles to their subordinates. The capital city of Palembang was a cosmopolitan place, where even the parrots were said to speak four languages. Buddhism in particular provided a "higher level of magic" for rulers as well as the prestige of association with Indian civilization.[14] These rulers sponsored the creation of images of the Buddha and various bodhisattvas whose faces resembled those of deceased kings and were inscribed with traditional curses against anyone who would destroy them. Srivijaya grew into a major center of Buddhist observance and teaching, attracting thousands of monks and students from throughout the Buddhist world. The seventh-century Chinese monk Yi Jing was so impressed that he advised Buddhist monks headed for India to study first in Srivijaya for several years.[15]

Srivijaya was not the only part of Southeast Asia to be influenced by Indian culture. The Sailendra kingdom in central Java, an agriculturally rich region closely allied with Srivijaya, mounted a massive building program between the eighth and tenth centuries featuring Hindu temples and Buddhist monuments. The most famous, known as Borobudur, is an enormous mountain-shaped structure of ten levels, with a three-mile walkway and elaborate carvings illustrating the spiritual journey from ignorance and illusion to full enlightenment. The largest Buddhist monument anywhere in the world, it is nonetheless a distinctly Javanese creation, whose carved figures have Javanese features and whose scenes are clearly set in Java, not India. Its

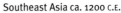

Southeast Asia ca. 1200 C.E.

Borobudur

This huge Buddhist monument, constructed probably in the ninth century C.E., was subsequently abandoned and covered with layers of volcanic ash and vegetation as Java came under Islamic influence. It was rediscovered by British colonial authorities in the early nineteenth century and has undergone several restorations over the past two centuries. Although Indonesia is a largely Muslim country, its Buddhist minority (about 1 percent of the country's population) still celebrates the Buddha's birthday at Borobudur. (Robert Harding World Imagery/Alamy)

shape resonated with an ancient Southeast Asian veneration of mountains as sacred places and the abode of ancestral spirits. Borobudur represents the process of Buddhism becoming culturally grounded in a new place.

Temple complexes such as Borobudur and others constructed in Burma, in the Khmer state of Angkor, and elsewhere illustrate vividly the penetration of Indian culture—in both Hindu and Buddhist forms—throughout mainland and island Southeast Asia. Some scholars have spoken of the "Indianization" of the region, similar perhaps to the earlier spread of Greek culture within the empires of Alexander the Great and Rome. In the case of Southeast Asia, however, no imperial control accompanied Indian cultural influence. It was a matter of voluntary borrowing by independent societies that found Hindu or Buddhist ideas useful and were free to adapt those ideas to their own needs and cultures. Somewhat later, but in much the same way, Islam too began to penetrate Southeast Asia, as the world of Indian Ocean commerce brought yet another religious tradition to the region.

Sea Roads as a Catalyst for Change: East Africa and Swahili Civilization

■ **Connection**

What was the role of Swahili civilization in the world of Indian Ocean commerce?

On the other side of the Indian Ocean, the transformative processes of long-distance trade were likewise at work, giving rise to an East African civilization known as

Swahili. Emerging in the eighth century C.E., this civilization took shape as a set of commercial city-states stretching all along the East African coast, from present-day Somalia to Mozambique.

The earlier ancestors of the Swahili lived in small farming and fishing communities, spoke Bantu languages, and traded with the Arabian, Greek, and Roman merchants who occasionally visited the coast during the classical era. But what stimulated the growth of Swahili cities was the far more extensive commercial life of the western Indian Ocean following the rise of Islam. As in Southeast Asia, local people and aspiring rulers found opportunity for wealth and power in the growing demand for East African products associated with an expanding Indian Ocean commerce. Gold, ivory, quartz, leopard skins, and sometimes slaves acquired from interior societies, as well as iron and processed timber manufactured along the coast, found a ready market in Arabia, Persia, India, and beyond. In response to such opportunities, an African merchant class developed, villages turned into sizable towns, and clan chiefs became kings. A new civilization was in the making.

Between 1000 and 1500, that civilization flourished along the coast, and it was a very different kind of society than the farming and pastoral cultures of the East African interior. It was thoroughly urban, centered in cities of 15,000 to 18,000 people, such as Lamu, Mombasa, Kilwa, Sofala, and many others. Like the city-states of ancient Greece, each Swahili city was politically independent, generally governed by its own king, and in sharp competition with other cities. No imperial system or larger territorial states unified the world of Swahili civilization. Nor did any of them control a critical choke point of trade, as Srivijaya did for the Straits of Malacca. Swahili cities were commercial centers that accumulated goods from the interior and exchanged them for the products of distant civilizations, such as Chinese porcelain and silk, Persian rugs, and Indian cottons. While the transoceanic journeys occurred largely in Arab vessels, Swahili craft navigated the coastal waterways, concentrating goods for shipment abroad. Swahili cities were class-stratified societies with sharp distinctions between a mercantile elite and commoners.

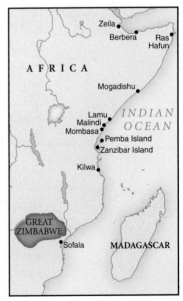

The Swahili Coast of East Africa

Culturally as well as economically, Swahili civilization participated in the larger Indian Ocean world. Arab, Indian, and perhaps Persian merchants were welcome visitors, and some settled permanently. Many ruling families of Swahili cities claimed Arab or Persian origins as a way of bolstering their prestige, even while they dined off Chinese porcelain and dressed in Indian cottons. The Swahili language, widely spoken in East Africa today, was grammatically an African tongue within the larger Bantu family of languages, but it was written in Arabic script and contained a number of Arabic loan words. A small bronze lion found in the Swahili city of Shanga and dating to about 1100 illustrates the distinctly cosmopolitan character of Swahili culture. It depicted a clearly African lion, but it was created in a distinctly Indian artistic style and was made from melted-down Chinese copper coins.[16]

Most important, however, Swahili civilization rapidly became Islamic. Introduced by Arab traders, Islam was voluntarily and widely adopted within the Swahili world. Like Buddhism in Southeast Asia, Islam linked Swahili cities to the larger Indian Ocean world. These East African cities were soon dotted with substantial mosques. When Ibn Battuta, a widely traveled Arab scholar, merchant, and public official, visited the Swahili coast in the early fourteenth century, he found altogether Muslim societies in which religious leaders often spoke Arabic, and all were eager to welcome a learned visitor from the heartland of Islam. But these were African Muslims, not colonies of transplanted Arabs. "The rulers, scholars, officials, and big merchants as well as the port workers, farmers, craftsmen, and slaves, were dark-skinned people speaking African tongues in everyday life."[17]

Islam sharply divided the Swahili cities from their African neighbors to the west, for neither the new religion nor Swahili culture penetrated much beyond the coast until the nineteenth century. Economically, however, the coastal cities acted as intermediaries between the interior producers of valued goods and the Arab merchants who carried them to distant markets. Particularly in the southern reaches of the Swahili world, this relationship extended the impact of Indian Ocean trade well into the African interior. Hundreds of miles inland, between the Zambezi and Limpopo rivers, lay rich sources of gold, much in demand on the Swahili coast. The emergence of a powerful state, known as Great Zimbabwe, seems clearly connected to the growing trade in gold to the coast as well as to the wealth embodied in its large herds of cattle. At its peak between 1250 and 1350, Great Zimbabwe had the resources and the labor power to construct huge stone enclosures entirely without mortar, with walls sixteen feet thick and thirty-two feet tall. "[It] must have been an astonishing sight," writes a recent scholar, "for the subordinate chiefs and kings who would have come there to seek favors at court."[18] Here in the interior of southeastern Africa lay yet another example of the reach and transforming power of Indian Ocean commerce.

Sand Roads: Exchange across the Sahara

In addition to the Silk Roads and the Sea Roads, another important pattern of long-distance trade—this one across the vast reaches of the Sahara—linked North Africa and the Mediterranean world with the land and peoples of interior West Africa. Like the others, these Sand Road commercial networks had a transforming impact, stimulating and enriching West African civilization and connecting it to larger patterns of world history during the postclassical era.

Commercial Beginnings in West Africa

Trans-African trade, like the commerce of the Silk Roads and the Sea Roads, was rooted in environmental variation. The North African coastal regions, long part of Roman or later Arab empires, generated cloth, glassware, weapons, books, and other manufactured goods. The great Sahara held deposits of copper and especially salt, while its oases produced sweet and nutritious dates. Although the sparse populations of the desert were largely pastoral and nomadic, farther south lived agricultural peoples who grew a variety of crops, produced their own textiles and metal products, and mined a considerable amount of gold. The agricultural regions of sub-Saharan Africa are normally divided into two ecological zones: the savanna grasslands immediately south of the Sahara, which produced grain crops such as millet and sorghum; and the forest areas farther south, where root and tree crops such as yams and kola nuts predominated. These quite varied environments provided the economic incentive for the exchange of goods.

The earliest long-distance trade within this huge region was not across the Sahara at all, but largely among the agricultural peoples themselves in the area later known to Arabs as the Sudan, or "the land of black people." During the first millennium B.C.E., the peoples of Sudanic West Africa began to exchange metal goods, cotton textiles, gold, and various food products across considerable distances using boats along the Niger River and donkeys overland. On the basis of this trade, a number of independent urban clusters emerged by the early centuries of the Common Era. The most well known was Jenne-jeno, which was located at a crucial point on the Niger River where goods were transshipped from boat to donkey or vice versa.[19] This was the Niger Valley civilization, described in Chapter 7.

Gold, Salt, and Slaves: Trade and Empire in West Africa

A major turning point in African commercial life occurred with the introduction of the camel to North Africa and the Sahara in the early centuries of the Common Era. This remarkable animal, which could go for ten days without water, finally made possible the long trek across the Sahara. It was camel-owning dwellers of desert oases who initiated regular trans-Saharan commerce by 300 to 400 C.E. Several centuries later, North African Arabs, now bearing the new religion of Islam, also organized caravans across the desert.

■ **Connections**
What changes did trans-Saharan trade bring to West Africa?

What they sought, above all else, was gold, which was found in some abundance in the border areas straddling the grasslands and the forests of West Africa. From its source, it was transported by donkey to transshipment points on the southern edge of the Sahara and then transferred to camels for the long journey north across the desert. African ivory, kola nuts, and slaves were likewise in considerable demand in the desert, the Mediterranean basin, and beyond. In return, the peoples of the Sudan received horses, cloth, dates, various manufactured goods, and especially salt from the rich deposits in the Sahara.

Thus the Sahara was no longer simply a barrier to commerce and cross-cultural interaction; it quickly became a major international trade route that fostered new relationships among distant peoples. The caravans that made the desert crossing could be huge, with as many as 5,000 camels and hundreds of people. Traveling mostly at night to avoid the daytime heat, the journey might take up to seventy days, covering fifteen to twenty-five miles per day. For well over 1,000 years, such caravans traversed the desert, linking the interior of West Africa with lands and people far to the north.

Map 8.3 The Sand Roads

For a thousand years or more, the Sahara was an ocean of sand that linked the interior of West Africa with the world of North Africa and the Mediterranean but separated them as well.

As in Southeast Asia and East Africa, long-distance trade across the Sahara provided both incentive and resources for the construction of new and larger political structures. It was the peoples of the western and central Sudan, living between the forests and the desert, who were in the best position to take advantage of these new opportunities. Between roughly 500 and 1600, they constructed a series of states, empires, and city-states that reached from the Atlantic coast to Lake Chad, including Ghana, Mali, Songhay, Kanem, and the city-states of the Hausa people (see Map 8.3).

All of them were monarchies with elaborate court life and varying degrees of administrative complexity and military forces at their disposal. All drew upon the wealth of trans-Saharan trade, taxing the merchants who conducted it. In the wider world, these states soon acquired a reputation for great riches. An Arab traveler in the tenth century C.E. described the ruler of Ghana as "the wealthiest king on the face of the earth because of his treasures and stocks of gold."[20] At its high point in the fourteenth century, Mali's rulers monopolized the import of strategic goods such as horses and metals; levied duties on salt, copper, and other merchandise; and reserved large nuggets of gold for themselves while permitting the free export of gold dust.

As in all civilizations, slavery found a place in West Africa. Early on, most slaves had been women, working as domestic servants and concubines. As West African civilization crystallized, however, male slaves were put to work as state officials, porters, craftsmen, miners harvesting salt from desert deposits, and especially agricultural laborers producing for the royal granaries on large estates or plantations. Most came from non-Islamic and stateless societies farther south, which were raided during the dry season by cavalry-based forces of West African states, though some white slave women from the eastern Mediterranean also made an appearance in Mali. A song in honor of one eleventh-century ruler of Kanem boasted of his slave-raiding achievements.

> The best you took (and sent home) as the first fruits of battle. The children crying on their mothers you snatched away from their mothers. You took the slave wife from a slave, and set them in lands far removed from one another.[21]

Most of these slaves were used within this emerging West African civilization, but a trade in slaves also developed across the Sahara. Between 1100 and 1400, perhaps 5,500 slaves per year made the perilous trek across the desert. When the famous Muslim traveler Ibn Battuta visited Mali in the fourteenth century, he returned home to Morocco with a caravan that included 600 female slaves, who walked across the burning desert, while he rode a camel. Most such slaves were put to work in the homes of the wealthy in Islamic North Africa, but a small number were sold in Europe. Those who arrived in Ireland, for example, were termed "blue men." Far more significant in Europe were slaves from the Slavic-speaking regions along the northern coast of the Black Sea. They were so numerous that the word "slave" in many European languages derives from the term "Slav." Not until the Atlantic slave trade developed after the 1440s did Africans become the major source of slaves for Europeans.

These states of Sudanic Africa developed substantial urban and commercial centers—such as Koumbi-Saleh, Jenne, Timbuktu, Gao, Gobir, and Kano—where traders congregated and goods were exchanged. Some of these cities also became centers of manufacturing, creating finely wrought beads, iron tools, or cotton textiles, some of which entered the circuits of commerce. Visitors described them as cosmopolitan places where court officials, artisans, scholars, students, and local and foreign merchants all rubbed elbows. As in East Africa, Islam accompanied trade and became an important element in the urban culture of West Africa. The growth of long-distance trade had stimulated the development of an African civilization, which was linked to the wider networks of exchange in the Eastern Hemisphere.

The Gold of Mali
This detail from the *Catalan Atlas*, a series of maps issued in Spain in 1375, illustrates Mali's reputation in Europe for its great wealth in gold. This reputation later propelled Portuguese voyages down the west coast of Africa in search of direct access to that wealth. (Bibliothèque nationale de France)

An American Network: Commerce and Connection in the Western Hemisphere

Before the voyages of Columbus, the world of the Americas developed quite separately from that of the Eastern Hemisphere. Despite intriguing hints of occasional contacts, no sustained interaction between the peoples of these two great landmasses took place.[22] But if the Silk, Sea, and Sand Roads linked the diverse peoples of the Afro-Eurasian world, did a similar network of interaction join and transform the various societies of the Western Hemisphere?

Clearly, direct connections among the various civilizations and cultures of the Americas were less densely woven than in the Afro-Eurasian region. The llama and the potato, both domesticated in the Andes, never reached Mesoamerica; nor did the writing system of the Maya diffuse to Andean civilizations. The Aztecs and the

■ **Comparison**
In what ways did networks of interaction in the Western Hemisphere differ from those in the Eastern Hemisphere?

Incas, contemporary civilizations in the fifteenth century, had little if any direct contact with each other. The limits of these interactions owed something to the absence of horses, donkeys, camels, wheeled vehicles, and large oceangoing vessels, all of which facilitated long-distance trade and travel in Afro-Eurasia.

Geographic or environmental differences added further obstacles. The narrow bottleneck of Panama, largely covered by dense rain forests, surely inhibited contact between South and North America. Furthermore, the north/south orientation of the Americas—which required agricultural practices to move through, and adapt to, quite distinct climatic and vegetation zones—slowed the spread of agricultural products. By contrast, the east/west axis of Eurasia meant that agricultural innovations could diffuse more rapidly because they were entering roughly similar environments. Thus nothing equivalent to the long-distance trade of the Silk, Sea, or Sand Roads of the Eastern Hemisphere arose in the Americas, even though local and regional commerce flourished in many places. Nor did distinct cultural traditions such as Buddhism, Christianity, and Islam spread so widely to integrate distant peoples.

Nonetheless, scholars have discerned "a loosely interactive web stretching from the North American Great Lakes and upper Mississippi south to the Andes."[23] (See Map 8.4.) Partly, it was a matter of slowly spreading cultural elements, such as the gradual diffusion of maize from its Mesoamerican place of origin to the southwestern United States and then on to much of eastern North America as well as to much of South America in the other direction. A game played with rubber balls on an outdoor court has left traces in the Caribbean, Mexico, and northern South America. The spread of particular pottery styles and architectural conventions likewise suggests at least indirect contact over wide distances.

Commerce too played an important role in the making of this "American web." A major North American chiefdom at Cahokia, near

Map 8.4   The American Web

Transcontinental interactions within the American web were more modest than those of the Afro-Eurasian hemisphere. The most intense areas of exchange and communication occurred within the Mississippi valley, Mesoamerican, and Andean regions.

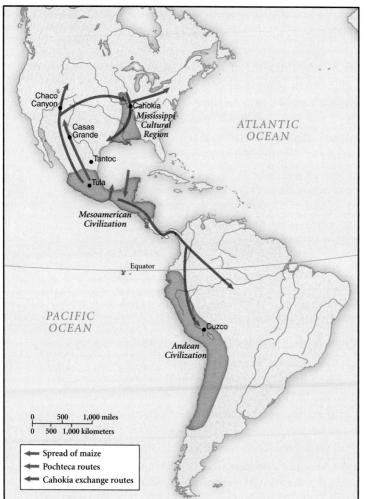

present-day St. Louis, flourished from about 900 to 1250 at the confluence of the Mississippi, Illinois, and Missouri rivers (see Chapter 7). Cahokia lay at the center of a widespread trading network that brought it shells from the Atlantic coast, copper from the Lake Superior region, buffalo hides from the Great Plains, obsidian from the Rocky Mountains, and mica from the southern Appalachian Mountains. Sturdy dugout canoes plied the rivers of the eastern woodlands, connecting their diverse but related societies. Construction in the Tantoc region of northeastern Mexico resembled the earlier building styles of Cahokia, suggesting the possibility of some interaction between the two regions.[24] Many items from Mesoamerica—copper bells, macaw feathers, tons of shells—have been found in the Chaco region of the southwestern United States, while turquoise flowed in the other direction.

Early European explorers and travelers along the Amazon and Orinoco rivers of South America reported active networks of exchange that may well have operated for many centuries. Caribbean peoples using large oceangoing canoes had long conducted an interisland trade, and the Chincha people undertook ocean-based exchange in copper, beads, and shells along the Pacific coast of Peru and Ecuador on large seagoing rafts.[25] But the most active and dense networks of communication and exchange in the Americas lay within, rather than between, the regions that housed the two great civilizations of the Western Hemisphere—Mesoamerica and the Andes.

During the classical era of Mesoamerican civilization (200–900 C.E.), both the Maya cities in the Yucatán area of Mexico and Guatemala and the huge city-state of Teotihuacán in central Mexico maintained commercial relationships with one another and throughout the region. In addition to this land-based trade, the Maya conducted a seaborne commerce, using large dugout canoes holding forty to fifty people, along both the Atlantic and Pacific coasts.[26] Although most of this trade was in luxury goods rather than basic necessities, it was critical to upholding the position and privileges of royal and noble families. Items such as cotton clothing, precious jewels, and feathers from particular birds marked the status of elite groups and served to attract followers. Controlling access to such high-prestige goods was an important motive for war among Mesoamerican states.[27] Among the Aztecs of the fifteenth century, professional merchants, known as *pochteca,* undertook large-scale trading expeditions both within and well beyond the borders of their empire, sometimes as agents for the

Inca Roads
Used for transporting goods by pack animal or sending messages by foot, the Inca road network included some 2,000 inns where travelers might find food and shelter. Messengers, operating in relay, could cover as many as 150 miles a day. Here a modern-day citizen of Peru walks along an old Inca trail road. (Loren McIntyre/lorenmcintyre.com)

state or for members of the nobility, but more often acting on their own as private businessmen.

Unlike the Aztec Empire, in which private traders largely handled the distribution of goods, economic exchange in the Andean Inca Empire during the fifteenth century was a state-run operation, and no merchant group similar to the Aztec *pochteca* emerged there. Instead, great state storehouses bulged with immense quantities of food, clothing, military supplies, blankets, construction materials, and more, all carefully recorded on *quipus* (knotted cords used to record numerical data) by a highly trained class of accountants. From these state centers, goods were transported as needed by caravans of human porters and llamas across the numerous roads and bridges of the empire. Totaling some 20,000 miles, Inca roads traversed the coastal plain and the high Andes in a north/south direction, while lateral roads linked these diverse environments and extended into the eastern rain forests and plains as well. Despite the general absence of private trade, local exchange took place at highland fairs and along the borders of the empire with groups outside the Inca state.

Reflections: Economic Globalization— Ancient and Modern

The densely connected world of the modern era, linked by ties of commerce and culture around the planet, certainly has roots in much earlier patterns. Particularly in the era of third-wave civilizations from 500 to 1500, the Silk, Sea, and Sand roads of the Afro-Eurasian world and the looser networks of the American web linked distant peoples both economically and culturally, prompted the emergence of new states, and sustained elite privileges in many ancient civilizations. In those ways, they resembled the globalized world of modern times.

In other respects, though, the networks and webs of the premodern millennium differed sharply from those of more recent centuries. By and large, most people still produced largely for their own consumption rather than for the market, and a much smaller range of goods was exchanged in the marketplaces of the world. Far fewer people then were required to sell their own labor for wages, an almost universal practice in modern economies. Because of transportation costs and technological limitations, most trade was in luxury goods rather than in necessities. In addition, the circuits of commerce were rather more limited than the truly global patterns of exchange that emerged after 1500.

Furthermore, the world economy of the modern era increasingly had a single center—industrialized Western European countries—which came to dominate much of the world both economically and politically during the nineteenth century. Though never completely equal, the economic relationships of earlier times occurred among much more equivalent units. For example, no one region dominated the complex pattern of Indian Ocean exchange, although India and China generally offered manufactured goods, while Southeast Asia and East Africa contributed agricultural products or raw materials. And with the exception of the brief Mongol control of the Silk Roads and the Inca domination of the Andes for a century, no single power exercised political control over the other major networks of world commerce.

The world of third-wave civilizations, in short, was a more balanced, multicentered world than that of the modern era. Although massive inequalities occurred within particular regions or societies, relationships among the major civilizations operated on a rather more equal basis than in the globalized world of the past several centuries. With the rise of China and India as major players in the world economy of the twenty-first century, are we perhaps returning to that earlier pattern?

Second Thoughts

What's the Significance?

Silk Roads

Black Death

Indian Ocean trading
  network

Srivijaya

Borobudur

Swahili civilization

Great Zimbabwe

Sand Roads

Ghana, Mali, Songhay

trans-Saharan slave trade

American web

To assess your mastery of the material in this chapter, see the **Online Study Guide** at bedfordstmartins.com/strayer.

Big Picture Questions

1. What motivated and sustained the long-distance commerce of the Silk Roads, Sea Roads, and Sand Roads?
2. Why did the Eastern Hemisphere develop long-distance trade more extensively than did the societies of the Western Hemisphere?
3. In what ways did commercial exchange foster other changes?
4. In what ways was Afro-Eurasia a single interacting zone, and in what respects was it a vast region of separate cultures and civilizations?

Next Steps: For Further Study

Jerry Bentley, *Old World Encounters* (1993). A wonderfully succinct and engaging history of cross-cultural interaction all across Afro-Eurasia before 1500.

E. W. Bovill, *The Golden Trade of the Moors* (1970). A classic account of the trans-Saharan trade.

Rainer Buschmann, *Oceans in World History* (2007). A brief study of communication and exchange across the world's oceans.

K. N. Chaudhuri, *Trade and Civilization in the Indian Ocean* (1985). A well-regarded study that treats the Indian Ocean basin as a single region linked by both commerce and culture during the postclassical era.

Philip Curtin, *Cross-Cultural Trade in World History* (1984). Explores long-distance trade as a generator of social change on a global level.

Liu Xinru and Lynda Shaffer, *Connections across Eurasia* (2007). A brief, accessible, and up-to-date account by two major scholars of the Silk Road trading network.

Bridging World History, http://www.learner.org/channel/courses/worldhistory. Units 9 and 10 of this Web-based guide to world history provide an illustrated examination of global trade in the postclassical millennium.

For Web sites and documents related to this chapter, see **Make History** at bedfordstmartins.com/strayer.

CHAPTER NINE

China and the World

East Asian Connections

500–1300

"China will be the next superpower."[1] That was the frank assertion of an article in the British newspaper *The Guardian* in June 2006. Nor was it alone in that assessment. As the new millennium dawned, headlines with this message appeared with increasing frequency in public lectures, in newspaper and magazine articles, and in book titles all across the world. China's huge population, its booming economy, its massive trade surplus with the United States, its entry into world oil markets, its military potential, and its growing presence in global political affairs—all of this suggested that China was headed for a major role, perhaps even a dominant role, in the world of the twenty-first century. Few of these analyses, however, paused to recall that China's prominence on the world stage was hardly something new or that its nineteenth- and twentieth-century position as a "backward," weak, or dependent country was distinctly out of keeping with its long history. Is China perhaps poised to resume in the twenty-first century a much older and more powerful role in world affairs?

IN THE WORLD OF THIRD-WAVE CIVILIZATIONS, even more than during the classical era that preceded it, China cast a long shadow. Its massive and powerful civilization, widely imitated by adjacent peoples, gave rise to a China-centered "world order" encompassing most of eastern Asia.[2] China extended its borders deep into Central Asia, while its wealthy and cosmopolitan culture attracted visitors from all over Eurasia. None of its many neighbors—whether nomadic peoples to the

---

Chinese Astronomy: During classical and postclassical times, the impressive achievements of Chinese astronomy included the observation of sunspots, supernovae, and solar and lunar eclipses as well as the construction of elaborate star maps and astronomical devices. Since the time of the Han dynasty, armillary spheres, such as the one depicted in this seventeenth-century painting, assisted Chinese scholars in representing the position and motion of the earth, sun, moon, planets, and stars. (Courtesy of the Trustees of the British Museum) north and west or smaller peripheral states such as Tibet, Korea, Japan, and Vietnam—could escape its gravitational pull. All of them had to deal with China. Far beyond these near neighbors, China's booming economy and many technological innovations had ripple effects all across Eurasia.

Even as China so often influenced the world, it too was changed by its many interactions with non-Chinese peoples. Northern nomads—"barbarians" to the Chinese—frequently posed a military threat and on occasion even conquered and ruled parts of China. The country's growing involvement in international trade stimulated important social, cultural, and economic changes within China itself. Buddhism, a religion of Indian origin, took root in China, and, to a lesser extent, so did Christianity and Islam. In short, China's engagement with the wider world became a very significant element in a global era of accelerating connections.

The Reemergence of a Unified China

The collapse of the Han dynasty around 220 C.E. ushered in more than three centuries of political fragmentation in China and signaled the rise of powerful and locally entrenched aristocratic families. It also meant the incursion of northern nomads, many of whom learned Chinese, dressed like Chinese, married into Chinese families, and governed northern regions of the country in a Chinese fashion. Such conditions of disunity, unnatural in the eyes of many thoughtful Chinese, discredited Confucianism and opened the door to a greater acceptance of Buddhism and Daoism among the elite.

Those centuries also witnessed the beginning of Chinese migration southward toward the Yangzi River valley, a movement of people that gave southern China some 60 percent of the country's population by 1000. That movement of Chinese people, accompanied by their intensive agriculture, set in motion a vast environmental transformation, marked by the destruction of the old-growth forests that once covered much of the country and the retreat of the elephants that had inhabited those lands. Around 800 C.E., the Chinese official and writer Liu Zongyuan lamented what was happening.

> A tumbled confusion of lumber as flames on the hillside crackle
> Not even the last remaining shrubs are safeguarded from destruction
> Where once mountain torrents leapt—nothing but rutted gullies.[3]

A "Golden Age" of Chinese Achievement

■ Change
Why are the centuries of the Tang and Song dynasties in China sometimes referred to as a "golden age"?

Unlike the fall of the western Roman Empire, where political fragmentation proved to be a permanent condition, China regained its unity under the Sui dynasty (589–618). Its emperors solidified that unity by a vast extension of the country's canal system, stretching some 1,200 miles in length and described by one scholar as "an engineering feat without parallel in the world of its time."[4] Those canals linked northern and southern China economically and contributed much to the prosperity that followed. But the ruthlessness of Sui emperors and a futile military campaign to conquer Korea exhausted the state's resources, alienated many people, and prompted the overthrow of the dynasty.

This dynastic collapse, however, witnessed no prolonged disintegration of the Chinese state. The two dynasties that followed—the Tang (618–907) and the Song (960–1279)—built on the Sui foundations of renewed unity (see Map 9.1). Together they established patterns of Chinese life that endured into the twentieth century, despite a fifty-year period of disunity between the two dynasties.

Map 9.1   Tang and Song Dynasty China
During the postclassical millennium, China interacted extensively with its neighbors. The Tang dynasty extended Chinese control deep into Central Asia, while the Song dynasty witnessed incursions by the nomadic Jurchen people, who created the Jin Empire, which ruled parts of northern China.

Culturally, this era has long been regarded as a "golden age" of arts and literature, setting standards of excellence in poetry, landscape painting, and ceramics. Particularly during the Song dynasty, an explosion of scholarship gave rise to Neo-Confucianism, an effort to revive Confucian thinking while incorporating into it some of the insights of Buddhism and Daoism.

Politically, the Tang and Song dynasties built a state structure that endured for a thousand years. Six major ministries—personnel, finance, rites, army, justice, and public works—were accompanied by the Censorate, an agency that exercised surveillance over the rest of the government, checking on the character and competence of public officials. To staff this bureaucracy, the examination system was revived and made more elaborate, encouraged by the ability to print books for the first time in world history. Efforts to prevent cheating on the exams included searching candidates entering the examination hall and placing numbers rather than names on their papers. Schools and colleges proliferated to prepare candidates for the rigorous exams, which became a central feature of upper-class life. A leading world historian has described Tang dynasty China as "the best ordered state in the world."[5]

Selecting officials on the basis of merit represented a challenge to established aristocratic families' hold on public office. Still, a substantial percentage of official positions went to the sons of the privileged, even if they had not passed the exams. Moreover, because education and the examination system grew far more rapidly than the number of official positions, many who passed lower-level exams could not be accommodated with a bureaucratic appointment. Often, however, they were able to combine landowning and success in the examination system to maintain an immense cultural prestige and prominence in their local areas. Despite the state's periodic efforts to redistribute land in favor of the peasantry, the great families of large landowners continued to encroach on peasant plots. This has been a recurring pattern in rural China from classical times to the present.

Underlying these cultural and political achievements was an "economic revolution" that made Song dynasty China "by far the richest, most skilled, and most populous country on earth."[6] The most obvious sign of China's prosperity was its rapid growth in population, which jumped from about 50 million or 60 million during the Tang dynasty to 120 million by 1200. Behind this doubling of the population were remarkable achievements in agricultural production, particularly the adoption of a fast-ripening and drought-resistant strain of rice from Vietnam.

Many people found their way to the cities, making China the most urbanized country in the world. Dozens of Chinese cities numbered over 100,000, while the Song dynasty capital of Hangzhou was home to more than a million people. A Chinese observer in 1235 provided a vivid description of that city.[7] Specialized markets abounded for meat, herbs, vegetables, books, rice, and much

Kaifeng
This detail comes from a huge watercolor scroll, titled *Upper River during Qing Ming Festival,* originally painted during the Song dynasty. It illustrates the urban sophistication of Kaifeng and other Chinese cities at that time and has been imitated and copied many times since then. (Palace Museum, Beijing)

more, with troupes of actors performing for the crowds. Restaurants advertised their unique offerings—sweet bean soup, pickled dates, juicy lungs, meat pies, pigs' feet—and some offered vegetarian fare for religious banquets. Inns of various kinds appealed to different groups. Those that served only wine, a practice known as "hitting the cup," were regarded as "unfit for polite company." "Luxuriant inns," marked by red lanterns, featured prostitutes, and "the wine chambers [were] equipped with beds." Specialized agencies managed elaborate dinner parties for the wealthy, complete with a Perfume and Medicine Office to "help sober up the guests." Schools for musicians offered thirteen different courses. Numerous clubs provided companionship for poets, fishermen, Buddhists, physical fitness enthusiasts, antiques collectors, horse lovers, and many other groups. No wonder that the Italian visitor Marco Polo described Hangzhou later in the thirteenth century as "beyond dispute the finest and noblest [city] in the world."[8]

Supplying these cities with food was made possible by an immense network of internal waterways—canals, rivers, and lakes—stretching perhaps 30,000 miles. They provided a cheap transportation system that bound the country together economically and created the "world's most populous trading area."[9]

Industrial production likewise soared. In both large-scale enterprises employing hundreds of workers and in smaller backyard furnaces, China's iron industry increased its output dramatically. By the eleventh century, it was providing the government with 32,000 suits of armor and 16 million iron arrowheads annually, in addition to supplying metal for coins, tools, construction, and bells in Buddhist monasteries. Technological innovation in other fields also flourished. Inventions in printing, both woodblock and movable type, generated the world's first printed books, and by 1000 relatively cheap books on religious, agricultural, mathematical, and medical topics became widely available in China. Its navigational and ship-building technologies led the world. The Chinese invention of gunpowder created within a few centuries a revolution in military affairs that had global dimensions.

Most remarkably, perhaps, all of this occurred within the world's most highly commercialized society, in which producing for the market, rather than for local consumption, became a very widespread phenomenon. Cheap transportation allowed peasants to grow specialized crops for sale, while they bought rice or other staples on the market. In addition, government demands for taxes paid in cash rather than in kind required peasants to sell something in order to meet their obligations. The growing use of paper money as well as financial instruments such as letters of credit and promissory notes further contributed to the commercialization of Chinese society. Two prominent scholars have described the outcome: "Output increased, population grew, skills multiplied, and a burst of inventiveness made Song China far wealthier than ever before—or than any of its contemporaries."[10]

Women in the Song Dynasty

■ **Change**
In what ways did women's lives change during the Tang and Song dynasties?

The "golden age" of Song dynasty China was perhaps less than "golden" for many of the country's women, for that era marked yet another turning point in the history of Chinese patriarchy. Under the influence of steppe nomads, whose women led less restricted lives, elite Chinese women of the Tang dynasty era, at least in the north, had participated in social life with greater freedom than in classical times. Paintings and statues from that time show aristocratic women riding horses, while the Queen Mother of the West, a Daoist deity, was widely worshipped by female Daoist priests and practitioners (see Chapter 6). By the Song dynasty, however, a reviving Confucianism and rapid economic growth seemed to tighten patriarchal restrictions on women and to restore some of the earlier Han dynasty images of female submission and passivity.

Once again Confucian writers highlighted the subordination of women to men and the need to keep males and females separate in every domain of life. The Song dynasty historian and scholar Sima Guang (1019–1086) summed up the prevailing view: "The boy leads the girl, the girl follows the boy; the duty of husbands to be resolute and wives to be docile begins with this."[11] Women were also frequently viewed as a distraction to men's pursuit of a contemplative and introspective life. The remarriage of widows, though legally permissible, was increasingly condemned, for "to walk through two courtyards is a source of shame for a woman."[12]

The most compelling expression of a tightening patriarchy lay in foot binding. Beginning apparently among dancers and courtesans in the tenth or eleventh century C.E., this practice involved the tight wrapping of young girls' feet, usually breaking the bones of the foot and causing intense pain. During the Tang dynasty, foot binding spread widely among elite families and later became even more widespread in Chinese society. It was associated with new images of female beauty and eroticism that emphasized small size, delicacy, and reticence, all of which were necessarily produced by foot binding. It certainly served to keep women restricted to the "inner quarters," where Confucian tradition asserted that they belonged. Many mothers imposed this painful procedure on their daughters, perhaps to assist them in competing with concubines for the attention of their husbands.[13]

A rapidly commercializing economy undermined the position of women in the textile industry. Urban workshops and state factories, run by men, increasingly took over the skilled tasks of weaving textiles, especially silk, which had previously been the work of rural women. But as their economic role in textile production declined, other opportunities emerged in an increasingly prosperous Song China. In the cities, women operated restaurants, sold fish and vegetables, and worked as maids, cooks, and dressmakers. The growing prosperity of elite families funneled increasing numbers of women into roles as concubines, entertainers, courtesans, and prostitutes. Their ready availability surely reduced the ability of wives to negotiate as equals with their husbands. It set women against one another and created endless household jealousies.

Foot Binding
The two young women pictured in this late-nineteenth-century photograph have bound feet, while the boy standing between them does not. A girl of a similar age would likely have begun this painful process already. The practice, dating back to around 1000 C.E., lasted into the twentieth century, when it was largely eliminated by reformist and Communist governments. (Photograph courtesy Peabody Essex Museum; image #A9392)

In other ways, the Song dynasty witnessed more positive trends in the lives of women. Their property rights expanded, in terms of both controlling their own dowries and inheriting property from their families. "Neither in earlier nor in later periods," writes one scholar, "did as much property pass through women's hands" as during the Song dynasty.[14] Furthermore, lower-ranking but ambitious officials strongly urged the education of women, so that they might more effectively raise their sons and increase the family's fortune. Song dynasty China, in short, offered a mixture of tightening restrictions and new opportunities to its women.

China and the Northern Nomads: A Chinese World Order in the Making

Chinese history has been subjected to two enduring misconceptions, in popular thinking, if not in scholarly writing. First, it was often viewed as the story of an impressive but largely static civilization. In fact, however, China changed substantially over the centuries as its state structures evolved, as its various cultural traditions mixed and blended, as its economy expanded, as its population grew and migrated to the south, and as its patriarchy altered in tone and emphasis. A second

Snapshot   **Key Moments in the History of Postclassical China**

Collapse of Han dynasty; end of classical era	220
Political fragmentation of China; incursion of nomads in the north; Buddhism takes root	220–581
Sui dynasty; reunification of China	589–618
Reign of Emperor Wendi; state support for Buddhism	581–604
Tang dynasty; golden age of Chinese culture; expansion into Central Asia; high point of Chinese influence in Japan	618–907
Withdrawal of Chinese military forces from Korea	688
Reign of Empress Wu, China's only female emperor	690–705
State action against Buddhism	9th century
Political breakdown between dynasties	907–960
Vietnam establishes independence from China	939
Song dynasty; China's economic revolution; northern China ruled by peoples of nomadic background (Khitan, Jurchen)	960–1279
Yuan dynasty; Mongol rule of China	1271–1368
Ming dynasty; Chinese rule resumed	1368–1644
Maritime expeditions in the Indian Ocean	1405–1433

misconception has portrayed China as a self-contained civilization. The balance of this chapter challenges this impression by showing how China's many interactions with a larger Eurasian world shaped both China's own development and that of classical and postclassical world history more generally.

■ **Connection**
How did the Chinese and their nomadic neighbors to the north view each other?

From early times to the nineteenth century, China's most enduring and intense interaction with foreigners lay to the north, involving the many nomadic pastoral or semi-agricultural peoples of the steppes. Living in areas unable to sustain Chinese-style farming, the northern nomads had long focused their economies around the raising of livestock (sheep, cattle, goats) and the mastery of horse riding. Organized locally in small, mobile, kinship-based groups, sometimes called tribes, these peoples also periodically created much larger and powerful states or confederations that could draw upon the impressive horsemanship and military skills of virtually the entire male population of their societies. Such specialized pastoral societies needed grain and other agricultural products from China, and their leaders developed a taste for Chinese manufactured and luxury goods—wine and silk, for example—with which they could attract and reward followers. Thus the nomads were drawn like a magnet toward China, trading, raiding, and extorting in order to obtain the resources so vital to their way of life. For 2,000 years or more, pressure from the steppes and the intrusion of nomadic peoples were constant factors in China's historical development.

From the nomads' point of view, the threat often came from the Chinese, who periodically directed their own military forces deep into the steppes, built the Great Wall to keep the nomads out, and often proved unwilling to allow pastoral peoples easy access to trading opportunities within China.[15] And yet the Chinese needed the nomads. Their lands were the source of horses, so essential for the Chinese military. Other products of the steppes and the forests beyond, such as skins, furs, hides, and amber, were also of value in China. Furthermore, pastoral nomads controlled much of the Silk Road trading network, which funneled goods from the West into China. The continuing interaction between China and the northern nomads brought together peoples occupying different environments, practicing different economies, governing themselves with different institutions, and thinking about the world in quite different ways.

The Tribute System in Theory

An enduring outcome of this cross-cultural encounter was that the Chinese developed a particular view of themselves, fully articulated by the time of the Han dynasty (200 B.C.E.–200 C.E.) and lasting for more than two millennia. That understanding cast China as the "middle kingdom," the center of the world, infinitely superior to the "barbarian" peoples beyond its borders. With its long history, great cities, refined tastes, sophisticated intellectual and artistic achievements, bureaucratic state, literate elite, and prosperous economy, China represented "civilization." All of this, in Chinese thinking, was in sharp contrast to the rude cultures and primitive life of the northern nomads, who continually moved about "like beasts and birds," lived in tents, ate mostly meat and milk, and practically lived on their horses, while making war on everyone within reach. Educated Chinese saw their own society as self-sufficient, requiring little from the outside world, while barbarians, quite understandably, sought access to China's wealth and wisdom. Furthermore, China was willing to permit that access under controlled conditions, for its sense of superiority did not preclude the possibility that barbarians could become civilized Chinese. China was a "radiating civilization," graciously shedding its light most fully to nearby barbarians and with diminished intensity to those farther away.[16]

Such was the general understanding of literate Chinese about their own civilization in relation to northern nomads and other non-Chinese peoples. That worldview also took shape as a practical system for managing China's relationship with these people. Known to us as the "tribute system," it was a set of practices that required non-Chinese authorities to acknowledge Chinese superiority and their own subordinate place in a Chinese-centered world order. Foreigners seeking access to China had to send a delegation to the Chinese court, where they would perform the kowtow, a series of ritual bowings and prostrations, and present their tribute— produce of value from their countries—to the Chinese emperor. In return for these

■ **Connection**
What assumptions underlay the tribute system?

The Tribute System
This Qing dynasty painting shows an idealized Chinese version of the tribute system. The Chinese emperor receives barbarian envoys, who perform rituals of subordination and present tribute in the form of a horse. (Réunion des Musées Nationaux/Art Resource, NY)

expressions of submission, he would grant permission for foreigners to trade in China's rich markets and would provide them with gifts or "bestowals," often worth far more than the tribute they had offered. This was the mechanism by which successive Chinese dynasties attempted to regulate their relationships with northern nomads; with neighboring states such as Korea, Vietnam, Tibet, and Japan; and, after 1500, with those European barbarians from across the sea.

Often, this system seemed to work. Over the centuries, countless foreign delegations proved willing to present their tribute, say the required words, and perform the necessary rituals in order to gain access to the material goods of China. Aspiring non-Chinese rulers also gained prestige as they basked in the reflected glory of even this subordinate association with the great Chinese civilization. The official titles, seals of office, and ceremonial robes they received from China proved useful in their local struggles for power.

The Tribute System in Practice

■ **Connection**
How did the tribute system in practice differ from the ideal Chinese understanding of its operation?

But the tribute system also disguised some realities that contradicted its assumptions. Frequently, China was confronting not separate and small-scale barbarian societies, but large and powerful nomadic empires able to deal with China on at least equal terms. An early nomadic confederacy was that of the Xiongnu, established about the same time as the Han dynasty and eventually reaching from Manchuria to Central Asia. Devastating Xiongnu raids into northern China persuaded the Chinese emperor to negotiate an arrangement that recognized the nomadic state as a political equal, promised its leader a princess in marriage, and, most important, agreed to supply him annually with large quantities of grain, wine, and silk. Although these goods were officially termed "gifts," granted in accord with the tribute system, they were in fact tribute in reverse or even protection money. In return for these goods, so critical for the functioning of the nomadic state, the Xiongnu agreed to refrain from military incursions into China. The basic realities of the situation were summed up in this warning to the Han dynasty in the first century B.C.E.:

> Just make sure that the silks and grain stuffs you bring the Xiongnu are the right measure and quality, that's all. What's the need for talking? If the goods you

deliver are up to measure and good quality, all right. But if there is any deficiency or the quality is no good, then when the autumn harvest comes, we will take our horses and trample all over your crops.[17]

Something similar occurred during the Tang dynasty as a series of Turkic empires arose in Mongolia. Like the Xiongnu, they too extorted large "gifts" from the Chinese. One of these peoples, the Uighurs, actually rescued the Tang dynasty from a serious internal revolt in the 750s. In return, the Uighur leader gained one of the Chinese emperor's daughters as a wife and arranged a highly favorable exchange of poor-quality horses for high-quality silk that brought half a million rolls of the precious fabric annually into the Uighur lands. Despite the rhetoric of the tribute system, the Chinese were clearly not always able to dictate the terms of their relationship with the northern nomads.

Steppe nomads were generally not much interested in actually conquering and ruling China. It was easier and more profitable to extort goods from a functioning Chinese state. On occasion, though, that state broke down, and various nomadic groups moved in to "pick up the pieces," conquering and governing parts of China. Such a process took place following the fall of the Han dynasty and again after the collapse of the Tang dynasty, when the Khitan (907–1125) and then the Jurchen (1115–1234) peoples established states that encompassed parts of northern China as well as major areas of the steppes to the north. Both of them required the Chinese Song dynasty, located farther south, to deliver annually huge quantities of silk, silver, and tea, some of which found its way into the Silk Road trading network. The practice of "bestowing gifts on barbarians," long a part of the tribute system, allowed the proud Chinese to imagine that they were still in control of the situation even as they were paying heavily for protection from nomadic incursion. Those gifts, in turn, provided vital economic resources to nomadic states.

Cultural Influence across an Ecological Frontier

When nomadic peoples actually ruled parts of China, some of them adopted Chinese ways, employing Chinese advisers, governing according to Chinese practice, and, at least for the elite, immersing themselves in Chinese culture and learning. This process of "becoming Chinese" went furthest among the Jurchen, many of whom lived in northern China and learned to speak Chinese, wore Chinese clothing, married Chinese husbands and wives, and practiced Buddhism or Daoism. On the whole, however, Chinese culture had only a modest impact on the nomadic people of the northern steppes. Unlike the native peoples of southern China, who were gradually absorbed into Chinese culture, the pastoral societies north of the Great Wall generally retained their own cultural patterns. Few of them were incorporated, at least not for long, within a Chinese state, and most lived in areas where Chinese-style agriculture was simply impossible. Under these conditions, there were few incentives for adopting Chinese culture wholesale. But various modes of interaction—peaceful trade, military conflict, political negotiations,

■ **Connection**
In what ways did China and the nomads influence each other?

economic extortion, some cultural influence—continued across the ecological frontier that divided two quite distinct and separate ways of life. Each was necessary for the other.

On the Chinese side, elements of steppe culture had some influence in those parts of northern China that were periodically conquered and ruled by nomadic peoples. The founders of the Sui and Tang dynasties were in fact of mixed nomad and Chinese ancestry and came from the borderland region where a blended Chinese/Turkic culture had evolved. High-ranking members of the imperial family personally led their troops in battle in the style of Turkic warriors. Furthermore, Tang dynasty China was awash with foreign visitors from all over Asia—delegations bearing tribute, merchants carrying exotic goods, bands of clerics or religious pilgrims bringing new religions such as Christianity, Islam, Buddhism, and Manichaeism. For a time in the Tang dynasty, almost anything associated with "western barbarians"—Central Asians, Persians, Indians, Arabs—had great appeal among northern Chinese elites. Their music, dancing, clothing, foods, games, and artistic styles found favor among the upper classes. The more traditional southern Chinese, feeling themselves heir to the legacy of the Han dynasty, were sharply critical of their northern counterparts for allowing women too much freedom, for drinking yogurt rather than tea, for listening to "western" music, all of which they attributed to barbarian influence. Around 800 C.E., the poet Yuan Chen gave voice to a growing backlash against this too easy acceptance of things "western":

> Ever since the Western horsemen began raising smut and dust,
> Fur and fleece, rank and rancid, have filled Hsien and Lo.
> Women make themselves Western matrons by the study of Western makeup.
> Entertainers present Western tunes, in their devotion to Western music.[18]

Coping with China: Comparing Korea, Vietnam, and Japan

Also involved in tributary relationships with China during the postclassical era were the newly emerging states and civilizations of Korea, Vietnam, and Japan. Unlike the northern nomads, these societies were thoroughly agricultural and sedentary. During the first millennium C.E., they were part of a larger process—the globalization of civilization—which produced new city- and state-based societies in various parts of the world. Proximity to their giant Chinese neighbor decisively shaped the histories of these new East Asian civilizations, for all of them borrowed major elements of Chinese culture. But unlike the native peoples of southern China, who largely became Chinese, the peoples of Korea, Vietnam, and Japan did not. They retained distinctive identities, which have lasted into modern times. While resisting Chinese political domination, they also appreciated Chinese culture and sought the source of Chinese wealth and power. In such ways, these smaller East Asian civilizations anticipated the "developing" Afro-Asian societies of the twentieth century, which embraced "modernity" and elements of Western culture, while trying to maintain their political and cultural independence from the European and American centers of that modern way of life. Korea, Vietnam, and Japan, however, encountered China and responded to it in quite different ways.

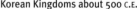

■ **Comparison**

In what different ways did Korea, Vietnam, and Japan experience and respond to Chinese influence?

Korea and China

Immediately adjacent to northeastern China, the Korean peninsula and its people have long lived in the shadow of their imposing neighbor. Temporary Chinese conquest of northern Korea during the Han dynasty and some colonization by Chinese settlers provided an initial channel for Chinese cultural influence, particularly in the form of Buddhism. Early Korean states, which emerged in the fourth through seventh centuries C.E., all referred to their rulers with the Chinese term *wang* (king). Bitter rivals with one another, these states strenuously resisted Chinese political control, except when they found it advantageous to join with China against a local enemy. In the seventh century, one of these states—the Silla kingdom—allied with Tang dynasty China to bring some political unity to the peninsula for the first time. But Chinese efforts to set up puppet regimes and to assimilate Koreans to Chinese culture provoked sharp military resistance, persuading the Chinese to withdraw their military forces in 688 and to establish a tributary relationship with a largely independent Korea.

Under a succession of dynasties—the Silla (688–900), Koryo (918–1392), and Yi (1392–1910)—Korea generally maintained its political independence while participating in China's tribute system. Its leaders actively embraced the connection with China and, especially during the Silla dynasty, sought to turn their small state into a miniature version of Tang China.

Tribute missions to China provided legitimacy for Korean rulers and knowledge of Chinese court life and administrative techniques, which they sought to replicate back home. A new capital city of Kumsong was modeled directly on the Chinese capital of Chang'an. Tribute missions also enabled both official and private trade, mostly in luxury goods such as ceremonial clothing, silks, fancy teas, Confucian and Buddhist texts, and artwork—all of which enriched the lives of a Korean aristocracy that was becoming increasingly Chinese in culture. Thousands of Korean students were sent to China, where they studied primarily Confucianism but also natural sciences and the arts. Buddhist monks visited centers of learning and pilgrimage in China and brought back popular forms of Chinese Buddhism, which quickly took root in Korea. Schools for the study of Confucianism, using texts in the Chinese language, were established in Korea. In these ways, Korea became a part of the expanding world of Chinese culture, and refugees from the peninsula's many wars carried Chinese culture to Japan as well.

These efforts to plant Confucian values and Chinese culture in Korea had what one scholar has called an "overwhelmingly negative" impact on

Korean Kingdoms about 500 C.E.

Korean women, particularly after 1300.[19] Early Chinese observers noticed, and strongly disapproved of, "free choice" marriages in Korea as well as the practice of women singing and dancing together late at night. With the support of the Korean court, Chinese models of family life and female behavior, especially among the elite, gradually replaced the more flexible Korean patterns. Earlier a Korean woman had generally given birth and raised her young children in her parents' home, where she was often joined by her husband. This was now strongly discouraged, for it was deeply offensive to Confucian orthodoxy, which held that a married woman belonged to her husband's family. Some Korean customs—funeral rites in which a husband was buried in the sacred plot of his wife's family, the remarriage of widowed or divorced women, and female inheritance of property—eroded under the pressure of Confucian orthodoxy. So too did the practice of plural marriages for men. In 1413, a legal distinction between primary and secondary wives required men to identify one of their wives as primary. Because she and her children now had special privileges and status, sharp new tensions emerged within families. Korean restrictions on elite women, especially widows, came to exceed even those in China itself.

Still, Korea remained Korean. After 688, the country's political independence, though periodically threatened, was largely intact. Chinese cultural influence, except for Buddhism, had little impact beyond the aristocracy and certainly did not penetrate the lives of Korea's serflike peasants or its large slave population. A Chinese-style examination system to recruit government officials, though encouraged by some Korean rulers, never assumed the prominence that it gained in Tang and Song dynasty China. Korea's aristocratic class was able to maintain an even stronger monopoly on bureaucratic office than their Chinese counterparts. And in the 1400s, Korea moved toward greater cultural independence by developing a phonetic alphabet, known as *hangul*, for writing the Korean language. Although resisted by male conservative elites, who were long accustomed to using the more prestigious Chinese characters to write Korean, this new form of writing gradually took hold, especially in private correspondence, in popular fiction, and among women. Clearly part of the Chinese world order, Korea nonetheless retained a distinctive culture as well as a separate political existence.

Vietnam

← Route of Vietnamese expansion

— Present-day boundaries of Vietnam

Vietnam and China

At the southern fringe of the Chinese cultural world, the people who eventually came to be called Vietnamese had a broadly similar historical encounter with China. As in Korea, the elite culture of Vietnam borrowed heavily from China—adopting Confucianism, Daoism, Buddhism, administrative techniques, the examination system, artistic and literary styles—even as its popular culture remained distinctive. And, like Korea, Vietnam achieved political independence, while participating fully in the tribute system as a vassal state.

But there were differences as well. The cultural heartland of Vietnam in the Red River valley was fully incorporated into the Chinese state for more than a thousand years (111 B.C.E.–939 C.E.), far longer than corresponding parts of Korea. Regarded by the Chinese as "southern barbarians," the Vietnamese were ruled by Chinese officials who expected to fully assimilate this rich rice-growing region into China culturally as well as administratively. To these officials, it was simply a further extension of the southward expansion of Chinese civilization. Thus Chinese-style irrigated agriculture was introduced; Vietnamese elites were brought into the local bureaucracy and educated in Confucian-based schools; Chinese replaced the local language in official business; Chinese clothing and hairstyles became mandatory; and large numbers of Chinese, some fleeing internal conflicts at home, flooded into the relative security of what they referred to as "the pacified south," while often despising the local people.[20]

The heavy pressure of the Chinese presence generated not only a Vietnamese elite thoroughly schooled in Chinese culture but also periodic rebellions. In 39 C.E., a short-lived but long-remembered uprising was launched by two sisters, daughters of a local leader deposed by the Chinese. One of them, Trung Trac, whose husband had been executed, famously addressed some 30,000 soldiers, while dressed in full military regalia.

> Foremost I will avenge my country.
> Second I will restore the Hung lineage.
> Third I will avenge the death of my husband.
> Lastly I vow that these goals will be accomplished.[21]

When the rebellion was crushed several years later, the Trung sisters committed suicide rather than surrender to the Chinese, but in literature, monuments, and public memory, they long remained powerful symbols of Vietnamese resistance to Chinese aggression.

The weakening of the Tang dynasty in the early tenth century C.E. finally enabled a particularly large rebellion to establish Vietnam as a separate state, though one that carefully maintained its tributary role, sending repeated missions to do homage at the Chinese court. Nonetheless, successive Vietnamese dynasties found the Chinese approach to government useful, styling their rulers as emperors, claiming the Mandate of Heaven, and making use of Chinese court rituals, while expanding their state

The Trung Sisters Although it occurred nearly 2,000 years ago, the revolt of the Trung sisters against Chinese occupation remains a national symbol of Vietnam's independence, as illustrated by this modern Vietnamese painting of the two women, astride war elephants, leading their followers into battle against the Chinese invaders. (From William J. Duiker, *Sacred War: Nationalism and Revolution in a Divided Vietnam* [New York: The McGraw-Hill Companies, 1995])

steadily southward. More so than in Korea, a Chinese-based examination system in Vietnam functioned to undermine an established aristocracy, to provide some measure of social mobility for commoners, and to create a merit-based scholar-gentry class to staff the bureaucracy. Furthermore, the Vietnamese elite class remained deeply committed to Chinese culture, viewing their own country less as a separate nation than as a southern extension of a universal civilization, the only one they knew.[22]

Beyond the elite, however, there remained much that was uniquely Vietnamese, such as a distinctive language, a fondness for cockfighting, chewing betel nuts, and a greater role for women in social and economic life. Female nature deities and even a "female Buddha" continued to be part of Vietnamese popular religion, even as Confucian-based ideas took root among the elite. These features of Vietnamese life reflected larger patterns of Southeast Asian culture that distinguished it from China. And like Korea, the Vietnamese developed a variation of Chinese writing called *chu nom* ("southern script"), which provided the basis for an independent national literature.

Japan and China

Unlike Korea and Vietnam, the Japanese islands were physically separated from China by 100 miles or more of ocean and were never successfully invaded or conquered by their giant mainland neighbor. Thus Japan's very extensive borrowing from Chinese civilization was wholly voluntary, rather than occurring under conditions of direct military threat or outright occupation. The high point of that borrowing took place during the seventh to the ninth centuries C.E., as the first more or less unified Japanese state began to emerge from dozens of small clan-based aristocratic chiefdoms. That state found much that was useful in Tang dynasty China and set out, deliberately and systematically, to transform Japan into a centralized bureaucratic state on the Chinese model.

Japan

The initial leader of this effort was Shotoku Taishi (572–622), a prominent aristocrat from one of the major clans. He launched a series of large-scale missions to China, which took hundreds of Japanese monks, scholars, artists, and students to the mainland, and when they returned, they put into practice what they had learned. He issued the Seventeen Article Constitution, proclaiming the Japanese ruler as a Chinese-style emperor and encouraging both Buddhism and Confucianism. In good Confucian fashion, that document emphasized the moral quality of rulers as a foundation for social harmony.

When wise men are entrusted with office, the sound of praise arises. If unprincipled men hold office, disasters and tumults are multiplied. In this world few men are born with knowledge: wisdom is the product of earnest meditation. In all things, great or small, find the right man and they will surely be well managed.[23]

In the decades that followed, court rituals and a system of court rankings for officials also were based on Chinese models, and the Chinese calendar was adopted. Subsequently, Chinese-style taxation systems, law codes, government ministries, and provincial administration were established, at least on paper. Two capital cities, first Nara and then Heian (Kyoto), arose, both modeled on the Chinese capital of Chang'an.

Chinese culture, no less than its political practices, also found favor in Japan. Various schools of Chinese Buddhism took root, first among the educated and literate classes and later more broadly in Japanese society, affecting, according to one scholar, "nearly every aspect of Japanese life." Art, architecture, education, medicine, views of the afterlife, attitudes toward suffering and the impermanence of life—all of this and more reflected the influence of Buddhist culture in Japan.[24] The Chinese writing system—and with it an interest in historical writing, calligraphy, and poetry—likewise proved attractive among the elite.

The absence of any compelling threat from China made it possible for the Japanese to be selective in their borrowing. By the tenth century, deliberate efforts to absorb additional elements of Chinese culture diminished, and formal tribute missions to China stopped, although private traders and Buddhist monks continued to make the difficult journey to the mainland. Over many centuries, the Japanese combined what they had assimilated from China with elements of their own tradition into a distinctive Japanese civilization, which differed from Chinese culture in many ways.

In the political realm, for example, the Japanese never succeeded in creating an effective centralized and bureaucratic state to match that of China. Although the court and the emperor retained an important ceremonial and cultural role, their real political authority over the country gradually diminished in favor of competing aristocratic families, both at court and in the provinces. A Chinese-style university trained officials, but rather than serving as a mechanism for recruiting talented commoners into the political elite, it enrolled students who were largely the sons of court aristocrats.

As political power became increasingly decentralized, local authorities developed their own military forces, the famous *samurai* warrior class of Japanese society. With their exquisite curved swords, the samurai developed a distinctive set of values featuring great skill in martial arts, bravery, loyalty, endurance, honor, and a preference for death over surrender. This was *bushido*, the way of the warrior. Japan's celebration of the samurai and of military virtues contrasted sharply with China's emphasis on intellectual achievements and political officeholding, which were accorded higher prestige than bearing arms. "The educated men of the land," wrote a Chinese minister in the eleventh century, "regard the carrying of arms as a disgrace."[25] The Japanese, clearly, did not agree.

Religiously as well, Japan remained distinctive. Although Buddhism in many forms took hold in the country, it never completely replaced the native beliefs and practices, which focused attention on numerous *kami*, sacred spirits associated with

The Samurai of Japan
This twelfth-century painting depicts the famous naval battle of Dan-no-ura (1185), in which the samurai warriors of two rival clans fought to the death. Many of the defeated Taira warriors, along with some of their women, plunged into the sea rather than surrender to their Minamoto rivals. The prominence of martial values in Japanese culture was one of the ways in which Japan differed from its Chinese neighbor, despite much borrowing. (Tokyo National Museum. Image: TNM Images Archives. Source: http://TnmArchives.jp/)

■ Comparison
In what different ways did Japanese and Korean women experience the pressures of Confucian orthodoxy?

human ancestors and various natural phenomena. Much later referred to as Shinto, this tradition provided legitimacy to the imperial family, based on claims of descent from the sun goddess. Because veneration of the kami lacked an elaborate philosophy or ritual, it conflicted very little with Buddhism. In fact, numerous kami were assimilated into Japanese Buddhism as local expressions of Buddhist deities or principles.

Japanese literary and artistic culture likewise evolved in distinctive ways, despite much borrowing from China. As in Korea and Vietnam, there emerged a unique writing system that combined Chinese characters with a series of phonetic symbols. A highly stylized Japanese poetic form, known as *tanka*, developed early and has remained a favored means of expression ever since. Particularly during the Heian period of Japanese history (794–1192), a highly refined esthetic culture found expression at the imperial court, even as the court's real political authority melted away. Court aristocrats and their ladies lived in splendor, composed poems, arranged flowers, and conducted their love affairs. "What counted," wrote one scholar, "was the proper costume, the right ceremonial act, the successful turn of phrase in a poem, and the appropriate expression of refined taste."[26] Much of our knowledge of this courtly culture comes from the work of women writers, who composed their diaries and novels in the vernacular Japanese script, rather than in the classical Chinese used by elite men. *The Tale of Genji*, a Japanese novel written by the woman author Murasaki Shikibu around 1000, provides an intimate picture of the intrigues and romances of court life.

At this level of society, Japan's women, unlike those in Korea, largely escaped the more oppressive features of Chinese Confucian culture, such as the prohibition of remarriage for widows, seclusion within the home, and foot binding. Perhaps this is because the most powerful Chinese influence on Japan occurred during the Tang dynasty, when Chinese elite women enjoyed considerable freedom. Japanese women continued to inherit property; Japanese married couples often lived apart or with the wife's family; and marriages were made and broken easily. None of this corresponded to Confucian values. When Japanese women did begin to lose status in the twelfth century and later, it had less to do with Confucian pressures than with the rise of a warrior culture. As the personal relationships of samurai warriors to their lords replaced marriage alliances as a political strategy, the influence of women in political life was reduced, but this was an internal Japanese phenomenon, not a reflection of Chinese influence.

Japan's ability to borrow extensively from China while developing its own distinctive civilization perhaps provided a model for its encounter with the West in the nineteenth century. Then, as before, Japan borrowed selectively from a foreign culture without losing either its political independence or its cultural uniqueness.

China and the Eurasian World Economy

Beyond China's central role in East Asia was its economic interaction with the wider world of Eurasia generally. On the one hand, China's remarkable economic growth, taking place during the Tang and Song dynasties, could hardly be contained within China's borders and clearly had a major impact throughout Eurasia. On the other hand, China was recipient as well as donor in the economic interactions of the postclassical era, and its own economic achievements owed something to the stimulus of contact with the larger world.

Spillovers: China's Impact on Eurasia

One of the outcomes of China's economic revolution lay in the diffusion of its many technological innovations to peoples and places far from East Asia as the movements of traders, soldiers, slaves, and pilgrims conveyed Chinese achievements abroad. Chinese techniques for producing salt by solar evaporation spread to the Islamic world and later to Christian Europe. Papermaking, known in China since the Han dynasty, spread to Korea and Vietnam by the fourth century C.E., to Japan and India by the seventh, to the Islamic world by the eighth, to Muslim Spain by 1150, to France and Germany in the 1300s, and to England in the 1490s. Printing, likewise a Chinese invention, rapidly reached Korea, where movable type became a highly developed technique, and Japan as well. Both technologies were heavily influenced by Buddhism, which accorded religious merit to the act of reproducing sacred texts. The Islamic world, however, valued handwritten calligraphy highly and generally resisted printing as impious until the nineteenth century. The adoption of printing in Europe was likewise delayed because of the absence of paper until the fourteenth century. Then movable type was reinvented by Johannes Gutenberg in the fifteenth century, although it is unclear whether he

■ **Connection**

In what ways did China participate in the world of Eurasian commerce and exchange, and with what outcomes?

was aware of Chinese and Korean precedents. With implications for mass literacy, bureaucracy, scholarship, the spread of religion, and the exchange of information, papermaking and printing were Chinese innovations of revolutionary and global dimensions.

Chinese technologies were seldom simply transferred from one place to another. More often a particular Chinese technique or product stimulated innovations in more distant lands in accordance with local needs.[27] For example, as the Chinese recipe for gunpowder, invented around 1000, became available in Europe, together with some early and simple firearms, these innovations triggered the development of cannons in the early fourteenth century. Soon cannons appeared in the Islamic world and by 1356 in China itself, which first used cast iron rather than bronze in their construction. But the highly competitive European state system drove the "gunpowder revolution" much further and more rapidly than in China's imperial state. Chinese textile, metallurgical, and naval technologies likewise stimulated imitation and innovation all across Eurasia. An example is the magnetic compass, a Chinese invention eagerly embraced by mariners of many cultural backgrounds as they traversed the Indian Ocean.

In addition to its technological influence, China's prosperity during the Song dynasty greatly stimulated commercial life and market-based behavior all across the Eurasian trading world. China's products—silk, porcelain, lacquerware—found eager buyers from Japan to East Africa, and everywhere in between. The immense size and wealth of China's domestic economy also provided a ready market for hundreds of commodities from afar. For example, the lives of many thousands of people in the spice-producing islands of what is now Indonesia were transformed as they came to depend on Chinese consumers' demand for their products. "[O]ne hundred million [Chinese] people," wrote historian William McNeill, "increasingly caught up within a commercial network, buying and selling to supplement every day's livelihood, made a significant difference to the way other human beings made their livings throughout a large part of the civilized world."[28] Such was the ripple effect of China's economic revolution.

On the Receiving End: China as Economic Beneficiary

Chinese economic growth and technological achievements significantly shaped the Eurasian world of the postclassical era, but that pattern of interaction was surely not a one-way street, for China too was changed by its engagement with a wider world. During this period, for example, China had learned about the cultivation and processing of both cotton and sugar from India. From Vietnam, around 1000, China gained access to the new, fast-ripening, and drought-resistant strains of rice that made a highly productive rice-based agriculture possible in the drier and more rugged regions of southern China. This marked a major turning point in Chinese history as the frontier region south of the Yangzi River grew rapidly in population, overtaking the traditional centers of Chinese civilization in the north.

Technologically as well, China's extraordinary burst of creativity owed something to the stimulus of cross-cultural contact. Awareness of Persian windmills, for example, spurred the development of a distinct but related device in China. Printing arose from China's growing involvement with the world of Buddhism, which put a spiritual premium on the reproduction of the Buddha's image and of short religious texts that were carried as charms. It was in Buddhist monasteries during the Tang dynasty that the long-established practice of printing with seals was elaborated by Chinese monks into woodblock printing. The first printed book, in 868 C.E., was a famous Buddhist text, the Diamond Sutra. Gunpowder too seems to have had an Indian and Buddhist connection. An Indian Buddhist monk traveling in China in 644 C.E. identified soils that contained saltpeter and showed that they produced a purple flame when put into a fire. This was the beginning of Chinese experiments, which finally led to a reliable recipe for gunpowder.

A further transforming impact of China's involvement with a wider world derived from its growing participation in Indian Ocean trade. By the Tang dynasty, thousands of ships annually visited the ports of southern China, and settled communities of foreign merchants—Arabs, Persians, Indians, Southeast Asians—turned some of these cities into cosmopolitan centers. Buddhist temples, Muslim mosques and cemeteries, and Hindu phallic sculptures graced the skyline of Quanzhou, a coastal city in southern China. Occasionally the tensions of cultural diversity erupted in violence, such as the massacre of tens of thousands of foreigners in Canton during the 870s when Chinese rebel forces sacked the city. Indian Ocean commerce also contributed much to the transformation of southern China from a subsistence economy to one more heavily based on producing for export. In the process, merchants achieved a degree of social acceptance not known before, including their frequent appointment to high-ranking bureaucratic positions. Finally, much-beloved stories of the monkey god, widely popular even in contemporary China, derived from Indian sources transmitted by Indian Ocean commerce.[29]

China and Buddhism

By far the most important gift that China received from India was neither cotton, nor sugar, nor the knowledge of saltpeter, but a religion, Buddhism. The gradual assimilation of this South Asian religious tradition into Chinese culture illustrates the process of cultural encounter and adaptation and invites comparison with the spread of Christianity into Europe. Until the adoption of Marxism in the twentieth century, Buddhism was the only large-scale cultural borrowing in Chinese history. It also made China into a launching pad for Buddhism's dispersion to Korea and from there to Japan as well. Thus, as Buddhism faded in the land of its birth, it became solidly rooted in much of East Asia, providing an element of cultural commonality for a vast region (see Map 9.2).

Map 9.2   The World of Asian Buddhism
Born in India, Buddhism later spread widely throughout much of Asia to provide a measure of cultural or religious commonality to this vast region.

Making Buddhism Chinese

■ Change
What facilitated the rooting of Buddhism within China?

Buddhism initially entered China via the Silk Road trading network during the first and second centuries C.E. The stability and prosperity of the Han dynasty, then at its height, ensured that the new "barbarian" religion held little appeal for native

Chinese. Furthermore, the Indian culture from which Buddhism sprang was at odds with Chinese understandings of the world in many ways. Buddhism's commitment to a secluded and monastic life for monks and nuns seemed to dishonor Chinese family values, and its concern for individual salvation or enlightenment appeared selfish, contradicting the social orientation of Confucian thinking. Its abstract philosophy ran counter to the more concrete, "this-worldly" concerns of Chinese thinkers; and the Buddhist concept of infinite eons of time, endlessly repeating themselves, was quite a stretch for the Chinese, who normally thought in terms of finite family generations or dynastic cycles. No wonder that for the first several centuries C.E., Buddhism was largely the preserve of foreign merchants and monks living in China.

In the half millennium between roughly 300 and 800 C.E., however, Buddhism took solid root in China within both elite and popular culture, becoming a permanent, though fluctuating, presence in Chinese life. How did this remarkable transformation unfold? It began, arguably, with the collapse of the Han dynasty around 200 C.E. The chaotic, violent, and politically fragmented centuries that followed seriously discredited Confucianism and opened the door to alternative understandings of the world. Nomadic rulers, now governing much of northern China, found Buddhism useful in part because it was foreign. "We were born out of the marches," declared one of them, "and though we are unworthy, we have complied with our appointed destiny and govern the Chinese as their prince. . . . Buddha being a barbarian god is the very one we should worship."[30] Rulers and elite families provided money and land that enabled the building of many Buddhist monasteries, temples, and works of art. In southern China, where many northern aristocrats had fled following the disastrous decline of the Han dynasty, Buddhism provided some comfort in the face of a collapsing society. Its emphasis on ritual, morality, and contemplation represented an intellectually and esthetically satisfying response to times that were so clearly out of joint.

Meanwhile, Buddhist monasteries increasingly provided an array of social services for ordinary people. In them, travelers found accommodation; those fleeing from China's many upheavals discovered a place of refuge; desperate people received charity; farmers borrowed seed for the next planting; the sick were treated; children learned to read. And for many, Buddhism was associated with access to magical powers as reports of miracles abounded. Battles were won, rain descended on drought-ridden areas, diseases were cured, and guilt was relieved—all through the magical ministrations of charismatic monks.

Accompanying all of this was a serious effort by monks, scholars, and translators to present this Indian religion in terms that Chinese could relate to. Thus the Buddhist term *dharma*, referring to the Buddha's teaching, was translated as *dao*, or "the way," a notion long familiar in both Daoist and Confucian thinking (see Chapter 5). The Buddhist notion of "morality" was translated with the Confucian term that referred to "filial submission and obedience." Some Indian concepts were modified in the process of translation. For example, the idea that "husband supports wife," which reflected a considerable respect for women and mothers in early Indian Buddhism, became in translation "husband controls wife."[31]

As Buddhism took hold in China, it was primarily in its broader Mahayana form—complete with numerous deities, the veneration of relics, many heavens and hells, and bodhisattvas to aid the believer—rather than the more psychological and individualistic Theravada Buddhism (see Chapter 5). One of the most popular forms of Buddhism in China was the Pure Land School, in which faithfully repeating the name of an earlier Buddha, the Amitabha, was sufficient to ensure rebirth in a beautifully described heavenly realm, the Pure Land. In its emphasis on salvation by faith, without arduous study or intensive meditation, Pure Land Buddhism became a highly popular and authentically Chinese version of the Indian faith.

China's reunification under the Sui and early Tang dynasties witnessed growing state support for Buddhism. The Sui emperor Wendi (reigned 581–604 C.E.) had monasteries constructed at the base of China's five sacred mountains, further identifying the imported religion with traditional Chinese culture. He even used Buddhism to justify his military campaigns. "With a hundred victories in a hundred battles," he declared, "we promote the practice of the ten Buddhist virtues."[32] With state support and growing popular acceptance, monasteries became centers of great wealth, largely exempt from taxation, owning large estates; running businesses such as oil presses, water mills, and pawn shops; collecting gems, gold, and lavish works of art; and even employing slaves. But Buddhism, while solidly entrenched in Chinese life by the early Tang dynasty, never achieved the independence from state authorities that the Christian church acquired in Europe. The examinations for becoming a monk were supervised by the state, and education in the monasteries included the required study of the Confucian classics. And in the mid-ninth century, the state showed quite dramatically just how much control it could exercise over the Buddhist establishment.

Losing State Support: The Crisis of Chinese Buddhism

■ Change
What were the major sources of opposition to Buddhism within China?

The impressive growth of Chinese Buddhism was accompanied by a persistent undercurrent of resistance and criticism. Some saw the Buddhist establishment, at least potentially, as a "state within a state" and a challenge to imperial authority. More important was a deepening resentment of its enormous wealth. One fifth-century critic, referring to monks, put the issue squarely: "Why is it that their ideals are noble and far-reaching and their activities still are base and common? [They] become merchants and engage in barter, wrangling with the masses for profit."[33] When state treasuries were short of funds, government officials cast a covetous eye on wealthy and tax-exempt monasteries. Furthermore, Buddhism was clearly of foreign origin and offensive for that reason to some Confucian and Daoist thinkers. The celibacy of the monks and their withdrawal from society, the critics argued, undermined the Confucian-based family system of Chinese tradition.

Such criticisms took on new meaning in the changed environment of China after about 800 C.E. After centuries of considerable foreign influence in China, a growing resentment against foreign culture, particularly among the literate classes, increasingly took hold. The turning point may well have been the An Lushan rebellion (755–763), in which a general of foreign origin led a major revolt against the Tang dynasty. Whatever its origins, an increasingly xenophobic reaction set in among the upper classes, reflected in a desire to return to an imagined "purity" of earlier times.[34] In this setting, the old criticisms of Buddhism became more sharply focused. In 819, Han Yu, a leading figure in the Confucian counterattack on Buddhism, wrote a scathing memorial to the emperor, criticizing his willingness to honor a relic of the Buddha's finger.

> Now the Buddha was of barbarian origin. His language differed from Chinese speech; his clothes were of a different cut; his mouth did not pronounce the prescribed words of the Former Kings. . . . He did not recognize the relationship between prince and subject, nor the sentiments of father and son. . . . I pray that Your Majesty will turn this bone over to the officials that it may be cast into water or fire.[35]

Several decades later, the Chinese state took direct action against the Buddhist establishment as well as against other foreign religions. A series of imperial decrees between 841 and 845 ordered some 260,000 monks and nuns to return to normal life as tax-paying citizens. Thousands of monasteries, temples, and shrines were either destroyed or turned to public use, while the state confiscated the lands, money, metals, and serfs belonging to monasteries. Buddhists were now forbidden to use gold, silver, copper, iron, and gems in constructing their images. These actions dealt a serious blow to Chinese Buddhism. Its scholars and monks were scattered, its creativity diminished, and its institutions came even more firmly under state control.

Despite this persecution, Buddhism did not vanish from China. At the level of elite culture, its philosophical ideas played a role in the reformulation of Confucian thinking that took place during the Song dynasty. At the village level, Buddhism became one element of Chinese popular religion, which also included the veneration of ancestors, the honoring of Confucius, and Daoist shrines and rituals. Temples frequently included statues of Confucius, Laozi, and the Buddha, with little sense of any incompatibility among them. "Every black-haired son of Han," the Chinese have long said, "wears a Confucian thinking cap, a Daoist robe, and Buddhist sandals." Unlike Europe, where an immigrant religion triumphed over and excluded all other faiths, Buddhism in China became assimilated into Chinese culture alongside its other traditions.

Reflections: Why Do Things Change?

The rapidity of change in modern societies is among the most distinctive features of recent history, but change and transformation, though at various rates, have been constants in the human story since the very beginning. Explaining how and why human societies change is perhaps the central issue that historians confront, no matter which societies or periods of time they study. Those who specialize in the history of some particular culture or civilization often emphasize sources of change operating within those societies, although there is intense disagreement as to which are most significant. The ideas of great thinkers, the policies of leaders, struggles for power, the conflict of classes, the impact of new technologies, the growth or decline in population, variations in local climate or weather—all of these and more have their advocates as the primary motor of historical transformation.

Of course, it is not necessary to choose among them. The history of classical and postclassical China illustrates the range of internal factors that have driven change in that civilization. The political conflicts of the "era of warring states" provided the setting and the motivation for the emergence of Confucianism and Daoism, which in turn have certainly shaped the character and texture of Chinese civilization over many centuries. The personal qualities and brutal policies of Shihuangdi surely played a role in China's unification and in the brief duration of the Qin dynasty. The subsequent creation of a widespread network of canals and waterways as well as the country's technological achievements served to maintain that unity over very long periods of time. But the massive inequalities of Chinese society generated the peasant upheavals, which periodically shattered that unity and led to new ruling dynasties. Sometimes natural events, such as droughts and floods, triggered those rebellions.

World historians, more so than those who study particular civilizations or nations, have been inclined to find the primary source of change in contact with strangers, in external connections and interactions, whether direct or indirect. The histories of China and East Asia provide plenty of examples for this point of view as well. Conceptions of China as the "middle kingdom," infinitely superior to all surrounding societies, grew out of centuries of involvement with its neighbors. Some of those neighbors became Chinese as China's imperial reach grew, especially to the south. Even those that did not, such as Korea, Vietnam, and Japan, were decisively transformed by proximity to the "radiating civilization" of China. China's own cuisine, so distinctive in recent centuries, may well be a quite recent invention, drawing heavily on Indian and Southeast Asian cooking. Buddhism, of course, is an obvious borrowing from abroad, although its incorporation into Chinese civilization and its ups and downs within China owed much to internal cultural and political realities.

In the end, clear distinctions between internal and external sources of change in China's history—or that of any other society—are perhaps misleading. The boundary between "inside" and "outside" is itself a constantly changing line. Should the borderlands of northern China, where Chinese and Turkic peoples met and mingled, be regarded as internal or external to China itself? And, as the histories of Chinese Buddhism and of Japanese culture so clearly indicate, what comes from beyond is always transformed by what it encounters within.

Second Thoughts

What's the Significance?

Sui dynasty	tribute system	Shotoku Taishi
Tang dynasty	Xiongnu	*bushido*
Song dynasty economic revolution	Khitan/Jurchen people	Chinese Buddhism
Hangzhou	Silla dynasty (Korea)	Emperor Wendi
foot binding	*hangul/chu nom*	
	Trung sisters	

To assess your mastery of the material in this chapter, see the **Online Study Guide** at bedfordstmartins.com/strayer.

Big Picture Questions

1. In what ways did Tang and Song dynasty China resemble the classical Han dynasty period, and in what ways had China changed?
2. Based on this chapter, how would you respond to the idea that China was a self-contained or isolated civilization?
3. In what different ways did nearby peoples experience their giant Chinese neighbor, and how did they respond to it?
4. How can you explain the changing fortunes of Buddhism in China?
5. How did China influence the world beyond East Asia? How was China itself transformed by its encounters with a wider world?

Next Steps: For Further Study

Samuel Adshead, *Tang China: The Rise of the East in World History* (2004). Explores the role of China within the larger world.

Patricia Ebrey, *The Inner Quarters* (1993). A balanced account of the gains and losses experienced by Chinese women during the changes of the Song dynasty.

Mark Elvin, *The Pattern of the Chinese Past* (1973). A classic account of the Chinese economic revolution.

Edward Shaffer, *The Golden Peaches of Samarkand* (1985). Examines the interaction between China and Central Asia during the Tang dynasty.

Murasaki Shikibu, *The Tale of Genji*, translated by Royall Tyler (2002). Written around 1000, this saga of Japanese court life is sometimes called the world's first novel.

Arthur F. Wright, *Buddhism in Chinese History* (1959). An older account filled with wonderful stories and anecdotes.

Upper River during the Qing Ming Festival, http://www.ibiblio.org/ulysses/gec/painting/qingming/full.htm. A scrolling reproduction of a huge Chinese painting, showing in detail the Song dynasty city of Kaifeng.

For Web sites and documents related to this chapter, see **Make History** at bedfordstmartins.com/strayer.

CUM SEDEAT KAROLUS MAGNO COORONATUS HONORE
EST IOSIA SIMILLS PARQUE THLODOS

CHAPTER TEN

The Worlds of European Christendom

Connected and Divided

500–1300

"We embraced each other once, then again and again. We were like brothers meeting after a long separation."[1] That is how the Eastern Orthodox patriarch Athenagoras described his historic meeting with Roman Catholic Pope Paul VI in early 1964 near the Mount of Olives in Jerusalem, the very site where Jesus had spent the night before his arrest. Not for more than 500 years had the heads of these two ancient branches of Christianity personally met. Now they held each other and exchanged gifts, including a representation of two of Christ's disciples embracing. Then they lifted mutual decrees of excommunication that representatives of their respective churches had imposed in 1054. It was a small step in a still very incomplete process of overcoming this deep rift within Christianity, which had been in the making for well over a thousand years. How had the world of Christendom come to be so sharply divided, both religiously and politically, as well as in terms of the larger historical trajectories of its eastern and western halves?

DURING THE POSTCLASSICAL ERA, CHRISTIANITY PROVIDED a measure of cultural commonality for the diverse societies of western Eurasia, much as Chinese civilization and Buddhism did for East Asia. By 1300, almost all of these societies—from Spain and England in the west to Russia in the east—had embraced in some form the teachings of the Middle Eastern Jewish carpenter called Jesus, but the world of European Christendom was deeply divided, both politically and

---

Charlemagne: This fifteenth-century manuscript painting depicts Charlemagne, King of the Franks, who was crowned Emperor by the pope in 800 C.E. His reign illustrates the close and sometimes conflicted relationship of political and religious authorities in postclassical Europe. It also represents the futile desire of many in Western Europe to revive the old Roman Empire, even as a substantially new civilization was taking shape in the aftermath of the Roman collapse several centuries earlier. (Victoria & Albert Museum, London, UK/The Bridgeman Art Library) religiously, in a way that the Chinese world was not. Its eastern half, known as the Byzantine Empire or Byzantium, continued the traditions of the Roman Empire, though on a smaller scale, until its conquest by the Muslim Turks in 1453. Centered on the magnificent city of Constantinople, Byzantium gradually evolved a distinctive civilization, all the while claiming to be Roman and seeking to preserve the heritage of the classical Mediterranean. With a particular form of Christianity known as Eastern Orthodoxy, the Byzantine Empire housed one of the major third-wave civilizations.

In Western or Latin Christendom, encompassing what we now know as Western Europe, political and religious leaders also tried to maintain links to the classical world, as illustrated by the spread of Christianity, the use of Latin in elite circles, and various efforts to revive or imitate the Roman Empire. The setting, however, was far different. In the West, the Roman imperial order had largely vanished by 500 C.E., accompanied by the weakening of many features of Roman civilization. Roads fell into disrepair, cities decayed, and long-distance trade shriveled. What replaced the old Roman order was a highly localized society—fragmented, decentralized, and competitive—in sharp contrast to the unified state of Byzantium. Like Byzantium, the Latin West ultimately became thoroughly Christian, but it was a gradual process lasting centuries, and its Roman Catholic Church, increasingly centered on the pope, had an independence from political authorities that the Eastern Orthodox Church did not. Moreover, the western church in particular and its society in general were far more rural than Byzantium and certainly had nothing to compare to the splendor of Constantinople. However, slowly at first and then with increasing speed after 1000, Western Europe emerged as an especially dynamic, expansive, and innovative third-wave civilization, combining elements of its classical past with the culture of Germanic and Celtic peoples to produce a hybrid civilization.

Europe eventually became the global center of Christianity, but that destiny was far from clear in 500 C.E. At that time, only about one-third of the world's Christians lived in Europe, while the rest found their homes in various parts of Africa, the Middle East, and Asia.[2] There they often followed distinct forms of Christianity, such as Nestorianism, which was regarded as heretical in Europe for its belief that Jesus had two quite distinct natures, one human and one divine. In Egypt, India, and Persia, remnants of earlier and larger Christian communities have survived as tolerated minorities into the present. By contrast, in early Armenia and Ethiopia (Axum), Christianity became the faith of the majority and has continued to express the national identity of peoples long cut off from contact with other Christian societies. Finally, the early Christian communities of North Africa, Nubia, Central Asia, and western China were largely eliminated as these regions subsequently embraced alternative religious traditions, such as Islam, Buddhism, or Confucianism. In this chapter, however, the historical spotlight falls on those regions that became the center of the Christian world—Byzantium and Western Europe.

Eastern Christendom: Building on the Past

Unlike most empires, Byzantium has no clear starting point. Its own leaders, as well as its neighbors and enemies, viewed it as simply a continuation of the Roman Empire. Some historians date its beginning to 330 C.E., when the Roman emperor Constantine, who became a Christian during his reign, established a new capital, Constantinople, on the site of an ancient Greek city called Byzantium. At the end of that century, the Roman Empire was formally divided into eastern and western halves, thus launching a division of Christendom that has lasted into the twenty-first century. Although the western Roman Empire collapsed during the fifth century, the eastern half persisted for another thousand years. Housing the ancient civilizations of Egypt, Greece, Syria, and Anatolia, the eastern Roman Empire (Byzantium) was far wealthier, more urbanized, and more cosmopolitan than its western counterpart; it possessed a much more defensible capital in the heavily walled city of Constantinople; and it had a shorter frontier to guard. Byzantium also enjoyed access to the Black Sea and command of the eastern Mediterranean. With a stronger army, navy, and merchant marine as well as clever diplomacy, its leaders were able to deflect the Germanic and Hun invaders who had overwhelmed the western Roman Empire.

Much that was late Roman—its roads, taxation system, military structures, centralized administration, imperial court, laws, Christian church—persisted in the east for many centuries. Like Tang dynasty China seeking to restore the glory of the Han era, Byzantium consciously sought to preserve the legacy of classical civilization and the Roman Empire. Constantinople was to be a "New Rome," and Byzantines referred to themselves as "Romans." Fearing contamination by "barbarian" customs, emperors forbade the residents of Constantinople from wearing boots, trousers, clothing made from animal skins, and long hairstyles, all of which were

■ **Continuity and Change**

In what respects did Byzantium continue the patterns of the classical Roman Empire? In what ways did it diverge from those patterns?

$\mathcal{S}$napshot   **Key Moments in Byzantine History**

Founding of Constantinople	330
Final division of Roman Empire into eastern and western halves	ca. 395
Reign of Justinian; attempted reconquest of western empire	527–565
Loss of Syria/Palestine, Egypt, and North Africa to Arab forces	7th century
Iconoclastic controversy	726–843
Conversion of Vladimir, prince of Kiev, to Christianity	988
Mutual excommunication of pope and patriarch	1054
Crusaders sack Constantinople	1204
Ottomans seize Constantinople; end of Byzantine Empire	1453

associated with Germanic peoples, and insisted instead on Roman-style robes and sandals. But much changed as well over the centuries, marking the Byzantine Empire as the home of a distinctive civilization.

The Byzantine State

Perhaps the most obvious change was one of scale, as the Byzantine Empire never approximated the size of its Roman predecessor (see Map 10.1). The western Roman Empire was permanently lost to Byzantium, despite Emperor Justinian's (reigned 527–565) impressive but short-lived attempt to reconquer the Mediterranean basin. The rapid Arab/Islamic expansion in the seventh century resulted in the loss of Syria/Palestine, Egypt, and North Africa. Nonetheless, until roughly 1200, a more compact Byzantine Empire remained a major force in the eastern Mediterranean, controlling Greece, much of the Balkans (southeastern Europe), and Anatolia. A reformed administrative system gave appointed generals civil authority

Map 10.1 The Byzantine Empire

The Byzantine Empire reached its greatest extent under Emperor Justinian in the mid-sixth century C.E. It subsequently lost considerable territory to various Christian European powers as well as to Muslim Arab and Turkic invaders.

in the empire's provinces and allowed them to raise armies from the landowning peasants of the region. From that territorial base, the empire's naval and merchant vessels were active in both the Mediterranean and Black seas.

In its heyday, the Byzantine state was an impressive creation. Political authority remained tightly centralized in Constantinople, where the emperor claimed to govern all creation as God's worldly representative, styling himself the "peer of the Apostles" and the "sole ruler of the world." The imperial court tried to imitate the awesome grandeur of what they thought was God's heavenly court, which in fact resembled ancient Persian imperial splendor. Aristocrats trained in classical Greek rhetoric and literature took jobs in the administration in order to participate in court ceremonies that maintained their elite status. Parades of these silk-clad administrators added splendor to the imperial court, which also included mechanical lions that roared, birds that sang, and an immense throne that quickly elevated the emperor high above his presumably awestruck visitors. Nonetheless, this centralized state touched only lightly on the lives of most people, as it focused primarily on collecting taxes, maintaining order, and suppressing revolts. "Personal freedom in the provinces was constrained more by neighbors and rival households," concluded one historian, "than by the imperial government."[3]

After 1085, Byzantine territory shrank, owing to incursions by aggressive Christian European powers, by Catholic Crusaders, and later by Turkic Muslim invaders. The end came in 1453 when the Turkic Ottoman Empire, then known as the "sword of Islam," finally took Constantinople. One eyewitness to the event wrote a moving lament to his fallen city.

> And the entire city was to be seen in the tents of the [Turkish] camp, the city deserted, lying lifeless, naked, soundless, without either form or beauty. O city, head of all cities, center of the four corners of the world, pride of the Romans, civilizer of the barbarians.... Where is your beauty, O paradise...? Where are the bodies of the Apostle of my Lord...? Where are the relics of the saints, those of the martyrs? Where are the remains of Constantine the Great and the other emperors?... Oh, what a loss![4]

The Byzantine Church and Christian Divergence

Intimately tied to the state was the Church, a relationship that became known as *caesaropapism*. Unlike Western Europe, where the Roman Catholic Church maintained some degree of independence from political authorities, in Byzantium the emperor assumed something of the role of both "Caesar," as head of state, and the pope, as head of the Church. Thus he appointed the patriarch, or leader, of the Orthodox Church; sometimes made decisions about doctrine; called church councils into session; and generally treated the Church as a government department. "The [Empire] and the church have a great unity and community," declared a twelfth-century patriarch. "Indeed they cannot be separated."[5] A dense network of bishops and priests brought the message of the Church to every corner of the empire, while numerous

■ **Comparison**

How did Eastern Orthodox Christianity differ from Roman Catholicism?

monasteries accommodated holy men, whose piety, self-denial, and good works made them highly influential among both elite and ordinary people.

Orthodox Christianity had a pervasive influence on every aspect of Byzantine life. It legitimated the supreme and absolute rule of the emperor, for he was a God-anointed ruler, a reflection of the glory of God on earth. It also provided a cultural identity for the empire's subjects. Even more than being "Roman," they were orthodox, or "right-thinking," Christians for whom the empire and the Church were equally essential to achieving eternal salvation. Constantinople was filled with churches and the relics of numerous saints. And the churches were filled with icons—religious paintings of Jesus, Mary, and the other saints—some of them artistic masterpieces, that many believed conveyed the divine presence to believers. Obscure theological issues about the Trinity and especially about the relationship of God and Jesus engaged the attention of ordinary people. One fourth-century bishop complained: "I wish to know the price of bread; one answers 'The Father is greater than the Son.' I inquire whether my bath is ready; one answers 'The Son has been made out of nothing.' "[6] Partisans of competing chariot-racing teams, known as the Greens and the Blues, vigorously debated theological issues as well as the merits of their favorite drivers.

As Eastern Orthodoxy evolved, it came to define itself against an emerging Latin Christianity centered on papal Rome, as a deepening divide opened within the world of Christendom. Both had derived, of course, from the growth of Christianity in the Roman Empire and therefore had much in common—the teachings of Jesus; the Bible; the sacraments; a church hierarchy of patriarchs, bishops, and priests; a missionary impulse; and intolerance toward other religions. Despite these shared features, a general sense of a single widespread Christian community was increasingly replaced by an awareness of difference, competition, and outright hostility that even a common fear of Islam could not overcome. In part, this growing religious divergence reflected the political separation and rivalry between the Byzantine Empire and the emerging kingdoms of Western Europe. As the growth of Islam in the seventh century (described more fully in Chapter 11) submerged earlier centers of Christianity in the Middle East and North Africa,

St. Mark's Basilica
Consecrated in 1094, this ornate cathedral, although located in Venice, Italy, is a classic example of Byzantine architecture. Such churches represented perhaps the greatest achievement of Byzantine art and were certainly the most monumental expressions of Byzantine culture. (Erich Lessing/Art Resource, NY)

Constantinople and Rome alone remained as alternative hubs of the Church. But they were now in different states that competed with each other for territory and for the right to claim the legacy of imperial Rome.

Beyond such political differences were those of language and culture. Although Latin remained the language of the Church and of elite communication in the West, it was abandoned in the Byzantine Empire in favor of Greek, which remained the basis for Byzantine education. More than in the West, Byzantine thinkers sought to formulate Christian doctrine in terms of Greek philosophical concepts.

Differences in theology and church practice likewise widened the gulf between Orthodoxy and Catholicism, despite agreement on fundamental doctrines. Disagreements about the nature of the Trinity or the relative importance of faith and reason gave rise to much controversy. One major issue involved the veneration of icons, popular paintings of saints and biblical scenes, usually painted on small wooden panels. Between 726 and 843, the Eastern Orthodox Church, on orders from Byzantine emperors, took the offensive against the use of icons in worship, arguing that they too easily became "idols," distracting believers from the adoration of God himself. Perhaps influenced by Islam's prohibition on the representation of the human form, this effort, known as *iconoclasm*, involved the actual destruction of much-loved icons and generated considerable opposition within Byzantium itself until it was ended in the mid-ninth century. But while it lasted, iconoclasm was highly offensive within Roman Catholic circles as well, for most of the Roman popes were fervent supporters of icon veneration.

Other more modest differences also occasioned mutual misunderstanding and disdain. Priests in the West shaved and, after 1050 or so, were supposed to remain celibate, while those in Byzantium allowed their beards to grow long and were permitted to marry. Orthodox ritual called for using bread leavened with yeast in the Mass, but Catholics used unleavened bread. More significant was the question of authority. Eastern Orthodox leaders sharply rejected the growing claims of Roman popes to be the sole and final authority for all Christians everywhere.

The rift in the world of Christendom grew gradually from the seventh century on, punctuated by various efforts to bridge the mounting divide between the western and eastern branches of the Church. A sign of this continuing deterioration occurred in 1054 when representatives of both churches mutually excommunicated each other, declaring in effect that those in the opposing tradition were not true Christians. The Crusades, launched in 1095 by the Catholic pope against the forces of Islam, made things worse. Western Crusaders, passing through the Byzantine Empire on their way to the Middle East, engaged in frequent conflict with local people and thus deepened the distrust between them. From the western viewpoint, Orthodox practices were "blasphemous, even heretical." One western observer of the Second Crusade noted that the Greeks "were judged not to be Christians and the Franks [French] considered killing them a matter of no importance."[7] During the Fourth Crusade in 1204, western forces seized and looted Constantinople and ruled Byzantium for the next half century. Their brutality only confirmed Byzantine views of their Roman Catholic despoilers as nothing more than barbarians. According to one Byzantine account, "they sacked the sacred places and trampled on divine things . . . they tore children from their mothers . . . and they defiled virgins in the holy chapels, fearing neither God's anger nor man's vengeance."[8] After this, the rupture in the world of Christendom proved irreparable.

Byzantium and the World

■ **Connection**

In what ways was the Byzantine Empire linked to a wider world?

Beyond its tense relationship with Western Europe, the Byzantine Empire, located astride Europe and Asia, also interacted intensively with its other neighbors. On a political and military level, Byzantium continued the long-term Roman struggle with the Persian Empire. That persisting conflict weakened both of them and was one factor in the remarkable success of Arab armies as they poured out of Arabia in the seventh century. Although Persia quickly became part of the Islamic world, Byzantium held out, even as it lost considerable territory to the Arabs. A Byzantine military innovation, known as "Greek fire"—a potent and flammable combination of oil, sulfur, and lime that was launched from bronze tubes—helped to hold off the Arabs. It operated something like a flamethrower and subsequently passed into Arab and Chinese arsenals as well. Byzantium's ability to defend its core regions delayed for many centuries the Islamic advance into southeastern Europe, which finally occurred at the hands of the Turkish Ottoman Empire in the fifteenth and sixteenth centuries.

Economically, the Byzantine Empire was a central player in the long-distance trade of Eurasia, with commercial links to Western Europe, Russia, Central Asia, the Islamic world, and China. Its gold coin, the bezant, was a widely used currency in the Mediterranean basin for more than 500 years, and wearing such coins as pendants was a high-status symbol in the less developed kingdoms of Western Europe.[9] The luxurious products of Byzantine craftspeople—jewelry, gemstones, silver and gold work, linen and woolen textiles, purple dyes—were much in demand. Its silk industry, based on Chinese technology, supplied much of the Mediterranean basin with this precious fabric.

The cultural influence of Byzantium was likewise significant. Preserving much of ancient Greek learning, the Byzantine Empire transmitted this classical heritage to the Islamic world as well as to the Christian West. In both places, it had an immensely stimulating impact among scientists, philosophers, theologians, and other intellectuals. Some saw it as an aid to faith and understanding of the world, while others feared it as impious and distracting (see the section on "Reason and Faith").

Byzantine religious culture also spread widely among Slavic-speaking peoples in the Balkans and Russia. As lands to the south and the east were overtaken by Islam, Byzantium looked to the north. By the early eleventh century, steady military pressure had brought many of the Balkan Slavic peoples, especially the Bulgars, under Byzantine control. Christianity and literacy accompanied this Byzantine offensive. Already in the ninth century, two Byzantine missionaries, Cyril and

Methodius, had developed an alphabet, based on Greek letters, with which Slavic languages could be written. This Cyrillic script made it possible to translate the Bible and other religious literature into these languages and greatly aided the process of conversion.

The Conversion of Russia

The most significant expansion of Orthodox Christianity occurred among the Slavic peoples of what is now Ukraine and western Russia. In this culturally diverse region, which also included Finnic and Baltic peoples as well as Viking traders, a modest state known as Kievan Rus—named after the most prominent city, Kiev—emerged in the ninth century C.E. Like many of the new third-wave civilizations, the development of Rus was stimulated by trade, in this case along the Dnieper River, linking Scandinavia and Byzantium. Loosely led by various princes, especially the prince of Kiev, Rus was a society of slaves and freemen, privileged people and commoners, dominant men and subordinate women. This stratification marked it as a third-wave civilization in the making (see Map 10.3 on page 283).

■ **Connection**

How did links to Byzantium transform the new civilization of Kievan Rus?

Religion reflected the region's cultural diversity, with the gods and practices of many peoples much in evidence. Small numbers of Christians, Muslims, and Jews were part of the mix. Then, in the late tenth century, a decisive turning point occurred. The growing interaction of Rus with the larger world prompted Prince Vladimir of Kiev to affiliate with one of the major religions of the area. He was searching for a faith that would unify the diverse peoples of his region, while linking Rus into wider networks of communication and exchange. According to ancient chronicles, he actively considered Judaism, Islam, Roman Catholicism, and Greek Orthodoxy before finally deciding on the religion of Byzantium. He rejected Islam, the chronicles tell us, because it prohibited alcoholic drink and "drinking is the joy of the Russes." The splendor of Constantinople's Orthodox churches apparently captured the imagination of Rus's envoys, for there they reported, "we knew not whether we were in heaven or on earth."[10] Political and commercial considerations no doubt also played a role in Vladimir's decision, and he acquired a sister of the Byzantine emperor as his bride, along with numerous Byzantine priests and advisers. Whatever the precise process, it was a freely made decision. Eastern Orthodox Christianity thus came to Rus without the pressure of foreign military defeat or occupation. Eventually, it took deep root among the Russian people.

It was a fateful choice with long-term implications for Russian history, for it brought this fledgling civilization firmly into the world of Orthodox Christianity, separating it from both the realm of Islam and the Roman Catholic West. Like many new civilizations, Rus borrowed extensively from its older and more sophisticated neighbor. Among these borrowings were Byzantine architectural styles, the Cyrillic alphabet, the extensive use of icons, a monastic tradition stressing prayer and service, and political ideals of imperial control of the Church, all of which became part of a transformed Rus. Orthodoxy also provided a more unified identity for this emerging civilization and religious legitimacy for its rulers. Centuries later, when Byzantium had fallen to the Turks, a few Russian church leaders proclaimed the doctrine of a "third Rome." The original Rome had betrayed the faith, and the second Rome, Constantinople, had succumbed to Muslim infidels. Moscow was now the third Rome, the final protector and defender of true Orthodox Christianity. Though not widely proclaimed in Russia itself, such a notion reflected the "Russification" of Eastern Orthodoxy and its growing role as an element of Russian national identity. It was also a reminder of the enduring legacy of a thousand years of Byzantine history, long after the empire itself had vanished.

Western Christendom: Constructing a Hybrid Civilization

The western half of the Christian world followed a rather different path than that of the Byzantine Empire. For much of the postclassical millennium, it was distinctly on the margins of world history, partly because of its geographic location at the far western end of the Eurasian landmass. Thus it was far removed from the growing routes of world trade—by sea in the Indian Ocean and by land across the Silk Roads to China and the Sand Roads to West Africa. Not until the Eastern and Western hemispheres were joined after 1500 did Western Europe occupy a geographically central position in the global network. Internally, Europe's geography made political unity difficult. It was a region in which population centers were divided by mountain ranges and dense forests as well as by five major peninsulas

Snapshot   Key Moments in the Evolution of Western Civilization

End of the western Roman Empire	476
Papacy of Gregory I	590–604
Muslim conquest of Spain	711
Charlemagne crowned as emperor	800
Otto I crowned as Holy Roman Emperor	962
Viking colony in Newfoundland	1000
Investiture conflict	1059–1152
Crusades begin	1095
Translations of Greek and Arab works available in Europe	12th–13th centuries
Thomas Aquinas	1225–1274
Marco Polo visits China	1271–1295

and two large islands (Britain and Ireland). However, its extensive coastlines and interior river systems facilitated exchange within Europe, while a moderate climate, plentiful rainfall, and fertile soils enabled a productive agriculture that could support a growing population.

In the Wake of Roman Collapse: Political Life in Western Europe, 500–1000

In the early centuries of the postclassical era, history must have seemed more significant than geography, for the Roman Empire, long a fixture of the western Mediterranean region, had collapsed. The traditional date marking the fall of Rome is 476, when the German general Odoacer overthrew the last Roman emperor in the West. In itself not very important, this event has come to symbolize a major turning point in the West, for much that had characterized Roman civilization also weakened, declined, or disappeared in the several centuries before and after 476. Any semblance of large-scale centralized rule vanished. Disease and warfare reduced Europe's population by more than 25 percent. Land under cultivation contracted, while forests, marshland, and wasteland expanded. Urban life too diminished sharply, as Europe reverted to a largely rural existence. Rome at its height was a city of 1 million people, but by the tenth century it numbered perhaps 10,000. Public buildings crumbled from lack of care. Outside Italy, long-distance trade dried up as Roman roads deteriorated, and money exchange gave way to barter in many places. Literacy lost ground as well. Germanic peoples, whom the Romans had viewed as barbarians—Goths, Visigoths, Franks, Lombards, Angles, Saxons—now emerged as the dominant peoples of Western Europe. In the process, Europe's center of gravity moved away from the Mediterranean toward the north and west.

■ **Comparison**

How did the historical development of the European West differ from that of Byzantium in the postclassical era?

Yet much that was classical or Roman persisted, even as a new order emerged in Europe. On the political front, a series of regional kingdoms—led by Visigoths in Spain, Franks in France, Lombards in Italy, and Angles and Saxons in England—arose to replace Roman authority, but many of these Germanic peoples, originally organized in small kinship-based tribes with strong warrior values, had already been substantially Romanized. Contact with the Roman Empire in the first several centuries C.E. generated more distinct ethnic identities among them, militarized their societies, and gave greater prominence to Woden, their god of war. As Germanic peoples migrated into or invaded Roman lands, many were deeply influenced by Roman culture, especially if they served in the Roman army. On the funeral monument of one such person was the telling inscription: "I am a Frank by nationality, but a Roman soldier under arms."[11]

■ **Change**

What replaced the Roman order in Western Europe?

The prestige of things Roman remained high, even after the empire itself had collapsed. Now as leaders of their own kingdoms, the Germanic rulers actively embraced written Roman law, using fines and penalties to provide order and justice in their new states in place of feuds and vendettas. One Visigoth ruler named

Athaulf (reigned 410–415), who had married a Roman noblewoman, gave voice to the continuing attraction of Roman culture and its empire.

> At first I wanted to erase the Roman name and convert all Roman territory into a Gothic empire. . . . But long experience has taught me that . . . without law a state is not a state. Therefore I have more prudently chosen the different glory of reviving the Roman name with Gothic vigour, and I hope to be acknowledged by posterity as the initiator of a Roman restoration.[12]

Several of the larger, though relatively short-lived, Germanic kingdoms also had aspirations to re-create something of the unity of the Roman Empire. Charlemagne (reigned 768–814), ruler of the Carolingian Empire, occupying what is now France, Belgium, the Netherlands, and parts of Germany and Italy, erected an embryonic imperial bureaucracy, standardized weights and measures, and began to act like an imperial ruler. On Christmas Day of the year 800, he was crowned as a new Roman emperor by the pope, although his realm splintered shortly after his death (see Map 10.2). Later Otto I of Saxony (reigned 936–973) gathered much of Germany under his control, saw himself as renewing Roman rule, and was likewise invested with the title of emperor by the pope. Otto's realm, subsequently known as the Holy Roman Empire, was largely limited to Germany and soon proved little more than a collection of quarreling principalities. Though unsuccessful in reviving anything approaching Roman authority, these efforts testify to the continuing appeal of the classical world, even as a new political system of rival kingdoms blended Roman and Germanic elements.

Map 10.2 Western Europe in the Ninth Century
Charlemagne's Carolingian Empire brought a temporary unity to parts of Western Europe, but it was subsequently divided among his three sons, who waged war on one another.

In the Wake of Roman Collapse: Society and the Church, 500–1000

Within these new kingdoms, a highly fragmented and decentralized society with great local variation emerged. In thousands of independent, self-sufficient, and largely isolated landed estates or manors, power—political, economic, and social—was exercised by a warrior elite of landowning lords. In the constant competition of these centuries, lesser lords and knights swore allegiance to greater lords or kings and thus became their vassals, frequently receiving lands and booty in return for military service.

Such reciprocal ties between superior and subordinate were also apparent at the bottom of the social hierarchy, as Roman-style slavery gradually gave way to serfdom. Unlike slaves, serfs were not the personal property of their masters, could not be arbitrarily thrown off their land, and were allowed to live in families. However, they were bound to their masters' estates as peasant laborers and owed various payments and services to the lord of the manor. One family on a manor near Paris in the ninth century owed four silver coins, wine, wood, three hens, and fifteen eggs per year. Women generally were required to weave cloth and make clothing for the lord, while men labored in the lord's fields. In return, the serf family received a small farm and such protection as the lord could provide. In a violent and insecure world adjusting to the absence of Roman authority, the only security available to many individuals or families lay in these communities, where the ties to kin, manor, and lord constituted the primary human loyalties. It was a world apart from the stability of life in imperial Rome or its continuation in Byzantium.

Also filling the vacuum left by the collapse of empire was the Roman Catholic Church, yet another link to the now defunct Roman world. Its hierarchical organization of popes, bishops, priests, and monasteries was modeled on that of the Roman Empire and took over some of its political, administrative, educational, and welfare functions. Like the Buddhist establishment in China, the Church later became extremely wealthy, with reformers often accusing it of forgetting its central spiritual mission. It also provided a springboard for the conversion of Europe's many "pagan" peoples. Numerous missionaries, commissioned by the pope, monasteries, or already converted rulers, fanned out across Europe, generally pursuing a "top-down" strategy. Frequently it worked, as local kings and warlords found status and legitimacy in association with a literate and "civilized" religion that still bore something of the grandeur of Rome. With "the wealth and protection of the powerful," ordinary people followed their rulers into the fold of the Church.[13] This process was similar to Buddhism's appeal for the nomadic rulers of northern and western China following the collapse of the Han dynasty. Christianity, like Buddhism, also bore the promise of superior supernatural powers, and its spread was frequently associated with reported miracles of healing, rainfall, fertility, and victory in battle.

But it was not an easy sell. Outright coercion was sometimes part of the process. For example, when Charlemagne conquered the Saxons of northern Germany, he converted them to Christianity through mass baptisms, under the threat of death for anyone who refused. More often, softer methods prevailed. The Church proved willing to accommodate a considerable range of earlier cultural practices, absorbing them into an emerging Christian tradition. Pope Gregory (reigned 590-604) famously instructed his missionaries in England

> that the temples of the idols in that nation ought not to be destroyed; but let the idols that are in them be destroyed; let holy water be made and sprinkled in

the said temples; let altars be erected and relics placed; . . . that the nation, seeing that their temples are not destroyed . . . , may the more familiarly resort to the places to which they have been accustomed.[14]

Thus amulets and charms to ward off evil became medals with the image of Jesus or the Virgin Mary; traditionally sacred wells and springs became the sites of churches; festivals honoring ancient gods became Christian holy days. December 25 was selected as the birthday of Jesus, for it was associated with the winter solstice, the coming of more light, and the birth or rebirth of various deities in pre-Christian European traditions. By 1100, most of Europe had embraced Christianity. Even so, priests and bishops had to warn their congregations against the worship of rivers, trees, and mountains, and for many people, ancient gods, monsters, trolls, and spirits still inhabited the land. The spreading Christian faith, like the new political framework of European civilization, was a hybrid.

Church authorities and the nobles/warriors who exercised political influence reinforced each other. Rulers provided protection for the papacy and strong encouragement for the faith. In return, the Church offered religious legitimacy for the powerful and the prosperous. "It is the will of the Creator," declared the teaching of the Church, "that the higher shall always rule over the lower. Each individual and class should stay in its place [and] perform its tasks."[15] But Church and nobility competed as well as cooperated, for they were rival centers of power in post-Roman Europe. Particularly controversial was the right to appoint bishops and the pope himself; this issue, known as the investiture conflict, was especially prominent in the eleventh and twelfth centuries. Was the right to make appointments the responsibility of the Church alone, or did kings and emperors also have a role? In the compromise that ended the conflict, the Church won the right to appoint its own officials, while secular rulers retained an informal and symbolic role in the process.

Accelerating Change in the West, 1000–1300

The pace of change in this emerging civilization picked up considerably in the several centuries after 1000. For the preceding 300 years, Europe had been subject to repeated invasions from every direction. Muslim armies had conquered Spain and threatened Europe. Magyar (Hungarian) invasions from the east and Viking incursions from the north likewise disrupted and threatened post-Roman Europe. But by the year 1000, these invasions had been checked and the invaders absorbed into settled society. The greater security and stability that came with relative peace arguably opened the way to an accelerating tempo of change. The climate also seemed to cooperate. A generally warming trend after 750 reached its peak in the eleventh and twelfth centuries, enhancing agricultural production.

■ Change
In what ways was European civilization changing after 1000?

Whatever may have launched this new phase of European civilization, commonly called the High Middle Ages, the signs of expansion and growth were widely evident. The population of Europe grew from perhaps 35 million in 1000 to about

Map 10.3   Europe in the High Middle Ages
By the eleventh century, the national monarchies—of France, Spain, England, Poland, and Germany—that would organize European political life had begun to take shape. The earlier external attacks on Europe from Vikings, Magyars, and Muslims had largely ceased, although it was clear that European civilization was developing in the shadow of the Islamic world.

80 million in 1340. With more people, many new lands had to be opened for cultivation in a process paralleling that of China at the same time. Great lords, bishops, and religious orders organized new villages on what had recently been forest or wasteland. Marshes were drained; land was reclaimed from the sea in the Netherlands; everywhere trees were felled. By 1300, the forest cover of Europe had

been reduced to about 20 percent of the land area. "I believe that the forest . . . covers the land to no purpose," declared a German abbot, "and hold this to be an unbearable harm."[16]

The increased production associated with this agricultural expansion stimulated a considerable growth in long-distance trade, much of which had dried up in the aftermath of the Roman collapse. One center of commercial activity lay in Northern Europe from England to the Baltic coast and involved the exchange of wood, beeswax, furs, rye, wheat, salt, cloth, and wine. The other major trading network centered on northern Italian towns such as Florence, Genoa, and Venice. Their trading partners were the more established civilizations of Islam and Byzantium, and the primary objects of trade included the silks, drugs, precious stones, and spices from Asia. At great trading fairs, particularly those in the Champagne area of France near Paris, merchants from Northern and Southern Europe met to exchange the products of their respective areas, such as northern woolens for Mediterranean spices. Thus the self-sufficient communities of earlier centuries increasingly forged commercial bonds among themselves and with more distant peoples.

The population of towns and cities likewise grew, on the sites of older Roman towns, at trading crossroads and fortifications, and around cathedrals all over Europe. Some had only a few hundred people, but others became much larger. In the early 1300s, London had about 40,000 people, Paris had approximately 80,000, and Venice by the end of the fourteenth century could boast perhaps 150,000. To keep these figures in perspective, Constantinople housed some 400,000 people in 1000, Córdoba in Muslim Spain about 500,000, the Song dynasty capital of Hangzhou more than 1 million in the thirteenth century, and the Aztec capital of Tenochtitlán perhaps 200,000 by 1500. Nonetheless, urbanization was proceeding apace in Europe. These towns gave rise to and attracted new groups of people, particularly merchants, bankers, artisans, and university-trained professionals such as lawyers, doctors, and scholars. Many of these groups, including university professors and students, organized themselves into guilds (associations of people pursuing the same line of work) in order to regulate their respective professions. In doing so, they introduced a new and more productive division of labor into European society.

Between the eleventh and thirteenth centuries, economic growth and urbanization offered European women substantial new opportunities. Women were active in a number of urban professions, such as weaving, brewing, milling grain, midwifery, small-scale retailing, laundering, spinning, and, of course, prostitution. In twelfth-century Paris, for example, a list of 100 occupations identified 86 as involving women workers, of which 6 were exclusively female. In England, women worked as silk weavers, hatmakers, tailors, brewers, and leather processors and were entitled to train female apprentices in some of these trades. In Frankfurt, about one-third of the crafts and trades were entirely female, another 40 percent were dominated by men, and the rest were open to both. Widows of great merchants sometimes continued their husbands' businesses, and one of them, Rose Burford, lent a large sum of money to the king of England to finance a war against Scotland in 1318.

European Women at Work This manuscript painting from the Middle Ages shows women and men cooperating in the baking of bread, long a staple of European diets. (Bibliothèque nationale de France)

By the fifteenth century, such opportunities were declining. Most women's guilds were gone, and women were restricted or banned from many others. Even brothels were run by men. Technological progress may have been one reason for this change. Water- and animal-powered grain mills replaced the hand-grinding previously done by women, and larger looms making heavier cloth replaced the lighter looms that women had worked. Men increasingly took over these professions and trained their sons as apprentices, making it more difficult for women to remain active in these fields.

If urban work roles were diminishing for women, religious life provided other possibilities. As in Buddhist lands, substantial numbers of women, particularly from aristocratic families, were attracted to the secluded life of poverty, chastity, and obedience within a nunnery for the relative freedom from male control that it offered. Here was one of the few places where some women could exercise authority and obtain a measure of education. Operating outside of monastic life, the Beguines were groups of laywomen, often from poorer families in Northern Europe, who lived together, practiced celibacy, and devoted themselves to weaving and to working with the sick, the old, and the poor. Another religious role was that of anchoress, a woman who withdrew to a locked cell, usually attached to a church, where she devoted herself wholly to prayer and fasting. Some of them gained reputations for great holiness and were much sought after for spiritual guidance. For a few women—the nun Hildegard of Bingen and the anchoress Julian of Norwich, for example—religious life brought considerable public prominence and spiritual influence.

A further sign of accelerating change in the West lay in the growth of territorial states with more effective institutions of government commanding the loyalty, or at least the obedience, of their subjects. Since the disintegration of the Roman Empire, Europeans' loyalties had focused on the family, the manor, or the religious community, but seldom on the state. Great lords may have been recognized as kings, but their authority was extremely limited and was exercised through a complex network of feudal relationships with earls, counts, barons, and knights, who often felt little obligation to do the king's bidding. But in the eleventh through the thirteenth century, the nominal monarchs of Europe gradually and painfully began to consolidate their authority, and the outlines of French, English, Spanish, Scandinavian, and other states began to appear, each with its own distinct language and culture (see Map 10.3). Royal courts and embryonic bureaucracies were established, and groups of professional administrators appeared. Territorial kingdoms were not universal, however. In Italy, city-states flourished as urban areas grew wealthy and powerful, whereas the Germans remained loyal to a large number of small principalities within the Holy Roman Empire.

Europe Outward Bound: The Crusading Tradition

■ Change
What was the impact of the Crusades in world history?

Accompanying the growth of European civilization after 1000 were efforts to engage more actively with both near and more distant neighbors. This "medieval expansion" of Western Christendom took place as the Byzantine world was contracting under pressure from the West, from Arab invasion, and later from Turkish conquest. The western half of Christendom was on the rise, while the eastern part was in decline. It was a sharp reversal of their earlier trajectories.

Expansion, of course, has been characteristic of virtually every civilization and has taken a variety of forms—territorial conquest, empire building, settlement of new lands, vigorous trading initiatives, and missionary activity. European civilization was no exception. As population mounted, settlers cleared new land, much of it on the eastern fringes of Europe. The Vikings of Scandinavia, having raided much of Europe, set off on a maritime transatlantic venture around 1000 that briefly established a colony in Newfoundland in North America, and more durably in Greenland and Iceland. As Western economies grew, merchants, travelers, diplomats, and missionaries brought European society into more intensive contact with more distant peoples and with Eurasian commercial networks. By the thirteenth and fourteenth centuries, Europeans had direct, though limited, contact with India, China, and Mongolia. Europe clearly was outward bound.

Nothing more dramatically revealed European expansiveness and the religious passions that informed it than the Crusades, a series of "holy wars" that captured the imagination of Western Christendom for more than four centuries, beginning in 1095. In European thinking and practice, the Crusades were wars undertaken at God's command and authorized by the pope as the Vicar of Christ on earth. They required participants to swear a vow and in return offered an indulgence, which removed the penalties for any confessed sins, as well as various material benefits, such as immunity from lawsuits and a moratorium on the repayment of debts. Any number of political, economic, and social motives underlay the Crusades, but at their core they were religious wars. Within Europe, the amazing support for the Crusades reflected an understanding of them "as providing security against mortal enemies threatening the spiritual health of all Christendom and all Christians."[17] Crusading drew upon both Christian piety and the warrior values of the elite, with little sense of contradiction between these impulses.

The most famous Crusades were those aimed at wresting Jerusalem and the holy places associated with the life of Jesus from Islamic control and returning them to Christendom (see Map 10.4). Beginning in 1095, wave after wave of Crusaders from all walks of life and many countries flocked to the eastern Mediterranean, where they temporarily carved out four small Christian states, the last of which was recaptured by Muslim forces in 1291. Led or supported by an assortment of kings, popes, bishops, monks, lords, nobles, and merchants, the Crusades demonstrated a growing European capacity for organization, finance, transportation, and recruitment, made all the more impressive by the absence of any centralized direction for the project. They also demonstrated an amazing cruelty. The seizure of Jerusalem in 1099 was

Map 10.4   The Crusades
Western Europe's crusading tradition reflected the expansive energy and religious impulses of an emerging civilization. It was directed against Muslims in the Middle East, Sicily, and Spain as well as the Eastern Orthodox Christians of the Byzantine Empire. The Crusades also involved attacks on Jewish communities, probably the first organized mass pogroms against Jews in Europe's history.

Christians and Muslims
This fourteenth-century painting illustrates the Christian seizure of Jerusalem during the First Crusade in 1099. The crowned figure in the center is Godefroi de Bouillon, a French knight and nobleman who played a prominent role in the attack and was briefly known as the king of Jerusalem. (Snark/Art Resource, NY)

accompanied by the slaughter of many Muslims and Jews as the Crusaders made their way, according to perhaps exaggerated reports, through streets littered with corpses and ankle deep in blood to the Sepulcher of Christ.

Crusading was not limited to targets in the Islamic Middle East, however. Those Christians, both Spanish and foreign, who waged war for centuries to reclaim the Iberian Peninsula from Muslim hands were likewise declared "crusaders," with a similar set of spiritual and material benefits. So too were Scandinavian and German warriors who took part in wars to conquer, settle, and convert lands along the Baltic Sea. The Byzantine Empire and Russia, both of which followed Eastern Orthodox Christianity, were also on the receiving end of Western crusading, as were Christian heretics and various enemies of the pope in Europe itself. Crusading, in short, was a pervasive feature of European expansion, which persisted as Europeans began their oceanic voyages in the fifteenth century and beyond.

Surprisingly perhaps, the Crusades had little lasting impact, either politically or religiously, in the Middle East. European power was not sufficiently strong or long-lasting to induce much conversion, and the small European footholds there had come under Muslim control by 1300. The penetration of Turkic-speaking peoples from Central Asia and the devastating Mongol invasions of the thirteenth century were far more significant in Islamic history than were the temporary incursions of European Christians. In fact, Muslims largely forgot about the Crusades until the late nineteenth and early twentieth centuries, when their memory was revived in the context of a growing struggle against European imperialism.

In Europe, however, interaction with the Islamic world had very significant long-term consequences. Spain, Sicily, and the Baltic region were brought permanently into the world of Western Christendom, while a declining Byzantium was further weakened by the Crusader sacking of Constantinople of 1204 and left even more vulnerable to Turkish conquest. In Europe itself, popes strengthened their position, at least for a time, in their continuing struggles with secular authorities. Tens of thousands of Europeans came into personal contact with the Islamic world, from which they picked up a taste for the many luxury goods available there, stimulating a demand for Asian goods. They also learned techniques for producing sugar on large plantations using slave labor, a process that had incalculable consequences in later centuries as Europeans transferred the plantation system to the Americas.

Muslim scholarship, together with the Greek learning that it incorporated, also flowed into Europe, largely through Spain and Sicily.

If the cross-cultural contacts born of crusading opened channels of trade, technology transfer, and intellectual exchange, they also hardened cultural barriers between peoples. The rift between Eastern Orthodoxy and Roman Catholicism deepened further and remains to this day a fundamental divide in the Christian world. Christian anti-Semitism was both expressed and exacerbated as Crusaders on their way to Jerusalem found time to massacre Jews in a number of European cities. European empire building, especially in the Americas, continued the crusading notion that "God wills it." Crusading's impact has been felt even in more recent times. In the past two centuries, as the worlds of Europe and Islam collided, both sides found many occasions in which images of the Crusades, however distorted, proved politically or ideologically useful.[18]

The West in Comparative Perspective

At one level, the making of Western civilization in the postclassical era was unremarkable. Civilizations had risen, fallen, renewed themselves, and evolved at many times and in many places. The European case has received extraordinary scrutiny, not so much because of its special significance at the time, but because of its later role as a globally dominant region. Historians have sometimes sought to account for Western Europe's global influence after 1500 in terms of some unique feature of its earlier history. However we might explain Europe's later rise to prominence on the world stage, its development in the several centuries after 1000 made only modest ripples beyond its own region. In some respects, Europe was surely distinctive, but it was not yet a major player in the global arena. Comparisons, particularly with China, help to place European developments in a world history context.

Catching Up

As the hybrid civilization of the West evolved, it was clearly less developed in comparison to Byzantium, China, India, and the Islamic world. Its cities were smaller, its political authorities weaker, its economy less commercialized, its technology inferior to the more established civilizations. Muslim observers who encountered Europeans saw them as barbarians. "Their bodies are large, their manners harsh, their understanding dull, and their tongues heavy. . . . Those of them who are farthest to the north are the most subject to stupidity, grossness and brutishness."[19] That was the opinion of a tenth-century Arab geographer. Muslim travelers over the next several centuries saw more to be praised in West African kingdoms, where Islam was practiced and gold was plentiful.

Furthermore, thoughtful Europeans who directly encountered other peoples often acknowledged their comparative backwardness. "In our time," wrote a twelfth-century European scholar, "it is in Toledo [a Spanish city long under

Muslim rule] that the teaching of the Arabs . . . is offered to the crowds. I hastened there to listen to the teaching of the wisest philosophers of this world."[20] The Italian traveler Marco Polo in the thirteenth century proclaimed Hangzhou in China "the finest and noblest [city] in the world." In the sixteenth century, Spanish invaders of Mexico were stunned at the size and wealth of the Aztec capital, especially its huge market, claiming that "we had never seen such a thing before."[21]

■ **Change**
In what ways did borrowing from abroad shape European civilization after 1000?

Curious about the rest of the world, Europeans proved quite willing to engage with and borrow from the more advanced civilizations to the east. Growing European economies, especially in the northwest, reconnected with the Eurasian trading system, with which they had lost contact after the fall of Rome. Now European elites eagerly sought spices, silks, porcelain, sugar, and much else that was available on the world market. Despite their belief in Christianity as the "one true religion," Europeans embraced scientific treatises and business practices from the Arabs, philosophical and artistic ideas from the pagan Greeks, and mathematical concepts from India. It was China, however, that was the most significant source of European borrowing, although often indirectly. From that East Asian civilization, Europeans learned about the compass, papermaking, gunpowder, nautical technology, iron casting, a public postal service, and more. When the road to China opened in the thirteenth and fourteenth centuries, many Europeans, including the merchant-traveler Marco Polo, were more than willing to make the long and difficult journey, returning with amazing tales of splendor and abundance far beyond what was available in Europe. When Europeans took to the oceans in the fifteenth and sixteenth centuries, they were seeking out the sources of African and Asian wealth. Thus the accelerating growth of European civilization was accompanied by its reintegration into the larger Afro-Eurasian networks of exchange and communication.

In this willingness to borrow, Europe resembled several other third-wave civilizations of the time. Japan, for example, took much from China; West Africa drew heavily on Islamic civilization; and Russia actively imitated Byzantium. All of them were then developing civilizations, in a position similar to the developing countries of the third world in the twentieth century. The whole process, of course, was then rather less deliberate and self-conscious than it became in the last century.

Technological borrowing required adaptation to the unique conditions of Europe and was accompanied by considerable independent invention as well. Together these processes generated a significant tradition of technological innovation that allowed Europe by 1500 to catch up with, and in some areas perhaps to surpass, China and the Islamic world. That achievement bears comparison with the economic revolution of Tang and Song dynasty China, although Europe began at a lower level and depended more on borrowing than did its Chinese counterpart. But in the several centuries surrounding 1000 at both ends of Eurasia, major processes of technological innovation were under way.

In Europe, technological breakthroughs first became apparent in agriculture as Europeans adapted to the very different environmental conditions north of the Alps in the several centuries following 500 C.E. They developed a heavy-wheeled plow, which could handle the dense soils of Northern Europe far better than the light or "scratch" plow used in Mediterranean agriculture. To pull the plow, Europeans began to rely increasingly on horses rather than oxen and to use iron horseshoes and a more efficient collar, which probably originated in China or Central Asia and could support much heavier loads. In addition, Europeans developed a new three-field system of crop rotation, which allowed considerably more land to be planted at any one time. These were the technological foundations for a more productive agriculture that could support the growing population of European civilization, and especially its urban centers, far more securely than before.

Beyond agriculture, Europeans began to tap nonanimal sources of energy in a major way, particularly after 1000. A new type of windmill, very different from an earlier Persian version, was widely used in Europe by the twelfth and thirteenth centuries. The water-driven mill was even more important. The Romans had used that type of mill largely to grind grain, but their development was limited, given that few streams flowed all year and many slaves were available to do the work. By the ninth century, however, water mills were rapidly becoming more evident in Europe. In the early fourteenth century, a concentration of sixty-eight mills dotted a one-mile stretch of the Seine River near Paris. In addition to grinding grain, these mills provided power for sieving flour, tanning hides, making beer, sawing wood, manufacturing iron, and making paper. Devices such as cranks, flywheels, camshafts, and complex gearing mechanisms, when combined with water or wind power, enabled Europeans of the High Middle Ages to revolutionize production in a number of industries and to break with the ancient tradition of depending almost wholly on animal or human muscle as sources of energy. So intense was the interest of European artisans and engineers in tapping mechanical sources of energy that a number of them experimented with perpetual-motion machines, an idea borrowed from Indian philosophers.

Technological borrowing also was evident in the arts of war. Gunpowder was invented in China, but Europeans were probably the first to use it in cannons, in the early fourteenth century, and by 1500 they had the most advanced arsenals in the world. In 1517, one Chinese official, upon first encountering European ships and weapons, remarked with surprise, "The westerns are extremely dangerous because of their artillery. No weapon ever made since memorable antiquity is superior to their cannon."[22] Advances in

European Technology

Europeans' fascination with technology and their religious motivation for investigating the world are apparent in this thirteenth-century portrayal of God as a divine engineer, laying out the world with a huge compass. (Erich Lessing/Art Resource, NY)

shipbuilding and navigational techniques—including the magnetic compass and stern-post rudder from China and adaptations of the Arab lateen sail, which enabled vessels to sail against the wind—provided the foundation for European mastery of the seas.

Europe's passion for technology was reflected in its culture and ideas as well as in its machines. About 1260, the English scholar and Franciscan friar Roger Bacon wrote of the possibilities he foresaw, and in doing so, he expressed the confident spirit of the age.

> Machines of navigation can be constructed, without rowers...which are borne under the guidance of one man at a greater speed than if they were full of men. Also a chariot can be constructed, that will move with incalculable speed without any draught animal....Also flying machines may be constructed so that a man may sit in the midst of the machine turning a certain instrument by means of which wings artificially constructed would beat the air after the manner of a bird flying...and there are countless other things that can be constructed.[23]

Pluralism in Politics

■ **Comparison**
Why was Europe unable to achieve the kind of political unity that China experienced? What impact did this have on the subsequent history of Europe?

Unlike the large centralized states of Byzantium, the Islamic world, and China, post-Roman European civilization never regained the unity it had under Roman rule. Rather, political life gradually crystallized into a system of competing states (France, Spain, England, Sweden, Prussia, the Netherlands, and Poland, among others) that has persisted into the twenty-first century and that the European Union still confronts. Geographic barriers, ethnic and linguistic diversity, and the shifting balances of power among its many states prevented the emergence of a single European empire, despite periodic efforts to re-create something resembling the still-remembered unity of the Roman Empire.

This multicentered political system shaped the emerging civilization of the West in many ways. It gave rise to frequent wars, enhanced the role and status of military men, and drove the "gunpowder revolution." Thus European society and values were militarized far more than in China, which gave greater prominence to scholars and bureaucrats. Intense interstate rivalry, combined with a willingness to borrow, also greatly stimulated European technological development. By 1500, Europeans had gone a long way toward catching up with their more advanced Asian counterparts in agriculture, industry, war, and sailing.

But endemic warfare did not halt European economic growth. Capital, labor, and goods found their way around political barriers, while the common assumptions of Christian culture and the use of Latin and later French by the literate elite fostered communication across political borders. Europe's multistate system thus provided enough competition to be stimulating but also sufficient order and unity to allow economic endeavors to prosper.

The states within this emerging European civilization also differed from those to the east. Their rulers generally were weaker and had to contend with competing sources of power. Unlike the Orthodox Church in Byzantium, with its practice of caesaropapism, the Roman Catholic Church in the West maintained a degree of independence from state authority that served to check the power of kings and lords. European vassals had certain rights in return for loyalty to their lords and kings. By the thirteenth century, this meant that high-ranking nobles, acting through formal councils, had the right to advise their rulers and to approve new taxes.

This three-way struggle for power among kings, warrior aristocrats, and church leaders, all of them from the nobility, enabled urban-based merchants in Europe to achieve an unusual independence from political authority. Many cities, where wealthy merchants exercised local power, won the right to make and enforce their own laws and appoint their own officials. Some of them—Venice, Genoa, Pisa, and Milan, for example—became almost completely independent city-states. In the case of other cities, kings granted charters that allowed them to have their own courts, laws, and governments, while paying their own kind of taxes to the king instead of feudal dues. Powerful, independent cities were a distinctive feature of European life after 1100 or so. By contrast, Chinese cities, which were far larger than those of Europe, were simply part of the empire and enjoyed few special privileges. Although commerce was far more extensive in China than in a developing Europe, the powerful Chinese state favored the landowners over merchants, monopolized the salt and iron industries, and actively controlled and limited merchant activity far more than the new and weaker royal authorities of Europe were able to do.

The relative weakness of Europe's rulers allowed urban merchants more leeway and, according to some historians, paved the way to a more thorough development of capitalism in later centuries. It also led to the development of representative institutions or parliaments through which the views and interests of these contending forces could be expressed and accommodated. Intended to strengthen royal authority by consulting with major social groups, these embryonic parliaments did not represent the "people" or the "nation" but instead embodied the three great "estates of the realm"—the clergy (the first estate), the landowning nobility (the second estate), and urban merchants (the third estate).

Reason and Faith

A further feature of this emerging European civilization was a distinctive intellectual tension between the claims of human reason and those of faith. Christianity, of course, had developed in a classical world suffused with Greek rationalism. Some early Christian thinkers sought to maintain a clear separation between the new religion and the ideas of Plato and Aristotle. "What indeed has Athens to do with Jerusalem?" asked Tertullian (150–225 C.E.), an early church leader from North Africa. More common, however, was the notion that Greek philosophy could serve as a "handmaiden" to faith, more fully disclosing the truths of Christianity. In the reduced circumstances of Western Europe after the collapse of the Roman Empire,

■ **Comparison**

In what different ways did classical Greek philosophy and science have an impact in the West, in Byzantium, and in the Islamic world?

European University Life in the Middle Ages
This fourteenth-century manuscript painting shows a classroom scene from the University of Bologna in Italy. Note the sleeping and disruptive students.
(Bildarchiv Preussischer Kulturbesitz/Art Resource, NY)

the Church had little direct access to the writings of the Greeks, although some Latin translations and commentaries provided a continuing link to the world of classical thought.

But intellectual life in Europe changed dramatically in the several centuries after 1000, amid a rising population, a quickening commercial life, growing towns and cities, and the Church's growing independence from royal or noble authorities. Moreover, the West was developing a legal system that guaranteed a measure of independence for a variety of institutions—towns and cities, guilds, professional associations, and especially universities. An outgrowth of earlier cathedral schools, these European universities—in Paris, Bologna, Oxford, Cambridge, Salamanca—became "zones of intellectual autonomy" in which scholars could pursue their studies with some freedom from the dictates of religious or political authorities, although that freedom was never complete and was frequently contested.[24]

This was the setting in which European Christian thinkers, a small group of literate churchmen, began to emphasize, quite self-consciously, the ability of human reason to penetrate divine mysteries and to grasp the operation of the natural order. An early indication of this new emphasis occurred in the late eleventh century when students in a monastic school in France asked their teacher, Anselm, to provide them a proof for the existence of God based solely on reason, without using the Bible or other sources of divine revelation.

The new interest in rational thought was applied first and foremost to theology, the "queen of the sciences" to European thinkers. Here was an effort to provide a rational foundation for faith, not to replace faith or to rebel against it. Logic, philosophy, and rationality would operate in service to Christ. Of course, some people opposed this new emphasis on human reason. Bernard of Clairvaux, a twelfth-century French abbot, declared, "Faith believes. It does not dispute."[25] His contemporary and intellectual opponent, the French scholar William of Conches, lashed out: "You poor fools. God can make a cow out of a tree, but has he ever done so? Therefore show some reason why a thing is so or cease to hold that it is so."[26]

European intellectuals also applied their newly discovered confidence in human reason to law, medicine, and the world of nature, exploring optics, magnetism, astronomy, and alchemy. Slowly and never completely, the scientific study of nature, known as "natural philosophy," began to separate itself from theology. In

European universities, natural philosophy was studied in the faculty of arts, which was separate from the faculty of theology, although many scholars contributed to both fields.

This mounting enthusiasm for rational inquiry stimulated European scholars to seek out original Greek texts, particularly those of Aristotle. They found them in the Greek-speaking world of Byzantium and in the Arab world, where they had long ago been translated into Arabic. In the twelfth and thirteenth centuries, an explosion of translations from Greek and Arabic into Latin gave European scholars direct access to the works of ancient Greeks and to the remarkable results of Arab scholarship in astronomy, optics, medicine, pharmacology, and more. Much of this Arab science was now translated into Latin and provided a boost to Europe's changing intellectual life, centered in the new universities. One of these translators, Adelard of Bath (1080–1142), remarked that he had learned, "under the guidance of reason from Arabic teachers," not to trust established authority.[27]

It was the works of the prolific Aristotle, with his logical approach and "scientific temperament," that made the deepest impression. His writings became the basis for university education and largely dominated the thought of Western Europe in the five centuries after 1200. In the work of the thirteenth-century theologian Thomas Aquinas, Aristotle's ideas were thoroughly integrated into a logical and systematic presentation of Christian doctrine. In this growing emphasis on human rationality, at least partially separate from divine revelation, lay one of the foundations of the later Scientific Revolution and the secularization of European intellectual life (see Chapter 16).

Surprisingly, nothing comparable occurred in the Byzantine Empire, where knowledge of the Greek language was widespread and access to Greek texts was easy. Although Byzantine scholars kept the classical tradition alive, their primary interest lay in the humanities (literature, philosophy, history) and theology rather than in the natural sciences or medicine. Furthermore, both state and church had serious reservations about classical Greek learning. In 529, the emperor Justinian closed Plato's Academy in Athens, claiming that it was an outpost of paganism. Its scholars dispersed into lands that soon became Islamic, carrying Greek learning into the Islamic world. Church authorities as well were suspicious of classical Greek thought, sometimes persecuting scholars who were too enamored with the ancients. Even those who did study the Greek writers did so in a conservative spirit, concerned to preserve and transmit the classical heritage rather than using it as a springboard for creating new knowledge. "The great men of the past," declared the fourteenth-century Byzantine scholar and statesman Theodore Metochites, "have said everything so perfectly that they have left nothing for us to say."[28]

In the Islamic world, classical Greek thought was embraced "with far more enthusiasm and creativity" than in Byzantium.[29] A massive translation project in the ninth and tenth centuries made Aristotle and many other Greek writers available in Arabic. That work contributed to a flowering of Arab scholarship, especially in the sciences and natural philosophy, between roughly 800 and 1200 (see Chapter 11), but it also stimulated a debate about faith and reason among Muslim thinkers, many of whom greatly admired Greek philosophical, scientific, and medical texts. As in the Christian world, the issue was whether secular Greek thought was an aid or a threat to the faith. Western European church authorities after the thirteenth century had come to regard natural philosophy as a wholly legitimate enterprise and had thoroughly incorporated Aristotle into university education, but learned opinion in the Islamic world swung the other way. Though never completely disappearing from Islamic scholarship, the ideas of Plato and Aristotle receded after the thirteenth century in favor of teachings that drew more directly from the Quran or from mystical experience. Nor was natural philosophy a central concern of Islamic higher education as it was in the West. The integration of political and religious life in the Islamic world, as in Byzantium, contrasted with their separation in the West, where there was more space for the independent pursuit of scientific subjects.

Reflections: Remembering and Forgetting: Continuity and Surprise in the Worlds of Christendom

Many of the characteristic features of Christendom, which emerged during the era of third-wave civilizations, have had a long life, extending well into the modern era. The crusading element of European expansion was prominent among the motives of Spanish and Portuguese explorers. Europe's grudging freedom for merchant activity and its eagerness to borrow foreign technology arguably contributed to the growth of capitalism and industrialization in later centuries. The endemic military conflicts of European states, unable to recover the unity of the Roman Empire, found terrible expression in the world wars of the twentieth century. The controversy about reason and faith resonates still, at least in the United States, in debates about the authority of the Bible in secular and scientific matters. The rift between Eastern Orthodoxy and Roman Catholicism remains one of the major divides in the Christian world. Modern universities and the separation of religious and political authority likewise have their origins in the European Middle Ages. Such a perspective, linking the past with what came later, represents one of the great contributions that the study of history makes to human understanding.

Yet that very strength of historical study can be misleading, particularly if it suggests a kind of inevitability, in which the past determines the future. Some historians have argued, looking backward from the present, that Europe's industrial transformation and global domination in the nineteenth century grew inexorably out of its unique character as a changing civilization after 1000. This kind of thinking, however, misses the great surprise of Europe's more recent historical trajectory, and it minimizes the way people at the time understood their world.

Surely in 1000, few people would have predicted the startling reversal of roles between the Eastern and Western wings of Christendom, which the next several centuries witnessed. At that time, the many small, rural, unsophisticated, and endlessly quarreling warrior-based societies of Western Europe would hardly have borne comparison with the powerful Byzantine Empire and its magnificent capital of Constantinople. Even in 1500, when Europe had begun to catch up with China and the Islamic world in various ways, there was little to predict its remarkable transformation over the next several centuries and the dramatic change in the global balance of power that this transformation produced. To recapture the unexpectedness of the historical process and to allow ourselves to be surprised, it may be useful on occasion to forget the future and to see the world as contemporaries viewed it.

Second Thoughts

What's the Significance?

Byzantine Empire	Vladimir, prince of Kiev	system of competing	To assess your mastery of the material in this chapter, see the **Online Study Guide** at bedfordstmartins.com/strayer.
Justinian	Roman Catholic	states	
Constantinople	Christianity	Crusades	
caesaropapism	Charlemagne	European cities	
Eastern Orthodox	Holy Roman Empire	Aristotle and classical	
Christianity	the West as a "hybrid	Greek learning	
iconoclasm	civilization"		
Kievan Rus			

Big Picture Questions

1. How did the histories of the Byzantine Empire and Western Europe differ during the era of third-wave civilizations?
2. What accounts for the different historical trajectories of these two expressions of Christendom?
3. How did Byzantium and Western Europe interact with each other and with the larger world of the postclassical era?
4. Was the civilization of the Latin West distinctive and unique, or was it broadly comparable to other third-wave civilizations?
5. How does the history of the Christian world in the postclassical era compare with that of Tang and Song dynasty China?

Next Steps: For Further Study

For Web sites and documents related to this chapter, see **Make History** at bedfordstmartins.com/strayer.

Renate Bridenthal et al., eds., *Becoming Visible: Women in European History* (1998). A series of essays that reflects recent scholarship on women.

Edward Grant, *Science and Religion from Aristotle to Copernicus* (2004). Demonstrates the impact of Greek philosophy and science in Europe, with comparisons to Byzantium and the Islamic world.

Barbara A. Hanawalt, *The Middle Ages: An Illustrated History* (1999). A brief and beautifully illustrated introduction to the Middle Ages in European history.

Rowena Loverance, *Byzantium* (2004). A lavishly illustrated history of the Byzantine Empire, drawing on the rich collection of artifacts in the British Museum.

Christopher Tyerman, *Fighting for Christendom: Holy Wars and the Crusades* (2005). A very well-written, up-to-date history of the Crusades designed for nonspecialists.

Mark Whittow, *The Making of Byzantium, 600–1025* (1996). An engaging account of Byzantium at its height, with an emphasis on its external connections.

"Middle Ages," http://www.learner.org/exhibits/middleages. An interactive Web site with text and images relating to life in Europe after the collapse of the Roman Empire.

وَكَادَ يَنْزِعُ الجِمالَ النَّمَرُ وَأَنشَدَ

مَا الحَجُّ سَيْرُكَ تَأَوِيباً وَإِدلاجاً وَلا اعْتِيامُكَ أَجمالاً وَأَحداجا

الحَجُّ أَنْ تَقصِدَ البَيْتَ الحَرامَ عَلى تَحصيلِ بِرٍّ لِلحَجِّ لا تَبغي بِهِ حاجا

وَتَشْتَطي كَاهِلَ الإِنصافِ مُنتَخباً رَدعَ الهَوى هادِياً وَالجَورَ مِنهاجا

CHAPTER ELEVEN

The Worlds of Islam

Afro-Eurasian Connections

600-1500

"There were tens of thousands of pilgrims, from all over the world. They were of all colors, from blue-eyed blondes to black-skinned Africans. But we were all participating in the same ritual, displaying a spirit of unity and brotherhood that my experiences in America had led me to believe never could exist between the white and non-white. . . . I have never before seen sincere and true brotherhood practiced by all colors together, irrespective of their color."[1] So said Malcolm X, the American black radical leader and convert to Islam, following his participation in 1964 in the *hajj*, or pilgrimage, to Mecca. That experience persuaded him to abandon his earlier commitment to militant black separatism, for he was now convinced that racial barriers could indeed be overcome within the context of Islam.

As the twenty-first century dawned, Islam had acquired a serious presence in the United States, with more than 1,200 mosques and an estimated 8 million Muslims, of whom some 2 million were African Americans. Here was but one sign of the growing international influence of the Islamic world. Independence from colonial rule, the Iranian Revolution of 1979, repeated wars between Israel and its Arab neighbors, the rising price of oil—all of this focused global attention on the Islamic world in the second half of the twentieth century. Osama bin Laden and the September 11, 2001, attacks on the United States, U.S. military action in Afghanistan and Iraq, and the increasing assertiveness of Muslims in Europe likewise signaled the growing role of Islam in world affairs in the first decade of the new millennium.

The Hajj: The pilgrimage to Mecca, known as the *hajj*, has long been a central religious ritual in Islamic practice. It also embodies the cosmopolitan character of Islam as pilgrims from all over the vast Islamic realm assemble in the city where the faith was born. This painting shows a group of joyful pilgrims, led by a band, on their way to Mecca. (Bibliothèque nationale de France)

PROMINENCE ON THE WORLD STAGE, OF COURSE, was nothing new for Muslim societies. For a thousand years (roughly 600–1600), peoples claiming allegiance to Islam represented a highly successful, prosperous, and expansive civilization, encompassing parts of Africa, Europe, the Middle East, and Asia. While Chinese culture and Buddhism provided the cultural anchor for East Asia during the postclassical millennium and Christianity did the same for western Eurasia, the realm of Islam touched on both of them and decisively shaped the history of the entire Afro-Eurasian world.

The significance of a burgeoning Islam was enormous. It thrust the previously marginal and largely nomadic Arabs into a central role in world history, for it was among them and in their language that the newest of the world's major religions was born. The sudden emergence and rapid spread of that religion in the seventh century C.E. was accompanied by the creation of a huge empire that stretched from Spain to India. Both within that empire and beyond it, a new and innovative civilization took shape, drawing on Arab, Persian, Turkish, Greco-Roman, South Asian, and African cultures. It was clearly the largest and most influential of the new third-wave civilizations. Finally, the broad reach of Islam generated many of the great cultural encounters of this age of accelerating connections, as that civilization challenged and provoked Christendom, penetrated and was transformed by African cultures, and also took root in India, Central Asia, and Southeast Asia. The spread of Islam continued in the modern era so that by the beginning of the twenty-first century, perhaps 1.2 billion people, or 22 percent of the world's population, identified as Muslims.

The Birth of a New Religion

Most of the major religious or cultural traditions of the classical era had emerged from the core of established civilizations—Confucianism and Daoism from China, Hinduism and Buddhism from India, Greek philosophy from the Mediterranean world, and Zoroastrianism from Persia. Christianity and Islam, by contrast, emerged more from the margins of Mediterranean and Middle Eastern civilizations. The former, of course, appeared among a small Middle Eastern people, the Jews, in a remote province of the Roman Empire, while Islam took hold in the cities and deserts of the Arabian Peninsula.

The Homeland of Islam

■ **Description**
In what ways did the early history of Islam reflect its Arabian origins?

The central region of the Arabian Peninsula had long been inhabited by nomadic Arabs, known as Bedouins, who herded their sheep and camels in seasonal migrations. These peoples lived in fiercely independent clans and tribes, which often engaged in bitter blood feuds with one another. They recognized a variety of gods, ancestors, and nature spirits; valued personal bravery, group loyalty, and hospitality; and greatly treasured their highly expressive oral poetry. But there was more to Arabia than camel-herding nomads. Scattered oases, the highlands of Yemen, and interior mountains supported sedentary village-based agriculture, and in the northern and southern regions of Arabia, small kingdoms had flourished in earlier times. Arabia also sat astride increasingly important trade routes, which connected the Indian Ocean world with that of the Mediterranean Sea and gave rise to more cosmopolitan commercial cities, whose values and practices were often in conflict with those of traditional Arab tribes.

Arabia at the Time of Muhammad

One of those cities, Mecca, came to occupy a distinctive role in Arabia. Though somewhat off the major long-distance trade routes, Mecca was the site of the Kaaba, the most prominent religious shrine in Arabia, which housed representations of some 360 deities and was the destination for many pilgrims. Mecca's dominant tribe, the Quraysh, had come to control access to the Kaaba and grew wealthy by taxing the local trade that accompanied the annual pilgrimage season. By the sixth century C.E., Mecca was home to people from various tribes and clans as well as an assortment of individual outlaws, exiles, refugees, and foreign merchants, but much of its growing wealth was concentrated in the hands of a few ruling Quraysh families.

Furthermore, Arabia was located on the periphery of two established and rival civilizations of that time—the Byzantine Empire, heir to the Roman world, and the Sassanid Empire, heir to the imperial traditions of old Persia. This location, coupled with long-distance trade, ensured some familiarity with the larger world, particularly in the cities and settled farming regions of the peninsula. Many Jews and Christians as well as some Zoroastrians lived among the Arabs, and their monotheistic ideas became widely known. By the time of Muhammad, most of the settled Arabs had acknowledged the preeminent position of Allah, the supreme god of the Arab pantheon, although they usually found the lesser gods, including the three daughters of Allah, far more accessible. Moreover, they increasingly identified Allah with Yahweh, the Jewish High God, and regarded themselves too as "children of Abraham." A few Arabs were beginning to explore the possibility that Allah/Yahweh was the only God and that the many others, residing in the Kaaba and in shrines across the peninsula, were nothing more than "helpless and harmless idols."[2]

To an outside observer around 600, it might well have seemed that Arabs were moving toward Judaism religiously or that Christianity, the most rapidly growing religion in western Asia, would encompass Arabia as well. Any such expectations, however, were thoroughly confounded by the dramatic events of the seventh century.

The Messenger and the Message

The catalyst for those events and for the birth of this new religion was a single individual, Muhammad Ibn Abdullah (570–632 C.E.), who was born in Mecca. Orphaned early in life, he was adopted by an uncle, became a widely traveled trader, and married a wealthy widow, Khadija, herself a prosperous merchant, who provided him with financial and emotional support. A highly reflective man deeply troubled by the religious corruption and social inequalities of Mecca, he often undertook

■ **Comparison**
How does the core message of Islam compare with that of Judaism and Christianity?

Snapshot   **Key Moments in the Early History of Islam**

Birth of Muhammad	570
Beginning of Muhammad's revelations	610
Hijra (the emigration from Mecca to Medina)	622
Muhammad returns to Mecca in triumph	630
Death of Muhammad	632
Rightly Guided Caliphs	632–661
Arab victories against Byzantine and Persian forces	636–637
Conquest of Egypt	640
Compilation of the Quran	650s
Umayyad caliphate	661–750
Conquest of Spain	711–718
Abbasid caliphate	750–1258
Battle of Talas River	751

periods of withdrawal and meditation in the arid mountains outside the city. There, like the Buddha and Jesus, Muhammad had a powerful, overwhelming religious experience that left him convinced, albeit reluctantly, that he was Allah's messenger to the Arabs, commissioned to bring to them a scripture in their own language.

According to Muslim tradition, the revelations began in 610 and continued periodically over the next twenty-two years. Those revelations, recorded in the Quran, became the sacred scriptures of Islam, which to this day Muslims everywhere regard as the very words of God and the core of their faith. Intended to be recited rather than simply read for information, the Quran, Muslims claim, when heard in its original Arabic, conveys nothing less than the very presence of the divine. One of the earliest converts testified to its power: "When I heard the Quran, my heart was softened and I wept and Islam entered into me."[3]

In its Arabian setting, the Quran's message, delivered through Muhammad, was revolutionary. Religiously, it was radically monotheistic, presenting Allah as the only God, the all-powerful Creator, good, just, and merciful; rejecting as utterly false and useless the many gods housed in the Kaaba; and scorning the Christian notion of the Trinity. Allah was the "Lord sustainer of the worlds, the Compassionate, the Caring, master of the day of reckoning."[4] Here was an exalted conception of the Deity that drew heavily on traditions of Jewish and Christian monotheism. As "the Messenger of God," Muhammad presented himself in the line of earlier prophets—Abraham, Moses, Jesus, and many others. He was the last, "the seal of the prophets," bearing God's final revelation to humankind. It was not so much a call to a new faith as an invitation to return to the old and pure religion of Abraham from which Arabs, Jews, and Christians alike had deviated.

Submission to Allah ("Muslim" means "one who submits") was the primary obligation of believers and the means of achieving a place in paradise after death. According to the Quran, however, submission was not merely an individual or spiritual act, for it involved the creation of a whole new society. Over and again, the Quran denounced the prevailing social practices of an increasingly prosperous Mecca: the hoarding of wealth, the exploitation of the poor, the charging of high rates of interest on loans, corrupt business deals, the abuse of women, and the neglect of the widows and orphans. Like the Jewish prophets of the Old Testament, the Quran demanded social justice and laid out a prescription for its implementation. It sought a return to the older values of Arab tribal life—solidarity, equality, concern for the poor—which had been undermined, particularly in Mecca, by growing wealth and commercialism.

Muslims, Jews, and Christians The close relationship of three Middle Eastern monotheistic traditions is illustrated in this fifteenth-century Persian painting, which portrays Muhammad leading Moses, Abraham, and Jesus in prayer. The fire surrounding the prophet's head represents his religious fervor. The painting reflects the Islamic belief that the revelations granted to Muhammad built upon and completed those given earlier to Jews and Christians. (Bibliothèque nationale de France)

The message of the Quran challenged not only the ancient polytheism of Arab religion and the social injustices of Mecca but also the entire tribal and clan structure of Arab society, which was so prone to war, feuding, and violence. The just and moral society of Islam was the *umma*, the community of all believers, replacing tribal, ethnic, or racial identities. Such a society would be a "witness over the nations," for according to the Quran, "You are the best community evolved for mankind, enjoining what is right and forbidding what is wrong."[5] In this community, women too had an honored and spiritually equal place. "The believers, men and women, are protectors of one another," declared the Quran.[6] The umma, then, was to be a new and just community, bound by a common belief, rather than by territory, language, or tribe.

The core message of the Quran—following the law of God—was effectively summarized as a set of five requirements for believers, known as the Pillars of Islam. The first pillar affirmed the central tenets of Islam—absolute monotheism and a final revelation—in a simple but fundamental profession of faith: "There is no god but Allah, and Muhammad is the messenger of God." The second pillar was prayer, preferably five times a day at prescribed times and performed while facing toward Mecca. The accompanying rituals, including cleansing, bowing, kneeling, and prostration, expressed believers' submission to Allah and provided a frequent reminder, amid the busyness of daily life, that they were living in the presence of the divine. The third pillar, requiring believers to generously give their wealth to maintain the community and to help the needy, reflected the Quran's repeated demands for social justice. The fourth pillar called for a month of fasting—no food, drink, or sexual relations—from the first light of dawn to sundown during Ramadan, the ninth lunar month of the Islamic calendar. It provided an occasion for self-purification and a reminder of the needs of the hungry. The fifth pillar urged a pilgrimage to Mecca, where believers from all over the Islamic world assembled once a year and put on identical simple white clothing as they performed rituals reminding them of key events in Islamic history. A moving display of religious devotion, the hajj or pilgrimage expressed in a compelling fashion the unity of the umma.

A further requirement for believers, sometimes called the sixth pillar, was "struggle," or *jihad* in Arabic. Its more general meaning, which Muhammad referred to as the "greater jihad," was the personal effort of each Muslim against greed and selfishness, a spiritual striving toward living a God-conscious life. In its "lesser" form, the "jihad of the sword," the Quran authorized armed struggle against the forces of unbelief and evil as a means of establishing Muslim rule and of defending the umma from the threats of infidel aggressors. The understanding and use of the jihad concept varied widely within the history of Islam and remains a matter of controversy in the twenty-first century.

The Transformation of Arabia

■ **Change**

In what ways was the rise of Islam revolutionary, both in theory and in practice?

As the revelations granted to Muhammad became known in Mecca, they attracted a small following of some close relatives, a few prominent Meccan leaders, and an assortment of lower-class dependents, freed slaves, and members of poorer clans. Those teachings also soon attracted the vociferous opposition of Mecca's elite families, particularly those of Muhammad's own tribe, the Quraysh. Muhammad's claim to be a "messenger of Allah," his rigid monotheism, his call for social reform, his condemnation of Mecca's business practices, and his apparent disloyalty to his own tribe enraged the wealthy and ruling families of Mecca. So great had this opposition become that in 622 Muhammad and his small band of followers emigrated to the more welcoming town of Yathrib, soon to be called Medina, the city of the Prophet. This agricultural settlement of mixed Arab and Jewish population had invited Muhammad to serve as an arbitrator of their intractable conflicts. The emigration to Yathrib, known in Arabic as the *hijra*, was a momentous turning point in the early history of Islam and thereafter marked the beginning of a new Islamic calendar.

The Islamic community, or umma, that took shape in Medina was a kind of "supertribe," but very different from the traditional tribes of Arab society. Membership was a matter of belief rather than birth, allowing it to expand rapidly. Furthermore, all authority, both political and religious, was concentrated in the hands of Muhammad, who proceeded to introduce radical changes. Usury was outlawed, tax-free marketplaces were established, and a mandatory payment to support the poor was imposed.

In Medina, Muhammad not only began to create a new society but also declared Islam's independence from its earlier affiliation with Judaism. In the early years, he had anticipated a warm response from Jews and Christians, based on a common monotheism and prophetic tradition, and had directed his followers to pray facing Jerusalem. But when some Jewish groups allied with his enemies, Muhammad acted harshly to suppress them, exiling some and enslaving or killing others. This was not, however, a general suppression of Jews, since others among them remained loyal to Muhammad's new state. But the prophet now redirected Muslims' prayer toward Mecca, essentially declaring Islam an Arab religion, though one open to all.

From its base in Medina, the Islamic community rapidly extended its reach throughout Arabia. Early military successes against Muhammad's Meccan opponents convinced other Arab tribes that the Muslims and their God were on the rise, and they sought to negotiate alliances with the new power. Growing numbers, though not all, converted. The religious appeal of the new faith, its promise of material gain, the end of incessant warfare among feuding tribes, periodic military actions skillfully led by Muhammad, and the Prophet's willingness to enter into marriage alliances with leading tribes—all of this contributed to the consolidation of Islamic control throughout Arabia. In 630, Mecca itself voluntarily surrendered, and Muhammad purged the Kaaba of its idols, declaring it a shrine to the one God, Allah. By the time Muhammad died in 632, most of Arabia had come under the control of this new Islamic state, and many had embraced the new faith.

Thus the birth of Islam differed sharply from that of Christianity. Jesus' teaching about "giving to Caesar what is Caesar's and to God what is God's" reflected the minority and subordinate status of the Jews within the Roman Empire. Early Christians found themselves periodically persecuted by Roman authorities for more than three centuries, requiring them to work out some means of dealing with an often hostile state. The answer lay in the development of a separate church hierarchy and the concept of two coexisting authorities, one religious and one political, an arrangement that persisted even after the state became Christian.

The young Islamic community, by contrast, found itself constituted as a state, and soon a huge empire, at the very beginning of its history. Muhammad was not only a religious figure but also, unlike Jesus or the Buddha, a political and military leader able to implement his vision of an ideal Islamic society. Nor did Islam give rise to a separate religious organization, although tension between religious and political goals frequently generated conflict. No professional clergy mediating between God and humankind emerged within Islam. Teachers, religious scholars, prayer leaders, and judges within an Islamic legal system did not have the religious role that priests held within Christianity. No distinction between religious law and civil law, so important in the Christian world, existed within the realm of Islam. One law, known as the *sharia*, regulated every aspect of life. The sharia (literally, a path to water, which is the source of life) evolved over the several centuries following the birth of this new religion and found expression in a number of separate schools of Islamic legal practice.

In little more than twenty years (610–632), a profound transformation had occurred in the Arabian Peninsula. A new religion had been born, though one that had roots in earlier Middle Eastern traditions. A new and vigorous state had emerged, bringing peace to the warring tribes of Arabia. Within that state, a distinctive society, which served ever after as a model for Islamic communities everywhere, had begun to take shape. In his farewell sermon, Muhammad described the outlines of this community.

> All mankind is from Adam and Eve, an Arab has no superiority over a non-Arab nor a non-Arab has any superiority over an Arab; also a white has no superiority over a black nor a black has any superiority over a white—except by piety and good action. Learn that every Muslim is a brother to every Muslim and that the Muslims constitute one brotherhood.[7]

The Making of an Arab Empire

It did not take long for the immense transformations occurring in Arabia to have an impact beyond the peninsula. In the centuries that followed, the energies born of those vast changes profoundly transformed much of the Afro-Eurasian world. The new Arab state became a huge empire, encompassing all or part of Egyptian, Roman/Byzantine, Persian, Mesopotamian, and Indian civilizations. The Islamic faith spread widely within and outside that empire. So too did the culture and language of Arabia, as many Arabs migrated far beyond their original homeland. From the mixing and blending of these many peoples emerged the new and distinctive third-wave civilization of Islam, bound by the ties of a common faith but divided by differences of culture, class, politics, gender, and religious understanding. These enormously consequential processes—the making of a new religion, a new empire, and a new civilization—were central to world history during the postclassical millennium.

War and Conquest

■ Change
Why were Arabs able to construct such a huge empire so quickly?

Within a few years of Muhammad's death in 632, Arab armies engaged the Byzantine and Persian Sassanid empires, the great powers of the region. It was the beginning of a process that rapidly gave rise to an Islamic/Arab empire that stretched from Spain to India, penetrating both Europe and China and governing most of the lands between them (see Map 11.1). In creating that empire, Arabs were continuing a long pattern of tribal raids into surrounding civilizations, but now the Arabs were newly organized in a state of their own with a central command able to mobilize the military potential of the entire Arab population. The Byzantine and Persian empires, weakened by decades of war with each other and by internal revolts, continued to view the Arabs as a mere nuisance rather than a serious threat. But the Sassanid Empire was defeated by Arab forces during the 650s, while Byzantium soon lost the southern half of its territories. Beyond these victories, Arab forces, operating on both land and sea, swept westward across North Africa, conquered Spain in the early 700s, and attacked southern France. To the east, Arab forces reached the Indus River and seized some of the major oases towns of Central

Map 11.1   The Arab Empire and the Initial Expansion of Islam, 622–900 C.E.
Far more so than with Buddhism or Christianity, the initial spread of Islam was both rapid and extensive. And unlike the other two world religions, Islam gave rise to a huge empire, ruled by Muslim Arabs, which encompassed many of the older civilizations of the region.

Asia. In 751, Arab armies inflicted a crushing defeat on Chinese forces in the Battle of Talas River, which had lasting consequences for the cultural evolution of Asia, for it checked the further expansion of China to the west and made possible the conversion of Central Asia's Turkic-speaking people to Islam.

The motives driving the creation of the Arab Empire were in many ways similar to those of other empires. The merchant leaders of the new Islamic community wanted to capture profitable trade routes and wealthy agricultural regions. Individual Arabs found in military expansion a route to wealth and social promotion. The need to harness the immense energies of the Arabian transformation was also important. The fragile unity of the umma threatened to come apart after Muhammad's death, and external expansion provided a common task for the community.

Also apparent in the making of the Arab Empire was a distinctly religious dimension. To the Arabs themselves, the only possible explanation for their amazing, indeed miraculous, success was that "God gave us the victory over them, allowing us to take their countries and to settle in their lands, their homes, and their property, we having no strength or force other than the truth."[8] Many viewed the mission of empire in terms of jihad, bringing righteous government to the peoples they conquered, but this did not mean imposing Islam on individuals at the point of a sword. Initially, Arabs regarded Islam as a revelation uniquely their own and discouraged conversion. By the middle of the eighth century, however, they had come to view it as a universal religion actively seeking converts, but even then they recognized Jews, Christians, and Zoroastrians as "people of the book," giving them the status of *dhimmis* (protected subjects). Such people were permitted to freely practice their own religion, so long as they paid a special tax known as the *jizya*. Theoretically the tax was a substitute for military service, supposedly forbidden to non-Muslims. In practice, many dhimmis served in the highest offices within Muslim kingdoms and in their armies as well.

In other ways too, the Arab rulers of an expanding empire sought to limit the disruptive impact of conquest. To prevent indiscriminate destruction and exploitation of conquered peoples, occupying Arab armies were restricted to garrison towns, segregated from the native population. Local elites and bureaucratic structures were incorporated into the new Arab Empire. Nonetheless, the empire worked many changes on its subjects, the most enduring of which was the mass conversion of Middle Eastern peoples to Islam.

Conversion to Islam

■ **Explanation**
What accounts for the widespread conversion to Islam?

Becoming a Muslim was for some people no doubt a profound spiritual or psychological transformation, but far more often it was "social conversion," defined as "movement from one religiously defined social community to another."[9] It happened at various rates and in different ways, but in the four centuries or so after the death of Muhammad, millions of individuals and many whole societies within the Arab Empire found their cultural identity bound up with a belief in Allah and the message of his prophet as they came to associate themselves with a community of people known as Muslims. How had this immense cultural change occurred?

In some ways, perhaps, the change was not so dramatic, as major elements of Islam—monotheism; ritual prayer and cleansing ceremonies; fasting; divine revelation; the ideas of heaven, hell, and final judgment—were quite familiar to Jews, Christians, and Zoroastrians. Furthermore, Islam was from the beginning associated with the sponsorship of a powerful state, quite unlike the experience of early Buddhism or Christianity. Conquest called into question the power of old gods, while the growing prestige of the Arab Empire attracted many to Allah. Although deliberately forced conversion was rare, living in an Islamic-governed state provided a variety of incentives for claiming Muslim identity.[10] Slaves and prisoners of war were among the early converts, particularly in Persia. Converts could also avoid the jizya, a tax imposed on non-Muslims. In Islam, merchants found a religion friendly to commerce, and in the Arab Empire they enjoyed a huge and secure arena for trade. People aspiring to official positions found conversion to Islam an aid to social mobility.

Conversion was not an automatic or easy process. Vigorous resistance delayed conversion for centuries among the Berbers of North Africa; a small group of zealous Spanish Christians in the ninth century provoked their own martyrdom by publicly insulting the Prophet; and some Persian Zoroastrians fled to avoid Muslim rule. More generally, though, a remarkable and lasting religious transformation occurred throughout the Arab Empire. In Persia, for example, between 750 and 900, about 80 percent of the population had made the transition to a Muslim religious identity, while retaining their own ancient language.[11] In places where large-scale Arab migration had occurred, such as Egypt, North Africa, and Iraq, Arabic culture and language, as well as the religion of Islam, took hold. Such areas are today both Muslim and Arab, while Iran, Turkey, and Pakistan, for example, have "Islamized" without "Arabizing."

Divisions in the Islamic World

The ideal of a unified Muslim community, so important to Muhammad, proved difficult to realize as conquest and conversion vastly enlarged the Islamic umma. A central problem was that of leadership and authority in the absence of Muhammad's towering presence. Who should hold the role of caliph, the successor to Muhammad as the political leader of the umma, the protector and defender of the faith? That issue crystallized a variety of emerging conflicts within the Islamic world—between early and later converts, among various Arab tribes and factions, between Arabs and non-Arabs, between privileged and wealthy rulers and their far less fortunate subjects. Many of these political and social conflicts found expression in religious terms as various understandings of the Quran and of Muhammad's life and teachings took shape within the growing Islamic community.

The first four caliphs, known among most Muslims as the Rightly Guided Caliphs (632–661), were close "companions of the Prophet," selected by the Muslim elders of Medina. Division surfaced almost immediately as a series of Arab tribal rebellions and new "prophets" persuaded the first caliph, Abu Bakr, to suppress them forcibly. The third and fourth caliphs, Uthman and Ali, were both assassinated, and by 656, less than twenty-five years after Muhammad's death, civil war pitted Muslim against Muslim.

Out of that conflict emerged one of the deepest and most enduring rifts within the Islamic world. On one side were the Sunni Muslims, who held that the caliphs were rightful political and military leaders, selected by the Islamic community. On the other side of this sharp divide was the Shia (an Arabic word meaning "party" or "faction") branch of Islam. Its adherents felt strongly that leadership in the Islamic world should derive from the line of Ali and his son Husayn, blood relatives of Muhammad, both of whom died at the hands of their political or religious enemies.

In the beginning, therefore, this divide was simply a political conflict without serious theological or religious meaning, but over time the Sunni/Shia split acquired deeper significance. For Sunni Muslims, religious authority in general

■ Comparison

What is the difference between Sunni and Shia Islam?

The Kaaba
Located in Mecca, this stone structure covered with a black cloth and known as the Kaaba, was originally home to the numerous deities of pre-Islamic Arabia. Cleansed by Muhammad, it became the sacred shrine of Islam and the destination of countless pilgrims undertaking the hajj. Part of that ritual involves circling the Kaaba seven times, as shown here in a photograph from 2004. (Dan Mohiuddin, photographer)

emerged from the larger community, particularly from the religious scholars known as *ulama*. Shia Muslims, on the other hand, invested their leaders, known as *imams*, with a religious authority that the caliphs lacked, allowing them alone to reveal the true meaning of the Quran and the wishes of Allah. For much of early Islamic history, Shia Muslims saw themselves as the minority opposition within Islam. They felt that history had taken a wrong turn and that they were "the defenders of the oppressed, the critics and opponents of privilege and power," while the Sunnis were the advocates of the established order.[12] Various armed revolts by Shias over the centuries, most of which failed, led to a distinctive conception of martyrdom and to the expectation that their defeated leaders were merely in hiding and not really dead and that they would return in the fullness of time. Thus a messianic element entered Shia Islam. The Sunni/Shia schism was a lasting division in the Islamic world, reflected in conflicts among various Islamic states, and was exacerbated by further splits among the Shia. Those divisions echo still in the twenty-first century.

As the Arab Empire grew, its caliphs were transformed from modest Arab chiefs into absolute monarchs of the Byzantine or Persian variety, complete with elaborate court rituals, a complex bureaucracy, a standing army, and centralized systems of taxation and coinage. They were also subject to the dynastic rivalries and succession disputes common to other empires. The first dynasty, following the era of the Rightly Guided Caliphs, came from the Umayyad family (ruled 661–750). Under its rule, the Arab Empire expanded greatly, caliphs became hereditary rulers, and the capital moved from Medina to the cosmopolitan Roman/Byzantine city of Damascus in Syria. Its ruling class was an Arab military aristocracy, drawn from various tribes. But Umayyad rule provoked growing criticism and unrest. The Shia viewed the Umayyad caliphs as illegitimate usurpers, and non-Arab Muslims resented their second-class citizenship in the empire. Many Arabs protested the luxurious living and impiety of their rulers. The Umayyads, they charged, "made God's servants slaves, God's property something to be taken by turns among the rich, and God's religion a cause of corruption."[13]

Such grievances lay behind the overthrow of the Umayyads in 750 and their replacement by a new Arab dynasty, the Abbasids. With a splendid new capital in Baghdad, the Abbasid caliphs presided over a flourishing and prosperous Islamic civilization in which non-Arabs, especially Persians, now played a prominent role.

Persian cultural influence was reflected in a new title for the caliph, "the shadow of God on earth." But the political unity of the Abbasid Empire did not last long. Beginning in the mid-ninth century, many local governors or military commanders effectively asserted the autonomy of their regions, while still giving formal allegiance to the caliph in Baghdad. Long before Mongol conquest put an official end to the Abbasid Empire in 1258, the Islamic world had fractured politically into a series of "sultanates," many ruled by Persian or Turkish military dynasties.

A further tension within the world of Islam, though seldom a violent conflict, lay in different answers to the central question: What does it mean to be a Muslim, to submit wholly to Allah? That question took on added urgency as the expanding Arab Empire incorporated various lifestyles, customs, and practices that had been unknown during Muhammad's lifetime. One answer lay in the development of an extensive body of Islamic law, known as the sharia. It was the work of religious scholars, the ulama, primarily in the eighth and ninth centuries.

■ **Comparison**

In what ways were Sufi Muslims critical of mainstream Islam?

Based on the Quran, the life and teachings of Muhammad, deductive reasoning, and the consensus of scholars, the emerging sharia addressed in great detail practically every aspect of religious and social life. While Christendom focused on correct belief, the sharia was far more concerned with correct behavior. It was a blueprint for an authentic Islamic society, providing detailed guidance for prayer and ritual cleansing; marriage, divorce, and inheritance; business and commercial relationships; the treatment of slaves; political life; and much more. Debates among the ulama led to the creation of four schools of law among Sunni Muslims and still others in the lands of Shia Islam. To the ulama and their followers, living as a Muslim meant following the sharia and thus participating in the creation of an Islamic society.

A second and quite different understanding of the faith emerged among those who saw the worldly success of Islamic civilization as a distraction and deviation from the purer spirituality of Muhammad's time. Known as *Sufis*, they represented Islam's mystical dimension, in that they sought a direct and personal experience of the divine. Through renunciation of the material world, meditation on the words of the Quran, the use of music and dance, the veneration of Muhammad and various "saints," Sufis pursued the obliteration of the ego and spiritual union with Allah. To describe that inexpressible experience, they often resorted to metaphors of drunkenness or the embrace of lovers. "Stain your prayer rug with wine," urged the famous Sufi poet Hafiz, referring to the intoxication of the believer with the divine presence. Rabia, an eighth-century woman and Sufi master, conveyed something of the fervor of early Sufi devotion in her much-repeated prayer:

> O my Lord, if I worship Thee from fear of Hell, burn me in Hell; and if I worship Thee from hope of Paradise, exclude me thence; but if I worship Thee for Thine own sake, then withhold not from me Thine Eternal Beauty.[14]

This mystical tendency in Islamic practice, which became widely popular by the ninth and tenth centuries, was sharply critical of the more scholarly and legalistic practitioners of the sharia. To Sufis, establishment teachings about the law and correct behavior, while useful for daily living, did little to bring the believer into the presence of God. For some, even the Quran had its limits. Why spend time reading a love letter (the Quran), asked one Sufi master, when one might be in the very presence of the Beloved who wrote it?[15] Furthermore, they felt that many of the ulama had been compromised by their association with worldly and corrupt governments. Sufis therefore often charted their own course to God, implicitly challenging the religious authority of the ulama. For these orthodox religious scholars, Sufi ideas and practice verged on heresy, as Sufis claimed to be one with God, to receive new revelations, or to incorporate religious practices from outside the Islamic world.

Despite their differences, the legalistic emphasis of the ulama and the Sufis' spirituality never became irreconcilable versions of Islam. A major Islamic thinker, al-Ghazali (1058–1111), himself both a legal scholar and a Sufi practitioner, in fact worked out an intellectual accommodation among different strands of Islamic thought. Rational philosophy alone could never enable believers to know Allah, he argued. Nor were revelation and the law sufficient, for Muslims must know God in their hearts, through direct personal encounter with Allah. Thus al-Ghazali incorporated Sufism into mainstream Islamic thinking. Nonetheless, differences in emphasis remained an element of tension and sometimes discord within the world of Islam.

Women and Men in Early Islam

■ Change

How did the rise of Islam change the lives of women?

What did the rise of Islam and the making of the Arab Empire mean for the daily lives of women and their relationship with men? Virtually every aspect of this question has been and remains highly controversial. The debates begin with the Quran itself. Did its teachings release women from earlier restrictions, or did they impose new limitations? At the level of spiritual life, the Quran was quite clear and explicit: men and women were equal.

> Those who surrender themselves to Allah and accept the true faith; who are devout, sincere, patient, humble, charitable, and chaste; who fast and are ever mindful of Allah—on these, both men and women, Allah will bestow forgiveness and rich reward.[16]

But in social terms, and especially within marriage, the Quran, like the written texts of almost all civilizations, viewed women as inferior and subordinate.

> Men have authority over women because Allah has made the one superior to the other, and because they spend their wealth to maintain them. Good women are obedient. They guard their unseen parts because Allah has guarded them. As for those from whom you fear disobedience, admonish them and send them to beds apart and beat them. Then if they obey you, take no further action against them.[17]

More specifically, the Quran provided a mix of rights, restrictions, and protections for women. The earlier Arab practice of female infanticide, for example, was forbidden. Women were given control over their own property, particularly their dowries, and were granted rights of inheritance, but at half the rate of their male counterparts. Marriage was considered a contract between consenting parties, thus making marriage by capture illegitimate. Within marriage, women were expected to enjoy sexual satisfaction and could sue for divorce if they had not had sexual relations for more than four months. Divorce was thus possible for both parties, although it was far more readily available for men. The practice of taking multiple husbands, which operated in some pre-Islamic Arab tribes, was prohibited, while polygyny (the practice of having multiple wives) was permitted, though more clearly regulated than before. Men were limited to four wives and required to treat each of them equally. The difficulty of doing so has been interpreted by some as virtually requiring monogamy. Men were, however, permitted to have sexual relations with consenting female slaves, but any children born of those unions were free, as was the mother once her owner died. Furthermore, men were strongly encouraged to marry orphans, widows, and slaves.

Such Quranic prescriptions were but one factor shaping the lives of women and men. At least as important were the long-established practices of the societies into which Islam spread and the growing sophistication, prosperity, and urbanization of Islamic civilization. As had been the case in Athens and China during their "golden ages," women, particularly in the upper classes, experienced growing restrictions as Islamic civilization flourished culturally and economically in the Abbasid era. In early Islamic times, a number of women played visible public roles, particularly Muhammad's youngest wife, Aisha. Women prayed in the mosques, although separately, standing beside the men. Nor were women generally veiled or secluded. As the Arab empire grew in size and splendor, however, the position of women became more limited. The second caliph, Umar, asked women to offer prayers at home. Now veiling and the seclusion of women became standard practice among the upper and ruling classes, removing them from public life. Separate quarters within the homes of the wealthy were the domain of women, from which they could emerge only completely veiled. The caliph Mansur (ruled 754–775) carried this separation of the sexes even further when he ordered a separate bridge for women to be built over the Euphrates in the new capital of Baghdad. Such seclusion was less possible for lower-class women, who lacked the servants of the rich and had to leave the home for shopping or work.

Such practices derived far more from established traditions of Middle Eastern cultures than from the Quran itself, but they soon gained an Islamic rationale in the

Men and Women at Worship This sixteenth-century Persian painting of a mosque service shows older men with beards toward the front, younger men behind them, and veiled women and children in a separate area. (Bodleian Library, University of Oxford, Ms. Ouseley. Add 24, fol. 55v)

writings of Muslim thinkers. The famous philosopher and religious scholar al-Ghazali clearly saw a relationship between Muslim piety and the separation of the sexes.

> It is not permissible for a stranger to hear the sound of a pestle being pounded by a woman he does not know. If he knocks at the door, it is not proper for the woman to answer him softly and easily because men's hearts can be drawn to [women] for the most trifling [reason]. . . . However, if the woman has to answer the knock, she should stick her finger in her mouth so that her voice sounds like that of an old woman.[18]

Other signs of a tightening patriarchy—such as "honor killing" of women by their male relatives for violating sexual taboos and, in some places, clitorectomy (female circumcision)—likewise derived from local cultures, with no sanction in the Quran or Islamic law. Where they were practiced, such customs often came to be seen as Islamic, but they were certainly not limited to the Islamic world. In many cultures, concern with family honor, linked to women's sexuality, dictated harsh punishments for women who violated sexual taboos.

Negative views of women, presenting them variously as weak, deficient, and a sexually charged threat to men and social stability, emerged in the *hadiths*, traditions about the sayings or actions of Muhammad, which became an important source of Islamic law. A changing interpretation of the Adam and Eve story illustrates the point. In the Quran, equal blame attaches to both of them for yielding to the temptation of Satan, and both alike ask for and receive God's forgiveness. Nothing suggests that Eve tempted or seduced Adam into sin. In later centuries, however, several hadiths and other writings took up Judeo-Christian versions of the story that blamed Eve, and thus women in general, for Adam's sin and for the punishment that followed, including expulsion from the garden and pain in childbirth.[19]

Even as women faced growing restrictions in society generally, Islam, like Buddhism and Christianity, also offered new outlets for them in religious life. The Sufi practice of mystical union with Allah allowed a greater role for women than did mainstream Islam. Some Sufi orders had parallel groups for women, and a few welcomed women as equal members. Within the world of Shia Islam, women teachers of the faith were termed *mullahs*, the same as their male counterparts. Islamic education, either in the home or in Quranic schools, allowed some to become literate and a few to achieve higher levels of learning. Visits to the tombs of major Islamic figures as well as the ritual of the public bath provided some opportunity for women to interact with other women beyond their own family circle.

Islam and Cultural Encounter: A Four-Way Comparison

In its earliest centuries, the rapid spread of Islam had been accompanied by the creation of an immense Arab Empire, very much in the tradition of earlier Mediterranean and Middle Eastern empires. By the tenth century, however, little

Map 11.2 The Growing World of Islam (900–1500) Islam as a religion, a civilization, and an arena of commerce continued to grow even as the Arab Empire fragmented.

political unity remained, and in 1258 even the powerless symbol of that earlier unity vanished as Mongol forces sacked Baghdad and killed the last Abbasid caliph. But even as the empire disintegrated, the civilization that was born within it grew and flourished. Perhaps the most significant sign of a flourishing Islamic civilization was the continued spread of the religion both within and beyond the boundaries of a vanishing Arab Empire (see Map 11.2), although that process differed considerably from place to place. The examples of India, Anatolia, West Africa, and Spain illustrate the various ways that Islam penetrated these societies as well as the rather different outcomes of these epic cultural encounters.

The Case of India

In South Asia, Islam found a permanent place in a long-established civilization as invasions by Turkic-speaking warrior groups from Central Asia, recently converted to Islam, brought the faith to India. Thus the Turks became the third major carrier

■ **Comparison**
What similarities and differences can you identify in the spread of Islam to India, Anatolia, West Africa, and Spain?

The Sultanate of Delhi

of Islam, after the Arabs and Persians, as their conquests initiated an enduring encounter between Islam and a Hindu-based Indian civilization. Beginning around 1000, those conquests gave rise to a series of Turkic and Muslim regimes that governed much of India until the British takeover in the eighteenth and nineteenth centuries. The early centuries of this encounter were violent indeed, as the invaders smashed Hindu and Buddhist temples and carried off vast quantities of Indian treasure. With the establishment of the Sultanate of Delhi in 1206, Turkic rule became more systematic, although their small numbers and internal conflicts allowed only a very modest penetration of Indian society.

In the centuries that followed, substantial Muslim communities emerged in India, particularly in regions less tightly integrated into the dominant Hindu culture. Disillusioned Buddhists as well as low-caste Hindus and untouchables found the more egalitarian Islam attractive. So did peoples just beginning to make the transition to settled agriculture. Others benefited from converting to Islam by avoiding the tax imposed on non-Muslims. Sufis were particularly important in facilitating conversion, for India had always valued "god-filled men" who were detached from worldly affairs. Sufi missionaries, willing to accommodate local gods and religious festivals, helped to develop a "popular Islam" that was not always so sharply distinguished from Hinduism.

Unlike the earlier experience of Islam in the Middle East, North Africa, and Persia, where it rapidly became the dominant faith, in India it was never able to claim more than 20 to 25 percent of the total population. Furthermore, Muslim communities were especially concentrated in the Punjab and Sind regions of northwestern India and in Bengal to the east. The core regions of Hindu culture in the northern Indian plain were not seriously challenged by the new faith, despite centuries of Muslim rule. One reason perhaps lay in the sharpness of the cultural divide between Islam and Hinduism. Islam was the most radically monotheistic of the world's religions, forbidding any representation of Allah, while Hinduism was surely among the most prolifically polytheistic, generating endless statues and images of the divine in many forms. The Muslim notion of the equality of all believers contrasted sharply with the hierarchical assumptions of the caste system. The sexual modesty of Muslims was deeply offended by the open eroticism of some Hindu religious art.

Although such differences may have limited the appeal of Islam in India, they also may have prevented it from being absorbed into the tolerant and inclusive embrace of Hinduism as had so many other religious ideas, practices, and communities. The religious exclusivity of Islam, born of its firm monotheistic belief and the idea of a unique revelation, set a boundary that the great sponge of Hinduism could not completely absorb.

Certainly not all was conflict across that boundary. Many prominent Hindus willingly served in the political and military structures of a Muslim-ruled India. Mystical seekers after the divine blurred the distinction between Hindu and

Muslim, suggesting that God was to be found "neither in temple nor in mosque." "Look within your heart," wrote the great fifteenth-century mystic poet Kabir, "for there you will find both [Allah] and Ram [a famous Hindu deity]."[20] In fact, during the early sixteenth century, a new and distinct religious tradition emerged in India, known as Sikhism, which blended elements of Islam, such as devotion to one universal God, with Hindu concepts, such as karma and rebirth. "There is no Hindu and no Muslim. All are children of God," declared Guru Nanak (1469–1539), the founder of Sikhism.

Nonetheless, Muslims, usually living quite separately, remained a distinctive minority within an Indian civilization, which they now largely governed but which they proved unable to completely transform.

The Case of Anatolia

At the same time that India was being subjected to Turkic invasion, so too was Anatolia, where the largely Christian and Greek-speaking population was governed by the Byzantine Empire. Here, as in India, the invaders initially wreaked havoc as Byzantine authority melted away in the eleventh century. Sufi missionaries likewise played a major role in the process of conversion. The outcome, however, was a far more profound cultural transformation than in India. By 1500, the population was 90 percent Muslim and largely Turkic-speaking, and Anatolia was the heartland of the powerful Turkish Ottoman Empire that had overrun Christian Byzantium. Why did the Turkic intrusion into Anatolia generate a much more thorough Islamization than in India?

One factor clearly lies in a very different demographic balance. The population of Anatolia—perhaps 8 million—was far smaller than India's roughly 48 million people, but far more Turkic-speaking peoples settled in Anatolia, giving them a much greater cultural weight than the smaller colonizing force in India. Furthermore, the disruption of Anatolian society was much more extensive. Massacres, enslavement, famine, and flight led to a sharp drop in the native population. The Byzantine state had been fatally weakened. Church properties were confiscated, and monasteries were destroyed or deserted. Priests and bishops were sometimes unable to serve their congregations. Christians, though seldom forced to convert, suffered many discriminations. They had to wear special clothing and pay special taxes, and they were forbidden to ride saddled horses or carry swords. Not a few Christians came to believe that these disasters represented proof that Islam was the true religion.[21] Thus Byzantine civilization in Anatolia, focused on the centralized institutions of church and state, was rendered leaderless and dispirited, whereas India's decentralized civilization, lacking a unified political or religious establishment, was better able to absorb the shock of external invasion while retaining its core values and identity.

The Turkish rulers of Anatolia built a new society that welcomed converts and granted them material rewards and opportunity for high office. Moreover, the

■ **Comparison**
Why was Anatolia so much more thoroughly Islamized than India?

Map 11.3 The Ottoman Empire by the Mid-Fifteenth Century

As Turkic-speaking migrants bearing the religion of Islam penetrated Anatolia, the Ottoman Empire took shape, reaching into southeastern Europe and finally displacing the Christian Byzantine Empire. Subsequently, it came to control much of the Middle East and North Africa as well.

cultural barriers to conversion were arguably less severe than in India. The common monotheism of Islam and Christianity, and Muslim respect for Jesus and the Christian scriptures, made conversion easier than crossing the great gulf between Islam and Hinduism. Such similarities lent support to the suggestion of some Sufi teachers that the two religions were but different versions of the same faith. Sufis also established schools, mills, orchards, hospices, and rest places for travelers and thus replaced the destroyed or decaying institutions of Christian Anatolia.[22] All of this contributed to the thorough religious transformation of Anatolia and laid a foundation for the Ottoman Empire, which by 1500 became the most impressive and powerful state within the Islamic world (see Map 11.3).

Islamization did not completely eliminate the influence of Turkish culture. For example, their tradition of a freer, more gender-equal life for women, common among pastoral people, persisted well after conversion to Islam, much to the distress of the Moroccan visitor Ibn Battuta during his travels among them in the fourteenth century: "A remarkable thing that I saw . . . was the respect shown to women by the Turks, for they hold a more dignified position than the men. . . . The windows of the tent are open and her face is visible, for the Turkish women do not veil themselves."[23] He was not pleased.

The Case of West Africa

Still another pattern prevailed in West Africa. Here Islam accompanied Muslim traders across the Sahara rather than being brought by invading Arab or Turkic armies. Its acceptance in the emerging civilization of West African states in the centuries after 1000 was largely peaceful and voluntary, lacking the incentives associated elsewhere with foreign conquest. Introduced by Muslim merchants from an already Islamized North Africa, the new faith was accepted primarily in the urban centers of the West African empires—Ghana, Mali, Songhay, Kanem-Bornu, and others (see Map 11.4). For African merchant communities, Islam provided an important link to Muslim trading partners, much as Buddhism had done in Southeast Asia. For the monarchs and their courts, it offered a source of literate officials to assist in state administration as well as religious legitimacy, particularly for

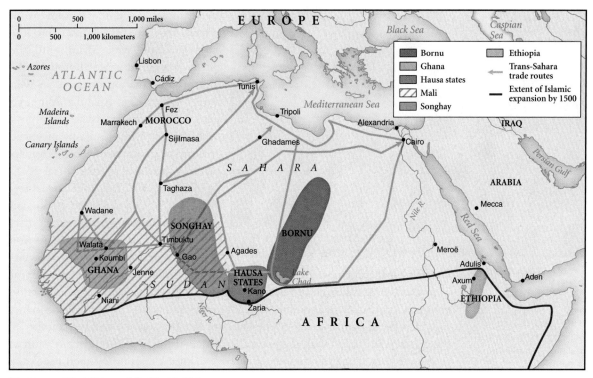

Map 11.4   West Africa and the World of Islam
Both trans-Saharan commerce and Islam linked the civilization of West Africa to the larger Muslim world.

those who gained the prestige conferred by a pilgrimage to Mecca. Islam was a world religion with a single Creator-God, able to comfort and protect people whose political and economic horizons had expanded well beyond the local realm where ancestral spirits and traditional deities might be effective. It had a religious appeal for societies that were now participating in a wider world.

By the sixteenth century, a number of West African cities had become major centers of Islamic religious and intellectual life, attracting scholars from throughout the Muslim world. Timbuktu boasted more than 150 lower-level Quranic schools and several major centers of higher education with thousands of students from all over West Africa and beyond. Libraries held tens of thousands of books and scholarly manuscripts. Monarchs subsidized the construction of mosques as West Africa became an integral part of a larger Islamic world. Arabic became an important language of religion, education, administration, and trade, but it did not become the dominant language of daily life. West Africa did not experience the massive migration of Arab peoples that had promoted the Arabization of North Africa and the Middle East. Moreover, in contrast to India and Anatolia, Sufi holy men played little role until at least the eighteenth century. Scholars, merchants, and rulers, rather than mystic preachers, initially established Islam in West Africa.

The Great Mosque at Jenne
This mosque in the city of Jenne, initially constructed in the thirteenth century, illustrates the assimilation of Islam into West African civilization. (Bildagentur/TIPS Images)

Islam remained the culture of an urban elite and spread little into the rural areas of West Africa until the nineteenth century. No thorough religious transformation occurred in West Africa as it had in Anatolia. Although many rulers adopted Islam, they governed people who steadfastly practiced African religions and whose sensibilities they had to respect if social peace were to prevail. Thus they made few efforts to impose the new religion on their rural subjects or to govern in strict accordance with Islamic law. Ibn Battuta, a fourteenth-century Arab visitor, was appalled that practicing Muslims in Mali permitted their women to appear in public almost naked and to mingle freely with unrelated men. "The association of women with men is agreeable to us," he was told, "and a part of good conduct to which no suspicion attaches. They are not like the women of your country."[24] Ibn Battuta also noted with disapproval a "dance of the masks" on the occasion of an Islamic festival and the traditional practice of sprinkling dust on their heads as a sign of respect for the king. Sonni Ali, a fifteenth-century ruler of Songhay, observed Ramadan and built mosques, but he also consulted traditional diviners and performed customary sacrifices. In such ways, Islam became Africanized even as parts of Africa became Islamized.

The Case of Spain

The chief site of Islamic encounter with Catholic Europe occurred in Spain (called al-Andalus by Muslims), which was conquered by Arab and Berber forces in the early eighth century during the first wave of Islamic expansion. But Islam did not overwhelm Christianity as it did later in Anatolia. In fact, Muslim Spain in the several centuries that followed conquest has often been portrayed as a vibrant civilization characterized by harmony and tolerance between its Muslim rulers and its Christian and Jewish subjects.

Certainly Spain's agricultural economy was the most prosperous in Europe during the ninth and tenth centuries, and at that time its capital of Córdoba was among the largest and most splendid cities in the world. Muslims, Christians, and Jews alike contributed to a brilliant high culture in which astronomy, medicine, the arts, architecture, and literature flourished. It was largely from Spain that the rich heritage of Islamic learning became available to Christian Europe.

Furthermore, social relationships among upper-class members of different faiths were easy and frequent. More than a few Christians converted to Islam, and many others, known as *Mozarabs* (would-be Arabs), learned Arabic, veiled their women, stopped eating pork, appreciated Arabic music and poetry, and sometimes married Muslims. One Christian bishop complained that Spanish Christians knew the rules of Arabic grammar better than those of Latin. During the reign of Abd al-Rahman III (912–961), freedom of worship was declared as well as the opportunity for all to rise in the bureaucracy of the state.

Even assimilated or Arabized Christians, however, remained infidels in the eyes of their Muslim counterparts, and by the late tenth century the era of toleration began to erode. Warfare with the remaining Christian states in northern Spain picked up in the tenth and eleventh centuries, and more puritanical and rigid forms of Islam entered Spain from North Africa. In these circumstances, the golden age of religious harmony faded. Under the rule of Abu Amir al-Mansur (981–1002), an official policy of tolerance turned to one of overt persecution against Christians, which now included the plundering of churches. Social life also changed. Devout Muslims avoided contact with Christians; Christian homes had to be built lower than those of Muslims; priests were forbidden to carry a cross or a Bible, lest they offend Muslim sensibilities; and Mozarabs were permitted to live only in particular places. Thus, writes one scholar, "the era of harmonious interaction between Muslim and Christian in Spain came to an end, replaced by intolerance, prejudice, and mutual suspicion."[25]

That intolerance was perpetuated as the Christian reconquest of Spain gained ground after 1200. Many Muslims were then forced out of Spain, while those who remained could no longer give the call to prayer, go on pilgrimage, or publicly practice their faith. When the reconquest was completed in 1492, all Jews, some 200,000 of them, were likewise expelled from the country. Thus, as Christianity was displaced by Islam in Anatolia, the opposite process was taking place in Spain.

The World of Islam as a New Civilization

As the religion spread and the Abbasid dynasty declined, the civilization of Islam, like Western Christendom and the Hindu world, operated without a single political center, bound more by a shared religious culture than by a shared state. Unlike the other civilizations, however, the Islamic world by 1500 embraced at least parts of virtually every other civilization in the Afro-Eurasian hemisphere. It was in that sense "history's first truly global civilization," although the Americas, of course, were not involved.[26] What held the Islamic world together? What enabled many people to feel themselves part of a single civilization despite its political fragmentation, religious controversies, and cultural and regional diversity?

Networks of Faith

At the core of that vast civilization was a common commitment to Islam. No group was more important in the transmission of those beliefs and practices than the ulama. These learned scholars were not "priests" in the Christian sense, for in Islam,

■ Description
What makes it possible to speak of the Islamic world as a distinct and coherent civilization?

at least theoretically, no person could stand between the believer and Allah. Rather they served as judges, interpreters, administrators, prayer leaders, and reciters of the Quran, but especially as preservers and teachers of the sharia. Supported mostly by their local communities, some also received the patronage of *sultans*, or rulers, and were therefore subject to criticism for corruption and undue submission to state authority. In their homes, mosques, shrines, and Quranic schools, the ulama passed on the core teachings of the faith. Beginning in the eleventh century, formal colleges called *madrassas* offered more advanced instruction in the Quran and the sayings of Muhammad; grammar and rhetoric; sometimes philosophy, theology, mathematics, and medicine; and, above all else, law. Teaching was informal, mostly oral, and involved much memorization of texts. It was also largely conservative, seeking to preserve an established body of Islamic learning.

The ulama were an "international elite," and the system of education they created served to bind together an immense and diverse civilization. Common texts were shared widely across the world of Islam. Students and teachers alike traveled great distances in search of the most learned scholars. From Indonesia to West Africa, educated Muslims inhabited a "shared world of debate and reference."[27]

Paralleling the educational network of the ulama were the emerging religious orders of the Sufis. By the tenth century, particular Sufi *shaykhs*, or teachers, began to attract groups of disciples who were eager to learn their unique devotional practices and ways of achieving union with Allah. The disciples usually swore eternal allegiance to their teacher and valued highly the chain of transmission by which those teachings and practices had come down from earlier masters. In the twelfth and thirteenth centuries, Sufis began to organize in a variety of larger associations, some limited to particular regions and others with chapters throughout the Islamic world. The Qadiriya order, for example, began in Baghdad but spread widely throughout the Arab world and into sub-Saharan Africa. Sufi orders were especially significant in the frontier regions of Islam because they followed conquering armies or traders into Central and Southeast Asia, India, Anatolia, West Africa, and elsewhere. Their passionate preaching, exemplary living, and reputation for supernatural powers gained a hearing for the new faith. Their emphasis on devotion rather than law allowed the Sufis to accommodate elements of local belief and practice and encouraged the growth of a popular or blended Islam. But that flexibility also often earned them the enmity of the ulama, who were sharply critical of such deviations from the sharia.

Like the madrassas and the sharia, Sufi religious ideas and institutions spanned the Islamic world and were yet another thread in the cosmopolitan web of Islamic civilization. Particular devotional teachings and practices spread widely, as did the writings of such famous Sufi poets as Hafiz and Rumi. Devotees made pilgrimages to the distant tombs of famous teachers, who, they often believed, might intercede with God on their behalf. Wandering Sufis, in search of the wisdom of renowned shaykhs, found fellow seekers and welcome shelter in the compounds of these religious orders.

In addition to the networks of the Sufis and the ulama, many thousands of people, from kings to peasants, made the grand pilgrimage to Mecca—the hajj—each year, no doubt gaining some sense of the umma. There men and women together, hailing from all over the Islamic world, joined as one people to rehearse the central elements of their faith. The claims of local identities based on family, clan, tribe, ethnicity, or state never disappeared, but now overarching them all was the inclusive unity of the Muslim community. For at least the few days of the hajj, the many worlds of Islam must surely have seemed a single realm.

Networks of Exchange

The world of Islamic civilization cohered not only as a network of faith but also as an immense arena of exchange in which goods, technologies, food products, and ideas circulated widely. It rapidly became a vast trading zone of hemispheric dimensions. In part, this was due to its central location in the Afro-Eurasian world and the breaking down of earlier political barriers between the Byzantine and Persian empires. Furthermore, commerce was valued positively within Islamic teaching: Muhammad himself had been a trader, and the pilgrimage to Mecca likewise fostered commerce. The extraordinary spurt of urbanization that accompanied the growth of Islamic civilization also promoted trade. Baghdad, established in 756 as the capital of the Abbasid Empire, soon grew into a magnificent city of half a million people. The appetite of urban elites for luxury goods stimulated both craft production and the desire for foreign goods.

■ **Connection**
In what ways was the world of Islam a "cosmopolitan civilization"?

Thus Muslim merchants, Arabs and Persians in particular, quickly became prominent and sometimes dominant players in all of the major Afro-Eurasian trade routes of the postclassical era—in the Mediterranean Sea, along the revived Silk Roads, across the Sahara, and throughout the Indian Ocean basin (see Chapter 8). By the eighth century, Arab and Persian traders had established a commercial colony in Canton in southern China, thus linking the Islamic heartland with Asia's other giant and flourishing economy. Various forms of banking, partnerships, business contracts, and instruments for granting credit facilitated these long-distance economic relationships and generated a prosperous, highly developed, "capitalist" economy that spanned the Old World.[28]

The vast expanses of Islamic civilization also facilitated a substantial exchange of agricultural products and practices from one region to another, the largest such transfer in world history prior to Europe's encounter with the Americas. The Muslim conquest of northwestern India opened the Middle East to a veritable treasure trove of crops that had been domesticated long before in South and Southeast Asia, including rice, sugarcane, new strains of sorghum, hard wheat, bananas, lemons, limes, watermelons, coconut palms, spinach, artichokes, and cotton. Some of these subsequently found their way into the Middle East and Africa and by the thirteenth century to Europe as well.[29] Both cotton and sugarcane, associated with complex production processes and slave labor, came to play central roles in the formation of the modern global system after 1500. These new crops and the development of the intensified agricultural techniques that often accompanied them contributed to increased food production, population growth, urbanization, and industrial development characteristic of the Muslim Middle East in early Abbasid times.

Technology too diffused widely within the Islamic world. Ancient Persian techniques for obtaining water by drilling into the sides of hills now spread across North Africa as far west as Morocco. Muslim technicians made improvements on rockets, first developed in China, by developing one that carried a small warhead and another used to attack ships.[30] Papermaking techniques entered the Abbasid Empire from China in the eighth century, with paper mills soon operating in Persia, Iraq, and Egypt. This revolutionary technology, which everywhere served to strengthen bureaucratic governments, spread from the Middle East into India and Europe over the following centuries.

Ideas likewise circulated across the Islamic world. The religion itself drew heavily and quite openly on Jewish and Christian precedents. Persia also contributed much in the way of bureaucratic practice, court ritual, and poetry, with Persian becoming the primary literary language of elite circles. Scientific, medical, and philosophical texts, especially from ancient Greece, the Hellenistic world, and India, were systematically translated into Arabic, for several centuries providing an enormous boost to Islamic scholarship and science. In 830, the Abbasid caliph al-Mamun, himself a poet and scholar with a passion for foreign learning, established the House of Wisdom in Baghdad as an academic center for this research and translation. Stimulated by Greek texts, a school of Islamic thinkers, known as Mutazalites ("those who stand apart"), argued that reason, rather than revelation, was the "surest way to truth."[31] In the long run, however, the philosophers' emphasis on logic, rationality, and the laws of nature was subject to increasing criticism by those who held that only the Quran, the sayings of the Prophet, or mystical experience represented a genuine path to God.

But the realm of Islam was much more than a museum of ancient achievements from the civilizations that it encompassed. Those traditions mixed and blended to generate a distinctive Islamic civilization with many new contributions to the world of learning.[32] (See the Snapshot.) Using Indian numerical notation, for example, Arab scholars developed algebra as a novel mathematical discipline. They also undertook much original work in astronomy and optics. They built upon earlier Greek and Indian practice to create a remarkable tradition in medicine and pharmacology. Arab physicians

A Muslim Astronomical Observatory
Drawing initially on Greek, Indian, and Persian astronomy, the Islamic world after 1000 developed its own distinctive tradition of astronomical observation and prediction, reflected in this Turkish observatory constructed in 1557. Muslim astronomy subsequently exercised considerable influence in both China and Europe. (University Library, Istanbul, Turkey/The Bridgeman Art Library)

$Snapshot$ **Key Achievements in Islamic Science and Scholarship**

Person/Dates	Achievement
al-Khwarazim (790–840)	Mathematician; spread use of Arabic numerals in Islamic world; wrote first book on algebra
al-Razi (865–925)	Discovered sulfuric acid; wrote a vast encyclopedia of medicine drawing on Greek, Syrian, Indian, and Persian work and his own clinical observation
al-Biruni (973–1048)	Mathematician, astronomer, cartographer; calculated the radius of the earth with great accuracy; worked out numerous mathematical innovations; developed a technique for displaying a hemisphere on a plane
Ibn Sina (Avicenna) (980–1037)	Prolific writer in almost all fields of science and philosophy; especially known for *Canon of Medicine*, a fourteen-volume work that set standards for medical practice in Islamic and Christian worlds for centuries
Omar Khayyam (1048–1131)	Mathematician; critic of Euclid's geometry; measured the solar year with great accuracy; Sufi poet; author of *The Rubaiyat*
Ibn Rushd (Averroës) (1126–1198)	Translated and commented widely on Aristotle; rationalist philosopher; made major contributions in law, mathematics, and medicine
Nasir al-Din Tusi (1201–1274)	Founder of the famous Maragha observatory in Persia (data from Maragha probably influenced Copernicus); mapped the motion of stars and planets
Ibn Khaldun (1332–1406)	Greatest Arab historian; identified trends and structures in world history over long periods of time

such as al-Razi and Ibn Sina accurately diagnosed many diseases, such as hay fever, measles, smallpox, diphtheria, rabies, diabetes, and more. In addition, treatments such as using a mercury ointment for scabies, cataract and hernia operations, and filling teeth with gold emerged from Arab doctors. The first hospitals, traveling clinics, and examinations for physicians and pharmacologists also were developed within the Islamic world. In the eleventh and twelfth centuries, this enormous body of Arab medical scholarship entered Europe via Spain, and it remained at the core of European medical practice for many centuries.[33]

Reflections: Learning from Outsiders: A Tale of Two Travelers

Historians generally prefer to rely on "insiders" for understanding the societies and cultures they study. Documents, artifacts, and images created by people actually living in those times and places have an authenticity that accounts from foreigners may lack. Nonetheless, scholars often find it necessary, and helpful, to make use of records written by outsiders as well. In describing the interacting worlds of Afro-Eurasia in the postclassical millennium, historians frequently draw on the experience and observations of those travelers who traversed that vast space. Their writings reveal much about themselves and their home cultures as well as about the distant peoples and places they visited. Among these travelers, none have been more useful to historians than Ibn Battuta, a Moroccan Muslim, and Marco Polo, an Italian Christian.

Nothing more effectively conveys the extent and the unity of the Islamic world than the travels of Ibn Battuta (1304–1368). Born in Morocco, he traversed nearly 75,000 miles during his extraordinary journeys, which took him to Spain and Anatolia; West and East Africa; Arabia, Iraq, and Persia; Central and Southeast Asia; India and China. He traveled at various times as a pilgrim, making the hajj twice; as a Sufi devotee; as a legal scholar who served for a time as a judge in India; and frequently in the company of Muslim merchants.

Remarkably, almost all of his extensive travels occurred within the "house of Islam," where he moved among people who shared his faith and often his language, and where the sharia provided, at least in theory, the basis of social life. As a visitor from a more established Islamic society, he was often highly critical of the quality of Islamic observance. In West Africa, in Turkish lands, and in the Maldive Islands of the Indian Ocean, Ibn Battuta was appalled at the freedom of women and the scanty clothing they wore. In India, he ordered eighty lashes for Muslims found drinking wine. Still, they were Muslims. Only China seemed wholly foreign, for there he could not explain the country's prosperity and security in terms of Islam.

> China was beautiful, but it did not please me.... I was greatly troubled thinking about the way paganism dominated this country.... That disturbed me so much that I stayed indoors most of the time and only went out when necessary. During my stay in China, whenever I saw any Muslims I always felt as though I were meeting my own family and close kinsmen.[34]

Ibn Battuta has frequently been compared with the European traveler Marco Polo (1254–1324), who had made his way a few decades earlier from Italy to China, where he served at the court of Khubilai Khan for seventeen years. Returning to Italy in 1295, Marco Polo wrote an account of his travels and the lands he visited, which became widely popular in Europe as a source of information about the mysterious East. Christopher Columbus carried a marked-up copy of the book on his transatlantic journeys, believing that he was seeking by sea the places Marco Polo had visited by land.

Marco Polo's travels were but the best-known example of a European civilization newly reaching out to reconnect with a wider world. Unlike Ibn Battuta, Polo felt himself constantly an outsider, "a stranger in a strange land," for he was traveling almost everywhere beyond the borders of Christendom. Perhaps because he was an outsider, Polo did not register the kind of disapproval or culture shock that Ibn Battuta experienced in the face of deviations from heartland Islamic practice. He reported prolifically on the strange ways and peoples he encountered, but without the disdain that often characterized Ibn Battuta's commentaries.

The respective journeys of these two travelers reveal much about the world of the thirteenth and fourteenth centuries. Most important, they show that Islamic civilization was then the central fact of the Afro-Eurasian world, while Europe was still on the margins. Memories of that earlier prominence and achievement both sustained and frustrated Muslims when, in the centuries after 1700, Europeans increasingly assumed the central role in world affairs. Those memories also inspired resistance to Western dominance in the twentieth century and beyond.

Second Thoughts

What's the Significance?

Quran	Umayyad caliphate	Timbuktu
umma	Abbasid caliphate	al-Andalus
Pillars of Islam	sharia	madrassas
hijra	al-Ghazali	House of Wisdom
jizya	Sikhism	Ibn Sina
ulama	Anatolia	Ibn Battuta

To assess your mastery of the material in this chapter, see the **Online Study Guide** at bedfordstmartins.com/strayer.

Big Picture Questions

1. What distinguished the first centuries of Islamic history from the early history of Christianity and Buddhism? What similarities and differences characterized their religious outlooks?
2. How might you account for the immense religious and political/military success of Islam in its early centuries?
3. In what ways can Islamic civilization be described as "cosmopolitan"?
4. "Islam was simultaneously both a single world of shared meaning and interaction and a series of separate and distinct communities, often in conflict with one another." What evidence could you provide to support both sides of this argument?
5. What changes did Islamic expansion generate in those societies that encountered it, and how was Islam itself transformed by those encounters?

Next Steps: For Further Study

For Web sites and documents related to this chapter, see **Make History** at bedfordstmartins.com/strayer.

Reza Aslan, *No God but God* (2005). A well-written and popular history of Islam by an Iranian immigrant to the United States.

Richard Bulliet, *Conversion to Islam in the Medieval Period* (1979). A scholarly study of the meaning and process of conversion in the early history of Islam and in several distinct places.

Richard Eaton, *Islamic History as Global History* (1990). A short account by a major scholar that examines Islam in a global framework.

John Esposito, ed., *The Oxford History of Islam* (1999). Up-to-date essays on various periods and themes in Islamic history. Beautifully illustrated.

Francis Robinson, ed., *Cambridge Illustrated History of the Islamic World* (1996). A series of essays by major scholars, with lovely pictures and maps.

Judith Tucker, *Gender and Islamic History* (1994). A brief overview of the changing lives of Islamic women.

"The Travels of Ibn Battuta: A Virtual Tour with the Fourteenth Century Traveler," http://www.sfusd.k12.ca.us/schwww/sch618/Ibn_Battuta/Battuta's_Trip_Twelve.html. A beautifully illustrated journey across the Islamic world in the early 1300s.

CHAPTER TWELVE

Pastoral Peoples on the Global Stage

The Mongol Moment

1200–1500

In 1937, the great Mongol warrior Chinggis Khan lost his soul, some seven centuries after his death. According to Mongol tradition, a warrior's soul was contained in his spirit banner, consisting of strands of hair from his best horses attached to a spear. For many centuries, Chinggis Khan's spirit banner had been housed in a Buddhist monastery in central Mongolia, where lamas (religious teachers) had tended it.[1] But in the 1930s, Mongolia, then under Communist control and heavily dominated by Stalin's Soviet Union, launched a brutal antireligious campaign that destroyed many monasteries, executed some 2,000 monks, and led to the vanishing of Chinggis Khan's spirit banner and thus his soul.

By the end of the twentieth century, as communism faded away, the memory of Chinggis Khan, if not his spirit banner, made a remarkable comeback in the land of his birth. Vodka, cigarettes, a chocolate bar, two brands of beer, the country's best rock band, and the central square of the capital city all bore his name, while his picture appeared on Mongolia's stamps and money. Rural young people on horseback sang songs in his honor, and their counterparts in urban Internet cafés constructed Web sites to celebrate his achievements. The country organized elaborate celebrations in 2006 to mark the 800th anniversary of his founding of the Mongol Empire.

ALL OF THIS IS A REMINDER OF THE ENORMOUS AND SURPRISING ROLE that the Mongols played in the Eurasian world of the thirteenth and fourteenth centuries and of the continuing echoes of that long-vanished empire. More generally, the story of the Mongols serves as a useful

---

Chinggis Khan at Prayer: This sixteenth-century Indian painting shows Chinggis Khan at prayer in the midst of battle. He is perhaps praying to Tengri, the great sky god, on whom the Mongol conqueror based his power. (Werner Forman/Art Resource, NY)

corrective to the almost exclusive focus that historians often devote to agricultural peoples and their civilizations, for the Mongols, and many other such peoples, were pastoral nomads who disdained farming while centering their economic lives around their herds of animals. Normally they did not construct elaborate cities, enduring empires, or monumental works of art, architecture, and written literature. Nonetheless, they left an indelible mark on the historical development of the entire Afro-Eurasian hemisphere, and particularly on the agricultural civilizations with which they so often interacted.

Looking Back and Looking Around: The Long History of Pastoral Nomads

The "revolution of domestication," beginning around 11,500 years ago, involved both plants and animals. People living in more favored environments were able to combine farming with animal husbandry and on this economic foundation generated powerful and impressive civilizations with substantial populations. But on the arid margins of agricultural lands, where productive farming was difficult or impossible, an alternative kind of food-producing economy emerged around 4000 B.C.E., focused on the raising of livestock. Peoples practicing such an economy learned to use the milk, blood, wool, hides, and meat of their animals to occupy lands that could not support agricultural societies. Some of those animals also provided new baggage and transportation possibilities. Horses, camels, goats, sheep, cattle, yaks, and reindeer were the primary animals that separately, or in some combination, enabled the construction of pastoral or herding societies. Such societies took shape in the vast grasslands of inner Eurasia and sub-Saharan Africa, in the Arabian and Saharan deserts, in the subarctic regions of the Northern Hemisphere, and in the high plateau of Tibet. Pastoralism emerged only in the Afro-Eurasian world, for in the Americas the absence of large animals that could be domesticated precluded a herding economy. But where such animals existed, their domestication shaped unique societies adapted to diverse environments.

The World of Pastoral Societies

■ Comparison

In what ways did pastoral societies differ from their agricultural counterparts?

Despite many differences among pastoral societies, they shared several important features that distinguished them from settled agricultural communities and civilizations. Pastoral societies' generally less productive economies and their need for large grazing areas meant that they supported far smaller populations than did agricultural societies. People generally lived in small and widely scattered encampments of related kinfolk rather than in the villages, towns, and cities characteristic of agrarian civilizations. Beyond the family unit, pastoral peoples organized themselves in kinship-based groups or clans that claimed a common ancestry, usually through the male line. Related clans might on occasion come together as a tribe, which could also absorb unrelated people into the community. Although values stressing equality

Snapshot **Varieties of Pastoral Societies[2]**

Region and Peoples	Primary Animals	Features
Inner Eurasian steppes (Xiongnu, Yuezhi, Turks, Uighurs, Mongols, Huns, Kipchaks)	Horses; also sheep, goats, cattle, Bactrian (two-humped) camel	Domestication of horse by 4000 B.C.E.; horseback riding by 1000 B.C.E.; site of largest nomadic empires
Southwestern and Central Asia (Seljuks, Ghaznavids, Mongol Il-khans, Uzbeks, Ottomans)	Sheep and goats; used horses, camels, and donkeys for transport	Close economic relationship with neighboring towns; provided meat, wool, milk products, and hides in exchange for grain and manufactured goods
Arabian and Saharan deserts (Bedouin Arabs, Berbers, Tuareg)	Dromedary (one-humped) camel; sometimes sheep	Camel caravans made possible long-distance trade; camel-mounted warriors central to early Arab/Islamic expansion
Grasslands of sub-Saharan Africa (Fulbe, Nuer, Turkana, Masai)	Cattle; also sheep and goats	Cattle were a chief form of wealth and central to ritual life; little interaction with wider world until nineteenth century
Subarctic Eurasia (Lapps)	Reindeer	Reindeer domesticated only since 1500 C.E.; little impact on world history
Tibetan plateau (Tibetans)	Yaks; also sheep, cashmere goats, some cattle	Tibetans supplied yaks as baggage animal for overland caravan trade; exchanged wool, skins, and milk with valley villagers and received barley in return

and individual achievement were strong, in some pastoral societies clans were ranked as noble or commoner, and considerable differences emerged between wealthy aristocrats owning large flocks of animals and poor herders.

Furthermore, nomadic societies generally offered women a higher status, fewer restrictions, and a greater role in public life than their sisters in agricultural civilizations enjoyed. Everywhere they were involved in productive labor as well as having domestic responsibility for food and children. The care of smaller animals such as sheep and goats usually fell to women, although only rarely did women own or control their own livestock. Among the Mongols, the remarriage of widows carried none of the negative connotations that it did among the Chinese, and women could initiate divorce. Mongol women frequently served as political advisers and were active in military affairs as well. A thirteenth-century European visitor, the Franciscan friar Giovanni DiPlano Carpini, recorded his impressions of Mongol women:

> Girls and women ride and gallop as skillfully as men. We even saw them carrying quivers and bows, and the women can ride horses for as long as the men; they have shorter stirrups, handle horses very well, and mind all the property. [Mongol] women make everything: skin clothes, shoes, leggings, and everything made of leather. They drive carts and repair them, they load camels, and are quick and vigorous in all their tasks. They all wear trousers, and some of them shoot just like men.[3]

Certainly literate observers from adjacent civilizations noticed and clearly disapproved of the freedom granted to pastoral women. Ancient Greek writers thought that the pastoralists with whom they were familiar were "women governed." To Han Kuan, a Chinese Confucian scholar in the first century B.C.E., China's northern nomadic neighbors "[made] no distinction between men and women."[4]

The most characteristic feature of pastoral societies was their mobility. As people frequently on the move, they are often referred to as nomads because they shifted their herds in regular patterns. These movements were far from aimless wanderings, as popular images often portray them, but rather sought to systematically follow the seasonal changes in vegetation and water supply. It was a life largely dictated by local environmental conditions and based on turning grass, which people cannot eat, into usable food and energy. Nor were nomads homeless; they took their homes, often elaborate felt tents, with them. According to a prominent scholar of pastoral life, "They know where they are going and why."[5]

Even though nomadic pastoralists represented an alternative to the agricultural way of life that they disdained, they were almost always deeply connected to, and often dependent on, their agricultural neighbors. Few nomadic peoples could live solely from the products of their animals, and most of them actively sought access to the foodstuffs, manufactured goods, and luxury items available from the urban workshops and farming communities of adjacent civilizations. Particularly among the nomadic peoples of inner Eurasia, this desire for the fruits of civilization periodically stimulated the creation of tribal confederations or nomadic states that could more effectively deal with the powerful agricultural societies on their

■ **Connection**
In what ways did pastoral societies interact with their agricultural neighbors?

The Scythians
An ancient horse-riding nomadic people during the classical era, the Scythians occupied a region in present-day Kazakhstan and southern Russia. Their pastoral way of life is apparent in this detail from an exquisite gold necklace from the fourth century B.C.E. (Private Collection/Photo Boltin Picture Library/The Bridgeman Art Library)

borders. The Mongol Empire of the thirteenth century was but the most recent and largest in a long line of such efforts, dating back to the first millennium B.C.E.

Constructing a large state among nomadic pastoralists was no easy task. Such societies generally lacked the wealth needed to buy the professional armies and bureaucracies that everywhere sustained the states and empires of agricultural civilizations. And the fierce independence of widely dispersed pastoral clans and tribes as well as their internal rivalries made any enduring political unity difficult to achieve. Nonetheless, charismatic leaders, such as Chinggis Khan, were periodically able to weld together a series of tribal alliances that for a time became powerful states. In doing so, they often employed the device of "fictive kinship," designating allies as blood relatives and treating them with a corresponding respect.

Despite their limited populations, such states had certain military advantages in confronting larger and more densely populated civilizations. They could draw upon the horseback-riding and hunting skills of virtually the entire male population and some women as well. Easily transferred to the role of warrior, these skills, which were practiced from early childhood, were an integral part of pastoral life. But what sustained nomadic states was their ability to extract wealth, through raiding, trading, or extortion, from agricultural civilizations such as China, Persia, and Byzantium. As long as that wealth flowed into pastoral states, rulers could maintain the fragile alliances among fractious clans and tribes. When it was interrupted, however, those states often fragmented.

Pastoral nomads interacted with their agricultural neighbors not only economically and militarily but also culturally as they "became acquainted with and tried on for size all the world and universal religions."[6] At one time or another, Judaism, Buddhism, several forms of Christianity, and Islam all found a home somewhere among the nomadic peoples of inner Eurasia. So did Manichaeism, a religious tradition born in third-century Persia and combining elements of Zoroastrian, Christian, and Buddhist practice. Usually conversion was a top-down process as nomadic elites and rulers adopted a foreign religion for political purposes, sometimes changing religious allegiance as circumstances altered. Nomadic peoples, in short, did not inhabit a world totally apart from their agricultural and civilized neighbors.

Surely the most fundamental contribution of pastoralists to the larger human story was their mastery of environments unsuitable for agriculture. Through the creative use of their animals, they brought a version of the food-producing revolution and a substantial human presence to the arid grasslands and desert fringes of Afro-Eurasia. As the pastoral peoples of the Inner Asian steppes learned the art of horseback riding, by roughly 1000 B.C.E., their societies changed dramatically. Now they could accumulate and tend larger herds of horses, sheep, and goats and move more rapidly over a much wider territory. New technologies, invented or adapted by pastoral societies, added to the mastery of their environment and spread widely across the Eurasian steppes, creating something of a common culture in this vast region. These innovations included complex horse harnesses, saddles with iron stirrups,

The Xiongnu Confederacy

■ **Significance**
In what ways did the Xiongnu, Arabs, and Turks make an impact on world history?

a small compound bow that could be fired from horseback, various forms of armor, and new kinds of swords. Agricultural peoples were amazed at the centrality of the horse in pastoral life. As one observer noted, "From their horses, by day and night every one of that [nomadic] nation buys and sells, eats and drinks, and bowed over the narrow neck of the animal relaxes in a sleep so deep as to be accompanied by many dreams."[7]

The Xiongnu: An Early Nomadic Empire

What enabled pastoral peoples to make their most visible entry onto the stage of world history was the military potential of horseback riding, and of camel riding somewhat later. Their mastery of mounted warfare made possible a long but intermittent series of nomadic empires across the steppes of inner Eurasia and elsewhere. For 2,000 years, those states played a major role in Eurasian history and represented a standing challenge to and influence upon the agrarian civilizations on their borders.

During the classical era, one such large-scale nomadic empire was associated with the people known as the Xiongnu, who lived in the Mongolian steppes north of China (see Chapter 9). Provoked by Chinese penetration of their territory, the Xiongnu in the third and second centuries B.C.E. created a huge military confederacy that stretched from Manchuria deep into Central Asia. Under the charismatic leadership of Modun (reigned 210–174 B.C.E.), the Xiongnu Empire effected a revolution in nomadic life. Earlier fragmented and egalitarian societies were now transformed into a far more centralized and hierarchical political system in which power was concentrated in a divinely sanctioned ruler and differences between "junior" and "senior" clans became more prominent. "All the people who draw the bow have now become one family," declared Modun. Tribute, exacted from other nomadic peoples and from China itself, sustained the Xiongnu Empire and forced the Han dynasty emperor Wen to acknowledge, unhappily, the equality of people he regarded as barbarians. "Our two great nations," he declared, no doubt reluctantly, "the Han and the Xiongnu, stand side by side."[8]

Although it subsequently disintegrated under sustained Chinese counterattacks, the Xiongnu Empire created a model that later Turkic and Mongol empires emulated. Even without a powerful state, various nomadic or seminomadic peoples played a role in the collapse of already weakened classical Chinese and Roman empires and the subsequent rebuilding of those civilizations (see Chapter 4).

The Arabs and the Turks

It was during the era of third-wave civilizations (500–1500 C.E.) that nomadic peoples made their most significant mark on the larger canvas of world history. Arabs,

Berbers, Turks, and Mongols—all of them of nomadic origin—created the largest and most influential empires of that postclassical millennium. The most expansive religious tradition of the era, Islam, derived from a largely nomadic people, the Arabs, and was carried to new regions by another nomadic people, the Turks. In that millennium, most of the great civilizations of outer Eurasia—Byzantium, Persia, India, and China—had come under the control of previously nomadic people, at least for a time. But as pastoral nomads entered and shaped the arena of world history, they too were transformed by the experience.

The first and most dramatic of these nomadic incursions came from Arabs. In the Arabian Peninsula, the development of a reliable camel saddle somewhere between 500 and 100 B.C.E. enabled nomadic Bedouin (desert-dwelling) Arabs to fight effectively from atop their enormous beasts. With this new military advantage, they came to control the rich trade routes in incense running through Arabia. Even more important, these camel nomads served as the shock troops of Islamic expansion, providing many of the new religion's earliest followers and much of the military force that carved out the Arab Empire. Although intellectual and political leadership came from urban merchants and settled farming communities, the Arab Empire was in some respects a nomadic creation that subsequently became the foundation of a new and distinctive civilization.

Even as the pastoral Arabs encroached on the world of Eurasian civilizations from the south, Turkic-speaking nomads were making inroads from the north. Never a single people, various Turkic-speaking clans and tribes migrated from their homeland in Mongolia and southern Siberia generally westward and entered the historical record as creators of a series of nomadic empires between 552 and 965 C.E., most of them lasting little more than a century. Like the Xiongnu Empire, they were fragile alliances of various tribes headed by a supreme ruler known as a *kaghan*, who was supported by a faithful corps of soldiers called "wolves." From their base in the steppes, these Turkic states confronted the great civilizations to their south—China, Persia, Byzantium—alternately raiding them, allying with them against common enemies, trading with them, and extorting tribute payments from them. Turkic language and culture spread widely over much of Inner Asia, and elements of that culture entered the agrarian civilizations. In the courts of northern China, for example, yogurt thinned with water, a drink derived from the Turks, replaced for a time the traditional beverage of tea, and at least one Chinese poet wrote joyfully about the delights of snowy evenings in a felt tent.[9]

A major turning point in the history of the Turks occurred with their conversion to Islam between the tenth and fourteenth centuries. This extended process represented a major expansion of the faith and launched the Turks into a new role as the third major carrier of Islam, following the Arabs and the Persians. It also brought the Turks into an increasingly important position within the heartland of an established Islamic civilization as they migrated southward into the Middle East. There they served first as slave soldiers within the Abbasid caliphate, and then, as the caliphate declined, they increasingly took political and military power themselves.

In the Seljuk Turkic Empire of the eleventh and twelfth centuries, centered in Persia and present-day Iraq, Turkic rulers began to claim the Muslim title of *sultan* rather than kaghan. Although the Abbasid caliph remained the formal ruler, real power was exercised by Turkic sultans.

Not only did Turkic peoples become Muslims themselves, but they carried Islam to new areas as well. Their invasions of northern India solidly planted Islam in that ancient civilization. In Anatolia, formerly ruled by Christian Byzantium, they brought both Islam and a massive infusion of Turkic culture, language, and people, even as they created the Ottoman Empire, which by 1500 became one of the great powers of Eurasia. In both places, Turkic dynasties governed and would continue to do so well into the modern era. Thus Turkic people, many of them at least, had transformed themselves from pastoral nomads to sedentary farmers, from creators of steppe empires to rulers of agrarian civilizations, and from polytheistic worshippers of their ancestors and various gods to followers and carriers of a monotheistic Islam.

The Masai of East Africa

■ **Comparison**

Did the history and society of the East African Masai people parallel that of Asian nomads?

In East African history as well, the relationship between nomads and settled farmers worked itself out over many centuries, although solid historical information in this case largely dates to after 1500. Unlike Inner Asia, no large states or chiefdoms developed among either agricultural or pastoral peoples in present-day Kenya and Tanzania. Instead the nomadic cattle-keeping Masai and their settled agricultural neighbors found another way to bind their people together beyond the ties of village and clan. Adolescent boys from a variety of villages or lineages were initiated together in a ritual that often included circumcision, an experience that produced a profound bond among them. This ceremony created an "age-set," which then moved through a series of "age-grades" or ranks, from warrior through elder, during their lives. Such a system provided an alternative to the state as a means of mobilizing young men for military purposes, for integrating outsiders into the community, and for establishing a larger social identity.

The Masai of East Africa

Sharp distinctions and strong views separated people practicing different economies. From the viewpoint of the Masai, who composed songs and poems in honor of their cattle, pastoralism was a vastly superior way of life, whereas farming was seen as demeaning and as destroying land that could be much better used for grazing. Farmers were fit only to provide beer, wives, and occasionally food for herding peoples. Conversely, agricultural peoples often saw the Masai as arrogant, aggressive, and lazy, stubbornly unwilling to engage in the hard work of cultivation or even to eat the products of the land.[10]

But ways of life were hardly static in East Africa. Earlier in their history, the proudly pastoral Masai had in fact raised sorghum and millet, fully abandoning cultivation only in the eighteenth and nineteenth centuries as they migrated southward from the upper Nile Valley into the more arid regions of central Kenya. Later several Masai groups returned to agriculture after bitter conflicts in the mid-nineteenth century drove them to the periphery of Masai territory. Furthermore, the Masai, while trumpeting the superiority of their culture, were altogether willing to admit others into its charmed circle, much like the Chinese in relation to surrounding barbarians. Outsiders could become Masai, and many did so by obtaining a herd of cattle, by joining a Masai age-set, by learning the language, or by giving a woman in marriage to a Masai man and receiving "bride-wealth" in cattle in return.

The Masai
This contemporary Masai woman from Tanzania is milking goats while carrying a child on her back, in much the same fashion as her ancestors have done for centuries. (The Africa Image Library, photographersdirect .com. Photographer: Ariadne Van Zandbergen)

The Masai were also dependent on those practicing other ways of life. Although they despised hunters as "poor people without cattle," the Masai relied on them for animal skins, bows and arrows, shields, and, most of all, honey, which was required in their ritual ceremonies. They were even more involved with neighboring agricultural peoples. Despite a great deal of mutual raiding and warfare, that relationship also involved substantial economic exchange as women conducted frequent trade to supplement the diet of milk, meat, and blood derived from their cattle. Elaborate peace negotiations after periods of conflict, frequent intermarriage, and occasional military alliances against a common enemy also brought the Masai into close contact with nearby farmers, such as the Gikuyu. And in times of desperation owing to drought or disease, the Masai might find refuge with hunters or farmers with whom they had long-established relationships.[11]

The prestige and the military success of the Masai encouraged those agricultural societies to borrow elements of Masai culture, such as hairstyles, shield decorations, terms referring to cattle, and the name for their High God. Farming societies also adopted elements of Masai military organization, the long Masai spear, and the practice of drinking cow's milk before battle.[12] Peaceful interaction and mutual dependence as well as conflict and hostility characterized the relationship of nomadic herders and settled farmers in East Africa, much as it did in Eurasia.

Breakout: The Mongol Empire

Of all the pastoral peoples who took a turn on the stage of world history, the Mongols made the most stunning entry. Their thirteenth-century breakout from Mongolia gave rise to the largest land-based empire in all of human history, stretching

Map 12.1 The Mongol Empire
Encompassing much of Eurasia, the Mongol Empire was divided into four khanates after the death of Chinggis Khan.

from the Pacific coast of Asia to Eastern Europe (see Map 12.1). This empire joined the nomadic peoples of the inner Eurasian steppes with the settled agricultural civilizations of outer Eurasia more extensively and more intimately than ever before. It also brought the major civilizations of Eurasia—Europe, China, and the Islamic world—into far more direct contact than in earlier times. Both the enormous destructiveness of the process and the networks of exchange and communication that it spawned were the work of the Mongols, numbering only about 700,000 people. It was another of history's unlikely twists.

For all of its size and fearsome reputation, the Mongol Empire left a surprisingly modest cultural imprint on the world it had briefly governed. Unlike the Arabs, the Mongols bequeathed to the world no new religion or civilization. Whereas the Islamic community offered a common religious home for all converts—conquerors and conquered alike—the Mongols never tried to spread their own faith among subject peoples. At the level of family life, that religion centered on rituals invoking the ancestors, which were performed around the hearth. Rulers sometimes consulted religious specialists, known as *shamans*, who might predict the future, offer sacrifices, and communicate with the spirit world, and particularly with Tengri, the supreme sky god of the Mongols. There was little in this tradition to attract outsiders, and in any event the Mongols proved uninterested in religious imperialism.

The Mongols offered the majority of those they conquered little more than the status of defeated, subordinate, and exploited people, although people with skills were put to work in ways useful to Mongol authorities. Unlike the Turks, whose languages and culture flourish today in many places far from the Turkic homeland, Mongol culture remains confined largely to Mongolia. Furthermore, the Mongol Empire, following in the tradition of Xiongnu and Turkic state building, proved to be "the last, spectacular bloom of pastoral power in Inner Eurasia."[13] Some Mongols themselves became absorbed into the settled societies they conquered. After the decline and disintegration of the Mongol Empire, the tide turned against the pastoralists of inner Eurasia, who were increasingly swallowed up in the expanding Russian or Chinese empires. Nonetheless, while it lasted and for a few centuries thereafter, the Mongol Empire exercised an enormous impact throughout the entire Eurasian world.

Snapshot   Key Moments in Mongol History

Birth of Temujin	1162
Temujin gains title of Chinggis Khan ("universal ruler")	1206
Reign of Chinggis Khan	1206–1227
Beginning of Mongol conquests	1209
Conquest of China	1209–1279
Initial assault on Persia	1219–1221
Conquest of Russia	1237–1240
Attacks in Eastern Europe; then withdrawal	1241–1242
Mongol seizure of Baghdad	1258
Khubilai Khan as ruler of China	1271–1294
Failed Mongol attacks on Japan	1274, 1281
Conversion of Il-khan Ghazan to Islam	1295
High point of plague in Europe	1348–1350
Ming dynasty established; end of Mongol rule in China	1368
End of "Mongol yoke" in Russia; Moscow emerges as center of Russian state	1480

From Temujin to Chinggis Khan: The Rise of the Mongol Empire

■ **Description**
Identify the major steps in the rise of the Mongol Empire.

World historians are prone to focus attention on large-scale and long-term processes of change in explaining "what happened in history," but in understanding the rise of the Mongol Empire, most scholars have found themselves forced to look closely at the role of a single individual—Temujin (1162–1227), later known as Chinggis Khan ("universal ruler"). The twelfth-century world into which he was born found the Mongols an unstable and fractious collection of tribes and clans, much reduced from a somewhat earlier and more powerful position in the shifting nomadic alliances in what is now Mongolia. "Everyone was feuding," declared a leading Mongol shaman. "Rather than sleep, they robbed each other of their possessions. . . . There was no respite, only battle. There was no affection, only mutual slaughter."[14]

The early life of Temujin showed few signs of a prominent future. The boy's father had been a minor chieftain of a noble clan, but he was murdered by tribal rivals before Temujin turned ten, and the family was soon deserted by other members of the clan. As social outcasts, Temujin's small family, headed by his resourceful mother, was forced to live by hunting, fishing, and gathering wild foods. Without livestock, they had fallen to the lowest level of nomadic life. In these desperate circumstances, Temujin's remarkable character came into play. His personal magnetism and courage and his inclination to rely on trusted friends rather than ties of kinship allowed him to build up a small following and to ally with a more powerful tribal leader. This alliance received a boost from Chinese patrons, who were always eager to keep the nomads divided. Military victory over a rival tribe resulted in Temujin's recognition as a chief in his own right with a growing band of followers.

Temujin's rise to power amid the complex tribal politics of Mongolia was never a sure thing. What contributed to his growing power were shifting alliances and betrayals, a mounting string of military victories, the indecisiveness of his enemies, a reputation as a leader generous to friends and ruthless to enemies, and the incorporation of warriors from defeated tribes into his own forces. In 1206, a Mongol tribal assembly recognized Temujin as Chinggis Khan, supreme leader of a now unified Great Mongol Nation. It was a remarkable achievement, but one little noticed beyond the highland steppes of Mongolia. That would soon change.

The unification of the Mongol tribes raised an obvious question: What was Chinggis Khan to do with the powerful army he had assembled? Without a common task, the new and fragile unity of the Mongols would surely dissolve into quarrels and chaos; and without external resources to reward his followers, Chinggis Khan would be hard pressed to maintain his supreme position. Both considerations pointed in a single direction—expansion, particularly toward China, long a source of great wealth for nomadic peoples.[15]

In 1209, the first major attack on the settled agricultural societies south of Mongolia set in motion half a century of a Mongol world war, a series of military campaigns, massive killing, and empire building without precedent in world history. In the process, Chinggis Khan, followed by his sons and grandsons (Ogodei, Mongke, and Khubilai), constructed an empire that contained China, Korea, Central Asia, Russia, much of the Islamic Middle East, and parts of Eastern Europe (see Map 12.1). "In a flash," wrote a recent scholar, "the Mongol warriors would defeat every army, capture every fort, and bring down the walls of every city they encountered. Christians, Muslims, Buddhists, and Hindus would soon kneel before the dusty boots of illiterate young Mongol horsemen."[16]

Various setbacks—the Mongols' withdrawal from Eastern Europe (1242), their defeat in Egypt (1260), the failure of their invasion of Japan owing to violent typhoons (1274, 1281), and the difficulty of penetrating the tropical jungles of Southeast Asia—marked the outer limits of the Mongol Empire. But what an empire it was! How could a Mongol confederation, with a total population of less than 1 million people and few resources beyond their livestock, assemble an imperial structure of such staggering transcontinental dimensions?

Explaining the Mongol Moment

Like the Roman Empire but far more rapidly, the Mongol Empire grew of its own momentum without any grand scheme or blueprint for world conquest. Each fresh victory brought new resources for making war and new threats or insecurities that seemed to require further expansion. As the empire took shape and certainly by the end of his life, Chinggis Khan came to see his career in terms of a universal mission. "I have accomplished a great work," he declared, "uniting the whole world in one empire."[17] Thus the Mongol Empire acquired an ideology in the course of its construction.

■ **Explanation**
What accounts for the political and military success of the Mongols?

What made this "great work" possible? The odds seemed overwhelming, for China alone, after all, outnumbered the Mongols 100 to 1 and possessed incomparably greater resources. Nor did the Mongols enjoy any technological superiority over their many adversaries. Clearly the key to the Mongols' success lay in their army. According to one scholar, "Mongol armies were simply better led, organized, and disciplined than those of their opponents."[18] In an effort to diminish a divisive tribalism, Chinggis Khan reorganized the entire social structure of the Mongols into military units of 10, 100, 1,000, and 10,000 warriors, an arrangement that allowed for effective command and control. Conquered tribes especially were broken up and their members scattered among these new units, which enrolled virtually all nomadic men and supplied the cavalry forces of Mongol armies. A highly prestigious imperial guard, also recruited across tribal lines, marked the further decline of the old tribalism as a social revolution, imposed from above by Chinggis Khan, reshaped Mongol society.

An impressive discipline and loyalty to their leaders characterized Mongol military forces, and discpline was reinforced by the provision that should one or two members of a unit desert in battle, all were subject to the death penalty. More positively, loyalty was cemented by the leaders' willingness to share the hardships of their men. "I eat the same food and am dressed in the same rags as my humble herdsmen," wrote Chinggis Khan. "I am always in the forefront, and in battle I am never at the rear."[19] Such discipline and loyalty made possible the elaborate tactics of encirclement, retreat, and deception that proved decisive in many a battle. Furthermore, the enormous flow of wealth from conquered civilizations benefited all Mongols, though not equally. Even ordinary Mongols could now dress in linens and silks rather than hides and felt, could own slaves derived from the many prisoners of war, and had far greater opportunities to improve their social position in a constantly expanding empire.

To compensate for their own small population, the Mongols incorporated huge numbers of conquered peoples into their military forces. "People who lived in felt tents"—mostly Mongol and Turkic nomads—were conscripted en masse into the cavalry units of the Mongol army, while settled agricultural peoples supplied the infantry and artillery forces. As the Mongols penetrated major civilizations, with their walled cities and elaborate fortifications, they quickly acquired Chinese techniques and technology of siege warfare. Some 1,000 Chinese artillery crews, for example, took part in the Mongol invasion of distant Persia. Beyond military recruitment, Mongols demanded that their conquered people serve as laborers, building roads and bridges and ferrying supplies over long distances. Artisans, craftsmen, and skilled people generally were carefully identified, spared from massacre, and often sent to distant regions of the empire where their services were required.

A Mongol Warrior
Horseback-riding skills, honed in herding animals and adapted to military purposes, were central to Mongol conquests, as illustrated in this Ming-dynasty Chinese painting of a mounted Mongol archer. (Victoria and Albert Museum, London/V & A Picture Library)

A French goldsmith, captured by Mongol forces in Hungary, wound up as a slave in the Mongol capital of Karakorum, where he constructed an elaborate silver fountain that dispensed wine and other intoxicating drinks.

A further element in the military effectiveness of Mongol forces lay in a growing reputation for a ruthless brutality and utter destructiveness. Chinggis Khan's policy was clear: "whoever submits shall be spared, but those who resist, they shall be destroyed with their wives, children and dependents . . . so that the others who hear and see should fear and not act the same."[20] The Central Asian kingdom of Khwarizm, whose ruler had greatly offended Chinggis Khan by murdering and mutilating Mongol envoys and merchants, was among the first, but by no means the last, to feel the full effects of Mongol terror. City after city was utterly destroyed, and their soldiers were passed out in lots to Mongol troops for execution, while women and skilled craftsmen were enslaved. Unskilled civilians served as human shields for attacks on the next city or were used as human fill in the moats surrounding those cities.

One scholar explained such policies in this way: "Extremely conscious of their small numbers and fearful of rebellion, Chinggis often chose to annihilate a region's entire population, if it appeared too troublesome to govern."[21] These policies also served as a form of psychological warfare, a practical inducement to surrender for those who knew of the Mongol terror. Historians continue to debate the extent and uniqueness of Mongol brutality, but their reputation for unwavering harshness proved a military asset.

Underlying the purely military dimensions of the Mongols' success was an impressive ability to mobilize both the human and material resources of their growing empire. Elaborate census taking allowed Mongol leaders to know what was available to them and made possible the systematic taxation of conquered people. An effective system of relay stations, about a day's ride apart, provided rapid communication across the empire and fostered trade as well. Marco Polo, the Italian trader who traveled through Mongol domains in the thirteenth century, claimed that the Mongols maintained some 10,000 such stations, together with 200,000 horses available to authorized users. The beginnings of a centralized bureaucracy with various specialized offices took shape in the new capital of Karakorum. There scribes translated official decrees into the various languages of the empire, such as Persian, Uighur, Chinese, and Tibetan.

Other policies appealed to various groups among the conquered peoples of the empire. Interested in fostering commerce, Mongol rulers often offered merchants 10 percent or more above their asking price and allowed them the free use of the relay stations for transporting their goods. In administering the conquered regions, Mongols held the highest decision-making posts, but Chinese and Muslim officials held many advisory and lower-level positions in China and Persia respectively. In religious matters, the Mongols welcomed and supported many religious traditions—Buddhist, Christian, Muslim, Daoist—as long as they did not become the focus of political opposition. This policy of religious toleration allowed Muslims to seek converts among Mongol troops and afforded Christians much greater freedom than they had enjoyed under Muslim rule.[22] Toward the end of his life and apparently feeling his approaching death, Chinggis Khan himself summoned a famous Daoist master from China and begged him to "communicate to me the means of preserving life." One of his successors, Mongke, arranged a debate among representatives of several religious faiths, after which he concluded: "Just as God gave different fingers to the hand, so has He given different ways to men."[23] Such economic, administrative, and religious policies provided some benefits and a place within the empire—albeit subordinate—for many of its conquered peoples.

Encountering the Mongols: Comparing Three Cases

The Mongol moment in world history represented an enormous cultural encounter between nomadic pastoralists and the settled civilizations of Eurasia. Differences among those civilizations—Confucian China, Muslim Persia, Christian Russia—ensured considerable diversity as this encounter unfolded across a vast realm. The process of conquest, the length and nature of Mongol rule, the impact on local people, and the extent of Mongol assimilation into the cultures of the conquered—all this and more varied considerably across the Eurasian domains of the empire. The experiences of China, Persia, and Russia provide brief glimpses into several expressions of this massive clash of cultures.

China and the Mongols

■ **Change**

How did Mongol rule change China? In what ways were the Mongols changed by China?

Long the primary target for nomadic steppe-dwellers in search of agrarian wealth, China proved the most difficult and extended of the Mongols' many conquests, lasting some seventy years, from 1209 to 1279. The invasion began in northern China, which had been ruled for several centuries by various dynasties of nomadic origin, and was characterized by destruction and plunder on a massive scale. Southern China, under the control of the native Song dynasty, was a different story, for there the Mongols were far less violent and more concerned to accommodate the local population. Landowners, for example, were guaranteed their estates in exchange for their support or at least their neutrality. By whatever methods, the outcome was the unification of a divided China, a treasured ideal among educated Chinese. This achievement persuaded many of them that the Mongols had indeed been granted the Mandate of Heaven and, despite their foreign origins, were legitimate rulers.

Having acquired China, what were the Mongols to do with it? One possibility, apparently considered by the Great Khan Ogodei in the 1230s, was to exterminate everyone in northern China and turn the country into pastureland for Mongol herds. That suggestion, fortunately, was rejected in favor of extracting as much wealth as possible from the country's advanced civilization. Doing so meant some accommodation to Chinese culture and ways of governing, for the Mongols had no experience with the operation of a complex agrarian society.

That accommodation took many forms. The Mongols made use of Chinese administrative practices, techniques of taxation, and their postal system. They gave themselves a Chinese dynastic title, the Yuan, meaning "great beginnings." They transferred their capital from Karakorum in Mongolia to what is now Beijing, building a wholly new capital city there known as Khanbalik, the "city of the khan." Thus the Mongols were now rooting themselves solidly on the soil of the world's most sophisticated civilization, well removed from their homeland on the steppes. Khubilai Khan, the grandson of Chinggis Khan and China's Mongol ruler from

Marco Polo and Khubilai Khan
In ruling China, the Mongols employed in high positions a number of Muslims and a few Europeans, such as Marco Polo, shown here kneeling before Khubilai Khan in a painting from the fifteenth century. (Ms 2810 f.5. Nicolo and Marco Polo before the Great Khan [vellum], Boucicaut Master, [fl. 1390–1430, and workshop]/Bibliothèque nationale de France, Paris, France/The Bridgeman Art Library)

1271 to 1294, ordered a set of Chinese-style ancestral tablets to honor his ancestors and posthumously awarded them Chinese names. Many of his policies evoked the values of a benevolent Chinese emperor as he improved roads, built canals, lowered some taxes, patronized scholars and artists, limited the death penalty and torture, supported peasant agriculture, and prohibited Mongols from grazing their animals on peasants' farmland. Mongol khans also made use of traditional Confucian rituals, supported the building of some Daoist temples, and were particularly attracted to a Tibetan form of Buddhism, which returned the favor with strong political support for the invaders.

Despite these accommodations, Mongol rule was still harsh, exploitative, and foreign. Marco Polo, who lived in China during the time of Khubilai Khan, observed the hostility between the Mongols and their Chinese subjects.

> The Cathayans [Chinese] detest the Grand Kaan's rule because he set over them governors who were Tartars [Mongols], or still more frequently Saracens [Muslims], and these they would not endure, for they were treated by them just like slaves.[24]

The Mongols did not become Chinese, nor did they accommodate every aspect of Chinese culture. Deep inside the new capital they established the so-called Forbidden City, where the royal family and court could continue to experience something of steppe life. Animals roamed freely in large open areas, planted with steppe grass. Many of the Mongol elite much preferred to live, eat, sleep, and give birth in the traditional tents that sprouted everywhere. In administering the country, the Mongols largely ignored the traditional Chinese examination system and relied heavily on foreigners, particularly Muslims from Central Asia and the Middle East, to serve as officials, as Marco Polo observed, while keeping the top decision-making posts for themselves. Few Mongols learned Chinese, and Mongol law discriminated against the Chinese, reserving for them the most severe punishments. In social life, the Mongols forbade intermarriage and prohibited Chinese scholars from learning the Mongol script. Mongol women never adopted foot binding and scandalized the Chinese by mixing freely with men at official gatherings and riding to the hunt with their husbands. Furthermore, the Mongols honored and supported merchants and artisans far more than Confucian bureaucrats had been inclined to do.

However one assesses Mongol rule in China, it was brief, lasting little more than a century. By the mid-fourteenth century, intense factionalism among the Mongols, rapidly rising prices, furious epidemics of the plague, and growing peasant rebellions combined to force the Mongols out of China. By 1368, rebel forces had triumphed, and thousands of Mongols returned to their homeland in the steppes. For several centuries, they remained a periodic threat to China, but during the Ming dynasty that followed, the memory of their often brutal and alien rule stimulated a renewed commitment to Confucian values and practices and an effort to wipe out all traces of the Mongols' impact.

Persia and the Mongols

■ Comparison

How was Mongol rule in Persia different from that in China?

A second great civilization conquered by the Mongols was that of an Islamic Persia. There the Mongol takeover was far more abrupt than the extended process of conquest in China. A first invasion (1219–1221), led by Chinggis Khan himself, was followed thirty years later by a second assault (1251–1258) under his grandson Hulegu, who became the first il-khan (subordinate khan) of Persia. More destructive than the conquest of Song dynasty China, the Mongol offensive against Persia and Iraq had no precedent in their history, although Persia had been repeatedly attacked, from the invasion of Alexander the Great to that of the Arabs. The most recent incursion had featured Turkic peoples, but they had been Muslims, recently converted, small in number, and seeking only acceptance within the Islamic world. The Mongols, however, were infidels in Muslim eyes, and their stunning victory was a profound shock to people accustomed to viewing history as the progressive expansion of Islamic rule. Furthermore, Mongol military victory brought in its train a degree of ferocity and slaughter that simply had no parallel in Persian experience. The Persian historian Juwayni described it in fearful terms:

> Every town and every village has been several times subjected to pillage and massacre and has suffered this confusion for years so that even though there be generation and increase until the Resurrection the population will not attain to a tenth part of what it was before.[25]

The sacking of Baghdad in 1258, which put an end to the Abbasid caliphate, was accompanied by the massacre of more than 200,000 people, according to Hulegu himself.

Beyond this human catastrophe lay the damage to Persian and Iraqi agriculture and their peasant farmers. Heavy taxes, sometimes collected twenty or thirty times a year and often under torture or whipping, pushed large numbers of peasants off their land. Furthermore, the in-migration of nomadic Mongols, together with their immense herds of sheep and goats, turned much agricultural land into pasture and sometimes into desert. In both cases, a fragile system of underground water channels that provided irrigation to the fields was neglected, and much good agricultural land was reduced to waste. Some sectors of the Persian economy gained, however. Wine production increased because the Mongols were fond of alcohol, and the Persian silk industry benefited from close contact with a Mongol-ruled China. In general, though, even more so than in China, Mongol rule in Persia represented "disaster on a grand and unparalleled scale."[26]

Nonetheless, the Mongols in Persia were themselves transformed far more than their counterparts in China. They made extensive use of the sophisticated Persian bureaucracy, leaving the greater part of government operations in Persian hands. During the reign of Ghazan (1295–1304), they made some efforts to repair the damage caused by earlier policies of ruthless exploitation, by rebuilding damaged cities and repairing neglected irrigation works. Most important, the Mongols who conquered Persia became Muslims, following the lead of Ghazan, who converted to Islam in 1295. No such widespread conversion to the culture of the conquered occurred in China or in Christian Russia. Members of the court and Mongol elites learned at least some Persian, unlike most of their counterparts in China. A number of Mongols also turned to farming, abandoning their nomadic ways, while some married local people. When the Mongol dynasty of Hulegu's descendants collapsed in the 1330s for lack of a suitable heir, the Mongols were not driven out of Persia as they had been from China. Rather they and their Turkic allies simply disappeared, through assimilation into Persian society. From a Persian point of view, the barbarians had been civilized.

Russia and the Mongols

When the Mongol military machine rolled over Russia between 1237 and 1240, it encountered a relatively new third-wave civilization, located on the far eastern fringe of Christendom (see Chapter 10). Whatever political unity this new civilization of Kievan Rus had earlier enjoyed was now gone, and various independent princes proved unable to unite even in the face of the Mongol onslaught. Although they had interacted extensively with nomadic people of the steppes north of the Black Sea, nothing had prepared them for the Mongols.

The devastation wrought by the Mongol assault matched or exceeded anything experienced by the Persians or the Chinese. City after city fell to Mongol forces,

■ **Comparison**

How was the Russian experience of Mongol domination different from that of Persia or China?

Mongol Russia
This sixteenth-century painting depicts the Mongol burning of the Russian city of Ryazan in 1237. Similar destruction awaited many Russian towns that resisted the invaders. (Sovfoto/Eastfoto)

which were now armed with the catapults and battering rams adopted from Chinese or Muslim sources. The slaughter that sometimes followed was described by Russian chroniclers, although twentieth-century historians often regard such accounts as exaggerated.

> They likewise killed the Prince and Princess, and men, women, and children, monks, nuns, and priests, some by fire, some by the sword, and violated nuns, priests' wives, good women and girls in the presence of their mothers and sisters.[27]

From the survivors and the cities that surrendered early, laborers and skilled craftsmen were deported to other Mongol lands or sold into slavery. A number of Russian crafts were so depleted of their workers that they did not recover for a century or more.

If the ferocity of initial conquest bore similarities to the experiences of Persia and China, Russia's incorporation into the Mongol Empire was very different. To the Mongols, it was the Kipchak Khanate, named after the Kipchak Turkic-speaking peoples north of the Caspian and Black seas, among whom the Mongols had settled. To the Russians, it was the "Khanate of the Golden Horde." By whatever name, the Mongols had conquered Russia, but they did not occupy it as they had China and Persia. Because there were no garrisoned cities, permanently stationed administrators, or Mongol settlement, the Russian experience of Mongol rule was quite different than elsewhere. From the Mongol point of view, Russia had little to offer. Its economy was not nearly as developed as that of more established civilizations; nor was it located on major international trade routes. It was simply not worth the expense of occupying. Furthermore, the availability of extensive steppe lands for pasturing their flocks north of the Black and Caspian seas meant that the Mongols could maintain their preferred nomadic way of life, while remaining in easy reach of Russian cities when the need arose to send further military expeditions. They could dominate and exploit Russia from the steppes.

And exploit they certainly did. Russian princes received appointment from the khan and were required to send substantial tribute to the Mongol capital at Sarai, located on the lower Volga River. A variety of additional taxes created a heavy burden, especially on the peasantry, while continuing border raids sent tens of thousands of Russians into slavery. The Mongol impact was highly uneven, however. Some Russian princes benefited considerably because they were able to manipulate their role as tribute collectors to grow wealthy. The Russian Orthodox Church likewise flourished under the Mongol policy of religious toleration, for it received exemption from many taxes. Nobles who participated in Mongol raids earned a share of the loot. Some cities, such as Kiev, resisted the Mongols and were devastated, while others collaborated and were left undamaged. Moscow in particular emerged as the primary collector of tribute for the Mongols, and its princes parlayed this position into a leading role as the nucleus of a renewed Russian state when Mongol domination receded in the fifteenth century.

The absence of direct Mongol rule had implications for the Mongols themselves, for they were far less influenced by or assimilated within Russian cultures than their counterparts in China and Persia had been. The Mongols in China had turned themselves into a Chinese dynasty, with the khan as a Chinese emperor. Some learned calligraphy, and a few came to appreciate Chinese poetry. In Persia, the Mongols had converted to Islam, with some becoming farmers. Not so in Russia. There "the Mongols of the Golden Horde were still spending their days in the saddle and their nights in tents."[28] They could dominate Russia from the adjacent steppes without in any way adopting Russian culture. Even though they remained culturally separate from Russia, eventually the Mongols assimilated to the culture and the Islamic faith of the Kipchak people of the steppes, and in the process they lost their distinct identity and became Kipchaks.

Despite this domination from a distance, "the impact of the Mongols on Russia was, if anything, greater than on China and Iran [Persia]," according to a leading scholar.[29] Russian princes, who were more or less left alone if they paid the required tribute and taxes, found it useful to adopt the Mongols' weapons, diplomatic rituals, court practices, taxation system, and military draft. Mongol policies facilitated, although not intentionally, the rise of Moscow as the core of a new Russian state, and that state made good use of the famous Mongol mounted courier service, which Marco Polo had praised so highly. Mongol policies also strengthened the hold of the Russian Orthodox Church and enabled it to penetrate the rural areas more fully than before. Some Russians, seeking to explain their country's economic backwardness and political autocracy in modern times, have held the Mongols responsible for both conditions, though most historians consider such views vastly exaggerated.

Divisions among the Mongols and the growing strength of the Russian state, centered now on the city of Moscow, enabled the Russians to break the Mongols' hold by the end of the fifteenth century. With the earlier demise of Mongol rule in China and Persia, and now in Russia, the Mongols had retreated from their brief but spectacular incursion into the civilizations of outer Eurasia. Nonetheless, they continued to periodically threaten these civilizations for several centuries, until their homelands were absorbed into the expanding Russian and Chinese empires. But the Mongol moment in world history was over.

The Mongol Empire as a Eurasian Network

During the postclassical millennium, Chinese culture and Buddhism provided a measure of integration among the peoples of East Asia; Christianity did the same for Europe, while the realm of Islam connected most of the lands in between. But it was the Mongol Empire, during the thirteenth and fourteenth centuries, that brought all of these regions into a single interacting network. It was a unique moment in world history and an important step toward the global integration of the modern era.

Toward a World Economy

■ **Connection**

In what ways did the Mongol Empire contribute to the globalization of the Eurasian world?

The Mongols themselves produced little of value for distant markets, nor were they active traders. Nonetheless, they consistently promoted international commerce, largely so that they could tax it and thus extract wealth from more developed civilizations. The Great Khan Ogodei, for example, often paid well over the asking price in order to attract merchants to his capital of Karakorum. The Mongols also provided financial backing for caravans, introduced standardized weights and measures, and gave tax breaks to merchants.

In providing a relatively secure environment for merchants making the long and arduous journey across Central Asia between Europe and China, the Mongol Empire brought the two ends of the Eurasian world into closer contact than ever before and launched a new phase in the history of the Silk Roads. Marco Polo was only the most famous of many European merchants, mostly Italians, who made their way to China through the Mongol Empire. So many traders attempted the journey that guidebooks were published with much useful advice about the trip. Merchants returned with tales of rich lands and prosperous commercial opportunities, but what they described were long-established trading networks of which Europeans had been largely ignorant.

The Mongol trading circuit was a central element in an even larger commercial network that linked much of the Afro-Eurasian world in the thirteenth century (see Map 12.2). Mongol-ruled China was the fulcrum of this vast system, connecting the overland route through the Mongol Empire with the oceanic routes through the South China Sea and Indian Ocean. Here, some historians have argued, lay the beginnings of those international economic relationships that have played such a major role in the making of the modern world.

Diplomacy on a Eurasian Scale

Not only did the Mongol Empire facilitate long-distance commerce, but it also prompted diplomatic relationships from one end of Eurasia to the other. As their invasion of Russia spilled over into Eastern Europe, Mongol armies destroyed Polish, German, and Hungarian forces in 1241–1242 and seemed poised to march

Map 12.2   Trade and Disease in the Fourteenth Century
The Mongol Empire played a major role in the commercial integration of the Eurasian world as well as in the spread of the plague across this vast area.

on Western Europe. But the death of the Great Khan Ogodei required Mongol leaders to return to Mongolia, and Western Europe lacked adequate pasture for Mongol herds. Thus Europe was spared the trauma of conquest, but fearing the possible return of the Mongols, both the pope and European rulers dispatched delegations to the Mongol capital, mostly led by Franciscan friars. They hoped to learn something about Mongol intentions, to secure Mongol aid in the Christian crusade against Islam, and, if possible, to convert Mongols to Christianity.

These efforts were largely in vain, for no alliance or widespread conversion occurred. In fact, one of these missions came back with a letter for the pope from the Great Khan Guyuk, demanding that Europeans submit to him. "But if you should not believe our letters and the command of God nor hearken to our counsel," he warned, "then we shall know for certain that you wish to have war. After that we do not know what will happen."[30] Perhaps the most important outcome of these diplomatic probings was the useful information about lands to the east that European missions brought back. Those reports contributed to a dawning European awareness of a wider world.

Somewhat later, in 1287, the Il-khanate of Persia sought an alliance with European powers to take Jerusalem and crush the forces of Islam, but the Persian Mongols' conversion to Islam soon put an end to any such anti-Muslim coalition. Within the Mongol Empire itself, close relationships developed between the courts of Persia and China. They regularly exchanged ambassadors, shared intelligence information, fostered trade between their regions, and sent skilled workers back and forth. Thus political authorities all across Eurasia engaged in diplomatic relationships with one another to an unprecedented degree.

Cultural Exchange in the Mongol Realm

Accompanying these transcontinental economic and diplomatic relationships was a substantial exchange of peoples and cultures. Mongol policy forcibly transferred many thousands of skilled craftsmen and educated people from their homelands to distant parts of the empire, while the Mongols' religious tolerance and support of merchants drew missionaries and traders from afar. The Mongol capital at Karakorum was a cosmopolitan city with places of worship for Buddhists, Daoists, Muslims, and Christians. Actors and musicians from China, wrestlers from Persia, and a jester from Byzantium provided entertainment for the Mongol court. Persian and Arab doctors and administrators were sent to China, while Chinese physicians and engineers found their skills in demand in the Islamic world.

This movement of people facilitated the exchange of ideas and techniques, a process actively encouraged by Mongol authorities. A great deal of Chinese technology and artistic conventions—such as painting, printing, gunpowder weapons, compass navigation, high-temperature furnaces, and medical techniques—flowed westward. Acupuncture, for example, was poorly received in the Middle East because it required too much bodily contact for Muslim taste, but Chinese techniques for diagnosing illness by taking the pulse of patients proved quite popular, as they involved minimal body contact. Muslim astronomers brought their skills and knowledge to China because Mongol authorities wanted "second opinions on the reading of heavenly signs and portents" and assistance in constructing accurate calendars, so necessary for ritual purposes.[31] Plants and crops likewise circulated within the Mongol domain. Lemons and carrots from the Middle East found a welcome reception in China, while the Persian Il-khan Ghazan sent envoys to India, China, and elsewhere to seek "seeds of things which are unique in that land."[32]

Europeans arguably gained more than most from these exchanges, for they had long been cut off from the fruitful interchange with Asia, and in comparison to the Islamic and Chinese worlds, they were less technologically developed. Now they could reap the benefits of much new technology, new crops, and new knowledge of a wider world. And almost alone among the peoples of Eurasia, they could do so without having suffered the devastating consequences of Mongol conquest. In these circumstances, some historians have argued, lay the roots of Europe's remarkable rise to global prominence in the centuries that followed.

The Plague: A Eurasian Pandemic

Any benefits derived from participation in Mongol networks of communication and exchange must be measured alongside the Eurasian catastrophe known as the "plague" or the "pestilence" and later called the Black Death. Originating most likely in Central Asia, the bacteria responsible for the disease spread across the trade routes of the vast Mongol Empire in the early fourteenth century (see Map 12.2). Carried by rodents and transmitted by fleas to humans, the plague erupted initially in 1331 in northeastern China and by 1347 had reached Western Europe. Its introduction to Europe is often attributed to a Mongol siege in 1346 of the Genoese city of Caffa in the Crimea, in which the Mongols, using catapults, hurled corpses infected with the plague into the city. It was perhaps the first recorded instance of biological warfare.

The disease itself was associated with swelling of the lymph nodes, most often in the groin; terrible headaches; high fever; and internal bleeding just below the skin. Infected people generally died within a few days. In the densely populated civilizations of China, the Islamic world, and Europe as well as in the steppe lands of the nomads, the plague claimed enormous numbers of human victims, causing a sharp contraction in Eurasian population for a century or more. Chroniclers reported rates of death that ranged from 50 to 90 percent of the affected population, depending on the time and place. Estimates for Europe suggest that between one-third and two-thirds of the population died within a few years. This intense first wave of the plague was followed by periodic visitations over the next several centuries. The plague, however, was not universal, for India and sub-Saharan Africa were much less affected than other regions of Eurasia.

Although the plague in the fourteenth century represented a crisis all across Eurasia, our best information about its impact comes from Western

■ **Change**
Disease changes societies. How might this argument apply to the plague?

The Plague
In this English painting from the fifteenth century, a priest offers last rites to a man dying of the plague, while a smiling death figure wounds him with a spear and God looks down from above. What message does this picture convey? (British Library/HIP/Art Resource, NY)

Europe.[33] In some places, such as city governments in Italy, authorities learned practical ways of dealing with the disease by establishing quarantines, hiring doctors, and organizing burials, but the response of most people, no doubt, was couched in religious terms. So great was the initial shock of this massive mortality that chroniclers described it in apocalyptic language. "So many have died," wrote an Italian observer in 1348, "that everyone believes it is the end of the world." Viewing the plague as God's judgment on a sinful world, many took part in the flagellant movement, in which people flogged themselves, sometimes almost to death, to atone for the sins that must have caused the pestilence. Attacks on Jews, who were sometimes held responsible for spreading the disease, sent many of them fleeing to Poland, where authorities welcomed their urban and commercial skills, leading to a flourishing of Jewish culture in the several centuries that followed. Still others fled into hedonism because life was so uncertain, while many joined mystical movements aimed at escaping from the world in an intense personal relationship with God. A clergyman in England expressed the dismay many must have felt.

> For God is deaf nowadays and will not hear us
> And for our guilt, he grinds good men to dust.[34]

Beyond its immediate devastation, the plague worked longer-term changes in European society. Labor shortages following the initial outburst provoked sharp conflict between scarce workers, who sought higher wages or better conditions, and the rich, who resisted such demands. A series of peasant revolts in the fourteenth century reflected this tension, which also undermined the practice of serfdom. That labor shortage also may have fostered a greater interest in technological innovation and created, at least for a time, more employment opportunities for women. Thus a resilient European civilization survived a cataclysm that had the power to destroy it. In a strange way, that catastrophe may have actually fostered its future growth.

Whatever its impact in particular places, the plague also had larger consequences. Ironically, that human disaster, born of the Mongol network, was a primary reason for the demise of that network in the fourteenth and fifteenth centuries. Population contracted, cities declined, and the volume of trade diminished all across the Mongol world. By 1350, the Mongol Empire itself was in disarray, and within a century the Mongols had lost control of Chinese, Persian, and Russian civilizations. The Central Asian trade route, so critical to the entire Afro-Eurasian world economy, largely closed.

This disruption of the Mongol-based land routes to the east, coupled with a desire to avoid Muslim intermediaries, provided incentives for Europeans to take to the sea in their continuing efforts to reach the riches of Asia. Their naval technology gave them military advantages on the seas, much as the Mongols' skill with the bow and their mobility on horseback gave these nomads a decisive edge in land battles. As Europeans penetrated Asian waters in the sixteenth century, they took on, in some ways, the role of the Mongols in organizing and fostering world trade and in creating a network of communication and exchange over an even larger area. Like the Mongols, Europeans were people on the periphery of the major established civilizations; they too were economically less developed in comparison to Chinese and Islamic civilizations; and both were prone to forcibly plundering the wealthier civilizations they encountered.[35] Europeans, of course, brought far more of their own culture and many more of their own people to the societies they conquered, as Christianity, European languages, settler societies, and their science and technology took root within their empires. Although their imperial presence lasted far longer and operated on a much larger scale, European actions at the beginning of their global expansion bore a striking resemblance to those of their Mongol predecessors. They were, as one historian put it, "the Mongols of the seas."[36]

Reflections: Changing Images of Nomadic Peoples

Until recently, nomads generally received "bad press" in history books. Normally they entered the story only when they were threatening or destroying established civilizations. In presenting a largely negative image of pastoral peoples, historians were reflecting the long-held attitudes of literate elites in the civilizations of Eurasia. Fearing and usually despising nomadic peoples, educated observers in China, the Middle East, and Europe often described them as bloodthirsty savages or barbarians, bringing only chaos and destruction in their wake. Han Kuan, a Chinese scholar of the first century B.C.E., described the Xiongnu people as "abandoned by Heaven ... in foodless desert wastes, without proper houses, clothed in animal hides, eating their meat uncooked and drinking blood."[37] To the Christian Saint Jerome (340–420 C.E.), the nomadic Huns "filled the whole earth with slaughter and panic alike as they flitted hither and thither on their swift horses."[38] Almost a thousand years later, the famous Arab historian Ibn Khaldun described nomads in a very similar fashion: "It is their nature to plunder whatever other people possess."[39]

Because nomadic peoples generally did not have written languages, the sources available to historians came from less-than-unbiased observers in adjacent agricultural civilizations. Furthermore, in the long-running conflict across the farming/pastoral frontier, agricultural civilizations ultimately triumphed. Over the centuries, some nomadic or barbarian peoples, such as the Germanic tribes of Europe and the Arabs, created new civilizations. Others, such as the Turkic and Mongol peoples, took over existing civilizations or were encompassed within established agrarian empires. By the early twentieth century, and in most places much earlier, nomadic peoples everywhere had lost their former independence and had often shed their nomadic life as well. Since "winners" usually write history, the negative views of nomads held by agrarian civilizations normally prevailed.

Reflecting more inclusive contemporary values, historians in recent decades have sought to present a more balanced picture of nomads' role in world history, emphasizing what they created as well as what they destroyed. These historians have highlighted the achievements of nomadic peoples, such as their adaptation to inhospitable environments; their technological innovations; their development of horse-, camel-, or cattle-based cultures; their role in fostering cross-cultural exchange; and their state-building efforts.

A less critical or judgmental posture toward the Mongols may also owe something to the "total wars" and genocides of the twentieth century, in which the mass slaughter of civilians became a strategy to induce enemy surrender. During the cold war, the United States and the Soviet Union were prepared, apparently, to obliterate each other's entire population with nuclear weapons in response to an attack. In light of this recent history, Mongol massacres may appear a little less unique. Historians living in the glass houses of contemporary societies are perhaps more reluctant to cast stones at the Mongols. In understanding the Mongols, as in so much else, historians are shaped by the times and circumstances of their own lives as much as by "what really happened" in the past.

Second Thoughts

What's the Significance?

To assess your mastery of the material in this chapter, see the **Online Study Guide** at bedfordstmartins.com/strayer.

pastoralism
Xiongnu
Modun
Turks
Masai

Temujin/Chinggis Khan
the Mongol world war
Yuan dynasty China
Khubilai Khan
Hulegu

Kipchak Khanate/Golden Horde
Black Death/plague

Big Picture Questions

1. Prior to the rise of the Mongols, in what ways had pastoral peoples been significant in world history?

2. What accounts for the often negative attitudes of settled societies toward the pastoral peoples living on their borders? Why have historians often neglected pastoral peoples' role in world history?

3. In what ways did the Mongol Empire resemble other empires, and in what ways did it differ from them? Why did it last a relatively short time?

4. In what different ways did Mongol rule affect the Islamic world, Russia, China, and Europe?

5. How would you define both the immediate and the long-term significance of the Mongols in world history?

6. How would you assess the perspective of this chapter toward the Mongols? Does it strike you as negative and critical of the Mongols, as "bending over backward" to portray them in a positive light, or as a balanced presentation?

Next Steps: For Further Study

John Aberth, *The First Horseman: Disease in Human History* (2007). A global study of the history of disease, with a fine chapter on the Black Death.

Thomas Allsen, *Culture and Conquest in Mongol Eurasia* (2001). A history of cultural exchange within the Mongol realm, particularly between China and the Islamic world.

Thomas J. Barfield, *The Nomadic Alternative* (1993). An anthropological and historical survey of pastoral peoples on a global basis.

Carter Finley, *The Turks in World History* (2005). The evolution of Turkic-speaking people, from their nomadic origins to the twentieth century.

Jack Weatherford, *Genghis Khan and the Making of the Modern World* (2004). A lively, well-written, and balanced account of the world the Mongols made and the legacy they left for the future.

"The Mongols in World History," http://afe.easia.columbia.edu/mongols. A wonderful resource on the Mongols generally, with a particular focus on their impact in China.

For Web sites and documents related to this chapter, see **Make History** at bedfordstmartins.com/strayer.

CHAPTER THIRTEEN

The Worlds of the Fifteenth Century

During 2005, Chinese authorities marked the 600th anniversary of the initial launching of their country's massive maritime expeditions in 1405. Some eighty-seven years before Columbus sailed across the Atlantic with three small ships and a crew of about ninety men, the Chinese admiral Zheng He had captained a fleet of more than 300 ships and a crew numbering some 27,000 people, which brought a Chinese naval presence into the South China Sea and the Indian Ocean as far as the East African coast. Now in 2005, China was celebrating. Public ceremonies, books, magazine articles, two television documentaries, an international symposium, a stamp in honor of Zheng He—all of this and more was part of a yearlong remembrance of these remarkable voyages.

Given China's recent engagement with the larger world, Chinese authorities sought to use Zheng He as a symbol of their country's expanding, but peaceful, role on the international stage. Until recently, however, his achievement was barely noticed in China's collective memory, and for six centuries Zheng He had been largely forgotten or ignored. Columbus, on the other hand, had long been highly visible in the West, celebrated as a cultural hero and more recently harshly criticized as an imperialist, but certainly remembered. The voyages of both of these fifteenth-century mariners were pregnant with meaning for world history. Why were they remembered so differently in the countries of their origin?

THE FIFTEENTH CENTURY, DURING WHICH BOTH ZHENG HE AND COLUMBUS undertook their momentous expeditions, proved in retrospect to mark a major turning point in the human story. At the time, of course,

The Meeting of Two Worlds: This famous sixteenth-century engraving by the Flemish artist Theodore de Bry shows Columbus landing in Hispaniola (Haiti), where the Taino people bring him presents, while the Europeans claim the island for God and queen. In light of its long-range consequences, this voyage was arguably the most important single event of the fifteenth century. (Bildarchiv Preussischer Kulturbesitz/Art Resource, NY)

Snapshot   **Major Developments around the World in the Fifteenth Century**

Region	Major Developments
Central, East, and Southeast Asia	Ming dynasty China, 1368–1644 Conquests of Timur, 1370–1406 Zheng He's maritime voyages, 1405–1433 Spread of Islam into Southeast Asia Rise of Malacca Civil war among competing warlords in Japan
South Asia/India	Timur's invasion of India, 1398 Various Muslim sultanates in northern India Rise of Hindu state of Vijayanagar in southern India Founding of Mughal Empire, 1526
Middle East	Expansion of Ottoman Empire Ottoman seizure of Constantinople, 1453 Founding of Safavid Empire in Persia, 1501 Ottoman siege of Vienna, 1529
Christendom/Europe	European Renaissance Portuguese voyages of exploration along West African coast Completion of reconquest of Spain, ending Muslim control End of the Byzantine Empire, 1453 End of Mongol rule in Russia; reign of Ivan the Great, 1462–1505
Africa	Songhay Empire in West Africa, 1464–1591 Kingdom of the Kongo in West Central Africa Expansion of Ethiopian state in East Africa Kingdom of Zimbabwe/Mwene Mutapa in southern Africa
The Americas/Western Hemisphere	Aztec Empire in Mesoamerica, 1345–1521 Inca Empire along the Andes, 1438–1533 Iroquois confederacy (New York State) "Complex" Paleolithic societies along west coast of North America
Pacific Oceania	Paleolithic persistence in Australia Chiefdoms and stratified societies on Pacific islands Yap as center of oceanic trading network with Guam and Palau

no one was aware of it. No one knew in 1405 that the huge armada under Zheng He's command would be recalled in 1433, never to sail again. And no one knew in 1492 that Columbus's minuscule fleet of three ships would utterly transform the world, bringing the people of two "old worlds" and two hemispheres permanently together, with enduring consequences for them all. The outcome of the processes set in motion by those three small ships included the Atlantic slave trade, the decimation of the native population of the Americas, the massive growth of world population, the Industrial Revolution, and the growing prominence of Europeans on the world stage. But none of these developments were even remotely foreseeable in 1492.

Thus the fifteenth century, as a hinge of major historical change, provides an occasion for a bird's-eye view of the world through a kind of global tour. This excursion around the world will serve to briefly review the human saga thus far and to establish a baseline from which the transformations of the modern era might be measured. How then might we describe the world, and the worlds, of the fifteenth century?

The Shapes of Human Communities

One way to describe the world of the fifteenth century is to identify the various types of societies that it contained. Bands of hunters and gatherers, villages of agricultural peoples, newly emerging chiefdoms or small states, nomadic/pastoral communities, established civilizations and empires—all of these social or political forms would have been apparent to a widely traveled visitor in the fifteenth century. They represented alternative ways of organizing human communities and responded to differences in the environment, in the historical development of various regions, and in the choices made by particular peoples. The balance among these distinctive kinds of societies at the end of the postclassical millennium (1500) was quite different than it had been at the beginning (500).

Paleolithic Persistence

Despite millennia of agricultural advance, substantial areas of the world still hosted gathering and hunting societies, known to scholars as Paleolithic ("old stone-age") peoples. All of Australia, much of Siberia, the arctic coastlands, and parts of Africa and the Americas fell into this category. These peoples were not simply relics of a bygone age, however. They too had changed over time, though more slowly than their agricultural counterparts, and they too interacted with their neighbors. In short, they had a history, although most history books largely ignore them after the age of agriculture arrived. Nonetheless, this most ancient way of life still had a sizable and variable presence in the world of the fifteenth century.

Consider, for example, Australia. That continent's many separate groups, some 250 of them, still practiced a gathering and hunting way of life in the fifteenth century, a pattern that continued well after Europeans arrived in the late eighteenth century.

■ **Comparison**

In what ways did the gathering and hunting people of Australia differ from those of the northwest coast of North America?

Over many thousands of years, these people had assimilated various material items or cultural practices from outsiders—outrigger canoes, fish hooks, complex netting techniques, artistic styles, rituals, and mythological ideas—but despite the presence of farmers in nearby New Guinea, no agricultural practices penetrated the Australian mainland. Was it because large areas of Australia were unsuited for the kind of agriculture practiced in New Guinea? Or did the peoples of Australia, enjoying an environment of sufficient resources, simply see no need to change their way of life?

Despite the absence of agriculture, Australia's peoples had mastered and manipulated their environment, in part through the practice of "firestick farming," a pattern of deliberately set fires, which they described as "cleaning up the country." These controlled burns served to clear the underbrush, thus making hunting easier and encouraging the growth of certain plant and animal species. In addition, native Australians exchanged goods among themselves over distances of hundreds of miles, created elaborate mythologies and ritual practices, and developed sophisticated traditions of sculpture and rock painting. They accomplished all of this on the basis of an economy and technology rooted in the distant Paleolithic past.

A very different kind of gathering and hunting society flourished in the fifteenth century along the northwest coast of North America among the Chinookan, Tulalip, Skagit, and other peoples. With some 300 edible animal species and an abundance of salmon and other fish, this extraordinarily bounteous environment provided the foundation for what scholars sometimes call "complex" or "affluent" gathering and hunting cultures. What distinguished the northwest coast peoples from those of Australia were permanent village settlements with large and sturdy houses, considerable economic specialization, ranked societies that sometimes included slavery, chiefdoms dominated by powerful clan leaders or "big men," and extensive storage of food.

Although these and other gathering and hunting peoples persisted still in the fifteenth century, both their numbers and the area they inhabited had contracted greatly as the Agricultural Revolution unfolded across the planet. That relentless advance of the farming frontier continued in the centuries ahead as the Russian, Chinese, and European empires encompassed the lands of the remaining Paleolithic peoples. By the early twenty-first century, what was once the only human way of life had been reduced to minuscule pockets of people whose cultures seemed doomed to a final extinction.

Agricultural Village Societies

■ Change
What kinds of changes were transforming West African agricultural village societies and those of the Iroquois as the fifteenth century dawned?

Far more numerous than hunters and gatherers were those many peoples who, though fully agricultural, had avoided incorporation into larger empires or civilizations and had not developed their own city- or state-based societies. Living usually in small village-based communities and organized in terms of kinship relations, such people predominated during the fifteenth century in much of North America, in Africa south of the equator, and in parts of the Amazon River basin and

Southeast Asia. They had created societies largely without the oppressive political authority, class inequalities, and seclusion of women that were so common in civilizations. Historians have largely relegated such societies to the periphery of world history, marginal to their overwhelming focus on large-scale civilizations. Viewed from within their own circles, though, these societies were of course at the center of things, each with its own history of migration, cultural change, social conflict, incorporation of new people, political rise and fall, and interaction with strangers.

In the forested region of what is now southern Nigeria in West Africa, for example, three quite different patterns of political development emerged in the centuries between 1000 and 1500 (see Map 13.3, p. 376). Each of them began from a base of farming village societies whose productivity was generating larger populations.

Among the Yoruba people, a series of city-states emerged, each within a walled town and ruled by an *oba*, or king (many of whom were women), who performed both religious and political functions. As in ancient Mesopotamia or classical Greece, no single state or empire encompassed all of Yorubaland. Nearby lay the kingdom of Benin, a small, highly centralized territorial state that emerged by the fifteenth century and was ruled by a warrior king named Ewuare, said to have conquered 201 towns and villages in the process of founding the new state. His administrative chiefs replaced the heads of kinship groups as major political authorities, while the ruler sponsored extensive trading missions and patronized artists who created the remarkable brass sculptures for which Benin is so famous.

East of the Niger River lay the lands of the Igbo peoples, where dense population and extensive trading networks might well have given rise to states, but the deliberate Igbo preference was to reject the kingship and state-building efforts of their neighbors, boasting on occasion that "the Igbo have no kings." Instead they relied on other institutions—title societies in which wealthy men received a series of prestigious ranks, women's associations, hereditary ritual experts serving as mediators, a balance of power among kinship groups—to maintain social cohesion beyond the level of the village. It was a "stateless society," famously described in Chinua Achebe's *Things Fall Apart*, the most widely read novel to emerge from twentieth-century Africa.

The Yoruba, Bini, and Igbo peoples did not live in isolated, self-contained societies, however. They traded actively among themselves and with more distant peoples, such as the large African kingdom of Songhay far to the north. Cotton cloth, fish, copper and iron goods, decorative objects, and more drew neighboring peoples into networks of exchange. Common artistic traditions reflected a measure of cultural unity in a politically fragmented region, and all of these peoples seem to have changed from a matrilineal to a patrilineal system of tracing their descent. Little of this registered in the larger civilizations of the Afro-Eurasian world, but to the peoples of the West African forest during the fifteenth century, these processes were central to their history and their daily lives. Soon, however, all of them would be caught up in the transatlantic slave trade and would be changed substantially in the process.

Benin Bronzes
British colonial forces in 1897 looted the palace of the king of Benin and seized more than 1,000 exquisite brass figures, most of which were associated with court ceremonies. Here is a sixteenth-century representation of the Queen Mother of Benin. (National Museum, Lagos, Nigeria/The Bridgeman Art Library)

Across the Atlantic in what is now central New York State, other agricultural village societies were also in the process of substantial change during the several centuries preceding their incorporation into European trading networks and empires. The Iroquois-speaking peoples of that region had only recently become fully agricultural, adopting maize- and bean-farming techniques that had origi- nated long ago in Mesoamerica. As this productive agriculture took hold by 1300 or so, the population grew, the size of settlements increased, and distinct peoples emerged, such as the Onondaga, Seneca, Cayuga, Oneida, and Mohawk. Frequent warfare also erupted among them. Some scholars have speculated that as agricul- ture, largely seen as women's work, became the primary economic activity, "war- fare replaced successful food getting as the avenue to male prestige."[1]

Whatever caused it, this increased level of conflict among Iroquois peoples trig- gered a remarkable political innovation—a loose alliance or confederation among five Iroquois peoples based on an agreement known as the Great Law of Peace (see Map 13.5, p. 383). It was an agreement to settle their differences peacefully through a confederation council of clan leaders, some fifty of them altogether, who had the authority to adjudicate disputes and set reparation payments. Operating by consen- sus, the Iroquois League of Five Nations effectively suppressed the blood feuds and tribal conflicts that had only recently been so widespread. It also coordinated their peoples' relationship with outsiders, including the Europeans, who arrived in grow- ing numbers in the centuries after 1500.

The Iroquois League also gave expression to values of limited government, social equality, and personal freedom, concepts that some European colonists found highly attractive. One British colonial administrator declared in 1749 that the Iroquois had "such absolute Notions of Liberty that they allow no Kind of Superiority of one over another, and banish all Servitude from their Territories."[2] Such equality extended to gender relationships, for among the Iroquois, descent was matrilineal (reckoned through the woman's line), married couples lived with the wife's family, and women controlled agriculture. While men were hunters, warriors, and the pri- mary political officeholders, women selected and could depose those leaders.

Wherever they lived in 1500, over the next several centuries independent agri- cultural peoples such as the Iroquois, Yoruba, and Igbo were increasingly encom- passed in expanding economic networks and conquest empires based in Western Europe or in Russia. In this respect, they repeated the experience of many other village-based farming communities that had much earlier found themselves forcibly included in the powerful embrace of Egyptian, Mesopotamian, Roman, Indian, Chinese, and other civilizations.

■ **Significance**

What role did Central Asian and West African pastoralists play in their respective regions?

Herding Peoples

Nomadic pastoral peoples impinged more directly and dramatically on civilizations than did hunting and gathering or agricultural village societies. The Mongol incur- sion, and the enormous empire to which it gave rise, was one in a long series of challenges from the steppes, but it was not the last. As the Mongol Empire disinte-grated, a brief attempt to restore it occurred in the late fourteenth and early fif-teenth centuries under the leadership of a Turkic warrior named Timur, known in the West as Tamerlane (see Map 13.1, p. 370).

With a ferocity that matched or exceeded that of his model, Chinggis Khan, Timur's army of nomads brought immense devastation yet again to Russia, Persia, and India. Timur himself died in 1405, while preparing for an invasion of China. Conflicts among his successors prevented any lasting empire, although his descen-dants retained control of the area between Persia and Afghanistan for the rest of the fifteenth century. That state hosted a sophisticated elite culture, particularly at its splendid capital of Samarkand, as its rulers patronized artists, poets, traders, and craftsmen. Timur's conquest proved to be the last great military success of nomadic peoples from Central Asia. In the centuries that followed, their homelands were swallowed up in the expanding Russian and Chinese empires, as the balance of power between steppe nomads of inner Eurasia and the civilizations of outer Eurasia turned decisively in favor of the latter.

In Africa, pastoral peoples stayed independent of established empires several centuries longer than the nomads of Inner Asia, for not until the late nineteenth century were they incorporated into European colonial states. The experience of the Fulbe, West Africa's largest pastoral society, provides a useful example of an African herding people with a highly significant role in the fifteenth century and beyond. From their homeland in the western fringe of the Sahara along the upper Senegal River, the Fulbe migrated gradually eastward in the centuries after 1000 C.E. (see Map 13.3, p. 376). Unlike the pastoral peoples of Inner Asia, they generally lived in small communities among agricultural peoples and paid various grazing fees and taxes for the privilege of pasturing their cattle. Relations with their farming hosts often were tense because the Fulbe resented their subordination to agricultural peoples, whose way of life they despised. That sense of cultural superiority became even more pronounced as the Fulbe, in the course of their eastward movement, slowly adopted Islam. Some of them in fact dropped out of a pastoral life and set-tled in towns, where they became highly respected religious leaders. In the eigh-teenth and nineteenth centuries, the Fulbe were at the center of a wave of reli-giously based uprisings, or jihads, that greatly expanded the practice of Islam and gave rise to a series of new states, ruled by the Fulbe themselves.

Civilizations of the Fifteenth Century: Comparing China and Europe

Beyond the foraging, farming, and herding societies of the fifteenth-century world were its civilizations, those city-centered and state-based societies that were far larger and more densely populated, more powerful and innovative, and much more unequal in terms of class and gender than other forms of human commu-nity. Since the First Civilizations had emerged between 3500 and 1000 B.C.E., both the geographic space they encompassed and the number of people they embraced had grown substantially. By the fifteenth century, a considerable majority of the world's population lived within one or another of these civilizations, although most of these people no doubt identified more with local communities than with a larger civilization. What might an imaginary global traveler notice about the world's major civilizations in the fifteenth century?

Ming Dynasty China

■ **Description**

How would you define the major achievements of Ming dynasty China?

Such a traveler might well begin his or her journey in China, heir to a long tradition of effective governance, Confucian and Daoist philosophy, a major Buddhist presence, sophisticated artistic achievements, and a highly productive economy. That civilization, however, had been greatly disrupted by a century of Mongol rule, and its population had been sharply reduced by the plague. During the Ming dynasty (1368–1644), however, China recovered (see Map 13.1). The early decades of that dynasty witnessed an effort to eliminate all signs of foreign rule, discouraging

Map 13.1   Asia in the Fifteenth Century
The fifteenth century witnessed the massive Ming dynasty voyages into the Indian Ocean as well as the last major eruption of nomadic power in Timur's empire.

the use of Mongol names and dress, while promoting Confucian learning based on earlier models from the Han, Tang, and Song dynasties. Emperor Yongle (reigned 1402–1422) sponsored an enormous *Encyclopedia* of some 11,000 volumes. With contributions from more than 2,000 scholars, this work sought to summarize or compile all previous writing on history, geography, ethics, government, and more. Culturally speaking, China was looking to its past.

Politically, the Ming dynasty reestablished the civil service examination system that had been neglected under Mongol rule and went on to create a highly centralized government. Power was concentrated in the hands of the emperor himself, while a cadre of eunuchs (castrated men) personally loyal to the emperor exercised great authority, much to the dismay of the official bureaucrats. The state acted vigorously to repair the damage of the Mongol years by restoring millions of acres to cultivation; rebuilding canals, reservoirs, and irrigation works; and planting, according to some estimates, a billion trees in an effort to reforest China. As a result, the economy rebounded, both international and domestic trade flourished, and the population grew. During the fifteenth century, China had recovered and was perhaps the best-governed and most prosperous of the world's major civilizations.

China also undertook the largest and most impressive maritime expeditions the world had ever seen. Since the eleventh century, Chinese sailors and traders had been a major presence in the South China Sea and in Southeast Asian port cities, with much of this activity in private hands. But now, after decades of preparation, an enormous fleet, commissioned by Emperor Yongle himself, was launched in 1405, followed over the next twenty-eight years by six more such expeditions. On board more than 300 ships of the first voyage was a crew of some 27,000, including 180 physicians, hundreds of government officials, 5 astrologers, 7 high-ranking or grand eunuchs, carpenters, tailors, accountants, merchants, translators, cooks, and thousands of soldiers and sailors. Visiting many ports in Southeast Asia, Indonesia, India, Arabia, and East Africa, these fleets, captained by the Muslim eunuch Zheng He, sought to enroll distant peoples and states in the Chinese tribute system (see Map 13.1). Dozens of rulers accompanied the fleets back to China, where they presented tribute, performed the required rituals of submission, and received in return abundant gifts, titles, and trading opportunities. Chinese officials were amused by some of the exotic products to be found abroad—ostriches, zebras, and giraffes, for example. Officially described as "bringing order to the world," Zheng He's expeditions served to establish Chinese power and prestige in the Indian Ocean and to exert Chinese control over foreign trade in the

Comparing Chinese and European Ships

Among the largest vessels in Zheng He's early-fifteenth-century fleet was this "treasure ship," measuring more than 400 feet long and carrying a crew of perhaps 1,000 men. The figure at the bottom right represents one of Columbus's ships. (© Dugald Stermer)

region. The Chinese, however, did not seek to conquer new territories, establish Chinese settlements, or spread their culture. On one of the voyages, Zheng He erected on the island of Ceylon (Sri Lanka) a tablet honoring alike the Buddha, Allah, and a Hindu deity.

The most surprising feature of these voyages was how abruptly and deliberately they were ended. After 1433, Chinese authorities simply stopped such expeditions and allowed this enormous and expensive fleet to deteriorate in port. "In less than a hundred years," wrote a recent historian of these voyages, "the greatest navy the world had ever known had ordered itself into extinction."[3] Part of the reason involved the death of the emperor Yongle, who had been the chief patron of the enterprise. Many high-ranking officials had long seen the expeditions as a waste of resources because China, they believed, was the self-sufficient "middle kingdom," requiring little from the outside world. In their eyes, the real danger to China came from the north, where nomadic barbarians constantly threatened. Finally, they viewed the voyages as the project of the court eunuchs, whom these officials despised. Even as these voices of Chinese officialdom prevailed, private Chinese merchants and craftsmen continued to settle and trade in Japan, the Philippines, Taiwan, and Southeast Asia, but they did so without the support of their government. The Chinese state quite deliberately turned its back on what was surely within its reach—a large-scale maritime empire in the Indian Ocean basin.

European Comparisons: State Building and Cultural Renewal

■ **Comparison**
What political and cultural differences stand out in the histories of fifteenth-century China and Western Europe? What similarities are apparent?

At the other end of the Eurasian continent, similar processes of demographic recovery, political consolidation, cultural flowering, and overseas expansion were under way. Western Europe, having escaped Mongol conquest but devastated by the plague, began to regrow its population during the second half of the fifteenth century. As in China, the infrastructure of civilization proved a durable foundation for demographic and economic revival.

Politically, too, Europe joined China in continuing earlier patterns of state building. In China, however, this meant a unitary and centralized government that encompassed almost the whole of its civilization, while in Europe a decidedly fragmented system of many separate, independent, and highly competitive states made for a sharply divided Christendom (see Map 13.2). Many of these states—Spain, Portugal, France, England, the city-states of Italy (Milan, Venice, and Florence), various German principalities—learned to tax their citizens more efficiently, to create more effective administrative structures, and to raise standing armies. A small Russian state centered on the city of Moscow also emerged in the fifteenth century as Mongol rule faded away. Much of this state building was driven by the needs of war, a frequent occurrence in such a fragmented and competitive political environment. England and France, for example, fought intermittently for more than a century in the Hundred Years' War (1337–1453) over rival claims to territory in France. Nothing remotely similar disturbed the internal life of Ming dynasty China.

Map 13.2 Europe in 1500
By the end of the fifteenth century, Christian Europe had assumed its early modern political shape as a system of competing states threatened by an expanding Muslim Ottoman Empire.

A renewed cultural blossoming, known in European history as the Renaissance, likewise paralleled the revival of all things Confucian in Ming dynasty China. In Europe, however, that blossoming celebrated and reclaimed a classical Greek tradition that earlier had been obscured or viewed through the lens of Arabic or Latin translations. Beginning in the vibrant commercial cities of Italy between roughly 1350 and 1500, the Renaissance reflected the belief of the wealthy elite that they were living in a wholly new era, far removed from the confined religious world of feudal Europe. Educated citizens of these cities sought inspiration in the art and literature of ancient Greece and Rome—they were "returning to the sources," as they put it. Their purpose was not so much to reconcile these works with the ideas of Christianity, as the twelfth- and thirteenth-century university scholars had done, but to use them as a cultural standard to imitate and then to surpass. The elite patronized great Renaissance artists such as Leonardo da Vinci, Michelangelo, and Raphael, whose paintings and sculptures were far more naturalistic, particularly in portraying the human body, than those of their medieval counterparts.

Although religious themes remained prominent, Renaissance artists now included portraits and busts of well-known contemporary figures and scenes from ancient mythology. In the work of scholars, known as "humanists," reflections on secular topics such as grammar, history, politics, poetry, rhetoric, and ethics complemented more religious matters. For example, Niccolò Machiavelli's (1469–1527) famous work *The Prince* was a prescription for political success based on the way politics actually operated in a highly competitive Italy of rival city-states rather than on idealistic and religiously based principles. To the question of whether a prince should be feared or loved, Machiavelli replied:

> One ought to be both feared and loved, but as it is difficult for the two to go together, it is much safer to be feared than loved. . . . For it may be said of men in general that they are ungrateful, voluble, dissemblers, anxious to avoid danger, and covetous of gain. . . . Fear is maintained by dread of punishment which never fails. . . . In the actions of men, and especially of princes, from which there is no appeal, the end justifies the means.[4]

Heavily influenced by classical models, Renaissance figures were more interested in capturing the unique qualities of particular individuals and in describing the world as it was than in portraying or exploring eternal religious truths. In its focus on the affairs of this world, Renaissance culture reflected the urban bustle and commercial preoccupations of the Italian cities. Its secular elements challenged the otherworldliness of Christian culture, and its individualism signaled the dawning of a more capitalist economy of private entrepreneurs. A new Europe was in the making, rather more different from its own recent past than Ming dynasty China was from its pre-Mongol glory.

European Comparisons: Maritime Voyaging

■ **Comparison**
In what ways did European maritime voyaging in the fifteenth century differ from that of China? What accounts for these differences?

A global traveler during the fifteenth century might be surprised to find that Europeans, like the Chinese, were also launching outward-bound maritime expeditions. Initiated in 1415 by the small country of Portugal, those voyages sailed ever farther down the west coast of Africa, supported by the state and blessed by the pope (see Map 13.3). As the century ended, two expeditions marked major breakthroughs, although few suspected it at the time. In 1492, Christopher Columbus, funded by Spain, Portugal's neighbor and rival, made his way west across the Atlantic hoping to arrive in the East and, in one of history's most consequential mistakes, ran into the Americas. Five years later, in 1497, Vasco da Gama launched a voyage that took him around the tip of South Africa, along the East African coast, and, with the help of a Muslim pilot, across the Indian Ocean to Calicut in southern India.

Snapshot   **Key Moments in European Maritime Voyaging**

Portuguese seize Ceuta in Morocco	1415
Prince Henry the Navigator launches Portuguese exploration of the West African coast	1420
Portuguese settle the Azores	1430s
Chinese fleets withdrawn from Indian Ocean	1433
Portuguese reach the Senegal River; beginning of Atlantic slave trade	1440s
Portuguese contact with Kongo; royal family converts to Christianity	1480s
Sugar production begins in Atlantic islands (Canaries, São Tomé)	1480s
Establishment of trading station at Elmina (in present-day Ghana)	1480s
First transatlantic voyage of Columbus	1492
John Cabot sails across North Atlantic to North America	1496
Vasco da Gama enters Indian Ocean and reaches India	1497–1498
Portuguese attacks on various Swahili cities; establishment of Fort Jesus at Mombasa; Portuguese contacts with Christian Ethiopia	1497–1520s
Magellan's voyage to Asia via the Americas; first circumnavigation of the globe	1520–1523

The differences between the Chinese and European oceangoing ventures were striking, most notably perhaps in terms of size. Columbus captained three ships and a crew of about 90, while da Gama had four ships, manned by perhaps 170 sailors. These were minuscule fleets compared to Zheng He's hundreds of ships and crew in the many thousands. "All the ships of Columbus and da Gama combined," according to a recent account, "could have been stored on a single deck of a single vessel in the fleet that set sail under Zheng He."[5]

Motivation as well as size differentiated the two ventures. Europeans were seeking the wealth of Africa and Asia—gold, spices, silk, and more. They also were in search of Christian converts and of possible Christian allies with whom to continue their long crusading struggle against threatening Muslim powers. China, by contrast, faced no equivalent power, needed no military allies in the Indian Ocean basin, and required little that these regions produced. Nor did China possess an impulse to convert foreigners to Chinese culture or religion as the Europeans surely did. Furthermore, the confident and overwhelmingly powerful Chinese fleet sought neither conquests nor colonies, while the Europeans soon tried to monopolize by force the commerce of the Indian Ocean and violently carved out huge empires in the Americas.

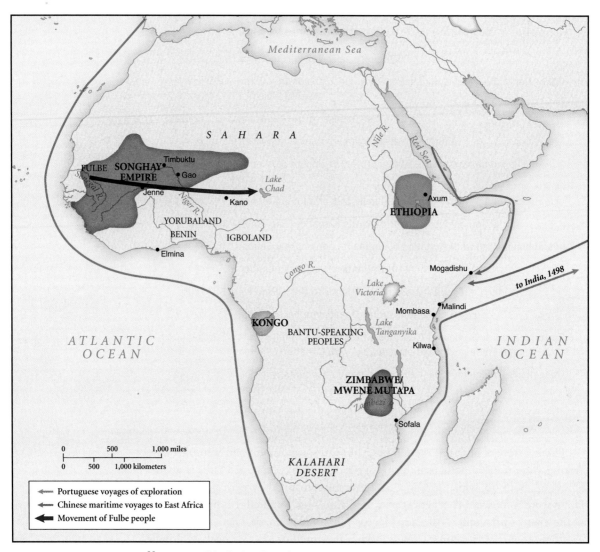

Map 13.3   Africa in the Fifteenth Century

By the 1400s, Africa was a virtual museum of political and cultural diversity, encompassing large empires, such as Songhay; smaller kingdoms, such as Kongo; city-states among the Yoruba, Hausa, and Swahili peoples; village-based societies without states at all, as among the Igbo; and nomadic pastoral peoples, such as the Fulbe. Both European and Chinese maritime expeditions touched on Africa during that century, even as Islam continued to find acceptance in the northern half of the continent.

The most striking difference in these two cases lay in the sharp contrast between China's decisive ending of its voyages and the continuing, indeed escalating, European effort, which soon brought the world's oceans and growing numbers of the world's people under its control. This is the reason that Zheng He's voyages were so long neglected in China's historical memory. They led nowhere, whereas the initial European expeditions, so much smaller and less promising, were but the initial steps on a journey to world power. But why did the Europeans continue a process that the Chinese had deliberately abandoned?

In the first place, of course, Europe had no unified political authority with the power to order an end to its maritime outreach. Its system of competing states, so unlike China's single unified empire, ensured that once begun, rivalry alone would drive the Europeans to the ends of the earth. Beyond this, much of Europe's elite had an interest in overseas expansion. Its budding merchant communities saw opportunity for profit; its competing monarchs eyed the revenue that could come from taxing overseas trade or from seizing overseas resources; the Church foresaw the possibility of widespread conversion; impoverished nobles might imagine fame and fortune abroad. In China, by contrast, support for Zheng He's voyages was very shallow in official circles, and when the emperor Yongle passed from the scene, those opposed to the voyages prevailed within the politics of the court.

Finally, the Chinese were very much aware of their own antiquity, believed strongly in the absolute superiority of their culture, and felt with good reason that, should they need something from abroad, others would bring it to them. Europeans too believed themselves unique, particularly in religious terms as the possessors of Christianity, the "one true religion." In material terms, though, they were seeking out the greater riches of the East, and they were highly conscious that Muslim power blocked easy access to these treasures and posed a military and religious threat to Europe itself. All of this propelled continuing European expansion in the centuries that followed.

The Waldseemüller Map of 1507
Just fifteen years after Columbus landed in the Western Hemisphere, this map, which was created by the German cartographer Martin Waldseemüller, reflected a dawning European awareness of the planet's global dimensions and location of the world's major landmasses. (Bildarchiv Preussischer Kulturbesitz/Art Resource, NY)

The Chinese withdrawal from the Indian Ocean actually facilitated the European entry. It cleared the way for the Portuguese to enter the region, where they faced only the eventual naval power of the Ottomans. Had Vasco da Gama encountered Zheng He's massive fleet as his four small ships sailed into Asian waters in 1498, world history may well have taken quite a different turn. As it was, however, China's abandonment of oceanic voyaging and Europe's embrace of the seas marked different responses to a common problem that both civilizations shared— growing populations and land shortage. In the centuries that followed, China's rice-based agriculture was able to expand production internally by more intensive use of the land, while the country's territorial expansion was inland toward Central Asia. By contrast, Europe's agriculture, based on wheat and livestock, expanded primarily by acquiring new lands in overseas possessions, which were gained as a consequence of a commitment to oceanic expansion.

Civilizations of the Fifteenth Century: The Islamic World

■ Comparison

What differences can you identify among the four major empires in the Islamic world of the fifteenth and sixteenth centuries?

Beyond the domains of Chinese and European civilization, our fifteenth-century global traveler would surely have been impressed with the transformations of the Islamic world. Stretching across much of Afro-Eurasia, the enormous realm of Islam experienced a set of remarkable changes during the fifteenth and early sixteenth centuries, as well as the continuation of earlier patterns. The most notable change lay in the political realm, for an Islamic civilization that had been severely fragmented since at least 900 now crystallized into four major states or empires (see Map 13.4). At the same time, a long-term process of conversion to Islam continued the cultural transformation in Afro-Eurasian societies both within and beyond these new states.

In the Islamic Heartland: The Ottoman and Safavid Empires

The most impressive and enduring of these new states was the Ottoman Empire, which lasted in one form or another from the fourteenth to the early twentieth century. It was the creation of one of the many Turkic warrior groups that had earlier migrated into Anatolia. By the mid-fifteenth century, these Ottoman Turks had already carved out a state that encompassed much of the Anatolian peninsula and had pushed deep into southeastern Europe (the Balkans), acquiring in the process a substantial Christian population. In the two centuries that followed, the Ottoman Empire extended its control to much of the Middle East, coastal North Africa, the lands surrounding the Black Sea, and even farther into Eastern Europe.

The Ottoman Empire was a state of enormous significance in the world of the fifteenth century and beyond. In its huge territory, long duration, incorporation of many diverse peoples, and economic and cultural sophistication, it was

Map 13.4 Empires of the Islamic World
The most prominent political features of the vast Islamic world in the fifteenth and sixteenth centuries were four large states: the Songhay, Ottoman, Safavid, and Mughal empires.

one of the great empires of world history. In the fifteenth century, only Ming dynasty China and the Incas matched it in terms of wealth, power, and splendor. The empire represented the emergence of the Turks as the dominant people of the Islamic world, ruling now over many Arabs, who had initiated this new faith more than 800 years before. In adding "caliph" (successor to the Prophet) to their other titles, Ottoman sultans claimed the legacy of the earlier Abbasid Empire. They sought to bring a renewed unity to the Islamic world, while also serving as protector of the faith, the "strong sword of Islam."

The Ottoman Empire represented a new phase in the long encounter between Christendom and the world of Islam. In the Crusades, Europeans had taken the aggressive initiative in that encounter, but now the rise of the Ottoman Empire reversed their roles. The seizure of Constantinople in 1453 marked the final demise of Christian Byzantium and allowed Ottoman rulers to see themselves as successors to the Roman Empire. In 1529, a rapidly expanding Ottoman Empire laid siege to Vienna in the heart of Central Europe. The political and military expansion of Islam, at the expense of Christendom, seemed clearly under way. Many Europeans spoke fearfully of the "terror of the Turk."

Des obriften samerling
Vnd Trüchses

Ottoman Janissaries
Originating in the fourteenth century, the Janissaries became the elite infantry force of the Ottoman Empire. Complete with uniforms, cash salaries, and marching music, they were the first standing army in the region since the days of the Roman Empire. When gunpowder technology became available, Janissary forces soon were armed with muskets, grenades, and handheld cannon. This image dates from the seventeenth century. (Austrian National Library, picture archive, Vienna: Cod. 8626, fol. 15r)

In the neighboring Persian lands to the east of the Ottoman Empire, another Islamic state was also taking shape in the late fifteenth and early sixteenth centuries—the Safavid Empire. Its leadership was also Turkic, but in this case it had emerged from a Sufi religious order founded several centuries earlier by Safi al-Din (1252–1334). The long-term significance of the Safavid Empire, which was established in the decade following 1500, was its decision to forcibly impose a Shia version of Islam as the official religion of the state. Over time, this form of Islam gained popular support and came to define the unique identity of Persian (Iranian) culture.

This Shia empire also introduced a sharp divide into the political and religious life of heartland Islam, for almost all of Persia's neighbors practiced a Sunni form of the faith. For a century (1534–1639), periodic military conflict erupted between the Ottoman and Safavid empires, reflecting both territorial rivalry and sharp religious differences. In 1514, the Ottoman sultan wrote to the Safavid ruler in the most bitter of terms:

You have denied the sanctity of divine law…you have deserted the path of salvation and the sacred commandments…you have opened to Muslims the gates of tyranny and oppression…you have raised the standard of irreligion and heresy…. [Therefore] the *ulama* and our doctors have pronounced a sentence of death against you, perjurer and blasphemer.[6]

This Sunni/Shia hostility has continued to divide the Islamic world into the twenty-first century.

On the Frontiers of Islam: The Songhay and Mughal Empires

While the Ottoman and Safavid empires brought both a new political unity and a sharp division to the heartland of Islam, two other states performed a similar role on the expanding African and Asian frontiers of the faith. In the West African savannas, the Songhay Empire rose in the second half of the fifteenth century. It was the most recent and the largest in a series of impressive states that operated at a crucial intersection of the trans-Saharan trade routes and that derived much of their revenue from taxing that commerce. Islam was a growing faith in Songhay but was limited largely to urban elites. This cultural divide within Songhay largely accounts for the religious behavior of its fifteenth-century monarch Sonni Ali (reigned 1465–1492), who gave alms and fasted during Ramadan in proper Islamic style but also enjoyed a reputation as a magician and possessed a charm thought to render his soldiers invisible to their enemies. Nonetheless, Songhay had become a major center of Islamic learning and commerce by the early sixteenth century. A North African traveler, known as Leo Africanus, remarked on the city of Timbuktu:

> Here are great numbers of [Muslim] religious teachers, judges, scholars, and other learned persons who are bountifully maintained at the king's expense. Here too are brought various manuscripts or written books from Barbary [North Africa] which are sold for more money than any other merchandise.... Here are very rich merchants and to here journey continually large numbers of negroes who purchase here cloth from Barbary and Europe.... It is a wonder to see the quality of merchandise that is daily brought here and how costly and sumptuous everything is.[7]

Sonni Ali's successor made the pilgrimage to Mecca and asked to be given the title "Caliph of the Land of the Blacks." Songhay then represented a substantial Islamic state on the African frontier of a still-expanding Muslim world.

The Mughal Empire in India bore similarities to Songhay, for both governed largely non-Muslim populations. Much as the Ottoman Empire initiated a new phase in the interaction of Islam and Christendom, so too did the Mughal Empire continue an ongoing encounter between Islamic and Hindu civilizations. Established in the early sixteenth century, the Mughal Empire was the creation of yet another Islamized Turkic group, which invaded India in 1526. Over the next century, the Mughals (a Persian term for Mongols) established unified control over most of the Indian peninsula, giving it a rare period of political unity and laying the foundation for subsequent British colonial rule. During its first several centuries, the Mughal Empire, a land of great wealth and imperial splendor, was the location of a remarkable effort to blend many Hindu groups and a variety of foreign Muslims into an effective partnership. The inclusive policies of the early Mughal emperors showed that Muslim rulers could accommodate their overwhelmingly Hindu subjects in somewhat the same fashion as Ottoman authorities provided religious autonomy for their Christian peoples. In southernmost India, however, the distinctly Hindu kingdom of Vijayanagara flourished in the fifteenth century, even as it borrowed architectural styles from the Muslim states of northern India and sometimes employed Muslim mercenaries in its military forces.

Together these four Muslim empires—Ottoman, Safavid, Songhay, and Mughal— brought to the Islamic world a greater measure of political coherence, military power, economic prosperity, and cultural brilliance than it had known since the early centuries of Islam. This new energy, sometimes called a "second flowering of Islam," impelled the continuing spread of the faith to yet new regions. The most prominent of these was oceanic Southeast Asia, which for centuries had been intimately bound up in the world of Indian Ocean commerce. By the fifteenth century, that trading network was largely in Muslim hands, and the demand for Southeast Asian spices was mounting as the Eurasian world recovered from the devastation of Mongol conquest and the plague. Growing numbers of Muslim traders, many of them from India, settled in Java and Sumatra, bringing their faith with them. Thus, unlike the Middle East and India, where Islam was established in the wake of Arab or Turkic conquest, in Southeast Asia, as in West Africa, it was introduced by traveling merchants and solidified through the activities of Sufi holy men.

The rise of Malacca, strategically located on the waterway between Sumatra and Malaya, was a sign of the times (see Map 13.1, p. 370). During the fifteenth century, it was transformed from a small fishing village to a major Muslim port city and became a springboard for the spread of Islam throughout the region. The Islam of Malacca, however, demonstrated much blending with local and Hindu/Buddhist traditions, while the city itself, like many port towns, had a reputation for "rough behavior." An Arab Muslim pilot in the 1480s commented critically:

> They have no culture at all....You do not know whether they are Muslim or not....They are thieves, for theft is rife among them and they do not mind....They appear liars and deceivers in trade and labor.[8]

Nonetheless, Malacca, like Timbuktu, became a center for Islamic learning, and students from elsewhere in Southeast Asia were studying there in the fifteenth century. As the more central regions of Islam were consolidating politically, the frontier of the faith continued to move steadily outward.

Civilizations of the Fifteenth Century: The Americas

■ Comparison
What distinguished the Aztec and Inca empires from each other?

Across the Atlantic, centers of civilization had long flourished in Mesoamerica and in the Andes. The fifteenth century witnessed new, larger, and more politically unified expressions of those civilizations in the Aztec and Inca empires. Both were the work of previously marginal peoples who had forcibly taken over and absorbed older cultures, giving them new energy, and both were decimated in the sixteenth century at the hands of Spanish conquistadores and their diseases. To conclude this global tour of world civilizations, we will send our weary traveler to the Western Hemisphere for a brief look at these American civilizations (see Map 13.5).

The Aztec Empire

The empire known to history as the Aztec state was largely the work of the Mexica people, a seminomadic group from northern Mexico who had migrated southward and by 1325 had established themselves on a small island in Lake Texcoco. Over the next century, the Mexica developed their military capacity, served as mercenaries

Map 13.5 The Americas in the Fifteenth Century

The Americas before Columbus represented a world almost completely separate from Afro-Eurasia. It featured similar kinds of societies, though with a different balance among them, but it completely lacked the pastoral economies that were so important in the Eastern Hemisphere.

for more powerful people, negotiated elite marriage alliances with them, and built up their own capital city of Tenochtitlán. In 1428, a Triple Alliance between the Mexica and two other nearby city-states launched a highly aggressive program of military conquest, which in less than 100 years brought more of Mesoamerica within a single political framework than ever before. Aztec authorities, eager to shed their rather undistinguished past, now claimed descent from earlier Mesoamerican peoples such as the Toltecs and Teotihuacán.

With a core population recently estimated at 5 to 6 million people, the Aztec Empire was a loosely structured and unstable conquest state, which witnessed frequent rebellions by its subject peoples. Conquered peoples and cities were required to regularly deliver to their Aztec rulers impressive quantities of textiles and clothing, military supplies, jewelry and other luxuries, various foodstuffs, animal products, building materials, rubber balls, paper, and more. The process was overseen by local imperial tribute collectors, who sent the required goods on to Tenochtitlán, a metropolis of 150,000 to 200,000 people, where they were meticulously recorded.

That city featured numerous canals, dikes, causeways, and bridges. A central walled area of palaces and temples included a pyramid almost 200 feet high. Surrounding the city were "floating gardens," artificial islands created from swamplands that supported a highly productive agriculture. Vast marketplaces reflected the commercialization of the economy. A young Spanish soldier who beheld the city in 1519 described his reaction:

> Gazing on such wonderful sights, we did not know what to say, or whether what appeared before us was real, for on one side, on the land there were great cities, and in the lake ever so many more, and the lake was crowded with canoes, and in the causeway were many bridges at intervals, and in front of us stood the great city of Mexico.[9]

Beyond tribute from conquered peoples, ordinary trade, both local and long-distance, permeated Aztec domains. The extent of empire and rapid population growth stimulated the development of markets and the production of craft goods, particularly in the fifteenth century. Virtually every settlement, from the capital city to the smallest village, had a marketplace that hummed with activity during weekly market days. The largest was that of Tlatelolco, near the capital city, which stunned the Spanish with its huge size, its good order, and the immense range of goods available. Hernán Cortés, the Spanish conquistador who defeated the Aztecs, wrote that "every kind of merchandise such as can be met with in every land is for sale there, whether of food and victuals, or ornaments of gold and silver, or lead, brass, copper, tin, precious stones, bones, shells, snails and feathers."[10] Professional merchants, known as *pochteca*, were legally commoners, but their wealth, often exceeding that of the nobility, allowed them to rise in society and become "magnates of the land."

Among the "goods" that the pochteca obtained were slaves, many of whom were destined for sacrifice in the bloody rituals so central to Aztec religious life. Long a part of Mesoamerican and many other world cultures, human sacrifice

■ **Description**

How did Aztec religious thinking support the empire?

assumed an unusually prominent role in Aztec public life and thought during the fifteenth century. Tlacaelel (1398–1480), who was for more than half a century a prominent official of the Aztec Empire, is often credited with crystallizing the ideology of state that gave human sacrifice such great importance.

In the Aztecs' cyclical understanding of the world, the sun, central to all of life and identified with the their patron deity Huitzilopochtli, tended to lose its energy in a constant battle against encroaching darkness. Thus the Aztec world hovered always on the edge of catastrophe. To replenish its energy and thus postpone the descent into endless darkness, the sun required the life-giving force found in human blood. Because the gods had shed their blood ages ago in creating humankind, it was wholly proper for people to offer their own blood to nourish the gods in the present. The high calling of the Aztec state was to supply this blood, largely through its wars of expansion and from prisoners of war, who were destined for sacrifice. The victims were "those who have died for the god." The growth of the Aztec Empire therefore became the means for maintaining

Aztec Women

Within the home, Aztec women cooked, cleaned, spun and wove cloth, raised their children, and undertook ritual activities. Outside the home, they served as officials in palaces, priestesses in temples, traders in markets, teachers in schools, and members of craft workers' organizations. This domestic image comes from the sixteenth-century Florentine Codex, which was compiled by the Spanish but illustrated by Aztec artists. (Templo Mayor Library Mexico/Gianni Dagli Orti/The Art Archive)

cosmic order and avoiding utter catastrophe. This ideology also shaped the techniques of Aztec warfare, which put a premium on capturing prisoners rather than on killing the enemy. As the empire grew, priests and rulers became mutually dependent, and "human sacrifices were carried out in the service of politics."[11] Massive sacrificial rituals, together with a display of great wealth, served to impress enemies, allies, and subjects alike with the immense power of the Aztecs and their gods.

Alongside these sacrificial rituals was a philosophical and poetic tradition of great beauty, much of which mused on the fragility and brevity of human life. Here are a few lines from the fifteenth-century work of Nezahualcoyotl (1402–1472), a poet and king of the city-state of Texcoco, which was part of the Aztec Empire:

Truly do we live on Earth?
Not forever on earth; only a little while here.
Be it jade, it shatters.

Be it gold, it breaks.
Be it a quetzal feather, it tears apart.
Not forever on earth; only a little while here

Like a painting, we will be erased.
Like a flower, we will dry up here on earth.
Like plumed vestments of the precious bird,
That precious bird with an agile neck,
We will come to an end.[12]

The Inca Empire

While the Mexica were constructing an empire in Mesoamerica, a relatively small community of Quechua-speaking people, known to us as the Inca, was building the Western Hemisphere's largest imperial state along the spine of the Andes Mountains, which run almost the entire length of the west coast of South America. Much as the Aztecs drew upon the traditions of the Toltecs and Teotihuacán, the Incas incorporated the lands and cultures of earlier Andean civilizations: the Chavín, Moche, Nazca, and Chimu. The Inca Empire, however, was much larger than the Aztec state; it stretched some 2,500 miles along the Andes and contained perhaps 10 million subjects. Although the Aztec Empire controlled only part of the Mesoamerican cultural region, the Inca state encompassed practically the whole of Andean civilization during its short life in the fifteenth and early sixteenth centuries.

Both the Aztec and Inca empires represent rags-to-riches stories in which quite modest and remotely located people very quickly created by military conquest the largest states ever witnessed in their respective regions, but the empires themselves were quite different. In the Aztec realm, the Mexica rulers largely left their conquered people alone, if the required tribute was forthcoming. No elaborate administrative system arose to integrate the conquered territories or to assimilate their people to Aztec culture.

■ **Description**
In what ways did Inca authorities seek to integrate their vast domains?

The Incas, on the other hand, erected a rather more bureaucratic empire, though with many accommodations for local circumstances. At the top reigned the emperor, an absolute ruler regarded as divine, a descendant of the creator god Viracocha and the son of the sun god Inti. In theory, the state owned all land and resources, and each of the some eighty provinces in the empire had an Inca governor. At least in the central regions of the empire, subjects were grouped into hierarchical units of 10, 50, 100, 500, 1,000, 5,000, and 10,000 people, each headed by local officials, who were appointed and supervised by an Inca governor or the emperor. A separate set of "inspectors" provided the imperial center with an independent check on provincial officials. Births, deaths, marriages, and other population data were carefully recorded on *quipus*, the knotted cords that served as an accounting device. A resettlement program moved one-quarter or more of the population to new locations, in part to disperse conquered and no doubt resentful people.

Efforts at cultural integration required the leaders of conquered peoples to learn Quechua. Their sons were removed to the capital of Cuzco for instruction in Inca culture and language. Even now, millions of people from Ecuador to Chile still speak Quechua, and it is the official second language of Peru after Spanish. While the Incas required their subject peoples to acknowledge major Inca deities, these subject peoples were then largely free to carry on their own religious traditions. Human sacrifice took place on great public occasions or at times of special difficulty, but nothing remotely on the scale of the Aztec practice.

Like the Aztec Empire, the Inca state represented an especially dense and extended network of economic relationships within the "American web," but these relationships took shape in quite a different fashion. Inca demands on their conquered people were expressed, not so much in terms of tribute, but as labor service, known as *mita*, which was required periodically of every household.[13] What people produced at home usually stayed at home, but almost everyone also had to work for the state. Some labored on large state farms or on "sun farms," which supported temples and religious institutions; others herded, mined, served in the military, or toiled on state-directed construction projects. Those with particular skills were put to work manufacturing textiles, metal goods, ceramics, and stonework. The most well known of these specialists were the "chosen women," who were removed from their homes as young girls, trained in Inca ideology, and set to producing corn beer and cloth at state centers. Later they were given as wives to men of distinction or sent to serve as priestesses in various temples, where they were known as "wives of the Sun." In return for such labor services, Inca ideology, expressed in terms of family relationships, required the state to provide elaborate feasts at which large quantities of food and drink were consumed.

The Inca state played a major role in the distribution of goods as well as their production. A sixteenth-century Spanish observer wrote that "in each of the many provinces there were many storehouses filled with supplies and other needful things.... When there was no war, this stock of supplies and food was divided up among the poor and widows.... If there came a lean year, the storehouses were opened and the provinces were lent what they needed."[14] Thus the authority of the state penetrated and directed the Incas' society and economy far more than did that of the Aztecs.

If the Inca and Aztec civilizations differed sharply in their political and economic arrangements, they resembled each other more closely in their

Machu Picchu
Machu Picchu, high in the Andes Mountains, was constructed by the Incas in the 1400s on a spot long held sacred by local people. Its 200 buildings stand at some 8,000 feet above sea level, making it truly a "city in the sky." According to scholars, it was probably a royal retreat or religious center, rather than serving administrative, commercial, or military purposes. The outside world became aware of Machu Picchu only in 1911, when it was discovered by a Yale University archeologist. (Crispin Rodwell/Alamy)

gender systems. Both societies practiced what scholars call "gender parallelism," in which "women and men operate in two separate but equivalent spheres, each gender enjoying autonomy in its own sphere."[15]

In both Mesoamerican and Andean societies, such systems had emerged long before their incorporation into the Aztec and Inca empires. In the Andes, men reckoned their descent from their fathers and women from their mothers, while Mesoamericans had long viewed children as belonging equally to their mothers and fathers. Parallel religious cults for women and men likewise flourished in both societies. Inca men venerated the sun, while women worshipped the moon, with matching religious officials. In Aztec temples, both male and female priests presided over rituals dedicated to deities of both sexes. Particularly among the Incas, parallel hierarchies of male and female political officials governed the empire, while in Aztec society, women officials exercised local authority under a title that meant "female person in charge of people." Social roles were clearly defined and different for men and women, but the domestic concerns of women—childbirth, cooking, weaving, cleaning—were not regarded as inferior to the activities of men. Among the Aztec, for example, sweeping was a powerful and sacred act with symbolic significance as "an act of purification and a preventative against evil elements penetrating the center of the Aztec universe, the home."[16] In the Andes, men broke the ground, women sowed, and both took part in the harvest.

None of this meant gender equality. Men occupied the top positions in both political and religious life, and male infidelity was treated more lightly than was women's unfaithfulness. As the Inca and Aztec empires expanded, military life, limited to men, grew in prestige, perhaps skewing an earlier gender parallelism. In other ways, the new Aztec and Inca rulers adapted to the gender systems of the people they had conquered. Among the Aztecs, the tools of women's work, the broom and the weaving spindle, were ritualized as weapons; sweeping the home was believed to assist men at war; and childbirth for women was regarded as "our kind of war."[17] Inca rulers did not challenge the gender parallelism of their subjects but instead replicated it at a higher level, as the *sapay Inca* (the Inca ruler) and the *coya* (his female consort) governed jointly, claiming descent respectively from the sun and the moon.

Webs of Connection

■ Connection

In what different ways did the peoples of the fifteenth century interact with one another?

Few people in the fifteenth century lived in entirely separate and self-contained communities. Almost all were caught up, to one degree or another, in various and overlapping webs of influence, communication, and exchange. Such interactions represent, of course, one of the major concerns of world history. What kinds of webs or networks linked the various societies and civilizations of the fifteenth century?[18]

Perhaps most obvious were the webs of empire, large-scale political systems that brought together a variety of culturally different people. Christians and Muslims encountered each other directly in the Ottoman Empire, as did Hindus and Muslims in the Mughal Empire. No empire tried more diligently to integrate its diverse peoples than the fifteenth-century Incas.

Religion too linked far-flung peoples, and divided them as well. Christianity provided a common religious culture for peoples from England to Russia, although the great divide between Roman Catholicism and Eastern Orthodoxy endured, and in the sixteenth century the Protestant Reformation would shatter permanently the Christian unity of the Latin West. Although Buddhism had largely vanished from its South Asian homeland, it remained a link among China, Korea, Tibet, Japan, and parts of Southeast Asia, even as it splintered into a variety of sects and practices. More than either of these, Islam actively brought together its many peoples. In the hajj, the pilgrimage to Mecca, Africans, Arabs, Persians, Turks, Indians, and many others joined as one people as they rehearsed together the events that gave birth to their common faith. And yet the divisions and conflicts within the umma persisted, as the violent hostility between the Sunni Ottoman Empire and the Shia Safavid Empire so vividly illustrates.

Long-established patterns of trade among peoples occupying different environments and producing different goods were certainly much in evidence during the fifteenth century, as they had been for millennia. Hunting societies of Siberia funneled furs and other products of the forest into the Silk Road trading network traversing the civilizations of Eurasia. In the fifteenth century, some of the agricultural peoples in southern Nigeria were receiving horses brought overland from the drier regions to the north, where those animals flourished better. The Mississippi River in North America and the Orinoco and Amazon rivers in South America facilitated a canoe-borne commerce along those waterways. Coastal shipping in large seagoing canoes operated in the Caribbean and along the Pacific coast between Mexico and Peru. In the Pacific, the Micronesian island of Yap by the fifteenth century was the center of an oceanic trading network, which included the distant islands of Guam and Palau and used large stone disks as money. Likewise the people of Tonga, Samoa, and Fiji intermarried and exchanged a range of goods, including mats and canoes.

The great long-distance trading patterns of the Afro-Eurasian world, in operation for a thousand years or more, likewise continued in the fifteenth century, although the balance among them was changing (see Map 13.6). The Silk Road overland network, which had flourished under Mongol control in the thirteenth and fourteenth centuries, contracted in the fifteenth century as the Mongol Empire broke up and the devastation of the plague reduced demand for its products. The rise of the Ottoman Empire also blocked direct commercial contact between Europe and China, but oceanic trade from Japan, Korea, and China through the islands of Southeast Asia and across the Indian Ocean picked up considerably. Larger ships made it possible to trade in bulk goods such as grain as well as luxury products, while more sophisticated partnerships and credit mechanisms greased the wheels of commerce. A common Islamic culture over much of this vast region likewise smoothed the passage of goods among very different peoples, as it also did for the trans-Saharan trade.

Map 13.6   Religion and Commerce in the Afro-Eurasian World

By the fifteenth century, the many distinct peoples and societies of the Eastern Hemisphere were linked to one another by ties of religion and commerce. Of course, not everyone was involved in long-distance trade, and many people in areas shown as Buddhist or Islamic on the map practiced other religions.

A Preview of Coming Attractions: Looking Ahead to the Modern Era, 1500–2000

Connections born of empire, culture, and commerce linked many of the peoples in the world of the fifteenth century, but none of them operated on a genuinely global scale. Although the densest webs of connection had been woven within the Afro-Eurasian zone of interaction, this huge region had no sustained ties with the Americas, and neither of them had meaningful contact with the peoples of Pacific Oceania. That situation was about to change as Europeans in the sixteenth century and beyond forged a set of genuinely global relationships that linked all of these regions. That enormous process and the many consequences that flowed from it marked the beginning of what historians commonly call the modern age—the more than five centuries that followed the voyages of Columbus starting in 1492.

Over those five centuries, the previously separate worlds of Afro-Eurasia, the Americas, and Pacific Oceania became inextricably linked, with enormous consequences for everyone involved. Global empires, a global economy, global cultural exchanges, global migrations, global disease, global wars, and global environmental changes have made the past 500 years a unique phase in the human journey. Those webs of communication and exchange have progressively deepened, so much so that by the end of the twentieth century few people in the world lived beyond the cultural influences, economic ties, or political relationships of a globalized world.

A second distinctive feature of the past five centuries involves the emergence of a radically new kind of human society, also called "modern," which took shape first in Europe during the nineteenth century and then in various forms elsewhere in the world. The core feature of such societies was industrialization, rooted in a sustained growth of technological innovation. The human ability to create wealth made an enormous leap forward in a very short period of time, at least by world history standards. Accompanying this economic or industrial revolution was an equally distinctive and unprecedented jump in human numbers, a phenomenon that has affected not only human beings but also many other living species and the earth itself (see the Snapshot).

Modern societies were far more urbanized and much more commercialized than ever before, as more and more people began to work for wages, to produce for the market, and to buy the requirements of daily life rather than growing or making those products for their own use. These societies gave prominence and power to holders of

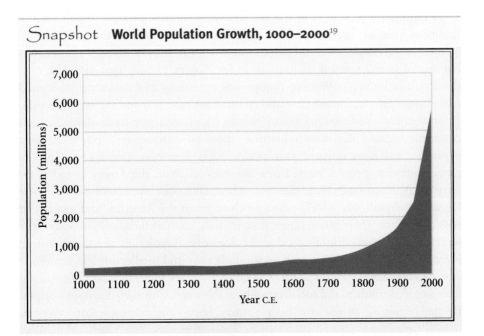

Snapshot   **World Population Growth, 1000–2000**[19]

urban wealth—merchants, bankers, industrialists, educated professionals—at the expense of rural landowning elites, while simultaneously generating a substantial factory working class and diminishing the role of peasants and handicraft artisans.

Modern societies were generally governed by states that were more powerful and intrusive than earlier states and empires had been, and they offered more of their people an opportunity to play an active role in public and political life. Literacy in modern societies was far more widespread than ever before, while new national identities became increasingly prominent, competing with more local loyalties. To the mix of established religious ideas and folk traditions were now added the challenging outlook and values of modern science, with its secular emphasis on the ability of human rationality to know and manipulate the world. Modernity has usually meant a self-conscious awareness of living and thinking in new ways that deliberately departed from tradition.

This revolution of modernity, comparable in its pervasive consequences only to the Agricultural Revolution of some 10,000 years ago, introduced new divisions and new conflicts into the experience of humankind. The ancient tensions between rich and poor within particular societies were now paralleled by new economic inequalities among entire regions and civilizations and a much-altered global balance of power. The first societies to experience the modern transformation—those in Western Europe and North America—became both a threat and a source of envy to much of the rest of the world. As modern societies emerged and spread, they were enormously destructive of older patterns of human life, even as they gave rise to many new ways of living. Sorting out what was gained and what was lost during the modern transformation has been a persistent and highly controversial thread of human thought over the past several centuries.

A third defining feature of the last 500 years was the growing prominence of European peoples on the global stage. In ancient times, the European world, focused in the Mediterranean basin of Greek culture and the Roman Empire, was but one of several classical civilizations in the Eastern Hemisphere. After 500 C.E., the area later known as Western Europe was something of a backwater, compared to the more prosperous and powerful civilizations of China and the Islamic world.

In the centuries following 1500, however, this western peninsula of the Eurasian continent became the most innovative, most prosperous, most powerful, most expansive, and most imitated part of the world. European empires spanned the globe. European peoples created new societies all across the Americas and as far away as Australia and New Zealand. Their languages were spoken and their Christian religion was widely practiced throughout the Americas and in parts of Asia and Africa. Their businessmen bought, sold, and produced goods around the world. It was among Europeans that the Scientific Revolution and the Industrial Revolution first took shape, with enormously powerful intellectual and economic consequences for the entire planet. The quintessentially modern ideas of liberalism, nationalism, feminism, and socialism all bore the imprint of their European origin. By the beginning of the twentieth century, Europeans or peoples of European descent exercised unprecedented influence and control over the earth's many other peoples, a wholly novel experience in human history.

For the rest of the world, growing European dominance posed a common task. Despite their many differences, the peoples of Asia, Africa, the Middle East, the Americas, and Pacific Oceania all found themselves confronted by powerful and intrusive Europeans. The impact of this intrusion and how various peoples responded to it—resistance, submission, acceptance, imitation, adaptation—represent critically important threads in the world history of the past five centuries.

Reflections: What If? Chance and Contingency in World History

Seeking meaning in the stories they tell, historians are inclined to look for deeply rooted or underlying causes for the events they recount. And yet, is it possible that, at least on occasion, history turns less on profound and long-term causes than on coincidence, chance, or the decisions of a few that might well have gone another way?

Consider, for example, the problem of explaining the rise of Europe to a position of global power in the modern era. What if the Great Khan Ogodei had not died in 1241, requiring the forces then poised for an assault on Germany to return to Mongolia? It is surely possible that Central and Western Europe might have been overrun by Mongol armies as so many other civilizations had been, a prospect that could have drastically altered the trajectory of European history. Or what if the Chinese had decided in 1433 to continue their huge maritime expeditions, creating an empire in the Indian Ocean basin and perhaps moving on to "discover" the Americas and Europe? Such a scenario suggests a wholly different future for world history than the one that in fact occurred. Or what if the forces of the Ottoman Empire had taken the besieged city of Vienna in 1529? Might they then have incorporated even larger parts of Europe into their expanding domain, calling a halt to Europe's overseas empire-building enterprise?

None of this necessarily means that the rise of Europe was merely a fluke or an accident of history, but it does raise the issue of "contingency," the role of unforeseen or small events in the unfolding of the human story. An occasional "what if" approach to history reminds us that alternative possibilities existed in the past and that the only certainty about the future is that we will be surprised.

Second Thoughts

What's the Significance?

Paleolithic persistence	Iroquois	Ming dynasty China	To assess your mastery of the material in this chapter, see the **Online Study Guide** at bedfordstmartins.com/strayer.
Benin	Timur	Zheng He	
Igbo	Fulbe	European Renaissance	

Ottoman Empire
seizure of Constantinople
(1453)
Safavid Empire

Songhay Empire
Timbuktu
Mughal Empire
Malacca

Aztec Empire
Inca Empire

Big Picture Questions

1. Assume for the moment that the Chinese had *not* ended their maritime voyages in 1433. How might the subsequent development of world history have been different? Is there value in asking this kind of "what if" or counterfactual question? Or is it an irrelevant waste of time?

2. How does this chapter distinguish among the various kinds of societies that comprised the world of the fifteenth century? Are there other ways of categorizing the world's peoples that might work as well or better?

3. What would surprise a knowledgeable observer from 500 C.E., were he or she to make a global tour in the fifteenth century? What features of that earlier world might still be recognizable?

4. What predictions about the future might a global traveler of the fifteenth century reasonably have made? Would it depend on precisely when those predictions were made?

Next Steps: For Further Study

For Web sites and documents related to this chapter, see **Make History** at bedfordstmartins.com/strayer.

Terence N. D'Altroy, *The Incas* (2002). A history of the Inca Empire that draws on recent archeological and historical research.

Edward L. Dreyer, *Zheng He: China and the Oceans in the Early Ming Dynasty* (2006). The most recent scholarly account of the Ming dynasty voyages.

Halil Inalcik and Donald Quataert, *An Economic and Social History of the Ottoman Empire, 1300–1914* (1994). A classic study of the Ottoman Empire.

Robin Kirkpatrick, *The European Renaissance, 1400–1600* (2002). A beautifully illustrated history of Renaissance culture as well as the social and economic life of the period.

Charles Mann, *1491: New Revelations of the Americas before Columbus* (2005). A review of Western Hemisphere societies and academic debates about their pre-Columbian history.

J. R. McNeill and William H. McNeill, *The Human Web* (2003). A succinct account of the evolving webs or relationships among human societies in world history.

Michael Smith, *The Aztecs* (2003). A history of the Aztec Empire, with an emphasis on the lives of ordinary people.

"Ming Dynasty," http://www.metmuseum.org/toah/hd/ming/hd_ming.htm. A sample of Chinese art from the Ming dynasty from the collection of the Metropolitan Museum of Art.

"Renaissance Art in Italy," http://witcombe.sbc.edu/ARTHrenaissanceitaly.html. An extensive collection of painting and sculpture from the Italian Renaissance.

The Early Modern World

1450–1750

Contents

Debating the Character of an Era

For the sake of clarity and the coherence of the stories they tell, historians often characterize a particular period of time in a brief phrase—the age of First Civilizations, the classical era, the age of empires, the era of revolutions, and so on. Though useful and even necessary, such capsule descriptions leave a lot out and vastly oversimplify what really happened. Historical reality is always more messy, more complicated, and more uncertain than any shorthand description can convey. Such is surely the case when we examine the three centuries spanning the years from roughly 1450 to 1750.

An Early Modern Era?

Those three centuries, which are addressed in Chapters 14 through 16, are conventionally labeled as "the early modern era." In using this term, historians are suggesting that during these three centuries we can find signs or markers of the modern era, such as those described at the end of Chapter 13: the beginnings of genuine globalization, elements of distinctly modern societies, and a growing European presence in world affairs.

The most obvious expression of globalization, of course, lay in the oceanic journeys of European explorers and the European conquest and colonial settlement of the Americas. The Atlantic slave trade linked Africa permanently to the Western Hemisphere, while the global silver trade allowed Europeans to use New World precious metals to buy their way into ancient Asian trade routes. The massive transfer of plants, animals, diseases, and people, known to scholars as the Columbian exchange, created wholly new networks of interaction across both the Atlantic and Pacific oceans, with enormous global implications. Missionaries carried Christianity far beyond Europe, allowing it to become a genuinely world religion, with a presence in the Americas, China, Japan, the Philippines, and south-central Africa. Other threads in the emerging global web were also woven as Russians marched across Siberia to the Pacific, as China expanded deep into Inner Asia, and as the Ottoman Empire encompassed much of the Middle East, North Africa, and southeastern Europe (see Chapter 14).

Scattered signs of what later generations thought of as "modernity" appeared in various places around the world. China, Japan, India, and Europe experienced the beginnings of modern population growth as the foods of the Americas—corn and potatoes, for example—provided nutrition to support larger numbers. World population more than doubled between 1400 and 1800 (from about 374 million to 968 million), even as the globalization of disease produced a demographic catastrophe in the Americas and the slave trade limited African population growth. More highly commercialized economies centered in large cities developed in various parts of Eurasia and the Americas. By the early eighteenth century, for example, Japan was one of the most urbanized societies in the world, with Edo (Tokyo) housing more than a million inhabitants and ranking as the world's largest city. In China, Southeast Asia, India, and across the Atlantic basin, more and more people found themselves, sometimes willingly and at other times involuntarily, producing for distant markets rather than for the use of their local communities.

Stronger and more cohesive states also emerged in various places, incorporating many local societies into larger units that were both able and willing to actively promote trade, manufacturing, and a common culture within their borders. France, the Dutch Republic, Russia, Morocco, the Mughal Empire, Vietnam, Burma, Siam, and Japan all represent this kind of state.[1] Their military power likewise soared as the "gunpowder revolution" kicked in around the world. Large-scale empires proliferated, and various European powers carved out new domains in the Americas. The most obviously modern cultural development took place in Europe, where the Scientific Revolution transformed, at least for members of a small educated elite, their view of the world, their approach to knowledge, and their understanding of traditional Christianity.

A Late Agrarian Era?

All of these developments give some validity to the notion of an early modern era. But this is far from the whole story, and it may be misleading if it suggests that European world domination and more fully modern societies were a "sure thing," an inevitable outgrowth of early modern developments. In fact, that future was far from clear in 1750.

Although Europeans ruled the Americas and controlled the world's sea routes, their political and military power in mainland Asia and Africa was very limited. Eighteenth-century China and Japan strictly controlled the European missionaries and merchants who operated in their societies, and African authorities frequently set the terms under which the slave trade was conducted. Islam, not Christianity, was the most rapidly spreading faith in much of Asia and Africa, and in 1750 Europe, India, and China were roughly comparable in their manufacturing output. In short, it was not obvious that Europeans would soon dominate the planet. Moreover, populations and economies had surged at various points in the past, only to fall back again in a cyclical pattern. Nothing guaranteed that the early modern surge would be any more lasting than the others.

Nor was there much to suggest that anything approaching modern industrial society was on the horizon. Animal and human muscles, wind, and water still provided almost all of the energy that powered human economies. Handicraft techniques of manufacturing had nowhere been displaced by factory-based production or steam power. Long-established elites, not middle-class upstarts, everywhere provided leadership and enjoyed the greatest privileges, while rural peasants, not urban workers, represented the primary social group in the lower classes. Kings and nobles, not parliaments and parties, governed. Male dominance was assumed to be natural almost everywhere. Modern society, with its promise of liberation from ancient inequalities and the end of poverty for most, hardly seemed around the corner.

Most of the world's peoples, in fact, continued to live in long-established ways, and their societies operated according to traditional principles. Kings ruled most of Europe, and landowning aristocrats remained at the top of the social hierarchy. Another change in ruling dynasties occurred in China, while that huge country affirmed Confucian values and a social structure that privileged landowning and officeholding elites. Most Indians practiced some form of Hinduism and owed their most fundamental loyalty to local castes, even as South Asia continued its centuries-long incorporation into the Islamic world. The realm of Islam maintained its central role in the Eastern Hemisphere as the Ottoman Empire revived the political fortunes of Islam and the religion sustained its long-term expansion into Africa and Southeast Asia.

For the majority of humankind, the three centuries between 1450 and 1750 marked less an entry into the modern era than the continuing development of older agrarian societies. It was as much a late agrarian era as an early modern age. Persistent patterns rooted in the past characterized that period, along with new departures and sprouts of modernity. Nor was change always in the direction of what we now regard as "modern." In European, Islamic, and Chinese societies alike, some people urged a return to earlier ways of living and thinking rather than embracing what was new and untried. Although Europeans were increasingly prominent on the world stage, they certainly did not hold all of the leading roles in the global drama of these three centuries.

From this mixture of what was new and what was old during the early modern era, the three chapters that follow highlight the changes. Chapter 14 turns the spotlight on the new empires of those three centuries—European, Middle Eastern, and Asian. New global patterns of long-distance trade in spices, sugar, silver, fur, and slaves represent the themes of Chapter 15. New cultural trends—both within the major religious traditions of the world and in the emergence of modern science—come together in Chapter 16. With the benefit of hindsight, we may see many of these developments as harbingers of a modern world to come, but from the viewpoint of 1700 or so, the future was open and uncertain, as it almost always is.

Landmarks in the Early Modern Era, 1450–1750

1400	1450	1500	1550

Europe

■ **1492** Columbus's first voyage to the Americas

■ **1543** Copernicus publishes heliocentric view of the universe

1400–1600 Renaissance

1400s Portuguese maritime voyages

■ **1517** Beginnings of Protestant Reformation

Africa

■ **1441** Beginnings of Atlantic slave trade

1464–1591 Songhay Empire (West Africa)

■ **1505** Portuguese attacks on Swahili cities

■ **1516** Benin begins to restrict slave trade

1506–1542 Reign of King Afonso (Kongo)

1500–1530 Christian-Muslim conflict in Ethiopia

The Americas

■ **1494** Treaty of Tordesillas divides New World between Spain and Portugal

■ **1541** Discovery of silver near Potosí

1530s First Portuguese plantations in Brazil

1532–1540 Spanish conquest of Inca Empire

1519–1521 Spanish conquest of Aztec Empire

Islamic World

■ **1453** Ottoman conquest of Constantinople

1501–1722 Safavid Empire in Persia

1534–1639 Conflict between Ottoman and Safavid empires

1526–1707 Flourishing of Mughal Empire

1556–1605 Reign of Mughal emporer Akbar

1520–1566 Reign of Ottoman emporer Suleiman

■ **1529** Ottoman siege of Vienna

Asia

■ **1433** Withdrawal of Chinese fleet from Indian Ocean

■ **1498** Vasco da Gama arrives in India

■ **1550** Russian expansion across Siberia begins

■ **1582** Jesuit missionary Matteo Ricci arrives in China

■ **1565** Spanish takeover of Philippines begins

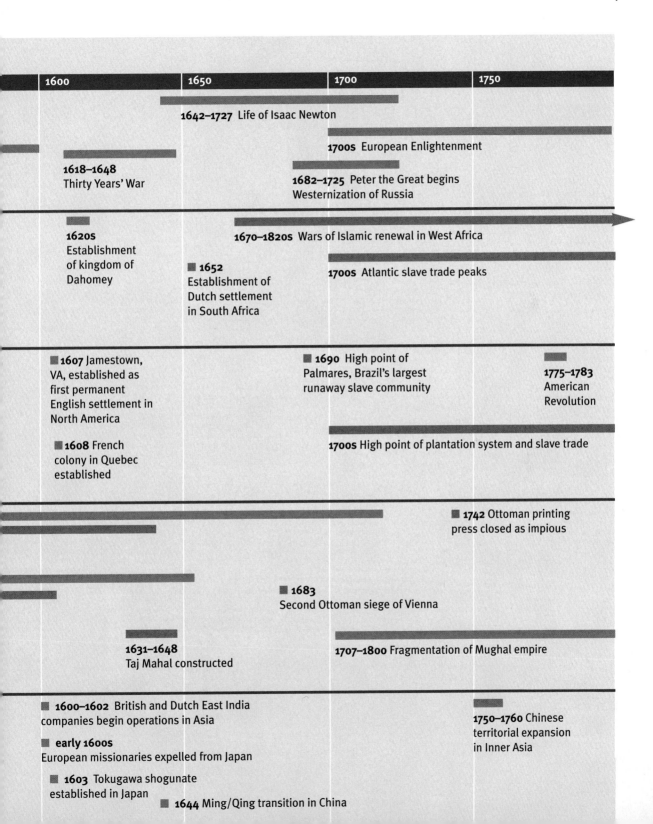

1600   1650   1700   1750

1642–1727 Life of Isaac Newton

1700s European Enlightenment

1618–1648
Thirty Years' War

1682–1725 Peter the Great begins
Westernization of Russia

1620s
Establishment
of kingdom of
Dahomey

1670–1820s Wars of Islamic renewal in West Africa

1652
Establishment of
Dutch settlement
in South Africa

1700s Atlantic slave trade peaks

1607 Jamestown,
VA, established as
first permanent
English settlement in
North America

1690 High point of
Palmares, Brazil's largest
runaway slave community

1775–1783
American
Revolution

1608 French
colony in Quebec
established

1700s High point of plantation system and slave trade

1742 Ottoman printing
press closed as impious

1683
Second Ottoman siege of Vienna

1631–1648
Taj Mahal constructed

1707–1800 Fragmentation of Mughal empire

1600–1602 British and Dutch East India
companies begin operations in Asia

1750–1760 Chinese
territorial expansion
in Inner Asia

early 1600s
European missionaries expelled from Japan

1603 Tokugawa shogunate
established in Japan

1644 Ming/Qing transition in China

Empires and Encounters

1450-1750

"We will not yield to the Chinese authorities, no matter what brutal means they will take against us. We are preparing our fight."[1] So stated Muhammet Tursun, a forty-year-old Uighur businessman from the far western province of China known as Xinjiang, in 1999. That territory had been brought under Chinese control in the early eighteenth century as part of a huge expansion of China's imperial state. Now in the late twentieth and early twenty-first centuries, some Uighurs were seeking independence from what they regarded as centuries of Chinese colonial rule. Nor was this the only echo of early modern empire building to find expression in recent times. The breakup of the Soviet Union in 1991 represented the partial end of the Russian Empire, which was initially constructed in the sixteenth and seventeenth centuries. In 1992, many Native Americans strenuously objected to any celebration of the 500th anniversary of Columbus's arrival in the Americas. Winona LaDuke, president of the Indigenous Women's Network, declared: "Columbus was a perpetrator of genocide..., a slave trader, a thief, a pirate, and most certainly not a hero. To celebrate Columbus is to congratulate the process and history of the invasion."[2]

IN CHINA, RUSSIA, AND THE UNITED STATES ALIKE, the legacy of early modern empire building continued to provoke both debate and action as a new millennium dawned. Of those empires, none were more significant than the European colonies—Spanish, Portuguese, British, French, and Dutch—constructed all across the Western Hemisphere.

The Mughal Empire: Among the most magnificent of the early modern empires was that of the Mughals in India. In this painting by an unknown Mughal artist, the seventeenth-century emperor Shah Jahan is holding a *durbar*, or ceremonial assembly, in the audience hall of his palace. The overall material splendor of the setting shows the immense wealth of the court, while the halo around Shah Jahan's head indicates the special spiritual grace or enlightenment associated with emperors. (© British Library Board, Add or 385)

Within those empires, vast transformations took place, old societies were destroyed, and new societies arose as indigenous peoples, Europeans, and Africans came into sustained contact with one another for the first time in world history. It was a revolutionary encounter with implications that extended far beyond the Americas themselves.

But European empires in the Americas were not alone on the imperial stage of the early modern era. Across the immense expanse of Siberia, the Russians constructed what was then the world's largest territorial empire, making Russia an Asian as well as a European power. Qing dynasty China penetrated deep into Inner Asia, doubling the size of the country while incorporating millions of non-Chinese people who practiced Islam, Buddhism, or animistic religions. On the South Asian peninsula, the Islamic Mughal Empire brought Hindus and Muslims into a closer relationship than ever before, sometimes quite peacefully and at other times with great conflict. In the Middle East, the Turkish Ottoman Empire reestablished something of the earlier political unity of heartland Islam and posed an ominous military and religious threat to European Christendom.

Thus the early modern era was an age of empire. Within their borders, those empires mixed and mingled diverse peoples in a wide variety of ways. Those relationships represented a new stage in the globalization process and new arenas of cross-cultural encounter. The transformations they set in motion echo still in the twenty-first century.

European Empires in the Americas

Among the early modern empires, those of Western Europe were distinctive because they were initiated by maritime expansion and because the conquered territories lay an ocean away from the imperial heartland, rather than adjacent to it. Following the breakthrough voyages of Columbus, the Spanish focused their empire-building efforts in the Caribbean and then in the early sixteenth century turned to the mainland, with stunning conquests of the powerful Aztec and Inca empires. Meanwhile the Portuguese established themselves along the coast of present-day Brazil. In the early seventeenth century, the British, French, and Dutch launched colonial settlements along the eastern coast of North America. From these beginnings, Europeans extended their empires to encompass most of the Americas, at least nominally, by the mid-eighteenth century (see Map 14.1). It was a remarkable achievement. What had made it possible?

The European Advantage

■ Connection
What enabled Europeans to carve out huge empires an ocean away from their homelands?

Geography provides a starting point for explaining Europe's American empires. It was countries on the Atlantic rim of Europe (Portugal, Spain, Britain, and France) that led the way to empire in the Western Hemisphere. They were simply closer to the Americas than was any possible Asian competitor. Furthermore, the fixed winds of the Atlantic blew steadily in the same direction. Once these air currents were understood

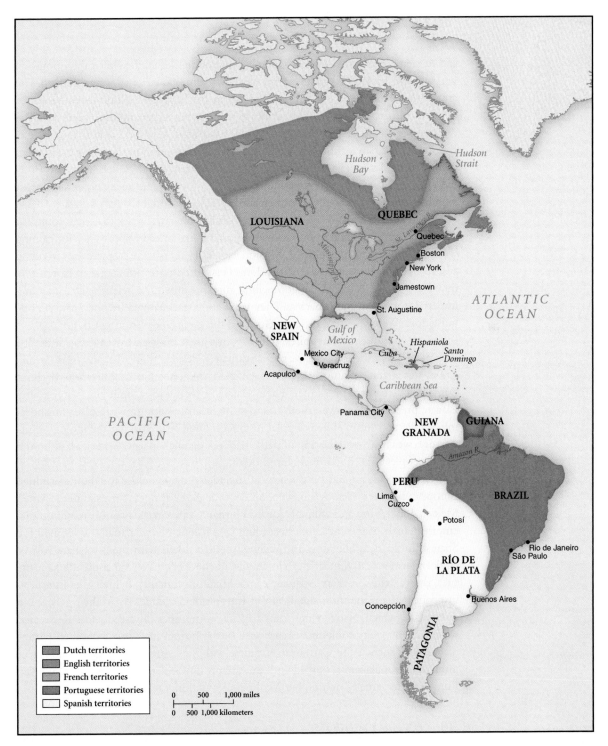

Map 14.1 **European Colonial Empires in the Americas**
By the beginning of the eighteenth century, European powers had laid claim to most of the Western Hemisphere. Their wars and rivalries during that century led to an expansion of Spanish and English claims, at the expense of the French.

and mastered, they provided a far different environment than the alternating monsoon winds of the Indian Ocean, in which Asian maritime powers had long operated. The enormously rich markets of the Indian Ocean world provided little incentive for its Chinese, Indian, or Muslim participants to venture much beyond their own waters.

Europeans, however, were powerfully motivated to do so. After 1200 or so, Europeans were increasingly aware of their marginal position in the world of Eurasian commerce and were determined to gain access to that world. Rulers were driven by the enduring rivalries of competing states. The growing and relatively independent merchant class in a rapidly commercializing Europe sought direct access to Asian wealth in order to avoid the reliance on Muslim intermediaries that they found so distasteful. Impoverished nobles and commoners alike found opportunity for gaining wealth and status in the colonies. Missionaries and others were inspired by crusading zeal to enlarge the realm of Christendom. Persecuted minorities were in search of a new start in life. All of these compelling motives drove the relentlessly expanding imperial frontier in the Americas. They were aptly summarized by one Spanish con-quistador: "We came here to serve God and the King, and also to get rich."[3]

In carving out these empires, often against great odds and with great difficulty, Europeans nonetheless bore certain advantages, despite their distance from home. Their states and trading companies enabled the effective mobilization of both human and material resources. Their seafaring technology, built on Chinese and Islamic precedents, allowed them to cross the Atlantic with growing ease, transport-ing people and supplies across great distances. Their ironworking technology, gun-powder weapons, and horses initially had no parallel in the Americas, although many peoples subsequently acquired them.

Divisions within and between local societies provided allies for the determined European invaders. Various subject peoples of the Aztec Empire, for example, resented Mexica domination and willingly joined Hernán Cortés in the Spanish assault on that empire. Much of the Inca elite, according to a recent study, "actually welcomed the Spanish invaders as liberators and willingly settled down with them to share rule of Andean farmers and miners."[4] A violent dispute between two rival contenders for the Inca throne, the brothers Atahualpa and Huáscar, certainly helped the European invaders. Perhaps the most significant of European advantages lay in their germs and diseases, to which Native Americans had no immunities. Those diseases decimated society after society, sometimes in advance of the Europeans' actual arrival. In partic-ular regions such as the Caribbean, Virginia, and New England, the rapid buildup of immigrant populations, coupled with the sharply diminished native numbers, allowed Europeans to actually outnumber local peoples within a few decades.

■ Change

What large-scale transformations did European empires generate?

The Great Dying

Whatever combination of factors explains the European acquisition of their empires in the Americas, there is no doubting their global significance. Chief among those consequences was the demographic collapse of Native American societies, a phenomenon that one prominent scholar described as "surely the greatest tragedy in the history of the human species."[5] Although precise figures remain the subject of much debate, scholars generally agree that the pre-Columbian population of the Western Hemisphere was substantial, on the order of that of Europe, perhaps 60 million to 80 million. The greatest concentrations of people lived in the Mesoamerican and Andean zones, which were dominated by the Aztec and Inca empires. Long isolation from the Afro-Eurasian world and the lack of most domesticated animals meant the absence of acquired immunities to Old World diseases, such as smallpox, measles, typhus, influenza, malaria, and yellow fever.

Therefore, when they came into contact with these European and African diseases, Native American peoples died in appalling numbers, in many cases up to 90 percent of the population. The densely settled peoples of Caribbean islands virtually vanished within fifty years of Columbus's arrival. Central Mexico, with a population estimated at some 10 million to 20 million, declined to about 1 million by 1650. A native Nahuatl account depicted the social breakdown that accompanied the smallpox pandemic: "A great many died from this plague, and many others died of hunger. They could not get up to search for food, and everyone else was too sick to care for them, so they starved to death in their beds."[6]

The situation was similar in North America. A Dutch observer in New Netherlands (later New York) reported in 1656 that "the Indians…affirm that before the arrival of the Christians, and before the small pox broke out amongst them, they were ten times as numerous as they are now, and that their population had been melted down by this disease, whereof nine-tenths of them have died."[7] To Governor Bradford of Plymouth colony (in present-day Massachusetts), such conditions represented the "good hand of God" at work, "sweeping away great multitudes of the natives…that he might make room for us."[8] Not until the late seventeenth century did native numbers begin to recuperate somewhat from this catastrophe, and even then not everywhere.

The Columbian Exchange

In sharply diminishing the population of the Americas, this "great dying" created an acute labor shortage and certainly did make room for immigrant newcomers, both colonizing Europeans and enslaved Africans. Over the several centuries of the colonial era and beyond, various combinations of indigenous, European, and African peoples created entirely new societies in the Americas, largely replacing the many and varied cultures that had flourished before 1492. To those colonial societies, Europeans and Africans brought not only their germs and their people but also their plants and animals. Wheat, rice, sugarcane, grapes, and many garden vegetables and fruits, as well as numerous weeds, took hold in the Americas, where they transformed the landscape and made possible a recognizably European diet and way of life. Even more revolutionary were their animals — horses, pigs, cattle, goats, sheep — all of which were new to the Americas and multiplied spectacularly in an environment largely free of natural predators. These domesticated animals made possible the ranching economies, the cowboy cultures, and the transformation of many Native American societies that were seen in both North and South America. Environmentally speaking, it was nothing less than revolutionary.

In the other direction, American food crops such as corn, potatoes, and cassava spread widely in the Eastern Hemisphere, where they provided the nutritional foundation for the immense population growth that became everywhere a hallmark of the modern era. In Europe, calories derived from corn and potatoes helped push human numbers from some 60 million in 1400 to 390 million in 1900. Those Amerindian crops later provided cheap and reasonably nutritious food for millions of industrial workers. Potatoes especially allowed Ireland's population to grow enormously and then condemned many of them to starvation or emigration when an airborne fungus, also from the Americas, destroyed the crop in the mid-nineteenth century. In China, corn, peanuts, and especially sweet potatoes supplemented the traditional rice and wheat to sustain China's modern population explosion. By the early twentieth century, American food plants represented about 20 percent of total Chinese food production. In Africa, corn took hold quickly and was used as a cheap food for the human cargoes of the transatlantic trade. Scholars have speculated that corn, together with peanuts and cassava, underwrote some of Africa's population growth and partially offset the population drain of the slave trade. Never before in human history had such a large-scale and consequential exchange of plants and animals operated to remake the biological environment of the planet.

Furthermore, the societies that developed within the American colonies drove the processes of globalization and reshaped the world economy of the early modern era (see Chapter 15 for a more extended treatment). The silver mines of Mexico and Peru fueled both transatlantic and transpacific commerce,

Plants and Animals of the Columbian Exchange
This eighteenth-century Peruvian painting illustrates two of the many biological species that crossed the Atlantic. Cattle from Europe flourished in the Americas, while cassava (also known as manioc), shown in the bottom of the picture, was native to South America but spread widely in Asia, and especially Africa, where its edible root provided a major source of carbohydrates. (Martinez Campañon, Trujillo del Peru, v. II, courtesy of the Biblioteca del Palacio Real/Oronoz Archives)

encouraged Spain's unsuccessful effort to dominate Europe, and enabled Europeans to buy the Chinese tea, silk, and porcelain that they valued so highly. The plantation owners of the tropical lowland regions needed workers and found them by the millions in Africa. The slave trade, which brought these workers to the colonies, and the sugar and cotton trade, which distributed the fruits of their labor abroad, created a lasting link among Africa, Europe, and the Americas, while scattering peoples of African origin throughout the Western Hemisphere.

This enormous network of communication, migration, trade, the spread of disease, and the transfer of plants and animals, all generated by European colonial empires in the Americas, has been dubbed "the Columbian exchange." It gave rise to something wholly new in world history: an interacting Atlantic world connecting four continents. Millions of years ago, the Eastern and Western hemispheres had physically drifted apart, and, ecologically speaking, they had remained largely apart. Now these two "old worlds" were joined, increasingly creating a single biological regime, a "new world" of global dimensions.

The long-term benefits of this Atlantic network were very unequally distributed. Western Europeans were clearly the dominant players in the Atlantic world, and their societies reaped the greatest rewards. Mountains of new information flooded into Europe, shaking up conventional understandings of the world and contributing to a revolutionary new way of thinking known as the Scientific Revolution. The wealth of the colonies—precious metals, natural resources, new food crops, slave labor, financial profits, colonial markets—provided one of the foundations on which Europe's Industrial Revolution was built. The colonies also provided an outlet for the rapidly growing population of European societies and represented an enormous extension of European civilization. In short, the colonial empires of the Americas greatly facilitated a changing global balance of power, which now thrust the previously marginal Western Europeans into an increasingly central and commanding role on the world stage. "[W]ithout a New World to deliver economic balance in the Old," concluded a prominent world historian, "Europe would have remained inferior, as ever, in wealth and power, to the great civilizations of Asia."[9]

Comparing Colonial Societies in the Americas

What the Europeans had discovered across the Atlantic was a second "old world," but their actions surely gave rise to a "new world" in the Americas. Their colonial empires did not simply conquer and govern established societies but rather generated wholly new societies. In at least one respect, these various colonial empires— Spanish, Portuguese, British, and French—had something in common. Each of them was viewed through the lens of the prevailing economic theory known as mercantilism. This view held that European governments served their countries' economic interests best by encouraging exports and accumulating bullion (precious metals such as silver and gold), which were believed to be the source of national prosperity. Colonies, in this scheme of things, provided closed markets for the manufactured goods of the "mother country" and, if they were lucky, supplied great quantities of bullion as well.

Beyond this shared mercantilism, though, the various colonial societies that grew up in the Americas differed sharply from one another, varying with the cultures and policies of the colonizing power. The character of the Native American cultures—the more densely populated and urbanized Mesoamerican and Andean civilizations versus the more sparsely populated rural villages of North America, for example—also shaped the new colonial societies. The kind of economy established in particular regions—settler-dominated agriculture, slave-based plantations, ranching, or mining—likewise influenced their development. Three examples indicate the differences among these new colonial societies.

In the Lands of the Aztecs and the Incas

■ Change

What was the economic foundation of colonial rule in Mexico and Peru? How did it shape the kinds of societies that arose there?

The Spanish conquest of the Aztec and Inca empires in the early sixteenth century gave Spain access to the most wealthy, urbanized, and densely populated regions of the Western Hemisphere. Within a century and well before the British had even begun their colonizing efforts in North America, the Spanish in Mexico and Peru had established nearly a dozen major cities; several impressive universities; hundreds of cathedrals, churches, and missions; an elaborate administrative bureaucracy; and a network of regulated international commerce. The economic foundation for this emerging colonial society lay in commercial agriculture, much of it on large rural estates, and in silver and gold mining. In both cases, native peoples, rather than African slaves or European workers, provided the labor, despite their much-diminished numbers. Almost everywhere it was forced labor, often directly required by colonial authorities. The loss of land to European settlers represented another incentive for wage labor, as did the growing need to repay debts to employers.

On this economic base, a distinctive social order grew up, replicating something of the Spanish class hierarchy while accommodating the racially and culturally different Indians and Africans as well as growing numbers of racially mixed people. At the top of this colonial society were the Spanish settlers, who were politically and economically dominant and seeking to become a landed aristocracy. One Spanish official commented in 1619: "The Spaniards, from the able and rich to the humble and poor, all hold themselves to be lords and will not serve [do manual labor]."[10] Politically, they increasingly saw themselves, not as colonials, but as residents of a Spanish kingdom, subject to the Spanish monarch, yet separate and distinct from Spain itself and deserving of a large measure of self-government. Therefore, they chafed under the heavy bureaucratic restrictions imposed by the Crown. "I obey but I do not enforce" was a slogan that reflected local authorities' resistance to orders from Spain.

But the Spanish minority, never more than 20 percent of the population, was itself a divided community. Descendants of the original *conquistadores* sought to protect their privileges against immigrant newcomers; Spaniards born in the Americas (creoles) resented the pretensions to superiority of those born in Spain (*peninsulares*); landowning Spaniards felt threatened by the growing wealth of commercial and mercantile groups practicing less prestigious occupations. Spanish missionaries and church authorities were often sharply critical of how these settlers treated native peoples. "By what right…do you keep these Indians in such a cruel and horrible servitude?" demanded a Dominican priest in 1511 to a Spanish audience in Santo Domingo that included the son of Columbus himself. "Why do you keep those who survive so oppressed and weary, not giving them enough to eat, not caring for them in their illness?"[11]

The most distinctive feature of these new colonial societies in Mexico and Peru was the emergence of a *mestizo*, or mixed-race, population, the product of unions between Spanish men and Indian women. Rooted in the sexual imbalance among Spanish immigrants (seven men to one woman in early colonial Peru, for example), the emergence of a mestizo population was facilitated by the desire of many surviving Indian women for the relative security of life in a Spanish household, where their children would not be subject to the abuse and harsh demands made on native peoples. The Spanish Crown encouraged settlers to marry into elite Indian families, and Cortés, the conqueror of Mexico, fathered children with two of Moctezuma's daughters. Over the 300 years of the colonial era, mestizo numbers grew substantially, becoming the majority of the population in Mexico sometime during the nineteenth century.

Mestizos were largely Hispanic in culture, but Spaniards looked down on them during much of the colonial era, regarding them as illegitimate, for many were not born of "proper" marriages. Despite this attitude, their growing numbers and their economic usefulness as artisans, clerks, supervisors of labor gangs, and lower-level officials in both church and state bureaucracies led to their recognition as a distinct social group. Particularly in Mexico, mestizo

Mestizos

This eighteenth-century painting by the famous Zapotec artist Miguel Cabrera shows a Spanish man, a Native American woman, and their child, who was termed a *mestizo* in Mexico. By the twentieth century, such mixed-race mestizos represented the majority of the population of Mexico, and cultural blending had become a central feature of the country's identity. (Scala/Art Resource, NY) identity blurred the sense of sharp racial difference between Spanish and Indian peoples and became a major element in the identity of modern Mexico.

At the bottom of Mexican and Peruvian colonial societies were the indigenous peoples, known to Europeans as "Indians." Traumatized by "the great dying," they were subject to gross abuse and exploitation as the primary labor force for the mines and estates of the Spanish Empire and were required to render tribute payments to their Spanish overlords. Their empires dismantled by Spanish conquest, their religions attacked by Spanish missionaries, and their diminished numbers forcibly relocated into larger settlements, many Indians gravitated toward the world of their conquerors. Many learned Spanish; converted to Christianity; moved to cities to work for wages; ate the meat of cows, chickens, and pigs; used plows and draft animals rather than traditional digging sticks; and took their many grievances to Spanish courts.

But much that was native persisted. At the local level, Indian authorities retained a measure of autonomy, and traditional markets operated regularly. Maize, beans, and squash continued as the major elements of Indian diets in Mexico. Christian saints in many places blended easily with specialized indigenous gods, while belief in magic, folk medicine, and communion with the dead remained strong. Memories of the past also persisted, and the Tupac Amaru revolt in Peru during 1780–1781 was made in the name of the last independent Inca emperor.

Thus Spaniards, mestizos, and Indians represented the major social groups in the colonial lands of what had been the Inca and Aztec empires, while African slaves and freemen were far less numerous than elsewhere in the Americas. Despite the sharp divisions among these groups, some movement was possible. Indians who acquired an education, wealth, and some European culture might "pass" as mestizo. Likewise more fortunate mestizo families might be accepted as Spaniards over time. Colonial Spanish America was a vast laboratory of ethnic mixing and cultural change. It was dominated by Europeans to be sure, but with a rather more fluid and culturally blended society than in the racially rigid colonies of North America.

Colonies of Sugar

■ Comparison
How did the plantation societies of Brazil and the Caribbean differ from those of southern colonies in British North America?

A second and quite different kind of colonial society emerged in the lowland areas of Brazil, ruled by Portugal, and in the Spanish, British, French, and Dutch colonies in the Caribbean. These regions lacked the great civilizations of Mexico and Peru. Nor did they provide much mineral wealth until the Brazilian gold rush of the 1690s and the discovery of diamonds a little later. Still, Europeans found a very profitable substitute in sugar, which was much in demand in Europe, where it was used as a medicine, a spice, a sweetener, a preservative, and in sculptured forms as a decoration that indicated high status. Although commercial agriculture in the Spanish Empire served a domestic market in its towns and mining camps, these sugar-based colonies produced almost exclusively for export, while importing their food and other necessities.

Large-scale sugar production had been pioneered by Arabs, who introduced it into the Mediterranean. Europeans learned the technique and transferred it to their Atlantic island possessions and then to the Americas. For a century (1570–1670), Portuguese planters along the northeast coast of Brazil dominated the world market for sugar. Then the British, French, and Dutch turned their Caribbean territories into highly productive sugar-producing colonies, breaking the Portuguese and Brazilian monopoly.

Sugar decisively transformed Brazil and the Caribbean. Its production, which involved both growing the sugarcane and processing it into usable sugar, was very labor intensive and could most profitably occur in a large-scale, almost industrial setting. It was perhaps the first modern industry in that it produced for an international and mass market, using capital and expertise from Europe, with production facilities located in the Americas. However, its most characteristic feature—the massive use of slave labor—was an ancient practice. In the absence of a Native American population, which had been almost totally wiped out in the Caribbean or had fled inland in Brazil, European sugarcane planters turned to Africa and the Atlantic slave trade for an alternative workforce. The vast majority of the African captives transported across the Atlantic, some 80 percent or more, ended up in Brazil and the Caribbean.

Plantation Life in the Caribbean
This painting from 1823 shows the use of slave labor on a plantation in Antigua, a British-ruled island in the Caribbean. Notice the overseer with a whip supervising the tilling and planting of the field. (British Library/HIP/Art Resource, NY)

Snapshot **Ethnic Composition in Colonial Societies in Latin America (1825)**[12]

	Highland Spanish America	Portuguese America (Brazil)
Europeans	18.2 percent	23.4 percent
Mixed-race	28.3 percent	17.8 percent
Africans	11.9 percent	49.8 percent
Native Americans	41.7 percent	9.1 percent

Slaves worked on sugar-producing estates in horrendous conditions. The heat and fire from the cauldrons, which turned raw sugarcane into crystallized sugar, reminded many visitors of scenes from hell. These conditions, combined with disease, generated a high death rate, perhaps 5 to 10 percent per year, which required plantation owners to constantly import fresh slaves. A Jesuit observer in 1580 aptly summarized the situation: "The work is great and many die."[13]

The extensive use of African slave labor gave these plantation colonies a very different ethnic and racial makeup than that of highland Spanish America, as the Snapshot indicates. Thus, after three centuries of colonial rule, a substantial majority of Brazil's population was either partially or wholly of African descent. In the French Caribbean colony of Haiti in 1790, the corresponding figure was 93 percent.

As in Spanish America, a considerable amount of racial mixing took place in Brazil. Cross-racial unions accounted for only about 10 percent of all marriages in Brazil, but the use of concubines and informal liaisons among Indians, Africans, and Portuguese produced a substantial mixed-race population. From their ranks derived much of the urban skilled workforce and supervisors in the sugar industry. *Mulattoes*, the product of Portuguese-African unions, predominated, but as many as forty separate and named groups, each indicating a different racial mixture, emerged in colonial Brazil.

The plantation complex of the Americas, based on African slavery, extended beyond the Caribbean and Brazil to encompass the southern colonies of British North America, where tobacco, cotton, rice, and indigo were major crops, but the social outcomes of these plantation colonies were quite different than those farther south. Because European women had joined the colonial migration to North America at an early date, these colonies experienced less racial mixing and certainly demonstrated less willingness to recognize the offspring of such unions and accord them a place in society. A sharply defined racial system (with black Africans, red Native Americans, and white Europeans) evolved in North America, whereas both Portuguese and Spanish colonies acknowledged a wide variety of mixed-race groups.

Slavery too was different, being perhaps less harsh in North America than in the sugar colonies. By 1750 or so, slaves in the United States had become self-reproducing, and a century later almost all North American slaves had been born in the New World. That was never the case in Latin America, where importation of new slaves continued well into the nineteenth century. Brazilian slave owners in fact calculated the useful life of their slaves at just seven years. Nonetheless, many more slaves were voluntarily set free by their owners in Brazil than was ever the case in North America, and free blacks and mulattoes in Brazil had far greater opportunities than did their counterparts in North America. At least a few among them found positions as political leaders, scholars, musicians, writers, and artists. Some were even hired as slave catchers.

Does this mean then that racism was absent in colonial Brazil? Certainly not, but it was different than in North America. For one thing, in North America, any African ancestry, no matter how small or distant, made a person "black"; in Brazil, a person of African and non-African ancestry was considered, not black, but some other mixed-race category. Racial prejudice clearly existed in the sense that white characteristics and features were prized more highly than those of blacks, and people regarded as white had enormously greater privileges and opportunities than others. Nevertheless, color in Brazil, and in Latin America generally, was only one criterion of class status, and the perception of color changed with the educational or economic standing of individuals. A light-skinned mulatto who had acquired some wealth or education might well "pass" as a white. One curious visitor to Brazil expressed surprise upon finding a darker-skinned man serving as a local official. "Isn't the governor a mulatto?" inquired the visitor. "He was, but he isn't any more," was the reply. "How can a governor be a mulatto?"[14]

Settler Colonies in North America

A third and distinctive type of colonial society emerged in the northern British colonies of New England, New York, and Pennsylvania. Because the British were the last of the European powers to establish a colonial presence in the Americas, a full century after Spain, they found that "only the dregs were left."[15] The lands they acquired were widely regarded in Europe as the unpromising leftovers of the New World, lacking the obvious wealth and sophisticated cultures of the Spanish possessions. Until at least the eighteenth century, these British colonies remained far less prominent on the world stage than those of Spain or Portugal.

■ Comparison
What distinguished the British settler colonies of North America from their counterparts in Latin America?

The British settlers came from a more rapidly changing society than did those from an ardently Catholic, semifeudal, authoritarian Spain. When Britain launched its colonial ventures in the seventeenth century, it had already experienced considerable conflict between Catholics and Protestants, the rise of a merchant capitalist class, the growth of a major cloth industry, the emergence of parliament as a check on the authority of kings, and the breakdown of feudalism in general.

Although they brought much of their English culture with them, many of the British settlers—Puritans in Massachusetts and Quakers in Pennsylvania, for example—sought to escape aspects of an old European society rather than to re-create it, as was the case for most Spanish and Portuguese colonists. The easy availability of land, the climate and geography of North America, and the "outsider" status of many British settlers made it even more difficult to follow the Spanish or Portuguese colonial pattern of sharp class hierarchy, large rural estates, and dependent laborers.

The British settlers also were far more numerous. By 1750, they outnumbered Spanish settlers by five to one. This disparity was the most obvious distinguishing feature of the New England and middle Atlantic colonies. By the time of the American Revolution, some 90 percent or more of these colonies' populations were Europeans. Devastating diseases and a highly aggressive military policy had largely cleared the colonies of Native Americans, and their numbers did not rebound in subsequent centuries as they did in the lands of the Aztecs and the Incas. Moreover, slaves were not needed in an agricultural economy dominated by numerous small-scale independent farmers working their own land, although elite families, especially in urban areas, sometimes employed household slaves. These were almost pure settler colonies, without the racial mixing that was so prominent in Spanish and Portuguese territories.

Other differences likewise emerged. A largely Protestant England was far less interested in spreading Christianity among the remaining native peoples than were the large and well-funded missionary societies of Catholic Spain. Although religion loomed large in the North American colonies, the church and colonial state were not so intimately connected as they were in Latin America. The Protestant emphasis on reading the Bible for oneself led to a much greater mass literacy than in Latin America, where three centuries of church education still left some 95 percent of the population illiterate at independence. Furthermore, far more so than in Latin America, British settler colonies evolved traditions of local self-government. Preferring to rely on joint stock companies or wealthy individuals operating under a royal charter, Britain had nothing resembling the elaborate bureaucracy that governed Spanish colonies. For much of the seventeenth century, a prolonged power struggle between the English king and parliament meant that the British government paid little attention to the internal affairs of the colonies. Therefore, elected colonial assemblies, seeing themselves as little parliaments defending "the rights of Englishmen," vigorously contested the prerogatives of royal governors sent to administer their affairs.

The grand irony of the modern history of the Americas lay in the reversal of long-established relationships between the northern and southern continents. For thousands of years, the major centers of wealth, power, commerce, and innovation lay in Mesoamerica and the Andes. That pattern continued for much of the colonial era, as the Spanish and Portuguese colonies seemed far more prosperous and successful than their British or French counterparts. In the nineteenth and twentieth centuries, however, the balance shifted. What had once been the "dregs" of the colonial world became the United States, which was more politically stable, more democratic, more economically successful, and more internationally powerful than a divided, unstable, and economically less developed Latin America.

The Steppes and Siberia: The Making of a Russian Empire

At the same time as Western Europeans were building their empires in the Americas, the Russian Empire, which subsequently became the world's largest state, was beginning to take shape. When Columbus crossed the Atlantic, a small Russian state, centered on the city of Moscow, was emerging from two centuries of Mongol rule. That state soon conquered a number of neighboring Russian-speaking cities and incorporated them into its expanding territory. Located on the remote, cold, and heavily forested eastern fringe of Christendom, it was perhaps an unlikely candidate for constructing one of the great empires of the modern era. And yet, over the next three centuries, it did precisely that, extending Russian domination over the vast tundra, forests, and grasslands of northern Asia that lay to the south and east of Moscow. Furthermore, Russian expansion westward brought numerous Poles, Germans, Ukrainians, Belorussians, and Baltic peoples into the Russian Empire.

■ **Description**
What motivated Russian empire building?

Russian attention was drawn first to the grasslands south and east of the Russian heartland, which had long been inhabited by various nomadic pastoral peoples, who were organized in feuding tribes and clans and adjusting to the recent disappearance of the Mongol Empire. From the viewpoint of the emerging Russian state, the problem was security because these pastoral peoples, like the Mongols before them, frequently raided their agricultural Russian neighbors and sold many of them into slavery. To the east across the vast expanse of Siberia, Russian motives were quite different, for the scattered peoples of its endless forests and tundra posed no threat to Russia. Numbering only some 220,000 in the seventeenth century and speaking more than 100 languages, they were mostly hunting, gathering, and herding people, living in small-scale societies and largely without access to gunpowder weapons. What drew the Russians across Siberia was opportunity—found primarily in the "soft gold" of fur-bearing animals, whose pelts were in great demand on the world market.

Whatever motives drove it, the enormous Russian Empire, stretching to the Pacific, took shape in the three centuries between 1500 and 1800 (see Map 14.2). A growing line of wooden forts offered protection to frontier towns and trading centers as well as to mounting numbers of Russian farmers. Empire building was an extended process, involving the Russian state and its officials as well as a variety of private interests—merchants, hunters, peasant agricultural settlers, churchmen, exiles, criminals, and adventurers. For the Russian migrants to these new lands, the

Map 14.2   The Russian Empire

From its beginnings as a small principality under Mongol control, Moscow became the center of a vast Russian Empire during the early modern era.

empire offered "economic and social improvements over what they had known at home—from more and better land to fewer lords and officials."[16] Political leaders and educated Russians generally defined the empire in grander terms: defending Russian frontiers; enhancing the power of the Russian state; and bringing Christianity, civilization, and enlightenment to savages. But what did that empire mean to those on its receiving end?

Experiencing the Russian Empire

■ **Change**

How did the Russian Empire transform the life of its conquered people and of the Russian homeland itself?

First, of course, creating an empire meant conquest, based on the precedent of Mongol domination. Although resistance was frequent, especially from nomadic peoples, in the long run Russian military might, based in modern weaponry and the organizational capacity of a powerful state, brought both the steppes and Siberia under Russian control. Everywhere Russian authorities demanded an oath of allegiance by which native peoples swore "eternal submission to the grand tsar," the monarch of the Russian Empire. They also demanded *yasak*, or tribute, paid in cash or in kind. In Siberia, this meant enormous quantities of furs, especially the extremely valuable sable, which Siberian peoples were compelled to produce. As in the Americas, devastating epidemics accompanied conquest, particularly in the more remote regions of Siberia, where local people had little immunity to smallpox or measles. Also accompanying conquest was an intermittent pressure to convert to Christianity. Tax breaks, exemptions from paying tribute, and the promise of land or cash provided incentives for conversion, while the destruction of many mosques and the forced resettlement of Muslims added to the pressures. Yet the Russian state did not pursue conversion with the single-minded intensity that Spanish authorities exercised in Latin America, particularly if missionary activity threatened political and social stability. The empress Catherine the Great, for example, established religious tolerance for Muslims in the late eighteenth century and created a state agency to oversee Muslim affairs.

The most profoundly transforming feature of the Russian Empire was the influx of Russian settlers, whose numbers by the end of the eighteenth century overwhelmed native peoples, thus giving their lands a distinctively Russian character. By 1720, some 700,000 Russians lived in Siberia, thus reducing the native Siberians to 30 percent of the total population, a figure that dropped to 14 percent in the nineteenth century. The loss of hunting grounds and pasturelands to Russian agricultural settlers undermined long-standing economies and rendered local people dependent on Russian markets for grain, sugar, tea, tobacco, and alcohol. Pressures to encourage pastoralists to abandon their nomadic ways included the requirement to pay fees and to obtain permission to cross agricultural lands. Kazakh herders responded with outrage: "The grass and the water belong to Heaven, and why should we pay any fees?"[17] Intermarriage, prostitution, and sexual abuse resulted in some mixed-race offspring, but these were generally absorbed as Russians rather than identified as distinctive communities, as happened in Latin America.

Over the course of three centuries, both Siberia and the steppes were incorporated into the Russian state. Their native peoples were not driven into reservations or eradicated as in the

A Cossack Jail
In the vanguard of Russian expansion across Siberia were the Cossacks, bands of fiercely independent warriors consisting of peasants who had escaped serfdom as well as criminals and other adventurers. This seventeenth-century jail was part of an early Cossack settlement on the Kamchatka Peninsula at the easternmost end of Siberia. It illustrates Russian wooden architecture. (Sovfoto/Eastfoto)

Americas. Many of them, though, were Russified, adopting the Russian language and converting to Christianity, even as their traditional ways of life—hunting and herding—were much disrupted. The Russian Empire represented the final triumph of an agrarian civilization over the hunting societies of Siberia and over the pastoral peoples of the grasslands.

Russians and Empire

If the empire transformed the conquered peoples, it also fundamentally changed Russia itself. As it became a multiethnic empire, Russians diminished as a proportion of the overall population (see the Snapshot), although they remained politically dominant. Among the growing number of non-Russians in the empire, Slavic-speaking Ukrainians and Belorussians predominated, while the vast territories of Siberia and the steppes housed numerous separate peoples, but with quite small populations. The wealth of empire—rich agricultural lands, valuable furs, mineral deposits—played a major role in making Russia one of the great powers of Europe by the eighteenth century, and it has enjoyed that position ever since. This European and Christian state also became an Asian power, bumping up against China, India, Persia, and the Ottoman Empire. It was on the front lines of the encounter between Christendom and the world of Islam.

This straddling of Asia and Europe was the source of a long-standing identity problem that has troubled educated Russians for 300 years. Was Russia a backward European country, destined to follow the lead of more highly developed Western European societies? Or was it different, uniquely Slavic or even Asian, shaped by its Mongol legacy and its status as an Asian power? It is a question that Russians have not completely answered even in the twenty-first century. Either way, the very size of that empire, bordering on virtually all of the great agrarian civilizations of outer Eurasia, turned Russia, like many empires before it, into a highly militarized state, "a society organized for continuous war," according to one scholar.[18] It also reinforced the highly autocratic character of the Russian Empire because such a huge state required a powerful monarchy to hold its vast domains and highly diverse peoples together.

Clearly the Russians had created an empire, similar to those of Western Europe in terms of conquest, settlement, exploitation, religious conversion, and feelings of superiority. Like the others, the Russians recognized and distinguished among their conquered and incorporated peoples. "The All-Russian empire is unique in the world," declared an official document from 1785, "on account of its far-flung lands," which it then proceeded to enumerate one by one.[19]

Nonetheless, the Russians acquired their empire under different circumstances than did the Western Europeans. The Spanish and the British had conquered and colonized the New World, an ocean away and wholly unknown to them before 1492. They acquired those empires only after establishing themselves as distinct European states. The Russians, on the other hand, entered adjacent territories with which they had long interacted, and they did so *at the same time* that a modern

$\mathcal{S}$napshot   **Demographics of the Russian Empire**[20]

Percentage of Russians in the Empire over Time

YEAR	TOTAL POPULATION (IN MILLIONS)	RUSSIANS (PERCENT OF TOTAL POPULATION)
1600	—	90
1719	15.8	71
1795	37	53
1897	125.6	44
1989 (Soviet Union)	285.7	51
2002 (Russian Federation)	145	80

Ethnic Composition of the Population in 1719 (percent)

Russians	71
Ukrainians	13
Volga/Urals peoples	6
Baltics/Scandinavians	4
Belorussians	2.4
Steppe peoples	2
Northern peoples	1
Siberians	1

Russian state was taking shape. "The British had an empire," wrote historian Geoffrey Hosking. "Russia *was* an empire."[21] Perhaps this helps explain the unique longevity of the Russian Empire. Whereas the Spanish, Portuguese, and British colonies in the Americas long ago achieved independence, the Russian Empire remained intact until the collapse of the Soviet Union in 1991. So thorough was Russian colonization that Siberia and much of the steppes remain still an integral part of the Russian state. But many internal administrative regions, which exercise a measure of autonomy, reflect the continuing presence of some 160 non-Russian peoples who were earlier incorporated into the Russian Empire.

Asian Empires

Even as Europeans were building their empires in the Americas and across Siberia, other imperial projects were likewise under way. The Chinese pushed deep into central Eurasia; Turko-Mongol invaders from Central Asia created the Mughal Empire, bringing much of Hindu South Asia within a single Muslim-ruled political system; and the Ottoman Empire brought Muslim rule to a largely Christian population in southeastern Europe and Turkish rule to largely Arab populations in North Africa and the Middle East. None of these empires had the global reach or worldwide impact of Europe's American colonies; they were regional rather than global in scope. Nor did they have the same devastating and transforming impact on their conquered peoples, for those peoples were not being exposed to new diseases. Nothing remotely approaching the catastrophic population collapse of Native American peoples occurred in these Asian empires. Moreover, the process of building these empires did not transform the imperial homeland as fundamentally as did the wealth of the Americas and to a lesser extent Siberia for European imperial powers. Nonetheless, these expanding Asian empires reflected the energies and vitality of their respective civilizations in the early modern era, and they gave rise to profoundly important cross-cultural encounters, with legacies that echoed for many centuries.

Making China an Empire

■ **Description**

What were the major features of Chinese empire building in the early modern era?

In the fifteenth century, China had declined an opportunity to construct a maritime empire in the Indian Ocean, as Zheng He's massive fleet was withdrawn and left to wither away (see Chapter 13). In the seventeenth and eighteenth centuries, however, China built another kind of empire on its northern and western frontiers that vastly enlarged the territorial size of the country and incorporated a number of non-Chinese peoples. Undertaking this enormous project of imperial expansion was China's Qing, or Manchu, dynasty (1644–1912). Strangely enough, the Qing dynasty was itself of foreign and nomadic origin, hailing from Manchuria, north of the Great Wall. Having conquered China, the Qing rulers sought to maintain their ethnic distinctiveness by forbidding intermarriage between themselves and Chinese. Nonetheless, their ruling elites also mastered the Chinese language and Confucian teachings and used Chinese bureaucratic techniques to govern the empire.

For many centuries, the Chinese had interacted with the nomadic peoples, who inhabited the dry and lightly populated regions now known as Mongolia, Xinjiang, and Tibet. Trade, tribute, and warfare ensured that these ecologically and culturally different worlds were well known to each other, quite unlike the New World "discoveries" of the Europeans. Chinese authority in the area had been intermittent and actively resisted. Then, in the early modern era, Qing dynasty China undertook an eighty-year military effort (1680–1760) that brought these huge regions solidly and permanently under Chinese control. It was largely security concerns that motivated this aggressive posture. During the late seventeenth century, the creation of a substantial state among the western Mongols, known as the Zunghars, revived Chinese memories of an earlier Mongol conquest. As in so many other

China's Qing Dynasty Empire

cases, Chinese expansion was viewed as a defensive necessity. The eastward movement of the Russian Empire likewise appeared potentially threatening, but this danger was resolved diplomatically, rather than militarily, in the Treaty of Nerchinsk (1689), which marked the boundary between Russia and China.

Although undertaken by the non-Chinese Manchus, the Qing dynasty campaigns against the Mongols marked the evolution of China into a Central Asian empire. The Chinese, however, have seldom thought of themselves as an imperialist power. Rather they spoke of the "unification" of the peoples of central Eurasia within a Chinese state. Nonetheless, historians have seen many similarities between Chinese expansion and other cases of early modern empire building, while noting some clear differences as well.[22]

Clearly the Qing dynasty takeover of central Eurasia was a conquest, making use of China's more powerful military technology and greater resources. Furthermore, the area was ruled separately from the rest of China through a new office called the Court of Colonial Affairs. Like other colonial powers, the Chinese made active use of local notables—Mongol aristocrats, Muslim officials, Buddhist leaders—as they attempted to govern the region as inexpensively as possible. Sometimes these native officials abused their authority, demanding extra taxes or labor service from local people and thus earning their hostility. In places, those officials imitated Chinese ways by wearing peacock feathers, decorating their hats with gold buttons, or adopting a Manchu hairstyle that was much resented by many Chinese who were forced to wear it.

More generally, however, Chinese or Qing officials did not seek to assimilate local people into Chinese culture and showed considerable respect for the Mongolian, Tibetan, and Muslim cultures of the region. People of noble rank, Buddhist monks, and those associated with monasteries were excused from the taxes and labor service required of ordinary people. Nor was the area flooded with Chinese settlers. In parts of Mongolia, for example, Qing authorities sharply restricted the entry of Chinese merchants and other immigrants in an effort to preserve the area as a source of recruitment for the Chinese military. They feared that the "soft" and civilized Chinese ways might erode the fighting spirit of the Mongols.

The long-term significance of this new Chinese imperial state was tremendous. It greatly expanded the territory of China and added a small but important minority of non-Chinese people to the empire's vast population. The borders of contemporary China are essentially those created during the Qing dynasty. Some of those peoples in the late twentieth century, particularly those in Tibet and Xinjiang, have retained their older identities and have actively sought greater autonomy or even independence from China.

Even more important, Chinese conquests, together with the expansion of the Russian Empire, utterly transformed Central Asia. For centuries, that region had been the cosmopolitan crossroads of Eurasia, hosting the Silk Road trading network, welcoming all of the major world religions, and generating an enduring encounter between the nomads of the steppes and the farmers of settled agricultural regions.

Now under Russian or Chinese rule, it became the backward and impoverished region known to nineteenth- and twentieth-century observers. Land-based commerce across Eurasia increasingly took a backseat to oceanic trade. Indebted Mongolian nobles lost their land to Chinese merchants, while nomads, no longer able to herd their animals freely, fled to urban areas, where many were reduced to begging. The incorporation of the heartland of Eurasian nomads into the Russian and Chinese empires "eliminated permanently as a major actor on the historical stage the nomadic pastoralists, who had been the strongest alternative to settled agricultural society since the second millennium B.C.E."[23] It was the end of a long era.

Muslims and Hindus in the Mughal Empire

■ **Change**

How did Mughal attitudes and policies toward Hindus change from the time of Akbar to that of Aurangzeb?

If the creation of a Chinese imperial state in the early modern era provoked a final clash of nomadic pastoralists and settled farmers, India's Mughal Empire hosted a different kind of encounter—a further phase in the long interaction of Islamic and Hindu cultures in South Asia. That empire was the product of Central Asian warriors, who were Muslims in religion and Turkic in culture and who claimed descent from Chinggis Khan and Timur (see Chapter 13). Their brutal conquests in the sixteenth century provided India with a rare period of relative political unity (1526–1707), as Mughal emperors exercised a fragile control over a diverse and fragmented subcontinent, which was divided into a bewildering variety of small states, principalities, tribes, castes, sects, and ethnolinguistic groups.

The central division within Mughal India was religious. The ruling dynasty and perhaps 20 percent of the population were Muslims; most of the rest practiced some form of Hinduism. Mughal India's most famous emperor, Akbar (ruled 1556–1605), clearly recognized this fundamental reality and acted deliberately to accommodate the Hindu majority. After conquering the warrior-based and Hindu Rajputs of northwestern India, Akbar married several of their princesses but did not require them to convert to Islam. He incorporated a substantial number of Hindus into the political-military elite of the empire and supported the building of Hindu temples as well as mosques, palaces, and forts.

The Mughal Empire

In directly religious matters, Akbar imposed a policy of toleration, deliberately restraining the more militantly Islamic ulama (religious scholars) and removing the special tax (jizya) on non-Muslims. His son Jehangir wrote proudly of his father: "He associated with the good of every race and creed and persuasion.... The professors of various faiths had room in the broad expanse of his incomparable sway."[24] Akbar went so far as to create his own state cult, a religious faith aimed at the Mughal elite. This cult drew on Islam, Hinduism, and Zoroastrianism and emphasized loyalty to the emperor himself. The overall style of the Mughal Empire was that of a blended elite culture in which both Hindus and various Muslim groups could feel comfortable. Thus Persian artists and writers were welcomed into the empire, and the Hindu epic *Ramayana* was translated into Persian, while various Persian classics appeared in Hindi and Sanskrit. In short, Akbar and his immediate successors downplayed a distinctly Islamic identity for the Mughal Empire in favor of a cosmopolitan and hybrid Indian-Persian-Turkic culture.

Such policies fostered sharp opposition among some Muslims. The philosopher Shayk Ahmad Sirhindi (1564–1624), claiming to be a "renewer" of authentic Islam in his time, strongly objected to this cultural synthesis. The worship of saints, the sacrifice of animals, and support for Hindu religious festivals all represented impure intrusions of Sufi Islam or Hinduism that needed to be rooted out. It was the duty of Muslim rulers to impose the sharia, to enforce the jizya on nonbelievers, and to remove non-Muslims from high office. This strain of Muslim thinking found a champion in the emperor Aurangzeb (1658–1707), who reversed Akbar's policy of accommodation and sought to impose Islamic supremacy. He forbade the Hindu practice of *sati*, in which a widow followed her husband to death by throwing herself on his funeral pyre. Music and dance were now banned at court, and previously tolerated vices such as gambling, drinking, prostitution, and narcotics were actively suppressed. Some Hindu temples were destroyed, and the jizya was reimposed. "Censors of public morals," posted to large cities, enforced Islamic law.

Aurangzeb's religious policies, combined with intolerable demands for taxes to support his many wars of expansion, antagonized Hindus and prompted various movements of opposition to the Mughals. "Your subjects are trampled underfoot," wrote one anonymous protester. "Every province of your empire is impoverished.... God is the God of all mankind, not the God of Mussalmans [Muslims] alone."[25] These opposition movements, some of them self-consciously Hindu, fatally fractured the Mughal Empire, especially after Aurangzeb's death in 1707, and opened the way for a British takeover in the second half of the eighteenth century.

Thus the Mughal Empire was the site of a highly significant encounter between two of the world's great religious traditions. It began with an experiment in multicultural empire building and ended in growing antagonism between Hindus and Muslims. In the centuries that followed, both elements of the Mughal experience would be repeated.

Muslims, Christians, and the Ottoman Empire

Like the Mughal state, the Ottoman Empire was also the creation of Turkic warrior groups, whose aggressive raiding of agricultural civilization was now legitimized in Islamic terms. Beginning around 1300 from a base area in northwestern Anatolia, these Ottoman Turks over the next three centuries swept over much of the Middle East, North Africa, and southeastern Europe to create the Islamic world's most significant empire (see Map 14.3). During those centuries, the Ottoman state was transformed from a small frontier principality to a prosperous, powerful, cosmopolitan empire, heir to both the Byzantine Empire and to leadership within the Islamic world. Its sultan combined the roles of a Turkic warrior

Map 14.3 The Ottoman Empire

At its high point in the mid-sixteenth century, the Ottoman Empire encompassed a vast diversity of peoples; straddled Europe, Africa, and Asia; and battled both the Austrian and Safavid empires.

prince, a Muslim caliph, and a conquering emperor, bearing the "strong sword of Islam" and serving as chief defender of the faith.

Within the Islamic world, the Ottoman Empire represented the growing prominence of Turkic people, for their empire now incorporated a large number of Arabs, among whom the religion had been born. Mecca, Medina, and Jerusalem—the holy cities of Islam—now lay in Turkic hands, while the responsibility and the prestige of protecting them belonged to the Ottoman Empire. A century-long conflict (1534–1639) between the Ottoman Empire, espousing the Sunni version of Islam, and the Persian Safavid Empire, holding fast to the Shia form of the faith, expressed a deep and enduring division within the Islamic world. Nonetheless, Persian culture, especially its poetry, painting, and traditions of imperial splendor, occupied a prominent position among the Ottoman elite.

The Ottoman Empire, like its Mughal counterpart, was the site of a highly significant cross-cultural encounter in the early modern era, adding yet another chapter to the long-running story of interaction between the Islamic world and Christendom. As the Ottoman Empire expanded across Anatolia, its largely Christian population converted in large numbers to Islam as the Byzantine state visibly weakened and large numbers of Turks settled in the region. By 1500, some 90 percent of Anatolia's inhabitants were Muslims and Turkic speakers. The climax of this Turkic assault on the Christian world of Byzantium occurred in 1453, when Constantinople fell to the invaders. Renamed Istanbul, that splendid Christian city became the capital of the Ottoman Empire. Byzantium, heir to the glory of Rome, was no more.

In the empire's southeastern European domains, known as the Balkans, the Ottoman encounter with Christian peoples unfolded quite differently than it had in Anatolia. In the Balkans, Muslims ruled over a large Christian population, but the scarcity of Turkish settlers and the willingness of the Ottoman authorities to accommodate the region's Christian churches led to far less conversion. By the early sixteenth century, only about 19 percent of the area's people were Muslims, and 81 percent were Christians.

Many of these Christians had welcomed Ottoman conquest because taxes were lighter and oppression less pronounced than under their former Christian rulers. Christian communities such as the Eastern Orthodox and Armenian churches were granted considerable autonomy in regulating their internal social, religious, educational, and charitable affairs. A substantial number of these Christians—Balkan landlords, Greek merchants, government officials, and high-ranking clergy—became part of the Ottoman elite, without converting to Islam. Jewish refugees, fleeing Christian persecution in a Spain recently "liberated" from Islamic rule, likewise found greater opportunity in the Ottoman Empire, where they became prominent in trade and banking circles. In these ways, Ottoman dealings with the Christian and Jewish populations of their empire broadly resembled Akbar's policies toward the Hindu majority of Mughal India.

In another way, however, Turkish rule bore heavily on Christians. Through a process known as the *devshirme* (the collecting or gathering), Balkan Christian communities were required to hand over a quota of young boys, who were then removed from their families, required to learn Turkish, usually converted to Islam, and trained for either civil administration or military service in elite Janissary units. Although it was a terrible blow for families who lost their children, the *devshirme* also represented a means of upward mobility within the Ottoman Empire. Nonetheless, this social gain occurred at a high price.

Even though Ottoman authorities were relatively tolerant toward Christians within their borders, the empire itself represented an enormous threat to Christendom generally. The seizure of Constantinople, the conquest of the Balkans, Ottoman naval power in the Mediterranean, and the siege of Vienna in 1529 and again in 1683 raised anew "the specter of a Muslim takeover of all of Europe."[26]

■ **Significance**
In what ways was the Ottoman Empire important for Europe in the early modern era?

One European ambassador reported fearfully in 1555 from the court of the Turkish ruler Suleiman:

> He tramples the soil of Hungary with 200,000 horses, he is at the very gates of Austria, threatens the rest of Germany, and brings in his train all the nations that extend from our borders to those of Persia.[27]

Indeed, the "terror of the Turk" inspired fear across much of Europe and placed Christendom on the defensive, even as Europeans were expanding aggressively across the Atlantic and into the Indian Ocean.

The Ottoman encounter with Christian Europe spawned admiration and cooperation as well as fear and trembling. The sixteenth-century French philosopher Jean Bodin praised the religious tolerance of the Ottoman sultan in contrast to Christian intolerance: "The King of the Turks who rules over a great part of Europe safeguards the rites of religion as well as any prince in this world. Yet he constrains no-one, but on the contrary permits everyone to live as his conscience

The Ottoman Seige of Vienna, 1683
In this late-seventeenth-century painting by artist Frans Geffels, the last Ottoman incursion into the Austrian Empire was pushed back with French and Polish help, marking the end of a serious Muslim threat to Christian Europe. (Historisches Museum der Stadt Wien/Gianni Dagli Orti/The Art Archive)

dictates."[28] The French government on occasion found it useful to ally with the Ottoman Empire against their common enemy of Habsburg Austria, while European merchants willingly violated a papal ban on selling firearms to the Turks. In the early eighteenth century, the wife of an English diplomat posted to Istanbul praised the morality of Ottoman women as well as their relative freedom: "It is easy to see they have more liberty than we do."[29] Cultural encounter involved more than conflict.

⊞ Reflections: Countering Eurocentrism... or Reflecting It?

With an emphasis on empires and cross-cultural encounter, this chapter deliberately places the more familiar narrative of European colonization in the Americas along-side the less well-known stories of Russian, Chinese, Mughal, and Ottoman empire building. The chief purpose in doing so is to counteract a Eurocentric understanding of the early modern age, in which European initiatives dominate our view of this era. It reminds us that Western Europe was not the only center of vitality and expansion and that the interaction of culturally different peoples, so characteristic of the modern age, derived from multiple sources. How often do we notice that a European Christendom creating empires across the Atlantic was also the victim of Ottoman empire building in the Balkans?

A critic of this chapter, however, might well argue that it is nonetheless a Eurocentric narrative, for it allots rather more space to the Western European empires than to the others, and it tells the European story first. What led to such an ordering of this material?

Underlying the organization of this chapter is the notion that Western European empires in the Americas were in some ways both different from and more significant than the others. They represented something wholly new in human history, an interacting Atlantic world, while the Russian, Chinese, Mughal, and Ottoman empires continued older patterns of historical development. Furthermore, the European empires had a far heavier impact on the peoples they incorporated than did the others. After all, the great tragedies of the early modern era—the population collapse of Native American societies and the Atlantic slave trade—both grew out of these European empires. Moreover, they had, arguably, a far wider impact on the world as a whole, as they extended European civilization to the vast areas of the Americas, laid the nutritional foundation for the global population explosion of modern times, and contributed to both the Scientific Revolution and the Industrial Revolution.

Counteracting Eurocentrism, while acknowledging the unique role of Europe, continues to generate controversy among both scholars and students of modern world history. It is an issue that will recur repeatedly in the chapters that follow.

Second Thoughts

What's the Significance?

To assess your mastery of the material in this chapter, see the **Online Study Guide** at bedfordstmartins.com/strayer.

"the great dying"

Columbian exchange

peninsulares

mestizo

mulattoes

plantation complex

settler colonies

Siberia

yasak

Qing dynasty empire

Mughal Empire

Akbar

Aurangzeb

Ottoman Empire

Constantinople, 1453

devshirme

Big Picture Questions

1. In comparing the European empires in the Americas with the Russian, Chinese, Mughal, and Ottoman empires, should world historians emphasize the similarities or the differences? What are the implications of each approach?

2. In what different ways was European colonial rule expressed and experienced in the Americas?

3. Why did the European empires in the Americas have such an enormously greater impact on the conquered people than did the Chinese, Mughal, and Ottoman empires?

4. In what ways did the empires of the early modern era continue patterns of earlier empires? In what ways did they depart from those patterns?

Next Steps: For Further Study

For Web sites and documents related to this chapter, see **Make History** at bedfordstmartins.com/strayer.

Jorge Canizares-Esguerra and Erik R. Seeman (eds), *The Atlantic in Global History* (2007). A collection of essays that treats the Atlantic basin as a single interacting region.

Alfred W. Crosby, *The Columbian Voyages, the Columbian Exchange, and Their Historians* (1987). A brief and classic account of changing understandings of Columbus and his global impact.

John Kicza, *Resilient Cultures: America's Native Peoples Confront European Colonization, 1500–1800* (2003). An account of European colonization in the Americas that casts the native peoples as active agents rather than passive victims.

Peter Perdue, *China Marches West: The Qing Conquest of Central Eurasia* (2005). Describes the process of China becoming an empire as it incorporated the non-Chinese people of Central Asia.

John F. Richards, *The Mughal Empire* (1996). A well-regarded summary by a major scholar in the field.

David R. Ringrose, *Expansion and Global Interaction, 1200–1700* (2001). A world history perspective on empire building that bridges the postclassical and early modern eras.

Willard Sutherland, *Taming the Wild Fields: Colonization and Empire on the Russian Steppe* (2004). An up-to-date account of Russian expansion in the steppes.

"1492: An Ongoing Voyage," http://www.ibiblio.org/expo/1492.exhibit/Intro.html. An interactive Web site based on an exhibit from the Library of Congress that provides a rich context for exploring the meaning of Columbus and his voyages.

Global Commerce

1450–1750

"I have come full circle back to my destiny: from Africa to America and back to Africa. I could hear the cries and wails of my ancestors. I weep with them and for them."[1] This is what an African American woman from Atlanta wrote in 2002 in the guest book of the Cape Coast Castle, one of the many ports of embarkation for slaves located along the coast of Ghana in West Africa. There she no doubt saw the whips and leg irons used to discipline the captured Africans as well as the windowless dungeons in which hundreds of them were crammed while waiting for the ships that would carry them across the Atlantic to the Americas. Almost certainly she also caught sight of the infamous "gate of no return," through which the captives departed to their new life as slaves.

THIS VISITOR'S EMOTIONAL ENCOUNTER WITH THE LEGACY OF THE ATLANTIC SLAVE TRADE reminds us of the enormous significance of this commerce in human beings for the early modern world and of its continuing echoes even at the beginning of the twenty-first century. The slave trade, however, was only one component of those international trading networks that shaped human interactions during the centuries between 1450 and 1750. Europeans now smashed their way into the ancient spice trade of the Indian Ocean, developing new relationships with Asian societies as a result. Silver, obtained from mines in Spanish America, enriched Western Europe, even as much of it made its way to China, where it allowed Europeans to participate more fully in the rich commerce of East Asia. Furs from North America and Siberia found a

The Atlantic Slave Trade: Among the threads of global commerce during the early modern era, none has resonated more loudly in historical memory than the Atlantic slave trade. This eighteenth-century French painting shows the sale of slaves at Goree, a major slave trading port in what is now Dakar in Senegal. A European merchant and an African authority figure negotiate the arrangement, while the shackled victims themselves wait for their fate to be decided. (Bibliothèque des Arts Décoratifs, Paris/Archives Charmet/The Bridgeman Art Library) ready market in Europe and China, while the hunting and trapping of those fur-bearing animals transformed both natural environments and human societies. Despite their growing prominence in long-distance exchange, Europeans were far from the only active traders. Southeast Asians, Chinese, Indians, Armenians, Arabs, and Africans likewise played major roles in the making of the world economy of the early modern era.

Thus commerce joined empire as the twin drivers of globalization during these centuries. Together they created new relationships, disrupted old patterns, brought distant peoples into contact with one another, enriched some, and impoverished or enslaved others. From the various "old worlds" of the premodern era, a single "new world" emerged—slowly, with great pain, and accompanied by growing inequalities. What was gained and what was lost in the transformations born of global commerce have been the subject of great controversy ever since.

Europeans and Asian Commerce

Schoolchildren everywhere know that European empires in the Western Hemisphere grew out of an accident—Columbus's unknowing encounter with the Americas—and that new colonial societies and new commercial connections across the Atlantic were the result. In Asia, it was a very different story. The voyage (1497–1499) of the Portuguese mariner Vasco da Gama, in which Europeans sailed to India for the first time, was certainly no accident. It was the outcome of a deliberate, systematic, century-long Portuguese effort to explore a sea route to the East, by creeping slowly down the West African coast, around the tip of South Africa, up the East African coast, and finally to Calicut in southern India in 1498. There Europeans encountered an ancient and rich network of commerce that stretched from East Africa to China. They were certainly aware of the wealth of that commercial network, but largely ignorant of its workings.

■ **Causation**

What drove European involvement in the world of Asian commerce?

The most immediate motivation for this massive effort was the desire for tropical spices—cinnamon, nutmeg, mace, cloves, and, above all, pepper—which were widely used as condiments and preservatives and were sometimes regarded as aphrodisiacs. Other products of the East, such as Chinese silk, Indian cottons, rhubarb for medicinal purposes, emeralds, rubies, and sapphires, also were in great demand.

Underlying this growing interest in Asia was the more general recovery of European civilization following the disaster of the Black Death in the early fourteenth century. During the fifteenth century, Europe's population was growing again, and its national monarchies—in Spain, Portugal, England, and France—were learning how to tax their subjects more effectively and to build substantial military forces equipped with gunpowder weapons. Its cities were growing too. Some of them—in England, the Netherlands, and northern Italy, for example—were becoming centers of international commerce, giving birth to a more capitalist economy based on market exchange, private ownership, and the accumulation of capital for further investment.

For many centuries, Eastern goods had trickled into the Mediterranean through the Middle East from the network of Indian Ocean trade. From the viewpoint of an increasingly dynamic Europe, several major problems accompanied this pattern of commerce. First, of course, the source of supply for these much-desired goods lay solidly in Muslim hands. Most immediately, Muslim Egypt was the primary point of transfer into the Mediterranean basin and its European customers. The Italian commercial city of Venice largely monopolized the European trade in Eastern goods, annually sending convoys of ships to Alexandria in Egypt. Venetians resented the Muslim monopoly on Indian Ocean trade, and other European powers disliked relying on Venice as well as on Muslims. Circumventing these monopolies was yet another impetus—both religious and political—for the Portuguese to attempt a sea route to India that bypassed both Venetian and Muslim middlemen. In addition, many Europeans of the time were persuaded that a mysterious Christian monarch, known as Prester John, ruled somewhere in Asia or Africa. Joining with his mythical kingdom to continue the Crusades and combat a common Islamic enemy was likewise a goal of the Portuguese voyages.

A final problem lay in paying for Eastern goods. Few products of an economically less developed Europe were attractive in Eastern markets. Thus Europeans were required to pay cash—gold or silver—for Asian spices or textiles. This persistent trade deficit contributed much to the intense desire for precious metals that attracted early modern European explorers, traders, and conquerors. Portuguese voyages along the West African coast, for example, were seeking direct access to African goldfields. The enormously rich silver deposits of Mexico and Bolivia provided at least a temporary solution to this persistent European problem.

First the Portuguese and then the Spanish, French, Dutch, and British found their way into the ancient Asian world of Indian Ocean commerce (see Map 15.1). How they behaved in that world and what they created there differed considerably among the various European countries, but collectively they contributed much to the new regime of globalized trade.

A Portuguese Empire of Commerce

The arena of Indian Ocean commerce into which Vasco da Gama and his Portuguese successors sailed was a world away from anything they had known. It was a vast world, both in geographic extent and in the diversity of those who participated in it. East Africans, Arabs, Persians, Indians, Malays, Chinese, and others traded freely. Most of them were Muslims, though hailing from many separate communities, but Hindus, Christians, Jews, and Chinese likewise had a role in this commercial network. Had the Portuguese sought simply to participate in peaceful trading, they certainly could have done so, but it was quickly apparent that European trade goods were crude and unattractive in Asian markets and that Europeans would be unable to compete effectively. Moreover, the Portuguese soon learned that most Indian Ocean merchant ships were not heavily armed and certainly lacked the

■ **Connection**
To what extent did the Portuguese realize their own goals in the Indian Ocean?

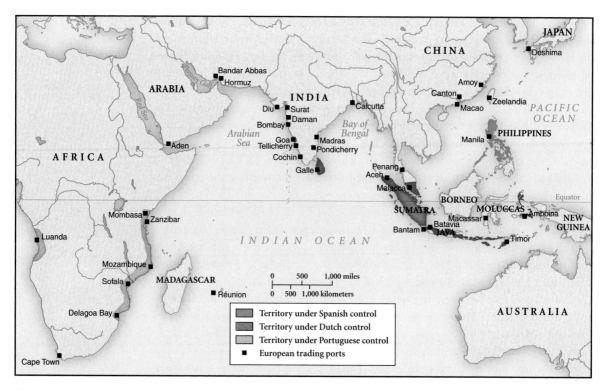

Map 15.1 Europeans in Asia in the Early Modern Era
The early modern era witnessed only very limited territorial control by Europeans in Asia. Trade, rather than empire, was the chief concern of the Western newcomers, who were not, in any event, a serious military threat to major Asian states.

onboard cannons that Portuguese ships carried. Since the withdrawal of the Chinese fleet from the Indian Ocean early in the fifteenth century, no major power was in a position to dominate the sea-lanes, and the many smaller-scale merchants generally traded openly, although piracy was sometimes a problem.

Given these conditions, the Portuguese saw an opening, for their ships could outgun and outmaneuver competing naval forces, while their onboard cannons could devastate coastal fortifications. Although their overall economy lagged behind that of Asian producers, Europeans had more than caught up in the critical area of naval technology and naval warfare. This military advantage enabled the Portuguese to quickly establish fortified bases at several key locations within the Indian Ocean world—Mombasa in East Africa, Hormuz at the entrance to the Persian Gulf, Goa on the west coast of India, Malacca in Southeast Asia, and Macao on the south coast of China. With the exception of Macao, which had been obtained through bribery and negotiations with Chinese authorities, these Portuguese bases were obtained forcibly against small and weak states. In Mombasa, for example, the commander of a Portuguese fleet responded to local resistance in 1505 by burning and sacking the city, killing some 1,500 people, and seizing large quantities of cotton and silk textiles and carpets. The king of Mombasa wrote a warning to a neighboring city:

> This is to inform you that a great lord has passed through the town, burning it and laying it waste. He came to the town in such strength and was of such a

cruelty that he spared neither man nor woman, or old nor young—nay, not even the smallest child. . . . Nor can I ascertain nor estimate what wealth they have taken from the town.[2]

What the Portuguese created in the Indian Ocean is commonly known as a "trading post empire," for they aimed to control commerce, not large territories or populations, and to do so by force of arms rather than by economic competition. Seeking to monopolize the spice trade, the Portuguese king grandly titled himself "Lord of the Conquest, Navigation, and Commerce of Ethiopia, Arabia, Persia, and India." Portuguese authorities in the East tried to require all merchant vessels to purchase a *cartaz*, or pass, and to pay duties of 6 to 10 percent on their cargoes. They partially blocked the traditional Red Sea route to the Mediterranean and for a century or so monopolized the highly profitable route around Africa to Europe. Even so, they never succeeded in controlling much more than half of the spice trade to Europe.[3]

Failing to dominate Indian Ocean commerce as they had hoped, the Portuguese gradually assimilated themselves to its ancient patterns. They became heavily involved in carrying Asian goods to Asian ports, selling their shipping services because they were largely unable to sell their goods. Even in their major settlements, the Portuguese were outnumbered by Asian traders, and many married Asian women. Hundreds of Portuguese escaped the control of their government altogether and settled in Asian or African ports, where they learned local languages, sometimes converted to Islam, and became simply one more group in the diverse trading culture of the East.

By 1600, the Portuguese trading post empire was in steep decline. This small European country was overextended, and rising Asian states such as Japan, Burma, Mughal India, Persia, and the sultanate of Oman actively resisted Portuguese commercial control. Unwilling to accept a dominant Portuguese role in the Indian Ocean, other European countries also gradually contested Portugal's efforts to monopolize the rich spice trade to Europe.

The Spice Trade
For thousands of years, spices were a major trade item in the Indian Ocean commercial network, as this fifteenth-century French depiction of the gathering of pepper in southern India illustrates. In the early modern era, Europeans gained direct access to this ancient network for the first time. (Bibliothèque nationale de France)

Spain and the Philippines

Spain was the first to challenge Portugal's position. As precious and profitable spices began to arrive in Europe on Portuguese ships in the early sixteenth century, the Spanish soon realized that they were behind in the race to gain access to the riches of the East. In an effort to catch up, they established themselves on what became the Philippine Islands, named after the Spanish king Philip II. The Spanish first

■ **Comparison**
How did the Portuguese, Spanish, Dutch, and British initiatives in Asia differ from one another?

Snapshot   Key Moments in the European Encounter with Asia

Vasco da Gama's arrival in India	1498
Portuguese trading post empire established	early 1500s
Spanish takeover of Philippines begins	1565
China establishes taxes payable in silver	1570s
Beginning of silver shipments from Mexico to Manila	1570s
British and Dutch East India companies begin operation in Asia	1601–1602
Missionaries expelled from Japan	early 1600s
Dutch conquest of nutmeg-producing Banda Islands	1620
French East India Company established	1664
British begin military conquest of India	1750s

encountered the region during the famous round-the-world voyage (1519–1521) of Ferdinand Magellan, a Portuguese mariner sailing on behalf of the Spanish Crown. There they found an archipelago of islands, thousands of them, occupied by culturally diverse peoples and organized in small and highly competitive chiefdoms. One of the local chiefs later told the Spanish: "There is no king and no sole authority in this land; but everyone holds his own view and opinion, and does as he prefers."[4] Some were involved in tribute trade with China, and a small number of Chinese settlers lived in the port towns. Nonetheless, the region was of little interest to the governments of China and Japan, the major powers in the area.

These conditions—proximity to China and the spice islands, small and militarily weak societies, the absence of competing claims—encouraged the Spanish to establish outright colonial rule on the islands, rather than to imitate a Portuguese-style trading post empire. Small-scale military operations, gunpowder weapons, local alliances, gifts and favors to chiefs, and the pageantry of Catholic ritual all contributed to a relatively easy and often bloodless Spanish takeover of the islands in the century or so after 1565. They remained a Spanish colonial territory until the end of the nineteenth century, when the United States assumed control following the Spanish-American War of 1898.

Accompanying Spanish rule was a major missionary effort, which turned Filipino society into the only major outpost of Christianity in Asia. That effort also opened up a new front in the long encounter of Christendom and Islam, for on the southern island of Mindanao, Islam was gaining strength and provided an ideology of resistance to Spanish encroachment for 300 years. Indeed Mindanao remains a contested part of the Philippines into the twenty-first century.

Beyond the missionary enterprise, other features of Spanish colonial practice in the Americas found expression in the Philippines. People living in scattered settlements were persuaded or forced to relocate into more concentrated Christian communities. Tribute, taxes, and unpaid labor became part of ordinary life. Large landed estates emerged, owned by Spanish settlers, Catholic religious orders, or prominent Filipinos. Women who had played a major role as ritual specialists, healers, and midwifes were now displaced by male Spanish priests, and their ceremonial instruments were deliberately defiled and disgraced. Short-lived revolts and flight to interior mountains were among the Filipino responses to colonial oppression.

Yet others fled to Manila, the new capital of the colonial Philippines. By 1600, it had become a flourishing and culturally diverse city of more than 40,000 inhabitants and was home to many Spanish settlers and officials and growing numbers of Filipino migrants. Its rising prosperity also attracted some 3,000 Japanese and more than 20,000 Chinese. Serving as traders, artisans, and sailors, the Chinese in particular became an essential element in the Spanish colony's growing economic relationship with China; however, their economic prominence and their resistance to conversion earned them Spanish hostility and clearly discriminatory treatment. Periodic Chinese revolts, followed by expulsions and massacres, were the result. On one occasion in 1603, the Spanish killed about 20,000 people, nearly the entire Chinese population of the island.

The East India Companies

Far more important than the Spanish as European competitors for the spice trade were the Dutch and English, both of whom entered Indian Ocean commerce in the early seventeenth century. Together they quickly overtook and displaced the Portuguese, often by force, even as they competed vigorously with each other as well. These rising Northern European powers were both militarily and economically stronger than the Portuguese. For example, during the sixteenth century, the Dutch had become a highly commercialized and urbanized society, and their business skills and maritime shipping operations were the envy of Europe. Around 1600, both the British and the Dutch, unlike the Portuguese, organized their Indian Ocean ventures through private trading companies, which were able to raise money and share risks among a substantial number of merchant investors. The British East India Company and the Dutch East India Company received charters from their respective governments granting them trading monopolies and the power to make war and to govern conquered peoples. Thus they established their own parallel and competing trading post empires, with the Dutch focused on the islands of Indonesia and the English on India. Somewhat later, a French company also established settlements in the Indian Ocean basin.

Operating in a region of fragmented and weak political authority, the Dutch acted to control not only the shipping but also the production of cloves, cinnamon, nutmeg, and mace. With much bloodshed, the Dutch seized control of a number of small spice-producing islands, forcing their people to sell only to the Dutch and destroying the crops of those who refused. On the Banda Islands, famous for their

■ Change
To what extent did the British and Dutch trading companies change the societies they encountered in Asia?

A European View of Asian Commerce
The various East India companies (British, French, and Dutch) represented the major vehicle for European commerce in Asia during the early modern era. This wall painting, dating from 1778 and titled *The East Offering Its Riches to Britannia*, hung in the main offices of the British East India Company. (© British Library Board)

nutmeg, the Dutch killed, enslaved, or left to starve virtually the entire population of some 15,000 people and then replaced them with Dutch planters, using a slave labor force to produce the nutmeg crop. For a time in the seventeenth century, the Dutch were able to monopolize the trade in nutmeg, mace, and cloves and to sell these spices in Europe and India at fourteen to seventeen times the price they paid in Indonesia.[5] While Dutch profits soared, the local economy of the Spice Islands was shattered, and their people were impoverished.

The British East India Company operated differently than its Dutch counterpart. Less well financed and less commercially sophisticated, the British were largely excluded from the rich Spice Islands by the Dutch monopoly. Thus they fell back on India, where they established three major trading settlements during the seventeenth century: Bombay, on India's west coast, and Calcutta and Madras, on the east coast. Although British naval forces soon gained control of the Arabian Sea and the Persian Gulf, largely replacing the Portuguese, on land they were no match for the powerful Mughal Empire, which ruled most of the Indian subcontinent. Therefore, the British were not in a position to practice "trade by warfare," as the Dutch did in Indonesia.[6] Rather they secured their trading bases with the permission of Mughal authorities or local rulers, with substantial payments and bribes as the price of admission to the Indian market. When some independent English traders plundered a Mughal ship in 1636, local authorities detained British East India Company officials for two months and forced them to pay a whopping fine. Although pepper and other spices remained important in British trade, British merchants came to focus much more heavily on Indian cotton textiles, which were becoming widely popular in England and its American colonies. Hundreds of villages in the interior of southern India became specialized producers for this British market.

Like the Portuguese before them, both the Dutch and English became heavily involved in trade within Asia. The profits from this "carrying trade" enabled them to purchase Asian goods without paying for them in gold or silver from Europe. Dutch and English traders also began to deal in bulk goods for a mass market—pepper, textiles, and later tea and coffee—rather than just luxury goods for an elite market. In the second half of the eighteenth century, both the Dutch and British trading post empires slowly evolved into a more conventional form of colonial domination, in which the British came to rule India and the Dutch controlled Indonesia.

Asian Commerce

Although European commerce in the Indian Ocean and the South China Sea created new linkages between East and West, historians have sometimes exaggerated their impact on Asian societies during the early modern era. Certainly the European presence was far less significant in Asia than it was in the Americas or Africa during these centuries. European political control was limited to the Philippines and a few of the Spice Islands. To the great powers of South and East Asia—Mughal India, China, and Japan—Europeans represented no real military threat and played minor roles in their large and prosperous economies. Japan provides a fascinating case study in the ability of major Asian powers to control the European intruders.

When Portuguese traders and missionaries first arrived on that island nation in the mid-sixteenth century, soon followed by Spanish, Dutch, and English traders, Japan was plagued by endemic conflict among numerous feudal lords, known as *daimyo*, each with his own cadre of *samurai* warriors. In these circumstances, the European newcomers found a hospitable welcome, for their military technology, shipbuilding skills, geographic knowledge, commercial opportunities, and even religious ideas proved useful or attractive to various elements in Japan's fractious and competitive society. The second half of the sixteenth century, for example, witnessed the growth of a substantial Christian movement, with some 300,000 converts and a Japanese-led church.

By the early seventeenth century, however, a series of remarkable military figures had unified Japan politically, under the leadership of a supreme military commander known as the *shogun*, who hailed from the Tokugawa clan. With the end of Japan's civil wars, successive shoguns came to view Europeans as a threat to the country's newly established unity rather than an opportunity. They therefore expelled Christian missionaries and violently suppressed the practice of Christianity. This policy included the execution, often under torture, of some sixty-two missionaries and thousands of Japanese converts. Shogunate authorities also forbade Japanese from traveling abroad and banned most European traders altogether, permitting only the Dutch, who appeared less interested in spreading Christianity, to trade at a single site. Thus, for two centuries (1650–1850), Japanese authorities of the Tokugawa shogunate largely closed their country off from the emerging world of European commerce, although they maintained their trading ties to China and Korea.

Despite the European naval dominance in Asian waters, Asian merchants did not disappear. Arab, Chinese, Javanese, Malay, and other traders benefited from the upsurge in seaborne commerce. Chinese merchants, for example, continued to carry most of the spice trade from Southeast Asia to China. Overland trade within Asia remained wholly in Asian hands and grew considerably. Christian merchants from Armenia were particularly active in the overland commerce linking Europe, the Middle East, and Central Asia. Tens of thousands of Indian merchants and moneylenders, mostly Hindus representing sophisticated family firms, lived through-out Central Asia, Persia, and Russia, thus connecting this vast region to markets in India. These commercial networks, equivalent in their sophistication to those of Europe, continued to operate successfully even as Europeans militarized the seaborne commerce of the Indian Ocean.

Silver and Global Commerce

■ **Significance**
What was the world historical importance of the silver trade?

Even more than the spice trade of Eurasia, it was the silver trade that gave birth to a genuinely global network of exchange (see Map 15.2). As one historian put it, silver "went round the world and made the world go round."[7] The mid-sixteenth-century discovery of enormously rich silver deposits in Bolivia, and simultaneously in Japan, suddenly provided a vastly increased supply of that precious metal. Spanish America alone produced perhaps 85 percent of the world's silver during the early modern era. Spain's sole Asian colony, the Philippines, provided a critical link in this emerging network of global commerce. Manila, the colonial capital of the Philippines, was the destination of annual Spanish shipments of silver, which were drawn from the rich mines of Bolivia, transported overland to Acapulco in Mexico, and from there shipped across the Pacific to the Philippines. This trade was the first direct and sustained link between the Americas and Asia, and it initiated a web of Pacific commerce that grew steadily over the centuries.

At the heart of that Pacific web, and of early modern global commerce gener-ally, was China's huge economy, and especially its growing demand for silver. In the

Map 15.2 The Global Silver Trade
Silver was one of the first major commodities to be exchanged on a genuinely global scale.

1570s, Chinese authorities consolidated a variety of tax levies into a single tax, which its huge population was now required to pay in silver. This sudden new demand for the white metal caused its value to skyrocket. It meant that foreigners with silver could now purchase far more of China's silks and porcelains than before.

This demand set silver in motion around the world, with the bulk of the world's silver supply winding up in China and much of the rest elsewhere in Asia. The routes by which this "silver drain" operated were numerous. Chinese, Portuguese, and Dutch traders flocked to Manila to sell Chinese goods in exchange for silver. European ships carried Japanese silver to China. Much of the silver shipped across the Atlantic to Spain was spent in Europe generally and then used to pay for the Asian goods that the French, British, and Dutch so greatly desired. Silver paid for some African slaves and for spices in Southeast Asia. The standard Spanish silver coin, known as a piece of eight, was used by merchants in North America, Europe, India, Russia, and West Africa as a medium of exchange. By 1600, it circulated widely in southern China. A Portuguese merchant in 1621 noted that silver "wanders throughout all the world . . . before flocking to China, where it remains as if at its natural center."[8]

In its global journeys, silver transformed much that it touched. At the world's largest silver mine in what is now Bolivia, the city of Potosí arose from a barren landscape high in the Andes, a ten-week mule trip away from Lima. "New people arrive by the hour, attracted by the smell of silver," commented a Spanish observer in the 1570s. With 160,000 people, Potosí became the largest city in the Americas and equivalent in size to London, Amsterdam, or Seville. Its wealthy European elite lived in luxury, with all the goods of Europe and Asia at their disposal. Meanwhile, the city's Native American miners worked in conditions so horrendous that some families held funeral services for men drafted to work the mines. One Spanish priest referred to Potosí as a "portrait of hell."[9]

In Spain itself, which was the initial destination for much of Latin America's silver, the precious metal vastly enriched the Crown, making Spain the envy of its European rivals during the sixteenth century. Spanish rulers could now pursue military and political ambitions in both Europe and the Americas far beyond the country's own resource base. "New World mines," concluded one scholar, "supported the Spanish empire."[10] Nonetheless, this vast infusion of wealth did not fundamentally transform the Spanish economy, because it generated more inflation of prices than

Potosí

This colonial-era painting shows the enormously rich silver mines of Potosí, then a major global source of the precious metal and the largest city in the Americas. Brutally hard work and poisonous exposure to mercury, which was used in the refining process, led to the deaths of many thousands of workers, even as the silver itself contributed to European splendor in the early modern era. (Courtesy, The Hispanic Society of America)

real economic growth. A rigid economy laced with monopolies and regulations, an aristocratic class that preferred leisure to enterprise, and a crusading insistence on religious uniformity all prevented the Spanish from using their silver windfall in a productive fashion. When the value of silver dropped in the early seventeenth century, Spain lost its earlier position as the dominant Western European power.

Japan, another major source of silver production in the sixteenth century, did better. Its military rulers, the Tokugawa shoguns, used silver-generated profits to defeat hundreds of rival feudal lords and unify the country. Unlike their Spanish counterparts, the shoguns allied with the country's vigorous merchant class to develop a market-based economy and to invest heavily in agricultural and industrial enterprises. Japanese state and local authorities alike acted vigorously to protect and renew Japan's dwindling forests, while millions of families in the eighteenth century took steps to have fewer children by practicing late marriages, contraception, abortion, and infanticide. The outcome was the dramatic slowing of Japan's population growth, the easing of an impending ecological crisis, and a flourishing, highly commercialized economy. These conditions were the foundations for Japan's remarkable nineteenth-century Industrial Revolution.

In China, silver deepened the already substantial commercialization of the country's economy. In order to obtain the silver needed to pay their taxes, more and more people had to sell something—either their labor or their products. Areas that devoted themselves to growing mulberry trees, on which silkworms fed, had to buy their rice from other regions. Thus the Chinese economy became more regionally specialized. Particularly in southern China, this surging economic growth resulted in the loss of about half the area's forest cover as more and more land was devoted to cash crops. No Japanese-style conservation program emerged to address this growing problem. An eighteenth-century Chinese poet, Wang Dayue, gave voice to the fears that this ecological transformation wrought.

> Rarer, too, their timber grew, and rarer still and rarer
> As the hills resembled heads now shaven clean of hair.
> For the first time, too, moreover, they felt an anxious mood
> That all their daily logging might not furnish them with fuel.[11]

China's role in the silver trade is a useful reminder of Asian centrality in the world economy of the early modern era. Its large and prosperous population, increasingly operating within a silver-based economy, fueled global commerce, vastly increasing the quantity of goods exchanged and the geographic range of world trade. Despite their obvious physical presence in the Americas, Africa, and Asia, economically speaking Europeans were essentially middlemen, funneling American silver to Asia and competing with one another for a place in the rich markets of Asia. The productivity of the Chinese economy was evident in Spanish America, where cheap and well-made Chinese goods easily outsold those of Spain. In 1594, the Spanish viceroy of Peru observed that "a man can clothe his wife in Chinese silks for [25 pesos], whereas he could not provide her with clothing of

Spanish silks with 200 pesos."[12] Indian cotton textiles likewise outsold European woolen or linen textiles in the seventeenth century to such an extent that French laws in 1717 prohibited the wearing of Indian cotton or Chinese silk clothing as a means of protecting French industry.

The "World Hunt": Fur in Global Commerce[13]

In the early modern era, furs joined silver, textiles, and spices as major items of global commerce. Their production had an important environmental impact as well as serious implications for the human societies that generated and consumed them. Furs, of course, had long provided warmth and conveyed status in colder regions of the world, but the integration of North America and of northern Asia (Siberia) into a larger world economy vastly increased their significance in global trade.

■ **Change**
Describe the impact of the fur trade on North American native societies.

By 1500, European population growth and agricultural expansion had sharply diminished the supply of fur-bearing animals, such as beaver, rabbits, sable, marten, and deer. Furthermore, much of the early modern era witnessed a period of cooling temperatures and harsh winters, known as the Little Ice Age, which may well have increased the demand for furs. "The weather is bitterly cold and everyone is in furs although we are almost in July," observed a surprised visitor from Venice while in London in 1604.[14] These conditions pushed prices higher. The cost of a good-quality beaver pelt, for example, quadrupled in France between 1558 and 1611. This translated into strong economic incentives for European traders to tap the immense wealth of fur-bearing animals found in North America.

Like other aspects of imperial expansion, the fur trade was a highly competitive enterprise. The French were most prominent in the St. Lawrence valley, around the Great Lakes, and later along the Mississippi River; British traders pushed into the Hudson Bay region; and the Dutch focused their attention along the Hudson River in what is now New York. They were frequently rivals for the great prize of North American furs. In the southern colonies of British North America, deerskins by the hundreds of thousands found a ready market in England's leather industry (see Map 15.3).

Only a few Europeans directly engaged in commercial trapping or hunting. They usually waited for Indians to bring the furs or skins initially to their coastal settlements and later to their fortified trading posts in the interior of North America. European merchants paid for the furs with a variety of trade goods, including guns, blankets, metal tools, rum, and brandy, amid much ceremony, haggling over prices, and ritualized gift-giving. Native Americans represented a cheap labor force in this international commercial effort, but they were not a directly coerced labor force.

Over the three centuries of the early modern era, enormous quantities of furs and deerskins found their way to Europe, where they considerably enhanced the standard of living in those cold climates. The environmental price was paid in the

Map 15.3   The North American Fur Trade
North America, as well as Russian Siberia, funneled an apparently endless supply of furs into the circuits of global trade during the early modern era.

Americas, and it was high. A consistent demand for beaver hats led to the near extinction of that industrious animal in much of North America by the early nineteenth century. Many other fur-bearing species were seriously depleted as the trade moved inexorably westward. By the 1760s, hunters in southeastern British colonies took about 500,000 deer every year, seriously diminishing the deer population of the region.

For the Native American peoples who hunted, trapped, processed, and trans- ported these products, the fur trade bore various benefits, particularly at the beginning. The Hurons, for example, who lived on the northern shores of Lakes Erie and Ontario in the early seventeenth century, annually exchanged some 20,000 to 30,000 pelts, mostly beaver, and in return received copper pots, metal axes, knives, cloth, firearms, and alcohol. Many of these items were of real value, which strengthened the Hurons in their relationship with neighboring peoples. These goods also enhanced the authority of Huron chiefs by providing them with gifts to distribute among their followers. At least initially, competition among Europeans ensured that Native American leaders could negotiate reason- able prices for their goods. Furthermore, their important role in the lucrative fur trade protected them for a time from the kind of extermination, enslavement, or displacement that was the fate of native peoples in Portuguese Brazil.

Nothing, however, protected them against the diseases carried by Europeans. In the 1630s and 1640s, to cite only one example of many, about half of the Hurons perished from influenza, smallpox, and other European-borne diseases. Furthermore, the fur trade generated warfare beyond anything previously known. Competition among Native American societies became more intense as the eco- nomic stakes grew higher. Catastrophic population declines owing to disease stim- ulated "mourning wars," designed to capture people who could be assimilated into much-diminished societies. A century of French-British rivalry for North America (1664–1763) forced Native American societies to take sides, to fight, and to die in these European imperial conflicts. Firearms, of course, made warfare far more deadly than before.

As many Native American peoples became enmeshed in commercial relation- ships with Europeans, they grew dependent on European trade goods. Among the Algonquians, for example, iron tools and cooking pots replaced those of stone, wood, or bone; gunpowder weapons took the place of bows and arrows; European textiles proved more attractive than traditional beaver and deerskin clothing; flint and steel were more effective for starting fires than wooden drills. A wide range of traditional crafts were thus lost, without the native peoples gaining a corresponding ability to manufacture the new items for themselves. Enthusiasm for these imported goods and continued European demands for furs and skins frequently eroded the customary restraint that characterized traditional hunting practices, resulting in the depletion of many species. One European observer wrote of the Creek Indians: "[They] wage eternal war against deer and bear . . . which is indeed carried to an unreasonable and perhaps criminal excess, since the white people have dazzled their senses with foreign superfluities."[15]

Beyond germs and guns, the most destructive of the imported goods was surely alcohol—rum and brandy, in particular. Whiskey, a locally produced grain-based alcohol, only added to the problem. With no prior experience of alcohol and little time to adjust to its easy availability, these drinks "hit Indian societies with explosive force."[16] Binge drinking, violence among young men, promiscuity, and addiction followed in many places. In 1753, Iroquois leaders complained bitterly to European authorities in Pennsylvania: "These wicked Whiskey Sellers, when they have once got the Indians in liquor, make them sell their very clothes from their backs. . . . If this practice be continued, we must be inevitably ruined."[17] In short, it was not so much the fur trade itself that decimated Native American societies, but all that accompanied it—disease, dependence, guns, alcohol, and the growing encroachment of European colonial empires.

■ **Comparison**
How did the North American and Siberian fur trades differ from each other? What did they have in common?

Much the same could be said about the other fur trade that was simultaneously taking shape within a rapidly expanding Russian Empire. As a new Russian state emerged from Mongol rule around the city of Moscow in the late fifteenth century, it became a major source of furs for both Western Europe and the Ottoman Empire. The profitability of that trade in furs was the chief incentive for Russia's rapid expansion during the sixteenth and seventeenth centuries across Siberia, where the "soft gold" of fur-bearing animals was abundant. With growing markets in both China and Europe, the fur trade greatly enriched the Russian state as well as many private merchants, trappers, and hunters. Here the silver trade and the fur trade intersected, as Europeans paid for Russian furs largely with American gold and silver.

The consequences for native Siberians were similar to those in North America as disease took its toll, as indigenous people became dependent on Russian goods, as the settler frontier encroached on native lands, and as many species of fur-bearing mammals were seriously depleted. In several ways, however, the Russian fur trade was unique. Whereas several European nations competed in North America and generally obtained their furs through commercial negotiations with Indian societies, no such competition accompanied Russian expansion across Siberia. Russian authorities imposed a tax or tribute, payable in furs, on every able-bodied Siberian male between eighteen and fifty years of age. To enforce the payment, they took hostages from Siberian societies, with death as a possible outcome if the required furs were not forthcoming. A further difference lay in the large-scale presence of private Russian hunters and trappers, who competed directly with their Siberian counterparts.

Fur and the Russians
This colored engraving shows a sixteenth-century Russian ambassador and his contingent arriving at the court of the Holy Roman Emperor and bearing gifts of animal pelts, the richest fruit of the expanding Russian Empire. (RIA Novosti)

Commerce in People: The Atlantic Slave Trade

Of all the commercial ties that linked the early modern world into a global network of exchange, none had more profound or enduring human consequences than the Atlantic slave trade. During the 400 years from the mid-fifteenth to the mid-nineteenth century, that trade in humankind took an estimated 11 million people from African societies, shipped them across the Atlantic in the infamous Middle Passage, and deposited them in the Americas, where they lived out their often brief lives as slaves. Countless millions more died in the process of capture and transport, before ever reaching American shores (see Map 15.4).

Beyond the multitude of individual tragedies that it spawned—capture and sale, displacement from home cultures, forced labor, beatings and brandings, broken families—the Atlantic slave trade transformed the societies of all of its participants. Within Africa itself, some societies were thoroughly disrupted; others were strengthened; many were corrupted. Elites were often enriched, while the slaves themselves, of course, were victimized beyond imagination.

In the Americas, the slave trade added a substantial African presence to the mix of European and Native American peoples. This African diaspora (the transatlantic

Map 15.4   The Atlantic Slave Trade Stimulated by the plantation complex of the Americas, the Atlantic slave trade represented an enormous extension of the ancient practice of people owning and selling other people.

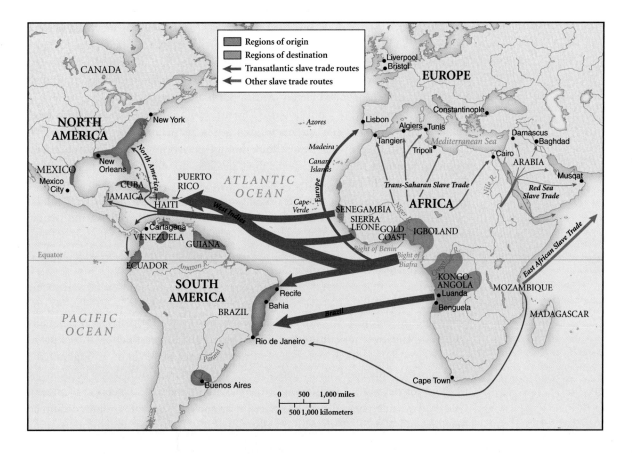

spread of African peoples) injected into these new societies issues of race that endure still in the twenty-first century. It also introduced elements of African culture, such as religious ideas, musical and artistic traditions, and cuisine, into the making of American cultures. The profits from the slave trade and the forced labor of African slaves certainly enriched European and Euro-American societies, even as the practice of slavery contributed much to the racial thinking of European peoples. Finally, slavery became a metaphor for many kinds of social oppression, quite different from plantation slavery, in the centuries that followed. Workers protested the slavery of wage labor; colonized people rejected the slavery of imperial domination; and feminists identified slavery with patriarchy.

The Slave Trade in Context

■ Comparison
What was distinctive about the Atlantic slave trade? What did it share with other patterns of slave owning and slave trading?

The Atlantic slave trade and slavery in the Americas represented the most recent large-scale expression of an almost universal human practice—the owning and exchange of human beings. With origins that go back to the earliest civilizations, slavery was widely accepted as a perfectly normal human enterprise and was closely linked to warfare and capture. Before 1500, the Mediterranean and Indian Ocean basins were the major arenas of the Old World slave trade, and southern Russia was a major source of slaves. Many African societies likewise both practiced slavery themselves and sold slaves into these international commercial networks. A trans-Saharan slave trade had long funneled African captives into Mediterranean slavery, and an East African slave trade brought Africans into the Middle East and the Indian Ocean basin. Both operated largely within the Islamic world.

Furthermore, slavery came in many forms. Although slaves were everywhere vulnerable "outsiders" to their masters' societies, in many places they could be assimilated into their owners' households, lineages, or communities. In some places, children inherited the slave status of their parents; elsewhere those children were free persons. Within the Islamic world, the preference was for female slaves by a two-to-one margin, while the later Atlantic slave trade favored males by a similar margin. Not all slaves, however, occupied degraded positions. Some in the Islamic world acquired prominent military or political status. Most slaves in the premodern world worked in their owners' households, farms, or shops, with smaller numbers laboring in large-scale agricultural or industrial enterprises.

The slavery that emerged in the Americas was distinctive in several ways. One was simply the immense size of the traffic in slaves and its centrality to the economies of colonial America. Furthermore, this New World slavery was largely based on plantation agriculture and treated slaves as a form of dehumanized property, lacking any rights in the society of their owners. Slave status throughout the Americas was inherited across generations, and there was little hope of eventual freedom for the vast majority. Nowhere else, with the possible exception of ancient Greece, was widespread slavery associated with societies affirming values of human freedom and equality. Perhaps most distinctive was the racial dimension: Atlantic slavery came to be identified wholly with Africa and with "blackness." How did this exceptional form of slavery emerge?

The origins of Atlantic slavery clearly lie in the Mediterranean world and with that now common sweetener known as sugar. Until the Crusades, Europeans knew nothing of sugar and relied on honey and fruits to sweeten their bland diets. However, as they learned from the Arabs about sugarcane and the laborious techniques for producing usable sugar, Europeans established sugar-producing plantations within the Mediterranean and later on various islands off the coast of West Africa. Sugar production was perhaps the first "modern" industry in that it required huge capital investment, substantial technology, an almost factory-like discipline among workers, and a mass market of consumers. The immense difficulty and danger of the work, the limitations attached to serf labor, and the general absence of wage workers all pointed to slavery as a source of labor for sugar plantations.

Initially, Slavic-speaking peoples from the Black Sea region furnished the bulk of the slaves for Mediterranean plantations, so much so that "Slav" became the basis for the word "slave" in many European languages. In 1453, however, when the Ottoman Turks seized Constantinople, the supply of Slavic slaves was effectively cut off. At the same time, Portuguese mariners were exploring the coast of West Africa; they were looking primarily for gold, but they also found there an alternative source of slaves available for sale. Thus, when sugar, and later tobacco and cotton, plantations took hold in the Americas, Europeans had already established links to a West African source of supply.

Largely through a process of elimination, Africa became the primary source of slave labor for the plantation economies of the Americas. Slavic peoples were no longer available; Native Americans quickly perished from European diseases; marginal Europeans were Christians and therefore supposedly exempt from slavery; and European indentured servants were expensive and temporary. Africans, on the other hand, were skilled farmers; they had some immunity to both tropical and European diseases; they were not Christians; they were, relatively speaking, close at hand; and they were readily available in substantial numbers through African-operated commercial networks.

Moreover, Africans were black. The precise relationship between slavery and European

■ **Causation**
What explains the rise of the Atlantic slave trade?

The Middle Passage
This mid-nineteenth-century painting of slaves held below deck on a Spanish slave ship illustrates the horrendous conditions of the transatlantic voyage, a journey experienced by many millions of captured Africans. (The Art Archive)

racism has long been a much-debated subject. Historian David Brion Davis has suggested the controversial view that "racial stereotypes were transmitted, along with black slavery itself, from Muslims to Christians."[18] For many centuries, Muslims had drawn on sub-Saharan Africa as one source of slaves and in the process had developed a form of racism. The fourteenth-century Tunisian scholar Ibn Khaldun wrote that black people were "submissive to slavery, because Negroes have little that is essentially human and have attributes that are quite similar to those of dumb animals."[19]

Other scholars find the origins of racism within European culture itself. For the English, argues historian Audrey Smedley, the process of conquering Ireland had generated by the sixteenth century a view of the Irish as "rude, beastly, ignorant, cruel, and unruly infidels," perceptions that were then transferred to Africans enslaved on English sugar plantations of the West Indies.[20] Whether Europeans borrowed such images of Africans from their Muslim neighbors or developed them independently, slavery and racism soon went hand in hand. "Europeans were better able to tolerate their brutal exploitation of Africans," writes a prominent world historian, "by imagining that these Africans were an inferior race, or better still, not even human."[21]

The Slave Trade in Practice

■ Connection
What roles did Europeans and Africans play in the unfolding of the Atlantic slave trade?

The European demand for slaves was clearly the chief cause of this tragic commerce, and from the point of sale on the African coast to the massive use of slave labor on American plantations, the entire enterprise was in European hands. Within Africa itself, however, a different picture emerges, for over the four centuries of the Atlantic slave trade, European demand elicited an African supply. A few early efforts by the Portuguese at slave raiding along the West African coast convinced Europeans that such efforts were unnecessary and unwise, for African societies were quite capable of defending themselves against European intrusion, and many were willing to sell their slaves peacefully. Furthermore, Europeans died like flies when they entered the interior because they lacked immunities to common tropical diseases. Thus the slave trade quickly came to operate largely with Europeans waiting on the coast, either on their ships or in fortified settlements, to purchase slaves from African merchants and political elites. Certainly Europeans tried to exploit African rivalries to obtain slaves at the lowest possible cost, and the firearms they funneled into West Africa may well have increased the warfare from which so many slaves were derived. But from the point of initial capture to sale on the coast, the entire enterprise was normally in African hands. Almost nowhere did Europeans attempt outright military conquest; instead they generally dealt as equals with local African authorities.

One English merchant in 1693 reported on his negotiations with the king of Whydah, a small kingdom on the coast of what is now Benin: "We attended his majesty with samples of our goods, and made our agreement about the prices, though not without much difficulty."[22] Those goods included both European and Indian textiles, cowrie shells (widely used as money in West Africa), European metal goods, firearms and gunpowder, tobacco and alcohol, and various decorative items such as beads. Europeans purchased some of these items—cowrie shells and Indian textiles, for example—with silver mined in the Americas. Thus the slave trade connected with commerce in silver and textiles as it became part of an emerging worldwide network of exchange. In most places most of the time, a leading scholar concluded, the slave trade took place "not unlike international trade anywhere in the world of the period."[23]

If African authorities and elite classes in many places controlled their side of the slave trade, on occasion they were almost overwhelmed by it. Many small-scale kinship-based societies, lacking the protection of a strong state, were thoroughly disrupted by raids from more powerful neighbors. Even some sizable states were destabilized. In the early sixteenth century, the kingdom of Kongo, located mostly in present-day Angola, had been badly damaged by the commerce in slaves, and the authority of its ruler had been severely undermined. In 1526, the Kongo king Afonso, himself a convert to Christianity, begged the Portuguese to halt the slave trade altogether. "We cannot calculate how great the damage is," he wrote to the king of Portugal. "[M]erchants are taking everyday our natives, sons of the land and the sons of our noblemen and vassals and our relatives."[24]

An incident along the so-called Slave Coast of West Africa during the final decades of the slave trade illustrates how even African slave traders themselves could be victimized. On this occasion in 1856, a "Yankee captain" bought some 500 slaves and then invited twenty-five "headmen or traders" aboard his ship for a drink. An American chaplain recounted what happened next as he heard the story from local people: "He [the ship's captain] was profuse in his hospitality, made them all drunk, put them in irons, sank their canoes, pocketed their money, and got under weigh. Two of the twenty five thus taken jumped overboard shortly after, and were drowned; the remainder he sold in Cuba for four hundred dollars each."[25]

Whatever the relationship between European buyers and African sellers, for the slaves themselves—who were seized in the interior, often sold several times on the harrowing journey to the coast, sometimes branded, and held in squalid slave dungeons while awaiting transportation to the New World—it was anything but a normal commercial transaction. One European engaged in the trade noted that "the negroes are so willful and loath to leave their own country, that they have often leap'd out of the canoes, boat, and ship, into the sea, and kept under water till they were drowned, to avoid being taken up and saved by our boats."[26]

Over the four centuries of the slave trade, millions of Africans underwent some such experience, but their numbers varied considerably over time. For the first 150 years (1450–1600), fewer than 4,000 slaves annually were shipped to Europe or across the Atlantic. During those years, the Portuguese were at least as much interested in African gold, spices, and textiles. Furthermore, as in Asia, they became involved in transporting African goods, including slaves, from one African port to another, thus becoming the "truck drivers" of coastal West African commerce.[27] In the seventeenth century, the pace picked up, with an average of about 10,000 slaves

Snapshot   **The Slave Trade in Numbers**

The Rise and Decline of the Slave Trade[28]

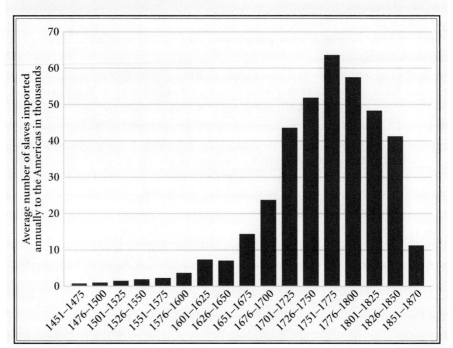

The Destination of Slaves in the Eighteenth Century[29]

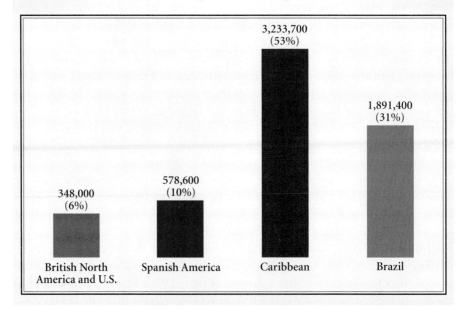

per year shipped to the Americas. By this time, the slave trade was becoming highly competitive, with the British, Dutch, and French contesting the earlier Portuguese monopoly. The eighteenth century was the high point of the slave trade as the plantation economies of the Americas boomed. By the 1750s, more than 60,000 people per year left Africa in chains, bound for the Americas and slavery.

Where did these Africans come from, and where did they go? Geographically, the slave trade drew on the societies of West Africa, from present-day Mauritania in the north to Angola in the south. Initially focused on the coastal regions, the slave trade progressively penetrated into the interior as the demand for slaves picked up. Socially, slaves were mostly drawn from various marginal groups in African societies— prisoners of war, criminals, debtors, people who had been "pawned" during times of difficulty. Thus Africans did not generally sell "their own people" into slavery. Divided into hundreds of separate, usually small-scale, and often rival communities—cities, kingdoms, microstates, clans, and villages—the various peoples of West Africa had no concept of an "African" identity. Those whom they captured and sold were normally outsiders, vulnerable people who lacked the protection of membership in an established community. When short-term economic or political advantage could be gained, such people were sold. In this respect, the Atlantic slave trade was little different from the experience of enslavement elsewhere in the world.

The destination of enslaved Africans, half a world away in the Americas, was very different. Some 80 percent wound up in Brazil or the Caribbean, where the labor demands of the plantation economy were most intense. About 5 to 6 percent found themselves in North America, with the balance in mainland Spanish America or in Europe itself (see the Snapshot). The journey across the Atlantic was horrendous almost beyond description, with the Middle Passage having an overall mortality rate of about 15 percent.

Comparing Consequences: The Impact of the Slave Trade in Africa

From the viewpoint of world history, the chief outcome of the slave trade lay in the new transregional linkages that it generated. Both commercially and demographically, Africa became a permanent part of an interacting Atlantic world. Millions of its people were now compelled to make their lives in the New World. West African economies were increasingly connected to an emerging European-centered world economy. These vast processes set in motion a chain of consequences that have transformed the lives and societies of people on both sides of the Atlantic.

■ **Change**
In what different ways did the Atlantic slave trade transform African societies?

Although the slave trade did not result in the kind of population collapse that occurred in the Americas, it certainly slowed Africa's growth at a time when Europe, China, and other regions were expanding demographically. Scholars have estimated that sub-Saharan Africa represented about 18 percent of the world's population in 1600, but only 6 percent in 1900.[30] A portion of that difference reflects the slave trade's impact on Africa's population history.

That impact derived not only from the loss of millions of people over four centuries but also from the economic stagnation and political disruption that the slave trade generated. Economically, the slave trade stimulated little positive change in Africa because those Africans who benefited most from the traffic in people were not investing in the productive capacities of African societies. Although European imports generally did not displace traditional artisan manufacturing, no technological breakthroughs in agriculture or industry increased the wealth available to these societies. Maize and manioc (cassava), introduced from the Americas, added a new source of calories to African diets, but the international demand was for Africa's people, not its agricultural products.

Within particular African societies, the impact of the slave trade differed considerably from place to place and over time. Particularly in small-scale societies that were frequently subjected to slave raiding and that had little centralized authority, insecurity was pervasive. Oral traditions in southern Ghana, for example, reported that "there was no rest in the land," that people went about in groups rather than alone, and that mothers kept their children inside when European ships appeared.[31] Some larger kingdoms such as Kongo and Oyo slowly disintegrated as access to trading opportunities and firearms enabled outlying regions to establish their independence. However, African authorities also sought to take advantage of the new commercial opportunities and to manage the slave trade in their own interests, as the contrasting experience of the neighboring kingdoms of Benin and Dahomey illustrates.[32]

The kingdom of Benin, in the forest area of present-day Nigeria, was one of the oldest and most highly developed states in the coastal hinterland of West Africa, dating perhaps to the eleventh century C.E. Its capital was a large, walled city with wide avenues, a lavish court, a wealthy elite, and a powerful monarch, or *oba*, who strictly controlled the country's trade. Benin's uniqueness lay in its relatively successful efforts to avoid a deep involvement in the slave trade and to diversify the exports with which it purchased European firearms and other goods. As early as 1516, the oba began to restrict the slave trade and soon forbade the export of male slaves altogether, a ban that lasted until the early eighteenth century. By then, the oba's authority over outlying areas had declined, and the country's major exports of pepper and cotton cloth had lost out to Asian and then European competition. In these circumstances, Benin felt compelled to resume limited participation in the slave trade. But even at the height of the trade, in the late eighteenth century, Benin exported fewer than 1,000 slaves a year.

Among the Aja-speaking peoples to the west of Benin, the situation was very different. There the slave trade had thoroughly disrupted a series of small and weak states along the coast. Some distance inland, the kingdom of Dahomey arose in the early eighteenth century, at least in part as an effort to contain the constant raiding and havoc occasioned by the coastal trade. It was a unique and highly authoritarian state in which commoners and chiefs alike were responsible directly to the king and in which the power of lineages and secret societies was considerably weakened.

For a time, Dahomey tried to limit the external slave trade, to import European craftsmen, and to develop plantation agriculture within the kingdom, but all this failed. In view of hostile relations with the neighboring kingdom of Oyo and others, Dahomey instead turned to a vigorous involvement in the slave trade, under strict royal control. The army conducted annual slave raids, and the government soon came to depend on the trade for its essential revenues. Unlike in Benin, the slave trade in Dahomey became the chief business of the state and remained so until well into the nineteenth century.

Reflections: Economic Globalization— Then and Now

The study of history reminds us of two quite contradictory truths. One is that our lives in the present bear remarkable similarities to those of people long ago. We are perhaps not as unique as we might think. The other is that our lives are very different from theirs and that things have changed substantially. This chapter about global commerce—long-distance trade in spices and textiles, silver and gold, beaver pelts and deerskins, slaves and sugar—provides both perspectives.

If we are accustomed to think about globalization as a product of the late twentieth century, early modern world history provides a corrective. Those three centuries reveal much that is familiar to people of the twenty-first century—the global circulation of goods; an international currency; production for a world market; the growing economic role of the West on the global stage; private enterprise, such as the British and Dutch East India companies, operating on a world scale; national governments eager to support their merchants in a highly competitive environment. By the eighteenth century, many Europeans dined from Chinese porcelain dishes called "china," wore Indian-made cotton textiles, and drank chocolate from Mexico, tea from China, and coffee from Yemen while sweetening these beverages with sugar from the Caribbean or Brazil. The millions who worked to produce these goods, whether slave or free, were operating in a world economy. Some industries were thoroughly international. New England rum producers, for example, depended on molasses imported from the Caribbean, while the West Indian sugar industry used African labor and European equipment to produce for a global market.

Nonetheless, early modern economic globalization was a far cry from that of the twentieth century. Most obvious perhaps were scale and speed. By 2000, immensely more goods circulated internationally and far more people produced for and depended on the world market than was the case even in 1750. Back-and-forth communications between England and India that took eighteen months in the eighteenth century could be accomplished in an hour by telegraph in the late nineteenth century and almost instantaneously via the Internet in the late twentieth century. Moreover, by 1900 globalization was firmly centered in the economies of

Europe and North America. In the early modern era, by contrast, Asia in general and China in particular remained major engines of the world economy, despite the emerging presence of Europeans around the world. By the end of the twentieth century, the booming economies of India and China suggested at least a partial return to that earlier pattern.

Early modern globalization differed in still other ways from that of the contemporary world. Economic life then was primarily preindustrial, still powered by human and animal muscles, wind, and water and lacking the enormous productive capacity that accompanied the later technological breakthrough of the steam engine and the Industrial Revolution. Finally, the dawning of a genuinely global economy in the early modern era was tied unapologetically to empire building and to slavery, both of which had been discredited by the late twentieth century. Slavery lost its legitimacy during the nineteenth century, and formal territorial empires largely disappeared in the twentieth. Most people during the early modern era would have been surprised to learn that a global economy, as it turned out, could function effectively without either of these long-standing practices.

Second Thoughts

What's the Significance?

Indian Ocean commercial network	British/Dutch East India companies	Potosí
trading post empires	Tokugawa shogunate	"soft gold"
Spanish Philippines	"silver drain"	African diaspora
		Benin/Dahomey

Big Picture Questions

1. In what specific ways did trade foster change in the world of the early modern era?
2. To what extent did Europeans transform earlier patterns of commerce, and in what ways did they assimilate into those older patterns?
3. Describe and account for the differing outcomes of European expansion in the Americas (see Chapter 14), Africa, and Asia.
4. How should we distribute the moral responsibility or blame for the Atlantic slave trade? Is this a task appropriate for historians?
5. What lasting legacies of early modern globalization are evident in the early twenty-first century? Pay particular attention to the legacies of the slave trade.

Next Steps: For Further Study

Glenn J. Ames, *The Globe Encompassed: The Age of European Discovery, 1500–1700* (2007). An up-to-date survey of European expansion in the early modern era.

Andre Gunder Frank, *ReOrient: Global Economy in the Asian Age* (1998). An account of the early modern world economy that highlights the centrality of Asia.

Erik Gilbert and Jonathan Reynolds, *Trading Tastes: Commodity and Cultural Exchange to 1750* (2006). A world historical perspective on transcontinental and transoceanic commerce.

David Northrup, ed., *The Atlantic Slave Trade* (2002). A fine collection of essays about the origins, practice, impact, and abolition of Atlantic slavery.

John Richards, *The Endless Frontier* (2003). Explores the ecological consequences of early modern commerce.

John Thornton, *Africa and Africans in the Making of the Atlantic World* (1998). A well-regarded but somewhat controversial account of the slave trade, with an emphasis on African authorities as active and independent players in the process.

"Atlantic Slave Trade and Slave Life in the Americas: A Visual Record," http://hitchcock.itc.virginia .edu/Slavery/index.php. An immense collection of maps and images illustrating the slave trade and the life of slaves in the Americas.

CHAPTER SIXTEEN

Religion and Science

1450–1750

"This country wasn't founded on Muslim beliefs or evolution. This country was founded on Christianity, and our students should be taught as such."[1] That was the view of one member of a rural school board in Dover, Pennsylvania, in 2004. It reflected a long-running tension between modern science and some Christian believers within the United States. The school board had mandated the teaching of "intelligent design"—the notion that life is so complex that it must have been created by some higher power—alongside evolutionary biology. A federal judge subsequently struck down the school board's policy, arguing that it violated the separation of church and state, and board members who mandated teaching intelligent design were defeated for reelection.

Few observers of the controversy paused to reflect on the historical processes of the early modern era that provide a context for this contemporary debate. It was during those three centuries that Christianity first achieved a global presence, including, of course, its transplantation to the Americas. That a religion of Middle Eastern origin should come to dominate the Western Hemisphere surely ranks high among the strange twists of world history. At the same time, the Scientific Revolution was generating among European thinkers a very different approach to the world, and it too took root in the Americas. The relationship between religion and science in the West has been long and complex, and by no means always antagonistic. But the controversy in this small Pennsylvania community in the early twenty-first century illustrates the continuing tension, at least in some places, between these alternative ways of understanding the universe. That tension has been an important

---

The Virgin of Guadalupe: According to Mexican tradition, a dark-skinned Virgin Mary appeared to an indigenous peasant named Juan Diego in 1531, an apparition reflected in this Mexican painting from 1720. Belief in the Virgin of Guadalupe represented the incorporation of Catholicism into the emerging culture and identity of Mexico. (National Palace Mexico City/Gianni Dagli Orti/The Art Archive) thread in the cultural history of the Christian world, and much of the rest of the world as well, over the past five centuries.

ALONGSIDE NEW EMPIRES AND NEW PATTERNS OF COMMERCE, the early modern centuries also witnessed novel cultural transformations that likewise connected distant peoples. Riding the currents of European empire building and commercial expansion, Christianity was solidly established in the Americas and the Philippines; far more modestly in Siberia, China, Japan, and India; and hardly at all within the vast and growing domains of Islam. A cultural tradition largely limited to Europe now became a genuine world religion, generating a multitude of cultural encounters. While this ancient faith was spreading, a new understanding of the universe and a new approach to knowledge were taking shape among European thinkers of the Scientific Revolution, giving rise to another kind of cultural encounter—that between science and religion. In certain respects, science was a new and competing worldview, and for some it was almost a new religion. It challenged the established outlooks of many European Christians and, over the next several centuries, of other religious or cultural traditions as well. In time, science became a defining feature of global modernity, achieving a worldwide acceptance that exceeded that of Christianity or any other religious tradition.

Although Europeans were central players in the globalization of Christianity and the emergence of modern science, they did not act alone in the cultural transformations of the early modern era. Asian, African, and Native American peoples largely determined how Christianity would be accepted, rejected, or transformed as it entered new cultural environments. Science emerged within an international and not simply a European context, and it met varying receptions in different parts of the world. Islam continued a long pattern of religious expansion and renewal, even as Christianity began to compete with it as a world religion. Buddhism maintained its hold in much of East Asia, as did Hinduism in South Asia and various smaller-scale religious traditions in Africa. And Europeans themselves were certainly affected by the many "new worlds" that they now encountered. The cultural interactions of the early modern era, in short, were not a "one-way street."

The Globalization of Christianity

Despite its Middle Eastern origins, Christianity was largely limited to Europe at the beginning of the early modern era. In 1500, the world of Christendom stretched from Spain and England in the west to Russia in the east, with small and beleaguered communities of various kinds in Egypt, Ethiopia, southern India, and Central Asia. Internally, Christianity was seriously divided between the Roman Catholics of Western and Central Europe and the Eastern Orthodox of Eastern Europe and Russia. Externally, it was very much on the defensive against an expansive Islam. Muslims had ousted Christian Crusaders from their toeholds in the Holy

Land by 1300, and with the Ottoman seizure of Constantinople in 1453, they had captured the prestigious capital of Eastern Orthodoxy. The Ottoman siege of Vienna in 1529 marked a Muslim advance into the heart of Central Europe. Except in Spain, which had recently been reclaimed for Christendom after centuries of Muslim rule, the future, it must have seemed, lay with Islam rather than Christianity.

Western Christendom Fragmented: The Protestant Reformation

As if these were not troubles enough, in the early sixteenth century the Protestant Reformation shattered the unity of Roman Catholic Christianity, which for the previous 1,000 years had provided the cultural and organizational foundation of Western European civilization. The Reformation began in 1517 when a German priest, Martin Luther, publicly invited debate about various abuses within the Roman Catholic Church by posting a document, known as the Ninety-five Theses, on the door of a church in Wittenberg. In itself, this was nothing new, for many people were critical of the luxurious life of the popes, the corruption and immorality of some clergy, the Church's selling of indulgences (said to remove the penalties for sin), and other aspects of church life and practice.

What made Luther's protest potentially revolutionary, however, was its theological basis. A troubled and brooding man who was anxious about his relationship with God, Luther recently had come to a new understanding of salvation, which held that it came through faith alone. Neither the good works of the sinner nor the sacraments of the Church had any bearing on the eternal destiny of the soul, for faith was a free gift of God, graciously granted to his needy and undeserving people. To Luther, the source of these beliefs, and of religious authority in general, was not the teaching of the Church, but the Bible alone, interpreted according to the individual's conscience. All of this challenged the authority of the Church and called into question the special position of the clerical hierarchy and of the pope in particular. In sixteenth-century Europe, this was the stuff of revolution.

Contrary to Luther's original intentions, his ideas ultimately provoked a massive schism within the world of Catholic Christendom, for they came to express a variety of political, economic, and social tensions as well as religious differences. Some kings and princes, many of whom had long disputed the political authority of the pope, found in

■ **Change**
In what ways did the Protestant Reformation transform European society, culture, and politics?

The Protestant Reformation This sixteenth-century painting by the well-known German artist Lucas Cranach the Elder shows Martin Luther and his supporters using a giant quill to write their demands for religious reform on a church door. It memorializes the posting of the Ninety-five Theses in 1517, which launched the Protestant Reformation. (Dr. Henning Schleifenbaum, Siegen, Germany/Visual Connection Archive)

Snapshot   **Catholic/Protestant Differences in the Sixteenth Century**

	Catholic	Protestant
Religious authority	Pope and church hierarchy	The Bible, as interpreted by individual Christians
Role of the pope	Ultimate authority in faith and doctrine	Denied the authority of the pope
Ordination of clergy	Apostolic succession: direct line between original apostles and all subsequently ordained clergy	Apostolic succession denied; ordination by individual congregations or denominations
Salvation	Importance of church sacraments as channels of God's grace	By faith alone; God's grace is freely and directly granted to believers
Status of Mary	Highly prominent, ranking just below Jesus; provides constant intercession for believers	Less prominent; denied Mary's intercession on behalf of the faithful
Prayer	To God, but often through or with Mary and saints	To God alone; no role for Mary and saints
Holy Communion	Transubstantiation: bread and wine become the actual body and blood of Christ	Denied transubstantiation; bread and wine have a spiritual or symbolic significance
Role of clergy	Generally celibate; sharp distinction between priests and laypeople; mediators between God and humankind	Ministers may marry; priesthood of all believers; clergy have different functions (to preach, administer sacraments) but no distinct spiritual status

these ideas a justification for their own independence and an opportunity to gain the lands and taxes previously held by the Church. In the Protestant idea that all vocations were of equal merit, middle-class urban dwellers found a new religious legitimacy for their growing role in society, since the Roman Catholic Church was associated in their eyes with the rural and feudal world of aristocratic privilege. For common people, who were offended by the corruption and luxurious living of some bishops, abbots, and popes, the new religious ideas served to express their opposition to the entire social order, particularly in a series of German peasant revolts in the 1520s.

Although large numbers of women were attracted to Protestantism, Reformation teachings and practices did not offer them a substantially greater role in the church or society. In Protestant-dominated areas, the veneration of Mary and female saints ended, leaving the male Christ figure as the sole object of worship. Protestant opposition to celibacy and monastic life closed the convents, which had offered some women an alternative to marriage. Nor were Protestants (except the Quakers) any more willing than Catholics to offer women an official role within their churches. The importance that Protestants gave to reading the Bible for oneself stimulated education and literacy for women, but given the emphasis on women as wives and mothers subject to male supervision, they had little opportunity to use that education outside of the family.

Reformation thinking spread quickly both within and beyond Germany, thanks in large measure to the recent invention of the printing press. Luther's many pamphlets and his translation of the New Testament into German were soon widely available. "God has appointed the [printing] Press to preach, whose voice the pope is never able to stop," declared one Reformation leader.[2] As the movement spread to France, Switzerland, England, and elsewhere, however, it also splintered, amoeba-like, into a variety of competing Protestant churches—Lutheran, Calvinist, Anglican, Quaker, Anabaptist—many of which subsequently subdivided, producing a bewildering array of Protestant denominations. Each was distinctive, but none gave allegiance to Rome or the pope.

Thus to the divided societies and the fractured political system of Europe was now added the potent brew of religious difference, operating both within and between states (see Map 16.1). For more than thirty years (1562–1598), French society was torn by violence between Catholics and the Protestant minority known as Huguenots. On a single day, August 24, 1572, Catholic mobs in Paris massacred some 3,000 Huguenots, and thousands more perished in provincial towns in the weeks that followed. Finally, a war-weary monarch, Henry IV, issued the Edict of Nantes (1598), which granted a substantial measure of religious toleration to French Protestants, though with the intention that they would soon return to the Catholic Church. The culmination of European religious conflict took shape in the Thirty Years' War (1618–1648), a Catholic-Protestant struggle that began in the Holy Roman Empire but eventually engulfed most of Europe. It was a horrendously destructive war, during which, scholars estimate, between 15 and 30 percent of the German population perished from violence, famine, or disease. Finally, the Peace of Westphalia (1648) brought the conflict to an end, with some reshuffling of boundaries and an agreement that each state was sovereign, authorized to control religious affairs within its own territory. Whatever religious unity Catholic Europe had once enjoyed was now permanently broken.

The Protestant breakaway, combined with reformist tendencies within the Catholic Church itself, provoked a Catholic Counter-Reformation. In the Council of Trent (1545–1563), Catholics clarified and reaffirmed their unique doctrines and practices, such as the authority of the pope, priestly celibacy, the veneration of saints and relics, and the importance of church tradition and good works, all of which Protestants had rejected. Moreover, they set about correcting the abuses and corruption that had stimulated the Protestant movement in the first place by

Map 16.1 Reformation Europe in the Sixteenth Century

The rise of Protestantism added yet another set of religious divisions, both within and between states, to European Christendom, which was already sharply divided between the Roman Catholic Church and the Eastern Orthodox Church.

Protestant dominant
Some Protestant influence
Catholic
Eastern Orthodox Christian
━━━ Boundary of the Holy Roman Empire

placing a new emphasis on the education of priests and their supervision by bishops. A crackdown on dissidents included the censorship of books, fines, exile, penitence, and occasionally the burning of heretics. Renewed attention was given to individual spirituality and personal piety. New religious orders, such as the Society of Jesus (Jesuits), provided a dedicated brotherhood of priests committed to the renewal of the Catholic Church and its extension abroad.

Although the Reformation was profoundly religious, it encouraged a skeptical attitude toward authority and tradition, for it had, after all, successfully challenged the immense prestige and power of the pope and the established Church. Protestant reformers fostered religious individualism as people were now encouraged to read and interpret the scriptures for themselves and to seek salvation without the mediation of the Church. For some in the centuries that followed, that skepticism and the habit of thinking independently were turned against revealed religion itself. Thus the Protestant Reformation opened some space for new directions in European intellectual life.

In short, it was a more highly fragmented but also a renewed and revitalized Christianity that established itself around the world in the several centuries after 1500.

Christianity Outward Bound

Christianity motivated European political and economic expansion and also benefited from it. The resolutely Catholic Spanish and Portuguese both viewed their movement overseas as a continuation of a long crusading tradition, which only recently had completed the liberation of their countries from Muslim control. When Vasco da Gama's small fleet landed in India in 1498, local authorities understandably asked, "What brought you hither?" The reply: they had come "in search of Christians and of spices."[3] Likewise, Columbus, upon arriving in the Americas, expressed the no doubt sincere hope that the people "might become Christians," even as he promised his Spanish patrons an abundant harvest of gold, spice, cotton, aloe wood, and slaves.[4] Neither man sensed any contradiction or hypocrisy in this blending of religious and material concerns.

■ **Connection**
How was European imperial expansion related to the spread of Christianity?

If religion drove and justified European ventures abroad, it is difficult to imagine the globalization of Christianity without the support of empire. Colonial settlers and traders, of course, brought their faith with them and sought to replicate it in their newly conquered homelands. New England Puritans, for example, planted a distinctive Protestant version of Christianity in North America, with an emphasis on education, moral purity, personal conversion, civic responsibility, and little tolerance for competing expressions of the faith. They did not show much interest in converting native peoples but sought rather to push them out of their ancestral territories. It was missionaries, mostly Catholic, who actively spread the Christian message beyond European communities. Organized in missionary orders such as the Dominicans, Franciscans, and Jesuits, Portuguese missionaries took the lead in Africa and Asia, while Spanish and French missionaries were most prominent in the Americas. Missionaries of the Russian Orthodox Church likewise accompanied the expansion of the Russian Empire across Siberia, where priests and monks ministered to Russian settlers and trappers, who often donated their first sable furs to a church or monastery.

Missionaries had their greatest success in Spanish America and in the Philippines, areas that shared two critical elements beyond their colonization by Spain. Most

Japanese Christian Martyrs
Christianity was beginning to take root in sixteenth-century Japan, but intensive persecution by Japanese authorities in the early seventeenth century largely ended that process. This monument was later erected in memory of twenty-six martyrs, Japanese and European alike, who were executed during this suppression of Christianity. (Photo Agency MH Martin Hladik, Photographer)

■ **Connection**
In what ways was European Christianity assimilated into the Native American cultures of Spanish America?

important, perhaps, was an overwhelming European presence, experienced variously as military conquest, colonial settlement, missionary activity, forced labor, social disruption, and disease. Surely it must have seemed as if the old gods had been bested and that any possible future lay with the powerful religion of the European invaders. A second common factor was the absence of a literate world religion in these two regions. Throughout the modern era, peoples solidly rooted in Confucian, Buddhist, Hindu, or Islamic traditions proved far more resistant to the Christian message than those who practiced more localized, small-scale, orally based polytheistic religions.

Conversion and Adaptation in Spanish America

Spanish America and China illustrate the difference between those societies in which Christianity became widely practiced and those that largely rejected it. Both cases, however, represent major cultural encounters of a kind that was becoming more frequent as European expansion brought the Christian faith to distant peoples with very different cultural traditions.

The decisive conquest of the Aztec and Inca empires and all that followed from it—disease, population collapse, loss of land to Europeans, forced labor, resettlement into more compact villages—created a setting in which the religion of the victors took hold in Spanish American colonies. Europeans saw their political and military success as a demonstration of the power of the Christian God. Native American peoples generally agreed, and by 1700 or earlier the vast majority had been baptized and saw themselves in some respects as Christians. After all, other conquerors such as the Aztecs and the Incas had always imposed their gods in some fashion on defeated peoples. It made sense, both practically and spiritually, to affiliate with the Europeans' God, saints, rites, and rituals. Many millions accepted baptism, contributed to the construction of village churches, attended services, and embraced images of Mary and other saints.

Earlier conquerors, however, had made no attempt to eradicate local deities and religious practices. The flexibility and inclusiveness of Mesoamerican and Andean religions had made it possible for subject people to accommodate the gods of their new rulers while maintaining their own traditions. But Europeans were different. They claimed an exclusive religious truth and sought the utter destruction of local gods and everything associated with them. Operating within a Spanish colonial regime that actively encouraged conversion, missionaries often proceeded by persuasion and patient teaching. At times, though, their frustration with the persistence of "idolatry, superstition, and error" boiled over into violent campaigns designed to uproot old religions once and for all. In 1535, the bishop of Mexico boasted that he had destroyed 500 pagan shrines and 20,000 idols. During the seventeenth and early eighteenth centuries, church authorities in the Andean region periodically launched movements of "extirpation," designed to fatally undermine native religion. They smashed religious images and ritual objects, publicly urinated on native "idols," desecrated the remains of ancestors, held religious trials and "processions of shame" aimed at humiliating offenders, and flogged "idolaters."[5]

Occasionally, overt resistance erupted. One such example was the religious revivalist movement in central Peru in the 1560s, known as Taki Onqoy ("dancing sickness"). Possessed by the spirits of local gods, or *huacas*, traveling dancers and teachers predicted that an alliance of Andean deities would soon overcome the Christian God, inflict the intruding Europeans with the same diseases that they had brought to the Americas, and restore the world of the Andes to an imagined earlier harmony. They called on native peoples to cut off all contact with the Spanish, to reject Christian worship, and to return to traditional practices. "The world has turned about," one member declared, "and this time God and the Spaniards [will be] defeated and all the Spaniards killed and their cities drowned; and the sea will rise and overwhelm them, so that there will remain no memory of them."[6]

More common than such frontal attacks on Christianity, which were quickly smashed by colonial authorities, were efforts at blending two religious traditions, reinterpreting Christian practices within an Andean framework, and incorporating local elements into an emerging Andean Christianity. Even female dancers in the Taki Onqoy movement sometimes took the names of Christian saints, seeking to appropriate for themselves the religious power of Christian figures. Within Andean Christian communities, people might offer the blood of a llama to strengthen a village church or make a cloth covering for the Virgin Mary and a shirt for an image of a huaca with the same material. Although the state cults of the Incas faded away, missionary attacks did not succeed in eliminating the influence of local huacas. Images and holy sites might be destroyed, but the souls of the huacas remained, and their representatives gained prestige. One resilient Andean resident inquired of a Jesuit missionary: "Father, are you tired of taking our idols from us? Take away that mountain if you can, since that is the God I worship."[7]

In Mexico as well, an immigrant Christianity was assimilated into patterns of local culture. Parishes were organized largely around precolonial towns or regions. Churches built on or near the sites of old temples became the focus of community identity. *Cofradias*, church-based associations of laypeople, organized community processions and festivals and made provision for a proper funeral and burial for their members. Central to an emerging Mexican Christianity were the saints who closely paralleled the functions of precolonial gods. Saints were imagined as parents of the local community and the true owners of its land, and their images were paraded through the streets on the occasion of great feasts and were collected by individual households. Although parish priests were almost always Spanish, the *fiscal*, or leader of the church staff, was a native Christian of great local prestige, who carried on the traditions and role of earlier religious specialists.

Throughout the colonial period and beyond, many Mexican Christians also took part in rituals derived from the past, with little sense that this was incompatible with Christian practice. Incantations to various gods for good fortune in hunting, farming, or healing; sacrifices of self-bleeding; offerings to the sun; divination; the use of hallucinogenic drugs—all of these rituals provided spiritual assistance in those areas of everyday life not directly addressed by Christian rites. Conversely, these practices also showed signs of Christian influence. Wax candles, normally used in Christian services, might now appear in front of a stone image of a precolonial god. The anger of a neglected saint, rather than that of a traditional god, might explain someone's illness and require offerings, celebration, or a new covering to regain his or her favor.[8] In such ways did Christianity take root in the new cultural environments of Spanish America, but it was a distinctly Andean or Mexican Christianity, not merely a copy of the Spanish version.

An Asian Comparison: China and the Jesuits

■ Comparison

Why were missionary efforts to spread Christianity so much less successful in China than in Spanish America?

The Chinese encounter with Christianity was very different from that of Native Americans in Spain's New World empire. The most obvious difference was the political context. The peoples of Spanish America had been defeated, their societies thoroughly disrupted, and their cultural confidence sorely shaken. China, on the other hand, encountered European Christianity between the sixteenth and eighteenth centuries during the powerful and prosperous Ming (1368–1644) and Qing (1644–1912) dynasties. Although the transition between these two dynasties occasioned several decades of internal conflict, at no point was China's political independence or cultural integrity threatened by the handful of European missionaries and traders operating in the country.

The reality of a strong, independent, confident China required a different missionary strategy, for Europeans needed the permission of Chinese authorities to operate in the country. Whereas Spanish missionaries working in a colonial setting sought primarily to convert the masses, the leading missionary order in China, the Jesuits, took deliberate aim at the official Chinese elite. Following the lead of their most famous missionary, Matteo Ricci (in China 1582–1610), many Jesuits learned Chinese, became thoroughly acquainted with classical Confucian texts, and dressed like Chinese scholars. Initially, they downplayed their mission to convert and instead emphasized their interest in exchanging ideas and learning from China's ancient culture. As highly educated men, the Jesuits carried the recent secular knowledge of Europe—science, technology, mapmaking—to an audience of curious Chinese scholars. In presenting Christian teachings, Jesuits were at pains to be respectful of Chinese culture, pointing out parallels between Confucianism and

Christianity rather than portraying it as something new and foreign. They chose to define Chinese rituals honoring the emperor or venerating ancestors as secular or civil observances rather than as religious practices that had to be abandoned. Such efforts to accommodate Chinese culture contrast sharply with the frontal attacks on Native American religions in the Spanish Empire.

The religious and cultural outcomes of the missionary enterprise likewise differed greatly in the two regions. Nothing approaching the mass conversion to Christianity of Native American peoples took place in China. During the sixteenth and seventeenth centuries, a modest number of Chinese scholars and officials—who were attracted by the personal lives of the missionaries, by their interest in Western science, and by the moral certainty that Christianity offered—did become Christians. Jesuit missionaries found favor for a time at the Chinese imperial court, where their mathematical, astronomical, technological, and mapmaking skills rendered them useful. For more than a century, they were appointed to head the Chinese Bureau of Astronomy. Among ordinary people, Christianity spread very modestly amid tales of miracles attributed to the Christian God, while missionary teachings about "eternal life" sounded to some like Daoist prescriptions for immortality. At most, though, missionary efforts over the course of some 250 years (1550–1800) resulted in 200,000 to 300,000 converts, a minuscule number in a Chinese population approaching 300 million by 1800. What explains the very limited acceptance of Christianity in early modern China?

Fundamentally, the missionaries offered little that the Chinese really needed. Confucianism for the elites and Buddhism, Daoism, and a multitude of Chinese gods and spirits at the local level adequately supplied the spiritual needs of most Chinese. Furthermore, it became increasingly clear that Christianity was an "all or nothing" faith that required converts to abandon much of traditional Chinese culture. Christian monogamy,

Jesuits in China

In this seventeenth-century Dutch engraving, two Jesuit missionaries hold a map of China. Their mapmaking skills were among the reasons that the Jesuits were initially welcomed among the educated elite of that country. (Frontispiece to *China Illustrated* by Athanasius Kircher [1601–80] 1667 [engraving], Dutch School, [17th century]/Private Collection, The Stapleton Collection/The Bridgeman Art Library)

for example, seemed to require Chinese men to put away their concubines. What would happen to these deserted women?

By the early eighteenth century, the papacy and competing missionary orders came to oppose the Jesuit policy of accommodation. The pope claimed authority over Chinese Christians and declared that sacrifices to Confucius and the veneration of ancestors were "idolatry" and thus forbidden to Christians. The pope's pronouncements represented an unacceptable challenge to the authority of the emperor and an affront to Chinese culture. In 1715, an outraged Emperor Kangxi wrote:

> I ask myself how these uncultivated Westerners dare to speak of the great precepts of China. . . . [T]heir doctrine is of the same kind as the little heresies of the Buddhist and Taoist monks. . . . These are the greatest absurdities that have ever been seen. As from now I forbid the Westerners to spread their doctrine in China; that will spare us a lot of trouble.[9]

This represented a major turning point in the relationship of Christian missionaries and Chinese society. Many were subsequently expelled, and missionaries lost favor at court.

In other ways as well, missionaries played into the hands of their Chinese opponents. Their willingness to work under the Manchurian Qing dynasty, which came to power in 1644, discredited them with those Chinese scholars who viewed the Qing as uncivilized foreigners and their rule in China as disgraceful and illegitimate. Missionaries' reputation as miracle workers further damaged their standing as men of science and rationality, for elite Chinese often regarded miracles and supernatural religion as superstitions, fit only for the uneducated masses. Some viewed the Christian ritual of Holy Communion as a kind of cannibalism. Others came to see missionaries as potentially subversive, for various Christian groups met in secret, and such religious sects had often provided the basis for peasant rebellion. Nor did it escape Chinese notice that European Christians had taken over the Philippines and that their warships were active in the Indian Ocean. Perhaps the missionaries, with their great interest in maps, were spies for these aggressive foreigners. All of this contributed to the general failure of Christianity to secure a prominent presence in China.

Persistence and Change in Afro-Asian Cultural Traditions

Although Europeans were central players in the globalization of Christianity, theirs was not the only expanding or transformed culture of the early modern era. African religious ideas and practices, for example, accompanied slaves to the Americas. Common African forms of religious revelation—divination, dream interpretation, visions, spirit possession—found a place in the Africanized versions of Christianity that emerged in the New World. Europeans frequently perceived these practices as evidence of sorcery, witchcraft, or even devil worship and tried to suppress them.

Nonetheless, syncretic (blended) religions such as Vodou in Haiti, Santeria in Cuba, and Candomble and Macumba in Brazil persisted. They derived from various West African traditions and featured drumming, ritual dancing, animal sacrifice, and spirit possession. Over time, they incorporated Christian beliefs and practices such as church attendance, the search for salvation, and the use of candles and crucifixes and often identified their various spirits or deities with Catholic saints.

Expansion and Renewal in the Islamic World

The early modern era likewise witnessed the continuation of the "long march of Islam" across the Afro-Asian world. In sub-Saharan Africa, in the eastern and western wings of India, and in Central and Southeast Asia, the expansion of the Islamic frontier, a process already almost 1,000 years in the making, extended farther still. Conversion to Islam generally did not mean a sudden abandonment of old religious practices in favor of the new. Rather it was more often a matter of "assimilating Islamic rituals, cosmologies, and literatures into . . . local religious systems."[10]

■ Explanation
What accounts for the continued spread of Islam in the early modern era and for the emergence of reform or renewal movements within the Islamic world?

Continued Islamization usually was not the product of conquering armies and expanding empires. It depended instead on wandering Muslim holy men, Islamic scholars, and itinerant traders, none of whom posed a threat to local rulers. In fact, such people often were useful to those rulers and their village communities. They offered literacy in Arabic, established informal schools, provided protective charms containing passages from the Quran, served as advisers to local authorities and healers to the sick, often intermarried with local people, and generally did not insist that new converts give up their older practices. What they offered, in short, was connection to the wider, prestigious, prosperous world of Islam. Islamization extended modestly even to the Americas, where enslaved African Muslims planted their faith, particularly in Brazil. There Muslims led a number of slave revolts in the early nineteenth century.

To more orthodox Muslims, this religious syncretism, which accompanied Islamization almost everywhere, became increasingly offensive, even heretical. Such sentiments played an important role in movements of religious renewal and reform that emerged throughout the vast Islamic world of the eighteenth century. Scholars and religious leaders frequently called attention to the ways in which the practice of Islam had come to deviate from the original teachings of Muhammad and the Quran. For example, in India, which was governed by the Muslim Mughal Empire, religious resistance to official policies that accommodated Hindus found concrete expression during the reign of the emperor Aurangzeb (1658–1707) (see Chapter 14). A series of religious wars in West Africa during the eighteenth and early nineteenth centuries took aim at corrupt Islamic practices and the rulers, Muslim and non-Muslim alike, who permitted them. In Southeast and Central Asia, tension grew between practitioners of localized and blended versions of Islam and those who sought to purify such practices in the name of a more authentic and universal faith.

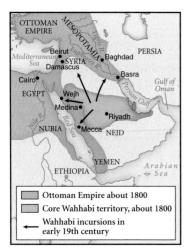

The Expansion of Wahhabi Islam

The most well known and widely visible of these Islamic renewal movements took place during the mid-eighteenth century in Arabia itself, where the religion had been born 1,000 years earlier. A young Muslim theologian, Abd al-Wahhab (1703–1792), argued that the declining fortunes of the Islamic world were the result of a gradual process of decay that had crept in over the centuries, as Muslims allowed themselves to be drawn away from the essentials of the faith. He was particularly upset by common religious practices in central Arabia that seemed to him idolatry—the widespread veneration of Sufi saints and their tombs, the adoration of natural sites, and even the respect paid to Muhammad's tomb at Mecca. All of this was a dilution of the absolute monotheism of authentic Islam.

Abd al-Wahhab began preaching among the tribes of the Arabian Desert, calling for a return to a doctrinaire Islam with an austere and puritanical lifestyle, in strict accordance with the sharia (Islamic law). When in the 1740s he joined forces with Muhammad Ibn Saud, a sympathetic local chieftain, the movement took on a political dimension and soon led to the creation of a state. Within that state, women were expected to subject themselves strictly to the traditional patronage of husbands and male relatives. Offending tombs were razed; "idols" were eliminated; books on logic were destroyed; the use of tobacco, hashish, and musical instruments was forbidden; and certain taxes not authorized by religious teaching were abolished. By the early nineteenth century, this new reformist state encompassed much of central Arabia, with Mecca itself coming under Wahhabi control in 1806. Although an Egyptian army broke the power of the Wahhabis in 1818, the movement's influence continued to spread across the Islamic world.

Together with the ongoing expansion of the religion, these movements of reform and renewal signaled the continuing cultural vitality of the "abode of Islam," even as the European presence on the world stage assumed larger dimensions. In the nineteenth and twentieth centuries, such movements persisted and became associated with resistance to the political, military, and cultural intrusion of the European West into the affairs of the Islamic world.

China: New Directions in an Old Tradition

■ **Comparison**

In what ways did Asian cultural changes in the early modern era parallel those of Europe, and in what ways were they different?

Neither China nor India experienced cultural or religious change as dramatic as that of the Reformation in Europe, nor did Confucian or Hindu cultures during the early modern era spread widely, as did Christianity and Islam. Nonetheless, neither of these traditions remained static. As in Christian Europe, challenges to established orthodoxies in China and India emerged as commercial and urban life, as well as political change, fostered new thinking.

China during the Ming and Qing dynasties continued to operate broadly within a Confucian framework, enriched now by the insights of Buddhism and Daoism to generate a system of thought called Neo-Confucianism. Chinese Ming dynasty rulers, in their aversion to the despised Mongols, embraced and actively supported this native Confucian tradition, whereas the foreign Manchu or Qing rulers did so in order to woo Chinese intellectuals to support the new dynasty. Within this context, a considerable amount of controversy, debate, and new thinking emerged during the early modern era.

During late Ming times, for example, the influential thinker Wang Yangmin (1472–1529) argued that truth and moral knowledge were innate to the human person. Thus anyone could achieve a virtuous life by introspection, without the extended education and constant striving for improvement that traditional Confucianism prescribed for an elite class of "gentlemen." Such ideas figured prominently among Confucian scholars of the sixteenth century, although critics later contended that the individualism that such thinking promoted had undermined the Ming dynasty and contributed to China's conquest by the foreign Manchus. Some Chinese Buddhists as well sought to make their religion more accessible to ordinary people, by suggesting that laypeople at home could undertake practices similar to those performed by monks in monasteries. Withdrawal from the world was not necessary for enlightenment. This kind of moral or religious individualism bore some similarity to the thinking of Martin Luther, who argued that individuals could seek salvation by "faith alone," without the assistance of a priestly hierarchy.

Another new direction in Chinese elite culture took shape in a movement known as *kaozheng*, or "research based on evidence." Intended to "seek truth from facts," kaozheng was critical of the unfounded speculation of conventional Confucian philosophy and instead emphasized the importance of verification, precision, accuracy, and rigorous analysis in all fields of inquiry. During the late Ming years, this emphasis generated works dealing with agriculture, medicine, pharmacology, botany, craft techniques, and more. In the Qing era, kaozheng was associated with a recovery and critical analysis of ancient historical documents, which sometimes led to sharp criticism of Neo-Confucian orthodoxy. It was a genuinely scientific approach to knowledge, but it was applied more to the study of the past than to the natural world of astronomy, physics, or anatomy, as in the West.

While such matters occupied the intellectual elite of China, in the cities a lively popular culture emerged among the less well educated. For city-dwellers, plays, paintings, short stories, and especially novels provided diversion and entertainment that were a step up from what could be found in teahouses and wine shops. Numerous "how-to" painting manuals allowed a larger public to participate in this favorite Chinese art form. Even though Confucian scholars disdained popular fiction, a vigorous printing industry responded to the growing demand for exciting novels. The most famous was Cao Xueqin's mid-eighteenth-century novel *The Dream of the Red Chamber*, a huge book that contained 120 chapters and some 400 characters, most of them women. It explored the social life of an eighteenth-century elite family with connections to the Chinese court.

India: Bridging the Hindu/Muslim Divide

In a largely Hindu India, ruled by the Muslim Mughal Empire, several significant cultural departures took shape in the early modern era that brought Hindus and Muslims together in new forms of religious expression. One was the flourishing of a devotional form of Hinduism known as *bhakti*. Through songs, prayers, dances, poetry, and rituals, devotees sought to achieve union with one or another of India's many deities. Appealing especially to women, the bhakti movement provided an avenue for social criticism. Its practitioners often set aside caste distinctions and disregarded the detailed rituals of the Brahmin priests in favor of direct contact with the divine. This emphasis had much in common with the mystical Sufi form of Islam and helped blur the distinction between these two traditions in India.

Among the most beloved of bhakti poets was Mirabai (1498–1547), a high-caste woman from northern India who abandoned her upper-class family and conventional Hindu practice. Upon her husband's death, tradition asserts, she declined to burn herself on his funeral pyre (a practice known as *sati*). She further offended caste restrictions by taking as her guru (religious teacher) an old untouchable shoemaker. To visit him, she apparently tied her saris together and climbed down the castle walls at night. Then she would wash his aged feet and drink the water from these ablutions. Much of her poetry deals with her yearning for union with Krishna, a Hindu deity she regarded as her husband, lover, and lord.

> What I paid was my social body, my town body, my family body, and all my inherited jewels.
> Mirabai says: The Dark One [Krishna] is my husband now.[11]

Yet another major cultural change that blended Islam and Hinduism emerged with the growth of Sikhism as a new and distinctive religious tradition in the Punjab region of northern India. Its founder, Guru Nanak (1469–1539), had been involved in the bhakti movement but came to believe that "there is no Hindu; there is no Muslim; only God." His teachings and those of subsequent gurus also set aside caste distinctions and untouchability and ended the seclusion of women, while proclaiming the "brotherhood of all mankind" as well as the essential equality

Guru Nanak
In this early-eighteenth-century manuscript painting, Guru Nanak, the founder of Sikhism, and his constant companion Mardana (with a musical instrument) encounter a robber (the man with a sword) along the road. According to the story accompanying the painting, that experience persuaded the robber to abandon his wicked ways and become a follower of the Sikh path. (© British Library Board)

of men and women. Drawing converts from Punjabi peasants and merchants, both Muslim and Hindu, the Sikhs gradually became a separate religious community. They developed their own sacred book, known as the Guru Granth (teacher book); created a central place of worship and pilgrimage in the Golden Temple of Amritsar; and pre-scribed certain dress requirements for men, including keeping hair and beards uncut, wearing a turban, and carrying a short sword. During the seventeenth century, Sikhs encountered hostility from both the Mughal Empire and some of their Hindu neigh-bors. In response, Sikhism evolved from a peaceful religious movement, blending Hindu and Muslim elements, into a militant community whose military skills were highly valued by the British when they took over India in the late eighteenth century.

A New Way of Thinking: The Birth of Modern Science

While some Europeans were actively attempting to spread the Christian faith to distant corners of the world, others were nurturing an understanding of the cos-mos very much at odds with traditional Christian teaching. These were the makers of Europe's Scientific Revolution, a vast intellectual and cultural transformation that took place between the mid-sixteenth and early eighteenth centuries. No longer would men of science rely on the external authority of divinely revealed scripture or the speculations of ancient philosophers or the received wisdom of cul-tural tradition. Instead a combination of careful observations, controlled experi-ments, and the formulation of general laws, expressed in mathematical terms, became the standard means of obtaining knowledge and understanding in every domain of life. Those who created this revolution—Copernicus from Poland, Galileo from Italy, Descartes from France, Newton from England, and many oth-ers—saw themselves as departing radically from older ways of thinking. They were the "moderns" combating the "ancients." "The old rubbish must be thrown away," wrote a seventeenth-century English scientist. "These are the days that must lay a new Foundation of a more magnificent Philosophy."[12]

The long-term significance of the Scientific Revolution can hardly be overes-timated. Within early modern Europe, it fundamentally altered ideas about the place of humankind within the cosmos and sharply challenged both the teachings and the authority of the Church. Over the past several centuries, it has substantially eroded religious belief and practice in the West. When applied to the affairs of human society, scientific ways of thinking challenged ancient social hierarchies and political systems and played a role in the revolutionary upheavals of the modern era. But science also was used to legitimize racial and gender inequalities, by defining people of color and women as inferior by nature. When married to the technolog-ical innovations of the Industrial Revolution, science fostered both the marvels of modern production and the horrors of modern means of destruction. By the twen-tieth century, science had become so widespread that it largely lost its association with European culture and became the chief symbol of global modernity.

The Question of Origins: Why Europe?

■ Comparison

Why did the Scientific Revolution occur in Europe rather than in China or the Islamic world?

Why did that breakthrough occur first in Europe and during the early modern era? The realm of Islam, after all, had generated the most advanced science in the world during the centuries between 800 and 1400. Arab scholars could boast of remarkable achievements in mathematics, astronomy, optics, and medicine, and their libraries far exceeded those of Europe.[13] And what of China? Its elite culture of Confucianism was both sophisticated and secular, less burdened by religious dogma than in the Christian or Islamic worlds; its technological accomplishments and economic growth were unmatched anywhere in the several centuries after 1000. In neither civilization, however, did these achievements lead to the kind of intellectual breakthrough that occurred in Europe.

Europe's historical development as a reinvigorated and fragmented civilization (see Chapter 10) arguably gave rise to conditions uniquely favorable to the scientific enterprise. By the twelfth and thirteenth centuries, Europeans had evolved a legal system that guaranteed a measure of independence for a variety of institutions—the Church, towns and cities, guilds, professional associations, and universities. This legal revolution was based on the idea of a "corporation," a collective group of people that was treated as a unit, a legal person, with certain rights to regulate and control its own members. Thus the Roman Catholic Church achieved some measure of autonomy from secular authorities, making Europe quite different from the Islamic world, where the separation of religious and secular law gained little traction.

Most important for the development of science in the West was the autonomy of its emerging universities. By 1215, the University of Paris was recognized as a "corporation of masters and scholars," which could admit and expel students, establish courses of instruction, and grant a "license to teach" to its faculty. Such universities—for example, in Paris, Bologna, Oxford, Cambridge, and Salamanca—became "neutral zones of intellectual autonomy" in which scholars could pursue their studies in relative freedom from the dictates of church or state authorities. Within them, the study of the natural order began to slowly separate itself from philosophy and theology and to gain a distinct identity. Their curricula featured "a basically scientific core of readings and lectures" that drew heavily on the writings of the Greek thinker Aristotle, which had only recently become available to Western Europeans. Most of the major figures in the Scientific Revolution had been trained in and were affiliated with these universities.

In the Islamic world, by contrast, science was patronized by a variety of local authorities, but it occurred largely outside the formal system of higher education. Within colleges known as madrassas, Quranic studies and religious law held the central place, whereas philosophy and natural science were viewed with great suspicion. To religious scholars, the Quran held all wisdom, and scientific thinking might well challenge it. An earlier openness to free inquiry and religious toleration was increasingly replaced by a disdain for scientific and philosophical inquiry, for it seemed to lead only to uncertainty and confusion. "May God protect us from useless knowledge" was a saying that reflected this outlook. Nor did Chinese authorities permit independent institutions of higher learning in which scholars could conduct their studies in relative freedom. Instead Chinese education focused on preparing for a rigidly defined set of civil service examinations and emphasized the humanistic and moral texts of classical Confucianism. "The pursuit of scientific subjects," one recent historian concluded, "was thereby relegated to the margins of Chinese society."[14]

Muslim Astronomy and the Scientific Revolution
This diagram of the eclipses of the moon by the eleventh-century Muslim mathematician and astronomer al-Biruni is a reminder of Muslim scientific achievements, some of which stimulated European scientific thinking. (Roland and Sabrina Michaud/Rapho/Eyedea)

Beyond its distinctive institutional development, Western Europe was in a position to draw extensively upon the knowledge of other cultures, especially that of the Islamic world. Arab medical texts, astronomical research, and translations of Greek classics played a major role in the birth of European natural philosophy (as science was then called) between 1000 and 1500. In constructing his proofs for a sun-centered solar system, Copernicus in the sixteenth century almost certainly drew upon astronomical work and mathematical formulations undertaken 200 to 300 years earlier in the Islamic world, particularly at the famous Muslim observatory of Maragha in present-day Iran.

In the sixteenth through the eighteenth centuries, Europeans found themselves at the center of a massive new exchange of information as they became aware of lands, peoples, plants, animals, societies, and religions from around the world. This tidal wave of new knowledge, uniquely available to Europeans, clearly shook up older ways of thinking and opened the way to new conceptions of the world. The sixteenth-century Italian doctor, mathematician, and writer Girolamo Cardano (1501–1576) clearly expressed this sense of wonderment: "The most unusual [circumstance of my life] is that I was born in this century in which the whole world became known; whereas the ancients were familiar with but a little more than a third part of it." He worried, however, that amid this explosion of knowledge, "certainties will be exchanged for uncertainties."[15] It was precisely those uncertainties—skepticism about established views—that provided such a fertile cultural ground for the emergence of modern science.

Science as Cultural Revolution

Before the Scientific Revolution, educated Europeans held a view of the world that derived from Aristotle, perhaps the greatest of the ancient Greek philosophers, and from Ptolemy, a Greco-Egyptian mathematician and astronomer who lived in

■ Change
What was revolutionary about the Scientific Revolution?

Snapshot   **Major Thinkers and Achievements of the Scientific Revolution**

Thinker/Scientist	Achievements
Nicolaus Copernicus (Polish; 1473–1543)	Posited that sun is at the center of solar system, earth rotates on its axis, and earth and planets revolve around the sun
Andreas Vesalius (Flemish; 1514–1564)	"Father of anatomy"; made detailed drawings of human body based on dissection
Francis Bacon (English; 1561–1626)	Emphasized observation and experimentation as the key to modern science
Galileo Galilei (Italian; 1564–1642)	Developed an improved telescope; discovered sunspots, mountains on the moon, and Jupiter's moons; performed experimental work on the velocity of falling objects
Johannes Kepler (German; 1571–1630)	Posited that planets follow elliptical, not circular, orbits; described laws of planetary motion
William Harvey (English; 1578–1657)	Described the circulation of the blood and the function of the heart
René Descartes (French; 1596–1650)	Emphasized the importance of mathematics and logical deduction in understanding the physical world; invented analytical geometry
Isaac Newton (English; 1642–1727)	Synthesized earlier findings around the concept of universal gravitation; invented calculus; formulated concept of inertia and laws of motion

Alexandria during the second century C.E. To medieval European thinkers, the earth was stationary and at the center of the universe, and around it revolved the sun, moon, and stars embedded in ten spheres of transparent crystal. This understanding coincided well with the religious purpose of the Catholic Church because the attention of the entire universe was centered on the earth, where the drama of salvation took place, and on its human inhabitants. It was a universe of divine purpose, with angels guiding the hierarchically arranged spheres along their way while God watched over the whole from his realm beyond the spheres. The Scientific Revolution was revolutionary because it fundamentally challenged this understanding of the universe.

The initial breakthrough came from the Polish mathematician and astronomer Nicolaus Copernicus, whose famous book *On the Revolutions of the Heavenly Spheres* was published in the year of his death, 1543. Its essential argument was that "at the middle of all things lies the sun" and that the earth, like the other planets, revolved around it. Thus the earth was no longer unique or at the center of God's attention.

Other European scientists built on Copernicus's central insight, and some even argued that other inhabited worlds and other kinds of humans existed. Less speculatively, in the early seventeenth century Johannes Kepler, a German mathematician, showed that the planets followed elliptical orbits, undermining the ancient belief that they moved in perfect circles. The Italian Galileo Galilei developed an improved telescope, with which he observed sunspots, or blemishes, moving across the face of the sun. This called into question the traditional notion that no change or imperfection marred the heavenly bodies. His discovery of the moons of Jupiter and many new stars suggested a cosmos far larger than the bounded or finite universe of traditional astronomy. Some thinkers began to discuss the notion of an infinite universe in which humankind occupied a mere speck of dust in an unimaginable vastness. The French mathematician and philosopher Blaise Pascal (1623–1662) perhaps spoke for many when he wrote: "The eternal silence of infinite space frightens me."[16]

The culmination of the Scientific Revolution came in the work of Sir Isaac Newton, the Englishman who formulated the modern laws of motion and mechanics, which were scarcely modified until the twentieth century. Central to Newton's thinking was the concept of universal gravitation. "All bodies whatsoever," Newton declared, "are endowed with a principle of mutual gravitation."[17] Here was the grand unifying idea of early modern science. The radical implication of this view was that the heavens and the earth, long regarded as separate and distinct spheres, were not so different after all, for the motion of a cannonball on earth or the falling of an apple from a tree obeyed the same natural laws that governed the orbiting planets.

By the time Newton died, the view of the physical universe held by educated Europeans had substantially changed. It was no longer propelled by angels and spirits but functioned on its own according to timeless principles that could be described mathematically. In Kepler's view, "the machine of the universe is not similar to a divine animated being but similar to a clock."[18] Furthermore, it was a machine that regulated itself, requiring neither God nor angels to account for its normal operation. Knowledge of that universe could be obtained through human reason alone—by observation, deduction, and experimentation—without the aid of ancient authorities or divine revelation. The French philosopher René Descartes resolved "to seek no other knowledge than that which I might find within myself, or perhaps in the book of nature."[19]

Like the physical universe, the human body also lost some of its mystery. The careful dissections of cadavers and animals enabled doctors and scientists to describe the human body with much greater accuracy and to understand the circulation of the blood throughout the body. The heart was no longer the mysterious center of the body's heat and the seat of its passions; instead it was just another machine, a complex muscle that functioned as a pump.

Much of this thinking developed in the face of strenuous opposition from the Catholic Church, for both its teachings and its authority were under attack. The

Italian philosopher Giordano Bruno, proclaiming an infinite universe and many worlds, was burned at the stake in 1600. Galileo too was compelled by the Church to publicly renounce his belief that the earth moved around an orbit and rotated on its axis.

But not all was conflict between the Church and an emerging science. None of the early scientists rejected Christianity. Galileo himself proclaimed the compatibility of science and faith when he wrote that "God is no less excellently revealed in Nature's actions than in the sacred statements of the Bible."[20] Newton was a serious biblical scholar and saw no necessary contradiction between his ideas and belief in God. "This most beautiful system of the sun, planets, and comets," he declared, "could only proceed from the counsel and dominion of an intelligent Being."[21] The Church gradually accommodated as well as resisted the new ideas, admitting that science was competent in its limited sphere but insisting that religion held the key to ultimate questions concerning human salvation and the larger purpose of the universe.

Science and Enlightenment

■ Change

In what ways did the Enlightenment challenge older patterns of European thinking?

Initially limited to a small handful of scholars, the ideas of the Scientific Revolution spread to a wider European public during the eighteenth century. That process was aided by novel techniques of printing and book-making, by a popular press, and by a host of scientific societies. Moreover, the new approach to knowledge—rooted in human reason, skeptical of authority, expressed in natural laws—was now applied to human affairs, not just to the physical universe. The Scottish professor Adam Smith (1723–1790), for example, formulated laws that accounted for the operation of the economy and which, if followed, would generate inevitably favorable results for society. Growing numbers of people believed that the long-term outcome of scientific development would be "enlightenment," a term that has come to define the eighteenth century in European history. If human reason could discover the laws that governed the universe, surely it could uncover ways in which humankind might govern itself more effectively.

"What is Enlightenment?" asked the prominent German intellectual Immanuel Kant (1724–1804). "It is man's emergence from his self-imposed . . . inability to use one's own understanding without another's guidance. . . . Dare to know! 'Have the courage to use your own understanding' is therefore the motto of the enlightenment."[22] Although they often disagreed sharply with one another, Enlightenment thinkers shared this belief in the power of knowledge to transform human society. They also shared a satirical, critical style, a commitment to open-mindedness and inquiry, and in various degrees a hostility to established political and religious authority.

Many took aim at arbitrary governments, the "divine right of kings," and the aristocratic privileges of European society. The English philosopher John Locke (1632–1704) offered principles for constructing a constitutional government, a contract between rulers and ruled that was created by human ingenuity rather than divinely prescribed. Any number of writers, including many women, advocated education for women as a means of raising their status in society.

Much of Enlightenment thinking was directed against the superstition, ignorance, and corruption of established religion. In his *Treatise on Toleration*, the French writer Voltaire (1694–1778) reflected the outlook of the Scientific Revolution as he commented sarcastically on religious intolerance.

> This little globe, nothing more than a point, rolls in space like so many other globes; we are lost in its immensity. Man, some five feet tall, is surely a very small part of the universe. One of these imperceptible beings says to some of his neighbors in Arabia or Africa: "Listen to me, for the God of all these worlds has enlightened me; there are nine hundred million little ants like us on the earth, but only my anthill is beloved of God; He will hold all others in horror through all eternity; only mine will be blessed, the others will be eternally wretched."[23]

Voltaire's own faith, like many others among the "enlightened," was deism. Deists believed in a rather abstract and remote Deity, sometimes compared to a clockmaker, who had created the world, but not in a personal God who intervened in history or tampered with natural law. Others became *pantheists*, who believed that God and nature were identical. Among the most radical were the several Dutchmen who wrote the *Treatise of Three Imposters*, which claimed that Moses, Jesus, and Muhammad were fraudulent imposters who based their teachings on "the ignorance of Peoples [and] resolved to keep them in it."[24]

Though solidly rooted in Europe, Enlightenment thought was influenced by the growing global awareness of its major thinkers. Voltaire, for example, idealized China as an empire governed by an elite of secular scholars selected for their talent, which stood in sharp contrast to continental Europe, where aristocratic birth and military prowess were far more important. Throughout much of the eighteenth century, a fad for things Chinese—furniture styles, decorative arts, dishes, lacquerware, wallpaper—shaped the tastes of European elites.

The central theme of the Enlightenment—and what made it potentially revolutionary—was the idea of progress. Human society was not fixed by tradition or divine command but could be changed, and improved, by human action guided by reason. This view was a sharp departure from much of premodern social thinking, and it inspired those who later made the American, French, Haitian, and Latin American revolutions (see Chapter 17). No one expressed this soaring confidence in the "real improvement of humanity" more effectively than the French thinker the Marquis de Condorcet (1743–1794). The future, in his view,

Uncovering the Human Skeleton
This drawing by the sixteenth-century Flemish anatomist Andreas Vesalius suggests a rational and philosophical approach to the human predicament, even as it presents the human skeleton with scientific precision. (Courtesy, National Library of Medicine)

promised the end of slavery, racism, gender inequality, supernatural religion, political tyranny, and contagious disease. "The day will come when the sun will shine only on free men, born knowing no other master but their reason," he declared. "The perfectibility of humanity is indefinite."[25] Born of the Scientific Revolution, that was the faith of the Enlightenment. For some, it was virtually a new religion.

The age of the Enlightenment also witnessed a reaction against too much reliance on human reason. Jean-Jacques Rousseau (1712–1778) minimized the importance of book learning for the education of children and prescribed instead an immersion in nature, which taught self-reliance and generosity rather than the greed and envy fostered by "civilization." The Romantic movement in art and literature appealed to emotion, intuition, passion, and imagination rather than cold reason and scientific learning. Religious awakenings—complete with fiery sermons, public repentance, and intense personal experience of sin and redemption—shook Protestant Europe and North America. Science and the Enlightenment surely challenged religion, and for some they eroded religious belief and practice. Just as surely, though, religion persisted, adapted, and revived for many others.

Looking Ahead: Science in the Nineteenth Century

■ Change
How did nineteenth-century developments in the sciences challenge the faith of the Enlightenment?

The perspectives of the Enlightenment were challenged not only by romanticism and religious "enthusiasm" but also by the continued development of science itself. This remarkable phenomenon justifies a brief look ahead at several scientific developments in the nineteenth century.

Modern science was a cumulative and self-critical enterprise, which in the nineteenth century and after was applied to new domains of human inquiry in ways that undermined some of the assumptions of the Enlightenment. In the realm of biology, for example, Charles Darwin (1809–1882) laid out a complex argument that all of life was in flux, that over millions of years new species of plants and animals were continuously emerging and becoming extinct. Human beings were not excluded from this vast process, for they too were the work of evolution operating through natural selection. Darwin's famous books *The Origin of Species* (1859) and *The Descent of Man* (1871) were as shattering to traditional religious views as Copernicus's ideas about a sun-centered universe had been several centuries earlier.

At the same time, Karl Marx (1818–1883) articulated a view of human history that likewise emphasized change and struggle. Conflicting social classes—slave owners and slaves, nobles and peasants, capitalists and workers—successively drove the process of historical transformation. Although he was describing the evolution of human civilization, Marx saw himself as a scientist. He based his theories on extensive historical research; like Newton and Darwin, he sought to formulate general laws that would explain events in a rational way. Nor did he believe in heavenly intervention, chance, or the divinely endowed powers of kings. The coming of socialism, in this view, was not simply a good idea; it was inscribed in the laws of historical development.

Like the intellectuals of the Enlightenment, Darwin and Marx believed strongly in progress, but in their thinking, conflict and struggle rather than reason and education were the motors of progress. The image of the tranquil, rational, and autonomous individual created by the Enlightenment was fading. Individuals of all species were now viewed as caught in vast systems of biological, economic, and social conflict.

The work of the Viennese doctor Sigmund Freud (1856–1939) applied scientific techniques to the operation of the human mind and emotions and in doing so cast further doubt on Enlightenment conceptions of human rationality. At the core of each person, Freud argued, lay primal impulses toward sexuality and aggression, which were only barely held in check by the thin veneer of social conscience derived from civilization. Our neuroses arose from the ceaseless struggle between our irrational drives and the claims of conscience. This too was a far cry from the Enlightenment conception of the human condition.

European Science beyond the West

In the long run, the achievements of the Scientific Revolution spread globally, becoming the most widely sought-after product of European culture and far more desired than Christianity, democracy, socialism, or Western literature. In the early modern era, however, the level of interest in European scientific thinking within major Asian societies was both modest and selective.

In China, for example, Qing dynasty emperors and scholars were most interested in European astronomy and mathematics, derived largely from Jesuit missionaries, because those disciplines proved useful in predicting eclipses, reforming the calendar, and making accurate maps of the empire. European medicine, however, held little interest for Chinese physicians before the nineteenth century. But the reputation of the Jesuits suffered when it became apparent in the 1760s that for two centuries the missionaries had withheld information about Copernican views of a sun-centered solar system because those ideas had been condemned by the Church. Nonetheless, European science had a substantial impact on a number of Chinese scholars as it interacted with the data-based kaozheng movement, described by one participant as "an ant-like accumulation of facts."[26] European mathematics was of particular interest to kaozheng researchers who were exploring the history of Chinese mathematics. To encourage their skeptical colleagues that the barbarian Europeans had something to offer in this field, some Chinese scholars argued that European mathematics had in fact grown out of much earlier Chinese ideas and could therefore be adopted with comfort.[27] In such ways, early modern Chinese thinkers selectively assimilated Western science very much on their own terms.[28]

Although Japanese authorities largely closed their country off from the West in the early seventeenth century (see Chapter 15), one window remained open. Alone among Europeans, the Dutch were permitted to trade in Japan at a single location

■ **Connection**
In what ways was European science received in the major civilizations of Asia in the early modern era?

near Nagasaki, but not until 1720 did the Japanese lift the ban on importing Western books. Then a number of European texts in medicine, astronomy, geography, mathematics, and other disciplines were translated and studied by a small group of Japanese scholars. They were especially impressed with Western anatomical studies, for in Japan dissection was work fit only for outcasts. Returning from an autopsy conducted by Dutch physicians, several Japanese observers reflected on their experience: "We remarked to each other how amazing the autopsy had been, and how inexcusable it had been for us to be ignorant of the anatomical structure of the human body."[29] Nonetheless, this small center of "Dutch learning," as it was called, remained isolated amid a pervasive Confucian-based culture. Not until the mid-nineteenth century, when Japan was forcibly opened to Western penetration, would European science assume a prominent place in Japanese culture.

Like China and Japan, the Ottoman Empire in the sixteenth and seventeenth centuries was an independent, powerful, successful society whose intellectual elites saw no need for a wholesale embrace of things European. Ottoman scholars were conscious of the rich tradition of Muslim astronomy and chose not to translate the works of major European scientists such as Copernicus, Kepler, or Newton, although they were broadly aware of European scientific achievements by 1650. Insofar as they were interested in these developments, it was for their practical usefulness in making maps and calendars rather than for their larger philosophical implications. In any event, the notion of a sun-centered solar system did not cause the kind of upset that it did in Europe.[30]

More broadly, theoretical science of any kind—Muslim or European—faced an uphill struggle in the face of a conservative Islamic educational system. In 1580, for example, a highly sophisticated astronomical observatory was dismantled under pressure from conservative religious scholars and teachers, who interpreted an outbreak of the plague as God's displeasure with those who were seeking to penetrate his secrets. As in Japan, the systematic embrace of Western science would have to await the nineteenth century, when the Ottoman Empire was under far more intense European pressure and reform seemed more necessary.

Reflections: Cultural Borrowing and Its Hazards

Ideas are important in human history. They shape the mental or cultural worlds that people everywhere inhabit, and they often influence behavior as well. Many of the ideas developed or introduced during the early modern era have had enormous and continuing significance in the centuries that followed. The Western Hemisphere was solidly incorporated into Christendom. A Wahhabi version of Islam remains the official faith of Saudi Arabia into the twenty-first century and has influenced many contemporary Islamic revival movements. Modern science and the associated notions of progress have become for many people something approaching a new religion.

Accompanying the development of these ideas has been a great deal of cultural borrowing. Filipinos, Siberians, and many Native American peoples borrowed Christianity from Europeans. Numerous Asian and African peoples borrowed Islam from the Arabs. Northern Indian Sikhs drew upon both Hindu and Muslim teachings. Europeans borrowed scientific ideas from the Islamic world.

In virtually every case, though, that borrowing was selective rather than wholesale, even when it took place under conditions of foreign domination or colonial rule. Many peoples who appropriated Christianity or Islam certainly did not accept the rigid exclusivity and ardent monotheism of those faiths. Elite Chinese were far more interested in European astronomy and mathematics than in Western medicine, while Japanese scholars became fascinated with the anatomical work of the Dutch. Neither, however, adopted Christianity in a widespread manner.

Borrowing was frequently the occasion for serious conflict. Some objected to much borrowing at all, particularly when it occurred under conditions of foreign domination or foreign threat. Thus members of the Taki Onqoy movement in Peru sought to wipe out Spanish influence and control, while Chinese and Japanese authorities clamped down firmly on European missionaries, even as they maintained some interest in European technological and scientific skills. Another kind of conflict derived from the efforts to control the terms of cultural borrowing. For example, European missionaries and Muslim reformers alike sought to root out "idolatry" among native converts.

To ease the tensions of cultural borrowing, efforts to "domesticate" foreign ideas and practices proliferated. Thus the Jesuits in China tried to point out similarities between Christianity and Confucianism, and Native American converts identified Christian saints with their own gods and spirits. By the late seventeenth century, some local churches in central Mexico had come to associate Catholicism less with the Spanish than with ancient pre-Aztec communities and beliefs that were now restored to their rightful position.

The pace of global cultural borrowing and its associated tensions stepped up even more as Europe's modern transformation unfolded in the nineteenth century and as its imperial reach extended and deepened around the world.

Second Thoughts

What's the Significance?

Protestant Reformation	Wang Yangmin	Newton
Catholic Counter-Reformation	kaozheng	the European Enlightenment
Taki Onqoy	Mirabai	Voltaire
Jesuits in China	Sikhism	Condorcet and the idea of
Wahhabi Islam	Copernicus	progress

To assess your mastery of the material in this chapter, see the **Online Study Guide** at bedfordstmartins.com/strayer.

Big Picture Questions

1. Why did Christianity take hold in some places more than in others?
2. In what ways was the missionary message of Christianity shaped by the cultures of Asian and American peoples?
3. Compare the processes by which Christianity and Islam became world religions.
4. In what ways did the spread of Christianity, Islam, and modern science give rise to culturally based conflicts?
5. Based on Chapters 13 through 16, how does the history of Islam in the early modern era challenge a Eurocentric understanding of those centuries?

Next Steps: For Further Study

For Web sites and documents related to this chapter, see **Make History** at bedfordstmartins.com/strayer.

Natana J. Delong-Bas, *Wahhabi Islam: From Revival and Reform to Global Jihad* (2004). A careful study of the origins of Wahhabi Islam and its subsequent development.

Patricia B. Ebrey et al., *East Asia: A Cultural, Social, and Political History* (2005). A broad survey by major scholars in the field.

Geoffrey C. Gunn, *First Globalization: The Eurasian Exchange, 1500–1800* (2003). Explores the two-way exchange of ideas between Europe and Asia in the early modern era.

Toby E. Huff, *The Rise of Early Modern Science* (2003). A fascinating and controversial explanation as to why modern science arose in the West rather than in China or the Islamic world.

Steven Shapin, *The Scientific Revolution* (1996). A brief, accessible, and scholarly account of the emergence of modern science.

Paul R. Spickard and Kevin M. Cragg, *A Global History of Christians* (1994). A broad-brush account of the global spread of Christianity and its various expressions in different cultures.

Internet Modern History Sourcebook, "The Scientific Revolution," http://www.fordham.edu/halsall/mod/modsbook09.html. A collection of primary-source documents dealing with the breakthrough to modern science in Europe.

PART FIVE

The European Moment in World History

1750–1914

Contents

European Centrality and the Problem of Eurocentrism

During the century and a half between 1750 and 1914, sometimes referred to as the "long nineteenth century," two new and related phenomena held center stage in the global history of humankind and represent the major themes of the four chapters that follow. The first of these, explored in Chapters 17 and 18, was the creation of a new kind of human society, commonly called "modern," which was the outgrowth of the Scientific, French, and Industrial revolutions, all of which took shape in Western Europe. Those societies generated many of the ideas that have guided human behavior over the past several centuries—notions of progress, constitutional government, political democracy, socialism, nationalism, feminism, and opposition to slavery.

The second theme of this long nineteenth century, which is addressed in Chapters 19 and 20, was the growing ability of these modern societies to exercise enormous power and influence over the rest of humankind. In some places, this occurred within growing European empires, such as those that governed India, Southeast Asia, and Africa. Elsewhere, it took place through less formal means—economic penetration, military intervention, diplomatic pressure, missionary activity—in states that remained officially independent, such as China, Japan, the Ottoman Empire, and various countries in Latin America.

Together, these two phenomena thrust Western Europe, and to a lesser extent North America, into a new and far more prominent role in world history than ever before, for it was in those European societies that modern ways of living emerged most fully. Those societies, and their North American offspring, also came to exercise a wholly unprecedented role in world affairs, as they achieved, collectively, something approaching global dominance by the early twentieth century.

Eurocentric Geography and History

That unprecedented power included the ability to rewrite geography and history in ways that centered the human story on Europe and to impose those views on other people. Thus maps placed Europe at the center of the world, while dividing Asia in half. Europe was granted continental status, even though it was more accurately only the western peninsula of Asia, much as India was its southern peninsula. Other regions of the world, such as the Far East or the Near (Middle) East, were defined in terms of their distance from Europe. The entire world came to measure

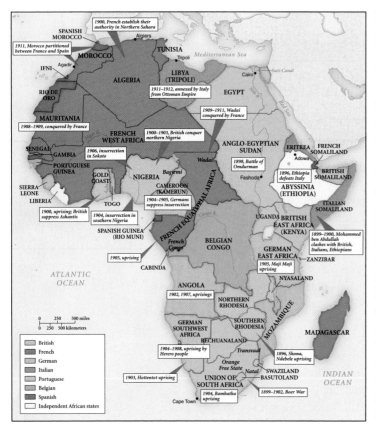

Conquest and Resistance in Colonial Africa (p. 593)

longitude from a line, known as the prime meridian, that passes through the Royal Astronomical Observatory in Greenwich, England.

History textbooks as well often reflected a Europe-centered outlook, sometimes blatantly. In 1874, the American author William O. Swinton wrote *An Outline of the World's History*, a book intended for use in high school and college classes, in which he flatly declared that "the race to which we belong, the Aryan, has always played the leading part in the great drama of the world's progress."[1] Other peoples and civilizations, by contrast, were long believed to be static and unchanging, thus largely lacking any real history. Most Europeans assumed that these "backward" peoples and regions were either headed in the European direction or doomed to extinction. Until the mid-twentieth century, such ideas went largely unchallenged in the Western world. Their implication was that history was a race toward the finish line of modernity. That Europeans arrived there first seemed to suggest something unique, special, or superior about them or their culture, while everyone else struggled to overcome their inadequacy and catch up.

As the discipline of world history took shape in the decades after World War II, scholars and teachers actively sought to counteract such a Eurocentric understanding of the past, but they faced a special problem in dealing with recent centuries. How can we avoid an inappropriate Eurocentrism when dealing with a phase of world history in which Europeans were in fact central? The long nineteenth century, after all, was "the European moment," a time when Europeans were clearly the most powerful, most innovative, most prosperous, most expansive, and most widely imitated people on the planet.

Countering Eurocentrism

At least five answers to this dilemma are reflected in the chapters that follow. You may want to look for examples of them as you read. The first is simply to remind ourselves how recent and perhaps how brief the European moment in world history has been. Other peoples too had times of "cultural flowering" that granted them a period of primacy or influence—for example, the Greeks (500 B.C.E.–200 C.E.), Indians of South Asia (200–600 C.E.), Arabs (600–1000), Chinese (1000–1500), Mongols (1200–1350), Incas and Aztecs (fifteenth century)—but all of these were limited to particular regions of Afro-Eurasia or the Americas.[2] Even though the European moment operated on a genuinely global scale, Western peoples have enjoyed their worldwide primacy for at most two centuries. Some scholars have suggested that the events of the late twentieth and early twenty-first centuries—the end of colonial empires,

Railroads (p. 534)

the rise of India and especially China, and the assertion of Islam—mark the end, or at least the erosion, of the age of Europe.

Second, we need to remember that the rise of Europe occurred within an international context. It was the withdrawal of the Chinese naval fleet that allowed Europeans to dominate the Indian Ocean in the sixteenth century, while Native Americans' lack of immunity to European diseases and their own divisions and conflicts greatly assisted the European takeover. Europe's Scientific Revolution drew upon earlier Islamic science and was stimulated by the massive amounts of new information pouring in from around the world. The Industrial Revolution, which is explored in Chapter 18, likewise benefited from New World resources and markets and from the stimulus of superior Asian textile and pottery production. Chapters 19 and 20 make clear that European control of other regions everywhere enlisted the cooperation of local elites. None of this diminishes the remarkable—indeed revolutionary—transformations of the European moment in world history. Rather it suggests that they did not derive wholly from some special European genius or long-term advantage but emerged from a unique intersection of European historical development with that of other peoples, regions, and cultures.

A third reminder is that the rise of Europe to a position of global dominance was not an easy or automatic process. Frequently it occurred in the face of ferocious resistance and rebellion, which often required Europeans to modify their policies and practices. The so-called Indian mutiny in mid-nineteenth-century South Asia, a massive uprising against British colonial rule, did not end British control, but it substantially transformed the character of the colonial experience. In

Africa, fear of offending Muslim sensibilities persuaded the British to keep European missionaries and mission schools out of northern Nigeria during the colonial era. Even when Europeans exercised political power, they could not do so precisely as they pleased. Empire, formal and informal alike, was always in some ways a negotiated arrangement.

Fourth, peoples the world over made active use of Europeans and European ideas for their own purposes, seeking to gain advantage over local rivals or to benefit themselves in light of new conditions. In Southeast Asia, for example, a number of highland minority groups, long oppressed by the dominant lowland Vietnamese, viewed the French invaders as liberators and assisted in their takeover of Vietnam. Hindus in India used the railroads, which had been introduced by the British, to go on pilgrimages to holy sites more easily, while the printing press made possible the more widespread distribution of their sacred texts. During the Haitian Revolution, which is explored in Chapter 17, enslaved Africans made use of radical French ideas about "the rights of man" in ways that most Europeans never intended. The leaders of a massive Chinese peasant upheaval in the mid-nineteenth century adopted a unique form of Christianity to legitimate their revolutionary assault on an ancient social order. Recognizing that Asian and African peoples remained active agents, pursuing their own interests even in oppressive conditions, is another way of countering residual Eurocentrism.

What was borrowed from Europe was always adapted to local circumstances. Thus Japanese or Russian industrial development did not wholly follow the pattern of England's Industrial Revolution. The Christianity that took root in the Americas or later in Africa evolved in culturally distinctive ways. Ideas of nationalism, born in Europe, were used to oppose European imperialism throughout Asia and Africa. Chinese socialism in the twentieth century departed in many ways from the vision of Karl Marx. The most interesting stories of modern world history are not simply those of European triumph or the imposition of Western ideas and practices, but of encounters, though highly unequal, among culturally different peoples. It was from these encounters, not just from the intentions and actions of Europeans, that the dramatic global changes of the modern era arose.

A fifth and final antidote to Eurocentrism in an age of European centrality lies in the recognition that although Europeans gained an unprecedented prominence on the world stage, they were not the only game in town, nor were they the sole preoccupation of Asian, African, and Middle Eastern peoples. While China confronted Western aggression in the nineteenth century, it was also absorbing a huge population increase and experiencing massive peasant rebellions that grew out of distinctly Chinese conditions. The long relationship of Muslim and Hindu cultures in India continued to evolve under British colonial rule as it had for centuries under other political systems. West African societies in the nineteenth century experienced a wave of religious wars that created new states and extended and transformed the practice of Islam, and that faith continued its centuries-long spread on the continent even under European colonial rule. A further wave of wars and state formation in southern Africa transformed the political and ethnic landscape, even as European penetration picked up speed.

None of this diminishes the significance of the European moment in world history, but it sets that moment in a larger context of continuing patterns of historical development and of interaction and exchange with other peoples.

Landmarks of the European Moment in World History, 1750–1914

1750	1775	1800	1825

Europe

1780s Beginnings of British Industrial Revolution

1799–1814 Reign of Napoleon

1848 Publication of Karl Marx's *Communist Manifesto*

1789–1799 French Revolution

1780s Beginnings of antislavery movement

North America

1775–1783 American Revolution

1787 U.S. Constitutional Convention

1803 Louisiana Purchase

1845–1848 Mexican-American War

1848 Women's Rights Convention, Seneca Fall, New York

1849 California gold rush

Latin America

1783–1830 Life of Simón Bolívar

1791–1803 Haitian Revolution

1810–1825 Latin American wars of independence

1810 Hidalgo-Morelos rebellion in Mexico

Africa

1798 Napoleon's invasion of Egypt

1815–1840 Rise of Zulu kingdom in South Africa

1804–1817 Fulbe wars and establishment of Sokoto caliphate in West Africa

1805–1848 Reign of Muhammad Ali in Egypt

1830 French invasion of Algeria

East Asia

1793 Chinese rejection of British request for open trade

1830s Famines and rebellions in Japan

1838–1842 First Opium War

South, Southwest, and Southeast Asia

1839–1876 Tanzimat reforms in Ottoman Empire

1740s–1818 Wahhabi movement of Islamic renewal in Arabia

1750s Beginnings of British takeover in India

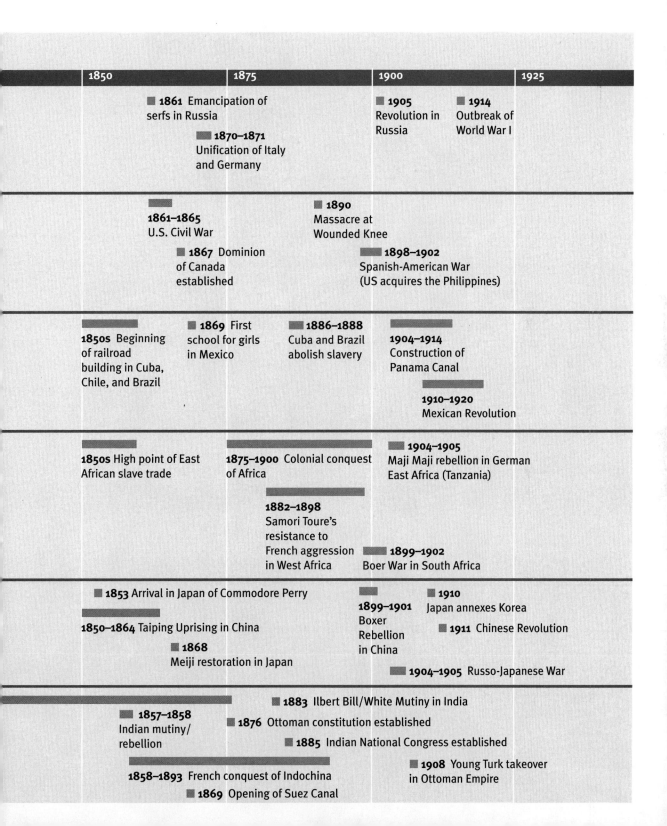

| 1850 | 1875 | 1900 | 1925 |

1861 Emancipation of serfs in Russia

1870–1871 Unification of Italy and Germany

1905 Revolution in Russia

1914 Outbreak of World War I

1861–1865 U.S. Civil War

1890 Massacre at Wounded Knee

1867 Dominion of Canada established

1898–1902 Spanish-American War (US acquires the Philippines)

1850s Beginning of railroad building in Cuba, Chile, and Brazil

1869 First school for girls in Mexico

1886–1888 Cuba and Brazil abolish slavery

1904–1914 Construction of Panama Canal

1910–1920 Mexican Revolution

1850s High point of East African slave trade

1875–1900 Colonial conquest of Africa

1904–1905 Maji Maji rebellion in German East Africa (Tanzania)

1882–1898 Samori Toure's resistance to French aggression in West Africa

1899–1902 Boer War in South Africa

1853 Arrival in Japan of Commodore Perry

1850–1864 Taiping Uprising in China

1868 Meiji restoration in Japan

1899–1901 Boxer Rebellion in China

1910 Japan annexes Korea

1911 Chinese Revolution

1904–1905 Russo-Japanese War

1883 Ilbert Bill/White Mutiny in India

1857–1858 Indian mutiny/ rebellion

1876 Ottoman constitution established

1885 Indian National Congress established

1858–1893 French conquest of Indochina

1908 Young Turk takeover in Ottoman Empire

1869 Opening of Suez Canal

CHAPTER SEVENTEEN

Atlantic Revolutions
and Their Echoes

1750–1914

On July 14, 1989, France celebrated the bicentennial of its famous revolution with a huge parade in Paris. At the head of that parade, strangely enough, were a number of Chinese students, pushing empty bicycles. Just a few weeks earlier, those students had been part of massive demonstrations in Beijing's Tiananmen Square, demanding from their communist government the kind of democratic political rights that the French Revolution had inspired two centuries before. In the process, they had created a thirty-foot-tall papier-mâché Goddess of Democracy, which resembled the Statue of Liberty, a French gift to the United States. Chinese authorities had violently crushed those demonstrations, and now a few students who had escaped to France were paying tribute to the ideals that the French Revolution had unleashed. Their empty bicycles symbolized thousands of their colleagues who had been killed or jailed during the Chinese struggle for democracy. Thus the reverberations of the French Revolution of 1789 still echoed two centuries later and half a world away.

ESSENTIAL AS IT WAS TO THE HISTORY OF EUROPE, the French Revolution holds an even larger significance as the centerpiece of a more extensive revolutionary process that unfolded all around the Atlantic world in the century or so following 1775. The upheaval in France was, of course, preceded by the American Revolution, which gave birth to the United States. It was followed by the Haitian Revolution, the first successful slave revolt in history, and by the Latin American revolutions, in

The Three Estates of Old-Regime France: This satirical eighteenth-century illustration represents the three estates of prerevolutionary French society as women, with the peasant woman carrying a nun and an aristocratic lady on her back. Such social tensions contributed much to the making of the French Revolution. (Réunion des Musées Nationaux/Art Resource, NY) which Spanish and Portuguese colonial rule was ended and the modern states of Latin America emerged. Further revolutionary outbreaks shook various European societies in 1830, 1848, and 1870. These upheavals also had an impact well beyond the Atlantic world. The armies of revolutionary France, for example, invaded Egypt, Poland, and Russia, carrying seeds of change. The ideals that animated these Atlantic revolutions inspired efforts in many countries to abolish slavery, to extend the right to vote, and to secure greater equality for women. Nationalism, perhaps the most potent ideology of the modern era, was nurtured in the Atlantic revolutions and shaped much of nineteenth- and twentieth-century world history. And the principles of equality that were articulated in these revolutions later found expression in social-ist and communist movements.

Comparing Atlantic Revolutions

■ **Causation**

In what ways did the ideas of the Enlighten-ment contribute to the Atlantic revolutions?

Writing to a friend in 1772, before any of the Atlantic revolutions had occurred, the French intellectual Voltaire asked, "My dear philosopher, doesn't this appear to you to be the century of revolutions?"[1] He was certainly on target: in the century that followed, revolutionary outbreaks punctuated the histories of three continents, with influences and echoes even farther afield. Nor were these various revolutions— in North America, France, Haiti, and Latin America—entirely separate and distinct events, for they clearly influenced one another. The American revolutionary leader Thomas Jefferson was the U.S. ambassador to France on the eve of the French Revolution, and while there he provided advice and encouragement to French reformers and revolutionaries. Simón Bolívar, a leading figure in Spanish American struggles for independence, twice visited Haiti, where he received military aid from the first black government in the Americas.

Beyond such direct connections, the various Atlantic revolutionaries shared a set of common ideas. The Atlantic basin had become a world of intellectual and cultural exchange as well as one of commercial and biological intercourse. The ideas that animated the Atlantic revolutions derived from the European Enlightenment and were shared across the ocean in newspapers, books, and pam-phlets. At the heart of these ideas was the radical notion that human political and social arrangements could be engineered, and improved, by human action. Thus conventional and long-established ways of living and thinking—the divine right of kings, state control of trade, aristocratic privilege, the authority of a single church— were no longer sacrosanct and came under repeated attack. New ideas of liberty, equality, free trade, religious tolerance, republicanism, and human rationality were in the air. Politically, the core notion was "popular sovereignty," which meant that the authority to govern derived from the people rather than from God or from established tradition. As the Englishman John Locke (1632–1704) had argued, the "social contract" between ruler and ruled should last only as long as it served the people well. In short, it was both possible and desirable to start over in the con-struction of human communities.

$\mathcal{S}$napshot **Key Moments in the History of Atlantic Revolutions**

American Declaration of Independence	1776
British recognition of American independence	1783
U.S. Constitutional Convention	1787
Tupac Amaru revolt in Peru	1780s
Outbreak of French Revolution	1789
Haitian Revolution	1791–1804
French Terror, execution of Louis XVI	1793–1794
Napoleon's rise to power	1799
High point of Napoleon's empire	1810–1811
Hidalgo-Morales rebellion in Mexico	1810–1813
Wars of Spanish American independence	1810–1825
Final defeat of Napoleon	1815
Independence of Brazil from Portugal	1822

Such ideas generated endless controversy. Were liberty and equality compatible? What kind of government—unitary and centralized or federal and decentralized—best ensured freedom? And how far should liberty be extended? Except in Haiti, the chief beneficiaries of these revolutions were propertied white men of the "middling classes." Although women, slaves, Native Americans, and men without property did not gain much from these revolutions, the ideas that accompanied these upheavals gave them ammunition for the future. Because their overall thrust was to extend political rights further than ever before, these Atlantic movements have often been referred to as "democratic revolutions."

Beneath a common political vocabulary and a broadly democratic character, the Atlantic revolutions differed substantially from one another. They were triggered by different circumstances, expressed quite different social and political tensions, and varied considerably in their outcomes. Liberty, noted Simón Bolívar, "is a succulent morsel, but one difficult to digest."[2] "Digesting liberty" occurred in quite distinct ways in the various sites of the Atlantic revolutions.

The North American Revolution, 1775–1787

Every schoolchild in the United States learns early that the American Revolution was a struggle for independence from oppressive British rule. That struggle was launched with the Declaration of Independence in 1776, resulted in an unlikely military victory by 1781, and generated a federal constitution in 1787, joining thirteen

■ **Change**
What was revolutionary about the American Revolution, and what was not?

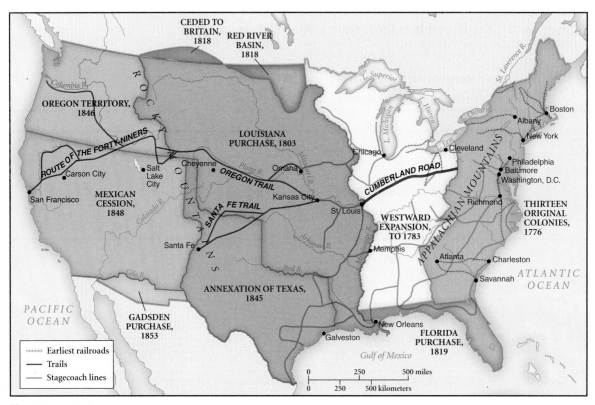

Map 17.1   The Expansion of the United States

The union of the thirteen British colonies in North America provided the foundation for the westward and transcontinental expansion of the United States during the nineteenth century, a process that turned the country into a global power by the early twentieth century.

formerly separate colonies into a new nation (see Map 17.1). It was the first in a series of upheavals that rocked the Atlantic world and beyond in the century that followed. But was it a genuine revolution? What, precisely, did it change?

In its break with Britain, the American Revolution marked a decisive political change, but in other ways it was, strangely enough, a conservative movement, because it originated in an effort to preserve the existing liberties of the colonies rather than to create new ones. For much of the seventeenth and eighteenth centuries, the British colonies in North America enjoyed a considerable degree of local autonomy as the British government was embroiled in its own internal conflicts and various European wars. Furthermore, Britain's West Indian colonies seemed more profitable and of greater significance than those of North America. In these circumstances, local elected assemblies in North America, dominated by the wealthier property-owning settlers, achieved something close to self-government. Colonists came to regard such autonomy as a birthright and part of their English heritage. Thus, until the mid-eighteenth century, almost no one in the colonies thought of breaking away from England because participation in the British Empire provided many advantages—protection in war, access to British markets, and confirmation of their continuing identity as "Englishmen"—and few drawbacks.

Within these colonies, English settlers had developed societies described by a leading historian as "the most radical in the contemporary Western world." Certainly class distinctions were real and visible, and a small class of wealthy "gentlemen"—the Adamses, Washingtons, Jeffersons, and Hancocks—wore powdered wigs, imitated the latest European styles, were prominent in political life, and were generally deferred to by ordinary people. But the ready availability of land following the elimination of Native Americans, the scarcity of people, and the absence of both a titled nobility and a single established church meant that social life was far more open than in Europe. No legal distinctions differentiated clergy, aristocracy, and commoners, as they did in France. All free people, which of course excluded black slaves, enjoyed the same status before the law. These conditions made for less poverty, more economic opportunity, fewer social differences, and easier relationships among the classes than in Europe. The famous economist Adam Smith observed that British colonists were "republican in their manners . . . and their government" well before their independence from England.[3]

Thus the American Revolution did not grow out of social tensions within the colonies, but from a quite sudden and unexpected effort by the British government to tighten its control over the colonies and to extract more revenue from them. As Britain's global struggle with France drained its treasury and ran up its national debt, British authorities, beginning in the 1760s, looked to America to make good these losses. Abandoning its neglectful oversight of the colonies, Britain began to act like a genuine imperial power, imposing a variety of new taxes and tariffs on the colonies without their consent, for they were not represented in the British parliament. By challenging their economic interests, their established traditions of local autonomy, and their identity as true Englishmen, such measures infuriated many of the colonists. Armed with the ideas of the Enlightenment—popular sovereignty, natural rights, the consent of the governed—they went to war, and by 1781 they had prevailed, with considerable aid from the French.

What was revolutionary about the American experience was not so much the revolution itself but the kind of society that had already emerged within the colonies. Independence from Britain was not accompanied by any wholesale social transformation. Rather the revolution accelerated the established democratic tendencies of the colonial societies. Political authority remained largely in the hands of existing elites who had led the revolution, although property requirements for voting were lowered and more white men of modest means, such as small farmers and urban artisans, were elected to state legislatures.

This widening of political participation gradually eroded the power of traditional gentlemen, but no women or people of color shared in these gains. Land was not seized from its owners, except in the case of pro-British loyalists who had fled the country. Although slavery was gradually abolished in the northern states, where it counted for little, it remained firmly entrenched in the southern states, where it counted for much. Chief Justice John Marshall later gave voice to this conservative understanding of the American Revolution: "All contracts and rights, respecting property, remained unchanged by the Revolution."[4] In the century that followed independence, the United States did become the world's most democratic country, but it was less the direct product of the revolution and more the gradual working out in a reformist fashion of earlier practices and the principles of equality announced in the Declaration of Independence.

Nonetheless, many American patriots felt passionately that they were creating "a new order for the ages." James Madison in the *Federalist Papers* made the point clearly: "We pursued a new and more noble course ... and accomplished a revolution that has no parallel in the annals of human society." Supporters abroad agreed. On the eve of the French Revolution, a Paris newspaper proclaimed that the United States was "the hope and model of the human race."[5] In both cases, they were referring primarily to the political ideas and practices of the new country. The American Revolution, after all, initiated the political dismantling of Europe's New World empires. The "right to revolution," proclaimed in the Declaration of Independence and made effective only in a great struggle, inspired revolutionaries and nationalists from Simón Bolívar in nineteenth-century Latin America to Ho Chi Minh in twentieth-century Vietnam. Moreover, the new U.S. Constitution—with its Bill of Rights, checks and balances, separation of church and state, and federalism—was one of the first sustained efforts to put the political ideas of the Enlightenment into practice. That document, and the ideas that it embraced, echoed repeatedly in the political upheavals of the century that followed.

The French Revolution, 1789–1815

■ Comparison
How did the French Revolution differ from the American Revolution?

Act Two in the drama of the Atlantic revolutions took place in France, beginning in 1789, although it was closely connected to Act One in North America. Thousands of French soldiers had provided assistance to the American colonists and now returned home full of republican enthusiasm. Thomas Jefferson, the U.S. ambassador in Paris, reported that France "has been awakened by our revolution."[6] More immediately, the French government, which had generously aided the Americans in an effort to undermine its British rivals, was teetering on the brink of bankruptcy and had long sought reforms that would modernize the tax system and make it more equitable. In a desperate effort to raise taxes against the opposition of the privileged classes, the French king, Louis XVI, had called into session an ancient parliamentary body, the Estates General. It consisted of representatives of the three "estates," or legal orders, of prerevolutionary France: the clergy, the nobility, and the commoners. The first two estates comprised about 2 percent of the population, and the Third Estate included everyone else. When that body convened in 1789, representatives of the Third Estate soon organized themselves as the National Assembly, with the sole authority to make laws for the country. A few weeks later they drew up the Declaration of the Rights of Man and Citizen, which forthrightly declared that "men are born and remain free and equal in rights." These actions, unprecedented and illegal in the *ancien régime* (the Old Regime), launched the

French Revolution and radicalized many of the participants in the National Assembly.

That revolution was quite different from its North American predecessor. Whereas the American Revolution expressed the tensions of a colonial relationship with a distant imperial power, the French insurrection was driven by sharp conflicts within French society. Members of the titled nobility—privileged, prestigious, and wealthy—resented and resisted the monarchy's efforts to subject them to new taxes. Educated middle-class groups, such as doctors, lawyers, lower-level officials, and merchants, were growing in numbers and sometimes in wealth and were offended by the remaining privileges of the aristocracy, from which they were excluded. Ordinary urban residents, many of whose incomes had declined for a generation, were particularly hard-hit in the late 1780s by the rapidly rising price of bread and widespread unemployment. Peasants in the countryside, though largely free of serfdom, were subject to a variety of hated dues imposed by their landlords, taxes from the state, obligations to the Church, and the requirement to work without pay on public roads. As Enlightenment ideas penetrated French society, more and more people, mostly in the Third Estate but including some priests and nobles, found a language with which to articulate these grievances. The famous French writer Jean-Jacques Rousseau had told them that it was "manifestly contrary to the law of nature . . . that a handful of people should gorge themselves with superfluities while the hungry multitude goes in want of necessities."[7]

These social conflicts gave the French Revolution, especially during its first five years, a much more violent, far-reaching, and radical character than its American counterpart. It was a profound social upheaval, more comparable to the revolutions of Russia and China in the twentieth century than to the earlier American Revolution. Initial efforts to establish a constitutional monarchy gave way to more radical measures, as internal resistance and foreign opposition produced a fear that the revolution might be overturned. In the process, urban crowds organized insurrections. Some peasants attacked the castles of their lords, burning the documents that recorded their dues and payments. The National Assembly decreed the end of all legal privileges and abolished what remained of feudalism in France. Even slavery was abolished, albeit briefly. Church lands were sold to raise revenue, and priests were put under government authority.

In early 1793, King Louis XVI and his queen, Marie Antoinette, were executed, an act of regicide that shocked traditionalists all across Europe and marked a new stage in revolutionary violence. What followed was the Terror of 1793–1794. Under the leadership of Maximilien Robespierre and his Committee of Public Safety, tens of thousands deemed enemies of the revolution lost their lives on the guillotine. Shortly thereafter, Robespierre himself was arrested and guillotined, accused of leading France into tyranny and dictatorship. "The revolution," remarked one of its victims, "was devouring its own children."

Accompanying attacks on the old order were efforts to create a wholly new society, symbolized by a new calendar with the Year 1 in 1792, marking a fresh start for

The Execution of Robespierre
The beheading of the radical leader Robespierre, who had himself brought thousands of others to the guillotine, marked a decisive turning point in the unfolding of the French Revolution and the end of its most violent phase. (Musée de la Revolution Française, Vizille, France/ Bridgeman Art Library)

France. Unlike the Americans, who sought to restore or build upon earlier freedoms, French revolutionaries perceived themselves to be starting from scratch and looked to the future. For the first time in its history, the country became a republic and briefly passed universal male suffrage, although it was never implemented. The old administrative system was rationalized into eighty-three territorial departments, each with a new name. As revolutionary France prepared for war against its threatened and threatening neighbors, it created the world's largest army, with some 800,000 men, and all adult males were required to serve. Led by officers from the middle and even lower classes, this was an army of citizens representing the nation.

The impact of the revolution was felt in many ways. Streets got new names; monuments to the royal family were destroyed; titles vanished; people referred to one another as "citizen so-and-so." Real politics in the public sphere emerged for the first time as many people joined political clubs, took part in marches and demonstrations, served on local committees, and ran for public office. Common people, who had identified primarily with their local community, now began to think of themselves as belonging to a nation. The state replaced the Catholic Church as the place for registering births, marriages, and deaths, and revolutionary festivals substituted for church holidays.

More radical revolutionary leaders deliberately sought to convey a sense of new beginnings. A Festival of Unity held in 1793 to mark the first anniversary of the end of monarchy burned the crowns and scepters of the royal family in a huge bonfire while releasing a cloud of 3,000 white doves. The Cathedral of Notre Dame was temporarily turned into the Temple of Reason, while a "Hymn to Liberty" combined traditional church music with the explicit message of the Enlightenment:

Oh Liberty, sacred Liberty
Goddess of an enlightened people
Rule today within these walls.
Through you this temple is purified.

Liberty! Before you reason chases out deception,
Error flees, fanaticism is beaten down.
Our gospel is nature
And our cult is virtue.
To love one's country and one's brothers,
To serve the Sovereign People—
These are the sacred tenets
And pledge of a Republican.[8]

The French Revolution differed from the American Revolution also in the way its influence spread. At least until the United States became a world power at the end of the nineteenth century, what inspired others was primarily the example of its revolution and its constitution. French influence, by contrast, spread through conquest, largely under the leadership of Napoleon Bonaparte (ruled 1799–1814). A highly successful general who seized power in 1799, Napoleon is often credited with taming the revolution in the face of growing disenchantment with its more radical features and with the social conflicts it generated. He preserved many of its more moderate elements, such as civil equality, a secular law code, religious freedom, and promotion by merit, while reconciling with the Catholic Church and suppressing the revolution's more democratic elements in a military dictatorship. In short, Napoleon kept the revolution's emphasis on social equality but dispensed with liberty.

Like many of the revolution's ardent supporters, Napoleon was intent on spreading its benefits far and wide. In a series of brilliant military campaigns, his forces subdued most of Europe, thus creating the continent's largest empire since the days of the Romans (see Map 17.2). Within that empire, Napoleon imposed such revolutionary practices as ending feudalism, proclaiming equality of rights, insisting on religious toleration, codifying the laws, and rationalizing government administration. In many places, these reforms were welcomed, and seeds of further change were planted. But French domination was also resented and resisted, stimulating national consciousness throughout Europe. That too was a seed that bore fruit in the century that followed. More immediately, national resistance, particularly from Russia and Britain, brought down Napoleon and his amazing empire by 1815 and marked an end to the era of the French Revolution, though not to the potency of its ideas.

The Haitian Revolution, 1791–1804

Nowhere did the example of the French Revolution echo more loudly than in the French Caribbean colony of Saint Domingue, later renamed Haiti (see Map 17.3, p. 511). Widely regarded as the richest colony in the world, Saint Domingue boasted 8,000 plantations, which in the late eighteenth century produced some 40 percent of the world's sugar and perhaps half of its coffee. Slaves, about 500,000 of them, made up the vast majority of its population. Whites numbered about 40,000, sharply divided between very well-to-do plantation owners, merchants, and lawyers and those known as *petits blancs*, or poor whites. A third social group consisted of some 30,000 *gens de*

■ Comparison
What was distinctive about the Haitian Revolution, both in world history generally and in the history of Atlantic revolutions?

Map 17.2 Napoleon's European Empire

The French Revolution spawned a French empire, under Napoleon's leadership, that encompassed most of Europe and served to spread the principles of the revolution.

couleur libres, or free people of color, many of them of mixed-race background. Saint Domingue was a colonial society very different from the New England colonies or even the southern colonies of British North America. Given its enormous inequalities and its rampant exploitation, this Caribbean colony was primed for explosion.

In such a volatile setting, the ideas and example of the French Revolution lit several fuses and set in motion a spiral of violence that engulfed the colony for more than a decade. The principles of the revolution, however, meant different things to different people. To the *grands blancs*—the rich white landowners—it suggested greater autonomy for the colony and fewer economic restrictions on trade, but they resented the demands of the *petits blancs,* who sought equality of citizenship for all whites. Both white groups were adamantly opposed to the insistence of free people of color that the "rights of man" meant equal treatment for all free people regardless of race. To the slaves, the promise of the French Revolution's ideas was a personal freedom that threatened the entire slave labor system. In a massive slave revolt beginning in 1791, triggered by rumors that the French king had already declared an end to slavery, they burned 1,000 plantations and killed hundreds of whites as well as mixed-race people.

Soon warring factions of slaves, whites, and free people of color battled one another. Spanish and British forces, seeking to enlarge their own empires at the expense of the French, only added to the turmoil. Amid the confusion, brutality, and massacres of the 1790s, power gravitated toward the slaves, now led by the astute Toussaint Louverture, himself a former slave. He and his successor overcame internal resistance, outmaneuvered the foreign powers, and even defeated an attempt by Napoleon to reestablish French control.

When the dust settled in the early years of the nineteenth century, it was clear that something remarkable and unprecedented had taken place, a revolution unique in the Atlantic world and in world history. Socially, the last had become first. In the only completely successful slave revolt in world history, "the lowest order of the society—slaves—became equal, free, and independent citizens."[9] Politically, they had thrown off French colonial rule, becoming the second independent republic in the Americas and the first non-European state to emerge from Western colonialism. They renamed their country Haiti, a term meaning "mountainous" or "rugged" in the language of the original Taino people. It was a symbolic break with Europe and represented some connection with the long-deceased native inhabitants of the land. Some, in fact, referred to themselves as "Incas." At the formal declaration of Haiti's independence on January 1, 1804, Jean-Jacques Dessalines, the new country's first head of state, declared: "I have given the French cannibals blood for blood; I have avenged America."[10] In defining all Haitians as "black," Haiti directly confronted an emerging racism, even as they declared all citizens legally equal regardless of race, color, or class. Economically, the country's plantation system, oriented wholly toward the export of sugar and coffee, had been largely destroyed. As whites fled or were killed, both private and state lands were redistributed among former slaves and free blacks, and Haiti became a nation of small-scale farmers producing mostly for their own needs, with a much smaller export sector.

PL. VII.

Wraak door het leger der zwarten genomen van de wreedheden, hun door de Franschen aangedaan.

The Haitian Revolution
This early-nineteenth-century engraving, entitled *Revenge Taken by the Black Army*, illustrates both the violence and the racial dimension of the upheaval in Haiti. (Schomburg Center, NY/Art Resource, NY)

The destructiveness of the Haitian Revolution; its bitter internal divisions of race, color, and class; and continuing external opposition contributed much to Haiti's abiding poverty as well as to its authoritarian and unstable politics. In the early nineteenth century, however, it was a source of enormous hope and of great fear. Within weeks of the Haitian slave uprising in 1791, Jamaican slaves had composed songs in its honor, and it was not long before slave owners in the Caribbean and North America observed a new "insolence" in their slaves. Certainly its example inspired other slave rebellions, gave a boost to the dawning abolitionist movement, and has been a source of pride for people of African descent ever since.

To whites throughout the hemisphere, the cautionary phrase "remember Haiti" reflected a sense of horror at what had occurred there and a determination not to allow political change to reproduce that fearful outcome again. Particularly in Latin America, it injected a deep caution and social conservatism in the elites that led their countries to independence in the early nineteenth century. Ironically, though, the Haitian Revolution also led to a temporary expansion of slavery elsewhere. Cuban plantations and their slave workers considerably increased their production of sugar as that of Haiti declined. Moreover, Napoleon's defeat in Haiti persuaded him to sell to the United States the French territories known as the Louisiana Purchase, from which a number of "slave states" were carved out. In such contradictory ways did the echoes of the Haitian Revolution reverberate in the Atlantic world.

Spanish American Revolutions, 1810–1825

■ Connection
How were the Spanish American revolutions shaped by the American, French, and Haitian revolutions that happened earlier?

The final act in a half century of Atlantic revolutionary upheaval took place in the Spanish and Portuguese colonies of mainland Latin America (see Map 17.3). Their revolutions were shaped by preceding events in North America, France, and Haiti as well as by their own distinctive societies and historical experience. As in British North America, native-born elites in the Spanish colonies (known as *creoles*) were offended and insulted by the Spanish monarchy's efforts during the eighteenth century to exercise greater power over its colonies and to subject them to heavier taxes and tariffs. Creole intellectuals also had become familiar with ideas of popular sovereignty, republican government, and personal liberty derived from the European Enlightenment. Why did these conditions, similar to those in North America, lead initially only to scattered and uncoordinated protests rather than to outrage, declarations of independence, war, and unity, as had occurred in the British colonies? Why, in short, did Spanish American struggles for independence occur decades later than those of British North America?

The settlers in the Spanish colonies had little tradition of local self-government such as had developed in North America. Their society was far more authoritarian and divided by class, and their culture was informed by the strict Catholicism of the Counter-Reformation. In addition, whites throughout Latin America were vastly outnumbered by Native Americans, people of African ancestry, or those of mixed race.

All of these factors help explain the delayed movement for independence, despite the example of North America and similar provocations.

Despite their growing disenchantment with Spanish rule, creole elites did not so much generate a revolution as have one thrust upon them by events in Europe. In 1808, Napoleon invaded Spain and Portugal, deposing the Spanish king Ferdinand VII and forcing the Portuguese royal family into exile in Brazil. With legitimate royal authority now in disarray, Latin Americans were forced to take action. The outcome, ultimately, was independence for the various states of Latin America, established almost everywhere by 1826. But the way in which it occurred and the kind of societies it generated differed greatly from the experience of both North America and Haiti.

The process lasted more than twice as long as it did in North America, partly because Latin American societies were so conflicted and divided by class, race, and region. In North America, violence was directed almost entirely

Map 17.3 Latin American Independence
With the exception of Haiti, Latin American revolutions brought independence to new states but offered little social change or political opportunity for the vast majority of people.

against the British and seldom spilled over into domestic disputes, except for some bloody skirmishes with loyalists. Even then, little lasting hostility occurred, and some loyalists were able to reenter U.S. society after independence was achieved. In Mexico, by contrast, the move toward independence began in 1810 in a peasant insurrection, driven by hunger for land and by high food prices and led successively by two priests, Miguel Hidalgo and José Morelos. Alarmed by the social radicalism of the Hidalgo-Morelos rebellion, creole landowners, with the support of the Church, raised an army and crushed the insurgency. Later that alliance of clergy and creole elites brought Mexico to a more socially controlled independence in 1821. Violent conflict among Latin Americans, along lines of race, class, and ideology, accompanied the struggle against Spain in many places.

The entire independence movement in Latin America took place under the shadow of a great fear—the dread of social rebellion from below—that had little counterpart in North America. The great violence of the French and Haitian revolutions was a lesson to Latin American elites that political change could easily get out of hand and was fraught with danger to themselves. An abortive rebellion of Native Americans in Peru in the early 1780s, made in the name of the last Inca emperor, Tupac Amaru, as well as the Hidalgo-Morelos rebellion in Mexico, reminded whites that they sat atop a potentially explosive society, most of whose members were exploited and oppressed people of color.

And yet the creole sponsors of independence movements, both regional military leaders such as Simón Bolívar and José de San Martín and their civilian counterparts, required the support of "the people," or at least some of them, if they were to prevail against Spanish forces. The answer to this dilemma was found in nativism, which cast all of those born in the Americas—creoles, Indians, mixed-race people, free blacks—as *Americanos*, while the enemy was defined as those born in Spain or Portugal.[11] This was no easy task, because many whites and mestizos saw themselves as Spanish and because great differences of race, culture, and wealth separated the Americanos. Nonetheless, nationalist leaders made efforts to mobilize people of color into the struggle with promises of freedom, the end of legal restrictions, and social advancement. Many of these leaders were genuine liberals, who had been influenced by the ideals of the Enlightenment, the French Revolution, and Spanish liberalism. In the long run, however, few of those promises were kept. Certainly the lower classes, Native Americans, and slaves benefited little from independence. "The imperial state was destroyed in Spanish America," concluded one historian, "but colonial society was preserved."[12]

A further difference in the Latin American situation lay in the apparent impossibility of uniting the various Spanish colonies, despite several failed efforts to do so. Thus no United States of Latin America emerged. Distances among the colonies and geographic obstacles to effective communication were certainly greater than in the eastern seaboard colonies of North America, and their longer colonial experience had given rise to distinct and deeply rooted regional identities. Shortly before his death in 1830, the "great liberator" Bolívar, who so admired George Washington and had so ardently hoped for greater unity, wrote in

Simón Bolívar
Among the heroic figures of Spanish American independence movements, none was more significant than Simón Bolívar (1783–1830), shown here in a moment of triumph entering his hometown of Caracas in present-day Venezuela. But Bolívar was immensely disappointed in the outcomes of independence as his dream of a unified South America perished amid the rivalries of separate countries. (akg-images)

despair to a friend: "[Latin] America is ungovernable. Those who serve the revolution plough the sea."[13]

The aftermath of independence in Latin America marked a reversal in the earlier relationship of the two American continents. The United States, which began its history as the leftover "dregs" of the New World, grew increasingly wealthy, industrialized, democratic, internationally influential, and generally stable, with the major exception of the Civil War. The Spanish colonies, which in their beginnings had occupied the wealthiest areas and the most sophisticated cultures of the Americas, were widely regarded as the more promising region compared to the backwater reputation of England's North American territories. But in the nineteenth century, as newly independent countries in both regions launched a new phase of their histories, those in Latin America became relatively underdeveloped, impoverished, undemocratic, politically unstable, and dependent on foreign technology and investment (see Chapter 18). Begun in broadly similar circumstances, the Latin American and North American revolutions occurred in very different societies and gave rise to very different historical trajectories.

Echoes of Revolution

The core values of the Atlantic revolutions continued to reverberate well after those upheavals had been concluded. Within Europe, which was generally dominated by conservative governments following Napoleon's final defeat, smaller revolutions erupted in 1830, more widely in 1848, and in Paris in 1870. They expressed ideas of republicanism, greater social equality, and national liberation from foreign rule. Such ideas and social pressures pushed the major states of Western Europe, the United States, and Argentina to enlarge their voting publics, generally granting universal male suffrage by 1914. An abortive attempt to establish a constitutional regime even broke out in autocratic Russia in 1825. It was led by military officers who had been influenced by ideals of the Enlightenment and the French Revolution while campaigning in Europe against Napoleon.

Beyond this limited extension of political democracy, three movements arose to challenge continuing patterns of oppression or exclusion. Abolitionists sought the end of slavery; nationalists hoped to do away with disunity and foreign rule; and feminists tried to end, or at least mitigate, male dominance. Each of these movements bore the marks of the Atlantic revolutions, and although they took root first in Europe, each came to have a global significance in the centuries that followed.

The Abolition of Slavery

In little more than a century, from roughly 1780 to 1890, a remarkable transformation occurred in human affairs as slavery, widely practiced and little condemned since the beginning of civilization, lost its legitimacy and was largely ended. In this amazing process, the ideas and practices of the Atlantic revolutions played an important role.

■ Change
What accounts for the end of Atlantic slavery during the nineteenth century?

Enlightenment thinkers in eighteenth-century Europe had become increasingly critical of slavery as a violation of the natural rights of every person, and the public pronouncements of the American and French revolutions about liberty and equality likewise focused attention on this obvious breach of those principles. To this secular antislavery thinking was added an increasingly vociferous religious voice, expressed first by Quakers and then Protestant evangelicals in Britain and the United States. To them slavery was "repugnant to our religion" and a "crime in the sight of God."[14] What made these moral arguments more widely acceptable was the growing belief that, contrary to much earlier thinking, slavery was not essential for economic progress. After all, England and New England were among the most prosperous regions of the Western world in the early nineteenth century, and both were based on free labor. Slavery in this view was out of date, unnecessary in the new era of industrial technology and capitalism. Thus moral virtue and economic success were joined. It was an attractive argument.

The actions of slaves themselves likewise hastened the end of slavery. The dramatically successful Haitian Revolution was followed by three major rebellions in the British West Indies, all of which were harshly crushed, in the early nineteenth century. They demonstrated clearly that slaves were hardly "contented," and the brutality with which the revolts were suppressed appalled British public opinion. Growing numbers of the British public came to feel that slavery was "not only morally wrong and economically inefficient, but also politically unwise."[15]

These various strands of thinking—secular, religious, economic, and political—came together in abolitionist movements, most powerfully in Britain, which brought growing pressure on governments to close down the trade in slaves and then to ban slavery itself. In the late eighteenth century, such a movement gained wide support among middle- and working-class people in Britain. Its techniques included pamphlets with heartrending descriptions of slavery, numerous petitions to parliament, lawsuits, boycotts of slave-produced sugar, and frequent public meetings, some of which dramatically featured the testimony of Africans who had experienced the horrors of slavery firsthand. In 1807, Britain forbade the sale of slaves within its empire and in 1834 emancipated those who remained enslaved. Over the next half century, other nations—under growing international pressure, particularly from Britain, then the world's leading economic and military power—followed suit. British naval vessels patrolled the Atlantic, intercepted illegal slave ships, and freed their human cargoes in a small West African settlement called Freetown, in present-day Sierra Leone. Following their independence, most Latin American countries abolished slavery by the 1850s. Brazil, in 1888, was the last to do so, bringing more than four centuries of Atlantic slavery to an end. A roughly similar set of conditions—fear of rebellion, economic inefficiency, and moral concerns—persuaded the Russian tsar to free the many serfs of that huge country in 1861, although there it occurred by fiat from above rather than from growing public pressure.

None of this happened easily. Slave economies continued to flourish well into the nineteenth century, and plantation owners vigorously resisted the onslaught of

Abolitionism
This antislavery medallion was commissioned in the late eighteenth century by English Quakers, who were among the earliest participants in the abolitionist movement. Its famous motto, "Am I not a man and a brother," reflected both Enlightenment and Christian values of human equality. (The Art Archive)

abolitionists. So did slave traders, both European and African, who together shipped millions of additional captives, mostly to Cuba and Brazil, long after the trade had been declared illegal. Osei Bonsu, the powerful king of the West African state of Asante, was puzzled as to why the British would no longer buy his slaves. "If they think it bad now," he asked a local British representative in 1820, "why did they think it good before?"[16] Nowhere was the persistence of slavery more evident and resistance to abolition more intense than in the southern states of the United States. It was the only slaveholding society in which the end of slavery occurred through such a bitter, prolonged, and highly destructive civil war (1861–1865).

The end of Atlantic slavery during the nineteenth century surely marked a major and quite rapid turn in the world's social history and in the moral thinking of humankind. Nonetheless, the outcomes of that process were often surprising and far from the expectations of abolitionists or the newly freed slaves. In most cases, the economic lives of the former slaves did not improve dramatically. Nowhere in the Atlantic world, except Haiti, did a redistribution of land follow the end of slavery. But freedmen everywhere desperately sought economic autonomy on their own land, and in parts of the Caribbean such as Jamaica, where unoccupied land was available, independent peasant agriculture proved possible for some. Elsewhere, as in the southern United States, various forms of technically free but highly dependent labor, such as sharecropping, emerged to replace slavery and to provide low-paid and often indebted workers for planters. The understandable reluctance of former slaves to continue working in plantation agriculture created labor shortages and set in motion a huge new wave of global migration. Large numbers of indentured servants from India and China were imported into the Caribbean, Peru, South Africa, Hawaii, Malaya, and elsewhere to work in mines, on sugar plantations, and in construction projects. There they often toiled in conditions not far removed from slavery itself.

Newly freed people did not achieve anything close to political equality, except in Haiti. White planters, farmers, and mine owners retained local authority in the Caribbean. In the southern United States, a brief period of "radical reconstruction," during which newly freed blacks did enjoy full political rights and some power, was followed by harsh segregation laws, denial of voting rights, a wave of lynching, and a virulent racism that lasted well into the twentieth century. For most former slaves, emancipation usually meant, in the words of a well-known historian, "nothing but freedom."[17]

Unlike the situation in the Americas, the end of serfdom in Russia transferred to the peasants a considerable portion of the nobles' land, but the need to pay for this land with "redemption dues" and the rapid growth of Russia's rural population ensured that most peasants remained impoverished and politically volatile. In both West and East Africa, the closing of the external slave trade decreased the price of slaves and increased their use within African societies to produce the export crops that the world economy now demanded from them. Thus, as Europeans imposed colonial rule on Africa in the late nineteenth century, one of their justifications for doing so was the need to emancipate enslaved Africans. Europeans proclaiming the need to

■ **Change**
How did the end of slavery affect the lives of the former slaves?

end slavery in a continent from which they had extracted slaves for more than four centuries was surely among the more ironic outcomes of the abolitionist process.

Nations and Nationalism

■ Explanation
What accounts for the growth of nationalism as a powerful political and personal identity in the nineteenth century?

In addition to contributing to the end of slavery, the Atlantic revolutions also gave new prominence to a relatively recent kind of human community—the nation. By the end of the twentieth century, the idea that humankind was divided into separate nations, each with a distinct culture and territory and deserving an independent political life, was so widespread as to seem natural and timeless. And yet for most of human experience, states did not usually coincide with the culture of a particular people, for all of the great empires and many smaller states governed culturally diverse societies. Few people considered rule by foreigners itself a terrible offense because the most important identities and loyalties were local, limited to clan, village, or region, with only modest connection to the larger state or empire that governed them. People might on occasion consider themselves part of larger religious communities (such as Christians or Muslims) or ethnolinguistic groupings such as Greek, Arab, or Mayan, but such identities rarely provided the basis for enduring states.

All of that began to change during the era of Atlantic revolutions. Independence movements in both North and South America were made in the name of new nations. The French Revolution declared that sovereignty lay with "the people," and its leaders mobilized this people to defend the "French nation" against its many external enemies. In 1793, the revolutionary government of France declared a mass conscription (*levée en masse*) with this stirring call to service:

> Henceforth, until the enemies have been driven from the territory of the Republic, all the French are in permanent requisition for army service. The young men shall go to battle; the married men shall forge arms and transport provisions; the women shall make tents and clothes, and shall serve in the hospitals; the children shall turn old linen into lint; the old men shall repair to the public places, to stimulate the courage of the warriors and preach the unity of the Republic and the hatred of kings.[18]

Napoleon's conquests likewise stimulated national resistance in many parts of Europe. European states had long competed and fought with one another, but increasingly in the nineteenth century, those states were inhabited by people who felt themselves to be citizens of a nation, deeply bound to their fellows by ties of blood, culture, or common experience, not simply common subjects of a ruling dynasty. It was a novel form of political community.

Europe's modern transformation also facilitated nationalism, even as older identities and loyalties eroded. Science weakened the hold of religion on some. Migration to industrial cities or abroad diminished allegiance to local communities.

Snapshot   **Key Moments in the Growth of Nationalism**

Independence of colonies in the Americas	1776–1825
Mass conscription to defend the French Revolution	1793
Wars of resistance to Napoleonic empire	1800–1815
Greek independence from Ottoman Empire	1830
Polish insurrections against Russian rule	1830, 1863
Young Ireland movement begins	1842
First Ukrainian nationalist organization established	1846
Hungarian national uprising against Austrian Habsburg rule	1848
Unification of Italy and Germany	1870, 1871
Egyptian revolt against British and French imperialism	1880
Founding of Indian National Congress	1885
Political Zionism emerges, seeking a homeland in Palestine for Jews	1890s

At the same time, printing and the publishing industry standardized a variety of dialects into a smaller number of European languages, a process that allowed a growing reading public to think of themselves as members of a common linguistic group or nation. All of this encouraged political and cultural leaders to articulate an appealing idea of their particular nations and ensured a growing circle of people receptive to such ideas. Thus the idea of the "nation" was constructed or even invented, but it was often presented as a reawakening of older linguistic or cultural identities and certainly drew upon the songs, dances, folktales, historical experiences, and collective memories of earlier cultures (see Map 17.4).

Whatever its precise origins, nationalism proved to be an infinitely flexible and enormously powerful idea in the nineteenth-century Atlantic world and beyond. It inspired the political unification of both Germany and Italy, gathering their previously fragmented peoples into new states by 1871. It encouraged Greeks and Serbs to assert their independence from the Ottoman Empire; Czechs and Hungarians to demand more autonomy within the Austrian Empire; Poles and Ukrainians to become more aware of their oppression within the Russian Empire; and the Irish to seek "home rule" and separation from Great Britain. By the end of the nineteenth century, a small Zionist movement, seeking a homeland in Palestine, had emerged among Europe's frequently persecuted Jews. Popular nationalism made the normal rivalry among European states even more acute and fueled a highly competitive drive for colonies in Asia and Africa. The immensity of the suffering and sacrifice that nationalism generated in Europe was disclosed most vividly during the horrors of World War I.

Map 17.4 The Nations and Empires of Europe, ca. 1880
By the end of the nineteenth century, the national principle had substantially reshaped the map of Europe, especially in the unification of Germany and Italy. However, several major empires (Russian, Austro-Hungarian, and Ottoman) remained, each with numerous subject peoples who likewise sought national independence.

Governments throughout the Western world claimed now to act on behalf of their nations and deliberately sought to instill national loyalties in their citizens through schools, public rituals, the mass media, and military service. Russian authorities, for example, imposed the use of the Russian language, even in parts of the country where it was not widely spoken. They succeeded, however, only in producing a greater awareness of Ukrainian, Polish, and Finnish nationalism.

As it became more prominent in the nineteenth century, nationalism took on a variety of political ideologies. Some supporters of liberal democracy and representative government, as in France or the United States, saw nationalism, with its emphasis on "the people," as an aid to their aspirations toward wider involvement in political life. Often called "civic nationalism," such a view identified the nation with a particular territory and maintained that people of various cultural backgrounds could assimilate into the dominant culture, as in the process of "becoming American." Other versions of nationalism, in Germany for example, sometimes defined the nation in racial terms, which excluded those who did not share a common ancestry, such as Jews. In the hands of conservatives, nationalism could be used to combat socialism and feminism, for those movements only divided the nation along class or gender lines. Thus nationalism generated endless controversy because it provided no clear answer to the question of who belonged to the nation or who should speak for it.

Nor was nationalism limited to the Euro-American world in the nineteenth century. An "Egypt for the Egyptians" movement arose in the 1870s as British and

Nationalism in Poland
In the eighteenth century, Poland had been divided among Prussia, Austria, and Russia and disappeared as a separate and independent state. Polish nationalism found expression in the nineteenth century in a series of revolts, among which was a massive uprising in 1863, directed against Poland's Russian occupiers. This famous painting by Polish artist Jan Matejko shows a crowd of Polish prisoners awaiting transportation to imprisonment in Siberia, while Russian military officers supervise a blacksmith, who fastens fetters on a woman representing Poland. (Courtesy, Czartoryski Museum, Cracow)

French intervention in Egyptian affairs deepened. When Japan likewise confronted European aggression in the second half of the nineteenth century, its long sense of itself as a distinct culture was readily transformed into an assertive modern nationalism. Small groups of Western-educated men in British-ruled India began to think of their enormously diverse country as a single nation. The Indian National Congress, established in 1885, gave expression to this idea. The notion of the Ottoman Empire as a Turkish national state rather than a Muslim or dynastic empire took hold among a few people. By the end of the nineteenth century, some Chinese intellectuals began to think in terms of a Chinese nation beset both by a foreign ruling dynasty and by predatory Europeans. Along the West African coast, the idea of an "African nation" stirred among a handful of freed slaves and missionary-educated men. Although Egyptian and Japanese nationalism gained broad support, elsewhere in Asia and Africa such movements would have to wait until the twentieth century, when they exploded with enormous power on the stage of world history.

Feminist Beginnings

■ **Significance**
What were the achievements and limitations of nineteenth-century feminism?

A third echo of the Atlantic revolutions lay in the emergence of a feminist movement. Although scattered voices had earlier challenged patriarchy, never before had an organized and substantial group of women called into question this most fundamental and accepted feature of all preindustrial civilizations—the subordination of women to men. Then, in the century following the French Revolution, such a challenge took shape, especially in Europe and North America. In the twentieth century, feminist thinking transformed "the way in which women and men work, play, think, dress, worship, vote, reproduce, make love and make war."[19] How did this extraordinary process get launched in the nineteenth century?

Thinkers of the European Enlightenment had challenged many ancient traditions, including on occasion that of women's intrinsic inferiority. The French writer Condorcet, for example, called for "the complete destruction of those prejudices that have established an inequality of rights between the sexes." The French Revolution then raised the possibility of re-creating human societies on new foundations. Many women participated in these events, and a few insisted, unsuccessfully, that the revolutionary ideals of liberty and equality must include women. In her *Declaration of the Rights of Woman*, the French feminist Olympe de Gouges wrote in 1791: "Woman, wake up; the tocsin [warning bell] of reason is being heard throughout the whole universe; discover your rights."[20]

Within the growing middle classes of industrializing societies, more women found both educational opportunities and some freedom from household drudgery. Such women increasingly took part in temperance movements, charities, abolitionism, and missionary work, as well as socialist and pacifist organizations. Some of their working-class sisters became active trade unionists. On both sides of the Atlantic, small numbers of these women began to develop a feminist consciousness that viewed women as individuals with rights equal to those of men.[21] Others, particularly in France, based their claims less on abstract notions of equality and more on the distinctive role of women as mothers. "It is above all this holy function of motherhood . . . ," wrote one advocate of "maternal feminism," "which requires that women watch over the futures of their children and gives women the right to intervene not only in all acts of civil life, but also in all acts of political life."[22] The first organized expression of this new feminism took place at a women's rights conference in Seneca Falls, New York, in 1848. At that meeting, Elizabeth Cady Stanton drafted a statement that began by paraphrasing the Declaration of Independence: "We hold these truths to be self-evident, that all men and women are created equal."

From the beginning, feminism was a transatlantic movement in which European and American women attended the same conferences, corresponded regularly, and read one another's work. Access to schools, universities, and the professions were among their major concerns as growing numbers of women sought these previously unavailable opportunities. The more radical among them refused to take their husbands' surname or wore trousers under their skirts. Elizabeth Cady Stanton published a Women's Bible, eliminating the parts she found offensive. As heirs to the French Revolution, feminists ardently believed in progress and insisted that it must now include a radical transformation of the position of women.

By the 1870s, feminist movements in the West were focusing primarily on the issue of suffrage and were gaining a growing constituency. Now many ordinary middle-class housewives and working-class mothers joined their better-educated sisters in the movement. By 1914, some 100,000 women took part in French feminist organizations, while the National American Woman Suffrage Association claimed 2 million members. Most operated through peaceful protest and persuasion, but the British Women's Social and Political Union organized a campaign of violence that included blowing up railroad stations, slashing works of art, and smashing department store windows. One British activist, Emily Davison, threw herself in front of the king's horse during a race in Britain in 1913 and was trampled to death. By the beginning of the twentieth century in the most highly industrialized countries of the West, the women's movement had become a mass movement.

That movement had some effect. By 1900, upper- and middle-class women had gained entrance to universities, though in small numbers, and women's literacy rates were growing steadily. In the United States, a number of states passed legislation allowing women to manage and control their own property and wages, separate from their husbands. Divorce laws were liberalized in some places. Professions such as medicine opened to a few, and teaching beckoned to many more. In Britain, Florence Nightingale professionalized nursing and attracted thousands of women into it, while Jane Addams in the United States virtually invented social work, which also became a female-dominated profession. Progress was slower in the political domain. In 1893, New Zealand became the first country to give the vote to all adult women; Finland followed in 1906. Elsewhere widespread voting rights for women in national elections were not achieved until after World War I and in France not until 1945.

Women's Suffrage
What began as a few isolated voices of feminist protest in the early nineteenth century had become by the end of the century a mass movement in the United States and Western Europe. Here, in a photograph of an American suffrage parade in 1912, is an illustration of that movement in action. (The Granger Collection, New York)

Beyond these concrete accomplishments, the movement prompted an unprecedented discussion about the role of women in modern society. In Henrik Ibsen's play *A Doll's House* (1879), the heroine Nora, finding herself in a loveless and oppressive marriage, leaves both her husband and her children. European audiences were riveted, and many were outraged. Writers, doctors, and journalists addressed previously taboo sexual topics, including homosexuality and birth control. Socialists too found themselves divided about women's issues. Did the women's movement distract from the class solidarity that Marxism proclaimed, or did it provide added energy to the workers' cause? Feminists themselves disagreed about the proper basis for women's rights. Some took their stand on the modern idea of human equality: "whatever is right for a man is right for a woman." Others argued that women's traditional role as mothers, the guardians of family life and social virtue, provided the stronger case for women's rights.

Not surprisingly, feminism provoked bitter opposition. Some academic and medical experts argued that the strains of education and life in the world outside the home would cause serious reproductive damage and as a consequence depopulate the nation. Thus feminists were viewed as selfish, willing to sacrifice the family or even the nation while pursuing their individual goals. Some saw suffragists, like Jews and socialists, as "a foreign body in our national life." Never before in any society had such a passionate and public debate about the position of women erupted. It was a novel feature of Western historical experience in the aftermath of the Atlantic revolutions.

Like nationalism, a concern with women's rights spread beyond Western Europe and the United States, though less widely. An overtly feminist newspaper was established in Brazil in 1852, and an independent school for girls was founded in Mexico in 1869. A handful of Japanese women and men, including the empress Haruko, raised issues about marriage, family planning, and especially education as the country began its modernizing process after 1868, but the state soon cracked down firmly, forbidding women from joining political parties or even attending political meetings. In Russia, the most radical feminist activists operated within socialist or anarchist circles, targeting the oppressive tsarist regime. Within the Islamic world and in China, some modernists came to feel that education and a higher status for women strengthened the nation in its struggles for development and independence and therefore deserved support. Huda Sharawi, founder of the first feminist organization in Egypt, returned to Cairo in 1923 from an international conference in Italy and threw her veil into the sea. Many upper-class Egyptian women soon followed her example.

Nowhere did nineteenth-century feminism have really revolutionary consequences. But as an outgrowth of the French and Industrial revolutions, it raised issues that echoed repeatedly and more loudly in the century that followed.

⌐⌐ Reflections: Revolutions Pro and Con

Not long before he died in 1976, the Chinese revolutionary and communist leader Zhou Enlai was asked what he thought about the French Revolution. His famous reply—"It's too early to say"—highlights the endless controversies that revolutions everywhere have spawned. Long after the dust had settled from these Atlantic upheavals, their legacies have continued to provoke controversy. Were these revolutions necessary? Did they really promote the freedoms that they advertised? Did their benefits outweigh their costs in blood and treasure?

To the people who made these revolutions, benefited from them, or subsequently supported them, they represented an opening to new worlds of human possibility, while sweeping away old worlds of oppression, exploitation, and privilege. Modern revolutionaries acted on the basis of Enlightenment ideas—that the structure of human societies was not forever ordained by God or tradition and that it was both possible and necessary to reconstruct those societies. They also saw themselves as correcting ancient and enduring injustices. To those who complained about the violence of revolutions, supporters pointed to the violence that maintained the status quo and the unwillingness of privileged classes to accommodate changes that threatened those privileges. It was persistent injustice that made revolution necessary and perhaps inevitable.

To their victims, critics, and opponents, revolutions appeared quite different. Conservatives generally viewed human societies, not as machines whose parts could be easily rearranged, but as organisms that evolved slowly. Efforts at radical and sudden change only invited disaster, as the unrestrained violence of the French Revolution at its height demonstrated. The brutality and bitterness of the Haitian Revolution arguably contributed much to the unhappy future of that country. Furthermore, critics charged that revolutions were largely unnecessary, since societies were in fact changing. France was becoming a modern society and feudalism was largely gone well before the revolution exploded. Slavery was ended peacefully in many places, and democratic reform proceeded gradually throughout the nineteenth century. Was this not a preferable alternative to that of revolutionary upheaval?

Historians too struggle with the passions of revolution—both pro and con— as they seek to understand the origins and consequences of these momentous events. Were revolutions the product of misery, injustice, and oppression? Or did they reflect the growing weakness of established authorities, the arrival of new ideas, or the presence of small groups of radical activists able to fan the little fires of ordinary discontent into revolutionary conflagrations? The outcomes of revolutions have been as contentious as their beginnings. Did the American Revolution enable the growth of the United States as an economic and political "great power"? Did the Haitian Revolution stimulate the later end of slavery elsewhere in the Atlantic world? Did the French Revolution and the threat of subsequent revolutions encourage the democratic reforms that followed in the nineteenth century? Such questions have been central to an understanding of eighteenth-century revolutions as well as to those that followed in Russia, China, and elsewhere in the twentieth century.

Second Thoughts

To assess your mastery of the material in this chapter, see the **Online Study Guide** at bedfordstmartins.com/strayer.

What's the Significance?

North American Revolution
French Revolution
Declaration of the Rights of
   Man and Citizen
Napoleon Bonaparte

Haitian Revolution
Latin American
   revolutions
abolitionist movement
nationalism

*Declaration of the Rights of
   Woman*
maternal feminism
Elizabeth Cady Stanton

Big Picture Questions

1. Make a chart comparing the North American, French, Haitian, and Spanish American revolutions. What categories of comparison would be most appropriate to include?
2. Do revolutions originate in oppression and injustice, in the weakening of political authorities, in new ideas, or in the activities of small groups of determined activists?
3. "The influence of revolutions endured long after they ended." To what extent does this chapter support or undermine this idea?

4. In what ways did the Atlantic revolutions and their echoes give a new and distinctive shape to the emerging societies of nineteenth-century Europe and the Americas?

Next Steps: For Further Study

For Web sites and documents related to this chapter, see **Make History** at bedfordstmartins.com/strayer.

Benedict Anderson, *Imagined Communities: Reflections on the Origins and Spread of Nationalism* (1991). A now-classic though controversial examination of the process by which national identities were created.

Bonnie S. Anderson, *Joyous Greetings: The First International Women's Movement, 1830–1860* (2000). Describes the beginnings of transatlantic feminism.

Laurent Dubois and John Garrigus, *Slave Revolution in the Caribbean, 1789–1804* (2006). A brief and up-to-date summary of the Haitian Revolution, combined with a number of documents.

Susan Dunn, *Sister Revolutions* (1999). A stimulating comparative study of the American and French revolutions.

Eric Hobsbawm, *The Age of Revolution, 1789–1848* (1999). A highly respected survey by a well-known British historian.

Lynn Hunt, ed., *The French Revolution and Human Rights* (1996). A collection of documents, with a fine introduction by a prominent scholar.

"Liberty, Equality, Fraternity: Exploring the French Revolution," http://chnm.gmu.edu/revolution/browse/images/#. A collection of cartoons, paintings, and artifacts illustrating the French Revolution.

Revolutions of Industrialization

1750-1914

"Industrialization is, I am afraid, going to be a curse for mankind.... God forbid that India should ever take to industrialism after the manner of the West. The economic imperialism of a single tiny island kingdom (England) is today [1928] keeping the world in chains. If an entire nation of 300 millions took to similar economic exploitation, it would strip the world bare like locusts.... Industrialization on a mass scale will necessarily lead to passive or active exploitation of the villagers.... The machine produces much too fast."[1]

Such were the views of the famous Indian nationalist and spiritual leader Mahatma Gandhi, who subsequently led his country to independence from British colonial rule by 1947, only to be assassinated a few months later. However, few people anywhere have agreed with India's heroic figure. Since its beginning in Great Britain in the late eighteenth century, the idea of industrialization, if not always its reality, has been embraced in every kind of society, both for the wealth it generates and for the power it conveys. Even Gandhi's own country, once it achieved its independence, largely abandoned its founding father's vision of small-scale, village-based, handicraft manufacturing in favor of modern industry. As the twenty-first century dawned, India was moving rapidly to develop a major high-technology industrial sector. At that time, across the river from the site in New Delhi where Gandhi was cremated in 1948 was a large power plant belching black smoke.

FEW ELEMENTS OF EUROPE'S MODERN TRANSFORMATION HELD A GREATER SIGNIFICANCE for the history of humankind than the Industrial Revolution, which took place initially in the century and a

---

Industrial Britain: The dirt, smoke, and pollution of early industrial societies are vividly conveyed in this nineteenth-century engraving of a copper foundry in Wales. (Bibliothèque des Arts Décoratifs Paris/Gianni Dagli Orti/The Art Archive)

half between 1750 and 1900. It drew upon the Scientific Revolution and accompanied the unfolding legacy of the French Revolution to utterly transform European society and to propel Europe into a position of global dominance. Not since the breakthrough of the Agricultural Revolution some 12,000 years ago had human ways of life been so fundamentally altered. But the Industrial Revolution, unlike its agricultural predecessor, began independently in only one place, Western Europe and more specifically Great Britain. From there, it spread far more rapidly than agriculture, though very unevenly, to achieve a worldwide presence in less than 250 years. Far more than Europe's Christian religion, its democratic political values, or its capitalist economic framework, the techniques of its Industrial Revolution have been intensely sought after virtually everywhere.

In any long-term reckoning, the history of industrialization is very much an unfinished story. It is hard to know whether we are at the beginning of a movement leading to worldwide industrialization, stuck in the middle of a world permanently divided into rich and poor countries, or approaching the end of an environmentally unsustainable industrial era. Whatever the future holds, this chapter focuses on the early stages of an immense transformation in the global condition of humankind.

Explaining the Industrial Revolution

At the heart of the Industrial Revolution lay a great acceleration in the rate of technological innovation, leading to an enormously increased output of goods and services. Particularly significant were new sources of energy—coal-fired steam engines early on and petroleum-fueled engines later. In Britain, where that revolution began, industrial output increased some fiftyfold between 1750 and 1900. It was a wholly unprecedented and previously unimaginable jump in the capacity of human societies to produce wealth. Lying behind it was not simply this or that invention—the spinning jenny, power loom, steam engine, or cotton gin—but a "culture of innovation," a widespread and almost obsessive belief that things could be endlessly improved. Until 1750 or even 1800, however, Europeans held no across-the-board technological advantage over China, India, or the Islamic world. These major Eurasian civilizations existed then in a state of rough technological equilibrium.

Early signs of the technological creativity that spawned the Industrial Revolution appeared in eighteenth-century Britain, where a variety of innovations transformed cotton textile production. It was only in the nineteenth century, though, that Europeans in general and the British in particular more clearly forged ahead. The great breakthrough was the steam engine, which provided an inanimate and almost limitless source of power beyond that of wind, water, or muscle and could be used to drive any number of machines as well as locomotives and oceangoing ships. Soon the Industrial Revolution spread beyond the textile industry to iron and steel production, railroads and steamships, food processing, construction, chemicals, electricity, the telegraph and telephone, rubber, pottery, printing, and much more. Agriculture too was affected as mechanical reapers, chemical fertilizers, pesticides, and refrigeration transformed this most ancient of industries. Technical innovation occurred in more modest ways as well. Patents for horseshoes in the United States, for example, grew from fewer than five per year before 1840 to thirty to forty per year by the end of the century. Furthermore, industrialization spread beyond Britain to continental Western Europe and then in the second half of the century to the United States, Russia, and Japan.

In the twentieth century, the Industrial Revolution became global when a number of Asian and Latin American countries developed substantial industrial sectors. Oil, natural gas, and nuclear reactions became widely available sources of energy, and new industries emerged in automobiles, airplanes, consumer durable goods, electronics, computers, and on and on. It was a cumulative process that, despite periodic ups and downs, accelerated over time. More than anything else, this continuous emergence of new techniques of production and the economic growth that they made possible mark the past 250 years as a distinct phase of human history.

Why Europe?

The Industrial Revolution has long been a source of great controversy among scholars. Why did it occur first in Europe? Within Europe, why did it occur first in Great Britain? And why did it take place in the late eighteenth and nineteenth centuries? Earlier explanations that sought the answer in some unique and deeply rooted feature of European society, history, or culture have been challenged by world historians because such views seemed to suggest that Europe alone was destined to lead the way to modern economic life. This approach not only was Eurocentric and deterministic but also flew in the face of much recent research in at least three ways.

First, other areas of the world had experienced times of great technological and scientific flourishing. Between 750 and 1100 C.E., the Islamic world generated major advances in shipbuilding, the use of tides and falling water to generate power, papermaking, textile production, chemical technologies, water mills, clocks, and much more.[2] India had long been the world center of cotton textile production, the first place to turn sugarcane juice into crystallized sugar, and the source of many agricultural innovations and mathematical inventions. To the Arabs of the ninth century C.E., India was a "place of marvels."[3] More than either of these, China was clearly the world leader in technological innovation between 700 and 1400 C.E., prompting various scholars to suggest that China was on the edge of an industrial revolution by 1200 or so. For reasons much debated among historians, all of these flowerings of technological creativity had slowed down considerably or stagnated by the early modern era, when the pace of technological change in Europe began to pick up. But their earlier achievements certainly suggest that Europe was not alone in its capacity for technological innovation.

Nor did Europe enjoy any overall economic advantage as late as 1750. Over the past twenty years or so, historians have carefully examined the economic conditions

■ **Causation**
In what respects did the roots of the Industrial Revolution lie within Europe? In what ways did that transformation have global roots?

of various Eurasian societies in the eighteenth century and found them surprisingly alike. Economic indicators such as life expectancies, patterns of consumption and nutrition, wage levels, general living standards, widespread free markets, and prosperous merchant communities suggest broadly similar conditions across the major civilizations of Europe and Asia.[4] Thus Europe had no obvious economic lead, even on the eve of the Industrial Revolution. Rather, according to one leading scholar, "there existed something of a global economic parity between the most advanced regions in the world economy."[5]

A final reason for doubting any unique European capacity for industrial development lies in the relatively rapid spread of industrial techniques to many parts of the world over the past 250 years (a fairly short time by world history standards). Although the process has been highly uneven, industrialization has taken root, to one degree or another, in Japan, China, India, Brazil, Mexico, Indonesia, South Africa, Saudi Arabia, Thailand, South Korea, and elsewhere. Such a pattern weakens any suggestion that European culture or society was exceptionally compatible with industrial development.

Thus contemporary historians are inclined to see the Industrial Revolution erupting rather quickly and quite unexpectedly between 1750 and 1850 (see Map 18.1). Two intersecting factors help to explain why this process occurred in Europe rather than elsewhere. One lies in certain patterns of Europe's internal development that favored innovation. Its many small and highly competitive states, taking shape in the twelfth or thirteenth centuries, arguably provided an "insurance against economic and technological stagnation," which the larger Chinese, Ottoman, or Mughal empires perhaps lacked.[6] If so, then Western Europe's failure to re-create the earlier unity of the Roman Empire may have acted as a stimulus to innovation.

Furthermore, the relative newness of these European states and their monarchs' desperate need for revenue in the absence of an effective tax-collecting bureaucracy pushed European royals into an unusual alliance with their merchant classes. Small groups of merchant capitalists might be granted special privileges, monopolies, or even tax-collecting responsibilities in exchange for much-needed loans or payments to the state. It was therefore in the interest of governments to actively encourage commerce and innovation. Thus states granted charters and monopolies to private trading companies, and governments founded scientific societies and offered prizes to promote innovation. In this way, European merchants and other innovators from the fifteenth century onward gained an unusual degree of freedom from state control and in some places a higher social status than their counterparts in more established civilizations. In Venice and Holland, merchants actually controlled the state. In short, by the eighteenth century major Western European societies were highly commercialized and governed by states generally supportive of private commerce. Such internally competitive economies, coupled with a highly competitive system of rival states, fostered innovation in the new civilization taking shape in Western Europe.

Europe's societies, of course, were not alone in developing market-based economies by the eighteenth century. Japan, India, and especially China were likewise

Map 18.1 The Early Phase of Europe's Industrial Revolution
From its beginning in Great Britain, industrialization spread by 1850 across northwestern Europe to include parts of France, Germany, Belgium, Bohemia, and Italy.

highly commercialized. However, in the several centuries after 1500, Western Europe alone "found itself at the hub of the largest and most varied network of exchange in history."[7] Widespread contact with culturally different peoples was yet another factor that historically has generated extensive change and innovation. This new global network, largely the creation of Europeans themselves, greatly energized European commerce and brought Europeans into direct contact with peoples around the world.

For example, Asia, home to the world's richest and most sophisticated societies, was the initial destination of European voyages of exploration. The German philosopher Gottfried Wilhelm Leibniz (1646–1716) encouraged Jesuit missionaries in China "not to worry so much about getting things European to the Chinese but rather about getting remarkable Chinese inventions to us."[8] Inexpensive and well-made Indian textiles began to flood into Europe, causing one English observer to note:"Almost everything that used to be made of wool or silk, relating either to dress of the women or the furniture of our houses, was supplied by the Indian trade."[9] The competitive stimulus of these Indian cotton textiles was certainly one factor driving innovation in the British textile industry. Likewise, the popularity of Chinese porcelain and Japanese lacquerware prompted imitation and innovation in England, France, and Holland.[10] Thus competition from desirable, high-quality, and newly available Asian goods played a role in stimulating Europe's Industrial Revolution.

In the Americas, Europeans found a windfall of silver that allowed them to operate in Asian markets. They also found timber, fish, maize, potatoes, and much else to sustain a growing population. Later, slave-produced cotton supplied an emerging textile industry with its key raw material at low prices, while sugar, similarly produced with slave labor, furnished cheap calories to European workers. "Europe's Industrial Revolution," concluded historian Peter Stearns, "stemmed in great part from Europe's ability to draw disproportionately on world resources."[11] The new societies of the Americas further offered a growing market for European machine-produced goods and generated substantial profits for European merchants and entrepreneurs. None of the other empires of the early modern era enriched their imperial heartlands so greatly or provided such a spur to technological and economic growth.

Thus the intersection of new, highly commercialized, competitive European societies with the novel global network of their own making provides a context for understanding Europe's Industrial Revolution. Commerce and cross-cultural exchange, acting in tandem, provided the seedbed for the impressive technological changes of the first industrial societies.

Why Britain?

■ **Comparison**
What was distinctive about Britain that may help to explain its status as the breakthrough point of the Industrial Revolution?

If the Industrial Revolution was a Western European phenomenon generally, it clearly began in Britain in particular. The world's first Industrial Revolution unfolded spontaneously in a country that concentrated some of the more general features of European society. It was both unplanned and unexpected.

Britain was the most highly commercialized of Europe's larger countries. Its landlords had long ago "enclosed" much agricultural land, pushing out the small farmers and producing for the market. A series of agricultural innovations—crop rotation, selective breeding of animals, lighter plows, higher-yielding seeds—increased agricultural output, kept food prices low, and freed up labor from the countryside. The guilds, which earlier had protected Britain's urban artisans, had largely disappeared by the eighteenth century, allowing employers to run their manufacturing enterprises as they saw fit. Coupled with a rapidly growing population, these processes ensured a ready supply of industrial workers who had few alternatives available to them. Furthermore, British aristocrats, unlike their counterparts in

Europe, had long been interested in commerce, and some took part in new mining and manufacturing enterprises. British commerce, moreover, extended around the world, its large merchant fleet protected by the Royal Navy. The wealth of empire and global commerce, however, were not themselves sufficient for spawning the Industrial Revolution, especially when we consider that Spain, the earliest beneficiary of American wealth, remained one of the more slowly industrializing European countries into the twentieth century.

British political life encouraged commercialization and economic innovation. Its policy of religious toleration, formally established in 1688, welcomed people with technical skills regardless of their faith, whereas France's persecution of its Protestant minority had chased out some of its most skilled workers. The British government favored men of business with tariffs to keep out cheap Indian textiles, with laws that made it easy to form companies and to forbid workers' unions, with roads and canals that helped create a unified internal market, and with patent laws that served to protect the interests of inventors. Checks on royal authority—trial by jury and the growing authority of parliament, for example—provided a freer arena for private enterprise than elsewhere in Europe.

Europe's Scientific Revolution also took a distinctive form in Great Britain in ways that fostered technological innovation.[12] Whereas science on the continent was largely based on logic, deduction, and mathematical reasoning, in Britain it was much more concerned with observation and experiment, precise measurements, mechanical devices, and practical commercial applications. Discoveries about atmospheric pressure and vacuums, for example, played an important role in the invention and improvement of the steam engine. Even though most inventors were artisans or craftsmen rather than scientists, in eighteenth-century Britain they were in close contact with scientists, makers of scientific instruments, and entrepreneurs, whereas in continental Europe these groups were largely separate. The British Royal Society, an association of natural philosophers (scientists) established in 1660, saw its role as one of promoting "useful knowledge." To this end, it established "mechanics' libraries," published broadsheets and pamphlets on recent scientific advances, and held frequent public lectures and demonstrations. The integration of science and technology became widespread and permanent after 1850, but for a century before, it was largely a British phenomenon.

Finally, several accidents of geography and history contributed something to Britain's Industrial Revolution. The country had a ready supply of coal and iron ore, often located close to each other and within easy reach of major industrial centers. Although Britain took part in the wars against Napoleon, the country's island location protected it from the kind of invasions that so many continental European states experienced during the era of the French Revolution. Moreover, Britain's relatively fluid society allowed for adjustments in the face of social changes without widespread revolution. By the time the dust settled from the immense disturbance of the French Revolution, Britain was well on its way to becoming the world's first industrial society.

Railroads
The popularity of railroads, long a symbol of the Industrial Revolution, is illustrated in this early-nineteenth-century watercolor, which shows a miniature train offered as a paid amusement for enthusiasts in London's Euston Square. (Science Museum, London, UK/The Bridgeman Art Library)

The First Industrial Society

Wherever it took hold, the Industrial Revolution generated, within a century or less, an economic miracle, at least in comparison with earlier technologies. The British textile industry, which used 52 million pounds of cotton in 1800, consumed 588 million pounds in 1850. Britain's output of coal soared from 5.23 million tons in 1750 to 68.4 million tons a century later.[13] Railroads crisscrossed Britain and much of Europe like a giant spider web (see Map 18.1, p. 531). Most of this dramatic increase in production occurred in mining, manufacturing, and services. Thus agriculture, for millennia the overwhelmingly dominant economic sector in every civilization, shrank in relative importance. In Britain, for example, agriculture generated only 8 percent of national income in 1891 and employed fewer than 8 percent of working Britons in 1914. Accompanying this vast economic change was an epic transformation of social life. "In two centuries," wrote one prominent historian, "daily life changed more than it had in the 7,000 years before."[14] Nowhere were the revolutionary dimensions of industrialization more apparent than in Great Britain, the world's first industrial society.

The social transformation of the Industrial Revolution both destroyed and created. Referring to the impact of the Industrial Revolution on British society, historian Eric Hobsbawm said: "[I]n its initial stages it destroyed their old ways of living and left them free to discover or make for themselves new ones, if they could and knew how. But it rarely told them how to set about it."[15] For many people, it was an enormously painful, even traumatic process, full of social conflict, insecurity, and false starts as well as new opportunities, an eventually higher standard of living, and greater participation in public life. Scholars, politicians, journalists, and ordinary people have endlessly debated the gains and losses associated with the Industrial Revolution. Amid the controversy, however, one thing is clear: not everyone was affected in the same way.

The British Aristocracy

■ **Change**
How did the Industrial Revolution transform British society?

Individual landowning aristocrats, long the dominant class in Britain, suffered little in material terms from the Industrial Revolution. In the mid-nineteenth century, a few thousand families still owned more than half of the cultivated land in Britain,

$\mathcal{S}$napshot   **Measuring the Industrial Revolution**[16]

Railroads are one useful measure of industrial development. This graph illustrates both Britain's head start and the beginning catch-up efforts of other countries.

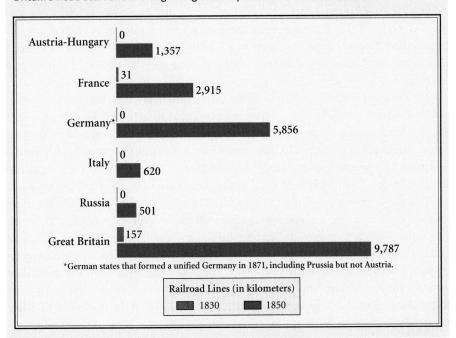

Austria-Hungary
0
1,357

France
31
2,915

Germany*
0
5,856

Italy
0
620

Russia
0
501

Great Britain
157
9,787

*German states that formed a unified Germany in 1871, including Prussia but not Austria.

Railroad Lines (in kilometers)
1830   1850

most of it leased to tenant farmers, who in turn employed agricultural wage laborers to work it. Rapidly growing population and urbanization sustained a demand for food products grown on that land. For most of the nineteenth century, landowners continued to dominate the British parliament.

As a class, however, the British aristocracy, like large landowners in every industrial society, declined. As urban wealth became more important, landed aristocrats had to make way for the up-and-coming businessmen, manufacturers, and bankers who had been newly enriched by the Industrial Revolution. The aristocracy's declining political clout was demonstrated in the 1840s when high tariffs on foreign agricultural imports, designed to protect the interests of British landlords, were finally abolished. By the end of the century, landownership had largely ceased to be the basis of great wealth, and businessmen, rather than aristocrats, led the major political parties. Even so, the titled nobility of dukes, earls, viscounts, and barons retained great social prestige and considerable personal wealth. Many among them found an outlet for their energies and opportunities for status and enrichment in the vast domains of the British Empire, where they went as colonial administrators or settlers. Famously described as a "system of outdoor relief for the aristocracy," the empire provided a cushion for a declining class.

The Middle Classes

■ Change
How did Britain's middle classes change during the nineteenth century?

Those who benefited most conspicuously from industrialization were members of that amorphous group known as the "middle classes." At its upper levels, the middle class contained extremely wealthy factory and mine owners, bankers, and merchants. Such rising businessmen readily assimilated into aristocratic life, buying country houses, obtaining seats in parliament, sending their sons to Oxford or Cambridge University, and gratefully accepting titles of nobility from Queen Victoria.

Far more numerous were the smaller businessmen, doctors, lawyers, engineers, teachers, journalists, scientists, and other professionals required in any industrial society. Such people set the tone for a distinctly middle-class society with its own values and outlooks. Politically they were liberals, favoring constitutional government, private property, free trade, and social reform within limits. Their agitation resulted in the Reform Bill of 1832, which broadened the right to vote to many men of the middle class, but not to middle-class women. Ideas of thrift and hard work, a rigid morality, and cleanliness characterized middle-class culture. The central value of that culture was "respectability," a term that combined notions of social status and virtuous behavior. Nowhere were these values more effectively displayed than in the Scotsman Samuel Smiles's famous book *Self-Help*, published in 1859. Individuals are responsible for their own destiny, Smiles argued. An hour a day devoted to self-improvement "would make an ignorant man wise in a few years." According to Smiles, this enterprising spirit was what distinguished the

The Industrial Middle Class
This late-nineteenth-century painting shows a prosperous French middle-class family, attended by a servant. (Chateau de Versailles/SuperStock, Inc.)

prosperous middle class from Britain's poor. The misery of the poorer classes was "voluntary and self-imposed—the results of idleness, thriftlessness, intemperance, and misconduct."[17]

Women in such middle-class families were increasingly cast as homemakers, wives, and mothers, charged with creating an emotional haven for their men and a refuge from a heartless and cutthroat capitalist world. They were also the moral center of family life and the educators of "respectability" as well as the managers of consumption in a setting in which "shopping," a new concept in eighteenth-century Britain, became a central activity. An "ideology of domesticity" defined the home and charitable activities as the proper sphere for women, while paid employment and public life beckoned to men.

The English poet Alfred, Lord Tennyson, aptly expressed this understanding in his poem "The Princess":

> Man for the field and woman for the hearth:
> Man for the sword and for the needle she:
> Man with the head and woman with the heart:
> Man to command and woman to obey.
> All else confusion.

Middle-class women played a very different role from women in the peasant farm or the artisan's shop, where wives, though clearly subordinate, worked productively alongside their husbands. By the late nineteenth century, however, some middle-class women began to enter the teaching, clerical, and nursing professions.

As Britain's industrial economy matured, it also gave rise to a sizable "lower middle class," which included people employed in the growing service sector as clerks, salespeople, bank tellers, hotel staff, secretaries, telephone operators, police officers, and the like. By the end of the nineteenth century, this growing class represented about 20 percent of Britain's population and provided new employment opportunities for women as well as men. In just twenty years (1881–1901), the number of female secretaries in Britain rose from 7,000 to 90,000. Almost all were single and expected to return to the home after marriage. For both men and women, such employment represented a claim on membership in the larger middle class and a means of distinguishing themselves clearly from a "working class" tainted by manual labor.

The Laboring Classes

The overwhelming majority of Britain's nineteenth-century population—some 70 percent or more—were, of course, neither aristocrats nor members of the middle classes. They were manual workers in the mines, ports, factories, construction sites, workshops, and farms of an industrializing Britain. Although their conditions varied considerably and changed over time, the laboring classes were the people who suffered most and benefited least from the epic transformations of the Industrial Revolution. Their efforts to accommodate, resist, protest, and change those conditions contributed much to the texture of the first industrial society.

The lives of the laboring classes were shaped primarily by the new working conditions of the industrial era. Chief among those conditions was the rapid urbanization of British society. Liverpool's population alone grew from 77,000 to 400,000 in the first half of the nineteenth century. By 1851, a majority of Britain's population lived in towns and cities, an enormous change from the overwhelmingly rural life of almost all previous civilizations. By the end of the century, London was the world's largest city, with more than 6 million inhabitants.

These cities were vastly overcrowded and smoky, with wholly inadequate sanitation, periodic epidemics, endless row houses and warehouses, few public services or open spaces, and inadequate water supplies. This was the environment in which

DEATH'S DISPENSARY.

OPEN TO THE POOR, GRATIS, BY PERMISSION OF THE PARISH.

The Urban Poor of Industrial Britain

This 1866 political cartoon shows an impoverished urban family forced to draw its drinking water from a polluted public well, while a figure of Death operates the pump. (The Granger Collection, New York)

most urban workers lived in the first half of the nineteenth century. Nor was there much personal contact between the rich and the poor of industrial cities. Benjamin Disraeli's novel *Sybil*, published in 1845, described these two ends of the social spectrum as "two nations between whom there is no intercourse and no sympathy; who are ignorant of each other's habits, thoughts and feelings, as if they were dwellers in different zones or inhabitants of different planets."

The industrial factories to which growing numbers of desperate people looked for employment offered a work environment far different from the artisan's shop or the tenant's farm. Long hours, low wages, and child labor were nothing new for the poor, but the routine and monotony of work, dictated by the factory whistle and the needs of machines, imposed novel and highly unwelcome conditions of labor. Also objectionable were the direct and constant supervision and the rules and fines aimed at enforcing work discipline. The ups and downs of a capitalist economy made industrial work insecure as well as onerous. Unlike their middle-class sisters, many girls and young women of the laboring classes worked in mills or as domestic servants in order to supplement meager family incomes, but after marriage they too usually left outside paid employment because a man who could not support his wife was widely considered a failure. Within the home, however, many working-class women continued to earn money by taking in boarders, doing laundry, or sewing clothes.

Social Protest among the Laboring Classes

For workers of the laboring classes, industrial life "was a stony desert, which they had to make habitable by their own efforts."[18] Such efforts took many forms. By 1815, about 1 million workers, mostly artisans, had created a variety of "friendly societies." With dues contributed by members, these working-class self-help groups provided insurance against sickness, a decent funeral, and an opportunity for social life in an otherwise bleak environment. Other skilled artisans, who had been displaced by machine-produced goods and forbidden to organize in legal unions, sometimes wrecked the offending machinery and burned the mills that had taken their jobs. The class consciousness of working people was such that one police informer reported that "most every creature of the lower order both in town and country are on their side."[19]

Others acted within the political arena by joining movements aimed at obtaining the vote for working-class men, a goal that was gradually achieved in the second half of the nineteenth century. When trade unions were legalized in 1824, growing numbers of factory workers joined these associations in their efforts to achieve better wages and working conditions. Initially their strikes, attempts at nationwide organization, and the threat of violence made them fearful indeed to the upper classes. One British newspaper in 1834 described unions as "the most dangerous institutions that were ever permitted to take root, under shelter of law, in any country,"[20] although they later became rather more "respectable" organizations.

Socialist ideas of various kinds gradually spread within the working class, challenging the assumptions of a capitalist society. Robert Owen (1771–1858), a wealthy British cotton textile manufacturer, urged the creation of small industrial communities, cooperatively run by the workers themselves. He established one such community, with a ten-hour workday, spacious housing, decent wages, and education for children, at his mill in New Lanark in Scotland.

Of more lasting significance was the socialism of Karl Marx (1818–1883). German by birth, Marx spent much of his life in England, where he witnessed the brutal conditions of Britain's Industrial Revolution and wrote voluminously about history and economics. To Marx, the story line of the human past and the motor of historical change had always been "class struggle," the bitter conflict of "oppressor and oppressed." In his own time, that struggle took the form of sharpening hostility between the *bourgeoisie*, who owned industrial capital, and the *proletariat*, his term for the industrial working class. For Marx, class struggle was the central dynamic of industrial capitalist societies.

■ **Change**
How did Karl Marx understand the Industrial Revolution? In what ways did his ideas have an impact in the industrializing world of the nineteenth century?

As a phase of human history, capitalism bore great promise, for it had unleashed, as Marx put it in the *Communist Manifesto*, "more massive and more colossal productive forces than have all preceding generations together," which meant, of course, that the end of poverty was in sight. And yet, according to Marx, capitalist societies could never deliver on that promise because private property, competition, and class hostility prevented those societies from distributing the abundance of industrial economies to the workers whose labor had created that abundance. Capitalism therefore was fatally flawed, doomed to inevitable collapse amid a working-class revolution as society polarized into rich and poor. After that revolution, Marx looked forward to a communist future in which the great productive potential of industrial technology would be placed in service to the entire community, thus ending forever the ancient conflict between rich and poor.

In the later decades of the nineteenth century, such ideas echoed among more radical trade unionists and some middle-class intellectuals in Britain, and even more so in a rapidly industrializing Germany and elsewhere, but the British working-class movement by then was not overtly revolutionary. When a working-class political party, the Labour Party, was established in the 1890s, it advocated a

reformist program and a peaceful democratic transition to socialism, largely rejecting the class struggle and revolutionary emphasis of Marxism.

A major factor producing a moderate working-class movement lay in the improv-
ing material conditions during the second half of the nineteenth century. Marx had
expected industrial capitalist societies to polarize into a small wealthy class and a huge
and increasingly impoverished proletariat. However, standing between "the captains
of industry" and the workers was a sizable middle and lower-middle class, constitut-
ing perhaps 30 percent of the population, most of whom were not really wealthy but
were immensely proud that they were not manual laborers. Marx had not foreseen
the development of this intermediate social group, nor had he imagined that workers could better their standard of living within a capitalist framework. But they did.
Wages rose under pressure from unions; cheap imported food improved working-class
diets; infant mortality rates fell; and shops and chain stores catering to working-class
families multiplied. As English male workers gradually obtained the right to vote,
politicians had an incentive to legislate in their favor, by abolishing child labor, regulating factory conditions, and even, in 1911, inaugurating a system of relief for the
unemployed. Sanitary reform considerably cleaned up the "filth and stink" of early-
nineteenth-century cities, and urban parks made a modest appearance. Contrary to
Marx's expectations, capitalist societies demonstrated some capacity for reform.

Socialist Protest
Socialism, a response to the injuctices and inequalities of industrial capitalism, spread throughout Europe in the nineteenth and early twenti-eth centuries. Here a group of French socialists in 1908 are demonstrating in mem-ory of an earlier uprising, the Paris commune of 1871. (Demonstration at Père-Lachaise for the commemoration of the Paris Commune, by Socialist party, French Section of the International Workingmen's Association, group of La Villette, 1st May 1908 [coloured photo], Gondry, [19th–early 20th century]/ Private Collection/The Bridgeman Art Library)

Manifestation du Père Lachaise
Parti Socialiste, Section Française de l'Internationale Ouvrière
Groupe de la Villette

Nonetheless, as the twentieth century dawned, industrial Britain could hardly be described as a stable or contented society. Immense inequalities still separated the classes. Some 40 percent of the working class continued to live in conditions then described as "poverty." A mounting wave of strikes from 1910 to 1913 testified to the intensity of class conflict. The Labour Party was becoming a major force in parliament. Some socialists and some feminists were becoming radicalized. "Wisps of violence hung in the English air," wrote Eric Hobsbawm, "symptoms of a crisis in economy and society, which the [country's] self-confident opulence…could not quite conceal."[21] The world's first industrial society remained a dissatisfied and conflicted society.

It was also a society in economic decline relative to industrial newcomers such as Germany and the United States. Britain paid a price for its early lead, for its businessmen became committed to machinery that became obsolete as the century progressed. Latecomers invested in more modern equipment and in various ways had surpassed the British by the early twentieth century.

Variations on a Theme: Comparing Industrialization in the United States and Russia

Not for long was the Industrial Revolution confined to Britain. It soon spread to continental Western Europe, and by the end of the nineteenth century, it was well under way in the United States, Russia, and Japan. The globalization of industrialization had begun. Everywhere it took hold, industrialization bore a range of outcomes broadly similar to those in Britain. New technologies and sources of energy generated vast increases in production and spawned an unprecedented urbanization as well. Class structures changed as aristocrats, artisans, and peasants declined as classes, while the middle classes and a factory working class grew in numbers and social prominence. Middle-class women generally withdrew from paid labor altogether, and their working-class counterparts sought to do so after marriage. Working women usually received lower wages than their male counterparts, had difficulty joining unions, and were subject to charges that they were taking jobs from men. Working-class frustration and anger gave rise to trade unions and socialist movements, injecting a new element of social conflict into industrial societies.

Nevertheless, different histories, cultures, and societies ensured that the Industrial Revolution unfolded variously in the diverse countries in which it became established. Differences in the pace and timing of industrialization, the size and shape of major industries, the role of the state, the political expression of social conflict, and many other factors have made this process rich in comparative possibilities. French industrialization, for example, occurred more slowly and perhaps less disruptively than did that of Britain. Germany focused initially on heavy industry—iron, steel, and coal—rather than on the textile industry with which Britain had begun. Moreover, German industrialization was far more highly concentrated in huge companies called cartels, and it generated a rather more militant and Marxist-oriented labor movement than in Britain.

Nowhere were the variations in the industrializing process more apparent than in those two vast countries that lay on the periphery of Europe. To the west across the Atlantic Ocean was the United States, a young, vigorous, democratic, expanding country, populated largely by people of European descent, along with a substantial number of slaves of African origin. To the east was Russia, with its Eastern Orthodox Christianity, an autocratic tsar, a huge population of serfs, and an empire stretching across all of northern Asia. In the early nineteenth century, the French observer Alexis de Tocqueville famously commented on these two emerging giants.

> The Anglo-American relies upon personal interest to accomplish his ends and gives free scope to the unguided strength and common sense of the people; the Russian centers all the authority of society in a single arm.... Their starting-point is different and their courses are not the same; yet each of them seems marked out by the will of Heaven to sway the destinies of half the globe.

By the early twentieth century, his prediction seemed to be coming true. Industrialization had turned the United States into a major global power and in Russia had spawned an enormous revolutionary upheaval that made that country the first outpost of global communism.

The United States: Industrialization without Socialism

■ Comparison
What were the differences between industrialization in the United States and that in Russia?

American industrialization began in the textile industry of New England during the 1820s but grew explosively in the half century following the Civil War (1861–1865) (see Map 18.2). The country's huge size, the ready availability of natural resources, its growing domestic market, and its relative political stability combined to make the United States the world's leading industrial power by 1914. At that time, it produced 36 percent of the world's manufactured goods, compared to 16 percent for Germany, 14 percent for Great Britain, and 6 percent for France. Furthermore, U.S. industrialization was closely linked to that of Europe. About one-third of the capital investment that financed its remarkable growth came from British, French, and German capitalists. Like many former colonies in the twentieth century, the United States initially relied on foreign capital for its development, although its overall economic strength was sufficient to avoid the dependency and underdevelopment that more recent emerging nations have so frequently experienced.

As in other second-wave industrializing countries, the U.S. government played an important role, though less directly than in Germany or Japan. Tax breaks, huge grants of public land to the railroad companies, laws enabling the easy formation of corporations, and the absence of much overt regulation of industry all fostered the rise of very large business enterprises. The U.S. Steel Corporation, for example, by 1901 had an annual budget three times the size of the federal government. In this

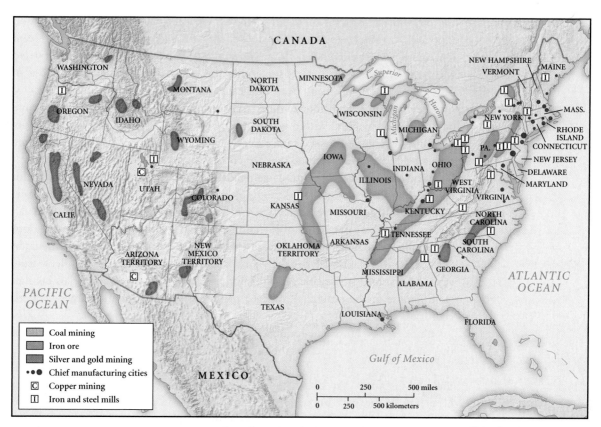

Map 18.2   The Industrial United States in 1900
By the early twentieth century, manufacturing industries were largely in the Northeast and Midwest, whereas mining operations were more widely scattered across the country.

respect, the United States followed the pattern of Germany but differed from that of France and Britain, where family businesses still predominated.

The United States also pioneered techniques of mass production, using interchangeable parts, the assembly line, and "scientific management" to produce for a mass market. The nation's advertising agencies, Sears Roebuck's and Montgomery Ward's mail-order catalogs, and urban department stores generated a middle-class "culture of consumption." When the industrialist Henry Ford in the early twentieth century began producing the Model T at a price that many ordinary people could afford, he famously declared: "I am going to democratize the automobile." More so than in Europe, with its aristocratic traditions, self-made American industrialists of fabulous wealth such as Henry Ford, Andrew Carnegie, and John D. Rockefeller became cultural heroes, widely admired as models of what anyone could achieve with daring and hard work in a land of endless opportunity.

Nevertheless, well before the first Model T rolled off the assembly line, serious social divisions of a kind common to European industrial societies mounted. Preindustrial America had prided itself on its lack of European-style slums, but by the 1850s, and even more so by the 1890s, a growing gap had opened between the poor and the working class on the one hand and the middle class and the rich on

■ **Explanation**
Why did Marxist socialism not take root in the United States?

the other hand. Around Carnegie's Homestead steel plant near Pittsburgh stood thousands of workers' shacks. Employees worked every day of the year except Christmas and the Fourth of July, often for twelve hours a day. In crowded Manhattan, often the first (and sometimes the last) stopping point for millions of European immigrants, many lived in the infamous "dumbbell" tenements: five- or six-story buildings with four families and two toilets on each floor. In every large city, these slums existed within walking distance of the mansions of the well-to-do. To some, the contrast was a disgrace to the economic system that produced it, while others held that it was a natural result of competition and "the survival of the fittest."

As elsewhere, such conditions generated much labor protest, the formation of unions, and strikes, sometimes leading to violence. In 1877, when the eastern railroads announced a 10 percent wage cut for their workers, strikers disrupted rail service across the eastern half of the country, smashed equipment, and rioted. Both state militias and federal troops were called out to put down the movement. In 1892, the entire National Guard of Pennsylvania was sent to suppress a violent strike at the Homestead steel plant near Pittsburgh. Class consciousness and class conflict were intense in the industrial America of the late nineteenth and early twentieth centuries.

Unlike many European countries, however, no major political party emerged in the United States to represent the interests of the working class. Nor did the ideas of socialism, and especially Marxism, appeal to American workers nearly as much as they did in Europe. At its high point, the Socialist Party of America garnered just 6 percent of the vote for its presidential candidate in the 1912 election, whereas socialists at the time held more seats in Germany's parliament than any other party. Even in the depths of the Great Depression of the 1930s, no major socialist movement emerged to champion American workers. How might we explain this distinctive feature of American industrial development?

One answer lies in the relative conservatism of major American union organizations, especially the American Federation of Labor. Its focus on skilled workers excluded the more radical unskilled laborers, and its refusal to align with any party limited its influence in the political arena. Furthermore, the immense religious, ethnic, and racial divisions of American society contrasted sharply with the more homogeneous populations of many European countries. Catholics and Protestants; English, Irish, Germans, Slavs, Jews, and Italians; whites and blacks—such differences undermined the class solidarity of American workers, making it far more difficult to sustain class-oriented political parties and a socialist labor movement. Moreover, the country's remarkable economic growth generated on average a higher standard of living for American workers than their European counterparts experienced. Land was cheaper, and home ownership was more available. Workers with property generally found socialism less attractive than those without. By 1910, a particularly large group of white-collar workers in sales, services, and offices outnumbered factory laborers. Their middle-class aspirations further diluted impulses toward radicalism.

The seamy side of American industrialization did not go unchallenged, however. "Populists," whose ideas echoed most loudly among small farmers in the U.S. South, West, and Midwest, systematically denounced banks, industrialists, monopolies, the existing money system, and both major political parties, which they saw as being controlled by the corporate interests of the eastern part of the country. But populism, after reaching a high point in the mid-1890s, found scant support in the growing industrial areas, even among the workers at whom some of its rhetoric was aimed. More successful, especially after 1900, were the Progressives, who sought to remedy the ills of industrialization through reforms such as wages-and-hours legislation, better sanitation standards, antitrust laws, and greater governmental intervention in the economy. Conservatives sometimes accused Progressives of being socialists and radicals, but nothing could have been further from the minds of men such as Presidents Theodore Roosevelt and Woodrow Wilson, both of whom championed their ideas. Socialism came to be defined as fundamentally "un-American" in a country that so valued individualism and so feared "big government." It was a distinctive feature of the American response to industrialization.

Russia: Industrialization and Revolution

As a setting for the Industrial Revolution, it would be hard to imagine two more different environments than the United States and Russia. If the United States was the Western world's most exuberant democracy in the nineteenth century, Russia remained the sole outpost of absolute monarchy, in which the state exercised far greater control over individuals and society than anywhere in the Western world. At the beginning of the twentieth century, Russia still had no national parliament, no legal political parties, and no nationwide elections. The tsar, answerable to God alone, ruled unchecked. Furthermore, Russian society was dominated by a titled nobility of various ranks, whose upper levels included great landowners, who furnished the state with military officers and leading gov-

Russian Serfdom
This nineteenth-century cartoon by the French artist Gustave Doré shows Russian noblemen gambling with tied bundles of stiff serfs. Serfdom was not finally abolished in Russia until 1861. (The Granger Collection, New York)

ernment officials. Until 1861, most Russians were peasant serfs, bound to the estates of their masters, subject to sale, greatly exploited, and largely at the mercy of their owners. In Russia at least, serfdom approximated slavery. A vast cultural gulf separated these two classes. Many nobles were highly Westernized, some speaking French better than Russian, whereas their serfs were steeped in a backwoods Orthodox Christianity that incorporated pre-Christian spirits, spells, curses, and magic.

A further difference between Russia and the United States lay in the source of social and economic change. In the United States, such change bubbled up from society as free farmers, workers, and businessmen sought new opportunities and operated in a political system that gave them varying degrees of expression. In autocratic Russia, change was far more often initiated by the state itself, in its continuing efforts to catch up with the more powerful and innovative states of Europe. This kind of "transformation from above" found an early expression in the reign of Peter the Great (reigned 1689–1725). His massive efforts included vast administrative changes, the enlargement and modernization of Russian military forces, a new educational system for the sons of noblemen, and dozens of manufacturing enterprises. Russian nobles were instructed to dress in European styles and to shave their sacred and much-revered beards. The newly created capital city of St. Petersburg was to be Russia's "window on the West." One of Peter's successors, Catherine the Great (reigned 1762–1796), followed up with further efforts to Europeanize Russian cultural and intellectual life, viewing herself as heir to the European Enlightenment.

■ **Change**
What factors contributed to the making of a revolutionary situation in Russia by the beginning of the twentieth century?

Such state-directed change continued in the nineteenth century with the freeing of the serfs in 1861, an action stimulated by military defeat at the hands of British and French forces in the Crimean War (1854–1856). To many thoughtful Russians, serfdom seemed incompatible with modern civilization and held back the country's overall development, as did its economic and industrial backwardness. Thus, beginning in the 1860s, Russia began a program of industrial development, which was more heavily directed by the state than was the case in Western Europe or the United States.

By the 1890s, Russia's Industrial Revolution was launched and growing rapidly. It focused particularly on railroads and heavy industry and was fueled by a substantial amount of foreign investment. By 1900, Russia ranked fourth in the world in steel production and had major industries in coal, textiles, and oil. Its industrial enterprises, still modest in comparison to those of Europe, were concentrated in a few major cities—Moscow, St. Petersburg, and Kiev, for example—and took place in factories far larger than in most of Western Europe.

All of this contributed to the explosive social outcomes of Russian industrialization. A growing middle class of businessmen and professionals increasingly took shape. As modern and educated people, many in the middle class objected strongly to the deep conservatism of tsarist Russia and sought a greater role in political life, but they were also dependent on the state for contracts and jobs and for suppressing the growing radicalism of the workers, which they greatly feared. Although factory workers constituted only about 5 percent of Russia's total population, they quickly developed an unusually radical class consciousness, based on harsh conditions and the absence of any legal outlet for their grievances. Until 1897, a thirteen-hour working day was common. Ruthless discipline and overt disrespect from supervisors created resentment, while life in large and unsanitary barracks added to workers' sense of injustice. In the absence of legal unions or political parties, these grievances often erupted in the form of large-scale strikes.

In these conditions, a small but growing number of educated Russians found in Marxist socialism a way of understanding the changes they witnessed daily and hope for the future in a revolutionary upheaval of workers. In 1898, they created an illegal Russian Social-Democratic Labor Party and quickly became involved in workers' education, union organizing, and, eventually, revolutionary action. By the early twentieth century, the strains of rapid change and the state's continued intransigence had reached the bursting point, and in 1905, following its defeat in a naval war with Japan, Russia erupted in spontaneous insurrection. Workers in Moscow and St. Petersburg went on strike and created their own representative councils, called soviets. Peasant uprisings, student demonstrations, revolts of non-Russian nationalities, and mutinies in the military all contributed to the upheaval. Recently formed political parties, representing intellectuals of various persuasions, came out into the open.

The 1905 Revolution in Russia

The 1905 revolution, though brutally suppressed, forced the tsar's regime to make more substantial reforms than it had ever contemplated. It granted a constitution, legalized both trade unions and political parties, and permitted the election of a national assembly, called the Duma. Censorship was eased, and plans were under way for universal primary education. Industrial development likewise continued at a rapid rate, so that by 1914 Russia stood fifth in the world in terms of overall output. But in the first half of that year, some 1,250,000 workers, representing about 40 percent of the entire industrial workforce, went out on strike.

Thus the tsar's limited political reforms, which had been granted with great reluctance and were often reversed in practice, failed to tame working-class radicalism or to bring social stability to Russia. In 1906–1907, when a newly elected and radically inclined Duma refused to cooperate with the tsar's new political system, Tsar Nicholas II twice dissolved that elected body and finally changed the electoral laws to favor the landed nobility. Consequently, in Russian political life, the people generally, and even the middle class, had only a limited voice. The representatives of even the privileged classes had become so alienated by the government's intransigence that many felt revolution was inevitable. Various revolutionary groups, many of them socialist, published pamphlets and newspapers, organized trade unions, and spread their messages among workers and peasants. Particularly in the cities, these revolutionary parties had an impact. They provided a language through which workers could express their grievances; they created links among workers from different factories; and they furnished leaders who were able to act when the revolutionary moment arrived.

World War I provided that moment. The enormous hardships of that war, coupled with the immense social tensions of industrialization within a still autocratic political system, sparked the Russian Revolution of 1917. That massive upheaval quickly brought to power the most radical of the socialist groups operating in the country—the Bolsheviks, led by the charismatic Vladimir Ulyanov, better known as Lenin. Only in Russia was industrialization associated with violent social revolution, and this was the most distinctive feature of Russia's modern historical development. And only in Russia was a socialist political party, inspired by the teachings of Karl Marx, able to seize power, thus launching the modern world's first socialist society, with enormous implications for the twentieth century.

The Industrial Revolution and Latin America in the Nineteenth Century

Beyond the world of Europe and North America, only Japan underwent a major industrial transformation during the nineteenth century, part of that country's overall response to the threat of European aggression. (See Chapter 19 for a more detailed examination of Japan in the nineteenth century.) Elsewhere—in colonial India, Egypt, the Ottoman Empire, China, and Latin America—very modest experiments in modern industry were undertaken, but nowhere did they drive the kind of major social transformation that had taken place in Britain, Europe, North America, and Japan. However, even in societies that did not experience their own Industrial Revolution, the profound impact of European and North American industrialization was hard to avoid. Such was the case in Latin America during the nineteenth century.

Snapshot   **The Industrial Revolution and the Global Divide**[22]

During the nineteenth century, the Industrial Revolution generated an enormous and unprecedented economic division in the world, as measured by the share of manufacturing output. What patterns can you see in this table?

SHARE OF TOTAL WORLD MANUFACTURING OUTPUT (PERCENT)

	1750	1800	1860	1880	1900
Europe as a Whole	**23.2**	**28.1**	**53.2**	**61.3**	**62.0**
UNITED KINGDOM	1.9	4.3	19.9	22.9	18.5
FRANCE	4.0	4.2	7.9	7.8	6.8
GERMANY	2.9	3.5	4.9	8.5	13.2
RUSSIA	5.0	5.6	7.0	7.6	8.8
United States	**0.1**	**0.8**	**7.2**	**14.7**	**23.6**
Japan	**3.8**	**3.5**	**2.6**	**2.4**	**2.4**
The Rest of the World	**73.0**	**67.7**	**36.6**	**20.9**	**11.0**
CHINA	32.8	33.3	19.7	12.5	6.2
SOUTH ASIA (INDIA/PAKISTAN)	24.5	19.7	8.6	2.8	1.7

After Independence in Latin America

The struggle for independence in Latin America had lasted far longer and proved far more destructive than in North America. Decimated populations, diminished herds of livestock, flooded or closed silver mines, abandoned farms, shrinking international trade and investment capital, and empty national treasuries were some of the conditions under which Latin American countries greeted independence. Furthermore, the four major administrative units (vice-royalties) of Spanish America ultimately dissolved into eighteen separate countries, and regional revolts wracked Brazil in the early decades of its independent life. A number of international wars in the postindependence century likewise shook these new nations. Mexico lost huge territories to the United States (1846–1848); an alliance of Argentina, Brazil, and Uruguay went to war with Paraguay (1864–1870) in a conflict that devastated Paraguay's small population; Peru and Bolivia briefly united and then broke apart in a bitter conflict (1836–1839).

Within these new countries, political life was turbulent and unstable. Conservatives favored centralized authority and sought to maintain the social status quo of the colonial era in alliance with the Catholic Church, which at independence owned perhaps half of all productive land. Their often bitter opponents were liberals, who attacked the Church in the name of Enlightenment values, sought at least modest social reforms, and preferred federalism. In many countries, conflicts between these factions, often violent, enabled military strongmen known as *caudillos* to achieve power as defenders of order and property, although they too succeeded one another with great frequency. One of them, Antonio López de Santa Anna of Mexico, was president of his country at least nine separate times between 1833 and 1855. Constitutions too replaced one another with bewildering speed. Bolivia had ten constitutions during the nineteenth century, while Ecuador and Peru each had eight.

Social life did not change fundamentally in the aftermath of independence. Slavery, it is true, was abolished in most of Latin America by midcentury, although it persisted in both Brazil and Cuba until the late 1880s. Most of the legal distinctions among various racial categories also disappeared, and all free people were considered, at least officially, equal citizens. Nevertheless, productive economic resources such as businesses, ranches, and plantations remained overwhelmingly in the hands of creole whites, who were culturally oriented toward Europe. The military provided an avenue of mobility for a few skilled and ambitious mestizo men, some of whom subsequently became *caudillos*. Other mixed-race people found a place in a small middle class as teachers, shopkeepers, or artisans. The vast majority—blacks, Indians, and many mixed-race people—remained impoverished, working small subsistence farms or laboring in the mines or on the *haciendas* (plantations) of the well-to-do. Only rarely did the poor and dispossessed actively rebel against their social betters. One such case was the Caste War of Yucatán (1847–1901), a prolonged struggle of the Maya people of Mexico, aimed at cleansing their land of European and mestizo intruders.

Facing the World Economy

■ Connection

In what ways and with what impact was Latin America linked to the global economy of the nineteenth century?

During the second half of the century, a measure of political consolidation took hold in Latin America, and countries such as Mexico, Peru, and Argentina entered periods of greater stability. At the same time, Latin America as a whole became more closely integrated into a world economy driven by the industrialization of Western Europe and North America. The new technology of the steamship cut the sailing time between Britain and Argentina almost in half, while the underwater telegraph instantly brought the latest news and fashions of Europe to Latin America.

The most significant economic outcome of this growing integration was a rapid growth of Latin American exports to the industrializing countries, which now needed the food products, raw materials, and markets of these new nations. Latin American landowners, businessmen, and governments proved eager to supply those needs, and in the sixty years or so after 1850, an export boom increased the value of Latin American goods sold abroad by a factor of ten.

Mexico continued to produce large amounts of silver, supplying more than half the world's new supply until 1860. Now added to the list of raw materials flowing out of Latin America were copper from Chile, a metal that the growing electrical industry required; tin from Bolivia, which met the mounting demand for tin cans; and nitrates from Chile and guano (bird droppings) from Peru, both of which were used for fertilizer. Wild rubber from the Amazon rain forest was in great demand for bicycle and automobile tires, as was sisal from Mexico, used to make binder twine for the proliferating mechanical harvesters of North America. Bananas from Central America, beef from Argentina, cacao from Ecuador, coffee from Brazil and Guatemala, and sugar from Cuba also found eager markets in the rapidly growing and increasingly prosperous world of industrializing countries. In return for these primary products, Latin Americans imported the textiles, machinery, tools, weapons, and luxury goods of Europe and the United States (see Map 18.3).

Accompanying this burgeoning commerce was large-scale investment of European capital in Latin America, $10 billion alone between 1870 and 1919. Most of this capital came from Great Britain, which invested more in Argentina in the late nineteenth century than in its colony of India, although France, Germany, Italy, and the United States also contributed to this substantial financial transfer. By 1910, U.S. business interests controlled 40 percent of Mexican property and produced half of its oil. Much of this capital was used to build railroads, largely to funnel Latin American exports to the coast, where they were shipped to overseas markets. Mexico had only 390 miles of railroad in 1876; it had 15,000 miles in 1910. By 1915, Argentina, with 22,000 miles of railroad, had more track per person than the United States.

■ Comparison

Did Latin America follow or diverge from the historical path of Europe during the nineteenth century?

Becoming like Europe?

To the economic elites of Latin America, who were intent on making their countries resemble Europe or the United States, all of this was progress. In some respects,

U.S. Interventions

Puerto Rico, 1898–on
Panama, 1903
Cuba, 1898–1902, 1905–09, 1917–21
Haiti, 1915–34
Mexico, 1914, 1916–17
Nicaragua, 1909, 1912–25, 1927–32
Dominican Republic, 1916–24

MEXICO
$1329

CUBA
$471

$11 $16 $44

$99 $42
$19 $12
$61 $28

VENEZUELA
$161

COLOMBIA
$77

ECUADOR
$41

PERU
$197

BOLIVIA
$59

BRAZIL
$1913

PARAGUAY
$27

ARGENTINA
$4001

CHILE
$668

$475

Legend

- Bananas
- Cacao
- Cattle
- Coffee
- Copper and tin
- Cotton
- Guano
- Henequen
- Nitrate
- Oil
- Rubber
- Sheep
- Silver
- Sugar
- Tobacco
- Wheat
- Yerba mate

$161   Foreign investment (in millions of U.S. dollars around 1914)

← European immigration

← U.S. intervention

Map 18.3   Latin America and the World, 1825–1935

During the nineteenth and early twentieth centuries, Latin American countries interacted with the industrializing world via investment, trade, immigration, and military intervention from the United States.

they were surely right. Economies were growing and producing more than ever before. The population also was burgeoning; it increased from about 30 million in 1850 to more than 77 million in 1912 as public health measures (such as safe drinking water, inoculations, sewers, and campaigns to eliminate mosquitoes that carried yellow fever) brought down death rates.

Urbanization also proceeded rapidly. By the early twentieth century, wrote one scholar, "Latin American cities lost their colonial cobblestones, white-plastered walls, and red-tiled roofs. They became modern metropolises, comparable to urban giants anywhere. Streetcars swayed, telephones jangled, and silent movies flickered from Montevideo and Santiago to Mexico City and Havana."[23] Buenos Aires, Argentina's metropolitan center, boasted 750,000 people in 1900 and billed itself the "Paris of South America." There the educated elite, just like the English, drank tea in the afternoon, while discussing European literature, philosophy, and fashion, usually in French.

To become more like Europe, Latin America sought to attract more Europeans. Because civilization, progress, and modernity apparently derived from Europe, many Latin American countries actively sought to increase their European populations by deliberately recruiting impoverished people with the promise, mostly unfulfilled, of a new and prosperous life in the New World. Argentina received the largest wave of European immigrants (some 2.5 million between 1870 and 1915), mostly from Spain and Italy. Brazil and Uruguay likewise attracted substantial numbers of European newcomers.

Only a quite modest segment of Latin American society saw any great benefits from the export boom and all that followed from it. Upper-class landowners certainly gained as exports flourished and their property values soared. Middle-class urban dwellers—merchants, office workers, lawyers, and other professionals—also grew in numbers and prosperity as their skills proved valuable in a modernizing society. As a percentage of the total population, however, these were narrow elites. In Mexico in the mid-1890s, for example, the landowning upper class made up no more than 1 percent and the middle classes perhaps 8 percent of the population. Everyone else was lower-class, and most of them were impoverished.[24]

A new but quite small segment of this vast lower class emerged among urban workers who labored in the railroads, ports, mines, and a few factories. They organized themselves initially in a variety of mutual aid societies, but by the end of the nineteenth century, they were creating unions and engaging in strikes. To authoritarian governments interested in stability and progress, such activity was highly provocative and threatening, and they acted harshly to crush or repress unions and strikes. In 1906, the Mexican dictator Porfirio Díaz invited the Arizona Rangers to suppress a strike at Cananea near the U.S. border, an action that resulted in dozens of deaths. The following year in the Chilean city of Iquique, more than 1,000 men, women, and children were slaughtered by police when nitrate miners protested their wages and working conditions.

The vast majority of the lower class lived in rural areas, where they suffered the most and benefited the least from the export boom. Government attacks on communal landholding and peasant indebtedness to wealthy landowners combined to push many farmers off their land or into remote and poor areas where they could barely make a living. Many wound up as dependent laborers or peons on the haciendas of the wealthy, where their wages were often too meager to support a family. Thus women and children, who had earlier remained at home to tend the family plot, were required to join their menfolk as field laborers. Many immigrant Italian farmworkers in Argentina and Brazil were unable to acquire their own farms, as they had expected, and so drifted into the growing cities or returned to Italy.

Although local protests and violence were frequent, only in Mexico did these vast inequalities erupt into a nationwide revolution. There, in the early twentieth century, middle-class reformers joined with workers and peasants to overthrow the long dictatorship of Porfirio Díaz (1876–1911). What followed was a decade of bloody conflict (1910–1920) that cost Mexico some 1 million lives, or roughly 10 percent of the population. Huge peasant armies under charismatic leaders such as Pancho Villa and Emiliano Zapata helped oust Díaz. Intent on seizing land and redistributing it to the peasants, they then went on to attack many of Mexico's large haciendas. But unlike the later Russian and Chinese revolutions, in which the most radical elements seized state power, Villa and Zapata proved unable to do so, in part because they were hobbled by factionalism and focused on local or regional issues. Despite this limitation and its own internal conflicts, the Mexican Revolution transformed the country. When the dust settled, Mexico had a new constitution (1917) that proclaimed universal suffrage; provided for the redistribution of land; stripped the Catholic Church of any role in public education and forbade it to own land; announced unheard-of rights for workers, such as a minimum wage and an eight-hour workday; and placed restrictions on foreign ownership of property. Much of Mexico's history in the twentieth century involved working out the implications of these nationalist and reformist changes. The revolution's direct influence, however, was largely limited to Mexico itself, without the wider international impact of the Russian and Chinese upheavals.

Perhaps the most significant outcome of the export boom lay in what did *not*

The Mexican Revolution
Women were active participants in the Mexican Revolution. They prepared food, nursed the wounded, washed clothes, and at times served as soldiers on the battlefield, as illustrated in this cover image from a French magazine in 1913. (© Archivo Iconografico, S.A./Corbis)

happen, for nowhere in Latin America did it jump-start a thorough Industrial Revolution, despite a few factories that processed foods or manufactured textiles, clothing, and building materials. The reasons are many. A social structure that relegated some 90 percent of its population to an impoverished lower class generated only a very small market for manufactured goods. Moreover, economically powerful groups such as landowners and cattlemen benefited greatly from exporting agricultural products and had little incentive to invest in manufacturing. Domestic manufacturing enterprises could only have competed with cheaper and higher-quality foreign goods if they had been protected for a time by high tariffs. But Latin American political leaders had thoroughly embraced the popular European doctrine of prosperity through free trade, and many governments depended on taxing imports to fill their treasuries.

Instead of its own Industrial Revolution, Latin Americans developed a form of economic growth that was largely financed by capital from abroad and dependent on European and North American prosperity and decisions. Brazil experienced this kind of dependence when its booming rubber industry suddenly collapsed in 1910–1911, after seeds from the wild rubber tree had been illegally exported to Britain and were used to start competing and cheaper rubber plantations in Malaysia.

Later critics saw this "dependent development" as a new form of colonialism, expressed in the power exercised by foreign investors. The influence of the U.S.-owned United Fruit Company in Central America was a case in point. Allied with large landowners and compliant politicians, the company pressured the governments of these "banana republics" to maintain conditions favorable to U.S. business. This indirect or behind-the-scenes imperialism was supplemented by repeated U.S. military intervention in support of American corporate interests in Cuba, Haiti, the Dominican Republic, Nicaragua, and Mexico. The United States also controlled the Panama Canal and acquired Puerto Rico as a territory in the aftermath of the Spanish-American War (see Map 18.3, p. 551).

Thus, despite its domination by people of European descent and its close ties to the industrializing countries of the Atlantic world, Latin America's historical trajectory in the nineteenth century diverged considerably from that of Europe and North America.

Reflections: History and Horse Races

Historians and students of history seem endlessly fascinated by "firsts"—the first breakthrough to agriculture, the first civilization, the first domestication of horses, the first use of gunpowder, the first printing press, and so on. Each of these firsts presents a problem of explanation: why did it occur in some particular time and place rather than somewhere else or at some other time? Such questions have assumed historical significance both because "first achievements" represent something new in the human journey and because many of them conveyed unusual power, wealth, status, or influence on their creators.

Nonetheless, the focus on firsts can be misleading as well. Sometimes those who accomplished something first have seen themselves as generally superior to those who embraced that innovation later. Historians too can sometimes adopt a winners-and-losers mentality, inviting a view of history as a horse race toward some finish line of accomplishment. Most first achievements in history, however, were not the result of intentional efforts but rather were the unexpected outcome of converging circumstances.

The Industrial Revolution is a case in point. Understanding the European beginnings of this immense breakthrough is certainly justified by its pervasive global consequences and its global spread over the past several centuries. In terms of our ability to dominate the natural environment and to extract wealth from it, the Industrial Revolution marks a decisive turning point in human history. But Europeans' attempts to explain their Industrial Revolution have at times stated or implied their own superiority. In the nineteenth century, many Europeans saw their technological mastery as a sure sign of their cultural and racial superiority as they came to use "machines as the measure of men."[25] In attempting to answer the "why Europe?" question, historians too have sometimes sought the answer in some distinct or even superior feature of European civilization.

In emphasizing the unexpectedness of the first Industrial Revolution, and the global context within which it occurred, world historians have attempted to avoid a "history as horse race" syndrome. Clearly the first industrial breakthrough in Britain was not a self-conscious effort to win a race; it was the surprising outcome of countless decisions by many people to further their own interests. Subsequently, however, other societies and their governments quite deliberately tried to catch up, seeking the wealth and power that the Industrial Revolution promised.

The rapid spread of industrialization across the planet, though highly uneven, promises to diminish the importance of the "why Europe?" issue. Just as no one views agriculture as a Middle Eastern phenomenon, even though it occurred first in that region, it seems likely that industrialization will be seen increasingly as a global process rather than one uniquely associated with Europe. If industrial society proves to be a sustainable future for humankind—and this is presently an open question—historians of the future will probably be more interested in the pattern of its global spread and in efforts to cope with its social and environmental consequences than with its origins in Western Europe.

Second Thoughts

What's the Significance?

steam engine	Karl Marx	Russian Revolution of 1905
Indian cotton textiles	proletariat	*caudillo*
British Royal Society	Labour Party	Latin American export boom
middle-class values	socialism in the United States	Mexican Revolution
lower middle class	Progressives	dependent development

To assess your mastery of the material in this chapter, see the **Online Study Guide** at bedfordstmartins.com/strayer.

Big Picture Questions

1. What was revolutionary about the Industrial Revolution?
2. What was common to the process of industrialization everywhere, and in what ways did it vary from place to place?
3. What did humankind gain from the Industrial Revolution, and what did it lose?
4. In what ways might the Industrial Revolution be understood as a global rather than simply a European phenomenon?

Next Steps: For Further Study

For Web sites and documents related to this chapter, see **Make History** at bedfordstmartins.com/strayer.

John Charles Chasteen, *Born in Blood and Fire* (2006). A lively and well-written account of Latin America's turbulent history since the sixteenth century.

David S. Landes, *The Wealth and Poverty of Nations* (1998). An argument that culture largely shapes the possibilities for industrialization and economic growth.

Robert B. Marks, *The Origins of the Modern World* (2007). An effective summary of new thinking about the origins of European industrialization.

Peter Stearns, *The Industrial Revolution in World History* (1998). A global and comparative perspective on the Industrial Revolution.

Peter Waldron, *The End of Imperial Russia, 1855–1917* (1997). A brief account of Russian history during its early industrialization.

Bridging World History, Units 18 and 19, http://www.learner.org/channel/courses/worldhistory. An innovative world history Web site that provides pictures, video, and text dealing with "Rethinking the Rise of the West" and "Global Industrialization."

CHAPTER NINETEEN

Internal Troubles, External Threats

China, the Ottoman Empire, and Japan

1800-1914

In the early twenty-first century, the issue of Japanese history textbooks became a serious matter in the relationship between Japan and its Chinese and Korean neighbors. From a Chinese point of view, those textbooks had minimized or whitewashed Japanese atrocities committed against China during World War II. In particular, many Chinese were outraged at the treatment of the so-called Rape of Nanjing, which witnessed the killing of perhaps 200,000 people, most of them civilians, and the rape of countless women. "Nanjing city was soaked with bloodshed and piles of bodies were everywhere," declared one survivor of those events. "Japanese rightist groups distort history and attempt to cover the truth of Nanjing Massacre. This makes me extremely angry."[1] For Koreans, the issue was the Japanese use of Korean "comfort women," sexual slaves forced to service Japanese troops. Japan, they argued, had not sufficiently acknowledged this outrage in their history textbooks, nor had the Japanese government adequately apologized for it.

To an observer from, say, the fifteenth century or even the eighteenth century, all of this—Japanese aggression during World War II, its enormous economic success after the war, and the continuing fear and resentment of Japan reflected in the textbook controversy—would have seemed strange indeed. For many centuries, after all, Japan had lived in the shadow of its giant Chinese neighbor, borrowing many elements of Chinese culture. Certainly it was never a threat to China. Beginning in the mid-nineteenth century, however, a remarkable reversal of roles occurred in East Asia when both China and Japan experienced a series of internal crises and, at the same time, had to confront

Carving Up the Pie of China: In this French cartoon from the late 1890s, the Great Powers of the day (from left to right: Great Britain's Queen Victoria, Germany's Kaiser Wilhelm, Russia's Tsar Nicholas II, a female figure representing France, and the Meiji emperor of Japan) participate in dividing China, while a Chinese figure behind them tries helplessly to stop the partition of his country. (Gianni Dagli Orti/The Art Archive) the novel reality of an industrialized, newly powerful, intrusive Europe. It was their very different responses to these internal crises and external challenges that led to their changed relationship in the century or more that followed and to the continuing suspicions and tensions that still characterize their relationship.

CHINA AND JAPAN WERE NOT ALONE IN FACING AN EXPANSIVE EUROPE. During the nineteenth century, and in some places earlier, most of the peoples of Asia, the Middle East, and Africa, as well as those living in the newly independent states of Latin America, were required to deal with European or American imperialism of one kind or another. Whatever their other differences, this was a common thread that gave these diverse peoples something of a shared history.

But—and this can hardly be emphasized too strongly—dealing with Europe was not the only item on their agendas. Islamic revival and the rise and fall of their own states occupied many African peoples; population growth and peasant rebellion wracked China; the great empires of the Islamic world shrank or disappeared; Hindus and Muslims persisted in their sometimes competitive and sometimes cooperative relationship in India; and rivalry among competing elites troubled Latin American societies. Encounters with an expansive Europe were conditioned everywhere by particular local circumstances. Those encounters provided a mirror in which the peoples of Asia and Africa viewed themselves, as they alternately celebrated, criticized, and sought to transform their own cultures.

This chapter examines the experience of societies that confronted these crises while retaining their formal independence, with China, the Ottoman Empire, and Japan as primary examples. The following chapter turns the spotlight on the colonial experience of those societies that fell under the official control of one or another of the European powers. In both cases, they were dealing with a new thrust of European expansion, one that drew its energy from the Industrial Revolution.

Four dimensions of European imperialism confronted these societies. First, they faced the immense military might and political ambitions of rival European states. Second, they became enmeshed in networks of trade, investment, and sometimes migration that radiated out from an industrializing and capitalist Europe to generate a new world economy. Third, they were touched by various aspects of traditional European culture, as some among them learned the French, English, or German language; converted to Christianity; or studied European literature and philosophy. Finally, Asians and Africans engaged with the culture of modernity—its scientific rationalism; its technological achievements; its belief in a better future; and its ideas of nationalism, socialism, feminism, and individualism. In that epic encounter, they sometimes resisted, at other times accommodated, and almost always adapted what came from the West. They were active participants in the global drama of nineteenth-century world history, not simply its passive victims or beneficiaries.

The External Challenge: European Industry and Empire

More than any other period, the nineteenth century was Europe's age of global expansion. During that century, Europe became the center of the world economy, with ties of trade and investment in every corner of the globe. Between 1812 and 1914, millions of Europeans migrated to new homes outside Europe. Missionaries and explorers penetrated the distant interiors of Asia and Africa. European states incorporated India, Africa, Southeast Asia, and the islands of the Pacific into their overseas colonial empires and seriously diminished the sovereignty and independence of the once proud domains of China, the Ottoman Empire, and Persia. Many newly independent states in Latin America became economically dependent on Europe and the United States (see Chapter 18). How can we explain such dramatic changes in the scope, character, and intensity of European expansion?

New Motives, New Means

Behind much of Europe's nineteenth-century expansion lay the massive fact of the Industrial Revolution. That process gave rise to new economic needs, many of which found solutions abroad. The enormous productivity of industrial technology and Europe's growing affluence now created the need for extensive raw materials and agricultural products. The demand for a wide variety of products—wheat from the American Midwest and southern Russia, meat from Argentina, bananas from Central America, rubber from Brazil, cocoa and palm oil from West Africa, tea from Ceylon, gold and diamonds from South Africa—radically changed patterns of economic and social life in the countries of their origin.

Furthermore, Europe needed to sell its own products. One of the peculiarities of industrial capitalism was that it periodically produced more manufactured goods than its own people could afford to buy. By 1840, for example, Britain was exporting 60 percent of its cotton-cloth production, annually sending 200 million yards to Europe, 300 million yards to Latin America, and 145 million yards to India. This last figure is particularly significant because for centuries Europe had offered little that Asian societies were willing to buy. Part of European and American fascination with China during the nineteenth and twentieth centuries lay in the enormous potential market represented by its huge population.

Much the same could be said for capital, for European investors often found it more profitable to invest their money abroad than at home. Between 1910 and 1913, Britain was sending about half of its savings abroad as foreign investment. In 1914, it had about 3.7 billion pounds sterling invested abroad, about equally divided between Europe, North America, and Australia on the one hand and Asia, Africa, and Latin America on the other hand.

■ **Change**
In what ways did the Industrial Revolution shape the character of nineteenth-century European imperialism?

Wealthy Europeans also saw social benefits to foreign markets, which served to keep Europe's factories humming and its workers employed. The English imperialist Cecil Rhodes confided his fears to a friend:

> Yesterday I attended a meeting of the unemployed in London and having listened to the wild speeches which were nothing more than a scream for bread, I returned home convinced more than ever of the importance of imperialism.... In order to save the 40 million inhabitants of the United Kingdom from a murderous civil war, the colonial politicians must open up new areas to absorb the excess population and create new markets for the products of the mines and factories.... The British Empire is a matter of bread and butter. If you wish to avoid civil war, then you must become an imperialist.[2]

Thus imperialism promised to solve the class conflicts of an industrializing society while avoiding revolution or the serious redistribution of wealth.

But what made imperialism so broadly popular in Europe, especially in the last quarter of the nineteenth century, was the growth of mass nationalism. By 1871, the unification of Italy and Germany made Europe's always competitive political system even more so, and much of this rivalry spilled over into the struggle for colonies or economic concessions in Asia and Africa. Colonies and spheres of influence abroad became a symbol of national "Great Power" status, and their acquisition was a matter of urgency, even if they possessed little immediate economic value. After 1875, it seemed to matter, even to ordinary people, whether some remote corner of Africa or some obscure Pacific island was in British, French, or German hands. Imperialism, in short, appealed on economic and social grounds to the wealthy or ambitious, seemed politically and strategically necessary in the game of international power politics, and was emotionally satisfying to almost everyone. It was a potent mix.

If the industrial era made overseas expansion more desirable or even urgent, it also provided new means for achieving those goals. Steam-driven ships, moving through the new Suez Canal, allowed Europeans to reach distant Asian and African ports more quickly and predictably and to penetrate the interior rivers as well. The underwater telegraph made possible almost instant communication with far-flung outposts of empire. The discovery of quinine to prevent malaria greatly reduced European death

The Gatling Gun
The Gatling gun, which was designed by the American Richard Gatling during the Civil War and named after him, was one of the earliest machine guns. By the late nineteenth century, this weapon gave European powers and the United States an enormous military advantage. (Courtesy, Royal Artillery Historical Trust)

rates in the tropics. Breech-loading rifles and machine guns vastly widened the military gap between Europeans and everyone else.

New Perceptions of the "Other"

Industrialization also occasioned a marked change in the way Europeans perceived themselves and others. In earlier centuries, Europeans had defined others largely in religious terms. "They" were heathen; "we" were Christian. Even as they held on to their sense of religious superiority, Europeans nonetheless adopted many of the ideas and techniques of more advanced societies. They held many aspects of Chinese and Indian civilization in high regard; they freely mixed and mingled with Asian and African elites and often married their women; some even saw the more technologically simple peoples of Africa and America as "noble savages."

■ **Change**
What contributed to changing European views of Asians and Africans in the nineteenth century?

With the advent of the industrial age, however, Europeans developed a secular arrogance that fused with or in some cases replaced their notions of religious superiority. They had, after all, unlocked the secrets of nature, created a society of unprecedented wealth, and used both to produce unsurpassed military power. These became the criteria by which Europeans judged both themselves and the rest of the world.

By such standards, it is not surprising that their opinions of other cultures dropped sharply. The Chinese, who had been highly praised in the eighteenth century, were reduced in the nineteenth century to the image of "John Chinaman," weak, cunning, obstinately conservative, and, in large numbers, a distinct threat, the "yellow peril" of late-nineteenth-century European fears. African societies, which had been regarded even in the slave-trade era as nations and their leaders as kings, were demoted in nineteenth-century European eyes to the status of tribes led by chiefs as a means of emphasizing their "primitive" qualities.

Increasingly, Europeans viewed the culture and achievements of Asian and African peoples through the prism of a new kind of racism, expressed now in terms of modern science. Although physical differences had often been a basis of fear or dislike, in the nineteenth century Europeans increasingly used the prestige and apparatus of science to support their racial preferences and prejudices. Phrenologists, craniologists, and sometimes physicians used allegedly scientific methods and numerous instruments to classify the size and shape of human skulls and concluded, not surprisingly, that those of whites were larger and therefore more advanced. Nineteenth-century biologists, who classified the varieties of plants and animals, applied these notions of rank to varieties of human beings as well. The result was a hierarchy of races, with the whites, naturally, on top and the less developed "child races" beneath them. Race, in this view, determined human intelligence, moral development, and destiny. "Race is everything," declared the British anatomist Robert Knox in 1850; "civilization depends on it."[3] Furthermore, as the germ theory of disease took hold in nineteenth-century Europe, it was accompanied by fears that contact with "inferior" peoples threatened the health and even the biological future of more advanced or "superior" peoples.

PROGRESSIVE DEVELOPMENT OF MAN.—(2) EVOLUTION ILLUSTRATED WITH THE SIX CORRESPONDING LIVING FORMS.

European Racial Images
This nineteenth-century chart, depicting the "Progressive Development of Man" from apes to modern Europeans, reflected the racial categories that were so prominent at the time. It also highlights the influence of Darwin's evolutionary ideas as they were applied to varieties of human beings. (The Granger Collection, New York)

These ideas influenced how Europeans viewed their own global expansion. Almost everyone saw it as inevitable, a natural outgrowth of a superior civilization. For many, though, this viewpoint was tempered with a genuine, if condescending, sense of responsibility to the "weaker races" that Europe was fated to dominate. "Superior races have a right, because they have a duty," declared the French politician Jules Ferry in 1883. "They have the duty to civilize the inferior races."[4] That "civilizing mission," as Europeans regarded it, included bringing Christianity to the heathen, good government to disordered lands, work discipline and production for the market to "lazy natives," a measure of education to the ignorant and illiterate, clothing to the naked, and health care to the sick, while suppressing "native customs" that ran counter to Western ways of living. All of this was defined as "progress" and "civilization."

Another, harsher side to the ideology of imperialism derived from an effort to apply, or perhaps misapply, the evolutionary thinking of Charles Darwin to an understanding of human history. The key concept of this "social Darwinism," though not necessarily shared by Darwin himself, was "the survival of the fittest," suggesting that European dominance inevitably involved the displacement or destruction of backward peoples or "unfit" races. Referring to native peoples of Australia, a European bishop declared:

Everyone who knows a little about aboriginal races is aware that those races which are of a low type mentally and who are at the same time weak in constitution rapidly die out when their country comes to be occupied by a different race much more rigorous, robust and pushing than themselves.[5]

Such views made imperialism, war, and aggression seem both natural and progressive, for they served to weed out the weaker peoples of the world, allowing the stronger to flourish. These were some of the ideas with which industrializing and increasingly powerful Europeans confronted the peoples of Asia and Africa in the nineteenth century. Among those confrontations, none was more important than Europe's encounter with China.

Reversal of Fortune: China's Century of Crisis

In 1793 in a famous letter to King George III, the Chinese emperor Qianlong sharply rebuffed British requests for a less restricted trading relationship with his country. "Our Celestial Empire possesses all things in great abundance," he declared.

"There was therefore no need to import the manufactures of outside barbarians." Qianlong's snub simply continued the pattern of the previous several centuries, during which Chinese authorities had strictly controlled and limited the activities of European missionaries and merchants. By 1912, little more than a century later, China's long-established imperial state had collapsed, and the country had been transformed from a central presence in the Afro-Eurasian world to a weak and dependent participant in a European-dominated world system. It was a stunning reversal of fortune for a country that in Chinese eyes was the civilized center of the entire world—in their terms, the Middle Kingdom.

The Crisis Within

In many ways, China was the victim of its own earlier success. Its robust economy and American food crops had enabled massive population growth, from about 100 million people in 1685 to some 430 million in 1853. Unlike Europe, though, where a similar population spurt took place, no Industrial Revolution accompanied this vast increase in the number of people, nor was agricultural production able to keep up. The result was growing pressure on the land, smaller farms for China's huge peasant population, and, in all too many cases, unemployment, impoverishment, misery, and starvation.

■ **Causation**
What accounts for the massive peasant rebellions of nineteenth-century China?

Furthermore, China's famed centralized and bureaucratic state did not enlarge itself to keep pace with the growing population. In 1400, the lowest administrative unit, a county, encompassed perhaps 50,000 people and was governed by a magistrate and a small staff. By 1800, that magistrate was responsible for 200,000 people, with no increase in his staff. Thus the state was increasingly unable to effectively perform its many functions, such as tax collection, flood control, social welfare, and public security. Gradually the central state lost power to provincial officials and local gentry. Among such officials, corruption was endemic, and harsh treatment of peasants was common. According to an official report issued in 1852, "[D]ay and night soldiers are sent out to harass taxpayers. Sometimes corporal punishments are imposed upon tax delinquents; some of them are so badly beaten to exact the last penny that blood and flesh fly in all directions."[6]

This combination of circumstances, traditionally associated with a declining dynasty, gave rise to growing numbers of bandit gangs roaming the countryside and, even more dangerous, to outright peasant rebellion. Beginning in the late eighteenth century, such rebellions drew upon a variety of peasant grievances and found leadership in charismatic figures proclaiming a millenarian religious message. Increasingly they also expressed opposition to the Qing dynasty on account of its foreign Manchurian origins. "We wait only for the northern region to be returned to a Han emperor," declared one rebel group in the early nineteenth century.[7]

The culmination of China's internal crisis lay in the Taiping Uprising, which set much of the country aflame between 1850 and 1864. This was a different kind of peasant upheaval. Its leaders rejected Confucianism, Daoism, and Buddhism alike, finding their ideology in a unique form of Christianity. Its leading figure, Hong

Xiuquan (1814–1864), proclaimed himself the younger brother of Jesus, sent to cleanse the world of demons and to establish a "heavenly kingdom of great peace." Nor were these leaders content to restore an idealized Chinese society; instead they insisted on genuinely revolutionary change. They called for the abolition of private property; a radical redistribution of land; the equality of men and women; the end of foot binding, prostitution, and opium smoking; and the organization of society into sexually segregated military camps of men and women. Hong fiercely denounced the Qing dynasty as foreigners who had "poisoned China" and "defiled the emperor's throne." His cousin, Hong Rengan, developed plans for transforming China into an industrial nation, complete with railroads, health insurance for all, newspapers, and widespread public education.

With a rapidly swelling number of followers, Taiping forces swept out of southern China and established their capital in Nanjing in 1853. For a time, the days of the Qing dynasty appeared to be over. But divisions and indecisiveness within the Taiping leadership and their inability to link up with other rebel groups also operating in China provided an opening for Qing dynasty loyalists to rally and by 1864 to crush this most unusual of peasant rebellions. Western military support for pro-Qing forces likewise contributed to their victory. It was not the imperial military forces of the central government that defeated the rebels, however. Instead provincial gentry landowners, fearing the radicalism of the Taiping program, mobilized their own armies, which in the end destroyed the revolutionary rebels.

Thus the Qing dynasty was saved, but it was also weakened as the provincial gentry consolidated their power at the expense of the central state. The intense conservatism of both imperial authorities and their gentry supporters postponed any resolution of China's peasant problem, delayed any real change for China's women, and deferred any vigorous efforts at modernization until the communists came to power in the mid-twentieth century. More immediately, the devastation and destruction occasioned by this massive civil war seriously disrupted and weakened China's economy. Vast expanses of the Yangzi River valley became virtual wastelands, and travelers reported walking for days in previously densely populated regions without seeing a living person. Estimates of the number of lives lost range from 20 million to 30 million. In human terms, it was the most costly conflict in the world of the nineteenth century, and it took China more than a decade to recover from that devastation. China's internal crisis in general and the Taiping Uprising in particular also provided a highly unfavorable setting for the country's encounter with a Europe newly invigorated by the Industrial Revolution.

Western Pressures

■ **Connection**
What was the impact of Western pressures on China during the nineteenth century?

Nowhere was the shifting balance of global power in the nineteenth century more evident than in China's changing relationship with Europe, a transformation that registered most dramatically in the famous Opium Wars. Derived from Arab traders in the eighth century or earlier, opium had long been used on a small scale as a

Snapshot   **Chinese/British Trade at Canton, 1835–1836**[8]

What do these figures suggest about the role of opium in British trade with China? Calculate opium exports as a percentage of British exports to China, Britain's trade deficit without opium, and its trade surplus with opium. What did this pattern mean for China?

	Item	Value (in Spanish dollars)
British Exports to Canton	Opium	17,904,248
	Cotton	8,357,394
	All other items (sandlewood, lead, iron, tin, cotton yarn and piece goods, tin plates, watches, clocks)	6,164,981
	Total	32,426,623
British Imports from Canton	Tea (black and green)	13,412,243
	Raw silk	3,764,115
	Vermilion	705,000
	All other goods (sugar products, camphor, silver, gold, copper, musk)	5,971,541
	Total	23,852,899

drinkable medicine, regarded as a magical cure for dysentery and described by one poet as "fit for Buddha."[9] It did not become a serious problem until the late eighteenth century, when the British began to use opium, grown and processed in India, to cover their persistent trade imbalance with China. By the 1830s, British, American, and other Western merchants had found an enormous, growing, and very profitable market for this highly addictive drug. From 1,000 chests (each weighing roughly 150 pounds) in 1773, China's opium imports exploded to more than 23,000 chests in 1832.

By then, Chinese authorities recognized a mounting problem on many levels. Because opium importation was illegal, it had to be smuggled into China, thus flouting Chinese law. Bribed to turn a blind eye to the illegal trade, many officials were corrupted. Furthermore, a massive outflow of silver to pay for the opium reversed China's centuries-long ability to attract much of the world's silver supply, and this imbalance caused serious economic problems. Finally, China found itself with many millions of addicts—men and women, court officials, students preparing for exams, soldiers going into combat, and common laborers seeking to overcome the pain and drudgery of their work. Following an extended debate at court in 1836—whether

Addiction to Opium
Throughout the nineteenth century, opium imports created a massive addiction problem in China, as this photograph of an opium den from around 1900 suggests. Not until the early twentieth century did the British prove willing to curtail the opium trade from their Indian colony. (Hulton-Deutsch Collection/Corbis)

to legalize the drug or to crack down on its use—the emperor decided on suppression. An upright official, Commissioner Lin Zexu, led the campaign against opium use as a kind of "drug czar." His measures included seizing and destroying, without compensation, more than 3 million pounds of opium from Western traders and expelling them from the country.

The British, offended by this violation of property rights and emboldened by their new military power, determined to teach the Chinese a lesson about the virtues of free trade and the "proper" way to conduct relations among countries—and so began the first Opium War in 1839. The Treaty of Nanjing, which ended the conflict in 1842, largely on British terms, imposed numerous restrictions on Chinese sovereignty. Besides agreeing to pay a $21 million indemnity to the British and ceding the island of Hong Kong, the treaty required China to open five ports to trade, fixed the tariff on imported goods at a low 5 percent, and granted foreigners the right to live in China under their own laws. Its provisions reflected the changed balance of global power that had emerged with Britain's Industrial Revolution. To the Chinese, that agreement represented the first of the "unequal treaties" that seriously eroded China's independence by the end of the century.

But it was not the last of these treaties. Britain's victory in a second Opium War (1856–1858) was accompanied by the brutal vandalizing of the emperor's exquisite Summer Palace outside Beijing, resulted in the opening of yet more treaty ports to foreign traders, allowed foreigners to travel and buy land in China, opened the country to Christian missionaries, and permitted Western powers to patrol some of China's interior waterways. Following military defeats at the hands of the French (1885) and Japanese (1895), China lost control of Vietnam, Korea, and Taiwan. By the end of the century, the Western nations plus Japan and Russia all had carved out spheres of influence within China, granting them special privileges to establish military bases, extract raw materials, and build railroads. Many Chinese believed that their country was being "carved up like a melon" (see Map 19.1).

Coupled with its internal crisis, China's encounter with European imperialism had reduced the proud Middle Kingdom to dependency on the Western powers as it became part of a European-based "informal empire." China was no longer the center of civilization to which barbarians paid homage and tribute, but just one nation in a world of nation-states, and a beleaguered one at that. The Qing dynasty remained in power, but in a weakened condition, which served

Map 19.1   China and the World in the Nineteenth Century
As China was reeling from massive internal upheavals during the nineteenth century, it also faced external assaults from Russia, Japan, and various European powers. By the end of the century, large parts of China were divided into spheres of influence, each affiliated with one of the major industrial powers of the day.

European interests well. Thus imperialism had enfeebled the Chinese state at precisely the time when China required a strong government to manage its entry into the modern world. Restrictions imposed by the unequal treaties also inhibited China's industrialization, as foreign goods and foreign investment flooded the country largely unrestricted. Chinese businessmen mostly served foreign interests rather than developing as an independent capitalist class able to lead the country's economic modernization.

The Failure of Conservative Modernization

■ **Connection**

Why was China unable to respond effectively to mounting pressures from the West in the nineteenth century?

Chinese authorities were not passive in the face of their country's mounting crises, both internal and external. Known as "self-strengthening," their efforts during the 1860s and 1870s represented an attempt to rejuvenate a sagging dynasty and a failing society by vigorous application of traditional Confucian principles combined with very limited and cautious borrowing from the West. A revamped examination system, designed to recruit qualified candidates for official positions, sought the "good men" who could cope with the massive reconstruction that China faced in the wake of the Taiping Uprising. Support for landlords and the repair of dikes and irrigation helped restore rural social and economic order. Some gentry leaders recognized the superiority of Western military technology and sought to obtain modern weapons. Thus China established a number of modern arsenals and shipyards and supported foreign-language schools, translation services, and scientific personnel. In addition, a few industrial factories producing textiles and steel were established, coal mines were expanded, and a telegraph system was initiated.

Self-strengthening as an overall program for China's modernization was inhibited by the fears of conservative leaders that urban, industrial, or commercial development would erode the power and privileges of the landlord class. Furthermore, the new industries remained largely dependent on foreigners for machinery, materials, and expertise. And these enterprises were largely controlled, not by the central government, but by regional Chinese officials seeking to strengthen their own position rather than that of the nation as a whole.

The general failure of "self-strengthening" became apparent by 1900, when an antiforeign movement known as the Boxer Rebellion erupted in northern China. Led by militia organizations calling themselves the Society of Righteous and Harmonious Fists, the "Boxers" killed numerous Europeans and Chinese Christians and laid siege to the foreign embassies in Beijing. When Western powers and Japan occupied Beijing to crush the rebellion and imposed a huge payment on China as a punishment, it was clear that China remained a dependent country, substantially under foreign control.

No wonder, then, that growing numbers of educated Chinese, including many in official elite positions, became highly disillusioned with the Qing dynasty, which was both foreign and ineffective in protecting China. By the late 1890s, such people were organizing a variety of clubs, study groups, and newspapers to examine China's desperate situation and to explore alternative paths. The names of these organizations reflect their outlook—the National Rejuvenation Study Society, Society to Protect the Nation, and Understand the National Shame Society. They admired not only Western science and technology but also Western political practices that limited the authority of the ruler and permitted wider circles of people to take part in public life. They believed that only a truly unified nation in which rulers and ruled were closely related could save China from dismemberment at the hands of foreign imperialists. Thus was born the immensely powerful force of Chinese nationalism, directed against both the foreign imperialists and the foreign Qing dynasty, which many held responsible for China's nineteenth-century disasters.

The Qing dynasty response to these new pressures proved inadequate. More extensive reform in the early twentieth century, including the end of the old examination system and the promise of a national parliament, was a classic case of "too little too late." In 1911, the ancient imperial order that had governed China for two millennia collapsed, with only a modest nudge from organized revolutionaries. It was the end of a long era in China and the beginning of an immense struggle over the country's future.

The Ottoman Empire and the West in the Nineteenth Century

Like China, the Islamic world represented a highly successful civilization that felt little need to learn from the "infidels" or "barbarians" of the West until it collided with an expanding and aggressive Europe in the nineteenth century. Unlike China, though, Islamic civilization had been a near neighbor to Europe for 1,000 years. Its most prominent state, the Ottoman Empire, had long governed substantial parts of the Balkans and posed a clear military and religious threat to Europe in the sixteenth and seventeenth centuries. But if its encounter with the West was less abrupt than that of China, it was no less consequential. Neither the Ottoman Empire nor China fell under direct colonial rule, but both were much diminished as the changing balance of global power took hold; both launched efforts at "defensive modernization" aimed at strengthening their states and preserving their independence; and in both societies, some people held tightly to old identities and values, even as others embraced new loyalties associated with nationalism and modernity.

"The Sick Man of Europe"

In 1750, the Ottoman Empire was still the central political fixture of a widespread Islamic world. From its Turkish heartland of Anatolia, it ruled over much of the Arab world, from which Islam had come. It protected pilgrims on their way to Mecca, governed Egypt and coastal North Africa, and incorporated millions of Christians in the Balkans. Its ruler, the sultan, claimed the role of caliph, successor to the Prophet Muhammad, and was widely viewed as the leader, defender, and primary representative of the Islamic world. But by the middle, and certainly by the end, of the nineteenth century, the Ottoman Empire was no longer able to deal with Europe from a position of equality, let alone superiority. Among the Great Powers of the West, it was now known as "the sick man of Europe." Within the Muslim world, the Ottoman Empire, once viewed as "the strong sword of Islam," was unable to prevent region after region—India, Indonesia, West Africa, Central Asia—from falling under the control of Christian powers.

■ **Change**
What lay behind the decline of the Ottoman Empire in the nineteenth century?

Map 19.2 The Contraction of the Ottoman Empire
Foreign aggression and nationalist movements substantially diminished the Ottoman Empire during the nineteenth century, but they also stimulated a variety of efforts to revive and reform Ottoman society.

The Ottoman Empire's own domains shrank considerably at the hands of Russian, British, Austrian, and French aggression (see Map 19.2). In 1798, Napoleon's invasion of Egypt, which had long been a province of the Ottoman Empire, was a particularly stunning blow. A contemporary observer, Abd al-Rahman al-Jabarti, described the French entry into Cairo:

> [T]he French entered the city like a torrent rushing through the alleys and streets without anything to stop them, like demons of the Devil's army.... And the French trod in the Mosque of al-Azhar with their shoes, carrying swords and rifles.... They plundered whatever they found in the mosque.... They treated the books and Quranic volumes as trash.... Furthermore, they soiled the mosque, blowing their spit in it, pissing and defecating in it. They guzzled wine and smashed bottles in the central court.[10]

When the French left, a virtually independent Egypt pursued a modernizing and empire-building program of its own and on one occasion came close to toppling the Ottoman Empire itself.

Beyond territorial losses to stronger European powers, other parts of the empire, such as Greece, Serbia, Bulgaria, and Romania, achieved independence based on their own surging nationalism and support from the British or the Russians. The continued independence of the core region of the Ottoman Empire owed much to the inability of Europe's Great Powers to agree on how to divide it up among themselves.

Behind the contraction of the Ottoman Empire lay other problems. As in China, the central Ottoman state had weakened, particularly in its ability to raise necessary revenue, as provincial authorities and local warlords gained greater power. Moreover, the once feared Janissaries, the elite military corps of the Ottoman state, had become reactionary defenders of the status quo whose military ineffectiveness was increasingly obvious. The technological gap with the West was clearly growing.

Economically, the earlier centrality of the Ottoman and Arab lands in Afro-Eurasian commerce diminished as Europeans achieved direct oceanic access to the treasures of Asia. Competition from cheap European manufactured goods hit Ottoman artisans hard and led to urban riots protesting foreign imports. Furthermore, a lengthening set of capitulations, similar to the unequal treaties later signed with China, gave foreign merchants immunity from Ottoman laws and legal procedures, exempted them from internal taxes, and limited import and export duties on their products. Foreign consuls could grant these privileges to Ottoman citizens, and hundreds of thousands of them, usually Jews, Greeks, and Armenians, received this privileged status, which effectively removed them from Ottoman control and greatly enhanced European penetration of the Ottoman economy. All of this gradually drained the proud sovereignty of the once mighty empire. So too did the growing indebtedness of the Ottoman Empire, which came to rely on foreign loans to finance its efforts at economic development. By 1882, its inability to pay the interest on those debts led to foreign control of much of its revenue-generating system and the outright occupation of Egypt by the British. Like China, the Ottoman Empire had fallen into a position of considerable dependency on Europe.

Reform

The leadership of the Ottoman Empire recognized many of its "illnesses" and during the nineteenth century mounted increasingly ambitious reforms designed to preserve and strengthen the state. Its program of defensive modernization was earlier, more sustained, and far more vigorous than the timid and half-hearted measures of self-strengthening in China. One reason perhaps lay in the absence of any internal upheaval, such as the Taiping Uprising in China, which threatened the very existence of the ruling dynasty. Nationalist revolts on the empire's periphery, rather than Chinese-style peasant rebellion at the center, represented the primary internal crisis of nineteenth-century Ottoman history. Nor did the Middle East in general experience the explosive population growth that contributed so much to China's nineteenth-century crisis. Furthermore, the long-established Ottoman leadership was Turkic and Muslim, culturally similar to its core population, whereas China's Qing dynasty rulers were widely regarded as foreigners from Manchuria.

■ **Change**
In what ways did the Ottoman state respond to its problems?

Ottoman reforms began in the late eighteenth century when Sultan Selim III attempted to set up new military and administrative structures alongside traditional institutions as a means of enhancing and centralizing state power. Selim sent ambassadors to the courts of Europe, studied their administrative methods, imported European advisers, and established technical schools to train future officials. More far-reaching measures, known as *Tanzimat* ("reorganization"), emerged in the several decades after 1839 as the Ottoman leadership sought to provide the economic, social, and legal underpinnings for a strong and newly recentralized state. Factories producing cloth, paper, and armaments; modern mining operations; reclamation and resettlement of agricultural land; telegraphs, steamships, railroads, and a modern postal service; Western-style law codes and courts; new elementary and secondary schools—all of these new departures began a long process of modernization and Westernization in the Ottoman Empire.

Even more revolutionary, at least in principle, were changes in the legal status of the empire's diverse communities. In an effort to integrate non-Muslim subjects more effectively into the state, the principle of equality of all citizens before the law was accepted. An imperial proclamation of 1839 declared:

> Every distinction or designation tending to make any class whatever of the subjects of my Empire inferior to another class, on account of their religion, language or race shall be forever effaced.... No subject of my Empire shall be hindered in the exercise of the religion that he professes.... All the subjects of my Empire, without distinction of nationality, shall be admissible to public employment.

The Ottoman Empire and the West
The intense interaction of the Ottoman Empire and the world of European powers is illustrated in this nineteenth-century Austrian painting, which depicts an elaborate gathering of Ottoman officials with members of the Austrian royal family around 1850. (Miramare Palace Trieste/Alfredo Dagli Orti/The Art Archive)

This declaration represented a dramatic change that challenged the fundamentally Islamic character of the state. Mixed tribunals with representatives from various religious groups were established to hear cases involving non-Muslims. More Christians were appointed to high office. A mounting tide of secular legislation and secular schools, drawing heavily on European models, now competed with traditional Islamic institutions.

Identity

The reform process raised profound and highly contested questions about political and cultural identity. What was the Ottoman Empire, and who were its people? Even the modest innovations of Selim III stirred the hostility of powerful factions among both the ulama (religious scholars) and the Janissaries, who saw them in conflict with Islam. Opposition to his measures was so strong that Selim was forced from power in 1807. Subsequent sultans, however, crushed this conservative opposition while bringing the ulama more thoroughly under state control than elsewhere in the Islamic world.

■ **Comparison**

In what different ways did various groups define the Ottoman Empire during the nineteenth century?

Outside the Ottoman Empire, movements of Islamic renewal (see Chapter 16) began to express opposition to European encroachment while providing a prescription for rebuilding threatened societies. In Sumatra (present-day Indonesia), an Islamic renewal movement that sought to correct immorality and to impose the veil on women and Arab dress on men became a war of resistance to Dutch penetration in the early nineteenth century. Prominent Muslim leaders in the Caucasus regions of Chechnya and Dagestan organized jihads against Russian intrusion and simultaneously sought to purify the practice of Islam by eliminating local religious traditions. The French invasion of Algeria in 1830 provoked a Muslim-based resistance movement, which was also an effort to create an Islamic state.

Such political expressions of Islamic renewal had little impact in the Ottoman Empire of the mid-nineteenth century, when the Tanzimat reforms were being implemented. To those who supported these reforms, the Ottoman Empire was a secular state whose people were loyal to the dynasty that ruled it, rather than a primarily Muslim state based on religious principles. This was the outlook of a new class spawned by the reform process itself—lower-level officials, military officers, writers, poets, and journalists, many of whom had a modern Western-style education. Dubbed the "Young Ottomans," they were active during the middle decades of the nineteenth century, when they urged the extension of Westernizing reforms to the political system. Rejecting the despotism of Ottoman rulers, they favored a constitutional regime like that of Great Britain. Only such a political system could mobilize the energies of the country to overcome backwardness and preserve the state against European aggression. Known as Islamic modernism, such ideas found expression in many parts of the Muslim world in the second half of the century. Muslim societies, they argued, needed to embrace Western technical and scientific knowledge, while rejecting its materialism. Moreover, they believed it was possible to find in Islam itself the basis for freedom, progress, rationality, and patriotism. It was not necessary to choose between Western-style modernity and Islam. The growing influence of the Young Ottomans was reflected in the adoption of a short-lived constitution for the empire in 1876, which limited the authority of the sultan and established a representative government.

No sooner had Sultan Abd al-Hamid II (ruled 1876–1909) accepted the constitution than he suspended it and purged his government of the more radical reformers, using the occasion of a Russian invasion to act decisively. For the next three decades, he ruled as a reactionary autocrat, suppressing liberal and nationalist sentiments among his diverse and restive subjects, though continuing many of the educational, economic, and technical reforms of the earlier era. He sought to bolster his authority by reactivating the old claim that the Ottoman rulers were caliphs, speaking for the entire Islamic world. This claim was yet another answer to the question of identity. The Ottoman Empire would be a despotic state with a pan-Islamic identity. Thus Abd al-Hamid II restored the ulama to a position of prestige, if not real power, and reintroduced the distinction between Muslim and non-Muslim subjects.

Opposition to this revived despotism soon surfaced among both military and civilian elites known as the Young Turks. Largely abandoning any reference to Islam, they advocated a militantly secular public life. Furthermore, some among them began to think about the Ottoman regime neither as a dynastic state nor as a pan-Islamic empire, but as a Turkish national state. This was a revolutionary notion, drawn from the growing nationalism of the empire's subject peoples and ultimately from Europe. It went against the grain of Islamic thinking, which focused loyalty on a community of faith, not of ethnicity. It also challenged the longtime Ottoman practice of incorporating a variety of cultural groups into a common political system. Moreover, at the time few people were aware of a distinctly Turkish ethnic identity. By the beginning of the twentieth century, however, a number of writers and intellectuals began to articulate the notion of a "Turkish nation" and to define its unique character. To the writer Ziya Gokalp, Turkish nationality was based fundamentally on language and was expressed in folk stories and popular songs.

A military coup in 1908 allowed the Young Turks to exercise real power. They pushed for a radical secularization of schools, courts, and law codes; permitted elections and competing parties; established a single Law of Family Rights for all regardless of religion; and encouraged Turkish as the official language of the empire. They also opened up modern schools for women, allowed them to wear Western clothing, restricted polygamy, and permitted women to obtain divorces in some situations. But the nationalist conception of Ottoman identity antagonized non-Turkic peoples and helped stimulate Arab and other nationalisms in response. For some, a secular nationality was becoming the most important public loyalty, with Islam relegated to private life. Such nationalist sentiments contributed to the complete disintegration of the Ottoman Empire following World War I, but the secularizing and Westernizing principles of the Young Turks informed the policies of the Turkish republic that replaced it.

Outcomes: Comparing China and the Ottoman Empire

By the beginning of the twentieth century, both China and the Ottoman Empire, recently centers of proud and vibrant civilizations, had experienced the consequences of a rapidly shifting balance of global power. Now they were "semicolonies" within the "informal empires" of Europe, although they retained sufficient independence for their governments to launch catch-up efforts of defensive modernization. But neither was able to create the industrial economies or strong states required to fend off European intrusion and restore their former status in the world. Despite their diminished power, both China and the Ottoman Empire gave rise to new nationalist conceptions of society, which were initially small and limited in appeal but of great significance for the future.

In the early twentieth century, that future witnessed the end of both the Chinese and Ottoman empires. In China, the collapse of the imperial system in 1911 was followed by a vast revolutionary upheaval that by 1949 led to a Communist regime within largely the same territorial space as the old empire. By contrast, the collapse of the Ottoman Empire following World War I led to the creation of a new but much smaller nation-state in the Turkish heartland of the old empire, having lost its vast Arab and European provinces.

China's twentieth-century revolutionaries rejected traditional Confucian culture far more thoroughly than the secularizing leaders of modern Turkey rejected Islam. Almost everywhere in the Islamic world, traditional religion retained its hold on the private loyalties of most people and later in the twentieth century became a basis for social renewal in many places. Islamic civilization, unlike its Chinese counterpart, had many independent centers and was never so closely associated with a single state. Furthermore, it was embedded in a deeply religious tradition that was personally meaningful to millions of adherents, in contrast to the more elitist and secular outlook of Confucianism. All of this perhaps facilitated the survival and renewal of Islamic civilization in the twentieth century in a way that was not possible for traditional Chinese civilization.

The Japanese Difference: The Rise of a New East Asian Power

Like China and the Ottoman Empire, the island country of Japan confronted the aggressive power of the West during the nineteenth century, most notably in the form of U.S. Commodore Matthew Perry's "black ships," which steamed into Tokyo Bay in 1853 and forcefully demanded that this reclusive nation open up to more "normal" relations with the world. However, the outcome of that encounter differed sharply from the others. In the second half of the nineteenth century, Japan undertook a radical transformation of its society—a "revolution from above," according to some historians—turning it into a powerful, modern, united, industrialized nation. It was an achievement that neither China nor the Ottoman Empire was able to duplicate. Far from succumbing to Western domination, Japan joined the club of imperialist countries by creating its own East Asian empire, largely at the expense of China. In building a society that was both modern and distinctly Japanese, Japan demonstrated that modernity was not a uniquely European phenomenon. This "Japanese miracle," as some have called it, was both promising and ominous for the rest of Asia. How had it occurred?

The Tokugawa Background

■ Comparison
How did Japan's historical development differ from that of China and the Ottoman Empire during the nineteenth century?

For 250 years prior to Perry's arrival, Japan had been governed by a shogun (a military ruler) from the Tokugawa family who acted in the name of a revered but powerless emperor, who lived in Kyoto, 300 miles away from the seat of power in Edo (Tokyo). The chief task of this Tokugawa shogunate was to prevent the return of civil war among some 260 rival feudal lords, known as daimyo, each of whom had a cadre of armed retainers, the famed samurai warriors of Japanese tradition.

Based on their own military power and political skills, successive shoguns gave Japan more than two centuries of internal peace (1600–1850). To control the restive daimyo, they strictly regulated internal travel and communication and required the daimyo to spend alternate years in the capital of Edo, leaving their families behind as hostages during their absence. Nonetheless, the daimyo, especially the more powerful ones, retained substantial autonomy in their own domains and behaved in some ways like independent states with separate military forces, law codes, tax systems, and currencies. With no national army, no uniform currency, and little central authority at the local level, Tokugawa Japan was "pacified...but not really unified."[11] To further stabilize the country, the Tokugawa regime issued highly detailed rules governing the occupation, residence, dress, hairstyles, and behavior of the four hierarchically ranked status groups into which Japanese society was divided—samurai at the top, then peasants, artisans, and, at the bottom, merchants.

■ Change
In what ways was Japan changing during the Tokugawa era?

Much was changing within Japan during these 250 years of peace in ways that belied the control and orderliness of Tokugawa regulations. For one thing, the samurai, in the absence of wars to fight, evolved into a salaried bureaucratic or administrative class amounting to 5 to 6 percent of the total population, but they were still fiercely devoted to their daimyo lords and to their warrior code of loyalty, honor, and self-sacrifice.

More generally, centuries of peace contributed to a remarkable burst of economic growth, commercialization, and urban development. Entrepreneurial peasants, using fertilizers and other agricultural innovations, grew more rice than ever before and engaged in a variety of rural manufacturing enterprises as well. By 1750, Japan had become perhaps the world's most urbanized country, with about 10 percent of its population living in sizable towns or cities. Edo, with a million residents, was the world's largest city. Well-functioning markets linked urban and rural areas, marking Japan as an emerging capitalist economy. The influence of Confucianism encouraged education and generated a remarkably literate population, with about

40 percent of men and 15 percent of women able to read and write. Although no one was aware of it at the time, these changes during the Tokugawa era provided a solid foundation for Japan's remarkable industrial growth in the late nineteenth century.

These changes also undermined the shogunate's efforts to freeze Japanese society in the interests of stability. Some samurai found the lowly but profitable path of commerce too much to resist. "No more shall we have to live by the sword," declared one of them in 1616 while renouncing his samurai status. "I have seen that great profit can be made honorably. I shall brew *sake* and soy sauce, and we shall prosper."[12] Many merchants, though hailing from the lowest-ranking status group, prospered in the new commercial environment and supported a vibrant urban culture, while not a few daimyo found it necessary, if humiliating, to seek loans from these social inferiors. Thus merchants had money, but little status, whereas samurai enjoyed high status but were often indebted to inferior merchants. Both resented their position.

Despite prohibitions to the contrary, many peasants moved to the cities, becoming artisans or merchants and imitating the ways of their social betters. A decree of 1788 noted that peasants "have become accustomed to luxury and forgetful of their status." They wore inappropriate clothing, used umbrellas rather than straw hats in the rain, and even left the villages for the city. "Henceforth," declared the shogun, "all luxuries should be avoided by the peasants. They are to live simply and devote themselves to farming."[13] This decree, like many others before it, was widely ignored.

More than social change undermined the Tokugawa regime. Corruption was widespread, to the disgust of many. The shogunate's failure to deal successfully with a severe famine in the 1830s eroded confidence in its effectiveness. At the same time, a mounting wave of local peasant uprisings and urban riots expressed the many grievances of the poor. The most striking of these outbursts left the city of Osaka in flames in 1837. Its leader, Oshio Heihachiro, no doubt spoke for many ordinary people when he wrote:

> We must first punish the officials who torment the people so cruelly; then we must execute the haughty and rich Osaka merchants. Then we must distribute the gold, silver, and copper stored in their cellars, and bands of rice hidden in their storehouses.[14]

From the 1830s on, one scholar concluded, "there was a growing feeling that the *shogunate* was losing control."[15]

American Intrusion and the Meiji Restoration

It was foreign intervention that brought matters to a head. Since the expulsion of European missionaries and the harsh suppression of Christianity in the early seventeenth century (see Chapter 15), Japan had deliberately limited its contact with the West to a single port, where only the Dutch were allowed to trade. By the early nineteenth century, however, various European countries and the United States

The "Opening" of Japan
This nineteenth-century Japanese woodblock print depicts Commodore Perry's meeting with a Japanese official in 1853. It was this encounter that launched Japan on a series of dramatic changes that resulted in the country's modernization and its emergence as one of the world's major industrialized powers by the early twentieth century. (Bettmann/Corbis)

were knocking at the door. All were turned away, and even shipwrecked sailors or whalers were expelled, jailed, or executed. As it happened, it was the United States that forced the issue, sending Commodore Perry in 1853 to demand humane treatment for castaways, the right of American vessels to refuel and buy provisions, and the opening of ports for trade. Authorized to use force if necessary, Perry presented his reluctant hosts, among other gifts, with a white flag for surrender should hostilities follow.

In the end, conflict was avoided. Aware of what had happened to China in resisting European demands, Japan agreed to a series of unequal treaties with various Western powers. That humiliating capitulation to the demands of the "foreign devils" further eroded support for the shogunate, triggered a brief civil war, and by 1868 led to a political takeover by a group of young samurai from southern Japan. This decisive turning point in Japan's history was known as the Meiji restoration, for the country's new rulers claimed that they were restoring to power the young emperor, then a fifteen-year-old boy whose throne name was Meiji, or Enlightened Rule. Having eliminated the shogunate, these patriotic young men soon made their goals clear—to save Japan from foreign domination, not by futile resistance, but by a thorough transformation of Japanese society, drawing upon all that the modern West had to offer. "Knowledge shall be sought throughout the world," they declared, "so as to strengthen the foundations of imperial rule."

Japan now had a government committed to a decisive break with the past, and it had acquired that government without massive violence or destruction. By contrast, the defeat of the Taiping Uprising had deprived China of any such opportunity for a fresh start, while saddling it with enormous devastation and massive loss of life. Furthermore, Japan was of less interest to Western powers than either China, with its huge potential market and reputation for riches, or the Ottoman Empire, with its strategic location at the crossroads of Asia and Europe. The American Civil War and its aftermath likewise deflected U.S. ambitions in the Pacific for a time, further reducing the Western pressure on Japan.

■ Change
Does Japan's nineteenth-century transformation deserve to be considered revolutionary?

Modernization Japanese Style

These circumstances gave Japan some breathing space, and its new rulers moved quickly to take advantage of that unique window of opportunity by directing a cascading wave of dramatic changes that rolled over the country in the last three decades of the nineteenth century. Those reforms, which were revolutionary in their cumulative effect, transformed Japan far more thoroughly than even the most radical of the Ottoman efforts, let alone the modest self-strengthening policies of the Chinese.

The first task was genuine national unity, which required an attack on the power and privileges of both the daimyo and the samurai. By 1871, the new regime had abolished the daimyo domains with their considerable autonomy, replacing them with a system of prefectures, whose appointed governors were responsible to the central government. That government now collected the nation's taxes and raised a national army based on conscription from all social classes.

Thus the samurai lost their ancient role as the country's warrior class and with it their cherished right to carry swords. The old Confucian-based social order was largely dismantled as class restrictions on occupation, residence, marriage, and clothing were abolished, and almost all Japanese became legally equal as commoners. Limitations on travel and trade likewise fell as a nationwide economy came to parallel the centralized state. Although there was some opposition to these measures, including a brief rebellion of resentful samurai in 1877, it was on the whole a remarkably peaceful process in which a segment of the old ruling class abolished its own privileges. Many, but not all, of these displaced elites found a "soft landing" in the army, bureaucracy, or business enterprises of the new regime, thus easing a painful transition.

Accompanying these social and political changes was a widespread and eager fascination with almost everything Western. Knowledge about the West—its science and technology; its various political and constitutional arrangements; its legal and educational systems; its dances, clothing, and hairstyles—was enthusiastically sought out by official missions to the West, by hundreds of students sent to study abroad, and by many ordinary Japanese at home. Western writers were translated into Japanese; for example, Samuel Smiles's *Self-Help*, which focused on "achieving success and rising in the world," sold a million copies. "Civilization and Enlightenment" was the slogan of the time, and both were to be found in the West. The most prominent popularizer of Western knowledge, Fukuzawa Yukichi, summed up the chief lesson of his studies in the mid-1870s—Japan was backward and needed to learn from the West. "If we compare the knowledge of the Japanese and Westerners, in letters, in technique, in commerce, or in industry, from the largest to the smallest matter, there is not one thing in which we excel.... In Japan's present condition there is nothing in which we may take pride vis-à-vis the West."[16]

After this initial wave of uncritical enthusiasm for everything Western receded, Japan proceeded to borrow more selectively and to combine foreign and Japanese elements in distinctive ways. For example, the constitution of 1889, drawing heavily on German experience, introduced an elected parliament, political parties, and democratic ideals, but that constitution was presented as a gift from a sacred emperor descended from the Sun Goddess. The parliament could advise, but ultimate power, and particularly control of the military, lay theoretically with the

Snapshot   **Key Moments in the Rise of Japan in the Nineteenth Century and Beyond**

Famines, urban and rural rebellions	1830s
Commodore Perry arrives in Japan	1853
Meiji restoration	1868
Government-run enterprises in railroad construction, manufacturing, and mining	1870s
Western dress prescribed for court and official ceremonies	1872
Samurai rebellion crushed	1877
Government sells state industries to private investors	1880s
Ito Hirobumi travels to Europe to study political systems	1882
Peak of peasant protest against high taxes and prices	1883–1884
Women banned from political parties and meetings	1887
Japan's modern constitution announced	1889
Sino-Japanese War	1894–1895
Japan's labor movement crushed	by 1901
Anglo-Japanese alliance marks Japan's acceptance as Great Power	1902
Russo-Japanese War	1904–1905
Universal primary education	1905
Japanese annexation of Korea	1910
Meiji emperor dies	1912

emperor and in practice with an oligarchy of prominent reformers acting in his name. Likewise, a modern educational system, which achieved universal primary schooling by the early twentieth century, was also laced with Confucian-based moral instruction and exhortations of loyalty to the emperor. Neither Western-style feminism nor Christianity made much headway in Meiji Japan, but Shinto, an ancient religious tradition featuring ancestors and nature spirits, was elevated to the status of an official state cult. Japan's earlier experience in borrowing massively but selectively from Chinese culture perhaps served it better in these new circumstances than either the Chinese disdain for foreign cultures or the reluctance of many Muslims to see much of value in the infidel West.

At the core of Japan's effort at defensive modernization lay its state-guided industrialization program. The government took over and modernized Tokugawa and daimyo enterprises, such as iron foundries, munitions plants, and dockyards. It

Japan's Modernization
In Japan, as in Europe, railroads quickly became a popular symbol of the country's modernization, as this woodblock print from the 1870s illustrates. (Visual Arts Library [London]/Alamy)

established model factories to produce cement, chemicals, glass, sugar, and silk and cotton goods. It also opened mines, built railroads, and established postal, telegraph, and banking systems. Subsequently many of these state enterprises were sold off to private investors. By the early twentieth century, Japan's industrialization was well under way. Its major cities enjoyed mass-circulation newspapers, movie theaters, and electric lights. All of this was accomplished through its own resources and without the massive foreign debt that so afflicted Egypt and the Ottoman Empire. Although the country was still overwhelmingly agrarian, Japan's factories were now producing not only textiles for export but also munitions for the military and industrial goods for private industry. No other country outside of Europe and North America had been able to launch its own Industrial Revolution in the nineteenth century. It was a distinctive feature of Japan's modern transformation.

Less distinctive, however, were the social results of that process. Taxed heavily to pay for Japan's ambitious modernization program, many peasant families slid into poverty. Their sometimes violent protests peaked in 1883–1884 with attacks on government offices and moneylenders' homes that were aimed at destroying records of debt. Despite substantial private relief efforts, the Japanese countryside witnessed infanticide, the sale of daughters, and starvation.

As elsewhere during the early stages of industrial growth, urban workers were treated harshly. The majority of Japan's textile workers were young women from poor families in the countryside. Their pay was at or below subsistence, and a combination of bad food, overwork, terrible working conditions, and jail-like dormitories left many cast-off employees in their twenties without mates but with terminal diseases such as tuberculosis and dependent for survival on degrading occupations such as prostitution. Resistance to these conditions was reflected in a high turnover rate, strikes, and efforts to organize unions. A series of repressive laws allowed the government and employers to treat unions and strikes as criminal activities. These laws were used so effectively that the budding labor movement had been crushed by the end of 1901. But the authorities also began to draw upon familiar themes of service to state and emperor and new ideas of the enterprise as a family, which would emerge after World War I as a primary means of eliciting worker loyalty to the firm.

Japan and the World

■ **Connection**
How did Japan's relationship to the larger world change during its modernization process?

Japan's modern transformation soon registered internationally. By the early twentieth century, its economic growth, openness to trade, and embrace of "civilization and enlightenment" from the West persuaded the Western powers to revise the unequal treaties in Japan's favor. This had long been a primary goal of the Meiji regime, and the Anglo-Japanese Treaty of 1902 now acknowledged Japan as an equal player among the Great Powers of the world.

Not only did Japan escape from its semicolonial entanglements with the West, but it also launched its own empire-building enterprise, even as European powers and the United States were carving up much of Asia and Africa into colonies or spheres of influence. It was what industrializing Great Powers did in the late nineteenth century, and Japan followed suit. Successful wars against China (1894–1895) and Russia (1904–1905) established Japan as a formidable military competitor in East Asia and the first Asian state to defeat a major European power. Through those victories, Japan also gained colonial control of Taiwan and Korea and a territorial foothold in Manchuria.

Japan's entry onto the broader global stage was felt in many places (see Map 19.3). It added yet one more imperialist power to those already burdening a beleaguered China. Defeat at the hands of Japanese upstarts shocked Russia and triggered the 1905 revolution in that country. To Europeans and Americans, Japan was now an economic, political, and military competitor in Asia.

In the world of subject peoples, the rise of Japan and its defeat of Russia generated widespread admiration among those who saw Japan as a model for their own modern development and perhaps as an ally in the struggle against imperialism. Some Poles, Finns, and Jews viewed the Russian defeat in 1905 as an opening for their own liberation from the Russian Empire and were grateful to Japan for the opportunity. Despite Japan's aggression against their country, many Chinese reformers and nationalists found in the Japanese experience valuable lessons for themselves. Thousands flocked to Japan to study its achievements. Newspapers throughout the Islamic world celebrated Japan's victory over Russia as an "awakening of the East," which might herald Muslims' own liberation. Some Turkish women gave their children Japanese names. Indonesian Muslims from Aceh wrote to the Meiji emperor asking for help in their struggle against the Dutch, and Muslim poets wrote odes in his honor. The Egyptian nationalist Mustafa Kamil spoke for many when he

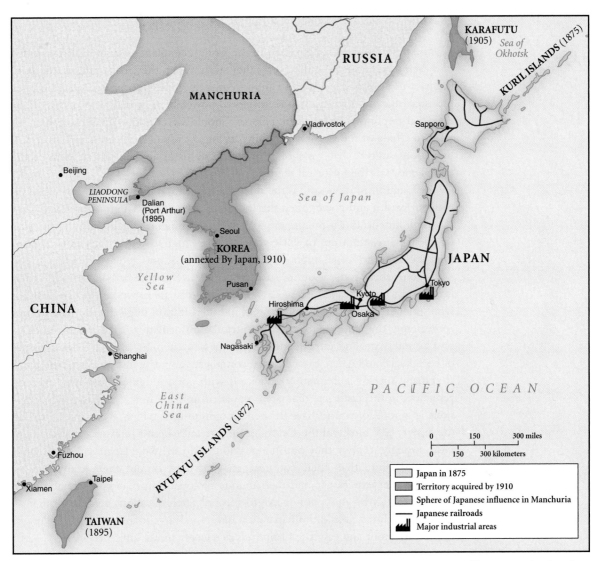

KARAFUTU (1905)   *Sea of Okhotsk*

KURIL ISLANDS (1875)

RUSSIA

MANCHURIA

Vladivostok

Sapporo

• Beijing

LIAODONG
PENINSULA   • Dalian
(Port Arthur)
(1895)

Sea of Japan

• Seoul

KOREA
(annexed By Japan, 1910)

JAPAN

*Yellow
Sea*

• Pusan

Tokyo

CHINA

Hiroshima

Kyoto

Osaka

Nagasaki

• Shanghai

*East
China
Sea*

PACIFIC OCEAN

RYUKYU ISLANDS (1872)

0   150   300 miles

0   150   300 kilometers

• Fuzhou

• Taipei

• Xiamen

TAIWAN
(1895)

Japan in 1875
Territory acquired by 1910
Sphere of Japanese influence in Manchuria
Japanese railroads
Major industrial areas

Map 19.3   The Rise of Japan

As Japan modernized after the Meiji restoration, it launched an empire-building program that provided a foundation for further expansion in the 1930s and during World War II.

declared: "We are amazed by Japan because it is the first Eastern government to utilize Western civilization to resist the shield of European imperialism in Asia."[17]

Those who directly experienced Japanese imperialism in Taiwan or Korea no doubt had a less positive view, for its colonial policies matched or exceeded the brutality of European practices. In the twentieth century, China and much of Southeast Asia suffered bitterly under Japanese imperial aggression. Nonetheless, both the idea of Japan as a liberator of Asia from the European yoke and the reality of Japan as an imperial power in its own right derived from the country's remarkable modern transformation and its unique response to the provocation of Western intrusion.

Reflections: Success and Failure in History

Beyond describing what happened in the past and explaining why, historians often find themselves evaluating the events they study. When they make judgments about the past, notions of success and failure frequently come into play. Should Europe's Industrial Revolution and its rise to global power be regarded as a success? If so, does that imply that others were failures? Should we consider Japan more successful than China or the Ottoman Empire during the nineteenth century? Three considerations suggest that we should be very careful in applying these ideas to the complexities of the historical record.

First, and most obviously, is the question of criteria. If the measure of success is national wealth and power, then the Industrial Revolution surely counts as a great accomplishment. But if preservation of the environment, spiritual growth, and the face-to-face relationships of village life are more highly valued, then industrialization, according to some, might be more reasonably considered as a disaster.

Second, there is the issue of "success for whom?" British artisans who lost their livelihood to industrial machines as well as those Japanese women textile workers who suffered through the early stages of industrialization might be forgiven for not appreciating the "success" of their countries' transformation, even if their middle-class counterparts and subsequent generations benefited. In cases such as this, issues of both social and generational justice complicate any easy assessment of the past.

Finally, success is frequently associated with good judgment and wise choices, yet actors in the historical drama are never completely free in making their decisions, and none, of course, have the benefit of hindsight, which historians enjoy. Did the leaders of China and the Ottoman Empire fail to push industrial development more strongly, or were they not in a position to do so? Were Japanese leaders wiser and more astute than their counterparts elsewhere, or did their knowledge of China's earlier experience and their unique national history simply provide them with circumstances more conducive to success? Such questions regarding the possibilities and limitations of human action have no clear-cut answers, but they might caution us about any easy use of notions of success and failure.

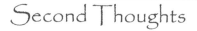

Second Thoughts

What's the Significance?

To assess your mastery of the material in this chapter, see the **Online Study Guide** at bedfordstmartins.com/strayer.

social Darwinism
Taiping Uprising
Opium Wars
unequal treaties
self-strengthening movement
Boxer Rebellion

China, 1911
"the sick man of Europe"
Tanzimat reforms
Young Ottomans
Sultan Abd al-Hamid II
Young Turks

informal empire
Tokugawa Japan
Meiji restoration
Russo-Japanese War,
    1904–1905

Big Picture Questions

1. How did European expansion in the nineteenth century differ from that of the early modern era (see Chapters 14–16)?

2. What differences can you identify in how China, the Ottoman Empire, and Japan experienced Western imperialism and confronted it? How might you account for those differences?

3. "The response of each society to European imperialism grew out of its larger historical development and its internal problems." What evidence might support this statement?

4. What kind of debates, controversies, and conflicts were generated by European intrusion within each of the societies examined in this chapter?

Next Steps: For Further Study

William Bowman et al., *Imperialism in the Modern World* (2007). A collection of short readings illustrating the various forms and faces of European expansion over the past several centuries.

Carter V. Finley, *The Turks in World History* (2004). Places the role of Turkish-speaking peoples in general and the Ottoman Empire in particular in a global context.

Maurice Jansen, *The Making of Modern Japan* (2000). A well-regarded account of Japan since 1600 by a leading scholar.

Jonathan Spence, *The Search for Modern China* (1999). Probably the best single-volume account of Chinese history from about 1600 through the twentieth century.

E. Patricia Tsurumi, *Factory Girls: Women in the Thread Mills of Meiji Japan* (1990). Examines the lives of women in Japan's nineteenth-century textile factories.

Arthur Waley, *The Opium War through Chinese Eyes* (1968). An older classic that views the Opium War from various Chinese points of view.

Justin Jesty, "Japanese History from 1868 to the Present," http://ceas.uchicago.edu/outreach/1868%20to%20Present.pdf. A guide to modern Japanese history, with many links to pictures, documents, and further information.

For Web sites and documents related to this chapter, see **Make History** at bedfordstmartins.com/strayer.

Colonial Encounters

1750–1914

In mid-1967, I was on summer break from a teaching assignment with the Peace Corps in Ethiopia and was traveling with some friends in neighboring Kenya, just four years after that country had gained its independence from British colonial rule. The bus we were riding on broke down, and I found myself hitchhiking across Kenya, heading for Uganda. Soon I was picked up by a friendly Englishman, one of Kenya's many European settlers who had stayed on after independence. At one point, he pulled off the road to show me a lovely view of Kenya's famous Rift Valley, and we were approached by a group of boys selling baskets and other tourist items. They spoke to us in perfect English, but my British companion replied to them in Swahili. He later explained that Europeans generally did not speak English with the "natives."

Several years later, while conducting research for my Ph.D. dissertation about British missionaries in Kenya in the early twentieth century, I came across a letter from one of them in which he argued against the teaching of English to Africans. Among his reasons were "the danger in which such a course would place our white women and girls" and "the danger of organizing against the government and Europeans."[1] Perhaps such fears—grounded in the intense colonial concern to maintain distance and distinction between whites and blacks, for both sexual and political reasons—were the origin of my helpful driver's reluctance to speak his own language with Kenyans. Maintaining racial boundaries was a central feature of many nineteenth- and early-twentieth-century colonial societies and, in the case of my new British acquaintance, one that persisted even after the colonial era had ended.

The Imperial Durbar of 1903: To mark the coronation of British monarch Edward VII and his installation as the Emperor of India, colonial authorities in India mounted an elaborate assembly, or *durbar*. The durbar was intended to showcase the splendor of the British Empire, and its pageantry included sporting events; a state ball; a huge display of Indian arts, crafts, and jewels; and an enormous parade in which a long line of British officials and Indian princes passed by on bejeweled elephants. (Topham/The Image Works)

FOR MANY MILLIONS OF AFRICANS AND ASIANS, colonial rule—by the British, French, Germans, Italians, Belgians, Portuguese, Russians, or Americans—was the major new element in their historical experience during the nineteenth century. Between roughly 1750 and 1950, much of the Afro-Asian-Pacific world was enveloped within this new wave of European empire building. The encounter with European power in these colonized societies was more immediate, and often more intense, than in those regions that were buffered by their own independent governments, such as Latin America, China, and the Ottoman Empire. Of course, no single colonial experience characterized these two centuries across this vast region. Much depended on the cultures and prior history of various colonized people. Policies of the colonial powers sometimes differed sharply and changed over time. Men and women experienced the colonial era differently, as did traditional elites, Western-educated classes, urban artisans, peasant farmers, and migrant laborers. Furthermore, the varied actions and reactions of such people, despite their oppression and exploitation, shaped the colonial experience, perhaps as much as the policies, practices, and intentions of their temporary European rulers. All of them—colonizers and colonized alike—were caught up in the flood of change that accompanied the Industrial Revolution and a new burst of European imperialism.

A Second Wave of European Conquests

■ Comparison

In what different ways did the colonial takeover of Asia and Africa occur?

If the sixteenth- and seventeenth-century takeover of the Americas represented the first phase of European colonial conquests, the century and a half between 1750 and 1900 was a second and quite distinct round of that larger process. Now it was focused in Asia and Africa rather than in the Western Hemisphere. It featured a number of new players—Germany, Italy, Belgium, the United States, Japan—who were not at all involved in the earlier phase, while the Spanish and Portuguese now had only minor roles. In mainland Asia and Africa, nineteenth-century European conquests nowhere had the devastating demographic consequences that had so sharply reduced the Native American populations. Furthermore, this second wave of European colonial conquests, at least by the mid-nineteenth century, was conditioned by Europe's Industrial Revolution. In both their formal colonies and their "informal empires" (Latin America, China, the Ottoman Empire, and for a time Japan), European motives and activities were shaped by the military capacity and economic power that the Industrial Revolution conveyed. In general, Europeans preferred informal control, for it was cheaper and less likely to provoke wars. But where rivalry with other European states made it impossible or where local governments were unable or unwilling to cooperate, Europeans proved more than willing to undertake the expense and risk of conquest and outright colonial rule.

The construction of these second-wave European empires in the Afro-Asian world, like empires everywhere, involved military force or the threat of using it. Initially, the European military advantage lay in organization, drill and practice, and command structure. Increasingly in the nineteenth century, the Europeans also

Map 20.1 Colonial Asia in the Early Twentieth Century
By the early 1900s, several of the great population centers of Asia had come under the colonial control of Britain, the Netherlands, France, the United States, or Japan.

possessed overwhelming advantages in firepower, deriving from the recently invented repeating rifles and machine guns. A much-quoted jingle by the English writer Hilaire Belloc summed up the situation:

> Whatever happens we have got
> The Maxim gun [an automatic machine gun] and they have not.

Nonetheless, Europeans had to fight, often long and hard, to create their new empires, as countless wars of conquest attest. In the end, though, they prevailed almost everywhere, largely against adversaries who did not have Maxim guns or in some cases any guns at all. Thus were African and Asian peoples of all kinds incorporated within one or another of the European empires. Gathering and hunting bands in Australia, agricultural village societies on Pacific islands and in Africa, pastoralists of the Sahara and Central Asia, residents of states large and small, and virtually everyone in the large and complex civilizations of India and Southeast Asia—all of them alike lost the political sovereignty and freedom of action they had previously exercised. For some, such as Hindus governed by the Muslim Mughal Empire, it was an exchange of one set of foreign rulers for another. But now all were subjects of a European colonial state.

The passage to colonial status occurred in various ways. For the peoples of India and Indonesia, colonial conquest grew out of earlier interaction with European trading firms. Particularly in India, the British East India Company, rather than the British government directly, played the leading role in the colonial takeover of South Asia. The fragmentation of the Mughal Empire and the absence of any overall sense of cultural or political unity both invited and facilitated European penetration. A similar situation of many small and rival states assisted the Dutch acquisition of Indonesia. However, neither the British nor the Dutch had a clear-cut plan for conquest. Rather it evolved slowly as local authorities and European traders made and unmade a variety of alliances over a long period of time, lasting roughly a century in India (1750–1850). In Indonesia, a few areas held out until the early twentieth century (see Map 20.1).

For most of Africa, mainland Southeast Asia, and the Pacific islands, colonial conquest came later, in the second half of the nineteenth century, and rather more abruptly and deliberately than in India or Indonesia. The "scramble for Africa," for example, pitted half a dozen European powers against one another as they partitioned the entire continent among themselves in only about twenty-five years (1875–1900). European leaders themselves were surprised by the intensity of their rivalries and the speed with which they acquired huge territories, about which they knew very little (see Map 20.2).

That process involved endless but peaceful negotiations among the competing Great Powers about "who got what" and extensive and bloody military action, sometimes lasting decades, to make their control effective on the ground. Among the most difficult to subdue were those decentralized societies without a formal state structure. In such cases, Europeans confronted no central authority with which they could negotiate or that they might decisively defeat. It was a matter of village-by-village conquest against extended resistance. As late as 1925, one British official commented on the process as it operated in central Nigeria: "I shall of course go on walloping them until they surrender. It's a rather piteous sight watching a village being knocked to pieces and I wish there was some other way, but unfortunately there isn't."[2]

The South Pacific territories of Australia and New Zealand, both of which were taken over by the British during the nineteenth century, were more similar to the earlier colonization of North America than to contemporary patterns of Asian and African conquest. In both places, conquest was accompanied by massive European settlement and diseases that reduced native numbers by 75 percent or more by 1900. Like Canada and the United States, these became settler colonies, "neo-European" societies in the Pacific. Aboriginal Australians constituted only about 2.4 percent of their country's population in the early twenty-first century, and the indigenous Maori were a minority of about 15 percent in New Zealand. With the exception

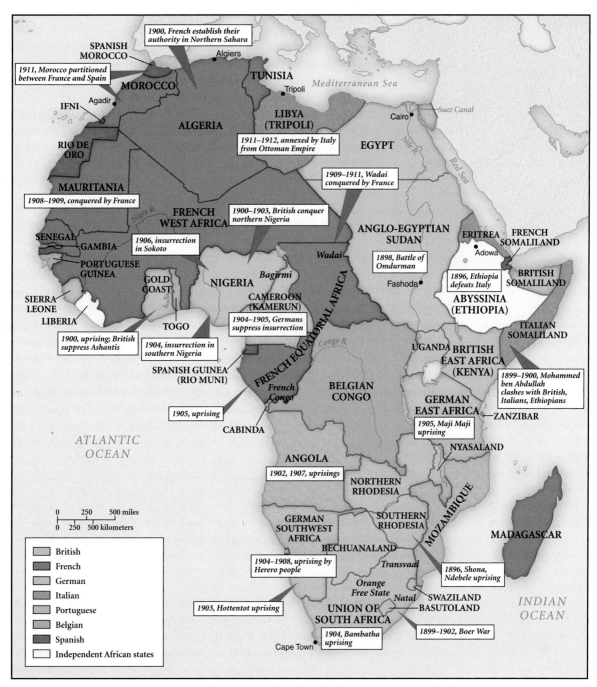

Map 20.2 Conquest and Resistance in Colonial Africa

By the early twentieth century, the map of Africa reflected the outcome of the "scramble for Africa," a conquest that was heavily resisted in many places. The boundaries established during that process still provide the political framework for Africa's independent states.

The following labels appear on the map:

1900, French establish their authority in Northern Sahara

1911, Morocco partitioned between France and Spain

1911–1912, annexed by Italy from Ottoman Empire

1909–1911, Wadai conquered by France

1900–1903, British conquer northern Nigeria

1908–1909, conquered by France

1906, insurrection in Sokoto

1898, Battle of Omdurman

1896, Ethiopia defeats Italy

1904–1905, Germans suppress insurrection

1900, uprising; British suppress Ashantis

1904, insurrection in southern Nigeria

1899–1900, Mohammed ben Abdullah clashes with British, Italians, Ethiopians

1905, uprising

1905, Maji Maji uprising

1902, 1907, uprisings

1904–1908, uprising by Herero people

1896, Shona, Ndebele uprising

1903, Hottentot uprising

1904, Bambatha uprising

1899–1902, Boer War

Legend:
- British
- French
- German
- Italian
- Portuguese
- Belgian
- Spanish
- Independent African states

of Hawaii, nowhere else in the nineteenth-century colonial world were existing populations so decimated and overwhelmed as they were in Australia and New Zealand.

Elsewhere other variations on the theme of imperial conquest unfolded. Japan's takeover of Taiwan and Korea bore marked similarities to European actions. The westward expansion of the United States and the Russian penetration of Central Asia brought additional millions under European control as these two states continued their earlier territorial growth. Filipinos acquired new colonial rulers when the United States took over from Spain following the Spanish-American War of 1898. Some 13,000 freed U.S. slaves, seeking greater freedom than was possible at home, migrated to West Africa, where they became, ironically, a colonizing elite in the land they named Liberia. Ethiopia and Siam (Thailand) were notable for avoiding the colonization to which their neighbors succumbed. Those countries' military and diplomatic skills, their willingness to make modest concessions to the Europeans, and the rivalries of the imperialists all contributed to these exceptions to the rule of colonial takeover in East Africa and Southeast Asia.

These broad patterns of colonial conquest dissolved into thousands of separate encounters as Asian and African societies were confronted with decisions about how to respond to encroaching European power in the context of their local circumstances. Many initially sought to enlist Europeans in their own internal struggles for power or in their external rivalries with neighboring states or peoples. As pressures mounted and European demands escalated, some tried to play off imperial powers against one another. Many societies were sharply divided between those who wanted to fight and those who believed that resistance was futile. After extended resistance against French aggression, the nineteenth-century Vietnamese emperor Tu Duc argued with those who wanted the struggle to go on.

> Do you really wish to confront such a power with a pack of [our] cowardly soldiers? It would be like mounting an elephant's head or caressing a tiger's tail. . . . With what you presently have, do you really expect to dissolve the enemy's rifles into air or chase his battleships into hell?[3]

Others negotiated, attempting to preserve as much independence and power as possible. The rulers of the East African kingdom of Buganda, for example, saw opportunity in the British presence and negotiated an arrangement that substantially enlarged their state and personally benefited the kingdom's elite class.

Under European Rule

In many places and for many people, incorporation into European colonial empires was a traumatic experience. Especially for small-scale societies, the loss of life, homes, cattle, crops, and land could be devastating. In 1902, a British soldier in East Africa described what happened in a single village: "Every soul was either shot or bayoneted. . . . We burned all the huts and razed the banana plantations to the ground."[4]

For the Vietnamese elite, schooled for centuries in Chinese-style Confucian thinking, conquest meant that the natural harmonies of life had been badly disrupted; it was a time when "water flowed uphill." Nguyen Khuyen (1835–1909), a senior Vietnamese official, retired to his ancestral village to farm and write poetry after the French conquest. There he expressed his anguish at the passing of the world he had known.

> Fine wine but no good friends,
> So I buy none though I have the money.
> A poem comes to mind, but I choose not to write it down.
> If it were written, to whom would I give it?
> The spare bed hangs upon the wall in cold indifference.
> I pluck the lute, but it just doesn't sound right.[5]

Many others also withdrew into private life, feigning illness when asked to serve in public office under the French.

Cooperation and Rebellion

Although violence was a prominent feature of colonial life both during conquest and after, various groups and many individuals willingly cooperated with colonial authorities to their own advantage. Many men found employment, status, and security in European-led armed forces. The shortage and expense of European administrators and the difficulties of communicating across cultural boundaries made it necessary for colonial rulers to rely heavily on a range of local intermediaries. Thus Indian princes, Muslim emirs, and African chiefs, often from elite or ruling families, found it possible to retain much of their earlier status and privileges while gaining considerable wealth by exercising authority, both legally and otherwise, at the local level. For example, in French West Africa, an area eight times the size of France itself and with a population of about 15 million in the late 1930s, the colonial state consisted of just 385 French administrators and more than 50,000 African chiefs. Thus colonial rule rested upon and reinforced the most conservative segments of Asian and African societies.

■ **Explanation**
Why might subject people choose to cooperate with the colonial regime? What might prompt them to rebel or resist?

Both colonial governments and private missionary organizations had an interest in promoting a measure of European education. From this process arose a small Western-educated class, whose members served the colonial state, European businesses, and Christian missions as teachers, clerks, translators, and lower-level administrators. A few received higher education abroad and returned home as lawyers, doctors, engineers, or journalists. As colonial governments and business enterprises became more sophisticated, Europeans increasingly depended on the Western-educated class at the expense of the more traditional elites.

If colonial rule enlisted the willing cooperation of some, it provoked the bitter opposition of many others. Thus periodic rebellions, both large and small, punctuated the history of colonial regimes everywhere. The most famous among them was

THE DEVILFISH IN EGYPTIAN WATERS.

An Egyptian View of British Imperialism
In this late-nineteenth-century Egyptian cartoon, the British Empire is portrayed as an octopus whose tentacles are already attached to many countries, while one tentacle is about to grasp still another one, Egypt. (The Granger Collection, New York)

the Indian Rebellion of 1857–1858, which was triggered by the introduction into the colony's military forces of a new cartridge smeared with animal fat from cows and pigs. The first animal was sacred to Hindus and the second deeply offensive to Muslims, and both groups viewed the innovation as a plot to render them defiled and to convert them to Christianity. Behind this incident were many groups of people with a whole series of grievances generated by the British colonial presence: local rulers who had lost power; landlords deprived of their estates or their rent; peasants overtaxed and exploited by urban moneylenders and landlords alike; unemployed weavers displaced by machine-manufactured textiles; and religious leaders threatened by missionary activities. A mutiny among Indian troops in Bengal triggered the rebellion, which soon spread to other regions of the colony and other social groups. Soon much of India was aflame. Rebel leaders presented their movement as an effort to revitalize the defunct Mughal Empire and thereby attracted many with strong resentments against the British. Although it was crushed in 1858, the rebellion greatly widened the racial divide in colonial India and eroded British tolerance for those they viewed as "nigger natives" who had betrayed their trust. It made the British more conservative and cautious about deliberately trying to change Indian society for fear of provoking another rebellion. Moreover, it convinced the British government to assume direct control over India, ending the era of British East India Company rule in the subcontinent.

Colonial Empires with a Difference

■ Comparison

What was distinctive about European colonial empires of the nineteenth century?

At one level, European colonial empires were but the latest in a very long line of imperial creations, all of which had enlisted cooperation and experienced resistance from their subject peoples, but the nineteenth-century European version of empire differed from the others in several remarkable ways. One was the prominence of race in distinguishing rulers and ruled, as the high tide of "scientific racism" in Europe coincided with the acquisition of Asian and African colonies (see Chapter 19). In East Africa, for example, white men were referred to as "bwana" (Swahili for "master"), whereas Europeans regularly called African men "boy." Education for colonial subjects was both limited and skewed toward practical subjects rather than scientific and literary studies, which were widely regarded as inappropriate for the "primitive mind" of "natives." Particularly affected by European racism were those whose Western education and aspirations most clearly threatened the racial divide. Europeans were exceedingly reluctant to allow even the most highly educated Asians and Africans to enter the higher ranks of the colonial civil service. A proposal in 1883 to allow Indian judges to hear cases involving whites provoked outrage and massive demonstrations among European inhabitants of India.

In those colonies that had a large European settler population, the pattern of racial separation was much more pronounced than in places such as Nigeria, which had few permanently settled whites. The most extreme case was South Africa, where a large European population and the widespread use of African labor in mines and industries brought blacks and whites into closer and more prolonged contact than elsewhere. The racial fears that were aroused resulted in extraordinary efforts to establish race as a legal, not just a customary, feature of South African society. This racial system provided for separate "homelands," educational systems, residential areas, public facilities, and much more. In what was eventually known as apartheid, South African whites attempted the impossible task of creating an industrializing economy based on cheap African labor, while limiting African social and political integration in every conceivable fashion.

A further distinctive feature of nineteenth-century European empires lay in the extent to which colonial states were able to penetrate the societies they governed. Centralized tax-collecting bureaucracies, new means of communication and transportation, imposed changes in landholding patterns, integration of colonial economies into a global network of exchange, public health and sanitation measures, and the activities of missionaries all touched the daily lives of many people far more deeply than in most earlier empires. Not only were Europeans foreign rulers, but they also bore the seeds of a very different way of life, which grew out of their own modern transformation.

Nineteenth-century European colonizers were extraordinary as well in their penchant for counting and classifying their subject people. With the assistance of anthropologists and missionaries, colonial governments collected a vast amount of information, sought to organize it "scientifically," and used it to manage the unfamiliar, complex, varied, and fluctuating societies that they governed. In India, the British found in classical texts and Brahmin ideology an idealized description of the caste system, based on the notion of four ranked and unchanging varnas, which made it possible to bring order out of the immense complexity and variety of caste as it actually operated. Thus the British invented or appropriated a Brahmin version of "traditional India" that they favored and sought to preserve, while scorning as "non-Indian" the new elite educated in European schools and enthusiastic about Western ways of life. This view of India reflected the great influence of Brahmins on British thinking and clearly served the interests of this Indian upper class.

Likewise within African colonies, Europeans identified, and sometimes invented, distinct tribes, each with its own clearly defined territory, language, customs, and chief. The notion of a "tribal Africa" expressed the Western view that African societies were primitive or backward, representing an earlier stage of human development. It was also a convenient idea, for it reduced the enormous complexity and fluidity of African societies to a more manageable state and thus made colonial administration easier.

Finally, European colonial policies contradicted their own core values and their practices at home to an unusual degree. While nineteenth-century Britain and France were becoming more democratic, their colonies were essentially dictatorships, offering perhaps order and stability, but certainly not democratic government, because few colonial subjects were participating citizens. Empire of course was wholly at odds with European notions of national independence, and ranked racial classifications went against the grain of both Christian and Enlightenment ideas of human equality. Furthermore, many Europeans were distinctly reluctant to encourage within their colonies the kind of modernization—urban growth, industrialization, individual values, religious skepticism—that was sweeping their own societies. They feared that this kind of social change, often vilified as "detribalization," would encourage unrest, challenging colonial rule. As a model for social development, they much preferred "traditional" rural society, with its established authorities and social hierarchies, though shorn of abuses such as slavery and sati (widow-burning). Such contradictions between what Europeans preached at home and what they practiced in the colonies became increasingly apparent to many Asians and Africans and played a major role in undermining the foundations of colonial rule in the twentieth century.

Ways of Working: Comparing Colonial Economies

Colonial rule affected the lives of its subject people in many ways, but the most pronounced change was in their ways of working. The colonial state—with its power to tax, to seize land for European enterprises, to compel labor, and to build railroads, ports, and roads—played an important role in these transformations. Even more powerful was the growing integration of Asian and African societies into a world economy that increasingly demanded their gold, diamonds, copper, tin, rubber, coffee, cotton, sugar, cocoa, and many other products. But the economic transformations born of these twin pressures were far from uniform. Various groups—migrant workers and cash-crop farmers, plantation laborers and domestic servants, urban elites and day laborers, men and women—experienced the colonial era differently as their daily working lives underwent profound changes.

To various degrees, old ways of working were eroded almost everywhere in the colonial world. Subsistence farming, in which peasant families produced largely for their own needs, diminished as growing numbers directed at least some of their energies to working for wages or selling what they produced for a cash income.

That money was both necessary to pay their taxes and school fees and useful for buying the various products—such as machine-produced textiles, bicycles, and kerosene—that the industrial economies of Europe sent their way. As in Europe, artisans suffered greatly when cheaper machine-manufactured merchandise displaced their own handmade goods. A flood of inexpensive textiles from Britain's new factories ruined the livelihood of tens of thousands of India's handloom weavers. Iron smelting largely disappeared in Africa, and occupations such as blacksmithing and tanning lost ground. Furthermore, Asian and African merchants, who had earlier handled the trade between their countries and the wider world, were squeezed out by well-financed European commercial firms.

Economies of Coercion: Forced Labor and the Power of the State

Many of the new ways of working that emerged during the colonial era derived directly from the demands of the colonial state. The most obvious was required and unpaid labor on public projects, such as building railroads, constructing government buildings, and transporting goods. In French Africa, all "natives" were legally obligated for "statute labor" of ten to twelve days a year, a practice that lasted through 1946. It was much resented. A resident of British West Africa, interviewed in 1996, bitterly recalled this feature of colonial life: "They [British officials] were rude, and they made us work for them a lot. They came to the village and just rounded us up and made us go off and clear the road or carry loads on our heads."[6]

■ Connection

How did the power of colonial states transform the economic lives of colonial subjects?

The most infamous cruelties of forced labor occurred during the early twentieth century in the Congo Free State, then governed personally by Leopold II of Belgium. Private companies in the Congo, operating under the authority of the state, forced villagers to collect rubber, which was much in demand for bicycle and automobile tires, with a reign of terror and abuse that cost millions of lives. One refugee from these horrors described the process.

> We were always in the forest to find the rubber vines, to go without food, and our women had to give up cultivating the fields and gardens. Then we starved. . . . We begged the white man to leave us alone, saying we could get no more rubber, but the white men and their soldiers said "Go. You are only beasts yourselves. . . ." When we failed and our rubber was short, the soldiers came to our towns and killed us. Many were shot, some had their ears cut off; others were tied up with ropes round their necks and taken away.[7]

Eventually such outrages were widely publicized in Europe, where they created a scandal, forcing the Belgian government to take control of the Congo in 1908 and ending Leopold's reign of terror.

A variation on the theme of forced labor took shape in the so-called cultivation system of the Netherlands East Indies (Indonesia) during the nineteenth century.

Colonial Violence in the Congo
These young boys with severed hands were among the victims of a brutal regime of forced labor undertaken in the Congo during the late nineteenth and early twentieth centuries. Such mutilation was punishment for their villages' inability to supply the required amount of wild rubber. (Courtesy, Anti-Slavery Organization, London)

Peasants were required to cultivate 20 percent or more of their land in cash crops such as sugar or coffee to meet their tax obligation to the state. Sold to government contractors at fixed and low prices, those crops, when resold on the world market, proved highly profitable for Dutch traders and shippers as well as for the Dutch state and its citizens. According to one scholar, the cultivation system "performed a miracle for the Dutch economy," enabling it to avoid taxing its own people and providing capital for its Industrial Revolution.[8] It also enriched and strengthened the position of those "traditional authorities" who enforced the system, often by using lashings and various tortures, on behalf of the Dutch. For the peasants of Java, however, it meant a double burden of obligations to the colonial state as well as to local lords. Many became indebted to moneylenders when they could not meet those obligations. Those demands, coupled with the loss of land and labor now excluded from food production, contributed to a wave of famines during the mid-nineteenth century in which hundreds of thousands perished.

The forced cultivation of cash crops was widely and successfully resisted in many places. In German East Africa, for example, colonial authorities in the late nineteenth century imposed the cultivation of cotton, which seriously interfered with production of local food crops. Here is how one man remembered the experience:

> The cultivation of cotton was done by turns. Every village was allotted days on which to cultivate. . . . After arriving you all suffered very greatly. Your back and your buttocks were whipped and there was no rising up once you stooped to dig. . . . And yet he [the German] wanted us to pay him tax. Were we not human beings?[9]

Such conditions prompted a massive rebellion in 1905 and persuaded the Germans to end the forced growing of cotton. In Mozambique, where the Portuguese likewise brutally enforced cotton cultivation, a combination of peasant sabotage, the planting of unauthorized crops, and the smuggling of cotton across the border to more profitable markets ensured that Portugal never achieved its goal of becoming self-sufficient in cotton production. In such ways did the actions of the colonized alter or frustrate the plans of the colonizers.

Economies of Cash-Crop Agriculture: The Pull of the Market

Many Asian and African peoples had produced quite willingly for an international market long before they were enclosed within colonial societies. They offered for trade items such as peanuts and palm oil in West Africa, cotton in Egypt, spices in Indonesia, and pepper and textiles in India. In some places, colonial rule created conditions that facilitated and increased cash-crop production to the advantage of local farmers. British authorities in Burma, for example, acted to encourage rice production among small farmers by ending an earlier prohibition on rice exports, providing irrigation and transportation facilities, and enacting land tenure laws that facilitated private ownership of small farms. Under these conditions, the population of the Irrawaddy Delta boomed, migrants from Upper Burma and India poured into the region, and rice exports soared. Local small farmers benefited considerably because they were now able to own their own land, build substantial houses, and buy imported goods. For several decades in the late nineteenth century, standards of living improved sharply. It was a very different situation from that of peasants forced to grow crops that seriously interfered with their food production.

Profitable cash-crop farming also developed in the southern Gold Coast (present-day Ghana), a British territory in West Africa. Unlike Burma, it was African farmers themselves who took the initiative to develop export agriculture. Planting cacao trees in huge quantities, they became the world's leading supplier of cocoa, used to make chocolate, by 1911. Cacao was an attractive crop because, unlike cotton, it was compatible with the continued production of foods and did not require so much labor time. In the early twentieth century, it brought a new prosperity to many local farmers. "A hybrid society was taking shape," wrote one scholar, "partly peasant, in that most members farmed their own land with family labor . . . and partly capitalist, in that a minority employed wage laborers, produced chiefly for the market, and reinvested profits."[10]

That success brought new problems in its wake. A shortage of labor fostered the employment of former slaves as dependent and exploited workers and also generated tensions between the sexes when some men married women for their labor power but refused to support them adequately. Moreover, the labor shortage brought a huge influx of migrants from the drier interior parts of West Africa, generating ethnic and class tensions. Furthermore, many colonies came to specialize in one or two cash crops, creating an unhealthy dependence when world market prices dropped. Thus African and Asian farmers were increasingly subject to the uncertain rhythms of the international marketplace as well as to those of the seasons and the weather.

Economies of Wage Labor: Working for Europeans

Yet another new way of working in colonial societies involved wage labor in some European enterprise. Driven by the need for money, by the loss of land adequate to support their families, or sometimes by the orders of colonial authorities, millions of

■ **Change**
How did cash-crop agriculture transform the lives of colonized peoples?

■ **Change**
What kinds of wage labor were available in the colonies? Why might people take part in it? How did doing so change their lives?

colonial subjects across Asia and Africa sought employment in European-owned plantations, mines, construction projects, and homes. All across Southeast Asia in the later nineteenth and early twentieth centuries, huge plantations sprouted, which were financed from Europe and which grew sugarcane, rubber, tea, tobacco, sisal (used for making rope), and more. Impoverished workers by the hundreds of thousands came from great distances—India, China, Java—finding their way to these plantations, where they were subject to strict control, often housed in barracks, and paid poorly, with women receiving 50 to 75 percent of a man's wage. Disease was common, and death rates were twice or more that of the colony as a whole. In southern Vietnam in 1927 alone, one in twenty plantation workers died. British colonial authorities in India facilitated the migration of millions of Indians to work sites elsewhere in the British Empire—Trinidad, Fiji, Malaysia, Ceylon, South Africa, Kenya, and Uganda, for example—with some laboring as indentured workers and others as independent merchants.

In Africa more than in Asia, people migrated to European farms or plantations because they had lost their own land. In the settler colonies of Africa—Algeria, Kenya, Southern Rhodesia (Zimbabwe), and South Africa, for example—permanent European communities, with the help of colonial governments, obtained huge tracts of land, much of which had previously been home to African societies. A 1913 law in South Africa legally defined 88 percent of the land as belonging to whites, who were then about 20 percent of the population. Much of highland Kenya, an

Economic Change in the Colonial World
These workers on a Ceylon tea plantation in the early twentieth century are moving sacks of tea into a drying house in preparation for export. The Lipton label on the bags is a reminder of the role of large-scale foreign investment in the economic transformations of the colonial era. (Hulton-Deutsch Collection/Corbis)

enormously rich agricultural region that was home to the Gikuyu and Kamba peoples, was taken over by some 4,000 white farmers. Some Africans stayed on the land as squatters, working for the new landowners as the price of remaining on what had been their own land. Others were displaced to "native reserves," limited areas that could not support their growing populations, thus forcing many to work for wages on European farms.

Mines were another source of wage labor for many. In the British-ruled Malay States (Malaysia), tin mining accelerated greatly in the late nineteenth century, and by 1895 that colony produced some 55 percent of the world's tin. Operated initially by Chinese and later by European entrepreneurs, these mines drew many millions of impoverished Chinese workers on strictly controlled three-year contracts. Appalling living conditions, disease, and accidents generated extraordinarily high death rates. The gold and diamond mines of South Africa likewise set in motion a huge pattern of labor migration that encompassed all of Africa south of the Belgian Congo. With skilled and highly paid work reserved for white miners, Africans were relegated largely to unskilled labor at a fraction of white wages. Furthermore, they were recruited on short-term contracts, lived in all-male prisonlike barracks that were often surrounded by barbed wire, and were forced to return home periodically to prevent them from establishing a permanent family life near the mines.

The rapidly swelling cities of the colonial world—Lagos, Nairobi, Cairo, Calcutta, Rangoon, Batavia, Singapore, Saigon—required no coercion to attract would-be wage earners, particularly from the late nineteenth century on. Racially segregated, often unsanitary, and greatly overcrowded, these cities nonetheless were seen as meccas of opportunity for people all across the social spectrum. Traditional elites, absentee landlords, and wealthy Chinese businessmen occupied the top rungs of Southeast Asian cities. Western-educated people everywhere found opportunities as teachers, doctors, and professional specialists, but more often as clerks in European business offices and government bureaucracies. Skilled workers on the railways or in the ports represented a working-class elite, while a few labored in the factories that processed agricultural goods or manufactured basic products such as beer, cigarettes, cement, and furniture. Far more numerous were the construction workers, rickshaw drivers, food sellers, domestic servants, prostitutes, and others who made up the urban poor of colonial cities. In 1955, a British investigating commission described life in Nairobi, the capital of Kenya, one of Britain's richest colonies.

> The wages of the majority of African workers are too low to enable them to obtain accommodation which is adequate to any standard. The high cost of housing relative to wages is in itself a cause of overcrowding, because housing is shared to lighten the cost. This, with the high cost of food in towns, makes family life impossible for the majority.[11]

Thus, after more than half a century of colonial rule, British authorities themselves acknowledged that normal family life in the colony's major urban center proved out of reach for the vast majority. It was quite an admission.

Women and the Colonial Economy: An African Case Study

■ Change
How were the lives of African women altered by colonial economies?

If economic life in European empires varied greatly from place to place, even within the same colony, it also offered a different combination of opportunities and hardships to women than it did to men, as the experience of colonial Africa shows.[12] In precolonial times, African women were almost everywhere active farmers, with responsibility for planting, weeding, and harvesting in addition to food preparation and child care. Men cleared the land, built houses, herded the cattle, and in some cases assisted with field work. Within this division of labor, women were expected to feed their own families and were usually allocated their own fields for that purpose. Many also were involved in local trading activity. Though clearly subordinate to men, African women nevertheless had a measure of economic autonomy.

As the demands of the colonial economy grew, women's lives diverged more and more from those of men. In colonies where cash-crop agriculture was dominant, men often withdrew from subsistence production in favor of more lucrative export crops. Among the Ewe people of southern Ghana, men almost completely dominated the highly profitable cacao farming, whereas women assumed near total responsibility for domestic food production. In neighboring Ivory Coast, women had traditionally grown cotton for their families' clothing; but when that crop acquired a cash value, men insisted that cotton grown for export be produced on their own personal fields. Thus men acted to control the most profitable aspects of cash-crop agriculture and in doing so greatly increased the subsistence workload of women. One study from Cameroon estimated that women's working hours increased from forty-six per week in precolonial times to more than seventy by 1934.

Further increasing women's workload and differentiating their lives from those of men was labor migration. As more and more men sought employment in the cities, on settler farms, or in the mines, their wives were left to manage the domestic economy almost alone. In many cases, women also had to supply food to men in the cities to compensate for very low urban wages. They often took over such traditionally male tasks as breaking the ground for planting, milking the cows, and supervising the herds, in addition to their normal responsibilities. In South Africa, where the demands of the European economy were particularly heavy, some 40 to 50 percent of able-bodied adult men were absent from the rural areas, and women headed 60 percent of households. In

Women in Colonial Africa
The movement of many African men into wage labor thrust even more of the domestic responsibilities onto women. Here in a photograph from colonial Kenya in 1936 a woman carries on the ancient craft of making clay pots. (Elspeth Huxley/Huxley Collection/Images of Empire, British Empire & Commonwealth Museum)

Botswana, which supplied much male labor to South Africa, married couples by the 1930s rarely lived together for more than two months at a time. In such situations, the lives and cultures of men and women increasingly diverged, with one focused on the cities and working for wages and the other on village life and subsistence agriculture.

Women coped with these difficult circumstances in a number of ways. Many sought closer relations with their families of birth rather than with their absent husbands' families, as would otherwise have been expected. Among the Luo of Kenya, women introduced laborsaving crops, adopted new farm implements, and earned some money as traders. In the cities, they established a variety of self-help associations, including those for prostitutes and for brewers of beer.

The colonial economy sometimes provided a measure of opportunity for enterprising women, particularly in small-scale trade and marketing. In some parts of West Africa, women came to dominate this sector of the economy by selling foodstuffs, cloth, and inexpensive imported goods, while men or foreign firms controlled the more profitable wholesale and import-export trade. Such opportunities sometimes gave women considerable economic autonomy. By the 1930s, for example, Nupe women in northern Nigeria had gained sufficient wealth as itinerant traders that they were contributing more to the family income than their husbands and frequently lent money to them. Among some Igbo groups in southern Nigeria, men were responsible for growing the prestigious yams, but women's crops—especially cassava—came to have a cash value during the colonial era, and women were entitled to keep the profits from selling it. "What is man? I have my own money" expressed the growing economic independence of such women.[13]

At the other end of the social scale, women of impoverished rural families, by necessity, often became virtually independent heads of household in the absence of their husbands. Others took advantage of new opportunities in mission schools, towns, and mines to flee the restrictions of rural patriarchy. Such challenges to patriarchal values elicited various responses from men, including increased accusations of witchcraft against women and fears of impotence. Among the Shona in Southern Rhodesia, and no doubt elsewhere, senior African men repeatedly petitioned the colonial authorities for laws and regulations that would criminalize adultery and restrict women's ability to leave their rural villages.[14] The control of women's sexuality and mobility was a common interest of European and African men.

Assessing Colonial Development

Beyond the many and varied changes that transformed the working lives of millions in the colonial world lies the difficult and highly controversial question of the overall economic impact of colonial rule on Asian and African societies. Defenders, both then and now, praise it for jump-starting modern growth, but numerous critics cite a record of exploitation and highlight the limitations and unevenness of that growth. Amid the continuing debates, three things seem reasonably clear. First,

■ **Change**
Did colonial rule bring "progress" in its wake?

colonial rule served, for better or worse, to further the integration of Asian and African economies into a global network of exchange, now centered in Europe. In many places, that process was well under way before conquest imposed foreign rule, and elsewhere it occurred without formal colonial control. Nonetheless, it is apparent that within the colonial world far more land and labor were devoted to production for the global market at the end of the colonial era than at its beginning.

Second, Europeans could hardly avoid conveying to the colonies some elements of their own modernizing process. It was in their interests to do so, and many felt duty bound to "improve" the societies they briefly governed. Modern administrative and bureaucratic structures facilitated colonial control; communication and transportation infrastructure (railroads, motorways, ports, telegraphs, postal services) moved products to the world market; schools trained the army of intermediaries on which colonial rule depended; and modest health care provisions fulfilled some of the "civilizing mission" to which many Europeans felt committed. These elements of modernization made an appearance, however inadequately, during the colonial era.

Third, nowhere in the colonial world did a breakthrough to modern industrial society of Japanese dimensions occur. When India became independent after two centuries of colonial rule by the world's first industrial society, it was still one of the poorest of the world's developing countries. The British may not have created Indian poverty, but neither did they overcome it to any substantial degree. Scholars continue to debate the reasons for that failure: was it the result of deliberate British policies, or was it due to the conditions of Indian society? The nationalist movements that surged across Asia and Africa in the twentieth century had their own answer. To their many millions of participants, colonial rule, whatever its earlier promise, had become an economic dead end, whereas independence represented a grand opening to new and more hopeful possibilities. Paraphrasing a famous teaching of Jesus, Kwame Nkrumah, the first prime minister of an independent Ghana, declared, "Seek ye first the political kingdom, and all these other things [schools, factories, hospitals, for example] will be added unto you."

Snapshot   **Long-Distance Migration in an Age of Empire, 1846–1940**[15]

The age of empire was also an age of global migration. Beyond the long-distance migration shown here, shorter migrations within particular regions or colonies set millions more into motion.

Origins	Destination	Numbers
Europe	Americas	55–58 million
India, southern China	Southeast Asia, Indian Ocean rim, South Pacific	48–52 million
Northeast Asia, Russia	Manchuria, Siberia, Central Asia, Japan	46–51 million

Believing and Belonging: Identity and Cultural Change in the Colonial Era

The experience of colonial rule—its racism, its exposure to European culture, its social and economic upheavals—contributed much to cultural change within Asian and African societies. Coping with these enormous disruptions induced many colonized peoples to alter the ways they thought about themselves and their communities. Cultural identities, of course, are never static, but the transformations of the colonial era catalyzed substantial and quite rapid changes in what people believed and in how they defined the societies to which they belonged. Those transformed identities continued to echo long after European rule had ended.

Education

For an important minority, it was the acquisition of Western education, obtained through missionary or government schools, that generated a new identity. To previously illiterate people, the knowledge of reading and writing of any kind often suggested an almost magical power. Within the colonial setting, it could mean an escape from some of the most onerous obligations of living under European control, such as forced labor. More positively, it meant access to better-paying positions in government bureaucracies, mission organizations, or business firms and to the exciting imported goods that their salaries could buy. Moreover, education often provided social mobility and elite status within their own communities and an opportunity to achieve, or at least approach, equality with whites in racially defined societies. An African man from colonial Kenya described an encounter he had as a boy in 1938 with a relative who was a teacher in a mission school.

> Aged about 25, he seems to me like a young god with his smart clothes and shoes, his watch, and a beautiful bicycle. I worshipped in particular his bicycle that day and decided that I must somehow get myself one. As he talked with us, it seemed to me that the secret of his riches came from his education, his knowledge of reading and writing, and that it was essential for me to obtain this power.[16]

Many such people ardently embraced European culture, dressing in European clothes, speaking French or English, building European-style houses, getting married in long white dresses, and otherwise emulating European ways. Some of the early Western-educated Bengalis from northeastern India boasted about dreaming in English and deliberately ate beef, to the consternation of their elders. In a well-known poem entitled "A Prayer for Peace," Léopold Senghor, a highly educated West African writer and political leader, enumerated the many crimes of colonialism and yet confessed, "I have a great weakness for France." Asian and African colonial societies now had a new cultural divide: between the small number who had mastered to varying degrees the ways of their rulers and the vast majority who had

■ **Change**
What impact did Western education have on colonial societies?

The Educated Elite
Throughout the Afro-Asian world of the nineteenth century, the European presence generated a small group of people who enthusiastically embraced the culture and lifestyle of Europe. Here King Chulalongkorn of Siam poses with the crown prince and other young students, all of them garbed impeccably in European clothing. (Hulton-Deutsch Collection/Corbis)

not. Literate Christians in the East African kingdom of Buganda referred with contempt to their "pagan" neighbors as "they who do not read."

Many among the Western-educated elite saw themselves as a modernizing vanguard who were leading the regeneration of their societies, in association with colonial authorities. For them, at least initially, the colonial enterprise was full of promise for a better future. The Vietnamese teacher and nationalist Nguyen Thai Hoc, while awaiting execution in 1930 by the French for his revolutionary activities, wrote about his earlier hopes: "At the beginning, I had thought to cooperate with the French in Indochina in order to serve my compatriots, my country, and my people, particularly in the areas of cultural and economic development."[17] Senghor too wrote wistfully about an earlier time when "we could have lived in harmony [with Europeans]."

In nineteenth-century India, Western-educated people organized a variety of reform societies, which sought a renewed Indian culture that was free of idolatry, child marriages, caste, and discrimination against women, while drawing inspiration from the classic texts of Hinduism. For them, European education was an instrument of progress and liberation from the stranglehold of tradition. Ram Mohan Roy (1772–1833), perhaps the foremost of these Indian reformers, sought from the colonial regime "European gentlemen of talent and education to instruct the natives of India in mathematics, natural philosophy, chemistry, anatomy and other useful sciences which the natives of Europe have carried to a degree of perfection that has raised them above the inhabitant of other parts of the world."[18]

Such fond hopes for the renewal of Asian and African societies through colonial rule would be bitterly disappointed. Europeans generally declined to treat their Asian and African subjects—even those with a Western education—as equal partners in the enterprise of renewal. The frequent denigration of their cultures as primitive, backward, uncivilized, or savage certainly rankled, particularly among the well-educated. "My people of Africa," wrote the West African intellectual James Aggrey in the 1920s, "we were created in the image of God, but men have made us think that we are chickens, and we still think we are; but we are eagles. Stretch forth your wings and fly."[19]

Religion

Religion too provided the basis for new or transformed identities during the colonial era. Most dramatic were those places where widespread conversion to Christianity took place, such as New Zealand, the Pacific islands, and especially

■ Change
What were the attractions of Christianity within some colonial societies?

non-Muslim Africa. Some 10,000 missionaries had descended on Africa by 1910; by the 1960s, about 50 million Africans, roughly half of the non-Muslim population, claimed a Christian identity. The attractions of the new faith were many. As in the Americas centuries earlier, military defeat shook confidence in the old gods and local practices, fostering openness to new sources of supernatural power that could operate in the wider world now impinging on their societies. Furthermore, Christianity was widely associated with modern education, and, especially in Africa, mission schools were the primary providers of Western education. The young, the poor, and many women—all of them oppressed groups in many African societies— found new opportunities and greater freedom in some association with missions. Moreover, the spread of the Christian message was less the work of

The Missionary Factor

Among the major change agents of the colonial era were the thousands of Christian missionaries who brought not only a new religion but also elements of European medicine, education, gender roles, and culture. Here is an assembly at a mission school for girls in New Guinea in the early twentieth century. (Rue des Archives/The Granger Collection, New York)

European missionaries than of those many thousands of African teachers, catechists, and pastors who brought the new faith to remote villages as well as the local communities that begged for a teacher and supplied the labor and materials to build a small church or school.

■ **Change**
How and why did Hinduism emerge as a distinct religious tradition during the colonial era in India?

As elsewhere, Christianity in Africa soon became Africanized. Within mission-based churches, many converts continued using protective charms and medicines and consulting local medicine men, all of which caused their missionary mentors to speak frequently of "backsliding." Other converts continued to believe in their old gods and spirits but now deemed them evil and sought their destruction. Furthermore, thousands of separatist movements established a wide array of independent churches, which were thoroughly Christian but under African rather than missionary control and which in many cases incorporated African cultural practices and modes of worship. It was a twentieth-century "African Reformation."

In India, where Christianity made only very modest inroads, leading intellectuals and reformers began to define their region's endlessly varied beliefs, practices, sects, rituals, and schools of philosophy as a more distinct, unified, and separate religion that we now know as Hinduism. It was in part an effort to provide for India a religion wholly equivalent to Christianity, "an accessible tradition and a feeling of historical worth when faced with the humiliation of colonial rule."[20] To Swami Vivekananda (1863–1902), one of nineteenth-century India's most influential religious figures, a revived Hinduism, shorn of its distortions, offered a means of uplifting the country's village communities, which were the heart of Indian civilization. Moreover, it could offer spiritual support to a Western world mired in materialism and militarism, a message that he took to the First World Parliament of Religions held in 1893 in Chicago. Here was India speaking back to Europe.

Hinduism in the West
The cultural interactions of the colonial era brought Asian traditions such as Hinduism to the attention of small groups in Europe and the United States. The visit of India's Swami Vivekananda to the First World Parliament of Religions in Chicago in 1893 was part of that process, illustrated here by a famous poster that circulated at that event. (Courtesy, Goes Lithographics, Chicago, after photo by Frank Parlato Jr. Image provided by www.vivekananda.net)

> Let the foreigners come and flood the land with their armies, never mind. Up, India and conquer the world with your spirituality. . . . The whole of the Western world is a volcano which may burst tomorrow, go to pieces tomorrow. . . . Now is the time to work so that India's spiritual ideas may penetrate deep into the West.[21]

This new notion of Hinduism provided a cultural foundation for emerging ideas of India as a nation, but it also contributed to a clearer sense of Muslims as a distinct community in India. Before the British takeover, little sense of commonality united the many diverse communities who practiced Islam—urban and rural dwellers; nomads and farmers; artisans, merchants, and state officials. But the British had created separate inheritance laws for all Muslims and all Hindus; in their census taking, they counted the numbers of people within these now sharply distinguished groups; and they allotted seats in local councils according to these artificial categories. As some anti-British patriots began to cast India in Hindu terms, the idea of Muslims as a separate community, which was perhaps threatened by the much larger number of Hindus, began to make sense to some who practiced Islam. In the early twentieth century, a young Hindu Bengali schoolboy noticed that "our Muslim school-fellows were beginning to air the fact of their being Muslims rather more consciously than before and with a touch of assertiveness."[22] Here were the beginnings of what became in the twentieth century a profound religious and political division within the South Asian peninsula.

"Race" and "Tribe"

In Africa as well, intellectuals and ordinary people alike forged new ways of belonging as they confronted the upheavals of colonial life. Central to these new identities were notions of race and ethnicity. By the end of the nineteenth century, a number of African thinkers, familiar with Western culture, began to define the idea of an "African identity." Previously, few if any people on the continent had regarded themselves as Africans. Rather they were members of particular local communities, usually defined by language; some were also Muslims; and still others inhabited some state or empire. Now, however, influenced by the common experience of colonial oppression and by a highly derogatory European racism, well-educated Africans began to think in broader terms, similar to Indian reformers who were developing the notion of Hinduism. It was an effort to revive the cultural self-confidence of their people by articulating a larger, common, and respected "African tradition," equivalent to that of Western culture.

■ Change
In what way were "race" and "tribe" new identities in colonial Africa?

This effort took many shapes. One line of argument held that African culture and history in fact possessed the very characteristics that Europeans exalted. Knowing that Europeans valued large empires and complex political systems, African intellectuals pointed with pride to the ancient kingdoms of Ethiopia, Mali, Songhay, and others. C. A. Diop, a French-educated scholar from Senegal, insisted that Egyptian civilization was in fact the work of black Africans. Turning European assumptions on their head, Diop argued that Western civilization owed much to Egyptian influence and was therefore derived from Africa. Black people, in short, had a history of achievement fully comparable to that of Europe and therefore deserved just as much respect and admiration.

An alternative approach to defining an African identity lay in praising the differences between African and European cultures. The most influential proponent of such views was Edward Blyden (1832–1912), a West African born in the West Indies and educated in the United States, who later became a prominent scholar and political official in Liberia. Blyden accepted the assumption that the world's various races were different but argued that each had its own distinctive contribution to make to world civilization. The uniqueness of African culture, Blyden wrote, lay in its communal, cooperative, and egalitarian societies, which contrasted sharply with Europe's highly individualistic, competitive, and class-ridden societies; in its harmonious relationship with nature as opposed to Europe's efforts to dominate and exploit the natural order; and particularly in its profound religious sensibility, which Europeans had lost in centuries of attention to material gain. Like Vivekananda in India, Blyden argued that Africa had a global mission "to be the spiritual conservatory of the world."[23]

In the twentieth century, such ideas resonated with a broader public. Hundreds of thousands of Africans took part in World War I, during which they encountered other Africans as well as Europeans. Some were able to travel widely. Contact with American black leaders such as Booker T. Washington, W. E. B. DuBois, and Marcus Garvey and with West Indian intellectuals further stimulated among a few a sense of belonging to an even larger pan-African world. Such notions underlay the growing nationalist movements that contested colonial rule as the twentieth century unfolded.

For the vast majority, however, the most important new sense of belonging that evolved from the colonial experience was not the notion of "Africa"; rather, it was the idea of "tribe" or, in the language of contemporary scholars, that of ethnic identity. African peoples, of course, had long recognized differences among themselves based on language, kinship, clan, village, or state, but these were seldom sharp or clearly defined. Boundaries fluctuated and were hazy; local communities often incorporated a variety of culturally different peoples. The idea of an Africa sharply divided into separate and distinct "tribes" was in fact a European notion that facilitated colonial administration and reflected Europeans' belief in African primitiveness. When the British, for example, began to govern the peoples living along the northern side of Lake Tanganyika, in present-day Tanzania, they found a series of communities that were similar to one another in language and customs but that governed themselves separately and certainly had not regarded themselves as a tribe. It was British attempts to rule them as a single people, first through a "paramount chief" and later through a council of chiefs and elders, that resulted in their being called, collectively, the Nyakyusa. A tribe had been born. By requiring people to identify their tribe on applications for jobs, schools, and identity cards, colonial governments spread the idea of tribe widely within their colonies.

New ethnic identities were not simply imposed by Europeans; Africans increasingly found ethnic or tribal labels useful. This was especially true in rapidly growing urban areas. Surrounded by a bewildering variety of people and in a setting where competition for jobs, housing, and education was very intense, migrants to the city found it helpful to categorize themselves and others in larger ethnic terms. Thus, in many colonial cities, people who spoke similar languages, shared a common culture, or came from the same general part of the country began to think of themselves as a single people—a new tribe. They organized a rich variety of ethnic or tribal associations to provide mutual assistance while in the cities and to send money back home to build schools or clinics. Migrant workers, far from home and concerned to protect their rights to land and to their wives and families, found a sense of security in being part of a recognized tribe, with its chiefs, courts, and established authority.

The Igbo people of southeastern Nigeria represent a case in point. Prior to the twentieth century, they were organized in a series of independently governed village groups. Although they spoke related languages, they had no unifying political system and no myth of common ancestry. Occupying a region of unusually dense population, many of these people eagerly seized on Western education and moved in large numbers to the cities and towns of colonial Nigeria. There they gradually discovered what they had in common and how they differed from the other peoples of Nigeria. By the 1940s, they were organizing on a national level and calling on Igbos everywhere to "sink all differences" in order to achieve "tribal unity, cooperation, and progress of all the Igbos." Fifty years earlier, however, no one had regarded himself or herself as an Igbo. One historian summed up the process of creating African ethnic identities in this way: "Europeans believed Africans belonged to tribes; Africans built tribes to belong to."[24]

Reflections: Who Makes History?

Winners may write history, but they do not make history, at least not alone. Dominant groups everywhere—slave owners, upper classes, men generally, and certainly colonial rulers—have found their actions constrained and their choices limited by the sheer presence of subordinated people and the ability of those people to act. Europeans who sought to make their countries self-sufficient in cotton by requiring colonized Africans to grow it generally found themselves unable to achieve that goal. Missionaries who tried to impose their own understanding of Christianity in the colonies found their converts often unwilling to accept missionary authority or the cultural framework in which the new religion was presented. In the twentieth century, colonial rulers all across Asia and Africa found that their most highly educated subjects became the leaders of those movements seeking to end colonial rule. Clearly this was not what they had intended.

In recent decades, historians have been at pains to uncover the ways in which subordinated people—slaves, workers, peasants, women, the colonized—have been able to act in their own interests, even within the most oppressive conditions. This kind of "history from below" found expression in a famous book about American slavery that was subtitled "The World the Slaves Made." Historians of women's lives have sought to depict women not only as victims of patriarchy but also as historical actors in their own right. Likewise, colonized people in any number of ways actively shaped the history of the colonial era. On occasion, they resisted and rebelled; in various times and places, they embraced, rejected, and transformed a transplanted Christianity; many eagerly sought Western education but later turned it against the colonizers; women both suffered from and creatively coped with the difficulties of colonial life; and everywhere people created new ways of belonging. None of this diminishes the hardships, the enormous inequalities of power, or the exploitation and oppression of the colonial experience. Rather it suggests that history is often made through the struggle of unequal groups and that the outcome corresponds to no one's intentions.

Perhaps we might let Karl Marx have the last word on this endlessly fascinating topic: "Men make their own history," he wrote, "but they do not make it as they please nor under conditions of their own choosing." In the colonial experience of the nineteenth and early twentieth centuries, both the colonizers and the colonized "made history," but neither was able to do so as they pleased.

Second Thoughts

What's the Significance?

To assess your mastery of the material in this chapter, see the **Online Study Guide** at bedfordstmartins.com/strayer.

scramble for Africa
Indian Rebellion, 1857–1858
Congo Free State/Leopold II
cultivation system

cash-crop agriculture
Western-educated elite
Africanization of Christianity
Swami Vivekananda

colonial racism
Edward Blyden
colonial tribalism

Big Picture Questions

1. Why were Asian and African societies incorporated into European colonial empires later than those of the Americas? How would you compare their colonial experiences?
2. In what ways did colonial rule rest upon violence and coercion, and in what ways did it elicit voluntary cooperation or generate benefits for some people?
3. In what respects were colonized people more than victims of colonial conquest and rule? To what extent could they act in their own interests within the colonial situation?
4. Was colonial rule a transforming, even a revolutionary, experience, or did it serve to freeze or preserve existing social and economic patterns? What evidence can you find to support both sides of this argument?

Next Steps: For Further Study

For Web sites and documents related to this chapter, see **Make History** at bedfordstmartins.com/strayer.

A. Adu Boahen, *African Perspectives on Colonialism* (1987). A prominent African scholar examines the colonial experience.

Alice Conklin and Ian Fletcher, *European Imperialism, 1830–1930* (1999). A collection of both classical reflections on empire and examples of modern scholarship.

Scott B. Cook, *Colonial Encounters in the Age of High Imperialism* (1996). Seven case studies of the late-nineteenth-century colonial experience.

Adam Hochschild, *King Leopold's Ghost* (1999). A journalist's evocative account of the horrors of early colonial rule in the Congo.

Douglas Peers, *India under Colonial Rule* (2006). A concise and up-to-date exploration of colonial India.

Bonnie Smith, ed., *Imperialism* (2000). A fine collection of documents, pictures, and commentary on nineteenth- and twentieth-century empires.

Margaret Strobel, *Gender, Sex, and Empire* (1994). A brief account of recent historical thinking about colonial life and gender.

"History of Imperialism," http://members.aol.com/TeacherNet/World.html. A Web site with dozens of links to documents, essays, maps, cartoons, and pictures dealing with modern empires.

PART SIX

The Most Recent Century

1914–2008

Contents

The Twentieth Century: A New Period in World History?

Dividing up time into coherent segments—periods, eras, ages—is the way historians mark major changes in the lives of individuals, local communities, social groups, nations, and civilizations and also in the larger story of humankind as a whole. Because all such divisions are artificial, imposed by scholars on a continuously flowing stream of events, they are endlessly controversial and never more so than in the case of the twentieth century.

Does this most recent 100-year period represent a separate phase of world history? Granting it that status has become conventional in many world history textbooks, including this one, but there are reasons to wonder whether future generations will view it in the same way. One problem, of course, lies in its brevity—less than 100 years, compared to the many centuries or millennia that comprise earlier periods. Furthermore, an immense overload of information about these decades makes it difficult to distinguish "the forest from the trees." We cannot be sure what will prove of lasting significance and what will later seem of only passing importance. Furthermore, because we are so close to the events we study and obviously ignorant of the future, we cannot know if or when this most recent period of world history will end. Or, as some have argued, has it ended already, perhaps with the collapse of the Soviet Union in 1991 or with the attacks of September 11, 2001? If so, are we now in yet another phase of historical development?

We are more certain about the beginning of the twentieth century than its end. For most historians, it was the outbreak of World War I in 1914 that marked the start of a new era. That terrible conflict, after all, represented a fratricidal civil war within Western civilization; it triggered the Russian Revolution and the beginning of world communism; it stimulated many in the colonial world to work for their own independence; and the way it ended set the stage for an even more terrible struggle in World War II.

Old and New in the Twentieth Century

Like most historical periods, the twentieth century both carried on from the past and developed distinctive characteristics. Whether that combination of the old and new merits the designation of a separate era in world history will likely be debated for a long time to come. For our purposes, it will be enough to highlight both the continuities with the past and the sharp changes of this most recent century.

Consider, for example, the world wars that played such an important role in the first half of the century. They grew out of Europeans' persistent inability to embody their civilization within a single state or empire, as China had long done. They also represent a further stage of European rivalries around the globe that had been going on for four centuries. Nonetheless, the world wars of the twentieth century were also new in the extent to which whole populations were mobilized to fight them and in the enormity of the destruction that they caused. During World War II, for example, Hitler's attempted extermination of the Jews in the Holocaust and the United States' dropping of atomic bombs on Japanese cities marked something new in the history of human conflict.

The communist phenomenon provides another illustration of the blending of old and new. The Russian (1917) and Chinese (1949) revolutions, both of which were enormous social upheavals, brought to power regimes committed to remaking their societies from top to bottom along socialist lines. They were the first large-scale attempts in modern world history to undertake such a gigantic task, and in doing so they broke sharply with the capitalist democratic model of the West. They also created a new and global division of humankind, expressed most dramatically in the cold war between the communist East and the capitalist West. On the other hand, the communist experience also drew much from the past. The great revolutions of the twentieth century derived from long-standing conflicts in Russian and Chinese society, particularly between impoverished and exploited peasants and dominant landlord classes. The ideology of those communist governments came from the thinking of the nineteenth-century German intellectual Karl Marx. Their intention, like that of their capitalist enemies, was modernization and industrialization. They simply claimed to do it better—more rapidly and more justly.

Another distinguishing feature of the twentieth century lay in the disintegration of its great empires—the Austro-Hungarian, Ottoman, Russian, British, French, Japanese, Soviet, and more—and in their wake the emergence of dozens of new nation-states. At one level, this is simply the latest turn of the wheel in the endless rise and fall of empires, dating back to the ancient Assyrians. But something new occurred this time, for the very idea of empire was rendered illegitimate in the twentieth century, much as slavery lost its international acceptance in the nineteenth century. The superpowers of the second half of the twentieth century—the Soviet Union and the United States—both claimed an anticolonial ideology, even as both of them constructed their own "empires" of a different kind. By the beginning of the twenty-first century, a world of more than 200 nation-states had come to pass, each claiming sovereignty and legal equality with all the others. This represented a distinctly new global ordering of peoples.

The less visible underlying processes of the twentieth century, just like the more dramatic wars, revolutions, and political upheavals, also had roots in the past as well as new expressions in the new century. Perhaps the most fundamental process was explosive population growth, as human numbers more than quadrupled since 1900, leaving the planet with about 6.7 billion people by 2008. This was an absolutely

Globalization in Action:
Trade and Investment in the
Early Twenty-first Century
(p. 726)

unprecedented rate of growth that conditioned practically every other feature of the century's history. Still, this new element of twentieth-century world history built upon earlier achievements, most notably the increased food supply deriving from the global spread of American crops such as corn and potatoes. Improvements in medicine and sanitation, which grew out of the earlier Scientific and Industrial revolutions, likewise drove down death rates and thus spurred population growth.

While global population increased fourfold in the twentieth century, industrial output grew fortyfold. This unprecedented economic growth, despite large variations over time and place, was associated with a cascading rate of scientific and technological innovation as well as with the extension of industrial production to many regions of the world. This too was a wholly novel feature of twentieth-century world history and, combined with population growth, resulted in an extraordinary and mounting human impact on the environment. Historian J. R. McNeill wrote that "this is the first time in human history that we have altered ecosystems with such intensity, on such a scale, and with such speed.... The human race, without intending anything of the sort, has undertaken a gigantic uncontrolled experiment on the earth."[1] From a longer-term perspective, of course, these developments represent a continued unfolding of the Scientific and Industrial revolutions. Both began in Europe, but in the twentieth century they largely lost their unique association with the West as they took hold in many cultures. Furthermore, the human impact on the earth itself and other living creatures has a history dating back to the extinction of some large mammals at the hands of Paleolithic hunters.

Much the same might be said about that other grand process of twentieth-century world history—globalization. It too has a genealogy reaching deep into the past, reflected in the Silk Road trading network; Indian Ocean and trans-Saharan commerce; the spread of Buddhism, Christianity, and Islam; and the Columbian exchange. But the twentieth century deepened and extended the connections among the distinct peoples, nations, and regions of the world in ways unparalleled in earlier centuries. A few strokes on a keyboard can send money racing around the planet; radio, television, and the Internet link the world in an unprecedented network of communication; the warming of the lower atmosphere due to the accumulation of greenhouse gases portends radical changes for the whole planet; far more people than ever before produce for and depend on the world market; and global inequalities increasingly surface as sources of international conflict. For good or ill, we live—all of us—in a new phase of an ancient process.

Three Regions—One World

The chapters that follow explore these themes of twentieth-century world history in a particular way. Chapters 21, 22, and 23 tell the separate stories of three major regions or groups of countries—the Western world; the communist world; and the third world, sometimes called the world of developing countries. Chapter 21, which focuses on the Western world of capitalist countries, highlights the dramatic changes that occurred at the center of the global network. The European heartland of the world system collapsed in war and economic depression during the first half of the century but recovered in the second half as leadership of the Western world passed to the United States.

Accompanying those changes internal to the West was the profound challenge of world communism. Chapter 22 addresses four features of the communist phenomenon: the revolutionary origins of communism, especially in Russia and China; the efforts of those two communist giants to build new and socialist societies; the global conflict of the cold war, which arose from the expansion of communism; and the amazing abandonment of communism as the century ended.

Chapter 23 turns the historical spotlight on the colonial world of Asia and Africa. Two major themes serve to structure the twentieth-century history of this vast region. The first focuses attention on the struggles for independence, the end of colonial empires, and the emergence of dozens of new nations. The second describes the increasingly important role on the global stage that these new states have played in the second half of the century. The assertion of African, Asian, and Middle Eastern peoples, joined by those of Latin America, made the world of 2000 a very different place from that of a century earlier.

These twentieth-century histories of the Western world, the communist world, and the third world not only paralleled one another but also frequently intersected and overlapped, as Chapters 21, 22, and 23 repeatedly indicate. All of them, however, were also part of an even larger story, known everywhere now as globalization. The post–World War II acceleration of this much older process is the grand theme of Chapter 24, which examines four dimensions of recent globalization—economic relationships, feminism, religious fundamentalism, and environmentalism.

Perhaps there is enough that is new about the twentieth century to treat it, tentatively, as a distinct era in human history, but only what happens next will determine how this most recent century will be understood by later generations. Will it be regarded as the beginning of the end of the modern age, as human demands upon the earth prove unsustainable? Or will it be seen as the midpoint of an ongoing process that extends a full modernity to the entire planet? Like all of our ancestors, every one of them, we too live in a fog when contemplating our futures and see more clearly only in retrospect. In this strange way, the future shapes the telling of the past, even as the past shapes the living of the future.

Landmarks of the Most Recent Century, 1914–2008

1910	1920	1930	1940	1950

The Western/ Developed World

■ **1919** Treaty of Versailles, ending World War I

■ **1933** Hitler's rise to power in Germany

■ **1945** Bombing of Hiroshima/Nagasaki (first use of nuclear weapons in combat)

1957 ■ European Economic Community established

1914–1918 World War I

■ **1929** Stock market crash and beginning of Great Depression

■ **1937** Japan invades China, beginning World War II in Asia

1939–1945 World War II/Holocaust in Europe

The Communist World

■ **1921** Founding of Chinese Communist Party

1945–1950 Expansion of communism in Eastern Europe

■ **1917** Russian Revolution

1929–1953 Stalin in power in USSR

■ **1949** Communist triumph in Chinese Revolution

1934–1935 Long March in China

1950–1953 Korean War

The Third World/ Developing World

1923–1938 Turkey's secular modernization/Kemal Atatürk

■ **1947** Independence of India/Pakistan

■ **1919** May Fourth movement in China

■ **1928** Muslim Brotherhood established in Egypt

■ **1949** Independence of Indonesia

1959 ■ Cuban Revolution

The Whole World (Markers of Globalization)

1919–1946 League of Nations

■ **1945** Founding of United Nations

■ **1945** World Bank/International Monetary Fund established

1946–1991 Cold war

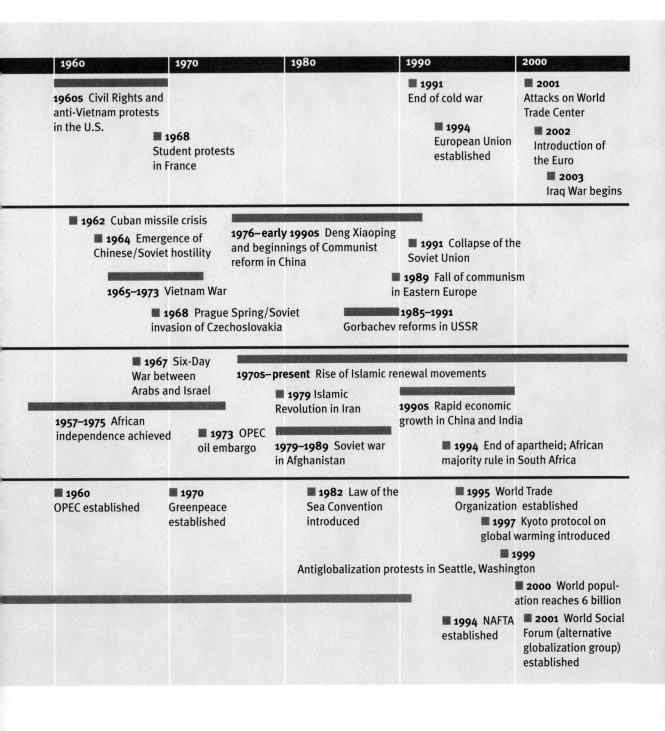

1960	1970	1980	1990	2000

1960s Civil Rights and anti-Vietnam protests in the U.S.

■ **1968** Student protests in France

■ **1991** End of cold war

■ **1994** European Union established

■ **2001** Attacks on World Trade Center

■ **2002** Introduction of the Euro

■ **2003** Iraq War begins

■ **1962** Cuban missile crisis

■ **1964** Emergence of Chinese/Soviet hostility

1976–early 1990s Deng Xiaoping and beginnings of Communist reform in China

■ **1991** Collapse of the Soviet Union

1965–1973 Vietnam War

■ **1989** Fall of communism in Eastern Europe

■ **1968** Prague Spring/Soviet invasion of Czechoslovakia

1985–1991 Gorbachev reforms in USSR

■ **1967** Six-Day War between Arabs and Israel

1970s–present Rise of Islamic renewal movements

■ **1979** Islamic Revolution in Iran

1990s Rapid economic growth in China and India

1957–1975 African independence achieved

■ **1973** OPEC oil embargo

1979–1989 Soviet war in Afghanistan

■ **1994** End of apartheid; African majority rule in South Africa

■ **1960** OPEC established

■ **1970** Greenpeace established

■ **1982** Law of the Sea Convention introduced

■ **1995** World Trade Organization established

■ **1997** Kyoto protocol on global warming introduced

■ **1999** Antiglobalization protests in Seattle, Washington

■ **2000** World population reaches 6 billion

■ **1994** NAFTA established

■ **2001** World Social Forum (alternative globalization group) established

The Collapse and Recovery of Europe

1914–1970s

In November 2005, at the age of 109, Alfred Anderson died in a nursing home in Scotland. He was one of a rapidly dwindling group of men who had served in World War I. He was also, apparently, the last survivor of the famous Christmas truce of 1914, when British and German soldiers, enemies on the battlefield of that war, briefly mingled, exchanged gifts, and played football in the "no-man's land" that lay between their entrenchments in Belgium. "I was told," he said several years before his death, "that I was fighting a war that would end all wars, but that wasn't the case." He was especially dismayed when in 2003 his own unit, the famous Black Watch regiment, was ordered into Iraq along with other British forces.[1] Despite his disappointment at the many conflicts that followed World War I, Anderson's own lifetime had witnessed the fulfillment of the promise of the Christmas truce. By the time he died, the major European nations had put aside their centuries-long hostilities, and war between Britain and Germany, which had erupted twice in the twentieth century, seemed unthinkable. What happened to Europe, and to the larger civilization of which it was a part, during the life of this one man is the focus of this chapter.

THE "GREAT WAR," WHICH CAME TO BE CALLED THE FIRST WORLD WAR (1914–1918), effectively launched the twentieth century, considered as a new phase of world history. That bitter conflict—essentially a European civil war with a global reach—was followed by the economic meltdown of the Great Depression, by the rise of Nazi Germany and the horror of

---

Over the Top: Among the most famous paintings to emerge from World War I, this work depicts the absurdity, futility, and despair that accompanied trench warfare during that conflict. More specifically, it reflects the experience of an eighty-man British unit that was sent "over the top" in late 1917; sixty-eight of them perished in the first few minutes of the battle. Three months later, John Nash, one of the twelve survivors, painted this haunting picture from his memory of that horrendous experience. (Imperial War Museum, London, UK/The Bridgeman Art Library) the Holocaust, and by an even bloodier and more destructive World War II. During those three decades, Western Europe, for more than a century the dominant and dominating center of the modern "world system," largely self-destructed, in a process with profound and long-term implications far beyond Europe itself. By 1945, an outside observer might well have thought that Western civilization, which for several centuries was in the ascendancy on the global stage, had damaged itself beyond repair.

In the second half of the century, however, that civilization proved quite resilient. Its Western European heartland recovered remarkably from the devastation of war, rebuilt its industrial economy, and set aside its war-prone nationalist passions in a loose European Union. But as Europe revived after 1945, it lost both its overseas colonial possessions and its position as the political, economic, and military core of Western civilization. That role now passed across the Atlantic to the United States. This was a major change in the historical development of the West. The offspring now overshadowed its parent.

Map 21.1   The World in 1914
A map of the world in 1914 shows an unprecedented situation in which one people—Europeans or those of European descent—exercised enormous control and influence over virtually the entire planet.

The First World War: European Civilization in Crisis, 1914–1918

Since 1500, Europe had assumed an increasingly prominent position on the global stage, driven by its growing military capacity and the marvels of its Scientific and Industrial revolutions. By 1900, Europeans, or people with a European ancestry, largely controlled the world's other peoples through their formal empires, their informal influence, or the weight of their numbers (see Map 21.1). That unique

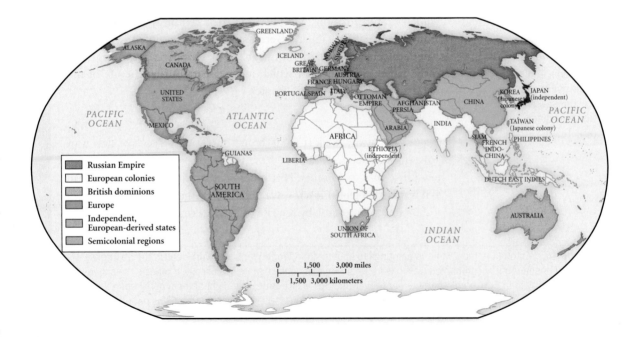

situation provided the foundation for Europeans' pride, self-confidence, and sense of superiority. Few could have imagined that this "proud tower" of European dominance would lie shattered less than half a century later. The starting point in that unraveling was the First World War.

An Accident Waiting to Happen

Europe's modern transformation and its global ascendancy were certainly not accompanied by a growing unity or stability among its own peoples—quite the opposite. The most obvious division was among its competing states, a long-standing feature of European political life. Those historical rivalries further sharpened as both Italy and Germany joined their fragmented territories into two major new powers around 1870. German unification had occurred in the context of a short war with France (the Franco-Prussian War of 1870–1871), which embittered relations between these two large countries for the next half century. More generally, the arrival on the international scene of a powerful and rapidly industrializing Germany, seeking its "place in the sun" as Kaiser Wilhelm put it, was a disruptive new element in European political life, especially for the more established powers, such as Britain, France, and Russia. Since the defeat of Napoleon in 1815, a fragile and fluctuating balance of power had generally maintained the peace among Europe's major countries. By the early twentieth century, that balance of power was expressed in two rival alliances, the Triple Alliance of Germany, Austria, and Italy and the Triple Entente of Russia, France, and Britain. It was those commitments, undertaken in the interests of national security, that transformed a minor incident in the Balkans into a conflagration that consumed all of Europe.

That incident occurred on June 28, 1914, when a Serbian nationalist assassinated the heir to the Austrian throne, Archduke Franz Ferdinand. To the rulers of Austria, the surging nationalism of Serbian Slavs was a mortal threat to the cohesion of their fragile multinational empire, which included other Slavic peoples as well, and they determined to crush it. But behind Austria lay its far more powerful ally, Germany; and behind tiny Serbia lay Russia, with its self-proclaimed mission of protecting other Slavic peoples; and allied to Russia were the French and the British. Thus a system of alliances intended to keep the peace created obligations that drew the Great Powers of Europe into a general war by early August 1914 (see Map 21.2).

The outbreak of that war was an accident, in that none of the major states planned or predicted the archduke's assassination or deliberately sought a prolonged conflict, but the system of rigid alliances made Europe prone to that kind of accident. Moreover, behind those alliances lay other factors that contributed to the eruption of war and shaped its character. One of them was a mounting popular nationalism (see Chapter 17). Slavic nationalism and Austrian opposition to it certainly lay at the heart of the war's beginning. More important, the rulers of the major countries of Europe saw the world as an arena of conflict and competition

■ **Explanation**
What aspects of Europe's nineteenth-century history contributed to the First World War?

Map 21.2   Europe on the Eve of World War I
Despite many elements of common culture, Europe in 1914 was a powder keg, with its major states armed to the teeth and divided into two rival alliances. In the early stages of the war, Italy changed sides to join the French, British, and Russians.

among rival nation-states. The Great Powers of Europe competed intensely for colonies, spheres of influence, and superiority in armaments. Schools, mass media, and military service had convinced millions of ordinary Europeans that their national identities were profoundly and personally meaningful. The public pressure of these competing nationalisms allowed statesmen little room for compromise and ensured widespread popular support, at least initially, for the decision to go to war. Men rushed to recruiting offices, fearing that the war might end before they could enlist. Celebratory parades sent them off to the front. For conservative governments, the prospect of war was a welcome occasion for national unity in the face of the mounting class- and gender-based conflicts of European society.

Also contributing to the war was an industrialized militarism. Europe's armed rivalries had long ensured that military men enjoyed great social prestige, and most heads of state wore uniforms in public. All of the Great Powers had substantial standing armies and, except for Britain, relied on conscription (compulsory military service) to staff them. One expression of the quickening rivalry among these states was a mounting arms race in naval warships, particularly between Germany and Britain. Furthermore, each of the major states had developed elaborate "war plans" spelling out in great detail the movement of men and materials that should occur immediately upon the outbreak of war. Such plans created a hair-trigger mentality, since each country had an incentive to strike first so that its particular strategy could be implemented on schedule and without interruption or surprise. The rapid industrialization of warfare had generated an array of novel weapons, including submarines, tanks, airplanes, poison gas, machines guns, and barbed wire. This new military technology contributed to the staggering casualties of the war, including some 10 million deaths; perhaps twice that number wounded, crippled, or disfigured; and countless women for whom there would be no husbands or children.

Europe's imperial reach around the world likewise shaped the scope and conduct of the war. It funneled colonial troops and laborers by the hundreds of thousands into the war effort, with men from Africa, India, China, Southeast Asia, Australia, New Zealand, Canada, and South Africa taking part in the conflict. Battles raged in Africa and the South Pacific as British and French forces sought to seize German colonies abroad. Japan, allied with Britain, took various German possessions in China and the Pacific and made heavy demands on China itself. The Ottoman Empire, which entered the conflict on the side of Germany, became the site of intense military actions and witnessed an Arab revolt against Ottoman control. Finally, the United States, after initially seeking to avoid involvement in European quarrels, joined the war in 1917 when German submarines threatened American shipping. Some 2 million Americans took part in the first U.S. military action on European soil and helped turn the tide in favor of the British and French. Thus the war, though centered in Europe, had global dimensions and certainly merited its familiar title as a "world war."

Legacies of the Great War

The Great War was a conflict that shattered almost every expectation. Most Europeans believed in the late summer of 1914 that "the boys will be home by Christmas," but instead the war ground relentlessly on for more than four years

■ Change
In what ways did World War I mark new departures in the history of the twentieth century?

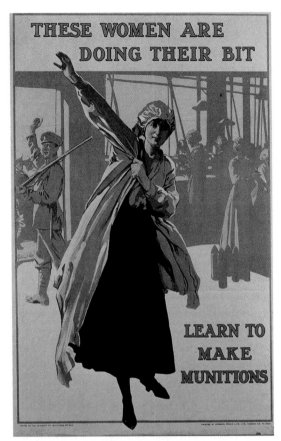

THESE WOMEN ARE DOING THEIR BIT

LEARN TO MAKE MUNITIONS

Women and the Great War
World War I temporarily brought a halt to the women's suffrage movement as well as to women's activities on behalf of international peace. Most women on both sides actively supported their countries' war efforts, as suggested by this British wartime poster, inviting women to work in the munitions industry. (Eileen Tweedy/The Art Archive)

before ending in a German defeat in November 1918. At the beginning, most military experts expected a war of movement and attack, but it soon bogged down on the western front into a war of attrition, in which "trench warfare" resulted in enormous casualties while gaining or losing only a few yards of muddy, blood-soaked ground. Extended battles lasting months—such as those at Verdun and the Somme—generated casualties of a million or more each, as the destructive potential of industrialized warfare made itself tragically felt. Moreover, everywhere it became a "total war," requiring the mobilization of each country's entire population. Thus the authority of governments expanded greatly. The German state, for example, assumed such control over the economy that its policies became known as "war socialism." Vast propaganda campaigns sought to arouse citizens by depicting a cruel and inhuman enemy who killed innocent children and violated women. In factories, women replaced the men who had left for the battlefront, while labor unions agreed to suspend strikes and accept sacrifices for the common good.

No less surprising were the outcomes of the war. In the European cockpit of that conflict, the unprecedented casualties, particularly among elite and well-educated groups, and the physical destruction, especially in France, led to a widespread disillusionment among intellectuals with their own civilization. The war seemed to mock the Enlightenment values of progress, tolerance, and rationality. Who could believe any longer that the West was superior or that its vaunted science and technology were unquestionably good things? In the most famous novel to emerge from the war, the German veteran Erich Remarque's *All Quiet on the Western Front*, one soldier expressed what many no doubt felt: "It must all be lies and of no account when the culture of a thousand years could not prevent this stream of blood being poured out."

Furthermore, from the collapse of the German, Russian, and Austrian empires emerged a new map of Central Europe with an independent Poland, Czechoslovakia, Yugoslavia, and other nations (see Map 21.3). Such new states were based on the principle of "national self-determination," a concept championed by the U.S. president Woodrow Wilson, but each of them also contained dissatisfied ethnic minorities, who claimed the same principle. In Russia, the strains of war triggered a vast revolutionary upheaval that brought the radical Bolsheviks to power in 1917 and took Russia out of the war. Thus was launched world communism, which was to play such a prominent role in the history of the twentieth century (see Chapter 22).

Map 21.3   Europe and the Middle East after World War I
The Great War brought into existence a number of new states that were carved out of the old German, Austro-Hungarian, Russian, and Ottoman empires. Turkey and the new states in Europe were independent, but those in the Middle East—Syria, Palestine, Iraq, and Transjordan—were administered by Britain or France as mandates of the League of Nations.

    The Treaty of Versailles, which formally concluded the war in 1919, proved in retrospect to have established conditions that generated a second world war only twenty years later. In that treaty, Germany lost its colonial empire and 15 percent of its European territory, was required to pay heavy reparations to the winners, had its military forces severely restricted, and had to accept sole responsibility for the outbreak of the war. All of this created immense resentment in Germany. One of the country's many demobilized and disillusioned soldiers declared in 1922: "It cannot be that two million Germans should have fallen in vain.... No, we do not pardon, we demand—vengeance."[2] His name was Adolf Hitler, and within two decades he had begun to exact that vengeance.

The Great War generated profound changes in the world beyond Europe as well. During the war itself, Ottoman authorities, suspecting that some of their Armenian population were collaborating with the Russian enemy, massacred or deported an estimated 1 million Armenians. Although the term had not yet been invented, those atrocities merit the label of "genocide" and established a precedent on which the Nazis later built. The war also brought a final end to a declining Ottoman Empire, creating the modern map of the Middle East, with the new states of Turkey, Syria, Iraq, Jordan, and Palestine. Thus Arabs emerged from Turkish rule, but many of them fell for a time under the control of the British or French, who were acting on behalf of the League of Nations (see Map 21.3). Conflicting British promises to both Arabs and Jews regarding Palestine set the stage for an enduring struggle over that ancient and holy land.

In the world of European colonies, the war echoed loudly. Millions of Asian and African men had watched Europeans butcher one another without mercy, had gained new military skills and political awareness, and returned home with less respect for their rulers and with expectations for better treatment as a reward for their service. To gain Indian support for the war, the British had publicly promised to put that colony on the road to self-government, an announcement that set the stage for the independence struggle that followed. In East Asia, Japan emerged strengthened from the war, with European support for its claim to take over German territory and privileges in China. That news enraged Chinese nationalists and among a few sparked an interest in Soviet-style communism, for only the new communist rulers of Russia seemed willing to end the imperialist penetration of China.

Finally, the First World War brought the United States to center stage as a global power. Its manpower had contributed much to the defeat of Germany, and its financial resources turned the United States from a debtor nation into Europe's creditor. When Woodrow Wilson arrived in Paris for the peace conference in 1919, he was greeted with an almost religious enthusiasm, for his famous Fourteen Points seemed to herald a new kind of international life, one based on moral principles rather than secret deals and imperialist machinations. Particularly appealing to many was his idea for the League of Nations, a new international peacekeeping organization based on the principle of "collective security" and intended to avoid any repetition of the horrors of the war just ended. Wilson's idealistic vision largely failed, however. Germany was treated more harshly than he had wished. And in his own country, the U.S. Senate refused to join the league, on which he had pinned his hopes for a lasting peace. Its opponents feared that Americans would be forced to bow to "the will of other nations." That refusal seriously weakened the League of Nations as a vehicle for a new international order.

Capitalism Unraveling: The Great Depression

The aftermath of war brought substantial social and cultural changes to the European and American victors in that conflict. Integrating millions of returning veterans into ordinary civilian life was no easy task, for they had experienced horrors almost beyond imagination. Governments sought to accommodate them—for example, with housing programs called "homes for heroes" and with an emphasis on traditional family values. French authorities proclaimed Mother's Day as a new holiday designed to encourage childbearing and thus replace the millions lost in the war.

Nonetheless, the war had loosened the hold of tradition in many ways. Enormous casualties promoted social mobility, allowing commoners to move into positions previously dominated by aristocrats. Women increasingly gained the right to vote. Young middle-class women, sometimes known as "flappers," began to flout convention by appearing at nightclubs, smoking, dancing, drinking hard liquor, cutting their hair short, wearing more revealing clothing, and generally expressing a more open sexuality. A new consumerism encouraged those who could to acquire cars, washing machines, vacuum cleaners, electric irons, gas ovens, and other newly available products. Radio and the movies now became vehicles of popular culture, transmitting American jazz to Europe and turning Hollywood stars into international celebrities.

Far and away the most influential change of the postwar decades lay in the Great Depression. If World War I represented the political collapse of Europe, this catastrophic downturn suggested that its economic system was likewise failing. During the nineteenth century, European industrial capitalism had spurred the most substantial economic growth in world history and had raised the living standards of millions, but to many people it was a troubling system. Its very success generated an individualistic materialism that seemed to conflict with older values of community and spiritual life. To socialists and many others, its immense social inequalities were unacceptable. Furthermore, its evident instability—with cycles of boom and bust, expansion and recession—generated profound anxiety and threatened the livelihood of both industrial workers and those who had gained a modest toehold in the middle class.

Never had the instabilities of capitalism been so evident or so devastating as during the decade that followed the outbreak of the Great Depression in 1929. All across the Euro-American heartland of the capitalist world, this vaunted economic system seemed to unravel. For the rich, it meant contracting stock prices that wiped out paper fortunes almost overnight. On the day that the American stock market initially crashed (October 24, 1929), eleven Wall Street financiers committed suicide, some by jumping out of skyscrapers. Banks closed, and many people lost their life's savings. Investment dried up, world trade dropped by 62 percent within a few years, and businesses contracted when they were unable to sell their products. For ordinary people, the worst feature of the Great Depression was the loss of work. Unemployment soared everywhere, and in both Germany and the United States it

■ **Connection**

In what ways was the Great Depression a global phenomenon?

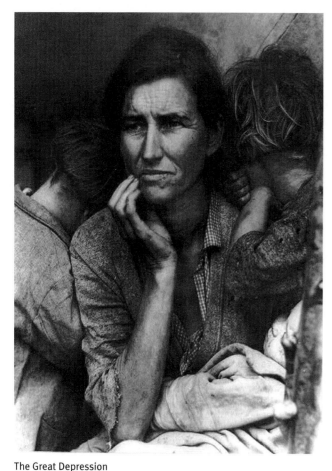

The Great Depression
This photograph of an impoverished American mother of three children, which was taken in 1936, came to symbolize the agonies of the Depression and the apparent breakdown of capitalism in the United States. (Library of Congress)

reached 30 percent or more by 1932 (see the Snapshot on p. 635). Vacant factories, soup kitchens, bread lines, shantytowns, and beggars came to symbolize the human reality of this economic disaster.

Explaining its onset, its spread from America to Europe and beyond, and its continuation for a decade has been a complicated task for historians. Part of the story lies in the United States' booming economy during the 1920s. In a country physically untouched by the war, wartime demand had greatly stimulated agricultural and industrial capacity. By the end of the 1920s, its farms and factories were producing more goods than could be sold because a highly unequal distribution of income meant that many people could not afford to buy the products that American factories were churning out. Nor were major European countries able to purchase those goods. Germany and Austria had to make huge reparation payments and were able to do so only with extensive U.S. loans. Britain and France, which were much indebted to the United States, depended on those reparations to repay their loans. Furthermore, Europeans generally had recovered enough to begin producing some of their own goods, and their expanding production further reduced the demand for American products. Meanwhile, a speculative stock market frenzy had driven up stock prices to an unsustainable level. When that bubble burst in late 1929, this intricately connected and fragile economic network across the Atlantic collapsed like a house of cards.

Much as Europe's worldwide empires had globalized the war, so too its economic linkages globalized the Great Depression. Countries or colonies tied to exporting one or two products were especially hard-hit. Chile, which was dependent on copper mining, found the value of its exports cut by 80 percent. In an effort to maintain the price of coffee, Brazil destroyed enough of its coffee crop to have supplied the world for a year. Colonial Southeast Asia, the world's major rubber-producing region, saw the demand for its primary export drop dramatically as automobile sales in Europe and the United States were cut in half. In Britain's West African colony of the Gold Coast (present-day Ghana), farmers who had staked their economic lives on producing cocoa for the world market were badly hurt by the collapse of commodity prices. Depending on a single crop or product rendered these societies extraordinarily vulnerable to changes in the world market.

The Great Depression sharply challenged the governments of capitalist countries, which generally had believed that the economy would regulate itself through the market. The market's apparent failure to self-correct led many people to look twice at the Soviet Union, a communist state whose more equal distribution of income and state-controlled economy had generated an impressive growth with no unemployment in the 1930s, even as the capitalist world was reeling. No Western country opted for the dictatorial and draconian socialism of the USSR, but in Britain, France, and Scandinavia, the Depression energized a "democratic socialism" that sought greater regulation of the economy and a more equal distribution of wealth through peaceful means and electoral politics.

The United States' response to the Great Depression came in the form of President Franklin Roosevelt's New Deal (1933–1942), a complex tangle of reforms intended to restore pre-Depression prosperity and to prevent future calamities. These measures reflected the thinking of John Maynard Keynes, a prominent British economist who argued that government actions and spending programs could moderate the recessions and depressions to which capitalist economies were prone. Although this represented a departure from standard economic thinking, none of it was really "socialist," even if some of the New Deal's opponents labeled it as such.

Nonetheless, Roosevelt's efforts permanently altered the relationship among government, the private economy, and individual citizens. Through immediate programs of public spending (for dams, highways, bridges, and parks), the New Deal sought to "prime the pump" of the economy and thus reduce unemployment. The

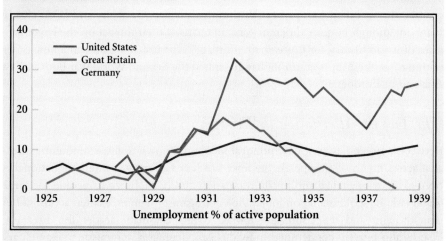

Snapshot **Comparing the Impact of the Depression**[3]

As industrial production dropped during the Depression, unemployment soared. Yet the larger Western capitalist countries differed considerably in the duration and extent of this unemployment. Note especially the differences between Germany and the United States. How might you account for this difference?

Unemployment % of active population

New Deal's longer-term reforms, such as the Social Security system, the minimum wage, and various relief and welfare programs, attempted to build an economic floor below which the poor, the unemployed, and the elderly could not fall. By supporting the organization of labor unions, the New Deal strengthened their hand against business. Through farm subsidies, it created a permanent agribusiness that made possible continued production without the risk of falling prices. Finally, the vast array of government agencies that were created during the New Deal instituted a new degree of federal regulation and supervision of the economy.

Ultimately, none of the New Deal's programs worked very well to end the Great Depression. Not until the massive government spending required by World War II kicked in did that economic disaster abate in the United States. The most successful efforts to cope with the Depression came from unlikely places—Nazi Germany and an increasingly militaristic Japan.

Democracy Denied: Comparing Italy, Germany, and Japan

Despite the victory of the democratic powers in World War I—Britain, France, and the United States—their democratic political ideals and cultural values of liberalism and individual freedom came under sharp attack in the aftermath of that bloody conflict. One challenge derived from communism, which was initiated in the Russian Revolution of 1917 and expressed most fully in the cold war during the second half of the twentieth century (see Chapter 22). In the 1920s and 1930s, however, the more immediate challenge to the victors in the Great War came from highly authoritarian, intensely nationalistic, territorially aggressive, and ferociously anti-communist regimes, particularly those that took shape in Italy, Germany, and Japan. The common features of these three countries drew them together by 1936–1937 in a political alliance directed against the Soviet Union and international communism. In 1940, they solidified their relationship in a formal military alliance, creating the so-called Axis powers. Within this alliance, Germany and Japan clearly stand out, though in quite different ways, in terms of their impact on the larger patterns of world history, for it was their efforts to "establish and maintain a new order of things," as the Axis Pact put it, that generated the Second World War both in East Asia and in Europe.

The Fascist Alternative in Europe

■ Change

In what ways did fascism challenge the ideas and practices of European liberalism and democracy?

Between 1919 and 1945, a new political ideology, known as fascism, found expression across much of Europe. At the level of ideas, fascism was intensely nationalistic, seeking to revitalize and purify the nation and to mobilize its people for some grand task. Its spokesmen condoned violence against enemies, exalted action rather than thought and reflection, and looked to a charismatic leader for direction. Fascists also bitterly condemned individualism, liberalism, feminism, parliamentary democracy, and communism, all of which, they argued, divided and weakened the nation. In their determination to overthrow existing regimes, they were revolutionary; in their celebration of traditional values and their opposition to much of modern life, however, they were conservative or reactionary.

Such ideas appealed to dissatisfied or unfulfilled people in all social classes. In the devastation that followed the First World War, the numbers of such people grew substantially. Some among the middle and upper classes feared the advance of socialism and communism; small-scale merchants, artisans, and farmers felt threatened with the loss of their independence to either big business or socialist revolution; demobilized soldiers had few prospects and nursed many resentments; intellectuals were appalled by the materialism and artificiality of modern life. Such people had lost faith in the capacity of liberal democracy and capitalism to create a good society and to protect their interests. Some among them proved a receptive audience for the message of fascism.

Small fascist movements appeared in many Western European countries, including France, Great Britain, and the Netherlands, but they had little political impact. More substantial movements took shape in Austria, Hungary, and Romania. In Spain, the rise of a fascist movement led to a bitter civil war (1936–1939) and a dictatorial regime that lasted into the 1970s. But in Italy and especially in Germany, such movements achieved prolonged power in major states, with devastating consequences for Europe and the world.

The fascist alternative took shape first in Italy. That nation had become a unified state only in 1870 and had yet to develop a thoroughly modern and democratic culture. Conservative landlords controlled most of the rural areas both economically and politically. In the north, however, a significant industrial society arose in the late nineteenth century, and with it came considerable tension between a factory working class and a substantial middle class. The First World War introduced still other social disruptions in the form of resentful veterans, who lacked both employment and popular respect, and patriots who believed that Italy had not gained the territory it deserved from the Treaty of Versailles. During the economic crisis following the war, trade unions, peasant movements, and various communist and socialist parties threatened the established social order with a wave of strikes and land seizures.

Into this setting stepped a charismatic orator and a former journalist with a socialist background, Benito Mussolini (1883–1945). With the help of a private army of disillusioned veterans and jobless men known as the Black Shirts, Mussolini swept to power in 1922, promising an alternative to both communism and ineffective democratic rule. Considerable violence accompanied Mussolini's rise to power as bands of Black Shirts destroyed the offices of socialist newspapers, attacked striking workers, and forced socialists to drink castor oil. Fearful of communism, big business threw its support to Mussolini, who promised order in the streets, an end to bickering party-based politics, and the maintenance of the traditional social order. That Mussolini's government allegedly made the trains run on time became

The Faces of European Fascism
Benito Mussolini (left) and Adolf Hitler came to symbolize fascism in Europe in the several decades between the two world wars. In this photograph from September 1937, they are reviewing German troops in Munich during Mussolini's visit to Germany, a trip that deepened the growing relationship between their two countries.
(Luce/Keystone/Getty Images)

evidence that these promises might be fulfilled. The symbol of this movement was the *fasces*, a bundle of birch rods bound together around an axe, which represented power and strength in unity and derived from ancient Rome. Thus fascism was born.

Mussolini promised his mass following a generous social program, but once he attained power, he concentrated instead on building state power. Democracy in Italy was suspended, and opponents were imprisoned, deported, or sometimes executed. Independent labor unions and peasant groups were disbanded, as were all political parties except the Fascist Party. In economic life, a "corporate state" took shape, at least in theory, in which workers, employers, and various professional groups were organized into corporations that were supposed to settle their disagreements and determine economic policy under the supervision of the state.

Culturally, fascists invoked various aspects of traditional Italian life. Mussolini, though personally an atheist, embraced the Catholic culture of Italy in a series of agreements with the Church (the Lateran Accords of 1929) that made the Vatican a sovereign state and Catholicism Italy's national religion. In fascist propaganda, women were portrayed in highly traditional terms as domestic creatures, particularly as mothers creating new citizens for the fascist state, with no hint of equality or liberation. Nationalists were delighted when Italy invaded Ethiopia in 1935, avenging the embarrassing defeat that Italians suffered at the hands of Ethiopians in 1896. In the eyes of Mussolini and fascist believers, all of this was the beginning of a "new Roman Empire" that would revitalize Italian society and give it a global mission.

Hitler and the Nazis

Far more important in the long run was the German expression of European fascism, which took shape as the Nazi Party under the leadership of Adolf Hitler (1889–1945). In many respects, it was similar to its Italian counterpart. Both espoused an extreme nationalism, openly advocated the use of violence as a political tool, generated a single-party dictatorship, were led by charismatic figures, despised parliamentary democracy, hated communism, and viewed war as a positive and ennobling experience.[4] The circumstances that gave rise to the Nazi movement

■ Comparison
What was distinctive about the German expression of fascism? What was the basis of popular support for the Nazis?

were likewise broadly similar to those of Italian fascism, although the Nazis did not achieve national power until 1933. As World War I ended, the German imperial state, itself less than a half century old, collapsed, and democratic politicians of a new government—known as the Weimar Republic—were left to negotiate the peace settlement. Traditional elites were either disgraced or had withdrawn from public life because their regime had lost the war. However, these defeated leaders never explicitly took responsibility for the defeat; instead they attacked the democratic politicians who had the unfortunate task of signing the peace settlement and enforcing it. In this atmosphere, there arose a myth that Germany had not really lost the war but that civilians, especially socialists, communists, and Jews, had betrayed the nation, "stabbing it in the back."

As in postwar Italy, liberal or democratic political leaders during the 1920s faced the active or silent animosity of much of the German population. Vigilante groups of veterans (the Freikorps) assassinated hundreds of liberal politicians, journalists, and supporters of the Weimar regime, and they received only mild punishments from conservative judges, who also detested the republic. These small groups of discontented veterans, hostile to democracy, gradually drew support from the middle classes as well as from conservative landowners because of the ruinous inflation of 1923 and then the Great Depression. The German economy largely ground to a halt in the early 1930s amid massive unemployment among workers and the middle class alike. Everyone demanded decisive governmental action. Many industrial workers turned to socialists and communists for answers; others looked to fascism. Large numbers of middle-class people deserted moderate political parties in favor of conservative and radical right-wing movements.

This was the context in which Adolf Hitler's National Socialist, or Nazi, Party gained growing public support. Founded shortly after the end of World War I, the Nazi Party under Hitler's leadership proclaimed a message of intense German nationalism cast in terms of racial superiority, bitter hatred for Jews as an alien presence, passionate opposition to communism, a determination to rescue Germany from the humiliating requirements of the Treaty of Versailles, and a willingness to decisively tackle the country's economic problems. Throughout the 1920s, the Nazis were a minor presence in German politics, gaining only 2.6 percent of the vote in the national elections of 1928. Just four years later, however, in the wake of the Depression's terrible impact and the Weimar government's inability to respond effectively, the Nazis attracted 37 percent of the vote. In 1933, Hitler was legally installed as the chancellor of the German government. Thus did the Weimar Republic, a democratic regime that never gained broad support, give way to the Third Reich.

Once in power, Hitler quickly suppressed all other political parties, abolished labor unions, arrested thousands of opponents, controlled the press and radio, and in general assumed police power over society far more thoroughly than Italian fascists were able to achieve. German workers, for example, never rose up to challenge the Nazi regime, whereas Italian workers engaged in mass strikes in early 1943 against the fascist state.[5]

By the late 1930s, Hitler apparently had the support of a considerable majority of the population, in large measure because his policies successfully brought Germany out of the Depression. The government invested heavily in projects such as superhighways, bridges, canals, and public buildings and, after 1935, in rebuilding and rearming the country's diminished military forces. These policies drove down the number of unemployed Germans from 6.2 million in 1932 to fewer than 500,000 in 1937. Two years later Germany had a labor shortage. Erna Kranz, a teenager in the 1930s, later remembered the early years of Nazi rule as "a glimmer of hope...not just for the unemployed but for everybody because we all knew that we were downtrodden....It was a good time...there was order and discipline."[6] Millions agreed with her.

For many countries still suffering from the Depression throughout the 1930s, Hitler seemed to have found the secret for recovery: economic planning, controlled wages and prices, government investment, and enforced peace between capital and labor. This was a radical departure from the principles of capitalism. Still, neither Hitler nor Mussolini chose to dispossess the capitalists so long as they cooperated by producing goods that the regime required.

Other factors as well contributed to Nazi popularity. Like Italian fascists, Hitler masterfully invoked rural and traditional values that many Germans feared losing in their increasingly urban and materialistic culture. Far more so than in Italy, he used Jews as a symbol of the urban, capitalist, and foreign influences that were corrupting "true" German culture. The Nazis reflected and reinforced a current of anti-Semitism that had deep roots in Germany and most of Europe. More than elsewhere, though, the Nazis projected their distaste for modern life and for recent German history onto the Jews. In his book *Mein Kampf* (*My Struggle*), Hitler outlined his case against the Jews and his call for the racial purification of Germany in vitriolic terms.

> The black-haired Jewish youth, with Satanic joy on his face, lurks in wait for hours for the innocent girls he plans to defile with his blood, and steal the young girl from her people. With every means at hand, he seeks to undermine the racial foundations of the people they would subjugate....[But] a people which is racially pure and is conscious of its blood will never be able to be subjugated by the Jews. The Jew in this world will forever only be the masters of a bastardized people.

This insistence on a racial revolution was a central feature of the Nazi program and differed

Nazi Hatred of the Jews
This picture served as the cover of a highly anti-Semitic book of photographs entitled *The Eternal Jew*, published by the Nazis in 1937. It effectively summed up many of the themes of the Nazi case against the Jews, showing them as ugly and subhuman, as the instigators of communism (the hammer and sickle on a map of Russia), as greedy capitalists (coins in one hand), and as seeking to dominate the world (the whip). (akg-images)

from the racial attitudes in Italy, where Jews were a tiny minority of the population and deeply assimilated into Italian culture. Early on Mussolini had ridiculed Nazi racism, but as Germany and Italy drew closer together, Italy too began a program of overt anti-Semitism, though nothing approaching the extremes that characterized Nazi Germany.

Soon after coming to power, Hitler implemented policies that increasingly restricted Jewish life, such as exclusion from universities, professional organizations, and civil employment. In 1935, the Nuremberg Laws forbade sexual relations or marriage between Jews and other Germans and forced Jews to identify themselves in public by wearing the Star of David. Ostracism escalated to terror on the night of November 9, 1938, known as *Kristallnacht*, when Nazis smashed and looted Jewish shops. Such actions made clear the Nazis' determination to rid Germany of its Jewish population, thus putting into effect the most radical element of Hitler's program, although it was not yet apparent that this "racial revolution" would mean the mass killing of Europe's Jews. That horrendous development emerged only in the context of World War II.

Meanwhile, in schools and in massive torchlight ceremonies, the Nazis celebrated the superiority of the German race, its folk culture, and its ancient heroes. Although Hitler relied on modern technology to create his war machine, in his public speeches he was the mystical leader, the Führer, whose deeds were beyond the rational understanding of his people. Intuition and force rather than reason and compromise should rule Germany. "The stronger must dominate," he declared, "and must not blend with the weaker orders and sacrifice their powers." Hitler's own power rested ultimately on the willingness of most Germans to surrender their right to question and analyze; instead they followed a mesmerizing orator, a leader who, they believed, would direct them to national greatness and personal fulfillment.

If World War I and the Great Depression brought about the political and economic collapse of Europe, the Nazi phenomenon represented a moral collapse within the West, deriving from a highly selective incorporation of earlier strands of European culture. On the one hand, the Nazis actively rejected some of the values—rationalism, tolerance, democracy, human equality—that for many people had defined the core of Western civilization since the Enlightenment. On the other hand, they claimed the legacy of modern science, particularly in their concern to classify and rank various human groups. Thus they drew heavily on the "scientific racism" of the nineteenth century and its expression in phrenology, which linked the size and shape of the skull to human behavior and personality. Moreover, in their effort to purify German society, the Nazis reflected the Enlightenment confidence in the perfectibility of humankind and in the social engineering necessary to achieve it.

Japanese Authoritarianism

In various ways, the modern history of Japan paralleled that of Italy and Germany. All three were newcomers to great power status, with Japan joining the club of

■ Comparison
How did Japan's experience during the 1920s and 1930s resemble that of Germany, and how did it differ?

industrializing and empire-building states only in the late nineteenth century as its sole Asian member (see Chapter 19). Like Italy and Germany, Japan had a rather limited experience with democratic politics, for its elected parliament was constrained by a very small electorate (only 1.5 million men in 1917) and by the exalted position of a semidivine emperor and his small coterie of elite advisers. During the 1930s, Japan too moved toward authoritarian government and a denial of democracy at home, even as it launched an aggressive program of territorial expansion in East Asia.

Despite these broad similarities, Japan's history in the first half of the twentieth century was clearly distinctive. In sharp contrast to Italy and Germany, Japan's participation in World War I was minimal, and its economy grew considerably as other industrialized countries were engaged in the European war. At the peace conference ending that war, Japan was seated as an equal participant, allied with the winning side of democratic countries such as Britain, France, and the United States.

During the 1920s, Japan seemed to be moving toward a more democratic politics and Western cultural values. Universal male suffrage was achieved in 1925; cabinets led by leaders of the major parties, rather than bureaucrats or imperial favorites, governed the country; and a two-party system began to emerge. Supporters of these developments generally embraced the dignity of the individual, free expression of ideas, and greater gender equality. Education expanded; an urban consumer society developed; middle-class women entered new professions; young women known as *moga* (modern girls) sported short hair and short skirts, while dancing with *mobo* (modern boys) at jazz clubs and cabarets. To such people, the Japanese were becoming world citizens and their country was becoming "a province of the world" as they participated increasingly in a cosmopolitan and international culture.

In this environment, the accumulated tensions of Japan's modernizing and industrializing processes found expression. "Rice riots" in 1918 brought more than a million people into the streets of urban Japan to protest the rising price of that essential staple. Union membership tripled in the 1920s as some factory workers began to think in terms of entitlements and workers' rights rather than the benevolence of their employers. In rural areas, tenant unions multiplied, and disputes with landowners increased amid demands for a reduction in rents. A mounting women's movement advocated a variety of feminist issues, including suffrage and the end of legalized prostitution. "All the sleeping women are now awake and moving," declared Yosano Akiko, a well-known poet, feminist, and social critic. Within the political arena, a number of "proletarian parties"—the Labor-Farmer Party, the Socialist People's Party, and a small Japan Communist Party—promised in various ways to "bring about the political, economic and social emancipation of the proletarian class."[7]

To many people in established elite circles—bureaucrats, landowners, industrialists, military officials—all of this was alarming, even appalling, and suggested echoes of the Russian Revolution of 1917. A number of political activists were arrested, and a few were killed. A Peace Preservation Law, enacted in 1925, promised long prison sentences or even the death penalty to anyone who organized against the existing imperial system of government or private property.

As in Germany, however, it was the impact of the Great Depression that paved the way for harsher and more authoritarian action. That worldwide economic catastrophe hit Japan hard. Shrinking world demand for silk impoverished millions of rural dwellers who raised silkworms. Japan's exports fell by half between 1929 and 1931, leaving a million or more urban workers unemployed. Many young workers returned to their rural villages only to find food scarce, families forced to sell their daughters to urban brothels, and neighbors unable to offer the customary money for the funerals of their friends. In these desperate circumstances, many began to doubt the ability of parliamentary democracy and capitalism to address Japan's "national emergency." Politicians and business leaders alike were widely regarded as privileged, self-centered, and heedless of the larger interests of the nation.

Such conditions energized a growing movement in Japanese political life known as Radical Nationalism or the Revolutionary Right. It was expressed in dozens of small groups and was especially appealing to younger army officers. The movement's many separate organizations shared an extreme nationalism, hostility to parliamentary democracy, a commitment to elite leadership focused around an exalted emperor, and dedication to foreign expansion. The manifesto of one of those organizations, the Cherry Blossom Society, expressed these sentiments clearly in 1930.

> As we observe recent social trends, top leaders engage in immoral conduct, political parties are corrupt, capitalists and aristocrats have no understanding of the masses, farming villages are devastated, unemployment and depression are serious. . . . The rulers neglect the long term interests of the nation, strive to win only the pleasure of foreign powers and possess no enthusiasm for external expansion. . . . The people are with us in craving the appearance of a vigorous and clean government that is truly based upon the masses, and is genuinely centered around the Emperor.[8]

Members of such organizations managed to assassinate a number of public officials and prominent individuals, in the hope of provoking a return to direct rule by the emperor, and in 1936 a group of junior officers attempted a military takeover of the government, which was quickly suppressed. In sharp contrast to developments in Italy and Germany, however, no right-wing party gained wide popular support, nor was any such party able to seize power in Japan. Although individuals and small groups sometimes espoused ideas similar to those of European fascists, no major fascist party emerged. Nor did Japan produce any charismatic leader on the order of Mussolini or Hitler. People arrested for political crimes were neither criminalized nor exterminated, as in Germany, but instead were subjected to a process of "resocialization" that brought the vast majority of them to renounce their "errors" and return to the "Japanese way." Japan's established institutions of government were sufficiently strong, and traditional notions of the nation as a family headed by the emperor were sufficiently intact, to prevent the development of a widespread fascist movement able to take control of the country.[9]

In the 1930s, though, Japanese public life clearly changed in ways that reflected the growth of right-wing nationalist thinking. Parties and the parliament continued to operate, and elections were held, but major cabinet positions now went to prominent bureaucratic or military figures rather than to party leaders. The military in particular came to exercise a more dominant role in Japanese political life, although military men had to negotiate with business and bureaucratic elites as well as party leaders. Censorship limited the possibilities of free expression, and a single news agency was granted the right to distribute all national and most international news to the country's newspapers and radio stations. An Industrial Patriotic Federation replaced independent trade unions with factory-based "discussion councils" to resolve local disputes between workers and managers.

Established authorities also adopted many of the ideological themes of the Radical Right. In 1937, the Ministry of Education issued a new textbook, *The Cardinal Principles of Our National Polity*, for use in all Japanese schools. That document proclaimed the Japanese to be "intrinsically quite different from the so-called citizens of Occidental [Western] countries." Those nations were "conglomerations of separate individuals" with "no deep foundation between ruler and citizen to unite them." In Japan, by contrast, an emperor of divine origin related to his subjects as a father to his children. It was a natural, not a contractual, relationship, expressed most fully in the "sacrifice of the life of a subject for the Emperor." In addition to studying this text, students were now required to engage in more physical training, in which Japanese martial arts replaced baseball in the physical education curriculum.

The erosion of democracy and the rise of the military in Japanese political life reflected long-standing Japanese respect for the military values of its ancient samurai warrior class as well as the relatively independent position of the military in Japan's Meiji constitution. The state's success in quickly bringing the country out of the Depression likewise fostered popular support. As in Nazi Germany, state-financed credit, large-scale spending on armaments, and public works projects enabled Japan to emerge from the Depression more rapidly and more fully than major Western countries. "By the end of 1937," noted one Japanese laborer, "everybody in the country was working."[10] By the mid-1930s, the government increasingly assumed a supervisory or managerial role in economic affairs that included subsidies to strategic industries; profit ceilings on major corporations; caps on wages, prices, and rents; and a measure of central planning. Private property, however, was retained, and the huge industrial enterprises called *zaibatsu* continued to dominate the economic landscape.

Although Japan during the 1930s shared some common features with fascist Italy and Nazi Germany, it remained, at least internally, a less repressive and more pluralistic society than either of those European states. Japanese intellectuals and writers had to contend with government censorship, but they retained some influence in the country. Generals and admirals exercised great political authority as the role of an elected parliament declined, but they did not govern alone. Political prisoners were few and were not subjected to execution or deportation as in European fascist states. Japanese conceptions of their racial purity and uniqueness were directed largely against foreigners rather than an internal minority. Nevertheless, like Germany and Italy, Japan developed extensive imperial ambitions. Those projects of conquest and empire building collided with the interests of established world powers such as the United States and Britain, launching a second, and even more terrible, global war.

A Second World War

World War II, even more than the Great War, was a genuinely global conflict with independent origins in both Asia and Europe. Their common feature lay in dissatisfied states in both continents that sought to fundamentally alter the international arrangements that had emerged from World War I. Many Japanese, like their counterparts in Italy and Germany, felt stymied by Britain and the United States as they sought empires that they regarded as essential for their national greatness and economic well-being.

The Road to War in Asia

World War II began in Asia before it occurred in Europe. In the late 1920s and the 1930s, Japanese imperial ambitions mounted as the military became more prominent and powerful in Japan's political life and as an earlier cultural cosmopolitanism gave way to more nationalist sentiments. An initial problem was the rise of Chinese nationalism, which seemed to threaten Japan's sphere of influence in Manchuria, which had been acquired after the Russo-Japanese War of 1904–1905. Acting independently of civilian authorities in Tokyo, units of the Japanese military seized control of Manchuria in 1931 and established a puppet state called Manchukuo. This action infuriated Western powers, prompting Japan to withdraw from the League of Nations, to break politically with its Western allies, and in 1936 to align more closely with Germany and Italy. By that time, relations with an increasingly nationalist China had deteriorated further, leading to a full-scale attack on heartland China in 1937 and escalating a bitter conflict that would last another eight years. World War II in Asia had begun (see Map 21.4).

■ **Comparison**

In what ways were the origins of World War II in Asia and in Europe similar to each other? How were they different?

As the war with China unfolded, the view of the world held by Japanese authorities and many ordinary people hardened. Increasingly, they felt isolated, surrounded, and threatened. A series of international agreements in the early 1920s that had granted Japan a less robust naval force than Britain or the United States as well as anti-Japanese immigration policies in the United States convinced some Japanese that European racism prevented the West from acknowledging Japan as an equal power. Furthermore, Japan was quite dependent on foreign and especially American sources of strategic goods. By the late 1930s, some 73 percent of Japan's scrap iron, 60 percent of its imported machine tools, 80 percent of its oil, and about half of its

Map 21.4 World War II in Asia
Japanese aggression temporarily dislodged the British, French, Dutch, and Americans from their colonial possessions in Asia, while inflicting vast devastation on China.

copper came from the United States, which was becoming increasingly hostile to Japanese ambitions in Asia. Western imperialist powers—the British, French, and Dutch—controlled resource-rich colonies in Southeast Asia. Finally, the Soviet Union, which was proclaiming an alien communist ideology, loomed large in northern Asia. To growing numbers of Japanese, their national survival was at stake.

Thus in 1940–1941, Japan extended its military operations to the French, British, Dutch, and American colonies of Indochina, Malaya, Burma, Indonesia, and the Philippines in an effort to acquire those resources that would free it from dependence on the West. In carving out this Pacific empire, the Japanese presented themselves as liberators and modernizers, creating an "Asia for Asians" and freeing their continent from European dominance. Experience soon showed that Japan's concern was far more for Asia's resources than for its liberation and that Japanese rule exceeded in brutality even that of the Europeans.

A decisive step in the development of World War II in Asia lay in the Japanese attack on the United States at Pearl Harbor in Hawaii in December 1941. Japanese authorities undertook that attack with reluctance and only after negotiations to end American hostility to Japan's empire-building enterprise proved fruitless and an American oil embargo was imposed on Japan in July 1941. American opinion in the 1930s increasingly saw Japan as aggressive, oppressive, and a threat to U.S. economic interests in Asia. In the face of this hostility, Japan's leaders felt that the alternatives for their country boiled down to either an acceptance of American terms, which they feared would reduce Japan to a second- or third-rank power, or a war with an uncertain outcome. Given those choices, the decision for war was made more with foreboding than with enthusiasm. A leading Japanese admiral made the case for war in this way in late 1941: "The government has decided that if there were no war the fate of the nation is sealed. Even if there is a war, the country may be ruined. Nevertheless a nation that does not fight in this plight has lost its spirit and is doomed."[11]

As a consequence of the attack on Pearl Harbor, the United States entered the war in the Pacific, beginning a long and bloody struggle that ended only with the use of atomic bombs against Hiroshima and Nagasaki in 1945. The Pearl Harbor action also joined the Asian theater of the war and the ongoing conflict in Europe into a single global struggle that pitted Germany, Italy, and Japan (the Axis powers) against the United States, Britain, and the Soviet Union (the Allies).

The Road to War in Europe

If Japan was the dissatisfied power in Asia, Nazi Germany occupied that role in Europe even more sharply. As a consequence of its defeat in World War I and the harsh terms of the Treaty of Versailles, many Germans harbored deep resentments about their country's position in the international arena. Taking advantage of those resentments, the Nazis pledged to rectify the treaty's perceived injustices. Thus, to most historians, the origins of World War II in Europe lie squarely in German aggression, although with many twists and turns and encouraged by the initial unwillingness of Britain, France, and the Soviet Union to confront that aggression forcefully and collectively. If World War I was accidental and unintended, World War II was more deliberate and planned, perhaps even desired by the German leadership and by Hitler in particular.

War was central to the Nazi phenomenon in several ways. Nazism was born out of World War I, the hated treaty that ended it, and the disillusioned ex-soldiers who emerged from it. Furthermore, the celebration of war as a means of ennobling humanity and enabling the rise of superior peoples was at the core of Nazi ideology. "Whoever would live must fight," Hitler declared. "Only in force lies the right of possession." He consistently stressed the importance for Germany of gaining "living space" in the east, in the lands of Slavic Poland and Russia. Inevitably, this required war.

Slowly at first and then more aggressively, Hitler prepared the country for war and pursued territorial expansion. A major rearmament program began in 1935. The next year, German forces entered the Rhineland, which the Treaty of Versailles had declared demilitarized. In 1938, Germany annexed Austria and the German-speaking parts of Czechoslovakia. At a famous conference in Munich in that year, the British and the French gave these actions their reluctant blessing, hoping that this "appeasement" of Hitler could satisfy his demands and avoid all-out war. But it did not. In the following year, 1939, Germany unleashed a devastating attack on Poland, an action that triggered the Second World War in Europe. Quickly defeating France, the Germans launched a destructive air war against Britain and in 1941 turned their war machine loose on the Soviet Union. By then, most of Europe was under Nazi control (see Map 21.5).

Although Germany was central to both world wars, the second one was quite different from the first. It was not welcomed with the kind of mass enthusiasm that had accompanied the opening of World War I in 1914. The bitter experience of the Great War suggested to most people that only suffering lay ahead. The conduct of the two wars likewise differed. The first war had quickly bogged down in trench warfare that emphasized defense, whereas in the second war the German tactic of *blitzkrieg* ("lightning war") coordinated the rapid movement of infantry, tanks, and airpower over very large areas.

Such military tactics were initially successful and allowed German forces, aided by their Italian allies, to sweep over Europe, the western Soviet Union, and North Africa. The tide began to turn in 1942 when the Soviet Union absorbed the German onslaught and counterattacked, sustaining some 25 million casualties in the process. The United States, with its enormous material and human resources, fully joined the struggle against Germany in 1942. Three more years of bitter fighting ensued before the German defeat in May 1945.

World War II: The Outcomes of Global Conflict

■ Comparison

How did World War II differ from World War I?

The Second World War was the most destructive conflict in world history, with total deaths estimated at around 60 million, some six times the deaths in World War I.

Map 21.5 World War II in Europe

For a brief moment during World War II, Nazi Germany came close to bringing all of Europe and much of the Mediterranean basin under its rule.

More than half of those casualties were civilians. Partly responsible for this horrendous toll were the new technologies of warfare—heavy bombers, jet fighters, missiles, and atomic weapons. Equally significant, though, was the almost complete blurring of the traditional line between civilian and military targets, as entire cities and whole populations came to be defined as the enemy.

Nowhere was that blurring more complete than in the Soviet Union, which accounted for more than 40 percent of the total deaths in the war—probably around 25 million, with an equal number made homeless and thousands of towns, villages, and industrial enterprises destroyed. German actions fulfilled Hitler's instructions to his leading generals: "The war against Russia will be such that it cannot be conducted in a knightly fashion; the struggle is one of ideologies and racial differences and will have to be conducted with unprecedented, unmerciful, and unrelenting harshness.... German soldiers guilty of breaking international law...will be excused."[12]

Snapshot   **Key Moments in the History of World War II**

Japanese invasion of Manchuria	1931
Hitler's rise to power	1933
Italian invasion of Ethiopia	1935
Anti-Comintern Pact (alliance of Germany, Japan, and Italy)	1936–1937
Japanese invasion of China/Rape of Nanjing	1937–1938
German takeover of Austria and Sudetenland in Czechoslovakia	1938
German invasion of Poland (beginning of World War II in Europe)	1939
The fall of France and German air war on Britain	1940
Japanese seizure of French, British, Dutch, and U.S. colonies in Asia	1940–1942
German invasion of USSR; Japanese attack on Pearl Harbor, Hawaii	1941
The Holocaust	1941–1945
U.S. victory in Battle of Midway (turning point in the Pacific war)	1942
Soviet victory in Battle of Stalingrad (turning point in European war)	1943
D-day: Allied forces invade France	1944
Yalta Conference (Britain, United States, Soviet Union) to determine fate of postwar Europe	1945
Soviets capture Berlin; atomic bombing of Hiroshima and Nagasaki; Germany and Japan surrender	1945

In China as well, perhaps 15 million deaths and uncounted refugees grew out of prolonged Chinese resistance and the shattering Japanese response, including the killing of every person and every animal in many villages. During the infamous Rape of Nanjing in 1937–1938, some 200,000 to 300,000 Chinese civilians were killed and often mutilated within a few months, and countless women were sexually assaulted. Indiscriminate German bombing of British cities and the Allied firebombing of Japanese and German cities likewise reflected the new morality of total war, as did the dropping of atomic bombs on Hiroshima and Nagasaki, which in a single instant vaporized tens of thousands of people. This was total war with a scale, intensity, and indiscriminate brutality that exceeded even the horrors of World War I.

A further dimension of total war lay in governments' efforts to mobilize their economies, their people, and their propaganda machines even more extensively than in World War I. Colonial resources were harnessed once again. The British in particular made extensive use of colonial troops and laborers from India and Africa. Japan compelled some 300,000 women from its Korean, Manchurian, and Taiwanese

Hiroshima
The dropping of atomic bombs on Hiroshima (August 6, 1945) and a few days later on Nagasaki marked the end of World War II in the Pacific and the opening of a nuclear arms race that cast an enormous shadow on the rest of the twentieth century. In this photograph from an utterly devastated Hiroshima, a group of survivors waits for help in the southern part of the city a few hours after the bomb was dropped. (AP Images/Wide World Photos)

possessions to serve the sexual needs of Japanese troops as "comfort women," who often accommodated twenty to thirty men a day.

Everywhere, the needs of the war drew large numbers of women into both industry and the military, although in Britain and the United States this was regarded as a temporary necessity. In the United States, "Rosie the Riveter" represented those women who now took on heavy industrial jobs, which previously had been reserved for men. In the USSR, women constituted more than half of the workforce by 1945. A much smaller percentage of Japanese women were mobilized for factory work, but a Greater Japan Women's Society enrolled some 19 million members, who did volunteer work and promised to lay aside their gold jewelry and abandon extravagant weddings. As always, war heightened the prestige of masculinity, and given the immense sacrifices that men had made, few women were inclined to directly challenge the practices of patriarchy immediately following the war.

Among the most haunting outcomes of the war was the Holocaust. The outbreak of the war closed off certain possibilities, such as forced emigration, for implementing the Nazi dream of ridding Germany of its Jewish population. It also brought millions of additional Jews in Poland and Russia under German control and triggered among Hitler's enthusiastic subordinates various schemes for a "Final Solution" to the Jewish question. From this emerged the death camps and gas chambers of Auschwitz, Dachau, Bergen-Belsen, and other concentration camps. Altogether, some 6 million Jews perished in a technologically sophisticated genocide that set a new standard for human depravity and has haunted the world's conscience ever since. Millions more whom the Nazis deemed inferior, undesirable, or danger-ous—Russians, Poles, and other Slavs; Gypsies, or the Roma; mentally or physically handicapped people; homosexuals; communists; and Jehovah's Witnesses—likewise perished in Germany's efforts at racial purification.

On an even larger scale than World War I, this second global conflict rearranged the architecture of world politics. As the war ended, Europe was impoverished, its industrial infrastructure was shattered, many of its great cities were in ruins, and millions of its people were homeless or displaced. Within a few years, this much-weakened Europe was effectively divided, with its western half operating under an American umbrella and the eastern half subject to Soviet control. It was clear that Europe's dominance in world affairs was finished.

Over the next two decades, Europe's greatly diminished role in the world reg-istered internationally when its Asian and African colonies achieved independence. Not only had the war weakened both the will and the ability of European powers to hold onto their colonies, but it had also emboldened nationalist and anticolonial movements everywhere (see Chapter 23). Japanese victories in Southeast Asia had certainly damaged European prestige, for British, Dutch, and American military forces fell to Japanese conquerors, sometimes in a matter of weeks. Japanese author-ities staged long and brutal marches of Western prisoners of war, partly to drive home to local people that the era of Western domination was over. Furthermore, tens of thousands of Africans had fought for the British or the French, had seen white people die, had enjoyed the company of white women, and had returned home with very different ideas about white superiority and the permanence of colonial rule. Colonial subjects everywhere were very much aware that U.S. presi-dent Franklin Roosevelt and British prime minister Winston Churchill had solemnly declared in 1941 that "we respect the right of all peoples to choose the form of government under which they will live." Many asked whether those prin-ciples should not apply to people in the colonial world as well as to Europeans.

A further outcome of World War II lay in the consolidation and extension of the communist world. The Soviet victory over the Nazis, though bought at an unimaginable cost in blood and treasure, gave immense credibility to the commu-nist regime and to its leader, Joseph Stalin. In the decades that followed, Soviet authorities nurtured a virtual cult of the war: memorials were everywhere; wedding parties made pilgrimages to them, and brides left their bouquets behind; May 9, Victory Day, saw elaborately orchestrated celebrations; veterans were honored and granted modest privileges. Furthermore, communist parties, largely dominated by the Soviet Union and supported by its armed forces, took power all across Eastern Europe, pushing the communist frontier deep into the European heartland. Even more important was a communist takeover in China in 1949. The Second World War allowed the Chinese Communist Party to gain support and credibility by lead-ing the struggle against Japan. By 1950, the communist world seemed to many in the West very much on the offensive (see Chapter 22).

The horrors of two world wars within a single generation prompted a renewed interest in international efforts to maintain the peace in a world of competing and sovereign states. The chief outcome was the United Nations (UN), established in 1945 as a successor to the moribund League of Nations. As a political body dependent on agreement among its most powerful members, the UN proved more effective as a forum for international opinion than as a means of resolving the major conflicts of the postwar world, particularly the Soviet/American hostility during the cold war decades. Further evidence for a growing internationalism lay in the creation in late 1945 of the World Bank and International Monetary Fund, whose purpose was to regulate the global economy, prevent another depression, and stimulate economic growth, especially in the poorer nations.

What these initiatives shared was the dominant presence of the United States. Unlike the aftermath of World War I, when an isolationist United States substantially withdrew from world affairs, the half century following the end of World War II witnessed the emergence of the United States as a global superpower. This was one of the major outcomes of the Second World War and a chief reason for the remarkable recovery of a badly damaged and discredited Western civilization.

The Recovery of Europe

The tragedies that afflicted Europe in the first half of the twentieth century—fratricidal war, economic collapse, the Holocaust—were wholly self-inflicted, and yet despite the sorry and desperate state of heartland Europe in 1945, that civilization had not permanently collapsed. In the twentieth century's second half, Europeans rebuilt their industrial economies and revived their democratic political systems, while the United States, a European offshoot, assumed a dominant and often dominating role both within Western civilization and in the world at large.

Three factors help to explain this astonishing recovery. One is the apparent resiliency of an industrial society, once it has been established. The knowledge, skills, and habits of mind that made industrial societies work remained intact, even if the physical infrastructure had been largely destroyed. Thus even the most terribly damaged countries—Germany, the Soviet Union, and Japan—had substantially recovered, both economically and demographically, within a quarter of a century. A second factor lay in the ability of the major Western European countries to integrate their recovering economies. After centuries of military conflict climaxed by the horrors of the two world wars, the major Western European powers were at last willing to put aside some of their prickly nationalism in return for prolonged peace and a general prosperity.

Perhaps most important, Europe had long ago spawned an overseas extension of its own civilization in what became the United States. In the twentieth century, that country served as a reservoir of military manpower, economic resources, and political leadership for the West as a whole. By 1945, the center of gravity within Western civilization had shifted decisively, relocated now across the Atlantic. With

■ **Change**

How was Europe able to recover from the devastation of war?

Europe diminished, divided, and on the defensive against the Communist threat, leadership of the Western world passed, almost by default, to the United States. It was the only major country physically untouched by the war. Its economy had demonstrated enormous productivity during that struggle and by 1945 was generating fully 50 percent of total world production. Its overall military strength was unmatched, and it was in sole possession of the atomic bomb, the most powerful weapon ever constructed. Thus the United States became the new heartland of the West as well as a global superpower. In 1941, the publisher Henry Luce had proclaimed the twentieth century as "the American century." As the Second World War ended, that prediction seemed to be coming true.

An early indication of the United States' intention to exercise global leadership took shape in its efforts to rebuild and reshape shattered European economies. Known as the Marshall Plan, that effort funneled into Europe some $12 billion, at the time a very large amount, together with numerous advisers and technicians. It was motivated by some combination of genuine humanitarian concern, a desire to prevent a new depression by creating overseas customers for American industrial goods, and an interest in undermining the growing appeal of European communist parties. This economic recovery plan was successful beyond anyone's expectations. Between 1948 and the early 1970s, Western European economies grew rapidly, generating a widespread prosperity and improving living standards; at the same time, Western Europe became both a major customer for American goods and a major competitor in global markets.

The Marshall Plan also required its European recipients to cooperate with one another. After decades of conflict and destruction almost beyond description, many Europeans were eager to do so. That process began in 1951 when Italy, France, West Germany, Belgium, the Netherlands, and Luxembourg created the European Coal and Steel Community to jointly manage the production of these critical items. In 1957, these six countries deepened their level of cooperation by establishing the European Economic Community (EEC), more widely known as the Common Market, whose members reduced their tariffs and developed common trade policies. Over the next half century, the EEC expanded its membership to include almost all of Europe, including many former communist states. In 1994, the EEC was renamed the European Union, and in 2002 twelve of its members adopted a common currency, the euro (see Map 21.6). All of this sustained Europe's remarkable economic recovery and expressed a larger European identity, although it certainly did not erase deeply rooted national loyalties. Nor did it lead, as some had hoped, to a political union, a United States of Europe.

Beyond economic assistance, the American commitment to Europe soon came to include political and military security against the distant possibility of renewed German aggression and the more immediate communist threat from the Soviet Union. Without that security, economic recovery was unlikely to continue. Thus was born the military and political alliance known as the North Atlantic Treaty Organization (NATO) in 1949. It committed the United States and its nuclear arsenal to the defense of Europe against the Soviet Union, and it firmly anchored West Germany within the Western alliance. Thus, as Western Europe revived economically,

Map 21.6 The Growth of European Integration

Gradually during the second half of the twentieth century, Europeans put aside their bitter rivalries and entered into various forms of economic cooperation with one another, although these efforts fell short of complete political union. This map illustrates the growth of what is now called the European Union (EU). Notice the eastward expansion of the EU following the collapse of communism in Eastern Europe and the Soviet Union.

it did so under the umbrella of U.S. political and military leadership, which Europeans generally welcomed. It was perhaps an imperial relationship, but to historian John Gaddis, it was "an empire by invitation" rather than by imposition.[13]

A parallel process in Japan, which was under American occupation between 1945 and 1952, likewise revived that country's devastated but already industrialized economy. In the two decades following the occupation, Japan's economy grew at the remarkable rate of 10 percent a year, and the nation became an economic giant on the world stage. This "economic miracle" received a substantial boost from some $2 billion in American aid during the occupation and even more from U.S. military purchases in Japan during the Korean War (1950–1953). Furthermore, the democratic constitution imposed on Japan by American occupation authorities required that "land, sea, and air forces, as well as other war potential, will never be maintained." This meant that Japan, even more so than Europe, depended on the United States for its military security. Because it spent only about 1 percent of its gross national product on defense, more was available for productive investment.

The Western world had changed dramatically during the twentieth century. It began that century with its European heartland clearly the dominant imperial center of a global network. That civilization substantially self-destructed in the first half of the century, but it revived during the second half in a changed form—without its Afro-Asian colonies and with a new and powerful core in the United States. Accompanying this process and intersecting with it was another major theme of twentieth-century world history—the rise and fall of world communism, which is the focus of the next chapter.

Reflections: War and Remembrance: Learning from History

When asked about the value of studying history, most students respond with some version of the Spanish-born philosopher George Santayana's famous dictum: "Those who cannot remember the past are condemned to repeat it." At one level, this notion of learning from the "lessons of history" has much to recommend it, for there is, after all, little else except the past on which we can base our actions in the present. And yet historians in general are notably cautious about drawing particular lessons from the past and applying them to present circumstances.

For one thing, the historical record, like the Bible or any sacred text, is sufficiently rich and complex to allow many people to draw quite different lessons from it. The world wars of the twentieth century represent a case in point, as writer Adam Gopnik has pointed out:

> The First World War teaches that territorial compromise is better than full-scale war, that an "honor-bound" allegiance of the great powers to small nations is a recipe for mass killing, and that it is crazy to let the blind mechanism of armies and alliances trump common sense. The Second teaches that searching for an accommodation with tyranny by selling out small nations only encourages the tyrant, that refusing to fight now leads to a worse fight later on. . . . The First teaches us never to rush into a fight, the Second never to back down from a bully.[14]

Did the lessons of the First World War lead Americans to ignore the rise of fascism until the country was directly threatened by Japanese attack? Did the lessons of World War II contribute to unnecessary wars in Vietnam and more recently in Iraq? There are no easy answers to such questions, for the lessons of history are many, varied, and changing.

Behind any such lesson is the common assumption that history repeats itself. This too is a notion to which historians bring considerable skepticism. They are generally more impressed with the complexity and particularity of major events such as wars rather than with their common features. Here is a further basis for caution in easily drawing lessons from the past.

But the wars of the past century perhaps share one broad similarity: all of them led to unexpected consequences. Few people expected the duration and carnage of

World War I. The Holocaust was literally unimaginable when Hitler took power in 1933 or even at the outbreak of the Second World War in 1939. Who would have expected an American defeat at the hands of the Vietnamese? And the invasion of Iraq in 2003 has generated a long list of surprises for the United States, including the absence of weapons of mass destruction and a prolonged insurgency. History repeats itself most certainly only in its unexpectedness.

Second Thoughts

What's the Significance?

World War I	fascism	total war
Treaty of Versailles	Mussolini	Holocaust
Woodrow Wilson/Fourteen Points	Nazi Germany/Hitler	Marshall Plan
	Revolutionary Right (Japan)	European Economic Community
Great Depression	World War II in Asia	
New Deal	World War II in Europe	NATO

To assess your mastery of the material in this chapter, see the **Online Study Guide** at bedfordstmartins.com/strayer.

Big Picture Questions

1. What explains the disasters that befell Europe in the first half of the twentieth century?
2. In what ways were the world wars a motor for change in the history of the twentieth century?
3. To what extent were the two world wars distinct and different conflicts, and in what ways were they related to each other? In particular, how did the First World War and its aftermath lay the foundations for World War II?
4. In what ways did Europe's internal conflicts between 1914 and 1945 have global implications?

Next Steps: For Further Study

Michael Burleigh, *The Third Reich: A New History* (2001). A fresh and thorough look at the Nazi era in Germany's history.

John Keegan, *The Second World War* (2005). A comprehensive account by a well-known scholar.

Bernd Martin, *Japan and Germany in the Modern World* (1995). A comparative study of these two countries' modern history and the relationship between them.

Mark Mazower, *Dark Continent* (2000). A history of Europe in the twentieth century that views the era as a struggle among liberal democracy, fascism, and communism.

Michael S. Nieberg, *Fighting the Great War: A Global History* (2006). Explores the origins and conduct of World War I.

Dietman Rothermund, *The Global Impact of the Great Depression, 1929–1939* (1996). Examines the origins of the Depression in America and Europe and its impact in Asia, Africa, and Latin America.

First World War.com, http://www.firstworldwar.com. A Web site rich with articles, documents, photos, diaries, and more that illustrate the history of World War I.

"Nazi Rule," http://www.ushmm.org/outreach/nrule.htm. A great Web site, sponsored by the U.S. Holocaust Memorial Museum, for exploring various aspects of the Nazi experience.

For Web sites, images, and documents related to this chapter, see **Make History** at bedfordstmartins.com/strayer.

ЛЕНИН —
ЖИЛ,
ЛЕНИН —
ЖИВ,
ЛЕНИН —
БУДЕТ ЖИТЬ

ВЛ. МАЯКОВСКИЙ.

CHAPTER TWENTY-TWO

The Rise and Fall of World Communism

1917–PRESENT

"I was living in Germany on the day the wall came down and well remember talking to my German neighbour. With tears streaming down his face he kept saying in English and German: 'I never thought I would live to see this.'

"For anyone who didn't experience the Wall, it will be hard to imagine what an overwhelming feeling of relief, of joy, of unreality filled one that this monster was dead, and people had conquered it."[1]

Both of these eyewitness comments referred to that remarkable day, November 9, 1989, when the infamous Berlin Wall in Germany was breached. Built in 1961 to prevent the residents of communist East Berlin from escaping to the West, that concrete barrier had become a potent symbol of communist tyranny. Its fall, amid the overthrow of communist governments all across Eastern Europe, was part of a larger process that marked the collapse or the abandonment of communism as the twentieth century entered its final decade. In the midst of that euphoria, it was hard to remember that earlier in the century communism had been greeted with enthusiasm by many people—in Russia, China, Cuba, Vietnam, and elsewhere—as a promise of liberation from inequality, oppression, exploitation, and backwardness.

IT WOULD BE HARD TO OVERESTIMATE THE SIGNIFICANCE OF COMMU-NISM IN THE WORLD OF THE TWENTIETH CENTURY. Communist regimes came to power almost everywhere in the tumultuous wake of war, revolution, or both. Once established, those regimes set about a thorough and revolutionary transformation of their societies—"building socialism," as they so often put it. Internationally, world communism posed a

Lenin: Vladimir Ulyanov, better known as Lenin, was the Bolshevik leader of the Russian Revolution. He became the iconic symbol of world communism and in his own country was the focus of a semireligious cult. This widely distributed Soviet propaganda poster reads "Lenin lived; Lenin lives; Lenin will live." (David King Collection) profound military and political/ideological threat to the Western world of capitalism and democracy, particularly during the decades of the cold war (1946–1991). That struggle divided continents, countries, and cities into communist and noncommunist halves. It also prompted a global rivalry between the United States and the Soviet Union (USSR) for influence in the third world. Most hauntingly, it spawned an arms race in horrendously destructive nuclear weapons that sent schoolchildren scrambling under their desks during air raid drills, while sober scientists speculated about the possible extinction of human life, and perhaps all life, in the event of a major war.

Then, to the amazement of everyone, it was over, more with a whimper than with a bang. The last two decades of the twentieth century witnessed the collapse of communist regimes or the abandonment of communist principles practically everywhere. The great global struggle of capitalism and communism, embodied in the United States and the Soviet Union, was resolved in favor of the former far more quickly and much more peacefully than anyone had imagined possible.

Global Communism

■ Description

When and where did communism exercise influence during the twentieth century?

Modern communism found its political and philosophical roots in nineteenth-century European socialism, inspired by the teachings of Karl Marx (see Chapter 18). Although most European socialists came to believe that they could achieve their goals peacefully and through the democratic process, those who defined themselves as communists in the twentieth century disdained such reformism and advocated uncompromising revolution as the only possible route to a socialist future. Russia was the first country to experience such a revolution. Other movements that later identified or allied with the Soviet Union, as the Russian Empire was renamed after its 1917 revolution, likewise defined themselves as communist. In Marxist theory, that term also referred to a final stage of historical development when social equality and collective living would be most fully developed, wholly without private property. Socialism was an intermediate stage along the way to that final goal.

At communism's high point in the 1970s, almost one-third of the world's population lived in societies governed by communist regimes. By far the most significant were the Soviet Union, the world's largest country in size, and China, the world's largest country in population. This chapter focuses primarily on a comparison of these two large-scale experiments in communism and their global impact.

Beyond the Soviet Union and China, communism also came to Eastern Europe in the wake of World War II and the extension of the Soviet military presence there. In Asia, following Japan's defeat in that war, its Korean colony was partitioned, with the northern half coming under Soviet and therefore communist control. In Vietnam, a much more locally based communist movement, under the leadership of Ho Chi Minh, embodied both a socialist vision and Vietnamese nationalism as it battled Japanese, French, and later American invaders and established communist control first in the northern half of the country and after 1975 throughout the whole country. The victory of the Vietnamese communists spilled over into neighboring Laos and Cambodia, where communist parties took power in the mid-1970s. In Latin America, Fidel Castro led a revolutionary nationalist movement against a repressive and American-backed government in Cuba. On coming to power in 1959, he moved toward communism and an alliance with the Soviet Union. Finally, a shaky communist regime took power in Afghanistan in 1979, propped up briefly only by massive Soviet military support. None of these countries had achieved the kind of advanced industrial capitalism that Karl Marx had viewed as a prerequisite for revolution and socialism. In one of history's strange twists, the great revolutions of the twentieth century took place instead in largely agrarian societies.

In addition to those countries where communist governments exercised state power, communist parties took root in still other places, where they exercised various degrees of influence. In the aftermath of World War II, such parties played important political roles in Greece, France, and Italy. In the 1950s, a small communist party in the United States became the focus of an intense wave of fear and political repression known as McCarthyism. Revolutionary communist movements threatened established governments in the Philippines, Malaya, Indonesia, Bolivia, Peru, and elsewhere, sometimes provoking brutal crackdowns by those governments. A number of African states in the 1970s proclaimed themselves Marxist for a time and aligned with the Soviet Union in international affairs. All of this was likewise part of global communism.

These differing expressions of communism were linked to one another in various ways. They shared a common ideology derived from European Marxism, although it was substantially modified in many places. That ideology minimized the claims of national loyalty and looked forward to an international revolutionary movement of the lower classes and a worldwide socialist federation. The Russian Revolution of 1917 served as an inspiration and an example to aspiring revolutionaries elsewhere, and the new Soviet Communist Party and government provided them aid and advice. Through an organization called Comintern (Communist International), Soviet authorities also sought to control their policies and actions.

During the cold war decades, the Warsaw Pact brought the Soviet Union and Eastern European communist states together in a military alliance designed to counter the threat from the Western capitalist countries of the NATO alliance. A parallel organization called the Council on Mutual Economic Assistance tied Eastern European economies tightly to the economy of the Soviet Union. A Treaty of Friendship between the Soviet Union and China in 1950 joined the two communist giants in an alliance that caused many in the West to view communism as a unified international movement aimed at their destruction. Nevertheless, rivalry, outright hostility, and on occasion military conflict marked the communist world as much or more than solidarity and cooperation. Eastern European resentment of their Soviet overlords was expressed in periodic rebellions, even as the Soviet Union and China came close to war in the late 1960s.

Although the globalization of communism found expression primarily in the second half of the twentieth century, that process began with two quite distinct and different revolutionary upheavals—one in Russia and the other in China—in the first half of that century.

Comparing Revolutions as a Path to Communism

■ Comparison

Identify the major differences between the Russian and Chinese revolutions.

Communist movements of the twentieth century quite self-consciously drew on the mystique of the earlier French Revolution, which suggested that new and better worlds could be constructed by human actions. Communist revolutions, like their French predecessor, ousted old ruling classes and dispossessed landed aristocracies. They too involved vast peasant upheavals in the countryside and an educated leadership with roots in the cities. All three revolutions—French, Russian, and Chinese—found their vision of the good society in a modernizing future, not in some nostalgic vision of the past. Communists also worried lest their revolutions end up in a military dictatorship like that of Napoleon following the French Revolution.

But the communist revolutions were distinctive as well. They were made by highly organized parties guided by a Marxist ideology, were committed to an industrial future, pursued economic as well as political equality, and sought the abolition of private property. In doing so, they mobilized, celebrated, and claimed to act on behalf of society's lower classes—exploited urban workers and impoverished rural peasants. The middle classes, who were the chief beneficiaries of the French Revolution, numbered among the many victims of the communist upheavals. The Russian and Chinese revolutions shared these features, but in other respects they differed sharply from each other.

Russia: Revolution in a Single Year

In Russia, the communists came to power on the back of a revolutionary upheaval that took place within a single year, 1917. The immense pressures of World War I, which was going very badly for the Russians, represented the catalyst for that revolution as the accumulated tensions of Russian society exploded (see Chapter 18). Much exploited and suffering from wartime shortages, workers, including many women, took to the streets to express their outrage at the incompetence and privileges of their social betters. Activists from various parties, many of them socialist, recruited members, organized demonstrations, published newspapers, and plotted revolution. By February 1917, Tsar Nicholas II had lost almost all support and was forced to abdicate the throne, thus ending the Romanov dynasty, which had ruled Russia for more than three centuries.

That historic event opened the door to a massive social upheaval. Ordinary soldiers, seeking an end to a terrible war and despising their upper-class officers, deserted in substantial numbers. In major industrial centers such as St. Petersburg and Moscow, new trade unions arose to defend workers' interests, and some workers

Map 22.1 Russia in 1917
During the First World War, the world's largest state, bridging both Europe and Asia, exploded in revolution in 1917. The Russian Revolution brought to power the twentieth century's first communist government and launched an international communist movement that eventually incorporated about one-third of the world's people.

seized control of their factories. Grassroots organizations of workers and soldiers, known as "soviets," emerged to speak for ordinary people. Peasants, many of whom had been serfs only a generation or two ago, seized landlords' estates, burned their manor houses, and redistributed the land among themselves. Non-Russian nationalists in Ukraine, Poland, Muslim Central Asia, and the Baltic region demanded greater autonomy or even independence (see Map 22.1).

This was social revolution, and it quickly demonstrated the inadequacy of the Provisional Government, which had come to power after the tsar abdicated. Consisting of middle-class politicians and some socialist leaders, that government was divided and ineffectual, unable or unwilling to meet the demands of Russia's revolutionary masses. Nor was it willing to take Russia out of the war, as many were now demanding. Impatience and outrage against the Provisional Government provided an opening for more radical groups. The most effective were the Bolsheviks, a small socialist party with a determined and charismatic leader, Vladimir Ulyanov, more commonly known as Lenin. He had long believed that Russia, despite its industrial backwardness, was nonetheless ready for a socialist revolution that would, he expected, spark further revolutions in the more developed countries of Europe. Thus backward Russia would be a catalyst for a more general socialist breakthrough.

■ Change
Why were the Bolsheviks able to ride the Russian Revolution to power?

It was a striking revision of Marxist thinking to accommodate the conditions of a largely agrarian Russian society.

In the desperate circumstances of 1917, his party's message—an end to the war, land for the peasants, workers' control of factories, self-determination for non-Russian nationalities—resonated with an increasingly rebellious public mood, particularly in the major cities. Lenin and the Bolsheviks also called for the dissolution of the Provisional Government and a transfer of state power to the new soviets. On the basis of this program, the Bolsheviks—claiming to act on behalf of the highly popular soviets, in which they had a major presence—seized power in late October during an overnight coup in the capital city of St. Petersburg. Members of the discredited Provisional Government fled or were arrested, even as the Bolsheviks also seized power elsewhere in the country.

Taking or claiming power was one thing; holding onto it was another. A three-year civil war followed in which the Bolsheviks, now officially calling their party "communist," battled an assortment of enemies—tsarist officials, landlords, disaffected socialists, and regional nationalist forces, as well as troops from the United States, Britain, France, and Japan, all of which were eager to crush the fledgling communist regime. Remarkably, the Bolsheviks held on and by 1921 had staggered to victory over their divided and uncoordinated opponents. One thing that helped the Bolsheviks was their signing of a separate peace treaty with Germany, thus taking Russia out of World War I, but at a great, though temporary, cost in terms of Russian territory.

During the civil war (1918–1921), the Bolsheviks had harshly regimented the economy, seized grain from angry peasants, suppressed nationalist rebellions, and perpetrated bloody atrocities, as did their enemies as well. But they also had integrated many lower-class men into the Red Army, as Bolshevik military forces were known, and into new local governments, providing them an avenue of social mobility not previously available. By battling foreign troops from the United States, Britain, France, and Japan, the Bolsheviks claimed to be defending Russia from imperialists and protecting the downtrodden masses from their exploiters. The civil war exaggerated even further the Bolsheviks' authoritarian tendencies and their inclination to use force. Shortly after that war ended, they renamed their country the Union of Soviet Socialist Republics and set about its transformation.

For the next twenty-five years, the Soviet Union remained a communist island in a capitalist sea. The next major extension of communist control occurred in Eastern Europe in the aftermath of World War II, but it took place quite differently than in Russia. The war had ended with Soviet military forces occupying much of Eastern Europe. Furthermore, Stalin, the USSR's longtime leader, had determined that Soviet security required "friendly" governments in the region so as to permanently end the threat of invasion from the West. When the Marshall Plan seemed to suggest American plans to incorporate Eastern Europe into a Western economic network, Stalin acted to install fully communist governments, loyal to himself, in Poland, East Germany, Czechoslovakia, Hungary, Romania, and Bulgaria. Backed by the pressure and presence of the Soviet army, communism was largely imposed on Eastern Europe from outside rather than growing out of a domestic revolution, as had happened in Russia itself.

Local communist parties had some domestic support, deriving from their role in the resistance against the Nazis and their policies of land reform. In Hungary and Poland, for example, communist pressures led to the redistribution of much land to poor or landless peasants, and in free elections in Czechoslovakia in 1946, communists received 38 percent of the vote. Furthermore, in Yugoslavia, a genuinely popular communist movement had played a leading role in the struggle against Nazi occupation and came to power on its own with little Soviet help. Its leader, Josef Broz, known as Tito, openly defied Soviet efforts to control it, claiming that "our goal is that everyone should be master in his own house."[2]

China: A Prolonged Revolutionary Struggle

Communism triumphed in the ancient land of China in 1949, about thirty years after the Russian Revolution, likewise on the heels of war and domestic revolution. But that revolution, which was a struggle of decades rather than a single year, was far different from its earlier Russian counterpart. The Chinese imperial system had collapsed in 1911, under the pressure of foreign imperialism, its own inadequacies, and mounting internal opposition (see Chapter 19). Unlike Russia, where intellectuals had been discussing socialism for half a century or more before the revolution, the ideas of Karl Marx were barely known in China in the early twentieth century. Not until 1921 was a small Chinese Communist Party (CCP) founded, aiming its efforts initially at organizing the country's minuscule urban working class.

Over the next twenty-eight years, that small party, with an initial membership of only sixty people, grew enormously, transformed its strategy, found a charismatic leader in Mao Zedong, engaged in an epic struggle with its opponents, fought the Japanese heroically, and in 1949 emerged victorious as the rulers of China. The victory was all the more surprising because the CCP faced a far more formidable foe than the weak Provisional Government over which the Bolsheviks had triumphed in Russia. That opponent was

■ **Change**
What was the appeal of communism in China before 1949?

Mao Zedong and the Long March
An early member of China's then minuscule Communist Party, Mao rose to a position of dominant leadership during the Long March of 1934–1935, when beleaguered communists from southeastern China trekked to a new base area in the north. This photograph shows Mao on his horse during that epic journey of some 6,000 miles. (Collection J.A. Fox/Magnum Photos)

the *Guomindang*, or Nationalist Party, which governed China after 1928. Led by a military officer, Chiang Kai-shek, that party promoted a measure of modern development (railroads, light industry, banking, airline services) in the decade that followed. However, the impact of these achievements was limited largely to the cities, leaving the rural areas, where most people lived, still impoverished. The Guomindang's base of support was also narrow, deriving from urban elites, rural landlords, and Western powers.

Chased out of China's cities in a wave of Guomindang-inspired anticommunist terror in 1927, the CCP groped its way toward a new revolutionary strategy, quite at odds with both classical Marxism and Russian practice. Whereas the Bolsheviks had found their primary audience among workers in Russia's major cities, Chinese communists increasingly looked to the country's peasant villages for support. Thus European Marxism was adapted once again, this time to fit the situation in a mostly peasant China. Still, it was no easy sell. Chinese peasants did not rise up spontaneously against their landlords, as Russian peasants had. However, years of guerrilla warfare, experiments with land reform in areas under communist control, efforts to empower women, and the creation of a communist military force to protect liberated areas from Guomindang attack and landlord reprisals—all of this slowly gained for the CCP a growing measure of respect and support among China's peasants. In the process, Chinese communists discovered an effective leader in Mao Zedong, the son of a prosperous Chinese peasant family and a professional revolutionary since the early 1920s.

It was Japan's brutal invasion of China that gave the CCP a decisive opening, for that attack destroyed Guomindang control over much of the country and forced it to retreat to the interior, where it became even more dependent on conservative landlords. The CCP, by contrast, grew from just 40,000 members in 1937 to more than 1.2 million in 1945, while the communist-led People's Liberation Army mushroomed to 900,000 men, supported by an additional 2 million militia troops (see Map 22.2). Much of this growing support derived from the vigor with which the CCP waged war against the Japanese invaders. Using guerrilla warfare techniques learned in the struggle against the Guomindang, communist forces established themselves behind enemy lines and, despite periodic setbacks, offered a measure of security to many Chinese faced with Japanese atrocities. The Guomindang, by contrast, sometimes seemed to be more interested in eliminating the communists than in actively fighting the Japanese. Furthermore, in the areas it controlled, the CCP reduced rents, taxes, and interest payments for peasants; taught literacy to adults; and mobilized women for the struggle. As the war drew to a close, more radical action followed. Teams of activists, called cadres, encouraged poor peasants to "speak bitterness" in public meetings, to "struggle" with landlords, and to "settle accounts" with them.

Thus the CCP frontally addressed both of China's major problems—foreign imperialism and peasant exploitation. It expressed Chinese nationalism as well as a demand for radical social change. It gained a reputation for honesty that contrasted

Map 22.2 The Rise of Communism in China Communism arose in China at the same time as the country was engaged in a terrible war with Japan and in the context of a civil war with Guomindang forces.

sharply with the massive corruption of Guomindang officials. It put down deep roots among the peasantry in a way that the Bolsheviks never did. And whereas the Bolsheviks gained support by urging Russian withdrawal from the highly unpopular First World War, the CCP won support by aggressively pursuing the struggle against Japanese invaders during World War II. In 1949, four years after the war's end, the Chinese communists swept to victory over the Guomindang, many of whose followers fled to Taiwan. Mao Zedong announced triumphantly in Beijing's Tiananmen Square that "the Chinese people have stood up."

Building Socialism in Two Countries

Once they came to power, the communist parties of the Soviet Union and China set about the construction of socialist societies. In the Soviet Union, this massive undertaking occurred under the leadership of Joseph Stalin in the 1920s and 1930s. The corresponding Chinese effort took place during the 1950s and 1960s with Mao Zedong at the helm.

To communist regimes, building socialism meant first of all the modernization and industrialization of their backward societies. In this respect, they embraced many of the material values of Western capitalist societies and were similar to the new nations of the twentieth century, all of which were seeking development. The communists, however, sought a distinctly socialist modernity. This involved a frontal attack on long-standing inequalities of class and gender, an effort to prevent the making of new inequalities as the process of modern development unfolded, and the promotion of cultural values of selflessness and collectivism that could support a socialist society.

Those imperatives generated a political system thoroughly dominated by the Communist Party. Top-ranking party members enjoyed various privileges but were expected to be exemplars of socialism in the making by being disciplined, selfless, and utterly loyal to their country's Marxist ideology. The party itself penetrated society in ways that Western scholars called "totalitarian," for other parties were forbidden, the state controlled almost the entire economy, and political authorities ensured that the arts, education, and the media conformed to approved ways of thinking. Mass organizations for women, workers, students, and various professional groups operated under party control, with none of the independence that characterized civil society in the West.

In undertaking these tasks, the Soviet Union and China started from different places. As the first successful communist revolution, the Bolsheviks faced almost universal hostility from the capitalist Great Powers and international intervention in their civil war. China, however, had a secure northern border with the Soviet Union and confronted an international environment in which one of the Great Powers was an established communist state. Unlike the Bolsheviks, who came to power virtually overnight, the Chinese communists had substantial administrative and governing experience; by the early 1940s, they already ruled an area with 100 million inhabitants. Finally, whereas the Bolsheviks had little presence among the peasantry and lacked experience in the countryside, the Chinese communists came to power as the champions of the rural masses, who constituted some 80 percent of China's population.

In economic terms, China faced even more daunting prospects than did the Soviet Union. Its population was far greater, its industrial base far smaller, and the availability of new agricultural land far more limited than in the Soviet Union. China's literacy and modern education as well as its transportation network were likewise much less developed. Even more than the Soviets, Chinese communists had to build a modern society from the ground up.

Communist Feminism

Among the earliest and most revolutionary actions of these new communist regimes were efforts at liberating and mobilizing their women. Communist countries in fact pioneered forms of "women's liberation" that only later were adopted in the West. This communist feminism was largely state-directed, with the initiative coming from the top rather than bubbling up from grassroots movements as in the West. In the Soviet Union, where a small women's movement had taken shape in pre–World War I Russia, the new communist government almost immediately issued a series of laws and decrees regarding women. They declared full legal and political equality for women; marriage became a civil procedure among freely consenting adults; divorce was legalized and made easier, as was abortion; illegitimacy was abolished; women no longer had to take their husbands' surnames; pregnancy leave for employed women was mandated; and women were actively mobilized as workers in the country's drive to industrialization.

In 1919, the party set up a special organization called Zhenotdel (Women's Department), whose radical leaders, all women, pushed a decidedly feminist agenda in the 1920s. They organized numerous conferences for women, trained women to run day-care centers and medical clinics, published newspapers and magazines aimed at a female audience, provided literacy and prenatal classes, and encouraged Muslim women to take off their veils. Much of this encountered opposition from male communist officials and from ordinary people as well, and Stalin abolished Zhenotdel in 1930. While it lasted, though, it was a remarkable experiment in women's liberation by means of state action, animated by an almost utopian sense of new possibilities set loose by the revolution.

Similar policies took shape in communist China. The Marriage Law of 1950 was a direct attack on patriarchal and Confucian traditions. It decreed free choice in marriage, relatively easy divorce, the end of concubinage and child marriage, permission for widows to remarry, and equal property rights for women. A short but intense campaign by the CCP in the early 1950s sought to implement these changes, often against strenuous opposition. The party also launched a Women's Federation, a mass organization that enrolled millions of women. Its leadership, however, was far less radical than that of the Bolshevik feminists who led Zhenotdel in the

■ **Change**
What changes did communist regimes bring to the lives of women?

Mobilizing Women for Communism
As the Soviet Union mobilized for rapid economic development in the 1930s, women entered the workforce in great numbers. Here two young women are mastering the skills of driving a tractor on one of the large collective farms that replaced the country's private agriculture. (Sovfoto/Eastfoto)

1920s. In China, there was little talk of "free love" or the "withering away of the family," as there had been in the USSR. Nevertheless, like their Soviet counterparts, Chinese women became much more actively involved in production outside the home. By 1978, 50 percent of agricultural workers and 38 percent of nonagricultural laborers were female. "Women can do anything" became a famous party slogan in the 1960s.

Still, women's liberation communist style had definite limits. Fearing that the women's question would detract from his emphasis on industrial production, Stalin declared it "solved" in 1930. Little direct discussion of women's issues was permitted in the several decades that followed. In neither the Soviet Union nor China did the Communist Party undertake a direct attack on male domination within the family. Thus the double burden of housework and child care plus paid employment continued to afflict most women. Moreover, women appeared only very rarely in the top political leadership of either country.

Socialism in the Countryside

■ **Comparison**
How did the collectivization of agriculture differ between the USSR and China?

In their effort to build socialism, both the Soviet Union and China first expropriated landlords' estates and redistributed that land on a much more equitable basis to the peasantry. Such actions were not socialist, for peasants initially received their land as private property, but they were thoroughly revolutionary. In Russia, the peasants had spontaneously redistributed the land among themselves, and the victorious Bolsheviks merely ratified their actions. In China after 1949, it was a more prolonged and difficult process. Hastily trained land reform teams were dispatched to the newly liberated areas, where they mobilized the poorer peasants in thousands of separate villages to confront and humiliate the landlords or the more wealthy peasants and seized their land, animals, tools, houses, and money for redistribution to the poorer members of the village. In the villages, the land reform teams encountered the age-old deference that peasants traditionally had rendered to their social superiors. One young woman activist described the confrontational meetings intended to break this ancient pattern.

> "Speak bitterness meetings," as they were called, would help [the peasants] to understand how things really had been in the old days, to realize that their lives were not blindly ordained by fate, that poor peasants had a community of interests, having suffered similar disasters and misery in the past—and that far from owing anything to the feudal landlords, it was the feudal landlords who owed them a debt of suffering beyond all reckoning.[3]

It was, as Mao Zedong put it, "not a dinner party." Approximately 1 million to 2 million landlords were killed in the process, which was largely over by 1952.

A second and more distinctly socialist stage of rural reform sought to end private property in land by collectivizing agriculture. In China, despite brief resistance from richer peasants, collectivization during the 1950s was a generally peaceful process, owing much to the close relationship between the Communist Party and the peasantry, which had been established during three decades of struggle. This contrasted markedly with the experience of the Soviet Union from 1928 to 1933, when peasants were forced into collective farms and violence was extensive. Russian peasants slaughtered and consumed hundreds of thousands of animals rather than surrender them to the collectives. Stalin singled out the richer peasants, known as *kulaks*, for exclusion from the new collective farms. Some were killed, and many others were deported to remote areas of the country. With little support or experience in the countryside, Soviet communists, who came mostly from the cities, were viewed as intrusive outsiders in Russian peasant villages. A terrible famine ensued, with some 5 million deaths from starvation or malnutrition.

China pushed the collectivization process further than the Soviet Union did, particularly in huge "people's communes" during the Great Leap Forward in the late 1950s. It was an effort to mobilize China's enormous population for rapid development and at the same time to move toward a more fully communist society with an even greater degree of social equality and collective living. Administrative chaos, disruption of marketing networks, and bad weather combined to produce a massive famine that killed an amazing 20 million people or more between 1959 and 1962, dwarfing even the earlier Soviet famine.

Communism and Industrial Development

Both the Soviet Union and China defined industrialization as a fundamental task of their regimes. That process was necessary to end humiliating backwardness and poverty, to provide the economic basis for socialism, and to create the military strength that would enable their revolutions to survive in a hostile world. Though strongly anticapitalist, communists everywhere were ardent modernizers.

■ **Change**
What were the achievements of communist efforts at industrialization? What problems did these achievements generate?

When the Chinese communists began their active industrialization efforts in the early 1950s, they largely followed the model pioneered by the Soviet Union in the late 1920s and the 1930s. That model involved state ownership of property, centralized planning embodied in successive five-year plans, priority to heavy industry, massive mobilization of the nation's human and material resources, and intrusive Communist Party control of the entire process. Both countries experienced major—indeed unprecedented—economic growth. The Soviet Union constructed the foundations of an industrial society in the 1930s that proved itself in the victory over Nazi Germany in World War II and which by the 1960s and 1970s generated substantially improved standards of living. China too quickly expanded its output (see the Snapshot). In addition, both countries achieved massive improvements in their literacy rates and educational opportunities, allowing far greater social mobility for millions of people than ever before. In both countries, industrialization fostered a similar set of social outcomes: rapid urbanization, exploitation of the countryside to provide for modern industry in the cities, and the growth of a privileged bureaucratic and technological elite intent on pursuing their own careers and passing on their new status to their children.

Snapshot **China under Mao, 1949–1976**

The following table reveals some of the achievements, limitations, and tragedies of China's communist experience during the era of Mao Zedong.[4]

Steel production	from 1.3 million to 23 million tons
Coal production	from 66 million to 448 million tons
Electric power generation	from 7 million to 133 billion kilowatt-hours
Fertilizer production	from 0.2 million to 28 million tons
Cement production	from 3 million to 49 million tons
Industrial workers	from 3 million to 50 million
Scientists and technicians	from 50,000 to 5 million
"Barefoot doctors" posted to countryside	1 million
Annual growth rate of industrial output	11 percent
Annual growth rate of agricultural output	2.3 percent
Total population	from 542 million to 1 billion
Average population growth rate per year	2 percent
Per capita consumption of rural dwellers	from 62 to 124 yuan annually
Per capita consumption of urban dwellers	from 148 to 324 yuan
Overall life expectancy	from 35 to 65 years
Counterrevolutionaries killed (1949–1952)	between 1 million and 3 million
People labeled "rightists" in 1957	550,000
Deaths from famine during Great Leap Forward	20 million or more
Deaths during Cultural Revolution	500,000
Officials sent down to rural labor camps during Cultural Revolution	3 million or more
Urban youth sent down to countryside (1967–1976)	17 million

Perhaps the chief difference in the industrial histories of the Soviet Union and China lies in the leadership's response to these social outcomes. In the Soviet Union under Stalin and his successors, they were largely accepted. Industrialization was centered in large urban areas, which pulled from the countryside its most ambitious and talented people. A highly privileged group of state and party leaders emerged in the Stalin era and largely remained the unchallenged ruling class of the country until the 1980s. Even in the 1930s, the outlines of a conservative society, which had discarded much of its revolutionary legacy, were apparent. Stalin himself endorsed Russian patriotism, traditional family values, individual competition, and substantial differences in wages to stimulate production, even as an earlier commitment to egalitarianism was substantially abandoned. Increasingly the invocation of revolutionary values was devoid of real content, and by the 1970s the perception of official hypocrisy was widespread.

The unique feature of Chinese history under Mao Zedong's leadership was a recurrent effort to combat these perhaps inevitable tendencies of any industrializing process and to revive and preserve the revolutionary spirit, which had animated the Communist Party during its long struggle for power. By the mid-1950s, Mao and some of his followers had become persuaded that the Soviet model of industrialization was leading China away from socialism and toward new forms of inequality, toward individualistic and careerist values, and toward an urban bias that privileged the cities at the expense of the countryside. The Great Leap Forward of 1958–1960 marked Mao's first response to these distortions of Chinese socialism. It promoted small-scale industrialization in the rural areas rather than focusing wholly on large enterprises in the cities; it tried to foster widespread and practical technological education for all rather than relying on a small elite of highly trained technical experts; and it envisaged an immediate transition to full communism in the "people's communes" rather than waiting for industrial development to provide the material basis for that transition. The disruptions and resentments occasioned by this Great Leap Forward, coupled with a series of droughts, floods, and typhoons, threw China into a severe crisis, including a massive famine that brought death and malnutrition to some 20 million people between 1959 and 1962.

In the mid-1960s, Mao launched yet another campaign—the Great Proletarian Cultural Revolution—to combat the capitalist tendencies that he believed had penetrated even the highest ranks of the Communist Party itself. The Cultural Revolution also involved new policies to bring health care and education to the countryside and to reinvigorate earlier efforts at rural industrialization under local rather than central control. In these ways, Mao struggled, though without great success, to overcome the inequalities associated with China's modern development and to create a model of socialist modernity quite distinct from that of the Soviet Union.

Substituting Manpower for Machinery
Lacking sophisticated equipment, Chinese communist leaders pursued a labor-intensive form of development, mobilizing the country's huge population in constructing the economic infrastructure for its industrial development. Here thousands of workers using ancient techniques participate in the building of a modern dam during China's Great Leap Forward in 1958. (Henry Cartier-Bresson/Magnum Photos)

The Search for Enemies

■ Explanation
Why did communist regimes generate terror and violence on such a massive scale?

Despite their totalitarian tendencies, the communist societies of the Soviet Union and China were laced with conflict. Under both Stalin and Mao, those conflicts erupted in a search for enemies that disfigured both societies. An elastic concept of "enemy" came to include not only surviving remnants from the old prerevolutionary elites but also, and more surprisingly, high-ranking members and longtime supporters of the Communist Party who allegedly had been corrupted by bourgeois ideas. Refracted through the lens of Marxist thinking, these people became class enemies who had betrayed the revolution and were engaged in a vast conspiracy, often linked to foreign imperialists, to subvert the socialist enterprise and restore capitalism. In the rhetoric of the leadership, the class struggle continued and in fact intensified as the triumph of socialism drew closer.

In the Soviet Union, that process culminated in the Terror, or the Great Purges, of the late 1930s, which enveloped tens of thousands of prominent communists, including virtually all of Lenin's top associates, and millions of more ordinary people. Based on suspicious associations in the past, denunciations by colleagues, connections to foreign countries, or simply bad luck, such people were arrested, usually in the dead of night, and then tried and sentenced either to death or to long years in harsh and remote labor camps known as the gulag. Many of the accused were linked, almost always falsely, to the Nazis, who were then a real and growing external threat to the Soviet Union. A series of show trials publicized the threat that these "enemies of the people" allegedly posed to the country and its revolution. Close to 1 million people were executed between 1936 and 1941. Perhaps an additional 4 million or 5 million were sent to the gulag, where they were forced to work in horrendous conditions and died in appalling numbers. Victimizers too were numerous: the Terror consumed the energies of a huge corps of officials, investigators, interrogators, informers, guards, and executioners, many of whom themselves were arrested, exiled, or executed in the course of the purges.

In the Soviet Union, the search for enemies occurred under the clear control of the state. In China, however, it became a much more public process, escaping the control of the leadership, particularly during the Cultural Revolution of 1966–1969. Mao had become convinced that many within the Communist Party had been seduced by capitalist values of self-seeking and materialism and were no longer animated by the idealistic revolutionary vision of earlier times. Therefore, he called for rebellion, against the Communist Party itself. Millions of young people responded, and, organized as Red Guards, they set out to rid China of those who were "taking the capitalist road." Following gigantic and ecstatic rallies in Beijing, they fanned out across the country and attacked local party and government officials, teachers, intellectuals, factory managers, and others they defined as enemies. Rival revolutionary groups soon began fighting with one another, violence erupted throughout the country, and civil war threatened China. Mao found himself forced to call in the military to restore order and Communist Party control. Both the Soviet Terror and the Chinese Cultural

Revolution badly discredited the very idea of socialism and contributed to the ultimate collapse of the communist experiment at the end of the century.

East versus West: A Global Divide and a Cold War

Not only did communist regimes bring revolutionary changes to the societies they governed, but they also launched a global conflict that restructured international life and touched the lives of almost everyone, particularly in the twentieth century's second half. That rift began soon after the Russian Revolution when the new communist government became the source of fear and loathing to many in the Western capitalist world. The common threat of Nazi Germany temporarily made unlikely allies of the Soviet Union, Britain, and the United States, but a few years after World War II ended, that division erupted again in what became known as the cold war. Underlying that conflict were the geopolitical and ideological realities of the postwar world. The Soviet Union and the United States were now the major political/military powers, replacing the shattered and diminished states of Western Europe, but they represented sharply opposed views of history, society, politics, and international relations. Conflict, in retrospect, seemed almost inevitable.

Military Conflict and the Cold War

The initial arena of the cold war was Europe, where Soviet insistence on security and control in Eastern Europe clashed with American and British desires for open and democratic societies with ties to the capitalist world economy. What resulted were rival military alliances (NATO and the Warsaw Pact), a largely voluntary American sphere of influence in Western Europe, and an imposed Soviet sphere in Eastern Europe. The heavily fortified border between Eastern and Western Europe came to be known as the Iron Curtain. Thus Europe was bitterly divided; tensions flared across this dividing line, particularly in Berlin; but no shooting war occurred between the two sides (see Map 22.3).

■ Connection

In what different ways was the cold war expressed?

By contrast, the extension of communism into Asia—China, Korea, and Vietnam—globalized the cold war and led to its most destructive and prolonged "hot wars." A North Korean invasion of South Korea in 1950 led to both Chinese and American involvement in a bitter three-year war (1950–1953), which ended in an essential standoff that left the Korean peninsula divided still in the early twenty-first century. Likewise in Vietnam, military efforts by South Vietnamese communists and the already communist North Vietnamese government to unify their country prompted massive American intervention in the 1960s, peaking at some 550,000 U.S. troops. To American authorities, a communist victory opened the door to further communist expansion in Asia and beyond. Armed and supported by the Soviets and Chinese and willing to endure enormous losses, the Vietnamese communists bested the Americans, who were hobbled by growing protest at home. The Vietnamese united their country under communist control by 1975.

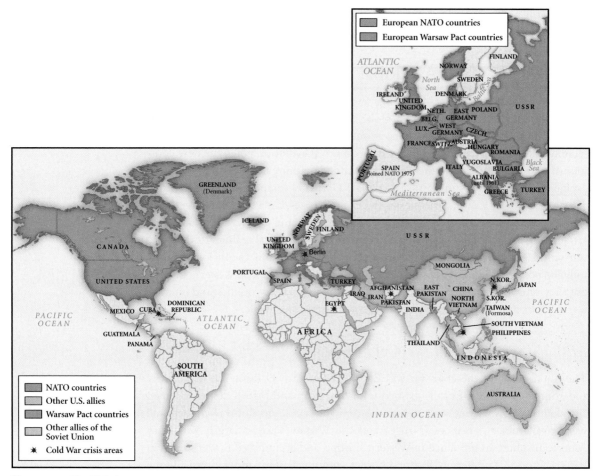

Map 22.3   The Global Cold War

The cold war sharply divided the world as a whole as well the continent of Europe; the countries of Korea, Vietnam, and Germany; and the city of Berlin. In many places, it also sparked crises that brought the nuclear-armed superpowers of the United States and the USSR to the brink of war, although in every case they managed to avoid direct military conflict between themselves.

A third major military conflict of the cold war era occurred in Afghanistan, where a Marxist party had taken power in 1978. Soviet leaders were delighted at this extension of communism on their southern border, but radical land reforms and efforts to liberate Afghan women soon alienated much of this conservative Muslim country and led to a mounting opposition movement. Fearing the overthrow of a new communist state and its replacement by Islamic radicals, Soviet forces intervened militarily and were soon bogged down in a war they could not win. For a full decade (1979–1989), that war was a "bleeding wound," sustained in part by U.S. aid to Afghan guerrillas. Under widespread international pressure, Soviet forces finally withdrew in 1989, and the Afghan communist regime soon collapsed. In Vietnam and Afghanistan, both superpowers painfully experienced the limits of their power.

The most haunting battle of the cold war era was the one that never happened. The setting was Cuba. When the revolutionary Fidel Castro came to power in 1959, his nationalization of American assets provoked great U.S. hostility and efforts to overthrow his regime. Such pressure only pushed this revolutionary nationalist closer to the Soviet Union, and gradually he began to think of himself and his revolution as Marxist. Soviet authorities were elated. "You Americans must realize what Cuba means to us old Bolsheviks," declared one high-ranking Soviet official. "We have been waiting all our lives for a country to go communist without the Red Army. It has happened in Cuba, and it makes us feel like boys again."[5] Fearing the loss of their newfound Caribbean ally to American aggression, the Soviet leader Nikita Khrushchev, who had risen to power after Stalin's death in 1953, secretly deployed nuclear-tipped Soviet missiles to Cuba, believing that this would deter further U.S. action against Castro. When the missiles were discovered in October 1962, the world held its breath for thirteen days as American forces blockaded the island and prepared for an invasion. A nuclear exchange between the superpowers seemed imminent, but that catastrophe was averted by a compromise between Khrushchev and U.S. president John F. Kennedy. Under the terms of that compromise, the Soviets removed their missiles from Cuba in return for an American promise not to invade the island.

Nuclear Standoff and Third World Rivalry

The Cuban missile crisis gave concrete expression to the most novel and dangerous dimension of the cold war—the arms race in nuclear weapons. An American monopoly on those weapons when World War II ended prompted the Soviet Union to redouble its efforts to acquire them, and in 1949 it succeeded. Over the next forty years, the world moved from a mere handful of nuclear weapons to a global arsenal of close to 60,000 warheads. Delivery systems included bomber aircraft and missiles that could rapidly propel numerous warheads across whole continents and oceans with accuracies measured in hundreds of feet. During those decades, the world's many peoples lived in the shadow of weapons whose destructive power is scarcely within the bounds of human imagination. A single bomb in a single instant could obliterate any major city in the world. The detonation of even a small fraction of the weapons then in the arsenals of the Soviet Union and the United States could reduce the target countries to radioactive rubble and social chaos. Responsible scientists seriously discussed the possible extinction of the human species under such conditions.

Awareness of this possibility is surely the primary reason that no shooting war of any kind occurred between the two

The Hydrogen Bomb
During the 1950s and early 1960s, tests in the atmosphere of ever larger and more sophisticated hydrogen bombs made images of enormous fireballs and mushroom-shaped clouds the universal symbol of these weapons, which were immensely more powerful than the atomic bombs dropped on Japan. The American test pictured here took place in 1957. (Image courtesy The Nuclear Weapon Archive)

superpowers. During the two world wars, the participants had been greatly surprised by the destructiveness of modern weapons. During the cold war, however, the leaders of the two superpowers knew beyond any doubt that a nuclear war would produce only losers and utter catastrophe. Already in 1949, Stalin had observed that "atomic weapons can hardly be used without spelling the end of the world."[6] Furthermore, the deployment of reconnaissance satellites made it possible to know with some clarity the extent of the other side's arsenals. Particularly after the frightening Cuban missile crisis of 1962, both sides carefully avoided further nuclear provocation, even while continuing the buildup of their respective arsenals. Moreover, because they feared that a conventional war would escalate to the nuclear level, they implicitly agreed to sidestep any direct military confrontation at all.

Still, opportunities for conflict abounded as the U.S.-Soviet rivalry spanned the globe. Using military and economic aid, educational opportunities, political pressure, and covert action, both sides courted third world countries just emerging from colonial rule. Cold war fears of communist penetration prompted U.S. intervention, sometimes openly and often secretly, in Iran, the Philippines, Guatemala, El Salvador, Chile, the Congo, and elsewhere, and in the process the United States frequently supported anti-communist but corrupt and authoritarian regimes. However, neither superpower was able to completely dominate its supposed third-world allies, many of whom resisted the role of pawns in superpower rivalries. Some countries, such as India, took a posture of nonalignment in the cold war, while others tried to play off the superpowers against each other. Indonesia received large amounts of Soviet and Eastern European aid, but that did not prevent it from destroying the Indonesian Communist Party in 1965, butchering half a million suspected communists in the process. When the Americans refused to assist Egypt in building the Aswan Dam in the mid-1950s, that country developed a close relationship with the Soviet Union. Later, in 1972, Egypt expelled 21,000 Soviet advisers and aligned more clearly with the United States.

The United States: Superpower of the West, 1945–1975

■ **Connection**
In what ways did the United States play a global role after World War II?

World War II and the cold war provided the context for the emergence of the United States as a global superpower, playing a role that has often been compared to that of Great Britain in the nineteenth century. Much of that effort was driven by the perceived demands of the cold war, during which the United States spearheaded the Western effort to contain a worldwide communist movement that seemed to be on the move. A series of global alliances and military bases sought to create a barrier against further communist expansion and to provide launching points for military action should it become necessary. By 1970, one writer observed, "the United States had more than 1,000,000 soldiers in 30 countries, was a member of four regional defense alliances and an active participant in a fifth, had mutual defense treaties with 42 nations, was a member of 53 international organizations, and was furnishing military or economic aid to nearly 100 nations across the face of the globe."[7]

The need for quick and often secret decision making gave rise in the United States to a strong or "imperial" presidency and a "national security state," in which defense and intelligence agencies acquired great power within the government and were often unaccountable to Congress. With power so focused in the executive branch, critics charged that democracy itself was undermined. Fear of internal subversion produced an intense anticommunism in the 1950s and in general narrowed the range of political debate in the country as both parties competed to appear "tough on communism." All of this served to strengthen the influence of what U.S. president Dwight Eisenhower (1953–1961) called the "military-industrial complex," a coalition of the armed services, military research laboratories, and private defense industries that both stimulated and benefited from increased military spending and cold war tensions.

Sustaining this immense military effort was a flourishing U.S. economy and an increasingly middle-class society. Private spending for houses, automobiles, and durable goods as well as public spending for schools, superhighways, and cold war armaments spurred this remarkable growth. The United States, of course, was the only major industrial society to escape the physical devastation of war on its own soil. As World War II ended, the United States was the world's largest creditor, controlled two-thirds of the world's gold, and accounted for half of its manufacturing and shipping. "The whole world is hungry for American goods," wrote one American economist in 1945. "Everyone would like to have the opportunity of riding in American automobiles, of drinking American fruit juices, and of possessing electric refrigerators and other conveniences of life."[8] Americans were a "people of plenty," ready and willing "to show to other countries the path that may lead them to plenty like our own."[9] Beyond their goods, Americans sent their capital abroad in growing amounts—from $19 billion in 1950 to $81 billion in 1965. Huge American firms such as General Motors, Ford, Mobil, Sears, General Electric, and Westinghouse established factories, offices, and subsidiaries in many countries and sold their goods locally. The U.S. dollar replaced the British pound as the most trusted international currency.

Accompanying the United States' political and economic penetration of the world was its popular culture. In musical terms, first jazz, then rock-and-roll, and most recently rap have found receptive audiences abroad, particularly among the young. Blacks in South Africa took up American "Negro spirituals." In the Soviet Union, American rock-and-roll became the music of dissent and a way of challenging the values of communist culture. Muslim immigrants to France as well as young Japanese have developed local traditions of rap. By the 1990s, American movies took about 70 percent of the market in Europe, and some 20,000 McDonald's restaurants in 100 countries served 30 million customers every day. Various American brand names—Kleenex, Coca-Cola, Jeep, Spam, Nike, Kodak—became common points of reference around the world. English became a global language, while American slang terms—"groovy," "crazy," "cool"—were integrated into many of the world's languages.

The Communist World, 1950s–1970s

■ **Description**
Describe the strengths
and weaknesses of the
communist world by the
1970s.

On the communist side, the cold war was accompanied by considerable turmoil both within and among the various communist states. Joseph Stalin, Soviet dictator and acknowledged leader of the communist world in general, died in 1953 as that global conflict was mounting. His successor, Nikita Khrushchev, stunned his country and communists everywhere with a lengthy speech delivered to a party congress in 1956 in which he presented a devastating but incomplete account of Stalin's crimes, particularly those against party members. "Everywhere and in everything, he [Stalin] saw 'enemies,' 'two-facers,' and 'spies,'" declared Khrushchev. "Possessing unlimited power, he indulged in great willfulness and choked a person morally and physically."[10] These revelations shocked many of the party faithful, for Stalin had been viewed as the "genius of all time." Now he was presented as a criminal.

In the Soviet Union, the superpower of the communist world, the cold war justified a continuing emphasis on military and defense industries after World War II and gave rise to a Soviet version of the military-industrial complex. Sometimes called a "metal-eater's alliance," this complex joined the armed forces with certain heavy industries to press for a weapons buildup that benefited both. Soviet citizens, even more than Americans, were subject to incessant government propaganda that glorified the Soviet system and vilified that of their American opponents.

As the communist world expanded, so too did divisions and conflicts among its various countries. Many in the West had initially viewed world communism as a monolithic force whose disciplined members meekly followed Soviet dictates in cold war solidarity against the West. And Marxists everywhere contended that revolutionary socialism would erode national loyalties as the "workers of the world" united in common opposition to global capitalism. Nonetheless, the communist world experienced far more bitter and divisive conflict than did the Western alliance, which was composed of supposedly warlike, greedy, and highly competitive nations.

Czechoslovakia, 1968
In August 1968, Soviet forces invaded Czechoslovakia, where a popular reform movement proclaiming "socialism with a human face" threatened to erode established communist control. The Soviet troops that crushed this so-called Prague Spring were greeted by thousands of peaceful street demonstrators begging them to go home. (Bettmann/Corbis)

In Eastern Europe, Yugoslav leaders early on had rejected Soviet domination of their internal affairs and charted their own independent road to socialism. Fearing that reform movements might lead to contagious defections from the communist bloc, Soviet forces actually invaded their supposed allies in Hungary (1956–1957) and Czechoslovakia (1968) to crush such groups. In the early 1980s, Poland was seriously threatened with a similar action. The brutal suppression of these reform movements gave credibility to Western perceptions of the cold war as a struggle between tyranny and freedom and badly tarnished the image of Soviet communism as a reasonable alternative to capitalism.

Even more startling, the two communist giants, the Soviet Union and China, found themselves sharply opposed, owing to territorial disputes, ideological differences, and rivalry for communist leadership. The Chinese bitterly criticized Khrushchev for backing down in the Cuban missile crisis, while to the Soviet leadership, Mao was insanely indifferent to the possible consequences of a nuclear war. In 1960, the Soviet Union backed away from an earlier promise to provide China with the prototype of an atomic bomb and abruptly withdrew all Soviet advisers and technicians, who had been assisting Chinese development. By the late 1960s, China on its own had developed a modest nuclear capability, and the two countries were at the brink of war, with the Soviet Union hinting at a possible nuclear strike on Chinese military targets. Their enmity certainly benefited the United States, which in the 1970s was able to pursue a "triangular diplomacy," easing tensions and simultaneously signing arms control agreements with the USSR and opening a formal relationship with China. Beyond this central conflict, a communist China in fact went to war against a communist Vietnam in 1979, while Vietnam invaded a communist Cambodia in the late 1970s. Nationalism proved more powerful than communist solidarity, even in the face of cold war hostilities with the West.

Despite its many internal conflicts, world communism remained a powerful global presence during the 1970s, reaching the greatest extent of its worldwide expansion. China was emerging from the chaos of the Cultural Revolution. The Soviet Union had achieved its long-sought goal of matching U.S. military might; in response, the Americans launched a major buildup of their own military forces in the early 1980s. Despite American hostility, Cuba remained a communist outpost in the Western Hemisphere, with impressive achievements in education and health care for its people. Communism triumphed in Vietnam, dealing a major setback to the United States. A number of African countries affirmed their commitment to Marxism. Few people anywhere expected that within two decades most of the twentieth century's experiment with communism would be gone.

Comparing Paths to the End of Communism

More rapidly than its beginning, and far more peacefully, the communist era came to an end during the last two decades of the twentieth century. It was a drama in three acts. Act One began in China during the late 1970s, following the death of its towering revolutionary leader Mao Zedong in 1976. Over the next several decades, the CCP gradually abandoned almost everything that had been associated with Maoist socialism, even as the party retained its political control of the country. Act Two took place in Eastern Europe in the "miracle year" of 1989, when popular movements toppled despised communist governments one after another all across the region. The final and climactic act in this "end of communism" drama occurred in 1991 in the Soviet Union, where the entire "play" had opened seventy-four years

■ **Change**
What explains the rapid end of the communist era?

earlier. There the reformist leader Mikhail Gorbachev had come to power in 1985 intending to revive and save Soviet socialism from its accumulated dysfunctions. Those efforts, however, only exacerbated the country's many difficulties and led to its political disintegration on Christmas Day of 1991. The curtain had fallen on the communist era and on the cold war as well.

Behind these separate stories lay two general failures of the communist experiment, measured both by their own standards and by those of the larger world. The first was economic. Despite their early successes, communist economies by the late 1970s showed no signs of catching up to the more advanced capitalist countries. The highly regimented Soviet economy in particular was largely stagnant; its citizens were forced to stand in long lines for consumer goods and complained endlessly about their poor quality and declining availability. This was enormously embarrassing, for it had been the proud boast of communist leaders everywhere that they had found a better route to modern prosperity than their capitalist rivals. Furthermore, these comparisons were increasingly well known, thanks to the global information revolution. They had security implications as well, for economic growth, even more than military capacity, was the measure of state power as the twentieth century approached its end.

The second failure was moral. The horrors of Stalin's Terror and the gulag, of Mao's Cultural Revolution, of something approaching genocide in communist Cambodia— all of this wore away at communist claims to moral superiority over capitalism. Moreover, this erosion occurred as global political culture more widely embraced democracy and human rights as the universal legacy of humankind, rather than the exclusive possession of the capitalist West. In both economic and moral terms, the communist path to the modern world was increasingly seen as a road to nowhere.

Communist leaders were not ignorant of these problems, and particularly in China and the Soviet Union, they moved aggressively to address them. But their approach to doing so varied greatly, as did the outcomes of those efforts. Thus, much as the Russian and Chinese revolutions differed and their approaches to building socialism diverged, so too did these communist giants chart distinct paths during the final years of the communist era.

China: Abandoning Communism and Maintaining the Party

As the dust settled from the political shakeout following Mao's death in 1976, Deng Xiaoping emerged as China's "paramount leader," committed to ending the periodic upheavals of the Maoist era while fostering political stability and economic growth. Soon previously banned plays, operas, films, and translations of Western classics reappeared, and a "literature of the wounded" exposed the sufferings of the Cultural Revolution. Some 100,000 political prisoners, many of them high-ranking communists, were released and restored to important positions. A party evaluation of Mao severely criticized his mistakes during the Great Leap Forward and the Cultural Revolution, while praising his role as a revolutionary leader.

Even more dramatic were Deng's economic reforms. In the rural areas, these reforms included a rapid dismantling of the country's system of collectivized farming and a return to something close to small-scale private agriculture. Impoverished Chinese peasants eagerly embraced these new opportunities and pushed them even further than the government had intended. Industrial reform proceeded more gradually. Managers of state enterprises were given greater authority and encouraged to act like private owners, making many of their own decisions and seeking profits. China opened itself to the world economy and welcomed foreign investment in special enterprise zones along the coast, where foreign capitalists received tax breaks and other inducements. Local governments and private entrepreneurs joined forces in thousands of flourishing "township and village enterprises" that produced food, clothing, building materials, and much more.

The outcome of these reforms was stunning economic growth, the most rapid and sustained in world history, and a new prosperity for millions. Better diets, lower mortality rates, declining poverty, massive urban construction, and surging exports accompanied China's rejoining of the world economy, contributed to a much-improved material life for many of its citizens, and prompted much commentary about China as the economic giant of the twenty-first century. On the other hand, the country's burgeoning economy also generated massive corruption among Chinese officials, sharp inequalities between the coast and the interior, a huge problem of urban overcrowding, terrible pollution in major cities, and periodic inflation as the state loosened its controls over the economy. Urban vices such as street crime, prostitution, gambling, drug addiction, and a criminal underworld, which had been largely eliminated after 1949, surfaced again in China's booming cities. Nonetheless, something remarkable had occurred in China: an essentially capitalist economy had been restored, and by none other than the Communist Party itself. Mao's worst fears had been realized, as China "took the capitalist road."

Although the party was willing to largely abandon communist economic policies, it was adamantly unwilling to relinquish its political monopoly or to promote democracy at the national level. "Talk about democracy in the abstract," Deng Xiaoping declared, "will inevitably lead to the unchecked spread of ultra-democracy and anarchism, to the complete disruption of political stability, and to the total failure of our modernization program. . . . China will once again be plunged into chaos, division, retrogression, and darkness."[11] Such attitudes associated democracy with the chaos and uncontrolled mass action of the Cultural Revolution. Thus, when a

After Communism in China Although the Communist Party still governed China in the early twenty-first century, communist values of selflessness, community, and simplicity had been substantially replaced for many by Western-style consumerism. Here a group of young people in Shanghai are eating at a Kentucky Fried Chicken restaurant, drinking Pepsi, wearing clothing common to modern youth everywhere, and using their ubiquitous cell phones. (Mike Kemp/Corbis)

democracy movement, spearheaded by university and secondary school students, surfaced in the late 1980s, Deng ordered the brutal crushing of its brazen demonstration in Beijing's Tiananmen Square before the television cameras of the world.

China entered the new millennium as a rapidly growing economic power with an essentially capitalist economy presided over by an intact and powerful Communist Party. Culturally, some combination of nationalism, consumerism, and a renewed respect for ancient traditions had replaced the collectivist and socialist values of the Maoist era. It was a strange and troubled hybrid.

The Soviet Union: The Collapse of Communism and Country

■ Comparison

How did the end of communism in the Soviet Union differ from communism's demise in China?

By the mid-1980s, the reformist wing of the Soviet Communist Party, long squelched by an aging conservative establishment, had won the top position in the party as Mikhail Gorbachev assumed the role of general secretary. Like Deng Xiaoping in China, Gorbachev was committed to aggressively tackling the country's many problems—economic stagnation, a flourishing black market, public apathy, and cynicism about the party. His economic program, launched in 1987 and known as *perestroika* ("restructuring"), paralleled aspects of the Chinese approach by freeing state enterprises from the heavy hand of government regulation, permitting small-scale private businesses called cooperatives, offering opportunities for private farming, and cautiously welcoming foreign investment in joint enterprises.

Heavy resistance to these modest efforts from entrenched party and state bureaucracies persuaded Gorbachev to seek allies outside of official circles. The vehicle was *glasnost* ("openness"), a policy of permitting a much wider range of cultural and intellectual freedoms in Soviet life. He hoped that glasnost would overcome the pervasive, long-standing distrust between society and the state and would energize Soviet society for the tasks of economic reform. "We need *glasnost*," Gorbachev declared, "like we need the air."[12]

In the late 1980s, glasnost hit the Soviet Union like a bomb. Newspapers and TV exposed social pathologies that previously had been presented solely as the product of capitalism. Stories about social problems such as crime, prostitution, child abuse, suicide, corruption, and homelessness flooded the public media. Viewers learned that the abortion rate in the USSR was the highest in the world, and they discovered something of the degrading process of obtaining one. Films broke the ban on nudity and explicit sex. TV reporters climbed the wall of a secluded villa to film the luxurious homes of the party elite. Soviet history was also reexamined as revelations of Stalin's crimes poured out of the media. Mass graves were uncovered, and a former executioner described on camera precisely how he had shot people. The Bible and the Quran became more widely available, atheistic propaganda largely ceased, and thousands of churches and mosques were returned to believers and opened for worship. Plays, poems, films, and novels that had long been buried "in the drawer" were now released to a public that virtually devoured them. "Like an excited boy reads a note from his girl," wrote one poet, "that's how we read the papers today."[13]

Beyond glasnost lay democratization and a new parliament with real powers, chosen in competitive elections. When those elections occurred in 1989, dozens of leading communists were rejected at the polls. And when the new parliament met and actually debated controversial issues, its televised sessions were broadcast to a transfixed audience of 100 million or more. In foreign affairs, Gorbachev moved to end the cold war by making unilateral cuts in Soviet military forces, engaging in arms control negotiations with the United States, and, most important, refusing to intervene as communist governments in Eastern Europe were overthrown. Thus the Soviet reform program was far more broadly based than that of China, for it embraced dramatic cultural and political changes, which Chinese authorities refused to consider.

Despite his good intentions, almost nothing worked out as Gorbachev had anticipated. Far from strengthening socialism and reviving a stagnant Soviet Union, the reforms led to its further weakening and collapse. In a dramatic contrast with China's booming economy, that of the Soviet Union spun into a sharp decline as its planned economy was dismantled before a functioning market-based system could emerge. Inflation mounted; consumer goods were in short supply, and ration coupons reappeared; many feared the loss of their jobs. Unlike Chinese peasants, few Soviet farmers were willing to risk the jump into private farming, and few foreign investors found the Soviet Union a tempting place to do business.

Furthermore, the new freedoms provoked demands that went far beyond what Gorbachev had intended. A democracy movement of unofficial groups and parties now sprang to life, many of them seeking a full multiparty democracy and a capitalist economy. They were joined by independent labor unions, which actually went on strike, something unheard of in the "worker's state." Most corrosively, a multitude of nationalist movements used the new freedoms to insist on greater autonomy, or even independence, from the Soviet Union. In the Baltic republics of Latvia, Lithuania, and Estonia, nationalists organized a human chain some 370 miles long, sending the word "freedom" along the line of a million people. Even in Russia, growing numbers came to feel that they too might be better off without the Soviet Union. In the face of these mounting demands, Gorbachev resolutely refused to use force to crush the protesters, another sharp contrast with the Chinese experience.

Events in Eastern Europe now intersected with those in the Soviet Union. Gorbachev's reforms had lit a fuse in these Soviet satellites, where communism had been imposed and maintained from outside. If the USSR could practice glasnost and hold competitive elections, why not Eastern Europe as well? This was the background for the "miracle year" of 1989. Massive demonstrations, last-minute efforts at reforms, the breaching of the Berlin Wall, the surfacing of new political groups—all of this and more quickly overwhelmed the highly unpopular communist regimes of Poland, Hungary, East Germany, Bulgaria, Czechoslovakia, and Romania, which were quickly swept away. This success then emboldened nationalists and democrats in the Soviet Union. If communism had been overthrown in Eastern Europe, perhaps it was possible to do so in the USSR as well. Soviet conservatives and patriots, however, were outraged. To them, Gorbachev had stood idly by while the political gains of World War II, for which the Soviet Union had paid in rivers of blood, vanished before their eyes. It was nothing less than treason.

Gorbachev's perceived betrayal was just one of the grievances that motivated a short-lived conservative attempt to restore the old order in August 1991. Leading state, party, and military officials placed Gorbachev under house arrest, occupied Moscow with tanks and troops, and prepared for mass arrests, but popular resistance ensured that this effort collapsed within three days. Ironically, this failed coup energized those who sought an end to both communism and the Soviet Union, and by the end of the year, the Soviet Union and its communist regime had passed into history. From the wreckage of the Soviet Union emerged fifteen new and independent states, following the internal political divisions of the USSR (see Map 22.4). Within Russia itself, the Communist Party was actually banned for a time in the place of its origin. Once again, nationalism had trumped socialism.

The Soviet collapse represented a unique phenomenon in the world of the late twentieth century. Simultaneously, the world's largest state and its last territorial empire vanished; the first Communist Party disintegrated; a powerful command

Map 22.4 The Collapse of the Soviet Empire
Soviet control over its Eastern European dependencies vanished as those countries threw off their communist governments in 1989. Then, in 1991, the Soviet Union itself disintegrated into fifteen separate states, none of them governed by communist parties.

economy broke down; an official socialist ideology was repudiated; and a forty-five-year global struggle between the East and the West ended. In Europe, Germany was reunited, and a number of former communist states joined NATO and the European Union, ending the division of that continent. At least for the moment, capitalism and democracy seemed to triumph over socialism and authoritarian governments. In many places, the end of communism allowed simmering ethnic tensions to explode into open conflict. Beyond the disintegration of the Soviet Union, both Yugoslavia and Czechoslovakia fragmented, the former amid terrible violence and the latter peacefully. Chechens in Russia, Abkhazians in Georgia, Russians in the Baltic states and Ukraine, Tibetans in China—all of these "minorities" found themselves in opposition to the states in which they lived.

As the twenty-first century dawned, the communist world had shrunk considerably from its high point just three decades earlier. In the Soviet Union and Eastern Europe, communism had disappeared entirely as the governing authority and dominant ideology, although communist parties continued to play a role in some countries. China had largely abandoned its communist economic policies as a market economy took shape. Like China, Vietnam and Laos remained officially communist, even while they pursued Chinese-style reforms, though more cautiously. Even Cuba, which was beset by economic crisis in the 1990s after massive Soviet subsidies ended, allowed small businesses, private food markets, and tourism to grow, while harshly repressing opposition political groups. An impoverished North Korea remained the most unreformed and Stalinist of the remaining communist countries.

International tensions born of communism remained only in East Asia and the Caribbean. North Korea's threat to develop nuclear weapons posed a serious international issue. Continuing tension between China and Taiwan as well as between the United States and Cuba were hangovers from the cold war era. But either as a primary source of international conflict or as a compelling path to modernity and social justice, communism was effectively dead. The communist era in world history had ended.

Reflections: To Judge or Not to Judge: The Ambiguous Legacy of Communism

Should historians or students of history make moral judgments about the people and events they study? On the one hand, some would argue, scholars do well to act as detached and objective observers of the human experience, at least as much as possible. The task is to describe what happened and to explain why things turned out as they did. Whether we approve or condemn the outcomes of the historical process is, in this view, beside the point. On the other hand, all of us, scholars and students alike, stand somewhere. We are members of particular cultures; we have values and outlooks on the world that inevitably affect the way we write or think about the past. Perhaps it is better to recognize and acknowledge these limitations than to pretend some unattainable objectivity that places us above it all. Furthermore, making judgments is a way of connecting with the past, of affirming our continuing relationship with those who have gone before us. It shows that we care.

The question of making judgments arises strongly in any examination of the communist phenomenon. In a United States without a strong socialist tradition, sometimes saying anything positive about communism or even noting its appeal to millions of people has brought charges of whitewashing its crimes. Within the communist world, even modest criticism was usually regarded as counterrevolutionary and was largely forbidden and harshly punished. Certainly few observers were neutral in their assessment of the communist experiment.

Were the Russian and Chinese revolutions a blow for human freedom and a cry for justice on the part of oppressed people, or did they simply replace one tyranny with another? Was Stalinism a successful effort to industrialize a backward country or a ferocious assault on its moral and social fabric? Do Chinese reforms that were initiated in the late twentieth century represent a return to sensible policies of modernization, a continued denial of basic democratic rights, or an opening to capitalist inequalities, corruption, and acquisitiveness? Passionate debate continues on all of these questions.

Communism, like many human projects, has been an ambiguous enterprise. On the one hand, communism brought hope to millions by addressing the manifest injustices of the past; by providing new opportunities for women, workers, and peasants; by promoting rapid industrial development; and by ending Western domination. On the other hand, communism was responsible for mountains of crimes—millions killed and wrongly imprisoned; massive famines partly caused by radical policies; human rights violated on an enormous scale; lives uprooted and distorted by efforts to achieve the impossible.

Studying communism challenges our inclination to want definitive answers and clear moral judgments. Can we hold contradictory elements in some kind of tension? Can we affirm our own values while acknowledging the ambiguities of life, both past and present? Doing so is arguably among the essential tasks of growing up and achieving intellectual maturity. That is the gift, both painful and enormously enriching, that the study of history offers to us all.

Second Thoughts

What's the Significance?

To assess your mastery of the material in this chapter, see the **Online Study Guide** at bedfordstmartins.com/strayer.

Russian Revolution	Zhenotdel	Nikita Khrushchev
Bolsheviks/Lenin	collectivization	Mikhail Gorbachev
Guomindang	Cultural Revolution	Deng Xiaoping
Chinese Revolution	Stalin	perestroika/glasnost
Mao Zedong	Great Purges/Terror	
building socialism	Cuban missile crisis	

Big Picture Questions

1. What was the appeal of communism, in terms of both its promise and its achievements? To what extent did it fulfill that promise?
2. Why did the communist experiment, which was committed to equality and a humane socialism, generate such oppressive, brutal, and totalitarian regimes?
3. What is distinctive about twentieth-century communist industrialization and modernization compared to the same processes in the West a century earlier?
4. What was the global significance of the cold war?
5. "The end of communism was as revolutionary as its beginning." Do you agree with this statement?
6. In what different ways did the Soviet Union and China experience communism during the twentieth century?

Next Steps: For Further Study

Archie Brown, *The Gorbachev Factor* (1996). A careful examination of Gorbachev's role in the collapse of the Soviet Union.

Jung Chang, *Wild Swans* (2004). A compelling view of twentieth-century Chinese history through the eyes of three generations of women in a single family.

Timothy Check, *Mao Zedong and China's Revolutions* (2002). A collection of documents about the Chinese Revolution and a fine introduction to the life of Mao.

John L. Gaddis, *The Cold War: A New History* (2005). An overview by one of the most highly regarded historians of the cold war.

Peter Kenez, *A History of the Soviet Union from the Beginning to the End* (1999). A thoughtful overview of the entire Soviet experience.

Maurice Meisner, *Mao's China and After* (1999). A provocative history of Mao's China and what followed.

Robert Strayer, *The Communist Experiment: Revolution, Socialism, and Global Conflict in the Twentieth Century* (2007). A comparative study of Soviet and Chinese communism.

"Mao Zedong Reference Archive," http://www.marxists.org/reference/archive/mao. A Web site offering the translated writings of Mao, including poetry and some images.

"Soviet Archives Exhibit," http://www.ibiblio.org/expo/soviet.exhibit/entrance.html. A rich Web site from the Library of Congress, focusing on the operation of the Soviet system and relations with the United States.

For Web sites and documents related to this chapter, see **Make History** at bedfordstmartins.com/strayer.

Independence and Development in the Global South

1914– PRESENT

"During my lifetime I have dedicated myself to this struggle of the African people. I have fought against white domination, and I have fought against black domination. I have cherished the ideal of a democratic and free society in which all persons live together in harmony and with equal opportunity. It is an ideal which I hope to live for and to achieve. But, if need be, it is an ideal for which I am prepared to die."[1]

Nelson Mandela, South Africa's nationalist leader, first uttered these words in 1964 at his trial for treason, sabotage, and conspiracy to overthrow the apartheid government of his country. Convicted of those charges, he spent the next twenty-seven years in prison, sometimes working at hard labor in a stone quarry. Often the floor was his bed, and a bucket was his toilet. For many years, he was allowed one visitor a year for thirty minutes and permitted to write and receive one letter every six months. When he was finally released from prison in 1990 under growing domestic and international pressure, he concluded his first speech as a free person with the words originally spoken at his trial. Four years later in 1994, South Africa held its first election in which blacks and whites alike were able to vote. The outcome of that election made Mandela the country's first black African president, and it linked South Africa to dozens of other countries all across Africa and Asia that had thrown off European rule or the control of white settlers during the second half of the twentieth century.

THAT PROCESS—VARIOUSLY CALLED THE STRUGGLE FOR INDEPENDENCE OR DECOLONIZATION—was immensely significant. It marked a dramatic

Nelson Mandela: In April 1994, the long struggle against apartheid and white domination in South Africa came to an end in the country's first democratic and nonracial election. The symbol of that triumph was Nelson Mandela, long a political prisoner, head of the African National Congress, and the country's first black African president. He is shown here voting in that historic election. (Peter Turnley/Corbis) change in the world's political architecture, as nation-states triumphed over the empires that had structured much of African and Asian life in the nineteenth and early twentieth centuries. It mobilized millions of people, thrusting them into political activity and sometimes into violence and warfare. Decolonization signaled the declining legitimacy of both empire and race as credible bases for political or social life. It promised not only national freedom but also personal dignity, abundance, and opportunity.

What followed in the decades after independence was equally significant. Political, economic, and cultural experiments proliferated across these newly independent nations, which during the cold war were labeled as the third world and now are often referred to as developing countries or the Global South. Their peoples, who represented the vast majority of the world's population, faced enormous challenges: the legacies of empire; their own deep divisions of language, ethnicity, religion, and class; their rapidly growing numbers; the competing demands of the capitalist West and the communist East; the difficult tasks of simultaneously building modern economies, stable politics, and coherent nations; and all of this in a world still shaped by the powerful economies of the wealthy, already industrialized nations. The emergence of the developing countries onto the world stage as independent and assertive actors has been a distinguishing feature of world history in this most recent century.

Toward Freedom: Struggles for Independence

In 1900, European colonial empires in Africa and Asia appeared as permanent features of the world's political landscape. Well before the end of the twentieth century, they were gone. The first major breakthroughs occurred in Asia and the Middle East in the late 1940s, when India, Pakistan, Burma, Indonesia, Iraq, Jordan, and Israel achieved independence. The period from the mid-1950s through the mid-1970s was the age of African independence as colony after colony, more than fifty in total, emerged into what was then seen as the bright light of freedom (see Map 23.1, p. 694).

The End of Empire in World History

■ Comparison
What was distinctive about the end of Europe's African and Asian empires compared to other cases of imperial disintegration?

At one level, this vast process was but the latest case of imperial dissolution, a fate that had overtaken earlier empires, including the Assyrian, Roman, Arab, and Mongol empires. But never before had the end of empire been so associated with the mobilization of the masses around a nationalist ideology; nor had these earlier cases generated a plethora of nation-states, each claiming an equal place in a world of nation-states. More comparable perhaps was that first decolonization, in which the European colonies in the Americas threw off British, French, Spanish, or Portuguese rule during the late eighteenth and early nineteenth centuries (see Chapter 17). Like their twentieth-century counterparts, these new nations claimed an international status equivalent to that of their former rulers. In the Americas, however, many of the colonized people were themselves of European origin, sharing much of their culture with their colonial rulers. In that respect, the African and Asian struggles of the twentieth century were very different, for they not only asserted political independence but also affirmed the vitality of their cultures, which had been submerged and denigrated during the colonial era.

The twentieth century witnessed the demise of many empires. The Austrian and Ottoman empires collapsed following World War I, giving rise to a number of new states in Europe and the Middle East. The Russian Empire also unraveled, although it was soon reassembled, under the auspices of the Soviet Union. World War II ended the German and Japanese empires. African and Asian movements for independence shared with these other "end of empire" stories the ideal of national self-determination. This novel idea—that humankind was naturally divided into distinct peoples or nations, each of which deserved an independent state of its own—was loudly proclaimed by the winning side of both world wars. The belief in national self-determination gained a global following in the twentieth century and rendered empire illegitimate in the eyes of growing numbers of people.

Empires without territory, such as the powerful influence that the United States exercised in Latin America and elsewhere, likewise came under attack from highly nationalist governments. An intrusive U.S. presence was certainly one factor stimulating the Mexican Revolution, which began in 1910. One of the outcomes of that upheaval was the nationalization in 1937 of Mexico's oil industry, much of which was owned by American and British investors. Similar actions accompanied Cuba's revolution of 1959–1960 and also occurred in other places throughout Latin America and elsewhere. National self-determination likewise lay behind the disintegration of the Soviet Union in 1991, when the last of the major territorial empires of the twentieth century came to an inglorious end with the birth of fifteen new states. Although the winning of political independence for Europe's African and Asian colonies was perhaps the most spectacular challenge to empire in the twentieth century, that achievement was part of a larger pattern in modern world history (see Map 23.1).

Explaining African and Asian Independence

As the twentieth century closed, the end of European empires seemed an almost "natural" phenomenon, for colonial rule had lost any credibility as a form of political order. What could be more natural than for people to seek to rule themselves? Yet at the beginning of the century, few observers were predicting the collapse of these empires, and the idea that "the only legitimate government is self-government" was not nearly so widespread as it subsequently became. This situation has presented historians with a problem of explanation—how to account for the fall of European colonial empires and the emergence of dozens of new nation-states.

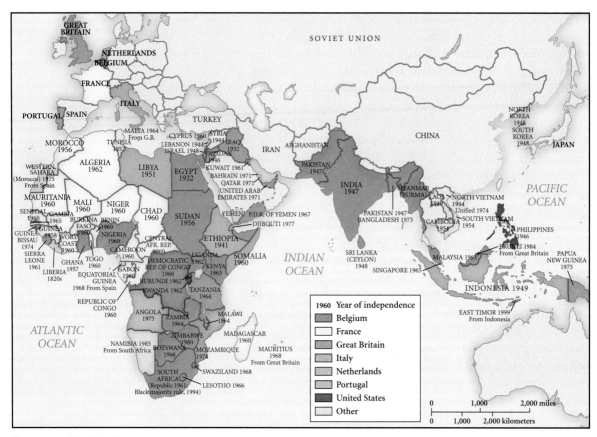

Map 23.1 The End of European Empires

In the second half of the twentieth century, under pressure from nationalist movements, Europe's Asian and African empires dissolved into dozens of new independent states.

■ **Change**

What international circumstances and social changes contributed to the end of colonial empires?

One approach to explaining the end of colonial empires focuses attention on fundamental contradictions in the entire colonial enterprise that arguably rendered its demise more or less inevitable. The rhetoric of both Christianity and material progress sat awkwardly with the realities of colonial racism, exploitation, and poverty. The increasingly democratic values of European states ran counter to the essential dictatorship of colonial rule. The ideal of national self-determination was profoundly at odds with the possession of colonies that were denied any opportunity to express their own national character. The enormously powerful force of nationalism, having earlier driven the process of European empire building, now played a major role in its disintegration. Colonial rule, in this argument, dug its own grave.

But why did this "fatal flaw" of European colonial rule lead to independence in the post–World War II era rather than earlier or later? In explaining the timing of the end of empire, historians frequently use the notion of "conjuncture," the coming together of several separate developments at a particular time. At the international level, the world wars had weakened Europe, while discrediting any sense of European moral superiority. Both the United States and the Soviet Union, the new global superpowers, generally opposed the older European colonial empires.

Meanwhile, the United Nations provided a prestigious platform from which to conduct anticolonial agitation. All of this contributed to the global illegitimacy of empire, a moral transformation that was enormously encouraging to Africans and Asians seeking political independence.

At the same time, social and economic circumstances within the colonies themselves generated the human raw material for anticolonial movements. By the early twentieth century in Asia and the mid-twentieth century in Africa, a second or third generation of Western-educated elites, largely male, had arisen throughout the colonial world. These young men were thoroughly familiar with European culture, were deeply aware of the gap between its values and its practices, no longer viewed colonial rule as a vehicle for their peoples' progress as their fathers had, and increasingly insisted on independence now. Moreover, growing numbers of ordinary people also were receptive to this message. Veterans of the world wars; young people with some education but no jobs commensurate with their expectations; a small class of urban workers who were increasingly aware of their exploitation; small-scale traders resentful of European privileges; rural dwellers who had lost land or suffered from forced labor; impoverished and insecure newcomers to the cities—all of these groups had reason to believe that independence held great promise.

A third approach to explaining the end of colonial empires puts the spotlight squarely on particular groups or individuals whose deliberate actions brought down the colonial system. Here the emphasis is on the "agency"—the deliberate initiatives—of historical actors rather than on impersonal contradictions or conjunctures. But which set of actors were most important in this end-of-empire drama?

Particularly in places such as West Africa or India, where independence occurred peacefully and through a negotiated settlement, the actions of colonial rulers have received considerable attention from historians. As the twentieth century wore on, these rulers were increasingly on the defensive and were actively planning for a new political relationship with their Asian and African colonies. With the colonies integrated into a global economic network and with local elites now modernized and committed to maintaining those links, outright colonial rule seemed less necessary to many Europeans. It was now possible to imagine retaining profitable economic interests in Asia and Africa without the expense and bother of formal colonial government. Deliberate planning for decolonization included gradual political reforms; investments in railroads, ports, and telegraph lines; the holding of elections; and the writing of constitutions. To some observers, it seemed as if independence was granted by colonial rulers rather than gained or seized by nationalist movements.

But these reforms and, ultimately, independence itself occurred only under considerable pressure from mounting nationalist movements. Creating such movements was no easy task. Political leaders, drawn from the ranks of the educated few, organized political parties, recruited members, plotted strategy, developed an ideology, and negotiated with one another and with the colonial state. The most prominent among them became the "fathers" of their new countries as independence

■ **Description**
What obstacles confronted the leaders of movements for independence?

dawned—Mahatma Gandhi and Jawaharlal Nehru in India, Sukarno in Indonesia, Ho Chi Minh in Vietnam, Kwame Nkrumah in Ghana, and Nelson Mandela in South Africa. In places where colonial rule was particularly intransigent—settler-dominated colonies and Portuguese territories, for example—leaders also directed military operations and administered liberated areas.

Agency within nationalist movements was not limited to leaders and the educated few. Millions of ordinary people decided to join Gandhi's nonviolent campaigns; tens of thousands of freedom fighters waged guerrilla warfare in Algeria, Kenya, Mozambique, and Zimbabwe; workers went on strike; market women in West Africa joined political parties, as did students, farmers, and the unemployed. In short, the struggle for independence did not happen automatically. It was deliberately made by the conscious personal choices of innumerable individuals across Asia and Africa.

In some places, that struggle produced independence within a few years, four in the case of the Belgian Congo. Elsewhere it was measured in decades. But everywhere it was a contested process. Those efforts were rarely if ever cohesive movements of uniformly oppressed people. More often they were fragile alliances of conflicting groups and parties representing different classes, ethnic groups, religions, or regions. Beneath the common goal of independence, they struggled with one another over questions of leadership, power, strategy, ideology, and the distribution of material benefits, even as they fought and negotiated with their colonial rulers. The very notion of "national self-government" posed obvious but often contentious questions: What group of people constituted the "nation" that deserved to rule itself? And who should speak for it?

Comparing Freedom Struggles

Two of the most extended freedom struggles—in India and South Africa—illustrate both the variations and the complexity of this process, which was so central to twentieth-century world history. India was among the first colonies to achieve independence and provided both a model and an inspiration to others, whereas South Africa, though not formally a colony, was among the last to throw off political domination by whites.

The Case of India: Ending British Rule

■ Change
How did India's nationalist movement change over time?

Surrounded by the Himalayas and the Indian Ocean, the South Asian peninsula, commonly known as India, enjoyed a certain geographic unity. But before the twentieth century few of its people thought of themselves as "Indians." Cultural identities were primarily local and infinitely varied, rooted in differences of family, caste, village, language, region, tribe, and religious practice. Various efforts in earlier centuries—during the Mauryan, Gupta, and Mughal empires, for example—had briefly brought large areas of the subcontinent within a single political system, but always these were imperial overlays, constructed on top of enormously diverse Indian societies.

So too was British colonial rule, but the British differed from earlier invaders in ways that promoted a growing sense of Indian identity. Unlike previous foreign rulers, the British never assimilated into Indian society because their acute sense of racial and cultural distinctiveness kept them apart. This served to intensify Indians' awareness of their collective difference from their alien rulers. Furthermore, British railroads, telegraph lines, postal services, administrative networks, newspapers, and schools as well as the English language bound India's many regions and peoples together more firmly than ever before and facilitated communication among its educated elite. Early-nineteenth-century cultural nationalists, seeking to renew and reform Hinduism, registered this sense of India as a cultural unit.

The most important political expression of an all-Indian identity took shape in the Indian National Congress (INC), which was established in 1885. This was an association of English-educated Indians—lawyers, journalists, teachers, business-men—drawn overwhelmingly from regionally prominent high-caste Hindu fami-lies. Its founding represented the beginning of a new kind of political protest, quite different from the rebellions, banditry, and refusal to pay taxes that had periodically erupted in the rural areas of colonial India. The INC was largely an urban phenom-enon and quite moderate in its demands. Initially, its well-educated members did not seek to overthrow British rule; rather they hoped to gain greater inclusion within the political, military, and business life of British India. From such positions of influence, they argued, they could better protect the interests of India than could their foreign-born rulers. The British mocked their claim to speak for ordinary Indians, referring to them as "babus," a derogatory term that implied a semiliterate "native" with only a thin veneer of modern education.

Even in the first two decades of the twentieth century, the INC remained largely an elite organization; as such, it had difficulty gaining a mass following among India's vast peasant population. That began to change in the aftermath of World War I. To attract Indian sup-port for the war effort, the British in 1917 had promised "the gradual devel-opment of self-governing institutions," a commitment that energized national-ist politicians to demand more rapid political change. Furthermore, British attacks on the Islamic Ottoman Empire antagonized India's Muslims. The end of the war was followed by a massive influenza epidemic, which cost the lives of millions of Indians. Finally, a series of repressive actions, including the killing of some 400 people who had defied a ban on public meetings to celebrate a

Mahatma Gandhi
The most widely recognized and admired figure in the global struggle against colo-nial rule was India's Mahatma Gandhi. In this famous photo-graph, he is sitting cross-legged on the floor, clothed in a traditional Indian gar-ment called a *dhoti*, while nearby stands a spinning wheel, symbolizing the inde-pendent and nonindustrial India that Gandhi sought. (Margaret Bourke-White/Time Life Pictures/Getty Images)

Hindu festival in the city of Amritsar, antagonized many. This was the context in which Mohandas Gandhi (1869–1948) arrived on the Indian political scene and soon transformed it.

Gandhi was born in the province of Gujarat in western India to a pious Hindu family of the Vaisya, or business, caste. He was married at the age of thirteen, had only a mediocre record as a student, and eagerly embraced an opportunity to study law in England when he was eighteen. He returned as a shy and not very success-ful lawyer, and in 1893 he accepted a job with an Indian firm in South Africa, where a substantial number of Indians had migrated as indentured laborers during the nineteenth century. While in South Africa, Gandhi personally experienced overt racism for the first time and as a result soon became involved in organizing Indians, mostly Muslims, to protest that country's policies of racial segregation. He also developed a concept of India that included Hindus and Muslims alike and pioneered strategies of resistance that he would later apply in India itself. His emerging political philosophy, known as *satyagraha* ("truth force"), was an active and confrontational, though nonviolent, approach to political action. As Gandhi argued,

> Non-violence means conscious suffering. It does not mean meek submission to the will of the evil-doer, but it means the pitting of one's whole soul against the will of the tyrant. . . . [I]t is possible for a single individual to defy the whole might of an unjust empire to save his honour, his religion, his soul.[2]

Returning to India in 1914, Gandhi quickly rose within the leadership ranks of the INC. During the 1920s and 1930s, he applied his approach in periodic mass campaigns that drew support from an extraordinarily wide spectrum of Indians—peasants and the urban poor, intellectuals and artisans, capitalists and socialists, Hindus and Muslims. The British responded with periodic repression as well as concessions that allowed a greater Indian role in political life. Gandhi's conduct and actions—his simple and unpretentious lifestyle, his support of Muslims, his frequent reference to Hindu religious themes—appealed widely in India and transformed the INC into a mass organization. To many ordinary people, Gandhi possessed mag-ical powers and produced miraculous events. He was the Mahatma, the Great Soul.

His was a radicalism of a different kind. He did not call for social revolution but sought the moral transformation of individuals. He worked to raise the status of India's untouchables (the lowest and most ritually polluting groups within the caste hierarchy), although he launched no attack on caste in general and accepted sup-port from capitalists and socialists alike. His critique of India's situation went far beyond colonial rule. "India is being ground down," he argued, "not under the English heel, but under that of modern civilization"—its competitiveness, its mate-rialism, its warlike tendencies, its abandonment of religion.[3] Almost alone among nationalist leaders in India or elsewhere, Gandhi opposed a modern industrial future for his country, seeking instead a society of harmonious self-sufficient vil-lages drawing on ancient Indian principles of duty and morality.

■ Change
What was the role of Gandhi in India's struggle for independence?

Gandhi and the INC or Congress Party leadership had to contend with a wide range of movements, parties, and approaches, whose very diversity tore at the national unity that they so ardently sought. Whereas Gandhi rejected modern industrialization, his own chief lieutenant, Jawaharlal Nehru, thoroughly embraced science, technology, and industry as essential to India's future. Nor did everyone accept Gandhi's nonviolence or his inclusive definition of India. A militant Hindu organization preached hatred of Muslims and viewed India as an essentially Hindu nation. To some in the Congress Party, movements to improve the position of women or untouchables seemed a distraction from the chief task of gaining independence from Britain. Whether to participate in British-sponsored legislative bodies without complete independence also became a divisive issue. Furthermore, a number of smaller parties advocated on behalf of particular regions or castes. India's nationalist movement, in short, was beset by division and controversy.

By far the most serious threat to a unified movement derived from the growing divide between the country's Hindu and Muslim populations. As early as 1906, the formation of an All-India Muslim League contradicted the Congress Party's claim to speak for all Indians. As the British allowed more elected Indian representatives on local councils, the League demanded separate electorates, with a fixed number of seats on local councils for Muslims. As a distinct minority within India, some Muslims feared that their voice could be swamped by a numerically dominant Hindu population, despite Gandhi's inclusive philosophy. Some Hindu politicians confirmed those fears when they cast the nationalist struggle in Hindu religious terms, hailing their country, for example, as a goddess, *Bande Mataram* (Mother India). When elections in 1937 gave the Congress Party control of many provincial governments, some of those governments began to enforce the teaching of Hindi in schools and to protect cows from slaughter, both of which antagonized Muslims.

As the movement for independence gained ground, the Muslim League and its leader, Muhammad Ali Jinnah, increasingly argued that those parts of India that had a Muslim majority should have a separate political status. They called it Pakistan, the land of the pure. In this view, India was not a single nation, as Gandhi had long argued. Jinnah put his case succinctly:

> The Muslims and Hindus belong to two different religious philosophies, social customs, and literatures. They neither intermarry nor interdine [eat] together and, indeed, they belong to two different civilizations.[4]

With great reluctance and amid mounting violence, Gandhi and the Congress Party finally agreed to partition as the British declared their intention to leave India after World War II.

Thus colonial India became independent in 1947 as two countries—a Muslim Pakistan, itself divided into two wings 1,000 miles apart, and a secular but mostly Hindu India. Dividing

■ **Description**
What conflicts and differences divided India's nationalist movement?

The Independence of British South Asia

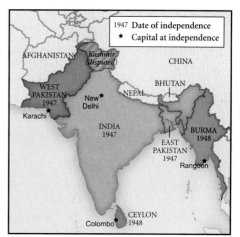

colonial India in this fashion was horrendously painful. A million people or more died in the communal violence that accompanied partition, and some 12 million refugees moved from one country to the other to join their religious compatriots. Gandhi himself, desperately trying to stem the mounting tide of violence in India's villages, refused to attend the independence celebrations. He was assassinated in 1948 by a Hindu extremist. The great triumph of independence, secured from the powerful British Empire, was shadowed by an equally great tragedy in the violence of partition.

■ Comparison

Why was African majority rule in South Africa delayed until 1994, whereas the overthrow of European colonialism had occurred much earlier in the rest of Africa and Asia?

The Case of South Africa: Ending Apartheid

The setting for South Africa's freedom struggle was very different from the situation in India. In the twentieth century, that struggle was not waged against an occupying European colonial power, for South Africa had in fact been independent of Great Britain since 1910. That independence, however, had been granted to a government wholly controlled by a white settler minority, which represented less than

Snapshot **Key Moments in South African History**

Earliest humans in South Africa	by 50,000 years ago
Arrival of iron-using, Bantu-speaking agricultural peoples	by 500 C.E.
First Dutch settlement	1652
Shaka and creation of a Zulu state	early 19th century
British takeover of South Africa	1806
Great Trek: Afrikaner migration to the interior to escape more liberal British rule	1830s
European conquest of interior African societies	mid- to late 19th century
Gold and diamond mining begins	late 19th century
Great Britain defeats Afrikaners in Boer War	1899–1902
South Africa independent under white minority government	1910
African National Congress established	1912
National Party comes to power; apartheid formally established	1948
Sharpville massacre	1960
ANC launches armed struggle	1961
Black Consciousness movement; urban insurrection	1970s
Nelson Mandela released from prison	1990
ANC comes to power following first all-race elections	1994

20 percent of the total population; the country's black African majority had no political rights whatever within the central state. Black South Africans' struggle therefore was against this internal opponent rather than against a distant colonial authority, as in India. Economically, the most prominent whites were of British descent; they or their forebears had come to South Africa during the nineteenth century, when Great Britain was the ruling colonial power. But the politically dominant section of the white community, known as Boers or Afrikaners, was descended from the early Dutch settlers, who had arrived in the mid-seventeenth century. The term "Afrikaner" reflected their image of themselves as "white Africans," permanent residents of the continent rather than colonial intruders. They had unsuccessfully sought independence from a British-ruled South Africa in a bitter struggle (the Boer War, 1899–1902), and a sense of difference and antagonism lingered. Despite a certain hostility between white South Africans of British and Afrikaner background, both felt that their way of life and standard of living were jeopardized by any move toward black African majority rule. The intransigence of this sizable and threatened settler community helps explain why African rule was delayed until 1994, while India, lacking any such community, had achieved independence almost a half century earlier.

Unlike a predominantly agrarian India, South Africa by the early twentieth century had developed a mature industrial economy, based initially in gold and diamond mining, but by midcentury including secondary industries such as steel, chemicals, automobile manufacturing, rubber processing, and heavy engineering. Particularly since the 1960s, the economy benefited from extensive foreign investment and loans. Almost all black Africans were involved in this complex modern economy, working in urban industries or mines, providing labor for white-owned farms, or receiving payments from relatives who did. The extreme dependence of most Africans on the white-controlled economy rendered individuals highly vulnerable to repressive action, but collectively the threat to withdraw their essential labor also gave them a powerful weapon.

A third unique feature of the South African situation was the overwhelming prominence of race, expressed most clearly in the policy of apartheid, which attempted to separate blacks from whites in every conceivable way while retaining their labor power in the white-controlled economy. An enormous apparatus of repression enforced that system. Rigid "pass laws" monitored and tried to control the movement of Africans into the cities, where they were subjected to extreme forms of social segregation. In the rural areas, a series of impoverished and overcrowded "native reserves," or Bantustans, served as ethnic homelands that kept Africans divided along tribal lines. Even though racism was present in colonial India, nothing of this magnitude developed there.

As in India, various forms of opposition—such as resistance to conquest, rural rebellions, urban strikes, and independent churches—arose to contest the manifest injustices of South African life. There too an elite-led political party provided an organizational umbrella for many of the South African resistance

■ **Change**
How did South Africa's struggle against white domination change over time?

efforts in the twentieth century. Established in 1912, the African National Congress (ANC), like its Indian predecessor, was led by educated, professional, and middle-class Africans who sought, not to overthrow the existing order, but to be accepted as "civilized men" within that society. They appealed to the liberal, humane, and Christian values that white society claimed. For four decades, its leaders pursued peaceful and moderate protest—petitions, multiracial conferences, delegations appealing to the authorities—even as racially based segregationist policies were implemented one after another. By 1948, when the Afrikaner-led National Party came to power on a platform of apartheid, it was clear that such "constitutional" protest had produced nothing.

During the 1950s, a new and younger generation of the ANC leadership, which now included Nelson Mandela, broadened its base of support and launched nonviolent civil disobedience—boycotts, strikes, demonstrations, and the burning of the hated passes that all Africans were required to carry. All of these actions were similar to and inspired by the tactics that Gandhi had used in India twenty to thirty years earlier. The government of South Africa responded with tremendous repression, including the shooting of sixty-nine unarmed demonstrators at Sharpville in 1960, the banning of the ANC, and the imprisonment of its leadership. This was the context in which Mandela was arrested and sentenced to his long prison term.

Independence in Kenya, East Africa

Almost everywhere in the colonial world, the struggle for independence climaxed in a formal and joyful ceremony in which power was transferred from the colonial authority to the leader of the new nation. Here a jubilant Jomo Kenyatta takes the oath of office in 1964 as Kenya's first president, while a dour and bewigged British official looks on. (Bettmann/Corbis)

At this point, the freedom struggle in South Africa took a different direction than it had in India. Its major political parties were now illegal. Underground nationalist leaders turned to armed struggle, authorizing selected acts of sabotage and assassination, while preparing for guerrilla warfare in camps outside the country. Active opposition within South Africa was now primarily expressed by student groups that were part of the Black Consciousness movement, an effort to foster pride, unity, and political awareness among the country's African majority. Such young people were at the center of an explosion of protest in 1976 in a sprawling, segregated, impoverished black neighborhood called Soweto, outside Johannesburg, in which hundreds were killed. The initial trigger for the uprising was the government's decision to enforce education for Africans in the hated language of the white Afrikaners rather than English. However, the momentum of the Soweto rebellion persisted, and by the mid-1980s, spreading urban violence and the radicalization of urban young people had forced the government to declare a state of emergency. Furthermore, South Africa's black labor movement, legalized only in 1979, became increasingly active and political. In June 1986, to commemorate the tenth anniversary of the Soweto uprising, the Congress of South African Trade Unions orchestrated a general strike involving some 2 million workers.

Beyond this growing internal pressure, South Africa faced mounting international demands to end apartheid as well. A variety of responses to apartheid—exclusion from most international sporting events, including the Olympics; the refusal of many artists and entertainers to perform in South Africa; economic boycotts; the withdrawal of private investment funds—isolated South Africa from a Western world in which its white rulers claimed membership. This was another feature of the South African freedom movement that had no parallel in India.

The combination of these internal and external pressures persuaded many white South Africans by the late 1980s that discussion with African nationalist leaders was the only alternative to a massive, bloody, and futile struggle to preserve white privileges. The outcome was the abandonment of key apartheid policies, the release of Nelson Mandela from prison, the legalization of the ANC, and a prolonged process of negotiations that in 1994 resulted in national elections, which brought the ANC to power. To the surprise of almost everyone, the long nightmare of South African apartheid came to an end without a racial bloodbath (see Map 23.2).

As in India, the South African nationalist movement that finally won freedom was divided and conflicted. Unlike India, though, these divisions did not occur along religious lines. Rather it was race, ethnicity, and ideology that generated dissension and sometimes violence. Whereas the ANC generally favored a broad alliance of everyone opposed to apartheid (black Africans, Indians, "coloreds" or mixed-race people, and sympathetic whites), a smaller group known as the Pan Africanist Congress rejected cooperation with other racial groups and limited its membership to black Africans. During the urban uprisings of the 1970s and 1980s, young people supporting the Black Consciousness movements and those following Mandela and the ANC waged war against each other in the townships of South African cities. Perhaps most threatening to the unity of the nationalist struggle were the separatist tendencies of the Zulu-based Inkatha Freedom Party. Its leader, Gatsha Buthelezi, had cooperated with the apartheid state and even received funding from it. As negotiations for a transition to African rule unfolded in the early 1990s, considerable violence between Inkatha followers, mostly Zulu migrant workers, and ANC supporters broke out in a number of cities. None of this, however, approached the massive killing of Hindus and Muslims that accompanied the partition of India. South Africa, unlike India, acquired its political freedom as an intact and unified state.

Map 23.2   South Africa after Apartheid

Under apartheid, all black Africans were officially designated as residents of small, scattered, impoverished Bantustans, shown on the inset map. Many black Africans, of course, actually lived in white South Africa, where they worked. The main map shows the new internal organization of the country as it emerged after 1994, with the Bantustans abolished and the country divided into nine provinces.

Experiments with Freedom

Africa's first modern nationalist hero, Kwame Nkrumah of Ghana, paraphrased a biblical quotation when he urged his followers, "Seek ye first the political kingdom and all these other things will be added unto you." However, would winning the political kingdom of independence or freedom from European rule really produce "all these other things"—opportunity for political participation, industrial growth and economic development, reasonably unified nations, and a better life for all? That was the central question confronting the new nations emerging from colonial rule. They were joined in that quest by already independent but nonindustrialized countries and regions such as China, Thailand, Ethiopia, Iran, Turkey, and Central and South America. Together they formed the bloc of nations known variously as the third world, the developing countries, or the Global South (see Map 23.3). In the second half of the twentieth century, these countries represented perhaps 75 percent of the world's population. They accounted for almost all of the fourfold increase in human numbers that the world experienced during the twentieth century. That immense surge in global population, at one level a great triumph for the human species, also underlay many of the difficulties these nations faced as they conducted their various experiments with freedom.

Almost everywhere, the moment of independence generated something close to euphoria. Having emerged from the long night of colonial rule, free peoples

Map 23.3 The "Worlds" of the Twentieth Century During the cold war, the term "third world" referred to those countries not solidly in either the Western or the Communist bloc of nations. Gradually it came to designate developing countries, those less wealthy and less industrialized societies seeking to catch up to the more developed countries of Europe, North America, and Japan. China, Vietnam, and Cuba, although governed by communist regimes, have been widely regarded as part of the developing world as well.

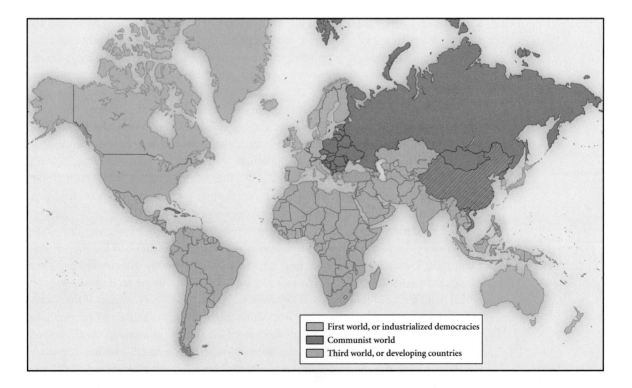

First world, or industrialized democracies
Communist world
Third world, or developing countries

were undertaking what Indian prime minister Nehru called a "tryst with destiny." The developing countries would be laboratories for new approaches to building states, nations, and modern economies. In the decades that followed, experiments with freedom multiplied, but the early optimism was soon tempered by the difficulties and disappointments of those tasks.

Experiments in Political Order: Comparing African Nations and India

All across the developing world, efforts to create political order had to contend with a set of common conditions. Populations were exploding. Expectations for independence ran very high, often exceeding the available resources. Most developing countries were culturally diverse, with little loyalty to the central state. Nonetheless, public employment mushroomed as the state assumed greater responsibility for economic development. In conditions of widespread poverty and weak private economies, groups and individuals sought to capture the state, or parts of it, both for the salaries and status it offered and for the opportunities for private enrichment that political office provided.

This was the formidable setting in which developing countries had to hammer out their political systems. The range of that effort was immense: Communist Party control in China, Vietnam, and Cuba; multiparty democracy in India and South Africa; one-party democracy in Tanzania and Senegal; military regimes for a time in much of Latin America and Africa; personal dictatorships in Uganda and the Philippines. In many places, one kind of political system followed another in kaleidoscopic succession. The political evolution of postindependence Africa illustrates the complexity and the difficulty of creating a stable political order in developing countries.

Although colonial rule had been highly authoritarian and bureaucratic with little interest in African participation, during the 1950s the British, the French, and the Belgians attempted, rather belatedly, to transplant democratic institutions to their colonies. They established legislatures, permitted elections, allowed political parties to operate, and in general anticipated the development of constitutional, parliamentary, multiparty democracies similar to their own. It was with such institutions that most African states greeted independence.

By the early 1970s, however, few such regimes were left among the new states of Africa. Many of the apparently popular political parties that had led the struggle for independence lost mass support and were swept away by military coups. When the army took power in Ghana in 1966, no one lifted a finger to defend the party that had led the country to independence only nine years earlier. Other states evolved into one-party systems, sometimes highly authoritarian and bureaucratic and sometimes more open and democratic. Still others degenerated into personal tyrannies or dictatorships. Freedom from colonial rule certainly did not automatically generate the internal political freedoms associated with democracy.

The contrast between Africa's political evolution and that of India has been particularly striking. In India, Western-style democracy, including regular elections, multiple parties, civil liberties, and peaceful changes in government, has been practiced almost continuously since independence. The struggle for independence in India had been a far more prolonged affair, thus providing time for an Indian political leadership to sort itself out. Furthermore, the British began to hand over power in a gradual way well before complete independence was granted in 1947. Thus a far larger number of Indians had useful administrative or technical skills than was the case in Africa. In sharp contrast to most African countries, the nationalist movement in India was embodied in a single national party (the Congress Party), which encompassed a wide variety of other parties and interest groups. Its leadership was genuinely committed to democratic practice. Even the tragic and painful partition of colonial India into two countries eliminated a major source of internal discord as independent India was born. Moreover, Indian statehood could be built on cultural and political traditions that were far more deeply rooted than in most African states.

Explaining the initial rejection of democracy in Africa has been a major concern of politicians and scholars alike. Some have argued, on the basis of paternalistic or even racist assumptions, that Africans were not ready for democracy or that they lacked some crucial ingredient for democratic politics—an educated electorate, a middle class, or perhaps a thoroughly capitalist economy. Others suggested that Africa's traditional culture, based on communal rather than individualistic values and concerned to achieve consensus rather than majority rule, was not compatible with the competitiveness of party politics.

Furthermore, some argued, Western-style democracy was simply inadequate for the tasks of development confronting the new states. Creating national unity was certainly more difficult when competing political parties identified primarily with particular ethnic or "tribal" groups, as was frequently the case in Africa. Similarly, the immense problems that inevitably accompany the early stages of economic development may be compounded by the heavy demands of a political system based on universal suffrage. Certainly Europe did not begin its modernizing process with such a system. Why, many Africans asked, should they be expected to do so?

Beyond these general considerations, more immediate conditions likewise undermined the popular support of many postindependence governments in Africa and discredited their initial democracies. One was widespread economic disappointment. By almost any measure, African economic performance since independence has been the poorest in the developing world. This has translated into students denied the white-collar careers they expected, urban migrants with little opportunity for work, farmers paid low prices for their cash crops, consumers resentful about shortages and inflation, and millions of impoverished and malnourished peasants pushed to the brink of starvation. These were people for whom independence was unable to fulfill even the most minimal of expectations, let alone the grandiose visions of a better life that so many had embraced in the early 1960s. Since modern governments everywhere staked their popularity on

■ **Comparison**
Why was Africa's experience with political democracy so different from that of India?

■ **Change**
What accounts for the ups and downs of political democracy in postcolonial Africa?

economic performance, it is little wonder that many Africans became disaffected and withdrew their support from governments they had enthusiastically endorsed only a few years earlier.

Nevertheless, economic disappointment did not affect everyone to the same extent, and for some, independence offered great opportunities for acquiring status, position, and wealth. Unlike the situation in Latin America and parts of Asia, those who benefited most from independence were not large landowners, for most African societies simply did not have an established class whose wealth was based in landed estates. Rather they were members of the relatively well-educated elite who had found high-paying jobs in the growing bureaucracies of the newly independent states. The privileges of this dominant class were widely resented. Government ministers in many countries earned the title "Mr. Ten Percent," a reference to the bribes or "gifts" they received from private contractors working for the state. This kind of resentment broke out in Zaire between 1964 and 1968 in the form of a widespread peasant rebellion calling for a "second independence" against the "new whites" of the elite class.

Frequently, however, the resentments born of inequality and of competition for jobs, housing, educational opportunities, development projects, and political position found expression in ethnic conflict, as Africa's immense cultural diversity became intensely politicized. In many places, a judicious balancing of appointments and budgetary allocations among major ethnic groups contained conflict within a peaceful political process. Elsewhere it led to violence. An ethnically based civil war in Nigeria during the late 1960s cost the lives of millions, while in the mid-1990s ethnic hatred led Rwanda into the realm of genocide.

Thus economic disappointment, class resentments, and ethnic conflict eroded support for the transplanted democracies of the early independence era. The most common alternative involved government by soldiers, a familiar pattern in Latin America as well. By the early 1980s, the military had intervened in at least thirty of Africa's forty-six independent states and actively governed more than half of them (see Map 23.4). Usually, the military took power in a crisis, after the civilian government had lost most of its popular support. The soldiers often claimed that the nation was in grave danger, that corrupt civilian politicians had led the country to the brink of chaos, and that only the military had the discipline and strength to put things right. And so they swept aside the old political parties and constitutions and vowed to begin anew, while promising to return power to civilians and restore democracy at some point in the future.

Since the early 1980s, a remarkable resurgence of Western-style democracy has brought popular movements, multiparty elections, and new constitutions to a number of African states, including Ghana, Kenya, Mali, Senegal, and Zambia (see Map 23.4). It was part of a late-twentieth-century democratic revival of global dimensions that included Southern and Eastern Europe, most of Latin America, and parts of Asia and the Middle East. How can we explain this rather sudden, though still fragile, resumption of democracy in Africa? Perhaps the most important internal

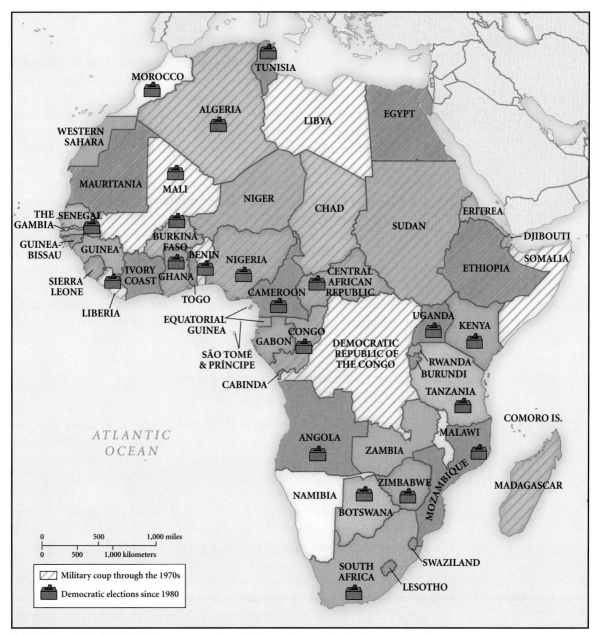

Map 23.4 Political Life in Postindependence Africa

The several decades after independence witnessed a wave of military regimes in Africa. However, since 1980 or so, a number of African countries have held reasonably free, multiparty elections, indicating a growing, but uncertain, interest in democratic practice.

factor was the evident failure of authoritarian governments to remedy the disastrous economic situation. Disaffected students, religious organizations, urban workers, and women's groups joined in a variety of grassroots movements to demand democratic change as a means to a better life. This pressure from below for political change reflected the growing strength of civil society in many African countries as organizations independent of the state provided a social foundation for the renewal of democracy.

Such movements found encouragement in the demands for democracy that accompanied the South African struggle against apartheid and the collapse of Soviet and Eastern European communism. The end of the cold war reduced the willingness of the major industrial powers to underwrite their authoritarian client states. For many Africans, democracy increasingly was viewed as a universal political principle to which they could also aspire rather than an alien and imposed system deriving from the West. None of this provided an immediate solution for the economic difficulties, ethnic conflicts, and endemic corruption of African societies, but it did suggest a willingness to continue the political experiments that had begun with independence.

Experiments in Economic Development: Changing Priorities, Varying Outcomes

At the top of the agenda everywhere in the Global South was economic development, a process that meant growth or increasing production as well as distributing the fruits of that growth to raise living standards. This quest for development, now operating all across the planet, represented the universal acceptance of beliefs unheard of not many centuries earlier—that poverty was no longer inevitable and that it was possible to deliberately improve the material conditions of life for everyone. Economic development was a central promise of all independence struggles, and it was increasingly the standard by which people measured and granted legitimacy to their governments.

■ **Change**
What obstacles impeded the economic development of third-world countries?

Achieving economic development, however, proved immensely difficult. It took place in societies sharply divided by class, religion, ethnic group, and gender and in the face of explosive population growth. In many places, colonial rule had provided only the most slender foundations for modern development to these newly independent nations, which had low rates of literacy, few people with managerial experience, a weak private economy, and transportation systems oriented to export rather than national integration. Furthermore, the entire effort occurred in a world split by rival superpowers and economically dominated by the powerful capitalist economies of the West. Despite their political independence, most developing countries had little leverage in negotiations with the wealthy nations of the Global North and their immense transnational corporations. It was hardly an auspicious environment in which to seek a fundamental economic transformation.

Beyond these structural difficulties, it was hard for leaders of developing countries to know what strategies to pursue. The academic field of "development economics" was new; its experts disagreed and often changed their minds; and conflicting political pressures, both internal and international, only added to the confusion. All of this resulted in considerable controversy, changing policies, and much experimentation.

One fundamental issue lay in the role of the state. All across the developing world and particularly in newly independent nations, most people expected that state authorities would take major responsibility for spurring the economic development of their countries. After all, the private economy was weakly developed; few entrepreneurs had substantial funds to invest; the example of rapid Soviet industrialization under state direction was hopeful; and state control held the promise of protecting vulnerable economies from the ravages of international capitalism. Some state-directed economies had real successes. China launched a major industrialization effort and massive land reform under the leadership of the Communist Party. A communist Cuba, even while remaining dependent on its sugar production, wiped out illiteracy and provided basic health care to its entire population, raising life expectancy to seventy-six years by 1992, equivalent to that of the United States. Elsewhere as well—in Turkey, India, South Korea, and much of Africa—the state provided tariffs, licenses, loans, subsidies, and overall planning, while most productive property was owned privately.

■ **Change**
In what ways did thinking about the role of the state in the economic life of developing countries change? Why did it change?

Yet in the last several decades of the twentieth century, an earlier consensus in favor of state direction largely collapsed, replaced by a growing dependence on the market to generate economic development. This was most apparent in the abandonment of much communist planning in China and the return to private farming (see Chapter 22). India and many Latin American and African states privatized their state-run industries and substantially reduced the role of the state in economic affairs. In part, this sharp change in economic policies reflected the failure, mismanagement, and corruption of many state-run enterprises, but it also was influenced by the collapse in the Soviet Union of the world's first state-dominated economy. Western pressures, exercised through international organizations such as the World Bank, likewise pushed developing countries in a capitalist direction. In China and India, the new approach generated rapid economic growth, but also growing inequalities and social conflict. As the new millennium dawned, a number of Latin American countries—Venezuela, Brazil, and Bolivia, for example—once again asserted a more prominent role for the state in their quests for economic development and social justice.

Other issues as well inspired debate. In many places, an early emphasis on city-based industrial development, stirred by visions of a rapid transition to modernity, led to a neglect or exploitation of rural areas and agriculture. This "urban bias" subsequently came in for much criticism and some adjustment in spending priorities. A growing recognition of the role of women in agriculture led to charges of "male bias" in development planning and to mounting efforts to assist women farmers

Snapshot   **Economic Development in the Global South by the Early Twenty-first Century[5]**

This table samples the economic performance of fourteen developing countries and five major regions of the Global South by the early twenty-first century. Similar data for the United States, Japan, and Russia are included for comparative purposes. Which indicators of development do you find most revealing? What aspects

Regions and Sample Countries	Average Annual Population Growth Rate, 2000–2004 (%)	Gross National Income per Capita, 2003–2004 (U.S. $)	Per Capita Purchasing Power 2004 (U.S. $)	Adult Literacy (%)
Russia	−0.5	3,410	9,620	99
East Asia	0.9	1,280	5,070	85
China	0.7	1,290	5,530	91
Philippines	2	1,170	4,890	93
Latin America	1.4	3,600	7,660	88
Mexico	1.4	6,770	9,590	90
Brazil	1.2	3,090	8,020	88
Guatemala	2.6	2,130	4,140	69
Middle East and North Africa	1.8	2,000	5,760	74
Egypt	1.8	1,310	4,120	80
Turkey	1.5	3,750	7,680	88
Iran	1.2	2,300	7,550	77
Saudi Arabia	2.8	10,430	14,010	79
South Asia	1.7	590	2,830	64
India	1.5	620	3,100	61
Indonesia	1.3	1,140	3,460	88
Subsaharan Africa	2.2	600	1,850	61
Nigeria	2.4	390	930	67
Congo	3	120	680	65
Tanzania	2	330	660	69
High-income countries	0.7	32,040	30,970	91
U.S.A.	1	41,000	39,710	99
Japan	0.2	37,180	30,040	99

of development does each of them measure? Based on these data, which countries or regions would you consider the most and the least successful? Does your judgment about "success" vary depending on which measure you use?

Life Expectancy in Years		Infant Mortality (Deaths under Age 5 per 1,000)		CO$_2$ Emission per Capita (Metric Tons)
MALE	FEMALE	1990	2003	
60	72	21	21	9.9
68	71	59	41	2.1
69	73	49	37	2.2
68	72	63	36	1
68	74	53	33	2.7
71	77	46	28	4.3
65	73	60	35	1.8
63	69	82	47	0.9
67	70	80	56	4.2
68	71	104	39	2.2
66	71	78	39	3.3
68	71	72	39	4.9
72	75	44	26	18.1
62	64	130	86	0.9
63	64	123	87	1.1
65	69	91	41	1.3
45	46	187	171	0.7
44	45	235	198	0.3
45	46	205	205	0.1
42	43	163	165	0.1
75	81	11	7	12.4
75	80	11	8	19.8
78	85	6	5	9.3

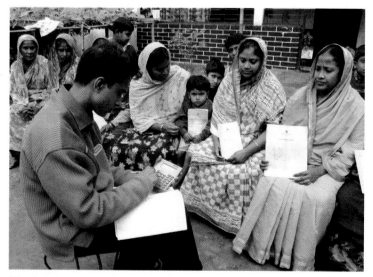

Microloans
Bangladesh's Grameen Bank pioneered an innovative approach to economic development by offering modest loans to poor people, enabling them to start small businesses. Here a group of women who received such loans meet in early 2004 to make an installment payment to an officer of the bank. (Rafiqur Rahman/Reuters/Corbis)

directly. Women also were central to many governments' increased interest in curtailing population growth. Women's access to birth control, education, and employment, it turned out, provided powerful incentives to limit family size. Another debate pitted the advocates of capital- and technology-driven projects (dams and factories, for example) against those who favored investment in "human capital," such as education, technical training, health care, and nutrition. The benefits and drawbacks of foreign aid, investment, and trade have likewise been contentious issues. Should developing countries seek to shield themselves from the influences of international capitalism, or are they better off vigorously engaging with the global economy?

Economic development was never simply a matter of technical expertise or deciding among competing theories. Every decision was political, involving winners and losers in terms of power, advantage, and wealth. Where to locate schools, roads, factories and clinics, for example, provoked endless controversies, some of them expressed in terms of regional or ethnic rivalries. It was an experimental process, and the stakes were high.

The results of those experiments have varied considerably, as the Snapshot indicates. East Asian countries in general have had the strongest record of economic growth. South Korea, Taiwan, Singapore, and Hong Kong were dubbed "newly industrialized countries," and China boasted the most rapid economic growth in the world by the end of the twentieth century, replacing Japan as the world's second-largest economy. In the 1990s, Asia's other giant, India, opened itself more fully to the world market and launched rapid economic growth with a powerful high-tech sector and an expanding middle class. Oil-producing countries reaped a bonanza when they were able to demand much higher prices for that essential commodity in the 1970s and after. Several Latin American states (Chile and Brazil, for example) entered the world market vigorously and successfully with growing industrial sectors. Limited principally to Europe, North America, and Japan in the nineteenth century, industrialization had become a global phenomenon in the twentieth century.

Elsewhere, the story was very different. In most of Africa, much of the Arab world, and parts of Asia—regions representing about one-third of the world's population—there was little sign of catching up and frequent examples of declining standards of living since the end of the 1960s. Between 1980 and 2000, the average income in forty-three of Africa's poorest countries dropped by 25 percent, pushing living standards for many below what they had been at independence.

Scholars and politicians alike argue about the reasons for such sharp variations. Variables such as geography and natural resources, differing colonial experiences, variations in regional cultures, the degree of political stability and social equality, state economic policies, population growth rates, and varying forms of involvement with the world economy have been invoked to explain the widely diverging trajectories among developing countries.

Experiments with Culture: The Role of Islam in Turkey and Iran

The quest for economic development represented the embrace of an emerging global culture of modernity—with its scientific outlook, its technological achievements, and its focus on material values. It also exposed developing countries to the changing culture of the West, including feminism, rock and rap, sexual permissiveness, consumerism, and democracy. But the peoples of the Global South also had inherited cultural patterns from the more distant past—Hindu, Confucian, Islamic, Aztec, or one of many African cultures, for example. A common issue all across the developing world involved the uneasy relationship between these older traditions and the more recent outlooks associated with modernity and the West. This tension provided the raw material for a series of cultural experiments in the twentieth century, and nowhere were they more consequential than in the Islamic world. No single answer emerged to the question of how Islam and modernity should relate to each other, but the experience of Turkey and Iran illustrate two quite different approaches to this fundamental issue.

In the aftermath of World War I, modern Turkey emerged from the ashes of the Ottoman Empire as a republic, led by a determined general, Mustafa Kemal Atatürk (1881–1938). During the 1920s and 1930s, he presided over a dramatic national cultural revolution, continuing in a more radical and single-minded fashion the modernizing reforms of the Ottoman Empire in the nineteenth century. Seeking far more than national independence, he wanted to create a thoroughly modern and Western Turkish society and viewed many traditional Islamic institutions, beliefs, and practices as obstacles to that goal. Within a few years, the caliphate had been officially ended, Sufi orders disbanded, religious courts abolished, and the sharia replaced by Swiss legal codes. Public education was completely secularized, and the Latin alphabet replaced the Arabic script for writing the Turkish language. Religious leaders (the ulama) were brought more firmly under state control. In 1932, the government even ordered that the call to prayer should be made in Turkish rather than Arabic, although this reform was later

Comparison

In what ways did cultural revolutions in Turkey and Iran reflect different understandings of the role of Islam in modern societies?

Iran, Turkey, and the Middle East

Westernization in Turkey
Mustafa Kemal Atatürk, the
founder of modern Turkey,
often appeared in public in
elegant European dress,
symbolizing for his people a
sharp break with traditional
Islamic ways of living. Here
he is dancing with his
adopted daughter at her
high-society wedding in
1929. (Hulton Archive/Getty
Images)

abandoned. Almost everything that had made Islam an official part of Ottoman public life was dismantled. In Atatürk's view, Islam should become a modernized personal religion, available to the individual citizens of a secular Turkish state.

The most visible symbols of Atatürk's revolutionary program occurred in the realm of dress. Turkish men were ordered to abandon the traditional headdress known as the *fez* and to wear brimmed hats. According to Atatürk,

> A civilized, international dress is worthy and appropriate for our nation, and we will wear it. Boots or shoes on our feet, trousers on our legs, shirt and tie, jacket and waistcoat—and of course, to complete these, a cover with a brim on our heads.[6]

Although women were not forbidden to wear the veil, many elite women abandoned it and set the tone for feminine fashion in Turkey. In other ways as well, women gained new legal rights. Polygamy was abolished, as was a husband's right to repudiate his wife or wives. Under the European-style legal codes, women achieved equal rights to divorce, child custody, inheritance, and education. By the mid-1930s, they had been granted the right to vote in national elections, a full decade before French women gained that right.

These reforms represented the most ambitious attempts at cultural transformation in the Middle East. Like Japan in the late nineteenth century, it was a "revolution from above" led by military and civilian officials unburdened by close ties to traditional landholding groups. State-organized enterprises were set up with centralized economic planning on the Soviet model, though without the redistribution of wealth and social revolution that was part of the Soviet experience. Landlords kept their lands, and most property was owned privately. In fact, there was considerable continuity with earlier patterns of Turkish life. Despite the imitation of Western European parliamentary politics, the Turkish government remained authoritarian. Despite the attacks on Islamic symbols, Turkish society at the local level remained firmly attached to Islamic traditions. Turkey underwent a cultural revolution in public life, but not a social or economic revolution.

After Atatürk's death in 1938, some of his more radical decrees were moderated, and a multiparty parliamentary system was allowed to develop. By the end of the twentieth century, a variety of other movements and parties emerged, some calling for the restoration of Islam to a more prominent role in society and the state. In early

2008, for example, the Turkish parliament voted to end the earlier prohibition of women wearing headscarves in universities. Nevertheless, the essential secularism of the Turkish state remained an enduring legacy of the Atatürk revolution. He and his successors had provided a distinctive answer to the question of what it meant to be modern in an Islamic setting. It entailed fully embracing modern culture and Western ways in public life and relegating Islam to the sphere of private life. Clearly, large numbers of Turkish and other Muslims did not find that solution satisfactory.

A very different answer emerged in Iran in the final quarter of the twentieth century. By that time all across the Islamic world, disappointments abounded with the social and economic results of political independence and secular development, while hostility to continuing Western cultural, military, and political intrusion grew apace. These conditions gave rise to numerous movements of Islamic revival or renewal that cast the religion as a guide to public as well as private life. If Western models of a good society had failed, it seemed reasonable to many people to turn their attention to distinctly Islamic solutions.

Iran became the epicenter of Islamic revival in the 1970s as opposition mounted to the modernizing, secularizing, American-supported government of the shah, Muhammad Reza Pahlavi (reigned 1941–1979). Some resented his close relationship with the Americans and the British as well as the heavy-handed brutality of his secret police. His land reform program had alienated landowners and upset traditional village life. Small merchants, shopkeepers, and artisans were threatened by modern stores, large government agencies, and imported foreign goods. Rural migrants to the rapidly growing cities, especially Tehran, lived an insecure life and were forced to cope with inflation, unemployment, and falling standards of living. Furthermore, the shah had provoked the Shia religious establishment by attempting to redistribute religious lands; by initiating reforms that offered women greater rights and a literacy program that threatened to replace religious schools; and by permitting the growth of Western political, economic, and cultural influences in the country. His decision to replace the Islamic calendar with one derived from Persian imperial history further alienated his subjects, as did the building of a Hyatt Hotel, which served foreign wines and liquors, near a religious sanctuary in the city of Meshed.

In a politically repressive Iran, opposition to the shah's regime came to focus on the mosque. Unlike their counterparts in Turkey, the Shia ulama in Iran had maintained their independence from the state and had often criticized both the shah's government and Western intervention in Iranian affairs. Thus the Shia leaders increasingly became the voice of opposition. One elderly cleric in particular, the Ayatollah Ruholla Khomeini, organized opposition from exile in Paris and became the center of a growing movement demanding the shah's removal. In the late 1970s, his taped messages, which were distributed through a network of local religious leaders, triggered massive urban demonstrations that paralyzed the government and strikes that shut down oil production. As the nation revolted and slipped into anarchy, the shah abdicated, and in early 1979 he and his family fled the country. The Ayatollah Khomeini returned to Iran to a hero's welcome and appointed his own government.

Khomeini believed that the purpose of government was to apply the law of Allah. Thus the sharia became the law of the land, and religious leaders themselves assumed the reins of government. Widespread purges ousted secular officials, who were replaced by Islamic activists. Actions of the parliament had to be approved by a clerical Council of Guardians. Culturally, the new regime sought the moral purification of the country under state control. Discos and bars were closed, and alcoholic drinks were forbidden. Boys and girls could no longer attend school together, and the curriculum was revised to emphasize Islamic studies and the Arabic language. An Islamic dress law required women to wear a veil and loose-fitting clothing to conceal their figures. In the early years, revolutionary guards patrolled the streets, while Islamic societies were established in many organizations; both groups served to enforce proper behavior. Khomeini made clear his posture toward much of Western culture.

> [J]ust what is the social life we are talking about? Is it those hotbeds of immorality called theatres, cinemas, dancing, and music? Is it the promiscuous presence in the streets of lusting young men and women with arms, chests, and thighs bared? Is it the ludicrous wearing of a hat like the Europeans or the imitation of their habit of wine drinking? . . . Let these shameful practices come to an end, so that the dawn of a new life may break![7]

Women and the Iranian Revolution
One of the goals of Iran's Islamic Revolution was to enforce a more modest and traditional dress code for the country's women. In this photo from 2004, a woman clad in a burka and talking on her cell phone walks past a poster of the Ayatollah Khomeini, who led that revolution in 1979. (AP Images)

In other respects, however, the new regime was less than revolutionary. Despite some efforts to respond to the demands of the poor for social justice, no class upheaval or radical redistribution of wealth followed; private property was maintained, and a new privileged elite emerged. Nor did an Islamic revolution mean the abandonment of economic modernity. The country's oil revenues continued to fund its development, and by the early twenty-first century, Iran was actively pursuing nuclear power and perhaps nuclear weapons, much to the consternation of the West. Like Turkey earlier in the century, Iran had experienced a cultural revolution without major social or economic change. But it was a cultural revolution that moved in precisely the opposite direction from that of Turkey—toward, rather than away from, the Islamization of public life.

Reflections: History in the Middle of the Stream

Historians are usually more at ease telling stories that have clear endings, such as those that describe ancient Egyptian civilization, Chinese maritime voyages, the collapse of the Aztec Empire, or the French Revolution. There is a finality to these stories and a distance from them, making it easier for historians to assume the posture of detached observer, even if their understandings of those events change over time. Finality, distance, and detachment are harder to come by when historians are narrating the history of the past century, for many of its processes are clearly not over. The United States' role as a global superpower and its war in Iraq, the fate of democracy in Latin America and Africa, the rise of China and India as economic giants, the position of Islam in Turkey and Iran—all of these are unfinished stories, their outcomes unknown and unknowable. In dealing with such matters, historians write from the middle of the stream, often uncomfortably, rather than from the banks, where they might feel more at ease.

In part, that discomfort arises from questions about the future that such issues inevitably raise. Can the spread of nuclear weapons be halted? Will democracy flourish globally? Are Islamic and Christian civilizations headed for a global clash? Can African countries replicate the economic growth experience of India and China? Historians in particular are uneasy about responding to such questions because they are so aware of the unexpectedness and surprising quality of the historical process. Yet those questions about the future are legitimate and important, for as the nineteenth-century Danish philosopher Søren Kierkegaard remarked: "Life can only be understood backward, but it is lived forward." History, after all, is the only guide we have to the possible shape of that future. So, like everyone before us, we stumble on, both individually and collectively, largely in the dark, using analogies from the past as we make our way ahead.

These vast uncertainties about the future provide a useful reminder that although we know the outcomes of earlier human stories—the Asian and African struggles for independence, for example—those who lived that history did not. Such awareness can perhaps engender in us a measure of humility, a kind of sympathy, and a sense of common humanity with those whose lives we study. However we may differ from our ancestors across time and place, we share with them an immense ignorance about what will happen next.

Second Thoughts

What's the Significance?

To assess your mastery of the material in this chapter, see the **Online Study Guide** at bedfordstmartins.com/strayer.

decolonization	Muhammad Ali Jinnah	democracy in Africa
Indian National Congress	African National Congress	economic development
Mahatma Gandhi	Nelson Mandela	Kemal Atatürk
satyagraha	Black Consciousness	Ayatollah Khomeini
Muslim League	Soweto	

Big Picture Questions

1. In what ways did the colonial experience and the struggle for independence shape the agenda of developing countries in the second half of the twentieth century?
2. To what extent did the experience of the former colonies and developing countries in the twentieth century parallel that of the earlier "new nations" in the Americas in the eighteenth and nineteenth centuries?
3. How would you compare the historical experience of India and China in the twentieth century?
4. From the viewpoint of the early twenty-first century, to what extent had the goals of nationalist or independence movements been achieved?

Next Steps: For Further Study

For Web sites and documents related to this chapter, see **Make History** at bedfordstmartins.com/strayer.

Chinua Achebe, *Anthills of the Savannah* (1989). A brilliant fictional account of postindependence Nigeria by that country's foremost novelist.

Fredrick Cooper, *Africa since 1940* (2002). A readable overview of the coming of independence and efforts at development by a leading historian of Africa.

Ramachandra Guha, *India after Gandhi: The History of the World's Largest Democracy* (2007). A thoughtful account of India's first six decades of independence.

John Isbister, *Promises Not Kept* (2006). A thoughtful consideration of the obstacles to and struggles for development in the Global South.

Nelson Mandela, *Long Walk to Freedom: The Autobiography of Nelson Mandela* (1995). Mandela's account of his own amazing life as nationalist leader and South African statesman.

W. David McIntyre, *British Decolonization, 1946–1997* (1998). A global history of the demise of the British Empire.

Complete site on Mahatma Gandhi, http://www.mkgandhi.org. A wealth of resources for exploring the life of Gandhi.

Accelerating Global Interaction

SINCE 1945

"I think every Barbie doll is more harmful than an American missile," declared Iranian toy seller Masoumeh Rahimi in early 2002. To Rahimi, Barbie's revealing clothing, her shapely appearance, and her close association with Ken, her longtime unmarried companion, were "foreign to Iran's culture." Thus she warmly welcomed the arrival of Sara and Dara, two Iranian Muslim dolls meant to counteract the negative influence of Barbie and Ken, who had long dominated Iran's toy market. Sara and her brother Dara depicted eight-year-old twins. Sara came complete with a headscarf to cover her hair in modest Muslim fashion and a full-length white chador enveloping her from head to toe. They were described as helping each other solve problems, while looking to their loving parents for guidance, hardly the message that Barbie and Ken conveyed.[1]

The widespread availability of Barbie in Muslim Iran provides one small example of the power of global commerce in the world of the early twenty-first century. The creation of Sara and Dara illustrates resistance to the cultural values associated with this American product. Still, Sara and Barbie had something in common: both were manufactured in China. This triangular relationship of the United States, Iran, and China neatly symbolized the growing integration of world economies and cultures as well as the divergences and conflicts that this process generated. Those linked but contrasting patterns are the twin themes of this final chapter.

DURING THE TWENTIETH CENTURY, AN INCREASINGLY DENSE WEB OF POLITICAL RELATIONSHIPS, economic transactions, and cultural influences cut across the world's many peoples, countries, and regions, binding them

One World: This NASA photograph, showing both the earth and the moon, reveals none of the national, ethnic, religious, or linguistic boundaries that have long divided humankind. Such pictures have both reflected and helped create a new planetary consciousness among growing numbers of people. (Image created by Reto Stockli, Nazmi El Saleous, and Marit Jentoft-Nilsen, NASA GSFC) more tightly, but also more contentiously, together. By the 1990s, this process of accelerating engagement among distant peoples was widely known as globalization.

Although the term was relatively new, the process was not. From the viewpoint of world history, the genealogy of globalization reaches far into the past. The Arab, Mongol, Russian, Chinese, and Ottoman empires; the Silk Road, Indian Ocean, and trans-Saharan trade routes; the spread of Buddhism, Christianity, and especially Islam—all of these connections had long linked the societies of the Eastern Hemisphere, bringing new rulers, religions, products, diseases, and technologies to many of its peoples. Later, in the centuries after 1500, European maritime voyages and colonizing efforts launched the Columbian exchange, incorporating the Western Hemisphere and inner Africa firmly and permanently into a genuinely global network of communication, exchange, and often exploitation. During the nineteenth century, as the Industrial Revolution took hold and Western nations began a new round of empire building in Asia and Africa, that global network tightened further, and its role as generator of social and cultural change only increased.

These were the foundations on which twentieth-century globalization was built. A number of prominent developments of the past century—the world wars, the Great Depression, communism, the cold war, the end of empire—which were explored in the last three chapters, operated on a global scale. But global interaction, while continuing earlier patterns, vastly accelerated its pace after World War II. Those contacts and interactions among geographically and culturally distant peoples gave rise to a world more densely connected and converging than ever before, but also to a world deeply divided, unequal, conflicted, and violent. To illustrate this accelerating globalization, this chapter examines four major processes: the transformation of the world economy, the emergence of a global feminism, the confrontation of world religions with modernity, and the growing awareness of humankind's enormous impact on the environment.

Global Interaction and the Transformation of the World Economy

■ **Change**

What factors contributed to economic globalization during the twentieth century?

When most people speak of globalization, they are referring to the immense growth in international economic transactions that took place in the second half of the twentieth century and that continues into the twenty-first. Many have come to see this process as almost natural, certainly inevitable, and practically unstoppable. Yet the first half of the twentieth century, particularly the decades between the two world wars, witnessed a deep contraction of global economic linkages as the aftermath of World War I and then the Great Depression wreaked havoc on the world economy. International trade, investment, and labor migration dropped sharply as major states turned inward, favoring high tariffs and economic autonomy in the face of a global economic collapse.

The aftermath of World War II was very different. The capitalist victors in that conflict, led by the United States, were determined to avoid any return to such

Depression-era conditions. At a conference in Bretton Woods, New Hampshire, in 1944, they forged a set of agreements and institutions (the World Bank and the International Monetary Fund) that laid the foundation for postwar globalization. This "Bretton Woods system" negotiated the rules for commercial and financial dealings among the major capitalist countries, while promoting relatively free trade, stable currency values linked to the U.S. dollar, and high levels of capital investment.

Technology also contributed to the acceleration of economic globalization. Containerized shipping, huge oil tankers, and air express services dramatically lowered transportation costs, while fiber optic cables and later the Internet provided the communication infrastructure for global economic interaction. Population growth, especially when tied to growing economies and modernizing societies, further fueled globalization as dozens of new nations, eager for modern development, entered the world economy.

A World Economy
Indian-based call centers that serve North American or European companies and customers have become a common experience of globalization for many. Here employees in one such call center in Patna, a major city in northeastern India, undergo voice training in order to communicate more effectively with their English-speaking callers. (Indiapicture/Alamy)

What kind of economic globalization was taking shape? In the 1970s and after, major capitalist countries such as the United States and Great Britain abandoned many earlier political controls on economic activity as their leaders and businesspeople increasingly viewed the entire world as a single market. Known as neoliberalism, this approach to the world economy favored the reduction of tariffs, the free global movement of capital, a mobile and temporary workforce, the privatization of many state-run enterprises, the curtailing of government efforts to regulate the economy, and both tax and spending cuts. Powerful international lending agencies such as the World Bank and the International Monetary Fund imposed such free-market and pro-business conditions on many poor countries if they were to qualify for much-needed loans. The collapse of the state-controlled economies of the communist world only furthered such unrestricted global capitalism. In this view, the market, operating both globally and within nations, was the most effective means of generating the holy grail of economic growth. By the end of the twentieth century, as economic historian Jeffrey Frieden put it, "capitalism was global and the globe was capitalist."[2]

Reglobalization

These were the foundations for a dramatic quickening of global economic transactions after World War II, a "reglobalization" of the world economy following the contractions of the 1930s. This immensely significant process was expressed in the accelerating circulation of goods, capital, and people.

■ **Connection**
In what ways has economic globalization linked the world's peoples more closely together?

World trade, for example, skyrocketed from a value of some $57 billion in 1947 to well over $7 trillion in 2001. Department stores and supermarkets around the world stocked their shelves with goods from every part of the globe. Twinings of London marketed its 120 blends of tea in more than 100 countries, and the Australian-based Kiwi shoe polish was sold in 180 countries. In 2005, about 70 percent of WalMart products reportedly included components from China. By then, Toyota had displaced Ford as the second-largest car seller in the United States and was edging up on the number one spot.

Money as well as goods achieved an amazing global mobility in three ways. The first was *foreign direct investment*, whereby a firm in, say, the United States opens a factory in China or Mexico (see Map 24.1). Such investment exploded after 1960 as companies in the rich countries sought to take advantage of cheap labor, tax breaks, and looser environmental regulations in the developing countries. A second form of money in motion has been the short-term movement of capital, in which investors annually spent trillions of dollars purchasing foreign currencies or stocks likely to increase in value and often sold them quickly thereafter, with unsettling consequences. A third form of capital movement involved the personal funds of individuals. By the end of the twentieth century, international credit cards had

Map 24.1 Globalization in Action: Trade and Investment in the Early Twenty-first Century
World trade has surged in the last half century, but the balance of trade among countries has made some nations net exporters and others net importers. Investment by transnational corporations around the world has been another major expression of globalization. Note that the United States and Europe are both major givers and receivers of foreign investment.

taken hold almost everywhere, allowing for easy transfer of money across national borders. In 2003, MasterCard was accepted at some 32 million businesses in 210 countries or territories.

Central to the acceleration of economic globalization have been huge global businesses known as transnational corporations (TNCs), which produce goods or deliver services simultaneously in many countries. For example, Mattel Corporation produced Barbie, that quintessentially American doll, in factories located in Indonesia, Malaysia, and China, using molds from the United States, plastic and hair from Taiwan and Japan, and cotton cloth from China. From distribution centers in Hong Kong, more than a billion Barbies were sold in 150 countries by 1999. Burgeoning in number since the 1960s, those TNCs, such as Royal Dutch Shell, Sony, and General Motors, often were of such an enormous size and economic clout that they dwarfed many countries. By 2000, 51 of the world's 100 largest economic units were in fact TNCs, not countries. In the permissive economic circumstances of recent decades, such firms have been able to move their facilities quickly from place to place in search of the lowest labor costs or the least restrictive environmental regulations. Nike, for example, during one five-year period closed twenty factories and opened thirty-five others, often thousands of miles apart.

More than ever workers too were on the move in a rapidly globalizing world economy. Examples included South Asians and West Indians seeking work and a better life in Great Britain; Algerians and West Africans in France; Yugoslavs in Germany and Switzerland; Mexicans, Cubans, and Haitians in the United States. By 2003, some 4 million Filipino domestic workers were employed in 130 countries. Young women by the hundreds of thousands from poor countries have been recruited as sex workers in wealthy nations, sometimes in conditions approaching slavery. Many highly educated professionals—doctors, nurses, engineers, computer specialists—left their homes in the Global South in a "brain drain" that clearly benefited the Global North. These flows of migrating laborers often represented a major source of income to their home countries. They also provided an inexpensive source of labor for their adopted countries, even as their presence generated mounting political and cultural tensions. Beyond those seeking work, millions of others sought refuge in the West from political oppression or civil war at home, and hundreds of millions of short-term international travelers and tourists joined the swelling ranks of people in motion.

Disparities and Resistance

What was the impact of these tightening economic links for nations and peoples around the world? That question has prompted enormous debate and controversy. Amid the swirl of contending opinion, one thing seemed reasonably clear: economic globalization accompanied, and arguably helped generate, the most remarkable spurt of economic growth in world history. On a global level, total world output grew from a value of $7.1 trillion in 1950 to $55.9 trillion in 2003 and on a per

■ Connection
What new or sharper divisions has economic globalization generated?

Snapshot   **Indicators of Reglobalization**[3]

Telephone lines	from 150 million in 1965 to 1.5 billion in 2000
Mobile telephones	from 0 in 1978 to more than 1 billion in 2004
Internet users	from 0 in 1985 to 934 million in 2004
International air travelers	from 25 million in 1950 to 400 million in 1996
Export processing zones	from 0 in 1957 to 3,000 in 2002
Daily foreign exchange turnover	from $15 billion in 1973 to $1.9 trillion in 2004
International bank loans	from $9 billion in 1972 to $1.465 trillion in 2000
World stock of foreign direct investment	from $66 billion in 1960 to $7.1 trillion in 2002
Value of international trade	from $629 billion in 1960 to $7.43 trillion in 2001
Number of transnational companies	from 7,000 in the late 1960s to 65,000 in 2001

capita basis from $2,835 to $8,753.[4] This represents an immense, rapid, and unprecedented creation of wealth with a demonstrable impact on human welfare. Life expectancies grew almost everywhere, infant mortality declined, and literacy increased. The UN Human Development Report in 1997 concluded that "in the past 50 years, poverty has fallen more than in the previous 500."[5]

Far more problematic has been the distribution of this new wealth. Since Europe's Industrial Revolution took hold in the early nineteenth century, a wholly new division appeared within the human community—between the rich industrialized countries, primarily in Europe and North America, and everyone else. In 1820, the ratio between the income of the top and bottom 20 percent of the world's population was three to one. By 1991, it was eighty-six to one.[6] The accelerated economic globalization of the twentieth century did not create this global rift, but it arguably has worsened the gap and certainly has not greatly diminished it. Even that well-known capitalist financier and investor George Soros, a billionaire many times over, acknowledged this reality in 2000: "The global capitalist system has produced a very uneven playing field. The gap between the rich and the poor is getting wider."[7] That gap has been evident, often tragically, in great disparities in incomes, medical care, availability of clean drinking water, educational and employment opportunities, access to the Internet, and dozens of other ways. It has shaped the life chances of practically everyone (see Map 24.2).

These disparities were the foundations for a new kind of global conflict. As the East/West division of capitalism and communism faded, differences between the rich nations of the Global North and the developing countries of the Global South assumed greater prominence in world affairs. Highly contentious issues have

World Population Distribution

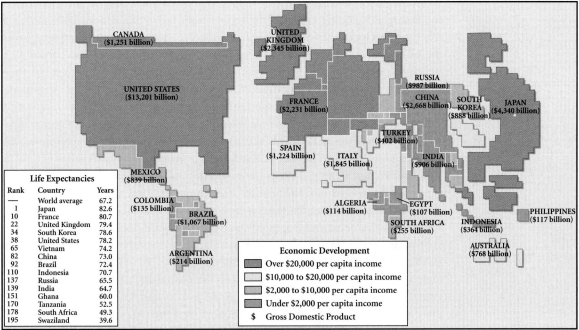

Life Expectancies		
Rank	Country	Years
—	World average	67.2
1	Japan	82.6
10	France	80.7
22	United Kingdom	79.4
34	South Korea	78.6
38	United States	78.2
65	Vietnam	74.2
82	China	73.0
92	Brazil	72.4
110	Indonesia	70.7
137	Russia	65.5
139	India	64.7
151	Ghana	60.0
170	Tanzania	52.5
178	South Africa	49.3
195	Swaziland	39.6

Economic Development

- Over $20,000 per capita income
- $10,000 to $20,000 per capita income
- $2,000 to $10,000 per capita income
- Under $2,000 per capita income
- $ Gross Domestic Product

Map 24.2   Global Inequality: Population and Economic Development

These two maps illustrate in graphic form the global inequalities of the early twenty-first century. The first shows the relative size of the world's population by region and country; the second shows the size of the economy measured by total gross domestic product and per capita income. Illustrating yet another indication of the global economic divide are figures for overall life expectancy, an indicator that has narrowed more sharply than have others.

included the rules for world trade, availability of and terms for foreign aid, representation in international economic organizations, the mounting problem of indebtedness, and environmental and labor standards. Such matters surfaced repeatedly in international negotiations during the last half of the twentieth century and into the twenty-first. In the 1970s, for example, a large group of developing countries joined together to demand a new international economic order that was more favorable to the poor countries. Not much success attended this effort. More recently, developing countries have contested protectionist restrictions on their agricultural exports imposed by the rich countries, which were eager to protect their own politically powerful farmers.

Beyond active resistance by the rich nations, a further obstacle to reforming the world economy in favor of the poor lay in growing disparities among the developing countries themselves (see Chapter 23). The oil-rich economies of the Middle East had little in common with the banana-producing countries of Central America. The rapidly industrializing states of China, India, and South Korea had quite different economic agendas than impoverished African countries. These disparities made common action difficult to achieve.

Economic globalization has generated inequalities not only at the global level and among developing countries, but also within individual nations, rich and poor alike. In the United States, for example, a shifting global division of labor required the American economy to shed millions of manufacturing jobs. With recent U.S. factory wages perhaps thirty times those of China, many companies moved their manufacturing operations offshore to Asia or Latin America. This left many relatively unskilled American workers in the lurch, forcing them to work in the low-wage service sector, even as other Americans were growing prosperous in emerging high-tech industries. Even some highly skilled work, such as computer programming, was outsourced to lower-wage sites in India, Ireland, Russia, and elsewhere.

Globalization divided Mexico as well. The northern part of the country, with close business and manufacturing ties to the United States, grew much more prosperous than the south, which was largely a rural agricultural area and had a far more slowly growing economy. Beginning in 1994, southern resentment boiled over in the Chiapas rebellion, which featured a strong antiglobalization platform. Its leader, Subcomandante Marcos, referred to globalization as a "process to eliminate that multitude of people who are not useful to the powerful."[8] China's rapid economic growth likewise fostered mounting inequality between its rural households and those in its burgeoning cities, where income by 2000 was three times that of the countryside. Economic globalization may have brought people together as never before, but it also divided them sharply.

The hardships and grievances of those left behind or threatened by the march toward economic integration have fueled a growing popular movement aimed at criticizing and counteracting globalization. Known variously as an antiglobalization, alternative globalization, or global justice movement, it emerged in the 1990s as an international coalition of political activists, concerned scholars and students, trade unions, women's and religious organizations, environmental groups, and others, hailing from rich and poor countries alike. Thus opposition to neo-liberal globalization was itself global in scope. That opposition, though reflecting a variety of viewpoints, largely agreed that free-trade, market-driven corporate globalization lowered labor standards, fostered ecological degradation, prevented poor countries from protecting themselves against financial speculators, ignored local cultures, disregarded human rights, and enhanced global inequality, while favoring the interests of large corporations and the rich countries.

This movement appeared dramatically on the world's radar screen in late 1999 in Seattle at a meeting of the World Trade Organization (WTO). An international body representing 149 nations and charged with negotiating the rules for global commerce and promoting free trade, the WTO had become a major target of globalization critics. "The central idea of the WTO," argued one of them, "is that *free trade*—actually the values and interests of global corporations—should supersede all other values."[9] Tens of thousands of protesters—academics, activists, farmers, labor union leaders from all over the world—descended on Seattle in what became a violent, chaotic, and much-publicized protest. At the city's harbor, protest organizers created a Seattle Tea Party around the slogan "No globalization without representation," echoing the Boston Tea Party of 1773. Subsequent meetings of the WTO and other high-level international economic gatherings were likewise greeted with large-scale protest and a heavy police presence. In 2001, alternative globalization activists created the World Social Forum, an annual gathering to coordinate strategy, exchange ideas, and share experiences, under the slogan "Another world is possible." It was an effort to demonstrate that neo-liberal globalization was not inevitable and that the processes of a globalized economy could and should be regulated and subjected to public accountability.

Globalization and an American Empire

For many people, opposition to this kind of globalization also expressed resistance to mounting American power and influence in the world. An "American Empire," some have argued, is the face of globalization (see Map 24.3), but scholars, commentators, and politicians have disagreed as to how best to describe the United States' role in the postwar world. Certainly it has not been a colonial territorial empire such as that of the British or the French in the nineteenth century. Americans generally, seeking to distinguish themselves from Europeans, have vigorously denied that they were an empire at all.

In some ways, the U.S. global presence might be seen as an "informal empire," similar to the ones that Europeans exercised in China and the Middle East during the nineteenth century. In both cases, economic penetration, political pressure, and periodic military action sought to create societies and governments compatible with the values and interests of the dominant power, but without directly governing large populations for long periods of time. In its economic dimension,

U.S. Bases Abroad: The Political/Military Face of the American Empire

U.S. Military Bases, 2003
Countries housing U.S. military bases in the early 21st century

Global McDonald's: The Economic/Cultural Face of the American Empire

Global McDonald's Restaurants by Country, 2003
1–19
20–99
100–499
500–999
1,000–1,999
2,000–9,999
10,000 +

Map 24.3 Two Faces of an "American Empire"
Those who argue that the United States constructed an empire in the second half of the twentieth century point both to its political/military alliances around the world and to U.S. economic and cultural penetration of many countries. The distribution of U.S. military bases and of McDonald's restaurants indicates something of the scope of America's global presence in the early twenty-first century.

American dominance has been termed an "empire of production," which uses its immense wealth to entice or intimidate potential collaborators.[10] Some scholars have emphasized the United States' frequent use of force around the world, while others have focused attention on the "soft power" of its cultural attractiveness, its political and cultural freedoms, the economic benefits of cooperation, and the general willingness of many to follow the American lead voluntarily.

With the collapse of the Soviet Union and the end of the cold war by the early 1990s, U.S. military dominance was now unchecked by any equivalent power. When the United States was attacked by Islamic militants on September 11, 2001, that power was unleashed first against Afghanistan (2001), which had sheltered the al-Qaeda instigators of that attack, and then against Iraq (2003), where Saddam Hussein allegedly had been developing weapons of mass destruction. In the absence of the Soviet Union, the United States could act unilaterally without fear of triggering a conflict with another major power. Although the Afghan and Iraqi regimes were quickly defeated, establishing a lasting peace and rebuilding badly damaged Muslim countries proved a difficult task. Thus, within a decade of the Soviet collapse, the United States found itself in yet another global struggle, an effort to contain or eliminate Islamic terrorism.

In the final quarter of the twentieth century, as its relative military strength peaked, the United States faced growing international economic competition. The recovery of Europe and Japan and the emergent industrialization of South Korea, Taiwan, China, and India substantially reduced the United States' share of overall world production from about 50 percent in 1945 to 20 percent in the 1980s. Accompanying this relative decline was a sharp reversal of the country's trade balance as U.S. imports greatly exceeded its exports. Once the world's leading creditor, the United States now became its leading debtor. Lee Iacocca, president of Chrysler Corporation, registered the dismay that many Americans felt at this turn in their fortunes: "We send Japan low-value soybeans, wheat, corn, coal, and cotton. They send us high-value autos, motorcycles, TV sets, and oil well casings. It's 1776 and we're a colony again."[11]

However it might be defined, the exercise of American power, like that of many empires, was resisted abroad and contested at home. In Vietnam, Cuba, Iraq, and elsewhere, armed struggle against U.S. intervention was both costly and painful. During the cold war, the governments of India, Egypt, and Ethiopia sought to diminish American influence in their affairs by turning to the Soviet Union or playing off the two superpowers against each other. Even France, resenting U.S. domination, withdrew from the military structure of NATO in 1967 and expelled all foreign-controlled troops from the country. Many intellectuals, fearing the erosion of their own cultures in the face of well-financed American media around the world, have decried American "cultural imperialism." By the early twenty-first century, the United States' international policies—such as its refusal to accept the jurisdiction of the International Criminal Court; its refusal to ratify the Kyoto protocol on global warming; its doctrine of preemptive war, which was exercised in Iraq; and its apparent use of torture—had generated widespread opposition.

Within the United States as well, the global exercise of American power generated controversy. The Vietnam War, for example, divided the United States more sharply than at any time since the Civil War. It split families and friendships, churches and political parties. It alienated the United States from many of its traditional allies. The war in Vietnam provided a platform for a growing number of critics, both at home and abroad, who had come to resent American cultural and economic dominance in the post-1945 world. It stimulated a new sense of activism among students in the nation's colleges and universities. Finally, the Vietnam War gave rise to charges that the cold war had undermined American democracy by promoting an overly powerful, "imperial" presidency, by creating a culture of secrecy and an obsession with national security, and by limiting political debate in the country. Not a few came to see America itself as an imperialist power. A similar set of issues, protests, and controversies followed the American invasion of Iraq in the early twenty-first century.

The Globalization of Liberation: Comparing Feminist Movements

More than goods, money, and people traversed the planet during the twentieth century. So too did ideas, and none was more powerful than the ideology of liberation. Communism promised workers and peasants liberation from capitalist oppression. Nationalism offered subject peoples liberation from imperialism. Advocates of democracy sought liberation from authoritarian governments.

The 1960s in particular witnessed an unusual convergence of protest movements around the world, suggesting the emergence of a global culture of liberation. Within the United States, the civil rights demands of African Americans and Hispanic Americans; the youthful counterculture of music, sex, and drugs; and the prolonged and highly divisive protests against the war in Vietnam gave the 1960s a distinctive place in the country's recent history. Across the Atlantic, swelling protests against unresponsive bureaucracy, consumerism, and middle-class values likewise erupted, most notably in France in 1968. There a student-led movement protesting conditions in universities attracted the support of many middle-class people, who were horrified at the brutality of the police, and stimulated an enormous strike among some 9 million workers. France seemed on the edge of another revolution. Related but smaller-scale movements took place in Germany, Italy, and elsewhere.

The communist world too was rocked by protest. In 1968, the new Communist Party leadership in Czechoslovakia, led by Alexander Dubcek, initiated a sweeping series of reforms aimed at creating "socialism with a human face." Censorship ended, generating an explosion of free expression in what had been a highly repressive regime; unofficial political clubs emerged publicly; victims of earlier repression were rehabilitated; secret ballots for party elections were put in place. To the conservative leaders of the Soviet Union, this "Prague Spring" seemed to challenge communist rule itself, and they sent troops and tanks to crush it. Across the world in communist

China, another kind of protest was taking shape in that country's Cultural Revolution (see Chapter 22).

In the developing countries, a substantial number of political leaders, activists, scholars, and students developed the notion of a "third world." Their countries, many of which had recently broken free from colonial rule, would offer an alternative to both a decrepit Western capitalism and a repressive bureaucratic Soviet communism. They claimed to pioneer new forms of economic development, of grassroots democracy, and of cultural renewal. By the late 1960s, the icon of this third world-ideology was Che Guevara, the Argentine-born revolutionary who had embraced the Cuban Revolution and subsequently attempted to replicate its experience of liberation through guerrilla warfare in parts of Africa and Latin America. Various aspects of his life story—his fervent anti-imperialism, which was cast as a global struggle; his self-sacrificing lifestyle; his death in 1967 at the hands of the Bolivian military—made him a heroic figure to third-world revolutionaries as well as to Western radicals, who were disgusted with the complacency and materialism of their own societies.

Che Guevara
In life, Che was an uncompromising but failed revolutionary, while in death he became an inspiration to third-world liberation movements and a symbol of radicalism to many in the West. His image appeared widely on T-shirts and posters, and in Cuba itself a government-sponsored cult featured schoolchildren chanting each morning "We will be like Che." This billboard image of Che was erected in Havana in 1988. (Tim Page/Corbis)

No expression of the global culture of liberation held a more profound potential for change than feminism, for it represented a rethinking of the most fundamental and personal of all human relationships—that between women and men. Feminism had begun in the West in the nineteenth century with a primary focus on suffrage and in several countries had achieved the status of a mass movement by the outbreak of World War I (see Chapter 17). The twentieth century witnessed the globalization of feminism as organized efforts to address the concerns of women took shape across the world. Communist governments—in the Soviet Union, China, and Cuba, for example—mounted vigorous efforts to gain the support of women and to bring them into the workforce by attacking major elements of older patriarchies (see Chapter 22). But feminism took hold in many cultural and political settings, where women confronted different issues, adopted different strategies, and experienced a range of outcomes.

Feminism in the West

In the West, organized feminism had lost momentum by the end of the 1920s, when most countries had achieved universal suffrage. When it revived in the 1960s in both Western Europe and the United States, it did so with a quite different agenda. In France, for example, the writer and philosopher Simone de Beauvoir in 1949 had

■ **Comparison**
What distinguished feminism in the industrialized countries from that of the Global South?

published *The Second Sex*, a book arguing that women had historically been defined as "other," or deviant from the "normal" male sex. The book soon became a central statement of a reviving women's movement. French feminists dramatized their concerns publicly in the early 1970s when some of them attempted to lay a wreath at the tomb of the unknown soldier in Paris, declaring, "Someone is even more unknown than the soldier: his wife." They staged a counter–Mother's Day parade under the slogan "Celebrated one day; exploited all year." To highlight their demand to control their own bodies, some 343 women signed a published manifesto stating that they had undergone an abortion, which was then illegal in France.

Across the Atlantic, millions of American women responded to Betty Friedan's book *The Feminine Mystique* (1963), which disclosed the identity crisis of educated women who were unfulfilled by marriage and motherhood. Some adherents of this second-wave feminism took up the equal rights agenda of their nineteenth-century predecessors, but with an emphasis now on employment and education rather than voting rights.

A more radical expression of American feminism took shape from the experience of women who had worked in other kinds of radical politics, such as the civil rights movement. Widely known as "women's liberation," this approach took broader aim at patriarchy as a system of domination, similar to those of race and class. One manifesto from 1969 declared:

> We are exploited as sex objects, breeders, domestic servants, and cheap labor. We are considered inferior beings, whose only purpose is to enhance men's lives.... Because we live so intimately with our oppressors, we have been kept from seeing our personal suffering as a political condition.[12]

Thus liberation for women meant becoming aware of their own oppression, a process that took place in thousands of consciousness-raising groups across the country. Many such women preferred direct action rather than the political lobbying favored by equal rights feminists. They challenged the Miss America contest of 1968 by tossing stink bombs in the hall, crowning a live sheep as their Miss America, and disposing of girdles, bras, high-heeled shoes, tweezers, and other "instruments of oppression" in a Freedom Trashcan. They also brought into open discussion issues involving sexuality, insisting that free love, lesbianism, and celibacy should be accorded the same respect as heterosexual marriage.

Yet another strand of Western feminism emerged from women of color. For many of them, the concerns of white, usually middle-class, feminists were hardly relevant to their oppression. Black women had always worked outside the home and so felt little need to be liberated from the chains of homemaking. Whereas white women might find the family oppressive, African American women viewed it as a secure base from which to resist racism. Solidarity with black men, rather than separation from them, was essential in confronting a racist America. Viewing mainstream feminism as "a family quarrel between White women and White men," many women of African descent in the United States and Britain established their own organizations, with a focus on racism and poverty.[13]

Feminism in the Global South

As women mobilized outside of the Western world during the twentieth century, they faced very different situations than did white women in the United States and Europe. For much of Asia, Africa, and Latin America, the predominant issues—colonialism, racism, the struggle for independence, poverty, development, political oppression, and sometimes revolution—were not directly related to gender. Women were affected by and engaged with all of these efforts and were welcomed by nationalist and communist leaders, mostly men, who needed their support. Once independence or the revolution was achieved, however, the women who had joined those movements often were relegated to marginal positions.

The different conditions within developing countries sometimes generated sharp criticism of Western feminism. To many African feminists in the 1970s and beyond, the concerns of their American or European sisters were too individualistic, too focused on sexuality, and insufficiently concerned with issues of motherhood, marriage, and poverty to be of much use. Furthermore, they resented Western feminists' insistent interest in cultural matters such as female circumcision and polygamy, which sometimes echoed the concerns of colonial-era missionaries and administrators. Western feminism could easily be seen as a new form of cultural imperialism. Moreover, many African governments and many African men defined feminism of any kind as "un-African" and associated with a hated colonialism.

Women's movements in the Global South took shape around a wide range of issues, not all of which were explicitly gender based. In the East African country of Kenya, a major form of mobilization was the women's group movement. Some 27,000 small associations of women, which were an outgrowth of traditional self-help groups, had a combined membership of more than a million by the late 1980s. They provided support for one another during times of need, such as weddings, births, and funerals; they took on community projects, such as building water cisterns, schools, and dispensaries; in one province, they focused on providing permanent iron roofing for their homes. Some became revolving loan societies or bought land or businesses. One woman testified to the sense of empowerment she derived from membership in her group.

> I am a free woman. I bought this piece of land through my group. I can lie on it, work on it, keep goats or cows. What more do I want? My husband cannot sell it. It is mine.[14]

Elsewhere, other issues and approaches predominated. In the North African Islamic kingdom of Morocco, a more centrally directed and nationally focused feminist movement targeted the country's Family Law Code, which still defined women as minors. In 2004, a long campaign by Morocco's feminist movement, often with the help of supportive men and a liberal king, resulted in a new Family Law Code, which recognized women as equals to their husbands and allowed them to initiate divorce and to claim child custody, all of which had previously been denied.

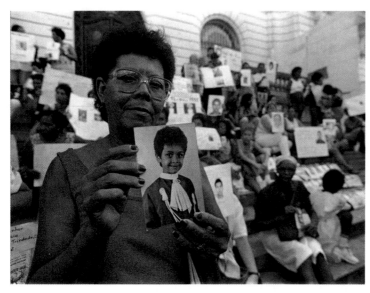

Mothers of Missing Children

This group of Brazilian mothers in Rio de Janeiro gathered every week during the mid-1990s to bring pressure on the government to find their missing children, generally believed to have been seized by criminal gangs engaged in child prostitution and illegal adoption. Often seeking loved ones who probably were executed by government or paramilitary death squads, such "mothers of the disappeared" have been active in many Latin American countries. (AP Images/Diego Guidice)

In Chile, a women's movement emerged as part of a national struggle against the military dictatorship of General Augusto Pinochet, who ruled the country from 1973 to 1990. Because they were largely regarded as "invisible" in the public sphere, women were able to organize extensively, despite the repression of the Pinochet regime. From this explosion of organizing activity emerged a women's movement that crossed class lines and party affiliations. Human rights activists, most of them women, called attention to the widespread use of torture and to the "disappearance" of thousands of opponents of the regime, while demanding the restoration of democracy. Poor urban women by the tens of thousands organized soup kitchens, craft workshops, and shopping collectives, all aimed at the economic survival of their families. Smaller numbers of middle-class women brought more distinctly feminist perspectives to the movement and argued pointedly for "democracy in the country and in the home." This diverse women's movement was an important part of the larger national protest that returned Chile to democratic government in 1990.

In South Korea as in Chile, women's mobilization contributed to a "mass people's movement" that brought a return to democracy by the late 1980s, after a long period of highly authoritarian rule. The women's movement in South Korea drew heavily on the experience of young female workers in the country's export industries. In those factories, they were poorly paid, were subjected to exhausting working conditions and frequent sexual harassment, and lived in crowded company dormitories, often called "chicken coops." Such women spearheaded a democratic trade union movement during the 1970s, and in the process many of them developed both a feminist and a class consciousness.

International Feminism

Perhaps the most impressive achievement of feminism in the twentieth century was its ability to project the "woman question" as a global issue and to gain international recognition for the view that "women's rights are human rights."[15] Like slavery and empire before it, patriarchy lost at least some of its legitimacy during this most recent century, although clearly it has not been vanquished.

Feminism registered as a global issue when the United Nations, under pressure from women activists, declared 1975 as International Women's Year and the next ten years as the Decade for Women. The United Nations also sponsored a series of World Conferences on Women over the next twenty years. By 2006, 183 nations had ratified a UN Convention to Eliminate Discrimination against Women, which committed them to promote women's legal equality, to end discrimination, to actively encourage women's development, and to protect women's human rights. Clearly this international attention to women's issues was encouraging to feminists operating in their own countries and in many places stimulated both research and action.

This growing international spotlight on women's issues also revealed sharp divisions within global feminism. One issue was determining who had the right to speak on behalf of women at international gatherings—the official delegates of male-dominated governments or the often more radical unofficial participants representing various nongovernmental organizations. North/South conflicts also surfaced at these international conferences. In preparing for the Mexico City gathering in 1975, the United States attempted to limit the agenda to matters of political and civil rights for women, whereas delegates from third-world and communist countries wanted to include issues of economic justice, decolonization, and disarmament. Feminists from the South resented the dominance and contested the ideas of their Northern sisters. One African group highlighted the differences.

> While patriarchal views and structures oppress women all over the world, women are also members of classes and countries that dominate others and enjoy privileges in terms of access to resources. Hence, contrary to the best intentions of "sisterhood," not all women share identical interests.[16]

Nor did all third-world groups have identical views. Some Muslim delegates at the Beijing Conference in 1995 opposed a call for equal inheritance for women, because Islamic law required that sons receive twice the amount that daughters inherit. In contast, Africans, especially in non-Muslim countries, were aware of how many children had been orphaned by AIDS and felt that girls' chances for survival depended on equal inheritance.

Beyond such divisions within international feminism lay a global backlash among those who felt that its radical agenda had undermined family life, the proper relationship of men and women, and civilization generally. To Phyllis Schlafly, a prominent American opponent of the Equal Rights Amendment, feminism was a "disease" that brought in its wake "fear, sickness, pain, anger, hatred, danger, violence, and all manner of ugliness."[17] In the Islamic world, Western-style feminism, with its claims of gender equality and open sexuality, was highly offensive to many and fueled movements of religious revivalism that invited or compelled women to wear the veil and sometimes lead a highly restricted life. The Vatican, some Catholic and Muslim countries, and at times the U.S. government took strong exception to aspects of global feminism, particularly its emphasis on reproductive rights, including access to abortion and birth control. Thus feminism was global as the twenty-first century dawned, but it was very diverse and much contested.

Religion and Global Modernity

Beyond liberation and feminism, a further dimension of cultural globalization took shape in the challenge that modernity presented to the world's religions. To the most "advanced" thinkers of the past several hundred years—Enlightenment writers in the eighteenth century, Karl Marx in the nineteenth, socialist intellectuals and secular-minded people in the twentieth—supernatural religion was headed for extinction in the face of modernity, science, communism, or globalization. In some places—Britain, France, the Netherlands, and the Soviet Union, for example—religious belief and practice had declined sharply. Moreover, the spread of a scientific culture around the world persuaded small minorities everywhere, often among the most highly educated, that the only realities worth considering were those that could be measured with the techniques of science. To such people, all else was superstition, born of ignorance. Nevertheless, the far more prominent trends of the last century have been those that involved the further spread of major world religions, their resurgence in new forms, their opposition to elements of a secular and global modernity, and their political role as a source of community identity and conflict. Contrary to earlier expectations, religion has played an unexpectedly powerful role in this most recent century.

Buddhism, Christianity, and Islam had long functioned as transregional cultures, spreading far beyond their places of origin. That process continued in the twentieth century. Buddhist ideas and practices such as meditation found a warm reception in the West, as did yoga, originally a mind-body practice of Indian origin. Christianity of various kinds spread widely in non-Muslim Africa and South Korea and less extensively in parts of India. By the end of the century, it was growing even in China, where perhaps 7 percent of China's population—some 82 million people—claimed allegiance to the faith. No longer a primarily European or North American religion, Christianity by the early twenty-first century found some 62 percent of its adherents in Asia, Africa, and Latin America. Moreover, millions of migrants from the Islamic world planted their religion solidly in Europe and North America. In the United States, for example, a substantial number of African Americans and smaller numbers of European Americans engaged in Islamic practice. More than ever before, religious pluralism characterized the world's societies, confronting people with the need to make choices in a domain of life previously regarded as given and fixed.

Fundamentalism on a Global Scale

■ Change

In what respect did the various religious fundamentalisms of the twentieth century express hostility to global modernity?

Religious vitality in the twentieth century was expressed not only in the spread of particular traditions to new areas but also in the vigorous response of those traditions to the modernizing and globalizing world in which they found themselves. One such response has been widely called "fundamentalism," a militant piety—defensive, assertive, and exclusive—that took shape to some extent in every major religious tradition. Many features of the modern world, after all, appeared threatening to established religion. The scientific and secular focus of global modernity directly challenged the core beliefs of supernatural religion. Furthermore, the social upheavals connected with capitalism, industrialization, and globalization thoroughly upset customary class, family, and gender relationships that had long been sanctified by religious tradition. Nation-states, often associated with particular religions, were likewise undermined by the operation of a global economy and challenged by the spread of alien cultures. In much of the world, these disruptions came at the hands of foreigners, usually Westerners, in the form of military defeat, colonial rule, economic dependency, and cultural intrusion.

To such threats, fundamentalism represented a religious response, characterized by one scholar as "embattled forms of spirituality...experienced as a cosmic war between the forces of good and evil."[18] Although fundamentalisms everywhere have looked to the past for ideals and models, their rejection of modernity was selective, not wholesale. What they sought was an alternative modernity, infused with particular religious values. Most, in fact, made active use of modern technology to communicate their message and certainly sought the potential prosperity associated with modern life. Extensive educational and propaganda efforts, political mobilization of their followers, social welfare programs, and sometimes violence ("terrorism" to their opponents) were among the means that fundamentalists employed.

The term "fundamentalism" derived from the United States, where religious conservatives in the early twentieth century were outraged by critical and "scientific" approaches to the Bible, by Darwinian evolution, and by liberal versions of Christianity that accommodated these heresies. They called for a return to the fundamentals of the faith, which included the inerrancy of the scriptures, the virgin birth and physical resurrection of Jesus, and a belief in miracles. After World War II, American Protestant fundamentalism came to oppose political liberalism and "big government," the sexual revolution of the 1960s, homosexuality and abortion rights, and secular humanism generally. Many fundamentalists saw the United States on the edge of an abyss. For one major spokesman, Francis Schaeffer (1912–1984), the West was about to enter

> an electronic dark age, in which the new pagan hordes, with all the power of technology at their command, are on the verge of obliterating the last strongholds of civilized humanity. A vision of darkness lies before us. As we leave the shores of Christian Western man behind, only a dark and turbulent sea of despair stretches endlessly ahead...unless we fight.[19]

And fight they did. At first, fundamentalists sought to separate themselves from the secular world in their own churches and schools, but from the 1970s on, they entered the political arena as the "religious right," determined to return America to a "godly path." "We have enough votes to run this country," declared Pat Robertson, a major fundamentalist evangelist and broadcaster, who ran for president in 1988. Conservative fundamentalist Christians, no longer willing to restrict their activities to personal conversion, had emerged as a significant force in American political life by the end of the century.

In the very different setting of independent India, another fundamentalist movement—known as *Hindutva*, or Hindu nationalism—took shape during the 1980s. Like American fundamentalism, it represented a politicization of religion within a democratic context. To its advocates, India was, and always had been, an essentially Hindu country, even though it had been overwhelmed in recent centuries by Muslim invaders, then by the Christian British, and most recently by the secular state of the postindependence decades. The leaders of modern India, they argued, and particularly its first prime minister, Jawaharlal Nehru, were "the self-proclaimed secularists who...seek to remake India in the Western image," while repudiating its basically Hindu religious character. The Hindutva movement took political shape in an increasingly popular party called the Bharatiya Janata Party (BJP), with much of its support coming from urban middle-class or upper-caste people who resented the state's efforts to cater to the interests of Muslims, Sikhs, and the lower castes. Muslims in particular were defined as outsiders, potentially more loyal to a Muslim Pakistan than to India. The BJP became a major political force in India during the 1980s and 1990s, winning a number of elections at both the state and national levels and promoting a distinctly Hindu identity in education, culture, and religion.

Creating Islamic Societies: Resistance and Renewal in the World of Islam

■ Change

From what sources did Islamic renewal movements derive?

The most prominent of the fundamentalisms that emerged in the late twentieth century was surely that of Islam, which was permanently etched in Americans' memory in the image of Osama bin Laden and the destruction of the World Trade Center on September 11, 2001. However, this violent event was only one expression of a much larger phenomenon—an effort among growing numbers of Muslims to create a new religious/political order centered on the teachings of Islam.

Emerging strongly in the last quarter of the century, this Islamic activism gained strength from the enormous disappointments that had accumulated in the Muslim world by the 1970s. Political independence had given rise to major states—Egypt, Iran, Algeria, and others—that pursued essentially Western and secular policies of nationalism, socialism, and economic development, often with only lip service to an Islamic identity. These policies were not very successful, however. A number of endemic problems—vastly overcrowded cities with few services, widespread unemployment, pervasive corruption, slow economic growth, a mounting gap between the rich and poor—flew in the face of the great expectations that had accompanied the struggle against European domination. Despite independence from a century or more of humiliating Western imperialism, foreign intrusion still persisted. Israel, widely regarded as an outpost of the West, had been reestablished as a Jewish state in the very center of the Islamic world in 1948. In 1967, Israel inflicted a devastating defeat on Arab forces in the Six-Day War and seized various Arab territories, including the holy city of Jerusalem. Furthermore, broader signs of

Map 24.4 The Islamic World in the Early Twenty-first Century
An Islamic world of well over a billion people incorporated much of the Afro-Asian landmass but was divided among many nations and along linguistic and ethnic lines as well. The long-term split between the majority Sunnis and the minority Shias also sharpened in the new millennium.

Western cultural penetration—secular schools, alcohol, Barbie dolls, European and American movies, scantily clad women—appeared frequently in the Muslim world.

This was the context in which the idea of an Islamic alternative to Western models of modernity began to take hold. The intellectual and political foundations of this Islamic renewal had been established earlier in the century. Its leading figures, such as the Indian Mawlana Mawdudi and the Egyptian Sayyid Qutb, insisted that the Quran and the sharia (Islamic law) provided a guide for all of life—political, economic, and spiritual—and a blueprint for a distinctly Islamic modernity not dependent on Western ideas. It was the departure from Islamic principles, they argued, that had led the Islamic world into decline and subordination to the West, and only a return to the "straight path of Islam" would ensure a revival of Muslim societies. That effort to return to Islamic principles was labeled "jihad," an ancient and evocative religious term that refers to "struggle" or "striving" to please God. In its twentieth-century political expression, jihad included the defense of an authentic Islam against Western aggression and vigorous efforts to achieve the Islamization of social and political life within Muslim countries. It was a posture that would enable Muslims to resist the seductive but poisonous culture of the West, which

Sayyid Qutb had witnessed during a visit to the United States in the late 1940s. He was shocked by what he saw.

> Look at this capitalism with its monopolies, its usury…at this individual free-dom, devoid of human sympathy and responsibility for relatives except under force of law; at this materialistic attitude which deadens the spirit; at this behavior like animals which you call "free mixing of the sexes"; at this vulgarity which you call "emancipation of women"; at this evil and fanatical racial discrimination.[20]

■ **Comparison**

In what different ways did Islamic renewal express itself?

Such ideas soon echoed widely all across the Islamic world and found expression in many ways. At the level of personal life, many people became more religiously obser-vant, attending mosque, praying regularly, and fasting. Substantial numbers of women, many of them young, urban, and well educated, adopted modest Islamic dress and the veil quite voluntarily. Participation in Sufi mystical practices increased. Furthermore, many governments sought to anchor themselves in Islamic rhetoric and practice. Under pressure from Islamic activists, the government of Sudan in the 1980s adopted Quranic punishments for various crimes (such as amputating the hand of a thief) and announced a total ban on alcohol, dramatically dumping thousands of bottles of beer and wine into the Nile. During the 1970s, President Anwar Sadat of Egypt claimed the title of "Believer-President," referred frequently to the Quran, and proudly displayed his "prayer mark," a callus on his forehead caused by touching his head to the ground in prayer.

All over the Muslim world, from North Africa to Indonesia, Islamic renewal movements spawned organizations that operated legally to provide social services—

Hamas in Action
The Palestinian militant organization Hamas, founded in 1987 as an offshoot of Egypt's Muslim Brotherhood, illustrates two dimensions of Islamic radicalism. On the one hand, Hamas repeatedly sent suicide bombers to target Israeli civilians and sought the elimination of the Israeli state. A group of would-be suicide bombers are shown here in white robes during the funeral of colleagues killed by Israeli security forces in late 2003. On the other hand, Hamas ran a network of social services, providing schools, clinics, orphanages, summer camps, soup kitchens, and libraries for Palestinians. The classroom pictured here was part of a school founded by Hamas. (Andrea Comas/Reuters/Corbis; Abid Katib/Getty Images)

schools, clinics, youth centers, legal-aid centers, financial institutions, publishing houses—that the state offered inadequately or not at all. Islamic activists took leadership roles in unions and professional organizations of teachers, journalists, engineers, doctors, and lawyers. Such people embraced modern science and technology but sought to embed these elements of modernity within a distinctly Islamic culture. Some served in official government positions or entered political life where it was possible to do so. The Algerian Islamic Salvation Front was poised to win elections in 1992, when a frightened military government intervened to cancel the elections, an action that plunged the country into a decade of bitter civil war. In Turkey, Egypt, Jordan, Iraq, Palestine, and Lebanon, Islamic parties made impressive electoral showings in the 1990s and the early twenty-first century.

Another face of Islamic renewal, however, sought the violent overthrow of what they saw as compromised regimes in the Muslim world. One such group, the Egyptian Islamic Jihad, assassinated President Sadat in 1981, following Sadat's brutal crackdown on both Islamic and secular opposition groups. One of the leaders of Islamic Jihad explained:

> We have to establish the Rule of God's Religion in our own country first, and to make the Word of God supreme.... There is no doubt that the first battlefield for jihad is the extermination of these infidel leaders and to replace them by a complete Islamic Order.[21]

Two years earlier in Mecca, members of another radical Islamic group sought the overthrow of the Saudi government. They despised its alliance with Western powers, the corrupt and un-Islamic lifestyle of its leaders, and the disruptive consequences of its oil-fueled modernization program. They even invaded the Grand Mosque, Islam's most sacred shrine. In Iran (1979) and Afghanistan (1996), Islamic movements succeeded in coming to power and began to implement a radical program of Islamization based on the sharia (see Chapter 23 for Iran).

Islamic revolutionaries also took aim at hostile foreign powers. Hamas in Palestine and Hezbollah in Lebanon, supported by the Islamic regime in Iran, targeted Israel with popular uprisings, suicide bombings, and rocket attacks in response to the Israeli occupation of Arab lands. For some, Israel's very existence was illegitimate. The Soviet invasion of Afghanistan in 1979 prompted widespread opposition aimed at liberating the country from atheistic communism and creating an Islamic state. Sympathetic Arabs from the Middle East flocked to the aid of their Afghan compatriots.

Among them was the young Osama bin Laden, a wealthy Saudi Arab, who created an organization, al-Qaeda (meaning "the base" in Arabic), to funnel fighters and funds to the Afghan resistance. At the time, bin Laden and the Americans were on the same side, both opposing Soviet expansion into Afghanistan, but they soon parted ways. Returning to his home in Saudi Arabia, bin Laden became disillusioned and radicalized when the government of his country allowed the stationing of "infidel" U.S. troops in Islam's holy land during and after the first American war against Iraq in 1991. By the mid-1990s, he had found a safe haven in Taliban-ruled Afghanistan, from which he and other leaders of al-Qaeda planned their now infamous attack on the World Trade Center and other targets. Although they had no standing as Muslim clerics, in 1998 they issued a *fatwa*, or religious edict, declaring war on America.

> [F]or over seven years the United States has been occupying the lands of Islam in the holiest of places, the Arabian Peninsula, plundering its riches, dictating to its rulers, humiliating its people, terrorizing its neighbors, and turning its bases in the Peninsula into a spearhead through which to fight the neighboring Muslim peoples.... [T]he ruling to kill the Americans and their allies—civilians and military—is an individual duty for every Muslim who can do it in any country in which it is possible to do it, in order to liberate the al-Aqsa Mosque in Jerusalem and the holy mosque (in Mecca) from their grip, and in order for their armies to move out of all the lands of Islam, defeated and unable to threaten any Muslim.[22]

Elsewhere as well—in East Africa, Indonesia, Great Britain, Spain, Saudi Arabia, and Yemen—al-Qaeda or groups associated with it launched scattered attacks on Western interests. At the international level, the great enemy was not Christianity itself or even Western civilization, but irreligious Western-style modernity, U.S. imperialism, and an American-led economic globalization so aptly symbolized by the World Trade Center. Ironically, al-Qaeda itself was a modern and global organization, many of whose members were highly educated professionals from a variety of countries. Despite their focus on the West, the struggles undertaken by politicized Islamic activists were as much within the Islamic world as they were with the external enemy. If Islamic fundamentalism represented a clash of cultures or civilizations, that collision took place among different conceptions of Islam at least as sharply as with the outlook and practices of the modern West.

Religious Alternatives to Fundamentalism

Militant revolutionary fundamentalism has certainly not been the only religious response to modernity and globalization within the Islamic world. Many who shared a concern to embed Islamic values more centrally in their societies have acted peacefully and within established political structures. Considerable debate among them has raised questions about the proper role of the state, the difference between the eternal law of God (sharia) and the human interpretations of it, the rights of women, the possibility of democracy, and many other issues. Some Muslim intellectuals and political leaders have called for a dialogue between civilizations; others have argued that traditions can change in the face of modern realities without losing their distinctive Islamic character. In 1996, Anwar Ibrahim, a major political and intellectual figure in Malaysia, insisted that

> [Southeast Asian Muslims] would rather strive to improve the welfare of the women and children in their midst than spend their days elaborately defining the nature and institutions of the ideal Islamic state. They do not believe it

makes one less of a Muslim to promote economic growth, to master the infor-mation revolution, and to demand justice for women.[23]

Within other religious traditions as well, believers found various ways of responding to global modernity. More liberal or mainstream Christian groups spoke to the ethical issues arising from economic globalization. Many Christian organizations, for example, were active in agitating for debt relief for poor coun-tries. Pope John Paul II was openly concerned about "the growing distance between rich and poor, unfair competition which puts the poor nations in a situ-ation of ever-increasing inferiority." "Liberation theology," particularly in Latin America, sought a Christian basis for action in the areas of social justice, poverty, and human rights, while viewing Jesus as liberator as well as savior. In Asia, a grow-ing movement known as "socially engaged Buddhism" addressed the needs of the poor through social reform, educational programs, health services, and peacemak-ing action during times of conflict and war. The Dalai Lama has famously advo-cated a peaceful resolution of Tibet's relationship with China. Growing interest in communication and exchange among the world's religions was expressed at a World Peace Summit in 2000, when more than 1,000 religious and spiritual leaders met to explore how they might more effectively confront the world's many conflicts. In short, religious responses to global modernity were articulated in many voices.

The World's Environment and the Globalization of Environmentalism

Even as world religions, fundamentalist and otherwise, challenged global modernity on cultural or spiritual grounds, burgeoning environmental movements in the 1960s and after did so with an eye to the human impact on the earth and its many living creatures, including ourselves. Among the distinctive features of the twenti-eth century, none has been more pronounced than humankind's growing ability to alter the natural order and the mounting awareness of this phenomenon. When the wars, revolutions, and empires of this most recent century have faded from mem-ory, environmental transformation and environmental consciousness may well seem to future generations the decisive feature of that century.

The Global Environment Transformed

Underlying the environmental changes of the twentieth century were three other factors that vastly magnified the human impact on earth's ecological systems far beyond anything previously known.[24] One was the explosion of human numbers, an unprecedented quadrupling of the world's population in a single century. Another lay in the amazing new ability of humankind to tap the energy potential of fossil fuels—coal in the nineteenth century and oil in the twentieth. Hydroelectricity, natural gas, and nuclear power added to the energy resources

■ Change
How can we explain the dramatic increase in the human impact on the environment in the twentieth century?

Snapshot **World Population Growth, 1950–2005**[25]

The great bulk of the world's population growth in the second half of the twentieth century occurred in the developing countries of Asia, Africa, the Middle East, and Latin America.

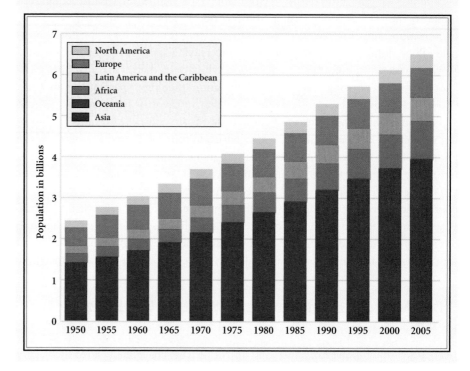

available to our species. These new sources of energy made possible a third contribution to environmental transformation—phenomenal economic growth—as modern science and technology immensely increased the production of goods and services. None of this occurred evenly across the planet. An average North American in the 1990s, for example, used 50 to 100 times more energy than an average Bangladeshi. But almost everywhere—in capitalist, communist, and developing countries alike—the idea of economic growth as something possible and desirable took hold as a part of global culture.

These three factors were the foundations for the immense environmental transformations of the twentieth century. Human activity had always altered the natural order, usually on a local basis, but now the scale of those disruptions assumed global proportions. The growing numbers of the poor and the growing consumption of the rich led to the doubling of cropland and a corresponding contraction of the world's forests and grasslands. With diminished habitats, numerous species of plants and animals either disappeared or were threatened with extinction. The human remaking of the environment also greatly increased the population of cattle, pigs, chickens, rats, and dandelions.

The global spread of modern industry, which was heavily dependent on fossil fuels, created a pall of air pollution in many major cities. By the 1970s, traffic police in Tokyo frequently wore face masks. In Mexico City, officials estimated in 2002 that air pollution killed 35,000 people every year. Industrial pollution in the Soviet Union rendered about half of the country's rivers severely polluted by the late 1980s, while fully 20 percent of its population lived in regions defined as "ecological disasters." The release of chemicals known as chlorofluorocarbons thinned the ozone layer, which protects the earth from excessive ultraviolet radiation.

The most critical and intractable environmental transformation was global warming. By the end of the twentieth century, a worldwide scientific consensus had emerged that the vastly increased burning of fossil fuels, which emit heat-trapping greenhouse gases, as well as the loss of trees that would otherwise remove carbon dioxide from the air, had begun to warm the atmosphere significantly. Although considerable disagreement existed about the rate and likely consequences of this process, concern about melting glaciers and polar ice caps, rising sea levels, thawing permafrost, extreme hurricanes, further species extinctions, and other ecological threats punctuated global discussion of this issue. It was clearly a global phenomenon, and it prompted a global awareness of the problem (see Map 24.5).

Green and Global

Environmentalism began in the nineteenth century as Romantic poets such as William Blake and William Wordsworth denounced the industrial era's "dark satanic mills," which threatened the "green and pleasant land" of an earlier England. The "scientific management" of nature, both in industrializing countries and in European colonies, represented another element of emerging environmental awareness among a few. So did the "wilderness idea," which aimed to preserve untouched areas from human disruption.[26] None of these strands of environmentalism attracted a mass following or provoked a global response. Not until the second half of the twentieth century, and then quite rapidly, did environmentalism achieve a worldwide dimension, although it was expressed in many quite different ways.

This second-wave environmentalism began in the West with the publication in 1962 of Rachel Carson's *Silent Spring*, an exposure of the chemical contamination of the environment that threatened both human health and the survival of many other species. She wrote of a "strange stillness" in a world where the songs of birds might no longer be heard. The book touched a nerve, generating an enormous response and effectively launching the environmental movement in the United States. Here, as virtually everywhere else, the impetus for action came from the grass roots and citizen protest. By the early 1990s, some 14 million Americans, one in seven adults, had joined one of the many environmental organizations—national or local—that aimed much of their effort at lobbying political parties and businesses. In Europe, the Club of Rome, a global think tank, issued a report in 1972 called *Limits to Growth*, which warned of resource exhaustion and the collapse of industrial society in the face of

■ **Comparison**
What differences emerged between environmentalism in the Global North and that in the Global South?

Map 24.5   Carbon Dioxide Emissions in the Twentieth Century

The source of carbon dioxide emissions, the chief human contribution to global warming, was distributed quite unevenly across the planet. Although the industrialized countries have been largely responsible for those emissions during the twentieth century, India and China in particular have assumed a much greater role in this process as their industrialization boomed in the early twenty-first century. The historically unequal distribution of those emissions has prompted much controversy between the countries of the Global North and the Global South about who should make the sacrifices required to address the problem of global warming.

unrelenting economic growth. The German environmental movement was distinctive in that its activists directly entered the political arena as the Green Party, which came to have a substantial role in German national politics. One of the Greens' main concerns was opposition to nuclear energy. Beyond addressing environmental pollution, Western activists focused much attention on wilderness issues, opposing logging, road building, and other development efforts in remaining unspoiled areas.

Quite quickly, during the 1970s and 1980s, environmentalism took root in the developing countries as well. There it often assumed a different character—it was more locally based and had fewer large national organizations than in the West; it involved poor people rather than affluent members of the middle class; it was less engaged in political lobbying and corporate strategies; it was more concerned with issues of food security, health, and basic survival than with the rights of nature or

Environmentalism in Action
These South Korean environmental activists are wearing death masks and holding crosses representing various countries during an antinuclear protest in Seoul in 1996, exactly ten years after a large-scale nuclear accident at Chernobyl in the Soviet Union. The lead protester holds a placard reading "Don't forget Chernobyl!" (AP Images/Yun Hai-Huoung)

wilderness protection; and it was more closely connected to movements for social justice.[27] Thus, whereas Western environmentalists defended forests where few people lived, the Chikpo or "tree-hugging" movement in India sought to protect the livelihood of farmers, artisans, and herders living in areas subject to extensive deforestation. A massive movement to prevent or limit the damming of India's Narmada River derived from the displacement of local people; similar anti-dam protests in the American Northwest were more concerned with protecting salmon runs.

Western environmentalists often called on individuals to change their values by turning away from materialism toward an appreciation of the intricate and fragile web of life that sustains us all. In the Philippines, by contrast, environmental activists confronting the operation of foreign mining companies have sought fundamental changes in the political and social structure of their country. Thus environmental protest has overlapped with other movements seeking to challenge established power structures and social hierarchies. Coalitions of numerous local groups—representing various religious, women's, human rights, indigenous peoples', peasant, and political organizations—frequently mobilized large-scale grassroots movements against the companies rather than seeking to negotiate with them. These movements have not been entirely nonviolent; occasionally they have included guerrilla warfare actions by "green armies." Such mass mobilization contributed to the decision of the Australian-based Western Mining Corporation in 2000 to abandon its plans for developing a huge copper mine in Mindanao.

By the late twentieth century, environmentalism had become a matter of global concern. Such an awareness motivated legislation aimed at pollution control in many countries; it pushed many businesses in a "green" direction; it fostered research on alternative and renewable sources of energy; it stimulated UN conferences on global warming; it persuaded millions of people to alter their way of life; and it generated a number of international agreements addressing matters such as whaling, ozone depletion, and global warming.

The globalization of environmentalism also disclosed sharp conflicts, particularly between the Global North and South. Both activists and governments in the developing countries have often felt that Northern initiatives to address atmospheric pollution and global warming would curtail their industrial development, leaving the North/South gap intact. "The threat to the atmospheric commons has been building over centuries," argued Indian environmentalist Vandana Shiva, "mainly because of industrial activity in the North. Yet... the North refuses to assume extra responsibility for cleaning up the atmosphere. No wonder the Third World cries foul when it is asked to share the costs." A Malaysian official put the dispute succinctly: "The developed countries don't want to give up their extravagant lifestyles, but plan to curtail our development."[28] The United States' refusal in the late 1990s to ratify the Kyoto protocol, aimed at reducing greenhouse gas emissions, seemed to confirm the unwillingness of the world's largest emitter to seriously limit those emissions and proved offensive to many of the 164 countries that had ratified it by 2006. Yet another North/South environmental issue arose over the export of hazardous wastes, generated in the rich countries, to disposal sites in the developing countries.

Beyond these and other conflicts, global environmentalism, more than any other widespread movement, came to symbolize "one-world" thinking, a focus on the common plight of humankind across the artificial boundaries of nation-states. It also marked a challenge to modernity itself, particularly its consuming commitment to endless growth. The ideas of sustainability and restraint, certainly not prominent in any list of modern values, entered global discourse and marked the beginnings of a new environmental ethic, though one based on concepts dating back to the Paleolithic era. This change in thinking was perhaps the most significant achievement of global environmentalism.

⊔ Final Reflections: Pondering the Uses of History

The end of a history book is an appropriate place to ask the fundamental question: just what is it good for, this field of study we call history? What, in short, are the uses of the past, and particularly of the global past?

At one level, philosophers, scholars, and thoughtful people everywhere have long used history to probe the significance of human experience. Does an examination of the past disclose any purpose, meaning, or pattern, or is it "just one damned thing after another"? Some sages, of course, have discerned divine purpose in the unfolding of the human story. To Saint Augustine, an early Christian thinker and writer, that purpose was the building of the "heavenly city," while events in this world were but steps in God's great plan. Chinese thinkers often viewed history as the source of moral lessons and related the behavior of rulers to the rise and fall of their dynasties. Europeans and others operating within the Enlightenment tradition have seen history in secular terms as a record of progress toward greater freedom or rationality in human affairs. Karl Marx viewed the past as a succession of economic changes and class struggles culminating in the creation of socialism, a secular utopia that would forever banish war, inequality, and social conflict.

Most contemporary historians are skeptical of such grand understandings of the human past, especially those that depend on some unseen hand directing the course of history to a defined end or those that reflect a particular set of values. But if "purpose" is hard to detect in the human story, some general "directions" over the long run are perhaps more evident.

One such trend lies in growing human numbers, which are linked to greater control over the natural environment as our ways of living moved from gathering and hunting, to agriculture, and most recently to industrial societies. Accompanying this broad direction in world history has been the growing complexity of human societies. Small hunting bands of a few dozen people gave way to agricultural villages of several thousands, to cities populated by tens or hundreds of thousands, to states and empires consisting of many millions. As the scale of human communities enlarged, so too did the pace of change in human affairs. In recent centuries, change has become both expected and valued in ways that would surely seem strange to most of the world's earlier inhabitants. A final possible direction in world history has been toward greater connection among the planet's diverse cultures and peoples. To early links among neighboring settlements or villages were later added networks of exchange and communication that operated among distant civilizations, across whole hemispheres, and after 1500 on a genuinely global level.

A word of caution, however, about finding direction in world history. None of this happened smoothly, evenly, or everywhere, and all of it was accompanied by numerous ups and downs, reversals, and variations. Furthermore, the notion of direction in history is quite different from that of progress. It is an observation rather than a judgment. One might consider growing populations, control over nature, increasing complexity, more rapid change, and global integration as great achievements and evidence of human "success." Alternatively, one might regard them as a burden or a curse, more of a disease than a triumph. We do well in studying the past to separate as much as possible our descriptions about what happened from our opinions about those events and processes.

In addition to discovering meaning or, even more modestly, direction in history, the uses of the past have long included efforts by political authorities to inculcate national, religious, civic, patriotic, or other values in their citizens. Furious debates in recent decades about history curricula in the schools of the United States, Japan, China, and elsewhere testify to the continuing impulse to use history in this way. In democratic societies, many people also express the hope that grounding in history will generate wiser public policies and more informed and effective partic-ipation by citizens. It is not always easy to find evidence for such outcomes of his-torical study, for the lessons of the past are many, varied, and conflicting, and the world, as always, hovers on the knife edge of possibility and disaster. Nonetheless, advocates for historical study continue to believe that probing the past enhances public life.

On a more personal level, many people have found in the study of history end-less material for musing, for pondering those matters of the heart and spirit that all of us must confront as we make our way in the world. Consider, for example, the question of suffering. History is, among other things, a veritable catalog of the vari-eties of human suffering. It provides ample evidence, should we need it, that suffer-ing is a common and bedrock human experience—and that none of us is exempt. But the study of history also highlights the indisputable fact that much of human suffering has come at our own hands in the shape of war, racism, patriarchy, exploitation, inequality, oppression, and neglect.

Is it possible that some exposure to the staggering sum of human suffering revealed in the historical record can soften our hearts, fostering compassion for our own suffering and that of others? In short, can the study of history generate kind-ness, both at the level of day-to-day personal interactions and at the wider level of acting to repair the brokenness of the world?

For those who choose to practice kindness or to seek justice in public life— overcoming global poverty, promoting equality between men and women, seeking understanding among religious traditions, encouraging environmental sustainabil-ity—history offers some encouragement. For one thing, it provides a record of those who have struggled long, hard, and on occasion with some success. Abolitionists contributed to the ending of slavery. Colonized peoples broke free of empire. Women secured the vote and challenged patriarchy. Socialists and commu-nists challenged the inequities of capitalism, while popular protest brought repres-sive communist regimes to their knees in the Soviet Union and Eastern Europe. Brave people have spoken truth to power. In short, things changed, and sometimes people changed things.

There is yet another way in which history might assist our personal journeys through life. We are, most of us, inclined to be insular, to regard our own ways as the norm, to be fearful of difference. Nor is this tendency largely our own fault. We all have limited experience. Few of us have had much personal encounter with cul-tures beyond our own country, and none of us, of course, knows personally what life was like before our birth. But we do know that a rich and mature life involves opening up to a wider world. If we base our understanding of life only on what we personally experience, we are impoverished indeed.

In this task of opening up, history in general and world history in particular have much to offer. They provide a marvelous window into the unfamiliar. They confront us with the whole range of human achievement, tragedy, and sensibility. They give context and perspective to our own limited experience. They allow us some modest entry into the lives of people far removed from us in time and place. They offer us company for the journeys of our own lives. If we take it seriously, historical study can assist us in enlarging and enriching our sense of self. In helping us open up to the wider experience of "all under heaven," as the Chinese put it, history can assist us in becoming wiser and more mature people. What more might one ask from any field of study?

Second Thoughts

What's the Significance?

neo-liberalism	Prague Spring	Islamic renewal
reglobalization	Che Guevara	Osama bin Laden/al-Qaeda
transnational corporations	second-wave feminism	global warming
North/South gap	fundamentalism	environmentalism
antiglobalization	Hindutva	

To assess your mastery of the material in this chapter, see the **Online Study Guide** at bedfordstmartins.com/strayer.

Big Picture Questions

1. To what extent did the processes discussed in this chapter (economic globalization, feminism, fundamentalism, environmentalism) represent something new in the twentieth century? In what respects did they have roots in the more distant past?

2. In what ways did the global North/South divide find expression in the twentieth century?

3. What have been the benefits and drawbacks of globalization since 1945?

4. Does the twentieth century as a whole confirm or undermine Enlightenment predictions about the future of humankind?

5. "The twentieth century marks the end of the era of Western dominance in world history." What evidence might support this statement? What evidence might contradict it?

6. To what extent do you think the various liberation movements of the twentieth century—communism, nationalism, democracy, feminism, internationalism—have achieved their goals?

7. Based on material in Chapters 21, 22, and 24, how might you define the evolving roles of the United States in the history of the twentieth century?

Next Steps: For Further Study

For Web sites and documents related to this chapter, see **Make History** at bedfordstmartins.com/strayer.

Karen Armstrong, *The Battle for God* (2000). A comparison of Christian, Jewish, and Islamic fundamentalism in historical perspective.

Nayan Chanda, *Bound Together: How Traders, Preachers, Adventurers, and Warriors Shaped Globalization* (2007). An engaging, sometimes humorous, long-term view of the globalization process.

Jeffrey Frieden, *Global Capitalism: Its Fall and Rise in the Twentieth Century* (2006). A thorough, thoughtful, and balanced history of economic globalization.

Michael Hunt, *The World Transformed* (2004). A thoughtful global history of the second half of the twentieth century.

J. R. McNeill, *Something New under the Sun: An Environmental History of the Twentieth Century World* (2001). A much-acclaimed global account of the rapidly mounting human impact on the environment during the most recent century.

Bonnie Smith, ed., *Global Feminisms since 1945* (2000). A series of essays about feminist movements around the world.

"No Job for a Woman," http://www.iwm.org.uk/upload/package/30/women/index.htm. A Web site illustrating the impact of war on the lives of women in the twentieth century.

Notes

Prologue

1. Adapted from Carl Sagan, *The Dragons of Eden* (New York: Random House, 1977), 13–17.
2. See David Christian, *Maps of Time* (Berkeley: University of California Press, 2004).
3. Voltaire, *Treatise on Toleration,* chap. 22.
4. See David Christian, "World History in Context," *Journal of World History* 14, no. 4 (December 2003), 437–58.

Part One

Chapter 1

1. Richard Rainsford, "What Chance, the Survival Prospects of East Africa's Last Hunting and Gathering Tribe," 1997, http://www.ntz.info/gen/n00757.html.
2. What follows comes from Sally McBreatry and Alison S. Brooks, "The Revolution That Wasn't: A New Interpretation of the Origin of Modern Human Behavior," *Journal of Human Evolution* 39 (2000), 453–563.
3. Peter Bogucki, *The Origins of Human Society* (Oxford: Blackwell, 1999), 94–95.
4. Paul G. Bahn and Jean Vertut, *Images of the Ice Age* (New York: Facts on File, 1988), chap. 7.
5. John Mulvaney and Johan Kaminga, *Prehistory of Australia* (Washington, D.C.: Smithsonian Institution Press, 1999), 93–102.
6. For a recent summary of this debate, see Charles C. Mann, *1491: New Revelations of the Americas before Columbus* (New York: Alfred Knopf, 2005), chap. 5.
7. Brian M. Fagan, *Ancient North America* (London: Thames and Hudson, 1995), 77–87.
8. Ben Finney, "The Other One-Third of the Globe," *Journal of World History* 5, no. 2 (Fall 1994): 273–85.
9. David Christian, *Maps of Time* (Berkeley: University of California Press, 2004), 143.
10. Richard B. Lee, *The Dobe Ju/'hoansi* (New York: Harcourt Brace, 1993), 58.
11. J. C. Beaglehole, *The Journals of Captain James Cook* (Cambridge: Hakluyt Society, 1968), 1:399.
12. Inga Clendinnen, *Dancing with Strangers* (Cambridge: Cambridge University Press, 2005), 159–67.
13. Marshall Sahlins, "The Original Affluent Society," in *Stone Age Economics* (London: Tavistock, 1972), 1–39.
14. Christopher Ehret, *The Civilizations of Africa* (Charlottesville: University of Virginia Press, 2002), chap. 2.
15. Marija Gimbutas, *The Language of the Goddess* (San Francisco: HarperCollins, 1989), 316–18.
16. D. Bruce Dickson, *The Dawn of Belief* (Tucson: University of Arizona Press, 1990), 210.
17. Derived from Christian, *Maps of Time*, 208.
18. Brian Fagan, *People of the Earth* (New York: HarperCollins, 1992), 200–201.
19. Jan Platvoet, "At War with God: Ju/'hoan Curing Dances," *Journal of Religion in Africa* 29, no. 1 (1999): 5.
20. J. David Lewis-Williams, *Believing and Seeing: Symbolic Meaning in Southern San Rock Paintings* (London: Academic Press, 1981).
21. Lee, *The Dobe Ju/'hoansi.* Unless otherwise noted, all information and quotes about the Ju/'hoansi come from this book.
22. Elizabeth Marshall Thomas, *The Harmless People* (New York: Vintage Books, 1989), 180.
23. For a contemporary account of a curing dance, see Bradford Keeney, "Ropes to God: Experiencing the Bushman Spiritual Universe," *Parabola* 27, no. 3 (2002), S1–S16.
24. Platvoet, "At War with God."
25. Brian Fagan, *Before California* (New York: Rowman and Littlefield, 2003), 153–55, 341–44.
26. Jeanne E. Arnold, *The Origins of a Pacific Coast Chiefdom* (Salt Lake City: University of Utah Press, 2001), 14.
27. Chester King, "Chumash Inter-Village Economic Exchange," in *Native Californians*, edited by Lowell John Bean and Thomas C. Blackburn (Menlo Park: Ballena Press, 1976), 289–318. The quote is on p. 297.

Chapter 2

1. "Population 1: The Town That's Been Reclaimed by the Prairie," *International Observer*, November 20, 2005, http://observer.guardian.co.uk/international/story/0,6903,1646659,00.html?gusrc=rss.
2. Peter Bellwood, *First Farmers* (London: Blackwood, 2005), 7.

3. Mark Nathan Cohen, *The Food Crisis in Prehistory* (New Haven: Yale University Press, 1977).

4. Bruce Smith, *The Emergence of Agriculture* (New York: Scientific American Library, 1995), 206–14.

5. Jared Diamond, *Guns, Germs, and Steel* (New York: Vintage, 1997), 132, 157–75.

6. Bellwood, *First Farmers*, 54–55.

7. Steven Mithen, *After the Ice* (Cambridge, Mass.: Harvard University Press, 2004), 87.

8. Neil Roberts, *The Holocene: An Environmental History* (Oxford: Blackwell, 1998), 116.

9. Nina V. Federoff, "Prehistoric GM Corn," *Science* 302 (November 2003): 1158.

10. Diamond, *Gun, Germs, and Steel*, 367.

11. The most recent summary of an immense literature on the spread of languages is found in Bellwood, *First Farmers*.

12. Many of these dates are much debated. See John Staller et al., *Histories of Maize* (Boston: Academic Press, 2006).

13. John A. Mears, "Agricultural Origins in Global Perspective," in *Agricultural and Pastoral Societies in Ancient and Classical History*, edited by Michael Adas (Philadelphia: Temple University Press, 2001), 63–64.

14. Elizabeth Wayland Barber, *Women's Work: The First 20,000 Years* (New York: W. W. Norton, 1994), chap. 3.

15. Andrew Sherrat, "The Secondary Exploitation of Animals in the Old World," *World Archeology* 15, no. 1 (June 1983): 90–104.

16. Clive Ponting, *A Green History of the World* (New York: St. Martin's Press, 1991), 69.

17. Anatoly M. Khazanov, *Nomads and the Outside World* (Madison: University of Wisconsin Press, 1994), 15.

18. Ian Hodder, "Women and Men at Catalhoyuk," *Scientific American* 15, no. 1 (2005): 35–41.

19. Allen W. Johnson and Timothy Earle, *The Evolution of Human Societies* (Stanford, Calif.: Stanford University Press, 2000), 281–94.

Chapter 3

1. http://www.utahoutventures.com/multiactivity/raftoffroadtours.htm.

2. Charles C. Mann, *1491: New Revelations of the Americas before Columbus* (New York: Alfred A. Knopf, 2005), 174–91; Proyecto Arqueológico Norte Chico, Project Description, 2005, http://www.fieldmuseum.org/research_collections/anthropology/anthro_sites/PANC/proj_desc.htm.

3. Jonathan Mark Kenoyer, *Ancient Cities of the Indus Valley Civilization* (Oxford: Oxford University Press, 1998), 83–84.

4. For a summary of many theories, see Stephen K. Sanderson, *Social Transformations* (Oxford: Blackwell, 1995), chap. 3.

5. Robert Carneiro, "A Theory of the Origin of the State," *Science* 169 (1970): 733–38.

6. Susan Pollock, *Ancient Mesopotamia* (Cambridge: Cambridge University Press, 1999), 48.

7. *The Epic of Gilgamesh*, translated and edited by Benjamin R. Foster (New York: W. W. Norton, 2001), 10, Tablet I:226–32.

8. Miriam Lichtheim, *Ancient Egyptian Literature* (Berkeley: University of California Press, 1975), 2:168–75.

9. Samuel Noah Kramer, *History Begins at Sumer* (Philadelphia: University of Pennsylvania Press, 1981), 3–4.

10. James Legge, trans., *The Chinese Classics* (London: Henry Frowde, 1893), 4:171–72.

11. Marija Gimbutas, *The Living Goddess* (Berkeley: University of California Press, 1999).

12. Margaret Ehrenberg, *Women in Prehistory* (London: British Museum Publications, 1989), 107.

13. David Christian, *Maps of Time* (Berkeley: University of California Press, 2004), 256–57, 263–64.

14. Sherry Ortner, "Is Female to Male as Nature Is to Culture?" in *Women, Culture, and Society*, edited by Michelle Rosaldo and Louise Lamphere (Stanford, Calif.: Stanford University Press, 1974), 67–88.

15. Gerda Lerner, *The Creation of Patriarchy* (New York: Oxford University Press, 1986), 70.

16. Lichtheim, *Ancient Egyptian Literature*, 2:184–85.

17. Lichtheim, *Ancient Egyptian Literature*, 2:168–75.

18. Prologue to *The Code of Hammurabi*, http://www.wsu.edu/~dee/MESO/CODE.HTM.

19. Gary Urton, "From Knots to Narratives: Reconstructing the Art of Historical Record-Keeping in the Andes from Spanish Transcriptions of Inka Khipus," *Ethnohistory* 45, no. 3 (1998): 409–38.

20. Adolf Erman, *The Literature of the Ancient Egyptians*, translated by Aylward M. Blackman (London: Methuen, 1927), 136–37.

21. H. and H. A. Frankfort, *Before Philosophy* (Baltimore: Penguin Books, 1963), 39, 138.

22. Quoted in Peter Stearns et al., *World Civilizations* (New York: Longman, 1996), 1:30.

23. *The Epic of Gilgamesh*, translated by N. K. Sandars (New York: Penguin Classics, 1972).

24. For both Egyptian quotes, see Lichtheim, *Ancient Egyptian Literature*, 1:41–42; 2:124–26.

25. See Clive Ponting, *A Green History of the World* (New York: St. Martin's Press, 1991), chap. 5.

26. Samuel Kramer, *The Sumerians* (Chicago: University of Chicago Press, 1963), 142.

27. Cyril Aldred, *The Egyptians* (London: Thames and Hudson, 1998), 138.

28. For a recent summary of a long debate about the relationship of Egypt and Africa, see David O'Connor and Andrew Reid, eds., *Ancient Egypt in Africa* (London: UCL Press, 2003).

29. James B. Pritchard, ed., *Ancient Near Eastern Texts Relating to the Old Testament* (Princeton: Princeton University Press, 1969), 647–48.

30. Lichtheim, *Ancient Egyptian Literature,* 1:25–27.

31. Joan Oates, *Babylon* (London: Thames and Hudson, 1986), 91.

32. Marvin Harris, ed., *Cannibals and Kings* (New York: Vintage, 1978), 102.

Part Two

1. Stephen K. Sanderson, *Social Transformation* (Oxford: Blackwell, 1995), chap. 4.

2. From Sanderson, *Social Transformation*, 103.

3. Colin Ronan and Joseph Needham, *The Shorter Science and Civilization in China* (Cambridge: Cambridge University Press, 1978), 58.

4. Sidney W. Mintz, *Sweetness and Power* (New York: Penguin Books, 1985), chap. 2.

5. William H. McNeill, *Plagues and Peoples* (New York: Doubleday, 1977), 94.

6. See world population estimates by region in Paul Adams et al., *Experiencing World History* (New York: New York University Press, 2000), 334.

Chapter 4

1. Cullen Murphy, *Are We Rome? The Fall of an Empire and the Fate of America* (Boston: Houghton Mifflin, 2007).

2. J. M. Cook, *The Persian Empire* (London: J. M. Dent & Sons, 1983), 76.

3. George Rawlinson, trans., *The Histories of Herodotus* (London: Dent, 1910), 1:131–40.

4. Erich F. Schmidt, *Persepolis I: Structures, Reliefs, Inscriptions,* OIP 68 (Chicago: University of Chicago Press, 1953), 63.

5. Quoted in Lynn Hunt et al., *The Making of the West* (Boston: Bedford/St. Martin's, 2005), 75.

6. Christian Meier, *Athens* (New York: Metropolitan Books, 1993), 93.

7. B. Jowett, trans., *Thucydides Translated into English* (Oxford: Oxford University Press, 1881) 1:115–29.

8. Arrian, *The Campaigns of Alexander*, translated by Aubrey de Selincourt, revised by J. R. Hamilton (London: Penguin, 1971), 395–96.

9. Stanley Burstein, *The Hellenistic Period in World History* (Washington, D.C.: American Historical Association, 1996), 12.

10. Norman F. Cantor, *Antiquity* (New York: HarperCollins, 2003), 25.

11. Greg Woolf, "Inventing Empire in Ancient Rome," in *Empires: Perspectives from Archeology and History*, edited by Susan Alcock et al. (Cambridge: Cambridge University Press, 2001), 314.

12. S. A. M. Adshead, *China in World History* (London: McMillan Press, 1988), 4–21.

13. See Padma Manian, "Harappans and Aryans: Old and New Perspectives on Ancient Indian History," *The History Teacher* 32, no. 1 (November 1998): 17–32.

14. Stanley Wolpert, *A New History of India* (New York: Oxford University Press, 1993), chap. 5.

15. Zhengyuan Fu, *Autocratic Tradition and Chinese Politics* (New York: Cambridge University Press, 1993), 188.

Chapter 5

1. S. N. Eisenstadt, ed., *The Origins and Diversity of Axial Age Civilizations* (Albany: SUNY Press, 1986), 1–4; Karen Armstrong, *The Great Transformation* (New York: Alfred A. Knopf, 2006).

2. Arthur Waley, *Three Ways of Thought in Ancient China* (Garden City, N.Y.: Doubleday, 1956), 159–60.

3. Nancy Lee Swann, trans., *Pan Chao: Foremost Woman Scholar of China* (New York: Century, 1932), 111–14.

4. Quoted in Huston Smith, *The Illustrated World's Religions* (San Francisco: HarperCollins, 1994), 123.

5. Lao Tsu, *Tao Te Ching*, translated by Gia-Fu Feng and Jane English (New York: Vintage Books, 1972), 80.

6. *Laws of Manu*, V, 146–48. Quoted in Swarna de Silva, "The Place of Women in Buddhism," 1994, http://www.enabling.org/ia/vipassana/Archive/D/DeSilva/WomenInBuddhism/womenInBuddhismSwarnaDeSilva.html.

7. Quoted in Karen Andrews, "Women in Theravada Buddhism," http://www.enabling.org/ia/vipassana/Archive/A/Andrews/womenTheraBudAndrews.html.

8. A. L. Basham, *The Wonder That Was India* (London: Sidgwick and Jackson, 1967), 309.

9. S. A. Nigosian, *The Zoroastrian Faith: Tradition and Modern Research* (Montreal: McGill–Queen's University Press, 1993), 95–97.

10. Isaiah 1:11–17.

11. Plato, *Apologia*.

12. Hippocrates, *On the Sacred Disease*, in *The Human Record*, edited by Alfred Andrea and James Overfield (Boston: Houghton Mifflin, 2005), 1:104–5.

13. Thanissaro Bhikkhu, trans., Karaniya Metta Sutta, 2004, http://www.accesstoinsight.org/tipitaka/kn/snp/snp.1.08.than.html.

14. Matthew 5:43–44.

15. See Marcus Borg, ed., *Jesus and Buddha: The Parallel Sayings* (Berkeley, Calif.: Ulysses Press, 1997).

16. For a popular summary of the voluminous scholarship on Jesus, see Stephen Patterson et al., *The Search for Jesus: Modern Scholarship Looks at the Gospels* (Washington, D.C.: Biblical Archeological Society, 1994).

17. Galatians 3:28.

18. Ephesians 5:22; 1 Corinthians 14:35.

19. Ekkehard W. Stegemann and Wolfgang Stegemann, *The Jesus Movement: A History of Its First Century* (Minneapolis: Fortress Press, 1999), 291–96.

20. Ramsay MacMullen, *Christianizing the Roman Empire* (New Haven: Yale University Press, 1984), chap. 4.

21. Peter Brown, *The Rise of Western Christendom* (London: Blackwell, 2003), 69–71.

22. Mary Ann Rossi, "Priesthood, Precedent, and Prejudice: On Recovering the Women Priests of Early Christianity," *Journal of Feminist Studies* 7, no. 1 (1991): 73–94.

23. Chai-Shin Yu, *Early Buddhism and Christianity* (Delhi: Motilal Banarsidass, 1981), 211.

Chapter 6

1. Po Chu-I, "After Passing the Examination," in Alfred Waley, *More Translations from the Chinese* (New York: Alfred A. Knopf, 1919), 37.

2. Quoted in Michael Lowe, *Everyday Life in Early Imperial China* (New York: Dorset Press, 1968), 38.

3. Selected Poems from the Tang Dynasty, http://www.lingshidao.net/hanshi/tang1.htm.

4. A. L. Basham, *The Wonder That Was India* (London: Sidgwick and Jackson, 1967), 138.

5. Karl Jacoby, "Slaves by Nature: Animals and Human Slaves," *Slavery and Abolition* 15 (1994): 89–97.

6. Orlando Patterson, *Slavery and Social Death* (Cambridge, Mass.: Harvard University Press, 1982).

7. Basham, *The Wonder That Was India*, 152.

8. Sarah Pomeroy et al., *Ancient Greece* (New York: Oxford University Press, 1999), 63, 239.

9. R. Zelnick-Abramovitz, *Not Wholly Free* (Leiden: Brill, 2005), 337, 343.

10. Keith Bradley, *Slavery and Society at Rome* (Cambridge: Cambridge University Press, 1994), 30.

11. 1 Peter 2:18.

12. Milton Meltzer, *Slavery: A World History* (New York: Da Capo Press, 1993), 189.

13. Quoted in Bret Hinsch, *Women in Early Imperial China* (Oxford: Rowman and Littlefield, 2002), 155.

14. Nancy Lee Swann, trans., *Pan Chao: Foremost Woman Scholar of China* (New York: Century Co., 1932), 111–14.

15. Lisa Raphals, *Sharing the Light: Representations of Women and Virtue in Early China* (Albany: SUNY Press, 1998).

16. Valerie Hansen, *The Open Empire* (New York: Norton, 2000), 183–84; Thomas Barfield, *The Perilous Frontier* (Cambridge: Blackwell Publishing, 1989), 140.

17. Vivian-Lee Nyitray, "Confucian Complexities," in Teresa A. Meade and Merry E. Weisner-Hanks, *A Companion to Gender History* (Oxford: Blackwell Publishing, 2004), 278.

18. Aristotle, *Politica*, ed. Loeb Classical Library, 1254b10–14.

19. Quoted in Pomeroy et al., *Ancient Greece*, 146.

Chapter 7

1. *Rethinking Schools on Line,* Fall 1999, http://www.rethinkingschools.org/archive/14_01/poor141.shtml.

2. Thomas Benjamin, "A Time of Reconquest: History, the Maya Revival, and the Zapatista Rebellion in Chiapas," *American Historical Review* 105, no. 2 (April 2000): 417.

3. Population figures are taken from Paul Adams et al., *Experiencing World History* (New York: New York University Press, 2000), 334.

4. Roderick J. McIntosh, *Ancient Middle Niger* (Cambridge: Cambridge University Press, 2005), 10.

5. Roderick J. McIntosh, *The Peoples of the Middle Niger* (Oxford: Blackwell, 1998), 177.

6. Kairn A. Klieman, *"The Pygmies Were Our Compass"* (Portsmouth, N.H.: Heinemann, 2003), chaps. 4, 5.

7. Christopher Ehret, *The Civilizations of Africa* (Charlottesville: University of Virginia Press, 2000), 175.

8. See Jan Vansina, *Paths in the Rainforest* (Madison: University of Wisconsin Press, 1990), 95–99.

9. Richard E. W. Adams, *Prehistoric Mesoamerica* (Norman: University of Oklahoma Press, 2005), 16.

10. Richard E. W. Adams, *Ancient Civilizations of the New World* (Boulder, Colo.: Westview Press, 1997), 53–56; T. Patrick Culbert, "The New Maya," *Archeology* 51, no. 5 (September–October 1998): 47–51.

11. William Haviland, "State and Power in Classic Maya Society," *American Anthropologist* 94, no. 4 (1992): 937.

12. Jared Diamond, *Collapse* (New York: Viking, 2005), chap. 5.

13. Esther Pasztory, *Teotihuacan: An Experiment in Living* (Norman: University of Oklahoma Press, 1997), 193.

14. George L. Cowgill, "The Central Mexican Highlands . . . ," in *The Cambridge History of the Native Peoples of the Americas*, vol. 2, part 1, *Mesoamerica*, edited by Richard E. W. Adams and Murdo J. MacLeod (Cambridge: Cambridge University Press, 2000), 289.

15. Karen Olsen Bruhns, *Ancient South America* (Cambridge: Cambridge University Press, 1994), 126–41; Sylvia R. Kembel and John W. Rick, "Building Authority at Chavin de Huantar," in *Andean Archeology*, edited by Helaine Silverman (Oxford: Blackwell, 2004), 59–76.

16. Garth Bawden, *The Moche* (Oxford: Blackwell, 1996), chaps. 9, 10.

17. John E. Kicza, *The Peoples and Civilizations of the Americas before Contact* (Washington, D.C.: American Historical Association, 1998), 43–44.

18. Much of this section draws on Brian Fagan, *Ancient North America* (London: Thames and Hudson, 2005), chaps. 14, 15. The quote is on p. 345.

19. George R. Milner, *The Moundbuilders* (London: Thames and Hudson, 2004).

20. David Hurst Thomas, *Exploring Ancient Native America* (New York: Routledge, 1999), 137–42.

21. Stephen H. Lekson and Peter N. Peregrine, "A Continental Perspective for North American Archeology," *The SAA Archeological Record* 4, no. 1 (January 2004): 15–19.

22. Fagan, *Ancient North America*, 475.

23. Quoted in Lynda Norene Shaffer, *Native Americans before 1492* (Armonk, N.Y.: M. E. Sharpe, 1992), 70.

Part Three

1. Marshall G. S. Hodgson, *The Venture of Islam* (Chicago: University of Chicago Press, 1974), 1:71.

2. Lynda Shaffer, "Southernization," *Journal of World History* 5, no. 1 (Spring 1994): 7.

Chapter 8

1. Somini Sengupta, "Sahara Journal," *New York Times*, November 25, 2003.

2. Seneca the Younger, *Declamations*, vol. 1.

3. Liu Xinru, "Silks and Religion in Eurasia, A.D. 600–1200," *Journal of World History* 6, no. 1 (Spring 1995): 25–48.

4. Jerry Bentley, "Hemispheric Integration, 500–1500 C.E.," *Journal of World History* 9, no. 2 (Fall 1998): 241–44.

5. See Jerry Bentley, *Old World Encounters* (New York: Oxford University Press, 1993), 42–53, 69–84.

6. Liu Xinru, *The Silk Road* (Washington, D.C.: American Historical Association, 1998), 10.

7. See William H. McNeill, *Plagues and Peoples* (New York: Doubleday, 1977), chaps. 3, 4.

8. Boccaccio, *The Decameron*, translated by M. Rigg (London: David Campbell, 1921), 1:5–11.

9. Kenneth McPherson, *The Indian Ocean* (Oxford: Oxford University Press, 1993), 15.

10. Janet L. Abu-Lughod, *Before European Hegemony* (Oxford: Oxford University Press, 1989), 269.

11. Nigel D. Furlonge, "Revisiting the Zanj and Revisioning Revolt," *Negro History Bulletin*, vol. 62 (December 1999).

12. Patricia Risso, *Merchants and Faith: Muslim Commerce and Culture in the Indian Ocean* (Boulder, Colo.: Westview, 1995), 54.

13. McPherson, *The Indian Ocean*, 97.

14. Kenneth R. Hall, *Maritime Trade and State Development in Early Southeast Asia* (Honolulu: University of Hawaii Press, 1985), 101.

15. Lynda Norene Shaffer, *Maritime Southeast Asia to 1500* (Armonk, N.Y.: M. E. Sharpe, 1996), 37, 46.

16. M. C. Horton and T. R. Burton, "Indian Metalwork in East Africa: The Bronze Lion Statuette from Shanga," *Antiquities* 62 (1988): 22.

17. Ross Dunn, *The Adventures of Ibn Battuta* (Berkeley: University of California Press, 1986), 124.

18. Christopher Ehret, *The Civilizations of Africa* (Charlottesville: University of Virginia Press, 2002), 255.

19. Ehret, *The Civilizations of Africa*, 227–32.

20. Nehemia Levtzion and Jay Spaulding, eds., *Medieval West Africa: Views from Arab Scholars and Merchants* (Princeton, N.J.: Marcus Wiener, 2003), 5.

21. Quoted in John Iliffe, *Africans: The History of a Continent* (Cambridge: Cambridge University Press, 1995), 75–76.

22. See Martin Raish and John L. Sorenson, *Pre-Columbian Contact with the Americas across the Oceans: An Annotated Bibliography* (Provo, Utah: Research Press, 1996).

23. J. R. McNeill and William McNeill, *The Human Web* (New York: W. W. Norton, 2003), 160.

24. Lauren Ristvet, *In the Beginning* (New York: McGraw-Hill, 2007), 165.

25. Maria Rostworowski de Diez Canseco, *History of the Inca Realm* (Cambridge: Cambridge University Press, 1999), 209–12.

26. Anthony Andrews, "America's Ancient Mariners," *Natural History*, October 1991, 72–75.

27. Richard Blanton and Gary Feinman, "The Mesoamerican World System," *American Anthropologist* 86, no. 3 (September 1984): 677.

Chapter 9

1. *The Guardian*, June 15, 2006.

2. John K. Fairbank, ed., *The Chinese World Order* (Cambridge, Mass.: Harvard University Press, 1968).

3. Mark Elvin, *The Retreat of the Elephants* (New Haven: Yale University Press, 2004), chap. 1. The quote is on p. 19.

4. Mark Elvin, *The Pattern of the Chinese Past* (London: Eyre Methuen, 1973), 55.

5. Samuel Adshead, *T'ang China: The Rise of the East in World History* (New York: Palgrave, 2004), 30.

6. Elvin, *The Pattern of the Chinese Past*, part 2; William McNeill, *The Pursuit of Power* (Chicago: University of Chicago Press, 1984), 50.

7. See "The Attractions of the Capital," in Patricia B. Ebrey, *Chinese Civilization: A Sourcebook* (New York: Free Press, 1993), 178–85.

8. Marco Polo, "The Glories of Kinsay," *Medieval Sourcebook*, http://www.fordham.edu/halsall/source/polo-kinsay.html.

9. John K. Fairbank, *China: A New History* (Cambridge, Mass.: Harvard University Press, 1992), 89.

10. J. R. McNeill and William H. McNeill, *The Human Web* (New York: W. W. Norton, 2003), 123.

11. Francesca Bray, *Technology and Gender: Fabrics of Power in Late Imperial China* (Berkeley: University of California Press, 1997), 116.

12. Patricia Ebrey, *The Inner Quarters* (Berkeley: University of California Press, 1993), 207.

13. Ebrey, *The Inner Quarters*, 37–43.

14. Ebrey, *The Inner Quarters*, 6.

15. See Nicolas DiCosmo, *Ancient China and Its Enemies* (Cambridge: Cambridge University Press, 2002), chap. 6.

16. DiCosmo, *Ancient China and Its Enemies*, 94.

17. Quoted in Thomas J. Barfield, "Steppe Empires, China, and the Silk Route," in *Nomads in the Sedentary World*, edited by Anatoly M. Khazanov and Andre Wink (Richmond: Kurzon Press, 2001), 237.

18. Quoted in Edward H. Shafer, *The Golden Peaches of Samarkand* (Berkeley: University of California Press, 1963), 28.

19. Susan Mann, "Women in East Asia," in *Women's History in Global Perspective*, edited by Bonnie Smith (Urbana: University of Illinois Press, 2005), 2:53–56.

20. Joseph Buttinger, *A Dragon Defiant: A Short History of Vietnam* (New York: Praeger, 1972), 32–34; Jerry Bentley, *Old World Encounters* (New York: Oxford University Press, 1993), 85–86.

21. Cited in "Trung Trac and Trung Nhi," http://www.viettouch.com/trungsis.

22. Liam C. Kelley, *Beyond the Bronze Pillars: Envoy Poetry and the Sino-Vietnamese Relationship* (Honolulu: University of Hawai'i Press, 2005).

23. "Chronicles of Japan," in *Nibongi*, translated by W. G. Aston (London: Kegan Paul, 1896), 2:128–33.

24. H. Paul Varley, "Japan, 550–838," in *Asia in Western and World History*, edited by Ainslee T. Embrey and Carol Gluck (Armonk, N.Y.: M. E. Sharpe, 1997), 353.

25. Quoted in McNeill, *The Pursuit of Power*, 40.

26. John Fairbank et al., *East Asia: Tradition and Transformation* (Boston: Houghton Mifflin, 1978), 353.

27. Arnold Pacey, *Technology in World Civilization* (Cambridge, Mass.: MIT Press, 1991), 50–53.

28. McNeill, *The Pursuit of Power*, 24–25.

29. Hugh Clark, "Muslims and Hindus in the Culture and Morphology of Quanzhou from the Tenth to the Thirteenth Century," *Journal of World History* 6, no. 1 (Spring 1995): 49–74.

30. Quoted in Arthur F. Wright, *Studies in Chinese Buddhism* (New Haven: Yale University Press, 1990), 16.

31. Arthur F. Wright, *Buddhism in Chinese History* (Stanford, Calif.: Stanford University Press, 1959), 36–39.

32. Quoted in Wright, *Buddhism in Chinese History*, 67.

33. Quoted in Eric Zurcher, *The Buddhist Conquest of China* (Leiden: E. J. Brill, 1959), 1:262.

34. Jacquet Gernet, *A History of Chinese Civilization* (Cambridge: Cambridge University Press, 1996), 291–96.

35. Edwin O. Reischauer, *Ennin's Travels in China* (New York: Ronald Press, 1955), 221–24.

Chapter 10

1. "East and West Churches Reconcile," http://chi.gospelcom.net/DAILYF/2002/12/daily-12-07-2002.shtml.

2. Paul R. Spickard and Kevin M. Cragg, *A Global History of Christians* (Grand Rapids, Mich.: Baker Academic, 1994), chap. 6.

3. Leonora Neville, *Authority in Byzantine Provincial Society, 950–1100* (Cambridge: Cambridge University Press, 2004), 2.

4. Deno John Geanakoplos, *Byzantium: Church, Society, and Civilization Seen through Contemporary Eyes* (Chicago: University of Chicago Press, 1984), 389.

5. Geanakoplos, *Byzantium*, 143.

6. Quoted in A. A. Vasiliev, *History of the Byzantine Empire* (Madison: University of Wisconsin Press, 1978), 79–80.

7. Geanakoplos, *Byzantium*, 362.

8. Geanakoplos, *Byzantium*, 369.

9. Rowena Loverance, *Byzantium* (Cambridge, Mass.: Harvard University Press, 2004), 43.

10. Daniel H. Kaiser and Gary Marker, *Reinterpreting Russian History* (Oxford: Oxford University Press, 1994), 63–67.

11. Quoted in Patrick J. Geary, *Before France and Germany* (New York: Oxford University Press, 1988), 79.

12. Quoted in Stephen Williams, *Diocletian and the Roman Recovery* (London: Routledge, 1996), 218.

13. Peter Brown, *The Rise of Western Christendom* (London: Blackwell, 1996), 305.

14. Karen Louise Jolly, *Tradition and Diversity: Christianity in a World Context to 1500* (Armonk, N.Y.: M. E. Sharpe, 1997), 195.

15. Quoted in John M. Hobson, *The Eastern Origins of Western Civilization* (New York: Cambridge University Press, 2004), 113.

16. Clive Ponting, *A Green History of the World* (New York: St. Martin's, 1991), 121–23.

17. Christopher Tyerman, *Fighting for Christendom: Holy Wars and the Crusades* (Oxford: Oxford University Press, 2004), 16.

18. Edward Peters, "The Firanj Are Coming—Again," *Orbis* 48, no. 1 (Winter 2004), 3–17.

19. See Peter Stearns, *Western Civilization in World History* (New York: Routledge, 2003), 52.

20. Quoted in Jean Gimple, *The Medieval Machine* (New York: Holt, 1976), 178.

21. Stuart B. Schwartz, ed., *Victors and Vanquished* (Boston: Bedford/St. Martin's, 2000), 147.

22. Quoted in Carlo Cipolla, *Before the Industrial Revolution* (New York: Norton, 1976), 207.

23. Quoted in S. Lilley, *Men, Machines, and History* (New York: International, 1965), 62.

24. See Toby Huff, *The Rise of Early Modern Science* (Cambridge: Cambridge University Press, 1993).

25. Quoted in Edward Grant, *Science and Religion from Aristotle to Copernicus* (Westport, Conn.: Greenwood Press, 2004), 158.

26. Quoted in L. Thorndike, *A History of Magic and Experimental Science* (New York: Columbia University Press, 1923), 2:58.

27. Quoted in Edward Grant, *God and Reason in the Middle Ages* (Cambridge: Cambridge University Press, 2001), 70.

28. Grant, *Science and Religion*, 228–29.

29. Marcia L. Colish, *Medieval Foundations of the Western Intellectual Tradition* (New Haven: Yale University Press, 1997), 128.

Chapter 11

1. Al-Hajj Malik El-Shabazz (Malcolm X), "The Pilgrimage to Mecca," Islam on Line, http://www.islamonline.net/English/hajj/2002/01/Exper- ience/article2.shtml.

2. Reza Aslan, *No God but God* (New York: Random House, 2005), 14

3. Quoted in Karen Armstrong, *A History of God* (New York: Ballantine Books, 1993), 146.

4. Quran 1:5.

5. Quran 3:110.

6. Quran 9:71.

7. "The Prophet's Farewell Sermon," Islam on Line, http://www.islamonline.net/English/In_Depth/mohamed/1424/kharitah/article02.shtml.

8. Quoted in Patricia Crone, "The Rise of Islam in the World," in the *Cambridge Illustrated History of the Islamic World*, edited by Francis Robinson (Cambridge: Cambridge University Press, 1996), 11.

9. Richard Bulliet, *Conversion to Islam in the Medieval Period* (Cambridge, Mass.: Harvard University Press, 1979), 33.

10. Nehemiah Levtzion, ed., *Conversion to Islam* (New York: Holmes and Meier, 1979), chap. 1.

11. Jerry Bentley, *Old World Encounters* (New York: Oxford University Press, 1993), 93.

12. Bernard Lewis, *Islam and the West* (New York: Oxford University Press, 1993), 157.

13. Quoted in Crone, "The Rise of Islam in the World," 14.

14. Quoted in Margaret Smith, *Readings from the Mystics of Islam* (London: Luzac, 1972), 11.

15. Aslan, *No God but God*, 201.

16. Quran 33:35.

17. Quran 4:34.

18. Quoted in Judith Tucker, "Gender and Islamic History," in *Islamic and European Expansion*, edited by Michael Adas (Philadelphia: Temple University Press, 1993), 46.

19. Nikki R. Keddie, "Women in the Middle East since the Rise of Islam," in *Women's History in Global Perspective*, edited by Bonnie G. Smith (Urbana: University of Illinois Press, 2005), 74–75.

20. William T. deBary, ed., *Sources of Indian Tradition* (New York: Columbia University Press, 1958), 2:355–57.

21. V. L. Menage, "The Islamization of Anatolia," in *Conversion to Islam*, edited by Nehemia Levtzion (New York: Holmes and Meier, 1979), chap. 4.

22. Ira M. Lapidus, *A History of Islamic Societies* (Cambridge: Cambridge University Press, 1988), 304–6.

23. Quoted in Keddie, "Women in the Middle East," 81.

24. Ross Dunn, *The Adventures of Ibn Battuta* (Berkeley: University of California Press, 1986), 300.

25. Jane I. Smith, "Islam and Christendom," in *The Oxford History of Islam*, edited by John L. Esposito (Oxford: Oxford University Press, 1999), 317–21.

26. Richard Eaton, "Islamic History as Global History," in *Islamic and European Expansion*, edited by Michael Adas (Philadelphia: Temple University Press, 1993), 12.

27. Francis Robinson, "Knowledge, Its Transmission and the Making of Muslim Societies," in the *Cambridge Illustrated History of the Islamic World*, edited by Francis Robinson (Cambridge: Cambridge University Press, 1996), 230.

28. Janet L. Abu-Lughod, *Before European Hegemony* (Oxford: Oxford University Press, 1989), 216–24.

29. Andrew Watson, *Agricultural Innovation in the Early Islamic World* (Cambridge: Cambridge University Press, 1983).

30. Arnold Pacey, *Technology in World History* (Cambridge, Mass.: MIT Press, 1991), 8, 74.

31. Robinson, "Knowledge, Its Transmission," 215.

32. Ahmad Dallal, "Science, Medicine, and Technology: The Making of a Scientific Culture," in *The Oxford History of Islam,* edited by John L. Esposito (Oxford: Oxford University Press, 1999), chap. 4.

33. David W. Tschanz, "The Arab Roots of European Medicine," *Aramco World,* May–June 1997, 20–31.

34. Dunn, *The Adventures of Ibn Battuta,* 258.

Chapter 12

1. Jack Weatherford, *Genghis Khan and the Making of the Modern World* (New York: Crown, 2004), xv.

2. Data derived from Thomas J. Barfield, "Pastoral Nomadic Societies," in *Berkshire Encyclopedia of World History* (Great Barrington: Berkshire, 2005), 4:1432–37.

3. Giovanni Carpini, *The Story of the Mongols,* translated by Erik Hildinger (Boston: Braden, 1996), 54.

4. Quoted in Peter B. Golden, "Nomads and Sedentary Societies in Eurasia," in *Agricultural and Pastoral Societies in Ancient and Classical History,* edited by Michael Adas (Philadelphia: Temple University Press, 2001), 73.

5. Thomas J. Barfield, *The Nomadic Alternative* (Englewood Cliffs, N.J.: Prentice Hall, 1993), 12.

6. Anatoly Khazanov, "The Spread of World Religions in Medieval Nomadic Societies of the Eurasian Steppes," in *Nomadic Diplomacy, Destruction and Religion from the Pacific to the Adriatic,* edited by Michael Gervers and Wayne Schlepp (Toronto: Joint Center for Asia Pacific Studies, 1994), 11.

7. Quoted in Gregory Guzman, "Were the Barbarians a Negative or Positive Factor in Ancient and Medieval History?" *The Historian* 50 (August 1988): 558–72.

8. Carter Finley, *The Turks in World History* (Oxford: Oxford University Press, 2005), 28–37.

9. Finley, *The Turks in World History,* 40.

10. Thomas Spear and Richard Waller, eds., *Being Maasai* (London: James Curry, 1993), 6, 12.

11. Richard Waller, "Ecology, Migration, and Expansion in East Africa," *African Affairs* 84 (1985): 347–70; Thomas Spear, *Kenya's Past* (London: Longman, 1981), 107.

12. Godfrey Muriuki, *A History of the Kikuyu* (Nairobi: Oxford University Press, 1974), chap. 4.

13. David Christian, *A History of Russia, Central Asia, and Mongolia* (London: Blackwell, 1998), 1:385.

14. Quoted in Christian, *A History of Russia,* 389.

15. David Morgan, *The Mongols* (Oxford: Blackwell, 1986), 63–67.

16. Weatherford, *Genghis Khan,* 86.

17. Chinggis Khan, "Letter to Changchun," in *The Human Record,* edited by Alfred J. Andrea and James Overfield (Boston: Houghton Mifflin, 2005), 1:431.

18. Thomas T. Allsen, *Mongol Imperialism* (Berkeley: University of California Press, 1987), 6.

19. Chinggis Khan, "Letter to Changchun."

20. Quoted in Weatherford, *Genghis Khan,* 111.

21. Barfield, *The Nomadic Alternative,* 166.

22. Peter Jackson, "The Mongols and the Faith of the Conquered," in *Mongols, Turks, and Others,* edited by Reuven Amitai and Michael Biran (Leiden: Brill, 2005), 262.

23. Quoted in Christian, *A History of Russia,* 425.

24. Quoted in Jerry Bentley, *Old World Encounters* (Oxford: Oxford University Press, 1993), 143.

25. Quoted in David Morgan, *Medieval Persia* (London: Longman, 1988), 79.

26. Morgan, *Medieval Persia,* 82.

27. Daniel H. Kaiser and Gary Marker, *Reinterpreting Russian History* (Oxford: Oxford University Press, 1994), 100.

28. Charles J. Halperin, *Russia and the Golden Horde* (Bloomington: Indiana University Press, 1985), 126.

29. Charles H. Halperin, "Russia in the Mongol Empire in Comparative Perspective," *Harvard Journal of Asiatic Studies* 43, no. 1 (June 1983): 261.

30. Quoted in Kevin Reilly, ed., *Worlds of History* (Boston: Bedford, 2004), 1:420.

31. Thomas Allsen, *Culture and Conquest in Mongol Eurasia* (Cambridge: Cambridge University Press, 2001), 211.

32. Quoted in Allsen, *Culture and Conquest,* 121.

33. See John Aberth, *The First Horseman: Disease in Human History* (Upper Saddle River, N.J.: Pearson Prentice Hall, 2007), chap. 1.

34. Quoted in Norman Cantor, *In the Wake of the Plague* (New York: Free Press, 2001), 6.

35. Andre Gunder Frank, *ReOrient* (Berkeley: University of California Press, 1998), 256.

36. Arnold Pacey, *Technology in World Civilization* (Cambridge, Mass.: MIT Press, 1990), 62.

37. Quoted in Golden, "Nomads and Sedentary Societies," 72–73.

38. Quoted in Guzman, "Were the Barbarians a Negative or Positive Factor?" 558–72.

39. Quoted in Barfield, *The Nomadic Alternative,* 3.

Chapter 13

1. Brian Fagan, *Ancient North America* (London: Thames and Hudson, 2005), 503.

2. Quoted in Charles C. Mann, *1491: New Revelations of the Americas before Columbus* (New York: Alfred A. Knopf, 2005), 334.

3. Louise Levanthes, *When China Ruled the Seas* (New York: Simon and Schuster, 1994), 175.

4. Niccolò Machiavelli, *The Prince* (New York: New American Library, 1952), 90, 94.

5. Frank Viviano, "China's Great Armada," *National Geographic*, July 2005, 34.

6. John J. Saunders, ed., *The Muslim World on the Eve of Europe's Expansion* (Englewood Cliffs, N.J.: Prentice Hall, 1966), 41–43.

7. Leo Africanus, *History and Description of Africa* (London: Hakluyt Society, 1896), 824–25.

8. Quoted in Patricia Risso, *Merchants and Faith* (Boulder, Colo.: Westview Press, 1995), 49.

9. Quoted in Stuart B. Schwartz, ed., *Victors and Vanquished* (Boston: Bedford/St. Martin's, 2000), 8.

10. Quoted in Michael E. Smith, *The Aztecs* (London: Blackwell, 2003), 108.

11. Smith, *The Aztecs*, 220.

12. Miguel León-Portilla, *Aztec Thought and Culture*, translated by Jack Emory Davis (Norman: University of Oklahoma Press, 1963), 7; Miguel León-Portilla, *Fifteen Poets of the Aztec World* (Norman: University of Oklahoma Press, 1992), 80–81.

13. Terence N. D'Altroy, *The Incas* (London: Blackwell, 2002), chaps. 11, 12.

14. Pedro de Cieza de León, *The Incas*, translated by Harriet de Onis (Norman: University of Oklahoma Press, 1959), 177–78.

15. For a summary of this practice among the Aztecs and Incas, see Karen Vieira Powers, *Women in the Crucible of Conquest* (Albuquerque: University of New Mexico Press, 2005), chap. 1.

16. Powers, *Women in the Crucible of Conquest*, 25.

17. Louise Burkhart, "Mexica Women on the Home Front," in *Indian Women of Early Mexico*, edited by Susan Schroeder et al. (Norman: University of Oklahoma Press, 1997), 25–54.

18. The "web" metaphor is derived from J. R. McNeill and William H. McNeill, *The Human Web* (New York: W. W. Norton, 2003).

19. Graph from David Christian, *Maps of Time* (Berkeley: University of California Press, 2004), 343.

Part Four

1. Victor Lieberman, "Transcending East–West Dichotomies," *Modern Asian Studies* 31 (1997): 463–546; John Richards, *The Unending Frontier* (Berkeley: University of California Press, 2003), 22–24.

Chapter 14

1. *Taipei Times*, October 11, 1999, http://uyghuramerican.org/articles/145/1/Fight-for-East-Turkestan/Fight-for-East-Turkestan.html.

2. Winona LaDuke, "We Are Still Here: The 500 Years Celebration," *Sojourners Magazine*, October 1991.

3. Quoted in Thomas E. Skidmore and Peter H. Smith, *Modern Latin America* (New York: Oxford University Press, 2001), 15.

4. George Raudzens, ed., *Technology, Disease, and Colonial Conquest* (Boston: Brill Academic, 2003), xiv.

5. Alfred W. Crosby, "The Columbian Voyages, the Columbian Exchange, and Their Historians," in *Islamic and European Expansion*, edited by Michael Adas (Philadelphia: Temple University Press, 1993), 160.

6. Quoted in Noble David Cook, *Born to Die: Disease and the New World Conquest* (Cambridge: Cambridge University Press, 1998), 202.

7. Quoted in Cook, *Born to Die*, 206.

8. Quoted in Charles C. Mann, *1491* (New York: Alfred A. Knopf, 2005), 56.

9. Felipe Fernandez-Armesto, "Empires in Their Global Context," in *The Atlantic in Global History*, edited by Jorge Canizares-Esguerra and Erik R. Seeman (Upper Saddle River, N.J.: Prentice-Hall, 2007), 105.

10. Quoted in Anthony Padgen, "Identity Formation in Spanish America," in *Colonial Identity in the Atlantic World, 1500–1800*, edited by Nicholas Canny and Anthony Padgen (Princeton, N.J.: Princeton University Press, 1987), 56.

11. Quoted in Marjorie Wall Bingham, *An Age of Empire, 1200–1750* (Oxford: Oxford University Press, 2005), 116.

12. Derived from Skidmore and Smith, *Modern Latin America*, 25.

13. Quoted in James Lockhart and Stuart B. Schwartz, *Early Latin America* (Cambridge: Cambridge University Press, 1983), 206.

14. From Kevin Reilly et al., eds., *Racism: A Global Reader* (Armonk, N.Y.: M. E. Sharpe, 2003), 136–37.

15. Felipe Fernandez-Armesto, *The Americas: A Hemispheric History* (New York: Modern Library, 2003), 58–59.

16. Willard Sutherland, *Taming the Wild Fields: Colonization and Empire on the Russian Steppe* (Ithaca, N.Y.: Cornell University Press, 2004), 223–24.

17. Quoted in Michael Khodarkovsky, *Russia's Steppe Frontier* (Bloomington: Indiana University Press, 2002), 216.

18. Khodarkovsky, *Russia's Steppe Frontier*, 222.

19. Quoted in Kappeler, *The Russian Empire*, 114.

20. Figures derived from Andreas Kappeler, *The Russian Empire* (New York: Longman, 2001), 115–17, 397–99.

21. Geoffrey Hosking, "The Freudian Frontier," *Times Literary Supplement*, March 10, 1995, 27.

22. Peter C. Perdue, *China Marches West* (Cambridge, Mass.: Harvard University Press, 2005); Nicola Di Cosmo, "Qing Colonial Administration in Inner Asia," *International History Review* 20, no. 2 (June 1998): 287–309.

23. Perdue, *China Marches West*, 10–11.

24. Quoted in Stephen F. Dale, "The Islamic World in the Age of European Expansion," in *The Cambridge Illustrated History of the Islamic World*, edited by Francis Robinson (Cambridge: Cambridge University Press, 1996), 80.

25. Quoted in Stanley Wolpert, *A New History of India* (New York: Oxford University Press, 1993), 160.

26. Jane I. Smith, "Islam and Christendom," in *The Oxford History of Islam*, edited by John Esposito (Oxford: Oxford University Press, 1999), 342.

27. Quoted in Alfred J. Andrea and James H. Overfield, *The Human Record* (New York: Houghton Mifflin Company, 2001), 2:91.

28. Jean Bodin, "The Rise and Fall of Commonwealths," chap. 7, http://www.constitution.org/bodin/bodin_4.htm.

29. Lord Wharncliffe, ed., *The Letters and Works of Lady Mary Wortley Montagu* (London: Henry G. Bohn, 1861), 1:298–300.

Chapter 15

1. Jacob Wheeler, "From Slave Post to Museum," *Christian Science Monitor*, December 31, 2002.

2. Quoted in Paul Lunde, "The Coming of the Portuguese," *Saudi Aramco World*, July–August 2005, 56.

3. Philip Curtin, *Cross Cultural Trade in World History* (Cambridge: Cambridge University Press, 1984), 144.

4. Quoted in Patricio N. Abinales and Donna J. Amoroso, *State and Society in the Philippines* (Lanham: Rowman and Littlefield, 2005), 50.

5. Anthony Reid, *Southeast Asia in the Age of Commerce, 1450–1680* (New Haven: Yale University Press, 1993), 2:274, 290.

6. Anthony Reid, *Charting the Shape of Early Modern Southeast Asia* (Chiang Mai: Silkworm Books, 1999), 227.

7. Andre Gunder Frank, *ReOrient: Global Economy in the Asian Age* (Berkeley: University of California Press, 1998), 131.

8. Quoted in Richard von Glahn, "Myth and Reality of China's Seventeenth Century Monetary Crisis," *Journal of Economic History* 56, no. 2 (June 1996): 132.

9. Kenneth Pomeranz and Steven Topik, *The World That Trade Created* (Armonk, N.Y.: M. E. Sharpe, 2006), 151–54.

10. Dennis O. Flynn and Arturo Giraldez, "Born with a 'Silver Spoon,'" *Journal of World History* 6, no. 2 (Fall 1995): 210.

11. Quoted in Mark Elvin, *The Retreat of the Elephant* (New Haven: Yale University Press, 2004), 37.

12. Quoted in Robert Marks, *The Origins of the Modern World* (Lanham: Rowman and Littlefield, 2002), 81.

13. See John Richards, *The Endless Frontier* (Berkeley: University of California Press, 2003), part 4. Much of this section is drawn from this source.

14. Elspeth M. Veale, *The English Fur Trade in the Later Middle Ages* (Oxford: Clarendon Press, 1966), 141.

15. Quoted in Richards, *The Endless Frontier*, 499.

16. Richards, *The Endless Frontier*, 504.

17. Quoted from "The Iroquois Confederacy," Portland State University, 2001, http://www.iroquoisdemocracy.pdx.edu/html/furtrader.htm.

18. David Brion Davis, *Challenging the Boundaries of Slavery* (Cambridge, Mass.: Harvard University Press, 2003), 13.

19. Quoted in Bernard Lewis, *Race and Slavery in the Middle East* (New York: Oxford University Press, 1990), 52–53.

20. Audrey Smedley, *Race in North America* (Boulder, Colo.: Westview Press, 1993).

21. Kevin Reilly et al., eds., *Racism: A Global Reader* (Armonk, N.Y.: M. E. Sharpe, 2003), 131.

22. Thomas Phillips, "A Journal of a Voyage Made in the Hannibal of London in 1694," in *Documents Illustrative of the History of the Slave Trade to America*, edited by Elizabeth Donnan (Washington, D.C.: Carnegie Institute, 1930), 399–410.

23. John Thornton, *Africa and Africans in the Making of the Atlantic World* (Cambridge: Cambridge University Press, 1998), 72.

24. Basil Davidson, trans., *The African Past* (London: Little Brown, 1964), 191–94.

25. Quoted in Anne Bailey, *African Voices in the Atlantic Slave Trade* (Boston: Beacon Press, 2005), 39.

26. Phillips, "A Journal of a Voyage," 399–410.

27. Erik Gilbert and Jonathan T. Reynolds, *Africa in World History* (Upper Saddle River, N.J.: Pearson, 2004), 160.

28. Adapted from Philip Curtin, *The Slave Trade: A Census* (Madison: University of Wisconsin Press, 1969).

29. Adapted from Lynn Hunt et al., *The Making of the West: Peoples and Cultures* (Boston: Bedford/St. Martin's, 2009), 521.

30. Paul Adams et al., *Experiencing World History* (New York: New York University Press, 2000), 334.

31. Bailey, *African Voices*, 153–54.

32. The present-day state of Benin was the location of the earlier kingdom of Dahomey. The ancient kingdom of Benin was located within present-day Nigeria.

Chapter 16

1. Michelle Goldberg, "The New Monkey Trial," January 10, 2005, http://www.salon.com/news/feature/2005/01/10/evolution/index.html.

2. Dr. Peter Hammond, "The Reformation," http://www.frontline.org.za/articles/thereformation_lectures.htm.

3. Glenn J. Ames, *Vasco da Gama: Renaissance Crusader* (New York: Pearson Education, 2005), 50.

4. Cecil Jane, ed. and trans., *Selected Documents Illustrating the Four Voyages of Columbus* (London: Hakluyt Society, 1930–1933), 2:2–18.

5. Kenneth Mills, *Idolatry and Its Enemies* (Princeton, N.J.: Princeton University Press, 1997), chap. 9.

6. Quoted in U.S. Library of Congress, *Country Studies: Peru*, http://countrystudies.us/peru/5.htm.

7. Quoted in Nicolas Griffiths, *The Cross and the Serpent* (Norman: University of Oklahoma Press, 1996), 263.

8. See James Lockhart, *The Nahuas after Conquest* (Stanford, Calif.: Stanford University Press, 1992), chap. 6.

9. Quoted in Joanna Waley-Cohen, *The Sextants of Beijing* (New York: W. W. Norton, 1999), 76–77.

10. Richard M. Eaton, "Islamic History as Global History," in *Islamic and European Expansion*, edited by Michael Adas (Philadelphia: Temple University Press, 1993), 25.

11. Robert Bly and Jane Hirshfield, trans., *Mirabai: Ecstatic Poems* (Boston: Beacon Press, 2004), ix–xi.

12. Quoted in Steven Shapin, *The Scientific Revolution* (Chicago: University of Chicago Press, 1996), 66.

13. This section draws heavily on Toby E. Huff, *The Rise of Early Modern Science* (Cambridge: Cambridge University Press, 2003), 48, 52, 76.

14. Huff, *The Rise of Early Modern Science*, 87, 288.

15. Jerome Cardano, *The Book of My Life*, translated by Jean Stoner (London: J. M. Dent, 1931), 189.

16. Quoted in Shapin, *The Scientific Revolution*, 28.

17. Quoted in Shapin, *The Scientific Revolution*, 61.

18. Quoted in Shapin, *The Scientific Revolution*, 33.

19. Quoted in Shapin, *The Scientific Revolution*, 68.

20. Stillman Drake, trans., *Discoveries and Opinions of Galileo* (Garden City, N.Y.: Doubleday, 1957).

21. H. S. Thayer, ed., *Newton's Philosophy of Nature: Selections from His Writings* (New York: Hafner Library of Classics, 1953), 42.

22. Immanuel Kant, "What Is Enlightenment?" translated by Peter Gay, in *Introduction to Contemporary Civilization in the West* (New York: Columbia University Press, 1954), 1071.

23. Voltaire, *A Treatise on Toleration* (1763), chap. 22.

24. Margaret C. Jacob, *The Enlightenment* (Boston: Bedford/St. Martin's, 2001), 103.

25. Marquis de Condorcet, *Historical View of the Progress of the Human Mind: The Tenth Stage* (1794).

26. Quoted in Jonathan Spence, *The Search for Modern China* (New York: Norton, 1999), 104.

27. Waley-Cohen, *The Sextants of Beijing*, 105–14.

28. Benjamin A. Elman, *On Their Own Terms: Science in China, 1550–1900* (Cambridge, Mass.: Harvard University Press, 2005).

29. Quoted in David R. Ringrose, *Expansion and Global Interaction, 1200–1700* (New York: Longman, 2001), 188.

30. Ekmeleddin Ihsanoglu, *Science, Technology, and Learning in the Ottoman Empire* (Burlington, Vt.: Ashgate, 2004).

Part Five

1. Quoted in Ross Dunn, *The New World History* (Boston: Bedford/St. Martin's, 2000), 17.

2. William H. McNeill, "*The Rise of the West* after 25 Years," *Journal of World History* 1, no. 1 (Spring 1990): 7.

Chapter 17

1. Quoted in Keith M. Baker, "A World Transformed," *Wilson Quarterly*, Summer 1989, 37.

2. Quoted in Thomas Benjamin et al., *The Atlantic World in the Age of Empire* (Boston: Houghton Mifflin, 2001), 205.

3. Jack P. Greene, "The American Revolution," *American Historical Review* 105, no. 1 (February 2000): 96–97.

4. Quoted in Greene, "The American Revolution," 102.

5. Quoted in Susan Dunn, *Sister Revolutions* (New York: Faber and Faber, 1999), 11, 12.

6. Quoted in Dunn, *Sister Revolutions*, 9.

7. Quoted in Lynn Hunt et al., *The Making of the West* (Boston: Bedford/St. Martin's, 2003), 625.

8. From James Leith, "Music for Mass Persuasion during the Terror," a collection of texts, tapes, and slides, copyright James A. Leith, Queen's University Kingston.

9. Franklin W. Knight, "The Haitian Revolution," *American Historical Review* 105, no. 1 (February 2000): 103.

10. Quoted in David P. Geggus, *Haitian Revolutionary Studies* (Bloomington: Indiana University Press, 2002), 27.

11. John C. Chasteen, *Born in Blood and Fire* (New York: Norton, 2006), 103.

12. Peter Winn, *Americas: The Changing Face of Latin America and the Caribbean* (Berkeley: University of California Press, 2006), 83.

13. Quoted in Thomas E. Skidmore and Peter H. Smith, *Modern Latin America* (New York: Oxford University Press, 2001), 33.

14. James Walvin, "The Public Campaign in England against Slavery," in *The Abolition of the Atlantic Slave Trade*, edited by David Eltis and James Walvin (Madison: University of Wisconsin Press, 1981), 76.

15. Michael Craton, "Slave Revolts and the End of Slavery," in *The Atlantic Slave Trade*, edited by David Northrup (Boston: Houghton Mifflin, 2002), 200.

16. Quoted in Northrup, *The Atlantic Slave Trade*, 175.

17. Eric Foner, *Nothing but Freedom* (Baton Rouge: Louisiana State University Press, 1983).

18. Quoted in Daniel Moran and Arthur Waldron, eds., *The People in Arms: Military Myth and National Mobilization since the French Revolution* (Cambridge: Cambridge University Press, 2003), 14.

19. Barbara Winslow, "Feminist Movements: Gender and Sexual Equality," in *A Companion to Gender History*, edited by Teresa A. Meade and Merry E. Weisner-Hanks (London: Blackwell, 2004), 186.

20. Olympe de Gouges, *The Declaration of the Rights of Woman*, 1791, http://www.pinn.net/~sunshine/book-sum/gouges.html.

21. Bonnie S. Anderson, *Joyous Greetings: The First International Women's Movement, 1830–1860* (Oxford: Oxford University Press, 2000).

22. Quoted in Claire G. Moses, *French Feminism in the Nineteenth Century* (Albany: SUNY Press, 1984), 135.

Chapter 18

1. "Mahatma Gandhi on Industrialization," http://www.tinytechindia.com/gandhi3.htm#1.

2. Joel Mokyr, *The Lever of Riches* (New York: Oxford University Press, 1990), 40–44.

3. Lynda Shaffer, "Southernization," *Journal of World History* 5, no. 1 (Spring 1994): 1–21.

4. Kenneth Pomeranz, *The Great Divergence* (Princeton, N.J.: Princeton University Press, 2000).

5. Pier Vries, "Are Coal and Colonies Really Crucial?" *Journal of World History* 12, no. 2 (Fall 2001): 411.

6. E. L. Jones, *The European Miracle* (Cambridge: Cambridge University Press, 1981), 119.

7. David Christian, *Maps of Time* (Berkeley: University of California Press, 2004), 390.

8. Quoted in Mokyr, *The Lever of Riches*, 188.

9. Quoted in Prasannan Parthansaranthi, "Rethinking Wages and Competitiveness in the Eighteenth Century," *Past and Present* 158 (February 1998): 79.

10. Maxine Berg, *Luxury and Pleasure in Eighteenth-Century Britain* (Oxford: Oxford University Press, 2005), 79–84.

11. Peter Stearns, *The Industrial Revolution in World History* (Boulder, Colo.: Westview Press, 1998), 36.

12. Jack Goldstone, "Efflorescences and Economic Growth in World History," *Journal of World History* 13, no. 2 (Fall 2002): 367–79.

13. Eric Hopkins, *Industrialization and Society* (London: Routledge, 2000), 2.

14. Mokyr, *The Lever of Riches*, 81.

15. Eric Hobsbawm, *Industry and Empire* (New York: New Press, 1999), 58. This section draws heavily on Hobsbawm's celebrated account of British industrialization.

16. Lynn Hunt et al., *The Making of the West: Peoples and Cultures* (Boston: Bedford/St. Martin's, 2009), 656.

17. Samuel Smiles, *Thrift* (London: John Murray, 1875), 30–40.

18. Hobsbawm, *Industry and Empire*, 65.

19. Peter Stearns and John H. Hinshaw, *Companion to the Industrial Revolution* (Santa Barbara: ABC-CLIO, 1996), 150.

20. http://www.workersliberty.org/node/view/3359?PHPSESSID=93d.

21. Hobsbawm, *Industry and Empire*, 171.

22. Derived from Paul Kennedy, *The Rise and Fall of the Great Powers* (New York: Random House, 1987), 149.

23. John Charles Chasteen, *Born in Blood and Fire* (New York: W. W. Norton, 2006), 181.

24. Peter Bakewell, *A History of Latin America* (Oxford: Blackwell, 1997), 425.

25. Michael Adas, *Machines as the Measure of Men* (Ithaca, N.Y.: Cornell University Press, 1990).

Chapter 19

1. *People's Daily*, April 6, 2001, http://english.peopledaily.com.cn/english/200104/06/eng20010406_66955.html.

2. Quoted in Heinz Gollwitzer, *Europe in the Age of Imperialism* (London: Thames and Hudson, 1969), 136.

3. Robert Knox, *Races of Man* (Philadelphia: Lea and Blanchard, 1850), v.

4. Quoted in Ralph Austen, ed., *Modern Imperialism* (Lexington, Mass.: D. C. Heath, 1969), 70–73.

5. Quoted in Julian Burger, "Echoes of History," *The New Internationalist*, August 1988, http://www.newint.org/issue186/echoes.htm.

6. Dun J. Li, ed., *China in Transition, 1517–1911* (New York: Van Nostrand Reinhold, 1969).

7. Quoted in Jonathan D. Spence, *The Search for Modern China* (New York: W. W. Norton, 1999), 169.

8. Hsin-Pao Chang, ed., *Commissioner Lin and the Opium War* (New York: Norton, 1970), 226–27.

9. Barbara Hodgson, *Opium: A Portrait of the Heavenly Demon* (San Francisco: Chronicle Books, 1999), 32.

10. Quoted in Magali Morsy, *North Africa: 1800–1900* (London: Longman, 1984), 79.

11. Marius B. Jansen, *The Making of Modern Japan* (Cambridge, Mass.: Harvard University Press, 2002), 33.

12. Quoted in Carol Gluck, "Themes in Japanese History," in *Asia in Western and World History*, edited by Ainslie T. Embree and Carol Gluck (Armonk, N.Y.: M. E. Sharpe, 1997), 754.

13. Quoted in S. Hanley and K. Yamamura, *Economic and Demographic Change in Pre-Industrial Japan* (Princeton, N.J.: Princeton University Press, 1977), 88–90.

14. Quoted in Harold Bolitho, "The Tempo Crisis," in *The Cambridge History of Japan,* vol. 5, *The Nineteenth Century*, edited by Maurice B. Jansen (Cambridge: Cambridge University Press, 1989), 230.

15. Kenneth Henshall, *A History of Japan* (New York: Palgrave, 2004), 67.

16. Quoted in James L. McClain, *Japan: A Modern History* (New York: W. W. Norton, 2002), 177.

17. Selcuk Esenbel, "Japan's Global Claim to Asia and the World of Islam," *American Historical Review,* October 2004, par. 1, 9, http://www.historycooperative.org/journals/ahr/109.4/esenbel.html.

Chapter 20

1. Quoted in Robert Strayer, *The Making of Mission Communities in East Africa* (London: Heinemann, 1978), 89.

2. Quoted in John Iliffe, *Africans: The History of a Continent* (Cambridge: Cambridge University Press, 1995), 191.

3. Quoted in Nicholas Tarling, "The Establishment of Colonial Regimes," in *The Cambridge History of Southeast Asia*, edited by Nicholas Tarling (Cambridge: Cambridge University Press, 1992), 2:76.

4. R. Meinertzhagen, *Kenya Diary* (London: Oliver and Boyd, 1957), 51–52.

5. Quoted in Neil Jamieson, *Understanding Vietnam* (Berkeley: University of California Press, 1993), 49–57.

6. Quoted in Donald R. Wright, *The World and a Very Small Place in Africa* (Armonk, N.Y.: M. E. Sharpe, 2004), 170.

7. Quoted in Scott B. Cook, *Colonial Encounters in the Age of High Imperialism* (New York: HarperCollins, 1996), 53.

8. D. R. SarDesai, *Southeast Asia: Past and Present* (Boulder, Colo.: Westview Press, 1997), 95–98.

9. Quoted in G. C. K. Gwassa and John Iliffe, *Records of the Maji Maji Rising*, part I (Nairobi: East African Publishing House, 1967), 4–5.

10. Iliffe, *Africans*, 216.

11. Quoted in Basil Davidson, *Modern Africa* (London: Longman, 1983), 79, 81.

12. This section draws heavily on Margaret Jean Hay and Sharon Stichter, eds., *African Women South of the Sahara* (London: Longman, 1984), especially chaps. 1–5.

13. Quoted in Robert A. Levine, "Sex Roles and Economic Change in Africa," in *Black Africa*, edited by John Middleton (London: Macmillan, 1970), 178.

14. Elizabeth Schmidt, *Peasants, Traders, and Wives: Shona Women in the History of Zimbabwe, 1870–1939* (Portsmouth, N.H.: Heinemann, 1992), chap. 4.

15. Derived from Adam McKeown, "Global Migration, 1846–1940," *Journal of World History* 15, no. 2 (June 2004): 156.

16. Josiah Kariuki, *Mau Mau Detainee* (London: Oxford University Press, 1963), 5.

17. Quoted in Harry Benda and John Larkin, *The World of Southeast Asia* (New York: Harper and Row, 1967), 182–85.

18. Rammohun Roy, *The English Works of Raja Rammohun Roy* (Allahabad: Panini Office, 1906), 471–74.

19. James Aggrey, "The Parable of the Eagle," in Edward W. Smith, *Aggrey of Africa* (London: SCM Press, 1929).

20. C. A. Bayly, *The Birth of the Modern World* (Oxford: Blackwell, 2004), 343.

21. William Theodore de Bary, ed., *Sources of Indian Tradition* (New York: Columbia University Press, 1958), 2:100.

22. Nirad Chaudhuri, *Autobiography of an Unknown Indian* (London: John Farquharson, 1968), 229.

23. Edward Blyden, *Christianity, Islam, and the Negro Race* (Edinburgh: Edinburgh University Press, 1967), 124.

24. John Iliffe, *A Modern History of Tanganyika* (Cambridge: Cambridge University Press, 1979), 324.

Part Six

1. J. R. McNeill, *Something New under the Sun* (New York: W. W. Norton, 2000), 3–4.

Chapter 21

1. "Scotland's Oldest Man Turns 107," *Scotsman,* June 25, 2003, http://www.aftermathww1.com/oldestscot.asp; MSNBC, November 21, 2005, http://www.msnbc.msn.com/id/10138446/.

2. Quoted in John Keegan, *The First World War* (New York: Vintage Books, 1998), 3.

3. Adapted from Lynn Hunt et al., *The Making of the West: Peoples and Cultures* (Boston: Bedford/St. Martin's, 2001), 1024.

4. Stanley Payne, *History of Fascism, 1914–1945* (Madison: University of Wisconsin Press, 1995), 208.

5. Richard Bessel, ed., *Fascist Italy and Nazi Germany: Comparisons and Contrasts* (Cambridge: Cambridge University Press, 1996), 8.

6. Quoted in Laurence Rees, *The Nazis: A Warning from History* (New York: New Press, 1997), 62.

7. James L. McClain, *Japan: A Modern History* (New York: W. W. Norton, 2002), 378.

8. Quoted in McClain, *Japan*, 414.

9. Bernd Martin, *Japan and Germany in the Modern World* (Providence: Berghahn Books, 1995), 155–81.

10. Quoted in Marius B. Jansen, *The Making of Modern Japan* (Cambridge, Mass.: Harvard University Press, 2000), 607.

11. Quoted in Jansen, *The Making of Modern Japan*, 639.

12. Quoted in John Keegan, *The Second World War* (New York: Viking Penguin, 1989), 186.

13. John Lewis Gaddis, *We Now Know: Rethinking Cold War History* (Oxford: Oxford University Press, 1997), 52.

14. Adam Gopnik, "The Big One: Historians Rethink the War to End All Wars," *The New Yorker*, August 23, 2004, 78.

Chapter 22

1. BBC, "On This Day," November 9, 1989, http://news.bbc.co.uk/onthisday/hi/witness/november/9/newsid_3241000/3241641.stm.

2. Quoted in Ronald Suny, *The Soviet Experiment* (Oxford: Oxford University Press, 1998), 357.

3. Yuan-tsung Chen, *The Dragon's Village* (New York: Penguin Books, 1980), 85.

4. Such figures are often highly controversial. See Maurice Meisner, *Mao's China and After* (New York: Free Press, 1999), 413–25; Roderick MacFarquhar, ed., *The Politics of China* (Cambridge: Cambridge University Press, 1997), 243–45.

5. Richard Rusk, *As I Saw It* (New York: Norton, 1990), 245.

6. Quoted in John L. Gaddis, *The Cold War: A New History* (New York: Penguin Press, 2005), 57.

7. Ronald Steel, *Pax Americana* (New York: Viking Press, 1970), 254.

8. Quoted in Donald W. White, *The American Century* (New Haven: Yale University Press, 1996), 164.

9. David Potter, *People of Plenty* (Chicago: University of Chicago Press, 1954), 139.

10. Quoted in John M. Thompson, *A Vision Unfulfilled* (Lexington, Mass.: D. C. Heath, 1996), 383.

11. Deng Xiaoping, "The Necessity of Upholding the Four Cardinal Principles in the Drive for the Four Modernizations," in *Major Documents of the People's Republic of China* (Beijing: Foreign Language Press, 1991), 54.

12. Mikhail Gorbachev, *Perestroika: New Thinking for Our Country and the World* (New York: Harper and Row, 1987), 64.

13. Quoted in Abraham Brumberg, *Chronicle of a Revolution* (New York: Pantheon Books, 1990), 225–26.

Chapter 23

1. "I Am Prepared to Die" (Nelson Mandela statement at the Rivonia trial, April 20, 1964), http://www.anc.org.za/ancdocs/history/rivonia.html.

2. Quoted in Jim Masselos, *Nationalism on the Indian Subcontinent* (Melbourne: Nelson, 1972), 122.

3. Mohandas Gandhi, *Hind Swaraj*, 1909, http://www.mkgandhi-sarvodaya.org/hindswaraj.htm.

4. Quoted in Stanley Wolpert, *A New History of India* (Oxford: Oxford University Press, 1993), 331.

5. This information is drawn from the World Bank, *World Development Report 2006* (Oxford: Oxford University Press, 2005), Tables 1, 2.

6. Quoted in Bernard Lewis, *The Emergence of Modern Turkey* (London: Oxford University Press, 1968), 268–69.

7. *The Sayings of Ayatollah Khomeini* (New York: Bantam Books, 1980), 3–29.

Chapter 24

1. BBC News, March 5, 2002, http://news.bbc.co.uk/2/hi/middle_east/1856558.stm.

2. Jeffrey Frieden, *Global Capitalism* (New York: W. W. Norton, 2006), 476.

3. Jan Aart Scholte, *Globalization: A Critical Introduction* (New York: Palgrave, 2005), 117.

4. Based on constant 2004 U.S. dollars. Earth Policy Institute, "Eco-Economy Indicators," http://www.earth-policy.org/Indicators/Econ/Econ_data.htm.

5. United Nations, *Human Development Report, 1997*, 2, http://hdr.undp.org/reports/global/1997/en.

6. Michael Hunt, *The World Transformed* (Boston: Bedford/St. Martin's, 2004), 442.

7. Quoted in Frieden, *Global Capitalism*, 408.

8. Quoted in Manfred B. Steger, *Globalization: A Very Short Introduction* (Oxford: Oxford University Press, 2003), 122.

9. Quoted in Frieden, *Global Capitalism*, 459.

10. Charles S. Maier, *Among Empires: American Ascendancy and Its Predecessors* (Cambridge, Mass.: Harvard University Press, 2006), chap. 5.

11. Quoted in Donald W. White, *The American Century: The Rise and Decline of the United States as a World Power* (New Haven: Yale University Press, 1996), 395.

12. Quoted in Sarah Shaver Hughes and Brady Hughes, *Women in World History* (Armonk, N.Y.: M. E. Sharpe, 1997), 2:268.

13. Susan Kent, "Worlds of Feminism," in *Women's History in Global Perspective*, edited by Bonnie G. Smith (Urbana: University of Illinois Press, 2004), 1:305–6.

14. Quoted in Wilhelmina Oduol and Wanjiku Mukabi Kabira, "The Mother of Warriors and Her Daughters: The Women's Movement in Kenya," in *Global Feminisms since 1945*, edited by Bonnie Smith (London: Routledge, 2000), 111.

15. Elisabeth Jay Friedman, "Gendering the Agenda," *Women's Studies International Forum* 26, no. 4 (2003): 313–31.

16. Quoted in Mary E. Hawkesworth, *Globalization and Feminist Activism* (New York: Rowman and Littfield, 2006), 124.

17. Phyllis Schlafly, *The Power of the Christian Woman* (Cincinnati: Standard, 1981), 117.

18. Karen Armstrong, *The Battle for God* (New York: Alfred A. Knopf, 2000), xi.

19. Quoted in Armstrong, *The Battle for God*, 273.

20. Quoted in John Esposito, *Unholy War* (Oxford: Oxford University Press, 2002), 57.

21. Quoted in Esposito, *Unholy War*, 63.

22. Text of Fatwah Urging Jihad against Americans, http://www.ict.org.il/articles/fatwah.htm.

23. Anwar Ibrahim, "The Ardent Moderates," *Time*, September 23, 1996, 24.

24. See J. R. McNeill, *Something New under the Sun: An Environmental History of the Twentieth Century World* (New York: Norton, 2001).

25. Adapted from Lynn Hunt et al., *The Making of the West: Peoples and Cultures* (Boston: Bedford/St. Martin's, 2009), 968.

26. Ramachandra Guha, *Environmentalism: A Global History* (New York: Longman, 2000), part 1.

27. Timothy Doyle, *Environmental Movements in Minority and Majority Worlds: A Global Perspective* (New Brunswick, N.J.: Rutgers University Press, 2005).

28. Quoted in Shiraz Sidhva, "Saving the Planet: Imperialism in a Green Garb," *The UNESCO Courier*, April 2001, 41–43.

Acknowledgments

Chapter 3

Benjamin R. Foster. "Come then, Enkidu, to ramparted Uruk." Excerpt (7 lines) from *The Epic of Gilgamesh*, translated by Benjamin R. Foster, p. 10. Tablet 1: 226–232. Copyright © 2001 by W.W. Norton & Company. Used by permission of W.W. Norton & Company, Inc.

Miriam Lichtheim. "Seven days to yesterday, I have not seen the 'sister.'" As appears in *Ancient Egyptian Literature*, volume 2, pp. 184–185 by Miriam Lichtheim, translator. Copyright © 1976 by University of California Press. Reproduced with permission of University of California Press, in the format Textbook via Copyright Clearance Center.

Miriam Lichtheim. "Now the scribe lands on the shore." From *Ancient Egyptian Literature,* volume 2, translated by Miriam Lichtheim, pp. 168–175. As appears in *A Book of Readings: the New Kingdom* by Miriam Lichtheim, translator. Copyright © 1976 by University of California Press. Reproduced with permission of University of California Press, in the format textbook via Copyright Clearance Center.

N. K. Sandars. "You will never find that life for which you are looking. . . ." Excerpts from *The Epic of Gilgamesh*, translated with an introduction by N. K. Sandars (Penguin Classics 1960, Third Edition 1972). Copyright © N.K. Sandars, 1960, 1964, 1972. Reproduced by permission of Penguin Books, Ltd.

Miriam Lichtheim. "The gatekeeper comes out to you." From *Ancient Egyptian Literature*, volume 2, translated by Miriam Lichtheim, pp. 124–126. As appears in *A Book of Readings: the New Kingdom* by Miriam Lichtheim, translator. Copyright © 1976 by University of California Press. Reproduced with permission of University of California Press, in the format textbook via Copyright Clearance Center.

Samuel Kramer. "After your city had been destroyed, how now can you exist!" From *The Sumerians*, translated by Samuel Kramer, p. 142. Copyright © 1963 by University of Chicago Press. Used by permission of University of Chicago Press.

Samuel Kramer. "In those days the dwellings of Agade were filled with gold." Translated by Samuel Kramer. As appears in *Ancient Near Eastern Texts Relating to the Old Testament* by James Pritchard, ed., pp. 647–648. Copyright © 1969 Princeton University Press. Used by permission of Princeton University Press.

Chapter 5

Lao Tsu. "A small country has few people." From *Tao Te Ching* by Lau Tsu, translated by Gia-Fu Feng and Jane English, p. 80. Copyright © 1972 by Gia-Fu Feng and Jane English. Translation copyright © 1997 by Jane English. Used by permission of Alfred A. Knopf, a division of Random House, Inc.

Sappho. "If you will come, I shall put out new pillows for you to rest on." From *Sappho: A New Translation* by Mary Bernard, translator. Copyright © 1958 by University of California Press. Reproduced with permission of University of California Press, in the format Textbook via Copyright Clearance Center.

Ovid. "Add gifts of mind to bodily language. . . ." From *The Art of Love and Other Poems*, translated by H. H. Mozley. Published by William Heinemann, 1929, pp. 73, 75.

Chapter 9

Yuan Chen. "Ever since the Western horsemen began raising smut and dust." Quoted in *The Golden Peaches of Samarkand: A Study of T'ang Exotics*, by Edward H. Shafer, translator. Copyright © 1963 by University of California Press. Reproduced by permission of University of California Press in the format Textbook via Copyright Clearance Center.

Chapter 13

Miguel Leon-Portilla. "Like a painting, we will be erased." From *Fifteen Poets of the Aztec World* by Miguel Leon-Portilla, editor and translator. Copyright © 1992 by the University of Oklahoma Press, Norman. Reprinted by permission.

Chapter 15

Mark Elvin. "Rarer too their timber grew." Excerpt (4 lines) from *Retreat of the Elephants* by Mark Elvin. Copyright © 2004 by Mark Elvin. Used by permission of Yale University Press.

Chapter 16

Mirabai. "What I paid was my social body. . . ." From *Mirabai: Ecstatic Poems* by Robert Bly and Jane Hirshfeld. Copyright © by Robert Bly and Jane Hirshfield. Reprinted by Beacon Press, Boston.

Chapter 20

Neil Jamieson. "Fine wine but no good friends." From *Understanding Vietnam* by Neil Jamieson, translator. Copyright © 1993 by University of California Press. Reproduced with permission of University of California Press in the format Textbook via Copyright Clearance Center.

Maps

Map 1.2 is adapted from Peter Bellwood, *First Farmers: The Origins of Agricultural Societies* (Blackwood, 2005). Spot Maps 2.1 and 12.1 are adapted from Jerry H. Bentley and Herbert F. Ziegler, *Traditions and Encounters,* Third Edition (McGraw-Hill, 2006). Maps 3.3, 5.1, and 19.1 are adapted from Jerry H. Bentley and Herbert F. Ziegler, *Traditions and Encounters,* Second Edition (McGraw-Hill, 2003). Maps 7.1 and 15.4 are adapted from Craig Lockard, *Societies, Networks, and Transitions: A Global History* (Houghton, 2008). Map 24.1 is adapted from Felipe Fernández-Armesto, *The World* (Prentice Hall, 2007). Map 18.2 is adapted from John Mack Faragher et al., *Out of Many: A History of the American People* (Prentice Hall, 1997). Map 18.3 is adapted from John Charles Chasteen, *Born in Blood and Iron: A Concise History of Latin America* (Norton, 2006). Map 24.3 (bottom) is adapted from http://www.princeton .edu/~ina/infographics/starbucks.html (2003).

Index

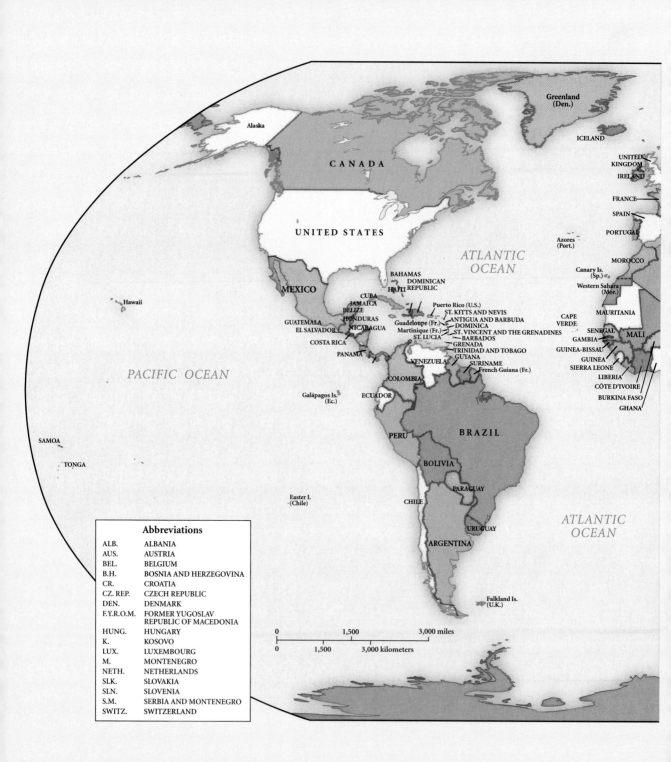

Greenland
(Den.)

Alaska

ICELAND

CANADA

UNITED
KINGDOM

IRELAND

FRANCE

SPAIN

PORTUGAL

Azores
(Port.)

UNITED STATES

ATLANTIC
OCEAN

MOROCCO

Canary Is.
(Sp.)

Western Sahara
(Mor.)

Hawaii

BAHAMAS

DOMINICAN
REPUBLIC

HAITI

MEXICO

CUBA

JAMAICA

BELIZE

HONDURAS

GUATEMALA

EL SALVADOR

NICARAGUA

COSTA RICA

PANAMA

Puerto Rico (U.S.)

ST. KITTS AND NEVIS

Guadeloupe (Fr.)

ANTIGUA AND BARBUDA

DOMINICA

Martinique (Fr.)

ST. VINCENT AND THE GRENADINES

ST. LUCIA

BARBADOS

GRENADA

TRINIDAD AND TOBAGO

GUYANA

MAURITANIA

CAPE
VERDE

SENEGAL

GAMBIA

GUINEA-BISSAU

GUINEA

SIERRA LEONE

LIBERIA

CÔTE D'IVOIRE

BURKINA FASO

GHANA

MALI

VENEZUELA

SURINAME

French Guiana (Fr.)

COLOMBIA

Galápagos Is.
(Ec.)

ECUADOR

PACIFIC OCEAN

SAMOA

TONGA

PERU

BRAZIL

BOLIVIA

PARAGUAY

Easter I.
(Chile)

CHILE

ATLANTIC
OCEAN

URUGUAY

ARGENTINA

Falkland Is.
(U.K.)

0		1,500		3,000 miles

0	1,500	3,000 kilometers

Abbreviations

ALB.	ALBANIA
AUS.	AUSTRIA
BEL.	BELGIUM
B.H.	BOSNIA AND HERZEGOVINA
CR.	CROATIA
CZ. REP.	CZECH REPUBLIC
DEN.	DENMARK
F.Y.R.O.M.	FORMER YUGOSLAV REPUBLIC OF MACEDONIA
HUNG.	HUNGARY
K.	KOSOVO
LUX.	LUXEMBOURG
M.	MONTENEGRO
NETH.	NETHERLANDS
SLK.	SLOVAKIA
SLN.	SLOVENIA
S.M.	SERBIA AND MONTENEGRO
SWITZ.	SWITZERLAND

ARCTIC OCEAN

NORWAY
SWEDEN
FINLAND
ESTONIA
LATVIA
LITHUANIA
DEN.
NETH.
GERMANY
BEL. POLAND BELARUS
LUX. CZ. REP.
AUS. SLK
MN. HUNG.
SWITZ. CR.
ITALY B.H. S. ROMANIA
M.F.Y.R.O.M.
ALB. BULGARIA
GREECE
MALTA
TUNISIA
CYPRUS
ISRAEL
Gaza Strip

RUSSIAN FEDERATION

KAZAKHSTAN

MONGOLIA

UKRAINE
MOLDOVA
GEORGIA
ARMENIA
AZERBAIJAN
TURKEY
SYRIA
LEBANON
IRAQ
West Bank
JORDAN

UZBEKISTAN
TURKMENISTAN
KYRGYZSTAN
TAJIKISTAN
AFGHANISTAN

CHINA

N. KOREA
S. KOREA
JAPAN

PACIFIC OCEAN

ALGERIA

LIBYA

EGYPT

IRAN
PAKISTAN
BAHRAIN
KUWAIT
SAUDI ARABIA
QATAR
UNITED ARAB
EMIRATES
OMAN
YEMEN

BHUTAN
NEPAL
BANGLADESH
INDIA
MYANMAR
(BURMA)

TAIWAN

LAOS
VIETNAM

THAILAND
CAMBODIA

PHILIPPINES

Mariana Is.
(U.S.)
Guam
(U.S.)

MARSHALL
IS.

NIGER
CHAD
SUDAN
ERITREA
DJIBOUTI

NIGERIA
BENIN
TOGO
CAMEROON
CENTRAL
AFRICAN REP.
ETHIOPIA
SOMALIA

SRI
LANKA

MALDIVES

BRUNEI

PALAU

FEDERATED STATES
OF MICRONESIA

NAURU
KIRIBATI

EQ.
GUINEA
GABON
CONGO
RWANDA
UGANDA
KENYA
DEM. REP. OF
THE CONGO
SÃO
TOMÉ
& PRÍNCIPE
BURUNDI
TANZANIA
COMOROS
SEYCHELLES

MALAYSIA

SINGAPORE

INDONESIA

PAPUA
NEW
GUINEA

SOLOMON
IS.

TUVALU

ANGOLA
ZAMBIA
MALAWI
ZIMBABWE
NAMIBIA
BOTSWANA
MADAGASCAR
MAURITIUS

INDIAN OCEAN

EAST
TIMOR

VANUATU
FIJI

SOUTH
AFRICA
MOZAMBIQUE
SWAZILAND
LESOTHO

AUSTRALIA

New Caledonia
(Fr.)

NEW
ZEALAND

Tasmania
(Aust.)

ANTARCTICA

ALPS

URAL MTS.

Volga R.

Ob R.

GOBI

Yellow R.

HIMALAYA MTS.

Yangzi R.

SYRIAN
DESERT

Mediterranean Sea

H A R A

Nile R.

Niger R.

Arabian
Sea

Bay of
Bengal

South
China
Sea

Tropic of Cancer

PACIFIC OCEAN

Equator

Congo R.

INDIAN OCEAN

Zambezi R.

KALAHARI
DESERT

Tropic of Capricorn

Vegetation Zones

- Tundra
- Northern forest
- Temperate forest
- Temperate grassland
- Desert and dry shrub
- Mediterranean shrub
- Mountain grassland
- Tropical grassland and savanna
- Tropical forest
- Permanent ice cover

About the Author

ROBERT W. STRAYER comes to the writing of this text with wide experience in the world history enterprise. With a Ph.D. in European and African history from the University of Wisconsin, he has taught world history at many levels, beginning with a two-year stint in high school history instruction in Ethiopia with the Peace Corps. Most of his academic career was spent at SUNY College at Brockport, where he taught world history as well as African and Soviet history for three decades and received both the Chancellor's Award for Excellence in Teaching and a similar award for Excellence in Scholarship. In 1998, he was a visiting professor of world history at the University of Canterbury in Christchurch, New Zealand. Since moving to California in 2002, he has taught world history at the University of California, Santa Cruz; California State University, Monterey Bay; and Cabrillo College. World history has been the primary intellectual focus of his career, during which he has served as a teacher, scholar, textbook author, consultant, and member of the Executive Committee of the World History Association.

Among his publications are works in African history, including *Kenya: Focus on Nationalism* (1975) and *The Making of Mission Communities in East Africa* (1978). More recently, he developed a specialty in Soviet history and wrote *Why Did the Soviet Union Collapse?* (1998) and *The Communist Experiment* (2007), comparing the experience of the Soviet Union with that of China. He was the senior author of an earlier world history textbook, *The Making of the Modern World* (1988; 1995), and has co-edited McGraw-Hill's Explorations in World History series. He has also published in a number of specialized journals, such as the *Journal of World History.*